Emerging Markets

The International Library of Critical Writings in Financial Economics

Series Editor: Richard Roll

Allstate Professor of Economics
The Anderson School at UCLA, USA

This major series presents by field outstanding selections of the most important articles across the entire spectrum of financial economics – one of the fastest growing areas in business schools and economics departments. Each collection has been prepared by a leading specialist who has written an authoritative introduction to the literature. A full list of published and future titles in this series is printed at the end of this volume.

Wherever possible, the articles in these volumes have been reproduced as originally published using facsimile reproduction, inclusive of footnotes and pagination to facilitate ease of reference.

For a list of all Edward Elgar published titles visit our site on the World Wide Web at
www.e-elgar.com

Emerging Markets

Edited by

Geert Bekaert

Leon G. Cooperman Professor of Finance and Economics
Columbia Business School, USA
and Research Associate
National Bureau of Economic Research, USA

and

Campbell R. Harvey

J. Paul Sticht Professor of International Business
Duke University, USA
and Research Associate
National Bureau of Economic Research, USA

THE INTERNATIONAL LIBRARY OF CRITICAL WRITINGS IN FINANCIAL ECONOMICS

An Elgar Reference Collection
Cheltenham, UK • Northampton, MA, USA

Published by
Edward Elgar Publishing Limited
Glensanda House
Montpellier Parade
Cheltenham
Glos GL50 1UA
UK

Edward Elgar Publishing, Inc.
136 West Street
Suite 202
Northampton
Massachusetts 01060
USA

ISBN   1 84376 105 X

Printed and bound in Great Britain by MPG Books Ltd, Bodmin, Cornwall

Contents

PART IV   CONTAGION

PART V   OTHER ISSUES

A   Corporate Finance

B   Microstructure of Equity Markets

C   Stock Selection of Equity Markets

Acknowledgements

The editors and publishers wish to thank the authors and the following publishers who have kindly given permission for the use of copyright material.

American Economic Association for articles: Maurice Obstfeld (1994), 'Risk-Taking, Global Diversification, and Growth', *American Economic Review*, **84** (5), December, 1310–29; Raghuram G. Rajan and Luigi Zingales (1998), 'Financial Dependence and Growth', *American Economic Review*, **88** (3), June, 559–86.

Blackwell Publishing Ltd for articles: René M. Stulz (1981), 'On the Effects of Barriers to International Investment', *Journal of Finance*, **XXXVI** (4), September, 923–34; Vihang Errunza and Etienne Losq (1985), 'International Asset Pricing under Mild Segmentation: Theory and Test', *Journal of Finance*, **XL** (1), March, 105–24; Geert Bekaert and Campbell R. Harvey (1995), 'Time-Varying World Market Integration', *Journal of Finance*, **L** (2), June, 403–44; Ian Domowitz, Jack Glen and Ananth Madhavan (1998), 'International Cross-Listing and Order Flow Migration: Evidence from an Emerging Market', *Journal of Finance*, **LIII** (6), December, 2001–27; Stephen R. Foerster and G. Andrew Karolyi (1999), 'The Effects of Market Segmentation and Investor Recognition on Asset Prices: Evidence from Foreign Stocks Listing in the United States', *Journal of Finance*, **LIV** (3), June, 981–1013; K. Geert Rouwenhorst (1999), 'Local Return Factors and Turnover in Emerging Stock Markets', *Journal of Finance*, **LIV** (4), August, 1439–64; Peter Blair Henry (2000), 'Stock Market Liberalization, Economic Reform, and Emerging Market Equity Prices', *Journal of Finance*, **LV** (2), April, 529–64; Geert Bekaert and Campbell R. Harvey (2000), 'Foreign Speculators and Emerging Equity Markets', *Journal of Finance*, **LV** (2), April, 565–613; Frans A. De Roon, Theo E. Nijman and Bas J.M. Werker (2001), 'Testing for Mean-Variance Spanning with Short Sales Constraints and Transaction Costs: The Case of Emerging Markets', *Journal of Finance*, **LVI** (2), April, 721–42.

Elsevier for articles: Graciela L. Kaminsky and Carmen M. Reinhart (2000), 'On Crises, Contagion, and Confusion', *Journal of International Economics*, **51**, 145–68; Thorsten Beck, Ross Levine and Norman Loayza (2000), 'Finance and the Sources of Growth', *Journal of Financial Economics*, **58**, 261–300; Enrico C. Perotti and Pieter van Oijen (2001), 'Privatization, Political Risk and Stock Market Development in Emerging Economies', *Journal of International Money and Finance*, **20**, 43–69; Geert Bekaert, Campbell R. Harvey and Christian Lundblad (2001), 'Emerging Equity Markets and Economic Development', *Journal of Development Economics*, **66**, 465–504; Geert Bekaert and Campbell R. Harvey (2003), 'Emerging Markets Finance', *Journal of Empirical Finance*, **10**, 3–55; Mitali Das and Sanket Mohapatra (2003), 'Income Inequality: The Aftermath of Stock Market Liberalization in Emerging Markets', *Journal of Empirical Finance*, **10**, 217–48.

Journal of Financial and Quantitative Analysis for article: William N. Goetzmann and Philippe Jorion (1999), 'Re-Emerging Markets', *Journal of Financial and Quantitative Analysis*, **34** (1), March, 1–32.

Oxford University Press for articles: Geert Bekaert (1995), 'Market Integration and Investment Barriers in Emerging Equity Markets', *World Bank Economic Review*, **9** (1), January, 75–107; Campbell R. Harvey (1995), 'Predictable Risk and Returns in Emerging Markets', *Review of Financial Studies*, **8** (3), Fall, 773–816.

University of Chicago Press for excerpt and article: René M. Stulz (1999), 'International Portfolio Flows and Security Markets', in Martin Feldstein (ed.), *International Capital Flows*, Chapter 5.2, 257–93; E. Han Kim and Vijay Singal (2000), 'Stock Market Openings: Experience of Emerging Economies', *Journal of Business*, **73** (1), January, 25–66.

Every effort has been made to trace all the copyright holders but if any have been inadvertently overlooked the publishers will be pleased to make the necessary arrangement at the first opportunity.

In addition the publishers wish to thank the Marshall Library of Economics, Cambridge University and the Library of Indiana University at Bloomington, USA for their assistance in obtaining these articles.

Foreword

Richard Roll

Over the past few decades, financial economists have devoted much attention to the financial aspects of emerging markets. Most modern finance has been erected in the context of large, developed economies and tested with data from such countries. Emerging markets seem to be either fundamentally different or else so far away from the norm of developed markets that they require unique theory and diverse empirical approaches.

Bekaert and Harvey (BH) have collected what they consider the most important contributions to the emerging markets literature. Moreover, their introductory essay is a comprehensive survey in the tradition of those in other volumes of the Elgar International Library of Critical Writings in Financial Economics. In addition to critical evaluations of the included papers, BH even take a further step by including new and original theoretical and empirical work in their essay.

Bekaert and Harvey categorize the existing literature into four major areas:

1.   Market integration and liberalization
2.   Financial effects of market integration
3.   Real effects of financial market integration
4.   Contagion.

The extent of market integration (or its opposite, segmentation) is a hotly debated issue. A theory has been emerging, a theory that predicts lower expected returns after integration. BH explain the effect as follows:

> The reason [for lower returns] is that the volatility of emerging market returns is much higher than their covariances with world market returns. Holding the variances and covariances constant, this implies that prices should rise (expected returns decrease) when a market moves from a segmented to an integrated state. However, when a market is opened to international investors, it may become more sensitive to world events (covariances with the world may increase). Even with this effect, it is likely that these covariances are still much smaller than the local variance, which would imply rising prices. (p. 8)

Even though theory provides some pointed implications, empirical work is thus far less than satisfactory because 'the degree of market integration is very difficult to measure'. There are several reasons for this, ranging from investment restrictions that can be more or less porous depending on the country, to tolerated innovations such as American Depositary Receipts (ADRs), which allow for trading even without direct access to the emerging market.

Moving now to the second major subject, the financial effects of market integration, BH further classify the literature into five sub-topics. These are: liberalization and the equity return generating process (means, volatility, etc.); liberalization and capital flows; liberalization and political risk; liberalization and the gains from international diversification; and, finally, an assessment of how well emerging market portfolios have performed.

In looking at possible real effects of financial market integration, BH first ask, 'Why would financial liberalization affect economic growth?' They go on to assess the literature that purports to measure the effect of liberalization on economic growth and they discuss intensity of liberalization and simultaneity problems in measuring real liberalization effects.

This is a controversial area fraught with problems of measurement and endogeneity (for example, growth might cause financial liberalization rather than the contrary). This section of BH's essay contains a lot of food for thought and suggestions for further research.

BH turn next to the literature on 'contagion', that is, the phenomenon that a crisis in one country spreads to other countries even without any underlying problems in the latter. Currency crises are the most notorious and familiar. One remembers Mexico in 1994 (the 'Tequila Crisis'), South-East Asia in 1997 (the 'Asian Flu' crisis), and Russia in 1998 (the 'Russian Virus' crisis). In each instance, perturbations appeared in other emerging markets far removed both geographically and economically from the originally infected countries.

BH also discuss contagion and equity markets, specifically the empirical finding that equity markets become more correlated during crises. Evidence for such increased correlation is provided in some papers, but thus far is not universally accepted.

Finally, in Section 6 of their essay, BH cover a miscellany of other topics that do not fall neatly into their main subject areas. Included here are discussions of research on corporate finance and corporate governance, fixed income markets, market microstructure, stock selection, and privatization. In each case, there are important distinctions, at least in degree, between emerging and developed markets.

Bekaert and Harvey have provided a valuable service, not only in the large number of original research publications they have themselves published about emerging markets, but in agreeing to compile their list of critical writings and to provide such an outstanding and comprehensive survey of the field. Their essay will, I predict, become required reading in most advanced courses on international finance and will be essential background reading for other scholars hoping to contribute to this rich emerging literature.

Introduction

ELSEVIER

Journal of Empirical Finance 10 (2003) 3–55

Journal of
EMPIRICAL
FINANCE

www.elsevier.com/locate/econbase

Emerging markets finance ☆

Geert Bekaert[a,b,*], Campbell R. Harvey[b,c]

[a] Columbia University, New York, NY 10027, USA
[b] National Bureau of Economic Research, Cambridge, MA 02138, USA
[c] Duke University, Durham, NC 27708, USA

Abstract

Emerging markets have long posed a challenge for finance. Standard models are often ill suited to deal with the specific circumstances arising in these markets. However, the interest in emerging markets has provided impetus for both the adaptation of current models to new circumstances in these markets and the development of new models. The model of market integration and segmentation is our starting point. Next, we emphasize the distinction between market liberalization and integration. We explore the financial effects of market integration as well as the impact on the real economy. We also consider a host of other issues such as contagion, corporate finance, market microstructure and stock selection in emerging markets. Apart from surveying the literature, this article contains new results regarding political risk and liberalization, the volatility of capital flows and the performance of emerging market investments.
© 2002 Elsevier Science B.V. All rights reserved.

Keywords: Market liberalization; Portfolio flows; Market reforms; Economic growth; Risk sharing; Contagion; Privatization; Capital flows; Market microstructure; Inequality; Productivity; Volatility of capital flows; Performance of emerging market investments

1. Introduction

In the early 1990s, developing countries regained access to foreign capital after a decade lost in the aftermath of the debt crisis of the mid-1980's. Not only did capital flows to emerging markets increase dramatically, but their composition changed substantially as

We have benefited from discussions with Karl Lins and Chris Lundblad. We appreciate the comments of Stijn Claessens, Vihang Errunza, Kristin Forbes, Andrew Frankel, Eric Ghysels, Angela Ng, Enrico Perotti, Roberto Rigobon, Frank Warnock. We thank Frank Warnock for providing us with an early release of his U.S. holdings estimates.
* Corresponding author.
E-mail address: gb241@columbia.edu (G. Bekaert).

4   *G. Bekaert, C.R. Harvey / Journal of Empirical Finance 10 (2003) 3–55*

well. Portfolio flows (fixed income and equity) and foreign direct investment replaced commercial bank debt as the dominant sources of foreign capital. This could not have happened without these countries embarking on a financial liberalization process, relaxing restrictions on foreign ownership of assets, and taking other measures to develop their capital markets, often in tandem with macroeconomic and trade reforms. New capital markets emerged as a result, and the consequences were dramatic. For example, in 1985, Mexico's equity market capitalization was 0.7% of gross domestic product (GDP) and the market was only accessible by foreigners through the Mexico Fund that traded on the New York Stock Exchange. In 2000, equity market capitalization had risen to 21.8% of GDP and U.S. investors alone were holding through a variety of channels about 25% of the market.[1]

These developments raise a number of intriguing questions. From the perspective of investors in developed markets, what are the diversification benefits of investing in these newly available emerging markets? And from the perspective of the developing countries themselves, what are the effects of increased foreign capital on domestic financial markets and ultimately on economic growth?

Market integration is central to both questions. In finance, markets are considered integrated when assets of identical risk command the same expected return irrespective of their domicile. In theory, liberalization should bring about emerging market integration with the global capital market, and its effects on emerging equity markets are then clear. Foreign investors will bid up the prices of local stocks with diversification potential while all investors will shun inefficient sectors. Overall, the cost of equity capital should go down, which in turn may increase investment and ultimately increase economic welfare.

Foreign investment can also have adverse effects, as the 1994 Mexican and 1997 South Asian crises illustrated. For example, foreign capital flows may complicate monetary policy, drive up real exchange rates and increase the volatility of local equity markets. Moreover, in diversifying their portfolios toward emerging markets, rational international investors should consider that the integration process might lower expected returns and increase correlations between emerging market and world market returns. To the extent that the benefits of diversification are severely reduced by the liberalization process, there may be less of an increase in the original equity price. Ultimately, all of these questions require empirical answers, which a growing body of research on emerging markets has attempted to provide.

Of course, it is unlikely that liberalization will lead to the full integration of any emerging market into the global capital market. After all, the phenomenon of home asset preference leads many international economists to believe that even developed markets are not well integrated. In fact, much of the literature has proceeded to compute the benefits of full market integration in the context of theoretical models of market integration and international risk sharing. The results of these counterfactual exercises depend very much on the model assumptions (see Lewis, 1996; Van Wincoop, 1999). The liberalization process in emerging markets offers an ideal laboratory to test directly some of the predictions of the market integration and risk sharing theoretical literature.

---

[1] See Thomas and Warnock (2002) for the estimates of U.S. holdings.

G. Bekaert, C.R. Harvey / Journal of Empirical Finance 10 (2003) 3- 55   5

In this article, we start in Section 2 by focusing on market integration and how it is related to the liberalization process in emerging markets. We discuss the theoretical effects of financial market liberalization and the problems in measuring when market integration has effectively taken place. Section 3 surveys the financial effects of market integration, from the cost of capital and equity return volatility to diversification benefits.

We also present some new results that examine the volatility of capital flows, the impact of financial liberalizations on country risk, and the performance of emerging market investments. Some of these results challenge conventional wisdom. For example, we find that capital flows to emerging markets as a group are less volatile than capital flows to developed countries as a group. We also find that despite growing reports on the irrational behavior of foreign investors in emerging markets, the emerging market portfolios of U.S. investors outperform a number of natural benchmarks.

Section 4 shifts attention to the real sector. We examine the effects of the liberalization process on economic growth, real exchange rates and income inequality. We present empirical evidence that suggests that for equity market liberalizations, there is a positive average effect. Nevertheless, a large literature stresses the disastrous effects freewheeling capital has had through severe currency, equity and banking crises in Mexico in 1995, Asia in 1997 and Russia in 1998. A comprehensive review of this evidence is beyond the scope of this article; however, in Section 5, we do offer a brief survey and suggest a somewhat different perspective on the rapidly growing contagion literature. In Section 6, we briefly review the important aspects of emerging market finance we do not discuss elsewhere in detail, including corporate finance and governance issues, the microstructure of emerging equity markets, the emerging fixed income markets and individual security analysis in emerging markets. Some concluding remarks are offered in Section 7.

2. Market integration and liberalization

2.1. The theory of market integration

It is important to be clear by what we mean by financial liberalization. In the development literature, it often refers to domestic financial liberalization (see Gelos and Werner, 2001; Beim and Calomiris, 2001 for example), which may include banking sector reforms or even privatizations. By financial liberalization, we mean allowing inward and outward foreign equity investment. In a liberalized equity market, foreign investors can, without restriction, purchase or sell domestic securities. In addition, domestic investors can purchase or sell foreign securities.

There are other forms of financial openness regarding bond market, banking sector and foreign exchange reforms. The popular International Monetary Fund (IMF) capital account openness measure lumps all of these together in a 0/1 variable (see below).

Even with our limited focus, the liberalization process is extremely complex and there is no established economic model that adequately describes the dynamics of the process. That is, while there are general equilibrium models of economies in integrated states and segmented states, there is no model that specifies the economic mechanism that moves a country from segmented to integrated status.[2]

To gain some intuition, we consider a simple model that traces the impact of market integration on security prices from the perspective of an emerging market. The model is a straightforward extension of the standard static integration/segmentation model; (see Errunza and Losq (1985), Eun and Janakiramanan (1986), Alexander, Eun and Janakiramanan and Errunza, Senbet and Hogan (1998), and Martin and Rey (2000)). Within the context of a simple quadratic utility specification, we examine a three-period problem for the world market and an emerging market. We assume that there is one share outstanding of each asset. In period three, dividends are paid out and, hence, there are only two trading periods. In period two, the government in the developing/emerging country may integrate the market with the world market or it may not. Each market has a price-taking agent, who only consumes in the third period. In period one, agents attach a probability, λ, to the government integrating the market with the world market in the second period.

For simplicity, the risk-free rate is set equal to zero and currency considerations are ignored. Risky assets in the world market (emerging market) yield a random per capita payoff of D_i^W (D_i^F) with, $i = 1, \ldots, N_W$, ($i = 1, \ldots, N_F$) in the third period. Denote the aggregate, market payoff as $D_M^W = \sum_{i=1}^{N_W} D_i^W$ and $D_M^E = \sum_{i=1}^{N_F} D_i^E$.

We focus on equity prices in the emerging markets. The second-period prices under perfect integration or perfect segmentation are well known:

$$P_2^S = E[D_M^E] - \rho \mathrm{Var}[D_M^E]$$

$$P_2^I = E[D_M^E] - \rho \mathrm{Cov}[D_M^E, D_M^{II}]$$

where ρ is the risk aversion coefficient and where we assumed the weight of the emerging market in the global world market to be negligible.

In period 1, agents know that prices in period 2 will either be P_2^S or P_2^I. The attraction of the quadratic utility framework is that in period 1, the price will be:

$$P_1 = \lambda P_2^I + (1 - \lambda) P_2^S$$

where λ is the probability (in period 1) that the government will integrate the market in period 2. It is important to realize that $P_2^S < P_2^I$, since the variability of local cash flows will be high whereas the covariance between local and world cash flows may be quite low.

Suppose the government announces a liberalization in period 1 to occur in period 2. The model predicts that prices will jump up and that the size of the jump is related both to the credibility of the government's announcement (and policies in general) as captured by the λ parameter, and the diversification benefits to be gained from integrating the market, as reflected in P_1^I. Foreign capital flows in when the market finally liberalizes (in period 2)

---

[2] One possibility is to model investments in international markets as being taxed by the host country (Stulz, 1981). A segmented (integrated) country is a country that imposes taxes (no taxes) on incoming and outgoing investments. A change in regime is a change in the tax rate. For a simple version of this idea, see Bacchetta and Wincoop (2000). The Errunza and Losq (1985) model, a limiting case of Stulz (1981), also lends itself to an analysis of a continuum of market structures.

G. Bekaert, C.R. Harvey / Journal of Empirical Finance 10 (2003) 3–55   7

and the price rises again since all uncertainty is resolved. This last price rise may be small if the announcement was credible.

Fig. 1 presents the implications of this simple model for equity prices and capital flows. Of course, this model is very stylized and ignores many dynamic effects. This simple model suggests that variables such as dividend yields and market capitalization to GDP may change significantly during liberalization as they embed permanent price changes. This simple story already reveals complex-timing issues. Market prices can change upon announcement of a liberalization or as soon as investors anticipate, liberalization may occur in the future. However, foreign ownership can only be established when allowed by the authorities. That is, capital flows may only occur after the "return to integration" has

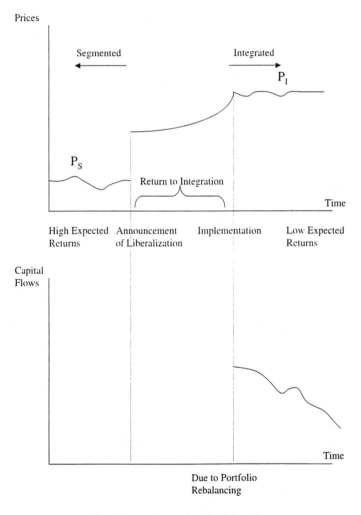

Fig. 1. Asset prices and market integration.

already taken place, so that foreign investors may not enjoy this return. (Note that we assume that capital inflows exceed capital outflows upon liberalization).

The model suggests that expected returns (cost of capital) should decrease. The reason is that the volatility of emerging market returns is much higher than their covariances with world market returns. Holding the variances and covariances constant, this implies that prices should rise (expected returns decrease) when a market moves from a segmented to an integrated state. However, when a market is opened to international investors, it may become more sensitive to world events (covariances with the world may increase). Even with this effect, it is likely that these covariances are still much smaller than the local variance, which would imply rising prices.

It also makes sense that the liberalization process may be reflected in activity in the local market. As foreigners are allowed to access the local market, liquidity may increase along with trading volume.

There could also be some structural changes in the market. For example, if the cost of capital decreases, new firms may present initial public offerings. Market concentration may decrease as a result of these new entrants. In addition, individual stocks may become less sensitive to local information and more sensitive to world events. This may cause the cross-correlation of individual stocks within a market to change. Morck et al. (2000) find that stock prices in poor economies move together more (that is, the cross-correlation is higher) than in rich countries, but they link this phenomenon to the absence of strong public investor property rights in emerging markets.

The liberalization process is intricately linked with the macro-economy. Liberalization of markets could coincide with other economic policies directed at inflation, exchange rates; or the trade sector (see Henry, 2000a for details) and it may be correlated with other financial reforms aimed at developing the domestic financial system. Liberalization may also be viewed as a positive step by international bankers that may lead to better country risk ratings. Hence, these ratings may contain valuable information regarding the integration process as well as the credibility of reforms.

2.2. Measuring market integration

Once we leave the pristine world of theory, it soon becomes clear that the degree of market integration is very difficult to measure. Investment restrictions may not be binding, or there may be indirect ways to access local equity markets for example, through country funds or American Depositary Receipts (ADRs). For example, the Korea Fund was launched in 1986, well before the liberalization of the Korean equity market. Also, there are many kinds of investment barriers, and the liberalization process is typically a complex and gradual one.

Bekaert (1995) distinguishes between three different kinds of barriers. First are legal barriers arising from the different legal status of foreign and domestic investors with regard to, for example, foreign ownership restrictions and taxes on foreign investment. Second are indirect barriers arising from differences in available information, accounting standards, and investor protection. Third are barriers arising from emerging market specific risks (EMSRs) that discourage foreign investment and lead to de facto segmentation. EMSRs include liquidity risk, political risk, economic policy risk, and perhaps currency

G. Bekaert, C.R. Harvey / Journal of Empirical Finance 10 (2003) 3–55   9

risk. Nishiotis (2002) uses country fund data to examine the differential pricing effects of these types of barriers and finds indirect barriers and EMSRs to have often more important pricing effects than direct barriers.

Some might argue that these risks, are in fact, diversifiable and not priced; however, World Bank surveys of institutional investors in developed markets found that liquidity problems were seen as major impediments to investing in emerging markets. Moreover, Bekaert, Erb, Harvey and Viskanta (1997) find political risk to be priced in emerging market securities. When Bekaert (1995) measures the three types of broadly defined investment barriers for nine emerging markets, he finds that direct barriers to investment are not significantly related to a return-based quantitative measure of market integration. However, indirect barriers, such as poor credit ratings and the lack of a high-quality regulatory and accounting framework, are strongly related cross-sectionally with the integration measure. These results reveal the danger in measuring market integration purely by investigating the market's regulatory framework. Nevertheless, many researchers have tried this, including Kim and Singal (2000), Henry (2000a) and Bekaert and Harvey (2000a). Bekaert and Harvey provide an Internet site with detailed time lines for 45 emerging markets that provided the basis for the dates in Bekaert and Harvey (2000a).[3] Bekaert (1995) and more recently, Edison and Warnock (2001) have proposed to use the ratio of market capitalization represented by the International Finance Corporation (IFC) Investable Indices, which correct for foreign ownership, to the market capitalization represented by the IFC Global Indices. This ratio has the advantage that it captures gradual liberalizations, as in South Korea where foreign ownership restrictions were relaxed gradually over time.[4]

There are a number of potential solutions to the problems posed in trying to date regulatory reforms.

First, Bekaert and Harvey (1995) measure the degree of integration directly from equity return data using a parameterized model of integration versus segmentation (a regime-switching model). The model yields a time-varying measure of the extent of integration between 0 and 1. Importantly, the model allows for the possibility of gradual integration, as in Korea where foreign ownership restrictions were gradually relaxed. In many countries, with Thailand as a stark example, variation in the integration measure coincides with capital market reforms. In contrast to general perceptions at the time of this article was written, its results suggest that some countries became less integrated over time.[5]

Carrieri et al. (2002) study eight emerging markets over the period 1976–2000. Their results suggest that although local risk is the most relevant factor in explaining time-variation in emerging market expected returns, global risk is also conditionally priced for three countries, while for two countries it exhibits marginal significance. Further, there are substantial cross-market differences in the degree of integration. More interestingly, they

---

[3] See http://www.duke.edu:80/~charvey/Country_risk/chronology/chronology_index.htm. Also see Bekaert and Harvey (2000b) and Bekaert, Harvey and Lundbland (2003a).

[4] De Jong and De Roon (2002) apply this measure to a model of emerging market expected returns. Bae et al. (2002a) use the measure to model time-varying volatility.

[5] The Bekaert and Harvey (1995) model has been extended in Bhattacharya and Daouk (2002), Hardouvelis et al. (2000), Carrieri et al. (2002) and Adler and Qi (2002). A related model in Bekaert and Harvey (1997) is extended by Rockinger and Urga (2001).

observe evolution towards more integrated financial markets. This conforms to our a priori expectations based on the reduction in barriers to portfolio flows, the general liberalization of capital markets, the increased availability of ADRs and country funds, better information and investor awareness. Finally, their results strongly suggest the impropriety of using correlations of market-wide index returns as a measure of market integration.

Laeven and Perotti (2001) argue that credibility of liberalizations evolves over time. Their evidence suggests that the positive impact of privatizations occurs during the actual privatization rather than the announcement period. This is consistent with the importance of allowing for gradual integration.

Second, Bekaert and Harvey (2000a,b) use bilateral capital flow data in conjunction with IFC index returns to construct measures of U.S. holdings of the emerging market equities as a percentage of local market capitalization. The use of more liquid securities represented in the IFC indices to compute the returns of foreign investors is consistent with Kang and Stulz (1997) who show that foreign investors in Japan mostly buy large and liquid stocks. Bekaert and Harvey then determine the time at which capital flows experienced a structural break as a proxy for when foreign investors may have become marginal investors in these markets. Although this measure avoids the necessity of having to specify an asset-pricing model and avoids noisy return data, the capital flow data that they use are complicated by the existence of financial intermediary centers (e.g. large flows to the UK are channeled to other countries), and by the fact that the United States is the only country for which we have detailed data on bilateral monthly flows with emerging markets.[6]

In Table 1, we show the U.S. holdings measure for various periods for 16 emerging markets. We contrast its value in the 1980s versus the 1990s and pre- and post-liberalization, where the liberalization date is the Official Liberalization date from Bekaert and Harvey (2000a). The message here is simple on average, liberalizations are associated with increased capital flows. In dollar terms, U.S. holdings increase 10-fold in the 5-years post-liberalization versus the 5-years pre-liberalization, but in percent of market capitalization, the increase is much more modest, but still quite substantial (from 6.2% to 9.4%). This modest percentage increase is influenced by the steep drop in holdings in the Philippines, where American capital was substantially present before the official liberalization. Also the dating of the liberalization may be incorrect. Finally the results are influenced by the fact that, comparing the 1980s to the 1990s, the U.S. share of the IFC market capitalization increased from 6.6% to 12.9%.

Third, Bekaert, Harvey, and Lumsdaine (2002b) exploit the idea that market integration is an all-encompassing event that should change the return-generating process, and with it the stochastic process governing other economic variables. They use a novel methodology both to detect breaks and to "date" them, looking at a wide set of financial and economic variables. The resulting break dates are mostly within 2 years of one of four alternative measures of a liberalization event: a major regulatory reform liberalizing foreign equity investments; the announcement of the first ADR issue; the first country fund launching; and a large increase in capital flows.[7]

---

[6] Also see Warnock and Cleaver (2002), and Tesar and Werner (1995) for an earlier study.

[7] Garcia and Ghysels (1998) also find strong evidence of structural change when applying different asset pricing models to emerging markets but they do not "date" the changes.

Table 1
Estimates of U.S. share of MSCI market capitalization around liberalizations

Country	U.S. holdings in millions		U.S. share of market capitalization		U.S. share of market capitalization	
	5-year pre-liberalization ($)	5-year post-liberalization ($)	5-year pre-liberalization (%)	5-year post-liberalization (%)	1980s (%)	1990s (%)
Argentina	193.5	3031.7	20.7	22.5	19.4	28.4
Brazil	243.9	6856.7	1.8	10.3	0.8	14.3
Chile	491.0	3261.8	7.6	10.3	7.1	10.6
Colombia	10.7	191.6	1.2	3.0	1.1	4.1
Greece	4.2	119.3	0.2	2.4	0.5	6.2
India	138.2	2779.1	0.7	5.4	0.6	5.4
Indonesia	46.7	776.0	NA	9.3	14.2	14.5
Jordan	NA	NA	NA	NA	NA	NA
Korea	754.0	6200.6	2.1	6.5	2.0	9.5
Malaysia	225.7	2128.8	1.5	4.7	1.7	8.1
Mexico	1184.5	16,197.8	18.0	26.0	17.0	29.9
Nigeria	NA	NA	NA	NA	NA	NA
Pakistan	NA	NA	NA	NA	NA	NA
Philippines	457.0	2219.1	16.8	12.7	18.8	16.3
Portugal	29.6	219.0	6.3	5.9	5.8	14.2
Taiwan	145.4	746.1	0.2	0.8	0.2	1.8
Thailand	107.3	1000.1	5.5	8.6	6.3	12.9
Turkey	44.4	425.5	3.8	6.3	3.8	13.7
Venezuela	47.5	444.9	6.9	15.2	6.9	16.6
Zimbabwe	NA	NA	NA	NA	NA	NA
Total average	4123.4	46,597.8	6.2	9.4	6.6	12.9

Finally, the macroeconomic and development literature has mostly focused on a broader concept of financial or capital market openness, using information in the IMF's Annual Report on Exchange Arrangements and Exchange Restrictions (AREAER). Within the AREAER, there is a category called 'capital account restrictions', which researchers have used to mark complete liberalization, that is, when the restrictions go to nil.[8] Unfortunately, as Eichengreen (2001) stresses, the IMF measure is an aggregate measure of many different types of capital controls and may be too coarse. Subcategories have only become available recently (see Miniane (2000)) and improvements in the measure for previous years (in particular, see Quinn (1997)) are available only for a few recent years.

3. Financial effects of market integration

There has been an extensive number of articles that measure the effects of the liberalization process on financial variables. We split the discussion into five parts. The first part focuses on the equity return generating process: moments of equity returns (mean, volatility, beta with respect to world returns, etc.). The second part addresses

---

[8] See Mathieson and Rojaz-Suarez (1992) as well as Edwards (1998) and Rodrik (1998).

12 *G. Bekaert, C.R. Harvey / Journal of Empirical Finance 10 (2003) 3–55*

capital flows, in particular equity flows. The third part focuses on political risk. The fourth part focuses, diversification benefits. We end this section evaluating the actual investment performance of U.S. investors in emerging markets.

Before we begin, it is important to realize that our analysis, from a historical perspective, is based only on the liberalizations that occurred over the last 20 years. Some emerging markets were thriving markets earlier in the 20th century (e.g. Argentina, see Taylor, 1998) and re-emerged. Goetzmann and Jorion (1999) study the bias in returns and betas that re-emergence might cause. For studies of the late 19th century globalization, see Taylor and Williamson (1994) and Williamson (1996).

3.1. Liberalization and returns

Bekaert and Harvey (2000a) measure how liberalization has affected the equity return-generating process in 20 emerging markets, focusing primarily on the cost of equity capital.[9] Given the complexity of the liberalization process, they define capital market liberalization using three alternative measures: official regulatory liberalization, the earliest date of either an ADR issue, country fund launch, or an official liberalization date, and the date denoting a structural break in capital flows (leading to increased flows). To measure the cost of capital, they use dividend yields. The integration process should lead to a positive return-to-integration (as foreign investors bid up local prices), but to lower post-liberalization returns. Given high return volatility and considerable uncertainty in timing equity market liberalization, average returns cannot be used to measure changes in the cost of capital. Dividend yields capture the permanent price effects of a change in the cost of capital better than noisy returns.

With a surprising robustness across specifications, they find that dividend yields decline after liberalizations, but that the effect is always less than 1% on average. The results are somewhat stronger when they use the liberalization dates from Bekaert, Harvey, and Lumsdaine (2002b) discussed earlier. Edison and Warnock (2003) find that the decrease in dividend yields is much sharper for those countries, that experienced more complete liberalizations. Henry (2000a) finds similar, albeit somewhat stronger, results using a different methodology and a slightly different sample of countries.

The impact of equity market liberalization on returns is presented in Figs. 2–7. First, consistent with Bekaert and Harvey (2000a) and Henry (2000a), Fig. 2 shows that average returns decrease after financial liberalizations. This is consistent with finance theory depicted in Fig. 1. Also it is possible that the pre-liberalization returns are upwardly biased from the affects of integration with the world market (the return to integration).[10]

Consistent with Bekaert and Harvey (1997), Fig. 3 shows that there is no significant impact on unconditional volatility. Indeed, it is not obvious from finance theory that volatility should increase or decrease when markets are opened. On the one hand, markets may become informationally more efficient leading to higher volatility as prices quickly

---

[9] Kawakatsu and Morey (1999) focus on market efficiency. Jain-Chandra (2002) examines efficiency after liberalizations.

[10] See also Errunza (2001) who shows that there is significant growth in market capitalization divided by GDP, trading volume divided by GDP, the turnover ratio and the number of listings after liberalization.

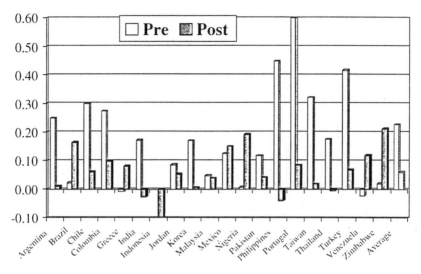

Data through April 2002. There are no pre-liberalization data for Indonesia.

Fig. 2. Average annual geometric returns. Pre and post Bekaert–Harvey Official Liberalization dates.

react to relevant information or hot speculative capital may induce excess volatility. On the other hand, in the pre-liberalized market, there may be large swings from fundamental values leading to higher volatility. In the long run, the gradual development and diversification of the market should lead to lower volatility.[11]

Bekaert and Harvey (2000a) argue that correlation and beta with the world market increase after equity market liberalizations. Figs. 4 and 5 show that unconditional correlations and betas both increase after liberalization. Indeed, of the 20 countries, only 3 countries experience a decrease in their correlations and betas—and the decrease is small. Figs. 6 and 7 present the time-series of rolling unconditional correlations and betas. Around the time of a clustering of equity market liberalizations in the late 1980s and early 1990s, both the average correlations and betas with the world increase. There is an even larger increase at the end of the 1990s, which may reflect further integration and overall higher market volatility (see Section 5), or the increase may be temporary, brought about by a potential bubble in global technology stocks (see Brooks and Del Negro, 2002). These results are corroborated in a recent study by Carrieri et al. (2002).

The analysis in Figs. 2–7 is unconditional. That is, we look at simple averages before and after liberalization. However, this type of analysis does not control for other financial and economic events that may coincide with equity market liberalization. Bekaert and Harvey (2000a) estimate panel regressions with a set of variables that are designed to control for coincidental financial and economic events. Interestingly, the message is similar to the unconditional analysis after liberalizations, expected returns decrease correlations and betas increase, and there is no particular impact on volatility.

---

[11] See also Richards (1996), De Santis and Imrohoroglu (1997), Aggarwal et al. (1999) and Kim and Singal (2000) for studies of the effects of liberalization on stock market volatility.

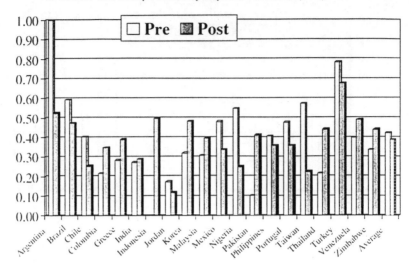

Data through April 2002. There are no pre-liberalization data for Indonesia.

Fig. 3. Average annualized standard deviation. Pre and post Bekaert–Harvey Official Liberalization dates.

There exists interesting corroborating evidence from the firm-level price effects of ADRs. An ADR from a country with investment restrictions can be viewed as investment liberalization. For example, when Chile had repatriation restrictions in place, it had to lift them for companies listing their shares overseas to make cross-market arbitrage possible. When the ADR is announced, we expect positive abnormal returns and presumably ex-

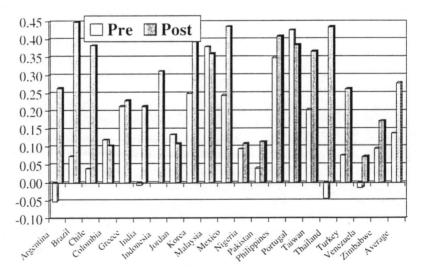

Data through April 2002. There are no pre-liberalization data for Indonesia.

Fig. 4. Correlation with world. Pre and post Bekaert–Harvey Official Liberalization dates.

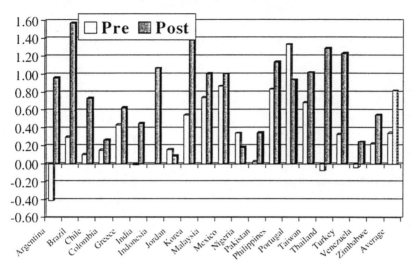

Data through April 2002. There are no pre-liberalization data for Indonesia.

Fig. 5. Beta with world. Pre and post Bekaert–Harvey Official Liberalization dates.

post under performance indicating lower expected returns after the liberalization. Of course, benchmarking ADR firms may be difficult, especially because the local market may experience significant spillover effects (see Urias, 1994). Overall, these predictions are borne out by the data and the announcement effect of ADR issuance is significant, being typically larger than 1% (see Miller, 1999; Foerster and Karolyi, 1999). Using a sample of 126 ADRs from 32 countries, Errunza and Miller (2000) document a very

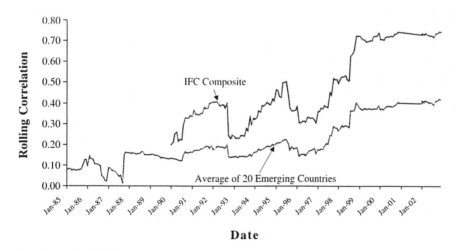

Data through April 2002.

Fig. 6. Evolution of world correlation. Five-year rolling window: 20 countries.

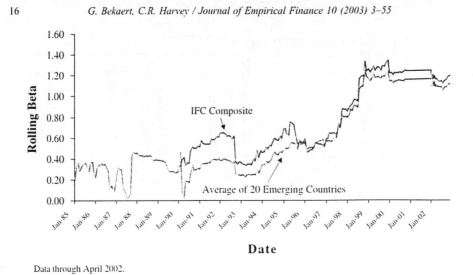

Data through April 2002.

Fig. 7. Evolution of world beta risk. Five-year rolling window: 20 countries.

significant decline in the cost of capital. In addition, they show that the decline is driven by the inability of U.S. investors to span the foreign security with domestic securities prior to cross-listing. Of course, there are many reasons, apart from liberalization, why ADR issues may induce a positive price effect, including additional liquidity and, the relaxation of capital constraints (Lins et al., 2001 for example). For further details, we refer to the excellent survey by Karolyi (1998). Recent studies by Chari and Henry (2001) and Patro and Wald (2002) also generally confirm the liberalization effects documented above using firm-specific data.

3.2. Liberalization and capital flows

With the emerging markets crises in the second half of the 1990s, the role of foreign capital in developing countries once again came under intense scrutiny. One country, Malaysia, imposed severe capital controls on October 1, 1998, in an effort to thwart the perceived destabilizing actions of foreign speculators. After a decade of capital market liberalizations and increased portfolio flows into developing countries, the process seemed to stall or even reverse. It is, therefore, important to develop an understanding of the dynamics, causes and consequences of capital flows in emerging markets. In particular, we need to understand the role of financial liberalization in these dynamics.

There is a growing body of research that studies the joint dynamics of capital flows and equity returns (see, for example, Warther, 1995; Choe et al., 1999; Froot et al., 2001; Clark and Berko, 1997; Edelen and Warner, 2001; Stulz, 1999; Edison and Warnock, 2001; Richards, 2002; Griffin et al., 2002). The first hypothesis of interest is whether foreign investors are "return chasers," in the terms of Bohn and Tesar (1996), that is, are flows caused by changes in expected returns? A related hypothesis is that international investors are momentum investors, leading to a positive relation between past returns and flows. A second set of hypotheses focuses on the effect of flows on returns. Both Froot et al. (2001)

G. Bekaert, C.R. Harvey / Journal of Empirical Finance 10 (2003) 3–55   17

(focusing on 28 emerging markets) and Clark and Berko (focusing on Mexico) find that increases in capital flows raise stock market prices, but the studies disagree on whether the effect is temporary or permanent. If the increase in prices is temporary, it may be just a reflection of "price pressure," which has also been documented in developed markets for mutual fund flows and stock indices (Warther, 1995; Shleifer, 1986). If the price increase is permanent, it may reflect a long-lasting decrease in the cost of equity capital associated with the risk-sharing benefits of capital market openings in emerging markets.

When focusing on emerging markets, the structural changes associated with capital market liberalization complicate any empirical analysis of capital flows, since these changes can cause permanent or at least long-lasting changes in the data-generating processes. Bekaert, Harvey and Lumsdaine (2002a) investigate the joint dynamics of returns and net U.S. equity flows acknowledging the important effects capital market liberalization may have. They precede their analysis with a detailed endogenous break-point analysis that helps define the relevant time-period over which to conduct the analysis. In general, they find sharply different results if their models are estimated over the entire sample—which ignores a fundamental nonstationarity in the data—versus a post-break (liberalization) sample. They find that net capital flows to emerging markets increase rapidly after liberalization as investors rebalance their portfolios, but that they level out after 3 years. As Fig. 1 indicates, if capital market liberalizations induce one-time portfolio rebalancing on the part of global investors, one may expect net flows to increase substantially after a liberalization and then to decrease again (see Bacchetta and Wincoop, 2000 for a formal model generating such dynamics). The empirical pattern appears consistent with this conclusion.

Furthermore, Bekaert, Harvey and Lumsdaine (2002a) add two variables to the bivariate vector autoregression set-up of returns and equity flows in Froot et al. (2001): the world interest rate and local dividend yields. The low level of U.S. interest rates has often been cited as one of the major reasons for increased capital flows to emerging markets in 1993 (see World Bank, 1997 as well as Calvo et al., 1993, 1994; Fernandez-Arias, 1996). However, Bekaert, Harvey and Lumsdaine (2002a) do not find a significant effect on capital flows to emerging markets from an unexpected reduction in world interest rates.

Other main findings include that unexpected equity flows are indeed associated with strong short-lived increases in returns. However, they also find that they lead to permanent reductions in dividend yields, which may reflect a change in the cost of capital. Hence, the reduction in the dividend yield suggests that additional flows reduce the cost of capital, and that the actual return effect is not a pure price pressure effect because it is partially permanent.

In more recent work, the focus has shifted towards detailed studies of the trading behavior of foreign investors in an effort to detect herding behavior and other behavioral biases. Two such studies, focusing on Korea before and during the currency crisis in 1997, are Choe et al. (1999) and Kim and Wei (2002a). Choe et al. find evidence of positive feedback trading and herding by foreign investors before the crisis, but not during the crisis period. They find no evidence that trades by foreign investors had a destabilizing effect on Korea's stock market and found the market to adjust quickly and efficiently to large sales by foreign investors. Kim and Wei find that foreign investors outside Korea are more likely to engage in positive feedback trading strategies and in herding than the branches and subsidiaries of foreign institutions in Korea or foreign individuals living in Korea. This difference in trading behavior is possibly related to the difference in possessed information by the two types of investors.

One problem that such studies face is that it is quite difficult to distinguish between irrational and rational trading in a country that is still liberalizing has stocks trading with and without associated ADRs, and is hit with an enormous economic crisis. Another problem is that however detailed the data; some foreign transactions are bound to be undetected and may undermine testing behavioral hypotheses. For example, hedge funds may hold Korean equity exposure through an asset swap with a local company, which will not be detected by the usual capital flow statistics. Apart from trades executed through derivatives, 1998 was also a very active ADR issue year for Korea, again making the determination of net positions difficult. Of course, such problems also complicate the interpretation of the more aggregate studies discussed earlier.

There is another related and rapidly growing literature that investigates the behavior of mutual funds investing in emerging markets. These include Borensztein and Gelos (2001), Kim and Wei (2002b), and Frankel and Schmukler (2000). Given that there already exists a survey article on this topic (Kaminsky et al., 2001), we do not further discuss these articles further.

Much has been made about the increased volatility of capital flows post liberalization (see Stiglitz, 2000). This discussion strikes us, in many ways, as odd. The emerging countries start with little or no capital flows and move to an environment (post liberalization) with significant capital flows which are, as expected, subject to portfolio rebalancing. Consequently, it is no mystery that the volatility of capital flows increases. In fact, if we revisit Fig. 1, the segmentation model predicts that volatility should spike around the time of market liberalization, but should then subside once the large capital inflow has occurred. Of course, there is always the worry that portfolio flows are not as "sticky" as foreign direct investment (FDI) and may disappear at a whim causing a crisis in the process (see Claessens et al., 1995) for an attempt to distinguish between hot and other forms of capital).

In Fig. 8, we provide a very simple measure of the evolution of capital flow volatility over time. We computed the coefficient of variation (volatility over mean) of the U.S. holdings measure previously referenced above for 16 emerging countries. Fig. 8 graphs the 3-year rolling window coefficient of variation for the aggregate U.S. holdings in these markets over time. Note that, the volatility measure starts to increase sharply in the early 1990s when many liberalizations take place and continues to increase, reaching its peak in 1995 at the time of the Mexican peso crisis. After falling sharply the volatility measure reaches another, but much lower peak at the end of 1997 around the time of the Asian crisis. Interestingly, 2000 was also a rather volatile year, but volatility in 2001 fell back to levels observed in the very early 1990s. It is very difficult to establish whether this volatility is excessive. Indeed, for comparison, we also consider the 3-year coefficient of variation of U.S. holdings in developed markets.[12] There is an even more substantial

---

[12] The set of developed countries follows Harvey (1991). We omit Hong Kong and Singapore/Malaysia from the set of MSCI developed markets. We also omit New Zealand because of lack of holdings data.

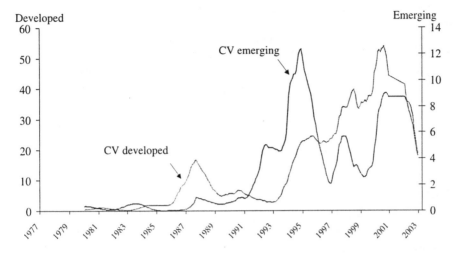

Fig. 8. Three-year rolling coefficient of variation of U.S. emerging and developed market equity holdings.

increase in the mid- to late-1990s in capital flows volatility for developed markets. In fact, both measures show similar patterns and capital flows to developed countries were more volatile than flows to emerging markets.

3.3. Liberalization and political risk

What is the relation between equity market liberalizations and political risk? Bekaert and Harvey (2000a) present some evidence that country ratings significantly increase (lower risk) with one of their measures of equity market liberalization. This is important because Erb et al. (1996a,b) show a significant cross-sectional relation between country rating and future equity returns and Bekaert Erb, Harvey and Viscanta (1997) make the case that political risk is a priced risk in emerging markets. That is, increased ratings lead to lower costs of capital.

Table 2 summarizes the behavior around liberalizations in 20 emerging markets studied in Bekaert and Harvey (2000a) with respect to the International Country Risk Guide's (ICRG's) measures of political, economic, and financial risk ratings. We report the rating at time t, which is the month of the official liberalization, reported in Bekaert and Harvey. We also report 1 year earlier, $t-1$, as well as 1 and 2 years after the liberalization $t+1$, and $t+2$. The results are striking. The ICRG measure of political risk rating increases by 10.8% from $t-1$ to $t+2$ (indicating lower political risk). During this same period, the largest change is with the financial risk rating measure, which increases by 26.8%, while the composite risk rating measure, which combines the three components, increases by 15.8%. This evidence is consistent with political risk and the cost of capital decreasing after equity market liberalizations. One market measure of political risk is the yield spread on dollar-denominated emerging market bonds, relative to dollar yields. Adler and Qi (2002) study market integration between the U.S. and Mexico using Brady bond spreads as an indicator of effective market integration and find that the spread significantly affects

Table 2
Equity market liberalization and political risk

(A) Political risk	$t-1$	t	$t+1$	$t+2$	(B) Financial risk	$t-1$	t	$t+1$	$t+2$
Argentina	56.0	61.0	64.0	66.0	Argentina	19.0	20.0	23.0	31.0
Brazil	69.0	64.0	69.0	66.0	Brazil	28.0	33.0	37.0	35.0
Chile	64.0	66.0	67.0	69.0	Chile	40.0	42.0	42.0	43.0
Colombia	54.0	59.0	61.0	58.0	Colombia	28.0	37.0	41.0	41.0
Greece	58.0	63.0	62.0	61.0	Greece	26.0	31.0	30.0	30.0
India	43.0	51.0	62.0	65.0	India	29.0	35.0	36.0	36.0
Indonesia	39.0	41.0	51.0	57.0	Indonesia	18.0	28.0	41.0	44.0
Jordan	73.0	76.0	70.0	73.0	Jordan	35.0	37.0	38.0	38.0
Korea	64.0	75.0	75.0	75.0	Korea	47.0	47.0	47.0	47.0
Malaysia	62.0	58.0	59.0	70.0	Malaysia	26.0	31.0	38.0	45.0
Mexico	69.0	68.0	70.0	71.0	Mexico	28.0	29.0	32.0	38.0
Nigeria	53.0	53.0	53.0	45.0	Nigeria	27.0	26.0	24.0	28.0
Pakistan	33.0	27.0	34.0	40.0	Pakistan	22.0	17.0	28.0	30.0
Philippines	37.0	41.0	44.0	55.0	Philippines	24.0	22.0	27.0	34.0
Portugal	70.0	71.0	67.0	76.0	Portugal	35.0	38.0	37.0	43.0
Taiwan	75.0	71.0	76.0	77.0	Taiwan	49.0	49.0	49.0	48.0
Thailand	54.0	55.0	60.0	59.0	Thailand	29.0	29.0	36.0	40.0
Turkey	48.0	45.0	45.0	52.0	Turkey	23.0	20.0	20.0	19.0
Venezuela	69.0	65.0	74.0	75.0	Venezuela	29.0	27.0	39.0	40.0
Zimbabwe	63.0	66.0	66.0	67.0	Zimbabwe	24.0	30.0	30.0	33.0
Average	57.7	58.8	61.5	63.9	Average	29.3	31.4	34.8	37.2
Increase from $t-1$		2.0%	6.6%	10.8%	Increase from $t-1$		7.2%	18.6%	26.8%

(C) Economic risk	$t-1$	t	$t+1$	$t+2$	(D) Composite risk	$t-1$	t	$t+1$	$t+2$
Argentina	18.0	14.0	25.5	24.5	Argentina	48.0	47.5	56.5	61.5
Brazil	20.0	23.5	26.5	25.0	Brazil	58.5	60.0	66.5	63.0
Chile	30.5	32.0	38.0	39.0	Chile	67.5	70.0	73.5	75.5
Colombia	29.5	34.0	35.0	38.0	Colombia	56.0	65.0	68.5	68.5
Greece	28.5	31.0	29.5	32.5	Greece	56.5	62.5	61.0	62.0
India	26.0	28.5	31.5	35.5	India	49.0	57.5	65.0	68.5
Indonesia	33.5	34.5	35.0	36.0	Indonesia	45.5	52.0	63.5	68.5
Jordan	38.5	38.0	38.0	39.5	Jordan	73.5	75.5	73.0	75.3
Korea	37.0	36.5	40.0	41.0	Korea	74.0	79.5	81.0	81.5
Malaysia	37.5	41.0	39.0	40.0	Malaysia	63.0	65.0	68.0	77.5
Mexico	27.5	27.5	25.5	29.0	Mexico	62.5	62.5	64.0	69.0
Nigeria	26.0	26.0	23.0	29.0	Nigeria	53.0	52.5	50.0	51.0
Pakistan	31.5	32.0	31.5	31.5	Pakistan	43.5	38.0	47.0	51.0
Philippines	29.5	29.0	31.0	34.0	Philippines	45.5	46.0	51.0	61.5
Portugal	34.0	34.5	36.0	38.0	Portugal	69.5	72.0	70.0	78.5
Taiwan	42.5	43.0	43.0	44.5	Taiwan	83.5	81.5	84.0	85.0
Thailand	33.0	36.5	35.5	36.0	Thailand	58.0	60.5	66.0	67.5
Turkey	26.0	28.0	28.0	27.5	Turkey	48.5	46.5	46.5	49.5
Venezuela	25.0	27.0	32.5	35.5	Venezuela	61.0	59.5	73.0	75.5
Zimbabwe	22.5	25.0	29.0	32.5	Zimbabwe	55.0	60.5	62.5	66.5
Average	29.8	31.1	32.7	34.4	Average	58.6	60.7	64.5	67.8
Increase from $t-1$		4.2%	9.5%	15.4%	Increase from $t-1$		3.6%	10.2%	15.8%

All ratings from International Country Risk Guide. 100 = maximum; 0 = minimum. t = Official Liberalization date from Bekaert and Harvey (2000a,b). We also report the ratings 1 year before as well as 1 and 2 years after the Official Liberalization.

G. Bekaert, C.R. Harvey / Journal of Empirical Finance 10 (2003) 3–55   21

expected returns. Country risk measures may reflect the credibility of the government's market-oriented reforms and its commitment to open capital markets. Perotti and van Oijen (2001) show that privatizations (see below) are significantly associated with lower political risk over time. Perotti (1995) presents the theoretical framework that links credible privatization and political risk.

3.4. Liberalization and diversification benefits

Although emerging market equity returns are highly volatile, they are relatively less correlated with equity returns in the developed world, making it possible to construct low-risk portfolios. Whereas the pioneering study of Errunza (1977) was largely ignored by both the academic and practitioner communities, interest in emerging market investments re-surfaced in the early 1990s. Early studies show very significant diversification benefits for emerging market investments, (Divecha et al., 1992; De Santis, 1993; Harvey, 1995). However, these studies used market indexes compiled by the (IFC) that generally ignore the high transaction costs, low liquidity, and investment constraints associated with emerging market investments.

Bekaert and Urias (1996, 1999) measure the diversification benefits from emerging equity markets using data on closed-end funds (country and regional funds), and (ADRs).[13] Unlike the IFC indexes, these assets are easily accessible to retail investors, and transaction costs are comparable to those for U.S.-traded stocks. The distinguishing feature of closed-end funds is that fund share prices generally deviate from the market value of all securities in the portfolio (known as "net asset value"); they may trade at a premium when the assets are invested in closed or restricted markets, or at a discount when the foreign market has unusual political risk. Historically, they provided access to restricted markets, while open-end funds and ADRs were relatively unimportant before 1993.

Bekaert and Urias (1996, 1999) generally find that investors give up a substantial part of the diversification benefits of investing in foreign markets when they do so by holding closed-end funds. Other studies, such as Bailey and Stulz (1990), Bailey and Lim (1992) and Chang et al. (1995) found larger diversification benefits but had not taken small sample biases in the statistical tests into account. Open-end funds, on the other hand, track the underlying IFC indices much better than other investment vehicles and prove to be the best diversification instrument in the Bekaert and Urias sample.

De Roon et al. (2001) and Li et al. (2003) take the transactions costs that investors in emerging markets face directly into account when measuring diversification benefits. De Roon et al. find that the diversification benefits of investing in emerging markets are eliminated when transactions costs and, in particular, short-sale constraints are introduced. However, they admit that there is some evidence of bias in their asymptotic spanning analysis. Unlike the asymptotic mean variance tests, Li et al. use a Bayesian approach, that incorporates the uncertainty of finite samples into their analysis. They argue that the diversification benefits to investing in emerging markets remain substantial even in the

---

[13] Also see Diwan et al. (1995).

22   *G. Bekaert, C.R. Harvey / Journal of Empirical Finance 10 (2003) 3–55*

presence of short-sale constraints. These two articles use the IFC indices to test for diversification benefits. Errunza et al. (1999) show that most of these diversification benefits can be obtained using domestically traded assets (ADRs and country funds).

By removing price segmentation, liberalizations may increase correlations and hence reduce diversification benefits. Using a model in which conditional correlations depend on world volatility and variables tracking the degree of integration, Bekaert and Harvey (1997) measure the time-variation in correlations for 17 emerging markets. For some countries, for example, Thailand, correlations increase markedly around the time of liberalization. The average response of these conditional correlations to liberalizations in 17 emerging markets is a small but statistically significant increase of 0.08 at most.

3.5. How well have emerging market portfolios done?

As we outlined before, there is some discussion in the literature suggesting that those who invest in emerging markets are subject to herding and other irrational behavior. Rather than focusing on one emerging market, we carry out two simple exercises to assess the overall performance of portfolio investment in emerging markets.

Our first exercise examines the performance of actual portfolio investments by U.S. investors in emerging countries. That is, the definition of U.S. investor is comprehensive, including all U.S. investments covered by the aggregate equity flow statistics, in contrast to studies such as Froot et al. (2001), who only focus on institutional investors. We compare their actual emerging market holdings through time to both an equally weighted and a value-weighted benchmark investment strategy as well as to the IFC Composite return. The difference between the U.S. portfolio weights and the benchmark investment weights represents U.S. investors 'over' or 'under' weighting in these markets. We compute these weights using the accumulated capital flow data from the U.S. Treasury and from Warnock and Cleaver (2002).

The results in Table 3 suggest that U.S. investors' country allocation led to substantially higher returns than all three benchmarks. For example, in the 1990s, the U.S. portfolio return was 11.4% compared to only 4.4% for the value-weighted benchmark of the 16 countries where we have U.S. holdings.[14] It is unlikely that this out performance would be overturned if additional countries were considered. During this period, the broader IFC Composite index returned only 0.1% on average.

The second exercise looks at aggregate investment in emerging markets versus developed markets. We conduct the following experiment. Using holdings data for both developed and emerging markets, we calculate the total U.S. foreign holdings. We determine the proportion of U.S. holdings in emerging markets versus developed markets (not including the U.S.). Using the same countries for which we have holdings data, we then calculate market capitalization weighted indices for both emerging and developed markets. Again, we can determine the proportion of total capitalization in emerging and developed markets.

---

[14] Holdings data are not available for Jordan, Nigeria and Zimbabwe. The revised data from Warnock and Cleaver (2002) also do not include data for Pakistan.

Table 3
Performance of U.S. investments in emerging equity markets

	IFC composite (%)	Value-weighted IFC 16 countries (%)	Equally weighted IFC 16 countries (%)	U.S. country allocation performance (%)
Mean from 1977		12.0	9.1	17.3
Std. dev. from 1977		22.6	19.2	25.9
Mean from 1981		11.2	7.0	14.2
Std. dev. from 1981		23.8	20.1	27.0
Mean from 1985	8.3	14.2	11.6	21.8
Std. dev. from 1985	23.9	25.2	21.1	28.0
Mean from 1990	0.1	4.4	2.6	11.4
Std. dev. from 1990	23.1	24.6	22.1	26.0

Data through December 2001. Mean represents the average compound return which is annualized in percent. Std. dev. is the annualized standard deviation in percent. The 16 country portfolios exclude: Jordan, Nigeria, Pakistan and Zimbabwe where holdings estimates are not available.

The results are in Table 4. The first two columns provide summary statistics for the U.S. holdings weight times both value and equally weighted developed and emerging market indices. That is, the portfolio mimics the actual allocation between emerging and developed markets but uses market indices within these broad groups. In the next two columns, we replace the holdings weights with market capitalization weights. The difference in performance is due to the difference in U.S. allocation to emerging markets relative to developed markets—rather than any particular country selection. That is, the weights, whether holdings-based or capitalization-based are multiplied by the same return indices. The results suggest that there is not much difference between the capitalization weights and the holdings weights in terms of the returns. For example, since 1990, the returns to the holdings-based weights and the market capitalization weights are both 4.4% per annum. The volatility is also very similar. Interestingly, even a fixed 90% weight in developed markets and 10% weight in emerging markets (see the last column) produces similar results. Hence, the overall U.S. allocation performance is quite similar to the performance that would have obtained from market capitalization weighting.

While the previous exercise is necessary for comparison, the analysis does not fairly represent the U.S. investor performance. We use the holdings to determine the aggregate weights in developed and emerging markets and then allocate to passive market capitalization benchmarks for these two groups of markets (that is, we ignore the country selection). But the results in Table 3 have already demonstrated some ability to choose the right countries. The fifth column of Table 4 allows for country selection. We use the weights in developed and emerging markets and create a developed and emerging market benchmark that reflects the country weighting chosen by U.S. investors. Consistent with the emerging market analysis, U.S. investors substantially outperform the market capitalization benchmark. For example, from 1990, the U.S. return is 7.6% per annum compared to a value-weighted benchmark return of 4.4%. The volatility of the U.S. strategy is 130 basis points lower than the volatility of the value weighted benchmark. Indeed, the U.S.

Table 4
Performance of US investment in developed and emerging equity markets

	EM Developed holdings weights times market cap weighted country indices (%)	EM Developed holdings weights times equally weighted country indices (%)	EM Developed market cap weights times market cap weighted country indices (%)	EM Developed market cap weights times equally weighted country indices (%)	EM Developed holdings weights times holdings weighted country indices (%)	MSCI world composite (%)	10% EM 90% Developed (%)
Mean from 1977	13.0	12.1	13.1	12.1	14.4	12.2	12.9
Std. dev. from 1977	16.0	14.7	16.1	14.9	15.4	14.1	15.8
Mean from 1981	11.7	11.5	11.9	11.6	12.5	11.9	11.7
Std. dev. from 1981	16.7	15.3	16.7	15.2	15.7	14.5	16.5
Mean from 1985	12.8	13.6	12.8	13.7	14.3	12.7	12.8
Std. dev. from 1985	17.1	15.8	17.0	15.7	15.8	14.9	16.9
Mean from 1990	4.4	6.7	4.4	6.8	7.6	7.5	4.3
Std. dev. from 1990	16.5	15.0	16.4	14.9	15.1	14.5	16.5

Data through December 2001. Mean represents the average compound return which is annualized in percent. Std. dev. is the annualized standard deviation in percent.

G. Bekaert, C.R. Harvey / Journal of Empirical Finance 10 (2003) 3–55   25

global return is even higher than the MSCI world market composite return—which includes a substantial weight for U.S. equity (which we know has done well over the past 12 years). All in all, the overall investment performance of U.S. investors is much rosier than the country-by-country results, which focus on behavioral biases. Disyatat and Gelos (2001) study the asset allocation of emerging market funds and find that it is not inconsistent with mean-variance optimizing behavior. Their results are similar in spirit to ours. However, Frankel and Schmukler's (2000) study on country funds suggests that the holders of the underlying assets (the portfolio managers) have more information than the country fund holders (the investors).

4. Real effects of financial market integration

From 1980 to 1997, Chile experienced average real GDP growth of 3.8% per year while the Ivory Coast had negative real growth of 2.4% per year. Why? Attempts to explain differences in economic growth across countries have again taken center stage in the macroeconomic literature. Although there is no agreement on what determines economic growth, most of the literature finds evidence of conditional convergence. Poorer countries grow faster than rich countries, once it is taken into account that poor countries tend to have lower long-run per capita GDPs, for example, because of the poor quality of their capital stock (both physical and human). Sachs and Warner (1995) have argued that policy choices, such as respect for property rights and open international trade, are important determinants of the long-run capacity for growth. Williamson (1996) has already argued that fast growth, globalization and convergence are positively correlated from the historical perspective of the end of the 19th century until now. Here, we focus on the real effects of the most recent wave of liberalizations.

There are some interesting differences between the two countries we mentioned. First, the Ivory Coast has a larger trade sector than Chile, but the role of trade openness remains hotly debated. Second, Chile liberalized its capital markets, in particular its equity market, to foreign investment in 1992. After the liberalization, the Chilean economy grew by 6.3% per year.

4.1. Why would financial liberalization affect economic growth?

There are a number of channels through which financial liberalization may affect growth. First, foreign investors, enjoying improved benefits of diversification, will drive up local equity prices permanently, thereby reducing the cost of equity capital. Consequently, the real variable most sensitive to the cost of capital should be real investment. Bekaert and Harvey (2000a), Bekaert, Harvey and Lundblad (2002c), and Henry (2000b) all find that investment increases post equity market liberalization. If this additional investment is efficient, then economic growth should increase. However, in the aftermath of the recent crises, some economists feel that foreign capital has been wasted on frivolous consumption and inefficient investment, undermining the benefits of financial liberalization. Bekaert, Harvey and Lundblad (2002c) show that not only does the ratio of investment to GDP actually increases, but also that the ratio of consumption to GDP does not increase after liberalization. The additional investment appears to be financed by foreign capital as the trade balance significantly decreases.

Second, there is now a large literature on how more developed financial markets and intermediation can enhance growth and how well-functioning equity markets may promote financial development [see, for example, Levine (1991); King and Levine (1993); Levine and Zervos (1996, 1998a,b); Levine et al. (2000)]. Furthermore, foreign investors may also demand better corporate governance to protect their investments, reducing the wedge between the costs of external and internal financial capital, and further increasing investment. There is, in fact, a large and growing literature on how the relaxation of financing constraints improves the allocation of capital and promotes growth [(see Rajan and Zingales (1998); Love [in press]; Wurgler (2000)). Lins et al. (2001)] show that firms in emerging markets listing on the U.S. exchanges are able to relax financing constraints. Since ADRs can be viewed as firm-specific investment liberalizations, this research directly establishes a link between liberalization and financing constraints. Galindo et al. (2001) show that financial liberalization improves the efficiency of capital allocation for individual firms in 12 developing countries. Laeven (2001) has examined the role of banking liberalization in relaxing financing constraints for emerging markets. Forbes (2002) finds that Chilean capital controls significantly increased financial constraints for smaller firms. The interplay between economic growth, financial development and corporate finance is likely to be an important area for future research, and is a topic to which we return to in Section 5.

4.2. Measuring the liberalization effect on economic growth

Bekaert, Harvey and Lundblad (2001) propose a time series panel methodology that fully exploits all the available data to measure how much an equity market liberalization increases growth. They regress future growth (in logarithmic form), averaged over periods ranging from 3 to 7 years, on a number of predetermined determinants of long-run steady state per capita GDP, including secondary school enrollment, the size of the government sector, inflation, trade openness, and on initial GDP (measured in logarithms) in 1980. The right-hand side variables also include an indicator of liberalization based primarily on an analysis of regulatory reforms in Bekaert and Harvey (2000a). To maximize the time-series content in their regressions, they use overlapping data. For example, they use growth from 1981 to 1986 and from 1982 to 1987 in the same regression. They correct for the resulting correlation in the model's residuals in the standard errors. Estimating the model by the Generalized Method of Moments, they can also adjust for the correlation of residuals across countries and different variances of residuals both across countries and over time (heteroskedasticity).

Bekaert, Harvey and Lundblad (2001) consider the liberalization effect in a small sample of 30 emerging and frontier markets as defined by the IFC and found that economic growth increased by 0.7% to 1.4% per year post liberalization.

Bekaert, Harvey and Lundblad (2002c) expand the sample to 95 countries, including to countries that may not even have financial markets, as well as to developed countries. The liberalization effect now has a cross-sectional component that measures the difference in growth between segmented and financially open countries, as well as a temporal

G. Bekaert, C.R. Harvey / Journal of Empirical Finance 10 (2003) 3–55   27

component (countries before and after liberalization). It is this cross-sectional dimension that has been the main focus of the trade openness literature.

Expanding the sample of countries strengthens the results. Taken by itself, financial liberalization leads to an increase in average annual per capita GDP growth of 1.5 to 2.3 percent per year. When they factor in a host of other variables that might also boost economic performance, improvements associated with financial liberalization still remain strong, 0.7% to 1.4% per year. In examining a number of different samples (whose size depends on the availability of control variables), the financial liberalization effect seems robust. They also consider an alternative set of liberalization dates. The main results are robust to these alternative dates. Further, they carry out a Monte Carlo experiment whereby one country's liberalization date is assigned randomly to another country. This allows them to test whether these results primarily reflect overall economic growth in the late 1980s and early 1990s (when the liberalization dates are concentrated). The Monte Carlo exercise shows that the liberalization dates do not really explain economic growth when they are decoupled from the specific country to which they apply, showing that the effect is not related to the world business cycle during these years.

4.3. Intensity and simultaneity problems in measuring real liberalization effects

4.3.1. Intensity of the reforms

There is a heated debate about the effect of capital account openness on economic growth and economic welfare, especially in developing countries [see, for example, Rodrik (1998); Edwards (2001); Arteta et al. (2001). Eichengreen (2001)] suggests that the weak and inconsistent results might be due to the fact that the IMF's AREAER was used as a measure of capital account restrictions. Because this measure does not differentiate between capital account restrictions, it is too coarse to yield meaningful results. When capital account restrictions are more finely measured, as in Quinn (1997), Quinn et al. (2001), and Edwards (2001), there does appear to be a growth effect, although it is fragile (see Arteta et al., 2001). Bekaert, Harvey and Lundblad (2001, 2002c), focusing on equity liberalization only, find a robust growth effect. Moreover, they also employ a measure that captures the intensity of the liberalization by taking the ratio of the market capitalization of the IFCs investable index versus the IFCs global index (see also Bekaert, 1995; Edison and Warnock, 2003) or the number of investable securities compared to the total number of securities. These measures also point to a strong positive growth effect from liberalization.

4.3.2. Financial liberalization and macroeconomic reforms

It is possible that financial liberalizations typically coincide with other more macro-oriented reforms which are the source of increased growth and not the financial liberalizations. However, when Bekaert, Harvey and Lundblad (2002c) add variables capturing macroeconomic reforms, such as inflation, trade openness, fiscal deficits and the black market premium, the liberalization effect remains intact. In some specifications, it does weaken somewhat suggesting that macroeconomic reforms may, indeed, account for some of the liberalization effect.

4.3.3. Financial liberalization and financial market development

Another possibility is that financial liberalization is the natural outcome of a financial development process, and that, consistent with many endogenous growth theories, it is financial development that leads to increased growth. When Bekaert, Harvey and Lundblad (2002c) add a number of banking and stock market development indicators to their regressions, the liberalization effect is reduced only marginally in most specifications but more substantially in a specification excluding the poorest countries. Moreover, they find that financial liberalization predicts additional financial development, but that the decision to liberalize does not seem to be affected by the degree of financial development. Hence, it is likely that one channel through which financial liberalization increases growth is by its impact on financial development.[15]

4.3.4. Functional capital markets

A final possibility acknowledges the imperfection of capital markets, which drives a wedge between the cost of internal and external capital and makes investment sensitive to the presence of internally generated cash flows. Foreigners may demand better corporate governance and financial liberalization, then, may coincide with security law reforms that enforce better corporate governance. Improved corporate governance may lead to lower costs of capital and increased investment (see Dahlquist et al., 2002). To capture this, Bekaert, Harvey and Lundblad (2002c) use a variable constructed by Bhattacharya and Daouk (2002), who trace the implementation and enforcement of insider trading laws in a large number of countries. Bekaert, Harvey and Lundblad (2003a) find that the enforcement of insider trading laws has a positive effect on growth and is statistically significant in three of their four samples. Importantly, it does not diminish the impact of financial liberalizations on economic growth. Another reason to suspect that corporate governance matters for growth prospects is that Bekaert, Harvey and Lundblad (2001) find larger liberalization effects for countries with an Anglo-Saxon legal system, which are thought to have better corporate governance systems (see Shleifer and Vishny, 1997). On a more basic level, it appears that more secure property rights lead to better capital accumulation and higher growth (see Claessens and Laeven, 2003).

4.4. Other real effects of financial liberalization

The positive growth effects are very surprising from the perspective of a large literature focusing on the detrimental effects of financial liberalization. Fig. 9 is taken from a World Bank document on private capital flows to emerging markets. The consensus view is simple. Financial integration naturally leads to increased capital inflows. This, in turn, increases asset prices (either rationally or irrationally), improves liquidity, and triggers a rapid expansion in bank credit. The lending boom then leads to a consumption binge, and potentially a real estate bubble. Apart from the appreciation in asset prices, the real exchange rate appreciates as well, aggravating macroeconomic vulnerability. A weak and inadequately regulated banking sector may aggravate this process by lending for spec-

---

[15] See Beck et al. (2000a,b), Demirgüç-Kunt and Levine (1996), Demirgüç-Kunt and Maksimovic (1996) and Rajan and Zingales (2001), for work on financial development and growth.

G. Bekaert, C.R. Harvey / Journal of Empirical Finance 10 (2003) 3–55   29

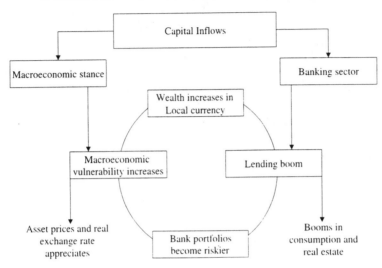

Fig. 9. Capital inflows can lead to a vicious circle that increases economic vulnerabilities. Source: World Bank (1997).

ulative purposes, consumption and frivolous investments, including the fuelling of a construction boom. When inflated assets are used as collateral to justify further borrowing, a boom–bust cycle is clearly in the making. The consensus view appears to be that liberalization dramatically increases financial sector vulnerability in many countries and that a weak banking sector played a large role in both the Mexican and Asian crises.

While this interpretation of how foreign capital can wreak havoc in the real economy of developing countries is widely accepted, it is surprising that empirical evidence for this view is very scarce. Bekaert, and Harvey (2000b) conduct a very simple exercise. First, they find the date at which foreign investors may have become marginal investors in the local equity market by using structural break tests applied to empirical measures of U.S. holdings of local market capitalization (see also, above). Second, they test for changes in a number of real variables, finding a larger trade sector, less long-term country debt, lower inflation and lower foreign exchange volatility. They also test whether the real exchange rate appreciates after the equity flow breaks and find that it does in 9 of 16 countries. However, there is a significant depreciation in four countries. Overall, panel estimates reveal a real appreciation of 5–10% that is statistically significant in about half of the specifications. Hence, the empirical evidence for the real appreciation story is not as strong as typically believed.

Finally, there is a clear sense that increased volatility in financial markets post liberalization (for which the empirical evidence is tenuous) also translates into real variability. Bekaert, Harvey and Lundblad (2002d) test this prediction directly. Investigating a large cross-section of liberalized and segmented markets and using information before and after liberalization for a large number of emerging market economies, they establish that the volatility of consumption and GDP growth did not significantly increase post-liberalization. When they focus on the years preceding the recent Asian crisis, volatility actually decreases, which is especially true for the volatility of consumption

30   *G. Bekaert, C.R. Harvey / Journal of Empirical Finance 10 (2003) 3–55*

growth. When they include the crises years (1997–2000) and focus on a subset of developing economies, this strong result is weakened. However, even with the crises' years, in no case does volatility significantly increase.

Bekaert, Harvey and Lundblad also strip out predictable consumption growth and focus on idiosyncratic consumption growth variability as in Athanasoulis and van Wincoop (2000, 2001).[16] They find that consumption growth volatility mostly significantly decreases post-liberalization. The analysis indicates that the drop in idiosyncratic volatility is economically large. The assertion that globalization has gone too far for emerging economies is not supported by their empirical analysis. Nevertheless, the crises that did occur do suggest that financial integration is best accompanied by vigorous reforms of the domestic financial sector.

5. Contagion

5.1. Currency crises and contagion

In the mid to late 1990s, a number of emerging markets experienced spectacular currency crises, first Mexico in 1994 (the "Tequila Crisis"), then Southeast Asia in 1997 (the "Asian Flu" crisis), and Russia in 1998 (the "Russian Virus" crisis). These crises not only rejuvenated research on speculative currency attacks, but also created a new buzzword: "contagion". We divide this literature roughly into two components. First, there is the work that explores why crises occur in the first place. Second, there is a large body of work on why crises spread. The literature is too vast to cover here adequately. For many more references, we refer to the survey articles of Claessens et al. (2001), Claessens and Forbes (2001), De Bandt and Hartmann (2000) and Krugman (2001). Of course, some articles examine both what causes currency crises and how they spread across countries.

5.1.1. Predictable currency crises?

There are two main explanations for why a currency may experience speculative pressures that can lead to a crisis and devaluation (or the floating of the currency).

The first explanation, building on the seminal work of Krugman (1979) and Flood and Garber (1984), simply argues that if governments follow policies inconsistent with the currency peg, a speculative attack is unavoidable. Speculators will sell the local currency and buy foreign currency. The central bank will lose foreign reserves defending the peg until a critical level of low reserves is reached, at which point the central bank will give up. Whereas initial models focused on expansionary fiscal policies, expansionary monetary policies can also lead to speculative attacks. Of course, this model has the strong implication that speculative attacks should be partially predictable. In fact, growing budget deficits, fast money growth and rising wages and prices should precede speculative attacks. If prices rise while the nominal exchange rate remains unchanged, the real exchange rate will appreciate. Hence, real exchange rate over-valuations should also signal an imminent crisis. The combination of budget deficits and real exchange rate over-

---

[16] Lewis (1996, 2000) provides an analysis of risk sharing in developed markets.

valuation may also lead to excessive current account deficits. Consequently, if Krugman is correct, speculative pressures should be predictable from economic data.

The second explanation recognizes that, sometimes, speculative attacks seem to come out of the blue. That is, the crises are self-fulfilling, caused by "animal spirits", as Keynes once phrased it. A significant group of investors simply starts speculating against the currency, provoking a large capital outflow that leads to the eventual collapse of the exchange rate, thereby validating the negative expectations regarding the survival chances of the peg. The authorities have no choice but to change their policies and accept the devalued currency, even though there are ex ante no fundamental reasons for dropping the peg.[17] The empirical prediction of these models is very strong, in that a currency crisis is essentially unpredictable; government policies will only become expansionary after the currency has been attacked and devalued.

More recent contributions to this literature [see Ozkan and Sutherland, 1998; Bensaid and Jeanne, 1997] introduce interaction with fundamental variables in this class of models. Basically, a deterioration of fundamentals (for instance in unemployment) may make defending the currency more costly (for instance, by raising interest rates) eventually leading to a crisis. However, the actual occurrence and timing of the crisis is still determined by the animal spirits of speculators.

Krugman (2001) distinguishes third-generation models in which currency crises lead to severe short-term real output declines. Inspired by the Asian crisis, these models may stress moral hazard driven excessive investment (Corsetti et al., 1999) or bank runs in a fragile banking system (Chang and Velasco, 2001) as the source of an eventual exchange rate collapse.

Because we have competing theories, with different empirical predictions, it would be nice if the data would provide a clear indication of which theory is correct, and definitively establish whether devaluations are predictable or not. Unfortunately, this is not the case. Although there have been many empirical studies, they differ in the countries and sample periods covered, as well as in the questions addressed. For example, it may be that a currency experiences speculative pressure but that the government successfully defends the currency and that no devaluation occurs. Some studies focus on predicting this kind of speculative pressure, (see, e.g. Eichengreen et al., 1995). One could also distinguish between actual devaluations, and regime transitions, like flotations.

Overall, there appear to be macro-economic signals that predict currency crises. Eichengreen et al. focusing on devaluations in OECD (developed) countries, find that monetary factors, current account deficits and inflation matter, but fiscal deficits do not matter. Past crises matter for current ones indicating that credibility is important. Esquivel and Larrain (2000) include also developing countries in their sample and find that real exchange rate misalignment, high monetary growth rates, low foreign exchange reserves and current account imbalances predict currency crises.

---

[17] Technically, such self-fulfilling attacks are possible in models with multiple equilibriums. There is a stable equilibrium, in which the government follows the right policies consistent with the peg, but there is also another equilibrium in which speculators attack the currency and the government accommodates the lower exchange rate, see, for example, Obstfeld (1986) or Masson (1999). Drazen (1998) provides a different approach in studying political contagion.

Klein and Marion (1997) and Goldfajn and Valdes (1997) also confirm that real exchange rate over-valuation is an important factor in predicting currency crises. Kaminsky et al. (1998) claim that a currency crisis is imminent when variables such as exports, output, the money/international reserves ratio and equity prices cross threshold levels. The empirical results therefore, fall some where between the first two models, there is some but rather weak, predictive power. The evidence on currency crisis predictability seems inconclusive.

5.1.2. Currency crisis contagion

It is from the perspective of the self-fulfilling attack literature that contagion seems easiest to understand. This literature defines contagion, in the context of currency crises, as the effect on the probability of a speculative attack, which stems from attacks on other currencies (see also De Gregorio and Valdés, 2001). When speculators attack one currency successfully, they may well try another. However, it is important to realize that contagion may also be truly rational and, perhaps, predictable, for a variety of reasons. For example, trade is a strong linkage between countries that has an obvious currency component (see Gerlach and Smets, 1994). When the British pound leaves the European Monetary System (EMS) in 1992 and depreciates, but the Irish punt remains in the EMS and does not devalue, it is likely that the Irish punt experiences a real exchange rate appreciation relative to the pound (unless inflation rapidly reacts to the changes in exchange rates, which, in 1992, it did not). Hence, the real exchange rate appreciation adversely affects the competitive position of Irish exporters, eventually causing economic and political pressure to devalue. A related channel of apparent contagion is an income effect—reduced growth and lower income levels after a crisis reduce the demand for imports from other countries. A third channel is the "wake up call". It may be that the second country experienced similar negative macroeconomic conditions or followed similar inconsistent policies.

In addition to these channels, Forbes (2000) analyzes two other channels by which crises spread: a credit crunch (banks affected by a crisis in one country reduce lending to other countries) and a forced-portfolio recomposition or liquidity effect (investors that suffer losses from a crisis in one country sell assets in other countries). Forbes uses data from over 10,000 firms to test for the relative importance of each of these five channels of "contagion" during the Asian and Russian crises and finds that the first two channels (based largely on trade) are the most important.

Esquivel and Larrain (2000) document some evidence of regional contagion, in that a currency is more likely to devalue if a neighboring country has experienced a devaluation even controlling for other determinants of devaluation. Eichengreen et al. (1996) also find that contagion is primarily due to trade links. More research seems warranted on the channels through which contagion may occur.

5.2. Contagion and equity markets

Contagion in equity markets refers to the notion that markets move more closely together during periods of crisis. A first problem in the literature is then to define what constitutes a crisis, especially given the extreme volatility of many emerging equity markets. Consider the simple exercise in Table 5 that details the five most severe negative returns in 17 emerging markets. In 9 of 17 markets, August 1998 (Russian default) was among the one of the five poorest performing months. For the Asian Crisis of July 1997 to May 1998, Indonesia, Korea, Malaysia and Thailand each have four representatives in the five worst returns during these months. On the other hand, none of the Latin American countries have any of their five worst return months during the Asian Crisis. Finally, the Mexican crisis of December 1994 shows up in a large negative return for Mexico. Interestingly, this month does not appear in any of the other Latin American or Asian worst return months. It should also be noted that October 1987 which is the date of a sharp

Table 5
The five largest negative log returns

	Largest	2nd largest	3rd largest	4th largest	5th largest
Argentina	Jul-89	Jan-90	Apr-81	Apr-84	Jan-82
	− 104.8%	− 77.6%	− 59.8%	− 52.7%	− 46.2%
Brazil	Mar-90	Jun-89	**Aug-98**	Jun-92	Jan-99
	− 84.2%	− 56.3%	**− 46.7%**	− 36.7%	− 34.5%
Chile	Jan-83	**Aug-98**	Sep-81	Oct-87	Sep-84
	− 32.9%	**− 30.9%**	− 21.2%	− 21.2%	− 18.6%
Colombia	**Aug-98**	Jan-99	Feb-92	Jun-99	May-00
	− 22.2%	− 20.5%	− 19.2%	− 19.0%	− 15.2%
Greece	Jan-88	**Aug-98**	Jan-83	Oct-92	Oct-85
	− 36.8%	**− 27.6%**	− 20.5%	− 18.9%	− 18.5%
India	May-92	Mar-93	Mar-01	Nov-86	Sep-01
	− 27.9%	− 19.6%	− 19.0%	− 17.6%	− 16.6%
Indonesia	**Aug-97**	**May-98**	**Dec-97**	**Jan-98**	Sep-98
	− 51.2%	**− 49.0%**	**− 44.8%**	**− 43.0%**	− 27.6%
Korea	**Dec-97**	**Oct-97**	**Nov-97**	**May-98**	Oct-00
	− 40.9%	**− 35.3%**	**− 32.7%**	**− 26.4%**	− 23.3%
Malaysia	**Aug-97**	Oct-87	**Aug-98**	**Nov-97**	**Jun-98**
	− 37.4%	− 36.5%	**− 30.9%**	**− 27.2%**	**− 24.4%**
Mexico	Nov-87	Dec-82	Oct-87	**Dec-94**	**Aug-98**
	− 89.9%	− 62.8%	− 55.3%	**− 43.1%**	**− 41.0%**
Pakistan	May-98	Oct-98	Jun-98	May-00	Jul-96
	− 43.3%	− 30.8%	− 29.1%	− 24.3%	− 17.5%
Philippines	Sep-90	**Aug-98**	**Aug-97**	Sep-87	Oct-00
	− 34.7%	**− 31.9%**	**− 28.2%**	− 27.5%	− 22.1%
Portugal	Nov-87	Dec-87	Oct-87	Feb-88	Oct-92
	− 34.7%	− 27.8%	− 23.2%	− 16.0%	− 15.3%
Taiwan	Oct-87	Aug-90	Jun-90	Oct-88	Dec-88
	− 43.9%	− 41.8%	− 30.7%	− 28.8%	− 28.7%
Thailand	Oct-87	**Aug-97**	**Oct-97**	**May-98**	**Dec-97**
	− 41.3%	**− 39.3%**	**− 38.1%**	**− 33.1%**	**− 29.1%**
Turkey	**Aug-98**	Feb-01	Nov-00	Sep-01	Nov-90
	− 52.2%	− 52.0%	− 43.2%	− 40.6%	− 37.8%
Venezuela	Dec-85	Nov-95	**Aug-98**	Mar-92	Jun-94
	− 68.9%	− 62.0%	**− 50.5%**	− 30.3%	− 29.2%
Composite	**Aug-98**	Oct-87	Aug-90	Sep-01	**Oct-97**
	− 29.3%	− 28.9%	− 19.0%	− 16.8%	**− 16.5%**

Bolded dates and log returns represent crisis periods.

drop in the U.S. stock market, shows up in the list for Mexico, Portugal, Taiwan and Thailand.[18]

The analysis in Table 5 is related to the recent work of Bae et al. (in press) who, using daily returns data in a number of emerging markets, look for the coincidences of extreme movements. Interestingly, they attempt to characterize (predict) the degree of coincidence using fundamental economic variables such as interest rates, exchange rate changes and conditional volatility (also see Karolyi and Stulz (1996) and Hartmann et al., 2001). The coincidence of extreme equity return movements may be one definition of contagion but Forbes and Rigobon (2002) declare, "there is no consensus on exactly what constitutes contagion or how it should be defined." Rigobon (in press) states, "paradoxically, ... there is no accordance on what contagion means."

Importantly, contagion is not simply increased correlation during a crisis period. From a completely statistical perspective, one would expect higher correlations during periods of high volatility.[19] Forbes and Rigobon (2002) present a statistical correction for this conditioning bias and argue that there was no contagion during the three most recent crises.[20]

Bekaert, Harvey and Ng (2003b) and Tang (2002) define contagion as excess correlation—correlation over and above what one would expect from economic funda-mentals and take an asset pricing perspective to studying contagion. For a given factor model, increased correlation is expected if the volatility of a factor increases. The size of the increased correlation will depend on the factor loadings. Contagion, therefore, is simply defined by the correlation of the model residuals. Tang restricts the underlying asset pricing model to a world capital asset pricing model (CAPM) whereas Bekaert et al. examine a more general factor model.

By defining the factor model, they effectively take a stand on the global, regional and country specific fundamentals as well as the mechanism that transfers fundamentals into correlation. Concretely, they apply a two-factor model with time-varying loadings to "small" stock markets in three different regions, Europe, Southeast Asia and Latin America. The two factors are the U.S. equity market return and a regional equity portfolio return. Their framework nests three models: a world capital asset pricing model (CAPM), a world CAPM with the U.S. equity return as the benchmark asset and a regional CAPM with a regional portfolio as the benchmark. They also add local factors to allow for the possibility of segmented markets. If the countries in a particular region are globally integrated for most of the sample period, but suddenly see their intra-regional correlations rise dramatically during a regional crisis, their contagion test would reject the null hypothesis of no contagion. On the other hand, if these countries expected returns are not well described by a global CAPM, but rather by a regional CAPM, the increased correlations may simply be a consequence of increased factor volatility.

---

[18] There is also some evidence that equity markets anticipate some currency crises (see Harvey and Roper, 1999; Becker et al., 2000; Glen, 2002).

[19] See Stambaugh (1995), Boyer et al. (1999), Loretan and English (2000) Forbes and Rigobon (2002) and early work by Pindyck and Rotemberg (1990, 1993). Work linking news, volatility and correlation includes King and Wadhwani (1990), Hamao et al. (1990) and King et al. (1994).

[20] As Forbes and Rigobon (2002) note, their methodology only works under a restrictive set of circumstances. An alternative is the test in Rigobon (in press (a)).

G. Bekaert, C.R. Harvey / Journal of Empirical Finance 10 (2003) 3–55

Equity return volatilities in the Bekaert, Harvey and Ng (2003b) model follow univariate generalized autoregressive conditional heteroskedasticity (GARCH) processes with asymmetry as in Bekaert, and Harvey (1997) and Ng (2000). Hence, negative news regarding the world or regional market may increase the volatility of the factor more than positive news and hence lead to increased correlations between stock markets.[21] Moreover, their model incorporates time-varying betas where the betas are influenced by trade patterns as in Chen and Zhang (1997). The results in Bekaert, Harvey and Ng (2003b) indicate the presence of contagion around the SouthEast Asian crisis, but not during the Mexican crisis. This contagion is not limited to SouthEast Asian, but extends to Latin America. These conclusions are broadly consistent with Rigobon (in press (b)) and Dungey and Martin (2001) who use a different methodology.

Finally, there are a number of recent papers that link contagion to liquidity and financial frictions (see Calvo, 1999; Calvo and Mendoza, 2000a,b; Kodres and Pritsker, 2002; Rigobon, 2002b; Yuan, 2002). Kyle and Xiong (2001) show how wealth effects can lead to contagion.

6. Other important issues

6.1. Corporate finance

Corporations in emerging markets provide an ideal testing ground for some important theories in corporate finance. For example, Lombardo and Pagano (2000) examine how legal institutions affect the return on equity. The cross-sectional variation in such institutions is particularly large for emerging markets. Similarly, it is often argued that the existence of a sufficient amount of debt helps mitigate the agency problems that arise as a result of the separation of ownership and control. In a number of emerging markets, the existence of multilevel ownership provides an environment, where there is an acute separation of cash flow and voting rights. Given the possibility of severe agency problems, emerging markets provide an ideal venue to test these theories. That is, powerful tests of these theories can be conducted in samples that have large variation in agency problems.

In order to compete in world capital markets, a number of countries are grappling with setting rules or formal laws with respect to corporate governance. There is a growing realization that inadequate corporate governance mechanisms will increase the cost of equity capital for emerging market corporations as they find it more difficult to obtain equity investors.

Overall, research has characterized the degree of external corporate governance in emerging markets as weak (Johnson et al. (2000b); Denis and Connell, 2002; Klapper and Love, 2002). Both shareholder rights and the legal enforcement of the rights that do exist are generally lacking in emerging markets (La Porta et al., 1998), and the use of corporate

---

[21] Longin and Solnik (1995) report an increase in cross-country correlation during volatile periods. Other empirical studies (for example, Erb et al., 1994; De Santis and Gerard, 1997) find different correlations in up and down markets while Longin and Solnik (2001), Ang and Bekaert (2002) and Das and Uppal (2001) document higher correlations in bear markets. Erb et al. (1995) document higher correlations during U.S. recessions.

takeovers as a disciplining mechanism is almost nonexistent. Further, as mentioned above, it is frequently the case that insiders possess control rights in excess of their proportional ownership. This is usually achieved through pyramid structures in which one firm is controlled by another firm, which may itself be controlled by some other entity, and so forth (Shleifer and Vishny, 1997; La Porta et al., 1998, 1999; Claessens et al., 2000; Lins, 2003). Finally, irrespective of pyramid structures, managers of emerging market firms sometimes issue and own shares with superior voting rights to achieve control rights that exceed their cash flow rights in the firm (Nenova, in press; Lins, 2003). Taken together, the net result is that a great number of firms in emerging markets have managers who possess control rights that exceed their cash flow rights in the firm, which, fundamentally, gives rise to potentially extreme managerial agency problems.

When external country-level corporate governance is weak, it is possible that internal governance in the form of concentrated ownership will step in to fill the void (see Himmelberg et al., 2002). Lins (2003) investigates whether management ownership structures and large non-management blockholders are related to firm value across a sample of 143 firms from 18 emerging markets. He finds that firm values are lower when a management group's control rights exceed its cash flow rights. Lins also finds that large non-management control rights blockholdings are positively related to firm value. Both of these effects are significantly more pronounced in countries with low shareholder protection. One interpretation of these results is that, in emerging markets, large non-management blockholders can act as a partial substitute for missing institutional governance mechanisms.

Lemmon and Lins (2003) use a sample of 800 firms in eight East Asian emerging markets to study the effect of ownership structure on value during the region's financial crisis. The crisis negatively impacted firms' investment opportunities, raising the incentives of controlling shareholders to expropriate minority investors. Further, because the crisis was for the most part unanticipated, it provides a "natural experiment" for the study of ownership and shareholder value that is less subject to endogeneity concerns. During the crisis, cumulative stock returns of firms in which managers have high levels of control rights, but have separated their control and cash flow ownership, are 10 to 20 percentage points lower than those of other firms. The evidence is consistent with the view that ownership structure plays an important role in determining the incentives of insiders to expropriate minority shareholders.

A related issue is the relation between the ownership structure and local authority. Johnson and Mitton (2003) examine Malaysian firms before and after the imposition of capital controls and find that firms with stronger ties to Prime Minister Mahatir benefited from the imposition of the capital controls. They interpret this as evidence that the capital controls provided a screen behind which favorable firms could be supported, as evidence of crony capitalism.

Claessens et al. (2003) examine the incidence of bankruptcy filings during the Asian crisis. They find after controlling for firm characteristics that bank-owned or group-affiliated firms were much less likely to file for bankruptcy. They also find that those countries with stronger creditor rights and better judicial systems have increased likelihood of bankruptcy filings. Johnson et al. (2000a) show that countries with lower quality corporate governance were hit harder during the Asian crisis.

Gibson (2000) examines the relation between CEO turnover and firm performance in emerging markets. In general, he finds a high turnover after poor performance, which is consistent with good corporate governance. However, when he isolates firms with a large domestic shareholder, such as a group-affiliated firm, there is no relation between performance and CEO turnover. This suggests that these ownership structures impede good corporate governance in emerging markets.

Lins and Servaes (2002) use a sample of over 1000 firms from seven emerging markets to study the effect of corporate diversification on firm value. They find that diversified firms trade at a discount of approximately 7% to single-segment firms. From a corporate governance perspective, Lins and Servaes find a discount only for those firms that are part of industrial groups, and for diversified firms with management ownership concentration between 10% and 30%. Further, the discount is most severe when management control rights substantially exceed management cash flow rights. Their results do not support internal capital market efficiency in economies with severe capital market imperfections.

Since management control and a separation of management ownership and control are associated with lower firm value in emerging markets, a question arises as to whether alternative external firm-level governance mechanisms exist that might improve the situation for minority shareholders. Several alternate governance mechanisms have the potential to lessen real or perceived agency problems between a firm's controlling shareholders and managers and its minority shareholders. Harvey et al. (2002) examine whether debt contracts can alleviate problems with potentially misaligned incentives that result when managers of emerging market firms have control rights in excess of their proportional ownership. Harvey et al. provide evidence that higher debt levels lessen the loss in value attributed to these managerial agency problems. When the authors investigate specific debt issues, they find that internationally syndicated term loans, which arguably provide the highest degree of firm-level monitoring, enhance value the most when issued by firms with high levels of expected managerial agency problems.[22]

Another potential firm-level governance mechanism that has received considerable research attention is a firm's decision to issue a cross-listed security, such as an (ADR). For firms in emerging markets and those with poor external governance environments, this allows the firm to "opt in" to a better external governance regime and to commit to a higher level of disclosure, both of which should increase shareholder value. Along this line of reasoning, Doidge et al. (2002) present evidence that non-U.S. firms with exchange-listed ADRs have higher Tobin's Q values and that this effect is most pronounced for firms from countries with the worst investor rights. Lang et al. (2002a) find that firms from emerging markets or non-English legal origin countries that have -listed ADRs show a greater improvement in their information environment (as measured by stock market analyst coverage and analyst forecast accuracy) than do developed markets firms with English legal origins that have exchange-listed ADRs. Lang et al. also show that

---

[22] Booth et al. (2001) find that the choice of debt ratios in emerging markets is more sensitive to country-specific factors than in developed markets. This is consistent with the existence of greater information asymmetries in developing markets. Demirgüç-Kunt and Maksimovic (1996) examine the link between firm financing and stock market development.

improvements in the information environment for firms with listed ADRs are positively related to firm valuations.

Lins et al. (2001) test directly whether improved access to capital is an important motivation for emerging market firms to issue an ADR. They find that, following a U.S. listing, the sensitivity of investment to free cash flow decreases significantly for emerging market firms, but does not change for developed market firms. Also, emerging market firms explicitly mention a need for capital in their filing documentation and annual reports more frequently than do developed market firms, whereas, in the post-ADR period, emerging market firms tout their liquidity rather than a need for capital access. Further, Lins et al. find that the increase in access to external capital markets following a U.S. listing is more pronounced for firms from emerging markets. Overall, these findings suggest that greater access to external capital markets is an important benefit of the U.S. stock market listing, especially for emerging market firms.

Research analysts have the potential to increase the scrutiny of controlling management groups endowed with private benefits of control, which should improve firm values. Controlling managers have incentives to hide information from the investing public in order to facilitate consumption of these private control benefits. Lang et al. (2002b) find that analyst coverage positively impacts Tobin's Q values and that there is an incremental valuation benefit to additional analysts coverage when the management/family group controls a firm. Further, these benefits of analysts' coverage are significantly more pronounced for firms from countries with poor shareholder rights and with non-English origin legal systems.

The private benefits of control are also studied in Dyck and Zingales (2002a). They find that the private benefits of control are higher when the buyer comes from a country that protects investors less (and, thus, is more willing or able to extract private benefits). In countries where private benefits of control are larger capital markets that are less developed, ownership is more concentrated, and privatizations are less likely to take place as public offerings. Dyck and Zingales (2002a,b) show that one important mechanism to minimize the negative impact of the private benefit of control and to enforce good corporate governance is the local media (as represented by the ratio of newspaper circulation to total population).

6.2. Fixed income

Emerging market equities have garnered a great deal more research attention than emerging market bonds. This is probably due to the availability of equity data versus bond data.[23] Although much of the research on emerging market bonds applies only to the last 15 years, global bond investing has a long and storied history. Through the First World War, London was the center of global finance. Indeed, the U. S. was for much of the 19th century considered as an emerging market. Not only was it emerging, but it also went through periodic eras of default. According to Chernow (1990), "During the depression of

---

[23] A historical analysis of the U.S. as an emerging market is found in Rousseau and Sylla (1999). Rousseau and Sylla (2001) examine the financial development of a number of countries.

the 1840s—a decade dubbed the Hungry Forties—state debt plunged to 50 cents on the dollar. The worst came when five American states—Pennsylvania, Mississippi, Indiana, Arkansas and Michigan—and the Florida Territory defaulted on their interest payments."

Latin American lending had already become quite widespread in the 19th century. Chernow states that "...as early as 1825 nearly every borrower in Latin America had defaulted on interest payments. In the 19th century, South America was already known for wild borrowing sprees, followed by waves of default." By the 1920s, foreign lending in the U. S. had once again become widespread. In fact, the sale of repackaged foreign bonds to individual investors, and the subsequent losses, was an impetus to the pasage of the Glass-Steagall Act in 1933, (see Chernow, 1990).

Erb et al. (2000) provide a historical analysis of emerging market bonds, using data from 1859 for Argentina, Brazil and the U.S. They find a similar level of volatility in emerging market bond and equity returns. Indeed, their correlation analysis (using more recent data) suggests that the correlation between emerging market bond returns and emerging market equity returns is over 0.70. Perhaps this is not surprising. Emerging market bonds are high-risk bonds, and often these types of bonds act like equity.

Considerable theoretical and empirical research has focused on understanding sovereign yield spreads (the spread between foreign government bond yields denominated in U.S. dollars and a similar maturity U.S. Treasury bond). The first branch of research tries to capture the strategic aspects of when a country should borrow and default (see Eaton and Gersovitz, 1981; Bulow and Rogoff, 1989a,b; Chowdhry, 1991). For example, the Bulow and Rogoff (1989b) model suggest that the threat of political and economic sanctions enforces the debt contracts between developing and developed nations. However, these models do not take a stand on what the sovereign credit spread should be. A second branch of research is cast in continuous-time, and focus on the likelihood of default and the determination of credit spreads in particular countries (see Kuilatilaka and Marcus, 1987; Claessens and Pennachi, 1996; Gibson and Sundaresan, 2001; Duffie et al., 2003). Gibson and Sundaresan derive a relation between sovereign yield spreads and the cost of sanctions. They show that the ability to punish the sovereign borrower leads to a lower sovereign spread. Duffie et al. show how to incorporate default, restructuring as well as illiquidity into a model of sovereign yield spreads. The final branch of research examines the cross-sectional relationship between fundamental variables in the economy and the size of the sovereign spreads (see Eichengreen and Mody, 2000; Cantor and Packer, 1996; Erb et al., 1997) For example, Erb et al. show that country risk ratings are positively associated with real per capita GDP, real per capita GDP growth, and the investment to GDP ratio. They find that ratings are negatively related to population growth. Given the strong negative correlation between ratings and sovereign spreads, these models provide a way to link the fundamental characteristics of an economy to the sovereign spread.

6.3. Market microstructure

The particular trading arrangements in an equity market may directly affect two key functions of that counytry's secondary stock market: price discovery, and liquidity. First, the trading process should lead to "fair" and correct prices; in other words, no investor should be able to manipulate market prices in his or her favor. Second, trading should occur at a, low transaction cost, high speed, and large quantities should trade without affecting the price. These issues are the topic of the field of market microstructure. It is clear that the large cross-sectional heterogeneity of emerging markets and the formidable changes they have undergone over time should make them an interesting laboratory for market microstructure research.

While a number of academics have looked at the issue of market segmentation using detailed data from one country (see, for example, Domowitz et al., 1997; Bailey and Chung, 1995 for Mexico, and Bailey and Jagtiani, 1994 for Thailand), there is surprisingly little genuine microstructure research on emerging markets, perhaps because accurate and detailed data are difficult to obtain. There are a few exceptions though, which we now discuss.

Domowitz et al. (1998) use detailed data on Mexican stocks to investigate whether the cross-listing of securities, although beneficial from a market integration perspective, may lead to order flow migration to the more liquid international (often US) market. Cho et al. (2003) use the Taiwanese market, with its unique price limits, to test the well-known magnet effect. The magnet effect postulates that prices accelerate towards the limits when getting closer to them. Cho et al. find strong evidence of a magnet, effect especially for the ceiling price.

Eventually, microstructure research is especially interested in transaction costs and liquidity, which differ greatly across emerging markets (see Glen, 2000 for an introduction to microstructure in emerging markets). Ghysels and Cherkaoui (2003) provide a detailed study of the Casablanca Stock Exchange in Morocco (CSE). The CSE is a typical emerging financial market that has gone through momentous change in the last 10 years. In the 1980s, the CSE in many ways a backwater. It was a state institution, on which very few stocks were listed and with almost no participation of individual investors. Institutional investors would often trade on the large "upstairs". The upstairs market was a negotiated market where trades were based on mutual agreements, and where transactions were established under circumstances that were neither transparent nor standardized. During this period, the number of Moroccan shareholders was probably less than 10,000. The exchange was extremely illiquid and most stocks did not trade for weeks. In 1989, Morocco announced an ambitious privatization and economic liberalization program, which also included financial market reforms that would greatly alter the operation of the stock exchange starting in 1993. The CSE was both privatized and reformed. The market reforms created a dealer/market maker structure under which more disclosure was required from both listing companies and market makers. Whereas Morocco never prevented foreign investors from buying Moroccan stock, CSE's pre-reform the archaic structure and low trading volume effectively kept foreigners from participating in the market. The new reforms changed this, and in 1996, the CSE was included in the IFC Emerging Market database. Even before then, the number of individual investors had increased considerably, reaching 300,000 in 1996. These reforms had a profound effect on the stock market. Trading volume and liquidity exploded. Finally, on December 17, 1996, the CSE adopted the screen-driven trading system used by the Bourse de Paris.

It is generally believed that such microstructural changes should greatly affect the quality of the market, which can best be approximated by the cost of trading. There is no doubt that reforms immediately increased turnover and liquidity in the Moroccan Market,

G. Bekaert, C.R. Harvey / Journal of Empirical Finance 10 (2003) 3–55   41

but did that also mean lower trading costs for the average trader on the market? Unfortunately, we do not have bid-ask spread data for the CSE. However, Ghysels and Cherkaoui (2003) obtained transactions data before and after the reforms for several stocks, and tried to infer the trading costs based on these data. Surprisingly, they find that, at least up until 1996, trading costs increased after the reforms. There are multiple interpretations of these results. First, on an absolute basis, although liquidity improved, the CSE remained a very thin, illiquid market with little trading. Second, foreign investors (especially new arrivals) may be among the least informed market participants. Possibly, CSE dealers possessed a tremendous amount of market power relative to foreign traders. This would imply that the high spreads were not a competitive equilibrium phenomenon, but rather indicated a fleecing opportunity, which disappeared, as foreign investors became more informed and the market developed. A third possibility is that the model used by Ghysels and Cherkaoui mis-estimates true trading costs. On the other hand, if the results are accurate a few important lessons may be drawn from this detailed study. First, jumps in turnover and trading need not necessarily be associated with lower trading costs (although they typically are). Second, microstructure reforms may be an important signal to foreign investors of the local stock exchange's genuine integration into the world financial markets. However, by themselves, such reforms do not seem to contribute to bringing down the effective costs of trading. Only after screen-driven trading was introduced in late 1996 did transaction costs CSE fall (see Derrabi et al., 2000).

Obtaining estimates of liquidity and transaction costs is important because: illiquid assets and assets with high transaction costs trade at low prices, relative to their expected cash flows. It follows that liquidity and trading costs may contribute both to the average equity premium in stocks and to the time-variation in expected returns if there is systematic variation in liquidity. Some recent research, most notably Amihud (2002) and Jones (2001), attempts to quantify the role of liquidity in U.S. expected stock returns. Using 100 years of annual data, Jones finds that bid-ask spreads and turnover predict U.S. stock returns one period ahead, whereas the decline in transaction costs may have contributed to a fall of about 1% in the equity premium. Amihud (2002), using a 1964–1997 NYSE sample, finds that expected market illiquidity has a positive effect on the ex ante excess return and unexpected illiquidity has a negative effect on the contemporaneous stock return.

Liquidity effects may be particularly acute in emerging markets. In a survey by Chuhan (1992), poor liquidity was mentioned as one of the main reasons for foreign institutional investors not investing in emerging markets. If the liquidity premium is an important feature of the data, emerging markets should yield particularly powerful tests and useful independent evidence. Moreover, the recent equity market liberalizations provide an additional verification of the importance of liquidity for expected returns, since, all else equal (including the price of liquidity risk), the importance of liquidity for expected returns should decline post liberalization. This is important, since when focusing on the U.S. alone, the finding of expected return variation due to liquidity can always be ascribed to an omitted variable correlated with liquidity. Another important question is whether improved liquidity contributes to the decline in the cost of capital post-liberalization which is documented by Bekaert and Harvey (2000a) and Henry (2000a).

Bekaert, Harvey and Lundblad (2002e) address these questions in a recent article using a measure that relies on the incidence of observed zero daily returns in these markets. Lesmond et al. (1999) and Lesmond (2002) argue that if the value of an information signal is insufficient to outweigh associated transaction costs, market participants will elect not to trade, resulting in an observed zero return. They propose zero returns as evidence of transaction costs. Using a simple empirical pricing model and limited dependent variable estimation techniques, they infer estimates of transaction and price impact costs. Lesmond (2002) applies this indirect approach to estimate the costs of equity trading in emerging markets. The advantage of this measure is that it requires only a time-series of daily equity returns.

Bekaert, Harvey and Lundblad (2002e) use the zero return measure as a proxy for illiquidity. They find that higher illiquidity is indeed associated with higher expected returns. Whereas liberalization overall improves liquidity, its effect on the relation between illiquidity and expected returns is somewhat inconsistent. However, it is invariably the case that the effect of illiquidity on expected returns is larger post-liberalization.

6.4. Stock selection

Most work on emerging market stock returns has focused on the IFC global index of IFC investible indices. However, there are a few papers that examine the characteristics of individual securities.

Stock selection is complicated by potentially extreme information asymmetry problems. Bhattacharya et al. (2000) provide evidence that Mexican stocks do not react contemporaneously to the usual types of news announcements. However, they find that the stocks react before such announcements, which is consistent with information leakage. In addition, they find that the price reaction of shares traded by foreigners lag those traded by nationals. This is consistent with information asymmetry.[24]

Fama and French (1998) collect information on size, book to market value, and price earnings ratios for 16 emerging markets. They find strong evidence of a value premium in these markets in both in-sample and out-of-sample tests. Rouwenhorst (1999) examines the characteristics of over 1700 firms in 20 emerging markets and finds that the cross-section of stock returns in emerging markets is driven by factors that also drive the cross-section in developed markets: size, momentum, and value.

Achour et al. (1999) examine a comprehensive list of 27 firm-specific factors to try to explain the cross-section of returns in three representative emerging markets. In contrast to previous work, Achour et al. examine both ex post and expectational firm characteristics. They find that measures, such as prospective earnings to price ratios, and analyst revision ratios, can differentiate between high and low expected return securities. While they document that some characteristics impact each market, there are considerable asymmetries across different markets. In addition, Achour et al. show that traditional measures of risk are unable to account for the differences in expected returns.

Van Der Hart et al. (2003) provide the most comprehensive analysis of individual stock returns in emerging markets by studying almost 3000 securities in 32 countries. Similar to

[24] Also see Choe et al. (2002) and Frankel and Schmukler (2000).

Achour et al. (1999), Van Der Hart et al. look at both ex post and expectational characteristics. They confirm the profitability of strategies based on value and momentum and show that the returns cannot be explained with traditional asset pricing models. In contrast to previous work, Van Der Hart et al. examine the ability to implement these strategies. They show that the profitability of these strategies is robust to the assumed transactions cost of a large institutional investor.

6.5. Privatization

In most emerging markets, privatization was intended to increase the productivity of state-owned economic enterprises (SOEs), and to help reduce government budget deficits. In some cases, governments actively sought to promote capital market development through privatization. Many governments intended to create a class of people with a stake in the new economy, therby making it more difficult for political changes to be reversed. Regardless of the goal, privatization was not initiated, in order to divest fully the government's interest in the real economy. Nevertheless, even the partial divestment under consideration was economically substantial.

Consider the evidence presented in Table 6. Between 1978 and 1991, SOEs in emerging markets controlled a significant proportion of (GDP). In our sample of 16

Table 6
The role of state-owned enterprises in emerging economies (1978–1991)

Country	SOE economic activity as % of GDP (1978–1991)[a]	Trade as % of GDP (1978–1991)[b]	Stock market capitalization as % of GDP (1978–1991)[c]
Argentina	4.7	15.4	1.8
Brazil	6.5	15.7	3.0
Chile	13.3	42.6	15.6
China	n.a.	n.a.	n.a.
Colombia	6.8	24.7	2.5
India	12.1	12.6	2.3
Indonesia	14.8	38.9	5.0
Jordan	n.a.	72.9	25.5
Malaysia	17.0	129.1	51.0
Mexico	11.6	21.5	4.3
Pakistan	10.3	29.4	2.5
Philippines	1.9	39.9	7.7
Portugal	18.2	53.0	8.4
Thailand	5.4	49.6	6.3
Turkey	7.5	22.2	3.5
Venezuela	23.1	40.9	4.0
Latin American average	11.0	26.8	5.2
Asian average	9.9	46.0	11.2
Average	10.9	40.6	9.6
United States[a]	1.2		

[a] Bureaucrats in Business: The Economics and Politics of Government Ownership (1995).
[b] Time series average of data available from World Development Indicators 1999 CDROM.
[c] Time series average of data available from IFC Emerging Markets Database. Sample size dependent upon data availability.

emerging economies, SOEs contributed to 10.9% of GDP during this time period. SOEs in developed economies contributed significantly less, 7.8%. Individual countries displayed significant cross-sectional variation in terms of the size of each country's SOE economic activity as a percent of GDP. For example, in the Philippines this figure was quite low, averaging 1.9% over the 14-year period. At the other extreme, SOEs in Venezuela contributed to just over 23% of GDP during the same period. Regardless of the country in question, the transfer of resources considered under any privatization program amounts to a non-trivial proportion of the wealth of the economy. Despite its importance, we provide only a short summary of the vast research on the topic because there already exists an extensive and excellent survey see Megginson and Netter (2001).

Privatization programs impact emerging capital markets through various mechanisms. For instance, share issued privatizations (SIPs) increase the market capitalization and the value traded on local exchanges. Moreover, SIPs can change the investment opportunity set of portfolio investors. Public offers of SOEs whose cash flows are not perfectly correlated with pre-existing companies help investors to achieve gains through diversification. Under this scenario, SIPs may help to lower the risk premium investors require for holding the market portfolio of publicly traded equity.

Other methods of privatization, including the direct sale of former SOEs, the direct sale of an SOE assets, or concessions of public sector monopolies, alter the dynamics of local capital markets in less obvious ways. Consider the direct sale of an SOE to a private investor. This sale does not increase the market capitalization or value traded on the local exchange. However, the sale may alter the real investment opportunity set of the private investor.

As viewed from this perspective, all forms of privatization can impact local capital market dynamics. The common component of privatization that impacts capital markets is the transfer of productive resources from the public sector to the private sector. This transfer may allow investors to achieve benefits through diversification and may effect the cost of capital in emerging markets.

Even if private investors do not benefit from the transfer of resources, i.e. their investment opportunity set does not change, privatization programs may still influence capital markets. Privatization programs can help the government signal its commitment to free market policies (see also Perotti, 1995; Biais and Perotti, 2002). For most emerging market governments, the implementation of a privatization program reverses decades of state-led economic development. Successful privatization of politically sensitive industries may convince investors to reduce the ex ante perceived risk of government interference in investment decisions and expropriation of productive assets. As a result of sustained privatization efforts, the sovereign risk premium inherent in the governments fixed income liabilities may be reduced. As this chain of events ripples through the economy, local market entrepreneurs eventually benefit in their ability to obtain debt financing at lower cost.

Bekaert, Harvey and Roper (2002f) find that the privatization of SOEs has increased local stock market capitalization and the value traded on these exchanges. They also find that privatization leads to a reduction in the dividend yield, which likely indicates a reduction in the cost of capital.

G. Bekaert, C.R. Harvey / Journal of Empirical Finance 10 (2003) 3–55   45

7. Conclusion

Most of our research on emerging equity markets has tried to draw inferences from a somewhat reluctant data set. Emerging market returns are highly non-normal (see Bekaert, Erb, Harvey and Viskanta, 1998; Susmel, 2001) and highly volatile, and the samples are short. Moreover, a dominating characteristic of the data is a potentially gradual, structural break. Although it is generally difficult to make inferences in such a setting, a few robust findings emerge: the liberalization process has led to a very small increase in correlations with the world market and a small decrease in dividend yields. This decrease could represent a decrease in the cost of capital or an improvement in growth opportunities; Bekaert, Harvey and Lundblad (2001, 2002c) find that economic growth increases post liberalization by about 1% per year on average over a 5-year period. Bekaert and Harvey (2000a), Henry (2000a), and Bekaert, Harvey and Lundblad (2002c) all find that aggregate investment increases significantly after liberalizations, providing one channel for this increased growth. Das and Mohapatra (2003) not only confirm the growth effect, but also investigate whether and how the reforms shifted the income distribution. They find an upward shift in the income share accruing to the top quintile of the income distribution at the expense of the middle class. The lowest income share remained unchanged. Such research counsels against drawing hasty inferences between economic growth and economic welfare.

Moreover, with a number of recent crises in emerging markets, the role of foreign capital in developing countries is again under intense scrutiny. Malaysia temporarily re-imposed capital controls, which deemed successful by some (see Kaplan and Rodrik, 2002). Thus, it is remarkable that we have so far failed to find negative effects of foreign investment on emerging markets. For example, although policy makers often complain about foreigners inducing excess volatility in local markets, our empirical tests never reveal a robust increase in volatility after liberalization. In other works, we cannot confirm the often-heard argument that foreign capital consistently drives up real exchange rates. We cannot even find increased real variability, that is, evidence of the variability of GDP and consumption growth rates increasing post liberalization (see Bekaert, Harvey and Lundblad). Despite very real problems in the financial and corporate sectors of the crisis countries in Southeast Asia, the current literature on the effects of capital flows on emerging markets reveals little reason for rich developed countries to discontinue their financing of emerging market country development. After all, one potential reason for the disappointingly small effect of the cost of capital that Bekaert, and Harvey (2000a) find, may be a combination of "segmentation risk"—foreign investors anticipating future policy reversals of foreign investment restrictions—and "home bias". "Home bias" refers to the fact that investors across the world have fairly small proportions of their assets allocated to foreign markets, and the proportion allocated to emerging markets is miniscule.[25] Portes and Rey (2002) find that the most important determinant of global equity transactions between two countries is geographical proximity.[26] We cannot help but wonder whether a world blessed with a vast pool of private, internationally active,

---

[25] See Lewis (1999) for a survey of the vast literature on this topic.
[26] Also see Ahearne et al. (in press).

speculative capital would have faced the kind of liquidity crises we have seen in recent years, and in the wake of these crisis the many proposals to limit capital flows.

There remain a number of important caveats, however. Most of our research has focused on equity market liberalization. Few dispute the beneficial effects of foreign direct investment (see Borensztein et al., 1998), and most of the work critical of foreign capital flows focuses on the banking sector and short-term bond flows (see, e.g. Kaminsky and Reinhart, 1999, 2000). For example, liberalizing debt flows in a weak institutional environment, including a poorly developed and supervised banking sector, may have negative consequences. Portfolio equity flows are somewhere in between and seem to have beneficial effects. Contrasting the real effects of equity market liberalizations and banking sector liberalizations appears to be an important topic for future research.[27] This, then, also naturally leads back to an old international economics and developmental economics question (see Edwards, 1987): what is the optimal sequencing of economic and financial liberalizations in developing countries?

References

Achour, D., Harvey, C.R., Hopkins, G., Lang, C., 1999. Stock selection in emerging markets: portfolio strategies for Malaysia, Mexico and South Africa. Emerging Markets Quarterly 3, 38–91.

Adler, M., Qi, R., 2002. Mexico's integration into the North American capital market. Working paper, Columbia University.

Aggarwal, R., Inclan, C., Leal, R., 1999. Volatility in emerging stock markets. Journal of Financial and Quantitative Analysis 34, 33–55.

Ahearne, A.G., Griever, W.L., Warnock, F.E., 2002. Information cost and home bias: an analysis of U.S. holdings of foreign equities. Journal of International Economics (in press).

Alexander, G., Eun, C.S., Janakiramanan, S., 1987. International listing and stock returns: some empirical evidence. Journal of Financial and Quantitative Analysis 23, 135–152.

Amihud, Y., 2002. Illiquidity and stock returns. Journal of Financial Markets 5, 31–56.

Ang, A., Bekaert, G., 2002. International asset allocation with regime shifts. Review of Financial Studies 15, 1137–1187.

Arteta, C., Eichengreen, B., Wyplosz, C., 2001. When does capital account liberalization help more than it hurts? Working paper, Graduate Institute of International Studies, Geneva.

Athanasoulis, S.G., van Wincoop, E., 2000. Growth uncertainty and risk sharing. Journal of Monetary Economics 45, 477–505.

Athanasoulis, S.G., van Wincoop, E., 2001. Risk sharing within the United States: what do financial markets and fiscal federalism accomplish. Review of Economics and Statistics 83, 688–698.

Bacchetta, P., Wincoop, E.V., 2000. Capital flows to emerging markets liberalization, overshooting and volatility. In: Edwards, S. (Ed.), Capital Inflows and the Emerging Economies. University of Chicago Press and NBER, Cambridge, MA, pp. 61–98.

Bae, K.-H., Chan, K., Ng, A., 2002a. Investibility and return volatility in emerging equity markets. Working paper, Hong Kong University of Science and Technology.

Bae, K.-H., Karolyi, G.A., Stulz, R.M., 2002b. A new approach to measuring financial contagion. Review of Financial Studies (in press).

Bailey, W., Chung, Y.P., 1995. Exchange rate fluctuations, political risk, and stock market returns: some evidence from an emerging market. Journal of Financial and Quantitative Analysis 30, 541–561.

Bailey, W., Jagtiani, J., 1994. Foreign ownership restrictions and stock prices in the Thai capital market. Journal of Financial Economics 36, 57–87.

---

[27] Bekaert and Harvey (2003) provide a list of possible directions for future research in emerging markets finance.

Bailey, W., Lim, J., 1992. Evaluating the diversification benefits of the new country funds. Journal of Portfolio Management, 74–80.

Bailey, W., Stulz, R.M., 1990. Benefits of international diversification: the case of Pacific Basin stock markets. Journal of Portfolio Management 4, 57–61.

Beck, T., Demirgüç-Kunt, A., Levine, R., 2000a. A new database on the structure and development of the financial sector. World Bank Economic Review 14, 597–605.

Beck, T., Levine, R., Loayza, N., 2000b. Finance and sources of growth. Journal of Financial Economics 58, 261–300.

Becker, R., Gelos, G., Richards, A., 2000. Devaluation expectations and the stock market—The case of Mexico in 1994/95. Working paper, International Monetary Fund.

Beim, D.O., Calomiris, C.W., 2001. Emerging Financial Markets. McGraw Hill Irwin, New York.

Bekaert, G., 1995. Market integration and investment barriers in emerging equity markets. World Bank Economic Review 9, 75–107.

Bekaert, G., Harvey, C.R., 1995. Time-varying world market integration. Journal of Finance 50, 403–444.

Bekaert, G., Harvey, C.R., 1997. Emerging equity market volatility. Journal of Financial Economics 43, 29–78.

Bekaert, G., Harvey, C.R., 2000a. Foreign speculators and emerging equity markets. Journal of Finance 55, 565–614.

Bekaert, G., Harvey, C.R., 2000b. Capital flows and the behavior of emerging market equity returns. In: Edwards, S. (Ed.), Capital Inflows to Emerging Markets. NBER and University of Chicago Press, pp. 159–194.

Bekaert, G., Harvey, C.R., 2003. Research in emerging market finance: looking to the future. Emerging Markets Review (in press).

Bekaert, G., Urias, M., 1996. Diversification, integration and emerging market closed-end funds. Journal of Finance 51, 835–869.

Bekaert, G., Urias, M., 1999. Is there a free lunch in emerging market equities? Journal of Portfolio Management 25, Spring, 83–95.

Bekaert, G., Erb, C.B., Harvey, C.R., Viskanta, T.E., 1997. What matters for emerging market investments? Emerging Markets Quarterly 1 (2), 17–46.

Bekaert, G., Erb, C.B., Harvey, C.R., Viskanta, T.E., 1998. Distributional characteristics of emerging market returns and asset allocation. Journal of Portfolio Management Winter, 102–116.

Bekaert, G., Harvey, C.R., Lundblad, C., 2001. Emerging equity markets and economic development. Journal of Development Economics 66, 465–504.

Bekaert, G., Harvey, C.R., Lumsdaine, R., 2002a. The dynamics of emerging market equity flows. Journal of International Money and Finance 21, 295–350.

Bekaert, G., Harvey, C.R., Lumsdaine, R., 2002b. Dating the integration of world capital markets. Journal of Financial Economics 65 (2), 203–248.

Bekaert, G., Harvey, C.R., Lundblad, C., 2002c. Does financial market liberalization spur growth? Working paper, Duke, Columbia and Indiana Universities.

Bekaert, G., Harvey, C.R., Lundblad, C., 2002d. Growth volatility and equity market liberalization? Working paper, Duke, Columbia and Indiana Universities.

Bekaert, G., Harvey, C.R., Lundblad, C., 2002e. Liquidity and expected returns: lessons from emerging markets. Working paper, Columbia, Duke and Indiana Universities.

Bekaert, G., Harvey, C.R., Roper, A., 2002f. Large-scale privatization and the dynamics of emerging market equity returns. Working paper, Columbia, Duke and Wisconsin.

Bekaert, G., Harvey, C.R., Lundblad, C., 2003a. Equity market liberalization in emerging markets. Federal Reserve Bank of St. Louis Review (in press).

Bekaert, G., Harvey, C.R., Ng, A., 2003b. Market integration and contagion. Journal of Business (in press).

Bensaid, B., Jeanne, O., 1997. The instability of fixed exchange rate systems when raising the nominal interest rate is costly. European Economic Review 41 (8), 1461–1478.

Bhattacharya, U., Daouk, H., 2002. The world price of insider trading. Journal of Finance 57, 75–108.

Bhattacharya, U., Daouk, H., Jorgenson, B., Kehr, C.-H., 2000. When an event is not an event: the curious case of an emerging market. Journal of Financial Economics 55, 69–101.

Biais, B., Perotti, E.C., 2002. Machiavellian privatization. American Economic Review 92, 240–258.

Bohn, H., Tesar, L.L., 1996. U.S. equity investment in foreign markets: portfolio rebalancing or return chasing? American Economic Review 86 (2), 77–81.

Booth, L., Aivazian, V., Demirguc-Kunt, A., Maksimovic, V., 2001. Capital structures in developing countries. Journal of Finance 56, 87–130.

Borensztein, E.R., Gelos, R.G., 2001. A panic-prone pack? The behavior of emerging market mutual funds. Working paper, International Monetary Fund.

Borensztein, E.R., De Gregario, J., Lee, J.W., 1998. How does foreign investment affect economic growth? Journal of International Economics 45, 115–135.

Boyer, B.H., Gibson, M.S., Loretan, M., 1999. Pitfalls in tests for changes in correlations. Federal Reserve Board, IFS Discussion Paper No. 597R, March.

Brooks, R., Del Negro, M., 2002. The rise in comovement across national stock markets: Market integration or IT bubble? Working paper, Federal Reserve Bank of Atlanta.

Bulow, J., Rogoff, K., 1989a. A constant recontracting model of sovereign debt. Journal of Political Economy 97, 155–178.

Bulow, J., Rogoff, K., 1989b. Is forgive to forget? American Economic Review 79, 43–50.

Calvo, G., 1999. Contagion in emerging markets: when wall street is a carrier. Working paper, University of Maryland.

Calvo, G., Mendoza, E., 2000a. Capital markets crises and economic collapse in emerging markets: an informational frictions approach. American Economic Review 90, 59–64.

Calvo, G., Mendoza, E., 2000b. Rational contagion and the globalization of securities markets. Journal of International Economics 51, 79–113.

Calvo, G., Leiderman, L., Reinhart, C., 1993. Capital inflows and real exchange rate appreciation in Latin America: the role of external factors. IMF Staff Papers 40, 108–151.

Calvo, G., Leiderman, L., Reinhart, C., 1994. The capital inflows problem: concepts and issues. Contemporary Economic Policy 12, 54–66.

Cantor, R., Packer, F., 1996. The determinants and impact of sovereign credit ratings. Journal of Fixed Income, 76–91.

Carrieri, F., Errunza, V., Hogan, K., 2002. Characterizing world market integration through time. Working paper, McGill University.

Chang, R., Velasco, A., 2001. A model of financial crises in emerging markets. Quarterly Journal of Economics 116, 489–517.

Chang, E.C., Eun, C., Kolodny, R., 1995. International diversification through closed end country funds. Journal of Banking and Finance 19, 1237–1263.

Chari, A., Henry, P.B., 2001. Stock market liberalizations and the repricing of systematic risk. Working paper, Stanford University.

Chen, N.-F., Zhang, F., 1997. Correlations, trades and stock returns of the Pacific Rim markets. Pacific Basin Finance Journal 5, 559–577.

Chernow, R., 1990. The House of Morgan. Simon & Schuster, New York.

Cho, D.C., Russell, J., Tiao, G.C., Tsay, R., 2003. The magnet effect of price limits: evidence from high frequency data on Taiwan Stock Exchange. Journal of Empirical Finance 10, 135–170.

Choe, H., Kho, B.-C., Stulz, R., 1999. Do foreign investors destabilize stock markets? The Korean experience in 1997. Journal of Financial Economics 54, 227–264.

Choe, H., Kho, B.-C., Stulz, R.M., 2002. Do domestic investors have more valuable information about individual stocks than foreign investors? Working paper, The Ohio State University, Columbus, OH.

Chowdhry, B., 1991. What is different about international lending? Review of Financial Studies 4, 121–148.

Chuhan, P., 1992. Sources of portfolio investment in emerging markets. Working Paper, International Economics Department, World Bank.

Claessens, S., Forbes, K., 2001. International Financial Contagion. Kluwer Academic Publishing, Boston, pp. 19–42.

Claessens, S., Laeven, L., 2003. Financial development, property rights, and growth. Journal of Finance (in press).

Claessens, S., Pennachi, G., 1996. Estimating the likelihood of Mexican default from the Mexican prices of Brady bonds. Journal of Financial and Quantitative Analysis 31, 109–126.

Claessens, S., Dooley, M., Warner, A., 1995. Portfolio flows: hot or cold? World Bank Economic Review 9, 53–174.

Claessens, S., Djankov, S., Lang, L.H.P., 2000. The separation of ownership and control in East Asian corporations. Journal of Financial Economics 58, 81–112.

Claessens, S., Dornbusch, R., Park, Y.C., 2001. Contagion: why crises spread and how this can be stopped. In: Classens, S., Forbes, K. (Eds.), International Financial Contagion. Kluwer Academic Publishing, Boston, pp. 19–52.

Claessens, S., Djankov, S., Klapper, L., 2003. Resolution of corporate distress in East Asia. Journal of Empirical Finance 10, 201–218.

Clark, J., Berko, E., 1997. Foreign investment fluctuations and emerging market stock returns: the case of Mexico. Staff Report, vol. 24. Federal Reserve Bank of New York, New York, NY.

Corsetti, G., Pesenti, P., Roubini, N., 1999. Paper tigers? A model of the Asian crisis. European Economic Review 43, 1211–1236.

Dahlquist, M., Pinkowitz, L., Stulz, R.M., Williamson, R., 2002. Corporate governance and the home bias. Working paper, Ohio State University, Columbus, OH.

Das, M., Mohapatra, S., 2003. Income inequality: the aftermath of stock market liberalization in emerging markets. Journal of Empirical Finance 10, 219–250.

Das, S., Uppal, R., 2001. Systemic risk and international portfolio choice. Working paper, London Business School.

De Bandt, O., Hartmann, P., 2000. Systematic risk: a survey. Working paper, European Central Bank.

De Gregorio, J., Valdés, R.G., 2001. Crisis transmission: evidence from the debt, tequila, and Asian flu crises. World Bank Economic Review 15, 289–324.

De Jong, F., De Roon, F.A., 2002. Time-varying expected returns and emerging markets integration. Working paper, University of Amsterdam.

Demirgüç-Kunt, A., Levine, R., 1996. Stock market development and financial intermediaries: stylized facts. World Bank Economic Review 10, 291–322.

Demirgüç-Kunt, A., Maksimovic, V., 1996. Stock market development and financing choices of firms. World Bank Economic Review 10, 341–370.

Denis, D.K., Connell, J.J., 2002. International corporate governance. Journal of Financial and Quantitative Analysis (in press).

De Roon, F., Nijman, Th.E., Werker, B.J.M., 2001. Testing for mean-variance spanning with short sales constraints and transaction costs: the case of emerging markets. Journal of Finance 56, 723–744.

Derrabi, M., de Bodt, E., Cobbaut, R., 2000. Microstructure changes and stock price behavior: evidence from Casablanca Stock Exchange. NASDAQ—Notre Dame Microstructure Conference.

De Santis, G., 1993. Asset pricing and portfolio diversification: evidence from emerging financial markets. World Bank Symposium on Portfolio Investment in Developing Countries, Washington, DC.

De Santis, G., Gerard, B., 1997. International asset pricing and portfolio diversification with time-varying risk. Journal of Finance 52, 1881–1912.

De Santis, G., Imrohoroglu, S., 1997. Stock returns and volatility in emerging financial markets. Journal of International Money and Finance 16, 561–579.

Disyatat, P., Gelos, R.G., 2001. The asset allocation of emerging market mutual funds. Working paper, International Monetary Fund, Washington, DC.

Divecha, A.B., Drach, J., Stefek, D., 1992. Emerging markets: a quantitative perspective. Journal of Portfolio Management 19, 41–50.

Diwan, I., Errunza, V., Senbet, L., 1995. Diversification benefits of country funds. In: Howell, M. (Ed.), Investing in Emerging Markets. Euromoney/World Bank, pp. 199–218.

Doidge, C., Karolyi, G.A., Stulz, R.M., 2002. Why are foreign firms listed in the U.S. worth more? Working paper, Ohio State University.

Domowitz, I., Glen, J., Madhavan, A., 1997. Market segmentation and stock prices: evidence from an emerging market. Journal of Finance 52, 1059–1085.

Domowitz, I., Glen, J., Madhavan, A., 1998. International cross listing and order flow migration: evidence from an emerging market. Journal of Finance 53, 2001–2028.

Drazen, A., 1998. Political contagion in currency crises. Working paper, University of Maryland.

Duffie, D., Pedersen, L.H., Singleton, K.J., 2003. Modeling sovereign yield spreads: a case study of Russian Debt. Journal of Finance (in press).

Dungey, M., Martin, V.L., 2001. Contagion across financial markets: an empirical assessment. Working paper, Australian National University.

Dyck, A., Zingales, L., 2002a. Private benefits of control: an international comparison. Working paper, National Bureau of Economic Research, Cambridge, MA.

Dyck, A., Zingales, L., 2002b. The corporate governance role of the media. Working paper, National Bureau of Economic Research, Cambridge, MA.

Eaton, J., Gersovitz, M., 1981. Debt with potential repudiation: theoretical and empirical analysis. Review of Economic Studies 48, 288–309.

Edelen, R.M., Warner, J.B., 2001. Aggregate price effects of institutional trading: a study of mutual fund flow and market returns. Journal of Financial Economics 59, 195–220.

Edison, H., Warnock, F., 2001. Cross-border listings, capital controls, and equity flows to emerging markets. International Finance Discussion Paper. Board of Governors of the Federal Reserve System, Washington, DC.

Edison, H., Warnock, F., 2003. A simple measure of the intensity of capital controls. Journal of Empirical Finance 10, 83–105.

Edwards, S., 1987. Sequencing of economic liberalization in developing countries. Finance and Development 24, 26–29.

Edwards, S., 1998. Openness, productivity, and growth: what do we really know? Economic Journal 108, 383–398.

Edwards, S., 2001. Capital mobility and economic performance: are emerging economies different? Working paper, University of California at Los Angeles.

Eichengreen, B., 2001. Capital account liberalization: what do the cross-country studies tell us? World Bank Economic Review 15, 341–365.

Eichengreen, B., Mody, A., 2000. What explains the changing spreads on emerging market debt? In: Edwards, S. (Ed.), The Economics of International Capital Flows. National Bureau of Economic Research and University of Chicago Press, Chicago, IL, pp. 107–134.

Eichengreen, B., Rose, A.K., Wyplosz, C., 1995. Exchange market mayhem: the antecedents and aftermaths of speculative attacks. Economic Policy 21, 251–312.

Eichengreen, B., Rose, A.K., Wyplosz, C., 1996. Contagious currency crises. Working paper 5681, National Bureau of Economic Research, Cambridge, MA.

Erb, C.B., Harvey, C.R., Viskanta, T.E., 1994. Forecasting international equity correlations. Financial Analysts, 32–45.

Erb, C.B., Harvey, C.R., Viskanta, T.E., 1995. Do world markets still serve as a hedge? Journal of Investing, 23–46.

Erb, C.B., Harvey, C.R., Viskanta, T.E., 1996a. Expected returns and volatility in 135 countries. Journal of Portfolio Management 22, 46–58.

Erb, C.B., Harvey, C.R., Viskanta, T.E., 1996b. Political risk, economic risk and financial risk. Financial Analysts Journal, 29–46.

Erb, C.B., Harvey, C.R., Viskanta, T.E., 1997. Country risk in global financial management. AIMR monograph.

Erb, C.B., Harvey, C.R., Viskanta, T.E., 2000. Understanding emerging market bonds. Emerging Markets Quarterly 4, 7–23.

Errunza, V., 1977. Gains from portfolio diversification into less developed countries' securities. Journal of International Business, 83–99.

Errunza, V., 2001. Foreign portfolio equity investments, financial liberalization and economic development. Special Issue of Review of International Economics, International Financial Liberalization, Capital Flows and Exchange Rate Regimes: Essays in Honor of Robert A. Mundell 9.

Errunza, V.R., Losq, E., 1985. International asset pricing under mild segmentation: theory and test. Journal of Finance 40, 105–124.

Errunza, V., Miller, D., 2000. Market segmentation and the cost of capital in international equity markets. Journal of Financial and Quantitative Analysis 35, 577–600.

Errunza, V.R., Senbet, L., Hogan, K., 1998. The pricing of country funds from emerging markets: theory and evidence. International Journal of Theoretical and Applied Finance, 111–143.

Errunza, V.R., Hogan, K., Hung, M.-W., 1999. Can the gains from international diversification be achieved without trading abroad? Journal of Finance 54, 2075–2107.

Esquivel, G., Larrain, F., 2000. Determinants of currency crises. Trimestre Economico 67, 191–237.

Eun, C.S., Janakiramanan, S., 1986. A model of international asset pricing with a constraint on the foreign equity ownership. Journal of Finance 41, 897–914.

Fama, E.F., French, K.R., 1998. Value versus growth: international evidence. Journal of Finance 53, 1975–2000.

Fernandez-Arias, E., 1996. The new wave of private capital inflows: push or pull? Journal of Development Economics 48, 389–418.

Flood, R., Garber, P., 1984. Collapsing exchange rate regimes, some linear examples. Journal of International Economics 17, 1–13.

Foerster, S., Karolyi, G.A., 1999. The effects of market segmentation and investor recognition on asset prices: evidence from foreign stocks listing in the U.S. Journal of Finance 54, 981–1014.

Forbes, K., 2000. The Asian flu and Russian virus: firm-level evidence on how crises are transmitted internationally. Working paper, National Bureau of Economic Research.

Forbes, K., 2002. One cost of the Chilean capital controls: increased financial constraints for small firms. Working paper, MIT.

Forbes, K., Rigobon, R., 2002. No contagion, only interdependence: measuring stock market co-movements. Journal of Finance 57, 2223–2261.

Frankel, J., Schmukler, S., 2000. Country funds and asymmetric information. International Journal of Finance and Economics 5, 177–195.

Froot, K.A., O'Connell, P.G.J., Seasholes, M.S., 2001. The portfolio flows of international investors. Journal of Financial Economics 59, 151–194.

Galindo, A., Schiantarelli, F., Weiss, A., 2001. Does financial liberalization improve the allocation of investment. Working paper, Boston College.

Garcia, R., Ghysels, E., 1998. Structural change and asset pricing in emerging markets. Journal of International Money and Finance 17, 455–473.

Gelos, R.G., Werner, A.M., 2001. Financial liberalization, credit constraints, and collateral: investment in Mexican manufacturing sector. Journal of Development Economics 67, 1–27.

Gerlach, S., Smets, F., 1994. Contagious speculative attacks. Centre for Economic Policy Research Discussion Paper Series 1055:1.

Ghysels, E., Cherkaoui, M., 2003. Emerging markets and trading costs: lessons from Casablanca. Journal of Empirical Finance 10, 171–200.

Gibson, M.S., 2000. Is corporate governance ineffective in emerging markets? Working paper, Board of Governors of the Federal Reserve System.

Gibson, R., Sundaresan, S.M., 2001. Sovereign borrowing and yield spreads. Working paper, University of Zurich.

Glen, J., 2000. An introduction to the microstructure of emerging markets. Working paper, International Finance Corporation.

Glen, J., 2002. Devaluations and emerging stock market returns. Working paper, International Finance.

Goetzmann, W., Jorion, P., 1999. Re-emerging markets. Journal of Financial and Quantitative Analysis 34, 1–32.

Goldfajn, I., Valdes, R.O., 1997. Are currency crises predictable? Staff Papers. International Monetary Fund, Washington, DC.

Griffin, J.M., Nardari, F., Stulz, R.M., 2002. Daily cross-border equity flows: Pushed or pulled? Working paper, The Ohio State University.

Hamao, Y., Masulis, R.W., Ng, V., 1990. Correlations in price changes and volatility across international stock markets. Review of Financial Studies 3, 281–307.

Hardouvelis, G., Malliaropoulos, D., Priestley, R., 2000. The EMU and European stock market integration. Working paper, Norwegian School of Management, Oslo.

Hartmann, P., Straetmans, S., de Vries, C.G., 2001. Asset market linkages in crisis periods. Working paper, European Central Bank.

Harvey, C.R., 1991. The world price of covariance risk. Journal of Finance 46, 111–157.

Harvey, C.R., 1995. Predictable risk and returns in emerging markets. Review of Financial Studies 8, 773–816.

Harvey, C.R., Roper, A.H., 1999. The Asian bet. In: Harwood, A., Litan, R.E., Pomerleano, M. (Eds.), The Crisis in Emerging Financial Markets. Brookings Institution Press, Washington, DC, pp. 29–115.

Harvey, C.R., Lins, K.V., Roper, A.H., 2002. The effect of capital structure when expected agency costs are extreme. Working paper, Duke University, Durham, NC.

Henry, P.B., 2000a. Stock market liberalization, economic reform, and emerging market equity prices. Journal of Finance 55, 529–564.

Henry, P.B., 2000b. Do stock market liberalizations cause investment booms? Journal of Financial Economics 58, 301–334.

Himmelberg, C.P., Hubbard, R.G., Love, I., 2002. Investor protection, ownership, and the cost of capital. Working paper, Columbia University.

Jain-Chandra, S., 2002. The impact of stock market liberalization on the efficiency of emerging stock markets. Working paper, Columbia University.

Johnson, S., Mitton, T., 2003. Cronyism and capital controls: evidence from Malaysia. Journal of Financial Economics (in press).

Johnson, S., Boone, P., Breach, A., Friedman, E., 2000a. Corporate governance in the Asian financial crisis. Journal of Financial Economics 58, 141–186.

Johnson, S., La Porta, R., Lopez-de-Salines, F., Shleifer, A., 2000b. Tunneling. American Economic Review 90 (2), 22–27.

Jones, C.M., 2001. A century of stock market liquidity and trading costs. Working paper, Columbia University.

Kaminsky, G.L., Reinhart, C.M., 1999. The twin crises: the causes of banking and balance of payments problems. American Economic Review 89, 473–500.

Kaminsky, G.L., Reinhart, C.M., 2000. On crises, contagion, and confusion. Journal of International Economics 51 (1), 145–168.

Kaminsky, G., Lizondo, S., Reinhart, C.M., 1998. Leading indicators of currency crises. IMF Staff Papers 45 (1), 1–48.

Kaminsky, G., Lyons, R., Schmukler, S., 2001. Mutual fund investment in emerging markets—an overview. World Bank Economic Review 15 (2), 315–340.

Kang, J.-K., Stulz, R.M., 1997. Why is there a home bias? An analysis of foreign portfolio equity ownership in Japan. Journal of Financial Economics 46, 3–28.

Kaplan, E., Rodrik, D., 2002. Did the Malaysian capital controls work? Working paper, National Bureau of Economic Research, Cambridge, MA.

Karolyi, G.A., 1998. Why do companies list their shares abroad? (A survey of the evidence and its managerial implications). Salomon Brothers Monograph Series, vol. 7:1. New York University, NY.

Karolyi, G.A., Stulz, R.M., 1996. Why do markets move together? An investigation of U.S.–Japan stock return comovements using ADRs. Journal of Finance, 951–986.

Kawakatsu, H., Morey, M.R., 1999. An empirical examination of financial liberalization and efficiency of emerging market stock prices. Journal of Financial Research 22 (4), 385–411.

Kim, E.H., Singal, V., 2000. Opening up of stock markets: lessons from emerging economies. Journal of Business 73, 25–66.

Kim, W., Wei, S.-J., 2002a. Foreign portfolio investors before and during a crisis. Journal of International Economic 56, 77–96.

Kim, W., Wei, S.-J., 2002b. Offshore investment funds: monsters in emerging markets? Journal of Development Economics 68, 205–224.

King, R.G., Levine, R., 1993. Finance, entrepreneurship and growth. Journal of Monetary Economics 32, 513–542.

King, M., Wadhwani, S., 1990. Transmission of volatility between stock markets. Review of Financial Studies 3, 5–33.

King, M., Sentana, E., Wadhwani, S., 1994. Volatility and links between national stock markets. Econometrica 62, 901–933.

Klapper, L., Love, I., 2002. Corporate governance, investor protection and performance in emerging markets. Working paper, World Bank, Washington, DC.

Klein, M.W., Marion, N.P., 1997. Explaining the duration of exchange-rate pegs. Journal of Development Economics 54, 387–404.

Kodres, L., Pritsker, M., 2002. A rational expectations model of financial contagion. Journal of Finance 52, 769–799.

Krugman, P., 1979. A model of balance of payments crises. Journal of Money, Credit and Banking 11, 311–325.

Krugman, P., 2001. Crisis: the next generation. Paper Presented at Conference Honoring Assaf Razin, Tel Aviv.

Kuilatilaka, N., Marcus, A., 1987. A model of strategic default of sovereign debt. Journal of Economic Dynamics and Control 11, 483–498.

Kyle, A.S., Xiong, W., 2001. Contagion as a wealth effect. Journal of Finance 56, 1401–1440.

Laeven, L., 2001. Financial liberalization and financing constraints: evidence from panel data on emerging economies. Working paper, World Bank, Washington. DC.

Laeven, L., Perotti, E.C., 2001. Confidence building in emerging stock markets. Working paper 3055, Centre for Economic Policy Research, London.

Lang, M.H., Lins, K.V., Miller, D.P., 2002a. ADRs, analysts, and accuracy: Does cross listing in the U.S. improve a firm's information environment and increase market value? Working paper, University of Utah.

Lang, M.H., Lins, K.V., Miller, D.P., 2002b. Do analysts matter most when investors are protected least? International evidence. Working paper, University of Utah.

La Porta, R., Lopez-de-Silanes, F., Shleifer, A., Vishny, R.W., 1998. Law and finance. Journal of Political Economy 106, 1113–1155.

La Porta, R., Lopez-de-Silanes, F., Shleifer, A., 1999. Corporate ownership around the world. Journal of Finance 54, 471–517.

Lemmon, M.L., Lins, K.V., 2003. Ownership structure, corporate governance, and firm value: evidence from the East Asian financial crisis. Journal of Finance (in press).

Lesmond, D.A., 2002. The costs of equity trading in emerging markets. Working paper, Tulane University, New Orleans, LA.

Lesmond, D.A., Ogden, J., Trzcinka, C., 1999. A new estimate of transaction costs. Review of Financial Studies 12, 1113–1142.

Levine, R., 1991. Stock markets, growth, and tax policy. Journal of Finance 46, 1445–1465.

Levine, R., Zervos, S., 1996. Stock market development and economic growth. World Bank Economic Review 10, 323–340.

Levine, R., Zervos, S., 1998a. Stock markets, banks, and economic growth. American Economic Review 88 (3), 537–558.

Levine, R., Zervos, S., 1998b. Capital control liberalization and stock market development. World Development, 1169–1183.

Levine, R., Loayza, N., Beck, T., 2000. Financial intermediation and growth: causality and causes. Journal of Monetary Economics 46, 31–77.

Lewis, K.K., 1996. What can explain the apparent lack of international consumption risk sharing? Journal of Political Economy 104, 267–297.

Lewis, K.K., 1999. Trying to explain home bias in equities and consumption. Journal of Economic Literature 37, 571–608.

Lewis, K.K., 2000. Why do stocks and consumption imply such different gains from international risk sharing? Journal of International Economics 52, 1–35.

Li, K., Sarker, A., Wang, Z., 2003. Diversification benefits of emerging markets subject to portfolio constraints. Journal of Empirical Finance 10, 59–82.

Lins, K.V., 2003. Equity ownership and firm value in emerging markets. Journal of Financial and Quantitative Analysis (in press).

Lins, K.V., Servaes, H., 2002. Is corporate diversification beneficial in emerging markets? Financial Management 31, 5–31.

Lins, K.V., Strickland, D., Zenner, M., 2001. Do non-U.S. firms issue equity on U.S. exchanges to relax capital constraints? Working paper, University of Utah.

Lombardo, D., Pagano, M., 2000. Legal determinants of the return on equity. Working paper, CEPR.

Longin, F., Solnik, B., 1995. Is correlation in international equity returns constant: 1960–1990. Journal of International Money and Finance 14, 3–26.

Longin, F., Solnik, B., 2001. Extreme correlation of international equity markets. Journal of Finance 56, 649–676.

Loretan, M., English, W.B., 2000. Evaluating "correlation breakdowns" during periods of market volatility. Federal Reserve Board, mimeo.

Love, I., 2002. Financial development and financing constraints: international evidence from the structural investment model. Review of Financial Studies (in press).

Martell, R., Stulz, R.M., 2003. Equity market liberalizations as country IPOs. Unpublished working paper, National Bureau of Economic Research, Cambridge, MA.

Martin, P., Rey, H., 2000. Financial integration and asset returns. European Economic Review 44, 1327–1350.

Masson, P., 1999. Contagion: macroeconomic models with multiple equilibria. Journal of International Money and Finance 18, 587–602.

Mathieson, D., Rojaz-Suarez, L., 1992. Liberalization of the capital account: experiences and issues. Staff papers. International Monetary Fund, Washington, DC.

Megginson, W.L., Netter, J.M., 2001. From state to market: a survey of empirical studies on privatization. Journal of Economic Literature 39, 321–389.

Miller, D.P., 1999. The impact of international market segmentation on securities prices: evidence from Depositary Receipts. Journal of Financial Economics 51, 103–123.

Miniane, J., 2000. A new set of measures on capital account restrictions. Working paper, Johns Hopkins University.

Morck, R., Yeung, B., Yu, W., 2000. The information content of stock markets: why do emerging markets have synchronous stock price movements? Journal of Financial Economics 58 (1), 215–260.

Nenova, T., 2003. The value of corporate votes and control benefits: cross-country analysis. Journal of Financial Economics (in press).

Ng, A., 2000. Volatility spillover effects from Japan and the U.S. to the Pacific-Basin. Journal of International Money and Finance 19, 207–233.

Nishiotis, G.P., 2002. Investment barriers and international asset pricing: Evidence from closed-end country funds. Working paper, Tulane University, New Orleans, LA.

Obstfeld, M., 1986. Rational and self-fulfilling balance of payments crises. American Economic Review 76, 72–81.

Ozkan, F.G., Sutherland, A., 1998. Currency crises model with an optimising policymaker. Journal of International Economics 44, 339–364.

Patro, D.K., Wald, J.K., 2002. Firm characteristics and the impact of emerging market liberalizations. Working paper, Rutgers University.

Perotti, E.C., 1995. Credible privatization. American Economic Review 85, 847–859.

Perotti, E., van Oijen, P., 2001. Privatization, political risk and stock market development in emerging economies. Journal of International Money and Finance 20 (1), 43–69.

Pindyck, R.S., Rotemberg, J.J., 1990. The excess co-movement of commodity prices. Economic Journal 100, 1173–1189.

Pindyck, R.S., Rotemberg, J.J., 1993. The comovement of stock prices. Quarterly Journal of Economics 108, 1073–1104.

Portes, R., Rey, H., 2002. The determinants of cross border equity flows. Working paper 7336, National Bureau of Economic Research, Cambridge, MA.

Quinn, D., 1997. The correlates of changes in international financial regulation. American Political Science Review 91, 531–551.

Quinn, D., Inclan, C., Toyoda, A.M., 2001. How and where capital account liberalization leads to growth. Working paper, Georgetown University.

Rajan, R.G., Zingales, L., 1998. Financial dependence and growth. American Economic Review 88, 559–586.

Rajan, R.G., Zingales, L., 2001. The great reversals: The politics of financial development in the 20th century. Working paper, University of Chicago, Chicago, IL.

Richards, A.J., 1996. Volatility and predictability in national markets: how do emerging and mature markets differ? Staff Papers. International Monetary Fund, Washington DC.

Richards, A.J., 2002. Big fish in small ponds: The momentum investing and price impact of foreign investors in Asian emerging equity markets. Working paper, Reserve Bank of Australia.

Rigobon, R., 2001. Contagion: how to measure it? In: Edwards, S., Frankel, J. (Eds.), Currency Crises Prevention. National Bureau of Economic Research and University of Chicago Press, Chicago, IL. In press.

Rigobon, R., 2002a. On the measurement of the international propagation of shocks: is it stable? Journal of International Economics (in press).

Rigobon, R., 2002b. The curse of non-investment grade countries. Journal of Development Economics (in press).

Rockinger, M., Urga, G., 2001. A time-varying parameter model to test for predictability and integration in the stock markets of transition economies. Journal of Business and Economic Statistics 19, 73–84.

Rodrik, D., 1998. Who needs capital account convertibility? Working paper, Department of Economics, Harvard University, Cambridge, MA.

Rousseau, P.L., Sylla, R., 1999. Emerging financial markets and early U.S. growth. Working paper, New York University.

Rousseau, P.L., Sylla, R., 2001. Financial systems, economic growth and globalization. Working paper 8323, National Bureau of Economic Research, Cambridge, MA.

Rouwenhorst, K.G., 1999. Local return factors and turnover in emerging stock markets. Journal of Finance 54, 1439–1464.

Sachs, J.D., Warner, A.M., 1995. Economic reform and the process of global integration. Brookings Papers on Economic Activity, 1–118.

Shleifer, A., 1986. Do demand curves for stocks slope down? Journal of Finance 41, 579–590.

Shleifer, A., Vishny, R.W., 1997. A survey of corporate governance. Journal of Finance 52, 737–783.

Stambaugh, R., 1995. Unpublished discussion of Karolyi and Stulz (1996). National Bureau of Economic Research Universities Conference on Risk Management, May.

Stiglitz, J.E., 2000. Capital market liberalization, economic growth and instability. World Development 25, 1075–1086.

Stulz, R.M., 1981. On the effects of barriers to international investment. Journal of Finance 36, 923–934.

Stulz, R.M., 1999. International portfolio flows and security markets. In: Feldstein, M. (Ed.), International Capital Flows. National Bureau of Economic Research and University of Chicago Press, pp. 257–293.

Susmel, R., 2001. Extreme observations and diversification in Latin American emerging equity markets. Journal of International Money and Finance 20, 971–986.

Tang, J.W., 2002. Contagion: An empirical test. Working paper, Duke University.

Taylor, A.M., 1998. Argentina and the world capital market: saving, investment, and international capital mobility in the twentieth century. Journal of Development Economics 57, 147–184.

Taylor, A.M., Williamson, J.G., 1994. Capital flows to the new-world as an intergenerational transfer. Journal of Political Economy 102, 348–371.

Tesar, L., Werner, I., 1995. U.S. equity investment in emerging stock markets. World Bank Economic Review 9, 109–130.

Thomas, C., Warnock, F.E., 2002. International equity and bond portfolios. Working paper, Board of Governors of the Federal Reserve System.

Urias, M., 1994. The impact of security cross-listing on the cost of capital in emerging markets. Unpublished dissertation, Stanford University, Stanford CA.

Van Der Hart, J.V., Slagter, E., van Dijk, D., 2003. Stock selection strategies in emerging markets. Journal of Empirical Finance 10, 107–134.

Van Wincoop, E., 1999. How big are potential welfare gains from international risk sharing? Journal of International Economics 47, 109–235.

Warnock, F.E., Cleaver, C., 2002. Financial centers and the geography of capital flows. Working paper, Board of Governors of the Federal Reserve System.

Warther, V.A., 1995. Aggregate mutual fund flows and security returns. Journal of Financial Economics 39, 209–235.

Williamson, J.G., 1996. Globalization, convergence, and history. Journal of Economic History 56, 277–306.

World Bank, 1997. Private Capital Flows to Developing Countries. The Road to Financial Integration. The World Bank and Oxford Univ. Press, Washington, DC.

Wurgler, J., 2000. Financial markets and the allocation of capital. Journal of Financial Economics 58, 187–214.

Yuan, Z.K., 2002. Asymmetric price movement and the borrowing constraint: A REE model of crises, contagion, and confusion. Working paper, University of Michigan.

Part I
Market Integration and Liberalization

A
Theoretical Effects of Market Integration

[1]

THE JOURNAL OF FINANCE • VOL. XXXVI, NO. 4 • SEPTEMBER 1981

On the Effects of Barriers to International Investment

RENÉ M. STULZ*

ABSTRACT

A simple model is presented in which it is costly for domestic investors to *hold* foreign assets. The implications of the model for the composition of optimal portfolios at home and abroad are derived. It is shown that all foreign assets with a beta larger than some beta β^* plot on either one of two security market lines. Some foreign assets with a beta smaller than β^* are not held by domestic investors even if their expected return is increased slightly.

WHILE IT IS OBVIOUSLY not true that asset markets are completely segmented between countries, there is evidence of barriers to international investment. Although reality seems to lie in that grey area between complete segmentation and no segmentation at all, most international asset pricing models are concerned with the extreme case of no barriers to international investment. No effort seems to have been made to study the effect on portfolio choice of such barriers, which make it costly to *hold* foreign securities, as opposed to domestic securities, but which do not, in general, render international diversification so onerous that investors avoid foreign securities completely.[1] Casual empiricism suggests that models without barriers to international investment should be suspect; those models cannot explain why it appears that in every country investors, on average, hold more domestic securities than would be required if they held the world market portfolio.[2]

This paper constructs a model of international asset pricing in which there is a cost associated with holding—either long or short—risky foreign securities. For the sake of simplicity, in most of the paper we assume that while domestic investors face barriers to international investment, foreign investors face no such barriers. It turns out that nothing significant is lost with such an assumption. The main conclusions of this paper for the case in which foreign investors face no barriers to international investment are:

1. In the presence of barriers to international investment, some risky foreign

The University of Rochester Graduate School of Management, Rochester, New York 14627.

* I am grateful to Fischer Black, Stanley Fischer, Donald Lessard, Fred Phillips-Patrick, Patricia Reagan, Clifford Smith, and Lee Wakeman for useful discussions and comments. I thank Michael Adler and the Editor for useful advice. I acknowledge generous financial help from the Swiss National Research Fund.

[1] The most important exception is Black [3]. Stapleton and Subrahmanyam [7] have a numerical example of incomplete segmentation. See also Adler and Dumas [2].

[2] Note that the fact that investors do not hold the world market portfolio is not very interesting. What is important is that everywhere investors have a bias towards domestic stocks. It is true, however, that this bias is not equally strong in all countries.

assets can be nontraded, in the sense that they are not held by domestic investors and would not be held if their expected return changed slightly.

2. In each country, all investors hold the same portfolio of risky assets.
3. Traded assets plot on well-defined security market lines. There is one security market line (SML) on which all domestic assets plot. Risky foreign assets held long (short) by domestic investors plot on an SML which lies above (below) and is parallel to the SML for risky domestic assets.
4. Nontraded risky assets plot between the two SML's for risky foreign assets.
5. For investors who face barriers to international investment, the world market portfolio is inefficient in that there cannot exist a mutual fund for domestic investors which would make them indifferent between choosing an appropriate combination of the safe asset, the mutual fund, and the world market portfolio, or holding their own portfolio.
6. There exists a (finite) beta β^* such that all assets which have a beta larger than β^* are traded.

As in Black [3], proportional taxes are used to model barriers to international investment. However, the only result we have summarized which also holds for the Black model is that in each country, all investors hold the same portfolio of risky assets. In the Black model, no *risky* asset can be nontraded.[3] We obtain very different results from those of the Black model because in our model an investor pays a tax proportional to the *absolute* value of his holdings of risky foreign assets, whereas in the Black model an investor has to pay taxes in proportion to his *net* holdings of risky foreign assets. The barriers to international investment in the Black model hinder *net* investment in risky foreign assets, whereas in our model they make it more difficult to *hold* risky foreign assets. In our model, if an investor pays a tax θ on each dollar held long in foreign assets, he also pays a tax θ on each dollar held short in foreign assets.

Barriers to international investment can take a variety of forms, some of them nonpecuniary, and taxes are a way, albeit imperfect, to represent them. The barriers to international investment we try to model are of a different type from those modeled by Black. In the Black model, an increase in barriers to international investment will never induce domestic investors to abstain from holding foreign risky securities. If the barriers to international investment modeled by Black were very high, one would not observe domestic investors holding few foreign securities, but rather would observe them holding large amounts of foreign securities short. One does not observe that whenever domestic investors have small long holdings in a foreign country, they also have large short holdings. This suggests that there must indeed exist barriers to international investment which make it difficult, for domestic investors, to hold—either long or short—foreign risky securities. The present paper tries to model such barriers.

Because exchange rate risks are irrelevant to our argument, we use a framework in which exchange rates do not appear at all. Introducing exchange rates in our model would *not* change our results; the effect of barriers to international

[3] In the Black model, it is possible for an investor to have zero holdings in a foreign risky asset. However, an infinitesimal change in the expected return of that asset would induce that investor to hold it—either short or long. In the Black model, the safe asset can be nontraded. The same result would obtain in our model if we introduced a tax on borrowing or lending abroad.

investment would be the same as in this study so long as those barriers to international investment were of a type which in the limit can produce complete segmentation. Formally, the portfolios which obtain in this paper would obtain in a world in which there is only one good, in which there is a safe real bond in each country, and in which there are neither transportation costs nor tariffs.

Finally, the model presented here is not a general equilibrium model, in the sense that the barriers to international investment are given and no attempt is made to explain those barriers. To the extent that those barriers correspond to taxes, no attempt is made to explain how the revenue from those taxes is spent.

I. The Model

Throughout this paper, we assume that there are only two countries, the domestic country D and the foreign country F. Let an investor k be a domestic (foreign) investor if we write $k \in D$ ($k \in F$). An asset i is a domestic (foreign) asset if we write $i \in D$ ($i \in F$). We assume that domestic investors face a very simple form of barriers to international investment, whereas foreign investors face no barriers to international investment. If a domestic investor k holds a foreign risky asset i long, his return is $\tilde{R}_i - \theta$, where $\tilde{R}_i$ is the return of asset i for a foreign investor and θ is the tax rate which represents barriers to international investment, whereas if he holds asset i short and keeps the proceeds in cash, his return is $-(\tilde{R}_i + \theta)$. Unlimited short-sales with full use of the proceeds are permitted. A portfolio which consists of one dollar sold short in one foreign security, with the proceeds of that short-sale invested long in another foreign risky asset, pays a tax of 2θ.[4] The barrier to international investment can usefully be thought of as a penalty for holding foreign shares long or short. Both domestic and foreign investors can buy or sell bonds which have a safe rate of return R. If domestic investors borrow or lend abroad at the safe rate, they do not pay a tax on their holdings of foreign bonds.[5]

Each investor is assumed to maximize a utility function which depends positively on expected end-of-period wealth and negatively on the variance of end-of-period wealth. With that assumption, the investor acts to minimize the variance of the return of his portfolio under the constraint that the expected return of his portfolio must be no less than an exogenously given return, $\bar{R}^k$. By convention, there are N risky assets and n risky domestic assets. $\bar{R}$ is the $N \times 1$ vector of expected returns of risky assets and V the $N \times N$ variance-covariance matrix of returns of risky assets. Let w^k be the $N \times 1$ vector of fractions of his wealth investor k holds long in risky assets. If $w_i^k = 0$, this means that investor k does

[4] In the Black model, because there is a subsidy on short-sales, the investor would not pay taxes on the portfolio we just described.

[5] Stulz [8] presents a more general model in which this assumption does not hold. Black [3] shows that if a tax is imposed on borrowing and lending abroad, it is possible that neither borrowing nor lending occurs between countries. Furthermore, when there is a tax on borrowing and lending abroad, it will never be the case that some domestic investors borrow abroad, whereas other domestic investors lend abroad. Either some domestic investors borrow abroad and none lend abroad, or vice versa. These results also hold in Stulz [8]. Introducing a tax on borrowing and lending abroad would complicate the present paper without offering any additional insight.

not hold a positive amount of risky asset i. Similarly, let $\underline{v}^k$ be the $N \times 1$ vector of fractions of his wealth the investor holds short in risky assets. $v_i^k > 0$ means that the investor k holds short risky asset i for an amount equal to $v_i^k W^k$, where W^k is the investor's wealth. The portfolio of risky assets of the investor is given by $(\underline{w}^k - \underline{v}^k)$. If $\underline{\varrho}$ is an $N \times 1$ vector which has zeros in its first n rows and ones everywhere else, the taxes a domestic investor k has to pay are equal to $(\underline{w}^k + \underline{v}^k)' \underline{\varrho} . \theta . W^k$, where a prime denotes a transpose. The elements of $\underline{w}^k$ and $\underline{v}^k$ must be nonnegative to guarantee that the investor cannot construct a portfolio which would transform taxes into subsidies. It will be convenient to define $\underline{l}$ as an $N \times 1$ vector of ones. It follows that the problem of investor k is to minimize the variance of his portfolio subject to a constraint on the expected rate of return of his portfolio and nonnegativity constraints on $\underline{w}^k$ and $\underline{v}^k$.[6]

$$\text{Min} \ \frac{1}{2} (\underline{w}^k - \underline{v}^k)' \ \underline{V}(\underline{w}^k - \underline{v}^k)$$

so that the following constraints are satisfied:

$$(\underline{w}^k - \underline{v}^k)' \ \bar{\underline{R}} - (\underline{w}^k + \underline{v}^k)' \underline{\varrho} . \theta + [1 - (\underline{w}^k - \underline{v}^k)' \underline{l}] R \geq R^k \tag{1}$$

$$\underline{w}^k \geq O \tag{2}$$

$$\underline{v}^k \geq O \tag{3}$$

The left-hand side of Expression (1) corresponds to the expected return of the portfolio of investor k, which is defined as the sum of (a) the expected return of his holdings of risky assets in the absence of barriers to international investment; (b) the total cost to the investor of the barriers to international investment, which is proportional to the absolute value of the investor's holdings of foreign risky assets; and (c) his holdings of safe bonds. If L^k is the Lagrangean function which corresponds to the investor's optimization problem and if λ^k is the multiplier associated with the constraint given by (1), then the investor's portfolio has to satisfy the following first-order conditions:

$$\frac{\partial L^k}{\partial \underline{w}_i^k} = \underline{V}(\underline{w}^k - \underline{v}^k) - \lambda^k \{ \bar{\underline{R}} - R.\underline{l} - \theta.\underline{\varrho} \} \geq O \tag{4}$$

$$\frac{\partial L^k}{\partial \underline{v}_i^k} = -\underline{V}(\underline{w}^k - \underline{v}^k) + \lambda^k \{ \bar{\underline{R}} - R.\underline{l} + \theta.\underline{\varrho} \} \geq O \tag{5}$$

$$(\underline{w}^k)' \frac{\partial L^k}{\partial \underline{w}_i^k} = 0 \tag{6}$$

$$(\underline{v}^k)' \frac{\partial L^k}{\partial \underline{v}_i^k} = 0 \tag{7}$$

To obtain the first-order conditions for the portfolio of a foreign investor, set θ

---

[6] Note that the optimization problem of the investor is very similar to the problem faced by investors in the literature dealing with transaction costs, except that here the initial allocation does not matter. Smith and Milne [5] derive equilibrium relationships in a model with transaction costs. For a discussion of optimal portfolios in the presence of transaction costs and references to the literature, see Abrams and Karmarkar [1].

equal to zero in (4) and (5). If we use $\underline{V}_i$ for the i-th row of $\underline{V}$, Expressions (4) and (5) can be rewritten as:

$$\lambda^k(\bar{R}_i - R + \theta) \geq \underline{V}_i(w^k - v^k) \geq \lambda^k(\bar{R}_i - R - \theta) \tag{8}$$

where $\underline{V}_i(w^k - v^k)$ is the covariance between the return on asset i and the return on the investor's portfolio of risky assets. Expression (8) has to be satisfied, for $\theta > 0$, for all risky foreign assets in the portfolio of domestic investor k. For $\theta = 0$, Expression (8) must be satisfied for all assets i, for all foreign investors, and for all domestic assets i, for all domestic investors. If the tax rate for an asset is equal to zero, i.e., $\theta = 0$, (8) reduces to:

$$\lambda^k(\bar{R}_i - R) = \underline{V}_i(w^k - v^k) \tag{9}$$

Expression (8) completely characterizes asset demands in our model. The implications of Expression (8) are discussed in detail in the next three sections.

II. Asset Demands and Non-Traded Assets

In this section, we prove two results. The first is that the proportion in which two risky assets are held is the same for each domestic investor. The second result is that for a given vector of expected excess returns and variance-covariance matrix of returns, some foreign assets can be nontraded. A foreign asset is nontraded if no domestic investor currently holds a nonzero number of shares of that asset and if no domestic investor would hold a nonzero number of shares of that asset if its expected return increased or decreased slightly.

First, we show that all domestic investors hold risky assets in identical proportions. (The same holds for foreign investors, but for them it is trivial, as they do not face any barriers to international investment.) From first-order conditions (4) to (7), it follows that both inequalities in (8) can hold strictly only if the investor does not hold that asset, i.e. $w_i = v_i = 0$. If we look only at the assets which satisfy (8) with one equality and one strict inequality and at the assets which satisfy (9), we can completely characterize an investor's portfolio. If we divide the first-order condition which an asset held in nonzero amount satisfies by the first-order condition a domestic asset j, such that $\bar{R}_j \neq R$, satisfies, we can write:

$$\frac{\underline{V}_i(w^k - v^k)}{\underline{V}_j(w^k - v^k)} = \frac{(\bar{R}_i - R - p\theta)}{\bar{R}_j - R} \tag{10}$$

where $p = 1$ if the asset is a foreign asset held long, $p = 0$ if the asset is a domestic asset, and $p = -1$ if the asset is a foreign asset held short. Because the right-hand side of (10) contains no taste variable, Equation (10) must hold for all domestic investors and for all assets i. (10) defines a system of $N - 1$ equations with $N - 1$ unknowns, where the unknowns are the ratios $(w_i^k - v_i^k)/(w_j^k - v_j^k)$ for any investor k. It follows necessarily that the ratios $(w_i^k - v_i^k)/(w_j^k - v_j^k)$, for all i's, must be the same for all domestic investors. This completes the proof of our result.

Our first result is important here because it implies that an asset which is nontraded for one domestic investor is nontraded for *all* domestic investors. We call a nontraded asset for domestic investor i an asset (a) of which the investor holds no share and (b) which the investor would not hold if the expected return of that asset increased or decreased slightly. For an asset to be nontraded, both inequalities in (8) have to hold strictly. We have just proved that if one inequality does not hold strictly in (8) for *one* domestic investor, it holds with equality for all domestic investors. It follows that a nontraded asset wil be nontraded for all domestic investors, which means that whether an asset is traded or not has nothing to do with an investor's preferences. If both inequalities in (8) hold strictly, there is a number ϵ such that if the expected return on the stock is either $\bar{R}_i + \epsilon$ or $\bar{R}_i - \epsilon$, those inequalities still hold strictly.

The fact that it is possible for nontraded assets to exist can be established easily. Choose the variance-covariance matrix of returns to be such that, in the last N^* rows, the only nonzero elements are the diagonal elements. For foreign assets, Expression (8) can be rewritten as:

$$\lambda^k(\bar{R}_i - R + \theta) \geq \sigma_i^2(w_i^k - v_i^k) \geq \lambda^k(\bar{R}_i - R - \theta) \tag{11}$$

where σ_i^2 is the variance of the return of the i-th asset. Suppose that $\bar{R}_i - R$ is approximately equal to zero. In this case, the investor will not hold the stock long, because the second inequality in (11) does not hold strictly, implying that w_i^k is negative, as θ is greater than zero. The investor will not hold the stock short, because this implies that v_i^k is negative. It follows that both inequalities hold strictly.

We have shown that for a given vector of expected excess returns and a given variance-covariance matrix of returns, it is possible for some assets to be non-traded and that if one asset is nontraded for a domestic investor, it will be nontraded for all domestic investors. Only empirical research can solve the question of whether or not some assets will be nontraded for some investors.

The *theoretical* result that nontraded assets *can* exist has, however, far-reaching implications. The first is that if there exist nontraded assets, the world portfolio of stocks cannot possibly be an efficient portfolio of stocks for all investors. In the next section, we will discuss the implication of that fact for what is usually thought of as the security market line. The result here that if the tax rate θ is positive the world market portfolio is not an efficient portfolio has the strong implication that if a mutual fund sells shares of the world market portfolio, no domestic investor wants to buy them. In our model, contrary to the model of Black [3], if a mutual fund sells claims to the world market portfolio, it is costly to undo its actions, (for instance, selling short an asset held long by the mutual fund involves paying the tax twice) and so investors are never indifferent between holding shares in that mutual fund and in some other portfolio, or holding their own portfolio of risky assets. In other words, contrary to the Black model, the world market portfolio cannot belong in a linear combination of portfolios which would produce an efficient portfolio for domestic investors. If there are nontraded assets, it is not true that adding foreign assets to a portfolio of domestic assets is necessarily a good thing. Finally, whereas proxies for the market portfolio are generally criticized for not including more risky assets, the theoretical possibility exists that, for some tests, some of those proxies can include too many assets.[7]

[7] See Roll [4] for a thorough discussion of the problems posed by the fact that we cannot observe the true market portfolio.

III. Is there a Security Market Line?

We have shown that some risky assets can be nontraded and that consequently the market portfolio is not even part of a linear combination of portfolios which yields an efficient portfolio for domestic investors. In this section, we show that a plot of expected returns of risky assets with respect to their betas computed using the world market portfolio is not arbitrary. In particular, all foreign traded assets plot along one of two straight lines whereas nontraded assets plot between those straight lines.

Let us look back at Expression (8) which gives bounds which a portfolio of risky assets must satisfy. This expression can be rewritten as (remember that if investor k is a foreign investor, $\theta = 0$):

$$\lambda^k(\bar{R}_i - R + \theta) - \lambda^k Q_i^k = \underline{V}_i(w^k - v^k) = \lambda^k(\bar{R}_i - R - \theta) + \lambda^k q_i^k \quad (12)$$

where Q_i^k and q_i^k are nonnegative numbers chosen so that the inequalities in (8) hold with equality signs. Q_i^k and q_i^k are not observable, but they facilitate considerably the derivation of our results. Q_i^k and q_i^k must take values so that they satisfy:

$$q_i^k + Q_i^k = 2\theta \quad i \in F \quad (13)$$

$$q_i^k = Q_i^k = 0 \quad i \in D \quad (14)$$

Let q^k be a $N \times 1$ vector whose representative element is q_i^k. We can write:

$$\underline{V}(w^k - v^k) = \lambda^k(\bar{R} - \underline{l}R - \theta\underline{e}) + \lambda^k q^k \quad (15)$$

Equation (15) is a restatement in matrix form of the right-hand side of the first equality in (12), for all i's. Define w^s as an $N \times 1$ vector whose element w_i^s is equal to the fraction of world wealth W^w supplied in the form of risky asset i. If $\lambda^k W^k$ is equal to T^k, $T^d(T^f)$ is equal to the sum of the T^k's for $k \in D$ ($k \in F$), π^k is equal to T^k/T^d and γ^d is equal to $T^d/(T^d + T^f)$, we get, after some rearranging:

$$\underline{V}w^s W^w = (T^d + T^f)(\bar{R} - R.\underline{l} - \gamma^d\theta\underline{e} + \gamma^d \sum_{k \in D} \pi^k q^k) \quad (16)$$

Equation (16) assumes that all markets for risky securities are in equilibrium. The last term on the right-hand side of (16) which we now write $\gamma^d q^d$, is a weighted average of the q^k's across all investors. If Equation (16) is premultiplied by $w^{s'}$, the left-hand side of the resulting expression is equal to the variance of portfolio w^s, which we write σ_w^2, multiplied by W^w:

$$\sigma_w^2 W^w = (T^d + T^f)\{\bar{R}_m - R - \theta_m + q_m\} \quad (17)$$

where $\bar{R}_m$ is equal to the expected return on portfolio w^s, θ_m is equal to γ^d times the amount of taxes domestic investors would have to pay on one dollar invested in portfolio w^s, and q_m is equal to $(w^s)'q^d\gamma^d$. Equation (17) is used to eliminate $(T^d + T^f)$ in (16):

$$\beta^m[\bar{R}_m - R - \theta_m + q_m] = \bar{R} - R.\underline{l} - \gamma^d\theta\underline{e} + \gamma^d q^d \quad (18)$$

Equation (18) is the fundamental asset pricing equation of this paper. β_i^m is the beta of common stock i computed using the *world* market portfolio, i.e. $\text{Cov}(\tilde{R}_i, \tilde{R}_m)/\text{Var}(\tilde{R}_m)$. With no barriers to international investment, (18) reduces to the usual Sharpe-Lintner pricing relationship.[8] We now look successively at the pricing of domestic stocks and foreign stocks when the tax rate θ is greater than zero.

Domestic stocks are equally easy to hold for foreign and domestic investors, because for foreign investors there are no barriers to international investment. We can rewrite (18) as it applies to domestic common stocks:

$$\beta_i^m[\bar{R}_m - R - \theta_m + q_m] = \bar{R}_i - R \qquad i \in D \tag{19}$$

If the capital asset pricing model held for domestic stocks, θ_m and q_m would be equal. With our assumptions, θ_m is a strictly positive number, whereas q_m is a nonnegative number. However, q_m can be larger than θ_m. If the value of foreign stocks is at least twice the value of foreign stocks which are nontraded, then q_m will be smaller than θ_m. In that case, domestic common stocks will plot on a security market line which has a smaller slope than the security market line which corresponds to the Sharpe-Lintner pricing relationship. If most foreign stocks are nontraded, no such statement can be made without restricting the variance-covariance matrix of asset returns. For instance, for a diagonal variance-covariance matrix, it can be shown that θ_m will always be larger than q_m. To interpret q_m, it is useful to ask the following question: suppose that *one* domestic investor is given the choice of having either the barrier on positive holdings or the barrier on negative holdings of foreign stocks removed, which barrier would he want to get rid of? As long as the investor prefers to have the barrier on positive holdings removed, which is not necessarily the case because of the distortions introduced by the barriers on foreign investment, q_m will be smaller than θ_m. In that case, the Sharpe-Lintner model will overpredict the returns of domestic risky assets and the expected prediction error will be an increasing function of beta.

The asset pricing relationship for foreign risky assets is:

$$\beta_i^m[\bar{R}_m - R - \theta_m + q_m] + \gamma^d\theta - q_i^d = \bar{R}_i - R \qquad i \in F \tag{20}$$

Whenever two risky foreign assets are held long by domestic investors, the expected returns of those two risky assets can differ only to the extent that the beta of those two assets differ, as for all risky foreign assets held long by domestic investors, $q_i^d = 0$. It follows that the expected returns of foreign risky assets held long by domestic investors must be a linear function of beta. For all risky foreign assets held short by domestic investors, $q_i^d = 2\gamma^d\theta$. This implies that all risky foreign assets held short by domestic investors must plot on a security market line, but that security market line lies below the security market line for domestic risky assets, whereas all risky foreign assets held long by domestic investors plot on a security market line which lies above the security market line for domestic risky assets.

---

[8] If foreign investors face barriers to international investment or if the tax on short holdings is different from the tax on long holdings, this affects θ_m and q_m.

   The two security market lines for foreign traded risky assets will be parallel to the security market line for domestic risky assets. Nontraded assets will plot *between* the two security market lines for foreign risky assets. Figure 1 illustrates those results for the case in which θ_m is larger than q_m. Asset 1 is a domestic risky asset; asset 2 is a foreign risky asset held long; asset 3 is a foreign risky asset held short; asset 4 is a foreign nontraded asset.

   Suppose that a researcher assumes that the Sharpe-Lintner pricing relationship holds when, in fact, Equation (20) holds. In that case, define α_i as the difference between the true expected return of risky asset i and the expected return which corresponds to the Sharpe-Lintner model:

$$\alpha_i = \gamma^d\theta - q_i^d + \beta_i^m(q_m - \theta_m) \qquad i \in F \tag{21}$$

If q_m is smaller than $\gamma^d\theta$, it immediately follows from (21) that traded foreign assets held long by domestic investors will have alphas which can be expressed as a decreasing function of beta. Zero-beta foreign assets held long by domestic investors will have positive alphas. Zero-beta foreign assets which are nontraded will have alphas between $\gamma^d\theta$ and $(-\gamma^d\theta)$. Finally, zero-beta foreign assets held short will have negative alphas. All *traded* assets, either foreign or domestic, will have alphas which can be expressed as a decreasing function of beta.

   The results of this section have important empirical implications. First, note that if there are barriers to international investment for domestic investors, but not for foreign investors, a portfolio of domestic risky assets with a beta of one will in general have an expected return different from the expected return of the world market portfolio. Furthermore, if it can be shown that a linear relationship exists for all assets of a country between their beta and their expected return, then no asset of that country is a nontraded asset. If there are no barriers to

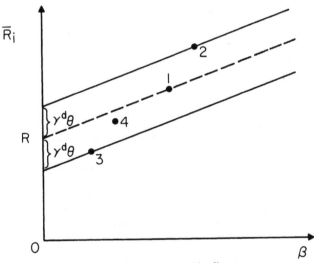

Figure 1. Security market lines

international investment for domestic assets, a domestic zero-beta portfolio would have an expected return equal to the rate of interest. Because a foreign zero-beta portfolio can include nontraded assets, its expected return can be greater than or smaller than the rate of interest.

IV. Which Assets are Non-Traded?

Section III showed that nontraded assets will plot between two security market lines which we described. It would be useful to find out more about nontraded assets. If we know which assets are likely to be nontraded by domestic investors, we have information from which to estimate the security markets lines. Furthermore, we can characterize more precisely efficient portfolios.

Aggregating Expression (8) across domestic investors, we get:

$$\bar{R} - R.\underline{l} + \theta.\varrho \geq \frac{1}{T^d} \, \underline{V} \sum\nolimits_{k \epsilon d} (w^k - v^k) W^k \geq \bar{R} - R.\underline{l} - \theta.\varrho \qquad (22)$$

For a nontraded asset, both inequalities in (22) must hold strictly. Define Ω^d as the proportion of domestic wealth W^d invested in risky assets:

$$\Omega^d = \frac{1}{W^d} \sum\nolimits_{\forall i} \sum\nolimits_{k \epsilon D} (w_i^k - v_i^k) W^k \qquad (23)$$

Let $(w^d - v^d)$ be a portfolio of risky assets whose weights sum up to one and such that the ratio of holdings of any two assets is the same as the ratio in which the domestic country holds these two risky assets. For a nontraded asset, Expression (22) can be rewritten as:

$$\bar{R}_i - R + \theta > \left(\frac{\Omega^d W^d}{T^d}\right) V_i(w^d - v^d) > \bar{R}_i - R - \theta \qquad (24)$$

$V_i(w^d - v^d)$ is equal to the covariance of the i-th asset with the *domestic* portfolio of risky assets. We can define Ω^f as the fraction of foreign wealth W^f invested in risky assets and $(w^f - v^f)$ as the portfolio of risky assets for foreign investors defined in the same way as $(w^d - v^d)$. With this notation, Expression (9) implies that if we write $\text{Cov}(\tilde{R}_i, \tilde{R}^F)$ for $V_i(w^f - v^f)$, the following relationship must hold:

$$\text{Cov}(\tilde{R}_i, \tilde{R}^F) = \frac{T^f}{\Omega^f W^f} (\bar{R}_i - R) \qquad (25)$$

Equation (25) can be used to eliminate the expected excess return in (24):

$$\theta > \left(\frac{\Omega^d w^d}{T^d}\right) \text{Cov}(\tilde{R}_i, \tilde{R}^D) - \left(\frac{\Omega^f W^f}{T^f}\right) \text{Cov}(\tilde{R}_i, \tilde{R}^F) > -\theta \qquad (26)$$

where i is a nontraded asset for domestic investors, and $\text{Cov}(\tilde{R}_i, \tilde{R}^D)$ is $V_i(w^d - v^d)$. From Expression (26), it follows that if there is an asset which is correlated neither with the domestic portfolio nor with the foreign portfolio of risky assets, that asset will necessarily be nontraded. A risky asset which is correlated neither with the portfolio of risky assets held by domestic investors, nor with the one held by foreign investors, must be an asset with a beta of zero. Looking at Expression (26), one would think that a risky asset with a beta different from zero in absolute value by some small number ϵ would still be a nontraded asset. It is shown in the appendix that (26) can be rewritten in such a way that it depends on the covariance of the asset being considered with the market portfolio and a constant. It immediately follows from that result that there must exist a beta β^* such that all assets with a larger beta must be traded. Because beta is a measure of the risk of an asset in a world without barriers to international investment, this result means that such barriers decrease trade in the least risky assets. Those assets do not provide an expected return large enough to offset the cost of holding them due to the barriers.

The fact that assets with low betas are those likely to be nontraded is important for empirical research. First, this result should make us very cautious about using portfolios which have a large proportion of assets with low beta in tests of international asset pricing models.[9] Secondly, this result suggests that, when estimating security market lines, it might be worthwhile to test whether a security market line estimated using only assets with a high beta has a different slope from one estimated using only assets with a low beta. Should the slope of these two security market lines be different, this could be used as evidence of the existence of barriers to international investment. Finally, one should be very careful in devising techniques to form a portfolio of foreign stocks. Buying the market portfolio in a foreign country might just be buying a highly inefficient portfolio for domestic investors.

V. Concluding Remarks

In this paper, we constructed a model of international asset pricing such that, for domestic investors, it is equally costly to hold foreign securities long or short. It can easily be shown that the results we obtained hold as long as barriers to international investment make it costly for a domestic investor to hold the same foreign security simultaneously long and short. Our results generalize in a natural way if foreign investors also face barriers to international investment.[10]

The model presented here holds if barriers to international investment can be represented as taxes on the *absolute* value of an investor's holdings of risky foreign assets. The Black model holds if barriers to international investment correspond to taxes on the *net* value of an investor's holdings of foreign risky assets. In the Black model, investors are indifferent between holding their portfolio of risky assets or their portfolio plus one foreign share held simultaneously long and short, whereas in our model investors offered this choice would never be indifferent. In our model, short-sales do not entail a subsidy. Both our model and the Black model offer well-defined null hypotheses against which the hypothesis of no barriers to international investment can be tested. Because earlier tests of models of international asset pricing were plagued by the lack of a well-defined null hypothesis,[11] our model leads to more powerful tests of models without barriers to international investment.

[9] For instance, Black [3] suggested looking at the minimum variance zero-beta portfolio. Clearly, in our model, that portfolio could have an expected return equal to the rate of interest in the presence of barriers to international investment.

[10] Stulz [8] contains a very general version of the present paper.

[11] See Solnik [6] and the comments following his paper.

The Journal of Finance
APPENDIX

Let h^f and h^d be two portfolios such that:

$$w^d - v^d + h^d = w^f - v^f + h^f = w^s \tag{A.1}$$

It follows that $(h^d)'l = (h^f)'l = 0$. It must be true that:

$$\Omega^d(w^d - v^d)W^d + \Omega^f(w^f - v^f)W^f = w^s W^w \tag{A.2}$$

From (A.2):

$$-\Omega^d h^d W^d = \Omega^f h^f W^f \tag{A.3}$$

From (9) and (A.3), after setting $-h^d = h$:

$$w^f - v^f = w^s + \left(\frac{\Omega^d W^d}{\Omega^f W^f}\right) h = Y^{-1}\left(\frac{T^f}{\Omega^f W^f}\right)(\bar{R} - Rl) \tag{A.4}$$

Substituting (17) and (18) in (9), we get:

$$\Omega^f = \frac{T^f}{W^f}\frac{W^w}{(T^d + T^f)} + \frac{T^f}{W^f}l'Y^{-1}(\gamma^d \varrho\theta - q^d\gamma^d) \tag{A.5}$$

Solving (A.4) for h yields, after using (18):

$$h = \frac{T^f}{\Omega^d W^d}\{-l'Y^{-'}(\gamma^d \varrho\theta - q^d\gamma^d)w^s\} + \frac{T^f}{\Omega^d W^d}\{Y^{-'}(\gamma^d \varrho\theta - q^d\gamma^d)\} \tag{A.6}$$

Substituting (A.6), in (26) using (A.1) and (A.5) yields an expression which can be written:

$$\theta > b \operatorname{Cov}(\tilde{R}_i, \tilde{R}_m) + d[\gamma^d\theta - q_i^d\gamma^d] > -\theta \tag{A.7}$$

where b and d can be zero only if $\theta = 0$.

REFERENCES

1. R. A. Abrams and U. S. Karmarkar. "Optimal Multiperiod Investment—Consumption Policies." *Econometrica* 48 (March 1980), 333–54.
2. M. Adler and B. Dumas. "Optimal International Acquisitions." *Journal of Finance* 30 (March 1975), 1–19.
3. F. Black. "International Capital Market Equilibrium with Investment Barriers." *Journal of Financial Economics* 1 (December 1974), 337–52.
4. R. Roll. "A Critique of the Asset Pricing Theory's Tests; Part I: On Past and Potential Testability of the Theory." *Journal of Financial Economics* 4 (March 1977), 129–76.
5. C. W. Smith and F. A. Milne. "Capital Asset Pricing with Proportional Transaction Costs." *Journal of Financial and Quantitative Analysis* 15 (June 1980), 253–65.
6. B. Solnik. "The International Pricing of Risk: An Empirical Investigation of the World Capital Market Structure." *Journal of Finance* 29 (May 1974), 365–79.
7. R. C. Stapleton and N. G. Subrahmanyam. "Market Imperfections, Capital Market Equilibrium and Corporation Finance." *Journal of Finance* 32 (May 1977), 307–19.
8. R. M. Stulz. "Essays on International Asset Pricing." PH.D. Dissertation, M.I.T., 1980.

[2]

THE JOURNAL OF FINANCE • VOL. XL, NO. 1 • MARCH 1985

International Asset Pricing under Mild Segmentation: Theory and Test

VIHANG ERRUNZA and ETIENNE LOSQ*

ABSTRACT

This paper conducts a theoretical and empirical investigation of the pricing (and portfolio) implications of investment barriers in the context of international capital markets. The postulated market structure—labelled "mildly segmented"—leads to the existence of "super" risk premiums for a subset of securities and to a breakdown of the standard separation result. The empirical study uses an extended data base including LDC markets and provides tentative support for the mild segmentation hypothesis.

THE QUESTION AS TO whether the international capital market is integrated or segmented appears particularly elusive. Indeed, the difficulties surrounding this important issue abound, as was made vividly clear by Solnik [20].

At the risk of tackling too ambitious a task, we undertake here to build a model and develop an empirical methodology to provide at least a partial answer to the segmentation-integration issue. To do so, we follow one of Solnik's recommendations [20, p. 505]:

> The efficient way to test for segmentation would seem to be to specify the type of imperfection which might create it and study its specific impact on portfolio optimality and asset pricing.

The specific imperfection we introduce relates to the assumed inability of a class of investors to trade in a subset of securities as a result of portfolio inflow restrictions imposed by some governments. From this starting point, we derive a valuation model and conduct an empirical analysis. As a whole, this paper has the following distinctive features:

1. Using a new concept of risk—conditional market risk—the model yields a closed-form solution for the equilibrium risk-return tradeoff in segmented markets.[1] Specifically, the securities inaccessible to a subset of investors

---

* Errunza is from McGill University and Losq is from McGill University and ESSEC, France. The authors wish to thank the International Finance Corporation, Washington, D.C. for funding the development of the LDC securities data bank. Research assistance of Prasad Padmanabhan and insightful comments of James Bicksler, Bernard Dumas, Dennis Logue, Lemma Senbet, René Stulz, Alex Whitmore, and Morty Yalovsky are greatly acknowledged. Financial support was provided by SSHRC and Faculty of Management, McGill University.

[1] By way of contrast, such an explicit representation of the risk-return tradeoff is generally missing in most of the well-known models of market segmentation. For example, in a recent paper on international asset pricing with barriers to entry, Stulz [24] fails to specify the risk-return tradeoff for at least one class of assets (those which are not traded by all investors). As for the oft cited paper of Adler and Dumas [1], the purpose is not really to characterize the equilibrium relationship between

105

    command a super risk premium that is proportional to the conditional market risk.

2. The model lends itself to the analysis of a continuum of market structures, with the two polar cases corresponding to complete (one-way) segmentation and complete integration, respectively. Although there exist a number of papers dealing with the segmentation-integration issue,[2] few accommodate intermediate—and more realistic—structures where the markets are neither completely segmented nor completely integrated. The paradigm which follows was designed to deal with this more realistic problem, and thus follows the lead of Black [3] and, more specifically, Stulz [24].[3]

3. The kind of imperfection which constitutes the source of segmentation in the model appears quite prevalent in the international arena.[4] Indeed, access to the capital markets of many countries is severely restricted for nonresidents; in contrast, intra-country restrictions on portfolio investment are typically much less stringent. A model of market segmentation would thus seem more appropriate in an international context than it would in a purely domestic setting.

4. Finally, this paper tests the segmentation hypothesis by using an expanded data base. This data base includes not only the standard U.S. securities but also the returns on selected common stocks heavily traded in Less Developed Countries (LDCs). On a priori grounds one would expect the degree of segmentation between LDC and U.S. markets to be higher than between European and U.S. markets. As a result, the ex ante probability of obtaining inconclusive results should be lower. The test results are not statistically inconsistent with the mild segmentation hypothesis.

    The analytical derivation of the asset pricing model under conditions of market segmentation is presented in Section I. In Section II, this valuation model is transformed to derive empirically testable hypotheses. Finally, Section III presents the test methodology and reports empirical results. A brief conclusion follows.

---

risk and return in markets which are neither fully segmented nor fully integrated. A similar comment can be made concerning the model of Lee and Sachdeva [12] where the focus is also more on the multinationals' investment policies than on asset pricing. In the paper of Stapleton and Subrahmanyam [21], asset prices are indeed determined for different market structures but only numerical, as opposed to analytical, solutions are provided. Finally, the model of market segmentation proposed by Glenn [10] in a domestic context also falls short of yielding a closed-form representation of the risk-return tradeoff since his pricing formula involves an endogenous variable (namely, the final wealth of those investors whose portfolio investments are restricted).

[2] See, for instance, Solnik [18], Grauer et al. [11], Stulz [23], and especially Stehle [22].

[3] The model of this paper can be seen as the limiting case of the more general framework developed by Stulz [24]. Indeed, while in Stulz the cost of investing abroad is finite, in this model it is prohibitively high, so that domestic (U.S.) investors trade primarily in U.S. securities. In this extreme case, the problem can be completely solved while in the more general case Stulz could only obtain partial results. Our model can also be contrasted to that of Mayers [15]; indeed, while Mayers focuses on the concept of nonmarketability, we introduce the more general notion of restricted marketability.

[4] In contrast, Black's model is premised on a type of imperfection which appears somewhat artificial. Indeed, one recalls that he assumes proportionality between the cost of investing abroad and the *net* foreign position, which amounts to assuming the existence of a subsidy for short-selling foreign securities.

I. A Model of International Market Segmentation

A. Model Set-Up

We consider an idealized representation of an international capital market characterized by the following:

(i) *Unequal Access Assumption.* A subset of the investing population—the unrestricted investors—can trade in all the securities available; the others, labelled the restricted investors, can trade only in a subset of the securities, those which are termed eligible; the noneligible or ineligible securities can thus be held only by the unrestricted investors.

(ii) *Perfect Capital Market Assumption.* The different national capital markets are perfect and frictionless (no taxes, no transaction costs, . . .).

(iii) *Mean-Variance Assumption.* The expected utility of each investor can be represented as a function of the expected value and the variance of the *real* returns on the investment portfolio.[5]

(iv) *Free Lending and Borrowing Assumption.* Each investor can freely lend and borrow at the same real rate of interest.[6]

(v) *Normality Assumption.* The real returns are assumed to be normally distributed.[7]

For the sake of illustration, we may focus on a two-country capital market where country 1 investors are restricted, country 2 investors are unrestricted, country 1 securities are eligible and country 2 securities are ineligible (for country 1 investors). Specifically, portfolio inflow restrictions imposed by the government of country 2 prevent country 1 investors from holding country 2 securities; whereas no such controls are imposed by the government of country 1. We shall characterize such a market structure by the term "mild segmentation."

B. Definitions and Notation

Before turning to the main results of the model, we need to introduce several notations and definitions.

---

[5] Explicit treatment of exchange risk is thus made unnecessary by the set of assumptions which are adopted in this paper for the sake of tractability. If it had to be recognized that the prices of consumption goods may vastly differ from one country to the rest, or that nationals of different countries do not necessarily share the same consumption preferences, or that tax systems may be highly discriminatory, then the problem of exchange risk could not be so conveniently dismissed. For a discussion of firm valuation under exchange risk and differential taxation, see Senbet [17]. A more modest objective is pursued in this paper which deals with only one imperfection of the international capital market. Also note that we deal only with the demand side. An equilibrium analysis in a framework that allows supply adjustments under barriers to capital flows is discussed in Errunza and Senbet [8].

[6] Clearly, in today's capital markets there does not exist a security which would be riskless in real terms. However, if the investment horizon is comparatively short, then, because of the low degree of uncertainty surrounding the short-term inflation rate, Treasury Bills might not constitute too unreasonable proxies for the riskless asset. For empirical treatment, see Section III.

[7] In the continuous time version of the model, the instantaneous returns are assumed to follow a stationary diffusion process which implies that the security prices are lognormally distributed. Preliminary results in Errunza and Losq [7] suggest that stock prices in various countries fit this specification reasonably well.

Notation—The subscript e (i) is used as a generic index to represent the eligible (ineligible) securities. The capital letter R stands for rate of return, the tilde denotes randomness, the prime the transposition operator, and the inferior bar a vector; thus R_f is the rate of interest and $\tilde{\underline{R}}$ the vector of rates of return on the risky securities. This vector $\tilde{\underline{R}}$, the variance-covariance matrix V, and the vector of aggregate market values $\underline{P}$ are partitioned as follows:

$$\tilde{\underline{R}} = \begin{bmatrix} \tilde{\underline{R}}_e \\ \tilde{\underline{R}}_i \end{bmatrix}; \qquad V = \begin{bmatrix} V_{ee} & V_{ei} \\ V_{ie} & V_{ii} \end{bmatrix}; \qquad \underline{P} = \begin{bmatrix} \underline{P}_e \\ \underline{P}_i \end{bmatrix}$$

Because of the mildly segmented structure of the market, we also need to introduce three market portfolios:

- The World Market Portfolio (WMP); market value: M; rate of return: $\tilde{R}_M$; representative vector: $\underline{\text{WMP}} = \underline{P}$.
- The Market Portfolio of Ineligible Securities (MPIS); market value: M_I: rate of return: $\tilde{R}_I$: representative vector: $\underline{\text{MPIS}} = \begin{bmatrix} 0 \\ \underline{P}_i \end{bmatrix}$.
- The Market Portfolio of Eligible Securities (MPES); market value: M_E; rate of return: $\tilde{R}_E$; representative vector: $\underline{\text{MPES}} = \begin{bmatrix} \underline{P}_e \\ 0 \end{bmatrix}$.

Finally, the subscripts u and r denote the unrestricted and the restricted investors, respectively. Thus A_u (A_r) stands for the absolute risk-aversion coefficient for the subset of unrestricted (restricted) investors. The capital letter A denotes the risk-aversion coefficient for the aggregate population of investors $(A^{-1} \equiv A_u^{-1} + A_r^{-1})$ and the greek letter μ the ratio A/A_r.

Definition 1: The *Diversification Portfolio* (DP) is a portfolio of eligible securities where the dollar amounts invested in the various securities are given by the vector $\underline{\text{DP}} \equiv \begin{bmatrix} V_{ee}^{-1} V_{ei} \underline{P}_i \\ 0 \end{bmatrix}$; it can be shown (see, for example, Dhrymes, Theorem

2, [4, p. 24]) that DP corresponds to that portfolio of eligible securities which is most highly correlated with the MPIS; hence, the name "Diversification Portfolio."

Definition 2: The *Hedged Portfolio* (HP) consists of a long position in MPIS and a short position in DP: $\underline{\text{HP}} \equiv \underline{\text{MPIS}} - \underline{\text{DP}}$; using the aforementioned theorem in Dhrymes, it can be verified that HP bears no correlation with any of the eligible securities, hence the name "Hedged Portfolio."

Definition 3: The *conditional market risk* of a security is defined as the conditional covariance between its return and the return on the market portfolio of all ineligible securities, the returns on all eligible securities being given. Thus, we characterize the conditional market risk as: $\text{Cov}[\tilde{R}_i, \{\tilde{R}_I \mid \{\tilde{R}_1 = R_1, \cdots, \tilde{R}_e = R_e, \cdots\}]$. For an eligible security, the risk is zero by construction; indeed,

$$\text{Cov}[\tilde{R}_e, \tilde{R}_I \mid \{\tilde{R}_1 = R_1, \cdots, \tilde{R}_e = R_e, \cdots\}] = \text{Cov}[R_e, \tilde{R}_i] = 0 \qquad (1)$$

Further, we recall from statistical theory (see, for example, Dhrymes, Theorem

2, [4, p. 24]) that in the case of a multivariate normal distribution, the conditional covariance does not depend on the given values $(\tilde{R}_e = {}_\Lambda R_1, \cdots, R_e, \cdots)$; hence, the more compact notation $\text{Cov}[\tilde{R}_i, \tilde{R}_I \mid \tilde{\underline{R}}_e]$. It is also a simple matter to verify that the conditional market risk is proportional to the covariance with the return on HP.[8]

C. Risk, Return, and Portfolio Composition under Mild Segmentation

PROPOSITION 1. *In a mildly segmented market under conditions* (i) *to* (v) *and at equilibrium*:

(a) *the eligible securities are priced as if the market was not segmented:*

$$E(\tilde{R}_e - R_f) = (AM)\text{Cov}[\tilde{R}_e, \tilde{R}_M] \qquad (2)$$

(b) *the ineligible securities command a "super" risk premium which is proportional to the conditional market risk:*

$$E(\tilde{R}_i - R_f) - (AM)\text{Cov}[\tilde{R}_i, \tilde{R}_M] = (A_u - A)M_I\text{Cov}[(\tilde{R}_i, \tilde{R}_I) \mid \tilde{\underline{R}}_e] \qquad (3)$$

with $(A_u - A)M_I \geq 0$.

(c) *the unrestricted investors hold the portfolio* D_u *defined by:* $\underline{D}_u \equiv (1 - \mu)$ WMP $+ \mu$HP.

(d) *the restricted investors hold the portfolio* D_r *defined by:* $\underline{D}_r \equiv \mu($MPES $+$ DP$)$.

Proof: Please refer to Appendix A.

Interpretation

1. Under mild segmentation, the eligible securities are priced as if the markets were completely integrated; this property should be contrasted with the results of Stulz [24] where it is not generally true that the eligible securities plot on a security market line which corresponds to the Sharpe-Lintner relationship (see Stulz [24, p. 930]).

2. The ineligible securities command a super risk premium which, on average, is positive. By aggregating Equation (3) over the set of ineligible securities, we obtain:

$$E(\tilde{R}_I - R_f) - (AM)\text{Cov}[\tilde{R}_I, \tilde{R}_M] = (A_u - A)M_I\text{Var}[\tilde{R}_I \mid \tilde{\underline{R}}_e] \geq 0 \qquad (4)$$

Further, if we denote by ρ the multiple correlation coefficient between $\tilde{R}_I$ and the random vector $\tilde{\underline{R}}_e$, we can show (see Dhrymes, Theorem 2, [4, p. 24]):

$$\text{Var}[\tilde{R}_I \mid \tilde{\underline{R}}_e] = (1 - \rho^2)\text{Var}[\tilde{R}_I] \qquad (5)$$

ρ can be interpreted here as the correlation coefficient between $\tilde{R}_I$ and that portfolio of eligible securities which is most correlated with $\tilde{R}_I$, i.e., the "Diversification Portfolio."

Equation (4) gives the super risk premium for the market portfolio of ineligible securities and thus provides us with a measure of the increase in required return which the ineligible securities must yield because of the segmented nature of the

---

[8] We are grateful to René Stulz for pointing out this interpretation to us.

110   *The Journal of Finance*

market. From the viewpoint of firms, this super risk premium also measures the effect of segmentation on the cost of supplying risky securities in the ineligible segment of the market. As is made clear by Equations (4) and (5), the effect of market segmentation becomes more pronounced as the risk aversion of the unrestricted investors increases and as the correlation between the two segments of the market decreases.[9]

3. The super risk premiums vanish only in two limiting cases, which we discuss in turn.

Limiting case no. 1: $A_r/A_u \to \infty$. As the unrestricted investors become much less risk-averse than the restricted investors, the following holds:

- $\mu \equiv (1 + A_r/A_u)^{-1} \to 0$. According to parts (c) and (d) of Proposition 1, the unrestricted investors tend to hold all of the risky securities and the restricted investors none of them.
- $(A_u - A)/A \equiv A_u/A_r \to 0$. According to part (b) of Proposition 1, the "super" risk premium becomes negligible relative to the "normal" risk premium.

Limiting case no. 2: $\rho \to 1$. As the multiple correlation coefficient ρ between $\tilde{R}_I$ and $\tilde{R}_e$ tends towards one, first, the return on the "Diversification Portfolio" becomes perfectly correlated with $\tilde{R}_I$; second, the "Hedged Portfolio" becomes riskless and, at equilibrium, yields the risk-free rate of interest R_f; and, third, the conditional market risk becomes negligible for all securities, so that the super risk premiums vanish.

In such a limiting case, the eligible segment of the market offers the same diversification opportunities as those offered by the whole market; consequently, the a priori constraint that denies the restricted investors access to the ineligible segment becomes ineffective. By holding DP as a perfect substitute for MPIS, the restricted investors can acquire a portfolio D_r, the return on which is perfectly correlated with $\tilde{R}_M$. As for the unrestricted investors, they view HP and the riskless asset as perfect substitutes; at equilibrium, they are thus willing to hold the fraction μ of HP and adjust their lending or borrowing accordingly. In any case, the return on their portfolio D_u is also perfectly correlated with $\tilde{R}_M$. Thus, it appears that the case where $\rho = 1$ does not essentially differ from the perfect integration case.

4. Because of segmentation, the restricted investors cannot hold the ineligible securities and thus properly diversify their holdings. As a second best solution,

---

[9] The extreme form of market segmentation takes place when $\rho = 0$, i.e., when no correlation exists between $\tilde{R}_I$ and the return on any eligible security. In this extreme case, the ineligible securities are priced as if there were two-way segmentation (no investment in either direction between the two segments); indeed, if $\rho = 0$, Equation (3) implies:

$$E(\tilde{R}_i - R_f) = (A_u M_I)\text{Cov}[\tilde{R}_i, \tilde{R}_I]$$

As for the eligible securities, however, they would still be priced as if the market was fully integrated.

In the two-country case, if the product and factor markets of the two countries were well integrated, we would expect some degree of correlation between the returns on the securities of the two countries; to that extent, we would thus not expect the extreme form of mild segmentation to prevail.

they hold the market portfolio of eligible securities plus a proxy for the market portfolio of ineligible securities—the portfolio DP—which is supplied to them by the unrestricted investors. The unrestricted investors thus play the role of financial intermediaries: they provide diversification services for which they receive an implicit remuneration; indeed, they supply securities for which no super risk premium exists, i.e., securities with a comparatively low return.

5. We have already seen that the super risk premium becomes negligible when the unrestricted investors have a comparatively small risk-aversion level or when a suitable proxy for MPIS exists in the eligible segment. Outside these two limiting cases (i.e., if $\mu > 0$ and $\rho < 1$), the super risk premiums must exist to induce the unrestricted, but risk-averse, investors to supply diversification services.

Indeed, in the absence of super risk premiums, the expected excess return on any security would be proportional to its covariance with the world market portfolio; in such a case, the risk-averse unrestricted investors would hold the fraction $A/A_u \equiv 1 - \mu < 1$ of the WMP, at the exclusion of any other risky investment. Since, by hypothesis, the restricted investors cannot hold the ineligible securities, these would be in excess supply. Consequently, for equilibrium to prevail, super risk premiums must exist, so that unrestricted investors are induced to acquire the residual fraction μ of MPIS (which the restricted investors would like to, but cannot, hold) and supply the same fraction μ of DP.

6. To conclude this section, we present Table I which summarizes the main features of three paradigms which may be used in the two-country case: perfect integration (no barrier to investments), mild segmentation (barriers in one direction only), and complete segmentation (barriers in both directions).

II. The Segmentation / Integration Issue: A Testable Hypothesis

The magnitude of the super risk premium depends on $A_u - A$, i.e., on risk-aversion coefficients that are not directly measurable. We must therefore rely on cross-sectional regressions in order to capture the degree of effective segmentation in the international capital market. We sketch below the specific procedure we have chosen to achieve that aim.

A. Estimation of Security-Specific Risk Characteristics

Without specifying a particular return generating model, the estimation of the conditional market risk for each ineligible security would be a formidable task. Thus, for the sake of tractability, we assume the following two-factor return generating model:[10]

$$\tilde{R}_e = \alpha_e + \beta_e \tilde{R}_M + \gamma_e \tilde{V}_E + \tilde{\varepsilon}_e \quad \text{with} \quad \text{Cov}[\tilde{\varepsilon}_e, \tilde{R}_M] = \text{Cov}[\tilde{\varepsilon}_e, \tilde{V}_E] = 0 \quad (6)$$

---

[10] Even though multivariate normality was assumed in the previous section, the two-factor return generating model does not require any assumption about the process generating returns (see Stehle [22]). In view of the significant world factor reported by Lessard [14] and Solnik [19], for the empirical tests, we use world market return ($\tilde{R}_W$) in place of $\tilde{R}_M$.

Table I

The Two-Country Case

Paradigm	Conditions	Expected Excess Returns		Portfolio Composition for	
		Eligible Securites	Ineligible Securities	Restricted Investors	Unrestricted Investors
Perfect Integration	No barrier to investment or $\mathrm{Var}[\tilde{R}_i \mid \tilde{R}_e] = 0$	$AM\,\mathrm{Cov}[\tilde{R}_e, \tilde{R}_M]$	$AM\,\mathrm{Cov}[\tilde{R}_i, \tilde{R}_M]$	World market portfolio	World market portfolio
Mild Segmentation	One-way barrier to investment; $A_u > A$ and $\mathrm{Var}[\tilde{R}_i \mid \tilde{R}_e] > 0$	$AM\,\mathrm{Cov}[\tilde{R}_e, \tilde{R}_M]$	$AM\,\mathrm{Cov}[\tilde{R}_i, \tilde{R}_M] + (A_u - A)M\,\mathrm{Cov}[\tilde{R}_i, \tilde{R}_i \mid \tilde{R}_e]$	Market portfolio of country 1 securities + "diversification" portfolio	World market portfolio + hedged market portfolio of country 2 securities
Special Case: Extreme Form of Mild Segmentation	$A_u > A$ and $\mathrm{Cov}[\tilde{R}_e, \tilde{R}_i] = 0$	$AM_E\,\mathrm{Cov}[\tilde{R}_e, \tilde{R}_E]$	$A_u M_I\,\mathrm{Cov}[\tilde{R}_i, \tilde{R}_I]$	Market portfolio of country 1 securities	World market portfolio + market portfolio of country 2 securities
Complete Segmentation	Two-way barriers to investment	$A_r M_E\,\mathrm{Cov}[\tilde{R}_e, \tilde{R}_E]$	$A_u M_I\,\mathrm{Cov}[\tilde{R}_i, \tilde{R}_I]$	Market portfolio of country 1 securities	Market portfolio of country 2 securities

Note: The subscripts r and u denote the investors of countries 1 and 2, respectively. The subscripts e and i denote the securities of countries 1 and 2, respectively.

where the second factor, $\tilde{V}_E$, is orthogonal to $\tilde{R}_M$ and defined by:

$$\tilde{R}_E = a_E + b_E \tilde{R}_M + \tilde{V}_E \quad \text{with} \quad \text{Cov}[\tilde{V}_E, \tilde{R}_M] = 0 \qquad (7)$$

A similar return generating model is assumed to apply to the ineligible segment of the market:

$$\tilde{R}_i = \alpha_i + \beta_i \tilde{R}_M + \gamma_i \tilde{V}_I + \tilde{\varepsilon}_i \quad \text{with} \quad \text{Cov}[\tilde{\varepsilon}_i, \tilde{R}_M] = \text{Cov}[\tilde{\varepsilon}_i, \tilde{V}_I] = 0 \qquad (8)$$

where the second factor, $\tilde{V}_I$, is orthogonal to $\tilde{R}_M$ and defined by:

$$\tilde{R}_I = a_I + b_I \tilde{R}_M + \tilde{V}_I \quad \text{with} \quad \text{Cov}[\tilde{V}_I, \tilde{R}_M] = 0 \qquad (9)$$

We further assume:

$$\text{Cov}[\tilde{\varepsilon}_i, \tilde{R}_e] = 0 \qquad e = 1, \cdots, E; \quad i = 1, \cdots, I \qquad (10)$$

an assumption which severely limits the sources of covariability between the returns of eligible and ineligible securities; for example, as in most empirical models of this type, industry effects are simply assumed away.

Given the above simplifying assumptions about the structure of returns in the two segments of the market, the unconditional and conditional market risks can be readily expressed in terms of the coefficients β and γ. In such a simplified context, the mild segmentation paradigm yields the following results:

PROPOSITION 2.

(a) *The unconditional market risk of any security is proportional to its beta coefficient:*

$$\text{Cov}[\tilde{R}_j, \tilde{R}_M] = \beta_j \text{Var}[\tilde{R}_M] \qquad j = i \text{ or } e \qquad (11)$$

(b) *The conditional market risk of any ineligible security is a linear function of the β and γ coefficients:*

$$\text{Cov}(\tilde{R}_i, \tilde{R}_I \mid \tilde{R}_e) = A\beta_i + B\gamma_i \qquad \text{with} \quad A \text{ and } B > 0 \qquad (12)$$

(c) *As a consequence, the risk-return tradeoff takes the following simplified forms:*

  • *for the eligible segment:*

$$E(\tilde{R}_e) = R_f + \lambda_E \beta_e + \theta_E \gamma_e \qquad \text{with} \quad \lambda_E \geq 0 \quad \text{and} \quad \theta_E = 0 \qquad (13)$$

  • *for the ineligible segment:*

$$E(\tilde{R}_i) = R_f + \lambda_I \beta_i + \theta_I \gamma_i \qquad \text{with} \quad \lambda_I \geq \lambda_E \geq 0 \quad \text{and} \quad \theta_I \geq 0 \qquad (14)$$

Proof: Please refer to Appendix B.

B. Testable Hypothesis

Assuming that the consensus expectations are unbiased, the expected return, $E(\tilde{R})$, can be proxied by the average historical return, $\bar{R}$; similarly, the beta and gamma coefficients can be estimated by means of time-series regressions conforming to Equations (6) and (8). Two cross-sectional regressions can then be run, one for each segment of the market:

- for the eligible segment:[11]

$$\bar{R}_e = a_E + \lambda_E \beta_e + \theta_E \gamma_e + u_e \tag{15}$$

- for the ineligible segment:

$$\bar{R}_i = a_I + \lambda_I \beta_i + \theta_I \gamma_i + u_i \tag{16}$$

The Hypothesis: Mild Segmentation Versus. Alternate of Not Mildly Segmented Market

If the mild segmentation paradigm holds, we can infer from Proposition 2:

$$\{a_E = a_I = R_f; \quad \lambda_I \geq \lambda_E \geq 0; \quad \theta_I \geq 0; \quad \theta_E = 0\}$$

Of course, the usual caveat applies: the empirical procedure cannot really test whether the markets are mildly segmented independently of the valuation model which was used to derive the test. Thus, if the mild segmentation hypothesis was to be rejected, it might mean either that the markets are not mildly segmented or that the valuation model does not apply. As usual, a joint hypothesis is involved; care should therefore be exercised in deriving implications from the results of the empirical tests which follow.

III. Test of the Mild Segmentation Hypothesis

A. Data

The data base consists of heavily traded securities from nine less developed countries (LDCs), and a random sample from the U.S.[12] Markets and securities included in the sample have monthly total return data for the period 1976–1980. The LDC markets are comparable to many European markets in terms of size, turnover, and liquidity (Errunza [6]). Similarly, tests of the random walk hypothesis suggest these markets to be comparable to some of the smaller developed markets (Errunza and Losq [7]).

B. A Simple Test

If markets are fully integrated, then the risk (World beta) adjusted average returns should be similar across national markets. Table II reports monthly realized returns in US$, β's on GNP and market capitalization weighted world

---

[11] For the sake of notational simplicity, we do not make an explicit distinction between the actual and estimated values of the beta and gamma coefficients.

[12] Information on LDC securities is obtained from the International Finance Corporation emerging markets data bank. COMPUSTAT data tapes are used for U.S. securities. Use of official exchange rates as reported by International Financial statistics of the International Monetary Fund to convert LDC returns into U.S. $ terms may induce bias. However, the problem does not appear to be serious in view of the extremely high correlations for U.S. $ returns based on official exchange rates and purchasing power parity relationships as reported by Errunza and Losq [7]. The nine LDCs are: Argentina (22), Brazil (18), Chile (21), Greece (9), India (23), Korea (22), Mexico (21), Thailand (7), and Zimbabwe (10). The number of securities in the sample is indicated in parentheses after each market.

Table II

Realized Returns, Expected Returns, and the National Factor (1976–1980)

	Average Monthly Realized Return in US$ %	GNP Wt. World Index		Mkt. Cap. Wt. World Index		Average Proportion of Variance Attributable to National Variations
		β	Monthly Expected Return in US$ %	β	Monthly Expected Return in US$ %	
Argentina	5.83	−0.035	0.49	−0.178	0.41	0.56
Brazil	0.39	0.392	0.65	0.162	0.58	0.43
Chile	6.9	−0.591	0.28	−0.623	0.19	0.50
Greece	0.26	0.213	0.58	0.139	0.57	0.41
India	2.45	0.742	0.78	0.637	0.82	0.42
Korea	2.23	0.876	0.83	0.753	0.88	0.40
Mexico	3.26	1.179	0.95	1.020	1.01	0.50
Thailand	1.64	−0.359	0.36	−0.621	0.19	0.60
Zimbabwe	2.24	−0.049	0.48	−0.024	0.49	0.32
U.S.	0.64	0.928	0.85	1.058	1.03	
GNP Wt. World Index	0.88	1.000				
Mkt. Cap. Wt. World Index	1.00			1.000		

Notes: 1. Assume $R_f = 0.5\%$ per month in US$.
2. Construction of world indices and national indices is described in Part E of Section III.

indices, as well as monthly expected returns in US\$. The realized returns in all cases are quite different from what one would anticipate under full integration. Further, for most LDCs, the ratio of realized to expected returns is substantially higher than that for the U.S. market, thereby providing some evidence of segmentation. Of course, this result should be construed as only the first step towards a formal asset pricing test of our model in view of the potential difficulties arising from country (sample) selection, use of official exchange rates, index construction procedure within each market, as well as the time period.

C. The National Factor

Before proceeding with the test of the mild segmentation hypothesis in an international asset pricing model, it would be prudent to investigate the importance of the country factor for our sample of newly emerging markets. The results have implications for the design of the test methodology as discussed below. Table II provides average proportion of security risk explained by the national factor.[13] Country factor seems to be very strong in most cases.[14]

In view of the strength of country effect, the cross-sectional tests of the mild segmentation hypothesis can be approached in two ways:

1. Deal explicitly with the country factor using a two-country design. For example, U.S. securities can be characterized as the eligible set and say Argentinean securities constitute the ineligible set with U.S. investors restricted and Argentinean investors unrestricted. The primary problem with such a design is the small LDC samples which would necessarily lead to formation of overlapping and/or differing size portfolios within each LDC market and hence violate OLS assumptions as suggested by Stehle [22]:
2. Pool securities and construct portfolios that are diversified across countries within each (eligible and ineligible) set. The increased sample size will avoid overlapping and eliminate selection bias that results from constructing portfolios by country in the presence of strong country effects (Adler and Horesh [2]). We will use this approach in the tests which follow.

D. Security and Investor Characterization[15]

Keeping in mind the existing capital flow controls and the patterns of portfolio investments which indirectly reflect perceptions of U.S. investors regarding feasibility or advisability of investments in LDC markets, the eligible (ineligible) segments will be further characterized as technically eligible (ineligible) or

---

[13] The proportions are average R^2 for the regressions of security returns on equally weighted national indices based on our sample of highly traded securities on each market.

[14] This result is consistent with those reported by Errunza [5] and Lessard [12] for LDC markets and is quite similar to the European findings of Solnik [19].

[15] Since published information on capital flow controls relates primarily to direct foreign investments and not to portfolio flows, the characterizations are based on in-house research by members of the capital markets department of the International Finance Corporation (IFC), the World Bank group, as well as personal conversations with various LDC stock exchange authorities by the IFC personnel and one of the authors of this paper. Details on IFC research as well as contact persons for each LDC exchange can be obtained from the authors.

perceived eligible (ineligible). A market (security) is considered technically eligible if there are no formal capital controls on foreign portfolio investments, i.e., if, technically, foreigners can freely invest in these markets (securities). Thus, the securities of U.S., Thailand, Zimbabwe, and open Mexican firms constitute the technically eligible segment. A market (security) is considered perceived eligible if it is characterized by no formal capital controls as well as significant foreign portfolio investments. Since foreign investors are not active in either Thailand or Zimbabwe, the perceived eligible set includes U.S. and open Mexican firms.

Technically Eligible Set:[16]	130 securities from U.S., Thailand, Zimbabwe, and Mexico (open firms).
Technically Ineligible Set:	130 securities from Argentina, Brazil, Chile, Greece, India, Korea, and Mexico (other than open firms).
Perceived Eligible Set:[16]	147 securities from U.S. and Mexico (open firms).
Perceived Ineligible Set:	147 securities from Argentina, Brazil, Chile, Greece, India, Korea, Mexico (other than open firms), Thailand, and Zimbabwe.

For our purpose, the nationals of markets constituting the eligible set(s) can trade only among each other and therefore are characterized as restricted investors, whereas the nationals of markets forming the ineligible set(s) can trade in all securities and hence are characterized as unrestricted investors. This nomenclature is confusing in view of our traditional perceptions of freewheeling U.S. investors and highly constrained LDC investors. A brief clarifying explanation would be valuable.

In practice, the U.S. investors can freely invest abroad but are not allowed to hold securities from the ineligible set. Thus, U.S. investors encounter portfolio inflow controls and could hold the World Market Portfolio (of eligible securities) excluding the ineligible set. In view of the restrictions placed on U.S. investors by the governments of ineligible set countries, we characterize them as restricted investors. On the other hand, LDC investors are not restricted by the governments of eligible set countries but cannot *easily* get funds out of their own countries. However, the official outflow controls on LDC investors do not appear to be prohibitive when one considers the participation of large (at times privileged) LDC investors in eligible markets (with or without home government knowledge). Thus, even though our characterization of LDC investors may not depict reality, it does approximate the current state of affairs as well as the implicit assumption of no outflow controls on LDC investors in our theoretical model. The assumption of free foreign portfolio investments among ineligible markets at both the theoretical and empirical levels is troublesome. An n-factor model to fully capture the pattern of international investment flows would be desirable but is left for further research because of the mathematical complications involved.

[16] The random U.S. (NYSE) sample size is chosen so as to match the appropriate eligible and ineligible sets.

E. The Test Procedure

Market Indices—The LDC market returns are equally weighted for our sample firms, the U.S. market return is a capitalization weighted NYSE index, and the other market returns are market capitalization weighted indices reported by Capital International Perspective. Following Solnik [19], the various compound indices (world, technically (in)eligible, and perceived (in)eligible) are based on GNP weights.

The Riskless Rate—The problem of assuming a riskless rate in an international context is well known (Adler and Horesch [2]) and is especially troublesome for LDCs where a domestic market determined short-term rate similar to U.S. T-bills is generally not available. We reluctantly use 30-day U.S. T-bill rate as a proxy. Of course, in the capital asset pricing context, the various stock price indices are also proxies for market rates of return and hence have their own shortcomings (Roll [16], Solnik [20]).

Portfolio Formation—For each security in each of the four segments (technically (in)eligible and perceived (in)eligible), β_e (β_i) and γ_e (γ_i) are calculated using monthly returns for the period 1976–1977. The β_e (β_i) and γ_e (γ_i) are estimated directly to avoid the measurement error problem associated with estimation of V_E (V_I) in an orthogonal design.[17] Following tradition, portfolio observations are used to minimize nonstationarity and measurement error problems. Since the optimal grouping procedure is not well defined in the case of three-variable linear regression and in view of limited data, we formed 16 nonoverlapping portfolios using a (4 × 4) matrix design to maximize intergroup variation of β_e (β_i) and γ_e (γ_i) using two alternate portfolio construction procedures.[18] Thus, we have 16 nonoverlapping portfolios for each of the four segments and for each of the two portfolio construction procedures using 1976–1977 as the portfolio formation period. Next, monthly portfolio rates of return are calculated for each portfolio for the following 12-month period. The procedure is repeated with 1977–1978

[17] The β_e and γ_e are estimated using:

$$\hat{\beta}_e = \frac{\text{Cov}(\tilde{R}_e, \tilde{R}_w)}{\text{Var}\, \tilde{R}_w} = \frac{\sum_t (R_{et} - \bar{R}_e)(R_{wt} - \bar{R}_w)}{\sum_t (R_{wt} - \bar{R}_w)^2}$$

and

$$\hat{\gamma}_e = \frac{\text{Cov}(\tilde{R}_e, \hat{V}_E)}{\text{Var}(\hat{V}_E)} = \frac{\text{Cov}(\tilde{R}_e, \tilde{R}_E)\text{Var}(\tilde{R}_w) - \text{Cov}(\tilde{R}_e, \tilde{R}_w) \cdot \text{Cov}(\tilde{R}_e, \tilde{R}_w)}{\text{Var}(\tilde{R}_w)\text{Var}(\tilde{R}_E) - [\text{Cov}(\tilde{R}_E, \tilde{R}_w)]^2}$$

Similar expressions are used to calculate β_i and γ_i.

[18] Two portfolio constructions procedures were used.

$\beta - \gamma$ *Portfolios.* Within each segment and during each portfolio formation period, securities were ranked by β to form four β-portfolios. Next, securities within each β-portfolio were ranked by γ to obtain four γ-portfolios, thereby yielding a total of sixteen $\beta - \gamma$ portfolios.

$\gamma - \beta$ *Portfolios.* Within each segment and during each portfolio formation period, securities were ranked by γ to form four γ-portfolios. Next, securities within each γ-portfolio were ranked by β to obtain four β-portfolios, thereby yielding a total of sixteen $\gamma - \beta$ portfolios.

and 1978–1979 as the portfolio formation periods and portfolio returns calculated for years 1979 and 1980, respectively. This provides us with 36 monthly portfolio returns on 16 portfolios for each of the four segments and for each of the two portfolio construction procedures.

Cross-Sectional Regressions—As discussed in the previous section, we have $\bar{r}_e = a_E + \lambda_E \hat{\beta}_e + \theta_E \hat{\gamma}_e + \mu_e$ for the eligible segments where r_{et} ($\bar{r}_e$) is the ex post (mean) excess rate of return for a given eligible portfolio during month t, $t = 1$, $\cdots$, 36; and $\bar{r}_i = a_I + \lambda_I \hat{\beta}_i + \theta_I \hat{\gamma}_i + \mu_i$ for the ineligible segments where r_{it} ($\bar{r}_i$) is the ex post (mean) excess rate of return for a given ineligible portfolio during month t, $t = 1$, $\cdots$, 36. Excess portfolio returns are used in cross-sectional regressions to obtain time series of estimated coefficients, a, λ, and θ for each of the four segments and for each of the two portfolio construction procedures. Following Stehle [22], the risk coefficients β and γ for period t are based on all portfolio returns excluding those during the portfolio formation period and the tth month. Using 1976–1977 as the portfolio formation period and using mean monthly portfolio returns during 1978–1980 as the dependent variable in cross-sectional regressions did not result in significantly different findings. Generalized Least Squares (GLS) procedure was used since the residuals were heteroscedastic.

F. Results

Table III reports GLS parameter estimates from cross-sectional regressions. The table also reports the averages of the month-by-month GLS values of a_t, λ_t, and θ_t; $s(a)$, $s(\lambda)$, and $s(\theta)$ the sample standard deviations of the monthly values of a_t, λ_t, and θ_t, respectively; relevant t-statistics; and the mean adjusted R^2 and its standard deviation $s(R^2)$ for month-by-month regressions of the 16 portfolio returns on the relevant risk measures. These statistics are reported for the four segments under two alternative portfolio construction methods.

The most striking feature of Table III is the consistency of results. Parameter estimates and their significance are quite similar across the two portfolio construction procedures. Further, the behavior of a given set (eligible or ineligible) across the differential characterization (perceived and technical) is also not very different.

The strength of the relationship between ex post returns and risk proxies is on average low and quite variable. Despite the use of a questionable proxy for the riskless return, the intercept estimates are not statistically significantly different from theoretical expectations. There are many months when λ_{Et}, λ_{It}, θ_{Et}, and θ_{It} are negative, indicating a negative relationship between return and risk during those months. This is neither very surprising nor contrary to the mild segmentation asset pricing model. Our theoretical model states the equilibrium relationship between expected return and risk. Thus, the postulated relationship should hold on average and not necessarily month by month. Following Fama [9], we use the average values and summary measures of the time-series properties of λ_{Et}, λ_{It}, θ_{Et}, and θ_{It} to test the mild segmentation hypothesis. We now discuss each of the four conditions associated with our hypothesis:

Table III

GLS Parameter Estimates—Mild Segmentation Model

Market Segment		α_i			λ_i			θ_i			R_i^2	
		$\bar{\alpha}$	$s(\alpha)$	$t(\bar{\alpha})$	$\bar{\lambda}$	$s(\lambda)$	$t(\bar{\lambda})$	$\bar{\theta}$	$s(\theta)$	$t(\bar{\theta})$	$\bar{R}^2$ Adj.	$s(R^2)$
$\beta - \gamma$ Portfolios												
Perceived	Eligible	-0.012	0.046	-1.5	0.010	0.052	1.14	0.010	0.032	1.84	0.217	0.205
	Ineligible	0.017	0.045	2.27	-0.020	0.051	-2.42	0.015	0.062	1.45	0.347	0.233
Technically	Eligible	0.002	0.036	0.33	0.019	0.062	1.87	-0.013	0.037	-2.18	0.335	0.237
	Ineligible	0.023	0.078	1.9	-0.019	0.077	-1.46	0.011	0.071	0.95	0.382	0.225
$\gamma - \beta$ Portfolios												
Perceived	Eligible	-0.011	0.050	-1.35	0.011	0.058	1.13	0.009	0.036	1.45	0.241	0.192
	Ineligible	0.017	0.044	2.32	-0.013	0.044	-1.83	0.013	0.063	1.20	0.338	0.224
Technically	Eligible	0.003	0.036	0.5	0.008	0.065	0.71	-0.001	0.037	-0.21	0.349	0.255
	Ineligible	0.022	0.067	1.95	-0.019	0.056	-2.08	0.011	0.067	1.02	0.350	0.242

Notes: The $t(\bar{\alpha})$ values are calculated based on the theoretical expected value of zero. The t-statistics for $\bar{\lambda}$ and $\bar{\theta}$ test the hypothesis that $E(\bar{\lambda}) = 0$ and $E(\bar{\theta}) = 0$, respectively.

$\bar{a}_E = \bar{a}_I = 0$ Even though the intercept estimates are not statistically significantly different from their theoretical value of 0, the subcondition of $\bar{a}_E = \bar{a}_I$ is rejected for the perceived set under $\beta - \gamma$ portfolio construction procedure.

$\overline{\lambda}_I \geq \overline{\lambda}_E \geq 0$ There is no evidence to support the hypothesis that $\overline{\lambda}_E$ and $\overline{\lambda}_I$ differ significantly.

$\overline{\theta}_E = 0$ We cannot reject this condition in all cases. The almost significantly negative $\overline{\theta}_E$ for technically eligible securities under $\beta - \gamma$ portfolio construction procedure is troublesome.

$\overline{\theta}_I \geq 0$ The $\overline{\theta}_I$ are not statistically significantly different from zero. Thus, one could claim that the mildly segmented CAPM cannot be rejected; but the same is true for the standard CAPM applied to all securities indiscriminately ($\overline{\theta}_I = 0$).[19] However, note that $\overline{\theta}_I$ are consistently greater than zero and large in practical terms.[20]

In summary, the results are not statistically inconsistent with the mild segmentation hypothesis. The weak results can be attributed to the kinds of restrictions imposed in the real world, use of various proxies including the risk-free rate, and small sample size. Further empirical research based on more realistic world capital market structure, alternate proxies, and larger sample size is suggested.

IV. Conclusion

In this paper, a formal model of international capital asset pricing was developed. The primary distinguishing feature of the model is the unequal access assumption which approximates the reality of a mildly segmented world market. The incidence of mild segmentation does not affect required return on an eligible security whereas the required return on an ineligible security is different from what the standard CAPM would suggest. The ineligible securities would generally command a super risk premium which is proportional to the differential risk aversion and the conditional market risk.

We then conduct a cross-sectional test of the mild segmentation hypothesis. The overall results are not statistically inconsistent with theoretical expectations and thus lend tentative support to the mild segmentation hypothesis. Further empirical work based on a richer data set with longer time period and larger sample size is needed to improve the power of the test.

Appendix A: Proof of Proposition 1

The proof consists of three steps:

Step 1: Check that, given (c) and (d), no security is in excess supply or in excess demand. By construction, the aggregate demand vector $\underline{D}_u + \underline{D}_r \equiv (1 - \mu)\underline{WMP} + \mu(\underline{MPIS} - \underline{DP} + \underline{MPES} + \underline{DP}) \equiv \underline{WMP}$ is indeed equal to the aggregate supply vector $\underline{P} \equiv \underline{WMP}$.

[19] We would like to thank the anonymous referee for pointing this out.

[20] In view of the major political risk factor associated with most of our sample LDCs during 1975–1980, the positive θ's may reveal political risk premia. We would like to thank the anonymous referee for this interpretation.

Step 2: Check the optimality of the portfolio D_r given (1) the constraint that restricted investors cannot acquire ineligible securities and (2) the postulated risk-return relationship in the eligible segment (Equation (2)).

This optimality condition is $E(\tilde{R}_e - R_f) = A_r\text{Cov}[\tilde{R}_e, \underline{D}_r'\tilde{R}]$ for any arbitrary eligible security. Given the definition of $\underline{D}_r$ in (d), we can write:

$$\text{Cov}[\tilde{\underline{R}}_e, \underline{D}_r'\tilde{R}] = \mu\{M_E\text{Cov}[\tilde{\underline{R}}_e, \tilde{R}_E] + V_{ee}V_{ee}^{-1}V_{ei}\underline{P}_i\} \tag{A1}$$

that is,

$$\text{Cov}[\tilde{\underline{R}}_e, \underline{D}_r'\tilde{R}] = \frac{A}{A_r}\text{Cov}[\tilde{\underline{R}}_e, M_E\tilde{R}_E + M_I\tilde{R}_I] = \frac{AM}{A_r}\text{Cov}[\tilde{\underline{R}}_e, \tilde{R}_M] \tag{A2}$$

Thus, given part (a) of the proposition, the portfolio $\underline{D}_r$ does realize the optimal compromise between risk and return.

Step 3. Check the optimality of the portfolio D_u given the postulated risk-return relationships in the ineligible and in the eligible segment (Equations (3) and (2)).

The first-order optimization condition can be written $E(\tilde{R} - R_f) = A_u\text{Cov}[\tilde{R}, \underline{D}_u'\tilde{R}]$. Given the definition of $\underline{D}_u$ in (c), we can write:

$$\text{Cov}[\tilde{\underline{R}}, \underline{D}_u'\tilde{R}] = (1 - \mu)\text{Cov}[\tilde{\underline{R}}, M\tilde{R}_M] + \mu\,\text{Cov}[\tilde{\underline{R}}, \underline{HP'}\tilde{R}] \tag{A3}$$

that is, given that $1 - \mu \equiv A/A_u$:

$$\text{Cov}[\tilde{\underline{R}}, \underline{D}_u'\tilde{R}] = \frac{AM}{A_u}\text{Cov}[\tilde{R}, \tilde{R}_M] + \mu\begin{bmatrix}\text{Cov}[\tilde{\underline{R}}_e, & \underline{HP'} & \tilde{R}] \\ \text{Cov}[\tilde{\underline{R}}_i, & \underline{HP'} & \tilde{R}]\end{bmatrix} \tag{A4}$$

We have already noted that $\text{Cov}[\tilde{\underline{R}}_e, \underline{HP'}\,\tilde{R}] = 0$; we can also assert from the definition of HP that:

$$\text{Cov}[\tilde{\underline{R}}_i, \underline{HP'}\,\tilde{R}] = \text{Cov}[\tilde{\underline{R}}_i, \underline{P}_i'\tilde{\underline{R}}_i - \underline{P}_i'V_{ie}V_{ee}^{-1}\tilde{\underline{R}}_e] = (V_{ii} - V_{ie}V_{ee}^{-1}V_{ei})\underline{P}_i \tag{A5}$$

Consequently, given Equation (A4) and the identity $\mu \equiv \dfrac{A_u - A}{A_u}$, we have:

$$A_u\text{Cov}[\tilde{\underline{R}}, \underline{D}_u'\tilde{R}] = (AM)\text{Cov}[\tilde{\underline{R}}, \tilde{R}_M] + (A_u - A)M_I\text{Cov}[\tilde{\underline{R}}, \tilde{R}_I \mid \tilde{\underline{R}}_e] \tag{A6}$$

so that the optimality condition is indeed satisfied by the portfolio D_u as long as Equations (2) and (3) represent the risk-return relationships in the two segments of the market.

Appendix B: Proof of Proposition 2

Part (a) of the proposition being a standard result, we proceed directly to prove part (b). To that end, we use Equation (8) to express the conditional market risk as:

$$\text{Cov}[\tilde{R}_i, \tilde{R}_I \mid \tilde{\underline{R}}_e] = \beta_i\text{Cov}[\tilde{R}_M, \tilde{R}_I \mid \tilde{\underline{R}}_e]$$
$$+ \gamma_i\text{Cov}[\tilde{V}_I, \tilde{R}_I \mid \tilde{\underline{R}}_e] + \text{Cov}[\tilde{\varepsilon}_i, \tilde{R}_I \mid \tilde{\underline{R}}_e] \tag{B1}$$

The last covariance term in Equation (B1) is null, since, by assumption,

$\text{Cov}[\tilde{\varepsilon}_i, \tilde{R}_I] = \text{Cov}[\tilde{\varepsilon}_i, \tilde{R}_M]b_I + \text{Cov}[\tilde{\varepsilon}_i, \tilde{V}_I] = 0$ and $\text{Cov}[\tilde{\varepsilon}_i, \tilde{R}_e] = 0$. Furthermore, recalling that $\tilde{R}_M \equiv (M_I/M)\tilde{R}_I + (M_E/M)\tilde{R}_E$, the coefficient of β_i in Equation (B1) can be written:

$$A \equiv \text{Cov}[\tilde{R}_M, \tilde{R}/\tilde{R}_e] = (M_I/M)\text{Var}[\tilde{R}_I \mid \tilde{R}_e] \geq 0 \tag{B2}$$

As for the coefficient of γ_i in Equation (B1), in view of Equation (9) in the text, it can be formulated as:

$$B \equiv \text{Cov}[\tilde{V}_I, \tilde{R}_I \mid \tilde{R}_e] = \text{Cov}[\tilde{R}_I - b_I[(M_I/M)\tilde{R}_I + (M_E/M)\tilde{R}_E], \tilde{R}_I \mid \tilde{R}_e] \tag{B3}$$

or, equivalently,

$$B = [1 - b_I(M_I/M)]\text{Var}[\tilde{R}_I \mid \tilde{R}_e] \tag{B4}$$

It is a simple matter to check that the expression $[1 - b_I(M_I/M)]$ is positive as long as the returns on WMP and the returns on MPES are positively correlated, a condition which is assumed to hold. This condition thus ensures that the coefficient B is positive or null. Part (c) of Proposition 2 then follows directly.

REFERENCES

1. M. Adler and B. Dumas. "Optimal International Acquisitions." *Journal of Finance* 30 (1975), 1–19.
2. M. Adler and R. Horesh. "The Relationship Among Equity Markets: Comment." *Journal of Finance* 29 (1974), 1311–17.
3. F. Black. "International Capital Market Equilibrium with Investment Barriers." *Journal of Financial Economics* 1 (1974), 337–52.
4. P. J. Dhrymes. *Econometrics.* Heidelberg, West Germany: Springer-Verlag, 1974.
5. V. Errunza. "Efficiency and the Program to Develop Capital Markets—The Brazilian Experience." *Journal of Banking and Finance* 3 (1979), 355–82.
6. ———. "Emerging Markets: A New Opportunity for Improving Global Portfolio Performance." *Financial Analysts Journal* 39 (September-October 1983), 51–58.
7. ——— and E. Losq. "The Behavior of Stock Prices on LDC Markets." Working Paper, McGill University, 1982.
8. ——— and L. Senbet. "The Effects of International Operations on the Market Value of the Firm: Theory and Evidence." *Journal of Finance* 36 (May 1981), 401–17.
9. E. Fama. *Foundations of Finance.* New York: Basic Books Inc., 1976.
10. D. Glenn. "Super Premium Security Prices and Optimal Corporate Financing." *Journal of Finance* 32 (1976), 479–92.
11. F. L. Grauer, R. H. Litzenberger, and R. E. Stehle. "Sharing Rules and Equilibrium in an International Capital Market Under Uncertainty." *Journal of Financial Economics* 3 (1976), 233–56.
12. W. Y. Lee and K. S. Sachdeva. "The Role of the Multinational Firm in the Integration of Segmented Capital Markets." *Journal of Finance* 32 (May 1977), 479–92.
13. D. Lessard. "International Portfolio Diversification: A Multivariate Analysis for a Group of Latin American Countries." *Journal of Finance* 28 (June 1973), 619–33.
14. ———. "World, National and Industry Factors in Equity Returns." *Journal of Finance* 29 (May 1974), 379–91.
15. D. Mayers. "Non-Marketable Assets and Capital Market Equilibrium Under Uncertainty." In M. Jensen (ed.), *Studies in the Theory of Capital Markets.* New York: Praeger, 1972.
16. R. Roll. "A Critique of the Asset Pricing Theory's Tests." *Journal of Financial Economics* 4 (1977), 129–76.
17. L. Senbet. "International Capital Market Equilibrium and the Multinational Firm Financing and Investment Policies." *Journal of Financial and Quantitative Analysis* 14 (September 1979), 455–80.

18. B. H. Solnik. "An Equilibrium Model of the International Capital Market." *Journal of Economic Theory* (1974), 500–24.
19. ——. "The International Pricing of Risk: An Empirical Investigation of the World Capital Market Structure." *Journal of Finance* 29 (1974), 365–78.
20. ——. "Testing International Asset Pricing: Some Pessimistic Views." *Journal of Finance* 32 (May 1977), 503–12.
21. R. C. Stapleton and M. G. Subrahmanyam. "Market Imperfections, Capital Market Equilibrium and Corporation Finance." *Journal of Finance* 32 (May 1977), 307–19.
22. R. Stehle. "An Empirical Test of the Alternative Hypotheses of National and International Pricing of Risky Assets." *Journal of Finance* 32 (May 1977), 493–502.
23. R. Stulz. "A Model of International Asset Pricing." *Journal of Financial Economics* 9 (1981), 383–403.
24. ——. "On the Effects of Barriers to International Investment." *Journal of Finance* 36 (1981), 923–34.

B
Measuring Market Integration

[3]

THE WORLD BANK ECONOMIC REVIEW, VOL. 9, NO. 1: 75–107

Market Integration and Investment Barriers in Emerging Equity Markets

Geert Bekaert

This article develops a return-based measure of market integration for nineteen emerging equity markets. It then examines the relation between that measure, other return characteristics, and broadly defined investment barriers. Although the analysis is exploratory, some clear conclusions emerge. First, global factors account for a small fraction of the time variation in expected returns in most markets, and global predictability has declined over time. Second, the emerging markets exhibit differing degrees of market integration with the U.S. market, and the differences are not necessarily associated with direct barriers to investment. Third, the most important de facto barriers to global equity-market integration are poor credit ratings, high and variable inflation, exchange rate controls, the lack of a high-quality regulatory and accounting framework, the lack of sufficient country funds or cross-listed securities, and the limited size of some stock markets.

Equity portfolio flows to developing economies, especially to the so-called emerging markets, have sharply increased in magnitude in recent years. The increase in financial flows to emerging markets raises three important questions:

- What are the expected return and diversification benefits of investing in these markets?
- How well are these markets integrated with the markets of industrial economies and to what extent is integration a function of identifiable barriers to investment?
- What are the opportunity costs, in terms of higher cost of capital, associated with these barriers?

These questions are closely related. The return properties and potential diversification benefits from investing in emerging markets have been investigated by

Geert Bekaert is with the Graduate School of Business at Stanford University. This article was commissioned by the Debt and International Division of the World Bank for its Conference on Portfolio Investment in Developing Countries, Washington, D.C., September 9–10, 1993. The author would like to thank Michael Urias for excellent research assistance and many useful comments; Stijn Claessens, Steve Grenadier, Bob Hodrick, Ingrid Werner, the discussant Cheol Eun, and three anonymous referees for suggestions and comments; Steve Gray and Rohit Kumar for their assistance with some of the computations; and Bob Korajzyek for providing part of the data.

76   THE WORLD BANK ECONOMIC REVIEW, VOL. 9, NO. 1

a number of authors, including Divecha, Drach, and Stefek (1992); Harvey (1993); Speidell and Sappenfield (1992); and Wilcox (1992). However, barriers to investment can make potential diversification benefits unattainable for foreign investors. As a consequence, capital flows from the industrial world, which might reduce domestic capital costs and increase economic welfare through more efficient resource mobilization, might not be forthcoming. This article will try to shed some light on the last two questions, with primary emphasis on market segmentation. The analysis is restricted to nineteen equity markets contained in the Emerging Markets Data Base (EMDB) of the International Finance Corporation (IFC).

There are two major approaches to testing and measuring the degree of market segmentation. The first approach assumes that markets are integrated and that a particular asset-pricing model holds (for example, Campbell and Hamao 1992). The second approach models the restrictions to integration explicitly and derives their effects on equilibrium returns (for example, Cooper and Kaplanis 1986, 1994; Errunza and Losq 1985; Eun and Janakiramanan 1986; Hietala 1989; Stulz 1981; and Wheatley 1988).

The second approach is unsatisfactory because I do not want to restrict the analysis to the effects of one particular barrier to investment and there are too many different barriers to consider. The first approach is hampered by the lack of a universally accepted international asset-pricing model. Recent research on international equity and foreign exchange markets, for instance, has uncovered considerable time variation in expected excess returns, but no consensus has emerged on what drives this apparent predictability. Some empirical papers show that common risk factors explain a large fraction of the time and cross-sectional variation in returns (for example, Harvey 1991). This suggests that markets in industrial economies, at least from 1980 onward, are relatively well integrated. In any case, the use of a formal asset-pricing model requires further research on capital market integration in general and is left for future work.

My approach consists of two steps. First, in section I, I examine whether predictable components in the excess returns from investing in emerging markets are similar to those observed in industrial equity markets. If the predictable components track time-varying risk premiums, examining these components can inform on market integration as well. I include both local factors (the lagged return and the dividend yield) and global factors (the lagged return on the U.S. market, the U.S. dividend yield, and the U.S. interest rate) in regression analysis to investigate the relative importance of global, compared with local, components in the predictability of excess returns in emerging markets. I interpret the predictive power of global factors as indicative of some degree of integration. Similarly, I interpret the lack of predictive power by the local instruments as indicative of integration, although some international asset-pricing models imply that economy-specific factors are priced (Adler and Dumas 1983).

Second, I use the regressions to compute correlations of expected returns in emerging markets with expected returns in equity markets in industrial economies. If there were only one source of risk and markets were perfectly integrated, expected returns would be perfectly correlated (see Cumby and Huizinga 1992). Bekaert (forthcoming), for instance, uses a vector autoregressive framework to compute correlations between expected returns on foreign exchange and finds that they are highly correlated. Although it seems unlikely that one risk factor explains all of the cross-sectional and time variation in equity returns, it is equally unlikely that expected returns in perfectly integrated markets would show low correlation. In fact, as shown in section II, the expected equity returns in the major industrial markets are highly correlated. This correlation is a measure of the common component in expected stock returns and hence, indirectly, of market integration (see also Campbell and Hamao 1992). However imperfect, the correlation of expected returns is the measure of market integration used in this article. To check for robustness, I have provided an alternative measure of market integration, based on the change in predictable variation in returns when an observable proxy for the world factor (the world market portfolio return) is added to the forecasting equations.

In section III, I discuss various other return characteristics and examine how they relate to the measure of market integration. The remainder of the article links the degree of market integration, as measured by the expected return correlation with the U.S. market, to various barriers to investment.

I distinguish between three kinds of barriers. First are legal barriers arising from the different legal status of foreign and domestic investors, for example, ownership restrictions and taxes. Second are indirect barriers arising from differences in available information, accounting standards, and investor protection. Third are barriers arising from emerging-market-specific risks (EMSRs) that discourage foreign investment and lead to de facto segmentation.

EMSRs include liquidity risk, political risk, economic policy risk, macroeconomic instability, and, perhaps, currency risk. Some might argue that these risks are in fact diversifiable and are not priced. However, such an argument seems inconsistent with the amount of resources spent on, for example, measuring political risk throughout the world. Chuhan (1992), for instance, on the basis of a survey of market participants in Canada, Germany, Japan, the United Kingdom, and the United States, reports liquidity problems as a major impediment to investing in emerging markets. But the survey yielded the surprising result that restrictions in host economies are not a crucial factor. The other EMSRs are related to the notion of country risk. For example, credit ratings not only reflect assessments of political stability but also incorporate factors related to the economic environment. Unstable macroeconomic policies, for instance, appear to have detrimental effects on stock market performance.

Barriers to investment are a direct function of the domestic policies pursued in the various economies. This article is intended as a preliminary empirical investigation into the association between a set of broadly defined barriers to investment and measures of market integration and other return characteristics. Because quantitative measures of these barriers to investment are necessarily crude, the association is simply measured through rank correlations. This approach has the obvious disadvantage of precluding strong quantitative policy implications, but it allows a broader analysis that can provide useful insights for further research. In section IV, I investigate the association between market integration and direct and indirect barriers to investment. I also examine whether any of the described return characteristics are related to measures of "openness" of the emerging markets, for example, the existence of country funds and cross-listed securities or the extent of ownership restrictions. Section V focuses on EMSRs.

Because I do not specify a formal asset-pricing model, I cannot make an explicit link between market integration and the cost of equity capital. The analysis here takes as a starting point the belief that a higher degree of market integration is necessarily accompanied by lower costs of capital and increased capital flows. Some of the return characteristics reported in section III are correlated with the cost of capital, but without a generally accepted asset-pricing model, estimating the cost of capital precisely is extremely difficult and is not formally attempted. A related disadvantage of the approach here is that the rankings are typically taken at a point in time or are based on averages. No dynamic relation between changes in barriers to investment and return properties is described. Some further implications for future research are discussed in section VI, which offers conclusions.

Finally, cost-of-capital issues cannot be fully analyzed without incorporating the configuration of the entire financial market in the developing economy, including bond, money, and informal markets, all of which are ignored in this analysis. Eventually, it would be fruitful to take the viewpoint of the developing economy, rather than a global asset-pricing perspective, as the basis of the analysis. A model of a developing economy with rudimentary financial markets could explicitly address how opening up the equity market to foreign investors would affect returns, the cost of capital, and ultimately social welfare.

I. THE PREDICTABILITY OF RETURNS IN EMERGING EQUITY MARKETS

To assess the predictability of excess returns earned on investments in emerging markets, I regressed the dollar index return in excess of the U.S. interest rate onto five instrumental variables (see also Bekaert and Harvey 1994, Buckberg 1995, and Harvey 1993). I used two local instruments, the local dividend yield and the lagged excess return, and three global instruments, the U.S lagged excess return, the U.S. dividend yield, and the U.S. interest rate relative to a one-year backward-moving average. These instruments were shown to predict excess returns on equities and foreign exchange in Germany, Japan, the United Kingdom, and the United States in Bekaert and Hodrick (1992). Because no reliable interest rate data are available for most emerging markets, I could not emulate Bekaert and Hodrick's specification, which uses the local excess return as the dependent variable and the forward premium as a predictor.

Table 1 reports the regression results for 1985–92, using data sampled at the end of each month for nineteen emerging markets.[1] The emerging-market indexes used are those compiled by the IFC as their so-called global indexes (IFC various issues). (Indonesia was excluded from the sample because of insufficient data.) The 1980s were a decade of increasing globalization and deregulation of financial markets. These developments, and the fact that the large financial flows to emerging equity markets only occurred near the end of the sample, motivated the choice of the sample period. Moreover, for some markets, data are only available since 1986. Several test statistics are reported. The $\chi^2(5)$ statistic is a Wald test of the joint predictive power of the five instruments, and the $\chi^2(2)$ and $\chi^2(3)$ statistics test the predictive power of the local and global instruments, respectively. The *l*-statistic is a test developed by Cumby and Huizinga (1993) for the remaining serial correlation in the residuals. It is robust to conditional heteroskedasticity and to the fact that the residuals are estimated.

The adjusted R^2 is greater than 10 percent in Chile, Colombia, Mexico, the Philippines, Portugal, Turkey, Venezuela, and Zimbabwe but is negative in Argentina, India, Nigeria, and Thailand. The joint predictability test for all five instruments rejects the null of no predictability at the 1 percent level for six economies: Chile, Colombia, the Philippines, Portugal, Venezuela, and Zimbabwe. Except for Portugal, this rejection appears to derive from the local instruments. For Malaysia the test for no predictability of the local instruments also rejects at the 1 percent level; for Brazil, the Republic of Korea, and Turkey, it rejects at the 5 percent level. Although this result could be construed as evidence of market inefficiency, it is important to point out that the predictive power of the dividend yield, not the lagged return, drives some of the rejections (see, for example, Brazil, Portugal, and Zimbabwe). The dividend yield predicts excess returns in the industrial equity markets as well (see, for example, Bekaert and Hodrick 1992). Campbell and Ammer (1993) use a log-linear decomposition of stock returns to show that the dividend yield should perform well as a proxy for the long-horizon expected excess return.

The predictive power of the global instruments is generally weak. The Wald test only rejects at the 1 percent level for Portugal, at the 5 percent level for Turkey, and at the 10 percent level for Chile. For Malaysia, the predictability is primarily caused by the local instruments. This does not necessarily mean that the Malaysian market is segmented, because the local instruments might partially track the common component in expected returns. This possibility will be examined in section II. Note that the return for the emerging-markets composite index is significantly predictable at the 1 percent level using all five instruments and at the 10 percent level using the global instruments.

The same type of analysis was done for four industrial economies: Germany, Japan, the United Kingdom, and the United States (not reported).[2] Surprisingly,

---

1. See the appendix for more details on all data used in the article.
2. Here and throughout the article, results that are not reported are available from the author on request.

Table 1. Predictable Components in Emerging Equity Markets, December 1985 to December 1992

	Coefficient estimates						Predictability statistics[b]			
Market	U.S. excess dollar returns, r_{1t}	Local excess dollar returns, r_{it}	U.S. dividend yield, dy_{1t}	Local dividend yield, dy_{it}	U.S. interest rate,[a] i_{1t}	Adjusted R^2	All five instruments, $\chi^2(5)$	Local interest instruments, $\chi^2(2)$	Global instruments, $\chi^2(3)$	Residual autocorrelation,[c] $l(5)$
Argentina	0.39 (0.37)	-0.19 (0.18)	-3.55 (88.79)	-0.65 (13.74)	8.18 (36.34)	-0.022	1.95 [0.86]	1.18 [0.55]	1.33 [0.72]	2.72 [0.74]
Brazil	0.34 (0.40)	-0.13 (0.10)	-37.3 (90.7)	29.2 (10.74)	1.96 (39.7)	0.025	9.66 [0.085]	7.60 [0.022]	1.44 [0.70]	6.67 [0.25]
Chile	0.38 (0.15)	0.25 (0.11)	45.3 (44.6)	0.67 (4.71)	-7.38 (14.82)	0.111	25.8 [0.0001]	5.67 [0.06]	6.68 [0.08]	7.39 [0.19]
Colombia	-0.005 (0.18)	0.40 (0.18)	-3.73 (37.3)	2.94 (2.80)	-11.04 (11.33)	0.166	20.13 [0.001]	14.94 [0.0006]	1.36 [0.71]	2.95 [0.71]
Greece	0.42 (0.27)	0.09 (0.08)	-50.8 (63.0)	2.14 (4.75)	8.74 (17.8)	0.003	9.12 [0.10]	1.98 [0.37]	5.66 [0.13]	5.12 [0.40]
India	-0.06 (0.18)	0.077 (0.14)	-34.3 (41.5)	41.5 (22.2)	-37.46 (19.6)	-0.011	4.78 [0.44]	4.03 [0.13]	4.23 [0.24]	2.98 [0.70]
Jordan	0.0017 (0.09)	-0.20 (0.14)	-3.73 (14.2)	-1.84 (2.13)	-11.75 (7.55)	0.003	5.43 [0.36]	3.02 [0.22]	3.04 [0.39]	8.22 [0.14]
Korea, Rep. of	0.26 (0.16)	-0.24 (0.12)	35.2 (33.64)	13.03 (5.15)	17.06 (10.81)	0.090	12.41 [0.029]	8.56 [0.014]	4.81 [0.19]	4.28 [0.51]
Malaysia	0.10 (0.20)	0.01 (0.13)	86.66 (52.22)	68.53 (22.15)	-24.27 (15.8)	0.088	10.95 [0.05]	9.93 [0.007]	2.85 [0.41]	3.77 [0.58]
Mexico	1.34 (0.60)	0.19 (0.15)	90.2 (85.14)	3.43 (5.58)	-24.5 (24.50)	0.259	8.04 [0.15]	2.40 [0.30]	5.22 [0.16]	7.99 [0.16]

Nigeria	0.26 (0.35)	0.08 (0.14)	-33.1 (71.1)	-0.83 (4.79)	16.1 (25.43)	-0.035	0.71 [0.98]	0.30 [0.86]	0.59 [0.90]	6.67 [0.25]
Pakistan	-0.13 (0.15)	0.21 (0.22)	-1.72 (23.9)	-0.92 (6.15)	8.39 (8.86)	0.015	3.83 [0.57]	0.88 [0.64]	1.79 [0.62]	10.37 [0.07]
Philippines	0.19 (0.19)	0.27 (0.10)	30.61 (56.26)	14.9 (6.22)	2.33 (16.97)	0.183	27.42 [0.00005]	19.1 [0.00007]	2.37 [0.50]	5.53 [0.35]
Portugal	0.72 (0.34)	-0.12 (0.17)	-279.2 (69.3)	-75.5 (23.2)	-4.04 (21.42)	0.299	29.8 [0.00002]	10.7 [0.005]	29.00 [0.0000002]	8.77 [0.12]
Taiwan (China)	0.64 (0.40)	-0.04 (0.14)	9.24 (87.6)	37.03 (23.6)	7.58 (26.24)	0.008	7.80 [0.17]	2.57 [0.28]	2.93 [0.40]	2.88 [0.72]
Thailand	0.33 (0.28)	0.02 (0.16)	14.9 (65.14)	2.87 (4.26)	-3.07 (19.03)	-0.018	3.41 [0.64]	0.45 [0.80]	1.63 [0.65]	11.4 [0.04]
Turkey	1.05 (0.46)	-0.01 (0.11)	-171.3 (109.0)	20.9 (8.21)	46.22 (30.96)	0.162	14.6 [0.01]	7.78 [0.02]	9.05 [0.03]	2.89 [0.72]
Venezuela	-0.37 (0.24)	0.21 (0.08)	-52.5 (45.7)	47.66 (18.5)	-7.98 (19.6)	0.116	14.6 [0.012]	9.83 [0.007]	2.81 [0.42]	1.59 [0.90]
Zimbabwe	-0.06 (0.13)	-0.008 (0.10)	24.72 (31.5)	12.5 (3.65)	12.44 (11.36)	0.207	25.3 [0.0001]	17.1 [0.0002]	3.08 [0.38]	2.53 [0.77]
Emerging-markets composite	0.41 (0.19)	-0.0026 (0.13)	11.13 (43.5)	14.93 (10.0)	2.60 (13.76)	0.057	17.38 [0.004]	2.24 [0.33]	6.40 [0.09]	7.16 [0.21]

Note: Figures in parentheses are heteroskedasticity-consistent standard errors; those in brackets are *p*-values.

a. In relation to a one-year backward-moving average.

b. Tests on the joint explanatory power of all five instruments, $\chi^2(5)$; the two local instruments, $\chi^2(2)$; and the three U.S. instruments, $\chi^2(3)$.

c. Tests for residual serial correlation using the first five autocorrelations of the residuals and is distributed $\chi^2(5)$ (Cumby and Huizinga 1993).

Source: Author's calculations.

Table 2. Predictable Components in Emerging Equity Markets, December 1976 to September 1985

	Coefficient estimates						Predictability statistics[b]				
Market	U.S. excess dollar returns, r_{1t}	Local excess dollar returns, r_{it}	U.S. dividend yield, dy_{1t}	Local dividend yield, dy_{it}	U.S. interest rate,[a] i_{1t}	Adjusted R^2	All five instruments, $\chi^2(5)$	Local instruments, $\chi^2(2)$	Global instruments, $\chi^2(3)$	Residual autocorrelation,[c] $l(5)$	Chow-type test for stability[d]
Argentina	0.08 (0.52)	0.07 (0.08)	−56.7 (45.7)	30.6 (29.1)	3.036 (11.7)	−0.021	5.05 [0.41]	2.25 [0.32]	1.82 [0.61]	1.54 [0.91]	7.39 [0.29]
Brazil	−0.37 (0.30)	0.13 (0.11)	−31.2 (24.8)	1.37 (3.49)	−2.40 (7.04)	−0.003	4.73 [0.45]	1.64 [0.44]	2.73 [0.43]	9.9 [0.08]	14.3 [0.027]
Chile	−0.04 (0.30)	0.04 (0.09)	−12.9 (19.1)	20.3 (7.11)	7.53 (5.70)	0.079	13.5 [0.02]	9.26 [0.01]	2.32 [0.51]	6.41 [0.27]	10.0 [0.13]
Greece	−0.12 (0.12)	0.02 (0.12)	−9.6 (12.2)	−3.62 (1.95)	−7.71 (3.75)	0.009	6.57 [0.25]	3.72 [0.15]	5.09 [0.16]	5.73 [0.33]	10.8 [0.094]
India	0.40 (0.10)	−0.06 (0.12)	−15.3 (9.54)	9.30 (8.34)	−0.66 (2.84)	0.092	23.7 [0.0002]	1.34 [0.51]	19.1 [0.0002]	9.16 [0.10]	14.4 [0.026]
Jordan	0.08 (0.17)	0.07 (0.12)	15.80 (18.24)	31.26 (20.48)	−3.53 (3.94)	−0.012	4.46 [0.48]	3.46 [0.18]	1.73 [0.63]	7.29 [0.20]	7.72 [0.259]
Korea, Rep. of	−0.34 (0.19)	0.04 (0.09)	−26.1 (13.9)	3.47 (9.68)	3.28 (4.71)	0.005	9.00 [0.11]	0.37 [0.83]	6.76 [0.08]	3.93 [0.56]	10.1 [0.12]
Mexico	0.62 (0.23)	−0.002 (0.14)	−34.7 (23.2)	0.59 (6.62)	12.45 (4.97)	0.034	12.4 [0.03]	0.01 [1.00]	11.77 [0.008]	5.95 [0.31]	4.33 [0.63]
Thailand	0.038 (0.16)	0.06 (0.10)	−26.3 (11.1)	−0.53 (2.92)	−4.14 (2.84)	0.039	18.7 [0.002]	0.40 [0.82]	16.8 [0.0008]	4.58 [0.47]	2.76 [0.84]
Zimbabwe	0.34 (0.30)	0.12 (0.11)	−10.0 (20.2)	−0.40 (2.84)	−2.97 (6.81)	−0.006	3.51 [0.62]	1.19 [0.55]	2.33 [0.51]	7.37 [0.19]	10.9 [0.091]

Note: Figures in parentheses are heteroskedasticity-consistent standard errors; those in brackets are p-values.
a. In relation to a one-year backward-moving average.
b. Tests on the joint explanatory power of all five instruments, $\chi^2(5)$; the two local instruments, $\chi^2(2)$; and the three U.S. instruments, $\chi^2(3)$.
c. Tests for residual serial correlation using the first five autocorrelations of the residuals and is distributed $\chi^2(5)$ (Cumby and Huizinga 1993).
d. Robust to heteroskedasticity on the six coefficients in the regressions, including the constant (see, for example, Hodrick and Srivastava 1984).
Source: Author's calculations.

there is only marginal evidence of predictability; for the excess returns on German, Japanese, and U.K. equity, all R^2s are negative and the Wald statistics never reject at the 5 percent level. This result is in sharp contrast to the large body of empirical literature on international predictability of equity returns (Bekaert and Hodrick 1992; Ferson and Harvey 1993; Harvey 1991). It is therefore of independent interest and deserves further scrutiny.

Because similar instruments were used in previous studies, it is probable that the lack of significant predictability is specific to the more recent sample period. The differences between the 1985–92 sample and the 1976–85 sample are striking. For the earlier period there is evidence of strong predictability that primarily derives from global instruments. The decrease in predictability for the later period complicates the interpretation of the predictable variation through global factors as an indicator of global-market integration. One possible explanation would be that the predictability is merely an indication of market inefficiency that was eliminated with increasing globalization at the end of the 1980s. Alternatively, the nature of time-varying risk premiums may have changed, making them more difficult to track with the instruments typically used in empirical studies. For Japan, for instance, including the local interest rate or the forward premium as an instrument improves predictability marginally, whereas in Germany changes that have occurred in the exchange rate help to predict future returns. However, formal tests for stability fail to reject the hypothesis that the coefficients have not changed for Germany, Japan, and the United Kingdom, but the tests reject at the 1 percent level for the United States. And, based on the *l*-tests, the forecasting variables used here suffice to eliminate all serial correlation in the residuals.

Table 2 reports the results for 1976–85 for ten emerging markets where data were available. The test for stability rejects for Greece and Zimbabwe at the 10 percent level and for India and Brazil at the 5 percent level. There is no clear pattern in how the predictability patterns move over time. For example, it is striking how the predictability arising from global factors was actually stronger in the early period for Greece, India, Korea, Mexico, and Thailand. The apparent decline of global predictability is not necessarily inconsistent with the fact that most markets became more open to foreign investment during the 1980s (see below).

In sum, expected returns generally vary through time, although predictability is stronger for both industrial and emerging markets before 1986 than it is in the late 1980s and early 1990s. I conclude that predictability tests do not yield much useful information on market segmentation.

II. A Measure of Market Integration

I interpret the fitted values of the regressions of excess returns on five predetermined variables to be estimates of expected returns. There are several asset-pricing models that justify this procedure. For example, suppose the returns satisfy a multifactor model with expected returns depending on the risk loadings (βs) with respect to risk factors and on the prices of these risks (their expected returns). In a K-factor model, the conditional expected value of an excess return, r_{it+1}, satisfies

$$(1) \qquad E_t(r_{it+1}) = \sum_{k=1}^{K} \beta_{ikt} \lambda_{kt}$$

where β_{ikt} is the factor loading of asset i for the kth factor at time t and λ_{kt} is the market price of risk for the kth factor at time t. To yield a projection equation on a number of forecasting variables as the reduced-form model, several auxiliary assumptions are needed. One sufficient set of assumptions is constant βs and time-varying prices of risk, with the time variation assumed to be a linear function of the information set (see, for example, Campbell and Hamao 1992). To see this, let Z_t be a vector of forecasting variables, $Z_t = (r_{1t}, r_{it}, dy_{1t}, dy_{it}, i_t)'$, where r_{1t} is the U.S. lagged excess return, r_{it} is the local lagged excess return, dy_{1t} is the U.S. dividend yield, dy_{it} is the local dividend yield, and i_t is the U.S. interest rate relative to a one-year backward-moving average. Let

$$(2) \qquad \lambda_{kt} = \sum_{l=1}^{L} \alpha_{lk} Z_{lt}, \qquad \beta_{ikt} = \beta_{ik}.$$

with α_{lk} the sensitivity of the kth price of risk to the lth variable in Z_t. Combining equations 1 and 2,

$$(3) \qquad E_t(r_{it+1}) = \sum_{k=1}^{K} \beta_{ik} \sum_{l=1}^{L} \alpha_{lk} Z_{lt} = \sum_{l=1}^{L} \delta_{il} Z_{lt}.$$

The δ_{il} coefficients can be recovered from a linear projection of r_{it+1} onto Z_t.

Alternatively, the βs could be assumed to be linear functions of the information set (see, for example, Ferson and Harvey 1993), which also would imply an equation such as equation 3. In either case, the coefficients on the forecasting variables are a function of coefficients that determine the βs or prices of risk in a multifactor model. The advantage of this reduced-form approach is that it is model free, and the factors do not have to be specified or measured. Allowing for time variation in expected returns is important, given the rapidly changing nature of the economies and stock markets. The evidence for predictability detected in the previous section confirms the presence of time variation in expected returns. My integration measure is the correlation of the regression estimates of the expected returns in the United States and the emerging markets. This correlation is an indicator of the common component in expected returns and hence, indirectly, of market integration.

A couple of caveats must be noted. First, because I compute the unconditional correlation coefficient, no changes in the degree of market integration are allowed over the sample period. This is another motivation for using the relatively short sample (1986–92) as opposed to the full sample available, which is longer for many economies. I examine whether integration changed over time by computing the correlations for an earlier sample as well. Harvey (1995) computes five-year rolling correlations between emerging-market returns and the world market. His results suggest that these correlations are increasing for many emerging markets.

Second, I want to stress that the measure is only a perfect measure of market integration in a one-factor world with constant risk exposures. Suppose the world equity market is fully integrated and assets are priced according to a multifactor model. Emerging markets might display dramatic cross-sectional differences in their risk exposures. These differences, in turn, might affect the correlation of expected returns with the U.S. market, without reflecting actual barriers to investment (broadly defined). For instance, the various emerging markets have different industrial structures, which might result in different exposures to "industry factors" (see Divecha, Drach, and Stefek 1992 on emerging markets, and Heston and Rouwenhorst 1994 and Roll 1992 on industrial markets). Moreover, some economies are dependent on a limited number of natural resources (for example, Nigeria on oil), which might give rise to different "commodity exposures." In section VI, I briefly assess the importance of these industry and commodity factors in the measurement of market segmentation.

In table 3, I report three different correlations. The regression decomposes the return into an expected and unexpected part. The reported correlations are then the correlation of the return, of the expected return, and of the unexpected return in economy i with its counterparts in the United States. The methodology borrows from Bekaert and Hodrick (1992) and Bekaert (forthcoming). Assume that Z_{it}, which includes the U.S. excess return, the emerging-market excess return, the two dividend yields, and the relative U.S. interest rate, follows a first-order vector autoregression:

$$(4) \qquad Z_{it+1} = \mu + A Z_{it} + u_{it+1}.$$

If the vector autoregressive framework is correctly specified, $E_t(u_{it+1}) = 0$. Let the variance-covariance matrix of the innovations u_{it} be V. Let Σ be the variance-covariance matrix of Z_{it}. As it is found from

$$(5) \qquad \text{vec}(\Sigma) = (I - A' \otimes A')^{-1} \text{vec}(V),$$

V and Σ are sufficient to compute the correlation of returns and unexpected returns. To compute the correlation of expected returns, the covariance matrix of $E_t(Z_{it+1})$, Σ_E, is derived to be

$$(6) \qquad \Sigma_E = A \Sigma A'.$$

Standard errors are obtained by estimating A and V using the general method of moments and applying the Mean Value Theorem. Note that this technique assumes that the vector autoregressive framework generates the expected returns correctly. If there is measurement error in the resulting expected-return estimates that is uncorrelated across the United States and emerging markets, the esti-

Table 3. Return Correlations with the U.S. market, 1976–85 and 1985–92

Market	1985:12–1992:12					1976:12—1985:09		
	Return, $\rho(r_{1t}, r_{it})$	Expected return, $\rho(rp_{1t}, rp_{it})$	Unexpected return, $\rho(u_{1t}, u_{it})$	Rank based on expected-return correlation estimate[a]	Rank based on a variance ratio[b]	Return, $\rho(r_{1t}, r_{it})$	Expected return, $\rho(rp_{1t}, rp_{it})$	Unexpected return, $\rho(u_{1t}, u_{it})$
Argentina	0.10 (0.09)	-0.14 (0.56)	0.12 (0.11)	12	12	0.03 (0.08)	-0.575 (0.45)	0.07 (0.075)
Brazil	0.13 (0.08)	-0.06 (0.38)	0.15 (0.09)	14	14	-0.07 (0.10)	-0.41 (0.33)	-0.04 (0.09)
Chile	0.32 (0.12)	0.485 (0.48)	0.30 (0.17)	5	11	-0.11 (0.08)	-0.47 (0.31)	-0.07 (0.08)
Colombia	0.11 (0.12)	-0.16 (0.46)	0.16 (0.08)	15	19	—	—	—
Greece	0.145 (0.11)	-0.38 (0.45)	0.19 (0.11)	18	20	0.04 (0.08)	0.57 (0.32)	0.005 (0.08)
India	-0.13 (0.075)	-0.57 (0.35)	-0.07 (0.08)	21	8	0.03 (0.08)	-0.14 (0.32)	0.06 (0.08)
Jordan	0.06 (0.13)	-0.44 (0.43)	0.10 (0.14)	19.5	22	0.05 (0.10)	0.13 (0.53)	0.04 (0.10)
Korea, Rep. of	0.21 (0.08)	0.135 (0.39)	0.21 (0.08)	11	7	0.04 (0.10)	-0.67 (0.34)	0.095 (0.10)
Malaysia	0.66 (0.07)	0.80 (0.24)	0.64 (0.10)	3	9	—	—	—
Mexico	0.49 (0.09)	0.33 (0.52)	0.54 (0.13)	7	10	0.125 (0.085)	-0.77 (0.21)	0.21 (0.09)
Nigeria	0.04 (0.08)	-0.33 (0.78)	0.06 (0.06)	13	21	—	—	—
Pakistan	-0.02 (0.10)	0.25 (0.37)	-0.05 (0.10)	10	16	—	—	—

Philippines	0.29 (0.16)	0.74 (0.34)	0.20 (0.14)	2	6	—	—	—
Portugal	0.26 (0.10)	-0.265 (0.45)	0.43 (0.11)	17	13	—	—	—
Taiwan (China)	0.195 (0.12)	0.12 (0.67)	0.20 (0.13)	9	5	—	—	—
Thailand	0.43 (0.14)	0.30 (0.68)	0.44 (0.16)	6	4	-0.09 (0.11)	-0.02 (0.46)	-0.10 (0.11)
Turkey	-0.16 (0.15)	-0.71 (0.34)	-0.08 (0.11)	22	15	—	—	—
Venezuela	-0.06 (0.07)	-0.35 (0.34)	-0.02 (0.10)	19.5	17	—	—	—
Zimbabwe	-0.14 (0.09)	-0.01 (0.28)	-0.18 (0.11)	16	18	0.13 (0.10)	0.28 (0.415)	0.12 (0.105)
Emerging-markets composite	0.40 (0.12)	0.19 (0.77)	0.42 (0.15)	—	—	—	—	—
Germany	0.42 (0.10)	0.73 (0.345)	0.43 (0.12)	4	1	0.25 (0.10)	0.31 (0.27)	0.24 (0.12)
Japan	0.23 (0.09)	0.34 (0.49)	0.23 (0.09)	8	3	0.21 (0.09)	-0.21 (0.445)	0.25 (0.10)
United Kingdom	0.67 (0.06)	0.96 (0.13)	0.67 (0.07)	1	2	0.39 (0.07)	0.56 (0.17)	0.37 (0.08)

—Not available.

Note: The correlations are computed using the dynamic structure of a vector autoregressive framework on the U.S. excess return, the emerging-market excess return, the two dividend yields, and the relative U.S. interest rate. Standard errors (in parentheses) are computed as in Bekaert (forthcoming) using three Newey-West lags.

a. The ranking is based on the sum of two ranks: one according to the point estimate of the correlation of expected returns estimated for the most recent sample, one based on the number of standard errors away from perfect correlation computed for the same sample.

b. Returns are regressed on the instruments plus the world market portfolio return. The statistic used for the rankings is the ratio of the predictable variation caused by the instruments in the model with the world market portfolio as an observable factor relative to the predictable variation in the regressions without the world market portfolio reported in tables 1 and 2. See Campbell and Hamao (1992).

Source: Author's calculations.

mated correlations will overestimate the true degree of expected-return correlation.

By far the highest expected-return correlation in table 3 is observed for the United Kingdom (0.96), as would be expected given the high degree of integration and the extent of cross-listing of securities between the London and New York markets. Germany, Malaysia, and the Philippines exhibit correlations of over 0.60. Japan has an expected return correlation of about 0.34, which is similar to the expected-return correlations of Chile, Mexico, and Thailand, which are 0.49, 0.33, and 0.30, respectively. Korea, Pakistan, and Taiwan (China) have expected-return correlations of 0.14, 0.25, and 0.12, respectively. All the other economies display negative expected-return correlations. Most markets show fairly large correlations for their unexpected returns. Hence, there must exist global news factors affecting many markets simultaneously, including the emerging markets.

The results for the 1976–85 sample conform to the trend toward increasing integration of equity markets. According to this measure, the industrial markets all became more integrated with the U.S. market during the last half of the 1980s, the change being most dramatic for Japan. Chile, Korea, and Mexico show negative correlation with the U.S. market in the early sample. In fact, before 1984, when the first Korean country fund was introduced, the Korean market was virtually closed to foreign investment. Some conundrums, however, do exist. For example, markets in Greece and Zimbabwe show high, albeit imprecisely measured, expected-return correlations with the U.S. market in the early sample.

In table 3 the rank based on the expected-correlation estimate is the sum of a ranking on the point estimate and a ranking on the size of the deviation from perfect correlation in number of standard errors. The expected-return correlations might not give an adequate picture of the common component in expected returns because the evidence for predictability is weak for some markets. To check the robustness of the results, I also provide an alternative measure of market integration based on the analysis in Campbell and Hamao (1992). Suppose that the emerging equity markets obey a multifactor model, where the first factor is international and the other factors are domestic; suppose that the international factor is well proxied by the world-stock-index return; and consider a regression of the excess equity returns on that world-market return and the forecasting variables. The variance of the predictable variation caused by the forecasting variables in that regression, in relation to the variance of the fitted values of the regressions reported in table 1, is a measure of the variation in risk prices of domestic factors relative to the variation in the risk prices of all factors. I interpret low ratios as indicative of more integration. In table 3, the column "Rank based on a variance ratio" ranks the markets on the basis of this ratio. For lack of space, further results are not reported.

There are some notable differences in the rankings based on the variance ratio compared with the earlier rankings (India and Nigeria are examples), but the rank correlation between the measures is 0.693, which is more than three standard errors from zero. The ratio is lower than 0.7 for only two emerging markets, Taiwan (China) and Thailand. I also checked whether inclusion of the world-market return changed the predictability tests. Significant rejections of the null of no predictability only disappeared for Greece (at the 10 percent level) and for Malaysia (at the 5 percent level). I also substituted a regional index for the world-market index to test whether there was any evidence of regional integration. (From Morgan Stanley Capital International I used the Pacific index for the Asian markets, the Europe index for the European and African markets, and the North America index for the Latin American markets.) The only markets for which the variance ratio dropped relative to the world-market regression were Chile and Korea. The regional βs were substantially higher only for Argentina, Chile, Mexico, and Venezuela. Hence there is weak evidence that regional integration is stronger than global integration in Latin America. In what follows, I will occasionally refer to results that use the ratio when they differ from the results that use the expected-return correlation measure.

III. Market Integration and Return Characteristics

In this section I provide a fuller picture of the properties of emerging-equity-market returns in order to relate them to various measures of barriers to investment. Some of the return properties might be correlated with popular cost-of-capital measures.

Tables 4 and 5 summarize some return properties for the two sample periods for nineteen emerging markets, an emerging-markets composite, and four major industrial markets. The first three columns report the mean, standard deviation, and Sharpe ratio. The Sharpe ratio is a measure of the risk-return tradeoff, computed as the excess return divided by the standard deviation of the excess return. Emerging markets offer higher but more variable returns compared with the industrial markets, although there are some notable exceptions to this rule (for example, in Jordan and Zimbabwe). The risk-return tradeoff during 1986–92 is most favorable in a number of Latin American markets (in Chile, Colombia, and Mexico), and it is generally better in emerging markets than in the industrial world. The composite index has a slightly higher mean return than the U.K stock market and a slightly higher risk. Its diversification potential stems from the relatively low correlation with the industrial markets. This is further illustrated in figure 1.

Tables 4 and 5 report the constant (α) and slope coefficient (β) of a regression of the excess return onto a constant and the world-market return. The Capital Asset Pricing Model (CAPM) would predict that the α coefficient equals zero. The major markets display very high βs with respect to the world-market portfolio and relatively small αs (pricing errors). In the emerging markets, high βs are found for Brazil, Korea, Malaysia, Mexico, the Philippines, Taiwan (China), and Thailand. Chile, Colombia, Mexico, the Philippines, and Thailand also

Table 4. *Properties of Emerging-Market Equity Returns, 1986–92*

	Dollar excess returns			World pricing error, α	World risk loading coefficient, β	First-order autocorrelation coefficient
Market	*Mean*	*Standard deviation*	*Sharpe ratio*[a]			
Argentina	62.048	104.396	0.594	64.735 (40.616)	−0.422 (0.638)	−0.082
Brazil	22.299	77.824	0.287	17.368 (28.419)	0.773 (0.504)	−0.030
Chile	41.186	28.508	1.445	39.593 (10.788)	0.250 (0.243)	0.310*
Colombia	43.069	33.524	1.285	41.899 (12.868)	0.184 (0.193)	0.479*
Greece	26.684	50.089	0.533	23.627 (18.720)	0.479 (0.285)	0.120
India	7.476	35.458	0.211	9.638 (13.473)	−0.339 (0.212)	0.103
Jordan	−2.369	17.139	−0.138	−3.113 (6.539)	0.117 (0.130)	−0.160
Korea, Rep. of	16.836	32.028	0.526	13.115 (11.388)	0.584 (0.178)	−0.099
Malaysia	11.782	26.520	0.444	6.789 (9.031)	0.783 (0.212)	0.031
Mexico	49.925	48.832	1.022	44.419 (18.239)	0.864 (0.374)	0.355*
Nigeria	−5.263	39.075	−0.135	−6.720 (15.132)	0.229 (0.217)	0.086
Pakistan	15.455	24.739	0.625	15.288 (9.408)	0.026 (0.151)	0.255*
Philippines	38.654	40.482	0.955	33.559 (14.575)	0.799 (0.278)	0.345*
Portugal	27.666	50.224	0.551	20.087 (17.364)	1.189 (0.242)	0.287*
Taiwan (China)	29.377	55.994	0.525	24.810 (21.190)	0.716 (0.429)	0.058
Thailand	29.567	30.964	0.955	25.247 (11.566)	0.678 (0.301)	0.114
Turkey[b]	30.815	74.146	0.416	30.212 (30.036)	0.247 (0.402)	0.114
Venezuela	32.684	46.452	0.704	34.454 (18.465)	−0.278 (0.337)	0.312*
Zimbabwe	1.245	26.669	0.047	1.428 (10.338)	−0.029 (0.195)	0.280*
Emerging-markets composite	10.453	25.249	0.414	7.215 (9.370)	0.508 (0.221)	0.130
Germany	2.909	25.113	0.116	−2.603 (7.678)	0.865 (0.152)	−0.083
Japan	8.156	29.528	0.276	−0.790 (6.959)	1.403 (0.174)	0.008
United Kingdom	10.372	23.173	0.448	3.374 (5.218)	1.098 (0.078)	−0.049
United States	8.210	17.091	0.480	3.563 (4.668)	0.729 (0.109)	−0.006

* Significant at the 5 percent level.
Note: All returns are annualized percentages. The reported mean is arithmetic. Standard errors are in parentheses.
a. The excess mean return scaled by the standard deviation.
b. Data begin January 1987.
Source: Author's calculations.

Table 5. *Properties of Emerging-Market Equity Returns, 1976–85*

Market	Dollar excess returns			World pricing error, α	World risk loading coefficient, β	First-order autocorrelation coefficient
	Mean	Standard deviation	Sharpe ratio[a]			
Argentina	61.236	105.525	0.580	60.265 (33.981)	0.321 (0.505)	0.151
Brazil	7.612	44.323	0.172	7.848 (14.115)	−0.078 (0.283)	0.116
Chile	16.977	46.527	0.365	17.223 (15.150)	−0.081 (0.353)	0.130
Greece	−21.814	20.119	−1.084	−22.769 (6.314)	0.315 (0.158)	0.077
India	11.502	19.721	0.583	10.258 (6.013)	0.411 (0.135)	−0.003
Jordan[b]	4.932	18.651	0.264	4.360 (6.996)	0.264 (0.170)	0.115
Korea, Rep. of	5.490	32.437	0.169	4.280 (10.158)	0.400 (0.265)	0.036
Mexico	−1.291	40.754	−0.032	−3.003 (12.873)	0.565 (0.310)	0.136
Thailand	3.547	21.519	0.165	3.571 (6.982)	−0.008 (0.122)	0.101
Zimbabwe	−3.601	39.089	−0.092	−5.420 (12.383)	0.601 (0.335)	0.099
Germany	2.307	17.995	0.128	0.315 (0.138)	0.750 (0.123)	0.022
Japan	9.150	18.807	0.487	0.309 (0.129)	0.910 (0.129)	−0.016
United Kingdom	7.583	23.053	0.329	0.607 (0.158)	1.171 (0.143)	0.038
United States	2.138	14.071	0.152	−0.849 (2.221)	0.987 (0.060)	−0.023

Note: All returns are annualized percentages. The reported mean is arithmetic. Standard errors are in parentheses.
    a. The excess return scaled by the standard deviation.
    b. Data begin January 1979.
Source: Author's calculations.

display significantly positive αs. Clearly, an unconditional world CAPM model does not explain much of the cross-sectional variation in emerging-equity-market returns. Hence, it would be incorrect to conclude that higher βs increase the cost of capital. On the contrary, high βs seem to indicate a higher degree of integration with the industrial world. Compared with the earlier sample, the βs and the Sharpe ratio have increased for most but not all emerging markets. The exceptions are Argentina, India, and Zimbabwe.[3]

Finally, tables 4 and 5 report the first-order autocorrelation coefficient for the various markets. This coefficient is clearly insignificantly different from zero for

3. It will be interesting to see whether the recent capital-market liberalization in India will have an effect on these statistics.

Figure 1. *Mean–Standard Deviation Frontiers of Monthly Dollar Total Returns of Selected Portfolios, January 1986–December 1992*
(percent)

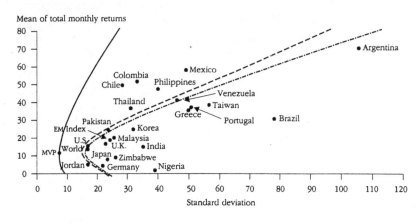

Mean of total monthly returns

——— Emerging Markets, Germany, Japan, United Kingdom, and United States.
– – – – Emerging Markets Index, Germany, Japan, United Kingdom, and United States.
–·–·–·– Germany, Japan, United Kingdom, and United States.

Note: MVP is the minimum-variance portfolio.
Source: IFC EMDB.

the major markets, but it is significantly positive for some emerging markets, potentially signaling market inefficiencies. However, not a single emerging market displays significant positive serial correlation in the early sample.

Table 6 contains information on dividend yields and price-earnings (P/E) ratios. Both variables exhibit large cross-sectional and time variation in the emerging markets. As Buckberg (1995) points out, P/E ratios typically increase substantially when a market is opened to foreign investment. By the same token, openness would result in lower dividend yields. Significant increases in P/E ratios coupled with significant decreases in dividend yields over the sample period are observed for Colombia, Mexico, and Pakistan. Both variables are factors in simple cost-of-capital computations and are likely to be affected by the degree of market segmentation. However, given the large differences in corporate and accounting practices, the absolute magnitude of dividend yields or P/E ratios may not be very informative on market segmentation.

Table 7 provides a matrix containing the rank correlations between all the return characteristics discussed above, including the measure of market integration. The ranking for all measures is such that the three industrial markets rank high. For example, markets with high values for mean return, volatility, Sharpe ratio, the α-pricing error from the world-market model, and dividend yield get a

Table 6. *Dividend Yields and Price-Earnings Ratios in Emerging Markets, 1986–92*
(percent, annual averages)

| | Dividend yields[a] | | | | | Price-earnings ratio[c] | | | | |
Market	1986–92	1986	1989	1992	Rank[b] 1992	1986–92	1986	1989	1992	Rank[b] 1992
Argentina	3.71	0.20	11.82	0.73	22	2.81	6.25	106.24	−25.19	23
Brazil	5.85	3.63	5.87	3.30	10	26.30	5.73	5.66	132.48	1
Chile	7.89	8.53	10.93	3.61	8	7.61	3.59	4.34	14.57	12
Colombia	8.19	15.39	7.62	3.50	9	6.71	−27.71	5.24	34.55	4
Greece	7.38	9.95	10.13	6.91	1	15.05	7.14	13.04	8.68	20
India	2.37	2.27	2.93	1.13	17	19.25	12.81	15.40	38.58	3
Jordan	4.82	3.00	3.63	4.23	5	11.56	12.13	13.66	12.22	17
Korea, Rep. of	2.04	6.20	1.08	0.02	23	21.71	16.43	31.18	19.17	11
Malaysia	2.42	2.26	2.64	2.62	13	28.05	21.40	29.65	20.78	8
Mexico	4.23	10.74	3.85	1.38	16	9.41	4.89	5.73	12.72	16
Nigeria	8.52	9.81	12.21	6.84	2	6.53	4.95	5.61	10.19	18
Pakistan	6.56	7.03	6.94	3.19	11	10.78	6.23	7.96	24.87	5
Philippines	2.75	7.75	1.82	0.91	20	12.62	—	13.13	13.99	14
Portugal[d]	2.27	1.59	1.79	3.76	7	15.11	10.85	16.75	9.82	19
Taiwan (China)	1.12	2.42	0.97	1.08	18	29.23	13.44	57.94	19.58	10
Thailand	4.71	9.77	3.87	2.44	14	12.47	8.47	14.01	13.73	15
Turkey	7.07	—	11.58	4.74	4	11.29	—	6.71	7.39	21
Venezuela	1.64	3.13	1.88	0.79	21	14.43	11.81	4.76	22.10	7
Zimbabwe	8.86	10.10	11.31	5.03	3	5.05	3.80	3.69	3.47	22
Germany	2.22	1.82	2.17	2.34	15	15.60	17.80	14.70	14.30	13
Japan	0.67	0.79	0.46	1.01	19	45.50	51.90	45.70	38.90	2
United Kingdom	3.60	4.03	3.41	3.80	6	14.93	11.70	13.40	19.70	9
United States	3.42	3.57	3.46	3.02	12	16.97	14.10	14.10	22.70	6

— Not available.
a. The dividend yield can be interpreted as a twelve-month reinvested average yield.
b. From high to low.
c. Twelve-month average computed by the IFC for IFC index stocks.
d. 1987 values substitute for 1986 values.
Source: Author's calculations. The earnings and dividend measures for the major markets are taken from Morgan Stanley and Company (various issues).

Table 7. Rank Correlations between Market Integration and Other Return Characteristics, 1986–92

Characteristic	Mean returns	Volatility	Sharpe ratio	Risk loading, β	Pricing error, α, from the world-market model	Expected-return correlation	Dividend yield	Price-earnings ratio
Market integration	−0.092	0.336	−0.268	0.610	−0.023	0.234	0.269	0.207
Mean returns		0.563	0.872	0.035	0.942	0.493	0.007	0.269
Volatility			0.209	0.054	0.472	0.051	−0.055	−0.010
Sharpe ratio				−0.027	0.905	0.612	0.028	0.251
Risk loading, β					0.175	0.228	0.403	0.557
Pricing error, α						0.584	0.156	0.366
First-order autocorrelation							0.357	0.503
Dividend yield								0.738

Note: The mean returns, volatility, Sharpe ratio, risk loading, pricing error, and autocorrelation coefficients are the return characteristics for the 1986–92 sample depicted in table 4. The 1986–92 sample averages for dividend yield and price-earnings ratio are given in table 6. The rank correlation coefficient is the Spearman rank correlation computed for nineteen emerging markets and Germany, Japan, and the United Kingdom. The standard error for each statistic is 0.22. The ranking for all measures is such that the three industrial countries rank high, that is, from low to high for the mean, volatility, Sharpe ratio, pricing error from the world-market model, and dividend yield and from high to low for the world-market risk loading and the price-earnings ratio. For the pricing error, the ranking is based on the sum of two ranks, one according to the absolute magnitude of the pricing error, another according to distance in the number of standard deviations away from zero. For the expected return correlation coefficients, countries with insignificantly small autocorrelations (smaller than 0.100 in absolute magnitude) are given the same rank.

Source: Author's calculations.

94

low rank for that particular statistic. The ranking is from low to high because the industrial markets typically display low values for these statistics. Likewise, the ranking is from high to low for expected-return correlation, world market β, and P/E ratio because the industrial markets typically have high values for these statistics. To help interpret the numbers, consider two examples. First, a positive rank correlation between the market-integration measure and volatility indicates that low volatility is associated with a high degree of market integration because industrial markets display low volatility. Second, a positive rank correlation between market integration and the P/E ratio indicates that higher P/E ratios typically imply higher degrees of market integration.

The only significant relation between the market-integration measure and other return characteristics is with the world β. As conjectured above, higher βs are associated with higher degrees of market integration and do not necessarily translate into higher expected returns. Although not significant, the rankings also reveal positive associations between market integration and P/E ratios and negative associations between market integration and dividend yields. This confirms the intuition that the capital flows associated with opening up markets tend to increase P/E ratios and decrease dividend yields.

Similarly, it would be expected that market integration contributes to domestic market efficiency. Because the autocorrelation ranking is from low to high, table 7 reveals the association between market-integration and the first-order autocorrelation coefficient to be negative but not significantly different from zero. The table also shows that the market-integration measure and volatility co-vary negatively. This supports my conjecture that concerns about excess price volatility in newly opened emerging stock markets might be unnecessary. The alternative market-integration measure yields similar results (not reported) with the exception that the associations with dividend yields and P/E ratios are significantly different from zero in this case.

There is no relation between mean returns and either the market-integration measures or the βs. Harvey (1995) examines the sensitivity of the emerging-market returns to measures of global risk, including the world-market portfolio. He finds that emerging markets have little or no sensitivity, which confirms the results of table 7. There is a strong positive rank correlation between average returns and volatility, the pricing error, and the autocorrelation coefficients. Consequently, high mean returns cannot be explained by the world-market model, but they might partially reflect inefficiencies in domestic markets.

IV. MARKET INTEGRATION AND BARRIERS TO INVESTMENT

Foreign investors face many barriers when investing in emerging markets. I distinguish two groups of direct barriers to investment and one group of indirect barriers. In the first group are direct restrictions on foreign ownership. For example, certain sectors may be closed to foreign investment, or limits may be imposed on direct ownership of equity.

Table 8. *Foreign Ownership Restrictions and Dates of Recent Liberalizations Affecting Foreign Investors*

Market	Exchange rate regime, 1991	Percent investable, 1992	Investable index/global index (ratio)	Liberalization	Date
Argentina	Free float	100	88.2	All limits on foreign capital abolished	December 1989
Brazil	Free float	49ᵃ	60.4	Group of foreign investment trusts approved	March 1987
				Interbank foreign exchange market allowed	March 1990
				Foreign ownership levels increased	May 1991
				Foreign portfolios without local custody allowed	July 1991
Chile	Pegged to basket	25	20.9	Non-Central Bank foreign exchange market authorization	April 1990
Colombia	Central Bank control	100	76.0	Made 100 percent investable	February 1991
Greece	Managed float	100	80.8	n.a.	n.a.
India	Free float	24	19.1	All shares made investable	November 1992
				Managed exchange rate abolished	March 1992
Jordan	Pegged to basket	49	29.0	n.a.	n.a.
Korea, Rep. of	Pegged to dollar	10ᵃ	9.6	Government-announced sweeping liberalization	December 1988
				Investment preapproval rules softened	January 1990
				Market average exchange rate system introduced	March 1990
Malaysia	Free float	30	67.4	Foreign ownership levels increased	January 1992
Mexico	Free float	100ᵃ	87.7	n.a.	n.a.
				Made 100 percent investable	May 1989
				Dual exchange rate system unified	November 1991
Nigeria	Pegged to French franc	0ᵃ	0.0	n.a.	n.a.
Pakistan	Pegged to dollar	100	29.3	Made 100 percent investable	February 1991
Philippines	Free float	40ᵃ	47.3	All shares made investable	November 1991
Portugal	European Monetary System	100ᵃ	54.1	n.a.	n.a.
Taiwan (China)	Central Bank control	10ᵃ	3.0	Equity market broadly opened, $5 billion maximum foreign holdings	January 1991
				Maximum foreign security holdings limit increased to $10 billion	March 1993
Thailand	Pegged to basket	100ᵃ	27.0	n.a.	n.a.
Turkey	Free float	100	97.3	n.a.	n.a.
Venezuela	Free float	100	36.3	Foreign ownership allowed with limits	December 1988
				All restrictions lifted	January 1990
Zimbabwe	Pegged to basket	—ᵃ	0.0	n.a.	n.a.

n.a. Not applicable.

a. Industry exceptions.

Source: IMF (1992), for foreign exchange policies; IFC (various issues), for foreign ownership levels and liberalizations; Park and van Agtmael (1993), for some liberalization dates.

In the second group are exchange and capital controls that affect investment in emerging markets and the repatriation of dividends and capital from emerging markets. For example, some economies have direct restrictions, such as a minimum investment period, on the remittance of profits. Taxes on dividends and capital gains are considered direct barriers in this second group (see Demirgüç-Kunt and Huizinga 1992). Some economies, such as Nigeria and Zimbabwe, are still completely closed to foreign investment. Overall, however, restrictions have been gradually relaxed, and this process has accelerated in the 1990s. Examples of economies in which restrictions have been recently lifted include Brazil, Colombia, India, Korea, and Taiwan (China). Table 8 gives some information on both groups of direct barriers. A more detailed survey of the existing restrictions on foreign investors at the end of 1992 is given in IFC (various issues).

In the third group are indirect barriers having to do with the regulatory and accounting environment. Investors might not have adequate information on these markets and on the financial health of the companies, the settlement systems might be inefficient and slow, accounting standards might be poor, and investor protection might be minimal. These factors might play a large role in the investment decisions of international investors. In her survey of market participants, Chuhan (1992) lists limited information on emerging markets as one of the key impediments to investing in emerging markets.

I considered several measures of "openness" and their relation to the market-integration measure. The difficulty was to quantify the extent of the restrictions in the various economies in order to make the computation of rank correlations possible. The IFC has recently launched indexes that take direct foreign ownership restrictions into account. The investable market capitalization of each stock is used for its weight in the index instead of the stock's total market capitalization, as in the IFC's regular global indexes.[4] Consequently, one measure of the extent of foreign ownership restrictions is the ratio of the IFC investable index to the IFC global index. That ratio is reported in table 8 and is the basis of my openness measure, Open I.

Unfortunately, the scarcity of available information prevented me from ranking the economies directly according to the severity of other capital and exchange restrictions. To gauge the effects of these restrictions indirectly, I computed a ranking based on the mean black-market premium and a ranking based on the sums of the ranks according to the mean and volatility of the premiums during 1988–92. The data used for these calculations are described in Chuhan, Claessens, and Mamingi (1993). Because some economies (Greece, Jordan, Nigeria, Portugal, Turkey, and Zimbabwe) are missing from the data set, the rank correlations have a standard error of 0.258. However, the rank correlation between black-market premiums (ranked from low to high) and the market-

---

4. For details on how a variety of restrictions on foreign ownership change the weights used to construct the index, see IFC (various issues).

integration measure is 0.711 if the ranking is based on the means and 0.697 if the ranking is based on the means and variances.

For indirect barriers, I used the EMDB table on the availability of market and company information, and the quality of accounting standards and investor protection, as reported by Harvey (1993). From this information, I computed a summary measure (unreported), which is the basis for my "Open II" ranking.

Despite the persistence of various restrictions on foreign investors, several emerging markets have been open to some form of foreign investment for a surprisingly long time. One of the first vehicles for foreign investment in emerging markets was country funds. Four Asian economies—Korea, Malaysia, Taiwan (China), and Thailand—individually have more than ten country funds listed abroad. There is of course potentially very useful information on market integration in the premiums that some of these closed-end funds command when traded in industrial markets (see, for instance, Bekaert and Urias 1994 and Diwan, Senbet, and Errunza 1992). More recently, some companies in emerging markets have begun to list their stock on the exchanges of industrial markets. No less than thirty Mexican companies are listed on American exchanges. I used the number of country funds and cross-listed securities to construct a third measure of openness, "Open III." The measure is imperfect because the lack of data has prevented me from weighting the funds and companies by market capitalization, and the cross-listings are restricted to the United States.

I calculated the rank correlations for the Open I, Open II, and Open III measures for the emerging markets (not reported). The rank correlations between market integration and the three measures are 0.214 for Open I, 0.601 for Open II, and 0.794 for Open III. The market-integration measure is most significantly positively associated with the Open III measure. This result indicates that the best way to effectively open up a market may be to mobilize foreign resources through country funds or cross-listed securities. Such an approach confirms the theoretical analysis of Diwan, Senbet, and Errunza (1992). They show that country funds, despite their small size, contribute significantly to capital mobilization and pricing efficiency in the originating capital markets. These results are robust to the use of the alternative measure of market segmentation; in fact, they are even stronger with the alternative measure than without it.

Somewhat surprisingly, the relation between the market-integration measure and the Open I measure is not significantly positive: either the ownership restrictions are circumvented or they are not binding. The Open I measure does correlate significantly with the world-market βs (not reported). Markets with less severe ownership restrictions tend to have high βs. In the theoretical analysis of Eun and Janakiramanan (1986) and Stulz and Wasserfallen (1992), the presence of ownership restrictions in a world CAPM leads to higher expected returns for foreign investors and to "home bias" in their portfolio holdings. How this super-risk premium affects the empirical estimates of α and β, however, is unclear. Again, the data reveal that openness goes hand in hand with higher βs.

The rank correlation between the world βs and the Open II and Open III measures is even higher than that between the world βs and the Open I measure. (The correlations with the world βs are 0.447 for Open I, 0.721 for Open II, and 0.700 for Open III.)

The Open II measure correlates significantly with the market-integration measure. The results suggest that providing more and better information on the markets and companies and improving accounting standards and investor protection should contribute to making emerging markets better integrated in the global equity market. In fact, such simple policy actions might be more important than fully abolishing ownership restrictions.

The Open II and Open III measures also correlate positively with P/E ratios and negatively with dividend yields. These results confirm that open markets tend to have lower dividend yields and higher P/E ratios. There are few other significant associations between return characteristics and the openness measures. In particular, there is no significant relation between the openness of a market and stock return volatility. Therefore, the fear that foreign-market access leads to more volatile markets might be ill-founded. In fact, the relatively high correlations with the autocorrelation measure, although not statistically significant, suggest that opening up markets is likely to improve domestic market efficiency.

V. Market Integration and Emerging-Market-Specific Risks

The first emerging-market-specific risk (EMSR) I investigated is political or, more broadly, country risk. Political instability and economic mismanagement might add substantial risk premiums to returns and deter some foreign investors. A crude and indirect measure of political risk is the secondary-market price of bank debt. Unfortunately, this is only available for a limited number of economies (unreported). Nevertheless, it is remarkable how the prices of Mexican and Chilean debt increased recently in conjunction with investors' renewed interest in these markets. Between 1989 and 1992, the price increased from 60.6 cents to 89.4 cents to the dollar for Chilean debt and from 39.7 cents to 64.3 cents to the dollar for Mexican debt. For all markets, a more direct measure of political risk is the Institutional Investor country credit rating. The credit rating did not change noticeably from 1986 to 1992 for most markets. However, the credit rating improved considerably for Chile (from 25.1 to 45.9) and for Mexico (from 30.8 to 42.6). By far, the credit rating for Taiwan (China) (77.5 in 1992) is the highest for the emerging markets.

The Economist regularly ranks the industrial countries according to three macroeconomic indicators: inflation, real gross domestic product (GDP) growth, and current account balance as a percentage of GDP. I computed this ranking for the emerging markets in the sample (not reported). The top performers are Korea and Malaysia. The United Kingdom's macroeconomic performance is only average in relation to that of the set of emerging markets; it ranks 10.5

100   THE WORLD BANK ECONOMIC REVIEW, VOL. 9, NO. 1

among the sample markets. Because a current account deficit does not necessarily signal instability but could be the healthy mirror image of large capital
inflows, I also computed a ranking based only on GDP growth and inflation.
Korea, Malaysia, and Thailand are the best performers. The variability, rather
than the level of inflation, might be a better indicator of the soundness of
economic policies. Inflation is even less variable in Malaysia and Thailand than
in the United Kingdom. I also computed a ranking of the economies based on
their performance with respect to both level and variability of inflation. Not
surprisingly, Latin American economies perform worst whereas Asian economies perform best.

Currency movements can have a dramatic impact on equity returns for foreign
investors. Many developing economies manage to keep exchange rate volatility
lower than that in the industrial economies. This is not surprising as many developing economies try to peg their exchange rates to the U.S. dollar or to a basket of
currencies (see table 8). Dramatic exceptions are Argentina, Brazil, and Nigeria.

The second EMSR I investigated is liquidity risk. Because liquidity might be correlated with the size of the stock market, I also investigated the relative size of the
market using locally compiled (not the IFC's) indexes. Most of the emerging markets are relatively small compared with the major industrial markets.[5] Mexico's
market, the largest emerging market, has a market capitalization value of $127.1
billion, about one-third the size of Germany's (market-capitalization value
$393.5 billion). Zimbabwe's market, the smallest (market-capitalization value
$869.2 million), is about 150 times smaller than Mexico's. Recently, some mar-
kets have grown tremendously. Between 1989 and 1992 the stock markets of
Chile, Colombia, Greece, India, Malaysia, Mexico, Pakistan, Thailand, Turkey,
and Venezuela all more than doubled in size in dollar terms. In percentage of GDP,
the markets of Chile and Malaysia, with market capitalization values of 82 percent of GDP in 1991 and 81 percent of GDP in 1989, respectively, have surpassed
the level of the U.S. market. The size of other markets, such as those of Colombia,
Nigeria, Turkey, and Venezuela, having market capitalization values of between 3
and 5 percent of GDP, is still tiny compared with the size of their economies.

I calculated a turnover measure (value traded as a percentage of market capitalization; not reported), which could serve as a liquidity indicator. Surprisingly, turnover is larger in many emerging markets than in the United Kingdom and Japan. Markets with particularly large turnover are those of Korea,
Taiwan (China), and Thailand.

Table 9 reports rank correlations between the return characteristics and the
EMSR measures. Macroeconomic performance, inflation volatility, size, and relative size all have an impact on the extent of market integration. Political risk is
positively associated with market segmentation, but the correlation is not signif-

---

5. Data on liquidity and size of markets in this and the next paragraph are from the Emerging Markets
Data Base for the emerging markets and from Allen and O'Connor (1992) for the industrial markets. GDP
data are from IMF (various issues).

icantly different from zero. Not surprisingly, these variables also correlate significantly with the βs and, except for the macroeconomic performance variable, with dividend yields and P/E ratios. The only marginally significant relation between mean returns and EMSRS involves the inflation variable. High and variable inflation also contributes to volatility in the stock markets.[6] Economies with relatively small stock market capitalization as a percentage of GDP and bad macroeconomic policies tend to have more-volatile stock markets. Exchange rate volatility is not significantly related to return characteristics. The turnover measure is positively correlated with volatility and mean returns, although the correlations are not significantly different from zero. Either the result is caused by some of the Asian markets, where trading is "excessive," or turnover is a bad proxy for liquidity and does not capture the liquidity problems mentioned by foreign investors in the Chuhan (1992) survey.

When the alternative measure of market integration is used, the rank correlation between liquidity and market integration is higher (0.390). The other results are robust; in particular, the relations between market integration and macroeconomic performance, inflation volatility, size, and relative size are invariably stronger. The alternative measure also exhibits a 0.698 rank correlation with the political-risk measure.

VI. Conclusions

In this article I have attempted to identify significant relations between a number of barriers to investment, broadly defined, and a return-based measure of market integration, as well as other return characteristics. The policy prescription is that an economy should try to eliminate or lessen the impact of those barriers that are most likely to effectively segment the local market from the global capital market. I have identified the following effective barriers to global equity-market integration: poor credit ratings, high and variable inflation, exchange rate controls, the lack of a high-quality regulatory and accounting framework, the lack of sufficient country funds or cross-listed securities, and the limited size of some stock markets. I have not found a significant link between return characteristics and ownership restrictions or a turnover measure.

My analysis has some major drawbacks. Foremost, I have simply assumed that my measure of capital-market integration is positively related to capital flows and negatively related to domestic capital costs. As to the former, I could not detect highly significant correlations between my market-integration measures and cumulative capital flows (as a percentage of market capitalization). The correlation between my market-integration measure and the capital-flow data (cumulated real net U.S. purchases of foreign equity studied in Chuhan, Claessens, and Mamingi 1993) is 0.542 with a standard error of 0.258, but it is

---

6. Although returns are measured in nominal terms, they are measured in dollars, so that high inflation should not necessarily lead to higher stock returns.

102   THE WORLD BANK ECONOMIC REVIEW, VOL. 9, NO. 1

Table 9. *Rank Correlations between Return Characteristics and Emerging-Market-Specific Risks*

Return characteristic	Political risk[a]	Macroeconomic performance[b]	Exchange rate volatility	Inflation volatility	Level and volatility of inflation	Size[c]	Relative size[d]	Liquidity[c]
Market integration	0.379	0.462	0.137	0.514	0.519	0.584	0.615	0.012
Mean returns	0.013	0.228	-0.078	0.238	0.410	-0.037	0.257	-0.258
Volatility	0.145	0.633	0.327	0.578	0.686	0.042	0.436	-0.263
Sharpe ratio	-0.069	-0.073	-0.298	-0.044	0.108	-0.016	0.173	-0.098
Risk loading, β	0.632	0.439	-0.021	0.535	0.504	0.632	0.557	0.199
Pricing error, α	0.138	0.215	-0.186	0.278	0.431	0.108	0.377	-0.153
Expected-return correlation	0.384	0.212	-0.090	0.173	0.271	0.516	0.437	0.332
Dividend yield	0.593	0.295	0.028	0.454	0.486	0.645	0.466	0.441
Price-earnings ratio	0.634	0.272	0.186	0.495	0.511	0.641	0.567	0.317

Note: Economies are ranked from high to low for size, relative size, and liquidity and from low to high for exchange rate volatility, inflation volatility, and level and volatility of inflation. The standard errors for the statistics are 0.22, except for relative size, for which it is 0.23; Argentina and Taiwan (China) are not included.

a. The ranking based on the Institutional Investor Credit Ratings for 1992.

b. Based on inflation and real GDP growth performance.

c. Based on 1992 data.

d. Average over 1986, 1989, and 1992.

Source: Author's calculations.

close to zero using the data reported in Tesar and Werner (1995). Note that both data sets involve somewhat different markets and time periods.

As for the cost of capital, I have demonstrated the difficulties associated with trying to measure the level of expected equity returns, and hence domestic capital costs. First, the lack of a relation between mean returns and any of the barriers to investment that I have considered does not bode well for approaches based on a history of returns. The market-integration measures correlate significantly with P/E ratios and dividend yields, which feature in some capital-cost calculations. Second, most efforts to measure expected returns use some version of the CAPM (see, for example, Demirgüç-Kunt and Huizinga 1992). However, my results show that high world market βs do not necessarily reflect higher expected returns but rather seem to reflect a higher degree of global capital-market integration.

There are a number of possible interpretations for this outcome. The CAPM could be a reasonable description of the returns but should be modified to allow for time-varying degrees of market segmentation. Bekaert and Harvey (1994), for instance, allow conditionally expected returns in emerging markets to depend on their covariance with a world benchmark portfolio and on the variance of the country return. The integration measure is a time-varying weight applied to these two moments, which arises from a conditional regime-switching model. It is also possible that the effect of the world-market factor is confounded by other factors in a multifactor world, where the risk exposures vary through time (Harvey 1993 makes a similar point). Additional factors that come to mind are industry factors and commodity factors.

The fact that my integration measure does not correct for different industry exposures and the general lack of diversification within indexes for emerging markets is another potential drawback. Divecha, Drach, and Stefek (1992) consider four "concentration measures": the proportion of capitalization in the top ten companies, an asset concentration factor (which is valued at one if the entire market capitalization is concentrated in one market), a sector concentration measure, and the average correlation between stocks in the index. To examine whether the industry and sectoral patterns affect my market-integration measure, I computed rank correlations between the four concentration measures as reported in Divecha, Drach, and Stefek (1992: 46) and my market-integration measure. If all markets were perfectly integrated and the correlation of expected returns only reflected different concentration or industry effects, one would expect to find positive correlations between the market integration measure and the concentration measures (ranked from low to high). I found the rank correlations to be 0.393 for the concentration measures based on the top ten companies, 0.399 for asset concentration, 0.448 for sector concentration, and −0.055 for the average correlation between stocks. Because data on Germany are not reported in Divecha, Drach, and Stefek, I used twenty-one countries, and the standard error was 0.224. When the alternative measure was used, the first three correlation coefficients were significantly different from zero. These results seem to contradict the conclusion of Divecha, Drach, and Stefek, who state that sector concentration is not important for explaining emerging-market returns. On the contrary, the results suggest that industry factors should be an important part of future analyses.

Finally, in this article I have ignored dynamic interactions between changes in barriers to investment and market returns. Future work should explore panel-data approaches that incorporate global and domestic risk factors jointly with quantitative indicators of barriers to investment. In such an analysis, the risk exposures should be made a function of the degree of market segmentation.

This article has implications for some other interesting policy questions. Genuine concern exists among policymakers about the impact of international investment on local-market turnover and the volatility of equity returns. Tesar and Werner (1995) find no evidence that U.S. investment activity contributes to either volatility in equity returns or to higher local turnover in emerging markets. This result is confirmed in the present article. Section IV has shown that volatility is unrelated to any measure of openness. In fact, volatility is actually negatively, although not significantly, correlated with the market-integration measure. Furthermore there is no association between turnover and the market-integration measures.

Policymakers might be concerned that increasing integration between the capital market and the economy will lead to lower diversification benefits. Lower diversification benefits, in turn, might reduce the appetite of the international investment community for stocks in emerging equity markets. Table 3 reports a correlation of the composite index with the United States that is 0.40, which is not unlike correlations noted between industrial countries. The more relevant correlation of expected returns is still only 0.19, which is fairly low. I would argue that these concerns are ill-founded for two reasons. First, as shown in this article, I have not detected any relation between the risk-return tradeoff of individual markets (as measured by the Sharpe ratio) and market integration or the openness measures. Second, capital-market integration might help secure long-lasting portfolio flows from institutional investors. The trend toward international diversification has caused an increasing number of money managers and institutional investors to practice global-asset-allocation strategies. Typically, asset-allocation models start from a neutral benchmark that is close to the world-market portfolio as, for instance, defined by Morgan Stanley Capital International. Emerging markets should eventually strive to become part of the global world-market portfolio, used as a benchmark by investors worldwide.

APPENDIX. DATA SOURCES

The stock return data for the emerging markets are from the IFC Emerging Markets Data Base. Annualized dividend yields are constructed as the sum of twelve monthly dividend yields. P/E ratios, market capitalizations, and turnover ratios are also taken from that data set. The stock return data for the

industrial countries are from Morgan Stanley Capital International. The U.S.
interest rate used in the article is the one-month Eurorate obtained from Data
Resources Incorporated (DRI) until mid-1988, from Citicorp Data Services between mid-1988 and July 1991, and from the *Financial Times* for the remainder
of the sample. Equity returns for Germany, Japan, and the United Kingdom
were computed using exchange rate data from Citicorp Data Services which
were updated from mid-1991 onward with data from the *Financial Times*.
Macroeconomic data were taken from IMF (various issues).

REFERENCES

The word "processed" describes informally reproduced works that may not be commonly available through library systems.

Adler, Michael, and Bernard Dumas. 1983. "International Portfolio Choice and Corporation Finance: A Synthesis." *Journal of Finance* 38(3, June):925–84.

Allen, S., and S. O'Connor, eds. 1992. *The GT Guide to World Equity Markets*. London, U.K.: Euromoney Publications.

Bekaert, Geert. Forthcoming. "The Time-Variation of Expected Returns and Volatility
in Foreign Exchange Markets." *Journal of Business and Economic Statistics*.

Bekaert, Geert, and Robert Hodrick. 1992. "Characterizing Predictable Components in
Excess Returns on Equity and Foreign Exchange Markets." *Journal of Finance*
47(2):467–509.

Bekaert, Geert, and Campbell R. Harvey. 1994. "Time-varying World Integration."
NBER Working Paper 4843. Cambridge, Mass.: National Bureau of Economic
Research.

Bekaert, Geert, and Michael Urias. 1994. "Diversification, Integration, and Emerging
Market Closed-End Funds." Stanford University, Graduate School of Business, Department of Finance, Stanford, Calif. Processed.

Buckberg, Elaine. 1995. "Emerging Stock Markets and International Asset Pricing." *The
World Bank Economic Review* 9(1):51–74.

Campbell, John, and John Ammer. 1993. "What Moves the Stock and Bond Markets? A
Variance Decomposition for Long-Term Asset Returns." *Journal of Finance* 48(1):
3–38.

Campbell, John Y., and Yasushi Hamao. 1992. "Predictable Stock Returns in the United
States and Japan: A Study of Long-Term Capital Market Integration." *Journal of
Finance* 47(1, March):43–69.

Capital International Perspective, S.A., and Morgan Stanley & Co. Various issues.
Morgan Stanley Capital International Perspective. New York: Morgan Stanley.

Chuhan, Punam. 1992. "Sources of Portfolio Investment in Emerging Markets." Working Paper, World Bank, International Economics Department, Washington, D.C.
Processed.

Chuhan, Punam, Stijn Claessens, and Nlandu Mamingi. 1993. "Equity and Bond Flows
to Latin America and Asia: The Role of Global and Country Factors." World Bank,
International Economics Department, Washington, D.C. Processed.

Cooper, Ian, and Evi Kaplanis. 1986. "Costs to Crossborder Investment and International Equity Market Equilibrium." In Jeremy Edwards, Julian Franks, Colin Mayer,

106 THE WORLD BANK ECONOMIC REVIEW, VOL. 9, NO. 1

and Stephen Schacter, *Recent Developments in Corporate Finance*. Cambridge, U.K.:
Cambridge University Press.

———. 1994. "Home Bias in Equity Portfolios, Inflation Hedging, and International
Capital Market Equilibrium." *Review of Financial Studies* 7(1, Spring):45–60.

Cumby, Robert E., and John Huizinga. 1993. "Investigating the Correlation of Unobserved Expectations: Expected Returns in Equity and Foreign Exchange Markets and
Other Examples." *Journal of Monetary Economics* 30(2, November):217–53.

———. 1992. "Testing the Autocorrelation Structure of Disturbances in Ordinary Least
Squares and Instrumental Variables Regressions." *Econometrica* 60(1, January):185–
95.

Demirgüç-Kunt, Asli, and Harry Huizinga. 1992. "Barriers to Portfolio Investments in
Emerging Stock Markets." Policy Research Working Paper WPS 984. World Bank,
Washington, D.C. Processed.

Divecha, Arjun B., Jaime Drach, and Dan Stefek. 1992. "Emerging Markets: A Quantitative Perspective." *Journal of Portfolio Management* 19(1, Fall):41–56.

Diwan, Ishac, Lemma Senbet, and Vihang Errunza. 1992. "Pricing of Country Funds
and Their Role in Capital Mobilization for Emerging Economies." University of
Maryland, Center for International Business Education and Research, College Park,
Md. Processed.

Errunza, Vihang, and Etienne Losq. 1985. "International Asset Pricing under Mild
Segmentation: Theory and Test." *Journal of Finance* 40(1, March):105–24.

Eun, Cheol S., and S. Janakiramanan. 1986. "A Model of International Asset Pricing
with a Constraint on the Foreign Equity Ownership." *Journal of Finance* 41(4,
September):897–914.

Ferson, Wayne E., and Campbell R. Harvey. 1993. "The Risk and Predictability of
International Equity Returns." *Review of Financial Studies.* 6(3):527–66.

Harvey, Campbell R. 1991. "The World Price of Covariance Risk." *Journal of Finance*
46(1, March):111–57.

———. 1993. "Predictable Risk and Returns in Emerging Markets." Duke University,
Fuqua School of Business, Raleigh, N.C. Processed.

———. 1995. "The Risk Exposure of Emerging Equity Markets." *The World Bank
Economic Review* 9(1):19–50.

Heston, Steve, and K. Geert Rouwenhorst. 1994. "Does Industrial Structure Explain the
Benefits of International Diversification?" *Journal of Financial Economics* 36(1):3–27.

Hietala, Pekka. 1989. "Asset Pricing in Partially Segmented Markets: Evidence from the
Finnish Market." *Journal of Finance* 44(3, July):697–718.

Hodrick, Robert, and Sanjay Srivastava. 1984. "An Investigation of Risk and Return in
Forward Foreign Exchange." *Journal of International Money and Finance* 3:5–29.

IFC (International Finance Corporation). Various issues. *IFC Index Methodology.* Washington, D.C.

IMF (International Monetary Fund). 1992. *1992 Annual Report.* Washington, D.C.

———. Various issues. *International Financial Statistics.* Washington, D.C.

Park, Keith K. H., and Antoine W. van Agtmael, eds. 1993. *The World's Emerging Stock
Markets: Structure, Developments, Regulations, and Opportunities.* Chicago, Ill.:
Probus Publications.

Roll, Richard. 1992. "Industrial Structure and the Comparative Behavior of International Stock Market Indices." *Journal of Finance* 47(1, March):3–41.

Speidell, Lawrence S., and Ross Sappenfield. 1992. "Global Diversification in a Shrinking World." *Journal of Portfolio Management* 19(1, Fall):57–67.

Stulz, René M. 1981. "On the Effects of Barriers to International Investment." *Journal of Finance* 36(4, September):923–34.

Stulz, René, and Walter Wasserfallen. 1992. "Foreign Equity Investment Restrictions and Shareholder Wealth Maximization: Theory and Evidence." Ohio State University, Department of Finance, Columbus, Ohio. Processed.

Tesar, Linda, and Ingrid Werner. 1995. "U.S. Portfolio Investment and Emerging Stock Markets." *The World Bank Economic Review* 9(1):109–30.

Wheatley, Simon. 1988. "Some Tests of International Equity Integration." *Journal of Financial Economics* 21(2, September):177–212.

Wilcox, Jarrod W. 1992. "Taming Frontier Markets." *Journal of Portfolio Management* 19(1, Fall):51–56.

[4]

Predictable Risk and Returns in Emerging Markets

Campbell R. Harvey
Duke University and National Bureau of Economic Research

The emergence of new equity markets in Europe, Latin America, Asia, the Mideast and Africa provides a new menu of opportunities for investors. These markets exhibit high expected returns as well as high volatility. Importantly, the low correlations with developed countries' equity markets significantly reduces the unconditional portfolio risk of a world investor. However, standard global asset pricing models, which assume complete integration of capital markets, fail to explain the cross section of average returns in emerging countries. An analysis of the predictability of the returns reveals that emerging market returns are more likely than developed countries to be influenced by local information.

In recent years, a number of new equity markets have emerged in Europe, Latin America, Asia, the Mideast, and Africa. Little is known about these markets other

I have benefited from the comments of Warren Bailey, Arjun Divecha, Vihang Errunza, Wayne Ferson, Pierre Hillion, Antti Ilmanen, Kees Koedijk, Harry Markowitz, James Moser, Jay Ritter, Rudi Shadt, Simon Wheatley, and Fernando Zapatero, as well as seminar participants at the University of California at Los Angeles, Virginia Polytechnic Institute, Stockholm School of Economics, Columbia, Carnegie-Mellon, Michigan, Chicago, Dartmouth, Duke, Georgia Institute of Technology, Board of Governors of the Federal Reserve System, CEPR Workshop in International Finance, Maastricht, May 1993, and the Western Finance Association, June 1993. Ahktar Siddique provided valuable research assistance. Peter Wall at the International Finance Corporation provided answers to a number of questions. I am especially indebted to Robert Stambaugh and an anonymous referee for their detailed suggestions. The emerging markets data are provided by the World Bank. This research was supported by the Batterymarch Fellowship. Address correspondence to Campbell R. Harvey, Fuqua School of Business, Duke University, Durham, NC 27708-0120, e-mail charvey@mail.duke.edu.

The Review of Financial Studies Fall 1995 Vol. 8, No. 3, pp. 773–816

The Review of Financial Studies / v 8 n 3 1995

than that the expected returns can be impressive and these markets are highly volatile. Importantly, the correlations of these equity returns with developed countries' equity returns are low. As a result, it may be possible to lower portfolio risk by participating in emerging markets.

This article has a number of goals. First, the average or unconditional risk of these equity returns is studied. While previous authors have documented low correlations of the emerging market returns with developed country returns, I test whether adding emerging market assets to the portfolio problem *significantly* shifts the investment opportunity set. I find that the addition of emerging market assets significantly enhances portfolio opportunities.

Second, I explore reasons why the emerging market equities have high expected returns. In the framework of asset pricing theory, high expected returns should be associated with large exposures to risk factors. However, I find that the exposures to the commonly used risk factors are low. The asset pricing model, as specified, is unable to explain the cross section of expected returns. One possible reason for this failure is the implicit assumption of complete integration of world capital markets. Some evidence is offered that points to a violation of this assumption.

Third, the time variation in the emerging market returns is studied. Emerging markets contrast with developed markets in at least two respects. I offer evidence that the emerging market returns are generally more predictable than the developed market returns. In addition, it is more likely that the emerging market returns are influenced by local rather than global information variables.

One interpretation of the influence of local information is that the emerging markets are segmented from world capital markets. A second interpretation is that there is important time variation in the risk exposures of the emerging markets. For countries with stable, developed industrial structures, many researchers studying time-varying asset returns have assumed that risk loadings are constant. This is a far less reasonable assumption for developing countries. The country risk exposure reflects the weighted average of the risk exposures of the companies that are included in the national index. As the industrial structure develops, both the weights and the risk exposures of the individual companies could change. This may induce time variation in risk exposures. In addition, the risk exposures are likely influenced by local rather than global information variables.

I study a conditional asset pricing model where the expected returns are functions of global and local information variables, the world risk premiums are dependent only on global information, and the conditional risk is a function of both global and local information.

In contrast to the unconditional models, this specification allows for time-variation in the risk exposures and the expected returns.

Tests of the conditional asset pricing model suggest that the risk exposures significantly change through time for a number of the countries. An examination of the time-varying risk functions suggests that the exposures in some countries move with the time-varying conditional correlations of the countries' returns and a benchmark world return. However, the asset pricing model's restrictions are rejected, which implies that this formulation is unable to explain the predictability of the returns nor the cross-section variation of the expected returns.

The article is organized as follows. The second section provides a description of the data and some summary statistics for the 20 emerging market index returns. In the third section, an analysis of the cross-country correlations of the emerging and developed returns is presented. The section includes tests of whether adding emerging markets to the portfolio problem significantly changes portfolio opportunities. The average risk exposures to prespecified world economic risk factors are also presented and interpreted. The rejection of the asset pricing theory is characterized in mean-variance space. The fourth section details the predictability of the emerging market returns. Conditional asset pricing models are estimated with the goal of trying to explain the predictability and to understand the sources of model rejection. Some concluding remarks are offered in the final section.

1. Characterizing the Returns and Volatility of Emerging Markets

1.1 Data sources

Data on more than 800 equities in six Latin American markets (Argentina, Brazil, Chile, Colombia, Mexico, Venezuela), eight Asian markets (India, Indonesia, Korea, Malaysia, Pakistan, Philippines, Taiwan, Thailand), three European markets (Greece, Portugal, Turkey), one Mideast market (Jordan), and two African markets (Nigeria, Zimbabwe) form the Emerging Market Data Base (EMDB) of the International Finance Corporation (IFC), which is part of the World Bank. Monthly value-weighted index returns are calculated, with dividend reinvestment, for these 20 countries. These markets are labeled "emerging" as a result of their low- or middle-income status by the World Bank. In 1991, a per capita GNP of US$635 or less implied low income and per capita GNP between US$636 and US$7910 defined middle income status.

Table 1 provides some basic statistics regarding the composition of the indices. For each market in June 1992, the market capitaliza-

The Review of Financial Studies / v 8 n 3 1995

Table 1
Summary statistics for emerging and developed markets' U.S. dollar returns through June 1992

Country	First month in sample	Market capitalization (US$ billion)	Firms in index	Annualized means US$ (%)	Annualized means Local currency (%)	Annualized std. dev. (%)	Autocorrelations ρ_1	ρ_2	ρ_{12}	Coefficients of skewness	Coefficients of excess kurtosis	p-value test of normality
Latin America												
Argentina	1976.02	25.5	27	71.79	155.22	105.06	0.05	0.06	-0.10	1.92	6.95	0.00
Brazil	1976.02	50.7	67	21.71	123.82	60.70	0.03	-0.03	0.03	0.53	0.99	0.00
Chile	1976.02	37.0	35	39.64	61.61	39.64	0.18	0.26	0.09	0.92	3.12	0.10
Colombia	1985.02	5.1	20	46.09	72.38	32.54	0.49	0.15	0.04	1.68	3.90	0.00
Mexico	1976.02	128.9	56	30.52	62.60	44.99	0.25	-0.08	-0.01	-0.83	3.60	0.05
Venezuela	1985.02	9.0	16	38.08	64.23	47.52	0.27	0.18	-0.07	0.08	3.18	0.00
Latin America	1985.02	256.2	221	35.67	—	39.39	0.25	-0.04	-0.10	-0.11	0.74	0.25
East Asia												
Korea	1976.02	85.9	77	18.52	21.41	31.38	0.01	0.07	0.11	0.99	2.26	0.00
Philippines	1985.02	15.8	30	49.90	54.44	38.64	0.34	0.02	0.06	0.37	2.07	0.01
Taiwan	1985.02	135.9	70	40.93	33.88	53.99	0.06	0.04	0.13	0.15	0.81	0.31
South Asia (U.S.$ returns)												
India	1976.02	69.9	60	20.45	24.02	26.56	0.09	-0.10	-0.09	0.74	2.65	0.04
Indonesia	1990.02	11.7	66	-11.40	-6.22	34.01	0.25	0.16	0.26	0.05	-0.38	0.73
Malaysia	1985.02	78.3	62	13.24	13.19	26.89	0.05	0.07	-0.10	-0.62	1.98	0.56
Pakistan	1985.02	8.3	54	25.86	32.47	22.37	0.27	-0.24	0.13	2.61	11.04	0.00
Thailand	1976.02	43.8	43	21.75	23.00	25.67	0.12	0.16	0.06	-0.12	3.42	0.00
Asia	1985.02	449.6	462	19.31	—	26.27	0.01	0.18	0.13	-0.74	1.26	0.20

(continued overleaf)

Predictable Risk and Returns in Emerging Markets

Table 1
Continued

Country	First month in sample	Market capitalization (US$ billion)	Firms in index	Annualized means US$ (%)	Local currency (%)	Annualized std. dev. (%)	Autocorrelations ρ_1	ρ_2	ρ_{12}	Coefficients of skewness	of excess kurtosis	p-value test of normality
Europe/Mideast/Africa												
Greece	1976.02	13.3	32	9.43	19.03	36.25	0.12	0.18	−0.05	1.87	7.37	0.01
Jordan	1979.02	2.8	25	10.29	16.12	18.03	0.00	0.03	−0.01	0.47	0.91	0.00
Nigeria	1985.02	1.1	24	2.44	35.02	37.19	0.09	−0.13	−0.08	−1.76	10.90	0.00
Portugal	1986.03	11.6	30	40.71	38.38	51.43	0.28	0.03	0.03	1.50	4.59	0.07
Turkey	1987.02	11.6	25	44.32	85.65	76.25	0.24	0.10	−0.18	0.98	0.68	0.00
Zimbabwe	1976.02	0.9	17	9.74	21.79	34.25	0.13	0.15	−0.04	0.26	1.93	0.14
Composite	1985.02	747.1	836	20.36	—	24.70	0.15	0.07	0.08	−0.71	1.27	0.10
Developed												
United Kingdom	1976.02	1030.1	145	18.69	18.85	22.80	−0.00	−0.08	−0.15	−0.02	0.80	0.25
Japan	1976.02	2119.7	266	17.69	11.49	23.35	0.01	−0.03	0.12	0.22	0.80	0.14
United States	1976.02	3707.3	332	13.63	—	15.24	−0.00	−0.07	−0.00	−0.48	2.91	0.17
Benchmarks												
MSCI World	1976.02	9,198.1	—	13.91	—	14.36	0.03	−0.07	0.02	−0.42	1.71	0.33
G–10 FX	1976.02	—	—	11.36	—	9.85	−0.05	0.12	−0.01	−0.02	0.29	0.63

All statistics based on monthly U.S. dollar returns except for one of the annualized means which is based on local currency returns. The emerging markets data are from the International Finance Corporation. The developed market returns are from Morgan Stanley Capital International (MSCI). The world market return is the U.S. dollar return on the MSCI value-weighted world market portfolio. G-10 FX is the U.S. dollar return to holding a trade-weighted portfolio of Eurocurrency deposits in 10 countries (G-10 countries minus United States plus Switzerland) [details of construction are found in Harvey (1993)]. Normality tests of the country returns are conducted using the generalized method of moments by imposing the restriction that the coefficients of skewness and excess kurtosis are jointly equal to zero. The χ^2 test statistic has two degrees of freedom. The probability values from the test statistic are reported in the final column. Multivariate tests were also conducted and are reported in the text.

777

The Review of Financial Studies / v 8 n 3 1995

tion in U.S. dollars is provided.[1] First, the emerging markets are small relative to the U.S., Japan, and U.K. equity markets. However, some emerging markets are larger than one might think. For example, capitalizations of Mexico and Taiwan are similar to those of the markets in Italy and the Netherlands. There are 10 emerging markets that are larger than the smallest European market (Finland US$13.6 billion). The total capitalization of the emerging markets is US$747.1 billion. This represents 8 percent of the Morgan Stanley Capital International (MSCI) world capitalization.

Similar to the MSCI method for calculating country equity indices, the IFC uses a subset of the stocks trading in the emerging market. Stocks are selected for inclusion in the index based on size, liquidity, and industry. The IFC targets 60 percent of the total market capitalization of the country and 60 percent of the total trading volume. The indices do not include stocks whose issuing company is headquartered in an emerging market but listed only on foreign stock exchanges. In addition, if several stocks meet the size and liquidity hurdle, the IFC selects stocks that represent industries that are not well represented in the index. A detailed description of the selection criteria and the index construction is contained in IFC (1993).

Table 1 contains the number of stocks used for each of the IFC country indices which ranges from 77 for Korea to 17 in Zimbabwe. These numbers seem small compared to the United Kingdom, Japan, and the United States. However, these portfolio sizes are comparable to the MSCI portfolios for developing countries. For example, Harvey (1991) reports that 15 of the 20 MSCI developed markets have fewer than 77 companies included in their indices.

Naturally, one might be concerned with the possibility of some biases being introduced as a result of infrequent trading of the some of the index stocks. However, the trading activity of many of the emerging markets is impressive compared to the developed markets. For example, Harvey (1995a) reports that five emerging markets have higher turnover than the average turnover in the United States, Japan, and the United Kingdom and 10 emerging markets have higher turnover than the United Kingdom. However, to mitigate the possible influences of infrequent trading, I concentrate the analysis on monthly rather than weekly data.

---

[1] For most markets, the exchange rate conversion is based on a rate quoted on the last day of the month in the *Wall Street Journal* or the *Financial Times*. When a number of exchange rates exist, the IFC uses the nearest equivalent "free market" rate or a rate that would apply to the repatriation of capital or income. In some cases, even the newspaper rates are not used and the IFC relies on their correspondents in the particular market. See IFC (1993).

1.2 Analysis of monthly returns

Some summary statistics of the 20 emerging market returns are presented in Table 1. All statistics are calculated in U.S. dollar terms (translated using the effective rate on the last trading day of the month) except for the means which are calculated in both U.S. and local currency terms. Annualized mean U.S. dollar returns range from 71.8 percent for Argentina to −11.4 percent for Indonesia (whose sample only begins in February 1990). High average returns are often associated with high volatility. For example, both Argentina and Turkey have annualized standard deviations over 75 percent. Taiwan, whose average return is 40.9 percent, has a standard deviation of 53.9 percent.[2]

In the overall sample, the average return on the emerging markets composite index is 20.4 percent with a standard deviation of 24.9 percent. The average returns are roughly 50 percent higher than the MSCI world composite index (13.9 percent arithmetic, same sample), and the standard deviation is about 80 percent higher than the MSCI world index (14.4 percent).

Although this study concentrates on U.S. dollar returns, it is informative to consider the magnitude of the local currency returns. In many countries, especially in Latin America, these returns are dramatically different as a result of high inflation. For example, the average annualized return in Argentina is 228.8 percent in local currency terms with a volatility of 155.2 percent. The average return in local currency for the Brazilian index is 155.5 percent.

Table 1 also reports the serial correlation of the monthly returns. In contrast to the developed markets, the first-order serial correlation coefficients are higher for the emerging markets. Twelve of the 20 emerging markets have serial correlation coefficients greater than 10 percent and 8 of the markets have coefficients above 20 percent. The first-order autocorrelation in Colombia is an astonishing 49 percent. The approximate standard error for those countries whose data begins in 1976:02 is 7.1 percent. These statistics are in sharp contrast to the three developed markets reported at the end of Table 1 whose first-order serial correlation averages less than 1 percent.[3]

To further investigate the properties of the data, the coefficients of skewness and excess kurtosis are reported. If the data are normally distributed, then these coefficients should be equal to zero. To test

---

[2] Given the high volatility, geometric and arithmetic average returns will be much different. The geometric mean represents the average return to a buy and hold strategy in the particular market with dividend reinvestment. For example, the arithmetic mean return for the Latin American Index is 35.7 compared to the geometric mean return of 27.6 percent. The arithmetic mean return for Brazil is 21.7 percent, whereas the geometric mean return is only 3.7 percent.

[3] Harvey (1995a) finds that some of the cross section of serial correlation can be explained by measures of the asset concentration within each index.

The Review of Financial Studies / v 8 n 3 1995

for normality, the following system of equations is estimated for each asset i:

$$e_{1it} = r_{it} - \mu_i$$
$$e_{2it} = (r_{it} - \mu_i)^2 - V_i$$
$$e_{3it} = [(r_{it} - \mu_i)^3]/V_i^{3/2}$$
$$e_{4it} = [(r_{it} - \mu_i)^4]/V_i^2 - 3 \tag{1}$$

where μ is the mean, V is the variance, $e_t = \{e_{1it}, e_{2it}, e_{3it}, e_{4it}\}$ represents the disturbances and $E[e_t] = 0$. There are two parameters and four orthogonality conditions leaving a χ^2 test with two degrees of freedom. The test statistic results from setting the coefficient of skewness and excess kurtosis equal to zero in the third and fourth equations. This forms a joint test of whether these higher moments are equal to zero.[4]

The results suggest that null hypothesis of normality can be rejected at the 5 percent level in 14 of the 20 emerging markets. However, normality cannot be rejected in any of the three developed markets reported. Multivariate tests not reported in the table suggest that the emerging markets are not normally distributed. For the eight emerging countries with data from 1976:02, the test statistic with 16 degrees of freedom is 68.52 (p-value < 0.1 percent). For the three developed countries over the same sample period, the statistic with six degrees of freedom is 9.36 (p-value = 15.4 percent). When the data are sampled from 1986:03, there are 18 emerging market indices and the test statistic is 75.79 (p-value < 0.1 percent). Over the same period, the test statistic for the developing countries is 12.99 (p-value = 4.3 percent).

The summary statistics provide a number of contrasts between emerging markets and developed markets. Emerging markets have higher average returns and volatility than developed markets. Many of the markets have serial correlation that is much higher than one would expect based on knowledge of the serial correlation in developed markets returns. Finally, the returns in the emerging markets depart from the normal distribution. These findings will be important in later sections when interpreting both the cross section of average returns and the predictability of the returns.

---

[4] A related test is presented in Richardson and Smith (1993). Their system contains parameters for the coefficients of skewness and excess kurtosis and the test statistic is analytically obtained by imposing the null distribution when calculating the asymptotic variance-covariance matrix of the estimators.

1.3 Survivorship bias in the emerging markets sample

There are a number of potential sources of survivorship bias in the sample of emerging markets. First, there are many possible countries that might have been included in the sample. Indeed, the World Bank considers any stock market in a developing country as an "emerging market." However, the small number of countries that are included in the sample are the winners.

The second source of bias arises from the methodology used in constructing the indices. While the IFC does not explicitly select stocks on the basis of historical financial performance or expected future performance, their size and liquidity criteria implicitly reveal information about the past history of the company. This type of survivorship bias in the index stocks, however, will also hold for more conventional indices, such as the MSCI or FT-Actuaries.

A more serious problem is the backtracking of some of the indices. The EMDB was established in early 1981 and the initial indices were based on stocks selected in 1981. For a number of countries, these indices were backtracked to December 1975. The first 60 months of data are potentially plagued with a lookback bias. That is, to be selected in 1981, the companies had to be successful (or at least solvent). As a result, one might expect the first 5 years of data to reveal high average returns. Indeed, some firms that may have existed in December 1975 and that dropped out of the market by January 1981 are not included in the IFC index. Fortunately, the backtracking problem is isolated to the pre-1981 data. Careful attention is paid later in the article to separately analyzing the full sample (1976–1992) and a 'no backtracking' sample.

2. Average Returns and Risks

2.1 Frontier intersection tests

A number of researchers have suggested that the low correlations between emerging markets and developed markets imply portfolio investment opportunities.[5] However, one obvious question arises: does the addition of emerging markets to the portfolio selection problem *significantly* shift the investment opportunity set?

First, consider the cross-country correlations of the emerging market stock returns in Table 2. The sample period is 1986:03 through 1992:06 (75 observations) for 18 markets, shorter samples are reported for Indonesia and Turkey. In contrast to the cross-country correlations

---

[5] For an early example, see Errunza (1983), and more recently the Fall 1992 *Journal of Portfolio Management.*

The Review of Financial Studies / v 8 n 3 1995

Table 2
Correlations of the emerging market U.S. dollar returns based on monthly data from March 1986 to June 1992 (75 observations)

	ARG	BRA	CHI	COL	MEX	VEN	KOR	PHI	TAI	IND	INO	MAL	PAK	THA	GRE	JOR	NGR	POR	TUR	ZIM	Lat Am	Asia	Comp
ARG	—																						
BRA	-.15	—																					
CHI	-.05	.15	—																				
COL	-.10	.11	-.02	—																			
MEX	.14	-.02	-.31	.00	—																		
VEN	.03	-.22	-.24	.11	-.10	—																	
KOR	-.16	.05	.03	-.05	.20	-.09	—																
PHI	-.10	.14	.15	.13	.09	-.16	.16	—															
TAI	-.03	.07	.30	.11	.34	-.22	.02	.04	—														
IND	.24	.04	.04	-.12	.06	.04	-.09	-.13	-.10	—													
INO	-.29	.06	.09	.25	.04	.01	.00	.50	.30	.07	—												
MAL	-.04	.12	.26	.06	.46	-.13	.17	.35	.25	.05	.46	—											
PAK	.02	-.03	-.13	.04	-.05	-.01	-.03	-.01	-.07	-.12	.05	-.08	—										
THA	.05	.07	.27	-.05	.39	-.19	.03	.28	.43	.07	.42	.52	.01	—									
GRE	.07	.02	.12	.22	.13	-.04	-.13	.12	.10	.02	.36	.08	-.10	.30	—								
JOR	-.10	-.10	.01	.14	-.02	-.05	-.14	.17	.16	-.01	.20	.08	.12	.15	.10	—							
NGR	.13	.00	-.03	.11	-.11	.12	.05	.09	-.15	-.16	-.10	-.17	.01	-.12	.12	-.03	—						
POR	-.02	.21	.14	.35	-.07	.10	.02	.02	-.39	-.11	.24	.24	.03	.35	.41	-.03	-.20	—					
TUR	.15	.07	.02	.17	-.10	.11	.10	.12	.17	.09	.28	.26	.04	.29	.28	-.12	.08	.27	—				
ZIM	-.19	-.05	-.09	-.02	.11	-.10	-.03	-.02	-.01	-.24	.04	-.04	-.11	-.10	.03	.00	.05	.12	.01	—			
Lat Am	-.03	.11	.33	.05	.44	-.26	.27	.20	.90	.05	.32	.48	-.07	.49	.03	.13	-.14	.29	.24	-.10	—		
Asia	.02	.81	.38	.07	.38	-.22	.14	.09	.23	.06	-.08	.27	-.04	.20	.02	-.12	-.02	.27	.13	-.14	.28	—	
Comp	.00	.39	.42	.09	.47	-.30	.26	.16	.82	.06	.31	.45	-.06	.46	.07	.08	-.11	.40	.27	-.16	.90	.63	—
Average	.03	.12	.15	.12	.20	-.04	.08	.15	.22	.04	.20	.22	.04	.24	.15	.07	.02	.20	.17	.00	.26	.19	.29
Developed	.01	.14	.15	.07	.24	-.09	.15	.24	.15	-.06	.26	.44	.04	.36	.15	.12	.06	.25	.10	-.06	.22	.24	.28
MSCI world	-.06	.18	.14	.08	.33	-.10	.33	.31	.21	-.21	.07	.55	.02	.41	.15	.13	.11	.40	.05	-.02	.30	.31	.36

The monthly returns for emerging markets are from the International Finance Corporation (IFC). Lat Am is the composite index for Latin American countries, Asia is the composite for Asian countries, and Comp is the IFC emerging markets composite index. Average denotes the average cross-correlation between the country and the other emerging markets. Developed is the average cross-correlation between the country and 18 Morgan Stanley Capital International (MSCI) developed market returns. MSCI world is the correlation with the MSCI value-weighted world market portfolio return.

of the developed market returns, most of the correlations are low
and many are negative. Harvey (1991) reports that the average cross-
country correlation in 17 developed markets is 41 percent over the
1970:02 to 1989:05 sample. The average cross-country correlation of
the emerging country returns is only 12 percent. Argentina, Venezuela,
Korea, India, Pakistan, Jordan, Nigeria, and Zimbabwe have about
zero average correlation with the other emerging countries. Surprisingly, Brazil has a negative correlation with Argentina, Venezuela, and
Mexico. Perhaps not surprisingly, India and Pakistan are negatively
correlated.

Table 2 also reports the average correlation of each of the emerging country returns with the 18 MSCI developed market returns. Similar to the results among the emerging markets, there are many low
average correlations between developed and emerging markets. Argentina, Colombia, Venezuela, India, Pakistan, Nigeria, and Zimbabwe
have effectively zero average correlation with developed markets. The
overall average correlation between emerging and developed markets
is only 14 percent. The final line reports the correlation of the emerging country returns with the MSCI world market return. Similar to the
results which equally weight the correlations in the 18 developed markets, the average correlation of the emerging markets and the world
market return is only 15 percent.

Figure 1 presents unconditional minimum standard deviation frontiers based on data from 1986:03 to 1992:06. In the first panel, the
dotted curve is based on 18 MSCI country indices. The solid curve
shows the effect of adding 18 emerging country indices to the problem. Indonesia and Turkey are not included in the sample because
of their short histories. At the global minimum variance portfolio, the
standard deviation is reduced by 6 percent (from 13 percent to 7 percent) by adding the emerging market assets.

The second panel of Figure 1 repeats the minimum standard deviation analysis with the constraint of no short selling imposed. This
may be a particularly appropriate constraint for the emerging market
sample where it could be operationally difficult to short a basket of securities. Interestingly, the analysis does not substantially change. The
minimum variance portfolio with 18 developed returns has a standard
deviation of 14.5 percent. When the 18 emerging market returns are
added, the minimum variance portfolio has a standard deviation of
7.5 percent.

The graphical analysis does not answer the question of whether
the frontier significantly shifts when the emerging market assets are
added to the problem. Following Shanken (1986), Huberman and
Kandel (1987), and Jobson and Korkie (1989), let $r = \{r_1, r_2\}$ where
r_1 is the matrix of returns in 18 developed markets and r_2 represents

The Review of Financial Studies / v 8 n 3 1995

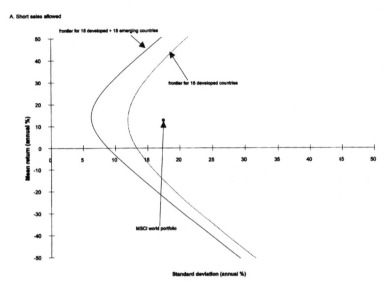

Figure 1
Minimum standard deviation frontier
The monthly returns for 18 emerging markets are from the International Finance Corporation. The 18 developed market returns are from Morgan Stanley Capital International (MSCI). The world market return is the MSCI value-weighted world market portfolio. All returns are computed in U.S. dollars. The sample is from 1986:03 to 1992:06. In panel A, unrestricted short sales are allowed. In panel B, short sales are prohibited.

the returns in the 18 emerging markets. The test is whether one set of assets (developed returns) spans the frontier of both developed and emerging markets by estimating the following moment condition:

$$\eta_t = r_{2t} - \alpha - \beta r_{1t} - \delta r_{0t} \qquad (2)$$

where r_0 is the return on the minimum variance portfolio constructed from r (all 36 assets), α and δ are 1×18 parameter vectors, β is a 18×18 parameter matrix, η defines the disturbances and $E[\eta|1, r_1, r_0] = \mathbf{0}$. Let the set of minimum-variance portfolios generated by r_1 be efficient with respect to the assets r. From Roll (1977), we know that a regression of r_2 on r_1 and the global minimum variance portfolio return should yield zero intercepts if r_2 intersects the efficient set. The slope coefficients should also sum to unity.

Table 3 reports the results of a test that the two frontiers intersect, based on the F-statistic proposed in Shanken (1986) and Jobson and

Predictable Risk and Returns in Emerging Markets

B. No short sales

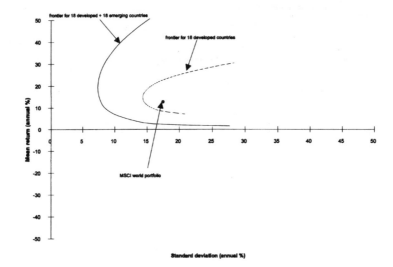

Figure 1
(continued)

Korkie (1989). I report three different versions of the test statistic, all of which use a heteroskedasticity-consistent variance-covariance matrix. The first does not correct for autocorrelation, whereas the second and third versions correct for a moving-average process of 15 months using Bartlett weights [Newey and West (1987)] and Parzen weights [Andrews (1991)]. All three versions of the test statistic provide evidence against the null with p-values less than 0.1 percent.

The F-test relies on the multivariate normality assumption for the returns. Yet the evidence in Table 1 strongly suggests departures from multivariate normality. In principle, Equation (2) could be directly estimated with the generalized method of moments. However, the dimension of the weighting matrix is over 300, which makes this method infeasible unless simplifying assumptions are made on the covariance structure.[6] An alternative is to conduct a Monte Carlo analysis to assess the empirical distribution of the test statistic.

---

[6] See the discussions in Ferson, Foerster, and Keim (1993) and Ferson (1993). De Santis (1993) presents an alternative approach that tests whether the stochastic discount factor that prices the developed country returns also prices the emerging country returns.

The Review of Financial Studies / v 8 n 3 1995

Table 3
Frontier intersection tests

A. Test statistic

Moving average structure	F-statistic (p-value)
None	6.943 (< 0.001)
15 lags Barlett	8.013 (< 0.001)
15 lags Parzen	8.183 (< 0.001)

B. Empirical distribution

Percentile	F-statistic
1%	0.80
5%	1.04
10%	1.15
90%	4.29
95%	4.78
99%	5.82

The test statistic reported in panel A is due to Shanken (1986) and Jobson and Korkie (1989) is

$$\phi_z = \frac{(T - N - 1)}{(N - N_1 - 1)} \frac{(\hat{a}_z - \hat{a}_{z1})}{(1 + \hat{a}_{z1})}$$

where

$$\hat{a}_z = (\bar{r} - \bar{r}_z \iota)' \hat{V}^{-1} (\bar{r} - \bar{r}_z \iota)$$

$$\hat{a}_{z1} = (\bar{r}_1 - \bar{r}_z \iota_1)' \hat{V}_{11}^{-1} (\bar{r}_1 - \bar{r}_z \iota_1)$$

$$\bar{r}_z = (\hat{b} - \hat{b}_1)/(\hat{c} - \hat{c}_1)$$

$$\hat{b} = \bar{r}' \hat{V}^{-1} \iota$$

$$\hat{c} = \iota' \hat{V}^{-1} \iota$$

and $\bar{r}$ represents the mean returns, $\hat{V}$ is a heteroskedasticity consistent estimator of the variance-covariance matrix and ι is a vector of ones. The p-value is computed by assuming that the test statistic follows an F-distribution with $(T - N - 1)$ and $(N - N_1 - 1)$ degrees of freedom where T is the number of observations, N is the total number of assets, and N_1 are the assets in r_1. The intuition behind the test is that a line originating from $\bar{r}_z$ in mean-variance space should have the same slope when it is tangent to the frontier of r_1 assets and when it is tangent to the frontier of all r assets. The test statistic essentially measures the difference in the slopes. A more detailed description can be found in Jobson and Korkie (1989).

The empirical distribution function of the Jobson and Korkie frontier intersection test is determined assuming that the asset returns have a 36-variate noncentral t distribution (matching the variance-covariance matrix as well as the skewness). Each sample has 1000 observations and 5000 replications are used. Similar results were also obtained with an alternative simulation (which is not reported) based on 76 observations and 100,000 replications.

The U.S. dollar monthly returns for emerging markets are from the International Finance Corporation. The developed U.S. dollar market returns are from Morgan Stanley Capital International (MSCI). The sample is from 1986:03 to 1992:06.

Table 3B reports the empirical distributions of the test statistic. I sample returns from a 36-variate noncentral t distribution. This distribution allows for the matching of the variance-covariance matrix, the skewness, and approximate matching of the kurtosis.[7] The Monte Carlo analysis confirms that the p-value for the test statistic is less than 0.1 percent. Hence, the intersection test tells us that the shift in the frontier in Figure 1 is genuine rather than an artifact of sampling variation.[8]

2.2 Risk exposure

Complete integration means that two assets with the same risk in different markets command the same expected returns. In the framework of a world capital asset pricing model with purchasing power parity, the covariance with the world portfolio is the risk and determines the cross section of expected returns.

However, it is reasonable to suspect that many emerging markets are not fully integrated into world markets. Factors such as taxes, investment restrictions, the timeliness of trading information, foreign exchange regulations, the availability and accuracy of accounting information, the number of securities cross-listed on developed exchanges, market liquidity, political risk, and the institutional structures that protect investors all contribute to the degree of integration. It is likely that the degree of integration varies across different countries and through time.[9] As such, it is unlikely that any asset pricing model that assumes complete integration of capital markets will be able to fully account for the behavior of security prices in these different markets. Nevertheless, it makes sense to first investigate the restrictions imposed by a model that imposes the null hypothesis of complete integration.

Table 4 provides tests of a single factor Sharpe (1964)–Lintner (1965) specification for the full sample. The single factor is the excess return on the MSCI world market portfolio. The null hypothesis is that this world portfolio is the Sharpe-Lintner tangency portfolio. All returns are calculated in U.S. dollars in excess of an Eurodollar deposit with 30 days to maturity. This model is consistent with the world CAPM investigated in Cumby and Glen (1990), Harvey (1991), and one of the models in Dumas and Solnik (1995).

---

[7] No attempt was made to match the coskewness or cokurtosis. The kurtosis is only approximate because one would need very large sample sizes to get close to the kurtosis in the data. The multivariate noncentral t is used because it can exhibit negative or positive skewness and the arbitrary kurtosis. The formula follows from Siddiqui (1967) and Johnson and Kotz (1970).

[8] Harvey (1994) examines the conditional mean-variance intersection tests.

[9] Bekaert (1995) and Harvey (1995b) detail investment restrictions in 20 emerging markets. Bekaert and Harvey (1994) offer evidence that the degree of market integration changes through time.

The Review of Financial Studies / v 8 n 3 1995

Table 4
Unconditional factor model tests

A. Single-equation results

Country	First month in sample	One factor model			Two factor model			
		Intercept (annualized)	β world return	$\bar{R}^2$	Intercept (annualized)	β_1 world return	β_2 FX return	$\bar{R}^2$
Latin America								
Argentina	1976.02	63.42 [2.40]	-0.17 [-0.40]	-0.00	64.06 [2.43]	-0.03 [-0.06]	-0.60 [-0.96]	-0.01
Brazil	1976.02	10.71 [0.73]	0.39 [1.20]	0.00	11.38 [0.78]	0.53 [1.59]	-0.63 [-1.41]	0.01
Chile	1976.02	29.66 [2.94]	0.17 [0.81]	-0.00	29.41 [2.91]	0.11 [0.47]	0.23 [0.77]	-0.00
Colombia	1985.02	37.34 [3.01]	0.15 [0.80]	-0.01	35.41 [2.84]	0.11 [0.60]	0.23 [0.72]	-0.01
Mexico	1976.02	17.60 [1.60]	0.79 [3.18]	0.06	18.70 [1.76]	1.03 [3.94]	-1.03 [-2.67]	0.10
Venezuela	1985.02	34.19 [1.86]	-0.38 [-1.12]	0.01	30.33 [1.68]	-0.46 [-1.31]	0.46 [1.31]	0.01
Latin America	1985.02	22.54 [1.60]	0.64 [2.08]	0.06	31.84 [2.42]	0.84 [3.07]	-1.10 [-2.89]	0.14
East Asia								
Korea	1976.02	6.93 [0.93]	0.51 [3.55]	0.05	7.23 [0.97]	0.58 [3.84]	-0.29 [-1.20]	0.05
Philippines	1985.02	35.69 [2.58]	0.76 [2.75]	0.09	37.92 [2.77]	0.80 [2.85]	-0.26 [-0.85]	0.09
Taiwan	1985.02	27.17 [1.34]	0.71 [1.67]	0.04	39.58 [2.01]	0.97 [2.51]	-1.47 [-3.42]	0.11
South Asia								
India	1976.02	11.53 [1.73]	-0.05 [-0.41]	-0.00	10.96 [1.68]	-0.18 [-1.30]	0.54 [2.70]	0.03
Indonesia	1990.02	-16.65 [-0.78]	0.21 [0.51]	-0.02	-12.97 [-0.57]	0.27 [0.66]	-0.41 [-0.56]	-0.05

(continued overleaf)

Predictable Risk and Returns in Emerging Markets

Table 4
(continued)

Country	First month in sample	One factor model			Two factor model			
		Intercept (annualized)	β world return	$\bar{R}^2$	Intercept (annualized)	β_1 world return	β_2 FX return	$\bar{R}^2$
Malaysia	1985.02	-0.81 [-0.09]	0.74 [3.51]	0.20	5.38 [0.65]	0.87 [4.61]	-0.73 [-3.01]	0.27
Pakistan	1985.02	18.01 [2.14]	0.05 [0.37]	-0.01	13.58 [1.76]	-0.04 [-0.27]	0.52 [2.28]	0.04
Thailand	1976.02	10.67 [1.63]	0.40 [2.06]	0.05	10.80 [1.67]	0.43 [1.83]	-0.12 [-0.46]	0.04
Asia	1985.02	7.76 [0.77]	0.46 [1.98]	0.07	14.63 [1.59]	0.61 [2.86]	-0.81 [-3.33]	0.17
Europe/Mideast/Africa								
Greece	1976.02	-1.57 [-0.18]	0.38 [2.09]	0.02	-2.30 [-0.26]	0.22 [1.05]	0.68 [2.47]	0.04
Jordan	1979.02	-0.29 [-0.06]	0.17 [1.67]	0.02	-0.23 [-0.05]	0.08 [0.78]	0.37 [2.38]	0.05
Nigeria	1985.02	-6.97 [-0.49]	0.23 [1.05]	-0.00	-9.98 [-0.64]	0.16 [0.83]	0.36 [1.21]	-0.00
Portugal	1986.03	26.79 [1.44]	1.20 [4.84]	0.15	27.12 [1.41]	1.21 [5.07]	-0.05 [-0.12]	0.14
Turkey	1987.02	36.95 [1.13]	0.10 [0.22]	-0.02	35.02 [1.07]	0.05 [0.10]	0.38 [0.40]	-0.03
Zimbabwe	1976.02	-0.43 [-0.05]	0.21 [1.11]	0.00	-1.13 [-0.13]	0.06 [0.29]	0.65 [2.62]	0.03
Composite	1985.02	8.44 [0.92]	0.50 [2.30]	0.10	15.71 [1.94]	0.66 [3.58]	-0.86 [-3.84]	0.23
Developed markets								
United Kingdom	1976.02	4.26 [1.06]	1.11 [14.78]	0.49	3.97 [1.00]	1.05 [11.89]	0.27 [2.29]	0.50
Japan	1976.02	2.92 [0.73]	1.18 [11.02]	0.53	2.46 [0.64]	1.08 [9.90]	0.43 [3.43]	0.56
United States	1976.02	0.47 [0.20]	0.84 [13.94]	0.63	0.98 [0.48]	0.95 [17.00]	-0.47 [-7.19]	0.71

789

The Review of Financial Studies / v 8 n 3 1995

Table 4
(continued)

B. Multivariate test that intercepts equal zero

Sample	Model	F-statistic (p-value)
8 countries 1976.02–1992.06	1 factor	2.449 (0.015)
8 countries 1976.02–1992.06	2 factor	2.493 (0.014)
18 countries 1986.03–1992.06	1 factor	2.625 (0.001)
18 countries 1986.03–1992.06	2 factor	3.012 (0.001)

The monthly returns for emerging markets are from the International Finance Corporation. The developed market returns are from Morgan Stanley Capital International (MSCI). All returns are calculated in U.S. dollars and are in excess of the 30-day Eurodollar deposit rate. In the one-factor model, the factor is the world market return is the U.S. dollar return on the MSCI value-weighted world market portfolio in excess of the 30-day Eurodollar deposit rate. In the two-factor model, the excess MSCI world return is used along with the U.S. dollar return to holding a trade-weighted portfolio of Eurocurrency deposits in 10 countries (G-10 countries minus United States plus Switzerland) [details of construction are found in Harvey (1993)] in excess of the 30-day Eurodollar deposit rate. Hetroskedasticity consistent t-statistics in brackets. Hetroskedasticity consistent multivariate tests are conducted with eight assets over the full sample (Argentina, Brazil, Chile, Mexico, Korea, India, Thailand, and Greece). In the subsample from 1986:03, 18 countries are used (all emerging markets except Indonesia and Turkey).

Table 4 also presents a two-factor specification, motivated by Adler and Dumas (1983), which augments the world market portfolio with the excess return on a trade-weighted portfolio of 10 currency deposits. Adler and Dumas's model allows for deviations from purchasing power parity. In their Equation 14 with L countries, expected returns in a numeraire currency are generated by the covariance with the world portfolio and by the covariances of the asset returns and inflation rates in all the countries. The weights on these inflation covariances depend on the wealth-weighted risk aversion in each country. The usual way to implement this model is to follow the Solnik (1974) assumption that the asset covariance with the numeraire country's inflation is zero. Expected returns can then be written in terms of their covariance with the world portfolio and their $L - 1$ covariances with exchange rate changes.[10]

Econometrically, this model is intractable unless a very small number of countries are examined. One possible simplification pursued in a number of articles[11] is to aggregate the exchange rate factor. Given

---

[10] See the discussions in Dumas (1993) and Stulz (1993).

[11] See Bodurtha (1990), Jorion (1991), Brown and Otsuki (1993), Bailey and Jagtiani (1994), Ferson and Harvey (1993, 1994a), Harvey, Solnik, and Zhou (1994), and Dumas and Solnik (1995).

that it is impossible to observe the wealth-weighted risk aversions of the $L - 1$ countries, trade weights (exports plus imports) are used as an aggregation method.

The aggregation of the exchange risk factor departs from the asset pricing theory but provides tractability. One may also view this as the prespecification of factors in some general multibeta model. Empirically, Ferson and Harvey (1993, 1994a) and Harvey, Solnik, and Zhou (1994) have found the aggregated exchange risk factor to be significant in both conditional and unconditional asset pricing tests. Indeed, Harvey, Solnik, and Zhou show that the loadings from these first two factors are able to explain 50 percent of the cross section of expected returns in developed markets.

In contrast to previous applications that use exchange rate changes, I calculate the excess return on the trade-weighted currency portfolio. The portfolio return is a trade-weighted sum of investments in 10 currencies (G-10 countries minus the United States and plus Switzerland). The investment includes both the change in the value of the currency *and* the country's 30-day Eurodeposit rate. While the measure does not include emerging markets, the trade weight on these markets would be very small.[12] The foreign currency portfolio return is measured in excess of the 30-day Eurodollar deposit rate. This procedure ensures that the factor return is a traded asset and avoids the two-step estimation problem for factor mimicking portfolios inherent in the Ferson and Harvey (1993) approach.

In contrast to the results of Cumby and Glen (1990) and Harvey (1991) for developed countries, the world market portfolio beta has little influence on the expected returns in emerging countries. Only one country, Portugal, has a beta greater than one.[13] The world market portfolio is significant in only seven countries: Mexico, Korea, Philippines, Malaysia, Thailand, Greece, and Portugal. Of the emerging markets sample, many conjecture that these countries are the most integrated in the world economy.

Looking across all the countries, the restrictions of the world CAPM are rejected. The intercepts in five countries, Argentina, Chile, Colombia, Philippines, and Pakistan, are significant at the 5 percent level, and the correlation among the stock returns in these countries is low.

---

[12] Although some emerging markets have had very large exchange rate swings, the factor is intended to measure the return on a currency deposit in each country. Presumably, a large depreciation in currency, say in Brazil, would be offset by a large local deposit interest rate. Additional details of the construction and the data used are provided in Harvey (1993).

[13] I also estimated (not reported) betas following Scholes and Williams (1977) using one lag and one lead of the world market return. In general, there is little difference between the Scholes-Williams betas (and intercepts) and the OLS parameters. However, three countries over the full sample have betas greater than one: Mexico, Philippines, and Portugal.

The Review of Financial Studies / v 8 n 3 1995

The multivariate test of the intercept restrictions of Gibbons, Ross, and Shanken (1989) adjusted for conditional heteroskedasticity and tested on the eight countries with data from 1976:02 provides convincing evidence against the null hypothesis that the intercepts are equal to zero.

Not only are the intercepts significantly different from zero, but the significant intercepts are all positive. Even if we use a different level of significance, say the one associated with t-ratios greater than 1.3 (10 percent level, one-sided), all 13 countries have positive intercepts. If the single factor CAPM describes world expected returns, this would imply that these countries' returns greatly exceeded expected levels of performance. Indeed, some of the unexpected returns are massive. For example, Argentina's unexpected return (or pricing error) is 63.4 percent per annum with a t-ratio of 2.4, and Chile has an annualized error of 29.7 percent with a t-ratio of 2.9. Another possible interpretation is that the intercepts are telling us something about survivorship bias. While the IFC started collecting data in 1981, the multivariate intercept tests reach back to 1976. However, an examination of the subperiod that does not include the look-back bias period suggests that survivorship does not completely explain the findings.

I also tested the restrictions (but do not report) over the most recent subperiod, 1986:03 to 1992:06. Five of the seven countries that had significant betas on the world index in the full sample have significant betas in the most recent subperiod. Intercepts are significant at the 5 percent level in 7 of the 20 countries. Eleven of the countries have intercepts with t-ratios greater than 1.3 and all of these intercepts are positive. Similar to the overall period, there are some countries with very large pricing errors. For example, Chile has an error of 43.9 percent per annum with a t-ratio of 3.9. The multivariate test of Gibbons, Ross, and Shanken (1989) provides evidence against the null hypothesis that the intercepts are zero for 18 countries at the 0.1 percent level.

The multivariate tests suggest that the world market portfolio is not the Sharpe-Lintner tangency portfolio. This is in contrast to the findings of Cumby and Glen (1990) and Harvey (1991) who consider only developed market returns. The intercept tests suggest that the shift in the mean-variance frontier documented in Table 3 was large enough to provide a rejection of the null hypothesis.

The two-factor estimates over the full sample are presented in the right-hand columns of Table 4. The world market beta remains significant at the 5 percent level in six countries: Mexico, Korea, Philippines, Malaysia, Thailand, and Portugal. The foreign exchange risk factor has some explanatory power in eight countries. It is especially important in explaining the aggregated index returns, Latin America, Asia, and the emerging markets composite.

The addition of this second factor, however, does not affect the intercepts. Five of the intercepts are significant (and positive) at the 5 percent level. Eleven have t-ratios greater than 1.3 and all of these are positive. The multivariate test provides evidence against the null hypotheses at the 1.4 percent level of significance.

The currency risk factor appears to have more of an influence in the most recent subperiod (not reported). The currency return significantly loads into seven countries' factor models: Chile, Mexico, Taiwan, Malaysia, Pakistan, Thailand, and Zimbabwe. Both factors are important for the aggregated indices with 29 percent of the variance of the composite index explained. However, 7 intercepts are significantly different from zero at the 5 percent level and 12 have t-ratios greater than 1.3. All of these intercepts are positive. The multivariate intercept test provides evidence against the null hypothesis of zero intercepts at the 0.1 percent level of significance.

It is possible that this analysis is sensitive to the assumption of a risk-free asset. Kandel and Stambaugh (1989) present a methodology to test whether the index portfolio or a combination of multiple index portfolios lies on the minimum variance boundary of risky assets. They characterize a critical hyperbola. If the index portfolio or a combination of factor portfolios lies to the right of the critical hyperbola, then we can reject the hypothesis that the portfolio or combination lies on the minimum-variance boundary. Importantly, this approach is different from the Gibbons, Ross, and Shanken (1989) approach which tests whether the index portfolio or combination of multiple index portfolios is the Sharpe-Lintner tangent portfolio. The Kandel and Stambaugh approach is graphical and, as such, one sees how close the given portfolio (portfolios) is to the critical hyperbola.

The Kandel and Stambaugh (1989) critical rejection regions are presented in Figure 2. The solid hyperbola in Figure 2 is the unconditional mean-variance frontier for 36 assets from 1986:03 to 1992:06. The dashed hyperbola in the first panel is the critical rejection region for a 5 percent significance level for the one-factor model. Notice that the world market portfolio is well to the right of the critical rejection region indicating that this benchmark portfolio is significantly off the minimum standard deviation frontier. The second panel of Figure 2 presents the critical rejection region for the two factor model. It is clear that portfolios of the world market return and the exchange rate return do not cross the critical rejection region drawn at the 5 percent significance level.

Two additional world risk factors were considered.[14] In contrast to

---

[14] These factors were examined after the factor models were estimated in Table 4, in response to a suggestion by a conference discussant, and, as such, should not be considered factor snooping.

The Review of Financial Studies / v 8 n 3 1995

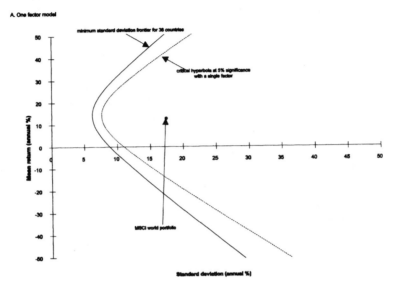

Figure 2
Minimum standard deviation frontier with critical rejection region for the one-factor model
The monthly returns for 18 emerging markets are from the International Finance Corporation. The 18 developed market returns are from Morgan Stanley Capital International (MSCI). The world market return is the MSCI value-weighted world market portfolio. The exchange rate portfolio is is the return to holding a trade-weighted portfolio of Eurocurrency deposits in 10 countries (G-10 countries minus the U.S. plus Switzerland). All returns are computed in U.S. dollars. The sample is from 1986:03 to 1992:06. The critical hyperbola follows Kandel and Stambaugh (1989). Define the efficient set constants $a = \bar{r}'\hat{V}^{-1}\bar{r}$, $b = \bar{r}'\hat{V}^{-1}\iota$, $c = \iota'\hat{V}^{-1}\iota$, and $d = ac - b^2$ where $\bar{r}$ are the expected returns, $\hat{V}$ is the estimated variance matrix and ι is a vector of ones. Let $\hat{\mu}_p$ be a target expected return and $\hat{\sigma}^{2*}(\hat{\mu}_p)$ be the minimum variance for expected return $\hat{\mu}_p$. Hence, $(\hat{\mu}_p, \hat{\sigma}^{2*}(\hat{\mu}_p))$ is a point in the expected return–minimum variance space. Let w^s be a central-F variate at a given significance level. Kandel and Stambaugh prove that $w(p) > w^s$, i.e., portfolio p's efficiency is rejected if and only if

$$\hat{\sigma}_p^2 > \delta_1(w^s) + \delta_2(w^s)\sigma^{2*}(\hat{\mu}_p)$$

where $\hat{\sigma}_p^2$ is the variance of p and

$$\delta_1(w) = \frac{w(w+1)}{cw-d} \qquad \delta_2(w) = \frac{-d(w+1)}{cw-d}$$

Thus, $\hat{\sigma}^2 = \delta_1(w^s) + \delta_2(w^s)\sigma^{2*}(\hat{\mu})$ defines a critical hyperbola in mean standard deviation space. If the given portfolio is to the right of the hyperbola, efficiency can be rejected at the significance level s. In panel A, the given portfolio is the MCSI world market portfolio. In panel B, the given portfolios are represented by the minimum standard deviation frontier formed from the MSCI world market portfolio and the exchange rate portfolio.

Predictable Risk and Returns in Emerging Markets

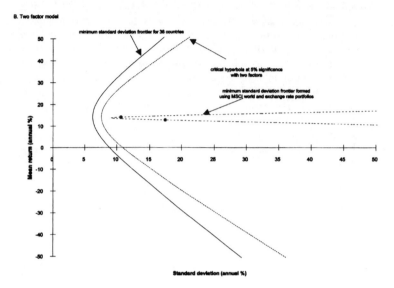

B. Two factor model

Figure 2
(continued)

developing countries, many of the emerging markets have undiversified industrial sectors. Given that many of these equities are resource
based, the emerging market equities may have significant exposure
to price fluctuations in an index of natural resources. Bivariate regressions are estimated using the percentage change in the Commodity
Research Bureau's (CRB) industrial inputs index in excess of a risk-
free rate. There was only one country, Indonesia, that had a significant
exposure to this factor.

   The emerging economies also have larger proportional agricultural
sectors than the developed economies. Factor models were estimated
using the percentage change CRB food price index in excess of a risk-
free rate. Similar to the industrial input series, no country exhibited a
significant sensitivity to this factor.

   Although the tests indicate that world market portfolio is inefficient,
what is the cross-sectional relation between the expected returns and
the risk sensitivities? Roll and Ross (1994) and Kandel and Stambaugh

---

Other specifications of global risk factors are investigated by Ferson and Harvey (1994a,b). The
general approach follows Chen, Roll, and Ross (1986).

The Review of Financial Studies / v 8 n 3 1995

(1994) have emphasized that a small degree of inefficiency could result in no relation between expected returns and risks.[15] The first panel of Figure 3 provides a scatter plot of the average returns and the world market betas over the recent subperiod. The cross-sectional regression line is also plotted and is insignificant. None of the cross-sectional variation is explained. If the loadings from the second risk factor are added to the estimation, the regression is still insignificant at the 5 percent level.

The second panel of Figure 3 presents the same average returns against their standard deviations. The cross-sectional regression line of the average returns on the volatilities is also presented with and without the influential Argentinian observation. The regression using all countries is significant at the 0.5 percent level. The country's variance has more explanatory power than the beta with respect to the world portfolio. These results support the interpretation that many of the emerging markets are not fully integrated into world capital markets.

There are other reasons why the unconditional CAPM could fail aside from the market integration issue. For example, the linear factor specification in Table 4 assumes that the risk exposures are constant over the estimation period. The differences in the magnitude of the some of the risk coefficients in the full and most recent subperiod (1986:03 to 1992:06, not reported) suggest that exposures may be time varying. Indeed, a rejection of the unconditional CAPM does not imply a rejection of the conditional CAPM.

3. Analysis of Conditional Risk

3.1 Predictable returns in emerging markets
Table 5 presents an analysis of the predictable variation in the emerging market returns. Linear regressions of the emerging market returns on three sets of information variables are detailed. The first set consists of common world information variables. The second includes only variables that are specific to the country being examined. The final set combines the local and country-specific information sets.

To provide a direct comparison to research on developed markets, the world information set follows Harvey (1991).[16] The set includes lagged values of the MSCI world return, the return on the U.S. 3-month Treasury bill minus the 1-month return, the yield spread between

---

[15] Kandel and Stambaugh (1994) also show that a high degree of inefficiency can accompany a near-perfect relation between expected returns and risk.

[16] Harvey's (1991) selection of variables was motivated by Keim and Stambaugh (1986), Campbell (1987), and Fama and French (1988).

Predictable Risk and Returns in Emerging Markets

A. Annual expected return vs. beta

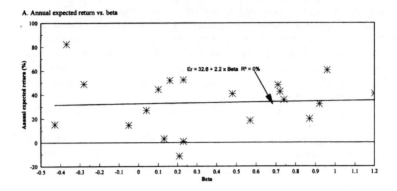

B. Annual expected return vs. standard deviation

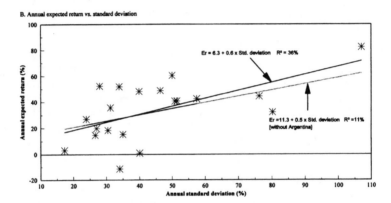

Figure 3
The cross section of expected returns, betas, and standard deviations
The monthly returns for 20 emerging markets are from the International Finance Corporation. The 18 developed market returns are from Morgan Stanley Capital International (MSCI). The world market return is the U.S. dollar return on the MSCI value-weighted world market portfolio. The sample is from 1986:03 to 1992:06 for all countries except Turkey and Indonesia. In panel A, the betas result from the least squares regression of the average returns on the world market return. The fitted line is a regression of the average returns on the estimated betas. In panel B, the solid line is a regression of the average returns on the estimated standard deviations. The dotted line excludes the influential Argentinian observation from the regression.

Moody's Baa and Aaa rated bonds, and the Standard and Poor's 500 dividend yield minus the 1-month U.S. Treasury bill return. The only difference between this information set and Harvey's is the exclusion of the January dummy variable.

The first column of adjusted R^2 results from regressions on the world information variables. Notice that the sample periods are slightly

The Review of Financial Studies / v 8 n 3 1995

Table 5
Analysis of predictable returns in emerging markets

A. Single-equation results

Country	First month in sample	$\overline{R}^2$ World information	$\overline{R}^2$ Local information	$\overline{R}^2$ Combined information	χ^2 exclude local	Proportion of variance due to World information	Proportion of variance due to Local information	Proportion of variance due to Covariance
Latin America								
Argentina	1977.04	0.003 [0.184]	−0.001 [0.638]	−0.000 [0.376]	2.499 [0.645]	0.551	0.456	−0.007
Brazil	1977.04	0.006 [0.196]	0.076 [0.000]	0.078 [0.000]	46.210 [0.000]	0.235	0.830	−0.065
Chile	1977.04	0.098 [0.000]	0.088 [0.000]	0.127 [0.000]	18.054 [0.001]	0.441	0.349	0.211
Colombia	1986.02	0.001 [0.200]	0.213 [0.001]	0.212 [0.001]	13.852 [0.008]	0.214	0.856	−0.070
Mexico	1977.04	0.110 [0.000]	0.072 [0.053]	0.145 [0.000]	12.021 [0.017]	0.652	0.361	−0.014
Venezuela	1985.02	−0.010 [0.422]	0.062 [0.039]	0.033 [0.064]	9.698 [0.046]	0.263	0.883	−0.145
East Asia								
Korea	1977.04	−0.011 [0.711]	0.036 [0.013]	0.021 [0.040]	11.837 [0.019]	0.110	0.856	0.034
Philippines	1985.02	0.150 [0.005]	0.121 [0.000]	0.201 [0.000]	15.016 [0.005]	0.427	0.512	0.061
Taiwan	1985.02	0.018 [0.081]	−0.019 [0.679]	−0.018 [0.242]	1.246 [0.871]	1.251	0.213	−0.464

(continued overleaf)

Predictable Risk and Returns in Emerging Markets

Table 5 (continued)

Country	First month in sample	$\bar{R}^2$ World information	$\bar{R}^2$ Local information	$\bar{R}^2$ Combined information	χ^2 exclude local	Proportion of variance due to World information	Proportion of variance due to Local information	Proportion of variance due to Covariance
South Asia								
India	1977.04	-0.011 [0.546]	-0.003 [0.740]	-0.003 [0.405]	3.677 [0.4511]	0.607	0.794	-0.401
Indonesia	1990.02	0.105 [0.002]	0.010 [0.341]	0.227 [0.000]	7.118 [0.130]	0.948	0.711	-0.659
Malaysia	1985.02	-0.014 [0.240]	0.046 [0.053]	0.045 [0.067]	10.888 [0.028]	0.346	0.889	-0.236
Pakistan	1985.02	0.018 [0.478]	0.134 [0.258]	0.114 [0.369]	5.842 [0.211]	0.144	0.719	0.138
Thailand	1977.04	0.067 [0.000]	0.003 [0.528]	0.055 [0.000]	1.371 [0.849]	0.795	0.117	0.088
Europe/Mideast/Africa								
Greece	1977.04	0.026 [0.004]	-0.002 [0.288]	0.018 [0.006]	3.343 [0.502]	0.754	0.230	0.016
Jordan	1979.02	0.003 [0.336]	-0.024 [0.978]	-0.020 [0.649]	0.868 [0.929]	0.990	0.114	-0.103
Nigeria	1985.02	-0.018 [0.853]	-0.026 [0.804]	-0.056 [0.937]	1.378 [0.848]	0.587	0.391	0.023
Portugal	1986.03	0.125 [0.003]	0.111 [0.005]	0.150 [0.001]	6.919 [0.140]	0.456	0.421	0.124
Turkey	1987.02	0.080 [0.033]	0.101 [0.001]	0.094 [0.000]	10.589 [0.032]	0.278	0.467	0.255
Zimbabwe	1978.01	0.051 [0.016]	0.038 [0.016]	0.159 [0.000]	24.384 [0.000]	0.946	0.803	-0.749
Global variables								
World return	1977.04	0.051 [0.002]	—	—	—	—	—	—
FX return	1977.04	0.063 [0.004]	—	—	—	—	—	—

799

The Review of Financial Studies / v 8 n 3 1995

Table 5
(continued)

B. Multivariate test of predictability

Sample	F-statistic
8 countries	2.1523
world information	[0.000]

The monthly returns for emerging markets are from the International Finance Corporation. The developed market returns are from Morgan Stanley Capital International (MSCI). All returns are calculated in U.S. dollars and are in excess of the 30-day Eurodeposit rate. The world information variables are the MSCI world return, the U.S. 3-month Treasury bill return minus the 1-month return, the spread between Moody's Baa rated bonds and Aaa bonds, and the Standard and Poor's 500 dividend yield minus the 30-day Treasury bill rate. The local information variables include the local U.S. dollar return, the change in the foreign currency rate versus the U.S. dollar, the local dividend yield, and a local interest rate. Heteroskedasticity consistent p-values are in brackets. The proportion of variance explained by the world information is the variance of the fitted values generated from the world information variables in the regression that includes both world and local information divided by the variance of the fitted values using both world and local information variables. A similar variance ratio is calculated using the local information in the numerator. The first two variance ratios do not sum to one because of the covariance between the local and world information.

The global variables include the U.S. dollar return on the MSCI value-weighted world market portfolio in excess of the 30-day Eurodollar deposit rate and the U.S. dollar return to holding a trade-weighted portfolio of Eurocurrency deposits in 10 countries (G-10 countries minus United States plus Switzerland) [details of construction are found in Harvey (1993)] in excess of the 30-day Eurodollar deposit rate.

Multivariate tests are conducted with eight assets over the full sample (Argentina, Brazil, Chile, Mexico, Korea, India, Thailand, and Greece). The heteroskedasticity consistent test is based on Pillai's trace. The F-statistic has degrees of freedom of 32 and 676.

different than the Table 4 regressions. This is due to the unavailability of some of the local information variables that will be used in later analysis. Heteroskedasticity consistent tests of significance (p-values) are reported beneath the R^2. The expected returns in 9 of the 20 countries are significantly (5 percent level) affected by the world information variables. A multivariate heteroskedasticity consistent test of predictability [see Kirby (1994)] provides strong evidence against the hypothesis of constant expected returns.

The second column of adjusted R^2 is obtained from regressions on the local information variables. The local information set includes the lagged country U.S. dollar returns, the change in the foreign exchange rate versus the U.S. dollar, the dividend yield and a local short-term interest rate.[17]

---

[17] I selected interest rates that were the 'most unregulated.' Deposit rates were used for Argentina, Chile, Colombia, Venezuela, Thailand, Greece, Jordan, and Nigeria. Call money rates were used in India, Indonesia, and Pakistan. Money market rates were used for Korea, Malaysia, and Turkey. Treasury bills were used for Mexico, Philippines, Portugal, and Zimbabwe. The bank rate was used for Brazil. The U.S. 3-month Treasury bill yield was used for Taiwan, who is not a member of the International Monetary Fund.

Local information is important for 11 of the 20 regressions at the 5 percent level of significance. When the local information is combined with the world information, 12 regressions are significant at the 5 percent level and 14 at the 10 percent level. A heteroskedasticity-consistent exclusion test of the local information variables provides evidence against the null hypothesis in 10 countries at the 5 percent level. That is, in the 12 countries with significant regressions, 10 are importantly influenced by local information. The variance ratios in the far right-hand columns suggest that more than half of the predictable variance in these emerging market returns is induced by local information.

From the evidence of serial correlation presented in Table 1, it may seem obvious that lagged country returns should predict future returns. Indeed, it is possible that this type of predictability could be induced by infrequent trading.[18] However, using a monthly frequency should diminish this influence. Interestingly, in the regressions with world and local information (not reported), only three countries—Colombia, Venezuela, and the Philippines—have significant coefficients on the lagged country returns.

These results contrast with the results on developed countries in three respects. First, the degree of explanatory power is greater in emerging markets. Using the combined information set, seven of the regression adjusted R^2 exceed 10 percent and three exceed 20 percent. Over the same period, the predictability of the world market portfolio is limited to 5 percent. Over the 1970.02 to 1989.5 period, Harvey (1991) reports that only 2 of 18 developed countries have adjusted R^2 that exceed 10 percent using world information variables. Using various combinations of world and local information only three countries have R^2 that exceed 10 percent.

The second difference concerns the importance of local information variables. In almost all of the significant regressions, local information played an important role. In contrast, Harvey (1991) found that most of the variation was being driven by global information variables. Using a different sample and different instruments, Ferson and Harvey (1993) report that local information is important in only 6 of 18 developed markets.

Some are skeptical of the predictability in asset returns because of the collective data snooping by many researchers [see, for example, Foster and Smith (1993)]. While most of the snooping is focused on U.S. returns, the use of international returns does not provide 'out-of-sample' evidence of predictability because of the correlation

---

[18] Serial correlation could be induced by persistence in country risk exposures or world risk premiums. It could also be induced by informational inefficiencies. Unfortunately there is no way to separate these possible causes and hence no attempt has been made to filter the data.

The Review of Financial Studies / v 8 n 3 1995

between the international returns and the U.S. return. For example, using the results in Harvey (1991), the rank-order correlation between the predictive R^2 and the squared correlation of the developed country returns with U.S. returns is 57.9 percent, which is significant at the 5 percent level (p-value $=$ 1.8 percent). That is, high correlation with the U.S. usually implies a high degree of predictability.

The final contrast with developed markets is that there is little or no relation between the predictability of emerging market returns and their unconditional correlations with the U.S. or world market return. The rank-order correlation between the predictive R^2 and the squared correlation with the U.S. return is only 29.5 percent (p-value $=$ 22.0 percent). A similar result is obtained when one considers the squared correlation with the world market return. In this case, the rank-order correlation drops to -3.7 percent (p-value $=$ 88.0 percent). While this evidence is informal, it suggests that the predictability may be genuine.

3.2 Conditional asset pricing tests

Following the unconditional analysis in Table 3, I examine the influences of two sources of risk, the world market return and the foreign exchange portfolio return, on conditionally expected returns. In this analysis, expected returns, risk premiums, and betas change through time as a function of the information variables.

Let Z^w, Z^ℓ, $Z^{w,\ell}$ be the world information, local information, and combined information respectively. The following model is estimated:

$$u_{1it} = r_{it} - Z_{t-1}^{w,\ell}\delta_i$$
$$u_{2t} = f_t - Z_{t-1}^{w}\theta$$
$$u_{3it} = \left[u_{2t}'u_{2t}(Z_{t-1}^{w,\ell}\kappa_i)' - f_t'u_{1it}\right]'$$
$$u_{4it} = \mu_i - Z_{t-1}^{w,\ell}\delta_i$$
$$u_{5it} = (-\alpha_i + \mu_i) - Z_{t-1}^{w,\ell}\kappa_i(Z_{t-1}^{w}\theta)' \qquad (3)$$

where r represents the return on asset i, δ are coefficients from a linear projection of the asset returns on the information, $Z^{w,\ell}\kappa_i$ are the fitted conditional betas, f are the factor returns, θ are the coefficients from a linear projection of the factor returns on the information, μ is the mean asset return, and α is the difference between the mean asset return and the model fitted mean asset return (pricing error). Conditioning u_1 and u_3 on $Z^{w,\ell}$, u_2 on Z^w, and u_4 and u_5 on ones produces an exactly identified system of equations.[19]

---

[19] For analysis of related systems, see Ferson (1990), Harvey (1991), Ferson and Korajzcyk (1995),

The following is the intuition behind the system. The first two equations are regressions of the asset and factor returns on the information. These are 'statistical' models of expected returns. I let the country returns be influenced by both local and world information variables. However, the world risk premiums are strictly a function of world information variables. Next, the definition of conditional beta is used:

$$\beta_{it} = (E[\mathbf{u}_{2t}'\mathbf{u}_{2t} \mid \mathbf{Z}_{t-1}^{w,\ell}])^{-1} E[\mathbf{f}_t'\mathbf{u}_{1it} \mid \mathbf{Z}_{t-1}^{w,\ell}] \qquad (4)$$

The conditional beta in Equation (4) is assumed to be a linear function of the combined world and local information.[20] The last two equations deliver the average pricing error. Parameter μ_i is the average expected return from the statistical model. The parameter α_i is the difference between the average 'statistical' model returns and the asset pricing model's fitted returns. It is analogous to the α_i reported in Table 3. However, in this analysis, both the betas and the premiums are changing through time. Furthermore, the focus is on the predictable portion of the returns.

This complicated system of equations can only be estimated one asset at a time. As such, not all the cross-sectional restrictions of asset pricing theory can be imposed. For example, it will not be possible to report a multivariate test of whether the α_i parameters are equal to zero. However, one important cross-sectional restriction has been imposed. Because the system is exactly identified, the world risk premium function, $\mathbf{Z}_{t-1}^w \theta$, is identical for every country examined.

The conditional risk function is simply $\mathbf{Z}^{w,\ell} \mathbf{\kappa}_i$. Wald tests are conducted to test for the significance of the beta and to test whether the beta changes through time.

As this system is exactly identified, there is no general test of the model's restrictions in the form of Hansen's (1982) J-statistic. However, the asset pricing model implies that the coefficient α_i should not be different from zero and this hypothesis can be tested. Another possible test involves analyzing the model disturbance:

$$u_{6it} = r_{it} - \mathbf{Z}_{t-1}^{w,\ell} \mathbf{\kappa}_i (\mathbf{Z}_{t-1}^w \theta)' \qquad (5)$$

According to the asset pricing model, $E[u_{6it} \mid \mathbf{Z}_{t-1}^{w,\ell}]$ should be zero. Diagnostics are reported by regressing u_{6it} on the three sets of infor-

---

and Ferson and Harvey (1995). Importantly, I ask the model to explain the predictability induced by both local *and* world information, whereas Ferson and Harvey (1993) only challenge the model to explain the predictability induced by the world information.

[20] The linear conditional beta formulation is used in Shanken (1990), Ferson and Harvey (1991, 1993), and Jagannathan and Wang (1994).

The Review of Financial Studies / v 8 n 3 1995

mation variables and comparing the predictability of the model errors to the predictability of the asset returns.

Estimates of Equation (3) are provided in Table 6 for the subset of eight countries with data available from 1977:04 (there are 183 observations).[21] Panel A details the results of the one factor model. Consistent with the unconditional results in Table 3, the annualized average pricing errors are more than two standard errors from zero for Chile and India and 1.5 standard errors from zero for Argentina, Mexico, and Thailand. The average pricing errors are of the same magnitudes as the average returns indicating that allowing for time-varying betas and premiums is not enough to get the mean returns right.

The Wald tests show that, in four of the countries, the conditional betas are significantly different from zero. In three of these countries, the betas exhibit significant time variation. However, the time variation in the betas does not help explain the predictability in the asset returns. For the countries that have significant time variation in their expected returns, not only are the pricing errors different from zero on average, they are correlated with the predetermined information. These correlations are sufficient to provide rejection of the asset pricing specification in Equation (3).

The results of the two-factor estimation are presented in panel B of Table 6. In six of the eight countries, the average pricing errors are worse with two factors rather than one. The betas are jointly significant in six of the countries. There is significant time variation in the betas of five of these six countries. The addition of the extra factor reduces the residual R^2 on the combined information in four of the five countries with time-varying betas. However, the correlation between the pricing errors and the combined information is still significant for three of the countries.

It is possible to further characterize these rejections either as a failure to model expected returns and/or as a rejection of the restriction of equal risk premiums. First, consider the restriction of equal world risk premiums. Given that the system in Equation (3) is exactly identified, equal risk premiums are enforced in the asset by asset estimation. It is possible to overidentify the system by adding orthogonality conditions based on the local information variables to the world risk premium disturbance, u_2. One interpretation of the χ^2 test of the overidentifying restriction is a test of the equality of the world risk premiums. That is, the unexpected part of the world risk premium should not

---

[21] For some of the countries, the interest rate data was not available before 1977:03. Zimbabwe is not included because the interest rate data begins later.

Predictable Risk and Returns in Emerging Markets

Table 6
An analysis of the conditional risk of emerging market returns

Country	Average Excess return	Average Error α_i	χ^2 Betas = 0	χ^2 Constant betas	χ^2 Equal risk premiums[a]	Returns on $Z^{w,t}$	$\bar{R}^2$ on Z^w	$\bar{R}^2$ Errors on Z^t	$\bar{R}^2$ on $Z^{w,t}$	Proportion of variance explained[b]
A: 1-factor model[c]										
Argentina[c]	45.956	41.888 (27.426)	11.678 [0.166]	11.566 [0.116]	2.807 [0.422]	0.005	0.011	0.003	0.014	0.111 (0.171)
Brazil	13.863	8.755 (16.020)	6.391 [0.700]	6.090 [0.637]	11.793 [0.019]	0.078	−0.000	0.073	0.075	0.033 (0.040)
Chile	24.436	26.971 (10.724)	10.462 [0.314]	10.357 [0.241]	2.847 [0.584]	0.127	0.096	0.150	0.150	0.082 (0.086)
Mexico	24.624	23.593 (12.028)	55.854 [0.000]	32.981 [0.000]	4.126 [0.389]	0.145	0.087	0.077	0.137	0.123 (0.092)
Korea	7.609	9.998 (8.325)	21.509 [0.011]	9.655 [0.290]	3.113 [0.539]	0.021	−0.015	0.024	0.010	0.171 (0.200)
India	11.513	15.760 (7.324)	19.714 [0.020]	19.380 [0.013]	2.814 [0.589]	−0.003	−0.015	0.002	−0.003	0.195 (0.237)
Thailand	11.874	12.340 (7.391)	47.419 [0.000]	45.730 [0.000]	1.124 [0.876]	0.055	0.064	0.045	0.053	0.148 (0.120)
Greece	0.716	−1.599 (9.337)	9.366 [0.404]	3.143 [0.925]	5.883 [0.208]	0.018	0.025	0.002	0.018	0.062 (0.104)

The Review of Financial Studies / v 8 n 3 1995

Table 6
(continued)

| | Average | | χ² | | | $\bar{R}^2$ | | | | Proportion |
	Excess return	Error α_t	Betas = 0	Constant betas	Equal risk premiums[a]	Returns on $Z^{w,t}$	Errors on Z^w	on Z^t	on $Z^{w,t}$	of variance explained[b]
Country										
B: 2-factor model										
Argentina[c]	45.956	47.300 (27.580)	44.891 [0.000]	44.446 [0.000]	13.487 [0.036]	0.005	0.008	0.003	0.011	0.110 (0.180)
Brazil	13.863	6.072 (16.967)	19.723 [0.349]	16.201 [0.439]	18.298 [0.019]	0.078	0.016	0.078	0.097	0.078 (0.082)
Chile	24.436	31.307 (9.638)	26.842 [0.082]	26.112 [0.052]	5.887 [0.659]	0.127	0.075	0.132	0.123	0.285 (0.231)
Mexico	24.624	27.365 (12.552)	114.147 [0.000]	64.523 [0.000]	5.965 [0.651]	0.145	0.091	0.081	0.131	0.131 (0.178)
Korea	7.609	6.351 (8.433)	74.269 [0.000]	28.267 [0.029]	4.519 [0.807]	0.021	-0.009	0.032	0.023	0.301 (0.268)
India	11.513	16.806 (7.554)	65.568 [0.000]	32.691 [0.008]	10.020 [0.201]	-0.003	-0.015	0.003	-0.003	0.408 (0.446)
Thailand	11.874	12.683 (7.197)	120.290 [0.000]	104.588 [0.000]	3.805 [0.874]	0.055	0.058	0.039	0.042	0.160 (0.144)
Greece	0.716	3.405 (10.030)	32.248 [0.021]	12.953 [0.676]	7.101 [0.526]	0.018	0.016	-0.002	0.007	0.270 (0.320)

The monthly returns for emerging markets are from the International Finance Corporation. All returns are calculated in U.S. dollars and are in excess of the 30-day Eurodeposit rate. The world information variables, Z^w, are the MSCI world return, the U.S. 3-month Treasury bill return minus the 1-month return, the spread between Moody's BAA rated bonds and AAA bonds, and the Standard and Poor's 500 dividend yield minus the 30-day Treasury bill rate. The local information variables, Z^t, include the local U.S. dollar return, the change in the foreign currency rate versus the U.S. dollar, the local dividend yield, and a local interest rate. The first factor is the U.S. dollar return on the MSCI value-weighted world market portfolio in excess of the 30-day Eurodollar deposit rate. The second factor is the U.S. dollar return to holding a trade-weighted portfolio of Eurocurrency deposits in 10 countries (G-10 countries plus Switzerland) [details of construction are found in Harvey (1993)] in excess of the 30-day Eurodollar deposit rate.

(continued overleaf)

Predictable Risk and Returns in Emerging Markets

Table 6
(continued)

The following system is estimated for each asset i:

Disturbance	Orthogonal to
$u_{1it} = r_{it} - Z_{t-1}^{w,\ell}\delta_i$	$Z_{t-1}^{w,\ell}$
$u_{2t} = f_t - Z_{t-1}^{w}\theta$	Z_{t-1}^{w}
$u_{3it} = [u_{2t}'u_{2t}(Z_{t-1}^{w,\ell}\kappa_i)' - f_t'u_{1it}]'$	$Z_{t-1}^{w,\ell}$
$u_{4it} = \mu_i - Z_{t-1}^{w,\ell}\delta_i$	1
$u_{5it} = (-\alpha_i + \mu_i) - Z_{t-1}^{w,\ell}\kappa_i(Z_{t-1}^{w}\theta)'$	1

where r represents the excess return on asset i, Z is the predetermined information, δ are coefficients from a linear projection of the asset returns on the information, $Z\kappa_i$ are the fitted conditional betas, f are the factor excess returns, θ are the coefficients from a linear projection of the factor returns on the information, μ is the mean asset return, and α is the difference between the mean asset return and the model fitted mean asset return (pricing error). The standard error of the pricing error parameter is reported in parentheses. Heteroskedasticity consistent Wald tests (with p-values in brackets) are reported for two hypotheses: the conditional betas equal zero and the conditional beta is constant. The last three columns report model diagnostics in the form of linear regressions of the pricing errors on the three information sets: world, local, and combined world and local. The sample is from 1977:04 to 1992:06 (183 observations).
[a] In the test of equal world risk premiums, the world risk premium disturbance u_2 is made orthogonal to $Z^{w,\ell}$. This provides overidentifying conditions that are tested with the reported statistic.
[b] The variance ratio is estimated by adding to the above system:

Disturbance	Orthogonal to
$u_{6it} = \Gamma_i(Z^{w,\ell} - \mu_i)^2 - (Z_{t-1}^{w,\ell}\kappa_i(Z_{t-1}^{w}\theta)' - (-\alpha_i + \mu_i))^2$	1

where Γ_i measures the proportion of predictable variation that the model explains. As in the original system of equation, this augmented model is exactly identified.
[c] Results are reported for a local information set that excludes the local short-term interest rate.

be related to local market information. The results in Table 6 suggest that the world risk premium restriction is rejected for Brazil in the one-factor model and for both Argentina and Brazil in the two-factor model. However, the results of this test do not help us understand the results in the other six countries.

A more likely explanation is that the model is not generating sufficient variation in the expected returns to match the baseline statistical predictability in the returns. The following condition is added to Equation (3):

$$u_{6it} = \Gamma_i(Z^{w,\ell} - \mu_i)^2 - (Z_{t-1}^{w,\ell}\kappa_i(Z_{t-1}^{w}\theta)' - (-\alpha_i + \mu_i))^2, \quad (6)$$

where Γ_i measures the proportion of predictable variation that the model explains. As in Equation (3), this augmented model is exactly identified.

The variance ratios are reported with heteroskedasticity-consistent standard errors in Table 6. The one-factor model explains, on average, 12 percent of the variation in the predictability across the eight coun-

The Review of Financial Studies / v 8 n 3 1995

Table 7
The relation between emerging market returns and the world market return

Country	Correlation with world	Tests of time-varying Correlation	Tests of time-varying Variance ratio
Argentina	−0.013 (0.062)	4.330 [0.826]	15.578 [0.035]
Brazil	0.094 (0.077)	7.337 [0.501]	12.701 [0.123]
Chile	0.052 (0.084)	11.741 [0.163]	20.275 [0.009]
Mexico	0.241 (0.087)	10.072 [0.260]	11.349 [0.183]
Korea	0.235 (0.064)	11.637 [0.168]	12.494 [0.130]
India	−0.044 (0.072)	9.080 [0.336]	14.882 [0.061]
Thailand	0.236 (0.110)	12.134 [0.145]	16.933 [0.031]
Greece	0.153 (0.081)	7.476 [0.486]	11.833 [0.159]

The monthly returns for emerging markets are from the International Finance Corporation. All returns are calculated in U.S. dollars and are in excess of the 30-day Eurodeposit rate. The world information variables, Z^w, are the MSCI world return, the U.S. 3-month Treasury bill return minus the 1-month return, the spread between Moody's Baa rated bonds and Aaa bonds, and the Standard and Poor's 500 dividend yield minus the 30-day Treasury bill rate. The local information variables, Z^t, include the local U.S. dollar return, the change in the foreign currency rate versus the U.S. dollar, the local dividend yield and a local interest rate. Correlation is measured against the U.S. dollar return on the MSCI value-weighted world market portfolio in excess of the 30-day Eurodollar deposit rate.

The test for constant correlation is estimated for each asset i:

Disturbance	Orthogonal to
$u_{1it} = r_{it} - \mu_i$	1
$u_{2it} = u_{1it}^2 - \sigma_i^2$	1
$u_{3it} = r_{wt} - \mu_w$	1
$u_{4it} = u_{3it}^2 - \sigma_w^2$	1
$u_{5it} = \rho\sigma_w\sigma_i - u_{1it}u_{3it}$	$Z_{t-1}^{w,t}$

where r_i represents the excess return on asset i, r_w represents the excess return on the world market portfolio, Z is the predetermined information, μ_i is the mean asset return, σ_i^2 is the variance of the asset return, μ_w is the mean world return, σ_w^2 is the variance of the world return, and ρ is the correlation. The correlation parameter reported in the first column is based on an exactly identified version of the above system of equations where the fifth equation is conditioned only on a vector of ones. The heteroskedasticity consistent standard error of the correlation is in parentheses. The test of the constant correlation, in the second column, is based on the overidentified system. The χ^2 statistic has eight degrees of freedom.

The test for constant ratio of world variance to country i variance is

Disturbance	Orthogonal to
$u_{1it} = r_{it} - Z_{t-1}^{w,t}\delta_i$	$Z_{t-1}^{w,t}$
$u_{2it} = r_{wt} - Z_{t-1}^{w}\theta$	Z_{t-1}^{w}
$u_{3it} = \phi_i u_{1it}^2 - u_{2it}^2$	$Z_{t-1}^{w,t}$

where ϕ_i is the ratio of the variance of the world to the variance of country i's excess returns. The χ^2 test of whether this ratio is constant has eight degrees of freedom. The sample is from 1977:04 to 1992:06 (183 observations).

Predictable Risk and Returns in Emerging Markets

tries. None of the individual variance ratios are significantly different from zero. The two-factor model is able to account for 22 percent of the predictable variation. However, consistent with the one-factor results, none of the individual variance ratios are significantly different from zero.

Hence, the explained variation in the expected returns is so small that there is little hope for the conditional model to yield any different conclusions than those of the unconditional model reported in Table 4. The variance ratio tests examine the product of the conditional risk function and the world risk premium. It is also potentially insightful to further decompose the model by examining the conditional risk function.

Figure 4 provides plots of the conditional betas from the one-factor estimation along with 60-month rolling correlations calculated with and without the October 1987 observation. For most of the countries, the general movements in the conditional betas are reflected in the rolling correlation measure (which is smoother due to the overlapping samples). This is especially true in the countries with the most significantly time-varying betas: Argentina, Mexico, India, and Thailand.

The behavior of the correlations and the relation between the correlations and market betas is important because some observers interpret increased correlation as evidence of increased market integration. From Figure 4, the numerical magnitude of the correlation has increased in five countries: Brazil, Chile, Mexico, Korea, and Thailand. However, there is no necessary link between correlation and integration. A country can have zero correlation with the world market and be perfectly integrated into world capital markets. The low correlation could be caused by the weighted average of the firm betas in the country index equaling zero.

Table 7 sheds some light on the relation between correlation and beta. Interestingly, the unconditional correlation is significantly different from zero in only three countries: Mexico, Korea, and Thailand. A test of whether this correlation is time varying produces no evidence against the null hypothesis of constant correlation, however, the lowest p-values are found for Chile, Mexico, Korea, India and Thailand.[22]

The correlation is related to beta by the ratio of the world and country standard deviations. Table 7 tests whether the ratio of variances is

---

[22] The test measures whether the unconditional correlation is constant. A different and more complex test is whether the conditional correlation is constant. This is more complex because it is necessary to model the dynamics of the conditional variance processes for both the country and the world portfolio.

The Review of Financial Studies / v 8 n 3 1995

constant in the following system:

$$u_{1it} = r_{it} - Z_{t-1}^{w,\ell}\delta_i$$
$$u_{2it} = r_{wt} - Z_{t-1}^{w}\theta$$
$$u_{3it} = \phi_i u_{1it}^2 - u_{2it}^2 \qquad (7)$$

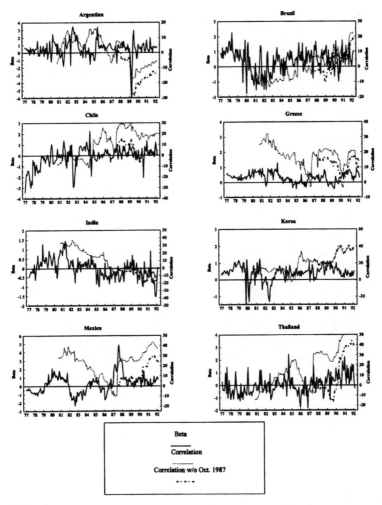

Figure 4
Time-varying conditional betas and correlations with the world market return

where ϕ_i is the ratio of the variance of the world to the variance of country i's excess returns. Conditioning u_1 and u_3 on $Z^{w,\ell}$ and u_2 on Z^w produces a χ^2 test of whether this ratio is constant with 8 degrees of freedom.

This decomposition helps interpret the observation that correlations of the emerging market returns and the world market return are shifting through time. For three of the countries—Argentina, Chile, and Thailand—there is evidence in Table 7 against the null hypothesis that the ratio of variances is constant. For two other countries—Mexico and India—the evidence in Table 6 suggests that the conditional betas are changing through time. Each or both of these two effects could cause time variation in correlations, or they could cancel each other out. But, importantly, the correlation measure, the ratio of volatilities, and the conditional betas are not sufficient to make inference about the degree of integration in these capital markets.

4. Conclusions

This article provides the first comprehensive analysis of 20 new equity markets in emerging economies. These markets have historically been characterized by high average returns and large volatility. However, given the low correlation with developed country returns, the evidence suggests that the emerging market returns are not spanned by the developed market returns. As a result, inclusion of emerging market assets in a mean-variance efficient portfolio will significantly reduce portfolio volatility and increase expected returns.

Figure 4
Facing page: The monthly U.S. dollar returns for eight emerging markets markets are from the International Finance Corpation. The world market return is the U.S. dollar return on the Morgan Stanley Capital International (MSCI) value-weighted world market portfolio. The sample is from 1977:04 to 1992:06. The dotted line denotes rolling unconditional correlations estimated with a 60-month window. The broken line represents rolling unconditional correlations estimated withou the October 1987 observation. The conditional betas result from the estimation of the following system for each asset i:

Disturbance	Orthogonal to
$u_{1it} = r_{it} - Z_{t-1}^{w,\ell}\delta_i$	$Z_{t-1}^{w,\ell}$
$u_{2t} = f_t - Z_{t-1}^{w}\theta$	Z_{t-1}^{w}
$u_{3it} = [u'_{2t}u_{2t}(Z_{t-1}^{w,\ell}\kappa_i)' - f'_t u_{1it}]'$	$Z_{t-1}^{w,\ell}$
$u_{4it} = \mu_i - Z_{t-1}^{w,\ell}\delta_i$	1
$u_{5it} = (-\alpha_i + \mu_i) - Z_{t-1}^{w,\ell}\kappa_i(Z_{t-1}^{w}\theta)'$	1

where r rerpesents the excess return on asset i, Z is the predetermined information, δ are coefficients from a linear projection of the asset returns on the information, f are the factor excess returns, θ are the coefficients from a linear projection of the factor returns on the information, μ is the mean asset return, and α is the difference between the mean asset return and the model fitted mean asset return (pricing error). The conditional betas are assumed to be linear functions of both the world and local information, $Z_{t-1}^{w,\ell}$. The fitted conditional betas are $Z_{t-1}^{w,\ell}\kappa_i$.

The Review of Financial Studies / v 8 n 3 1995

Next, the risk of emerging market equities is analyzed. Risk exposure is interlinked with asset pricing theory. That is, exposure is only meaningful if it is rewarded in equilibrium. However, equilibrium models of global asset pricing take, as given, the complete integration of world capital markets. Applying standard one- and two-factor global asset pricing paradigms leads to large pricing errors. The betas are unable to explain any of the cross-sectional variation in expected returns.

Finally, the predictability of the emerging market returns is investigated. Both world and local information variables are used to forecast the returns. There are three important differences between the predictability in emerging and in developed markets. First, in developed markets, the market's correlation with the U.S. return is closely linked to the degree of predictability. In emerging markets, there is no significant association between correlation with the U.S. portfolio and predictability. Second, the amount of predictability found in the emerging markets is greater than that found in developed markets. Third, local information variables play a much more important role in predicting emerging market returns. Indeed, over half of the predictable variance in the emerging market returns can be traced to local information.

Predictability can be induced by time-varying risk premiums, time-varying risk exposures, or a combination of the two. Given the nature of the predictability, in that it is strongly influenced by local information, it is most likely driven by time-varying risk exposures. When a model is estimated that allows for all of the moments to change through time, there is some evidence of time-varying risk exposures. However, the conditional asset pricing models fail to price the emerging market assets correctly on average and are unable to account for the time variation in expected returns.

The fact that much of the predictability is induced by local information is also consistent with the possibility that some of these countries are segmented from world capital markets. Future research will investigate an asset pricing framework that allows for the possibility of incomplete integration and for the degree of integration to change through time.

In contrast to the evidence in developed markets, the global unconditional asset pricing models are unable to explain the cross-section of expected returns in emerging markets. Also different from the evidence in developed markets, the analysis of conditional risk and risk premiums suggests that significant pricing errors persist and the standard asset pricing models do not account for the predictability in the emerging market returns.

While the null hypothesis of complete integration of the world capital markets is difficult to reject for many developed markets, it is likely a factor contributing to the failure of these models for the emerging markets. There are two other approaches. The first is to assume that the emerging markets are completely segmented. The second is to assume that emerging markets are partially integrated. These two approaches are problematic because they assume that the regime is fixed through time. That is, the partial integration models assume that the market can be characterized by the same degree of partial integration over the estimation period. However, intuition would suggest that integration is a dynamic concept. As regulations change and information becomes easier to access, the degree of integration may change through time.

In the context of a one-factor model, a specification that allows for time-varying integration should allow both the covariance with the world market and the variance of the local market return to affect the conditional mean. This research direction is being pursued in Bekaert and Harvey (1995).

References

Adler, M., and B. Dumas, 1983, "International Portfolio Selection and Corporation Finance: A Synthesis," *Journal of Finance*, 38, 925–984.

Andrews, D. W. K., 1991, "Heteroskedasticity and Autocorrelation Consistent Covariance Matrix Estimation," *Econometrica*, 59, 817–858.

Bailey, W., and J. Jagtiani, 1994, "Foreign Ownership Restrictions and Premiums for International Investment: Some Evidence from the Thai Capital Market," *Journal of Financial Economics*, 36, 57–87.

Bekaert, G., 1995, "Market Segmentation and Investment Barriers in Emerging Equity Markets," *World Bank Economic Review*, 9, 75–107.

Bekaert, G., and C. R. Harvey, 1995, "Time-Varying World Market Integration," forthcoming in *Journal of Finance*, 50.

Bodurtha, J. N., Jr., 1990, "International Factors and U.S. Equity Excess Returns," working paper, University of Michigan.

Brown, S. J., and T. Otsuki, 1993, "Risk Premia in Pacific Rim Capital Markets," *Pacific Basin Finance Journal*, 1, 235–262.

Campbell, J. Y., 1987, "Stock Returns and the Term Structure," *Journal of Financial Economics*, 18, 373–400.

Chen, N.-f., R. Roll, and S. A. Ross, 1986, "Economic Forces and the Stock Market," *Journal of Business*, 59, 383–403.

Cumby, R. E., and J. D. Glen, 1990, "Evaluating the Performance of International Mutual Funds," *Journal of Finance*, 45, 497–521.

De Santis, G., 1993, "Asset Pricing and Porfolio Diversification: Evidence from Emerging Financial Markets," working paper, University of Southern California.

The Review of Financial Studies / v 8 n 3 1995

Dumas, B., 1993, "Partial-Equilibrium vs. General Equilibrium Models of International Capital Market Equilibrium," forthcoming in R. van der Ploeg (ed.), *Handbook of International Macroeconomics*, Basil Blackwell, London.

Dumas, B., and B. Solnik, 1995, "The World Price of Exchange Rate Risk," forthcoming in *Journal of Finance*, 50.

Errunza, V. R., 1983, "Emerging Markets: New Opportunity for Improving Global Portfolio Performance," *Financial Analysts Journal*, 39, 51–58.

Fama, E. F., and K. R. French, 1988, "Dividend Yields and Expected Stock Returns," *Journal of Financial Economics*, 22, 3–26.

Ferson, W. E., 1990, "Are the Latent Variables in Time-Varying Expected Returns Compensation for Consumption Risk," *Journal of Finance*, 45, 397–430.

Ferson, W. E., 1993, "Theory and Empirical Testing of Asset Pricing Models," forthcoming in R. A. Jarrow, W. T. Ziemba, and V. Maksimovic (eds.), *The Finance Handbook*, North Holland, Amsterdam.

Ferson, W. E., S. R. Foerster, and D. B. Keim, 1993, "General Tests of Latent Variables Models and Mean-Variance Spanning," *Journal of Finance*, 48, 131–156.

Ferson, W. E., and C. R. Harvey, 1991, "The Variation of Economic Risk Premiums," *Journal of Political Economy*, 99, 285–315.

Ferson, W. E., and C. R. Harvey, 1993, "The Risk and Predictability of International Equity Returns," *Review of Financial Studies*, 6, 527–566.

Ferson, W. E., and C. R. Harvey, 1994a, "Sources of Risk and Expected Returns in Global Equity Markets," *Journal of Banking and Finance*, 18, 775–803.

Ferson, W. E., and C. R. Harvey, 1994b, "An Exploratory Investigation of the Fundamental Determinants of National Equity Market Returns," in Jeffrey Frankel (ed.), *The Internationalization of Equity Markets*, University of Chicago Press and NBER, 59–133.

Ferson, W. E., and R. A. Korajczyk, 1995, "Do Arbitrage Pricing Models Explain the Predictability of Stock Returns," forthcoming in *Journal of Business*, 68.

Foster, F. D., and T. Smith, 1993, "Assessing Goodness-of-Fit of Asset Pricing Models: The Distribution of the Maximal R^2," working paper, Duke University.

Gibbons, M. R., S. A. Ross, and J. Shanken, 1989, "A Test of the Efficiency of a Given Portfolio," *Econometrica*, 57, 1121–1152.

Hansen, L. P., 1982, "Large Sample Properties of Generalized Method of Moments Estimators," *Econometrica*, 50, 1029–1054.

Harvey, C. R., 1991, "The World Price of Covariance Risk," *Journal of Finance*, 46, 111–157.

Harvey, C. R., 1993, "Risk Exposure to a Trade-Weighted Index of Currency Investment," working paper, Duke University.

Harvey, C. R., 1994, "Conditional Asset Allocation in Emerging Markets," working paper, Duke University.

Harvey, C. R., 1995a, "The Cross-Section of Volatility and Autocorrelation in Emerging Stock Markets," forthcoming in *Finanzmarkt und Portfolio Management*.

Harvey, C. R., 1995b, "The Risk Exposure of Emerging Equity Markets," *World Bank Economic Review*, 9, 19–50.

Predictable Risk and Returns in Emerging Markets

Harvey, C. R., B. H. Solnik, and G. Zhou, 1994, "What Determines Expected International Asset Returns?," working paper, Duke University.

Huberman, G., and S. Kandel, 1987, "Mean-Variance Spanning," *Journal of Finance*, 42, 873–888.

International Finance Corporation, 1993, *IFC Index Methodology*, World Bank, Washington, D.C.

Jagannathan, R., and Z. Wang, 1994, "The CAPM is Alive and Well," working paper, University of Minnesota, Minneapolis.

Jobson, J. D., and R. Korkie, 1989, "A Performance Interpretation of Multivariate Tests of Asset Set Intersection, Spanning and Mean-Variance Efficiency," *Journal of Financial and Quantitative Analysis*, 24, 185–204.

Johnson, N. L., and S. Kotz, 1970, *Distributions in Statistics: Continuous Univariate Distributions*, Volume II, John Wiley and Sons, New York.

Jorion, P., 1991, "The Pricing of Exchange Rate Risk in the Stock Market," *Journal of Financial and Quantitative Analysis*, 26, 363–376.

Kandel, S., and R. F. Stambaugh, 1989, "A Mean-Variance Framework for Tests of Asset Pricing Models," *Review of Financial Studies*, 2, 125–156.

Kandel, S., and R. F. Stambaugh, 1994, "Portfolio Inefficiency and the Cross-Section of Expected Returns," forthcoming in *Journal of Finance*.

Keim, D. B., and R. F. Stambaugh, 1986, "Predicting Returns in the Bond and Stock Market," *Journal of Financial Economics*, 17, 357–390.

Kirby, C. M., 1994, "A Multivariate Analysis of Predictability in Stock and Bond Returns," working paper, Duke University.

Lintner, J., 1965, "The Valuation of Risk Assets and the Selection of Risky Investments in Stock Portfolios and Capital Budgets," *Review of Economics and Statistics*, 47, 13–37.

Newey, W. K., and K. D. West, 1987, "A Simple, Positive Semi-Definite, Heteroskedasticity-Consistent Covariance Matrix," *Econometrica*, 55, 703–708.

Richardson, M., and T. Smith, 1993, "A Test for Multivariate Normality in Stock Returns," *Journal of Business*, 66, 295–321.

Roll, R., 1977, "A Critique of the Asset Pricing Theory's Tests," *Journal of Financial Economics*, 4, 129–176.

Roll, R., and S. A. Ross, 1994, "On the Cross-Sectional Relation Between Expected Returns and Betas," *Journal of Finance*, 49, 101–121.

Ross, S. A., 1976, "The Arbitrage Theory of Capital Asset Pricing," *Journal of Economic Theory*, 13, 341–360.

Scholes, M., and J. Williams, 1993, "Estimating Betas from Nonsynchronous Data," *Journal of Financial Economics*, 5, 309–328.

Shanken, J., 1986, "Testing Portfolio Efficiency when the Zero Beta Rate is Unknown: A Note," *Journal of Finance*, 41, 269–276.

Shanken, J., 1990, "Intertemporal Asset Pricing: An Empirical Investigation," *Journal of Econometrics*, 45, 99–120.

Sharpe, W., 1964, Capital Asset Prices: A Theory of Market Equilibrium Under Conditions of Risk," *Journal of Finance*, 19, 425–442.

The Review of Financial Studies / v 8 n 3 1995

Siddiqui, M. M., 1967, "A Bivariate t-Distribution," *Annals of Mathematical Statistics*, 38, 162–166.

Solnik, B., 1974, "An Equilibrium Model of the International Capital Market," *Journal of Economic Theory*, 8, 500–524.

Stulz, R., 1993, "International Portfolio Choice and Asset Pricing: An Integrative Survey," working paper, Ohio State University.

[5]

THE JOURNAL OF FINANCE • VOL. L, NO. 2 • JUNE 1995

Time-Varying World Market Integration

GEERT BEKAERT and CAMPBELL R. HARVEY*

ABSTRACT

We propose a measure of capital market integration arising from a conditional regime-switching model. Our measure allows us to describe expected returns in countries that are segmented from world capital markets in one part of the sample and become integrated later in the sample. We find that a number of emerging markets exhibit time-varying integration. Some markets appear more integrated than one might expect based on prior knowledge of investment restrictions. Other markets appear segmented even though foreigners have relatively free access to their capital markets. While there is a perception that world capital markets have become more integrated, our country-specific investigation suggests that this is not always the case.

WHY DO DIFFERENT COUNTRIES' market indices command different expected returns? This question lies at the foundation of international finance. The answer follows from another question: What makes international finance different from finance in general? In studying assets in the United States, we would say that differing expected returns are due to differing risk exposures. In international markets, the answer is more difficult. Aside from the obvious complications arising from country-specific exchange rates, "risk" is hard to quantify if a country is not fully integrated into world capital markets.

Markets are completely integrated if assets with the same risk have identical expected returns irrespective of the market. Risk refers to exposure to some common world factor. If a market is segmented from the rest of the world, its covariance with a common world factor may have little or no ability to explain its expected return.

* Bekaert is from the Graduate School of Business, Stanford University and National Bureau of Economic Research. Harvey is from the Fuqua School of Business, Duke University and National Bureau of Economic Research. We have benefitted from the comments of Warren Bailey, Henning Bohn, Bob Cumby, Bernard Dumas, Charles Engel, Wayne Ferson, Steve Grenadier, Burton Hollifield, and Robert Hodrick, and from useful discussions with Bruno Solnik and René Stulz and seminar participants at the Ohio State University, the Board of Governors of the Federal Reserve Bank, the University of North Carolina at Chapel Hill, the University of Washington in Seattle, the Western Finance Association in Sante Fe, the National Bureau of Economic Research seminar at the University of Pennsylvania, the European Finance Association in Brussels, and the American Finance Association in Washington, D.C. We are especially indebted to our research assistants, Steve Gray and Michael Urias, for their comments and for the long hours they devoted to the nonlinear estimation. Both the Editor, René Stulz, and an anonymous referee provided many valuable insights which improved the article. Bekaert acknowledges the financial support of an NSF grant and the Financial Services Research Initiative and the Bass Faculty Fellowship of the Graduate School of Business at Stanford. Harvey's research was supported by the Batterymarch Fellowship.

The reward to risk is also an important consideration. In integrated world capital markets, there are common rewards to risk associated with risk exposures. In explaining the cross-section of expected returns, the reward to risk is not important because it is common to all the integrated countries. However, in segmented markets, the rewards to risk may not be the same because the sources of risk are different.

Asset pricing studies can be classified in three broad categories: segmented markets, integrated markets, or partially segmented markets. An example of an asset pricing study that assumes markets are segmented is one that "tests" a model like the Capital Asset Pricing Model (CAPM) of Sharpe (1964), Lintner (1965) and Black (1972), using one country's data. Indeed, all of the seminal U.S. asset pricing studies assume that the United States is a completely segmented market—or that the market proxy represents a broader world market return. While this might have been a reasonable working assumption through the 1970s, in the 1980s the U.S. equity capitalization dropped below 50 percent of the world market capitalization. Indeed, Japan's market capitalization exceeded the United States (albeit briefly) in 1989.

The second class of asset pricing studies assumes that world capital markets are perfectly integrated. These include studies of a world CAPM (see Harvey (1991) and references therein), a world CAPM with exchange risk (see Dumas and Solnik (1995) and Dumas (1994)), a world consumption-based model (Wheatley (1988)), world arbitrage pricing theory (see Solnik (1983) and Cho, Eun, and Senbet (1986)), world multibeta models (Ferson and Harvey (1993, 1994a, 1994b)) and world latent factor models (Campbell and Hamao (1992), Bekaert and Hodrick (1992) and Harvey, Solnik, and Zhou (1994)). Rejection of these models can be viewed as a rejection of the fundamental asset pricing model, inefficiency in the market, or rejection of market integration.

A good example of the difficulty in interpreting the joint hypotheses is presented in Harvey (1991). Using data through May 1989, Harvey finds that the conditionally expected returns in Japan are too high to be explained by asset pricing theory, or that the risk exposure was too small. In multivariate tests, the asset pricing model is not rejected. Is the rejection in Japan a result of using a one factor model, a function of Japanese stock prices deviating from their fundamental values (inefficiency), or an implication of imposing the null hypothesis of complete market integration?

Yet another strand of the literature falls in between segmentation and integration—the so-called mild segmentation model (see Errunza, Losq, and Padmanabhan (1992) and references therein). The advantage of these models is that the polar segmented/integrated cases are not assumed. The disadvantage of these models is that the degree of segmentation is fixed through time. This runs counter to the intuition (as do the polar cases) that some markets have become more integrated through time.

Our contribution is to propose a methodology that allows for the degree of market integration to change through time. While this method can be applied to a general multifactor model, the intuition can be readily obtained in a one factor setting. We allow conditionally expected returns in any country to be affected by their covariance with a world benchmark portfolio *and by* the variance of the country returns. In a perfectly integrated market, only the covariance counts. In segmented markets, the variance is the relevant measure of market risk. While our approach is not directly implied by any current asset pricing theory, it has the appeal of nesting, as special cases, two previous approaches to international asset pricing: complete segmentation and complete integration.

Our integration measure is a time-varying weight that is applied to the covariance and the variance. The model allows for a differing price of variance risk across countries, which depends on country-specific information, and a world price of covariance risk, which depends only on global information. The model is conditional in the sense that predetermined information is allowed to affect the expected returns, covariances, variances, and the integration measure.

Our procedure allows us to recover fitted values for the integration measure so that the degree and trend of a particular market's integration can be depicted through time. However, caution must be exercised in interpreting our results. First, our tests use the simplest asset pricing framework—the one factor model. Omitted factors may induce variation in the integration measure that is not related to market integration. Second, we conduct a battery of specification tests which suggest that the model is rejected in most countries. However, no one has ever attempted to estimate the degree and variation through time of capital market integration. In addition, the test rejections do not necessarily undermine the interpretation of our integration measure. Indeed, we think that our results are useful and interesting. In many countries, variation in the integration measure coincides with capital market reforms. In contrast to general perceptions that markets are becoming more integrated, our results suggest that some countries are becoming less integrated into the world market.

Our article is organized as follows. In Section I, the asset pricing framework is presented. An outline of the econometric model is also detailed. The data on 12 emerging equity markets are described in Section II. In Section III, the results are analyzed. Specification tests are conducted in Section IV. The final section explores the linkages between financial market integration and economic growth and offers some concluding remarks.

I. Asset Pricing with Time-Varying Market Integration

A. The Model

In completely integrated markets and in the absence of exchange risk, a conditional CAPM of Sharpe (1964) and Lintner (1965) imposes the restrictions:

$$E_{t-1}\left[r_{i,t}^A\right] = \lambda_{t-1}\mathrm{cov}_{t-1}\left[r_{i,t}^A, r_{w,t}\right], \tag{1}$$

where $E_{t-1}[r_{i,t}^A]$ is the conditionally expected excess return on security A's equity (in country i), r_w is the return on a value-weighted world portfolio, cov_{t-1} is the conditional covariance operator and λ_{t-1} is the conditionally expected world price of covariance risk for time t. The risk-free rate has zero conditional variance because the return is determined at $t-1$. This model is tested in Harvey (1991).

In completely segmented markets and under the same assumptions as equation (1):

$$E_{t-1}[r_{i,t}^A] = \lambda_{i,t-1}\mathrm{cov}_{t-1}[r_{i,t}^A, r_{i,t}]. \tag{2}$$

Security A is now priced with respect to its covariance with the return on the market portfolio in country i, r_i, and λ_i is the local price of risk. Aggregating (2) at the national level,

$$E_{t-1}[r_{i,t}] = \lambda_{i,t-1}\mathrm{var}_{t-1}[r_{i,t}]. \tag{3}$$

Merton (1980) argues that λ_i is a measure of the representative investor's relative risk aversion. The model suggests that the expected return in a segmented market is determined by the variance of return in that market times the price of variance. The price of variance will depend on the weighted relative risk aversions of the investors in country i.

Equations (1) and (3) focus on the conditions of complete market integration and segmentation, respectively. Suppose that markets are either fully integrated or fully segmented. When there is a change from market segmentation to market integration (or vice versa), the valuation of the payoffs and, hence, the stochastic process governing returns changes. The switch may be a complete surprise or it may be partially expected.

When market participants expect a switch from a segmented to integrated market in the future, or vice versa, equilibrium expected returns may reflect hedging demands against the switch. In that case, neither equation (1) nor equation (3) describes equilibrium expected returns. Furthermore, it may be incorrect to associate this switch with changes in investment restrictions, since the restrictions may not have been binding.

We approach this difficult problem empirically using a regime-switching model. Let S_t^i be an unobserved state variable that takes on the value of one when markets are integrated and a value of two when markets are segmented. In the first regime, returns are drawn from a distribution with conditional mean given by equation (1). In the second regime, the conditional mean of returns is given by equation (3). At each point in time, there may be a positive probability of a regime switch that is governed by switching probabilities.

From the viewpoint of the econometrician with information set $\mathcal{Z}_{t-1}$, the conditional mean return is given by:

$$E_{t-1}[r_{i,t}] = \phi_{i,t-1}\lambda_{t-1}\mathrm{cov}_{t-1}[r_{i,t}, r_{w,t}] + (1-\phi_{i,t-1})\lambda_{i,t-1}\mathrm{var}_{t-1}[r_{i,t}], \tag{4}$$

where the parameter $\phi_{i,t-1}$, which falls in the interval $[0,1]$, is the econometrician's time-varying assessment of the likelihood that the market is integrated. It can be interpreted as the conditional probability of being in regime 1, $\phi_{i,t-1} = \text{prob}[S_t^i = 1|\mathcal{Z}_{t-1}]$. Although equation 4 does not necessarily reflect equilibrium expected returns of the market participants, it may provide a reasonable approximation to expected returns in this setting.

To infer $\phi_{i,t-1}$ from the data, we explore two different regime switching models. The first is the standard Hamilton (1989, 1990) model. Here, S_t^i follows a Markov process with constant transition probabilities. Although the switching probabilities are time invariant, the regime probability, $\phi_{i,t-1}$, and hence the degree of market integration, varies through time as new information changes the econometrician's inference on the relative likelihood of the two regimes. Gray (1995a) derives the following recursive representation for the regime probability:

$$\phi_{t-1} = (1 - Q) + (P + Q - 1)\left[\frac{f_{1,t-1}\phi_{t-2}}{f_{1,t-1}\phi_{t-2} + f_{2,t-1}(1 - \phi_{t-2})}\right]. \quad (5)$$

where the country i subscript has been suppressed and

$$P = \text{prob}[S_t = 1|S_{t-1} = 1]$$

$$Q = \text{prob}[S_t = 2|S_{t-1} = 2]$$

and $f_{j,t}$ is the likelihood at time t conditional on being in regime j and time $t-1$ information, $\mathcal{Z}_{t-1}$.

Diebold, Lee, and Weinbach (1992), Ghysels (1993), and Gray (1995a, 1995b) extended the Hamilton model to allow for time-varying transition probabilities. In the second formulation, we allow the transition probabilities P and Q to be time varying, modeling them as logistic functions of $\mathbf{Z}_{t-1}^*$:

$$P_t = \frac{\exp(\beta_1'\mathbf{Z}_{t-1}^*)}{1 + \exp(\beta_1'\mathbf{Z}_{t-1}^*)}$$

$$Q_t = \frac{\exp(\beta_2'\mathbf{Z}_{t-1}^*)}{1 + \exp(\beta_2'\mathbf{Z}_{t-1}^*)} \quad (6)$$

where β_j, $j = 1, 2$, are vectors of parameters.

In implementing this model, we let $\mathbf{Z}_{t-1}^*$ be a subset of $\mathbf{Z}_{t-1}^i$ where $\mathbf{Z}_{t-1}^i$ is a collection of information variables specific to country i. $\mathbf{Z}_{t-1}^*$ includes lagged dividend yields and lagged equity market capitalization as a proportion of GDP. Since all of these variables might be influenced by a change in policies affecting market integration, they should influence the switching probabilities. For example, dividend yields typically decrease and market capitalization to GDP typically increases when markets become integrated. Although it is possible that global information variables are also important in determining the switching probabilities, we only allow the global variables to influence the probabilities indirectly—through their correlation with the local information variables.

Cumby and Khanthavit (1992) also investigate a standard Hamilton model for equity returns in Korea, Taiwan, and Thailand. Although they do not formulate an explicit model of time-varying integration, they attempt to relate their results to the capital market policies followed in these countries. Below, we will compare our results to theirs.

Following models like Stulz (1981b), the returns in equations (1) to (4) should be real. Given that reliable inflation data in many of the countries that we study are not available and given a lack of short-term interest rate data (to form local excess returns), we choose to calculate the local market volatility in U.S. dollar terms. The excess return should approximate a real return.

B. An Alternative Interpretation

There is another interpretation of equation (4). In addition to being used by an econometrician attempting to infer whether a certain capital market is integrated or segmented, (4) could be viewed within the context of a one-factor partially-segmented world asset pricing model. As Gray (1994a) emphasizes, the regime switching model in equation (5) is a special case of a general finite mixture distribution model with time-varying weights, i.e. $\phi_{i,t-1} = \phi_i(\mathbf{Z}_{t-1}^*)$ with $\phi_i(\cdot)$ a functional form that constrains $\phi_{i,t-1}$ to be between zero and one and $\mathbf{Z}_{t-1}^*$ a set of variables in $\mathscr{Z}_{t-1}$. Rather than the outcome of a regime switching model, equation (4) may be viewed as an imperfect approximation of expected returns in partially segmented markets.

Whether a market is integrated with world capital markets or segmented is greatly influenced by the economic and financial market policies followed by its government or other regulatory institutions. Barriers to investment (by foreigners in local markets or local participants in foreign markets) can take many forms. An obvious example is foreign ownership restrictions, often imposed by developing countries. However, not all barriers to foreign equity investment necessarily segment markets from the world capital market. For instance, Bekaert (1995) shows that the presence of country funds and/or cross-listed securities might serve to effectively integrate markets with the world capital market despite the existence of severe restrictions on direct foreign equity ownership. In general, it is hard to infer the actual degree of market segmentation from the complex set of capital market restrictions in place in a particular country at any one time.[1] However, the regime switching model allows us to infer the degree of market integration. Indeed, $\phi_{i,t-1}$ may be interpreted as a policy weight, varying with policies affecting the degree of market integration.

The nature of the approximation depends on the nature of the model of partial integration that one has in mind. Stulz (1981a), for example, assumes that world investors face a proportional tax on the (absolute) holdings of foreign equities. He shows that expected returns for individual stocks depend

---

[1] A similar argument is made in the development economics literature. A number of papers examine the relation between financial markets and economic growth. See, for example, King and Levine (1993), Pagano (1993), and Obstfeld (1994). The link between market integration and economic development is sketched in the conclusions.

on the covariance with the world market portfolio, and an intercept that depends on the world beta and on whether the local securities are held short or long by the world investors. Moreover, the model implies that some securities will not be traded internationally.

In models that incorporate foreign ownership restrictions, unrestricted stocks may be priced globally, whereas for restricted stocks both the covariance with the world market portfoilo and the covariance with part of the local market is priced. It is tempting to conclude that the parameter $\phi_{i,t-1}$ will reflect the relative market capitalization of unrestricted versus restricted shares. However, this is not necessarily true. The $\phi_{i,t-1}$ weight will depend on the covariance structure of the local stocks, since globally priced stocks might have spillover effects on correlated restricted stocks. Similarly, the importance of nontraded stocks in Stulz's (1981a) model, which he shows to be low world beta stocks, will affect the magnitude of $\phi_{i,t-1}$, since these stocks are likely to covary more with the local than with the global market. Importantly, our model lacks an intercept as is implied by the Stulz model. In our specification tests, however, we incorporate an intercept.

In general, the presence of unequal integration of individual shares makes it difficult to apply our model to the pricing of individual stocks. However, our methodology enables us to recover the fitted integration parameters for the market as a whole. This allows us to characterize the path of integration through time for each emerging equity market.

The idea that both the covariance with the world return and the covariance with the local market return affect securities' expected returns reaches back to Stehle (1977). He devises a test of local versus global pricing of individual stocks by modelling expected returns as a function of the covariance with the local market portfolio and of the covariance with the component of the world market portfolio which is orthogonal to the local market portfolio. A recent example of covariance and variance influencing conditionally expected national returns is proposed in Chan, Karolyi, and Stulz (1992) in their study of the United States and Japan. They use the definition of covariance to show, for example, that the conditionally expected U.S. market return is affected by both the covariance with other countries and its own variance. The weights they place on the second moments are derived from actual market shares of the U. S. and Japan in the world market portfolio. While this intuition is critical for modeling the United States and Japan, explicitly using the market share weights is less important for the countries in our emerging markets sample since they are so small.

C. Estimation Issues

C.1. The Likelihood Function

To complete the model described in equation (4), we need an auxiliary assumption on the movement of expected returns on the world equity portfolio. Consequently, we estimate a series of bivariate models for

$\mathbf{R}_{i,t} = [r_{i,t}, r_{w,t}]'$:

$$r_{i,t} = \phi_{i,t-1}\lambda_{t-1}\mathrm{cov}_{t-1}[r_{i,t}, r_{w,t}] + (1 - \phi_{i,t-1})\lambda_{i,t-1}\mathrm{var}_{t-1}[r_{i,t}] + e_{i,t} \quad (7)$$
$$r_{w,t} = \lambda_{t-1}\mathrm{var}_{t-1}[r_{w,t}] + e_{w,t}$$

Let $\mathbf{e}_t = [e_{i,t}, e_{w,t}]'$ and define $\mathbf{e}_t^I$ ($\mathbf{e}_t^S$) as the disturbance vector under integration (segmentation):

$$\mathbf{e}_t = \phi_{i,t-1}\mathbf{e}_t^I + (1 - \phi_{i,t-1})\mathbf{e}_t^S. \quad (8)$$

We assume that the residuals are heteroskedastic and that the variance processes under integration and segmentation differ:

$$E[\mathbf{e}_t^I\mathbf{e}_t^{I'}|\mathcal{Z}_{t-1}] = \mathbf{\Sigma}_t^I$$
$$E[\mathbf{e}_t^S\mathbf{e}_t^{S'}|\mathcal{Z}_{t-1}] = \mathbf{\Sigma}_t^S. \quad (9)$$

To relate equation (9) to our previous notation, $\mathrm{cov}_{t-1}[r_{i,t}, r_{w,t}]$ is the off-diagonal element of $\mathbf{\Sigma}_t^I$ while $\mathrm{var}_{t-1}[r_{it}]$ is the first diagonal element of $\mathbf{\Sigma}_t^S$. The conditional variance dynamics are modeled as ARCH(k) following Baba, Engle, Kraft, and Kroner (1989) (BEKK):[2]

$$\mathbf{\Sigma}_t^I = \mathbf{C}^I + (\mathbf{A}^I)'\left[\sum_{k=1}^{K} w_k(\mathbf{e}_{t-k}\mathbf{e}'_{t-k})\right]\mathbf{A}^I$$

$$\mathbf{\Sigma}_t^S = \mathbf{C}^S + (\mathbf{A}^S)'\left[\sum_{k=1}^{K} w_k(\mathbf{e}_{t-k}\mathbf{e}'_{t-k})\right]\mathbf{A}^S, \quad (10)$$

where $\mathbf{C}^I$ and $\mathbf{C}^S$ are symmetric 2×2 matrices, $\mathbf{A}^I$ and $\mathbf{A}^S$ are 2×2 matrices. An advantage of this model of conditional variances is that it guarantees positive definite conditional variance matrices under weak conditions. In addition, the model imposes restrictions across equations and thereby economizes on parameters relative to other multivariate ARCH models.

To further limit parameter proliferation, we impose the additional restrictions:

$$\mathbf{C}^I(2,2) = \mathbf{C}^S(2,2),$$
$$\mathbf{A}^I(j,j) = \mathbf{A}^S(j,j) \quad \text{for } j = 1,2,$$
$$\mathbf{A}^I(1,2) = \mathbf{A}^S(1,2) = 0, \quad (11)$$
$$\text{and}$$
$$\mathbf{A}^S(2,1) = 0.$$

The first, second, and third restrictions make the conditional variance of the world market return independent of the regime. The restriction $\mathbf{A}^I(1,2) = \mathbf{A}^S(1,2) = 0$ ensures that country-specific shocks do not affect the conditional variance of the world market return. The restriction $\mathbf{A}^S(2,1) = 0$ ensures that

---

[2] Frankel (1982) and Engel and Frankel (1984) are examples of ARCH-M models that impose similar restrictions to ours. However, these models assume perfect capital market integration.

the world market shocks do not affect the conditional variance of the country return when the market is segmented.[3] The dynamics of the conditional variances are constrained to be the same in both regimes. In the estimation, we set $K = 3$ and let $w_k = 2(K + 1 - k)/(K(K + 1))$ as in Engle, Lilien, and Robbins (1987). The resulting weights on the three past residual vectors are $1/2, 1/3$, and $1/6$, respectively.

The evidence presented in Campbell (1987) and Harvey (1989, 1991) suggests that the price of risk is time varying. In the most general version of the model, we let:

$$\lambda_{t-1} = \exp(\delta' \mathbf{Z}_{t-1})$$
$$\lambda_{i,t-1} = \exp(\delta'_i \mathbf{Z}^i_{i-1})$$
(12)

where $\mathbf{Z}$ represents global information variables and $\mathbf{Z}^i$ represents a set of local information variables. A similar assumption underlies much of the latent variables literature (Hansen and Hodrick (1983) and Gibbons and Ferson (1985)) and has recently been imposed by Dumas and Solnik (1995) and Dumas (1994). The exponentiation imposes one of the necessary conditions of the asset pricing theory—that the price of risk is positive.

The model is estimated by maximum likelihood assuming normally distributed error terms. The log-likelihood function, apart from some initial conditions, can be written:

$$\log L(\mathbf{R}_{i,T}) = \sum_{t=1}^{T} \log\{\phi_{i,t-1} g_{1,t} + (1 - \phi_{i,t-1}) g_{2,t}\}$$

$$\text{with} \quad g_{1,t} = (2\pi)^{-1} |\Sigma^I_t|^{-1/2} \exp\left\{-\frac{1}{2}\left(\mathbf{e}^{I'}_t (\Sigma^I_t)^{-1} \mathbf{e}^I_t\right)\right\},$$
(13)

$$g_{2,t} = (2\pi)^{-1} |\Sigma^S_t|^{-1/2} \exp\left\{-\frac{1}{2}\left(\mathbf{e}^{S'}_t (\Sigma^S_t)^{-1} \mathbf{e}^S_t\right)\right\}$$

$$\mathbf{R}_{i,T} = [R_{i,1}, R_{i,2}, \ldots, R_{i,T}]$$

where T is the sample size and $\phi_{i,t-1}$ is the integration measure previously specified. The parameter vector is given by

$$\Theta = \left[\delta', \delta'_i, \text{vech}(\mathbf{C}^I)', \mathbf{C}^S(1,1), \mathbf{C}^S(1,2), \mathbf{A}^I(1,1), \mathbf{A}^I(2,1), \mathbf{A}^I(2,2), \beta'\right]',$$

where β summarizes the parameters needed to estimate $\phi_{i,t-1}$. Under very weak assumptions, including misspecification of the error distribution function (see White (1982)), the vector of parameters, Θ, is asymptotically nor-

---

[3] The assumption that the world shocks do not affect the local variance in the segmented market is far stronger than the restriction that local shocks do not affect the world variance process. The plausibility of this restriction is explored in Bekaert and Harvey (1995a).

mally distributed with covariance matrix $\mathbf{A}^{-1}\mathbf{B}\mathbf{A}^{-1}$, where $\mathbf{A}$ is the Hessian form and $\mathbf{B}$ the outer product form of the information matrix. Below, we report "robust" standard errors.[4]

Rather than estimating the likelihood function in equation (13) directly, we proceed in two steps. First, we estimate $C^I(2,2)$, $A^I(2,2)$, and δ using the world market return and the world information variables, $\mathbf{Z}$. Second, we estimate equation (13) country by country imposing the parameter estimates from the first stage. This procedure imposes the restriction that the price of world market risk is the same in each country, which leads to more powerful tests. A disadvantage to this approach is that the usual standard errors are likely to be understated since we ignore the sampling error in the first-stage parameter estimates.

C.2. Specification Tests and Diagnostics

Many of the markets in our sample show predictable variation in returns. In contrast to previous work, our model has *three* sources of time-variation in expected returns: variation in the prices of risk (λ_{t-1}, $\lambda_{i,t-1}$), variation in the conditional risk measures (covariance with world and local market variances) and variation in the degree of market integration ($\phi_{i,t-1}$). Our estimation technique allows us to recover the time path of all three components. To gauge the ability of the model to capture the observed predictability of returns, we test whether the time t disturbance, $\mathbf{e}_t$, is orthogonal to information $\mathscr{Z}_{t-1}$ available at time $t-1$. The first set of diagnostics reports the R^2 and a heteroskedasticity-consistent Wald test of the joint significance of the coefficients of a linear regression of $e_{i,t}$ onto a set of information variables $\mathscr{Z}_{t-1}$. If the model fails to replicate the observed time-variation of expected returns, it is useful to track the source of the rejection. Hence, we set $\mathscr{Z} = \mathbf{Z}$, $\mathscr{Z} = \mathbf{Z}^i$, and $\mathscr{Z} = [\mathbf{Z}, \mathbf{Z}^i]$.

In addition to these informal diagnostics, we also perform a number of formal Lagrange Multiplier (LM) tests.[5] The alternative model that we consider is:

$$r_{i,t} = \zeta' \mathscr{Z}_{t-1} + \phi_{i,t-1}\lambda_{t-1}\text{cov}_{t-1}[r_{i,t}, r_{w,t}] + (1 - \phi_{i,t-1})\lambda_{i,t-1}\text{var}_{t-1}[r_{i,t}], \tag{14}$$

and we test whether $\zeta = \mathbf{0}$. The choices for $\mathscr{Z}$ are the same as above. We report the standard LM test computed as the uncentered R^2 from a regression of the unit vector on the matrix of scores under the null.

---

[4] The estimator is the quasi-maximum likelihood estimator (QMLE). For GARCH models, Bollerslev and Wooldridge (1992) show that the QMLE is generally consistent and has a limiting normal distribution as long as the first two conditional moments are correctly specified. Gray (1995a) has extended these results to standard regime switching models. Note that for ARCH-in-mean models the asymptotic properties of the maximum likelihood estimators have not been worked out.

[5] Computational difficulty in estimating even larger models prevents us from considering Wald or likelihood ratio tests.

We then estimate three alternative models embedded in the general specification equations (5) to (12). In the first alternative, we assume constant prices of risk and provide a likelihood ratio test of this restriction. The second alternative constrains the conditional variances to be constant over time (no ARCH). This produces a second likelihood ratio. Finally, in the third alternative, the degree of integration is constrained to be constant over time. In the standard Hamilton model, this alternative is nested by setting $1 - Q = P$.[6] It corresponds to a standard mixture of normals model (see Everitt and Hand (1981)). This delivers the final likelihood ratio.

Finally, we also report a likelihood ratio test of the standard Hamilton model versus a model with time-varying transition probabilities. When the Hamilton model is rejected, the constant prices of risk and no ARCH models are estimated using time-varying transition probabilities.

II. Data and Summary Statistics

A. The Data

Our sample of national equity markets includes data for both developed markets from Morgan Stanley Capital International (MSCI) and emerging markets from the International Finance Corporation (IFC) of the World Bank. The IFC provides value-weighted indices of a representative sample of equities in each country covering at least 60 percent of the market's capitalization. Our study focusses on twelve emerging markets: Chile, Colombia, Greece, India, Jordan, Korea, Malaysia, Mexico, Nigeria, Taiwan, Thailand, and Zimbabwe. These markets account for over 80 percent of the capitalization of all of the markets followed by the IFC.[7]

The summary statistics are presented in Table I for the total available data for each country. Most of the MSCI data begin in December 1969 and earliest available data for seven of the 12 emerging countries is December 1975. Our analysis will concentrate on the U.S. dollar returns.[8] The statistics include the average (annualized) arithmetic and geometric return, standard deviation, and autocorrelations. The developed market summary statistics are presented over different samples by other authors and appear for the purpose of comparison with the emerging market returns.

The range of average returns is much greater for the emerging than the developed markets. The mean U.S. dollar returns for the emerging markets vary from 43 percent (Colombia) to 3 percent (Nigeria). This sharply contrasts with the range of average returns in the developed markets. In the MSCI sample, no country has an average arithmetic return that exceeds 30 percent.

---

[6] Although we did not do this, in the model with time-varying transition probabilities, this restriction can be imposed by setting $\beta_1 = -\beta_2$.

[7] The appendix provides the details of the index construction and compares the IFC methodology to the MSCI methodology.

[8] Calculating the returns in U.S. dollars eliminates the location inflation. However, the U.S. inflation remains in the returns.

Table I
Summary Analysis of International Equity Returns

Means, standard deviations, and autocorrelations coefficients of 21 developed market returns based on the Morgan Stanley Capital International (MSCI) indices and 12 emerging market returns based on the International Finance Corporation (IFC) indices. Both arithmetic averages and geometric averages are reported. Both means and standard deviations are in annualized percentage terms. All returns are calculated in U.S. dollar terms. The sample ends in December 1992.

Country	Start	Arithmetic Mean	Geometric Mean	Std. Dev.	Autocorrelation					
					ρ_1	ρ_2	ρ_3	ρ_4	ρ_{12}	ρ_{24}
Panel A: Morgan Stanley Capital International										
Australia	70.01	11.40	7.56	26.95	0.00	-0.05	-0.00	-0.00	-0.04	0.04
Austria	70.01	14.20	11.81	21.97	0.15	0.03	0.05	0.10	0.03	0.02
Belgium	70.01	16.08	14.01	20.19	0.09	0.04	0.03	0.04	0.04	0.04
Canada	70.01	10.66	8.75	19.35	0.00	-0.09	0.07	-0.03	-0.04	0.05
Denmark	70.01	14.37	12.44	19.52	0.04	0.14	0.09	0.10	-0.11	0.07
Finland	88.01	-10.25	-13.18	24.05	0.14	-0.36	-0.17	-0.04	0.01	0.42
France	70.01	14.62	11.55	24.64	0.08	-0.00	0.12	0.03	-0.03	-0.00
Germany	70.01	12.78	10.47	21.36	0.01	-0.02	0.10	0.07	-0.05	0.02
Hong Kong	70.01	27.21	18.66	41.58	0.06	-0.04	-0.01	-0.05	-0.01	-0.02
Ireland	88.01	8.03	5.24	23.95	-0.14	-0.09	-0.10	0.19	-0.23	0.41
Italy	70.01	8.08	4.59	26.62	0.11	-0.01	0.09	0.08	0.03	0.04
Japan	70.01	18.00	15.32	22.97	0.06	0.00	0.10	0.04	0.06	0.01
Netherlands	70.01	15.69	13.91	18.53	0.04	-0.04	0.05	-0.10	0.06	-0.00
New Zealand	88.01	-2.20	-5.38	26.01	-0.05	-0.09	-0.11	-0.14	-0.10	0.07
Norway	70.01	14.92	10.88	28.30	0.16	-0.01	0.14	-0.05	0.02	0.04
Singapore/ Malaysia	70.01	18.84	14.08	30.95	0.17	-0.01	-0.08	0.05	0.04	0.00
Spain	70.01	9.80	7.19	22.75	0.12	-0.02	-0.03	0.07	-0.01	0.13
Sweden	70.01	15.67	13.13	22.31	0.08	-0.02	0.04	-0.01	0.03	0.05
Switzerland	70.01	13.36	11.38	19.73	0.05	-0.07	0.04	-0.00	0.01	-0.01
United Kingdom	70.01	15.42	12.04	26.52	0.09	-0.10	0.06	0.01	-0.01	0.05
United States	70.01	11.54	10.24	15.90	0.02	-0.04	0.00	-0.01	0.04	-0.01

(continued overleaf)

Table I—*Continued*

Country	Start	Arithmetic Mean	Geometric Mean	Std. Dev.	Autocorrelation					
					ρ_1	ρ_2	ρ_3	ρ_4	ρ_{12}	ρ_{24}
				Panel B: International Finance Corporation						
Chile	76.01	36.67	29.06	39.58	0.17	0.26	-0.01	-0.03	0.08	0.06
Colombia	85.01	43.64	38.48	32.14	0.49	0.15	-0.03	-0.16	-0.06	-0.08
Greece	76.01	7.47	1.54	36.22	0.13	0.18	0.03	-0.06	-0.04	0.06
India	76.01	20.20	16.54	27.23	0.08	-0.10	-0.03	-0.11	-0.08	-0.01
Jordan	79.01	10.75	9.15	17.89	0.00	0.02	0.18	0.00	-0.00	-0.00
Korea	76.01	21.26	16.27	32.34	-0.00	0.08	0.02	-0.02	0.09	0.05
Malaysia	85.01	13.84	10.24	26.35	0.05	0.06	-0.07	-0.01	-0.10	0.09
Mexico	76.01	30.39	19.20	44.56	0.25	-0.07	-0.04	0.04	-0.01	0.02
Nigeria	85.01	2.70	-5.49	36.50	0.09	-0.13	-0.21	0.03	-0.06	-0.02
Taiwan	85.01	34.02	20.21	52.90	0.07	0.05	-0.04	0.07	0.14	-0.08
Thailand	76.01	22.33	18.87	25.76	0.11	0.15	0.01	-0.12	0.04	-0.07
Zimbabwe	76.01	7.77	1.99	34.17	0.14	0.16	0.25	0.17	-0.01	-0.03

In the IFC sample, four countries (Chile, Colombia, Mexico, and Taiwan) have average returns above 30 percent.

Emerging market returns are characterized by high volatility. Standard deviations range from 18 percent (Jordan) to 53 percent (Taiwan). In contrast for the MSCI countries, volatility ranges between 15 percent and 42 percent. There are eight emerging markets with volatility higher than 30 percent.[9]

The emerging market returns are also more autocorrelated. In the MSCI sample of 18 countries with data from December 1969, there are only 5 countries with first-order autocorrelation that exceeds 10 percent. In contrast, six of the 12 emerging countries have autocorrelations greater than 10 percent. There are two countries with autocorrelations above 20 percent (Colombia and Mexico). This suggests that the returns in many of these countries are predictable (to some extent) based on past returns alone.

B. Predictability

A number of studies have documented the existence of predictable variation in developed country returns.[10] Recently, evidence of predictable variation in emerging market returns has been documented in Bekaert (1995) and Harvey (1993a, b, 1995).

In our econometric model, we separate the total information set, $\mathscr{Z}$, into local components, $\mathbf{Z}^i$, and global components, $\mathbf{Z}$. It is also necessary to be parsimonious with respect to the number of information variables presented. The global information variables include: a constant, the world market dividend yield in excess of the 30-day Eurodollar rate, the default spread (Moody's Baa minus Aaa bond yields), the change in the term structure spread (U.S. 10-year bond yield minus 3-month U.S. bill), and the change in the 30-day Eurodollar rate. These variables are designed to capture fluctuations in expectations of the world business cycle.[11]

The set of local information variables include a constant, local equity returns, local exchange rate changes, local dividend yields, and the ratio of equity market capitalization to GDP. These variables are designed to capture expectations about local economic conditions. Obviously, some of these variables will be correlated with the global variables—just as local economic growth may be correlated with world economic growth. However, the degree of correlation is small. For example, Ferson and Harvey (1994b) find less than 40 percent average correlation among dividend yields in the MSCI countries.

---

[9] Bekaert and Harvey (1995a) explore the reasons why volatility is different in emerging versus developed markets and detail the time-series characteristics of emerging market volatility.

[10] See Harvey (1991a), Bekaert and Hodrick (1992), Campbell and Hamao (1992), Ferson and Harvey (1993, 1994b), and Harvey, Solnik and Zhou (1994).

[11] While some of the variables are U.S. based, Harvey (1991b) shows that U.S. economic growth has 89 percent correlation with G-7 economic growth. He also finds that measures of the U.S. term structure have 87 percent correlation with GDP weighted measures of the world term structure.

Table II presents heteroskedasticity-consistent tests of the null hypothesis that expected returns are constant. In Panel A, tests are conducted on the developed markets. The multivariate test[12] of no predictability using the global information variables for 18 markets (Finland, Ireland, and New Zealand are excluded because their data begin in 1988) provides evidence against the null hypothesis. In addition, the table shows that the combination of global and local variables enhances the degree of predictability.

Panel B considers the 12 emerging markets. In more than half of these countries, the null hypothesis of no predictability is rejected at the 10 percent level. A multivariate test using the global information variables also provides a rejection of the null hypothesis at the 10 percent level of significance.

III. Empirical Results

A. The World Price of Covariance Risk

Table III presents the estimation of the ARCH-M model for the world price of covariance risk:

$$r_{w,t} = \lambda_{t-1}\mathrm{var}_{t-1}[r_{w,t}] + \varepsilon_{w,t}$$

$$\lambda_{t-1} = \exp(\delta' Z_{t-1})$$

where $\mathrm{var}_{t-1}[r_{w,t}]$, is given by:

$$h_t = c^2 + \alpha^2 \sum_{k=1}^{K} w_k \varepsilon_{w,t-k}^2$$

and Z represents the global information variables. Consistent with the evidence presented in Harvey (1991), the hypothesis that the world price of risk is constant is easily rejected. This is also seen in Figure 1 which plots the fitted prices of risk.

The price of risk displays a distinct business cycle pattern (NBER peaks and troughs of the U.S. business cycle are denoted by arrows). The price of risk is highest at economic troughs and lowest at economic peaks. This variation is consistent with the U.S. results of Fama and French (1989) who argue that risk premiums should be highest in recessions to lure investors into the market. Using the latent variables methodology and a sample of 18 MSCI country equity returns and eight fixed income returns, Harvey, Solnik, and Zhou (1994) also document business cycle variation in the world equity market risk premium.

The spikes in the world price of risk coincide with the deepest recessions: 1973–74, 1979, and 1981. Notably, there is no spike in March 1991 (NBER cyclical trough for the United States). However, the most recent recession was unusual in a number of respects. First, there was considerable debate about the nature of this recession. This is evidenced by the NBER waiting an unusually long time (over a year) before dating the business cycle trough.

---

[12] For a detailed analysis of this test and other multivariate tests of predictability, see Kirby (1994).

Table II

Predictability Using Local and Global Information

Heteroskedasticity-consistent tests of the null hypothesis that expected returns are constant. Tests are conducted on both the developed and emerging markets. Multivariate tests of no predictability using the global information variables for 18 developed markets with the longest samples and for the 9 emerging markets with the longest samples are presented. Individual country regressions are then estimated with both local and global information variables. Heteroskedasticity-consistent exclusion tests of global, local and global/local information are presented. The global information variables include a constant, the world market dividend yield in excess of the 30-day Eurodollar rate, the default spread (Moody's Baa minus Aaa bond yields), the change in the term structure spread (U.S. 10-year bond yield minus 3-month U.S. bill), and the change in the 30-day Eurodollar rate. The set of local information variables includes a constant, local equity returns, local exchange rate changes, local dividend yields, and the ratio of equity market capitalization to GDP. All returns are calculated in U.S. dollars.

Country	Exclude Global		Exclude Local		Exclude Global + Local	
	χ^2	p-value	χ^2	p-value	χ^2	p-value
Panel A: Morgan Stanley Capital International						
Australia	11.22	0.024	5.07	0.280	8.07	0.427
Austria	14.82	0.005	6.85	0.144	16.77	0.033
Belgium	7.62	0.107	4.86	0.302	8.73	0.366
Canada	6.32	0.177	6.70	0.153	18.46	0.018
Denmark	4.82	0.306	3.82	0.431	8.29	0.405
Finland	4.48	0.344	6.34	0.175	14.08	0.080
France	3.39	0.495	3.83	0.430	6.82	0.556
Germany	7.04	0.134	3.88	0.422	16.92	0.031
Hong Kong	1.35	0.853	4.52	0.341	6.24	0.620
Ireland	5.38	0.250	3.88	0.422	14.00	0.082
Italy	0.79	0.939	8.01	0.091	9.60	0.294
Japan	7.95	0.093	17.70	0.001	28.06	0.001
Netherlands	6.51	0.164	6.42	0.170	21.75	0.005
New Zealand	4.30	0.368	2.22	0.696	22.50	0.004
Norway	2.85	0.583	5.37	0.252	23.73	0.003
Singapore/Malaysia	10.39	0.034	5.41	0.248	8.63	0.375
Spain	9.88	0.043	2.62	0.624	23.40	0.003
Sweden	8.43	0.077	3.89	0.421	11.00	0.202
Switzerland	5.88	0.208	4.24	0.374	17.89	0.022
United Kingdom	3.63	0.459	3.68	0.451	4.95	0.763
United States	13.85	0.008	4.89	0.299	14.55	0.069
18 countries	—	0.086	—	—	—	—
Panel B: International Finance Corporation						
Chile	15.99	0.003	4.09	0.394	12.55	0.128
Colombia	3.01	0.556	5.43	0.246	15.10	0.057
Greece	8.29	0.082	16.28	0.003	181.63	0.000
India	5.96	0.202	3.13	0.537	6.38	0.604
Jordan	9.16	0.057	4.79	0.309	6.59	0.581
Korea	8.06	0.090	1.88	0.599	13.76	0.056
Malaysia	0.97	0.914	2.83	0.586	3.44	0.904
Mexico	15.83	0.003	3.09	0.542	18.55	0.018
Nigeria	2.16	0.707	0.96	0.916	6.96	0.541
Taiwan	21.24	0.000	3.18	0.529	16.06	0.042
Thailand	4.80	0.309	5.13	0.274	13.51	0.095
Zimbabwe	4.83	0.305	5.43	0.246	22.62	0.004
9 countries	—	0.049	—	—	—	—

Table III

The World Price of Covariance Risk

The model estimated is:

$$r_{w,t} = \lambda_{t-1}\text{var}_{t-1}[r_{w,t}] + \varepsilon_{w,t}$$

$$\lambda_{t-1} = \exp(\delta'Z_{t-1})$$

where r_w is the world market return, λ is the world price of covariance risk, ε_w is the return disturbance, and the conditional variance, $h_t = \text{var}_{t-1}[r_{w,t}]$, is given by:

$$h_t = c^2 + \alpha^2 \sum_{k=1}^{K} w_k \varepsilon_{w,t-k}^2$$

The conditioning information, Z, is a set of global information variables which include a constant, the world market dividend yield in excess of the 30-day Eurodollar rate, the default spread (Moody's Baa minus Aaa bond yields), the change in the term structure spread (U.S. 10-year bond yield minus 3-month U.S. bill), and the change in the 30-day Eurodollar rate. In the estimation, we set $K = 3$ and let $w_k = 2(K + 1 - k)/(K(K + 1))$ as in Engle, Lilien, and Robbins (1987). The resulting weights on the three past residual vectors are 1/2, 1/3 and 1/6, respectively. The χ^2 statistic in Panel B provides a test of whether the conditional variance is constant. It has one degree of freedom. The χ^2 statistic in Panel C provides a test of whether the price of risk is constant. It has 4 degrees of freedom.

Panel A: Full Model						
δ_1	δ_2	δ_3	δ_4	δ_5	c	α
0.217	−0.280	0.291	1.564	−0.123	0.039	0.345
(0.930)	(0.112)	(0.116)	(0.494)	(0.202)	(0.003)	(0.161)

Panel B: Constant Variance Model						
δ_1	δ_2	δ_3	δ_4	δ_5	c	χ^2
0.154	−0.351	0.343	1.656	−0.063	0.042	2.078
(0.712)	(0.124)	(0.163)	(0.474)	(0.176)	(0.003)	[0.149]

Panel C: Constant Price of Risk			
λ	c	α	χ^2
1.876	0.040	0.361	11.166
(1.535)	(0.004)	(0.152)	[0.025]

Second, the recession was less severe than the three previous ones. Third, and most importantly, the U.S. recession did not coincide with a world recession. Recessions in most European countries and Japan followed the U.S. recession. Presumably, variation in the world price of risk should reflect the world business cycle. The fact that the U.S. business cycle was out of phase with other major economies during the last U.S. recession could account for the lack of variation in the world price of risk.

There is only weak evidence that the variance dynamics follow an ARCH process. The α parameter is significant at standard levels (t-ratio of 2.1); however the χ^2 test of the null hypothesis that the variance is constant is not

420   *The Journal of Finance*

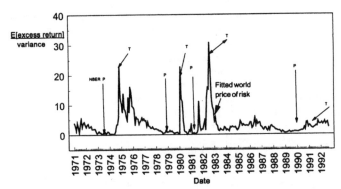

Figure 1. Time-variation in the world price of risk. The model estimated is:

$$r_{w,t} = \lambda_{t-1}\mathrm{var}_{t-1}[r_{w,t}] + \varepsilon_{w,t}$$

$$\lambda_{t-1} = \exp(\delta' \mathbf{Z}_{t-1})$$

where r_w is the world market return, λ is the world price of covariance risk, ε_w is the return disturbance, and the conditional variance, $h_t = \mathrm{var}_{t-1}[r_{w,t}]$, is given by:

$$h_t = c^2 + \alpha^2 \sum_{k=1}^{K} w_k \varepsilon_{w,t-k}^2$$

The conditioning information, $\mathbf{Z}$, is a set of global information variables which include a constant, the world market dividend yield in excess of the 30-day Eurodollar rate, the default spread (Moody's Baa minus Aaa bond yields), the change in the term structure spread (U.S. 10-year bond yield minus 3-month U.S. bill), and the change in the 30-day Eurodollar rate. In the estimation, we set $K = 3$ and let $w_k = 2(K + 1 - k)/(K(K + 1))$ as in Engle, Lilien, and Robbins (1987). The resulting weights on the three past residual vectors are 1/2, 1/3 and 1/6, respectively. The fitted values of λ_{t-1} are presented. P and T denote the National Bureau of Economic Research U.S. business cycle peaks and troughs, respectively.

rejected at conventional significance levels (*p*-value is 0.15). We examined the fitted values of the full model and the no ARCH model (full model in Figure 1). Both series exhibit the same time-series characteristics. However, the no ARCH model price of risk has some extreme values (over 100) at the beginning of 1980. Given the significance of the α coefficient and the higher volatility (and unreasonable values) implied by the no ARCH model, we choose to use the model with ARCH and time-varying prices of risk in the subsequent analysis.

B. Estimation

The results for estimating the standard Hamilton model are presented in Table IV. In this model, the transition probabilities are constant. The first column reports the probability of being in the integrated state given that the previous state was integration (P). The second column reports the probability of being in the segmented state given that the previous state was segmented

(Q). These transition probabilities along with the lagged regime probabilities
and the likelihood form the conditional measure of integration in equation
(4). The table also reports a likelihood ratio test of the null hypothesis that
the transition probabilities are constant.

Both the standard Hamilton model and the model with time-varying
transition probabilities are highly nonlinear and, as a result, special care
must be taken in the estimation. We first estimated the standard Hamilton
model and confirmed the optimum with at least ten different sets of starting
values. We use the parameters from the Hamilton model as a starting point
for the time-varying transition probability or full model. This model has the
most parameters, and up to 25 different sets of starting values were used to
confirm the global optimum.

For Chile, Greece, Jordan, Korea, Thailand, and Zimbabwe, the model with
constant transition probabilities is clearly rejected. For Colombia and Mexico,
there is some weak evidence against the constant transition probability
model. Table IV also reports the mean levels of the integration parameter
over the entire sample as well as over the last three years (post 1990). We
will now examine, in more detail, the results for each country.

B.1. Chile

The average value of the integration parameter for Chile is 0.59 and in
recent years the value has dropped to 0.26. The trend towards segmentation
is evident in Figure 2, which plots the ex ante probability of integration based
on the model with time-varying transition probabilities. The integration
parameter is equal to 1.0 between 1981 and 1984 and then drops sharply.

There are a priori reasons to expect some degree of segmentation in the
Chilean market. Foreign equity investors must pay a 35 percent tax on both
dividends and capital gains. Most importantly, there are currency controls
(see World Bank (1993)). The official rate often diverges from the market
rate, and most foreign investment flows are required to use the official rate.
The market is illiquid and dominated by only a few stocks (the top five stocks
account for over 50 percent of the market capitalization). To make things
worse, for most of the sample, capital repatriation was not allowed for five
years. This has recently been changed to one year.

Chile has one of the lowest percentages of equity that is investable among
the emerging markets, namely 25 percent. Bekaert (1995), who provides
detailed evidence of barriers to entry in emerging markets, ranks Chile 17th
out of 20 in terms of investability. The institutional barriers to investment
are consistent with the estimates of the degree of integration reported in
Table IV.

B.2. Colombia

The results for Colombia suggest that the market is more segmented than
integrated. Over the entire sample, the ex ante probability of integration
never exceeds 0.17. There is little variation in the integration measure for a
number of reasons. First, since a Hamilton model is estimated, the transition

Table IV

Estimation of the Model With Constant Transition Probabilities

The unobserved state variable, S_t^i, takes on the value of one when markets are integrated and a value of two when markets are segmented. Then, $\phi_{i,t-1}$ is the conditional probability of being integrated (regime 1), $\phi_{i,t-1} = \text{prob}[S_t^i = 1 | \mathcal{Z}_{t-1}]$. To infer $\phi_{i,t-1}$ from the data, we explore two different regime switching models. In the Hamilton (1989, 1990) model, the switching probabilities are time invariant but the regime probability and the degree of market integration varies through time as new information changes the econometrician's inference on the relative likelihood of the two regimes. The transition probabilities are:

$$P = \text{prob}[S_t = 1 | S_{t-1} = 1]$$

$$Q = \text{prob}[S_t = 2 | S_{t-1} = 2]$$

where $\mathcal{Z}_{t-1}$ is the conditioning information. In our model with time-varying transition probabilities, we allow P and Q to be logistic functions of $\mathbf{Z}_{t-1}^*$ (includes lagged dividend yields and lagged equity market capitalization as a proportion of GDP).

The χ^2 statistic is from a likelihood ratio test for constant transition probabilities and has 4 degrees of freedom. The transition probabilities are from the simple Hamilton model (constant transition probabilities). The mean degrees of integration are from the model with time-varying transition probabilities, unless the simple Hamilton model is not rejected. In the latter case, the degrees of integration are based on the Hamilton model estimates. All returns are measured in U.S. dollars.

Country	Transition Probabilities		χ^2 [*p*-value]	Degree of Integration Full Sample	Degree of Integration Post-1990
	P	*Q*			
Chile	0.9414 (0.0230)	0.8688 (0.0892)	12.198 [0.016]	0.59	0.26
Colombia	0.0000 (0.0000)	0.8322 (0.0202)	6.382 [0.172]	0.14	0.14
Greece	0.9868 (0.0011)	0.6244 (0.0155)	28.731 [0.000]	0.89	0.86
India	0.9962 (0.0054)	0.9941 (0.0081)	6.332 [0.176]	0.54	0.10
Jordan	0.9022 (0.0113)	0.1710 (0.0099)	14.570 [0.006]	0.85	0.79
Korea[a]	0.9573 (0.0028)	0.0000 (0.0000)	11.462 [0.022]	0.97	0.99
Malaysia[a]	0.8185 (0.0316)	0.3214 (0.0286)	4.123 [0.390]	0.79	0.79
Mexico	0.9363 (0.0427)	0.9839 (0.0113)	6.962 [0.155]	0.21	0.04
Nigeria	0.7402 (0.1486)	0.8941 (0.0847)	1.115 [0.892]	0.27	0.20

(continued overleaf)

Table IV—*Continued*

Country	Transition Probabilities		χ^2 [p-value]	Degree of Integration Full Sample	Degree of Integration Post-1990
	P	Q			
Taiwan	0.9309 (0.0090)	0.3086 (0.0312)	[b] —	0.89	0.90
Thailand[c]	0.9062 (0.0078)	0.9804 (0.0018)	14.369 [0.006]	0.77	1.00
Zimbabwe	0.9808 (0.0098)	0.9699 (0.0146)	10.387 [0.034]	0.47	0.52

[a] The estimation for Korea was extremely ill-behaved and the full model for Malaysia failed to satisfy all convergence criteria. The results for the full model have not been confirmed as the global optimum.
[b] We failed to find an optimum with a likelihood value higher than that of the Hamilton model.
[c] Due to an ill-conditioning problem, standard errors were computed from the inverse of the Hessian.

probabilities are not time-varying. Second, the estimated P parameter is very close to zero. As a result, ϕ cannot exceed 0.17.[13] Given that P is zero, the system will never spend more than one period in the integrated state. According to the estimates, Colombia looks very segmented. However, the pricing of world factors does have some influence on the equity returns.

The evidence of segmentation in Colombia is consistent with the investment environment. The Colombian market is one of the most illiquid among the emerging markets. It ranks third last (just ahead of Chile and Nigeria) in terms of value traded divided by market capitalization. In addition, four securities account for 50 percent of trading volume. The potential liquidity problems are also evident from the remarkable 49 percent serial correlation in returns reported in Table I.

While there are some recent positive developments in Colombia such as announcements of privatization programs, there is no evidence yet of increased integration. Colombia is a good example of why integration cannot be accurately measured by regulatory standing. The degree of investability is quite high in Colombia. However, the lack of liquidity, combined with the political risk induced by the ongoing war with the drug cartels, has kept this market largely segmented.

B.3. Greece

Greece is no longer an emerging market, with U.S. $5,500 GDP per capital in 1990 (the World Bank definition of emerging market is less than $2,200 per capita in 1990). However, when the IFC indices were formed in 1981,

[13] This is the case because $\phi_{t-1} = (1 - Q)(1 - W_{t-1})$ where W_{t-1} is implicitly defined in equation (5). Since $Q = 0.83$, and $0 < W_{t-1} < 1$, the maximum value ϕ can take is 0.17.

424   *The Journal of Finance*

Greece fell within the emerging markets category. The evidence presented in Table IV suggests that the Greek market is integrated into world capital markets. The integration parameter in the 1990s is 0.86.

The integration of Greece is consistent with the investment environment. Outside certain industries, such as banking, shipping, and insurance, there are no foreign investment restrictions. The market capitalization is \$U.S. 9.5 billion at the end of 1992. There is a large foreign participation in the stock market (about 20 percent of shares are owned by foreigners). Finally, there is reasonable liquidity with \$9 million in average daily trading in 1992.

B.4. India

It was difficult to develop a prior assessment of the degree of integration of the Indian market. Factors favoring integration include the long history of

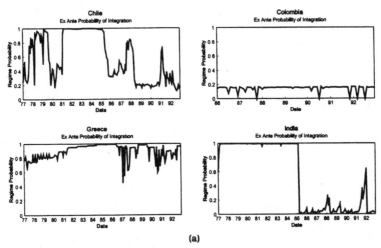

(a)

Figure 2. Time-varying integration measures. We use a regime-switching framework to estimate the ex ante probability of integration. The unobserved state variable, S_t^i, takes on the value of one when markets are integrated and a value of two when markets are segmented. Then, $\phi_{i,t-1}$ is the conditional probability of being integrated (regime 1), $\phi_{i,t-1} = \text{prob}[S_t^i = 1|\mathcal{Z}_{t-1}]$. To infer $\phi_{i,t-1}$ from the data, we use two different regime switching models. In the Hamilton (1989, 1990) model, the switching probabilities are time invariant but the regime probability and the degree of market integration vary through time as new information changes the econometrician's inference on the relative likelihood of the two regimes. The transition probabilities are:

$$P = \text{prob}[S_t = 1|S_{t-1} = 1]$$
$$Q = \text{prob}[S_t = 2|S_{t-1} = 2]$$

where $\mathcal{Z}_{t-1}$ is the conditioning information. In our model with time-varying transition probabilities, we allow P and Q to be logistic functions of $\mathbf{Z}_{t-1}^*$ (includes lagged dividend yields and lagged equity market capitalization as a proportion of GDP). The ex ante probabilities of integration for Chile, Greece, Jordan, Korea, Thailand, and Zimbabwe are based on the model with time-varying transition probabilities.

(continued overleaf)

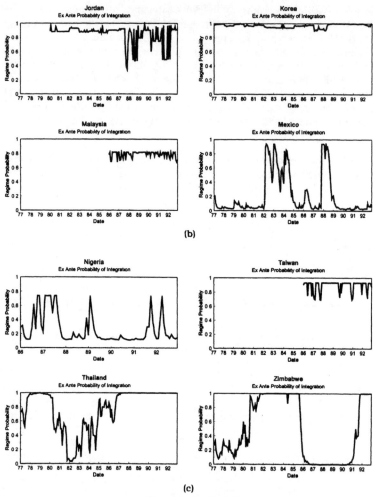

(b)

(c)

Figure 2.-*Continued.*

equity trading (the Bombay exchange is 115 years old) and the large number of stocks that trade (2556 securities were listed in 1991 on 19 exchanges). The capitalization at the end of 1992 was U.S. $65.1 billion with reasonable trading volume (U.S. $13.2 billion).

On the other hand, India is a very poor country, with only U.S. $300 of per capita GDP. Stock market investment is limited to authorized investors only. That is, foreigners need permission of the Reserve Bank of India to purchase shares. However, once approved there is complete freedom to repatriate.

Other factors such as political and religious strife and the the tensions with Pakistan could also work against foreign investors participating in the Indian market.

The results in Table IV suggest that India is not fully integrated into world capital markets. The average degree of integration has decreased. In Figure 1, the time-series patterns in the degree of integration are striking. The model suggests that India was fully integrated into world capital markets until the end of 1984. The integration parameter then plummets to close to zero. Interestingly, this closely coincides with the assassination of Prime Minister Indira Gandhi on October 31, 1984. There is some recent evidence of a movement towards higher levels of integration.

B.5. Jordan

The estimates suggest that Jordan is not fully integrated into world capital markets. In Table IV, the recent degree of integration is 79 percent. From Figure 2, the degree of integration has fluctuated between 40 percent and 90 percent over the past five years. The Jordanian market is small, with a market capitalization of U.S. $3.2 billion at the end of 1992. Foreigners are restricted to owning up to 49 percent of equity (with the exception of tourism and agriculture where there are no limits). Importantly, 85 percent of equities is owned by Jordanians. The remaining 15 percent is thought to be owned mainly by investors from other Arab states. There are no American Depository Receipts (ADRs) and no country funds. The only way to access the Jordanian market is to trade there directly. These factors are consistent with our evidence.

B.6. Korea

Korea also fails to qualify as an emerging market with per capita GDP exceeding U.S. $5,000 in 1990. The evidence suggests that this market is integrated. The ex ante probability of integration lies between 0.85 and 1.00 through the entire sample. Over the past three years, the integration parameter is 0.99.

The Korean market definitely clears the liquidity hurdle. It is the third most active emerging market (behind Taiwan and Thailand) with over 100 percent of its market capitalization turning over each year. In terms of total capitalization, Korea is also the third largest emerging market (behind Mexico and Taiwan) and the 15th largest equity market in the world.

However, if integration is measured by looking at the investment regulations, one would probably conclude that the market was segmented for most of our sample. Regulations on foreign participation prohibited direct access to the Korean market until January 1992. Even the recent liberalization does not seem that impressive. Foreign ownership is limited to 10 percent in so-called unlimited industries and 8 percent in limited industries (which includes communications and defense). Recently, the 10 percent ceiling was raised to 25 percent for 45 firms that hit the 10 percent cap.

But there are other ways for foreigners to access the Korean market. At last count, Korea has 17 U.S. dollar denominated country funds and 17 non-U.S. dollar country funds. Many of these country funds have a long history (Korea Trust began in 1981) and have allowed foreigners to participate, to some degree, in the Korean market.

Cumby and Khantavit (1992) also study a regime-switching model for the Korean stock market jointly with the world market. They allow a different mean and variance in each regime, but there is no time-variation allowed in either. Hence, it is difficult to compare their results to ours. Unlike our results, they find clearly distinguishable regimes in the Korean equity market, but find it difficult to attribute the regime switches to policies concerning capital market integration. However, consistent with our results, their graphs of the regime probabilities suggest that the regime associated with capital market integration dominates during the sample. Bae (1993) also studies the Korean equity market. He finds that both domestic and international factors are important in pricing Korean equities and that the Korean market has become more integrated with world capital markets in recent years.

B.7. Malaysia

For Malaysia, our priors tilted towards integration. The equity market is large (U.S. $94 billion at the end of 1992) with good trading volume (U.S. $21.8 billion in 1992). Malaysia has experienced very mild inflation averaging only 4.6 percent over the past 25 years. In addition, the currency is a free float and foreigners can have Ringgit accounts.

Importantly, foreigners play a large role in the Malaysian market. At the end of 1992, foreign participation in Malaysian equities was 27 percent. Although foreign investment is limited by the Foreign Investment Committee to 30 percent of equity, it is not clear that this constraint is binding in our sample. In addition, foreigners can access 11 closed-end funds, seven open-end funds, and 13 ADRs.

All of these factors suggest that the market is integrated. This is confirmed in the data. Although the estimation for Malaysia was difficult, the results in Table IV suggest that the market is integrated. The 1990s integration parameter is 0.79 and has been fairly stable from the start of our data.

B.8. Mexico

The results for Mexico seem surprising. The model estimates suggest that Mexico's equity market was segmented during most of our sample with the exception of the 1982–1985 period and the late 1980s. There is also a slight upturn since 1991 (see Figure 2). Today, Mexico has one of the highest capitalized markets (U.S. $139 billion at the end of 1992), with U.S. $171 million in average daily trading volume. There are 36 ADRs and six U.S. dollar based country funds. All of these factors point toward market integration.

While Mexican stocks get much attention in the United States, most observers do not realize that before 1991 only two Mexican ADRs were

428   *The Journal of Finance*

trading. In fact, the Mexican market was effectively closed to foreign investors until 1981. The upturn in our integration measure in Figure 2 occurs shortly after the initial public offering of the Mexican Fund on the New York Stock Exchange. While the debt crisis, starting in 1982, may have deterred foreign investment at first, debt conversion programs subsidized and encouraged foreign equity investments. From 1986 onwards, Mexico ran a large debt-equity swap problem while dismantling several important obstacles to foreign investment.[14] Nevertheless, the Mexican country fund remained the main vehicle of access to Mexican stocks for most of the eighties.

The major reforms are fairly recent. The Mexican stock market was made 100 percent investable (with the exception of certain key sectors such as banking) in May 1989, and the dual exchange rate was abolished in November 1991. In addition, there has been a lot of economic turmoil. Mexico had the fourth highest inflation rate over the past six years (behind Brazil, Argentina, and Turkey). Given that most of the liberalizations occurred at the end of our sample, the results appear more reasonable.

B.9. Nigeria

We chose to examine Nigeria because we had a strong prior that this is the most likely market to be segmented. Per capita GDP is only U.S. $295 in 1990 and over 80 percent of the economy is linked to petroleum. The results in Table IV confirm that this market is more segmented than integrated. Over the past three years, the ex ante probability of integration is only 0.20.

The evidence of segmentation is consistent with the investment environment. The IFC categorizes the market as 0 percent investable and ranks Nigeria last among the emerging markets. Liquidity is extremely thin. Only 1 percent of market capitalization traded in 1992 (the average daily trading volume was only U.S. $55,000). All direct investment must be preapproved by the government. There are no Nigerian country funds and no ADRs. While there was some reason for optimism about reform after Nigeria's first democratic elections in late 1992, the military changed their mind and decided not to recognize the results of the election.

B.10. Taiwan

Taiwan is another country where it was difficult to form a prior opinion about the degree of integration. Factors favoring integration included the high market capitalization (U.S. $101 billion at the end of 1992) and the very large trading volume (U.S. $214 billion in 1992). In addition, Taiwan no longer qualifies as an emerging market with 1992 GDP per capita of U.S. $8,815. The NT dollar is technically floating, but the Central Bank of China keeps close control, i.e, it is not freely traded. Foreign investors are allowed to repatriate once per quarter.

---

[14] We thank Jorge Calderon-Rossell for useful information on the development of Mexican capital markets.

Factors that work against integration are the regulations controlling the amount of foreign equity ownership. Foreign ownership was first allowed in 1983 (our sample begins in 1985) but restricted to four approved investment funds. In January 1991, direct investment by institutional investors was allowed. Foreign individuals cannot invest directly. In addition, some industries are not investable, others have investment limits. Furthermore, no single investor can own more than 5 percent of a firm's equity.

The model suggests that Taiwan is integrated. The average degree of integration in the 1990s is 0.89. Though foreign direct participation is limited, there are eight closed-end funds, nine open-end funds, and four investment trusts. These alternative ways to access the market along with the direct institutional participation could explain the estimated degree of integration.

Cumby and Khantavit (1992) also study the degree of integration in Taiwan and detail a stronger covariance between local returns and world returns in the integrated state than in the nonintegrated state. Similar to our experience, the short period of data availability (data begin in 1985) makes both estimation and inference difficult.

B.11. Thailand

The model estimates for Thailand show a dramatic increase in the ex ante probability of integration beginning in 1986. Using a different methodology, Cumby and Khantavit (1992) also show a large shift in the degree of integration in 1986 (from 0.1 to 1.0). This change coincides with the beginning of trading on the Alien board. Most Thai stocks have foreign ownership limits. When these limits are met, identical shares (in terms of dividends and voting rights) are traded on two exchanges, the Main board—for resident Thais, and the Alien board—for nonresidents (see Bailey and Jagtiani (1994)).

The existence of the Alien and Main boards implies some direct access barriers for foreigners. In addition, foreigners are not allowed to own property in Thailand. As a result of the property restrictions, a corporation cannot have greater than 49 percent foreign ownership. Although there are ownership restrictions, the foreigners have a long history of participation in the Thai market.

In addition, there are many ways to access the Thai market. As of December 1992, there were 26 closed-end and 11 open-end Thai funds trading world wide. Direct investment, even with the ownership restrictions, is also relatively easy. Foreigner holdings are estimated to represent up to 60 percent of the freely floating shares.[15] The market is large (U.S. $58.3 billion in December 1992, 5th largest of the emerging markets) and very liquid (U.S. $72.1 billion in 1992) with the second highest turnover ratio among the emerging markets. All of these factors increase the probability that the market is integrated.

---

[15] See Asiamoney (1994). The free float excludes the large blocks of shares owned by family groups and banks.

B.12. Zimbabwe

We chose to examine Zimbabwe, as we did Nigeria, because of a strong prior that the country is not integrated into world capital markets. Zimbabwe is the third poorest country in our sample with per capita GDP of U.S. $621 per year in 1991 (Nigeria is last with U.S. $295). The market capitalization is the smallest in the sample at U.S. $600 million and there is only U.S. $85,000 in average daily trading volume. While foreign investors are allowed in all but certain key sectors, the market is classified as uninvestable because of strict foreign exchange controls.

The evidence in Table IV confirms our prior that the market is not fully integrated. The average integration is 57 percent in the 1990s. However, much more information can be obtained from Figure 2. There is a sharp increase in the integration parameter in the late 1970s which coincides with the optimism leading to independence that was officially achieved on April 18, 1980.

In the mid 1980s, the integration parameter falls to zero. This coincides with the time that the strict exchange controls are implemented. Recently, there has been a sharp increase in the integration parameter that remains unexplained.

IV. Diagnostics

A. Robustness of the Specification

Table V presents three sets of model diagnostics. First, we regress the model errors (returns minus the model fitted values) for each country on the three sets of information variables. This produces an adjusted R^2 and a heteroskedasticity-consistent χ^2 test. The χ^2-statistic tests the hypothesis that the regression coefficients on the instruments are equal to zero. Finally, we present a Lagrange multiplier test of the alternative specified in equation (14). The test essentially adds a time-varying intercept to equation (4). The coefficient on the constant is the analogue to the Jensen (1969) "alpha." However, our alternative also tests for predictability of the pricing errors.

These tests are important for the interpretation of our results. There are many reasons why the model diagnostics might present evidence against the specification. Foremost on this list of reasons is that we choose to examine a single factor specification. Missing risk premiums could mask themselves in time-varying integration. Given a rejection of the specification, we need to exercise caution in interpreting the estimated degree of integration.

The specification tests suggest that the model specification is rejected for Chile, Greece, Korea, Mexico, and Zimbabwe. There is mixed evidence for India, Malaysia, Nigeria, Taiwan, and Thailand. We fail to reject the model for Colombia and Jordan.

First, consider the countries where the model is rejected. Chile's model errors are strongly correlated with local information. The R^2 is close to 10 percent when the errors are regressed on predetermined local information variables. While the R^2 is small on the world information, both the Wald and Lagrange multiplier tests present evidence against the specification with the common world information. A similar pattern is found for Greece. The errors are highly correlated with local information. However, the model is rejected by the Wald test with the common world information variables.

The rejections for Korea and Zimbabwe follow similar patterns. Parallel to Chile and Greece, model errors are more correlated with local information variables. But the correlations are much smaller with R^2s averaging only three percent. Consistent with the other countries, both the Wald and Lagrange multiplier test provide convincing evidence against the specification.

In contrast to the previous four countries, the Mexican rejection appears to be equally driven by both local and world information. The residual R^2s are about the same (6 percent) as are the p-values for the more formal statistical tests.

There is mixed evidence against the model for India and Taiwan. In all cases, the model R^2s are zero when measured against local information, world information or the combined world and local information sets. For both countries, the Wald test fails to reject the null hypothesis. However, when the time-varying intercept is injected into the estimation, the Lagrange multiplier test detects a misspecification.

The evidence for Thailand depends on the information set used. With the local information set, the Wald test fails to reject the null hypothesis and the Lagrange Multiplier test delivers a p-value of 3.6 percent. More convincing evidence against the model is furnished with the world information set.

We classify Malaysia as mixed because of the estimation problems that we encountered. Although the Wald tests do not reject the null hypothesis for any of the information specifications, we could not confirm that we achieved the global optimum.

Neither the Wald test nor Lagrange multiplier test provide any evidence against the null hypothesis for Nigeria. However, we classify the evidence as mixed in this country because of the large model residual R^2 with the local information.

Our diagnostic tests do not uncover evidence of misspecification for Colombia and Jordan. The residual R^2s are low in every case. Furthermore, both the Wald and Lagrange multiplier tests fail to reject the model specification.

These diagnostics suggest evidence against the model specification for a number of our sample countries. The strength of rejection and the source of the rejection generally differs across countries. A rejection does not imply that the model yields no useful information. Nevertheless, extreme caution should be exercised when interpreting the integration measure, $\phi_{i,t-1}$, in those countries where there is evidence against the model.

B. *Integration and Foreign Exchange Regimes*

It is possible that the estimated degree of integration is capturing changes in foreign exchange regimes rather than the broader notion of capital market

Table V
Model Diagnostics: Correlation of the Country Asset Pricing Errors with Information

The R^2 statistics are adjusted for degrees of freedom and result from a regression of the error term $e_{i,t}$ on the set of instruments: $\mathbf{Z}$ global information, $\mathbf{Z}^i$ local information, or $\mathcal{Z}$ global and local information. The W-statistics are heteroskedasticity-consistent Wald tests on the joint significance of the coefficients in that regression. The p-values are based on a χ^2 distribution with degrees of freedom equal to the number of included regressors. The LM tests are standard Lagrange multiplier tests of the alternative specified in equation 14. They are asymptotically distributed χ^2 with degrees of freedom equal to the number of elements in $\mathbf{Z}$, $\mathbf{Z}^i$, or $\mathcal{Z}$ if the error distribution is correctly specified. The asterisk indicates that the model is estimated with time-varying rather than constant transition probabilities. All returns are measured in U.S. dollars.

Country	World Information Z			Local Information Z'			World Plus Local $\mathcal{Z} = [\mathbf{Z}, \mathbf{Z}^i]$		
	$\bar{R}^2$	W	LM	$\bar{R}^2$	W	LM	$\bar{R}^2$	W	LM
Chile*	0.0097	38.64 [0.000]	21.32 [0.000]	0.0945	61.39 [0.000]	25.41 [0.000]	0.1004	83.51 [0.000]	28.33 [0.001]
Colombia	−0.0262	4.94 [0.423]	3.02 [0.697]	−0.0362	3.31 [0.652]	6.49 [0.261]	0.0234	8.48 [0.487]	10.53 [0.309]
Greece*	−0.0069	29.83 [0.000]	ª —	0.2726	42.06 [0.000]	ª —	0.2681	57.64 [0.000]	ª —
India	−0.0012	6.55 [0.257]	25.80 [0.000]	−0.0163	1.27 [0.938]	31.08 [0.000]	−0.0111	11.16 [0.265]	33.74 [0.000]
Jordan*	−0.0171	3.33 [0.648]	8.34 [0.138]	0.0444	3.74 [0.587]	9.99 [0.075]	0.0280	4.08 [0.906]	11.38 [0.251]
Korea*	0.0074	17.49 [0.004]	ª —	0.0243	30.71 [0.000]	ª —	0.0443	42.03 [0.000]	ª —
Malaysia	−0.0452	1.84 [0.871]	ª —	−0.0060	6.45 [0.265]	ª —	−0.0523	7.73 [0.562]	ª —
Mexico	0.0580	21.82 [0.001]	29.64 [0.000]	0.0657	13.38 [0.020]	33.72 [0.000]	0.1266	42.80 [0.000]	44.53 [0.000]

(continued overleaf)

Table V—*Continued*

Country	World Information Z			Local Information Z'			World Plus Local $\mathcal{Z} = [Z, Z']$		
	$\bar{R}^2$	W	LM	$\bar{R}^2$	W	LM	$\bar{R}^2$	W	LM
Nigeria	−0.0355	4.05 [0.543]	5.24 [0.388]	0.3830	7.11 [0.213]	3.28 [0.657]	0.3900	9.48 [0.395]	9.85 [0.363]
Taiwan	−0.0232	5.99 [0.307]	26.59 [0.000]	0.0290	4.10 [0.535]	20.81 [0.001]	0.0006	14.03 [0.121]	30.27 [0.000]
Thailand*	0.0394	19.55 [0.002]	13.23 [0.021]	0.0627	6.33 [0.275]	11.94 [0.036]	0.0793	25.86 [0.002]	20.58 [0.015]
Zimbabwe*	0.0106	9.44 [0.093]	19.44 [0.002]	0.0281	17.75 [0.003]	19.55 [0.002]	0.0720	28.86 [0.001]	25.16 [0.003]

* The moment matrix of the scores was singular.

The Journal of Finance

Table VI

The Interaction between Integration and Foreign Exchange Regimes

Two regressions are estimated for each country:

$$\Delta s_{t+1} = \alpha_0 + \alpha_1 \Delta s_t + \alpha_2 i_t + \alpha_3 \hat{\phi}_t + e_{t+1}$$
$$\Delta s_{t+1} = \alpha_0^* + \alpha_1^* \Delta s_t + \alpha_2^* i_t + e_{t+1}^*$$

where s_t is exchange rate versus the U.S. dollar, i_t is the interest rate, and $\hat{\phi}_t$ is the estimated degree of integration. We report the difference between the adjusted R^2s of the two models as well as the χ^2 and p-value associated with α_3 (coefficient on the estimated integration). The χ^2 test has one degree of freedom. All returns are measured in U.S. dollars.

Country	$\Delta \bar{R}^2$	χ^2
Chile	0.0197	4.081 [0.043]
Colombia	0.0093	4.344 [0.037]
Greece	0.0015	1.779 [0.182]
India	0.0072	2.964 [0.085]
Jordan	−0.0066	0.0013 [0.971]
Korea	0.0125	4.536 [0.033]
Malasia	0.0618	4.576 [0.032]
Mexico	0.0012	0.8513 [0.356]
Nigeria	0.0328	2.683 [0.101]
Taiwan	−0.0116	0.0436 [0.835]
Thailand	0.0005	2.512 [0.113]
Zimbabwe	0.0076	2.798 [0.094]

integration.[16] Table VI presents tests of the following regression models:

$$\Delta s_{t+1} = \alpha_0 + \alpha_1 \Delta s_t + \alpha_2 i_t + \alpha_3 \hat{\phi}_t + e_{t+1} \qquad (15)$$
$$\Delta s_{t+1} = \alpha_0^* + \alpha_1^* \Delta s_t + \alpha_2^* i_t + e_{t+1}^*$$

[16] We are grateful to Burton Hollifield for suggesting this possibility.

where s_t is U.S. dollar per local currency exchange rate, i_t is the interest rate, and $\hat{\phi}_t$ is the estimated degree of integration. We report the difference between the adjusted R^2s of the two models as well as the χ^2 and p-value associated with α_3 (coefficient on the estimated integration) which has one degree of freedom. To mitigate the generated regressor problem in equation (15) (see Pagan (1984)), we report heteroskedasticity-consistent standard errors.

The results in Table VI do not show strong evidence that exchange rate changes and the integration measure are interrelated. In only four of 12 countries, do the tests reject the hypothesis that $\alpha_3 = 0$ at the 5 percent level of significance (Chile, Colombia, Korea, and Malaysia). Moreover, the increases in the adjusted R^2 are small, except for Malaysia and Nigeria.

C. *Estimation of the Constrained Alternatives*

Table VII presents likelihood ratio tests of three specific alternative hypotheses: constant prices of risk, constant variance matrices, and constant degree of integration.

The hypothesis that the price of local volatility is constant is rejected at the 5 percent level in Chile, Colombia, Greece, India, Jordan, Korea, Mexico, and Taiwan. There is no evidence against the hypothesis for Nigeria, Thailand, or Zimbabwe. We also fail to reject the constant local price of risk for Malaysia. However, as mentioned earlier, the estimation for this country was ill-behaved and we should be cautious in drawing conclusions.

The hypothesis that the variance matrices are constant is also tested with a likelihood ratio in Table VII. Constant variance matrices are rejected for eight of the ten countries for which this test was feasible. The hypothesis is rejected at the 10 percent level for the remaining two countries.

The third likelihood ratio provides a test of the hypothesis that the degree of integration is constant. This hypothesis is rejected for Chile, Greece, India, Mexico, Nigeria, Taiwan, Thailand, and Zimbabwe. The rejection is informally confirmed by noticing the time variation in fitted integration measures in Figure 2. Constant integration is not rejected for Colombia, Jordan, Korea, and Malaysia. This can be confirmed by viewing the fitted integration measures.[17]

V. Conclusions and Further Research

Most would agree that the degree to which many countries are integrated into world capital markets has changed over time. However, all previous research has made one of three assumptions: all markets are perfectly integrated, individual markets are perfectly segmented, or local markets are

---

[17] In an other diagnostic exercise, we estimated our model for a developed market, Germany, which is most likely completely integrated into world capital markets. Our results (available on request) indicate that Germany is integrated throughout the sample.

Table VII

Estimation Results for the Constrained Alternatives

LR1 is the likelihood ratio statistic testing the restriction that the price of risk is constant and has 4 degrees of freedom. LR2 provides a test of constant variances and has 2 degrees of freedom. LR3 presents a test of whether the degree of integration is constant and has 1 degree of freedom.

Country	Constant Price of Risk LR1	Constant Variance LR2	Constant Degree of Integration LR3
Chile	28.95 [0.000]	6.93 [0.031]	6.49 [0.011]
Colombia	23.28 [0.000]	4.83 [0.090]	0.533 [0.466]
Greece	49.05 [0.000]	52.34 [0.000]	8.99 [0.003]
India	11.30 [0.023]	14.78 [0.001]	8.89 [0.003]
Jordan	17.75 [0.001]	8.90 [0.012]	0.34 [0.560]
Korea	27.34 [0.000]	27.21 [0.000]	1.17 [0.281]
Malaysia	7.10 [0.131]	5.62 [0.060]	0.77 [0.380]
Mexico	12.73 [0.013]	10.28 [0.036]	18.54 [0.000]
Nigeria	6.22 [0.183]	[a] —	9.93 [0.002]
Taiwan	23.92 [0.000]	18.21 [0.000]	4.08 [0.043]
Thailand	4.30 [0.367]	[a] —	21.32 [0.000]
Zimbabwe	4.51 [0.342]	8.51 [0.014]	10.25 [0.001]

[a] The likelihood value is higher in the constrained model. This is possible since the first-stage estimation prevents a complete nesting of the two models.

partially integrated with the degree of integration being constant. We provide a framework which allows for time-varying conditional market integration.

The degree that a national capital market is integrated into world capital markets is notoriously difficult to measure. Some have suggested that the correlation of the local market return with the world return is a measure of integration. However, this is flawed because a country could be perfectly integrated into world markets but have a low or negative correlation because its industry mix is much different from the average world mix.

Others have looked to investment restrictions as an indicator of integration. This measure is problematic because there are numerous types of restrictions, with some being more important than others across different countries. Importantly, the investment restrictions may not be binding. That is, investors may be able to access the national market in other ways. As a result, it may be a mistake to conclude that the market is segmented based on statutory investment restrictions.

We measure the degree of integration directly from the returns data. Our model nests the polar cases of complete integration and complete segmentation. The econometric method allows for the degree of integration to change through time. Our results indicate time-varying integration for a number of countries.

There are a number of possible extensions of our research. Our framework can be modified to allow for multiple sources of risk. An omitted risk factor could potentially mask itself through evidence of time-varying integration. One immediate modification, following Adler and Dumas (1983) and Dumas and Solnik (1995), involves the addition of foreign exchange risk. Indeed, strong assumptions (such as purchasing power parity) are needed in order to justify our basic model in equation (1) (see Stulz (1981b, 1993)).

Our modeling approach can be used to assess the effects of regulatory changes. It is possible to let the regime probabilities be functions of indicator variables that capture policy changes. For instance, Japan abolished many of its capital market restrictions in the 1980s (see Bonser-Neal, Brauer, Neal, and Wheatley (1990) and Gultekin, Gultekin, and Penati (1989)). A number of developing countries removed or relaxed restrictions on foreign equity ownership in the nineties (see Bekaert (1995) and Harvey (1993a)). However, we do not find overwhelming evidence pointing to increased integration (only four of the 12 countries have higher integration measures in the 1990s). Our framework will allow us to test directly whether these policy changes had a discernable affect on the degree of market integration and whether the cost of capital was altered. This research is currently being pursued in Bekaert and Harvey (1995b).

Finally, measuring the degree of financial market integration has implications beyond explaining why expected returns differ across different countries. There is a strong interest in development economics in models that relate capital market restrictions and the stage of financial market development to economic growth.

Economic growth is fundamentally linked to financial integration. A number of recent models show how improved risk sharing leads to higher economic growth.[18] Capital market integration provides the opportunity for better diversification. In a segmented economy, a consumer or a firm may only select low-risk low-expected return investments. With integrated mar-

---

[18] Examples are Levine (1991) and Saint-Paul (1992). Pagano (1993) presents a detailed review of the literature relating financial markets to economic growth.

kets, individuals shift to high-risk high-expected return projects because they are able to diversify their overall risk (see Obstfeld (1994)).

There is an expanding body of empirical work on the relation between capital market restrictions and economic growth. King and Levine (1993) detail a significant cross-sectional correlation between variables that proxy for both the depth of the financial sector and its development and economic growth. Atje and Jovanovic (1992) find significant correlations bewteen the ratio of stock market trading volume to GDP and economic growth. A problem with this empirical work, which is recognized by the authors, is that it is difficult to specify a set of variables that proxy for capital market restrictions (or capital market openness). Our article provides a new approach to assessing the degree of market integration. The empirical relation between integration and economic development is explored in Bekaert and Harvey (1995c).

Appendix

A. IFC Emerging Market Equity Indices

The International Finance Corporation (IFC) began calculating emerging market indices in 1981. The indices, known as the IFC Global (IFCG) Indices, do not take into consideration restrictions on foreign ownership. Recently, the IFC has introduced a second set of indices, the IFC Investable (IFCI) Indices. The IFCI Indices reflect restrictions on ownership limits. For example, if a firm had a market capitalization of U.S. $300 million and the national law restricts foreign ownership to 50 percent of any company, the IFCG uses the full $300 million as the market capitalization while the IFCI uses $150 million.

Since our article studies the integration of the emerging markets in world capital markets, we have chosen to use the IFCG. An additional reason for using the IFCG is the limited sample size of the IFCI (data begin in 1988). However, it is important to understand the restrictions in each market and the methodology used to construct the indices. The following description follows the International Finance Corporation (1993). (See Table AI.)

A.1. Selection Criteria

The IFC selects stocks for inclusion in the indices based on three criteria: size, liquidity, and industry. The indices include the largest and most actively traded stocks in each market, targeting 60 percent of total market capitalization at the end of each year. As a second objective, the index targets 60 percent of trading volume during the year. Size is measured by market capitalization and liquidity is measured by the total value of shares traded during the year.

Only stocks that are listed on one of the major exchanges in the emerging markets are included in the index. The index will not include stocks whose issuing company is headquartered in an emerging market but listed only on foreign markets.

Appendix Table AI

Market Weights in the IFC Indices at the End of March 1993

Total market capitalization is the number of shares multiplied by the end of March 1993 share value for each stock listed in 20 markets. The International Finance Corporation (IFC) creates value weighted indices of a smaller number of stocks within each country. The number of stocks included in each IFC index is also reported along with the market capitalization of the stocks included in the IFC index. Finally, we report the share that each country commands in the IFC emerging market composite index. The source of the data is IFC (1993).

Country	Total Market Capitalization (Millions US$)	Number of Stocks	Market Capitalization (Millions US$)	Weight in IFC Composite
Panel A: Latin America				
Argentina	19,101.8	30	14,994.8	2.9
Brazil	59,488.5	70	37,245.8	7.2
Chile	33,510.6	35	21,658.8	4.2
Colombia	6,571.0	20	4,156.1	0.8
Mexico	132,574.8	74	83,683.6	16.1
Venezuela	6,228.8	17	3,982.6	0.8
Panel B: East Asia				
Korea	105,929.0	134	71,016.7	13.7
Philippines	16,340.6	37	11,528.8	2.2
Taiwan	148,487.9	78	95,244.0	18.4
Panel C: South Asia				
India	59,793.1	108	29,987.8	5.8
Indonesia	14,385.0	41	9,469.1	1.8
Malaysia	100,142.6	66	68,153.6	13.1
Pakistan	7,198.9	64	4,607.5	0.9
Thialand	58,909.0	58	37,271.8	7.2
Panel D: Europe/Mideast/Africa				
Greece	9,928.9	36	6,304.7	1.2
Jordan	3,788.4	29	2,146.3	0.4
Nigeria	871.9	24	552.7	0.1
Portugal	9,988.2	38	7,255.3	1.4
Turkey	13,470.2	36	9,568.2	1.8
Zimbabwe	613.9	21	376.9	0.1
Panel E: IFC Regional Indices				
Composite	806,710.1	995	518,828.2	100.0
Latin America	257,475.4	246	165,721.7	31.9
Asia	511,187.1	586	327,299.3	63.1
Europe/Mideast/Africa	38,661.5	184	26,204.1	5.1

If many stocks meet the liquidity and size criteria, but only one or two are needed, IFC selects the stocks that represent industries that are not well represented in the IFC index.

In a few instances, particularly where multiple classes of stocks are common (e.g., Brazil and Mexico), IFC may include more than one class of stock for the same company even though they are not necessarily actively traded. The purpose is to give a balanced view of the capitalization of companies that have other classes of stock that are actively traded.

It is useful to compare and contrast the criteria used by Morgan Stanley Capital International (MSCI) (see Schmidt (1990)) and the IFC. In constructing the MSCI indices, 60 percent coverage of the total market capitalization of each market is also the first objective. In contrast to the IFC, there is no secondary objective regarding the volume of trading. The second MSCI criteria is that the companies included in the index replicate the industrial composition of the local market. In addition, the MSCI index tries to take a representative sample of large, medium, and small capitalization stocks (instead of just concentrating on the largest capitalization companies). MSCI uses liquidity as a consideration in choosing among the medium and small capitalization stocks. MSCI, like IFC, excludes nondomiciled companies and investment funds. MSCI excludes companies with restricted float due to dominant shareholders or cross-ownership. Similar to IFC, MSCI also publishes "Free" indices that exclude companies whose shares are not readily available to foreign investors.

A.2. Survivorship Bias and Time-Varying Inclusion Criteria

The IFC does not select stocks based on financial history or future expected performance. Nevertheless, any size or liquidity screen will tend to select stocks that have done well (or avoid poor performers). This is the case for all stock market indices. This selection criteria is not a problem if it is done on an ex ante basis. However, the IFC started their indices in 1981 and nine indices began in December 1975. This reconstruction induces an obvious survivorship bias. Harvey (1995) details the survivorship problem induced by the backtracking of the indices. He argues the survivorship problem is not that serious. In many countries, the very high return periods follow the lookback data in 1981.

Another issue focusses on time-varying criteria for including stocks in the indices. There is little publicly available information on how the original stocks were selected for index construction. However, from conversations with people that either worked at the World Bank, or still work at the World Bank, it is clear that the joint size, liquidity, and industry criteria were not used consistently through the years. Our conversations suggest that in 1981 size was the single criterion used in index construction.

A.3. Index Methodology

The IFC indices represent value-weighted portfolios of the stocks in each market. That is, each stock is weighted by its market capitalization in the same way that the Morgan Stanley Capital International (MSCI) country indices are formed (chained Paasche method).

Adjustments in the index divisor are initiated if new shares are issued or rights are declared. The change in the divisor neutralizes the effects of these two issues. The divisor will also change when a stock is added to or deleted from the index.

A.4. Currency Conversion

The IFC indices are calculated in local currencies as well as in U.S. dollars. For most markets, the indices use exchange rates taken from the *Wall Street Journal* or the *Financial Times*. When a multiple exchange rate system exists, the IFC uses the nearest equivalent "free market" rate or the rate that would apply to the repatriation of capital and income. In a few cases, the newspaper rates are inappropriate and the IFC uses rates provided by the IFC's correspondents in each market.

A.5. Price Information

The principal source of prices and changes in capitalization used for the IFC indices is a network of correspondents in each market, including local IFC brokers, investment banks, stock exchanges, and regulatory authorities.

When a stock is not traded on the date of the index, the last traded price is used. When a stock is traded on more than one local exchange, the price used by the IFC is taken from the exchange where the trading was most active.

Some markets, notably Thailand, maintain "Alien" boards to ensure that the total foreign ownership does not exceed a certain share of the total. The IFC has found that trading in stocks on the Alien board is generally thin and stocks often trade at different prices. The IFC asserts that price movements on the Alien board often lag behind those of the "Main" market. In the index construction, the IFC uses the Main Board prices. Additional analysis of the Thai market is presented in Bailey and Jagtiani (1994).

A.6. Index Revisions

Once a year, the individual component stocks are reviewed to see if the index meets the objective criteria. Additions and deletions are made as necessary. Although the target for the global indices is to attain 60 percent of market value, the actual coverage will vary. To ensure consistency, the IFC will not generally add or delete stocks unless the coverage of the global index drops below 50 percent or rises about 70 percent of the total market capitalization.

On a quarterly basis, the IFC will drop stocks that have been suspended, delisted, merged, dropped, or otherwise made irrelevant. Newly listed stocks that result from a merger or split of a stock already in the index will be added. The IFC may add a newly listed stock to the index between the regular quarterly revisions if it is unusually large. Such changes are announced one week prior to their actual inclusion in the indices.

REFERENCES

Adler, Michael, and Bernard Dumas, 1983, International portfolio selection and corporation finance: A synthesis, *Journal of Finance* 38, 925–984.

Atje, Raymond, and Boyan Javanovic, 1993, Stock markets and development, *European Economic Review* 37, 632–640.

Asiamoney, March 1994.

Baba, Yoshihisa, Robert F. Engle, Dennis F. Kraft, and Kenneth F. Kroner, 1989, Multivariate simultaneous generalized ARCH, Working paper, University of California, San Diego, California.

Bae, Kee-Hong, 1993, Time-variation in the price of risk and the international capital market structure, Unpublished dissertation, The Ohio State University.

Bailey, Warren, and Julapa Jagtiani, 1994, Foreign ownership restrictions and premiums for international investment: Some evidence from the Thai capital market, *Journal of Financial Economics* 36, 57–88.

Bekaert, Geert, 1995, Market integration and investment barriers in emerging equity markets, *World Bank Economic Review* 9, 75–107.

Bekaert, Geert, and Campbell R. Harvey, 1995a, Emerging equity market volatility, Working paper, Duke University and Stanford University.

———, 1995b, The cost of capital in emerging markets, Working notes, Duke University and Stanford University.

———, 1995c, Emerging capital markets and economic development, Working notes, Duke University and Stanford University.

Bekaert, Geert, and Robert Hodrick, 1992, Characterizing predictable components in excess returns on equity and foreign exchange markets, *Journal of Finance* 47, 467–509.

Black, Fischer, 1972, Capital market equilibrium with restricted borrowing, *Journal of Business* 45, 444–455.

Bollerslev, Tim, and Jeffrey M. Wooldridge, 1992, Quasi-maximum likelihood estimation and inference in dynamic models with time-varying covariance, *Econometric Reviews* 11, 143–172.

Bonser-Neal, Catherine, Gregory Brauer, Robert Neal, and Simon Wheatley, 1990, International investment restrictions and closed-end country fund prices, *Journal of Finance* 45, 523–548.

Campbell, John Y., 1987, Stock returns and the term structure, *Journal of Financial Economics* 18, 373–400.

Campbell, John Y., and Yasushi Hamao, 1992, Predictable bond and stock returns in the United States and Japan: A study of long-term capital market integration, *Journal of Finance* 47, 43–70.

Chan, K. C., G. Andrew Karolyi, and René Stulz, 1992, Global financial markets and the risk premium on U.S. equity, *Journal of Financial Economics* 32, 137–168.

Cho, Chinhyung, D., Cheol S. Eun, and Lemma W. Senbet, 1986, International arbitrage pricing theory: An empirical investigation, *Journal of Finance* 41, 313–330.

Cumby, Robert E., and Anya Khanthavit, 1992, A Markov switching model of market integration, Working paper, New York University.

Diebold, F. X., J.-H. Lee, and G. C. Weinbach, 1995, Regime switching with time-varying transition probabilities, in C. Hargreaves, Ed.: *Nonstationary Time Series Analysis and Cointegration* (Oxford University Press, London), Forthcoming.

Dumas, Bernard, 1994, A test of the international CAPM using business cycles indicators as instrumental variables, in Jeffrey Frankel, Ed.: *The Internationalization of Equity Markets* (University of Chicago Press, Chicago), pp. 23–50.

Dumas, Bernard, and Bruno Solnik, 1995, The world price of foreign exchange rate risk, *Journal of Finance*, 50, 445–479.

Engel, Charles, M., and Jeffrey A. Frankel, 1984, Do asset demand functions optimize over the mean and variance of real returns? A six currency test, *Journal of International Economics*, 17, 309–323.

Engle, Robert F., David, M. Lilien, and Russell P. Robbins, 1987, Estimating time varying risk premia in the term structure: The ARCH-M model, *Econometrica* 55, 391–407.

Errunza, Vihang R., and Etienne Losq, 1985, International asset pricing under mild segmentation: Theory and test, *Journal of Finance* 40, 105–124.

———, and Prasad Padmanabhan, 1992, Tests of integration, mild segmentation and segmentation hypotheses, *Journal of Banking and Finance* 16, 949–972.

Everitt, B. S., and O. J. Hand, 1981, *Finite Mixture Distributions* (London: Chapman and Hall).

Fama, Eugene F., and Kenneth R. French, 1989, Business conditions and the expected returns on stocks and bonds, *Journal of Financial Economics* 25, 23–50.

Ferson, Wayne E., and Campbell R. Harvey, 1993, The risk and predictability of international equity returns, *Review of Financial Studies* 6, 527–566.

———, 1994a, Sources of risk and expected returns in global equity markets, *Journal of Banking and Finance* 18, 775–803.

———, 1994b, An exploratory investigation of the fundamental determinants of national equity market returns, in Jeffrey Frankel, Ed.: *The Internationalization of Equity Markets*, (University of Chicago Press, Chicago, IL), 59–138.

Frankel, Jeffrey A., 1982, In search of the exchange risk premium: A six currency test assuming mean-variance optimization, *Journal of International Money and Finance* 1, 255–274.

Gibbons, Michael R., and Wayne E. Ferson, 1985, Tests of asset pricing models with changing expectations and an unobservable market portfolio, *Journal of Financial Economics* 14, 217–236.

Gray, Stephen F., 1995a, An analysis of conditional regime switching models, Working paper, Duke University.

———, 1995b, Modelling the conditional distribution of interest rates as a regime-switching process, Working paper, Duke University.

Ghysels, Eric, 1993, A time-series model with periodic stochastic regime switches, Working paper, University of Montréal.

Gultekin, N. Bulent, Mustafa N. Gultekin, and Alessandro Penati, 1989, Capital controls and international capital market segmentation: The evidence from the Japanese and American stock markets, *Journal of Finance* 44, 849–869.

Hamilton, J. D., 1989, A new approach of the economic analysis of nonstationary time series and the business cycle, *Econometrica* 57, 357–384.

———, 1990, Analysis of time series subject to changes in regime, *Journal of Econometrics* 45, 39–70.

Hansen, Lars P., and Robert J. Hodrick, 1983, Risk averse speculation in forward foreign exchange markets: An econometric analysis of linear models, in Jacob A. Frenkel, Ed.: *Exchange Rates and International Macroeconomics* (University of Chicago Press, Chicago), pp. 113–152.

Harvey, Campbell R., 1989, Time-varying conditional covariances in tests of asset pricing models, *Journal of Financial Economics* 24, 289–317.

———, 1991a, The world price of covariance risk, *Journal of Finance* 46, 111–157.

———, 1993a, Portfolio enhancement with emerging markets and conditioning information, in Stijn Claessens and Sudarshan Gooptu, Eds.: *Portfolio Investment in Developing Countries* (World Bank, Washington, D.C.), 110–144.

———, 1993b, Conditional asset allocation in emerging markets, Working paper, Duke University, Durham, N.C.

———, 1995, Predictable risk and returns in emerging markets, *Review of Financial Studies*, Forthcoming.

Harvey, Campbell R., Bruno H. Solnik, and Guofu Zhou, 1994, What determines expected international asset returns?, Working paper, Duke University, Durham, N.C.

International Finance Corporation, 1993, *IFC Index Methodology*, (World Bank, Washington, D.C.).

Jensen, Michael, 1969, Risk, the pricing of capital assets and the evaluation of portfolios, *Journal of Business* 42, 167–247.

King, Robert G., and Ross Levine, 1993, Finance, entrepreneurship, and growth: Theory and evidence, *Journal of Monetary Economics* 32, 513–542.

Kirby, Christopher M., 1994, A multivariate analysis of predictability in stock and bond returns, Working paper, University of Michigan, Ann Arbor, Mich.

Levine, Ross, 1991, Stock markets, growth and tax policy, *Journal of Finance* 46, 1445–1465.

Lintner, John, 1965, The valuation of risk assets and the selection of risky investments in stock portfolios and capital budgets, *Review of Economics and Statistics* 47, 13–37.

Merton, Robert C., 1980, On estimating the expected return on the market: An exploratory investigation, *Journal of Financial Economics* 8, 323–361.

Obstfeld, Maurice, 1994, Risk taking, global diversification, and growth, *American Economic Review* 84, 1310–1329.

Pagan, Adrian, 1984, Econometric issues in the analysis of regressions with generated regressors, *International Economic Review* 25, 221–247.

Pagano, Marco, 1993, Financial markets and growth: An overview, *European Economic Review* 37, 613–622.

Saint-Paul, G., 1992, Technological choice, financial markets and economic development, *European Economic Review* 36, 763–781.

Schmidt, Dana, 1990, *Morgan Stanley Capital International (MSCI) Indices* (Morgan Stanley, New York).

Sharpe, William, 1964, Capital asset prices: A theory of market equilibrium under conditions of risk, *Journal of Finance* 19, 425–442.

Solnik, Bruno, 1983, International arbitrage pricing theory, *Journal of Finance* 38, 449–457.

Stehle, Richard, 1977, An empirical test of the alternative hypotheses of national and international pricing of risky assets, *Journal of Finance* 32, 493–502.

Stulz, René, 1981a, On the effects of barriers to international investment, *Journal of Finance* 36, 923–934.

———, 1981b, A model of international asset pricing, *Journal of Financial Economics* 9, 383–406.

———, 1993, International portfolio choice and asset pricing: An integrative survey, Working paper, Ohio State University, Columbus, Oh.

Wheatley, Simon, 1988, Some tests of international equity integration, *Journal of Financial Economics* 21, 177–212.

White, Halbert, 1982, Maximum likelihood estimation of misspecified models, *Econometrica* 50, 1–26.

World Bank, 1993, *Emerging Stock Markets Factbook* (International Finance Corporation, Washington, D.C.).

Part II
Financial Effects of Market Integration

A
Liberalization and Returns

[6]

THE JOURNAL OF FINANCE • VOL. LV, NO. 2 • APRIL 2000

Foreign Speculators and Emerging Equity Markets

GEERT BEKAERT and CAMPBELL R. HARVEY*

ABSTRACT

We propose a cross-sectional time-series model to assess the impact of market liberalizations in emerging equity markets on the cost of capital, volatility, beta, and correlation with world market returns. Liberalizations are defined by regulatory changes, the introduction of depositary receipts and country funds, and structural breaks in equity capital flows to the emerging markets. We control for other economic events that might confound the impact of foreign speculators on local equity markets. Across a range of specifications, the cost of capital always decreases after a capital market liberalization with the effect varying between 5 and 75 basis points.

THROUGHOUT HISTORY AND IN MANY MARKET ECONOMIES, the speculator has been characterized as both a villain and a savior. Indeed, the reputation of the speculator generally depends on the country where he does business. In well-functioning advanced capital markets, such as the United States, the speculator is viewed as an integral part of the free-market system. In developing capital markets, the speculator, and in particular the international speculator, is looked upon with many reservations.

Recently, many so-called "emerging" markets have opened up their capital markets to foreign investors, creating an ideal laboratory for examining the impact of increased foreign portfolio investment in developing equity markets. Our main focus is the impact on expected equity returns—the cost of equity capital. However, we also examine the effects of increased foreign

* Bekaert is at Columbia University, Stanford University, and NBER; Harvey is at Duke University and NBER. This research was partially supported by the Davidson Institute at the University of Michigan. Bekaert acknowledges the support of a grant from the National Science Foundation. We have benefited from the comments of Stijn Claessens, Giorgio DeSantis, Bob Hodrick, Shinjun Liu, René Stulz (the editor), and seminar participants at the 1997 Conference on International Financial Markets at Georgia Tech, the International Monetary Fund, the University of Southern California, the University of California at Los Angeles Economics and Finance departments, Columbia University, the University of Limburg, the Stockholm School of Economics, the Swedish School of Economics, Tilburg University, the University of Virginia-Darden, the University of Maryland, the Wharton School, Yale University, Harvard Business School, the University of Miami, Barclays Global Investors in San Francisco, the 1997 European Finance Associate meetings in Vienna, the 1997 Western Finance Association meetings in San Diego, and the 1997 French Finance Association meetings in Grenoble. We have greatly benefited from the referee's comments. We appreciate the excellent research assistance of Rob Feldman, Han Hong, Fan Hu, Angela Ng, and especially Andrew Roper. We are grateful to Darius Miller for providing the ADR announcement dates.

investment activity and market integration on three other variables: volatility, the world beta, and the correlation between emerging markets and the
world market returns.

Excess volatility induced by foreign investors has often served as an argument in favor of stalling the liberalization process and is the topic of a
number of contemporaneous studies. Less is known about the effect of liberalization on emerging market correlations with the world market returns.
Recent evidence from country funds investing in emerging markets but priced
in the United States (Bailey and Lim (1992) and Bekaert and Urias (1996))
suggests that correlations may increase. If this finding is confirmed, it may
have an impact on the change we are likely to find in the cost of capital. A
reduction in the cost of capital is brought about by foreign investors bidding
up local prices in order to obtain the superior diversification benefits of
emerging market stocks. With higher correlations, these benefits are reduced and the corresponding price increase and cost of capital decrease is
smaller. Put together, evidence on changes in expected returns, volatility,
and correlations after capital market liberalizations may provide important
information which may help efforts to incorporate emerging markets into
global asset allocation models.

The outline of our paper is as follows. In Section I, we briefly survey the literature on the impact of speculative activity on price volatility and welfare,
focusing more specifically on the role of foreign speculators in emerging markets. We emphasize the *gradual* nature of the capital market integration process, identifying the event "increased foreign investment activity," with three
different indicators: the gradual introduction of American Depositary Receipts (ADRs) and country funds, the actual lifting of investment restrictions,
and the extent of U.S. capital flows into the emerging equity market.

Whereas our measures of conditional volatility, beta, and correlation build
on previous work, Section II presents a novel present value model, accommo-
dating time-varying expected returns, to motivate the use of dividend yields
as a measure of the cost of equity capital. Our work here is closely related to
that of Henry (2000) who measures the abnormal return to market liberalization in 12 emerging markets. Section III sets out the empirical framework, which
pools time-series and cross-sectional information to measure the economic impact of increased foreign investment activity while controlling for other factors that may affect local equity markets. Section IV reports the empirical results
on the costs of capital, in Section V we discuss the results for other variables,
and in Section VI we offer some concluding remarks.

I. The Role of Speculators in Emerging Markets

A. Speculation, Market Efficiency, and Volatility

Economic theory generally suggests that speculative activity enhances the
informational and allocational role of asset markets thereby making markets more efficient (see Grossman (1995) and Grossman and Stiglitz (1980)).
Foreign speculative activity in emerging markets can play a particularly

important role. First, the potential of market manipulation is acute in small emerging markets and liquidity is often poor. Although there are many policy initiatives that could increase liquidity and reduce the degree of collusion among large traders, there may not be a sufficient mass of domestic speculators to ensure market liquidity and efficiency. Second, opening the market to foreign speculators may increase the valuation of local companies, thereby reducing the cost of equity capital. The intuition is straightforward (see, e.g., Bekaert and Harvey (1995)). In segmented capital markets, the cost of equity capital is related to the local volatility of the particular market. In integrated capital markets, the cost of equity capital is related to the covariance with world market returns. Given that emerging economies have different industrial mixes and are less subject to macroeconomic shocks originating from developed economies, covariances with world factors are low (see Harvey (1995)). Since local market volatilities tend to be large, the cost of capital should decrease after capital market liberalizations.

In a more complex world, the magnitude and even the sign of the cost of capital effect is not a priori obvious. First, as Stulz (1999) indicates, the decrease in the equity risk premium depends critically on the diversification potential of the local market. In the context of our one-factor example, little effect should be expected when the local market is perfectly correlated with the world market. We incorporate this idea in one of our empirical specifications below. Second, though we believe risk premiums generally decrease (see also Subrahmanyam (1975)), there may be scenarios in which the real rate of interest may actually increase (see the examples in Obstfeld (1994), Basak (1996), and Basak and Cuoco (1998)).

The predictions for the effect of speculative activity on volatility are less clear cut. Moreover, there is no clear relation between volatility and market efficiency. In the models of Newbery (1987) and Ross (1989), for example, speculative activity increases volatility but is, at the same time, welfare improving. Correlations may increase because the discount rate becomes global or cash flows become more correlated but the magnitude of these effects is hard to predict.

A major problem in bringing theory to bear on our research here is our poor understanding of international portfolio choice. For example, in relatively open capital markets, we observe substantial cross-border flows but portfolios continue to display home-asset bias (see Tesar and Werner (1995a)). Therefore, we investigate empirically how the cost of capital, volatility, correlations, and betas are affected by foreign portfolio investors. To do so, we isolate cases in which the importance of foreign speculators in the local market increases.

B. Investing in Emerging Equities

B.1. Capital Market Liberalizations

Table I is based on the detailed chronology of capital market liberalizations for the 20 emerging markets in our sample presented in Bekaert and Harvey (1998) and summarized in Appendix B. Many liberalizations are

Table I
The Opening of Equity Markets in Emerging Countries

The official liberalization dates are based on the analysis in Bekaert and Harvey (1998). Appendices are available on the Internet that detail the ADR and country fund introduction dates. The estimate of the break point in cumulative net U.S. capital flows is obtained from the algorithm in Bai, Lumsdaine, and Stock (1998). The U.S. portfolio flows data are from the *U.S. Treasury Bulletin* and represent a fraction of the total portfolio flows to these countries. Market capitalizations are from the IFC. The cumulation of the capital flows takes into account the equity market returns in each country. n/a represents not available.

Country	Official Liberalization Date	First ADR Introduction	First Country Fund Introduction	Estimate of Increase in Net U.S. Capital Flows	Cumulative Net U.S. Flows to Market Cap Dec-95
Argentina	89.11	91.08	91.10	93.04	0.2181
Brazil	91.05	92.01	87.10	88.06	0.1114
Chile	92.01	90.03	89.09	88.01	0.0745
Colombia	91.02	92.12	92.05	93.08	0.0400
Greece	87.12	88.08	88.09	86.12	0.0357
India	92.11	92.02	86.06	93.04	0.0114
Indonesia	89.09	91.04	89.01	93.06	0.0669
Jordan	95.12	n/a	n/a	n/a	n/a
Korea	92.01	90.11	84.08	93.03	0.0480
Malaysia	88.12	92.08	87.12	92.04	0.0159
Mexico	89.05	89.01	81.06	90.05	0.1897
Nigeria	95.08	n/a	n/a	n/a	n/a
Pakistan	91.02	n/a	91.07	93.04	0.0123
Philippines	91.06	91.03	87.05	90.01	0.1232
Portugal	86.07	90.06	87.08	94.08	0.0637
Taiwan	91.01	91.12	86.05	92.08	0.0021
Thailand	87.09	91.01	85.07	88.07	0.0184
Turkey	89.08	90.07	89.12	89.12	0.0442
Venezuela	90.01	91.08	n/a	94.02	0.0005
Zimbabwe	93.06	n/a	n/a	n/a	n/a

clustered in the late 1980s or early 1990s. Although such an event may be considered a prime candidate for testing the impact of increased foreign speculative activity, there are a number of factors that could confound this experiment. First, the investment restrictions may not have been binding. Second, liberalizations can take many different forms—relaxing currency controls, reducing foreign ownership restrictions, etc.,—and not all market reforms take place at the same time. This makes the choice of the "liberalization date" in Table I open to debate. Third, despite the persistence of various restrictions on foreign investors, several emerging markets have been open to some form of foreign investment for a surprisingly long time. Two examples of such indirect participation of foreign speculators in local stock markets are Country Funds and American Depositary Receipts (ADRs). Although countries might enact official liberalizations of their capital markets, foreign investors still face many market imperfections, such as poor liquidity. Country Funds and ADRs provide the advantage of trading in transparent and liquid markets in New York and London. We review the theoretical and empirical evidence on the effects of these external financing vehicles in Sections I.B.2 and I.B.3. Fourth, a liberalization may not be enough to induce foreign investors to actually invest in the country, either because of other concerns or because of home bias. Therefore, we also use information from capital flows, which we discuss in Section I.B.4.

B.2. Country Funds

A closed-end country fund is an investment company that invests in a portfolio of assets in a foreign country (e.g., an emerging market) and issues a fixed number of shares domestically (e.g., in the United States). Each fund provides two distinct market-determined prices: the country fund's share price quoted on the market where it trades, and its net asset value determined by the prices of the underlying shares traded on the foreign market. Closed-end mutual funds were the original vehicles for foreign investment in emerging financial markets. For example, until the late 1980s the closed-end Mexico Fund was the only way U.S. investors could invest in the Mexican market. The Korea Fund partially opened up the Korean equity market to foreign investors in 1984, long before the capital market liberalizations of 1991. Table I presents the dates of the introduction of the first country fund for our sample of emerging markets.

Errunza, Senbet, and Hogan (1998) theoretically show that the introduction of country funds drives up the prices of local companies and reduces the cost of capital. The country fund essentially renders the local market partially integrated with global markets. These results hold even though the typical size of a country fund is very small relative to the total market capitalization of the emerging market. Using an event-study of returns around country fund launchings, Tandon (1997) presents empirical evidence that seems to support these claims.

B.3. American Depositary Receipts

American Depositary Receipts are rights to foreign shares that trade in dollars on a U.S. exchange or over-the-counter. Table I details the earliest ADR introduction for the emerging markets in our sample. ADRs overcome many of the investment restrictions, transaction costs, and informational problems associated with investing in foreign securities. For example, since ADRs are treated as U.S. securities in most legal situations, they enable mutual funds, pension funds, and other U.S. institutions to hold securities that are fungible with foreign shares.

The effects of ADRs on local stock market prices are theoretically similar to those of country funds (see Urias (1994)). Importantly, local stocks that are correlated with the newly cross-listed security respond as well, even though they are not themselves cross-listed. That is, there are *spill-over effects*. A variety of empirical studies[1] find mixed results, but mostly the local price effect of ADR introductions is positive.

B.4. Capital Flows

Arguably, the best measure of the foreign presence in an emerging market is the percentage of stocks held by foreign investors. However, the only available data are U.S. capital flows to emerging markets since 1985. These data are published monthly in the U.S. *Treasury Bulletin*.[2]

We accumulate the capital flows to obtain an approximate measure of the ratio of U.S. ownership to market capitalization. The accumulation takes into account the local market equity appreciation realized by the U.S. investor. That is, the dollar position of U.S. investors in emerging market i is

$$\text{Own}_{i,t} = \text{Flow}_{i,t} + \text{Own}_{i,t-1}(1 + R_{i,t}),$$

where $\text{Flow}_{i,t}$ is the net capital flow in period t and $R_{i,t}$ is the market i return in U.S. dollar terms from the IFC. The last column in Table I reports the U.S. percentage ownership at the end of 1995, which is largest in Mexico and Argentina.

These data are not without problems. First, although for most countries portfolio flows were zero before 1985, for others, not knowing the initial foreign ownership (in 1985) makes the resulting estimates hard to interpret. Second, it may be the case that foreigners hold portfolios different from the IFC index. Kang and Stulz (1997) show that foreign investors are more likely to invest in securities that are large and well known. The IFC indexes pos-

---

[1] See Foerster and Karolyi (1999), Miller (1999), the survey in Karolyi (1998), and Domowitz, Glen, and Madhavan (1997, 1998) for studies at the individual firm level and see Bekaert (1995) for a study at the market level.

[2] Table CM-V-4 reports on a monthly basis foreigners' gross purchases of foreign stocks (U.S. sales, column 7) and foreigners' gross sales of foreign stocks (U.S. purchases, column 14). See Tesar and Werner (1995b) for an early analysis and see Hamao and Mei (1997) for a study of the effects of foreign investment on Japanese equity pricing.

sess some advantage here over more comprehensive local indexes because of the IFC's focus on large, relatively liquid securities. Third, and perhaps most importantly, U.S. investors may invest in emerging markets through third countries, like the U.K. Hence, the large flows to the U.K. could partially reflect emerging market investment that we are unable to track. Fourth, the relation between the cost of capital and foreign ownership may be non-linear. That is, stocks will be priced differently when foreigners become the marginal investors. It is not clear at what level of foreign ownership this occurs.

Our approach is to test for a structural break in the U.S. ownership series to identify when the foreign investors' presence in the market increases significantly. We employ the endogenous break point tests detailed in Bai, Lumsdaine, and Stock (1998). Briefly, the test searches for a break in the mean within the context of an autoregressive model for the ownership series. Apart from a structural break test, the procedure yields a break date with a 90 percent confidence interval.[3] We report the results in the fourth column of Table I.

II. Measuring the Cost of Capital

The cost of capital is notoriously difficult to measure. The problems are compounded in our setting, since we believe that the cost of capital changes when markets integrate with world capital markets and that the process of integration is gradual. In such an environment, it is very difficult to use average returns to measure changes in the cost of capital. However, a change in the marginal investor and the different valuation it implies should have discrete effects on the price level of stocks (see also Korajczyk (1996) for similar arguments). Hence, it is likely that a technique exploiting information in price levels may be more powerful. Whereas Henry (2000), in effect, attempts to measure the discrete price change directly by estimating the abnormal return during the liberalization period, we use aggregate dividend yields to measure cost of capital changes.

Why dividend yields? First, shocks to prices should dominate its variation over time. Second, the dividend yield is intricately linked to the cost of capital in many asset pricing models, as we demonstrate below. Third, the dividend yield is directly measurable—that is, it need not be preestimated—and is a stationary random variable.[4] That is, in most rational expectations models, a transversality condition ensures that the price-dividend ratios (and hence the dividend yields) are stationary. The capital market liberalization process can be viewed as a structural break that renders dividend yields nonstationary over the full sample. Our empirical approach only requires

---

[3] We thank Robin Lumsdaine for the use of her program.

[4] With emerging markets, the dividend yield calculation is not straightforward. In our cost of capital regressions, we use the dividend yields provided by the IFC which are a 12-month moving average of dividends divided by the current price level. However, in high inflation countries, one can make the case that an average of the last 12 months' dividend yields is a more appropriate measure, since this assumes past dividends are reinvested in the stock market. We use this alternative dividend specification as one of our local instrumental variables.

them to be stationary before and after the liberalization.[5] In the United States, dividend yields have recently displayed a downward trend that is often partially ascribed to the marked increase in share repurchases, constituting an alternative means of dispensing cash to shareholders. Such repurchases are minor or entirely absent in emerging markets.[6]

A. *Dividend Yields versus Average Returns as a Cost of Capital Measure*

Consider first a simple example. Assume rational expectations and a discounted dividend model for the stock price, P_t:

$$P_t = E_t \left[\sum_{i=1}^{\infty} \delta_{t+i}^i D_{t+i} \right], \tag{1}$$

where D_t are the dividends and δ_t is the discount factor, and where the usual transversality condition holds. Let

$$Y_t^x = \begin{cases} 0, & \text{before liberalization;} \\ 1, & \text{after liberalization.} \end{cases}$$

The x superscript indicates different measures of liberalization (see below). We further assume that the liberalization is a one-time, unexpected event. When the market is segmented, the required rate of return is constant and equal to r. When the market opens up, the required rate of return drops to $\bar{r}$. We can represent this simple model for expected returns as

$$\delta_t = \frac{1}{1 + r - \eta Y_t^x}, \tag{2}$$

where $\eta = r - \bar{r}$, the drop in the cost of capital. Under this set of assumptions, the relation between the change in the dividend yield $\bar{D}_t/\bar{P}_t - D_t/P_t$ and the change in the cost of capital η depends on the dividend process.

In the standard Gordon model, which assumes that $E_t D_{t+i} = (1+g)E_t D_{t-1+i}$, this relation is virtually one to one. It is straightforward to show that

$$\eta = (1+g)\frac{D_t}{P_t} - (1+\bar{g})\frac{\bar{D}_t}{\bar{P}_t} + g - \bar{g}. \tag{3}$$

---

[5] This break complicates the interpretation of the notoriously powerless standard unit root and stationarity tests applied to dividend yields. This is especially the case for emerging markets which have short samples to begin with. A whole battery of tests yields the typical conclusion that it is about equally hard to reject the null of a unit root as to reject the null of stationarity. A Bayesian unit root test (Sims and Uhlig (1991)) overwhelmingly rejects the presence of a unit root in emerging market dividend yields.

[6] We searched the IFC database for negative changes in shares outstanding. Most of the negative numbers were traced to rights issues that were not fully subscribed. There is little evidence of share repurchases in emerging markets. Indeed, it is not uncommon for repurchases to be illegal in many emerging markets.

If the growth rate of dividends is not affected by the capital market liberalization, a regression of D_t/P_t onto Y_t^x yields $\eta/(1 + g)$. Hence, the slope coefficient provides a slight underestimate of the true response of the cost of capital.

The Gordon model is not a realistic model for stock price determination but its main intuition remains valid with more general models. Consider the following present value model. Dividend growth follows an autoregressive process with homoskedastic innovations:

$$\Delta d_t = \mu(1 - \rho) + \rho\Delta d_{t-1} + \epsilon_t$$

$$E_{t-1}[\epsilon_t^2] = \sigma_\epsilon^2, \tag{4}$$

where $d_t = \ell n(D_t)$ and $\epsilon_t \sim N(0, \sigma_\epsilon^2)$. This process for dividend growth is not entirely realistic, because there may be seasonal patterns in dividend growth rates and the innovations may be heteroskedastic (see Bollerslev and Hodrick (1995)). Nevertheless, a more general model in the log-linear class has implications similar to the model analyzed here. Moreover, we allow for time-varying log-discount rates, $\delta_t = \exp(-r_t)$ and assume that the continuously compounded expected return follows an autoregressive process:

$$r_t = q(1 - \phi) + \phi r_{t-1} + \eta_t$$

$$E_{t-1}[\eta_t^2] = \sigma_\eta^2 \tag{5}$$

and $\eta_t \sim N(0, \sigma_\eta^2)$. We also assume that η_t and ϵ_t are uncorrelated. This present value model bears some resemblance to the setup of Campbell and Shiller (1988) but we provide closed-form solutions for the price-dividend ratio. Although the current specification is quite simple, our solution technique would go through in the case of correlated residuals or a square root process for r_t (see Bekaert and Grenadier (1999) for more complex models in this framework).

Starting from

$$\frac{P_t}{D_t} = E_t\left[\sum_{i=1}^{\infty}\exp\left(\sum_{j=1}^{i} - r_{t+j-1} + \Delta d_{t+j}\right)\right], \tag{6}$$

Appendix A shows by induction

$$\frac{P_t}{D_t} = \sum_{i=1}^{\infty}\exp(a_i + b_i\,\Delta d_t + c_i\,r_t), \tag{7}$$

where

$$a_{i+1} = a_i + \bar{\mu}(1 + b_i) + \frac{\sigma_\epsilon^2}{2}(1 + b_i)^2 + c_i \bar{q} + \frac{\sigma_\eta^2}{2} c_i^2$$

$$b_{i+1} = \rho(1 + b_i) \tag{8}$$

$$c_{i+1} = -1 + \phi c_i,$$

and $\bar{\mu} = \mu(1 - \rho)$; $\bar{q} = q(1 - \phi)$ and $a_0 = b_0 = c_0 = 0$. The expressions for $\{a_{i+1}, b_{i+1}, c_{i+1}\}$ are Ricatti difference equations, which, for our simple specification, have closed-form solutions as a function of the model parameters:

$$a_{i+1} = i\left(\bar{\mu} + \frac{\sigma_\epsilon^2}{2}\right) + \sum_{j=1}^{i}\left[(\bar{\mu} + \sigma_\epsilon^2) + \frac{\sigma_\epsilon^2}{2}b_j\right]b_j + \sum_{j=1}^{i}\left(\bar{q} + \frac{\sigma_\eta^2}{2}c_j\right)c_j$$

$$b_{i+1} = \rho\,\frac{1 - \rho^{i+1}}{1 - \rho} \tag{9}$$

$$c_{i+1} = -\frac{1 - \phi^{i+1}}{1 - \phi}.$$

Hence, the price-dividend ratio at each point in time is a function of the two state variables r_t and Δd_t. In the constant expected returns case, the price-dividend ratio only depends on the current dividend growth rate (see Appendix A for more details). Returns are computed as

$$R_{t+1} = \exp(\Delta d_{t+1})\frac{D_t}{P_t}\left[1 + \frac{P_{t+1}}{D_{t+1}}\right]. \tag{10}$$

This simple model fits the data very well.[7] We calibrate the model parameters to annual U.S. data on real dividend growth, dividend yields, and real stock returns for the S&P 500. Appendix A reveals a close match with the first three moments of these series. For example, our model generates a standard deviation of 22.9 percent for real stock returns (20.0 percent in the data) and an average dividend yield of 5.0 percent (4.4 percent in the data).

Is the change in the dividend yield still a good proxy for the change in the cost of capital after a market liberalization? When expected returns are varying through time, dividend yields forecast both future dividend changes and future returns. Time variation in expected returns may therefore induce changes in dividend yields that do not reflect a change in the long-term cost

---

[7] This may surprise readers familiar with the excess volatility literature. The key feature that improves performance is the assumption of a unit root in the dividend process (see Kleidon (1986) and Cochrane (1992)).

of capital brought about by market integration. Such change is nevertheless likely to be near permanent and to have a larger effect on dividend yields than a transitory change in expected returns. Ideally, we would introduce a variable in our regressions that controls for time-variation in expected returns. The fact that this time-variation may be tracked by different variables before versus after liberalization (local versus global information variables) complicates this task. Nevertheless, since the change in the cost of capital induced by market integration is near permanent, investigating dividend yields is again superior to investigating returns.

What makes dividend yields superior in small samples is their lack of variability relative to returns. It is difficult to illustrate this superiority analytically given the persistence in dividend yields and returns. In Appendix A, we describe a Monte Carlo experiment that illustrates the relative performance of the two measures of cost of capital changes (average returns before and after the break versus changes in dividend yields) in the context of the present value model. We simulate samples of 40 data points (years) with the cost of capital (as measured by q) falling by two percent after 20 years. The results can be summarized as follows:

1. The distribution of the changes in average simple returns is so spread out that there is a larger than 10 percent probability one concludes that the cost of capital increased by more than five percent although it actually dropped by 2.19 percent in the population.[8] Dividend yields virtually always decrease.

2. When we investigate experiments where average returns just before liberalization are unusually high or low, the return measure is severely biased, whereas the dividend yield shows very little bias. This suggests that when there is endogeneity bias (for example, governments choosing to liberalize when it appears most advantageous to them, such as in times of depressed stock prices), the dividend yield measure is robust but the average return measure is not.

3. Cross-sectional pooling dramatically improves the performance of both the return and dividend yield measures, making the dividend yield measure extremely accurate.

B. Caveats

B.1. Growth Opportunities versus Cost of Capital Changes

Despite the gain in accuracy that the use of dividend yields brings, their use also creates some potential interpretation problems. First, the change in the dividend yield may overestimate the cost of capital because of its link to economic growth. A liberalization may enhance the growth prospects for a country (see Obstfeld (1994)), leading to increased prices. The Monte Carlo experiment described in Appendix A considers a case where in

---

[8] The change in expected return is computed from $E[\exp(r_t)] = \exp(q + \frac{1}{2}[\sigma_\eta^2/(1 - \phi^2)])$.

addition to a two percent reduction in the cost of capital, the permanent growth rate of dividends increases by one percent after a liberalization (see Appendix A, Table AII, Panels A and C, experiment 2). The dividend yield now drops by approximately 3.25 percent, of which 2.19 percent is due to a change in the cost of capital and the remainder is due to the change in the dividend growth rate. Hence, a decrease in the dividend yield may reflect a lower cost of capital or better growth opportunities. It is very hard to disentangle these two effects but we devote considerable attention to this problem.

First, in our cross-sectional analysis below, we add control variables that can pick up variation in D_t/P_t that is not accounted for by changes in the cost of capital. If these variables are correlated with better growth opportunities, they may alleviate the problem. For example, if the liberalization is accompanied by macroeconomic reforms and trade liberalization, the resulting increase in the growth potential of the country may be controlled for by a variable such as exports plus imports as a fraction of GDP or by country risk variables. Henry (2000) shows that trade and financial liberalization often are clustered in time and attempts to disentangle their effects on equity prices.

Second, following Henry (2000), we also use excess returns as the dependent variable in our regression analysis. When dividend yields drop by a large amount but excess returns do not, the dividend yield change is likely driven by an improvement in growth opportunities. Nevertheless, Section B of Appendix A shows that it remains the case that increases in average returns often are still consistent with a population decrease in the cost of capital.

Third, our experiments generally confirm that the response of dividend yields to cost of capital changes is indeed near linear (see Appendix A). Hence, we can simply attempt to "measure" the change in growth opportunities (for example, by reporting increased long-run GDP growth) and subtract it from the total dividend yield change to estimate the change in the cost of capital. We deliver a number of statistics on changes in growth opportunities after liberalizations in Section IV.A.5 below.

Fourth, since the linearity of dividend yield responses may not be general if other structural parameters change (e.g., dividend growth or return volatility), we also provide a calibration exercise of our structural model before and after liberalization, which yields direct estimates of changes in expected returns and dividend growth for an "average" emerging market (see Section C of Appendix A).

B.2. Corporate Finance Issues

Corporate finance theory also suggests that dividend yields may decrease for reasons other than a decrease in the cost of capital. If emerging market firms truly enjoy better growth opportunities after liberalizations, they may choose to distribute fewer dividends and invest more. Henry (1999) documents increased aggregate investment after financial market liberalizations. Of course, this increase may also be due to decreases in the cost of capital.

B.3. Other Caveats

Our analysis so far assumes there is one unexpected liberalization. When liberalizations are anticipated, prices adjust before the actual liberalization occurs. If some uncertainty remains about the liberalization, a positive price movement may still occur on the actual date. Since returns are likely to be positive in the period between anticipation and actual liberalization, expected liberalizations are another reason to be wary of the use of returns for testing the cost of capital effect. We attempt to take anticipated liberalizations into account in our measurement of the liberalization variable Y_t^x. One of our measures also reflects the gradual nature of capital market liberalizations.

Finally, emerging markets may be inefficient and illiquid and the arrival of foreign investors may enhance efficiency and liquidity, thereby reducing the cost of equity capital. We include control variables that measure stock market development which may partially capture this indirect liberalization effect.

III. Econometric Methodology

A. Defining the Liberalization Variables

We introduce two liberalization dummies, one based on the capital market liberalization dates and the other based on the capital flow break points in Table I. We split our sample into four parts: PRE (36 to seven months prior to liberalization), DURING (six months prior to three months after liberalization), POST (four months after liberalization to 34 months postliberalization), and AFTER (35 months after liberalization to the end of the sample). The PRE and POST periods are symmetric in duration. When liberalizations are preannounced or anticipated by market participants, expected returns may change some time before the liberalization date. By excluding nine months around the liberalization date, our procedure is hopefully robust to small errors in the dating of the liberalization. Moreover, we check the sensitivity of our results to the length and structure of the DURING window.

Our other measure uses launching data on ADRs and country funds to construct three indexes. First, $A_{t,i}$ counts the number of ADR issues in the United States or the U.K. for country i over time. Hence, for some countries this index may equal the zero vector. Second, $CF_{t,i}$ similarly "counts" the country fund launchings. Finally, $L_{t,i} = A_{t,i} + CF_{t,i}$. When attempting to measure how the cost of capital is affected by changes in these indexes, we face a number of immediate technical problems.

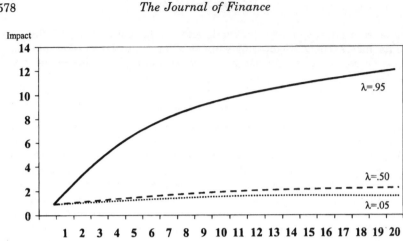

Figure 1. The decreasing impact of ADR and Country Fund launchings. The impact function is $(1 - \lambda^x)/(1 - \lambda)$ where x goes from 1 to 20. The size of λ determines how fast the additional impact of further launchings decline. For low λs, there is little effect of additional launchings.

First, the effect of the very first ADR and/or country fund is likely to be much larger than that of further ADR issues and/or country funds launchings. This is suggested by the theoretical analyses mentioned above and makes sense at an intuitive level. To accommodate that possibility, we introduce the variable

$$Y_t^x = \frac{1 - \lambda^{x_t}}{1 - \lambda}, \quad \text{for } x = A, \, CF, \text{ or } L, \tag{11}$$

where $0 < \lambda < 1$. The size of λ determines how fast the additional impact of further launchings declines. Figure 1 shows what happens for three different λs assuming the index goes from 1 to 20 continuously (in reality, Y_t^x will be a step function). As can be seen, for very low λs, the additional issues generate almost no additional effect.

Second, as indicated above, it is important to account for rational expectations of the market participants. Fortunately, for some ADRs, we have the actual announcement dates, using information provided by Miller (1999),[9]

---

[9] When announcement dates are unavailable, a proxy is used. For ADRs listed on the major stock exchanges (such as the NYSE, Nasdaq, and AMEX), a four-month period prior to the actual initial public offering (IPO) date is used; for OTC ADRs, a one-month period prior to the IPO is used; and for 144A ADRs, a two-month period prior to the IPO period is used. These are estimated from median announcement leads on the ADRs for which we have both announcement and listing dates.

but we only have the launching dates for the country funds. However, in earlier work, we found little impact on our results after introducing an announcement lead of three months for the country funds.

Expectations of future liberalizations may be partially captured by adjusting λ. For example, a second ADR issue would produce a reduction in the cost of capital by $\eta\lambda$, where $\lambda \leq 1$. However, it seems natural that ADR issues trigger expectations of further ADR issues and market openings. This implies that the jump on the liberalization date may be higher and λ smaller if expectational effects play an important role.[10]

More generally, if such expectation effects are important, what matters is the first signal of liberalization. This may occur in the form of a country fund, ADR, or a large-scale liberalization. Our final liberalization variable splits up the sample into four parts as was done for the capital market liberalization dummy. However, the date used is the date of the first sign of openness through whatever form.

B. Econometric Framework

Denote the variable of interest by Z_t^i, so $Z_t^i = D_t^i/P_t^i$ (dividend yield) or $Z_t^i = \ell n(P_t^i/P_{t-1}^i)$ (including dividends) less the U.S. Treasury bill rate (excess returns measure). Later we use the same model for conditional volatilities, correlations, and betas as the dependent variables. Our general model is

$$Z_t^i = \alpha^i + \beta' \mathbf{W}_t^i + \gamma Y_t^{x^i} + \epsilon_t^i$$

$$\epsilon_t^i = \rho^i \epsilon_{t-1}^i + u_t^i. \tag{12}$$

This model pools time-series and cross-sectional information and allows us to examine all observations simultaneously. The intercept specification allows for fixed effects. Fixed effects may capture cross-sectional differences in dividend yields due to differential tax regimes, for example. The set of variables that control for variation in Z_t^i, not accounted for by liberalizations, $\mathbf{W}_t^i$, is detailed below.

Notice that the liberalization variable is constrained to have the same slope coefficient, γ, across countries. This greatly enhances the power of our tests. In a sense, we measure the average impact of a market liberalization controlling for other variables, in the spirit of the event study methodology in finance. An alternative would be to write down the process for Z_t^i, assume that all parameters change after the liberalization, and test whether the parameter change is significant. Given the noise in the data, this approach is unlikely to be fruitful. Of course, there are reasons to expect that γ is not equal across countries. For example, the price response of a liberalization

---

[10] Another potential limitation is that we do not have data on the market capitalizations of the ADRs. It is possible that the first issue is "small" and relatively unimportant.

may depend on the nature of the existing restrictions or the size of the ADR or country fund. Some of these effects are controlled for by variables in $\mathbf{W}_t^i$ but not all. Underlying our approach is the view that the dominant effect of a market opening—a different marginal investor driving up the price— should be similar across countries. Hence, cross-sectional information effectively circumvents the peso-type problem that we only have one liberalization per country. It also allows us to make predictions about the likely effect of a capital market liberalization for countries that are as yet closed to international investors.

We conduct two experiments in which the liberalization variable is scaled by a country-specific variable so that country-specific responses are allowed for. The first variable is a correlation index, computed as $\ell n[2 - \rho^{\mathrm{pre}}]/\ell n[3]$, where ρ^{pre} is the correlation between the local excess return and the world market excess return before the liberalization. Consequently, whereas we still estimate a country invariant γ, the liberalization effect is country-specific and increases the lower is the correlation with the world market before the liberalization. In particular, the effect is zero if the preliberalization correlation is perfect and γ if the preliberalization correlation is -1. In another experiment, we weigh the dummies by the postliberalization five-year average value of foreign ownership in the case of the "Official Liberalizations" and "First Sign" measures and by the change in the five-year average of foreign ownership post- versus preliberalization for the capital flow break regressions. If the extent of foreign ownership significantly alters the cost of capital effect, γ ought to be large in such a regression.

Finally, in a previous version of the paper, we checked the robustness of our results to country-specific liberalization effects. To maintain power, we estimated one country at a time. That is, in the first regression, there was a country-specific coefficient for Argentina but the liberalization effect was restricted to be the same for the other countries. We found that the country-specific coefficients were rarely significant and generally insignificantly different from the overall coefficient.

C. *Estimation Issues*

We perform generalized least squares accounting for groupwise (country-by-country) heteroskedasticity, with a Prais–Winsten correction for serial correlation since it is unlikely that our control variables capture all serial correlation in dividend yields (and similarly in volatility below). We do not correct for potential endogeneity problems. If the government liberalizes when it is most needed (the cost of capital is temporarily high), policy endogeneity makes our estimates upper bounds on the true response. We also do not correct for correlation across residuals of different countries. First, given the low correlations between emerging market returns, it is unlikely that we will gain much efficiency by doing so. Second, it is technically nontrivial since the number of observations differs across countries.

D. Control Variables

The control variables generally fall into four categories: asset concentration, stock market development/economic integration, microstructure effects, and finally macroeconomic influences and political risk.

The asset concentration category includes the number of stocks in each of the country indexes followed by the International Finance Corporation (IFC). We also investigate a modified Herfindahl index of concentration. This index ranges from zero (equal market capitalization) to one (one dominant firm).

The stock market development/economic integration category includes two macroeconomic measures and one financial measure. The macroeconomic variables are the capitalization of the stock market relative to the country's GDP and the size of the trade sector (exports plus imports) relative to GDP. Our financial variable is the cross-sectional standard deviation of the stock returns within each index (at every month). As an economy becomes more developed and the stock market more mature, there is often less reliance on one particular sector (the correlation between stocks decreases), which increases the cross-sectional standard deviation.

We use cross-sectional standard deviation also as our main microstructure variable since other data, such as turnover and the number of stocks traded, are only available for a portion of the sample. This variable potentially wears two hats. In the model of Ross (1989), it measures the amount of information being revealed about the stocks traded in a particular country. However, as indicated above, it may also potentially reveal information about the diversity of the industrial sector. To account for these two interpretations in the volatility, correlation, and beta models, we also allow for the cross-sectional standard deviation to interact with the relative level of market development measured by the market capitalization to GDP ratio minus its cross-sectional mean. If $MC_t^i/GDP_t < \overline{(MC_t/GDP_t)}$ and the regression coefficient on the interaction variable is positive, then an increased cross-sectional standard deviation negatively affects market volatility. If $MC_t^i/GDP_t > \overline{(MC_t/GDP_t)}$, then the derivative of volatility with respect to the cross-sectional standard deviation is positive, which is what is predicted by the information flow model of Ross.

The final variables are linked to the condition of the macroeconomy. We examine the standard deviation of exchange rate changes as well as the average inflation rates. We also include a variable designed to proxy for political risk: the Institutional Investor country credit rating. Erb, Harvey and Viskanta (1996b) find that the Institutional Investor measure has high correlation with more direct measures of political risk that are available over shorter periods.

Table II presents country specific means of all the variables that we examine as well as some characteristics of the cross-sectional distribution of these variables. The large outliers in the inflation rates for Argentina and Brazil motivate a log transformation of the inflation data. It is also interesting to note the skewed nature of the market capitalization to GDP dis-

Table II
Summary Statistics

Sample averages for various variables are reported for each country. The bottom panel reports characteristics of the cross-sectional distribution using the data for all countries and all of the periods simultaneously. Volatility is the monthly standard deviation. Fitted volatility and correlations from the models are discussed in Bekaert and Harvey (1997). The number of companies in the index refers to the International Finance Corporation global indexes. The concentration ratio is a modified Herfindahl index based on market capitalization. The cross-sectional standard deviation is the standard deviation of the individual stock returns in the index at each month in time. FX volatility is a rolling three-year standard deviation of exchange rate versus U.S. dollar changes. Country credit rating is from the Institutional Investor's semiannual survey. The sample period depends on the country but ranges from January 1976 to December 1995. Unless mentioned, all data are from the IFC.

	Dividend Yield (annual)	Fitted Volatility (monthly)	Fitted Correlation	Market Capitalization to GDP	Inflation Rate (annual)	Number of Companies in Index	Concentration Ratio	Cross-Sectional Standard Deviation	FX Volatility (monthly)	Exports + Imports to GDP	Country Credit Rating (0–100 scale)
Argentina	1.53	0.277	0.122	0.034	579.28	25.0	0.250	0.199	0.220	0.152	32.4
Brazil	5.55	0.182	0.076	0.073	856.98	40.9	0.253	0.209	0.092	0.173	35.7
Chile	5.10	0.096	0.129	0.344	19.79	28.3	0.223	0.117	0.031	0.546	40.5
Colombia	4.06	0.077	0.016	0.102	25.97	21.4	0.195	0.119	0.016	0.336	38.7
Greece	6.42	0.099	0.142	0.064	17.94	20.6	0.386	0.097	0.033	0.480	51.6
India	2.40	0.081	−0.014	0.067	9.53	52.9	0.180	0.095	0.020	0.165	46.2
Indonesia	1.57	0.162	0.259	0.126	9.10	45.7	0.179	0.107	0.004	0.514	51.5
Jordan	3.70	0.047	0.173	0.349	6.31	21.2	0.534	0.067	0.019	1.223	31.0
Korean	3.51	0.084	0.139	0.153	7.98	60.7	0.184	0.092	0.011	0.672	63.1
Malaysia	1.95	0.063	0.481	1.157	3.60	71.2	0.189	0.091	0.012	1.569	61.6
Mexico	4.45	0.120	0.202	0.103	50.30	42.1	0.202	0.153	0.065	0.289	43.6
Nigeria	7.86	0.326	−0.030	0.035	45.00	23.1	0.176	0.094	0.183	0.519	18.9
Pakistan	4.10	0.090	0.053	0.085	10.17	58.9	0.160	0.097	0.012	0.357	29.5
Philippines	1.21	0.094	0.389	0.233	10.90	30.6	0.299	0.122	0.022	0.681	27.2
Portugal	3.00	0.071	0.506	0.115	8.89	29.7	0.220	0.084	0.036	0.618	64.5
Taiwan	0.76	0.195	0.064	0.591	3.91	70.2	0.176	0.099	0.012	0.903	77.8
Thailand	5.92	0.079	0.151	0.175	5.69	27.1	0.285	0.086	0.012	0.642	56.5
Turkey	4.41	0.189	0.022	0.120	75.14	28.9	0.243	0.173	0.043	0.352	42.7
Venezuela	1.64	0.151	0.044	0.089	47.57	15.3	0.262	0.142	0.061	0.535	35.7
Zimbabwe	8.36	0.089	0.076	0.138	19.60	14.5	0.278	0.148	0.037	0.587	25.0
Global means	4.16	0.143	0.137	0.189	118.48	35.6	0.254	0.122	0.051	0.535	43.4
Global minimum	0.00	0.023	−0.697	0.000	−4.55	7.0	0.107	0.005	0.000	0.115	15.8
Global maximum	27.26	1.994	0.819	2.414	8163.97	162.0	0.735	2.725	0.536	1.812	79.9
First quartile	1.66	0.067	0.041	0.028	6.28	20.0	0.181	0.071	0.012	0.301	29.1
Second quartile	3.09	0.087	0.106	0.091	13.81	25.0	0.214	0.100	0.024	0.498	41.9
Third quartile	5.85	0.129	0.213	0.230	32.48	47.0	0.286	0.144	0.047	0.636	54.9

tribution. There is relatively little difference between the first quartile and the median, but there is a sharp jump when moving from the median to the third quartile.

The role of control variables is complex in our framework. The regression that we specify in equation (12) is correct if the control variables reflect variation in dividend yields not associated with liberalizations. However, it is possible that the control variables may be correlated with growth opportunities or cost of capital changes induced by the liberalization. If we linearize our structural model around mean dividend growth rates and mean expected returns, we obtain a structural regression:

$$D_t/P_t = a(\theta) + b(\theta)Y_t^x + [c(\theta) + d(\theta)Y_t^x]\Delta d_t + [e(\theta) + f(\theta)Y_t^x]r_t \qquad (13)$$

where θs are the structural parameters, Y_t^x is the liberalization indicator, Δd_t is the log-dividend growth, and r_t represents the expected rate of return. If our control variables are correlated with structural changes in Δd_t and r_t, we may expect their data-generating process to change after financial liberalizations and we may find significant coefficients $d(\theta)$ and $f(\theta)$. We explore this below by examining whether control variables break around liberalization dates and whether they capture future growth opportunities. We also run regressions without control variables and we run "structural regressions," allowing for breaks in all the control variables.

An interesting and relevant special case is when dividend growth follows a white noise process, not an unreasonable approximation to the dividend growth rate process, and expected returns are constant. In that case, $c(\theta)$ and $d(\theta)$ are zero and, hence, the coefficient on Δd_t is also zero. As a consequence, any change in growth opportunities is absorbed in the constant $b(\theta)$, as is the change in the cost of capital. Given our previous Monte Carlo experiments, which suggest that the effect of growth opportunities on dividend yields is approximately linear, the change in the cost of capital would then be derived as $b(\theta)Y_t^x$ minus the change in the dividend growth, as we suggested earlier.

Finally, changes in control variables may be indirectly related to liberalizations, as in the case when foreign investment helps to improve liquidity and efficiency in the local market or amplifies the beneficial effect of a trade liberalization or macroeconomic reforms. After all, capital market liberalizations are often part of a broader reform package (see also Henry (2000)). More specifically, what matters is the general stock market development and openness of a country, which is proxied by a number of our right-hand-side variables.

To assess the economic significance of a liberalization from the regressions, we trace the effect on an emerging market of moving from a poorly developed capital market with poor economic performance to a median country following a capital market liberalization. To do this, we examine the cross-sectional distribution of all of the explanatory variables. We consider a change from the 25th percentile to the median for the number of companies in the IFC index, the size of the trade sector, the cross-sectional standard deviation, the country credit rating, and the country's equity capitalization. We look at a change from the 75th percentile to the median for the concentration ratio, inflation, and foreign currency volatility. We allow for a capital market liberalization.

We dissect the cumulative effect into three groups. Stock market development includes the number of companies in the index, the concentration ratio, the cross-sectional volatility, market capitalization, and the interaction between capitalization and cross-sectional volatility. Macroeconomic development includes the inflation rate, foreign exchange rate volatility, the size of the trade sector, and the political risk rating. Finally, the financial liberalization effect is constructed from the difference between the post- and pre-liberalization indicator variables. We construct such economic impact graphs for dividend yields, volatilities, correlations, and betas.

IV. Empirical Results: Cost of Capital

A. Regression Results

A.1. No Control Variables

Table III presents our estimates of the dividend yield model without control variables. This is roughly analogous to looking at mean dividend yields before and after liberalizations.

Panels A through C report the models for ADR and Country Fund introduction indexes with a single choice of the impact parameter, $\lambda = 0.90$. To arrive at this value, we grid search 17 different values of this parameter, from 0.01 to 0.99, and record the likelihood function value.[11] The size of λ determines the effect of additional ADRs or Country Funds. High values, such as 0.90, imply that additional introductions have important effects—that is, liberalization is a gradual process. For the dividend yield regressions, the likelihood is always maximized at 0.99. For the other variables (excess returns, betas, correlations, and volatility), the maximum occurs at a value higher than 0.80 in all but two cases. Although in many cases the likelihood function appears quite flat, the overwhelming evidence points toward high λs (gradual liberalization). We impose $\lambda = 0.90$ for all of our estimations.

The coefficient on the ADR announcement index in Table III, Panel A, is negative, implying that ADR introductions reduce the cost of capital. The coefficient is about 2.7 standard errors from zero. We also present results based on ADR effective dates (dates that the ADRs were launched in contrast to the announcement dates). The coefficient is also negative and two standard errors from zero.

---

[11] See http://www.afajof.org. This page contains links to all of the supplementary tables for this paper, including optimal_lambda.htm.

Table III
The Impact of Liberalizations on Dividend Yields: No Control Variables

The regressions include country specific intercepts and allow for panel specific heteroskedasticity and serial correlation. In Panels A–C, we estimate a time-series cross-sectional model with the dividend yields as the dependent variable. λ represents how fast the additional impact of further liberalizations declines. We perform a grid search of the λ parameter and find that 0.9 provides the best fit. With high λs, additional issues generate large additional effects, i.e. gradual liberalization. The Intro variable is defined in the panel title. In Panel A, we contrast the use of ADR announcements with effective ADR dates. In Panels D–F, we estimate a model with dummy variables around the liberalization definition. In the regressions in Panel E, we weight the dummy variables by a function of the correlation with the world market return before the liberalization. The function is $\ln(2-\text{correlation})/\ln(3)$. In the regressions in Panel F, the weights for 'Offical Liberalization' and 'First Sign' are constructed by multiplying the dummies by the five-year post average value of ownership. The weights for the 'Capital Flows' are constructed by differencing the five-year post minus five-year pre average value of ownership. The Wald test is whether the dividend yield declines from Pre to Post liberalization. The sample period ends December 1995.

	Panel A: Gradual Liberalization Model: Introduction of ADRs			Panel B: Gradual Model: Introduction of Country Funds		Panel C: Gradual Model: Introduction of ADRs and Country Funds	
	λ	Intro (Announc.)	Intro (Effective)	λ	Intro	λ	Intro
Coefficient	0.9	−0.097	−0.047	0.9	−0.218	0.9	−0.146
t-statistic		−2.731	−1.978		−5.187		−4.634

	Panel D: Simple Liberalization Indicators					Panel E: Liberalization Indicators Weighted by Correlation with World					Panel F: Liberalization Indicators Weighted by Degree of Foreign Ownership				
	PRE	DURING	POST	AFTER	WALD	wPRE	wDURING	wPOST	wAFTER	WALD	wPRE	wDURING	wPOST	wAFTER	WALD
Official Liberalization															
Coefficient	−0.455	−0.674	−0.766	−0.945	5.700	−1.336	−1.941	−2.091	−2.492	3.990	−0.735	−1.101	−1.264	−1.559	6.040
t-statistic	−4.13	−4.76	−4.65	−5.10	0.017	−4.14	−4.68	−4.32	−4.58	0.046	−3.95	−4.63	−4.61	−5.07	0.014
First Sign															
Coefficient	−0.476	−0.751	−1.196	−1.361	15.910	−1.566	−2.472	−3.692	−4.114	14.470	−0.706	−1.135	−1.835	−2.108	15.020
t-statistic	−2.78	−3.52	−5.14	−5.64	0.000	−2.88	−3.64	−5.08	−5.49	0.000	−2.47	−3.23	−4.86	−5.40	0.000
Capital Flows Break															
Coefficient	−0.116	−0.261	−0.285	−0.383	1.710	−0.164	−0.503	−0.523	−0.802	0.920	−0.198	−0.433	−0.468	−0.607	1.700
t-statistic	−1.05	−1.83	−1.76	−1.99	0.190	−0.52	−1.22	−1.11	−1.49	0.337	−1.12	−1.90	−1.80	−1.99	0.193

Country fund introductions have a more significant effect on dividend yields than the ADR introductions, both statistically and economically. In Panel B, the coefficient on the country fund index is always more than five standard errors away from zero and the immediate drop in the dividend yield is close to 20 basis points.

Panel C combines the ADR and country fund indexes. The results are consistent with Panels A and B. The index enters with a negative coefficient that is significantly less than zero.

Panels D, E, and F consider different definitions of capital market liberalizations. For "Official Liberalizations," the model implies a decrease in dividend yields of 31 basis points (comparing PRE with POST in Panel D). For the "First Sign" date (first date of ADR, Country Fund, or official liberalization), the decrease is 72 basis points. A Wald test reveals that these changes are statistically significant at the 5 percent level in both of these regressions. The "Capital Flows Break" regression suggests a decrease of only 17 basis points and this decrease is not significant even at the 10 percent level.

Generally, the economic effect of liberalization is larger than the direct impact of an ADR or Country Fund introduction in the gradual liberalization models. However, if we take into account further introductions, the effects are not that dissimilar. For example, the total effect of introducing five ADRs (Country Funds) is a 40 (89) basis point decrease in dividend yields.

Panel E uses the "weighted" correlation index-scaling described in Section III.B. The Wald tests for the Official Liberalizations and First Sign indicators are significant at the 5 percent level. The POST − PRE difference is now considerably larger in absolute value but this should be interpreted as the change occurring for a country with perfect negative correlation with the world market preliberalization. For example, for the First Sign regressions, the impact for a perfect negative correlation is −2.126 (POST − PRE). Argentina has a preliberalization correlation of −0.166, which translates into a correlation index of 0.703. Therefore, the country-specific impact on dividend yields is −1.49 (−2.126 × 0.703). Chile has a preliberalization correlation of 0.304, which implies a correlation index of 0.481. Chile's dividend yield is therefore predicted to change by −1.02. Lower correlations imply bigger valuation effects.

Panel F uses the foreign ownership weighting scheme, described in Section III.B. The results are similar. Dividend yields decrease and the Wald tests reveal that for both the Official Liberalization and the First Sign regression, the change is highly significant. Nevertheless, the economic impact of higher levels of foreign ownership seems relatively small. For the First Sign indicator, for example, five percent additional foreign ownership induces about a six basis point additional decrease in the cost of capital. The dividend yield change remains insignificant for the capital flow regression.

In sum, the weighted regressions suggest that countries with low correlations before the liberalization and/or higher degrees of foreign ownership (in the postliberalization period) experience larger reductions in the cost of capital. Strikingly, the cost of capital continues to decrease in the AFTER period, which is consistent with a pattern of very gradual liberalization.

A.2. Allowing for Control Variables

The problem with examining dividend yields before and after a liberalization is that the change may be linked to phenomena unrelated to the liberalization. There are a number of interesting patterns when the control variables enter the regressions. The results in Table IV show that their presence decreases the liberalization effect but not by much. In terms of statistical significance, the only effect is on the official liberalization measures, where the cost of capital change is no longer significant at the 5 percent level, but remains significant at the 10 percent level.

The log of the number of companies in the stock index enters with a negative coefficient (the more companies, the more developed the market, and the lower the dividend yield). The coefficient, with few exceptions, is borderline significant. The concentration ratio also enters with a negative, but insignificant, coefficient. This implies that as some large firms emerge in a country, the dividend yield decreases. It is possible that this result is being driven by privatizations in a few countries and we indeed find that asset concentration tends to increase after privatizations (see priv_conc.htm).

The size of the trade sector, which is a development indicator, enters strongly with a negative coefficient in all regressions. As the size of the trade sector increases, the dividend yield decreases. The cross-sectional standard deviation is also important in each regression. More industrial diversity (suggesting development of the market) tends to decrease the dividend yield. Indeed, this variable enters the regression with coefficients six standard errors from zero.[12] The political risk indicator fails to enter any of the regressions with a significant coefficient.

Finally, the macroeconomic climate variables have mixed effects. The volatility of the foreign exchange rate changes enters with a negative coefficient that is difficult to explain. However, inflation enters with a close to significant positive coefficient indicating that lower inflation is associated with lower dividend yields. It is possible that the inclusion of three variables, proxying for macroeconomic stability (inflation, exchange rate variability, and credit ratings) leads to the anomalous sign for exchange rate variability.

A.3. Interpretation Issues When Using Control Variables

We consider two issues. First, privatizations may affect both certain control variables and the liberalization effect we measure. Second, the control variables may be impacted by the capital market liberalization.

Policymakers may strategically time the liberalization process in an attempt to maximize the revenues from privatizations. This potential correlation between liberalizations and privatizations may affect our results through

---

[12] Nevertheless, omitting this variable has little impact on our results, both in terms of statistical significance and magnitude. This variable is also significant in the excess return regression with the opposite sign; see ret_control.htm for some additional tables and an interpretation of this result.

Table IV
The Impact of Liberalizations on Dividend Yields Allowing for Control Variables

Group-wise heteroskedasticity and autocorrelation-consistent *t*-statistics are reported below the coefficients. In Panels A–C, we estimate a time-series cross-sectional model with the dividend yields as the dependent variable. λ represents how fast the additional impact of further liberalizations declines. We perform a grid search of the λ parameter and find that 0.9 provides the best fit. With high λs, additional issues generate large additional effects—that is, gradual liberalization. NUMC represents the number of companies, CONCR the concentration ratio, STDL2 the cross-sectional standard deviation of stock returns within the local index, INFL past inflation, FXV the foreign exchange volatility, XMGDP the size of the trade sector, and CCR Institutional Investor's country credit rating. The Intro variable is defined in the panel title. In Panels D–F, we estimate a model with dummy variables around the liberalization definition. In the regressions labeled 'weighted', we weight the dummy variables by a function of the correlation with the world market return before the liberalization (see, also, Table III). The Wald test is whether the dividend yield declines from Pre- to Post-liberalization.

λ	NUMC	CONCR	STDL2	INFL	FXV	XMGDP	CCR	Intro	PRE	DURING	POST	AFTER	Wald Test
					Panel A: Gradual Liberalization Model: Introduction of ADRs								
0.9	−0.248	−0.944	−0.751	0.138	−3.088	−1.437	−0.057	−0.050					
Announc.	−2.19	−1.41	−6.46	1.77	−3.06	−3.53	−0.15	−1.42					
0.9	−0.296	−0.844	−0.750	0.150	−3.027	−1.410	−0.032	−0.012					
Effective	−2.61	−1.26	−6.42	1.94	−3.06	−3.34	−0.08	−0.51					
					Panel B: Gradual Liberalization Model: Introduction of Country Funds								
0.9	−0.204	−0.858	−0.746	0.173	−3.026	−1.326	−0.050	−0.156					
	−1.76	−1.24	−6.37	2.21	−2.97	−2.76	−0.12	−3.70					
					Panel C: Gradual Liberalization Model: Introduction of ADRs and Country Funds								
0.9	−0.201	−1.003	−0.749	0.149	−3.100	−1.291	−0.005	−0.089					
	−1.76	−1.48	−6.45	1.91	−2.94	−2.89	−0.01	−2.89					

Panel D: With Regulatory Liberalization Indicators

Correlation	-0.286	-1.093	-0.729	0.150	-2.902	-1.544	-0.134	-0.421	-0.573	-0.641	-0.655	2.840
	-2.46	-1.55	-6.15	1.79	-2.57	-3.27	-0.30	-3.86	-4.07	-3.91	-3.55	*0.092*
Weighted	-0.269	-1.069	-0.727	0.148	-2.862	-1.486	-0.196	-0.756	-1.027	-1.208	-1.300	3.620
	-2.33	-1.54	-6.16	1.78	-2.50	-3.35	-0.44	-3.82	-4.02	-4.08	-3.89	*0.057*

Panel E: With ADR, Country Fund, and Regulatory Liberalization Indicators

Correlation	-0.237	-1.101	-0.733	0.161	-2.820	-1.336	-0.076	-0.166	-0.347	-0.711	-0.940	9.200
	-2.13	-1.62	-6.34	1.98	-2.52	-3.09	-0.18	-0.98	-1.65	-3.06	-3.89	*0.002*
Weighted	-0.238	-1.112	-0.733	0.160	-2.820	-1.347	-0.080	-0.259	-0.537	-1.192	-1.596	9.090
	-2.14	-1.64	-6.33	1.96	-2.49	-3.21	-0.18	-0.91	-1.52	-3.01	-3.85	*0.003*

Panel F: With Cumulative Net Capital Flow Break Points

Correlation	-0.404	-1.022	-0.773	0.161	-3.198	-1.918	-0.129	0.047	-0.019	-0.030	-0.160	0.380
	-3.52	-1.45	-6.37	1.96	-3.05	-4.11	-0.33	0.50	-0.16	-0.21	-0.80	*0.537*
Weighted	-0.445	-0.938	-0.797	0.190	-3.969	-2.392	-0.058	0.050	-0.102	-0.122	-0.405	0.530
	-3.70	-1.26	-6.22	2.06	-3.46	-4.59	-0.14	0.28	-0.47	-0.46	-0.94	*0.468*

two channels. First, the control variables that measure stock market development are directly affected by privatizations. Second, the index composition change associated with privatizations may make dividend yields less informative as a cost of capital measure. Privatized firms may have high dividends as a result of commitments made during the privatization, biasing our liberalization coefficients upward.

To examine this, we collected data from the World Bank on all privatizations in emerging markets since 1988. This includes 14 of our 20 markets. We measure privatization in two ways. First, we examine the year-by-year value of privatization divided by market capitalization at $t - 1$; this value is kept constant throughout the year. Second, we use the indicator variable suggested by Perotti and van Oijen (1997) that comes on at the peak year of the privatization program and stays on to the end of the sample. Hence, the first measure looks for temporary effects of privatizations, whereas the second measure considers permanent effects.

With these two measures of privatization activity, we conduct a number of experiments that are fully described and documented on our Internet site. Here we offer only a brief summary of our findings. First, we reestimate the Table IV regressions interacting the value of privatizations with the number of companies, the cross-sectional standard deviation, and the concentration ratio, which are our stock market development variables. The p-values of the Wald tests for the decrease in dividend yields are not substantially affected and the estimated cost of capital change does not differ materially from our estimate in Table IV.

Second, we explore in more detail the relation between dividend yields and privatizations using various regression specifications. We find evidence of a weak negative relation between dividend yields and privatizations, which is strong when Perotti and van Oijen (1997) dummy variables are used. Our result of a more significant permanent effect is consistent both with Perotti and van Oijen who postulate that privatization signals political commitment to market-oriented policy reform, including financial liberalization, and with Henry (2000) who finds privatizations have a positive valuation effect.

Finally, we introduce the value of privatizations directly into the set of Table IV regressions with the liberalization indicator variables. The privatization variable is never significant. We conclude that our main results are not affected by privatizations.

A second issue that we face is the possibility that the control variables break at the liberalization dates. The resulting misspecification of our regression model is potentially important if any of these variables are correlated with the cost of capital or with growth opportunities. Table V presents an analysis of whether the control variables are different before and after Official Liberalizations, the First Sign, and the Capital Flows Break.

The results suggest that some of the control variables break. In all three liberalization definitions, the number of companies in the index increases significantly. In two of the three definitions, the concentration ratio signif-

Table V
Do the Control Variables Break at Liberalization Dates?

Regressions use the control variables as dependent variables with simple on/off liberalization indicators. In addition to the control variables, we examine, in the last row, Investment divided by GDP. Each panel represents a different definition of the liberalization indicator. All regressions allow for country specific intercepts and all standard errors are heteroskedasticity/serial correlation corrected. The sample is from January 1976 to December 1995.

	Panel A: Official Liberalization		Panel B: First Sign		Panel C: Capital Flows Break	
	Coefficient	t-statistic	Coefficient	t-statistic	Coefficient	t-statistic
Number of companies	0.0496	4.04	0.0310	2.49	0.1120	8.94
Concentration ratio	-0.0066	-2.74	-0.0041	-1.53	-0.0072	-2.71
Cross-sectional standard deviation	0.0071	1.90	0.0222	5.69	0.0019	0.58
Inflation rate	-0.0296	-2.12	-0.0084	-0.58	-0.0102	-0.81
Foreign exchange rate volatility	0.0004	1.22	0.0004	0.85	0.0000	-0.21
Trade sector to GDP	-0.0006	-0.36	-0.0014	-0.89	0.0009	0.58
Country credit rating	-0.0012	-0.51	-0.0023	-0.69	0.0048	2.55
Investment/GDP	0.7539	3.01	0.7330	3.12	0.6629	1.94

icantly decreases. There is weaker evidence of an increase in the cross-sectional standard deviation and decreases in inflation rates. Credit ratings significantly increase after the capital flows breaks.

Interestingly, the variables most obviously potentially correlated with growth opportunities or expected returns, such as trade sector to GDP and country credit rating, do not break, lessening the need for a structural regression as in equation (13). A possible exception here is the cross-sectional standard deviation, which may be an imperfect risk proxy in the more developed markets (see footnote 12). Moreover, since every control variable requires the estimation of five separate coefficients for the various windows, structural regressions may lack power. For example, when we estimate the structural counterpart of the regression with the First Sign liberalization measure, there are virtually no significant coefficients left. We fare somewhat better with the Official Liberalization measure regression (see div_struct.htm), where the regression detects a number of significant changes in the relation between the control variables and dividend yields induced by liberalizations. One example is that an increase in the number of companies leads to a smaller decrease in dividend yields BEFORE, DURING, and AFTER the liberalization compared to the early period. This is consistent with this relation being due to stock market development. Overall, however, the PRE, DURING, and POST coefficients fail to be significant. This is also true for the liberalization dummies. Although the decrease in the cost of capital now appears much larger, it is no longer statistically significant.

A.4. Liberalization and Returns

The simulation analysis shows that it is difficult to detect a change in the cost of capital by examining returns. This motivates our focus on dividend yields. Nevertheless, we might learn something from examining the behavior of the returns around liberalizations. Although this need not be generally true, in our structural model, changes in average returns are in fact not contaminated by changes in growth opportunities.

Table VI presents analysis analogous to Table IV except that excess returns are examined rather than dividend yields. In the gradual liberalization models, the coefficient on the introduction variable is negative for all three liberalization indexes. This implies a decrease in expected returns after liberalizations. However, it is not significantly different from zero. For the effective ADR case, the coefficient is 1.4 standard errors below zero.

In the liberalization indicator regressions, the message is different. In the First Sign regressions, average returns significantly increase (at the 5 percent level). For the Official Liberalization, the increase is only significant at the 10 percent level in the unweighted regression. In the Capital Flow Break regression, there is a small, insignificant decrease in average returns. These results remain largely unaltered when we introduce control variables in the regressions (see ret_control.htm). The gradual liberalization measures have

Table VI
The Impact of Liberalizations on Excess Returns: No Control Variables

The regressions include country-specific intercepts and allow for panel specific heteroscedasticity and serial correlation. In the regressions in Panel B, we weight the dummy variables by a function of the correlation with the world market return before the liberalization. The function is $\ln(2\text{-correlation})/\ln(3)$. In the regressions in Panel C, the weights for 'Offical Liberalization' and 'First Sign' are constructed by multiplying dummy variables by five-year post average value of ownership. The weights for 'Capital Flows' are constructed by differencing the five-year post minus five-year pre average value of foreign ownership. The Wald test is whether the excess return declines from PRE to POST liberalization. The sample ends in December 1995.

Panel A: Gradual Liberalization Model: Introduction of ADRs

	λ	Intro (Announc.)	Intro (Effective)
Coefficient	0.9	-0.00116	-0.001
t-statistic		-0.968	-1.386

Panel B: Gradual Model: Introduction of Country Funds

	λ	Intro
Coefficient	0.9	-0.00004
t-statistic		-0.038

Panel C: Gradual Model: Introduction of ADRs and Country Funds

	λ	Intro
Coefficient	0.9	-0.00029
t-statistic		-0.364

Panel D: Simple Liberalization Indicators

	PRE	DURING	POST	AFTER	WALD
Official Liberalization					
Coefficient	0.007	0.009	0.019	0.019	3.270
t-statistic	1.19	1.07	2.96	2.96	0.071
First Sign					
Coefficient	0.012	0.014	0.032	0.016	7.370
t-statistic	1.97	1.53	4.47	2.49	0.007
Capital Flows					
Coefficient	0.006	0.017	0.005	0.009	0.050
t-statistic	1.01	1.95	0.74	1.09	0.829

Panel E: Liberalization Indicators Weighted by Correlation with World

	wPRE	wDURING	wPOST	wAFTER	WALD
Official Liberalization					
Coefficient	0.020	0.029	0.053	0.008	2.330
t-statistic	1.16	1.14	2.65	0.39	0.127
First Sign					
Coefficient	0.042	0.046	0.094	0.055	5.390
t-statistic	2.17	1.62	4.35	2.82	0.020
Capital Flows					
Coefficient	0.013	0.045	0.015	0.019	0.010
t-statistic	0.80	1.95	0.85	0.89	0.935

Panel F: Liberalization Indicators Weighted by Degree of Foreign Ownership

	wPRE	wDURING	wPOST	wAFTER	WALD
Official Liberalization					
Coefficient	0.018	0.026	0.036	0.006	2.010
t-statistic	1.46	1.56	3.06	0.51	0.156
First Sign					
Coefficient	0.038	0.046	0.065	0.038	4.000
t-statistic	2.73	2.45	4.93	3.21	0.046
Capital Flows					
Coefficient	0.010	0.027	0.008	0.013	0.050
t-statistic	1.01	1.93	0.73	1.06	0.824

virtually no effect on returns, whereas the dummy variables record increases in returns that are now never significant at the 5 percent level. There are few significant relations with the control variables.

Why is it that the gradual liberalization regressions are suggesting a negative impact on expected returns and that some liberalization indicators are suggesting a positive impact on returns? One possibility is that the timing of the liberalization indicators is a problem. Indeed, in some cases in Table VI, we see a decrease in average returns in the AFTER period.

We investigate the sensitivity of our results to the definition of the DURING variable—which is defined as six months prior to a liberalization date to three months after. As indicated before, the DURING variable captures the period during which the "return to integration" is realized. That is, when markets open up, capital investment flows in and prices increase as investors take advantage of the diversification benefits. However, in the longer term, given the higher price level, expected returns should be lower than in the preliberalization period. How long the transition period lasts is hard to say. Henry (2000), who focuses on the excess returns during the liberalization, uses an eight-month window leading up to the implementation of the liberalization. Our analysis that allows for gradual liberalization suggests a very long period.

In results reported on the Internet, we present the sensitivity of the returns regressions to different windows for the DURING variable (see ret_window.htm). The results can be summarized as follows. First, the "return to integration" (DURING–PRE) ranges from 0.20 to 2.50 percent per month using official liberalizations, which is smaller than Henry's (1999a) findings. However, Henry examines 12 countries rather than 20 and his liberalization dates are not always the same as ours. Second, the results on returns depend on the definition of the liberalization variable, with small, insignificant increases for Official Liberalizations; a U-shaped pattern in the liberalization coefficients for the First Sign regression (PRE is low, DURING and POST are higher, and AFTER is low); and insignificant decreases in returns for the Capital Flow Break point regressions.

Whereas we find a consistent decrease in dividend yields, excess returns may increase or decrease from the pre- to postliberalization period depending on the specification. In the longer-term, average returns appear to be lower. Although the noisiness of returns most probably is the underlying factor in all of these results, there is another possibility. Our dividend yield decrease may reflect primarily an improvement in growth opportunities, leaving little room for cost of capital decreases.

A.5. Is It Growth or Lower Cost of Capital?

In the simple present value model, dividend yields are linked to both expected returns and growth opportunities. Some of our regressions could be picking up changes in growth opportunities rather than changes in the cost of capital. We conduct three exercises to address this issue.

First, we attempt to control for expectations of growth. To check whether our control variables might capture growth opportunities, we regress annual real GDP growth on lagged values of the control variables.[13] From all of our control variables, only one, the size of the trade sector, shows a significant association with future GDP growth. The coefficient for the size of the trade sector is positive (bigger trade sector, better growth prospects) and 2.9 standard errors from zero (see GDP_XMGDP.htm). The predictive power of the size of the trade sector variable holds up in a purely cross-sectional analysis, regressing average postliberalization GDP growth rates on the size of the trade sector at liberalization (see GDP_XMGDP_Post.htm).

We also investigate more direct measures of expected economic growth. Though data are available only from 1984, the International Country Risk Guide's Economic (ICRGE) rating variable is supposed to reflect future growth prospects. We find that the ICRGE rating predicts economic growth and enters the regression with a positive coefficient (higher rating, better prospects) which is 2.4 standard errors from zero (see GDP_ICRGE.htm).[14] We use the ICRGE as an additional variable in our regressions to control for growth prospects.

When we reestimate the dividend regressions with the ICRGE as an extra control variable, the results are similar to those in Table IV—even though the sample is shorter (see div_ICRGE.htm). Dividend yields decrease from PRE to POST and even more sharply from PRE to AFTER for Official Liberalizations. The change is significant at the 10 percent level. A similar pattern is found in the First Sign regressions, although the liberalization effect is now smaller, as would be expected if the original decrease we found is partially due to growth opportunities now controlled for by the ICRGE variable. The dividend yield change is also no longer significant.

Second, we attempt to directly measure the change in growth rates after liberalization. In a country-by-country examination, growth increases in 14 of 19 countries that experienced a liberalization. In a pooled GLS regression of GDP growth rates on the Official Liberalization indicator variable, the coefficient is positive and three standard errors from zero (see GDP_lib.htm). Growth increases on average by 1.26 percent. When the capital flows measure is used, the increase is smaller (61 basis points) and no longer significant. If we were to subtract this increase in growth opportunities from our estimate of the total dividend yield change, the drop in the cost of capital must have been economically very small or nonexistent.

Of course, this split-up of dividend yield changes into cost of capital changes and growth opportunity changes may be incorrect if all structural parameters change. In a third experiment, we calibrate the structural model

---

[13] Our discussion refers to pooled OLS estimates, but we also consider OLS with fixed effects and GLS with fixed effects regressions.

[14] Note that our other country risk variable, the Institutional Investor country credit rating, is more focused on the financial and political outlook. The ICRGE is more narrowly focused on anticipated economic performance. We did not use the ICRGE in our original regressions because of its shorter sample.

presented in Section II.A to an "average" emerging market before and after liberalizations. Appendix A contains details of the calibration procedure conducted for the capital flow liberalization measure. The output is the six structural parameters driving the present value model before and after the break, which can be used to characterize the dividend yield and log-return process before and after the break. We find a 61 basis point increase in the dividend growth rate (proxied by GDP growth) and a 75 basis point drop in the dividend yield. In the stylized simulations we conducted before, this would suggest a drop in the cost of capital of about 10 to 15 basis points. Indeed, the mean of logged returns drops from 7.16 percent to 7.05 percent, suggesting a very small drop in the cost of capital.

Our main conclusions continue to hold. Dividend yields decrease but not by more than 75 basis points. Our analysis here suggests that it is likely that part of this drop can be ascribed to improved growth opportunities making the actual drop in the cost of capital even smaller.

B. Economic Analysis of Cost of Capital Changes

Whereas the effects of capital market liberalization on the dividend yields seem small, economic integration, as measured by the size of the trade sector, does seem to have a significant effect (both economically and statistically) on the dividend yields. The economic experiment considers the global effect from stock market development, macroeconomic development, and a financial market liberalization.

Although we analyze the coefficients from three different definitions of liberalizations (Official Liberalizations, First Sign, and Capital Flow Breaks), we concentrate our discussion on the First Sign results. The economic impact is summarized in Figure 2.

Combining the coefficients from Panel E in Tables IV with the cross-sectional distribution of the control variables, we find that the dividend yield decreases by 87 basis points. Almost all of this effect is being driven by macroeconomic development and the actual liberalization.[15] Taken together, we argue that development has, at most, led to an economically small drop in the cost of capital that is often statistically insignificant.

---

[15] The returns results are hard to interpret given their lack of robustness but, in unreported results, we find that the macroeconomic development indicators continue to suggest a small drop in expected returns of 30 basis points. The credit rating variable implies a 1.6 percent decrease in expected returns. These results are consistent with those reported in Erb, Harvey, and Viskanta (1996a). However, this effect is offset by the financial development indicators and by the financial liberalization indicators, which suggest an overall increase in returns. The stock market development effect is primarily driven by the cross-sectional standard deviation, which experiences a break in its relation with returns postliberalization, and we have shown the returns results lack robustness.

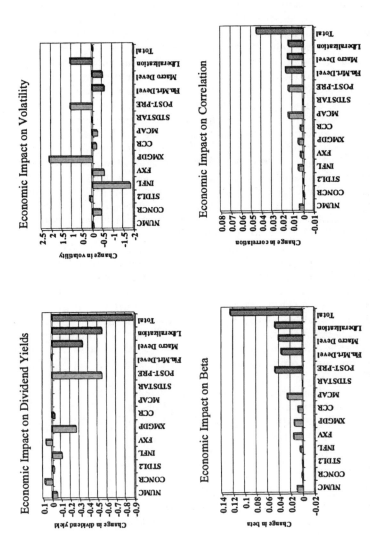

Figure 2. Country moving from 25th percentile to median after First Sign liberalization. Financial Development represents the sum of the number of companies (NUMC), the concentration ratio (CONCR), the cross-sectional standard deviation of stock returns within the local index (STDL2), the market capitalization (MCAP) and the interactive variable STDL2 and the mean adjusted MCAP (STDSTAR). Macroeconomic development is the sum of past inflation (INFL), foreign exchange volatility (FXV), the size of the trade sector (XMGDP) and Institutional Investor's country credit rating (CCR). Financial Liberalization is the difference between the coefficients on the dummy variables for the POST and PRE liberalization periods.

598 *The Journal of Finance*

V. Empirical Results: Volatility, Correlation, and Beta

A. Framework

Previous studies of emerging market volatility have relied on two approaches. Some studies, such as those by De Santis and İmrohoroğlu (1997) and Aggarwal, Inclan, and Leal (1999)), use a generalized autoregressive conditional heteroskedasticity (GARCH) model (see Bollerslev (1986)). The GARCH model is fit, country by country, and often includes dummy variables for regulatory shifts. This type of modeling has many limitations. The volatility process is only affected by past returns—that is, there is no other conditioning information. The parameters of the volatility model are assumed to be constant. Finally, the dummy variable approach lacks power to detect changes when information from only one country is used.

Other studies rely on an event study methodology (see, e.g., Kim and Singal (1999) and Richards (1996)). Volatility is modeled, following Schwert (1989a, 1989b), using residuals from an autoregressive model for returns controlling for calendar effects. Though this approach pools information from different countries, it does not control for other variables that affect volatility. This approach also ignores the changes in the stochastic process for returns that gradually integrating markets undergo.

We combine both methods and improve the econometric methodology along various dimensions. First, we estimate a time-series model for volatility for each country that allows both the conditional mean and the conditional variance to vary through time. We condition on both world and local information to capture changes in the degree of market integration. This model delivers a time-series of conditional volatilities for each country as well as conditional correlations and conditional betas of each country's return with the world market return.

Second, and as we discussed in Section III, we use these conditional volatility, correlation, and beta estimates in a pooled time-series/cross-sectional analysis. Although we can only estimate an "average" response to foreign speculative activity that way, the increase in power is essential.

Since our volatility model is fully described in Bekaert and Harvey (1997), we relegate a brief description of the model to an appendix that is available from the authors upon request.

B. Diversification and Liberalization

Table VII presents regressions that omit the control variables.[16] The results suggest an indeterminant effect of liberalizations on volatility. In only one specification, First Sign, is the change in volatility significant at the 10 percent level and it is only significant at the 5 percent level when the response is weighted by the foreign ownership variable. This particular regression suggests that volatility increases after liberalization.

[16] See vol_control.htm, corr_control.htm, and beta_control.htm for the results that include control variables.

Table VII
The Impact of Liberalizations on Volatility, Correlation and Beta: No Control Variables

The regressions include country-specific intercepts and allow for panel specific heteroskedasticity and serial correlation. In the regressions in Panel B, we weight the dummy variables by a function of the correlation with the world market return before the liberalization. The formula is ln(2-correlation)/ln(3). In the regressions in Panel C, the weights for Official Liberalization and First Sign are constructed by multiplying the dummy variables by the five-year average value of ownership. The weights for Capital Flows are constructed by differencing the five-year post minus five-year pre average value of foreign ownership. The Wald test is whether the volatility, correlation, or beta declines from PRE to POST liberalization. The sample ends in December 1995.

	Panel A: Simple Liberalization Indicators					Panel B: Liberalization Indicators Weighted by Correlation with World					Panel C: Liberalization Indicators Weighted by Degree of Foreign Ownership				
	PRE	DURING	POST	AFTER	WALD	wPRE	wDURING	wPOST	wAFTER	WALD	wPRE	wDURING	wPOST	wAFTER	WALD
Volatility															
Official Liberalization															
Coefficient	0.015	0.024	0.039	0.054	0.260	0.011	0.007	0.053	0.063	0.090	-0.023	0.043	0.043	0.076	0.500
t-statistic	0.39	0.48	0.75	0.88	0.607	0.09	0.05	0.33	0.34	0.768	-0.27	0.42	0.43	0.70	0.480
First Sign															
Coefficient	0.015	0.051	0.109	0.080	3.490	0.055	0.166	0.356	0.282	3.810	-0.046	0.085	0.182	0.127	5.160
t-statistic	0.37	0.97	1.89	1.30	0.062	0.44	1.02	2.01	1.51	0.051	-0.50	0.74	1.59	1.12	0.023
Capital Flows															
Coefficient	0.048	0.024	0.075	0.040	0.220	0.109	0.052	0.211	0.076	0.460	0.082	0.047	0.133	0.077	0.310
t-statistic	1.01	0.40	1.28	0.61	0.636	0.81	0.31	1.33	0.44	0.499	1.06	0.48	1.40	0.73	0.576
Correlation															
Official Liberalization															
Coefficient	0.007	0.027	0.049	0.040	31.800	0.023	0.088	0.150	0.121	31.890	0.010	0.050	0.087	0.073	35.270
t-statistic	1.16	3.59	5.57	4.03	0.000	1.29	3.78	5.66	4.02	0.000	1.00	3.65	5.74	4.33	0.000
First Sign															
Coefficient	0.007	0.019	0.023	0.040	5.280	0.019	0.055	0.065	0.113	3.780	0.011	0.033	0.041	0.067	5.580
t-statistic	1.20	2.53	2.69	4.13	0.022	1.13	2.34	2.34	3.65	0.052	1.18	2.56	2.74	4.12	0.018
Capital Flows															
Coefficient	0.013	0.020	0.039	0.051	10.450	0.044	0.068	0.126	0.175	11.020	0.020	0.030	0.060	0.080	9.610
t-statistic	2.10	2.40	4.04	4.49	0.001	2.34	2.69	4.33	5.11	0.001	2.04	2.28	3.88	4.32	0.002
Beta															
Official Liberalization															
Coefficient	0.028	0.071	0.133	0.161	39.080	0.092	0.226	0.429	0.507	42.740	0.033	0.125	0.229	0.272	44.620
t-statistic	2.15	4.16	6.99	7.43	0.000	2.28	4.31	7.44	7.81	0.000	1.30	3.89	6.74	7.25	0.000
First Sign															
Coefficient	0.021	0.054	0.079	0.177	11.510	0.069	0.177	0.256	0.577	11.950	0.018	0.087	0.125	0.285	13.210
t-statistic	1.56	3.06	3.98	8.44	0.001	1.64	3.18	4.11	8.86	0.001	0.69	2.62	3.57	7.92	0.000
Capital Flows															
Coefficient	0.053	0.094	0.135	0.225	20.150	0.165	0.287	0.418	0.675	20.980	0.085	0.150	0.213	0.348	18.590
t-statistic	3.64	4.97	6.54	8.31	0.000	3.73	5.03	6.82	8.85	0.000	3.61	4.88	6.35	7.89	0.000

Panel B of Table VII analyzes the behavior of correlations with world market returns around liberalizations. In all tests, correlations increase. For example, from PRE to POST for Official Liberalizations, correlation increases by 4.2 percent. This change is significant at the 1 percent level. Economically, the increase in correlation after liberalizations is too small to diminish any diversification benefits. Such benefits are likely large given that the average conditional correlation with the world market return is only 14 percent (see Table II). Panel B does show that countries which start out with low correlations experience much larger correlation increases.

The final panel examines changes in the beta with world markets. Increased correlations can come about because of cash flow or discount rate effects. In the latter case, we may expect an increase in beta. The results suggest a highly significant change in the beta. In each regression, the change from PRE to POST is significant at the 1 percent level. The size of the increase in beta ranges from 0.06 to 0.105. In the weighted regressions, the beta increases are substantially larger—in one case more than 0.33. Is the increase large enough to substantially impact the cost of capital? This analysis is complicated. Even if the beta with the world increases, this does not necessarily mean the cost of capital increases. The reason is that in the preliberalization regime the world CAPM should not hold. That is, expected returns in a segmented regime are related to the country's variance—not to its covariance with the world. Even if we were to assume that preliberalization emerging markets were integrated with the world market and the world CAPM held, the change in beta of 0.10 would imply an increase in the cost of capital of only 70 basis points (assuming a seven percent world risk premium).

C. Economic Analysis of Volatility, Correlation, and Beta

We repeat the economic analysis conducted on the dividend yields for volatility, beta, and correlation with world market returns (see Figure 2). Based on the estimates of the volatility model with control variables, we find that annualized volatility slightly decreases (by one basis point). In this case, both the financial and macroeconomic development indicators suggest a considerable decrease in volatility. This is offset by an increase in volatility attributed to the financial liberalization. These results are broadly consistent with those in Bekaert and Harvey (1997) who have a shorter sample and use a different methodology.

Correlation increases by 0.045, and all three categories contribute approximately equally to this increased correlation. Beta increases by 0.12. Similar to the analysis of correlation, financial market development, macroeconomic development, and liberalizations contribute about equally to the increase.

The economic exercise points to an insignificant change in volatility and a small increase in both correlation and beta with the world market. However, the increase in market capitalization to GDP that we use moving from the

25th percentile to the median is very small (2.8 percent to 9.1 percent). If we repeat the analysis using the 75th percentile (2.8 percent to 23.0 percent), volatility shows a more substantial decrease (0.6 percent). The increase in correlations is now 0.076 and the increase in beta is 0.182.

VI. Conclusions

There are many perceptions of the role of foreign speculators in emerging equity markets—many of which are negative. Our research looks at the various ways foreigners can access emerging market equity (ADRs, Country Funds, or direct participation in the local market) and tries to assess the impact on expected returns, volatility, beta, and correlation.

One of the major conclusions of our work is that the capital market integration process reduces the cost of capital but perhaps by less than we expected. In fact, there are reasons to believe that the effect we measure is upwardly biased. We have taken liberalizations as an exogenous event, whereas policymakers would probably choose to liberalize when it is most advantageous to do so. Although policy endogeneity would suggest our estimates are biased upward (see Henry (2000) for a similar point), the effect we measure is less than one percent. A positive effect of the liberalization on the growth potential of the country (as predicted by the new growth theory) should also decrease dividend yields, and we present some evidence in favor of a small growth effect.

In fact, one control variable that is very significant in our regressions is the economic openness of the country, which is known to be a reliable predictor of economic growth, a result confirmed in our data. Although we cannot disentangle the dividend yield changes precisely into the cost of capital changes versus changes in growth opportunities, the fact that dividend yields consistently decrease suggests some (albeit minor) beneficial effects of liberalizations. One macroeconomic variable that may be particularly sensitive to both cost of capital changes and growth opportunities is aggregate investment as a proportion of GDP. Henry (1999) already reports that financial and economic liberalization increases growth in aggregate investment. We repeat our analysis of Table V, regressing the investment to GDP ratio on the liberalization indicator. The results are striking. For the Official Liberalization, First Sign, and Capital Flows, we measure, respectively, 75, 73, and 66 basis point increases in the investment to GDP ratio—all of which are significant at the 5 percent level.

Our analysis details a small but mostly insignificant increase in the volatility of stock returns following capital market liberalizations. Moreover, the effect becomes negative when potentially concurrent movements in the control variables are taken into account. Interestingly, there is only a small increase in correlation with the world market return. Many foreign investors are attracted to emerging markets for the diversification benefits. Although correlations increase after markets open up, the magnitude of the increase is unlikely to deter investors seeking diversification.

The Journal of Finance

Our research comes at a time when a number of countries are pondering the wisdom of further liberalizing their capital markets or, in the case of some East Asian countries, reversing the process. Nevertheless, much research remains to be done. As this paper illustrates, it is extremely hard to identify when market integration really occurs. If we could use returns and other financial data to "date" market integration, we may be able to determine which liberalization initiatives (ADRs, Country Funds, large-scale capital market liberalizations) have proved most effective in bringing about market integration. Ongoing research by Bekaert, Harvey, and Lumsdaine (1998) offers some insight on this important question.

Appendix A. The Relation between Dividend Yields and the Cost of Capital

We explore in greater detail the present value model described in Section II.A. This includes a sketch of the price-dividend solution procedure, a Monte Carlo study pitting dividend yields versus average returns as a cost of capital measure, and, finally, a calibration to emerging market data before and after liberalization.

A. Model Solution

The model can be summarized by three equations:

$$\Delta d_t = \mu(1 - \rho) + \rho \Delta d_{t-1} + \epsilon_t; \tag{A1}$$

$$r_t = q(1 - \phi) + \phi r_{t-1} + \eta_t; \tag{A2}$$

$$\frac{P_t}{D_t} = E_t \left[\sum_{i=1}^{\infty} \exp\left(\sum_{j=1}^{i} -r_{t+j-1} + \Delta d_{t+j} \right) \right]. \tag{A3}$$

Introduce $v_{t,i} = E_t[\exp(\sum_{j=1}^{i}(-r_{t+j-1} + \Delta d_{t+j}))]$. Hence,

$$\frac{P_t}{D_t} = \sum_{i=1}^{\infty} v_{t,i}. \tag{A4}$$

Our conjecture is that

$$v_{t,i} = \exp(a_i + b_i \Delta d_t + c_i r_t) \tag{A5}$$

with the evolution of the $a_i, b_i,$ and c_i governed by the difference equations in equation (8) and $a_0 = b_0 = c_0 = 0$. It is easy to see that this works for $i = 1$. The induction step involves showing that

$$v_{t,i+1} = E_t[\exp(-r_t + \Delta d_{t+1})v_{t+1,i}] = \exp(a_{i+1} + b_{i+1} \Delta d_t + c_{i+1} r_t), \tag{A6}$$

which is straightforward.

A special case of this model is $q = -\ln\delta, \sigma_\eta^2 = 0, \phi = 0$, the case of constant expected returns. For this case, the solution can be rewritten as

$$\frac{P_t}{D_t} = Z_t \sum_{i=1}^{\infty} \delta^i \exp\left(v_i - \frac{\rho^i}{1 - \rho} \Delta d_t\right) \qquad \text{(A7)}$$

with

$$Z_t = \exp\left(\frac{\rho}{1 - \rho} \Delta d_t\right)$$

$$v_i = \frac{1}{2} \frac{\sigma^2}{(1 - \rho)^2} \left[i - 2\rho \frac{1 - \rho^i}{1 - \rho} + \rho^2 \frac{1 - \rho^{2i}}{1 - \rho^2}\right]. \qquad \text{(A8)}$$

B. Monte Carlo Study

We first calibrate the model to U.S. data. We fix the first three moments of dividend growth both to match the data and to guarantee reasonable implied moments for dividend yields. We set the unconditional mean of the time-varying expected return equal to 0.10 and its persistence equal to 0.75. Finally, the standard deviation of r_t is only 40 percent of that of dividend growth. With these parameters, the model delivers moments within one standard error of the mean, standard deviation, and autocorrelation of dividend growth rates, and the mean and autocorrelation of stock returns. It delivers stock returns that are slightly more variable than the data, but the implied moment remains within a two standard error band of the data moment. Although the dividend yield mean and volatility are not statistically close to the data moments, they are economically of similar magnitude. Further details are provided in Table AI.

Table AII describes a Monte Carlo experiment that illustrates the relative performance of the two measures of cost of capital changes (average returns before and after the break versus changes in dividend yields) in the context of the present value model. The table is presented in terms of cost of capital decreases; hence, a negative change implies an increase in the cost of capital. We simulate samples of 40 annual observations (which is double the number of observations we have for a typical emerging market) on $[\Delta d_t, r_t]$, but the mean of the r_t process permanently changes by two percent (from 10 percent to eight percent) midway through the sample. In population, the change in average returns ought to be approximately 2.19 percent (see footnote 8). The small sample distribution for the change in average simple returns is very spread out in that there is a 10 percent probability of concluding that the cost of capital went up by 5.44 percent or more, even though it actually dropped by 2.19 percent. The low variability of dividend yields implies that they virtually always decrease and the 10 percent quantile is still a 1.43 percent drop in the dividend yield.

604   *The Journal of Finance*

Table AI
A Comparison of Model and U.S. Data Moments

The annual data are from Ibbotson Associates spanning 1926–1996. The table reports the mean, standard deviation, and autocorrelation for the three series with a GMM-based standard error in parentheses. For more details, see Bekaert and Grenadier (1999). The third line is the moment implied by the present value model:

$$\Delta d_t = 0.032(1 - 0.1) + 0.1 \, \Delta d_{t-1} + 0.14 \, [1 - (0.1)^2]^{0.5} \times u_t,$$

$$r_t = 0.10(1 - 0.75) + 0.75 \, r_{t-1} + (0.4)0.14 \, [1 - (0.75)^2]^{0.5} \times v_t,$$

where u_t and v_t are jointly $N(0, I)$. To compute the model moments, we use a simulation of 100,000 observations. The model moments indicated by a * follow directly from the model parameters. The imposed and simulated moments are identical up to three digits.

Moment	Real Dividend Growth	Dividend Yields	Real Stock Returns
Mean			
Data	0.008	0.044	0.087
Data std. error	(0.0159)	(0.002)	(0.024)
PV model	0.032*	0.050	0.107*
Standard deviation			
Data	0.128	0.150	0.200
Data std. error	(0.023)	(0.002)	(0.018)
PV model	0.140*	0.010	0.229
Autocorrelation			
Data	0.185	0.667	0.001
Data std. error	(0.154)	(0.097)	(0.103)
PV model	0.100*	0.745	−0.050

Panel B illustrates the role of time-varying expected returns. We isolate cases in which expected returns are, at the time of the liberalization, low (left columns) or high (right columns). We define low (high) expected returns as five-year average returns before the liberalization of less (more) than eight percent (12 percent). When returns were already low in the preliberalization period, the drop in the cost of capital is less noticeable. Interestingly, the dividend yield measure remains fairly robust with the difference in mean across the distributions only being 30 basis points. For average returns, on the other hand, the differences are dramatic. In the low expected return case, no drop in the cost of capital is observed on average at all, and the decrease is upwardly biased in the high expected returns case. This is potentially important for empirical work since governments may choose to liberalize when it appears most advantageous to them, such as in times of depressed stock prices. Even then, dividend yields allow a rather accurate assessment of the long-run impact on the cost of capital.

So far we have examined one country at a time. Of course, cross-sectional pooling is what renders power to event studies. Unfortunately, we only have 20 emerging markets. In Panel C, we take our 20,000 Monte Carlo experi-

ments and construct cross-sectionally averaged changes in the cost of capital
over 20 experiments, yielding 1,000 observations. Although this is an idealized setup, the improvement is dramatic. The 10 percent quantile now suggests a 57 basis point decrease in the cost of capital. Nevertheless, whereas
the standard deviation of the returns measure distribution shrinks by a factor of almost four (6.04 percent to 1.27 percent), so does the standard deviation of the dividend yield change distribution, which drops to 12 basis points.
The actual change is now bounded between 1.78 percent and 2.56 percent for
our 1,000 experiments.

Experiment 2 investigates the effect of changing the mean dividend growth
rate, in addition to the change in q. Dividend yield changes now also reflect
this improvement in growth opportunities, and overestimate the true cost of
capital change. In another Monte Carlo experiment (not reported), we decrease the cost of capital by two percent, but increase dividend growth by
three percent. Dividend yields now decrease on average by 4.18 percent,
whereas returns decrease on average by 1.19 percent. However, the dispersion is large, with a 10 percent quantile of a 6.64 percent increase in returns.
Cross-sectional pooling reduces the 10 percent quantile to only slightly positive changes in average returns, but with the volatility of returns observed
in emerging markets much higher than in our experiments it remains unlikely that returns lead to statistically significant results. For dividend yields,
the effect of changes in μ and changes in q is close to additive and the range
is very tight.

C. The Cost of Capital and Growth

Our structural model requires the estimation of six parameters before and
after the structural break $(\mu,\rho,\sigma_\eta^2,\sigma_\epsilon^2,\phi,q)$, characterizing the properties of
dividend growth and expected returns. We identify these parameters in a
two-stage approach using data on real GDP growth (as a proxy to Δd_t in the
model), log returns (endogenous in the model), and dividend yields (also
endogenous in the model). We seek to estimate the mean, standard deviation, autocorrelation of real GDP growth, the mean dividend yield and its
autocorrelation, and the volatility of log returns for an "average" emerging
market. From the first three moments we can immediately infer the parameters for the dividend growth process. We then calibrate the remaining three
parameters for the expected return process so that they match the last three
moments. In practice, we conduct an exactly identified simulated GMM estimation with an identity weighting matrix, using 10,000 observations for
the simulated sample. Note that we do not use average returns because of
the imprecision with which they are measured. Expected returns are inferred indirectly from data on dividend yields, return volatility, and the structural restrictions imposed by the model.

We define an "average" emerging market consistent with the cross-
sectional regression framework. Let us illustrate for GDP growth. A similar
exercise is conducted for dividend yields and log returns. We consider a panel

Table AII
Small Sample Distribution of the Various Estimators of the Cost of Capital Decrease

Panel A reports characteristics of the small sample distribution for two experiments. We draw 20,000 samples of annual 40 observations on $\{q_t, \Delta d_t\}$ and then impute implied stock market returns. For the first 20 years, $q = 10$ percent, afterward, $q = 8$ percent. The cost of capital decrease measured in the simple returns is from 10.69 percent $[\exp(q + (\frac{1}{2})\sigma_\eta^2/(1 - \phi^2)) - 1]$ to 8.5 percent; a 2.19 percent decrease. In experiment 1, the only parameter change is the mean of q, in experiment 2, the mean of Δd_t, μ, increases by one percent as well. Panel B singles out samples with unusually low or high average returns five years before the break. Panel C shows results from cross-sectionally averaging 20 samples at a time.

Panel A: Standard Monte Carlo Distribution (20,000 experiments)

	Experiment 1 Reduce Cost of Capital, q, by 2%		Experiment 2 Reduce Cost of Capital, q, by 2% Increase Mean of Δd_t by 1%	
	Returns	Dividend Yields	Returns	Dividend Yields
Mean	2.28	2.18	2.25	3.25
σ	6.04	0.58	6.05	0.54
10% quantile	-5.44	1.43	-5.49	2.47
Minimum	-20.87	-0.03	-21.18	1.49
Maximum	28.12	4.82	28.19	3.25

Panel B: Restricted Monte Carlo Distribution (approximately 7250 experiments)

	Pre-Break Expected Return <8% (Low expected returns) Experiment 1		Pre-Break Expected Return >12% (High expected returns) Experiment 1	
	Returns	Dividend Yields	Returns	Dividend Yields
Mean	0.00	2.00	4.39	2.27
σ	5.74	0.57	5.75	0.59
10% quantile	-9.48	1.37	-0.15	1.52
Minimum	-20.87	-0.03	-15.40	0.36
Maximum	20.28	4.22	28.12	4.82

Panel C: Monte Carlo Distribution for Cross-Sectional Averages (1,000 experiments)

	Experiment 1 Reduce Cost of Capital, q, by 2%		Experiment 2 Reduce Cost of Capital, q, by 2% Increase Mean of Δd_t by 1%	
	Returns	Dividend Yields	Returns	Dividend Yields
Mean	2.28	2.18	2.25	3.25
σ	1.27	0.12	1.28	0.11
10% quantile	0.57	2.03	0.54	3.12
Minimum	-1.28	1.78	-1.36	2.86
Maximum	6.32	2.56	6.30	3.60

608   *The Journal of Finance*

regression with the dependent variable as real GDP growth, real GDP growth squared, or real GDP growth times past real GDP growth. The right-hand-side variables are simply a constant and the liberalization dummy. We run a cross-sectionally pooled regression with heteroskedasticity correction to obtain estimates of the constant and the liberalization effect for each moment. We use the estimated coefficients as our estimates of the corresponding uncentered moments from which we can construct the moments of interest. The regression approach has the advantage of making exactly the same assumptions about the cross section of emerging markets as our main regression framework, including the heteroskedasticity correction. The disadvantage of this approach is that the implied autocorrelation is not guaranteed to be between -1 and 1, and we experienced such a problem with the autocorrelation of the dividend yield for the Official Liberalization measure. We therefore focus the discussion on the Capital Flows measure, although the results for the Official Liberalization measure are qualitatively the same, when we fix the autocorrelation coefficient of the dividend yield at some high number.

The calibrated model fits the data moments very well. By construction, the first three moments of dividend (GDP) growth are matched exactly, as is the mean dividend yield and return volatility. The model has slightly lower dividend yield variability, 1.3 (1.0) percent before (after) the break, than is true in the data, 1.7 (1.2) percent before (after) the break. Dividend yield autocorrelation is slightly higher in the model but the overall fit is impressive. The main output is the estimate of the average decrease in log-returns versus dividend yields. Dividend yields decrease by 75 basis points, average log-returns decrease by 11 basis points.

Interestingly, it very much matters how the expected return is computed. When we investigate the mean of the expected return process (q), it *increases* from 11.72 percent to 11.98 percent and so does the mean of gross returns, from 13.60 percent to 13.99 percent. The main reason for these large differences between logged and nonlogged returns is of course the tremendous volatility characterizing emerging markets. Fama (1996) notes a similar problem in computing the cost of capital for individual stock returns in the United States, which display about the same volatility as emerging markets do.

Appendix B. Discussion of the Choices for Official Liberalization Dates[17]

Argentina: *November 1989.* New Foreign Investment regime put into place. All legal limits on foreign investment abolished. Capital gains and dividends allowed to be repatriated freely. No need for previous approval of transactions. No legal limits regarding type or nature of foreign investment. Introduction of a free exchange regime (free repatriation of capital, remittance of dividends and capital gains.) Also IFC liberalization date.

---

[17] This discussion is based on the chronology in Bekaert and Harvey (1998).

Brazil: *May 1991*. Foreign investment law changed. Resolution 1832 Annex IV stipulates that foreign institutions can now own up to 49 percent of voting stock and 100 percent of nonvoting stock. Economic Ministers approve rules allowing direct foreign investments; 15 percent on distributed earnings and dividends but no tax on capital gains. Foreign investment capital must remain in the country for six years as opposed to 12 under previous law. Bank debt restructuring agreement. Also IFC liberalization date. Note that until *July 1991* foreign portfolio investors could invest in Brazil only through Brazil investment funds. Now foreign investors are allowed to set up omnibus accounts which are essentially portfolios of one or more shares held in local custody. There are no minimum holding period restrictions.

Chile: *January 1992*. Regulation DL600 eases restrictions on foreign investment and repatriation of capital to minimum holding period of one year. Central Bank revalues the peso by five percent. DL600 also offers foreigners guaranteed access to the foreign exchange market. Coincides with a period of broad economic reform. For example, tariffs reduced to 11 percent across the board in *June 1991*. Note IFC liberalization date is *December 1988*. There are no particular regulatory events that coincide with this date. However, in 1987, Chile allowed, through LAN18657, Foreign Capital Investment Funds (FCIFs) to be set up outside Chile. An FCIF could neither invest more than 10 percent of its assets in a single stock nor own more than five percent of the voting shares of any stock. The funds require a local administrator.

Colombia: *February 1991*. At the end of *January 1991*, a new foreign investment code, Resolution 49, is made effective. Foreigners are given the same rights as domestic investors: remittances of up to 100 percent of most capital registered in the past year; equal access to local credit sources as well as to export incentives; and 100 percent foreign ownership of financial institutions. Also the IFC liberalization date.

Greece: *December 1987*. In 1987, there is a liberalization of currency controls. Europeans are allowed to participate in the equity market and to repatriate their capital gains. IFC considers 1987 the liberalization date for European investors but it dates the official liberalization in *December 1988* when the market is opened to non-European investors. 1987 also coincides with a number of significant macroeconomic reforms including the privatization of 190 of the largest state-controlled enterprises. Additionally, the government announces further privatization plans.

India: *November 1992*. In *September 1992*, the government announces that foreign portfolio investors will be able to invest directly in listed Indian securities. Simultaneously, the tax environment is made more conducive to foreign holdings of domestic securities. Also the IFC liberalization date.

Indonesia: *September 1989*. Minister of Finance allows foreigners to purchase up to 49 percent of all companies listing shares on the domestic exchange excluding financial firms. In *May 1989*, government accepted the IMF's conditions for currency convertibility. Also the IFC liberalization date.

610   *The Journal of Finance*

Jordan: *December 1995*. Foreign investment bylaws passed, allowing foreign investors to purchase shares without government approval. Note, IFC considers liberalization date to be *December 1988*. However, at this time and afterward, there is little foreign participation in the equity market.

Korea: *January 1992*. In *September 1991*, there is an announcement that the stock market will open to investors in January of 1992. The announced regulations are that a foreign investor cannot own more than three percent of a company's shares and foreigners cannot own collectively more than 10 percent of a company. The government later raised the limit to 25 percent for 45 companies that already had more than 10 percent ownership by foreigners. Also the IFC liberalization date. Important coincident events include Korea being admitted into the United Nations in *September 1991* and Republic of Korea and Democratic People's Republic of Korea concluding an agreement covering political reconciliation, military nonaggression, and economic cooperation in *December 1991*.

Malaysia: *December 1988*. In the budget introduced in *October 1988*, plans are detailed for the liberalization of foreign ownership policies to attract more foreign investors. Also the IFC liberalization date.

Mexico: *May 1989*. In 1989, a 1973 law promoting Mexican investment and foreign investment is relaxed. Amnesty in effect for repatriation of flight capital with a one-time two percent tax only. Also the IFC liberalization date. Important coincidental economic news includes the *March 1989* Brady plan (adjustment package that combined debt relief and market-oriented reforms).

Nigeria: *August 1995*. In 1995, the government budget repeals the Exchange Control Act of 1962 and the Enterprise Promotion Act of 1989. It also legalizes the autonomous foreign exchange market that was banned in *January 1994*. Repeal of the Exchange Control and Enterprises Promotion act clears the way for the stock exchange to be opened to foreign portfolio investment. In *August 1995*, the government releases the Nigerian Investment Promotion Decree and the Foreign Exchange Monitoring and Miscellaneous Provisions Decree. These decrees open the Nigerian market to foreign portfolio investment. There is no IFC liberalization date.

Pakistan: *February 1991*. In *November 1990*, several liberalization moves were announced that relaxed both domestic and foreign investment procedures. In *February 1991*, new foreign investment law passes. Now there is no restriction on foreigners or nonresident Pakistanis purchasing shares of a listed company or subscribing to public offerings of shares. There are, however, some approvals still necessary from the Investment Promotion Bureau, the government's project sanctioning and foreign investment regulatory body. Additionally, there still exist some exchange control restrictions imposed by the State Bank of Pakistan. The first foreign investment in listed shares takes place in *March 1991*. Also the IFC liberalization date.

Philippines: *June 1991*. A Foreign Investment Act is signed into law. The Act removes, over a period of three years, all restrictions on foreign investments. Under the provisions, foreign investors are required only to register with the Securities and Exchange Commission, and most sectors of the economy are opened to 100 percent foreign ownership. The IFC official date is *October 1989* but that is difficult to justify.

Portugal: *July 1986*. In 1986, Portugal enters the EC and agrees to eliminate all barriers to capital movements. In *July 1986*, all restrictions on foreign investment ownership are removed except for arms sector investments. The IFC official date is *December 1988*.

Taiwan: *January 1991*. Implementation date of the second phase of the liberalization plan. Eligible foreign institutional investors may now invest directly in Taiwan securities if they have applied for and received SEC approval as a qualified foreign institutional investor (QFII). Outward remittance is not allowed until three months after initial investment. Each foreign institution is limited to holding a maximum of five percent of any listed stock and total foreign holdings in any listed companies may not exceed 10 percent. Also the IFC liberalization date.

Thailand: *September 1987*. Inauguration of the Stock Exchange of Thailand's Alien Board. The Alien Board allows foreigners to trade stocks of those companies that have reached their foreign investment limits. Thais continue to trade stocks on the Main Board. The IFC liberalization date is *December 1988*, which is not associated with any particular regulatory changes.

Turkey: *July 1989*. Communiqué passes allowing foreign mutual funds to have access to equities market. Subsequently, a resolution, announced in the *Official Gazette*, declares the securities market in Turkey fully open to foreign institutional and individual investors. Also the IFC liberalization date.

Venezuela: *January 1990*. Decree 727 (January 16) opens foreign direct investment for all stocks except for bank stocks. Also the IFC liberalization date.

Zimbabwe: *June 1993*. In *April 1993*, Finance Minister Chidzero announces new investment guidelines and export incentives that effectively open the Zimbabwe Stock Exchange (ZSE) to foreign portfolio investment. Foreign investors are able to participate on the ZSE provided that: (1) they finance the purchase of shares by inward transfer of foreign currency through normal banking channels; (2) the purchase of shares is limited to 25 percent of the total equity of the company (excluding existing foreign shareholdings prior to May 1993) with the single investor limited to acquire at most five percent of the shares outstanding; and (3) investments (capital and capital gains) are freely remittable after capital gains taxes. Additionally, foreign investors participating in the stock market, under the new rules, are not required to obtain exchange control approval and can register share purchases either in their own names or names of nominee companies. These guidelines become effective on *June 23, 1993*. There is no official IFC liberalization date.

REFERENCES

Aggarwal, Reena, Carla Inclan, and Ricardo Leal, 1999, Volatility in emerging stock markets, *Journal of Financial and Quantitative Analysis* 34, 33–55.

Bai, Jushan, Robin Lumsdaine, and James H. Stock, 1998, Testing for and dating breaks in stationary and nonstationary multivariate time series, *Review of Economic Studies* 65, 395–432.

Bailey, Warren, and Joseph Lim, 1992, Evaluating the diversification benefits of the new country funds, *Journal of Portfolio Management* 18, 74–89.

Basak, Suleyman, 1996, An intertemporal model of international capital market segmentation, *Journal of Financial and Quantitative Analysis* 31, 161–188

Basak, Suleyman and Domenico Cuoco, 1998, An equilibrium model with restricted stock market participation, *Review of Financial Studies* 11, 309–341.

Bekaert, Geert, 1995, Market integration and investment barriers in emerging equity markets, *World Bank Economic Review* 9, 75–107.

Bekaert, Geert, and Steven R. Grenadier, 1999, Stock and bond pricing in an affine economy, Working paper, Stanford University.

Bekaert, Geert, and Campbell R. Harvey, 1995, Time-varying world market integration, *Journal of Finance* 50, 403–444.

Bekaert, Geert, and Campbell R. Harvey, 1997, Emerging equity market volatility, *Journal of Financial Economics* 43, 29–78.

Bekaert, Geert, and Campbell R. Harvey, 2000, Capital flows and the behavior of emerging equity market returns; in Sebastian Edwards, ed.: *Capital Inflows to Emerging Markets* (University of Chicago Press for the National Bureau of Economic Research, Chicago), forthcoming.

Bekaert, Geert, Campbell R. Harvey, and Robin Lumsdaine, 1998, Dating the integration of world capital markets, Working paper, Stanford University and Duke University.

Bekaert, Geert, and Michael S. Urias, 1996, Diversification, integration and emerging market closed-end funds, *Journal of Finance* 51, 835–870.

Bollerslev, Tim, 1986, Generalized autoregressive conditional heteroskedasticity, *Journal of Econometrics* 72, 307–327.

Bollerslev, Tim, and Robert J. Hodrick, 1995, Financial market efficiency tests; in M. Hashem Pesaran and Michael R. Wickens, eds.: *The Handbook of Applied Econometrics: Vol. 1. Macroeconometrics* (Blackwell, Oxford).

Campbell, John Y., and Robert J. Shiller, 1988, The dividend-price ratio and expectations of future dividends and discount factors, *Review of Financial Studies* 1, 195–228.

Cochrane, John, 1992, Explaining the variance of price-dividend ratios, *Review of Financial Studies* 5, 243–280.

De Santis, Giorgio, and Selahattin İmrohoroğlu, 1997, Stock returns and volatility in emerging financial markets, *Journal of International Money and Finance* 16, 561–579.

Domowitz, Ian, Jack Glen, and Ananth Madhavan, 1997, Market segmentation and stock prices: Evidence from an emerging market, *Journal of Finance* 52, 1059–1086.

Domowitz, Ian, Jack Glen, and Ananth Madhavan, 1998, International cross-listing, market segmentation and foreign ownership restrictions: The case of Mexico; in Richard Levich, ed.: *The Future of Emerging Market Capital Flows* (Kluwer Academic Publishers, Boston).

Erb, Claude B., Campbell R. Harvey, and Tadas E. Viskanta, 1996a, Expected returns and volatility in 135 countries, *Journal of Portfolio Management* 22, 46–58.

Erb, Claude B., Campbell R. Harvey, and Tadas E. Viskanta, 1996b, Political risk, economic risk and financial risk, *Financial Analysts Journal*, 29–46.

Errunza, Vihang, Lemma Senbet, and Ked Hogan, 1998, The pricing of country funds from emerging markets: Theory and evidence, *International Journal of Theoretical and Applied Finance* 1, 111–143.

Fama, Eugene F., 1996, Discounting under uncertainty, *Journal of Business* 69, 415–428.

Foerster, Stephen R., and G. Andrew Karolyi, 1999, The effects of market segmentation and investor recognition on asset prices: Evidence from foreign stocks listing in the United States, *Journal of Finance* 54, 981–1014.

Glosten, Lawrence R., Ravi Jagannathan, and David E. Runkle, 1993, On the relation between the expected value and the volatility of the nominal excess return on stocks, *Journal of Finance* 48, 1779–1802.

Grossman, Sanford, 1995, Dynamic asset allocation and the informational efficiency of markets, *Journal of Finance* 50, 773–788.

Grossman, Sanford, and Joseph Stiglitz, 1980, On the impossibility of informationally efficient markets, *American Economic Review* 70, 393–408.

Hamao, Yasushi, and Jianping Mei, 1997, Living with the "enemy": An analysis of investment in the Japanese equity market, Working paper, Columbia University.

Harvey, Campbell R., 1991, The world price of covariance risk, *Journal of Finance* 46, 111–157.

Harvey, Campbell R., 1995, Predictable risk and returns in emerging markets, *Review of Financial Studies* 8, 773–816.

Henry, Peter Blair, 1999, Do stock market liberalizations cause investment booms? *Journal of Financial Economics*, forthcoming.

Henry, Peter Blair, 2000, Stock market liberalization, economic reform, and emerging market equity prices, *Journal of Finance*, this issue, 529–564.

Karolyi, G. Andrew, 1998, *What Happens to Stocks That List Shares Abroad? A Survey of the Evidence and Its Managerial Implications*, Salomon Brothers Monograph Series (Salomon Brothers, New York).

Kang, Jun-Koo, and René M. Stulz, 1997, Why is there a home bias? An analysis of foreign portfolio equity ownership in Japan, *Journal of Financial Economics* 46, 1–28.

Kim, E. Han, and Vijay Singal, 2000, Stock market opening: Experience of emerging economies, *Journal of Business* 73, 25–66.

Kleidon, Allan W., 1986, Variance bounds tests and stock price valuation models, *Journal of Political Economy* 94, 953–1001.

Korajczyk, Robert A., 1996, A measure of stock market integration for developed and emerging markets, *World Bank Economic Review* 10, 267–290.

Miller, Darius P., 1999, The impact of international market segmentation on securities prices: Evidence from Depositary Receipts, *Journal of Financial Economics* 51, 103–124.

Newbery, David, 1987, When do futures stabilize spot prices, *International Economic Review* 28, 291–297.

Obstfeld, Maurice, 1994, Risk taking, global diversification and growth, *American Economic Review* 84, 1310–1329.

Perotti, Enrico C., and Pieter van Oijen, 1997, Privatization, stock market development and political risk in emerging economies, Working paper, University of Amsterdam.

Richards, Anthony J., 1996, Volatility and predictability in national markets: How do emerging and mature markets differ? Staff papers, International Monetary Fund, Washington, D.C.

Ross, Stephen A., 1989, Information and volatility: The no-arbitrage martingale approach to timing and resolution irrelevancy, *Journal of Finance* 44, 1–17.

Schwert, G. William, 1989a, Business cycles, financial crises and stock volatility, *Carnegie-Rochester Conference Series on Public Policy* 31, 83–126.

Schwert, G. William, 1989b, Why does stock market volatility change over time? *Journal of Finance* 44, 1115–1154.

Sims, Christopher A., and Harald Uhlig, 1991, Understanding unit rooters: A helicopter tour, *Econometrica* 59, 1591–1600.

Stulz, René M., 1999, International portfolio flows and security markets; in Martin Feldstein, ed.: *International Capital Flows* (University of Chicago Press, Chicago).

Subrahmanyam, Marti G., 1975, On the optimality of international capital market integration, *Journal of Financial Economics* 2, 3–28.

Tandon, Kishore, 1997, External financing in emerging markets: An analysis of market responses, *Emerging Markets Quarterly* 1, 63–74.

Tesar, Linda, and Ingrid Werner, 1995a, Home bias and high turnover, *Journal of International Money and Finance* 14, 467–492.

Tesar, Linda, and Ingrid Werner, 1995b, U.S. equity investment in emerging stock markets, *World Bank Economic Review* 9, 109–130.

Urias, Michael, 1994, The impact of security cross-listing on the cost of capital in emerging markets, Unpublished dissertation, Stanford University.

7

THE JOURNAL OF FINANCE • VOL. LV, NO. 2 • APRIL 2000

Stock Market Liberalization, Economic Reform, and Emerging Market Equity Prices

PETER BLAIR HENRY*

ABSTRACT

A stock market liberalization is a decision by a country's government to allow foreigners to purchase shares in that country's stock market. On average, a country's aggregate equity price index experiences abnormal returns of 3.3 percent per month in real dollar terms during an eight-month window leading up to the implementation of its initial stock market liberalization. This result is consistent with the prediction of standard international asset pricing models that stock market liberalization may reduce the liberalizing country's cost of equity capital by allowing for risk sharing between domestic and foreign agents.

A stock market liberalization is a decision by a country's government to allow foreigners to purchase shares in that country's stock market. Standard international asset pricing models (IAPMs) predict that stock market liberalization may reduce the liberalizing country's cost of equity capital by allowing for risk sharing between domestic and foreign agents (Stapleton and Subrahmanyan (1977), Errunza and Losq (1985), Eun and Janakiramanan (1986), Alexander, Eun, and Janakiramanan (1987), and Stulz (1999a, 1999b)).

This prediction has two important empirical implications for those emerging countries that liberalized their stock markets in the late 1980s and early 1990s. First, if stock market liberalization reduces the aggregate cost of equity capital then, holding expected future cash flows constant, we should observe an increase in a country's equity price index when the market learns that a stock market liberalization is going to occur. The second implication is

* Assistant Professor of Economics, Graduate School of Business, Stanford University, Stanford, CA 94305-5015. This paper is a revised version of Chapter 1 of my Ph.D. thesis at the Massachusetts Institute of Technology. I thank Christian Henry and Lisa Nelson for their support and encouragement. I am grateful to Steve Buser, Paul Romer, Andrei Shleifer, Jeremy Stein, René Stulz (the editor), and two anonymous referees for helpful comments on earlier drafts. I also thank Olivier Blanchard, Rudi Dornbusch, Stanley Fischer, Jeffrey Kling, Don Lessard, Tim Opler, Jim Poterba, Peter Reiss, Ken Singleton, Robert Solow, Ingrid Werner, and seminar participants at Harvard, MIT, Northwestern, Ohio State, Stanford, UNC-Chapel Hill, and the University of Virginia. I am grateful to Nora Richardson and Joanne Campbell for outstanding research assistance and to Charlotte Pace for superb editorial assistance. The International Finance Corporation and the Research Foundation of Chartered Financial Analysts generously allowed me to use the Emerging Markets Database. Ross Levine generously shared his extensive list of capital control liberalization dates. Finally, I would like to thank the National Science Foundation, The Ford Foundation, and the Stanford Institute for Economic Policy Research (SIEPR) for financial support. All remaining errors are my own.

that we should observe an increase in physical investment following stock market liberalizations, because a fall in a country's cost of equity capital will transform some investment projects that had a negative net present value (NPV) before liberalization into positive NPV endeavors after liberalization. This second effect of stock market liberalization should generate higher growth rates of output and have a broader impact on economic welfare than the financial windfall to domestic shareholders (see Henry (1999a)). This paper examines whether the data are consistent with the first of these two implications. Specifically, an event study approach is used to assess whether stock market liberalization is associated with a revaluation of equity prices and a fall in the cost of equity capital.

In the sample of 12 emerging countries examined in this paper, stock markets experience average abnormal returns of 4.7 percent per month in real dollar terms during an eight-month window leading up to the implementation of a country's initial stock market liberalization. After controlling for comovements with world stock markets, economic policy reforms, and macroeconomic fundamentals, the average abnormal return, 3.3 percent per month over the same horizon, is smaller but still economically and statistically significant. Estimates using five-month, two-month, and implementation-month-only windows are all associated with statistically significant stock price revaluation. The largest monthly estimate, 6.5 percent, is associated with the implementation-month-only estimate.

These facts are consistent with a fundamental prediction of the standard IAPM. If an emerging country's stock market is completely segmented from the rest of the world, then the equity premium embedded in its aggregate valuation will be proportional to the variance of the country's aggregate cash flows. Once liberalization takes place and the emerging country's stock market becomes fully integrated, its equity premium will be proportional to the covariance of the country's aggregate cash flows with those of a world portfolio. If, in spite of foreign ownership restrictions, the emerging market is not completely segmented (Bekaert and Harvey (1995)) then the emerging market's equilibrium valuation will incorporate an equity premium that lies somewhere between the autarky and fully integrated premium.[1]

The general consensus (see Stulz (1999a, 1999b), Tesar and Werner (1998), Bekaert and Harvey (2000), and Errunza and Miller (1998)) is that the local price of risk (the variance) exceeds the global price of risk (the covariance). Therefore, we expect the equity premium to fall when a completely or mildly segmented emerging country liberalizes its stock market.[2] Holding expected

---

[1] See also Errunza, Losq, and Padmanabhan (1992), who demonstrate that emerging markets are neither fully integrated nor completely segmented. Even if the emerging country prohibits developed-country investors from investing in its domestic equity market, developed-country investors may be able to construct portfolios of developed-country securities that mimic the returns on the emerging country's stock market.

[2] Markets that are mildly segmented ex ante should experience a smaller decline than fully segmented markets. See Errunza and Losq (1989).

future cash flows constant, this fall in the equity premium will cause a permanent fall in the aggregate cost of equity capital and an attendant revaluation of the aggregate equity price index.[3]

One of the key issues in constructing estimates of the cumulative abnormal returns associated with a country's initial stock market liberalization lies in establishing the date of the initial liberalization and picking an appropriate time interval around this date. After providing a detailed description of the dating procedure and the reasons for using an eight-month event window, the empirical analysis in this paper begins by focusing on the behavior of stock prices during the eight-month window. After controlling for comovements with world stock returns, macroeconomic reforms, and macroeconomic fundamentals, the average monthly revaluation effect associated with the eight-month stock market liberalization window is 3.3 percent, which implies a total revaluation of 26 percent.

Although these results suggest a revaluation of equity prices in anticipation of the initial stock market liberalization, using a relatively long window is problematic because policymakers may behave like managers who issue equity following a run-up in stock prices (Ritter (1991) and Loughran and Ritter (1995)). Using an eight-month event window may overstate the liberalization effect if policymakers try to liberalize during a period of unusually high returns. To address this problem, the paper also presents estimates based on shorter event windows. Estimates using five-month, two-month, and one-month (implementation-month-only) windows are all associated with a statistically significant stock price revaluation. The largest effect, 6.5 percent, is associated with the implementation-month-only estimate, which suggests that the revaluation associated with a country's initial stock market liberalization is not an artifact of using long windows. Further checks of robustness of the results are performed by estimating the revaluation effect using implementation-month-only windows and alternative liberalization dates that have been proposed by other authors. These results are quantitatively and qualitatively similar to the benchmark results. Finally, the paper also demonstrates that stock market liberalizations that follow the initial liberalization are associated with much smaller and statistically insignificant revaluations.

This paper presents the first careful empirical estimates of the impact of stock market liberalization on emerging market equity prices. A number of papers examine the effect of stock market liberalization on market integra-

---

[3] This is the case of an unanticipated liberalization. If the liberalization is announced before it actually occurs, then there will be a jump in price upon announcement followed by mild price appreciation until the liberalization is implemented. The reason for price appreciation between announcement and implementation is as follows: Let $P^* > P$ be the integrated capital market equilibrium price. Upon announcement of a future liberalization at time T, the current price will jump only part of the way to P^* because no risk sharing takes place until T^*. However, since the price at T^* must be P^* and there can be no anticipated price jumps, the price must gradually appreciate between T and T^*. Also, if there is uncertainty as to whether the announced stock market liberalization is going to occur, there may be significant price appreciation, as news confirming the liberalization becomes public knowledge.

tion (Errunza et al. (1992), Buckberg (1995), Bekaert (1995), and Bekaert and Harvey (1995)); however, none of these papers estimate the valuation impact of stock market liberalization. Kim and Singal's (2000) evidence that emerging market stock returns are abnormally high in the months leading up to liberalization provides crucial initial evidence on the valuation question, but they acknowledge that there were confounding events throughout the sample period for which they do not control. In a related paper, Bekaert and Harvey (2000) show that liberalization tends to decrease aggregate dividend yields and argue that the price change reflects a change in the cost of capital rather than a change in earnings or profits of firms.[4] They control for the potentially confounding effect of economic reforms by using proxy variables such as credit ratings.

An important contribution of this paper relative to Bekaert and Harvey (2000) is that rather than using ready-made proxy variables to control for economic reforms, I construct a novel data set of economic policy reforms (Henry (1999b)) for each of the 12 countries in my sample. Using this time series of economic policy changes to control explicitly for economic reforms provides transparent evidence on the impact of stock market liberalization.

Specifically, in addition to disentangling the effect of stock market liberalization from the effects of macroeconomic stabilization, trade liberalization, privatization, and the easing of exchange controls, the paper also provides a first set of estimates of the impact of these macroeconomic reforms on the stock market. For example, in the sample of countries considered here, stock markets experience average abnormal returns of 2.1 percent per month in real dollar terms during the eight months leading up to trade liberalization. The trade reform window frequently overlaps with the window for stock market liberalization. Therefore, estimating the effect of stock market liberalization without controlling for trade reforms may result in upward biased estimates. Moreover, the stock price responses to trade and other macroeconomic reforms are of independent interest.

The remainder of this paper proceeds as follows. Section I presents the data and descriptive findings. Section II describes the methodology that is used to identify a country's initial stock market liberalization and measure its valuation impact. Section III presents the empirical results. Section IV discusses some potential interpretation problems. Section V summarizes the main results and conclusions.

I. Data and Descriptive Findings

A. Stock Market Data

The sample examined in this paper includes 12 emerging markets: Argentina, Brazil, Chile, Colombia, Mexico, and Venezuela in Latin America, and India, Malaysia, Korea, the Philippines, Taiwan, and Thailand in Asia. These

---

[4] Errunza and Miller (1998) and Foerster and Karolyi (1999) provide firm level evidence on the related topic of ADR issuance.

countries were chosen because of the general interest in the two regions. Indonesia was excluded from the Asian list because Indonesian stock market data are available only after the date on which its stock market was liberalized. All emerging stock market data are taken from the International Finance Corporation's (IFC) Emerging Markets Data Base (EMDB). Returns for individual countries come from the *IFC Total Return Index* (U.S. dollar denominated). The Morgan Stanley Capital Index for Europe, Asia, and the Far East is also from the EMDB. Data on the S&P 500 come from the IMF's *International Financial Statistics* (IFS). Each country's U.S. dollar total return index is deflated by the U.S. consumer price index, which comes from the IFS. All of the data are monthly. All returns are logarithmic.

B. Stock Market Liberalization Dates

B.1. Implementation Dates

Testing the hypothesis that a country's first stock market liberalization causes equity price revaluation requires a systematic procedure for identifying the date of each country's first stock market liberalization. Official policy decree dates are used when they are available; otherwise, two alternatives are pursued. First, many countries initially permitted foreign ownership through country funds. Since government permission is presumably a necessary condition for establishment of these funds, the date when the first country fund is established is a proxy for the official implementation date. The second way of indirectly capturing official implementation dates is to monitor the IFC's Investability Index. The investability index is the ratio of the market capitalization of stocks that foreigners can legally hold to total market capitalization. A large jump in the investability index is evidence of an official liberalization. In what follows, the date of a country's first stock market liberalization is defined as the first month with a verifiable occurrence of any of the following: liberalization by policy decree, establishment of the first country fund, or an increase in the investability index of at least 10 percent.

Table I lists the date on which each of the 12 countries first liberalized its stock market, as well as the means by which it liberalized. In particular, where the initial liberalization is through a country fund, the specific name of the country fund is given. Table II provides a comparison of the liberalization dates in Table I with other liberalization dates in the literature. Specifically, column (2) of Table II lists the liberalization dates identified using the procedure outlined in the preceding paragraph. Columns (3) through (5) list the official liberalization dates of Bekaert and Harvey (2000), Kim and Singal (2000), and Buckberg (1995) respectively. Column (6) lists the earliest date of the preceding four columns. Three of the 12 dates in column (2) are preceded by dates in column (6). An investigation of the three dates preceding those given in column (2) yielded no confirmation of the September 1987 opening for Thailand or the December 1988 opening for Venezuela. The February 1991 date for Colombia actually refers to *La Apertura*, which was a trade liberalization not a stock market liberalization. Hence, the liberaliza-

534   *The Journal of Finance*

Table I
First Stock Market Liberalization
The stock market liberalization dates are based on information obtained from the following sources: Levine and Zervos (1994); The *Wilson Directory of Emerging Market Funds*; IFC Investable Indices; Park and Van Agtmael (1993); Price (1994); *The Economist Intelligence Unit*, various issues; *The Economist Guide to World Stock Markets* (1988); and the IMF's *Exchange Arrangements and Restrictions*, various issues.

Country	Date of First Stock Market Liberalization	Details about the Liberalization
Argentina	November 1989	Policy Decree: The liberalization began with the New Foreign Investment Regime in November 1989. Legal limits on the type and nature of foreign investments are reduced (Park and Van Agtmael (1993), p. 326).
Brazil	March 1988	Country Fund Introduction: "The Brazil Fund Incorporated" (*The Wilson Directory of Emerging Market Funds*, p. 17).
Chile	May 1987	Country Fund Introduction: "The Toronto Trust Mutual Fund" (*The Wilson Directory of Emerging Market Funds*, p. 17).
Colombia	December 1991	Policy Decree: Resolution 52 allowed foreign investors to purchase up to 100 percent of locally listed companies (Price (1994)).
India	June 1986	Country Fund Introduction: "The India Fund" (*The Wilson Directory of Emerging Market Funds*, p. 12).
Korea	June 1987	Country Fund Introduction: "The Korea Europe Fund Limited" (*The Wilson Directory of Emerging Market Funds*, p. 13).
Malaysia	May 1987	Country Fund Introduction: "The Wardley GS Malaysia Fund" (*The Wilson Directory of Emerging Market Funds*, p. 14).
Mexico	May 1989	Policy Decree: Restrictions on foreign portfolio inflows were substantially liberalized (Levine and Zervos (1994)).
The Philippines	May 1986	Country Fund Introduction: "The Thornton Philippines Redevelopment Fund Limited" (*The Wilson Directory of Emerging Market Funds*, p. 15).
Taiwan	May 1986	Country Fund Introduction: "The Taipei Fund" (*The Wilson Directory of Emerging Market Funds*, p. 15).
Thailand	January 1988	Country Fund Introduction: "The Siam Fund Limited" (*The Wilson Directory of Emerging Market Funds*, p. 16).
Venezuela	January 1990	Policy Decree: Decree 727 completely opened the market to foreign investors except for bank stocks ((Levine and Zervos (1994)).

Table II

Comparison of Official Liberalization Dates across Authors

The dates in column (2) are constructed using the dating procedure described in the paper. The dates in columns (3) through (5) are taken from Bekaert and Harvey (2000), Kim and Singal (2000), and Buckberg (1995), respectively. Column 6 shows the earliest date given for a country in the preceding four columns.

(1) Country	(2) Dating Procedure	(3) Bekaert & Harvey	(4) Kim & Singal	(5) Buckberg	(6) Earliest
Argentina	11-89	11-89	11-89	10-91	11-89
Brazil	3-88	5-91	5-91	5-91	3-88
Chile	5-87	1-92	9-87	10-89	5-87
Colombia	12-91	2-91	2-91	10-91	2-91
India	6-86	11-92	11-92	NA	6-86
Korea	6-87	1-92	1-92	NA	6-87
Malaysia	5-87	12-88	12-88	NA	5-87
Mexico	5-89	5-89	11-89	5-89	5-89
The Philippines	5-86	6-91	7-86	10-89	5-86
Taiwan	5-86	1-91	1-91	NA	5-86
Thailand	1-88	9-87	8-88	NA	9-87
Venezuela	1-90	1-90	1-90	12-88	12-88

tion dates in column (2) also represent the earliest verifiable stock market liberalization dates listed in Table I. This is important because the goal here is to identify the first stock market liberalization in any particular country. The empirical analysis in Section III begins with the dates in column (2) but, for comparison, results based on the other dates are also presented.

B.2. Announcement Dates

A search for announcement dates corresponding to the implementation dates listed in Table I was conducted using the database Lexis/Nexis Research Software version 4.06. Consultations with library science staff suggested that Lexis/Nexis offers two distinct advantages relative to Bloomberg and the Dow Jones News Retrieval. First, Bloomberg has relatively little coverage prior to 1991. Second, Dow Jones News Retrieval covers a subset of the news sources spanned by Lexis/Nexis. Lexis/Nexis covers more than 2,300 full-text information sources from U.S. and overseas newspapers, magazines, journals, newsletters, wire services, and broadcast transcripts. It also covers abstract material from more than 1,000 information sources.

The search algorithm used was as follows. If the initial stock market liberalization came via a country fund, the search was conducted using the name of the country fund. If the initial stock market liberalization was not a country fund, then the following search phrases were used: *stock market liberalization, stock market opening, capital market liberalization, capital market opening, restrictions on foreign capital, foreign investment,* and *foreign portfolio investment.*

536 *The Journal of Finance*

Table III presents the complete results of the search. The first column of the table lists the country and the implementation date of its first stock market liberalization. Column 2 lists all announcement dates that were uncovered by the search. For seven of 12 countries the earliest news of stock market liberalization comes on or after the actual implementation date. Of the five countries for which the announcement date precedes the actual liberalization date, three have announcements occurring only one month in advance. Given the legal, political, and logistical complexities of enacting such a policy, it is hard to believe that the market first learns of the undertaking only a month before it happens. By way of comparison, the average time between announcement and listing for American Depositary Receipts (ADRs) is three months, and ADRs are issued in markets that have already been liberalized. For the remaining two countries, Colombia and Taiwan, only Taiwan's announcement date seems reasonable. The headline for Colombia actually corresponds not to the stock market, but to its major trade liberalization, *La Apertura*. The central point of Table III is that announcement dates uncovered using a source such as Lexis/Nexis are likely to be poor proxies for the date at which information about the liberalization first reached market participants. In the absence of credible announcement dates, the only reliable way of capturing all of the price changes associated with the liberalization is to estimate abnormal returns over a generous window of time preceding the liberalization. A detailed discussion of the construction of such a window is postponed until Section II.

C. Descriptive Findings

Figure 1 motivates the analysis by plotting the average cumulative abnormal return (triangles) across all 12 countries in event time. T^* is the month in which the stock market liberalization was implemented (see the dates in Table I). Figure 1 suggests a revaluation of aggregate equity prices in anticipation of stock market liberalization; the cumulative abnormal return from $T^* - 12$ to T^* is on the order of 40 percent.[5]

As a way of checking the consistency of the cumulative abnormal return plot with other work, Figure 1 also plots the cumulative abnormal change in the log of the dividend yield (squares). As one would expect, the respective plots are near mirror images: Realized returns increase as the dividend yield decreases. The cumulative decline in dividend yields from $T^* - 12$ to T^* is on the order of 30 percent. Since the average level of the dividend yield in these countries prior to liberalization is about four percent, the 30 percent decline reported in Figure 1 suggests an average fall in the dividend yield of about 100 basis points.[6] This estimate of 100 basis points is slightly larger

[5] Kim and Singal (2000) also find that emerging countries experience positive abnormal returns in the months leading up to stock market liberalization. Errunza and Miller (1998) find similar results using firm level data.

[6] Ln(0.04) − Ln(0.03) is approximately equal to 0.3. Therefore, a 30 percent fall in the dividend yield from a level of four percent implies a fall of approximately 100 basis points.

Stock Market Liberalization   537

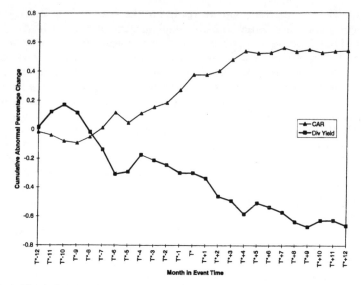

Figure 1. The behavior of stock returns and dividend yields around the first stock market liberalization. The variable on the y-axis is the continuously compounded abnormal percentage change. T^* is the month in which the stock market liberalization was implemented. The upward trending series (triangles) is a plot of the cumulative residuals from a panel regression of the real dollar return from all 12 countries on a constant and 11 country-specific dummies. The downward trending series (squares) is a plot of the cumulative residuals from a panel regression of the change in the natural log of the dividend yield on a constant and 11 country-specific dummies.

than the range of declines (5 to 90 basis points) reported by Bekaert and Harvey (2000), but once controls are introduced in Section III, this number falls well within the range of Bekaert and Harvey's estimates.

Though Figure 1 suggests a causal channel from stock market liberalization to stock prices and the cost of equity capital, the graph needs to be interpreted with caution because it does not control for any other reforms. In particular, note that there is a stock price revaluation of about 20 percent from T^* to $T^* + 4$. The dividend yield also continues to fall after implementation of the liberalization. Since there is no theoretical reason to expect a stock-market-liberalization-induced revaluation after implementation, Figure 1 suggests that favorable, unanticipated macroeconomic events tend to occur following stock market liberalizations. Macroeconomic reforms are the focus of the next subsection.

D. *Economic Reforms*

Conducting an event study is the most direct and transparent way of assessing the impact of stock market liberalization on emerging market equity prices. However, unlike the typical event study in finance where the econo-

Table III
Announcement Dates for First Stock Market Liberalizations

The announcements were procured via Lexis-Nexis Software version 4.06 using the search procedure described in the paper.

(1) Country and Implementation Date	(2) Announcement Date(s)	(3) Source	(4) Headline
Argentina (November 1989)	December 11, 1989	The Financial Times	Argentina fund aims at privatised companies.
Brazil (March 1988)	March 23, 1988	The Toronto Financial Post	Some like it hot: Shares in the fund will be offered to the public shortly by first Boston Corporation and Merrill Lynch Capital Markets
	March 31, 1988 April 4, 1988	PR Newswire Institutional Investor, Inc.	Brazil Fund Common Stock Offered Brazil Fund is Hot
Chile (May 1987)	February 7, 1996	The Reuter European Business Report	Micropal names best 1995 emerging market funds. The Toronto Trust Chile Fund, launched in 1987, is Micropal's best performing emerging market fund over the past seven years
Colombia (December 1991)	February, 1991	National Trade Data Bank Market reports	Colombia-Economic Policy and Trade Practices. The administration of President Gaviria has embarked on "la apertura" (the opening), a bold plan to lower tariffs and other barriers to foreign trade
India (June 1986)	May 12, 1986	The Financial Times	Maverick Brings in the Savings. The government approved the Unit trust of India's (UTI) collaboration with Merrill Lynch to launch the India Fund
	June 17, 1986	The Financial Times	More Details Given for India Fund. The Indian government last week approved the proposal which for the first time will allow foreigners to invest in the Indian stock markets

(continued overleaf)

Country	Date	Source	Headline / Details
Korea (June 1987)	March 21, 1987	*The Economist*	South Korean Securities; Authorised Entry Only
Malaysia (May 1987)	April 8, 1987	Jiji Press Limited	Arab-Malaysian Merchant Bank—IFC Move to Tap U.S. Market.
	May 11, 1987	U.P.I.	Malaysian Fund Offering Increased
Mexico (May 1989)	May 15, 1989	Reuters	Mexico Announces New Foreign Investment Rules
	July 8, 1989	*The New York Times*	Mexico Eases Foreign Curb. The government has opened Mexico's stock exchange to foreign investment
Philippines (May 1986)	September 22, 1986	*Business Week*	For Aquino, U.S. Business Will Be a Tough Sell. *Text*: Hong Kong-based Thornton Management (Asia) Ltd. recently launched the Philippines Redevelopment Fund which invests in Philippine stocks
Taiwan (May 1986)	July 3, 1985	Central News Agency	Local Securities Investment Company Formed in Taipei *Details*: A 25 million dollar investment fund to be called the Taipei Fund will be raised soon
	June 28, 1986	*The Economist*	Asian Funds *Details*: The Taipei Fund was formed on May 22nd
Thailand (January 1988)	April 27, 1988	*The Financial Times*	Another Thai Fund to Join the Market *Details*: the fund was established in January
Venezuela (January 1990)	December, 1989	*South Magazine*	Scramble at the Fringe; Third World Stock Markets *Details*: Liberalisation is proceeding in Argentina and Venezuela

metrician can be reasonably certain that the event in question is isolated from other influential events, the shift from closed to open capital markets usually coincides with four equally important changes in economic policy: macroeconomic stabilization, trade liberalization, privatization, and the easing of exchange controls.

Table IV, which lists all confounding macroeconomic events occurring within a 15-month window around the initial stock market liberalization, forcefully illustrates this point. Argentina provides a good illustration of why attention to concurrent economic reforms is a critical part of this event study. At least part of the dramatic increase in Argentine stock prices during 1989 was probably due to the implementation of a sweeping stabilization plan. There are many other conspicuous examples: IMF negotiations, a free trade agreement, and the overthrow of Marcos in the Philippines (1986); privatization in Malaysia (1987); a Brady debt reduction deal in Venezuela (1990); privatization and tariff reductions in Colombia (1992).[7]

The theory used to explain the stock price effects of a capital market liberalization assumes that everything else is held constant when this change is made. To construct an estimate that we can use to test the theory, it is necessary to hold constant the other reform measures and isolate a pure capital market effect. Additionally, the stock market's response to the other reforms is interesting in its own right. Using the full list of events allows for measurement of the price response to each of the four major reforms.

In addition to the problem of confounding macroeconomic reforms, four other methodological issues are involved in measuring the impact of stock market liberalization on equity prices: construction of the event windows in the absence of announcement dates, multiple stock market liberalizations, and accounting for macroeconomic fundamentals and policy endogeneity. The next section discusses these issues in detail.

II. Methodological Issues

A. *Construction of Event Windows*

In the absence of reliable announcement dates, the average time between announcement and listing for American Depositary Receipts (three months)[8] provides an announcement proxy. Suppose the government announces in month $T^* - 3$ that it will open the stock market to foreign investors in month T^*. Since there can be no anticipated price jumps, the price must jump on the announcement and then gradually appreciate in such a way that there is no jump in price when the liberalization occurs at T^*. Measuring the impact of stock market liberalization in this textbook world would be straightforward: Regress real returns on a constant, a set of control variables, and two dummies.

---

[7] For a complete chronological listing of events in each country see Henry (1999b). The complete list of events is also available at http://www.afajof.org.

[8] I thank an anonymous referee for bringing this fact to my attention.

The first dummy would pick up the level effect of the initial jump at $T^* - 3$, and the second dummy would measure the slope effect due to gradual price appreciation in months $T^* - 2$, $T^* - 1$, and T^*.[9]

Errunza and Miller (1998) argue that, unlike the canonical example where all market participants learn about the future opening at the same time, in practice there is likely to be widespread information leakage prior to any official announcement in emerging markets.[10] Given that learning about a future liberalization is a gradual process in which market participants receive the news at different times, and given the theoretical expectation of no revaluation implementation, an event window of $T^* - 7$ to T^* is used to test for a revaluation effect. Again, T^* refers to the implementation dates in Table I.

The magnitude and statistical significance of abnormal returns during the liberalization window are evaluated by estimating the following panel regression:

$$R_{it} = \alpha_i + \gamma \cdot Liberalize_{it} + \epsilon_{it}. \tag{1}$$

The α_i are country-specific dummies. $Liberalize_{it}$ is a dummy variable that takes on the value one in each of the eight months from $T^* - 7$ to T^* associated with country i's first stock market liberalization.[11] Hence, the parameter γ measures the average monthly abnormal return across all 12 countries during the eight-month stock market liberalization window.

B. Multiple Stock Market Liberalizations

Table AI shows that most countries' initial stock market liberalization did not constitute a complete opening to foreign investors. Rather, stock market liberalization is a gradual process generally involving several liberalizations subsequent to the first. Inasmuch as it is part of a broader set of economic reforms geared toward increased openness, news of the first stock market liberalization is also implicit news about the entire future schedule of stock market liberalizations. Consequently, future stock market liberalizations are

---

[9] Footnote 3 explains why there will be an initial jump followed by price appreciation.

[10] They give an example of the leakage problem in the context of Indian ADRs.

[11] If all market participants learned about the liberalization at the same time and there was no uncertainty about when the liberalization was going to occur, then the *Liberalize* variable would only need to be on during the month in which the announcement occurred. In reality, however, learning about an impending liberalization is a gradual process. The technique of allowing the dummy variable to be on during the entire announcement window is well established (see, e.g., MacKinlay (1997)). This dummy variable method is a variant of standard event study methodology. Standard event studies are unable to take into account exogenous shifts in the equation parameters that may occur during the event window. The dummy variable method avoids specification errors while yielding the same information on returns that would be obtained from the cumulative abnormal residual in event studies (see Ozler (1989) and Binder (1998)).

Table IV

First Stock Market Liberalizations and Contemporaneous Economic Reforms

T^* is the date of the country's stock market liberalization in event time. For example, in Argentina any event listed in the $T^* - 6$ box occurred on or between June and August of 1989. All events are taken from *The Economist Intelligence Unit: Quarterly Economic Reports*. A full chronology of events is presented in Henry (1999b).

Country, Date of Liberalization	Type of Liberalization	Event Time					
		$T^* - 12$	$T^* - 9$	$T^* - 6$	$T^* - 3$	T^*	$T^* + 3$
Argentina November 1989	Limits on foreign capital reduced	Airline privatization; dual exchange rate system fails	Structural adjustment funds frozen; economic team resigns	Privatization stabilization plan	IMF agreement	Exchange rate devalued by 35 percent	IMF agreement frozen
Brazil March 1988	Country Fund	Finance minister resigns	Second Cruzado Plan	New proposals submitted to creditors	None	Capital goods duties reduced	Tariffs reduced
Chile May 1987	Country Fund	None	Attempt on Pinochet's life	None	Largest banks privatized; new debt repayment terms	None	Two floods and an earthquake
Colombia December 1991	Investability Index jumps 46 percent	Restrictions on profit remittance eased	Tariffs reduced; external debt refinanced	Tariffs cut; credit controls relaxed	Exchange controls eased	Privatization of telecom industry begins	None
India June 1986	Country Fund	None	None	None	None	None	Attempt on Prime Minister's life

(continued overleaf)

Korea June 1987	Country Fund	None	None	False rumors of Kim Il Sung's death	Tariffs reduced on consumer durables	Protracted student protests	Tariff cuts announced
Malaysia February 1987	Country Fund	None	National Economic Plan (NEP) frozen	NEP to be extended past 1990	Privatization of telecom industry	Rubber price stabilization pact reached	None
Mexico May 1989	Investability index jumps 410 percent	Salinas elected; U.S. govt. gives $3.5B to boost reforms	Pacto extended	Privatization of two state mines	Brady Plan approved by U.S. Congress; IMF agreement	None	Brady agreement with creditors
The Philippines May 1986	Country Fund	Debt rescheduling signed	IMF targets missed	$2.9 billion of public debt rescheduled	Marcos overthrown	Import restrictions lifted	Talks open with IMF
Taiwan May 1986	Country Fund	None	None	Investment in foreign securities allowed	None	Import bans lifted	Exchange controls eased
Thailand January 1988	Country Fund	General Yongchaiyut calls for reforms	None	ASEAN free trade agreement extended	None	None	None
Venezuela January 1990	Full market access except bank stocks	Trade liberalization; adjustment loan approved	None	None	Easier profit remittance for foreign firms	$680 million structural adjustment loan	Brady deal; Agricultural tariffs reduced

probably anticipated at the time of the first stock market liberalization. Because subsequent liberalizations are probably anticipated, there are two relevant states of the world to consider:

State 1: When the first stock market liberalization occurs, future liberalizations are anticipated, and it is known that they will take place with a probability of 1.

State 2: When the first stock market liberalization occurs, future liberalizations are anticipated, but there is some positive probability that each of the subsequent liberalizations will not occur.

If State 1 is the true state of the world, then the only revaluation occurs when the first stock market liberalization is announced. Although there will be a gradual appreciation of prices until the entire liberalization process is completed, this slope effect[12] will be hard to detect given the noise in the data. If State 2 is the true state of the world, then in addition to the first price jump there may also be revaluations as each scheduled liberalization date approaches and market participants receive news confirming that it will take place according to schedule.

These two distinct states of the world raise the important question of how to measure the effects of the initial stock market liberalization versus those of subsequent liberalizations. Testing for revaluation effects by using a dummy variable that takes on the value one during the event window of each and every stock market liberalization is likely to understate the true effects of stock market liberalization if S1 is the true state of the world. On the other hand, it is also important to know whether subsequent stock market liberalizations induce revaluation effects. This discussion argues for creating two dummy variables. The first, called *Liberalize*, takes on the value one during the event window of the first stock market liberalization. The second, called *Liberalize2*, takes on the value one during all liberalization windows subsequent to the first.

C. Macroeconomic Fundamentals and Policy Endogeneity

As the ultimate goal is to estimate the size of the aggregate equity price response to stock market liberalization holding expected future cash flows constant, equation (1) will need augmentation. In Sections III.C and III.D I control for expected future cash flows by adding a set of economic reform dummies and macroeconomic fundamentals as right-hand-side variables. More generally, a fundamental concern with estimating the stock price response to liberalization is that policymakers have an incentive to liberalize the stock market when it is doing well. A policymaker who liberalizes the stock market when prices are depressed risks being accused of selling off the country at fire-sale prices. Summers (1994) makes a similar point in the context of

---

[12] Footnote 3 explains why there may be a slope effect.

privatization. To the extent that stock market performance depends on economic conditions, the decision to liberalize depends on the economy's current and expected future performance. Although controlling for macroeconomic fundamentals partially controls for this concern, the standard event study approach may yield upward-biased estimates if policymakers time liberalizations to coincide with news about positive future macroeconomic shocks. On the other hand, some liberalizations have been undertaken during crises. Nevertheless, the potential endogeneity of the liberalization decision requires cautious interpretation of the estimated revaluation effect. This issue is raised again in Section III.E.

III. Results

Sections A through D estimate the average cumulative impact of a country's first stock market liberalization on aggregate market returns over the eight-month liberalization window described in Section II. Section A begins with a benchmark specification, equation (1), that is comparable to Kim and Singal's (2000) earlier work. Sections B through D pose three alternative specifications that take seriously the notion that comovements with foreign stock markets, contemporaneous economic reforms, or a favorable shock to macroeconomic fundamentals might be responsible for the sharp increase in valuations. Section E discusses some of the interpretation difficulties involved in using a relatively long event window, and also presents results based on shorter windows. All of the estimates in Sections F and G use implementation-month-only windows. Section F also tests for a revaluation effect using alternative event dates. Specifically, the implementation dates of all the authors in Table II are used along with exactly the same battery of controls as in Sections A through E. Section G estimates the average effect of the second and all subsequent stock market liberalizations.

A. Benchmark Estimates

The results from estimating equation (1) are given in column (1a) of Table V. The coefficient of 0.047 on *Liberalize* is highly significant. On average, a country's first stock market liberalization is preceded by a total revaluation of 38 percent in U.S. dollar terms. The total revaluation number is calculated by multiplying the average monthly abnormal return during the window by the length of the window (4.7 percent per month × eight months = 37.6 percent). Panel B of Table V provides estimates of the impact of liberalization on dividend yields. The specification is identical to equation (1) except that the left-hand-side variable is the change in the log of the dividend yield. The dividend yield results are not as strong as those for returns. Specifically, the coefficient of −0.024 on *Liberalize* in the dividend yield specification implies an average fall in dividend yields of about 50 basis points. Again, this is consistent with Bekaert and Harvey (2000) who also

546   *The Journal of Finance*

Table V
Stock Market Reactions to First Stock Market Liberalization

The regressions are performed using monthly stock market data from December 1976 to December 1994 for Argentina, Brazil, Chile, India, Korea, Mexico, and Thailand. For the other countries the data are monthly from December 1984 to December 1994. The dividend yield data are also monthly and cover the period from December 1984 to December 1994. *Liberalize* is a dummy variable for the event window of the first stock market liberalization. The event window begins seven months prior to the implementation month and ends in the implementation month. For example, for a stock market liberalization that was implemented in November 1989, the event window begins in April 1989 and ends in November 1989. R^{LDC}, R^{US}, and R^{EAFE} are the dividend-inclusive monthly return on the IFC global index, the S&P 500, and the Morgan Stanley Capital Index for Europe, Asia, and the Far East, respectively. *Stabilize, Trade, Privatize,* and *Exchange* are dummy variables for the event windows of macroeconomic stabilization, trade opening, privatization, and exchange controls, respectively. Each of the event windows for these economic reform variables begins seven months prior to the implementation of the reform and ends in the implementation month. A constant plus 11 country dummies were also estimated but not reported. Heteroskedasticity-consistent (White) standard errors are in parentheses.

	Panel A: Stock Returns				Panel B: $\Delta\ln(D/P)$			
	(1a)	(2a)	(3a)	(4a)	(1b)	(2b)	(3b)	(4b)
Liberalize	0.047***	0.041***	0.039***	0.033***	−0.024*	−0.019	−0.015	−0.010
	(0.010)	(0.0124)	(0.012)	(0.011)	(0.015)	(0.015)	(0.015)	(0.017)
R^{LDC}		0.522***	0.517***	0.525***		−0.350***	−0.341***	−0.339***
		(0.148)	(0.015)	(0.142)		(0.114)	(0.110)	(0.115)
R^{US}		0.250***	0.278***	0.278***		−0.355*	−0.365*	−0.446**
		(0.102)	(0.109)	(0.109)		(0.200)	(0.205)	(0.200)
R^{EAFE}		−0.008	−0.006	−0.018		−0.043**	−0.045**	−0.027
		(0.044)	(0.044)	(0.042)		(0.020)	(0.022)	(0.024)
Stabilize			0.003	0.003			−0.003	0.003
			(0.010)	(0.010)			(0.010)	(0.010)
Trade			0.025***	0.021***			−0.039***	−0.037**
			(0.005)	(0.048)			(0.015)	(0.016)
Privatize			0.016**	0.010			−0.029	−0.030
			(0.007)	(0.008)			(0.019)	(0.021)
Exchange			−0.005	−0.002			0.010	0.007
			(0.015)	(0.015)			(0.049)	(0.045)
$\bar{R}^2$	0.007	0.076	0.083	0.147	0.000	0.018	0.023	0.027
No. of obs.	2292	2292	2292	2292	1569	1569	1569	1569

*, **, and *** indicate significant difference at the 10, 5, and 1 percent levels, respectively.

find a small fall in dividend yields around liberalization. Errunza and Miller (1998) also report dividend yield results that are not as significant as those for stock returns. Nevertheless, the negative coefficient on *Liberalize* in column (1b) of the dividend yield regressions is qualitatively consistent with a one-time equity price revaluation resulting from a fall in the cost of equity capital.

B. Controlling for World Stock Returns

A glaring omission associated with specification (1) is the effect of comovements with foreign stock markets. The following specification measures the abnormal return associated with a country's first stock market liberalization after controlling for the effects of foreign stock market fluctuations:

$$R_{it} = \alpha_i + \beta_1 R_t^{LDC} + \beta_2 R_t^{US} + \beta_3 R_t^{EAFE} + \gamma \cdot Liberalize_{it} + \epsilon_{it}, \qquad (2)$$

where R_t^{LDC} = the continuously compounded real dollar return on an index of emerging market funds at time t; R_t^{US} = the continuously compounded real return on the S&P 500 index at time t; and R_t^{EAFE} = the continuously compounded real dollar return on Morgan Stanley's Europe, Asia, and Far East (EAFE) stock market index at time t. If the run-up in emerging market equity prices is the result of booming foreign stock markets, then the coefficient on the *Liberalize* dummy in equation (2) should be significantly reduced relative to specification (1).

Column (2a) of Table V shows the results. As evidenced by the sharp increase in adjusted R^2 as compared with that in column (1a), the inclusion of world stock returns dramatically improves the regression fit. Not surprisingly, the largest beta is associated with other emerging market returns; own-country returns are most sensitive to movements in other emerging markets.[13] On average, when the aggregate emerging market index rises by one percentage point, an individual country's index will rise by 0.5 percentage points. The U.S. beta is smaller than the emerging market beta, but is also significant. The EAFE beta is not significant. Although comovements with foreign stock markets are an important explanatory factor for emerging market returns, their inclusion has little effect on the *Liberalize* coefficient. The monthly point estimate is now 0.041. The coefficient on *Liberalize* in the dividend yield specifications is still negative, but is no longer significant.

C. Controlling for Concurrent Economic Reforms

Four variables are constructed to control for the effect of the following economic reforms: macroeconomic stabilization, trade liberalization, privatization, and the easing of exchange controls. These variables are denoted *Stabilize*, *Trade*, *Privatize*, and *Exchange* respectively. The underlying data used to construct these variables are the policy events in Tables IV and V, and the full event list. For example, Table IV indicates that in May of 1986 the Philippines lifted import restrictions. Thus, May of 1986 is T^* for this particular trade liberalization, and the variable *Trade* takes on the value

---

[13] It is possible that the strong correlation results from the fact that each country in the sample is also a part of the emerging market index. Excluding the LDC returns from the right-hand side does not alter the sign or magnitude of the other betas.

one in each of the eight months from October 1985 through May 1986. The exact same methodology is followed for every occurrence of each type of reform in all 12 countries. The following panel model is then estimated:

$$R_{it} = \alpha_i + \beta_1 R_t^{LDC} + \beta_2 R_t^{US} + \beta_3 R_t^{EAFE} + \gamma_1 Liberalize_{it} + \gamma_2 Stabilize_{it}$$

$$+ \gamma_3 Trade_{it} + \gamma_4 Privatize_{it} + \gamma_5 Exchange_{it} + \epsilon_{it}. \qquad (3)$$

Column (3a) of Table V shows the results. After controlling for world stock returns and macroeconomic reforms, the *Liberalize* coefficient is now 0.039. Although they barely affect the *Liberalize* coefficient, the macroeconomic reforms are themselves associated with equity price revaluation. For instance, the coefficient on *Trade* is 0.025 and the *Privatize* coefficient is 0.016. This implies that trade liberalization and privatization are associated with cumulative revaluations of 20 percent and 13 percent respectively. The *Stabilize* coefficient also has the expected sign, but does not have a statistically significant effect on stock returns.[14] The coefficient on *Exchange* is negative, but also insignificant.

It is interesting to ask whether the estimated stock market revaluation effects of liberalization are statistically distinguishable from those of the economic reforms. The null hypothesis that the *Liberalize* coefficient is equal to the *Trade* and *Privatize* coefficients is rejected at the 10 percent level.

Given their magnitude and significance, the *Trade* and *Privatize* coefficients merit some further discussion. The *Trade* result is consistent with recent studies, such as that of Sachs and Warner (1995), which find trade liberalization to be the single economic reform most closely tied to future growth. Trade liberalization may reduce the cost of imported intermediate inputs, thereby increasing expected future profitability.[15] This interpretation, that trade liberalization signals higher future profitability, is also consistent with the negative and significant coefficient on *Trade* in the dividend yield specification in column (3b). The sign of the *Privatize* coefficient is consistent with a story that says placing state enterprises in private hands raises their efficiency and expected future profitability.[16] Indeed, this story is corroborated by Boubakri and Cosset (1998) who find evidence that privatization leads to improved firm performance.

---

[14] Every IMF agreement is counted as a stabilization plan, but in reality some agreements are not so much "news" in the sense of being a new stabilization plan as they are a continuation of an already existing plan. This may bias against finding a significant effect of stabilization, but is favorable to omitting some agreements and running the risk of attributing to liberalization that which is due to stabilization.

[15] For a formal model along these lines see Basu and Morey (1998).

[16] The efficiency argument is one of two competing effects of privatization on equity prices. The other effect is that the news that privatization is coming may increase the supply of shares in the country, driving down equity prices in some models. That privatization positively impacts the stock market would seem to suggest that the efficiency effect dominates.

D. Controlling for Macroeconomic Fundamentals

After controlling for comovements with foreign markets and concurrent economic reforms, the first stock market liberalization still has a point estimate of 0.039. However, macroeconomic factors have not been accounted for. This is a potentially serious problem because of the possibility that exogenous macroeconomic shocks unrelated to reform might cause a run-up in equity prices. Therefore, not accounting for country fundamentals might lead to an overstatement of the effects of stock market liberalization. This critique is addressed by adding distributed lags and leads of the growth rates of country macroeconomic fundamentals[17] to the right-hand side of regression (3) as in Fama (1981). Let F_{it} be a vector of country fundamentals. The following regression is estimated:

$$R_{it} = \alpha_i + \beta_1 R_t^{LDC} + \beta_2 R_t^{US} + \beta_3 R_t^{EAFE} + \gamma_1 Liberalize_{it} + \gamma_2 Stabilize_{it}$$
$$+ \gamma_3 Trade_{it} + \gamma_4 Privatize_{it} + \gamma_5 Exchange_{it} + \delta(L)\Delta(\ln F_{it}) + \epsilon_{it}. \quad (4)$$

The results are listed in column (4a) of Table V. (To conserve space, the estimates of the fundamentals are not included since they are not of direct interest.)

This time the story is substantially altered. After controlling for the fundamentals, the *Liberalize* coefficient falls to 0.033. At first glance this may not seem like much of a discrepancy from the 0.047 in specification (1). However, cumulated over the entire eight-month liberalization window, the new estimate implies a total revaluation of 26 percent, or two-thirds of the total revaluation implied by the original point estimate. Furthermore, the *Privatize* coefficient is no longer significant. One possible explanation for the attenuation of the *Privatize* coefficient is that governments decide to privatize when macroeconomic conditions are strong. In the absence of fundamentals on the right-hand side, the *Privatize* dummy simply picks up this correlation. Finally, the hypothesis that the *Liberalize* and *Trade* coefficients are the same can no longer be rejected. After accounting for the effects of macroeconomic activity on the stock market, trade opening has as large a revaluation effect as stock market liberalization. That the effects of stock market liberalization are substantially diminished by adding macroeconomic fundamentals to the right-hand side supports the argument in Section II that policymakers time market openings to coincide with good economic conditions.

E. Shorter Window Lengths

In the absence of verifiable announcement dates, the four preceding subsections (A–D) use an event window of eight months to capture potential announcement effects and to allow for the possibility of information leakage.

---

[17] The fundamentals are domestic industrial production, the U.S. Treasury bill rate, domestic inflation, the real exchange rate, and a political stability index. After trying a number of specifications I ended up including one-month lagged, current, and one-month leads of the fundamentals.

The use of this relatively long event window raises the following problem in interpreting the results. Policymakers may time stock market liberalization in the same way that managers time equity issuance to follow a period of significant run-up in their firm's equity price (Ritter (1991), Loughran and Ritter (1995)). If this is the case then the results in Table V may be an artifact of the relatively long event window. This section reestimates the response of equity prices to liberalization using shorter event windows. Specifically, equation (4) is reestimated using windows of three different lengths for the *Liberalize* variable: five months ($T^* - 4$ to T^*), two months ($T^* - 1$ to T^*), and one month (T^* only). The reform variables remain exactly as described in Section III.C.

The results, which are presented in Table VI, indicate that the equity price revaluation associated with stock market liberalization is relatively robust to the choice of window length. Although the statistical significance is not as strong as for the eight-month window, the *Liberalize* coefficient of 0.030 for the five-month window ($T^* - 4$ to T^*) is almost identical to the eight-month coefficient of 0.033. Interestingly, the point estimate for the two-month window ($T^* - 1$ to T^*), 0.050, is larger than that for both the five-month and eight-month windows. The implementation-month-only (T^*) point estimate, 0.065, is the largest of all. The fact that the strongest results are those for the window that is least susceptible to the market-timing critique is indeed suggestive of a revaluation effect of stock market liberalization. Given that the interpretation difficulties are least severe with the implementation-month-only estimation windows, all of the results in Sections III.F and III.G will rely on estimates using T^* only windows.

F. Other Initial Stock Market Liberalization Dates

Sections III.A through III.E present results based on the stock market liberalization dates in Table I. Now I estimate the impact of stock market liberalization using the other liberalization dates. The Appendix provides, in Table AII, a chronological listing of all the unique liberalization dates in Table II, columns (2) through (5). A variable called *LiberalizeAll*, which takes a value of one on each of the implementation dates listed in column (1) of Table AII, is created. The specifications given in equations (1) through (4) are reestimated, replacing *Liberalize* with *LiberalizeAll*. The *LiberalizeAll* coefficient can be interpreted as the average implementation-month-only revaluation across all the unique liberalization dates in Table II.

Table AIII, columns (1a) through (4a), presents the results. The *Liberalize* coefficient is highly significant in all stock return regressions. After controlling for all relevant factors, the coefficient of 0.052 on *LiberalizeAll* is slightly smaller than the coefficient of 0.065 on the *Liberalize* variable in Table VI.[18] The fall in dividend yields is only statistically significant in the first regression (1b), but the results in specifications (2b) through (4b) are qualitatively

---

[18] That the point estimate for *LiberalizeAll* is somewhat smaller than that for *Liberalize* is consistent with the fact that a number of the stock market liberalization dates used in constructing *LiberalizeAll* occur later than those used to construct *Liberalize*.

Table VI

Stock Market Reactions to First Stock Market Liberalization, Alternative Event Window Lengths

The regressions are performed using monthly stock market data from December 1976 to December 1994 for Argentina, Brazil, Chile, India, Korea, Mexico, and Thailand. For the other countries the data are monthly from December 1984 to December 1994. The dividend yield data are also monthly and cover the period from December 1984 to December 1994. *Liberalize* is a dummy variable for the event window of the first stock market liberalization. For $T^* - 4$ to T^*, the event window begins four months prior to the implementation month and ends in the implementation month. For example, for a stock market liberalization that was implemented in November 1989, the event window begins in July 1989 and ends in November 1989. For $T^* - 1$ to T^*, the event window begins in the month before the implementation month. For T^*, the event window is the implementation month only. R^{LDC}, R^{US}, and R^{EAFE} are the dividend-inclusive monthly return on the IFC Global Index, the S&P 500, and the Morgan Stanley Capital Index for Europe, Asia, and the Far East, respectively. *Stabilize, Trade, Privatize*, and *Exchange* are dummy variables for the event window of macroeconomic stabilization, trade opening, privatization, and exchange controls, respectively. Each of the event windows for these economic reform variables begins seven months prior to the implementation of the reform and ends in the implementation month. A constant plus 11 country dummies were also estimated but not reported. Heteroskedasticity-consistent (White) standard errors are in parentheses.

	Panel A: Stock Returns			Panel B: $\Delta\ln(D/P)$		
	$T^* - 4$ to T^*	$T^* - 1$ to T^*	T^*	$T^* - 4$ to T^*	$T^* - 1$ to T^*	T^*
Liberalize	0.030*	0.050*	0.065*	0.017	−0.008	−0.003
	(0.018)	(0.028)	(0.039)	(0.032)	(0.051)	(0.076)
R^{LDC}	0.520***	0.522***	0.522***	−0.340***	−0.340***	−0.339***
	(0.058)	(0.058)	(0.059)	(0.118)	(0.111)	(0.116)
R^{US}	0.283***	0.280***	0.281***	−0.451**	−0.367*	−0.448**
	(0.091)	(0.091)	(0.094)	(0.200)	(0.204)	(0.197)
R^{EAFE}	−0.016	−0.0150	−0.014	−0.028	−0.0276	−0.0281
	(0.036)	(0.036)	(0.033)	(0.024)	(0.021)	(0.024)
Stabilize	0.003	0.003	0.003	0.002	0.003	0.003
	(0.010)	(0.010)	(0.010)	(0.008)	(0.008)	(0.008)
Trade	0.021**	0.020**	0.020**	−0.037**	−0.037**	−0.037**
	(0.009)	(0.009)	(0.009)	(0.016)	(0.017)	(0.017)
Privatize	0.010	0.011	0.011	−0.030	−0.030	−0.030
	(0.009)	(0.009)	(0.009)	(0.021)	(0.021)	(0.0210
Exchange	−0.002	−0.002	−0.003	0.008	0.008	0.008
	(0.014)	(0.014)	(0.014)	(0.045)	(0.045)	(0.045)
$\bar{R}^2$	0.146	0.146	0.146	0.027	0.027	0.027
No. of obs.	2292	2292	2292	1569	1569	1569

*, **, and *** indicate significant difference at the 10, 5, and 1 percent levels, respectively.

consistent with the stock return results. As in Tables V and VI, the *Trade* coefficient is highly significant in all dividend yield regressions, indicating that a move toward freer trade is seen as improving future growth prospects. Column (2) of Table AII lists all of the unique dates in columns (3) through (5) of Table II. Column (5a) of Table AIII presents stock return estimates using these dates. The coefficient on *LiberalizeAll* in this case is 0.051.

G. Stock Market Liberalizations Subsequent to the First

Sections III.A through III.F analyze whether revaluations occur in anticipation of the first stock market liberalization. In order to test whether revaluations occur in anticipation of subsequent stock market liberalizations, a second set of regressions is run which no longer looks at countries' first stock market liberalization in isolation. A new variable called *Liberalize2* is created which takes on the value one during the implementation month of all the stock market liberalizations listed in Table AI. Again, as in Section III.F, since the dummy variable is on during the implementation month only, the total revaluation effect is the same as the point estimate. The analysis begins by estimating

$$R_{it} + \alpha_i + \gamma_1 Liberalize_{it} + \gamma_2 Liberalize2 + \epsilon_{it}, \tag{5}$$

and proceeds to augment specification (5) with the identical set of right-hand side variables used as controls in Sections III.B through III.D.

The results are reported in Table AIV in the Appendix. Regression (1a) indicates that the coefficient on *Liberalize2* is 0.030, but it is statistically insignificant. The *Liberalize* coefficient is now 0.101, and the hypothesis that the estimated *Liberalize* and *Liberalize2* coefficients are statistically the same is rejected at the 5 percent level. On average, subsequent stock market liberalizations have less of a valuation effect than the first. Regression (2a) illustrates that including world stock returns on the right-hand side does not change either set of coefficients very much.

Regression (3a) of Table AIV demonstrates that after including contemporaneous reforms the *Liberalize* coefficient is not affected much. *Liberalize2* continues to be statistically insignificant, and the *Trade* and *Privatize* coefficients are similar in magnitude to the estimates in Table V. Regression (4a), which includes the macroeconomic fundamentals, shows that the *Liberalize* coefficient has fallen from 0.101 in regression (1a) to 0.066. The true implementation-month-only revaluation effect of the first stock market liberalization is about two-thirds of what one is led to believe in the absence of controls. This corroborates the story that emerged from Table V where the true cumulative eight-month revaluation effect also was about two-thirds as large as in the absence of controls. The *Liberalize2* coefficient has fallen from 0.030 in regression (1a) to 0.022 and is still statistically insignificant.

The statistically insignificant *Liberalize2* coefficient lends itself to two possible interpretations. First, it could be that the revaluation effects of subsequent stock market liberalizations are not detectable at the time they occur because they are anticipated at the time of the first stock market liberalization (Urias (1994) makes a similar argument in the context of ADRs). Second, it is possible that once the initial liberalization occurs, new country funds (the majority of subsequent liberalizations) provide minimal diversification benefits because they are spanned by existing funds (Diwan, Errunza, and Senbet (1993)). In other words, it is possible that the first liberalization effectively integrates the market.

IV. Alternative Explanations

The central message from Sections III.A to III.F is that a substantial appreciation of aggregate share prices occurs both in the months leading up to the implementation of a country's initial stock market liberalization as well as in the implementation month itself. On average, in the eight-month window preceding its initial stock market liberalization, a country's aggregate share price index experiences a 38 percent increase in real dollar terms. After controlling for relevant factors, the revaluation is about 26 percent. About 6.6 percent of this revaluation takes place in the actual implementation month. The macroeoconomic reforms are themselves a significant source of share price revaluation. In particular, the stock market experiences a total revaluation of 2.1 percent per month in each of the eight months leading up to a trade liberalization. These results certainly suggest a revaluation of aggregate share prices in anticipation of future stock market liberalization and trade liberalization. Nevertheless, it is not clear that we can infer causation.

Suppose a trade reform occurs before a stock market liberalization. We might end up attributing any associated stock market revaluation to the trade reform and not to the stock market liberalization. However, the revaluation might really be due to the stock market liberalization, but the market knows that stock market liberalizations usually follow trade reforms. In fact, the sequencing literature (Dornbusch (1983), Edwards (1984), and McKinnon (1991)) advocates trade liberalization first, followed by capital account liberalization. Given the influence of this literature on the policy reform debate in developing countries during the 1980s, it is more than plausible that trade liberalizations were seen as a harbinger of future stock market liberalizations. Analogously, the possibility remains that when a stock market liberalization is implemented, equity prices jump because stock market liberalization is interpreted as a signal of future macroeconomic reforms.

V. Conclusions

The standard IAPM makes a salient prediction about an emerging country that does not allow foreigners to purchase shares in its stock market: The country's aggregate cost of equity capital will fall when it opens its stock market to foreign investors. Equivalently stated, holding expected future cash flows constant, we should see an increase in an emerging country's equity price index when the market learns of an impending future stock market liberalization. This paper examines whether the data are consistent with this theoretical prediction.

The paper attempts to hold expected future cash flows constant by augmenting the standard event study analysis with a set of right-hand-side variables that control for major economic policy changes such as macroeconomic stabilization programs, trade liberalizations, privatizations, and the easing of exchange controls. The analysis also controls for comovements with foreign stock markets and macroeconomic fundamentals. Finally, the paper confronts the potential endogeneity problem that arises out of policymakers' incentive to liberalize the stock market in response to a prolonged run-up in equity prices.

Bearing in mind all of the caveats about inferring causality, it is instructive to do some simple calculations. Suppose that the preliberalization discount rate on equity is 20 percent and that the entire revaluation effect is 26 percent—the size of the response to the first stock market liberalization. Since we are holding expected future cash flows constant and using logarithmic returns, this revaluation means that the cost of equity capital also falls by 26 percent. This implies a fall in the level of the discount rate to about 15 percent. If one uses the more conservative, implementation-month-only revaluation effect of 6.5 percent, the implied level of the postliberalization discount rate is on the order of 19 percent. Stulz (1999a, 1999b) argues that the magnitudes of the fall in the level of the discount rate implied by such estimates are small relative to what we would expect in a world where (1) there was no home bias and (2) liberalizations were implemented in a fully credible, once-and-for-all fashion.

An important question for future research lies in assessing whether what seems like a relatively small revaluation effect has any economic significance. At the macroeconomic level, Henry (1999a) finds that stock market liberalizations are consistently followed by a surge in the growth rate of private physical investment. Although this suggests significant economic effects of stock market liberalization, further research is needed. In particular, future research should work to uncover the sector-specific, valuation, cost of capital, and investment effects of stock market liberalization.

The fact that aggregate valuation seems to increase in anticipation of future trade liberalizations also points to a potentially fruitful line of research. Trade liberalization has heterogeneous effects on exporters and importers; an analysis of firm level data would deepen our understanding of the sector-specific valuation impacts of trade liberalization. More generally, if the goal is to understand emerging financial markets, then the fact that emerging stock markets respond to macroeconomic reforms suggests that there is positive value added to careful documentation and explicit statistical use of macroeconomic policy changes.

Appendix

Details of the stock market liberalization dates studied in addition to those in Table I are provided in the following four tables. Table AI shows that most countries' initial stock market liberalizations did not constitute a complete opening to foreign investors, Table AII provides a listing of all the unique liberalization dates in Table II, and Tables AIII and AIV provide details of regressions of stock market reactions to alternative initial liberalization dates and subsequent liberalization dates, respectively.

Table AI
Subsequent Stock Market Liberalizations and Contemporaneous Economic Reforms

T^* is the date of the country's stock market liberalization in event time. All events are taken from *The Economist Intelligence Unit: Quarterly Economic Reports*. A full chronology of events is presented in Henry (1999b).

Country, Opening Date	Type of Opening	T^*-12	T^*-9	T^*-6	T^*-3	T^*	T^*+3
Argentina							
January 91	Investable Index jumps 19 percent	None	Airline and ship privatizations begin	Structural adjustment funds unfrozen	IMF agreement; privatizations	Domingo Cavallo appointed finance minister	Tariff reductions
January 92	Country Fund	None	Privatizations	IMF stand by loan	None	IMF approves economic plan	IMF agreement; Brady deal
Brazil							
October 88	Country Fund	None	None	None	IMF approves economic program; import ban lifted	Creditors ratify new loan agreement	Third Cruzado Plan
April 90	Investability Index jumps 33 percent	IMF talks open; stock market scandal	Tariffs reduced	Privatization process frozen	None	Collor takes office, sweeping deregulations	Tariffs reduced; curb on profit remittance removed
January 91	Investability Index jumps 34 percent	None	None	IMF talks open	Deregulation measures announced; debt restructuring rejected	Second Collor Plan	None
July 91	Investability Index jumps 185 percent;	None	None	None	Agreement on payment of arrears	IMF negotiations begin; privatizations	None
May 92	Country Fund	None	None	IMF approves a new stand by loan	Negotiations begin on Brady deal	Brady debt deal signed; official charges of corruption against Collor	None

continued

Table AI—*Continued*

Country, Opening Date	Type of Opening	T^*-12	T^*-9	T^*-6	T^*-3	T^*	T^*+3
Chile							
June 88	Country Fund	None	None	Telefonos de Chile privatized	Privatization of state electricity company begins	Poll shows Pinochet to win plebiscite	None
January 89	Investability Index jumps 15 percent	None	None	None	Pinochet defeated in plebiscite	None	None
February 90	Country Fund	None	IMF mission visits	IMF loan; Central Bank independent	Patricio Alwyn takes over as President	Foreign exchange controls eased	Alwyn announces commitment to reforms
January 91	Investability Index jumps 42 percent	None	None	Debt rescheduling	None	None	Capital outflow restrictions eased
January 92	Investability Index jumps 46 percent	None	None	Free trade agreement with Mexcio	None	Peso revalued by 5 percent	Foreign exchange controls eased
India							
May 87	Country Fund	None	None	Stock market scandal	None	None	None
August 88	Country Fund	None	Talks on trade liberalization begin	Import liberalization package	Government declares support for privatization	None	None
December 88	Country Fund	None	None	None	None	None	None
October 89	Country Fund	None	None	None	None	Gandhi congress ousted	None
June 90	Country Fund	None	None	None	None	None	Import liberalization
May 92	Country Fund	Rao elected PM; rupee devalued	None	None	Exchange controls eased; import duties decreased	Illegal stock trading exposed	None

(*continued overleaf*)

Date							
India (continued) May 94	Country Fund	Government faces no confidence vote	None	None	None	Foreigners can enter telecom industry	None
September 94	Country Fund	None	None	None	None	None	None
Korea December 88	Government announces plan to open stock market	Roh Tae Woo elected president	Tariffs reduced on consumer durables	None	Minimum wage increased by 23 percent	Interest rates deregulated	Investment in foreign real estate allowed
July 90	Country Fund	None	None	None	North Korea proposes disarmament	Diplomatic relations with USSR	None
March 91	Country Fund	None	None	None	None	Bank bailout of $680 million	None
January 92	Foreigners allowed to hold up to 10 percent of market	None	None	Foreign firms allowed to hold retail outlets	Limit on foreign banks issue of cds eased	Kim Young Sam elected president	North Korea agrees to military inspection
October 92	Investability Index jumps 23 percent	None	None	None	Pension funds urged to buy more equity	Foreigners can buy convertible bonds	None
July 93	Country Fund	None	None	Governor of Bank of Korea is sacked	Financial reform plan published	GATT; tariff reduction agreements	Real name financial system decree
December 93	Country Fund	None	None	None	Lending rates liberalized	None	Foreign banks admitted
December 94	Foreign equity ceiling raised to 12 percent	None	Manufacturing firms can issue unlimited corporate bonds	Kim Il Sung dies	None	None	None
Malaysia December 87	Country Fund	None	None	Possible cut in corporate tax rate announced	90 arrests under Internal Security Act	None	$1 billion rescue plan for depositors
April 89	Country Fund	Most favored nation trade pact with China	None	ASEAN-Japan Development Fund loans	None	None	Hiatus on restructuring foreign equity
April 90	Country Fund	None	Banks allowed to purchase stock	152 firms delist from Singapore Stock Exchange	None	Plan for electricity privatization	None

Table AI—Continued

Country, Opening Date	Type of Opening	$T^* - 12$	$T^* - 9$	$T^* - 6$	$T^* - 3$	T^*	$T^* + 3$
Malaysia (continued)							
January 91	Investability Index jumps 29 percent	None	None	None	Prime Minister Mathir's party retains power in general elections	None	None
Mexico							
October 90	Country Fund	Brady term sheet submitted	None	Privatization of banks approved None	Salinas requests NAFTA talks; Telmex to be privatizatized	None	None
January 92	Investability Index jumps 51 percent	None	NAFTA talks begin; $2.2B of Telmex privatized	Election: strong PRI showing boosts reforms	Bancomer privatized	None	Environmental concerns about NAFTA
The Philippines							
May 87	Country Fund	None	Import controls lifted	Paris Club debt rescheduling of $870 million	$10.5 billion structural adjustment loan; debt rescheduling	Agrarian land reform plan is approved	Coup attempt; bombings of businesses in Makati
November 89	Country Fund	IMF approves stabilization plan	None	Debt rescheduling $2.2 billion	Brady deal reached in principle	Coup attempt	None
October 93	Country Fund	None	Airline privatization announced	IMF negotiations begin	Privatization of copper and shipyards	Privatization of steel company approved	IMF agreement reached
Taiwan							
December 86	Country Fund	None	None	None	Import tariffs reduced	None	Restrictions imposed on capital inflows
May 89	Country Fund	None	Capital gains tax imposed	Privatization of China Steel announced	More flexible exchange rate regime	Central bank governor resigns; trade restrictions lifted	Exchange controls lifted; privatizations

(continued overleaf)

Stock Market Liberalization   559

Taiwan (*continued*)						
January 91 — Foreigners allowed to hold up to 10 percent of market	Bank privatizations announced	Han Pei-Tsun elected prime minister	Pension funds allowed to invest in stock market	None	None	Privatizations
August 93 — Investability Index jumps 115 percent	None	Privatizations	Lien Chan becomes prime minister	None	None	None
March 94 — Investability Index jumps 33 percent	None	None	None	Tariffs cut by an average of 100 percent	288 million shares of China Steel sold	Banking opened to foreign banks
Thailand						
December 88 — Country Fund	None	None	Chartchai Choonhavan takes office	None	Ceiling on foreign borrowing raised	U.S. imposes restrictions on imports from Thailand
December 89 — Country Fund	None	None	Accusations of corruption	None	Strikes protesting privatization	Ceiling on loan rates raised
June 90 — Country Fund	None	None	None	None	None	Twenty ministers sacked in corruption scandal
January 91 — Investability Index jumps 35 percent	None	None	None	None	Coup overthrows government	Exchange controls eased
Venezuela						
January 94 — Investability Index jumps 33 percent	Perez accused of misusing public funds	Free trade agreement with Chile; rampant coup rumors	Perez suspended from presidency	Privatization process frozen	Price controls imposed; Banco Latino collapses	None

Table AII

Unique Stock Market Liberalization Dates

This table lists the unique liberalization dates from Table II. Column (1) lists all of the unique liberalization dates in Table II. Column (2) lists the unique liberalization dates from columns (3) through (5) of Table II.

Country	(1) All Unique Stock Market Liberalization Dates from Table II	(2) Unique Stock Market Liberalization Dates from Table II, Columns (3)–(5) only
Argentina	November 1989 October 1991	October 1991
Brazil	March 1988 /May 1991	May 1991
Chile	May 1987 September 1987 October 1989 January 1992	September 1987 October 1989 January 1992
Colombia	February 1991 October 1991 December 1991	February 1991 October 1991
India	June 1986 November 1992	November 1992
Korea	June 1987 January 1992	January 1992
Malaysia	May 1987 December 1988	December 1988
Mexico	May 1989 November 1989	November 1989
The Philippines	May 1986 July 1986 June 1991 October 1989	July 1986 June 1991 October 1989
Taiwan	May 1986 January 1991	January 1991
Thailand	January 1988 September 1987	September 1987
Venezuela	January 1990 December 1988	December 1988

Table AIII

Stock Market Reactions to First Stock Market Liberalization, Alternative Event Dates

The regressions are performed using monthly stock market data from December 1976 to December 1994 for Argentina, Brazil, Chile, India, Korea, Mexico, and Thailand. For the other countries the data are monthly from December 1984 to December 1994. The dividend yield data are also monthly and cover the period from December 1984 to December 1994. *Liberalize* is a dummy that takes on the value one during the implementation month of the first stock market liberalization. R^{LDC}, R^{US}, and R^{EAFE} are the dividend-inclusive monthly return on the IFC Global Index, the S&P 500, and the Morgan Stanley Capital Index for Europe, Asia, and the Far East, respectively. *Stabilize, Trade, Privatize,* and *Exchange* are dummy variables for the event windows of macroeconomic stabilization, trade opening, privatization, and exchange controls respectively. Each of the event windows for these variables begins seven months prior to the implementation of the reform and ends in the implementation month. A constant plus 11 country dummies were also estimated but not reported. Heteroskedasticity-consistent (White) standard errors are in parentheses.

	Panel A: Stock Returns					Panel B: Δln(D/P)				
	(1a)	(2a)	(3a)	(4a)	(5a)	(1b)	(2b)	(3b)	(4b)	(5b)
Liberalize	0.072*** (0.024)	0.057** (0.025)	0.056** (0.024)	0.052** (0.024)	0.051* (0.027)	-0.051* (0.029)	-0.041 (0.030)	-0.041 (0.030)	-0.034 (0.035)	-0.040 (0.041)
R^{LDC}		0.512*** (0.063)	0.507*** (0.062)	0.516*** (0.059)	0.519*** (0.143)		-0.343*** (0.103)	-0.334*** (0.103)	-0.334*** (0.104)	-0.335*** (0.116)
R^{US}		0.266*** (0.100)	0.272*** (0.100)	0.293*** (0.094)	0.293*** (0.108)		-0.363*** (0.140)	-0.372*** (0.140)	-0.452*** (0.156)	-0.453** (0.205)
R^{EAFE}		-0.004 (0.036)	-0.002 (0.036)	-0.014 (0.033)	-0.015 (0.042)		-0.045 (0.054)	-0.047 (0.055)	-0.029 (0.056)	-0.029 (0.024)
Stabilize			0.004 (0.013)	0.003 (0.011)	0.003 (0.005)			-0.003 (0.024)	0.003 (0.023)	0.003 (0.008)
Trade			0.025*** (0.008)	0.021*** (0.008)	0.021*** (0.005)			-0.039** (0.016)	-0.037** (0.017)	-0.037** (0.016)
Privatize			0.017* (0.010)	0.011 (0.008)	0.011 (0.001)			-0.030* (0.018)	-0.030 (0.017)	-0.030 (0.022)
Exchange			-0.007 (0.015)	-0.003 (0.014)	-0.003 (0.016)			0.008 (0.037)	0.008 (0.037)	0.008 (0.046)
$\bar{R}^2$	0.001	0.066	0.070	0.147	0.145	0.000	0.010	0.010	0.030	0.030
No. of obs.	2292	2292	2292	2292	2292	1569	1569	1569	1569	1569

*, **, and *** indicate significance at the 10, 5, and 1 percent levels, respectively.

Table AIV
Stock Market Reaction to First and All Subsequent Stock Market Liberalizations

The regressions are performed using monthly data from December 1984 to December 1994. *Liberalize* is a dummy variable that takes on the value one during the month that the first stock market liberalization is implemented. *Liberalize2* is a dummy variable that takes on the value 1 during the implementation month of all stock market liberalizations subsequent to the first. R^{LDC}, R^{US}, and R^{EAFE} are the monthly return on the IFC Global Index, the S&P 500, and the Morgan Stanley Capital Index for Europe, Asia, and the Far East, respectively. *Stabilize*, *Trade*, *Privatize*, and *Exchange* are dummy variables for the event windows of macroeconomic stabilization, trade opening, privatization, and exchange controls respectively. Each of the event windows for these variables begins seven months prior to the implementation of the reform and ends in the implementation month. A constant plus 11 country dummies were also estimated but not reported. Heteroskedasticity-consistent (White) standard errors are in parentheses.

	Panel A: Stock Returns				Panel B: $\Delta\ln(D/P)$			
	(1a)	(2a)	(3a)	(4a)	(1b)	(2b)	(3b)	(4b)
Liberalize	0.101*** (0.038)	0.082** (0.041)	0.078 (0.039)	0.066 (0.036)	-0.060 (0.049)	-0.043 (0.050)	-0.037 (0.049)	-0.003 (0.081)
Liberalize2	0.030 (0.022)	0.030 (0.022)	0.028 (0.021)	0.022 (0.018)	-0.056 (0.059)	-0.057 (0.060)	-0.055 (0.060)	-0.074 (0.062)
R^{LDC}		0.520*** (0.150)	0.514*** (0.147)	0.524*** (0.143)		-0.353*** (0.120)	-0.343*** (0.116)	-0.325*** (0.115)
R^{US}		0.251*** (0.102)	0.258*** (0.101)	0.280*** (0.110)		-0.349* (0.195)	-0.359* (0.200)	-0.385** (0.191)
R^{EAFE}		-0.002 (0.044)	-0.001 (0.044)	-0.013 (0.042)		-0.049 (0.021)	-0.051 (0.022)	-0.041 (0.025)
Stabilize			0.005 (0.011)	0.003 (0.010)			-0.003 (0.011)	-0.001 (0.005)
Trade			0.025*** (0.005)	0.021*** (0.005)			-0.040*** (0.015)	-0.039** (0.017)
Privatize			0.016** (0.006)	0.010* (0.007)			-0.027 (0.019)	-0.026 (0.021)
Exchange			-0.007 (0.015)	-0.003 (0.016)			0.008 (0.050)	0.009 (0.046)
$\bar{R}^2$	0.000	0.070	0.070	0.147	0.000	0.010	0.011	0.031
No. of obs.	2292	2292	2292	2292	1569	1569	1569	1569

*, **, and *** indicate significance at the 10, 5, and 1 percent levels, respectively.

Stock Market Liberalization 563

REFERENCES

Alexander, Gordon, Cheol Eun, and Sundaram Janakiramanan, 1987, Asset pricing and dual listing on foreign capital markets: A note, *Journal of Finance* 42, 151–158.

Basu, Parantap, and Matthew Morey, 1998, Trade liberalization and the behavior of emerging stock market prices, Working paper, Fordham Institute for Research in Economics.

Bekaert, Geert, 1995, Market integration and investment barriers in emerging equity markets, *World Bank Economic Review* 9, 75–107.

Bekaert, Geert, and Campbell R. Harvey, 1995, Time-varying world market integration, *Journal of Finance* 50, 403–444.

Bekaert, Geert, and Campbell R. Harvey, 2000, Foreign speculators and emerging equity markets, *Journal of Finance* 55, 565–613.

Binder, John, 1998, The event study methodology since 1969, *Review of Quantitative Finance and Accounting*, forthcoming.

Boubakri, Narjess, and Jean-Claude Cosset, 1998, The financial and operating performance of newly privatized firms: Evidence from developing countries, *Journal of Finance* 53, 1081–1111.

Buckberg, Elaine, 1995, Emerging stock markets and international asset pricing, *World Bank Economic Review* 9, 51–74.

Diwan, Ishac, Vihang Errunza, and Lemma Senbet, 1993, Empirical perspectives on national index funds, Working paper, World Bank, Washington, D.C.

Dornbusch, Rudiger, 1983, Panel discussion on the southern cone, *International Monetary Fund Staff Papers* 30, 164–184.

Edwards, Sebastian, 1984. The order of liberalization of the external sector in developing countries, *Princeton Essays in International Finance*, 156.

Errunza, Vihang, and Etienne Losq, 1985, International asset pricing under mild segmentation: Theory and test, *Journal of Finance* 40, 105–124.

Errunza, Vihang, and Etienne Losq, 1989, Capital flow controls, international asset pricing, and investors welfare: A multi-country framework, *Journal of Finance* 44, 1025–1037.

Errunza, Vihang, Etienne Losq, and Prasad Padmanabhan, 1992, Tests of integration, mild segmentation, and segmentation hypotheses, *Journal of Banking and Finance* 16, 949–972.

Errunza, Vihang, and Darius P. Miller, 1998, Market segmentation and the cost of capital in international equity markets, Working paper, McGill University and Texas A&M University.

Eun, Cheol, and Sundaram Janakiramanan, 1986, A model of international asset pricing with a constraint on foreign equity ownership, *Journal of Finance* 41, 897–914.

Fama, Eugene F., 1981, Stock returns, real activity, inflation, and money, *American Economic Review* 71, 545–565.

Foerster, Stephen R., and G. Andrew Karolyi, 1999, The effects of market segmentation and investor recognition on asset prices: Evidence from foreign stocks listing in the United States, *Journal of Finance* 54, 981–1013.

Henry, Peter Blair, 1999a, Do stock market liberalizations cause investment booms? *Journal of Financial Economics*, forthcoming.

Henry, Peter Blair, 1999b, Appendix of major policy changes in selected developing countries, mimeo, Stanford University Graduate School of Business.

Kim, E. Han, and Vijay Singal, 2000, Stock market openings: Experience of emerging economies, *Journal of Business* 73, 25–66.

Levine, Ross, and Sara Zervos, 1994, Capital control liberalization and stock market development: Data annex of country policy changes, World Bank, Washington, D.C.

Loughran, Timothy, and Jay Ritter, 1995, The new issues puzzle, *Journal of Finance* 50, 23–51.

McKinlay, A. Craig, 1997, Event studies in economics and finance, *Journal of Economic Literature* 35, 13–39.

McKinnon, Ronald I., 1991, *The Order of Economic Liberalization* (Johns Hopkins University Press, Baltimore).

Ozler, Sule, 1989, On the relationship between reschedulings and bank value, *American Economic Review* 12, 1117–1131.

Park, Keith, and Antoine W. Van Agtmael, 1993, *The World's Emerging Stock Markets: Structure, Development, Regulations and Opportunities* (Probus Publishing Company, Chicago).

Price, Margaret M., 1994, *Emerging Stock Markets* (McGraw Hill, Inc., New York).

Ritter, Jay, 1991, The long-run performance of initial public offerings, *Journal of Finance* 46, 3–27.

Sachs, Jeffrey, and Andrew Warner, 1995, Economic reform and the process of global integration, *Brookings Papers on Economic Activity* 1, 1–113.

Stapleton, Richard, and Marti Subrahmanyam, 1977, Market imperfections, capital market equilibrium, and corporate finance, *Journal of Finance* 32, 307–319.

Stulz, René M., 1999a, International portfolio flows and security markets, Working paper, Dice Center for Financial Economics, The Ohio State University.

Stulz, René M., 1999b, Globalization and the cost of equity capital, Working paper, The New York Stock Exchange.

Summers, Lawrence H., 1994, A changing course toward privatization; in Ahmed Galal and Mary Shirley, eds.: *Does Privatization Deliver?* (The World Bank, Washington, D.C.).

Tesar, Linda L., and Ingrid M. Werner, 1998, The internationalization of securities markets since the 1987 crash; in Robert E. Litan and Anthony M. Santomero, eds.: *Brookings-Wharton Papers on Financial Services* (Brookings Institution Press, Washington).

Urias, Michael, 1994, The impact of security cross-listing on the cost of capital in emerging markets, Unpublished dissertation, Stanford University.

[8]

E. Han Kim
University of Michigan

Vijay Singal
Virginia Tech

Stock Market Openings: Experience of Emerging Economies*

I. Introduction

The 1994 Mexican currency crisis and the recent turmoil in East Asian financial markets have prompted many academics and politicians to question the desirability of free flow of capital for emerging economies. They cite Chile's and China's success with restraints on capital flows. Even highly respected economists such as Joseph Stiglitz of the World Bank and Paul Krugman of MIT have championed capital controls as a way of coping with the financial crisis.[1] Perhaps heeding their advice, Malaysia closed its financial markets to foreign investors in September 1998. Around the same time, Taiwan announced that it was reconsidering its plans for full liberalization of capital flows in light of Asia's financial crisis.[2]

In contrast, economists such as Merton Miller (1998) reason that markets are not open enough. They argue that instead of limiting access to the markets, markets should be made more open by

This article is an exploratory examination of the benefits and risks associated with opening of stock markets. Specifically, we estimate changes in the level and volatility of stock returns, inflation, and exchange rates around market openings. We find that stock returns increase immediately after market opening without a concomitant increase in volatility. Stock markets become more efficient as determined by testing the random walk hypothesis. We find no evidence of an increase in inflation or an appreciation of exchange rates. If anything, inflation seems to decrease after market opening as do the volatility of inflation and volatility of exchange rates.

* This article has benefited from helpful discussions with Stijn Claessens, Josh Coval, Doug Diamond (the editor), Greg Kadlec, Bob Korajczyk, Raman Kumar, Yung Chul Park, Paul Seguin, and an anonymous referee. This project was partially supported by the Korea Institute of Finance, Mitsui Life Financial Research Center, and the World Bank. Singal acknowledges partial financial support from a Virginia Tech summer grant.
    1. Wilson (1998) and Krugman (1999).
    2. *Financial Times* (1998).

(*Journal of Business*, 2000, vol. 73, no. 1)

removing existing controls. Similarly, economists at the International Monetary Fund, such as Stanley Fischer and Michael Mussa, believe that currencies must be allowed to float so that markets, not governments, determine currency values. These economists are against any controls on capital flows. In fact, the Filipino central bank governor and the Philippine president declared that they will not restrain capital flows. Chile, long held up as the model of success with capital controls, eliminated a key capital restraint known as *encaje* because it caused a large increase in the borrowing cost for Chilean companies.[3]

The calls for capital controls also seem to be at odds with the move in recent years toward capital market liberalization by emerging economies. With the dissolution of the Soviet Union and a general decline in the number of centrally planned economies, politicians in developing countries could no longer ignore the global movement toward free markets. Partly to incorporate elements of market capitalism into their own economies and partly to satisfy their need for new capital, many countries have allowed a free flow of capital across their borders, including participation by foreign investors in their stock markets. Thus, before emerging economies reverse recent liberalization measures and implement regulatory restraints on capital flows, it is useful to consider the effects of such changes.

We hope to contribute to this debate on capital controls by examining the experience of emerging economies when they allow foreign investors to participate in their stock markets. Allowing foreign investment in domestic stock markets can be viewed as a removal of or reduction in constraints. By studying the effects of stock market openings, we also hope to provide insights into the opportunity cost of imposing capital constraints.

For emerging economies, there are several potential benefits of opening stock markets to foreign investors. Opening markets represent an important opportunity to attract foreign capital to finance economic growth. It also hastens the development of equity markets, which, as Boyd and Smith (1996) show theoretically and Levine and Zervos (1996, 1998) show empirically, is positively related to long-run economic growth. Furthermore, by comparing countries with differences in the development of financial markets, Rajan and Zingales (1998) find that development of financial markets facilitates economic growth by reducing the cost of external finance. Foreign equity flows result in global diversification that has other benefits for emerging economies. In Obstfeld's (1994) model, international risk sharing through global diversification results in improved resource allocation. Further, global diversification and stock market integration generate large steady-state welfare gains.[4]

---

3. Torres (1998). *Encaje* required 10% of foreign capital to be kept on deposit at the central bank.
4. For evidence on stock market integration, see Bekaert and Harvey (1995), Harvey (1995), and Korajczyk (1996).

In addition, foreign investors will demand transparency and improved disclosure rules that are crucial for improved allocational efficiency of capital. They will also demand accountability of management and shareholder rights in order to protect themselves against expropriation of wealth by controlling investors. A convincing and satisfactory response to these demands will decrease the risk of holding stocks, which, in turn, will lower the cost of capital.[5]

To policy makers of emerging economies, however, these benefits must be weighed against various uncertainties associated with the opening of markets. One issue of major concern is the movement of so-called hot money, that is, an international flow of funds allegedly highly sensitive to differences in interest rates, expectations of future economic growth, and expected returns from holding securities. Given the sensitivity of these investments, even a small shock to the economy can lead to a volatile change in fund flows, which exacerbates the shock and destabilizes the domestic economy. In addition, market opening means an exposure to foreign influence. If foreign stock prices are for some reason more volatile than domestic stock prices, domestic prices may also become more volatile. A greater volatility in stock prices would make investors more averse to holding stocks and lead them to demand a higher risk premium, which implies a higher cost of capital and less investment.

Some policy makers also believe that the economy cannot be left alone to react to unpredictable market forces and requires their guidance for controlled growth. For instance, capital inflows may cause the domestic currency to appreciate in real terms. For export-oriented economies, an appreciation of exchange rates may threaten the country's competitive position in the global marketplace. The government of such an economy may also worry that there may not be enough investment opportunities to absorb the inflow of money and that the ensuing excess capital will fuel inflation.[6]

This article examines changes in the economy that occur when a country liberalizes foreign portfolio investment so that foreign investors can more freely participate in the emerging stock markets. We estimate changes in the level and volatility of stock prices, exchange rates, and inflation rates around market openings. Briefly, we find that stock returns increase immediately after market opening but fall subsequently. There is no accompanying increase in the volatility of stock returns. We also find that stock markets tend to become more efficient, as determined by testing the random walk hypothesis. When we exam-

---

5. Disclosure in reporting is one of the two measures of financial development employed by Rajan and Zingales (1998).

6. A good example is Argentina, where capital inflows both increased inflation and strengthened the currency. For a discussion of the Argentine experience, see Rodriguez (1981) and Obstfeld (1985).

ine changes in inflation and exchange rates around market openings, we find neither an increase in inflation nor an appreciation in exchange rates. While the results vary across countries, on average, the evidence herein suggests that market openings have favorable effects on the emerging economies.

The article is organized as follows. After discussing the sample of emerging countries in Section II, Section III examines the effects of liberalization on the domestic stock market, including changes in stock returns, stock price volatility, and the incidence of rejection of the random walk hypothesis around market openings. Section IV focuses on inflation, changes in exchange rates, and the volatility of both. Section V contains the summary and concluding remarks.

II. Sample Description

Our sample consists of the emerging stock markets that are followed by the International Finance Corporation (IFC) in its Emerging Markets DataBase.[7] The number of countries covered by the IFC has continued to increase as the stock markets in other countries develop. As of September 1996 (the last month for which we have data available), there were 27 countries in the database. However, seven of those countries were recently added for which we do not have sufficient data for analysis. We study the remaining 20 countries. A similar sample is used in many other studies of emerging markets.[8]

The 20 countries in our sample are listed in the appendix. The appendix contains the market opening date, the maximum level of foreign participation allowed, and information relating to the process of liberalization for each country. The market opening dates reported in the appendix are important because much of the analysis in the article evaluates changes that took place around market openings. Recognizing the importance of these dates, many different sources have been consulted to ascertain and confirm the validity of opening dates.[9] One of the markets (Nigeria) is still considered closed, and another market (Malaysia) has been open to foreign investment in financial securities much before the availability of stock return data. Therefore, the sample of countries available for analysis around market openings drops to 18 from the original 20.

---

7. Emerging stock markets are defined by the International Finance Corporation to consist of stock markets in developing countries (low- and middle-income economies).

8. Aggarwal, Inclan, and Leal (1995); Bekaert and Harvey (1995, 1997); Buckberg (1995); Claessens, Dasgupta, and Glen (1995); Harvey (1995); Korajczyk (1996); and De-Santis and Imrohoroglu (1997).

9. See the appendix for a list of sources. Bekaert and Harvey (1999) have also documented the major political and economic events in the sample countries; most of that information is consistent with the information used in this study.

Some caveats regarding the opening dates are in order. First, market opening is a gradual process and the dates repoited represent only the most significant liberalization of the market. Therefore, changes measured around these dates will understate the true effect of market openings. Second, these are the actual opening dates, not the announcement dates. Since the announcement is typically made before the actual opening and the stock prices are likely to react to the announcement, the effects detected around the actual opening dates are due to foreign participation and to resolution of uncertainty regarding market opening. To control for the possibility of liberalization announcements affecting stock returns and exchange rates, the year prior to the actual opening is excluded from the analysis. Third, stock market liberalization is often accompanied by other economic reforms, such as relaxation of product market controls, trade liberalization, and privatization. These economic reforms will also affect the economic variables we examine in this article.[10]

While the focus in this article is on removal of restrictions on capital flows into the domestic market, there are often restrictions on capital flows out of the country. If domestic investors are allowed to own foreign securities prior to removal of restrictions on capital inflows, then the effect of the liberalization may differ as compared to the effect in countries where capital outflows are restricted. Thus, we distinguish market openings that are preceded by unrestricted capital outflows from those that had restrictions on outflows. Information related to restrictions on residents for owning foreign securities is given in the appendix for each country. There are four countries (Indonesia, Mexico, Taiwan, and Venezuela) where residents were allowed to own foreign securities prior to market opening as we have defined it.[11]

The database contains a monthly total return index for each market based on a representative set of stocks followed by the IFC, and adjusted for all distributions and stock splits.[12] The country indices allow computation of monthly return data up to September 1996. However, start of data differs by country. Monthly returns are available from January 1976 for nine countries (Argentina, Brazil, Chile, Mexico, India, Korea, Thailand, Greece, and Zimbabwe), from January 1985 for seven countries (Colombia, Venezuela, Malaysia, Pakistan, the Philip-

---

10. Henry (1998) controls for economic reforms and still finds a qualitatively similar effect of market liberalization on stock returns.

11. In three of the four countries, residents had been allowed to own foreign securities prior to the start of stock data (Indonesia, Mexico, and Venezuela).

12. The Emerging Markets DataBase of the International Finance Corporation (1975–) has a survivorship bias in the early part of the data (pre 1981). Although the data start from December 1975 for many countries, the companies were selected in 1981 when the Emerging Markets DataBase was established. Thus, better performing firms are likely to be selected for the period when the data are back-filled (see Harvey 1995). Fortunately, our analysis does not require use of pre-1981 data.

pines, Taiwan, and Nigeria), and from January 1979 for Jordan, February 1986 for Portugal, January 1987 for Turkey, and January 1990 for Indonesia.

To evaluate the impact of market liberalization on selected economic variables, we have chosen a long period, a total period of 10 years (5 years before market opening and 5 years after market opening), for our analysis. We believe this period is long enough to capture the effects related to market liberalization. Any changes in the economic variables that occur after that period are unlikely to be attributable to market openings.[13]

III. The Impact on Domestic Stock Markets

In this section, we investigate the effect of market openings on stock market returns, volatility, and market efficiency. The data are drawn from the Emerging Markets DataBase as explained above.

A. Stock Returns

To examine the effect of market opening on domestic stock markets, we compute and compare stock returns before market opening with the stock returns following market opening. The month of market opening is defined as month 0. Relative months -1, -2, and $+1$ represent 1 month before opening, 2 months before opening, and 1 month after market opening.

The stock returns for each country can be measured using a single reference currency, such as the U.S. dollar or the local currency. The advantage of using a local currency return is that the effect on the stock market can be measured from a local perspective rather than from a foreign perspective. For intercountry comparisons and from foreign investors' perspective, however, dollar returns are better to use because no transformation of local returns is required. For instance, the excess dollar returns can be computed from raw dollar returns by subtracting the 3-month Treasury-bill rate. But it is difficult to do the same for local currency returns for two reasons. First, risk-free rates are not available for all countries on a monthly basis because many countries do not issue risk-free debt or do not have active secondary markets.

---

13. An alternative would be to use all of the data available for the sample countries, in some cases those for as much as 20 years. However, this would result in using different amounts of data from different countries, which would tend to assign a higher weight to the country with more data because that country would appear in the analysis more often. It would also increase noise in the data as factors unrelated to market liberalization would affect the results. To guard against the possibility of extraneous factors affecting our results owing to the already long sample period chosen, we also report year-by-year comparisons in the relevant economic variables.

Second, excess local currency returns may vary due to differences in
the level of inflation; a 6% excess return based on a risk-free rate of
7% would be considered quite different from an excess return of 6%
based on a risk-free rate of 100%. Using the excess dollar returns will
partially mitigate the problems associated with different levels of inflation across countries. For these reasons, we use excess dollar returns
instead of local returns. Excess dollar returns are used in most studies of
emerging markets—see Bekaert (1995); Buckberg (1995); Claessens,
Dasgupta, and Glen (1995); and Harvey (1995).

An excess dollar return is computed as the change in the market
index expressed in U.S. dollars as reported by the IFC minus the
monthly riskless rate based on the 3-month Treasury-bill rate. These
excess dollar returns and standard deviations are reported for all 20
countries from the start date of data availability for each country to
September 1996 in table 1.[14]

The mean excess returns range from 0.12% per month to 4.32% per
month. By and large, the higher monthly returns are associated with
higher risk. Assuming U.S. stocks have a monthly excess return of
about 0.5%, most of the emerging stock markets generate a monthly
excess return greater than that level, which is consistent with the popular view that emerging stock markets generally have provided higher
returns albeit associated with higher risk.

To assess the effect of market opening on stock returns, the mean
excess returns are plotted in figure 1 for 15 countries for a period of
10 years (±60 months) around the month of market opening.[15] Relative
month 0 refers to the month of market opening as defined in the appendix. In addition to the mean excess return, we also compute a 12-month
moving average. Due to the high volatility of monthly returns, it is
easier to read the 12-month moving average graphs (the solid line) than
the mean excess return graphs. Looking at the individual markets, it
is easy to see that the returns are higher soon after market liberalization
in Brazil, Colombia, Greece, Pakistan, the Philippines, Turkey, Vene-

14. It should be noted that the returns reported in table 1 are arithmetic averages, not
geometric returns. Some would argue that, because of the volatile nature of emerging markets (many large negative returns and many large positive returns), the arithmetic returns
will overstate the true return. Others, like Fama (1998), disagree. However, for our purposes
the difference is not important as we do not rely on the mean level of returns for our
results; rather we focus on the significance of the change in returns.

15. We require that countries have at least 6 months of data before market opening and
6 months of data after market opening for comparison. Based on these criteria, five countries are excluded from the sample because Nigeria was closed as of 1998; Malaysia opened
before December 1984, the first month for which data are available for Malaysia; Indonesia
opened in September 1989, 3 months before the first set of data is available for Indonesia;
Jordan opened in January 1978, 12 months before the availability of the first return; and
Portugal has only 4 months of preopening data available.

TABLE 1   Descriptive Statistics of Monthly Excess Dollar Returns (January 1976–September 1996)

Country	Start Date of Monthly Data	Number of Months	Mean (%)	Standard Deviation (%)
			Excess Dollar Returns	
Argentina	January 1976	249	4.32	27.51
Brazil	January 1976	249	1.52	16.48
Chile	January 1976	249	2.23	10.83
Colombia	January 1985	141	2.34	8.87
Greece	January 1976	249	.12	9.74
India	January 1976	249	.80	8.02
Indonesia	January 1990	81	.26	8.78
Jordan	January 1979	213	.21	4.96
Korea	January 1976	249	.92	8.89
Malaysia	January 1985	141	.88	7.61
Mexico	January 1976	249	1.52	12.62
Nigeria	January 1985	141	1.28	15.12
Pakistan	January 1985	141	.76	7.21
Philippines	January 1985	141	2.84	10.32
Portugal	February 1986	128	1.98	12.03
Taiwan	January 1985	141	2.19	14.20
Thailand	January 1976	249	1.18	7.80
Turkey	January 1987	117	2.86	20.03
Venezuela	January 1985	141	1.67	13.76
Zimbabwe	January 1976	249	.71	9.80

NOTE.—An excess dollar return is the monthly dollar return minus the monthly riskless rate based on the 3-month Treasury-bill rate. A monthly dollar return is the change in the market index expressed for U.S. dollar investors as reported in the Emerging Markets DataBase of the International Finance Corporation (1975–). The index is adjusted for all distributions and stock splits.

zuela, and Zimbabwe. In the remaining countries, there is no discernible change in returns around market openings. The increase in returns probably reflects an increase in stock prices due to the additional demand created by foreign investors.

The returns are averaged across different markets by relative month for which individual country returns are available. This average return is plotted under the title "All Markets." Now the increase in return is clearly evident in the period following market opening. The return increases for about 12 months and then begins to fall to the preopening level. By month +24, the return seems to have returned to the preopening level. Another aggregate plot is under the title "Restricted Markets," which refers to markets where residents could not invest in foreign securities. The interpretation of the restricted markets plot is no different from the interpretation of the all markets plot. If we look at the individual country plots of the three countries excluded from the restricted markets' plot (the fourth country, Indonesia, has insufficient data), we find that Mexico and Taiwan show no change in returns

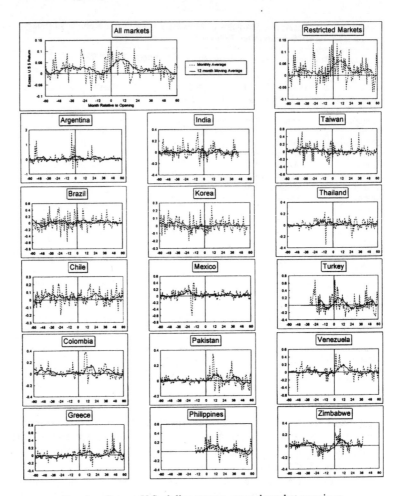

FIG. 1.—Excess U.S. dollar returns around market openings

around market opening, while Venezuela seems to display an effect similar to that of the restricted markets.[16]

16. One explanation for the similarity of the all markets and restricted markets plots is the relatively small difference in the sample of all markets and restricted markets. As indicated above, the all markets sample consists of 15 countries while the restricted markets sample consists of 12 countries. Another explanation might relate to the home country bias: although it is optimal for investors to invest in foreign securities, they do so only partially (see French and Poterba 1991; Cooper and Kaplanis 1994; and Baxter and Jermann 1997). Therefore, the freedom to invest in foreign securities does not motivate domestic investors to take full advantage of risk diversification provided by foreign securities. Why

TABLE 2   **Changes in Stock Returns, Inflation, and Exchange Rates around Market Openings**

Description	Return/Rate prior to Market Opening		Return/Rate after Market Opening		Change in the Return Rate	
	Mean (%)	Standard Deviation (%)	Mean (%)	Standard Deviation (%)	Change (%)	z-Statistic
Stock returns all markets*	2.05	4.04	2.26	3.88	.21	.26
Stock returns all markets, excluding 24 months*	1.97	3.75	1.21	3.23	−.76	−1.19
Inflation rate in low inflation markets†	1.67	.54	1.39	.41	−.28	−3.22
Change in nominal exchange rates in low inflation markets†	−1.44	.29	−.75	.27	.69	13.39
Change in real exchange rates in low inflation markets†	−2.66	.53	−1.67	.33	.99	12.34

Note.—Estimates are obtained for a portfolio of all the countries over a period of ±60 months around the month of market opening. Market opening dates are given in the appendix. Row 2 of the table reports stock returns after excluding 24 months centered on the month of market opening. It is better to exclude this period for comparison as changes may take place because of the uncertainty created by market opening.

* The following countries are not included: Jordan and Malaysia (no data before opening), Nigeria (closed as of 1998), and Indonesia and Portugal (insufficient data before opening).

† The following countries are not included: Malaysia (no data before opening), Nigeria (closed as of 1998) and Taiwan (no data in the International Financial Statistics of the International Monetary Fund 1997). Low inflation markets exclude Argentina and Brazil, both of which experienced inflation exceeding 10% per month.

In all of the subsequent analysis, we compare the results for all markets with results for restricted markets and find no perceptible difference between the two. Consequently, we drop discussions concerning the restricted versus nonrestricted markets from the remainder of this article.

We report the average pre– and post–market opening returns for a portfolio of 15 countries in the first two rows of table 2. Unlike figure 1, the first row of the table does not show the intertemporal changes in stock returns around market openings; that is, the increase in returns immediately after market opening is masked by the subsequent lower returns. Indeed, the second row of the table, which excludes returns for 1 year after opening, shows a decrease in the return from 1.97%

---

then should the opening of emerging stock markets induce foreign investors to invest in the emerging markets in a significant way? The answer lies in the relative size of these markets. The market capitalization of developed markets was more than eight times the capitalization of all emerging markets as of December 1996, and hence a small fraction of a developed market, if invested in an emerging market, would have constituted a large fraction of the emerging market.

to 1.21%. The decrease, though statistically insignificant, is consistent with the notion that domestic firms are able to access lower cost funds from international investors owing to the benefit of diversification. The result is consistent with Bekaert and Harvey (1999), who find that increases in equity flows are associated with a lower cost of capital. Similarly, Henry (1998) finds that liberalizing countries experience an upward revaluation of the domestic stocks, which reflects a reduction in the cost of equity capital.

To test more closely for changes in stock returns around market openings, excess dollar returns for a calendar month prior to opening are compared with the same calendar month postopening. Because of the anticipation of market opening and preopening announcements, the data for 1 year prior to opening are excluded.[17] The month-by-month comparison is made for each country, giving us a total of 170 country-month observations. For the 12 months after market opening (relative month +1 to +12), the returns are compared with the 12 months before market opening (relative month −13 to −24). Similarly, the second year after opening (relative month +13 to +24) is compared with the second year prior to market opening (relative month −13 to −24), the third year after opening (relative month +25 to +36) is compared with the third year prior to market opening (relative month −25 to −36), and so forth. In this manner, we can identify trends. If there is a trend, then as the observation period around market opening widens, we should see the changes increase or decrease monotonically.

Three statistical tests are conducted. The parametric test gives an estimate of the size of the average effect of market openings on changes in stock returns. Nonparametric tests are also used since the emerging market returns are nonnormal (see Claessens, Dasgupta, and Glen 1995). The first nonparametric test employs the binomial test (see Brown and Warner 1980) given by equation (1) to determine whether the percent of postopening returns greater than preopening returns is significantly different from 50%:

$$z = \frac{|P - 0.5| - (0.5/N)}{0.5/\sqrt{N}},\tag{1}$$

where P is the actual proportion of positive changes in returns, and N is the total number of observations for that event window. The last term in the numerator is a continuity correction since (1) is a continuous approximation of a discrete distribution. The expression z is positive when $p > .5$ and negative otherwise. The second nonparametric test is a simple sign test of no difference between the preopening and postopening returns.

---

17. A 1-year period is chosen so that comparison can be made by calendar month.

The results are presented in panel A of table 3 for the 15 countries with pre- and postopening data.[18] The overall impression is that, on average, the stock returns increase soon after opening of markets and this is followed by subsequent decreases in returns that are sometimes significant. The initial increase in returns suggests that stock prices increase initially due to greater demand for the domestic securities. The subsequent decrease in returns is consistent with the hypothesis that domestic firms are able to access lower cost funds from international investors. If expected returns (stock prices) decrease (increase) as a result of market integration, then the long-run average returns should be lower after market opening.[19] Stulz (1997), Bekaert and Harvey (1998, 1999), and Henry (1998) also find evidence consistent with a reduction in the cost of capital.

B. Stock Return Volatility

If integration with the world markets makes the equilibrating process more efficient for stocks in emerging markets, it is reasonable to expect a drop in stock return volatility and a concomitant drop in expected returns. One may argue, however, that foreign investors are quick to react to changes in short-term economic outlook in emerging economies, making unrestricted capital flows very volatile. This volatility of capital flows may increase the volatility of the stock market.

To explore this issue, we examine changes in stock return volatility around market openings. Recent research has demonstrated that stock return volatility is not time-invariant (see Schwert 1989). In particular, periods of extreme volatility are concentrated in time, that is, high volatility is followed by periods of high volatility. To account for the level of volatility in a previous period, we employ the autoregressive conditional heteroskedasticity model (ARCH), developed by Engle (1982), and variants thereof such as the generalized autoregressive conditional heteroskedasticity model (GARCH), developed by Bollerslev (1986). While volatility estimation is difficult, an evaluation of volatility forecasting techniques seems to suggest that the ARCH class of models

---

18. The number of observations (i.e., country-months) decreases as we move away from the date of opening due to nonavailability of data.

19. Greater integration of markets suggested by the lower long-run average returns in this article is consistent with the recent evidence on market integration. Buckberg (1995) finds evidence of integration of emerging markets with the world markets during the 1985–91 period. Bekaert and Harvey (1995), however, suggest that greater integration is not always evident for emerging markets. Korajczyk (1996) applies a new measure of deviations from the law of one price to estimate integration and obtains different results. He finds evidence consistent with the notion that adjusted mispricing tends to decrease through time, which to him suggests greater integration between emerging markets and the developed markets. Bekaert, Harvey, and Lumsdaine (1998) search for a common break in financial series for the emerging countries. In this way, they are able to identify the dates when the equity markets become financially integrated with world capital markets.

TABLE 3   Tests of Changes in Stock Returns, Inflation, and Exchange Rates around Market Openings

Description of Comparison	n	Nonparametric Test			Parametric Test	
		% Positive	z-Statistic	Sign Test of No Difference	Mean Change (%)	t-Statistic of Mean
Panel A: changes in monthly excess dollar returns:*						
Post 1st year versus pre 2d year	170	61.8	3.00	.00	+6.23	4.02
Post 2d year versus pre 2d year	170	52.9	.68	.49	+1.70	1.16
Post 3d year versus pre 3d year	163	46.6	−.79	.43	−3.03	−2.07
Post 4th year versus pre 4th year	144	42.4	−1.74	.08	−.49	−.34
Post 5th year versus pre 5th year	128	44.5	−1.16	.25	−1.47	−.82
Panel B: changes in inflation rates:†						
Post 1st year versus pre 2d year	179	40.8	−2.38	.02	−.75	−3.97
Post 2d year versus pre 2d year	179	40.8	−2.38	.02	−.76	−4.04
Post 3d year versus pre 3d year	168	38.1	−3.01	.00	−.65	−4.09
Post 4th year versus pre 4th year	159	59.7	2.37	.02	.14	1.02
Post 5th year versus pre 5th year	143	50.3	.01	1.00	.22	.91
Panel C: changes in nominal exchange rates:†						
Post 1st year versus pre 2d year	180	66.7	4.41	.00	1.01	8.35
Post 2d year versus pre 2d year	180	71.1	5.59	.00	1.10	8.64
Post 3d year versus pre 3d year	180	70.0	5.29	.00	1.04	6.78
Post 4th year versus pre 4th year	174	62.6	3.25	.00	.60	4.66
Post 5th year versus pre 5th year	158	55.7	1.35	.18	.09	.55
Panel D: changes in real exchange rates:†						
Post 1st year versus pre 2d year	169	62.1	3.06	.00	1.62	7.04
Post 2d year versus pre 2d year	169	66.9	4.32	.00	1.72	7.52
Post 3d year versus pre 3d year	168	64.9	3.79	.00	1.34	5.59
Post 4th year versus pre 4th year	159	56.0	1.43	.15	.66	3.23
Post 5th year versus pre 5th year	143	51.0	.16	.88	.05	.19

NOTE.—Preopening rates (excess dollar returns, inflation rates, and exchange rates) are compared with postopening rates in the following manner. First year after opening (relative months +1 to +12) is compared with the second year prior to opening (relative months −13 to −24). Since there is anticipation of market opening, the year immediately preceding the market opening is excluded. The second year after opening is compared with the second year before opening. The third year after opening is compared with the number of increases and decreases. Three tests are used to test for the difference between the two periods. The first nonparametric test is the z-statistic based on the number of increases and decreases. The second nonparametric test is the sign test for which the p-values are given. The last test is a parametric one that reports the difference in means. The significance is evaluated by a t-test that assumes independence.

* The following countries are not included: Jordan and Malaysia (no data before opening), Nigeria (closed as of 1998), and Indonesia and Portugal (less than 6 months of data before opening).

† The following countries are not included: Malaysia (no data before opening), Nigeria (closed as of 1998), Taiwan (no data in the International Financial Statistics of the International Monetary Fund 1997), and high inflation countries, Argentina and Brazil, both of which experienced inflation exceeding 10% per month.

provides superior forecasts of volatility (see Brailsford and Faff 1996). This method is used extensively in the literature.[20]

The first step in estimating conditional volatility is to specify a return-generating model.[21] Monthly stock index returns have been shown to include both seasonal and autoregressive components (see Bekaert and Harvey 1997). Although the conditional mean model can be specified in several ways, we choose the following model that allows for autocorrelation up to 12 lags because it has the best fit and superior autocorrelation properties. The other models we considered allowed for first-order autocorrelation only.[22] Schwert (1989) also uses this specification of the return-generating model:

$$\tilde{R}_t = \sum_{j=1}^{12} \alpha_j D_{jt} + \sum_{i=1}^{12} \beta_i R_{t-i} + \tilde{\epsilon}_t, \tag{2}$$

where R_t is the stock return during month t, D_{jt} are the 12 monthly dummies, and R_{t-i} are lagged returns.

We use ARCH and GARCH to fit the volatilities for each country. Different models ranging from ARCH(1) to ARCH(12) and GARCH(1,1) to GARCH(8,4) are fit for each country to estimate their volatilities. The best fit varies from ARCH(1) to ARCH(8) and GARCH(1,1) to GARCH(4,3) based on the log-likelihood estimates. The stock return volatility estimates by country are plotted in figure 2 for 10 years ($\pm$60 months) around market opening, and the aggregate volatility estimates for all markets are reported in the first two rows of table 4. In addition to the five countries excluded from the stock return computations, the Philippines is excluded because it has only four observations during the preperiod.

The first row of table 4 shows a marginally significant decrease in volatility after the market opens to foreign participation. Since the market opening itself as well as events leading to the policy change may affect volatility, we make another comparison after excluding $\pm$1 year around market opening. As shown in the second row of the table, excluding the 24 months around opening reveals a significant decrease in volatility from an average of 10.8% during the preperiod to 9.5% in the postopening period.

Panel A of table 5 reports the results of one parametric test and two nonparametric tests, which are similar to those reported in table 3. The parametric test assumes that stock return volatilities are normally distributed. Since this assumption may not be accurate, we also use the

---

20. See Bollerslev, Chou, and Kroner (1992) for an extensive overview of applications of conditional volatility models. Hargis (1994) and Aggarwal, Inclan, and Leal (1995) use the ARCH model for emerging markets.
21. In this article, we follow Frennberg and Hansson (1995).
22. For details pertaining to the selection of this model, please contact us.

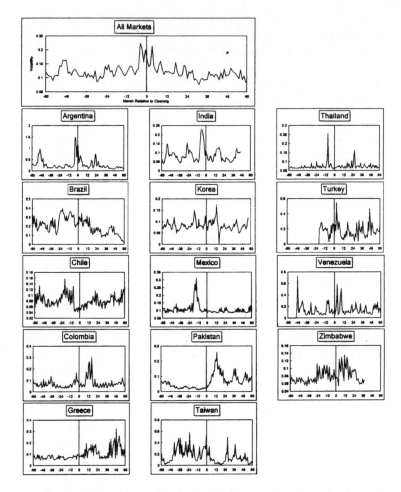

FIG. 2.—Change's in stock return volatility around market openings

ordinary sign test and a binomial test to evaluate changes in volatility.[23] Similar nonparametric tests are used by Ohlson and Penman (1985) and Skinner (1989) to test for changes in volatility. As stock return volatility may have a seasonal component, we compare the volatility of postopening months with the volatilities during the corresponding months in the preperiod. This is done for all countries in the sample.

23. One alternative is to use variance ratios. If returns are normally distributed, the ratio of the variances will have an *F* distribution. However, empirical evidence seems to indicate that variance ratios of returns do not follow an *F* distribution (see Skinner 1989).

TABLE 4   Changes in Volatility of Stock Returns, Inflation, and Exchange Rates around Market Openings

Country	Conditional Volatility prior to Market Opening		Conditional Volatility after Market Opening		Change in Volatility	
	Mean (%)	Standard Deviation (%)	Mean (%)	Standard Deviation (%)	Change (%)	z-Statistic
Volatility of stock returns— all markets*	12.48	2.71	11.63	2.27	−.85	−1.88
Volatility of stock returns— all markets, excluding 24 months*	10.82	2.44	9.45	2.59	−1.37	−4.53
Volatility of inflation in low inflation markets†	1.05	.24	.93	.21	−.12	−2.93
Volatility of changes in nominal exchange rates in low inflation markets†	.32	.12	.25	.10	−.06	−3.16
Volatility of changes in real exchange rates in low inflation markets†	.34	.11	.30	.12	−.04	−1.99

NOTE.—Volatility estimates are presented for a period of ±60 months around the month of market opening. Market opening dates are given in the appendix. The estimates are obtained by averaging across all the countries. Row 2 of the table reports the volatility after excluding 24 months centered on the month of market opening. It is better to exclude this period for comparison as changes may take place because of the uncertainty created by market opening.
 * The following countries are not included: Jordan and Malaysia (no data before opening), Nigeria (closed as of 1998), and Indonesia, Philippines, and Portugal (insufficient data before opening for volatility estimation).
 † The following countries are not included: Malaysia (no data before opening), Nigeria (closed as of 1998), and Taiwan (no data in the International Financial Statistics of the International Monetary Fund 1997). Low inflation markets exclude Argentina and Brazil, both of which experienced inflation exceeding 10% per month.

The results presented in table 5 show that changes in volatility during the first 2 years after opening are not significantly different from the volatility levels before opening. The parametric test, however, suggests that there is a significant decrease in stock return volatility in the fourth and fifth years after opening.

Two recent papers, Bekaert and Harvey (1997) and de Santis and Imrohoroglu (1997), have also examined changes in stock return volatility around liberalization. While de Santis and Imrohoroglu (1997) do not find any evidence of a systematic effect of market liberalization on stock return volatility similar to what we present in panel A of our table 5, Bekaert and Harvey (1997), find an overall decrease in volatility for the countries in their sample that is similar to what we show in our table 4. Since there is considerable variation in changes in stock return volatility across countries as shown in figure 2, the differences in results may be attributable to differences in sample countries and differences in the method of aggregation among the studies. Figure 2 illustrates that many countries have short periods of high volatility. For example,

TABLE 5   Tests of Changes in Conditional Volatility of Stock Returns, Inflation, and Exchange Rates around Market Openings

Description of Comparison	n	Nonparametric Test		Sign Test of No Difference	Parametric Test	
		% Positive	z-Statistic		Mean Change	t-Statistic of Mean
Panel A: changes in conditional volatility of stock returns:*						
Post 1st year versus pre 2d year	163	50.9	.15	.88	.78	.85
Post 2d year versus pre 2d year	163	49.7	-.02	1.00	-.48	-.50
Post 3d year versus pre 3d year	156	44.9	-1.19	.23	-.81	-1.37
Post 4th year versus pre 4th year	144	49.3	-.08	.93	-2.10	-2.24
Post 5th year versus pre 5th year	117	47.9	-.36	.71	-3.78	-2.66
Panel B: changes in conditional volatility of inflation rates:†						
Post 1st year versus pre 2d year	168	32.7	-4.41	.00	-.33	-4.20
Post 2d year versus pre 2d year	168	35.7	-3.62	.00	-.37	-4.36
Post 3d year versus pre 3d year	168	33.3	-4.24	.00	-.23	-4.44
Post 4th year versus pre 4th year	159	40.7	-2.28	.02	-.10	-3.09
Post 5th year versus pre 5th year	143	40.4	-2.24	.03	.05	.41
Panel C: changes in conditional volatility of nominal exchange rates:†						
Post 1st year versus pre 2d year	180	40.6	-2.45	.01	-.02	-.36
Post 2d year versus pre 2d year	180	37.2	-3.36	.00	-.09	-2.10
Post 3d year versus pre 3d year	180	36.1	-3.65	.00	-.17	-3.08
Post 4th year versus pre 4th year	165	47.3	-.62	.53	-.03	-1.32
Post 5th year versus pre 5th year	146	52.7	.57	.56	-.01	-.28
Panel D: changes in conditional volatility of real exchange rates:†						
Post 1st year versus pre 2d year	168	39.9	-2.54	.01	-.00	-.07
Post 2d year versus pre 2d year	168	27.4	-5.78	.00	-.08	-2.04
Post 3d year versus pre 3d year	168	38.7	-2.85	.00	-.14	-2.89
Post 4th year versus pre 4th year	159	47.5	-.56	.58	-.04	-1.81
Post 5th year versus pre 5th year	143	54.1	.91	.36	.02	.32

NOTE.—Preopening volatility of excess dollar returns, inflation rates, and exchange rates is compared with postopening volatility in the following manner. First year after opening (relative months +1 to +12) is compared with the second year prior to opening (relative months -13 to -24). Since there is anticipation of market opening, the year immediately preceding the market opening is excluded. The second year after opening is compared with the second year before opening. The third year after opening is compared with the third year before opening, et cetera. Three tests are used to test for the difference between the two periods. The first nonparametric test is the z-statistic based on the number of increases and decreases. The second nonparametric test is the sign test for which the p-values are given. The last test is a parametric one that reports the difference in means. The significance is evaluated by a t-test that assumes independence.

* The following countries are not included: Jordan and Malaysia (no data before opening), Nigeria (closed as of 1998), and Indonesia, Philippines, and Portugal (insufficient data before opening for volatility estimation).

† The following countries are not included: Malaysia (no data before opening), Nigeria (closed as of 1998), Taiwan (no data in the International Financial Statistics of the International Monetary Fund 1997), and high inflation countries, Argentina and Brazil, both of which experienced inflation exceeding 10% per month.

Argentina and India experienced high volatility around market opening. Mexico had a short period of high volatility prior to market opening, while Colombia had a period of high volatility after market opening. In contrast, some countries have long periods of high volatility: Greece and Pakistan both experienced extended periods of high volatility after market opening. From these results, the only unambiguous conclusion we can draw is that, contrary to popular belief, foreign investors do not add to stock market volatility.

C. Stock Market Efficiency

The third and last aspect of the stock markets examined relates to changes in stock market efficiency around market openings. To investigate these changes, we examine whether the stock returns become more random when markets open.[24] Although randomness of stock returns need not imply efficiency, it can generally be claimed that randomness is related to market efficiency.[25] Thus, while we test the random walk hypothesis, our conclusions relating to market efficiency are based on the randomness of stock returns.

The random walk hypothesis is tested using the variance ratio test proposed by Lo and MacKinlay (1988).[26] This method has been used by Claessens, Dasgupta, and Glen (1995) and Coppejans and Domowitz (1996) to evaluate stock market efficiency in emerging markets. We begin with the recursive relation

$$X_t = \mu + X_{t-l} + \varepsilon_t, \tag{3}$$

where $X_t \equiv \ln P_t$ and P_t is the stock price at time t. The variable μ denotes drift, and ε_t is the random disturbance. The expectation of ε_t is assumed to be zero. Variance ratio tests exploit the property of random walks that the variance is a linear function of period: $1/q$th of the variance of $X_t - X_{t-q}$ should be equal to the variance of $X_t - X_{t-1}$. Lo and MacKinlay (1988) develop two tests, a z-statistic under the assumption of homoskedasticity and a z^* statistic that allows for time-varying volatilities. The heteroskedasticity-corrected z-statistic is defined below:

$$z^*(q) = \sqrt{nq}\,\overline{M}_r(q)/\sqrt{\hat{\theta}} \quad \overset{a}{\sim} N(0,1), \tag{4}$$

---

24. Previous research has shown that stock prices do not follow a random walk in the emerging stock markets. See Harvey (1993) and Claessens, Dasgupta, and Glen (1995).
25. Stock return generating models could be consistent with both market efficiency and returns consisting of a nonrandom component.
26. Also see Lo and MacKinlay (1989), Liu and He (1991), and Ajayi and Karemera (1996). Jones and Kaul (1994) suggest that variance ratio tests do not suffer from known biases when used for testing for autocorrelation in portfolio returns.

where q is the number of overlapping base observations used for computing the variance, nq is the total number of base observations, and

$$\overline{M}_r(q) \equiv \frac{\overline{\sigma}_c^2(q)}{\overline{\sigma}_a^2} - 1;$$

$$\overline{\sigma}_a^2 = \frac{1}{nq - 1} \sum_{k=1}^{nq} (X_k - X_{k-1} - \hat{\mu})^2;$$

$$\overline{\sigma}_c^2 = \frac{1}{m} \sum_{k=q}^{nq} (X_k - X_{k-q} - q\hat{\mu})^2;$$

$$m = q(nq - q + 1)\left(1 - \frac{q}{nq}\right);$$

$$\hat{\theta}(q) \equiv \sum_{j=1}^{q-1} \left(\frac{2(q-j)}{q}\right)^2 \hat{\delta}(j);$$

and

$$\hat{\delta}(j) = \frac{\sum_{k=j+1}^{nq} (X_k - X_{k-1} - \hat{\mu})^2 (X_{k-j} - X_{k-j-1} - \hat{\mu})^2}{\left(\sum_{k=1}^{nq} (X_k - X_{k-1} - \hat{\mu})^2\right)^2}.$$

In addition to the monthly data described in Section I, weekly stock market indices are also available from December 1988 for 16 countries, from September 1990 for Indonesia, from March 1991 for Pakistan, and from July 1993 for Zimbabwe and Nigeria. There are trade-offs in choosing between weekly and monthly data. Monthly data are preferred because they cover longer periods (back to January 1976 in many cases) and because there would be smaller biases due to nonsynchronous trading. Weekly data are preferred because of the greater number of observations. Possibly, the bias due to nonsynchronous trading is limited even with weekly data as the IFC index is based on relatively large stocks. For each country, the ''Data Used'' column in table 6 indicates whether weekly or monthly data are used. The criteria for selection are the availability of data for both premarket opening and postmarket opening periods and increasing the minimum number of observations for both premarket and postmarket opening. Specific reasons for selecting the data type used for a specific country are given in the notes to the table.

TABLE 6   Tests of Random Walk around Market Openings

Country	Data Used	Preopening			Postopening			Difference	
		n	2-base	8-base	n	2-base	8-base	2-base	8-base
Argentina	Monthly (3)	160	1.16 [1.24]	1.40 [1.32]	80	.83 [-.84]	.93 [-.19]	-.33 [-1.37]	-.47 [-.99]
Brazil	Weekly (3)	120	1.34 [2.69]	1.66 [2.06]	272	.98 [-.92]	.96 [-.85]	-.36 [-2.81]	-.70 [-2.16]
Chile	Monthly (3)	160	1.17 [2.11]	1.81 [3.25]	80	1.29 [2.41]	1.73 [2.14]	.12 [.83]	-.08 [-.19]
Colombia	Weekly (2)	104	1.49 [3.45]	2.77 [4.91]	288	1.21 [2.41]	2.11 [4.07]	-.28 [-1.68]	-.66 [-1.46]
Greece	Monthly (1)	120	1.08 [.75]	1.03 [.11]	120	1.15 [1.72]	1.29 [.89]	.07 [.51]	.26 [.61]
India	Weekly (3)	192	1.11 [1.14]	1.71 [2.51]	200	1.12 [1.36]	1.23 [1.01]	.01 [.08]	-.48 [1.32]
Korea	Weekly (3)	152	.95 [-.51]	1.06 [.26]	240	1.07 [.80]	1.22 [.96]	.12 [.91]	.16 [.49]
Mexico	Monthly (3)	160	1.39 [2.55]	2.09 [2.79]	80	1.15 [1.06]	1.19 [.55]	-.24 [-1.15]	-.90 [-1.73]
Pakistan	Monthly (1)	72	1.00 [-.04]	.67 [-.91]	64	1.26 [1.57]	1.67 [1.62]	.26 [1.57]	1.00 [1.82]
Philippines	Monthly (1)	8	1.42 [3.68]	1.71 [2.51]	120	1.21 [2.11]	1.36 [1.23]	-.21 [-1.39]	-.35 [-.86]
Taiwan	Weekly (2)	96	1.02 [.15]	1.71 [1.75]	296	1.03 [.55]	1.37 [1.81]	.01 [.07]	-.34 [-.75]
Turkey	Weekly (2)	24	1.27 [1.37]	.87 [-.23]	368	1.04 [.61]	1.01 [.03]	-.23 [-1.11]	.14 [.21]
Venezuela	Weekly (2)	48	1.40 [2.43]	2.48 [3.20]	344	1.22 [3.08]	1.73 [3.91]	-.18 [-1.00]	-.75 [-1.50]
Zimbabwe	Monthly (1)	208	1.11 [1.29]	2.25 [5.32]	32	1.34 [1.60]	1.77 [1.35]	.23 [1.00]	-.48 [-.78]
Overall	...	...	...	...	...	...	...	[-1.48]	[-2.30]

NOTE.—The method used for the variance ratio test results reported here is described in the text. The tests are conducted using 2-base and 8-base observations. Reasons for selecting the periodicity of data include (1) no weekly data were available prior to opening, (2) equal or larger number of observations for both prior and post–market opening periods are available with weekly data, and (3) the periodicity of data used maximizes the minimum number of observations available for the prior market opening period and the post–market opening period. The numbers in parentheses in column 2 correspond to these three reasons. In the Argentinian row, e.g., (3) refers to the third reason given above. The heteroskedasticity-robust z-statistic is in brackets.

The tests are conducted using local currency returns. In this instance, it is not necessary to use U.S. dollar returns since raw returns across different countries are neither compared nor aggregated. The results for 14 countries prior to market opening and after market opening are presented in table 6.[27] Variance ratios are reported using 2-base and 8-base observations. The variance ratios should be equal to one for stock prices to follow a random walk.[28]

The preopening data in table 6 show that the returns were predictable in the 2-base test or the 8-base test or both for Brazil, Chile, Colombia, India, Mexico, the Philippines, Venezuela, and Zimbabwe. Several other studies have documented predictability of returns in emerging markets. Claessens, Dasgupta, and Glen (1995) find significant autocorrelations for many emerging markets. Based on variance ratios, they reject the null hypothesis of independently and identically distributed (i.i.d.) returns for seven countries. Harvey (1995) documents higher predictability for emerging market returns than for stock returns in developed markets.

The change in predictability of returns around market openings is given in the last two columns of table 6. There is a statistically significant reduction in predictability of returns for Brazil, Colombia, and Mexico. There is an increase in predictability only for Pakistan. For the remaining countries, the change is insignificantly different from zero. For the sample as a whole, however, stock markets tend to become more efficient in impounding information over longer periods: the heteroskedasticity corrected z-statistic for the overall sample is significantly negative for 8-base observations. For 2-base observations, the z-statistic is negative but not significantly different from zero. The results for the complete sample indicate that the stock returns become less predictable after market opening up to 8 periods in advance.

The improvement in market efficiency is consistent with increasing integration with the world markets as documented by Harvey (1995) and Korajczyk (1996). If markets are predictable and foreign investors are sophisticated, then foreign investors are likely to profit from the predictability of returns. As the foreign investors take advantage of market inefficiencies, those market inefficiencies will decrease and the prices will react more quickly to new information.

Another explanation for the observed decrease in predictability could be more frequent trading. If country indices include stocks that are infrequently traded, then index returns may give an impression of auto-

27. Indonesia, Jordan, Malaysia, Nigeria, Portugal, and Thailand are excluded due to insufficient data.

28. For instance, using 2-base observations for Argentina, the variance ratio prior to market opening is 1.16. However, the heteroskedasticity-robust z-statistic of 1.24 suggests that it is not statistically different from one. After market opening, the variance ratio decreases to 0.83, which is also insignificantly different from one.

TABLE 7   **Frequency of Trading**

	Preopening		Postopening		
Country	n	Days Traded	n	Days Traded	Difference
Argentina	43	17.69	60	18.64	.95
		(1.62)		(1.82)	[2.79]
Brazil	58	18.30	60	17.36	−.94
		(2.17)		(1.52)	[−2.72]
Chile	42	17.72	60	17.42	−.30
		(1.35)		(1.72)	[−.99]
Colombia	60	11.11	60	14.69	3.58
		(1.44)		(1.98)	[11.33]
Greece	4	13.40	60	17.14	3.74
		(1.29)		(2.17)	[5.32]
India	55	16.91	60	19.06	2.15
		(2.80)		(2.35)	[4.44]
Korea	60	24.19	44	24.58	.39
		(1.60)		(1.31)	[1.36]
Mexico	37	17.18	55	12.85	−4.33
		(2.86)		(2.03)	[−7.96]
Pakistan	60	14.61	60	12.76	−1.85
		(2.33)		(1.60)	[−5.07]
Philippines	16	9.77	60	16.67	6.90
		(1.86)		(2.45)	[12.27]
Taiwan	60	23.75	60	23.85	.10
		(2.73)		(2.24)	[.22]
Turkey	19	20.01	60	20.51	.50
		(1.42)		(1.77)	[1.26]
Venezuela	42	11.84	60	15.88	4.04
		(2.48)		(1.66)	[9.21]
Zimbabwe	60	7.69	37	12.71	5.02
		(1.48)		(2.05)	[12.96]

NOTE.—"Days Traded" refers to the average number of days traded per month across all securities in the index for each country during the pre- and postperiod; *n* refers to the number of months covered by the data. The standard deviation is given in the "Days Traded" columns in parentheses. The *z*-statistics are given in the "Difference" column in brackets.

correlation. Once stocks start trading more often, the nontrading bias in the autocorrelations will be eliminated, thereby enhancing the measured efficiency of the market even though there has been no change in the informational efficiency of the market. To examine this possibility, we study the change in the frequency of trading. The Emerging Markets DataBase has information on the number of days that a stock trades each month.[29] The frequencies of trading data are presented in table 7. The average number of days traded per month increases significantly after market opening for seven countries, decreases for three countries, and is not significantly different for the remaining four countries.

29. While we would have liked to have repeated this experiment with weekly data, frequency of trading data are not available in the weekly files of the Emerging Markets DataBase.

To compare how changes in trading frequency relate to efficiency improvements, we note the following: of the seven countries for which trading frequency increased, one country (Colombia) experienced an improvement in market efficiency; of the three countries for which trading frequency decreased, there are two countries for which market efficiency improved and one for which market efficiency deteriorated (Pakistan); of the four countries for which no significant change in trading frequency took place, there is no significant change in market efficiency. These data do not seem to indicate that the observed improvement in market efficiency is due to an increase in trading frequency. This result is also consistent with Mech (1993), who finds that the autocorrelation in NASDAQ stock portfolios cannot be explained by nontrading.

In sum, the results for both returns and volatilities around market openings reveal that market openings are good for domestic investors: the stock prices rise while the volatility does not increase. The subsequent drop in stock returns suggests that expected returns decrease and hence the domestic firms get access to lower cost capital. Furthermore, the test of the random walk hypothesis suggests that stock returns are less predictable over longer horizons. To the extent that less predictability in stock prices reflects greater stock market efficiency, open markets should result in a more efficient allocation of capital.

IV. Effect on Inflation and Exchange Rates

Policy makers of emerging economies are concerned that the inflow of capital after market opening may result in greater inflation and a stronger currency. They fear that if there are not enough investment opportunities to absorb the new inflow of foreign capital, excess capital may fuel inflation. Similarly, a strong currency may make exports more expensive and less competitive, thereby hurting the export sector of the economy. In addition, it is possible that large changes in portfolio capital flow (inflow and outflow) increase volatility of inflation and exchange rates. In this section, we analyze the effect of market opening on these macroeconomic variables.

A. Inflation

Monthly data relating to inflation have been obtained from the International Financial Statistics, which are published by the International Monetary Fund. For measuring inflation, the consumer price indices are used; these are available for all countries in the sample except Taiwan.[30] In addition to excluding Taiwan from our analyses of inflation

30. The consumer price index for each country is taken from line 64 of the International Financial Statistics on CD-ROM (International Monetary Fund 1997).

volatility, we also exclude Malaysia because of insufficient data prior to market opening and Nigeria because of insufficient data after market opening. Rates of inflation, as measured by changes in the consumer price index (CPI), are computed for 17 countries ±60 months around market opening. These are plotted in figure 3. Statistical tests for individual countries show that inflation seems to have increased significantly after market opening for Pakistan, Thailand, and Turkey and to have decreased significantly for Argentina, Chile, Korea, Mexico, the Philippines, and Portugal.[31]

To provide an overall picture of the effect of liberalization on inflation, inflation rates are aggregated across different countries. Since Argentina and Brazil have had very high rates of inflation, inflation rates of these countries will swamp the inflation rates of other countries. To overcome this problem, two different methods are used. First, we aggregate across countries but exclude those two countries with high inflation rates. These countries are called "low inflation markets." The third row in table 2 shows a significant decrease in inflation for the low inflation markets: inflation falls from 1.67% per month before market opening to 1.39% per month after market opening.

Second, we aggregate using standardized excess inflation rates. Specifically, we compute the excess inflation rate above the level of inflation rates for up to 5 years prior to market opening and standardize it by the sample standard deviation. Estimates of the mean inflation rate and the sample standard deviation are obtained for a period of 60 months immediately preceding the market opening. If 60 months of preopening data are not available, then all of the preopening data are used. The excess inflation (EI) is estimated as given by equation (5):

$$EI_{jt} = \frac{(\pi_{jt} - \bar{\pi})}{\hat{S}_j}, \tag{5}$$

where $\bar{\pi}$ is the average preopening inflation rate, and $\hat{S}_j$ is the standard deviation. The standardized excess inflation rates for each country are averaged across for each relative month. The standardized excess inflation rates are plotted for all countries ("All Markets–EI") and only for the low inflation countries ("Low Inflation Markets–EI"). All three aggregate plots in figure 3 imply that there is a decrease in the level of inflation rates after market opening.

Panel B of table 3 reports the month-by-month aggregate changes in inflation rates using only the low inflation markets. There is a significant decrease in inflation for all 3 years after market opening irre-

---

31. The statistical tests reported in table 2 for a portfolio of countries are also conducted for individual countries. The results are too voluminous to report here, but they are available from us upon request.

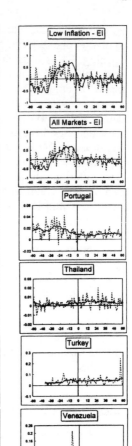

FIG. 3.—Rates of inflation around market openings

spective of whether parametric or nonparametric tests are used. Certainly, the evidence is consistent with the conclusion that inflation does not increase as a consequence of market openings.

B.   Exchange Rates

To measure relevant changes in exchange rates, we use the U.S. dollar as the reference currency.[32] An alternative is to use the currencies of the country's trading partners and competitors as the reference currency (referred to as effective exchange rates).[33] We do not use effective exchange rates for two reasons.[34] First, effective exchange rates are available only for eight countries in our sample (including Nigeria and Malaysia, which, as will be explained below, had to be dropped from this analysis for other reasons). Reliance on the effective exchange rates would reduce our sample size from 17 to six. Second, much of international trade is denominated in the U.S. dollar even when trading is not done with the United States.

Exchange rates are expressed as U.S. dollar per unit of local currency. An increase in the exchange rate implies an appreciation of the local currency, while a decrease in the exchange rate means a depreciation of the local currency. Changes in nominal exchange rates are computed for the 17 countries for which data are available. Taiwan is excluded because no exchange rate data are available, Malaysia because no data are available prior to opening, and Nigeria because no data are available after market opening.

The changes in nominal exchange rates around market openings are reported in the fourth row of table 2 and are plotted in figure 4. Many emerging economies had fixed exchange rates prior to market opening and still continue to have either fixed rate or managed floating rates. While the market eventually forces the countries to adjust exchange rates, the government-mandated changes tend to be infrequent but large. The large changes are smoothed by using the 12-month moving averages, which are shown in figure 4.

Individual country results (not reported) show that the currencies of Korea, Pakistan, and Turkey fell more rapidly after market opening than in the preopening period.[35] For all other countries, either the change is not significantly different from zero or the rate of depreciation is significantly lower in the postperiod than in the period preceding market opening. A striking feature of the data is that the changes in exchange rates show a persistent depreciation of the currency (i.e., the

32. Line ''AH..X'' from the International Financial Statistics on CD-ROM (International Monetary Fund 1997).
33. Lines ''rec'' and ''nec'' from the International Financial Statistics on CD-ROM (International Monetary Fund 1997).
34. Qualitatively similar results are obtained when effective exchange rates are used.
35. See n. 31 above.

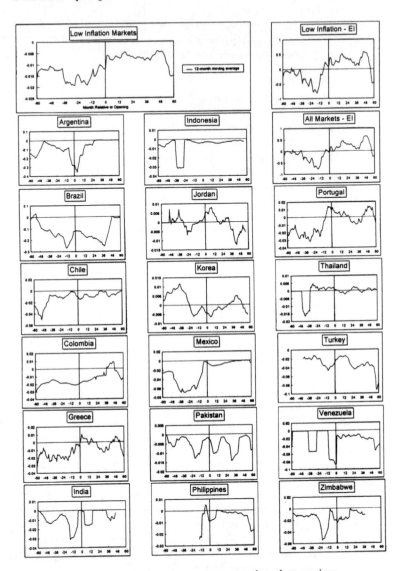

FIG. 4.—Nominal exchange rates around market openings

changes are negative) both before and after market opening. Currencies continue to fall in value but at a lower rate. The appreciation of the nominal exchange is not significant for any country during either the pre- or postopening period.

Aggregated over all markets (excluding Argentina and Brazil, which are high inflation countries) and reported in table 2, the rate of currency depreciation is significantly lower in the postperiod as compared to the preperiod, a decline in the rate of depreciation from −1.44% per month to −0.75% per month. This implies that while the currencies of emerging economies continued to depreciate, they did not depreciate nearly as much as they did in the preperiod.

The month-by-month test statistics for aggregate changes in exchange rates for low inflation markets are presented in panel C of table 3. The table confirms that there is a significant decrease in the rate of currency depreciation irrespective of whether the parametric or nonparametric tests are used.

Since the nominal exchange rates are unadjusted for relative inflation rates in the United States and the emerging economies, we also analyze changes in real exchange rates. The real exchange rate is calculated using the 1985 CPI for the United States and the emerging market. The results, given in the last row in table 2 and in panel D of table 3, are similar to those for the nominal exchange rates.

Overall, changes in exchange rates are negative prior to market opening, which implies a significant decrease in the currency value of emerging economies. This rate of currency depreciation falls significantly after market opening. The results do not present any evidence to suggest that there has been an appreciation in the currency values of emerging economies subsequent to market opening.

C. Volatility of Inflation Rates and Changes in Exchange Rates

The volatility of inflation rates, nominal exchange rates, and real exchange rates is estimated as described in Section III*B*. In all of the volatility calculations, equation (2) is estimated using ARCH or GARCH to model conditional volatilities in individual countries. The volatility estimates are presented individually for all countries with sufficient data in graphical form (data in tabular form are presented for a portfolio of countries). Aggregation across low inflation markets is attained by simple averages.[36]

Country-by-country volatility of inflation estimates are plotted in figure 5. Individual country test results (not reported here) reveal that no country experienced a significant increase in the volatility of inflation. The volatility decreased significantly in nine out of 17 countries:

---

36. There is no significant difference between standardized and simple average results for these countries.

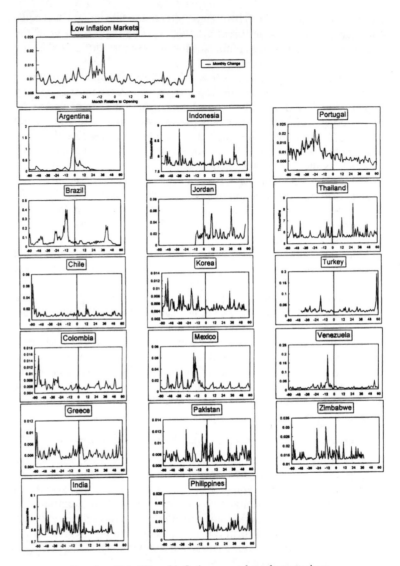

FIG. 5.—Volatility of inflation around market openings

Argentina, Brazil, Colombia, India, Korea, Mexico, the Philippines, Portugal, and Venezuela.

Aggregate results are presented as the third row of table 4 and in panel B of table 5 for 15 countries, excluding Argentina and Brazil. All of the results show a significant decrease in the volatility of inflation. Furthermore, the decrease in the volatility of inflation is not transitory—it decreases for the first, second, third, and fourth years after market opening.

Volatility of exchange rates is also important because it adds risk to cross-border transactions. Exchange-rate volatility is estimated for both nominal exchange rates and real exchange rates. Estimates for volatility of nominal exchange rates are presented in figure 6 and in the fourth row of table 4. The individual country test results (not reported) show that the volatility increased significantly in Colombia and Turkey and marginally in Pakistan, while it decreased significantly in seven countries. The aggregate test in table 4 shows that there was a significant decrease in volatility of nominal exchange rates after market opening. Month-by-month comparisons for the low inflation markets are presented in panel C of table 5. The nonparametric tests suggest that there was a significant decrease in volatility for 3 years after market opening when compared with the corresponding preopening periods. Results of the parametric test are also consistent with those of the nonparametric tests, except that the decreases in volatility are significant only for the second and third years after opening. However, none of the tests imply an increase in the volatility of nominal exchange rates. Volatility estimates of real exchange rates, reported as the last data row in table 4 and in panel D of table 5, are similar to those for nominal exchange rates.

Volatility of inflation, nominal exchange rates, and real exchange rates all show a decrease after market opening. There is certainly no hint of a substantial increase in volatility, though exceptions occur for a few individual countries. Overall, there is a distinctive pattern of a decrease in volatility after the opening of markets to foreign participation. The decrease in volatility suggests that capital inflows brought on by stock market openings are not disruptive to the economy.

V. Summary and Concluding Remarks

Our exploratory inquiry reveals that the opening of stock markets significantly increases stock prices without a concurrent increase in stock return volatility. The increase in stock prices is indicative of an increase in demand for domestic securities and the increased access of domestic firms to foreign capital at a lower cost. Once the stock prices adjust to new information, stock returns fall, reflecting lower expected returns.

When we test the random walk hypothesis, we find that the stock

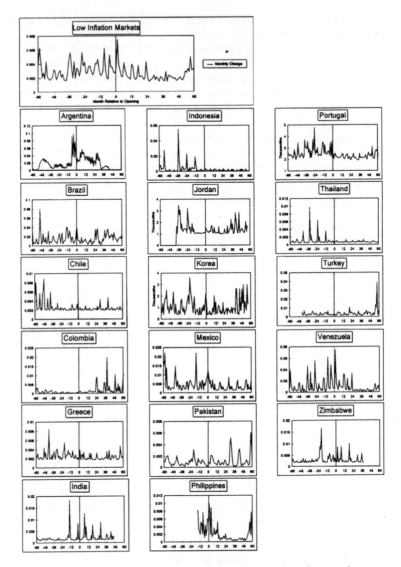

FIG. 6.—Volatility of nominal exchange rates around market openings

prices are less autocorrelated subsequent to market opening. The increased randomness of returns probably suggests an improvement in market efficiency. A more efficient market means better allocation of capital and an increase in the productivity of capital.

Policy makers are often concerned that these efficiency gains are offset by macroeconomic instability stemming from upward pressure on inflation and exchange rates. The results reveal no such upward pressure on inflation. Indeed, the results suggest that inflation rates, on average, fall after stock market liberalization.

The results regarding exchange rates are also comforting. We observe no evidence of an appreciation of the local currency that may adversely affect competition abroad. The evidence indicates that emerging market currencies had been depreciating relative to the U.S. dollar prior to market openings and that they continued to decline after the openings. But, the rate of depreciation declined significantly around the openings. This decrease in the rate of exchange rate depreciation seems to reflect increased investor confidence in the economy that is undergoing capital market liberalization.

The volatility of inflation also fell significantly after market openings as did the volatility of exchange rate changes. These reductions mean less inflation-related risk and less risk associated with international trade and international borrowing and lending.

What is the lesson that a country can draw from the experience of emerging markets, especially a country contemplating greater capital controls versus increased accessibility to foreign investors? As each country has its unique features that are different from our "average" country, it is difficult to argue that the country will only benefit from internationalization and that the risks associated with internationalization are irrelevant. However, by examining a sample of emerging economies instead of a single country, this study is better equipped to isolate the impact of market opening from country-specific factors. Thus, we conclude that the benefits are likely to outweigh the perceived risks associated with foreign portfolio flows.

Finally, some caveats are in order. The implications of this study are somewhat limited to the extent that it has not tried to control for other confounding factors. For example, countries often open stock markets as part of a broader liberalization package. Thus, the observed effects could be due to liberalization of economic policies and controls.[37] Further, most governments will attempt to control the potential ill effects of market openings by various policy measures. Thus, all we can safely say is that a majority of the emerging economies have

---

37. Henry (1998) finds an effect on stock returns that is similar to ours even after controlling for concurrent economic reforms.

successfully controlled the potential dangerous side effects of liberalization while reaping its benefits.

The evidence herein also has implications for the recent financial turmoil in emerging markets and the threatened reversion to capital controls. Based on the evidence provided in this article, we must agree with the advocates of the free flow of capital that, rather than imposing controls flows, capital markets should be made more open and transparent. Capital control enthusiasts should take note of the fact that liberalization took place more than 5 years (and as much as 10 years) before the Asian crisis began. It would certainly seem unlikely that the act of market liberalization was responsible for the crisis. Economic mismanagement and value destruction in the corporate sector are more likely causes.[38]

Perhaps it is time to recognize that we have now reached a stage of global economic development where capital users (sovereign countries) compete for capital in a competitive market environment. In such an environment, the only way to insure against a sudden outflow of capital and the ensuing financial crisis is to maintain the confidence of suppliers of capital, which in turn requires that the capital be used productively, investors treated fairly, and information flow freely.

Appendix

The Process of Liberalization in Sample Countries

Argentina

Start of monthly stock date.   January 1976.
Market opening date.   November 1989.
Details.   The liberalization began with the New Foreign Investment Regime in November 1989 (Park and Van Agtmael 1993, p. 326). Under this reform, all legal limits on the type and nature of foreign investments were abolished, and a free exchange regime was introduced. Capital, dividends, and capital gains could be repatriated freely. International Finance Corporation (1990) also lists Argentina as a free market for foreign investment on December 31, 1989. Bekaert (1995) reports that all limits on foreign capital were abolished by December 1989.

The market was fully opened in October 1991 (International Finance Corporation 1996*b*). The Deregulation Decree issued on October 31, 1991, eliminated most restrictions on foreign investment, including taxes on capital gains (Park and Van Agtmael 1993, p. 335). Buckberg (1995) lists October 1991 as the month of full opening.

Foreign portfolio investment by residents was unrestricted until October 1983 when it was suspended (Cowitt 1985, p. 66). Apparently residents could begin buying foreign securities from March 1990 when the currency was made fully convertible (Cowitt, Edwards, and Boyce 1996, pp. 218–19). Bentley (1986) also

---

38. See Kim (1998) for further discussion on this line of inquiry.

reports that foreign portfolio investment by residents is restricted and requires prior approval of the government.

Brazil

Start of monthly stock data. January 1976.

Market opening data. May 1991.

Details. From March 1987 to May 1991, foreign portfolio investment took place under CVM Resolution 1289, Annex II, which limited foreign portfolio investment to investment through special funds with onerous conditions. Since May 1991, foreign institutions were allowed to own up to 49% of voting stock and 100% of nonvoting stock under Resolution 1832, Annex IV. Some limitations apply—Petrobras common stock and banks' voting stock cannot be purchased. Bekaert (1995) reports that foreign investment trusts were approved in March 1987 and that foreign ownership levels were increased in May 1991. Buckberg (1995) reports that country funds were admitted in September 1987 but that the full opening took place in May 1991. International Finance Corporation (1996*b*) reports that foreign investors can invest 100% of nonvoting preferred stock and 49% of voting common stock as of May 1991. Park and Van Agtmael (1993, p. 302) have a slightly different date. They report that from March 1987 to July 1991, foreign investors could invest only through specialized funds. Price (1994, p. 96) reiterated the May 1991 opening date. Foreign portfolio investment by residents is restricted. See Bentley 1986; Cowitt 1991, p. 247; Cowitt, Edwards, and Boyce 1996, p. 244.

Chile

Start of monthly stock data. January 1976.

Market opening date. October 1989.

Details. Foreign investors are restricted under Law 18657 and DL 600. Law 18657 of 1987 requires capital to be retained for 5 years before it can be repatriated, while DL 600 of 1974 imposed a 1-year restriction only. Among other conditions, such restrictions were onerous. See Park and Van Agtmael (1993, pp. 317–18) and Price (1994, pp. 105, 106, and 119). Approvals under DL 600 have increased over time. Buckberg (1995) reports that the first country fund was admitted in October 1989. We use this date for initial opening of the market. The International Finance Corporation (1996*b*) considers the market as 100% open from January 1995.

Foreign portfolio investment by residents was allowed from April 1990 (Cowitt, Edwards, and Boyce 1996, p. 256). Prior to that time, residents could not own foreign securities (Cowitt 1991, p. 260).

Colombia

Start of monthly stock data. January 1985.

Market opening date. February 1991.

Details. The International Finance Corporation (1996*b*, p. 53) considers the Columbian market fully open from February 1991. Resolution 52, which was

Emerging Markets

adopted in December 1991, allowed foreign investors to buy up to 100% of the
shares of locally listed companies, thereby eliminating the previous cap of 10%.
It also abolished the requirement that investment funds remain in the country for
at least a year. See Price (1994, p. 129). Buckberg (1995) reports full opening
as occurring by October 1991. Foreign portfolio investment by residents is not
allowed (Cowitt, Edwards, and Boyce 1996, p. 263).

Greece

Start of monthly stock data.   January 1976.
Market opening date.   August 1986.
Details.   Until August 1986, only blocked accounts of nonresidents could be
used for purchase of local securities (Cowitt 1989, pp. 611–14). After August
1986, European Community nationals were free to invest in Greek securities.
International Finance Corporation (1988, p. 47) also reports that European Community investors could invest with no restrictions as of the end of 1987.
   As of 1989, Greek nationals could not send remittances abroad (de Caires and
Simmonds 1989; Cowitt 1991, p. 609). On May 14, 1994, the government lifted
all restrictions on capital movements, even for Greek nationals. Now they can
freely convert national currency into other currencies and borrow in other currencies. As a result of European Community directives, the foreign exchange restrictions were lifted in the summer of 1991 for investments in European Community
countries.

India

Start of monthly stock data.   January 1976.
Market opening date.   November 1992.
Details.   The International Finance Corporation (1996*b*, p. 53) considers the
market fully open from November 1992 when the Ministry of Finance established
regulations permitting the Securities and Exchange Board of India to register
Foreign Investment Institutions (FIIs) for investment in primary and secondary
markets. There is an overall limit of 24% foreign investment per company and
a per-FII limit of 5% per company. Foreign portfolio investment by residents is
not allowed (Cowitt, Edwards, and Boyce 1996, p. 432).

Indonesia

Start of monthly stock data.   January 1990.
Market opening date.   September 1989.
Foreign portfolio investment.   Residents were allowed to own foreign securi-
ties before the start of stock data.
Details.   Until December 1987, the market was closed to foreign investment.
In December 1987, the government introduced measures to allow foreigners to
purchase shares in eight non-joint-venture companies. The International Finance
Corporation (1996*b*, p. 53) considers the market open from September 16, 1989,
when the Ministry of Finance allowed foreigners to purchase up to 49% of all
companies' listed shares excluding bank shares. The Bank Act of 1992, enacted

October 30, 1992, allowed foreigners to invest up to 49% of listed shares of private national banks. See Park and Van Agtmael (1993, p. 166). Buckberg (1995) reports that there were minor restrictions on entry and exit in March 1989. Foreign portfolio investment by residents has been freely allowed since 1984 (or earlier), which is before the start of available data (Cowitt 1985, p. 357, 1989, p. 442, 1991, p. 446; Cowitt, Edwards, and Boyce 1996, p. 439).

Jordan

Start of monthly stock data.   January 1979.
Market opening date.   January 1978.
Details.   The Amman Stock Exchange opened in January 1978. Foreign investors have been allowed to own 49% of equity from the time that the market opened. See Economist Intelligence Unit (1978, p. 29). Foreign portfolio investment by residents is not allowed (Cowitt, Edwards, and Boyce 1996, p. 813).

Korea

Start of monthly stock data.   January 1976.
Market opening date.   January 1992.
Details.   Although the government intended to open the stock market to foreign investment in 1988, the opening was delayed due to a rapid increase in the money supply in the Korean economy. Eventually the market was opened on January 1, 1992. Foreign investors could own up to 10% of listed companies. The limit has been increased subsequently to 12% (January 1995), 15% (July 1, 1995), and 18% (April 1, 1996). See International Finance Corporation (1996b, p. 53).

Foreign portfolio investment by residents is restricted. See Bentley (1986) and Cowitt, Edwards, and Boyce (1996, p. 454).

Malaysia

Start of monthly stock data.   January 1985.
Market opening date.   Prior to availability of data.
Details.   The Malaysian market opened before December 1975. With the exception of bank and finance company stocks, most stocks are generally 100% available to foreign investors. Malaysian exchange control regulations are liberal. Foreign portfolio investment by residents has been freely allowed since 1984 (or earlier). See Cowitt (1985, p. 495) and Bentley (1986).

Mexico

Start of monthly stock data.   January 1976.
Market opening date.   May 1989.
Foreign portfolio investment.   Residents were allowed to own foreign securities before the start of stock data.
Details.   The 1989 revision of the 1973 Law to Promote Mexican Investment and Regulate Foreign Investment has relaxed restrictions on foreign ownership.

Foreign investment is now permitted up to 100% in 73% of Mexico's 754 economic sectors. The market is considered open from May 1989. See Bekaert (1995), Buckberg (1995), and International Financial Corporation (1996b, p. 53). Foreign portfolio investment by residents was freely allowed prior to January 1976. See *Pick's Currency Yearbook* (1976–77, p. 403), Cowitt (1985, p. 513), and Bentley (1986).

Nigeria

Start of data. January 1985.

Market opening date. Still considered closed.

Details. Nigeria was closed to foreign investors until mid-1995. Decree 16 (July 1995) allowed foreign investors to invest. However, the secondary market is virtually nonexistent. The International Finance Corporation (1996b, p. 53) still considers it closed. Foreign portfolio investment by residents is not allowed (Bentley 1986, and Cowitt, Edwards, and Boyce 1996, p. 142).

Pakistan

Start of monthly stock data. January 1985.

Market opening date. February 1991.

Details. A new Foreign Investment Law passed in February 1991 allows foreigners to own 100% equity in any industrial or business venture in Pakistan (Cowitt, Edwards, and Boyce 1996b, p. 502). The International Finance Corporation (1996b, p. 53) considers the Pakistani market 100% open from February 1991. Buckberg (1995) notes June 1991 as the full opening date, while Bekaert (1995) reaffirms the February 1991 date.

Foreign portfolio investment by residents is restricted and subject to government approval. See Bentley (1986) and Cowitt, Edwards, and Boyce (1996, p. 501).

Philippines

Start of monthly stock data. January 1985.

Market opening date. March 1986.

Details. At the end of 1984, up to 40% of local firms could be owned by foreign nationals (Cowitt 1985, p. 614). Two classes of shares exist—one for locals only (class A) and the other for foreigners and locals (class B). However, there was not much interest in the equity markets until the ouster of Ferdinand Marcos from office in March 1986. As of the end of 1987, there were few restrictions on repatriation of capital and income (International Financial Corporation 1988, p. 47). According to Buckberg (1995), the first country fund was admitted in October 1989. Bekaert (1995) lists November 1991 as the liberalization date.

Foreign portfolio investment by residents was not allowed as of the end of 1989 (Cowitt 1991, p. 511). However, by the end of 1993, residents could freely own foreign securities. See Cowitt, Edwards, and Boyce (1996, p. 510).

Portugal

Start of monthly stock data.   February 1986.

Market opening date.   July 1986.

Details.   The Foreign Investment Code of July 1986 places only the arms sector off limits to foreign capital. Foreign nationals can own all other Portuguese companies, and there are no longer restrictions on repatriation of capital or income. See Cowitt (1989, p. 663). Buckberg (1995) reports January 1986 as the month of full opening.

Foreign portfolio investment by residents was restricted and subject to government approval until the end of 1989. See Cowitt (1991, p. 663). These controls were relaxed during 1992 and 1993. Residents can now freely invest overseas. See Cowitt, Edwards, and Boyce (1996, p. 707).

Taiwan

Start of monthly stock data.   January 1985.

Market opening date.   January 1991.

Foreign portfolio investment.   Residents were allowed to own foreign securities beginning July 1987.

Details.   The stock market was closed until January 1, 1991 (except for closed-end funds). At that time, foreigners were allowed to invest up to 10% subject to an overall limit. The initial ceiling was $2.5 billion, which was raised to $5 billion on August 1, 1993, and to $7.5 billion on March 5, 1994. On July 8, 1995, the ceiling was eliminated and the limit was raised to 12%. The limit was raised further to 15% on September 1995 and to 20% on March 2, 1996. See International Finance Corporation (1996*b*, p. 53).

Taiwan nationals have been allowed to remit up to $3 million per year (inward or outward) since July 15, 1987. See Park and Van Agtmael (1993).

Thailand

Start of monthly stock date.   January 1976.

Market opening date.   August 1988.

Details.   According to the International Finance Corporation (1988), some restrictions existed on both entry and exit of foreign capital at the end of 1987. Beginning in 1988, several foreign country funds were allowed to invest in Thailand. In 1988, a ''Foreign Board'' was established as a parallel stock exchange for trading shares that could be held by foreigners to invest in Thailand (Park and Van Agtmael 1993, p. 128).

Foreign portfolio investment by residents is restricted and subject to government approval. See Cowitt, Edwards, and Boyce (1996b, p. 535) and de Caires and Simmonds (1989).

Turkey

Start of monthly stock data.   January 1987.

Market opening date.   August 1989.

Details. The market is considered 100% open from August 1989. (See International Finance Corporation 1996b, p. 53). Until then, purchases of securities by nonresidents required prior approval (Cowitt 1991, p. 687). Buckberg (1995) reports December 1989 as the liberalization date. As of 1989, investment in foreign securities have required governmental approval. See de Caires and Simmonds (1989) and Cowitt (1991, p. 687).

Venezuela

Start of monthly stock data.   January 1985.
Market opening date.   January 1990.
Foreign portfolio investment.   Residents were allowed to invest abroad before 1984, that is, before the Venezuelan market was opened.
Details.   The Venezuelan stock market was considered 100% open from January 1, 1990, under Decree 727, except for bank stocks. Since January 1994, bank stocks have also been fully open. In June 1994, the government fixed the exchange rate and effectively prohibited the repatriation of capital and income. Although Resolution 41 of November 1994 was intended to alleviate that constraint, it did not do so in practice. In June 1995, the government approved the trading of Brady bonds at the bolsa (stock exchange), creating de facto currency convertibility. See International Finance Corporation (1996b, p. 53). According to Bekaert (1995), too, the date of liberalization is January 1990, the date when all restrictions were lifted. Buckberg (1995) reports that minor restrictions on entry and exit existed in December 1988.

Foreign portfolio investment by residents has been freely allowed since 1976 (or earlier) (*Picks Currency Yearbook* 1976–77, p. 633; Cowitt 1985, p. 807, 1987, p. 891, 1989, p. 384, 1991, p. 389; Bentley 1986; Cowitt, Edwards, and Boyce 1996, p. 633), which is before the start of available data.

Zimbabwe

Start of monthly stock data.   January 1976.
Market opening date.   July 1993.
Details.   The stock market was effectively closed to foreign investment by virtue of severe exchange controls until June 1993. The regulations permitted foreigners to purchase up to 25% of listed shares. This limit was raised to 35% on January 1, 1996. See International Finance Corporation (1996b, p. 53).

Foreign portfolio investment by residents is not permitted. See Cowitt, Edwards, and Boyce (1996, p. 535).

The Data Sources

The dates and other information in this appendix are based on information obtained from the following sources: *Picks Currency Yearbook* (1976–77); *World Currency Yearbooks* (Cowitt 1985, 1987, 1989, 1991; Cowitt, Edwards, and Boyce 1996); Bentley (1986); Economist Publications (1988); International Finance Corporation, *Emerging Stock Markets Factbook* (1988, 1990, 1993, 1994, 1995, 1996a); de Caires and Simmonds (1989); O'Conner and Smith (1991); Park and Van Agtmael (1993); Price (1994); International Finance Corporation, *The IFC Indexes—Methodology, Definitions, and Practices* (1996*b*); Economist Intelligence Unit, Country Reports, various issues; International Finance Corporation, *Monthly Review of Emerging Stock Markets,* various issues. Complete details are in the reference list.

References

Aggarwal, Reena; Inclan, Carla; and Leal, Ricardo. 1995. Volatility in emerging markets. Working Paper. Washington, D.C.: Georgetown University.

Ajayi, Richard A., and Karemera, David. 1996. A variance ratio test of random walks in exchange rates. *Pacific-Basin Finance Journal* 4 (May): 77–91.

Baxter, Marianne, and Jermann, Urban J. 1997. The international diversification puzzle is worse than you think. *American Economic Review* 87 (March): 170–80.

Bekaert, Geert. 1995. Market integration and investment barriers in emerging equity markets. *World Bank Economic Review* 9 (January): 75–107.

Bekaert, Geert, and Harvey, Campbell R. 1995. Time-varying world market integration. *Journal of Finance* 50 (June): 403–44.

Bekaert, Geert, and Harvey, Campbell R. 1997. Emerging equity market volatility. *Journal of Financial Economics* 43 (January): 29–77.

Bekaert, Geert, and Harvey, Campbell R. 1998. Foreign speculators and emerging equity markets. Working Paper. Durham, N.C.: Duke University.

Bekaert, Geert, and Harvey, Campbell R. 1999. Capital flows and the behavior of emerging market equity returns. In S. Edwards (ed.), *Capital Inflows to Emerging Markets.* Chicago: National Bureau of Economic Research and University of Chicago Press, in press.

Bekaert, Geert; Harvey, Campbell R.; and Lumsdaine, Robin L. 1998. Dating the integration of world equity markets. Working Paper. Durham, N.C.: Duke University.

Bentley, Philip, ed. 1986. *World Guide to Exchange Control Regulations.* Wolfeboro, N.H.: Longwood.

Bollerslev, Tim. 1986. Generalized autoregressive conditional heteroscedasticity. *Journal of Econometrics* 31 (April): 307–27.

Bollerslev, Tim; Chou, Ray Y.; and Kroner, Kenneth F. 1992. ARCH modeling in finance. *Journal of Econometrics* 52 (April): 5–59.

Boyd, John, and Smith, Bruce. 1996. The coevolution of the real and financial sectors in the growth process. *World Bank Economic Review* 10 (May): 371–96.

Brailsford, Timothy J., and Faff, Robert W. 1996. An evaluation of volatility forecasting techniques. *Journal of Banking and Finance* 20 (April): 219–38.

Brown, Stephen J., and Warner, Jerold B. 1980. Measuring security price performance. *Journal of Financial Economics* 8 (September): 205–58.

Buckberg, Elaine. 1995. Emerging stock markets and international asset pricing. *World Bank Economic Review* 9 (January): 51–74.

Claessens, Stijn; Dasgupta, Susmita; and Glen, Jack. 1995. Return behavior in emerging stock markets. *World Bank Economic Review* 9 (January): 131–51.

Cooper, Ian, and Kaplanis, Evi. 1994. Home bias in equity portfolios, inflation hedging, and international capital market equilibrium. *Review of Financial Studies* 7 (Spring): 45–60.

Coppejans, Mark, and Domowitz, Ian. 1996. Liquidity-corrected variance ratios and the effect of foreign equity ownership on information in an emerging market. Working Paper. Evanstown, Ill.: Northwestern University.

Cowitt, Philip P., ed. 1985. *World Currency Yearbook, 1984.* New York: Currency Data & Intelligence, Inc.

Cowitt, Philip P., ed. 1987. *World Currency Yearbook, 1985.* New York: Currency Data & Intelligence, Inc.

Cowitt, Philip P., ed. 1989. *World Currency Yearbook, 1986–87.* New York: Currency Data & Intelligence, Inc.

Cowitt, Philip P., ed. 1991. *World Currency Yearbook, 1988–89.* New York: Currency Data & Intelligence, Inc.

Cowitt, Philip P.; Edwards, Carolyn A.; and Boyce, Elliot R., eds. 1996. *World Currency Yearbook, 1990–93*. New York: Currency Data & Intelligence, Inc.

de Caires, Bryan, and Simmonds, David., eds. 1989. *The GT Guide to World Stock Markets, 1989*. London: Euromoney Publications.

de Santis, Giorgio, and Imrohoroglu, Selahattin. 1997. Stock returns and volatility in emerging financial markets. *Journal of International Money and Finance* 16 (August): 561–79.

Economist Intelligence Unit. Country Reports. Various issues. London: Economist Intelligence Unit.

Economist Intelligence Unit. 1978. *Quarterly Economic Review of Syria and Jordan*. Annual Supplement, 1978. London: Economist Intelligence Unit.

Economist Publications. 1988. *The 1988 Directory of World Stock Exchanges*. Baltimore: Johns Hopkins University Press.

Engle, Robert F. 1982. Autoregressive conditional heteroscedasticity with estimates of the variance of United Kingdom inflation. *Econometrica* 50 (July): 987–1007.

Fama, Eugene. 1998. Market efficiency, long-term returns, and behavioral finance. *Journal of Financial Economics* 49 (September): 283–306.

Financial Times. 1998. Taiwan may retain some capital curbs. *Financial Times* (September 23), p. 10.

French, Kenneth, and Poterba, James. 1991. International diversification and international equity markets. *American Economic Review* 81 (May): 222–26.

Frennberg, Per, and Hansson, Bjorn. 1995. An evaluation of alternative models for predicting stock volatility: Evidence from a small stock market. *Journal of International Financial Markets, Institutions, and Money* 5 (January): 117–34.

Hargis, Kent. 1994. Time-varying transmission of prices and volatility: Latin-American equity markets. Working Paper. Urbana: University of Illinois at Urbana-Champaign.

Harvey, Campbell R. 1993. Portfolio enhancement using emerging markets and conditioning information. In Stijn Claessens and Sudarshan Gooptu (eds.), *Portfolio Investment in Developing Countries*. Washington, D.C.: World Bank.

Harvey, Campbell R. 1995. Predictable risk and returns in emerging markets. *Review of Financial Studies* 8 (Fall): 775–818.

Henry, Peter B. 1998. Stock market liberalization, economic reform, and emerging market equity prices. Research Paper 1505R. Stanford, Calif.: Stanford University.

International Finance Corporation. 1975–. Emerging Markets Database. [CD-ROM].

International Finance Corporation, Washington, D.C. (http://www.ifc.org/emdb/PUBS. HTM).

International Finance Corporation. 1988, 1990, 1993, 1994, 1995, 1996a. *Emerging Stock Markets Factbook*. Washington, D.C.: International Finance Corporation.

International Finance Corporation. 1996b. The IFC Indexes—Methodology, Definitions, and Practices. Washington, D.C.: World Bank, May.

International Finance Corporation. *Monthly Review of Emerging Stock Markets*. Washington, D.C., World Bank, various issues.

International Monetary Fund. 1997. International Financial Statistics, December 1997 [quarterly CD-ROM]. International Monetary Fund, Washington, D.C.

Jones, Charles M., and Kaul, Gautam. 1994. On the use of variance ratios. Working Paper. Ann Arbor: University of Michigan.

Kim, E. Han. 1998. Globalization of capital markets and the Asian financial crisis. *Journal of Applied Corporate Finance* 11 (Fall): 30–39.

Korajczyk, Robert A. 1996. A measure of stock market integration for developed and emerging markets. *World Bank Economic Review* 10 (May): 267–89.

Krugman, Paul. 1999. Saving Asia: It's time to get radical. *Fortune* (September 7), p. 74.

Levine, Ross, and Zervos, Sara. 1996. Stock market development and long-run growth. *World Bank Economic Review* 10 (May): 323–39.

Levine, Ross, and Zervos, Sara. 1998. Stock markets, banks and economic growth. *American Economic Review* 88 (June): 537–58.

Liu, Christina Y., and He, Jia. 1991. A variance-ratio test of random walks in foreign exchange rates. *Journal of Finance* 46 (June): 773–85.

Lo, Andrew W., and MacKinlay, A. Craig. 1988. Stock market prices do not follow random walks: Evidence from a simple specification test. *Review of Financial Studies* 1 (Spring): 41–66.

Lo, Andrew W., and MacKinlay, A. Craig. 1989. The size and power of the variance ratio test in finite samples: A Monte Carlo investigation. *Journal of Econometrics* 40 (February): 203–38.

Mech, Timothy S. 1993. Portfolio return autocorrelation. *Journal of Financial Economics* 34 (December): 307–44.

Miller, Merton. 1998. Financial markets and economic growth. *Journal of Applied Corporate Finance* 11 (Fall): 8–15.

O'Conner, Selina, and Smith, David, eds. 1991. *The GT Guide to World Stock Markets, 1991*. London: Euromoney Publications.

Obstfeld, Maurice. 1985. The capital inflows problem revisited: A stylized model of southern cone disinflation. *Review of Economic Studies* 52 (October): 605–25.

Obstfeld, Maurice. 1994. Risk-taking, global diversification, and growth. *American Economic Review* 84 (December): 1310–29.

Ohlson, James A., and Penman, Stephen H. 1985. Volatility increases subsequent to stock splits: An empirical aberration. *Journal of Financial Economics* 14 (June): 251–66.

Park, Keith K. H., and Van Agtmael, Antoine W., eds. 1993. *The World's Emerging Stock Markets: Structure, Development, Regulations and Opportunities*. Chicago: Probus.

Price, Margaret M. 1994. *Emerging Stock Markets*. New York: McGraw Hill.

Pick's Currency Yearbook. 1976–77. New York: Pick.

Rajan, Raghuram G., and Zingales, Luigi. 1998. Financial dependence and growth. *American Economic Review* 88 (June): 559–86.

Rodriguez, Carlos A. 1981. Managed float: An evaluation of alternative rules in the presence of speculative capital flows. *American Economic Review* 71 (March): 256–60.

Schwert, G. William. 1989. Why does stock market volatility change over time? *Journal of Finance* 44 (December): 1115–54.

Skinner, Douglas. 1989. Options markets and stock return volatility. *Journal of Financial Economics* 23 (June): 61–78.

Stulz, René. 1997. International portfolio flows and security markets. Working Paper no. 97-12. Columbus: Ohio State University, Charles A. Dice Center for Research in Financial Economics.

Torres, Craig. 1998. Chile's Massad discusses capital control. *Wall Street Journal* (October 1), p. A17.

Wilson, James. 1998. Delegates agree the state has a role to play in the financial sector. *Financial Times* (July 1), p. 6.

Re-Emerging Markets

William N. Goetzmann and Philippe Jorion*

Abstract

Recent research shows that emerging markets are distinguished by high returns and low covariances with global market factors. To check whether these results can be attributed to their recent emergence, we simulate a simple, general model of global markets with a realistic survival process. The simulations reveal a number of new effects. We find that pre-emergence returns are systematically lower than post-emergence returns, and that the brevity of a market history is related to the bias in returns as well as to the world beta. These patterns are confirmed by an empirical analysis of emerging and submerged markets.

I. Introduction

The last 20 years of capital market history have witnessed a dramatic expansion of opportunity for global investors, led primarily by *emerging markets* in Asia, South America, Africa, the Middle East, and Eastern Europe. In many countries, equity markets have grown rapidly from tiny, fledgling markets with little volume and limited international participation to important sources of capital with short but impressive track records of share price appreciation. Although the fundamental shift in the global political environment is undoubtedly a major factor in the growth of emerging markets, consideration of a longer term view is worthwhile.

In this paper, we show that markets tend to emerge, submerge, and re-emerge through time. Consider, for instance, the case of Argentina. Even though the Argentinian stock market is usually classified as emerging, it actually dates back to 1872. Since it emerged in 1975, this market has grown at an average compound rate of 27% per annum, measured in dollars. However, collecting data before the market disappeared reveals a less than stellar performance, with a real share price growth of -24% per annum from 1947 to 1965.

*Goetzmann, Yale University, School of Management, Box 208200, New Haven, CT 06520-8200; Jorion, University of California at Irvine, Graduate School of Management, 350 GSM, Irvine, CA 92697-3125. The authors thank Vihang Errunza, Campbell Harvey, N. Prabhala, Stephen Ross, Peter Bossaerts (the referee), and, especially, Stephen Brown (the editor) for helpful discussions on this topic. Thanks are also due to seminar participants at the Federal Reserve Board, INSEAD, the NBER Summer Workshop in Asset Pricing, Ohio State University, Rutgers University, the University of Southern California, the University of Lausanne, the University of Limburg, the University of Massachusetts at Amherst, the University of Vienna, Vanderbilt University, and the Wharton School for useful comments. This research received financial support from the Institute for Quantitative Research in Finance, for which the authors are grateful.

We argue that many of today's emerging markets are actually *re-emerging markets*, i.e., were large enough to be included in previous databases, but for one reason or another disappeared from sight. China, Malaysia, India, Egypt, Poland, Romania, Czechoslovakia, Colombia, Uruguay, Chile, Venezuela, and Mexico all had active equity markets in the 1920s. Many of these markets were large enough to attract foreign investors as well as significant enough to have share price indices reported in international publications. For various political, economic, and institutional reasons, investors lost interest in these markets, which then submerged (or disappeared), and re-emerged only recently. Not surprisingly, performance since the last emergence is invariably higher than before emergence. This disparity has serious implications for the performance evaluation of emerging markets.

For example, recent research using short-term, high quality emerging market data collected by the International Finance Corporation (IFC) shows that emerging markets are distinguished by, among other things, high returns and low co-variances with global market factors.[1] This is a striking result because of its immediate implications for the international investor. Emerging markets appear to be very attractive investments since they provide very large expected returns, with or without adjusting for systematic risk. Bekaert and Harvey (1995) suggest that the apparent contradiction between low factor loadings and high ex post market returns may be due to the pricing of local factors preceding full emergence and integration into the global market.[2] In other words, a global investor with the ability to diversify idiosyncratic risk may take advantage of higher returns demanded by local, poorly diversified investors. Perhaps this free lunch hypothesis explains why net private capital flows into emerging countries have reached $240 billion in 1996, a six-fold increase since 1990.[3] A contrasting view is that these stylized empirical facts may be due, in part, to conditioning the data analysis on recent emergence—the key issue addressed in this paper.

The potential for certain biases related to emerging markets has already been noted in the literature. In particular, Harvey (1995) observes that high means may be partially due to the practice of backfilling indices. Brown, Goetzmann, and Ross (1995) (BGR, hereafter) provide a general solution for the bias in the mean of a diffusion price path that survives any sample selection criterion as well as an analytical solution for the simple case of survival above an absorbing lower bound. In this model, markets all start at the same time, have the same expected returns, and disappear in a "down and out" process. They show that high ex post means and a convex price pattern are direct consequences of survival.[4]

---

[1] See, for example, Bekaert and Harvey (1995), Harvey (1995), and Divecha et al. (1992). More recently, however, Barry et al. (1998) argue that the performance of emerging markets has trailed that of U.S. stocks over longer periods.

[2] For prior theoretical and empirical evidence on local pricing, see Stulz (1981) and Errunza and Losq (1985).

[3] According to estimates from the World Bank debtor reporting system.

[4] In addition, survival induces other spurious relationships. Goetzmann and Jorion (1995), for instance, examine the predictability of stock returns based on dividend yields and find that survivorship biases the results toward finding spurious evidence of predictability. These effects are akin to the peso problem in the foreign exchange market, where forward rates appear to be systematically biased forecasts of future spot rates, essentially because they account for a non-zero probability of devaluation that may not be observed in the test sample period.

Unfortunately, there is no analytical result for more complex conditioning processes. We expect markets to start at various points in time, to display different expected returns, to have different risk characteristics, and to be censored after the last emergence. Thus, the current paper explores the effects of using a "last time up" survival process. In particular, we model a price threshold that does not eliminate markets, but instead simply determines how far back historically a time series can be constructed (or is kept) from the present. In other words, we condition upon the ability of the researcher to backfill a continuous series. Because of the lack of analytical solutions, we generate simulations of a global markets model that is quite general. The simulations also provide additional hypotheses which we test with historical data.

Our simulations also show that this type of conditioning induces additional effects of interest. We find that conditioning upon market history, where *history* is defined as the length of time since the market has emerged, should result in a number of empirical regularities. Among other things, the brevity of a market history should be closely related to the bias in annual returns imparted by survivorship, as well as to the low level of covariance with the rest of the markets. These findings are potentially useful for international investors, because *merely knowing that a market has recently emerged* contains information about the future distribution, as well as about its future prospects for survival. Our analysis combines the usual survival effects with new "sorting" effects that are due to inherent differences in expected returns across markets. Given that markets can, in theory, emerge at any point in time, markets that emerge late are more likely to have low true expected returns. Thus, time tends to sort markets by expected returns. These effects interact with each other to create a situation where recently emerged markets have a low unconditional mean.

Second, we provide historical evidence on the extent of survivor conditioning among global markets over the long term. We find that global market data from standard sources are typically characterized by interruptions, reflecting the fact that collecting return data on submerged markets is not an easy matter when investors have lost interest and/or the market has closed. Turning to recent, high quality IFC data, we provide evidence of empirical regularities consistent with the simulations. In particular, we find that returns are greatest and betas low when markets have just emerged. Cumulative returns after emergence display the convex pattern predicted from simulations. Alternatively, these results can be explained by a number of other hypotheses, such as structural changes in emerging economies or price pressures due to the attention brought by official recognition of a market. The common message, however, is that historical performance will be a poor guide to future returns.

This paper is organized as follows. To introduce the issue of survivorship, Section II reviews the literature and presents some evidence from long-term market histories. Section III discusses the process by which markets typically emerge and how this is modeled in our simulations. Results are presented in Section IV. In Section V, we provide performance results for the so-called emerging markets from the last 20 years. Section VI contains some concluding comments.

4   Journal of Financial and Quantitative Analysis

II.   Emergence and Survivorship

A.   Stock Market Histories

In this paper, we define an emerging market as a stock market in a developing country that is included in a current major database such as the one maintained by the IFC. In practice, the criterion for inclusion is related to an increase in market capitalization, which must have reached a minimum threshold. The time of emergence is defined as the first date for which an index is computed. This criterion corresponds to the actual performance reporting period for emerging markets. Many of these markets, however, have been around for much longer than is commonly assumed.

Table 1 provides a partial list of the founding dates of the world's stock exchanges. It is based upon information in two well-known guides to global stock markets, Park and Van Agtmael (1993) and O'Conner and Smith (1992). Both of these sources collect information about market histories from currently operating stock exchanges around the world. Because countries without current exchanges are not included, Table 1's list of the markets that existed at one time is presumably incomplete.[5] However, even this partial list is interesting because it tells us just how much *we do not know* about equity markets. Of the 40 markets that were founded before the twentieth century, only two, the U.S. and the U.K. markets, have been extensively analyzed over long investment horizons. This is not from lack of interest, but from lack of data. While econometricians in the U.S. and the U.K. have compiled reliable price information stretching back into the nineteenth and eighteenth centuries, comparable information has only recently become available for other markets such as Germany, France, and Switzerland, albeit with notable gaps due to wars. Even so, this table is informative.

Table 1 indicates that *most* of today's stock exchanges have long histories. Many non-European markets began under the aegis of colonial rule, including Hong Kong, India, Pakistan, Sri Lanka, Indonesia, South Africa, Egypt, and Singapore, and have continued with or without interruption to the present. Other markets only recently emerged from communist rule—Hungary, Czechoslovakia, Poland, Romania, and Yugoslavia. Perhaps most surprising is the number of South and Central American countries with long market histories; Argentina, Brazil, Colombia, Uruguay, Mexico, and Venezuela all have had equity markets for more than 60 years.

The League of Nations collected data on the capital appreciation of market indices in the period from 1929 through 1944. This collection effort was continued by the U.N. Using these and other sources, Jorion and Goetzmann (1999) collected a sample of long-term capital appreciation indices for 40 countries with histories from 1921 to 1996.

Interruptions in the series were due to a number of factors, including wars, expropriation, hyperinflation, and political changes. The early price data indicate that hyperinflation closed the Danish and German markets in the early 1920s. While most markets remained open and functional through the Great Depression,

---

[5]The actual starting date for France is 1720, but the bourse was closed due to the French Revolution, a time during which capital did not fare well.

TABLE 1

Time Line of Stock Market Founding Dates

Netherlands	1611	Brazil	1877	Philippines	1927
Germany	1685	India	1877	Colombia	1929
U.K.	1698	Norway	1881	Luxembourg	1929
Austria	1771	South Africa	1887	Malaysia	1929
U.S.	1792	Egypt	1890	Romania	1929
Ireland	1799	Hong Kong	1890	Israel	1934
Belgium	1801	Chile	1892	Pakistan	1947
Denmark	1808	Greece	1892	Venezuela	1947
Italy	1808	Venezuela	1893	Lebanon	1948
France	1826	Mexico	1894	Taiwan	1953
Switzerland	1850	Yugoslavia	1894	Kenya	1954
Spain	1860	Sri Lanka	1900	Nigeria	1960
Hungary	1864	Portugal	1901	Kuwait	1962
Turkey	1866	Sweden	1901	Thailand	1975
Australia	1871	Singapore	1911		
Czechoslovakia	1871	Finland	1912		
Poland	1871	Indonesia	1912		
Argentina	1872	Korea	1921		
New Zealand	1872	Slovenia	1924		
Canada	1874	Uruguay	1926		

This table compiles the founding dates of exchanges in cities currently within the borders of the identified countries, in chronological order up to 1975, when standard databases started. Only countries which today have significant equity markets are included in the group, so this sample is subject to selection bias. For instance, it contains no information about Russian exchange(s) and Baltic exchanges. Sources are O'Conner and Smith (1992) and Park and Van Agtmael (1993).

WWII caused many of them to shut down in the 1940s. Some Eastern European markets remained open through the war, only to suffer expropriation after 1945. In total, Austria, Belgium, Shanghai, Czechoslovakia, France, Hungary, Japan, Korea, Luxembourg, Malaysia, the Netherlands, Norway, Poland, Portugal, Uruguay, Venezuela, Yugoslavia, and Slovenia all experienced temporary or permanent shutdowns either in the war years, or in occupation following the war. Many of the markets that shut in mid-century re-emerged after the war or after occupation.

Wars were not the only factors that created discontinuities in the price records. Markets in Egypt, Lebanon, Portugal, and Chile, for instance, were shut down or barred to foreign investors due to political changes largely uncorrelated to outside global trends. Shifting legal factors have changed the attractiveness of markets such as Greece, Turkey, and India to outside investors, and thus caused them to be regarded as emerging markets, despite long histories as capital markets. A turn of political fortunes can make a long forgotten market suddenly of interest to outside investors.

A fair question is whether these events should be considered endogenous or exogenous. Clearly, some of these formerly emerged countries failed to maintain a social and political system that fostered steady industrial growth. While it is not the object of this paper to ask why these markets did not prosper in the same way as the U.S. and U.K. markets, it is reasonable to ask whether anything has changed. Have the political and economic forces that caused these markets to

6   Journal of Financial and Quantitative Analysis

submerge been fundamentally altered? Can we expect the next 60 years of capital markets to be different from the last 60 years?

B. Survivorship Effects

The issue of survivorship in financial markets is starting to attract much deserved attention among financial researchers. Survivorship occurs at various levels, among companies within an exchange, among exchanges within countries, and among countries.

At the level of company selection, Shumway (1997) provides a detailed analysis of what is probably the most comprehensive equity database in the world, the Center for Research in Security Prices (CRSP) database. The CRSP attempts to keep track of all outstanding stocks, even those that disappear. In theory, it does not suffer from survivorship bias. The problem is that the last returns for stocks that disappear for performance reasons are typically omitted because of lack of data. Shumway shows that such delisted firms typically experience returns around -30%. He even recommends setting the delisting return to -100%. This adjustment can have dramatic effects on stock index performance. For small firms (in the NYSE lowest decile), delisting reduces annual returns by 5%; for large firms, there is no effect. Thus, part of the small-firm effect may be due to survivorship.[6]

At the level of exchanges, it is interesting to note that, at some point, the U.S. had more than 250 stock exchanges. While consolidation of stock exchanges is driven by economies of scale, it is fair to surmise that exchanges that fail are not associated with the most successful firms or industries. At the level of countries, we contend in this paper that the selection process for emerging markets also suffers from serious selection biases.

BGR (1995) provide a detailed analysis of the effects of survival conditioning. They specify a model where markets all start at the same time with the logarithm of price p that follows an absolute diffusion process,

$$(1) \qquad\qquad dp \;=\; \mu dt + \sigma dz.$$

BGR show that under any sample selection criterion, the mean return is given by

$$(2) \qquad\qquad \mu^* \;=\; \mu + \sigma^2 \frac{\pi(p)}{\pi},$$

where $\pi(p)$ is the ex ante probability of surviving the criterion, given the current price level p. The volatility of the survived series, however, is the same as that of the original series,

$$(3) \qquad\qquad \sigma^* \;=\; \sigma.$$

---

[6]In a related paper, Stolin (1997) studies the hazard rate of times listed on the London Stock Exchange. He finds probability of disappearance of about 6% per annum, which is quite high.

BGR solve analytically for $\pi(p)/\pi$ in the case where markets are eliminated as soon as p falls below a performance threshold $\bar{p}$. For the survived series with an infinite horizon, the mean return is

$$(4) \quad \mu^* \; = \; \mu + \frac{2\mu \times \exp\left(\dfrac{-2\mu(p-\bar{p})}{\sigma^2}\right)}{1 - \exp\left(\dfrac{-2\mu(p-\bar{p})}{\sigma^2}\right)} \; = \; \mu + \frac{2\mu(1-\pi(p))}{\pi(p)}.$$

Perhaps the most interesting aspect of BGR's result is the positive bias imparted onto the mean. For small μ, this bias tends to $\sigma^2/(p-\bar{p})$. Thus, there is a functional relationship between the bias and the variance of the series. The more volatile markets have, ceteris paribus, a higher probability of failing, and thus have a larger bias in the mean. Ex post, in a world with survival conditioning, risk appears to be priced. Ex ante, of course, these high returns are illusory. This interpretation of emerging market returns is diametrically opposed to the explanation that high returns are due to the pricing of local risk under segmentation. Under the segmentation hypothesis, the first investors who have access to emerging markets reap the benefits of high returns.

Although we learn a lot from the simple BGR framework—particularly about the relationship between risk and conditional returns—analytical results for more complex survival rules such as a last time up emergence at a finite horizon are not easy to obtain. It is difficult, for instance, to adapt the deterministic absorbing barrier framework to the realities of historical market emergences and failures. The BGR solution also assumes that all market returns are independent and identically distributed. With a more general selection process, however, the ratio of probabilities in equation (2) is difficult to solve analytically and explains why we resort to numerical simulations.

C.   Emerging vs. Developed Markets

Are these results consistent with the empirical evidence on emerging markets? Table 2 reports performance numbers for the long-term sample of Jorion and Goetzmann (1999). Arithmetic capital appreciation returns are measured in dollar terms, over the longest sample period for which we have continuous data. This includes periods before breaks, but does not cover interruptions for which we could not measure volatility. Note that these data do not include dividends.

The table provides two group averages: developed and emerging markets. The sample of 11 emerging markets consists of countries in the long-term database that match the current IFC definition. Developed markets had an average dollar return of 6.9%, with a volatility of 19.8%; emerging markets had an average dollar return of 9.1%, with a volatility of 34.8%. For comparison, the table also reports the capital appreciation performance of all the IFC emerging markets, using the IFC indices since inception, from 1975 to 1996. The average dollar return for them was 18.4%, with a volatility of 41.6%.

These results are striking. We note first that emerging markets have much higher volatility than developed markets. As volatility plays a key role in the sample selection process, the BGR analysis indicates that returns should also be

8   Journal of Financial and Quantitative Analysis

TABLE 2

Performance Characteristics of Global Markets

Country	Period (Years)	Dollar Returns		Aver. Return	
		Average	Std. Dev.	Pre-IFC	Post-IFC
Developed					
U.S.	1920–96	8.1	16.2		
Canada	1920–96	6.9	18.2		
Austria	1924–96	7.2	21.5		
Belgium	1920–96	5.8	21.8		
Denmark	1925–96	6.1	14.4		
Finland	1930–96	8.2	20.5		
France	1920–96	7.8	25.5		
Germany	1920–44, 50–96	12.0	27.3		
Ireland	1933–96	6.4	16.7		
Italy	1928–96	3.2	25.7		
Netherlands	1920–96	5.9	16.5		
Norway	1927–96	8.0	19.3		
Spain	1920–96	2.4	28.9		
Sweden	1920–96	8.4	17.7		
Switzerland	1925–96	7.9	16.0		
U.K.	1920–96	6.7	17.6		
Australia	1930–96	7.7	18.1		
New Zealand	1930–96	5.0	16.0		
Japan	1920–44, 49–96	8.3	19.9		
Average =		6.9	19.8		
Emerging					
Portugal	1930–74, 77–96	11.3	28.8	10.1	18.3
India	1939–96	2.4	17.5	−1.4	8.8
Pakistan	1960–96	2.4	17.5	2.2	2.7
Philippines	1954–96	5.3	38.9	−7.4	37.6
Argentina	1947–65, 75–96	22.9	74.1	−18.2	57.9
Brazil	1961–96	18.5	53.4	18.0	18.3
Mexico	1934–96	10.5	29.1	4.0	23.0
Chile	1927–71, 73–96	8.8	32.4	1.0	26.7
Colombia	1936–96	1.7	23.4	−2.7	19.2
Peru	1941–52, 57–77, 88–96	11.5	40.4	7.8	28.9
Venezuela	1937–96	4.9	28.1	1.3	18.9
Average =		9.1	34.8	1.3	23.7
All IFC =	1975–96	18.4	41.6		

The table compares average stock returns and their standard deviations (Std. Dev.) for a group of developed and emerging markets. Monthly returns are computed from capital appreciation indices as collected by Jorion and Goetzmann (1998), measured in U.S. dollars. All data are converted to percent annual numbers. Average for each group is the arithmetic average of performance numbers for the group above. All IFC is average of all IFC markets. Average returns pre- and post-IFC are computed before and after the first IFC date of record.

higher. Indeed, they are. Over the last 20 years, IFC markets enjoyed average returns more than three times those of developed markets since the 1920s. Furthermore, the long-term performance of these so-called emerging markets is only 9%, which is half of that in recent history. This number would be even lower if the performance during the breaks was properly accounted for. Our results suggests that survival is an important issue and is why we turn to a stylized model that will be the basis for our simulations.

III.   A Stylized Model

A.   How Markets Emerge

Among the broad range of reasons for market emergence is the common presumption that markets emerge due to some fundamental economic or political shift. We do not develop an explanatory model for global market emergence because the effects are obviously numerous and complex. Rather, we focus on one likely characteristic of emergence—capital appreciation. In our simplified model, markets emerge because the market prices of existing firms increase, or submerge following price drops.[7] Alternatively, prices may be viewed as summary statistics for changing economic and political conditions.

Suppose a number of markets started trading at different times during the past 100 years, each starting with about the same capitalization (without loss of generality), but with differing expected returns. Later, this assumption will be relaxed. In our simple setting, markets with lower expected returns will have lower capitalization in the future than those with higher expected returns, on average. Thus, time will sort markets according to their respective drift processes.

The key feature of our analysis is the assumption that we only observe markets where market capitalization exceeds a barrier, or threshold, *at the end of the sample period.* Figure 1 illustrates the model. We define a market as an *emerged* market if it has crossed the barrier from below at least once since $t = 0$, and if the last crossing was from below.

In the BGR setup, markets all start above the barrier but are discarded as soon as they hit the barrier. In the case where the drift is known and the barrier is constant, analytical solutions are available to calculate the bias in the observed mean. In this paper, by conditioning upon last time up, we are also implicitly conditioning upon survival since last emergence, and thus, we expect post-emergence biases similar to those found in BGR. The survival bias in BGR, however, is not the whole story.

In our model, the time of emergence contains additional information about the market. When all markets start at the same time, for instance, markets that crossed recently (i.e., later than other markets) are likely to have lower expected returns.

Thus, historical information about when the market began, what its past capitalization was when it started, and what its capitalization was when it last emerged may all be useful inputs to estimating expected returns. Here, the "recentness" of emergence is related to its drift, in contrast to the conditioning process in the BGR analysis, which is "memoryless." In the current analysis, the long-term memory of when and where the process began is crucial.

---

[7]We ignore emergence due strictly to increases in the number of listed firms. A case in point is China, in which the growth of the market has been a function of many new firms listing. Unless appreciation and issues of new securities are uncorrelated, price appreciation can be treated as an instrument, and the results we obtain are qualitatively valid.

FIGURE 1

Emerging ... or Re-Emerging Markets?

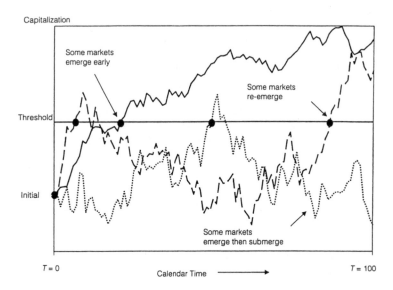

B.   Model Setup

We now present a simple model that formalizes the above arguments. As Harvey (1995) shows, world markets differ in their systematic as well as unsystematic risk components. Consider a single-factor model excess log return-generating process for the equity market of country k,

$$(5) \qquad R_{k,t} \;=\; \beta_k R_{m,t} + e_{k,t},$$

where $E[e_{k,t}] = 0$, $E[R_{m,t}e_{k,t}] = 0$, and $R_{m,t}$ is the excess log return on the global market portfolio at time t. The mean zero term need not be pure noise, but it could be a function of some asset class that has no covariance to the global wealth portfolio, such as gold, or physical assets such as commodities that are known to have nearly zero betas. The log price level of market k at time T can be expressed as $P_{k,T} = P_{k,0} + \sum_{t=1}^{T} R_{k,t}$, which converges to $P_{k,0} + TE[R_m]\beta_k$ as T increases. Thus, we expect prices to be distributed according to their beta values—for big enough T, it matters little whether initial capitalizations differ.

Note that under our baseline model, expected returns are driven by exposure to the world market. This setup is akin to a null hypothesis, where no market is mispriced. The only reason to invest in foreign markets is for diversification benefits—markets are perfectly integrated. An opposite view is segmentation, i.e., local factor(s) are priced, perhaps because of barriers to capital flows.[8]

Here we assume that expected returns are driven by outside investors who are able to diversify idiosyncratic risk sufficiently for the standard models to apply. In particular, the prospect of market disappearance for local reasons is not priced, i.e., does not enter expected returns. We will show that, even under our null hypothesis of no mispricing, survivorship creates situations where emerging markets appear attractive for the wrong reasons.

We want to emphasize that it is unlikely that this simple model fully captures the dynamics of emerging markets.[9] Additional factors could be added to the model. Time variation in risk and structural changes could also be incorporated. These additions, however, would obscure the main message from the simulations: a simplistic model can generate, when submitted to selection through survival, complex patterns of biases and time variation in returns.

C. Simulation Experiment

We simulate emergence among a group of markets as follows.

1. Annual returns for each simulated market are generated by the model in equation (1) in the following.

(a) We simulate 100-year histories of the global market $R_{m,t}$ using i.i.d. normal returns with an annual mean of 10% and an annual standard deviation of 20%, which are typical of stock market data.

(b) We simulate the local factor, $e_{k,t}$, with i.i.d. draws from a normal distribution with a mean of zero and a random standard deviation drawn from a uniform distribution between 10% and 30%.

(c) β_k, the constant loading on the global market index, is drawn randomly from a uniform distribution between zero and two.

2. Markets begin randomly with starting dates drawn from a random uniform distribution over the interval $t = 1$ to $t = 99$. This random starting date is more realistic than usual models where all markets start at a fixed point in time. All markets start at one standard deviation of $R_{k,t}$ below the capitalization threshold.

3. We construct capital appreciation returns for each market, assuming no dividend payments and cumulate each index from its inception until the last period, to create stock market indices for 100 markets.

4. We censor the markets by dropping those that are below the threshold *at the terminal date.*

---

[8]There is a long literature on integration vs. segmentation in international capital markets (see, for instance, Jorion and Schwartz (1986) or Stulz (1992)).

[9]One further caveat is that the truncations are imposed exogenously. In other words, we assume that the underlying CAPM model is unaffected by re-emergence or disappearance of individual markets. This assumes that the dormant markets are observable to investors (i.e., for the pricing of global markets) but not to the empirical researcher. This limitation of the model, however, is common for all econometric models of censoring. The exogenous imposition of selection bias imposes even more subtle effects, however. In a global market, we might expect pricing effects on other markets due to the disappearance of markets. A more fundamental model of the global economy with investors, speculators, and a rich specification of the information diffusion process might allow one to investigate this question. Bossaerts (1997) helps identify pricing effects due to updating of beliefs arising from news about market crises.

12   Journal of Financial and Quantitative Analysis

This model is quite general. Both beta and residual risk differ to make the model more realistic, as we would expect markets to differ in terms of expected returns and risk. The time of market founding is also random—markets start at any time within the 100-year interval. The important assumptions are that i) no market is mispriced, ii) expected returns differ across markets and are constant through time, and iii) markets are arbitrarily censored if they end up below the threshold.

This procedure is repeated 2,500 times for 100 markets each time, which results in 187,954 simulated price paths of survived series. For each simulation, we save a number of variables, including the year the market began t_1, the year it last emerged t_e, and conditional and unconditional summary statistics; *conditional* statistics are those recorded after the last emergence. Of particular interest to emerging market investors is the difference between the mean annual return of the series *since the time of last emergence* less the expected return of the series, i.e., the true market beta times the global market return realization since emergence. We define this as the bias in the annual mean return,

$$(6) \qquad \text{Bias}_k \;=\; \left[\frac{1}{T-t_e}\sum_{t=t_e+1}^{T} R_{k,t}\right] - \beta_k\left[\frac{1}{T-t_e}\sum_{t=t_e+1}^{T} R_{m,t}\right],$$

where β_k is the true beta (we found that using the beta estimated over the ex post period led to nearly identical results).

We also wish to examine the relationship between conditional beta and emergence, R^2 and emergence, and finally, the additional information provided by the start date of the series in relation to the emergence date of the series. This last issue is important because it may be possible to develop heuristics for correcting the bias in the mean returns for recently emerged markets. One potentially useful piece of information for this purpose is the length of time that the market has existed. For example, given any two markets that emerged 10 years ago, the market with a longer history should have a lower mean and, therefore, a greater bias than the market with a shorter history. We examine this issue via simulation results.

IV. Simulation Results

A. Survival Effects

The simulations reveal two effects: survival and sorting effects. Relative to the BGR results, the sorting effects are novel. First, we find that, the more recent the emergence of the market, the higher the bias in the mean return. Figure 2 shows the relationship between the bias in the mean and the time of last emergence.

The figure shows quantiles of the distribution of the bias, as defined in equation (6). Notice that for early emergence, that is, for markets that emerged in the early part of our hypothetical century (on the left side of the graph), there is virtually no bias in the distributions—the difference between the sample average annual return and the ex ante return is typically zero. For very recent emergence, that is for markets that last emerged only five years ago (on the right side of the graph), the bias is as high as 10% per year, with values more than 20% per year not unusual. Even for markets that emerged a decade ago, we still see a substantial return bias, averaging about 5% annually.

FIGURE 2

Bias vs. Year of Last Emergence

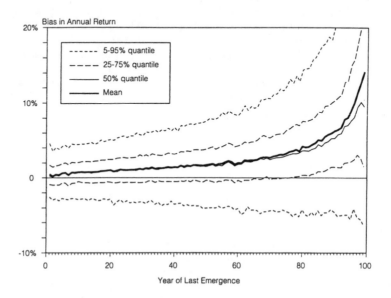

BGR find that survival bias is greater when the price level is near the lower bound. In the context of our simulations, recent emergence implies a proximity to the bound and, thus, a more acute survival bias, since we constructed the sample so that the price never fell below the threshold after emergence. BGR also show that the bias increases in the residual variance of the series. Our regressions confirm that the bias is positively related to the residual risk of the series. In addition, we find that the effect is greatest for recently emerged markets. This provides an interesting possible application. For two markets emerging at the same time, we expect the one with the highest residual variance to have the largest bias. Empirically, this relationship between bias and residual risk may appear as though the local market factor is priced, i.e., that the expected return is positively related to the portion of the variance not correlated to global factors.

B.   Sorting Effects

Our simulations reveal another effect, which differs from the usual survival story. By conditioning on last emergence, we are sorting markets according to their last crossing time through a barrier. Indeed, Figure 3 shows the average

14   Journal of Financial and Quantitative Analysis

beta of each market, sorted on the year of last emergence. It shows that recent emergence is negatively correlated with the loading on the global market factor. Markets that emerged near the beginning of the hypothetical century have an average beta of 1.2, while recently emerged markets have much lower average betas, around 0.9. Thus, the period of last emergence is informative about the unconditional expected return of the market—the more recent the last emergence, the lower the beta, and, consequently, the lower the unconditional expected return. This relation between global factor loading and recent emergence accords well with the observation that emerging markets have low betas.

FIGURE 3

Beta vs. Year of Last Emergence

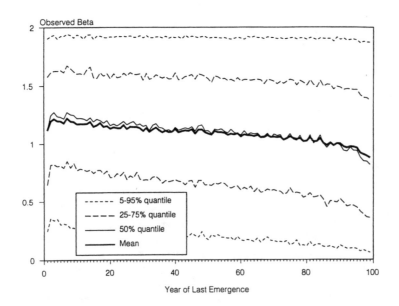

Year of Last Emergence

Our simulations reveal a second empirical regularity due to threshold-induced sorting. Figure 4 shows the R^2 from the market regression, sorted on period of last emergence. For markets that emerged early, the amount of variance explained by the market is high, about 60%. For markets that only recently emerged, the R^2 is lower than 50%. Thus, by conditioning upon recent emergence, we should expect to find markets with higher ratios of idiosyncratic risk, which corresponds exactly to the observation that emerging markets seem to have low R^2 with respect to worldwide factors. Indeed, emerging markets are often sold to institutional investors on the basis of their substantial diversification benefits. Our analysis suggests that this is a legitimate argument for emerging market investing, as opposed to claims of high alphas.

FIGURE 4

R^2 vs. Year of Last Emergence

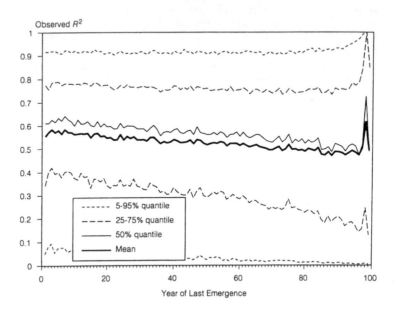

Recall from Figure 1 that last time up conditioning implies that the longer the market history before emergence, the greater the potential bias. The intuition is that markets that remain in the neighborhood of the boundary over time are also likely to be those that emerged and submerged repeatedly. When we condition upon having emerged early in the hypothetical century, we implicitly pick out those markets with positive drift, which, in turn, decreases the probability of being near the barrier for any length of time. This effect provides another possibly useful heuristic for adjusting mean bias for emerging markets. For any two markets that emerged at the same time, the one that began earlier should have the largest bias. The reason for this is that, if a market began a long time previously and still only recently crossed the barrier, it probably has a low beta, whereas a newly formed market that quickly crosses the barrier is likely to have a high beta and, thus, a high expected return.

Figure 5 shows precisely this effect. For each period, we select all the markets that last emerged at that time. We regress the bias in the mean upon the starting date for the series. We find the relationship negative for all periods. That is, *the earlier the starting date, the higher is the bias in the mean*. For new markets, the bias is lower. Therefore, the time since last emergence and the time since the market first began may be used to forecast expected returns.

The survival and sorting effects are related. When markets differ in terms of expected returns, sorting effects exacerbate survival effects. In the BGR analysis,

16   Journal of Financial and Quantitative Analysis

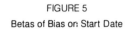

FIGURE 5

Betas of Bias on Start Date

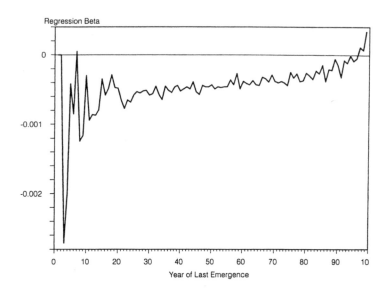

for instance, the bias can be shown to be functionally related to the true expected return. Thus, while sorting effects and survival can be considered separately in the simulations, they interact to increase the magnitude of the bias.

C.   Cumulative Average Returns: Emergence as an Event

Another approach to examining the effects of emergence conditioning is to treat the date of emergence as an event and to align the simulations around the event time. Figure 6 shows the cumulative and average returns for all markets that last emerged in a given year. The horizontal axis is aligned in event time, as opposed to calendar time, and market emergence is set to year zero. The figure shows a cumulative index of 10 years of returns preceding and following the emergence date.

Notice the strong effect of conditioning upon emergence. Returns are nearly flat before emergence, despite the fact that the average returns in the simulation are positive. Following emergence, cumulative returns follow a positive trajectory, which is slightly convex.

The returns comprising the price path are also shown in Figure 6. The difference between pre-emergence and post-emergence returns is dramatic. The low returns preceding emergence result from conditioning upon the market being below the capitalization threshold. Simply knowing that a market crossed the threshold from below, and remained above until the end of the sample period, helps to differentiate historical returns. Notice also that the largest return is in the year im-

FIGURE 6

Average Returns around Emergence

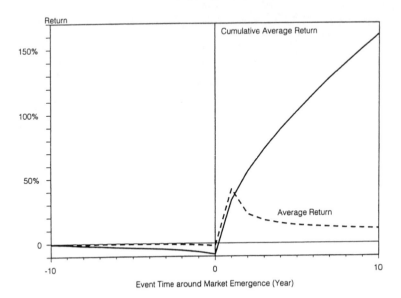

Event Time around Market Emergence (Year)

mediately following emergence. This is because year one is the year in which the market is closest to the boundary, thus most likely to fail, and yet has not failed in the subsequent period. As the market climbs away from the boundary, the chances of submerging decrease, and the survival-conditioned return decreases as well. If an econometrician only observes the history of a market since emergence, the simulation suggests that average returns will be greatest just after emergence.

These results are in line with theoretical work by Bossaerts (1996) who analyzes the dynamics of securities prices when investors have rational expectations but incomplete information. He shows that the dynamics of prices can be described when securities have payoffs that can be categorized into two states: an out-of-the-money state, where it pays zero, and an in-the-money state, where the payoff is random. He shows that for securities that end up in-the-money, i.e., that have survived, large returns are associated with low prices. Thus, the slope of the cumulative return line is greater when markets have just emerged.

D. Implications

The simulations, however stylized, provide some general guidance for investment practice. First, recent emergence by a market has the potential to be a strong conditioning factor that may affect ex post observed return distributions. Some of the effects are due to the fact that recently emerged markets are, by definition, near the lower threshold of capitalization. However, some of the effects are also due to actual differences in long-term expected returns, given differing betas. This sorting also underscores the importance of detecting changing betas for emerging markets. Local or recent changes in expected returns may be sufficient to help a market avoid plunging below the lower threshold. The econometrics of conditional betas would appear to be a crucial step in the analysis of expected returns.

These simulation results have strong implications for applications of mean-variance optimization to emerging market data, as is typically applied to strategic, or long-term, asset allocation. The brevity of emerging market histories induces a well-known uncertainty in the inputs to the mean-variance model, known as estimation risk.[10]

Our work shows that the problem extends beyond input uncertainty to input bias. Recently emerged markets typically have a positive bias in the mean and wider distribution. In a mean-variance framework, the *distribution* of the bias is as important as the average, because extreme values exert a large influence upon the composition of the optimal portfolio. Institutional investors seeking data on emerging markets for use in mean-variance optimization should use recently emerged market data with extreme caution.[11] As the number of emerging markets used in the optimization is increased, the likelihood of overweighing one with an extreme positive bias in the mean increases as well.

E.   Evidence from Long-Term Markets

Later on, we will examine the empirical evidence on emerging markets using recent IFC data. Since these high quality indices, unfortunately, have a rather short history, it is also useful to examine long-term histories of global stock markets.

Using the Jorion-Goetzmann (1999) dataset, all markets were followed continuously from the initial reporting period until 1996, at which time 32 were still included. These authors also compute a global index of stock returns weighted by GDP, which will be useful to compute the global beta. For comparison purposes, all series are measured in real terms, using a wholesale price index deflator.

Most of these series have experienced some breaks. Defining emergence as the first observation after the last break, the question is whether observed price patterns are consistent with the simulations. We can use the global stock index to verify a key prediction of the simulation—that the systematic exposure of emerging markets should be less than that of developed markets. Figure 7 plots the global beta against time since the last break.

The graph clearly shows a negative pattern, which is consistent with that in Figure 4. The U.S. market has the highest beta and also the longest continuous history, going back to the beginning of the sample in 1921. Other markets, such

---

[10]This problem is discussed in Michaud (1989). Jorion (1985) pointed out that the practical application of mean-variance optimization to international diversification is seriously hampered by estimation risk. Stambaugh (1996) provides a framework to analyze investments whose histories differ in length.

[11]For instance, Divecha et al. (1992) report that, over the five-year period ending in March 1991, the IFC Index returned 7.1% more than the FT World Index. With a correlation of 0.35 between the two indices, a mean-variance analysis reveals that investing 40% in EMs apparently would have increased returns by 4% annually relative to the World Index, with no greater risk.

FIGURE 7

Global Beta and Emergence

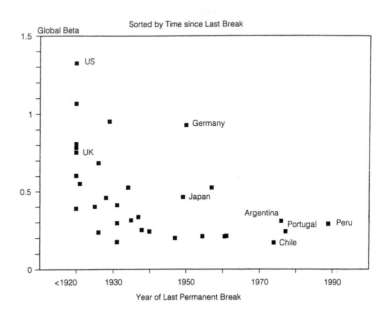

as Peru, Portugal, and Argentina, have had long histories but are only recently re-emerged. With their global betas only around 0.40, suggesting their true expected return is lower than that of other markets.

The other major prediction of the model is the relationship between bias and recent emergence. Figure 8 plots the average compound real return for each market against time since the last break and dramatically illustrates the importance of survival conditioning. As expected, markets with shorter histories have greater dispersion, but also much higher returns, while markets with long histories experienced real returns around 2% per annum. More recently emerged markets (with long histories) displayed much higher returns, reaching 35% for Peru. The figure would show even higher performance for recently emerged markets if the IFC data were included.

Figures 7 and 8 confirm the intuition behind the simulations: markets with long histories that only recently emerged are likely to have low betas and high returns. The simulations show that such results can be interpreted in terms of conditioning upon recent emergence.

V. Empirical Analysis of Emerging Markets

One of the obvious problems with evaluating survival issues in emerging markets is that the data may not be readily available before markets are considered to have emerged. Yet a number of empirical regularities should be expected from

20   Journal of Financial and Quantitative Analysis

FIGURE 8

Real Returns on Global Stock Markets

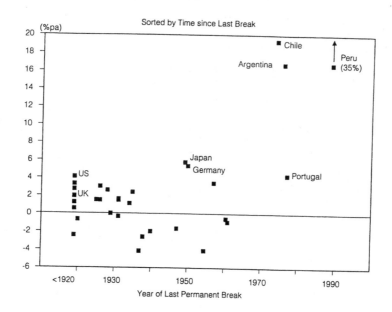

the simulations. For instance, right after emergence, the bias should be greatest if markets that perform badly do not appear in the sample. This hypothesis is analyzed using a variety of approaches.

A. Selection of Emerged Markets

The standard data source for emerging stock markets is from the IFC, which is part of the World Bank group. In its laudable quest for promoting private equity investment in less developed countries, the IFC has developed the most comprehensive and consistent database for emerging markets (EMs). The database started in December 1980 with nine markets, which were backfilled to December 1975, and has expanded to 25 markets as of December 1995 (Jordan was backfilled to 1978). Other markets are being watched by the IFC, then periodically added to their composite EM index. The IFC collects not only share prices, but also dividend and exchange rate information, allowing construction of a total return index that is consistent across all countries.

The term emerging stock market was coined by the IFC in 1981. The IFC defines an emerging stock market as one located in a developing country. Using the World Bank's definition, this includes all countries with a GNP per capita less than $8,625 in 1993. The IFC (1995) states that "although IFC has no predetermined criteria for selecting an emerging market for IFC index coverage, in practice most markets added have had at least 30 to 50 listed companies with market capitalization of U.S. $1 billion or more and annual value traded of U.S. $100 million or more at the start of IFC index coverage." This definition clearly defines a size threshold that markets have to reach before official inclusion in the database.

B.   Backfilling in IFC Indices

In practice, different types of biases are imparted to IFC indices. The first issue relates to the backfilling of IFC indices. The early IFC indices were started in 1980 using companies that were in existence at that time and backfilled to 1975; more recently, the first data points generally predate the decision to include a market by one year or more. Backfilling a market explicitly conditions upon exceeding a threshold as of the decision date. For example, markets that were in existence in 1975 but performed poorly in subsequent years are not included in the database. Therefore, markets that survived the backfilling period are likely to exhibit biases similar to those in the simulations.

Besides the country selection issue, there is the problem of company selection. In 1980, for instance, the IFC indices were constructed using companies that were in existence at that time. As noted by Harvey (1995), the backfilling of the series to December 1975 creates a company-specific bias. We do not address this problem in our simulations.

C.   Survival in IFC Indices

Another issue relates to using long-term market histories. To date, the IFC has never dropped a market from its sample. Does this mean that, absent the backfilling issue, the IFC database is not subject to survival issues? In other words, as long as the IFC keeps following all markets once they enter, would not any potential survival bias be eliminated? The answer is no. The fact that all the IFC markets have survived with continuous return records is not sufficient to prove that there is no survival effect in the series.

Two IFC markets that had near death experiences illustrate this point. Both the Zimbabwe and Nigerian markets became quite small after inclusion in the database. The market value of Zimbabwe began at $450 million in 1980, when it was introduced into the IFC database. It fell to $40 million during the next four years and then increased to $1.5 billion by the end of 1995. The drop in share prices after 1980 can reasonably be attributed to uncertainty regarding the future of the Zimbabwean economy in the early years of the new government. In 1984, there was a real possibility that the equity market would disappear or become so thin that share prices would not be meaningful. Instead, we do observe a continuous series for Zimbabwe because of the successful transition to democratic rule by 1995. However, we completely eliminated from this sample the possibility that the market would not survive this crisis.

A related example is the Nigerian market, which fell to about a fourth of its initial 1984 capitalization of $1.6 billion four years later. The Nigerian market emerged due to soaring oil prices in the early 1980s. The collapse of oil prices in 1986, however, certainly contributed to the subsequent economic crisis. President

22   Journal of Financial and Quantitative Analysis

Babangida addressed the crisis by implementing drastic policy changes. These measures, which included the liberalization of trade and the privatization of agricultural markets, ultimately proved successful, and the market recovered to $1.5 billion in 1995. Again, we have no record of what might have happened to the Nigerian equity market had the adjustment policy not worked.[12]

More generally, the fact that no market was dropped by the IFC does not imply that there is no survival effect. A sample of nine markets over 15 years may not adequately represent the possibility of disappearance. The number of markets and the time span may simply be too low. A lack of sufficient cross-sectional observations of disasters neither proves their non-existence, nor does it prove that the bias imparted by such conditioning is non-existent.

There is further evidence on this point. The IFC also follows stock markets in developing countries that have not yet been included into the official database. One of the largest ones was Kuwait, with $10 billion in market capitalization in the late 1980s. This market was close to making the grade to emerging market. Had Kuwait been included in the IFC indices, the series would no doubt have been interrupted during the 1990 Gulf War. Here, no matter how diligent the IFC researchers were, the interruption in price observations would not have been a matter of choice. Thus, with a larger sample, at least one market would have been dropped during the 1980–1995 period.

Our simulations should not be construed as a critique of the IFC database. In fact, the IFC has demonstrated an awareness of survival biases by following poorly performing markets, even when capitalization dropped sharply. This careful data collection certainly can reduce the magnitude of bias, although, as we have shown, it cannot eliminate it. Whenever a significant probability of market closure exists, any long-term historical series implicit conditions upon survival. This effect can be demonstrated in the context of the long-term history of the global markets, rather than from the perspective of an unusually placid 15-year period. Over the long term, how frequent is market closure?

To answer this question, Table 3 describes the distribution of lives of stock markets starting at two points in time, 1929 and 1953. These dates correspond to times at which the League of Nations and the U.N. collected a large sample of market indices, which happened to number 29 in both cases (although the markets are not the same). We compute life as the number of remaining years before an interruption in the series of at least one year using the same data sources.

The distributions show that, over long periods, markets do suffer disruptions. Out of 29 markets existing in 1929, 14 did not last until 1995 without major interruptions. Many markets, of course, were either closed or nationalized around WWII. But even more recently, starting in 1953, seven markets out of 29 did not make it until 1995.

---

[12] In fact, Nigeria is a country for which the IFC was unable to construct a reliable index of investor return over the period since emergence. In 1993, the IFC started a new series of investable indices that were designed to measure more precisely returns that were available to foreign investors, taking into account legal and practical restrictions. These series were reconstructed to 1988, but omitted Nigeria, which was considered closed to foreign investors. In other words, while the Nigerian market survived its late-1980s crisis and bounced back from the brink of disaster, the return record was not reliable enough to be considered a fair representation of investor returns over the period.

TABLE 3

Distribution of Stock Market Lives

1929–1995			1953–1995		
Life (years)	Count	Country	Life (years)	Count	Country
66	15	Others	42	22	Others
45	1	Mexico	32	1	Peru
44	1	Portugal	21	1	Mexico
42	1	Chile	20	1	Portugal
16	4	Germany, Hungary, Netherlands, Uruguay	18	1	Chile
14	1	Romania	9	1	Egypt
11	1	Greece	4	2	Argentina, Lebanon
10	3	Austria, Czechoslovakia, Poland			
9	1	Italy			
7	1	Spain			
Total:	29		Total:	29	

The table describes the distribution of lives or number of years a market has existed without interruption from a fixed starting date. The left column reports the lives of markets that existed in 1929 over the period 1929–1995. The right column starts in 1953.

In the long run, it is fair to predict that markets will disappear and reappear. The lack of censored observations over a brief period in the history of global capital markets is not sufficient to prove the absence of survival effects. The question is whether any of the regularities we find in the simulation also appear in recent actual data.

D. Performance of Emerged Markets

The IFC dataset has become the standard database for research on EMs and provides performance benchmarks for portfolio managers. As a result, the introduction of new markets is watched very closely by portfolio managers, given that it affects the return on their "bogey." We consider the first date at which the IFC compiles a market index as the date of emergence.

Table 4 presents start dates and market capitalizations for the markets covered by the IFC. Prior to the IFC, the International Monetary Fund (IMF) has also compiled stock index data, which are directly supplied by the central banks or the stock exchanges, and include no dividend data. The table also indicates the first date of record for monthly IMF data when it predated the IFC indices.

So, what is the performance of emerging markets? Table 5 displays risk and return characteristics of emerging markets, expressed in percent per annum. For each market, the period covers the inception date until December 1995. The table shows that returns on emerging markets have been very high, using both arithmetic and continuously compounded averages. The return on the equally-weighted index, for instance, was 24.8% per annum, on average, during the last 20 years, which is enormous. These markets, of course, display high volatility, but most of this risk is diversifiable by global investors, since correlations with the world market are generally very low, averaging 0.155. As a result, many of

24   Journal of Financial and Quantitative Analysis

TABLE 4

Emerging Markets Covered by IFC

Country	IFC Start Date	Capitalization ($ million)		IMF Coverage Start Date
		Start Date	As of Dec 95	
Argentina	Dec 75	83	22,148	
Brazil	Dec 75	8,469	94,615	
Chile	Dec 75	180	48,070	Jan 74
China	Dec 92	21,369	24,608	
Colombia	Dec 84	401	8,519	Jan 57
Greece	Dec 75	1,677	10,161	
Hungary	Dec 92	659	796	
India	Dec 75	527	57,753	Jan 57
Indonesia	Dec 89	2,254	27,610	
Jordan	Jan 78	335	3,484	
Korea	Dec 75	324	123,648	
Malaysia	Dec 84	9,523	142,494	
Mexico	Dec 75	677	60,419	
Nigeria	Dec 84	1,560	1,537	
Pakistan	Dec 84	498	6,482	Jul 60
Peru	Dec 92	2,081	7,353	Jan 88
Philippines	Dec 84	200	31,965	Jan 57
Poland	Dec 92	2,139	1,987	
Portugal	Jan 86	138	10,932	
Sri Lanka	Dec 92	1,082	1,249	
Taiwan	Dec 84	3,532	113,032	
Thailand	Dec 75	220	94,963	
Turkey	Dec 86	377	13,782	
Venezuela	Dec 84	505	2,483	Jan 57
Zimbabwe	Dec 75	215	1,517	

Historical information about the return series calculated for 25 equity markets designated emerging by the IFC. Start Date indicates the month the series begins in the IFC database. Capitalization at Start Date and as of Dec 95 indicate the IFC index market capitalization in millions of dollars at the start date and at the end of 1995. IMF Coverage Start Date is the date at which IMF data are available for the market.

these markets display superior alphas, many of which are statistically significant. Apparently, the combination of these two features, high returns and low correlations with developed markets, makes emerging markets quite appealing. Can these features be attributed to survival?

E.   Expected Returns after Emergence

In the first approach to measuring bias, we track the behavior of IFC indices right after emergence. Returns are measured in U.S. dollars, inclusive of dividends. As some of these markets have experienced hyperinflation, it is essential to measure returns either in a common foreign currency or in real terms, deflating by the local price index. Both approaches should give similar results in situations where purchasing power parity holds, which is likely to be the case in inflationary environments.

Hypothesis 1. Expected returns will be higher immediately following emergence than later on.

TABLE 5

Risk and Return of IFC Emerging Markets

Country	No. of Months	Returns		Risk			Abnorm.
		Arithm.	Compound	Volat.	β	ρ	α
Argentina	240	61.68	27.14	96.62	−0.07	−0.006	54.95*
Brazil	240	25.36	9.46	57.99	0.35	0.089	15.63
Chile	240	35.34	32.72	37.98	0.12	0.054	27.22*
China	36	1.83	−18.36	76.31	−0.04	−0.007	−1.69
Colombia	132	35.32	35.71	31.25	0.08	0.045	28.75*
Greece	240	8.34	3.00	34.39	0.45	0.191	−2.15
Hungary	36	−2.73	−8.40	36.89	0.80	0.292	−16.67
India	240	16.89	14.11	27.39	−0.03	−0.012	10.03
Indonesia	72	6.88	2.18	31.02	0.19	0.100	1.46
Jordan	215	12.27	11.22	18.12	0.16	0.129	3.70
Korea	240	22.62	19.78	30.80	0.52	0.243	11.65
Malaysia	132	15.73	12.74	26.91	0.73	0.423	2.21
Mexico	240	25.65	15.87	44.15	0.70	0.234	13.20
Nigeria	132	18.44	2.50	53.92	0.30	0.087	9.58
Pakistan	132	16.52	14.60	24.62	0.02	0.012	10.72
Peru	36	35.90	32.72	39.57	0.75	0.252	22.70
Philippines	132	40.61	40.24	36.66	0.71	0.299	27.41*
Poland	36	81.39	65.14	87.17	1.68	0.265	56.12
Portugal	119	29.66	23.71	43.23	1.06	0.392	14.80
Sri Lanka	36	5.68	0.75	32.08	−0.29	−0.111	4.94
Taiwan	132	31.09	20.93	50.05	0.73	0.227	17.60
Thailand	240	23.62	22.02	26.90	0.34	0.193	13.85*
Turkey	108	38.22	16.72	71.16	0.08	0.017	32.39
Venezuela	132	20.53	8.90	47.88	−0.37	−0.122	19.00
Zimbabwe	240	13.99	8.55	34.21	0.18	0.082	5.48
IFC Composite	132	17.03	15.42	22.76	0.46	0.317	6.42
EW Average	240	24.83	16.56	43.89	0.37	0.155	15.31

Annualized risk and returns of IFC emerging markets, using the earliest start month (in Table 4) until December 1995. The table reports sample size, arithmetic average, compound average, volatility, beta, and correlation with the world market, and alpha from a market model in excess returns. The sample consists of 25 IFC-covered countries plus the IFC Composite Index and an equally-weighted average of all countries. All data are presented in annual terms in percent. Arithmetic returns and abnormal alphas are multiplied by 1200; compound returns use annual compounding; monthly volatility measures are multiplied by $\sqrt{12} \times 100$.

*indicates significance at the 5% level.

To test this hypothesis, we adapt the event-study methodology used in the simulation above to the emergence of markets. We construct an equally-weighted index where returns are aligned on the emergence date. The advantage of this portfolio approach is that it fully accounts for cross-correlation between events, which is substantial in this case since nine markets out of 25 emerge on the same date. Figure 9 plots the time series of the emerging portfolio value; this portfolio is compared to that of a benchmark, which is constructed by replacing each market by the Morgan Stanley Capital International World Index.

Figure 9 shows that the slope of the line is greater immediately following emergence. This pattern is consistent with the simulation results. The emerging market portfolio also substantially outperforms the benchmark portfolio. The

26   Journal of Financial and Quantitative Analysis

FIGURE 9

Performance after Emergence

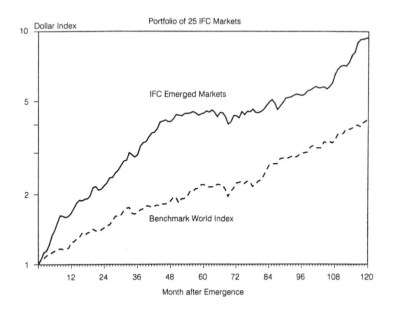

magnitude of the effect is confirmed in Table 6, which considers 36-, 48-, and 60-month windows after emergence. The portfolio performance is compared to that over the subsequent window of the same length. The table shows that the performance is significantly greater immediately after emergence. The difference is striking: 15% p.a. using a 60-month window, 29% p.a. with a 48-month window, and 24% p.a. with a 36-month window. These numbers are all statistically significant, as indicated by the t-statistics in the table.[13]

Among other explanations and competing theories for the price increase after emergence is the price pressure hypothesis. Official recognition of an emerging market by the IFC could induce purchases by foreign managers, leading to increased prices. These purchases convey no new information about the companies and, therefore, should have no permanent effect on stock prices. In a similar context, Harris and Gurel (1986) report that additions of stocks to the S&P 500 list led to price increases of about 3% during the 1978–1983 period. It is conceivable that, given the thinness of some emerging markets, foreign purchases drive prices by much greater amounts. The price pressure hypothesis, however, should lead to reversals after the initial buying, since the price pressure is temporary; however, reversals are not apparent.

---

[13]We also separated the sample into the initial pre-1980 group and others. In both cases, performance right after emergence is greater than later on, although the effect is most significant for the pre-1980 group.

TABLE 6

Returns after Emergence

	First Period	Next Period	Difference
60 months			
Mean	30.77	15.74	15.03
Std. Dev.	(10.42)	(11.30)	
t-Stat.			2.19*
48 months			
Mean	36.40	6.92	29.49
Std. Dev.	(10.66)	(10.11)	
t-Stat.			4.01*
36 months			
Mean	37.28	13.41	23.87
Std. Dev.	(10.97)	(10.75)	
t-Stat.			2.69*

This table reports statistics for returns for 25 IFC-covered markets in two equal-length se-
quential time periods following market emergence. Emergence is defined as the beginning
of the IFC total monthly return series. Data converted to annual measures by multiplying
monthly average by 12 and standard deviation by the square root of 12. The *t*-statistic tests
the equality of average returns in the first and second subperiods.

*indicates significance at the 5% level.

Another explanation is changing economic conditions. Some markets emerge
as a result of financial liberalization, which usually coincides with a changing political environment. We would then expect the best investment opportunities to
come to the market first, spurring an initial growth that slows down as less profitable investments later appear. On the other hand, emerging markets have been
characterized over time by regularly occurring sweeping economic reforms, many
of which have been often followed by equally sweeping changes in the opposite
direction. One would have to argue that the latest changes are of a permanent
nature. Whatever the explanation, it is clear that the long-run performance of
markets right after emergence is not sustainable.

F. Expected Returns around Emergence

An alternative approach to measuring bias is to recover market information
from a completely different source. We take a sample of markets for which equity
indices have been collected by the IMF since 1957. These indices are compiled by
the local stock exchange and may not be consistent across countries. In addition,
they often represent monthly averages, not end-of-month data. Still, comparisons
are appropriate as long as the same IMF series is used before and after emergence.
Additional data exist for a total of seven markets, which are listed in Table 4. The
shortest period before emergence is for Peru, for which we have data for only two
years.

Hypothesis 2. Expected returns will be higher after than before emergence.

To guard against hyperinflation, we measure returns both in dollars and in
real terms (deflated by the CPI as provided by the IMF). As before, returns are

28   Journal of Financial and Quantitative Analysis

aggregated into an equally-weighted portfolio of seven markets aligned on the date of emergence. Figure 10 displays the time series of cumulative returns. The picture clearly indicates a break in trend, with returns after emergence sharply moving upward. This pattern is also consistent with the simulation results reported from our hypothetical market subject to conditioning upon emergence. In fact, Figure 10 is quite similar to Figure 6, which aligns simulation returns on the emergence date.

FIGURE 10

Performance around Emergence

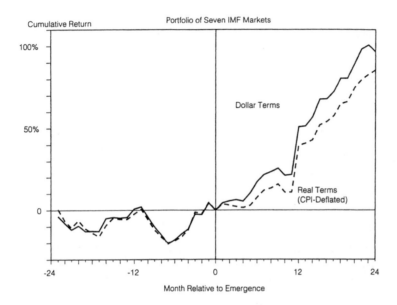

Formal tests of breaks in expected returns are presented in Table 7. Both real returns and dollar returns strongly indicate that average returns are higher right after emergence. The difference in real returns, for instance, averages 47% annually. Even with very large standard errors, two years of data are sufficient to bring strong rejections of the null. Again, these results strongly suggest that returns are biased upward once a market is considered emerged.

G.   Expected Returns before Emergence

A third approach considers markets that have not yet emerged. Besides its official list of emerged markets, the IFC also collects information on a sample of markets that have the potential to emerge. By the end of 1994, the IFC was watching 24 such markets. For these non-emerged markets, the IFC provides annual returns reported by local stock markets, exchange rates, and market capi-

TABLE 7

Returns around Emergence

	Before Emergence	After Emergence	Difference
Real Returns			
Average	−2.09	44.60	46.69
Std. Dev.	16.52	21.27	26.93
t-Stat.	−0.18	2.97	2.45*
Dollar Returns			
Average	1.23	50.43	49.20
Std. Dev.	15.00	22.82	27.30
t-Stat.	0.12	3.13	2.55*

This table reports statistics for returns for seven IMF-covered markets in two-year periods before and after market emergence. Emergence is defined as the beginning of the IFC total monthly return series. Returns are reported for real, CPI-deflated returns, and U.S. dollar-converted returns. Annual returns in percent.

*indicates significance at the 5% level.

talization.[14] Therefore, as suggested by the simulations, we find a significant bias due to recent emergence.

Annual returns were collected for this sample of markets varying from seven in 1985 to 19 in 1994. To compare their performance with those of established emerging markets, we constructed a value-weighted dollar return index that spanned 10 years.[15] This index was compared to the IFC composite index, which is also value weighted. To maintain comparability, both indices include only capital appreciation.

Hypothesis 3. Expected returns will be lower before emergence.

Table 8 compares the performance of the two groups of markets, non-emerged and emerged. The table shows that the non-emerged group returned an average of 12.5% over the 10 years, against 19.1% for the emerged index. Using an entirely different dataset, this difference confirms biases in the performance of emerged markets. Emerged markets, on average, return 6.6% more than other markets. For comparison purposes, the table also reports the performance of the MSCI World index, a value-weighted index of developed markets. Over this period, the average return was 14.0%, which also falls short of the performance of emerged markets. In our model, the 6.6% difference can be attributed either to the fact that non-emerged markets truly have low expected returns (low betas in our model) or to the fact that the sample selection process for defining emerged creates survivorship biases. Although the volatility of the series is such that the *t*-test is unable

---

[14]Countries watched by the IFC in 1994 include Bangladesh, Barbados, Botswana, Costa Rica, Ivory Coast, Cyprus, Ecuador, Egypt, Ghana, Honduras, Iran, Jamaica, Kenya, Kuwait, Mauritius, Morocco, Namibia, Oman, Panama, South Africa, Swaziland, Trinidad, Tunisia, and Uruguay. Of those, Costa Rica and Honduras have no stock price index, the series for Uruguay stops in 1991, and the series for Kuwait was interrupted from 1990 to 1993 because of the Gulf War.

[15]In the computation of the value-weighted index, we omit South Africa, because its market value would dwarf all others. As of December 1994, the market capitalization was $226 billion, while that of the next largest market is $10 billion.

30   Journal of Financial and Quantitative Analysis

to reject equality of mean returns, most portfolio managers would agree that an annual difference of 6.6% over a decade is economically important.

TABLE 8

Returns before and after Emergence

	Non-Emerged Market Index	Emerged IFC Composite Index	Difference	MSCIP World Index
Annual Returns				
Average	12.5	19.1	−6.6	14.0
Std. Dev.	18.1	28.0	40.0	17.0
t-Stat.	2.18	2.16	−0.52	2.61
Compound	11.2	15.7	−4.5	12.7

This table reports statistics for returns on IFC emerged markets and non-emerged markets. Returns are compared for the MSCIP world index, the IFC composite index, and a value-weighted index of returns on markets that have not yet emerged. Annual returns are measured in dollars, without dividends, over the period 1985–1994.

VI.   Conclusions

A general model of global markets that allows for differing expected returns and differing correlations to the world market provides the basis for simulations of selection of emerging markets. These simulations show that recently emerged markets have high observed returns. The model also shows that recently emerged countries have low covariances with the global market. These results are striking because they fit the empirical observation that emerging markets appear to have high returns and low correlations with other markets. In our baseline model, which assumes no mispricing of emerging markets, these high returns and low betas are simply due to recent emergence.

The findings of these simulations are confirmed by our empirical analysis, which shows that average returns on markets that have just emerged are temporarily high. The history of emerged markets provides an overly optimistic picture of future investment performance. Therefore, basing investment decisions on the past performance of emerging markets is likely to lead to disappointing results.

Another fruitful line of research would be to examine the predictive power of measures for the probability of market upheaval, such as credit risk ratings or default spreads.[16] Indeed, Erb, Harvey, and Viskanta (1995) find that, cross-sectionally, low credit ratings are associated with high average returns and low betas. As credit rating proxies for the probability of market failure, these results provide additional support for the survivorship story.

A major caveat of our analysis is that it is based upon a stationary model. Economies are never that simple. Global capital markets have been subject to

---

[16]Bailey and Chung (1995), for instance, show that the credit spread on Mexican sovereign bonds has predictive power for expected returns on the local stock market. They hypothesize that credit risk and political risk are positively correlated, which implies that credit spreads proxy for the probability of market upheaval.

dramatic changes during the twentieth century, and many nations with bright economic prospects in the 1920s subsequently failed to reward investors for their high expectations. It seems reasonable to condition expected returns in marginal markets on changing political, legal, and economic environments. It is also important to learn from history. Market contractions, banking failures, and expropriations have occurred in the past, and are likely to occur in the future, even in the absence of a major event such as a world war. If we fail to account for losers as well as winners in the global equity markets, we may be ignoring important information about actual investment risk.

One way to account for losers is to gather additional historical data. Financial economists are accustomed to working with abundant and accurate data, but, unfortunately, data are strongly conditioned upon survival. For instance, we do not as yet have a quality dataset for Argentina's equity market, even though it has existed for more than 100 years. Collecting long series of historical data will allow us to examine the behavior of markets in distress. Instead of blindly projecting returns from short-term historical data, investors should use the information in long-term histories to construct stress testing of portfolios. This parallels the trend in the financial services industry, where methods based on historical risk measures, such as value-at-risk, are widely recognized as unable to capture unusual but highly disruptive events. This is why traditional risk measurement techniques must be complemented by *scenario analysis,* which ideally should rely on long histories of stock markets.

Investors are always hungry for data. This has become especially true for the application of modern portfolio theory to the institutional asset allocation process, which requires quantitative estimates of risk and return. When long-term data series are unavailable for analysis, it has become common practice to use recent data only. The danger is that these data may not be representative of future performance. Although longer data series are of poorer quality, are difficult to obtain, and may reflect various political and economic regimes, they often paint a very different picture of emerging market performance.

References

Bailey, W., and P. Chung. "Exchange Rate Fluctuations, Political Risk and Stock Returns: Some Evidence from an Emerging Market." *Journal of Financial and Quantitative Analysis*, 30 (1995), 541–561.

Barry, C.; J. Peavy; and M. Rodriguez. "Performance Characteristics of Emerging Capital Markets." *Financial Analysts Journal*, 54 (1998), 72–80.

Bekaert, G., and C. Harvey. "Time-Varying World Market Integration." *Journal of Finance*, 50 (1995), 403–444.

Bossaerts, P. "The Dynamics of Equity Prices in Fallible Markets." Working Paper, California Institute of Technology (1997).

————. "Martingale Restrictions on Securities Prices under Rational Expectations and Consistent Beliefs." Working Paper, California Institute of Technology (1996).

Brown, S. J.; W. N. Goetzmann; and S. A. Ross. "Survival." *Journal of Finance*, 50 (1995), 853–873.

Divecha, A.; J. Drach; and D. Stefek. "Emerging Markets: A Quantitative Perspective." *Journal of Portfolio Management*, 19 (Fall 1992), 41–50.

Erb, C.; C. Harvey; and T. Viskanta. "Country Risk and Global Equity Selection." *Journal of Portfolio Management*, 21 (Winter 1995), 74–83.

Errunza, V., and E. Losq. "International Asset Pricing under Mild Segmentation: Theory and Tests." *Journal of Finance*, 40 (March 1985), 105–123.

Goetzmann, W., and P. Jorion. "A Longer Look at Dividend Yields." *Journal of Business*, 68 (1995), 483–508.

Harris, L., and E. Gurel. "Price and Volume Effects Associated with Changes in the S&P500 List: New Evidence for the Existence of Price Pressures." *Journal of Finance*, 41 (1986), 815–829.

Harvey, C. "Predictable Risk and Returns in Emerging Markets." *Review of Financial Studies*, 8 (1995), 773–816.

International Finance Corporation. *The IFC Indexes: Methodology, Definitions, and Practices*. Washington, DC: IFC (1995).

Jorion, P. "International Portfolio Diversification with Estimation Risk." *Journal of Business*, 58 (1985), 259–278.

Jorion, P., and E. Schwartz. "Integration vs. Segmentation in the Canadian Stock Market." *Journal of Finance*, 41 (1986), 603–616.

Jorion, P., and W. Goetzmann. "Global Stock Markets in the Twentieth Century." *Journal of Finance* (forthcoming 1999).

Michaud, R. "The Markowitz Optimization Enigma: Is Optimized Optimal?" *Financial Analysts Journal*, 45 (1989), 31–42.

O'Conner, S., and D. Smith. *The G.T. Guide to World Equity Markets*. London: Euromoney Publications (1992).

Park, K., and A. Van Agtmael, eds. *The World's Emerging Stock Markets*. Chicago, IL: Probus (1993).

Shumway, T. "The Delisting Bias in CRSP Data." *Journal of Finance*, 52 (1997), 327–340.

Stambaugh, R. "Analyzing Investments Whose Histories Differ in Length." Working Paper, The Wharton School (1996).

Stolin, D. "UK Share Delisting: A Survival Analysis." Working Paper, London Business School (1997).

Stulz, R. "International Asset Pricing Models: An Integrative Survey." Working Paper, Ohio State Univ. (1992).

––––––––––––. "On the Effects of Barriers to International Investment." *Journal of Finance*, 36 (Sept. 1981), 923–934.

[10]

THE JOURNAL OF FINANCE • VOL. LIV, NO. 3 • JUNE 1999

The Effects of Market Segmentation and Investor Recognition on Asset Prices: Evidence from Foreign Stocks Listing in the United States

STEPHEN R. FOERSTER and G. ANDREW KAROLYI*

ABSTRACT

Non-U.S. firms cross-listing shares on U.S. exchanges as American Depositary Receipts earn cumulative abnormal returns of 19 percent during the year before listing, and an additional 1.20 percent during the listing week, but incur a loss of 14 percent during the year following listing. We show how these unusual share price changes are robust to changing market risk exposures and are related to an expansion of the shareholder base and to the amount of capital raised at the time of listing. Our tests provide support for the market segmentation hypothesis and Merton's (1987) investor recognition hypothesis.

THE GLOBALIZATION OF U.S. CAPITAL MARKETS has accelerated dramatically in the past decade. Increasing numbers of companies from overseas have chosen to either raise capital through global equity issues or prepare for future capital raising by way of cross-listings on U.S. exchanges. As of 1997, about 1,300 non-U.S. companies have listed their shares for trading on the New York Stock Exchange (NYSE), the American Exchange (AMEX), the National Association of Securities Dealers' Automation Quotation (Nasdaq) system, or

*Foerster is with the Richard Ivey School of Business, University of Western Ontario, and Karolyi is with the Fisher College of Business at Ohio State University. We are grateful for data assistance from John Griffin, Rick Johnston, and Sonali Chalishazar; for background information from Jim Shapiro (NYSE), Mike Shokhouhi (NASD), Vince Fitzpatrick and Joe Velli (Bank of New York), Mark Bach (Citibank), and Rene Vanguestaine (JP Morgan); and for comments from Yakov Amihud, John McConnell, Darius Miller, René Stulz (editor), and an anonymous referee. Comments of conference participants at the 1997 NBER Market Microstructure Conference, the 1997 AFA, 1997 FMA International, 1997 Berkeley Program in Finance, the 1996 Vanderbilt Conference on Investing Internationally, and the 1996 Northern Finance Association meetings, and workshops at HKUST, Laval University, Queen's University, the University of Toronto, and the University of Waterloo greatly improved the paper. Nelson Mark kindly provided access to the Harris Bank interest rate data. We thank the Social Sciences and Humanities Research Council of Canada and the Richard Ivey School of Business Plan for Excellence for financial support, as well as Ohio State University's Dice Center and Summer Fellowship program. All remaining errors are our own.

over-the-counter (OTC), which represents a 75 percent increase since 1991. In 1996 alone, 162 new programs were created, raising $20 billion in new equity financing and generating exchange trading of over 7 billion shares.[1]

The goal of this paper is to study the stock price performance and changes in risk exposure associated with the cross-listing of non-U.S. stocks in U.S. markets. Our sample comprises first-time U.S. listings by 153 firms from Canada, Europe, and the Asia-Pacific Basin region from 1976 to 1992. We are motivated to study this phenomenon because important inferences pertaining to the issue of capital market integration and segmentation can be drawn from the reaction of stock prices to international listings.[2] Segmentation of markets due to investment barriers (e.g., regulatory barriers, taxes, information constraints) creates an incentive for firms to adopt financial policies to reduce their negative effects. Theory suggests that stock prices for firms that cross-list from segmented markets are expected to rise and their subsequent expected returns should fall as an additional built-in risk premium compensating for these barriers dissipates. Our overall evidence is consistent with this hypothesis. We also explore how these results extend earlier studies of cross-border listing in the United States, such as those by Alexander, Eun, and Janakiramanan (1988), Jayaraman, Shastri, and Tandon (1993), and Foerster and Karolyi (1993).[3]

We are also drawn to this question by a second branch of the finance literature that identifies significant changes in share prices for firms that choose to change the location for their traded shares. A number of studies have shown how share prices increase for firms that list on the NYSE from the Nasdaq OTC market and have attributed this outcome to increased investor recognition or superior liquidity.[4] Merton (1987), for example, provides a rationale for the effects of greater investor recognition in an extension to the Sharpe–Lintner Capital Asset Pricing Model (CAPM) which relaxes the assumption of equal information for investors. He shows that expected

---

[1] See "The Rise of ADRs," *Fortune* (March 6, 1995); "Four-year Surge in ADR and GDR Issues," *Financial Times* (November 10, 1994); "The Return of ADRs," *Euromoney* (December 1995); and Cochrane, Shapiro, and Tobin (1996).

[2] Survey papers by Adler and Dumas (1983) and more recently Stulz (1995) argue that an understanding of the extent of international capital market segmentation is a key challenge for research in international finance. Important studies with evidence of growing integration of financial markets include Jorion and Schwartz (1986), Gultekin, Gultekin, and Penati (1989), Campbell and Hamao (1992), Mittoo (1992), Chan, Karolyi, and Stulz (1992), Bailey and Chung (1995), and Bekaert and Harvey (1995).

[3] Karolyi (1998) surveys the literature on global exchange listings. He cites a number of studies that have examined stock price reactions for U.S. firms listing their shares abroad, including Howe and Kelm (1987), Howe and Madura (1990), Barclay, Litzenberger, and Warner (1990), Varela and Lee (1993), and Lau, Diltz, and Apilado (1994).

[4] Baker and Meeks (1991) and McConnell et al. (1996) survey the literature on domestic exchange listings and delistings. Important contributions include those of Sanger and McConnell (1986) and Dharan and Ikenberry (1995), who focus on the postlisting decline in stock prices following NYSE and AMEX listing, and that of Christie and Huang (1993), who examine the liquidity effects of Nasdaq and AMEX listings to the NYSE using transactions data.

returns decrease with the size of the firm's investor base, which he characterizes as "the degree of investor recognition." Amihud and Mendelson (1986)
develop the liquidity hypothesis in the context of an asset pricing model in
which gross returns are an increasing and concave function of liquidity measured by the bid-ask spread. Kadlec and McConnell (1994) show that these
two hypotheses can in part explain the abnormal returns to NYSE listings
from Nasdaq.

We propose that U.S. exchange listing by non-U.S. firms could also be
associated with share price changes that are not due to the effects of international investment barriers but rather to investor recognition and liquidity
factors, as experienced by purely domestic exchange listings. We test this
hypothesis using information available on changes in shareholder base and
capitalization changes due to new issues of equity around the listing period
for these firms and find that the abnormal returns before, around, and following listing are significantly related to these variables. We interpret this
finding as evidence consistent with Merton's investor recognition hypothesis. Finally, we indirectly test Amihud and Mendelson's (1986) liquidity hypothesis and show that the sensitivity of the abnormal returns, as well as
changing risk exposures, to changes in shareholder base is different for non-
U.S. stocks listing on the NYSE versus those listing on the AMEX and Nasdaq. The finding that stock returns around cross-border listings is related to
changes in the investor base and liquidity factors is new.

A primer on the cross-border listing process is presented in Section I. Section II provides a description of our methodology and data. Outlines of the
various hypotheses about stock price effects on international listings and the
main empirical results are presented in Sections III and IV. Conclusions
follow in Section V.

I. A Primer on ADRs

Almost all non-U.S. companies that list their shares on U.S. exchanges do
so by creating American Depositary Receipts (ADRs). ADRs were developed
by JP Morgan in 1927 as a vehicle for investors to register and earn dividends on non-U.S. stock without direct access to the overseas market itself.
U.S. depositary banks hold the overseas securities in custody in the country
of origin and convert all dividends and other payments into U.S. dollars to
receipt holders in the United States. Investors, therefore, bear all currency
risk and indirectly pay fees to the depositary bank. Each depositary receipt
denotes shares that represent a specific number of underlying shares in the
home market, and new receipts can be created by the bank for investors
when the requisite number of shares are deposited in their custodial account
in the home market. Cancellations or redemptions of ADRs simply reverse
the process.

There are a number of advantages to ADRs for issuers, including an en-
larged investor base, enhanced local market for shares, opportunity to raise
new capital, and a liquid secondary market in the United States. At the

same time, non-U.S. companies must satisfy two requirements to be listed in the United States. First, they have to arrange with a transfer agent and registrar for an exact replication of settlement facilities as for domestic securities. Second, to register with the U.S. Securities and Exchange Commission (SEC), the non-U.S. company must file a registration statement and furnish an annual report on a Form 20-F with a reconciliation of financial accounts with U.S. Generally Accepted Accounting Principles (GAAP). Several options are available to issuers to balance these advantages with the costs associated with increased scrutiny by the SEC and reconciliation with GAAP reporting requirements. ADRs must now be sponsored by a non-U.S. company seeking access to U.S. markets, but some pre-1983 programs were initially unsponsored, as an initiative by a U.S. securities broker with the depositary bank. The ADR issues can also be associated with new capital raised through the program, though usually this is not the case. Table I outlines the different options with listing, reporting, and GAAP requirements. Level I ADRs trade over-the-counter as Pink Sheet issues with limited liquidity and they require only minimal SEC disclosure and no GAAP compliance. These firms are exempt from SEC filing Form 20-F under Rule 12g3-2(b) allowing home country accounting statements with adequate English translation, if necessary. Level II ADRs are exchange-listed securities, but without a capital-raising element. Level III ADRs, the most prestigious and costly type of listing, require full SEC disclosure with Form 20-F and compliance with the exchange's own listing rules. Finally, Rule 144A, known as RADRs, are capital-raising issues in which the securities are privately placed to qualified institutional buyers (QIBs) and, as a result, do not require compliance with GAAP or SEC disclosure rules. These securities trade over the counter among QIBs with very limited liquidity. As of June 1995, Level I programs comprised 55 percent of new ADRs, 23 percent were private placements (RADRs), and 22 percent were exchange-listed on the NYSE, AMEX, or Nasdaq (Levels II and III).[5]

An alternative option is a direct "ordinary" listing. These ordinary listings must take place on a U.S. exchange. They require an exact replication of settlement facilities as for U.S. securities but have somewhat different GAAP reporting and SEC registration requirements. With rare exceptions, Canadian firms are the only firms that maintain ordinary listings.[6] For example, U.S. and Canadian companies file Form 10-K due within 90 days of their fiscal year-ends and Form 10-Q quarterly, whereas non-Canadian overseas issuers trading as ADRs file an annual Form 20-F within 180 days of fiscal year-end which is less extensive (e.g., fewer footnotes on income taxes, leases,

---

[5] More details are available from Bank of New York's *Global Offerings of Depositary Receipts; A Transaction Guide* (1996) and Citibank's *An Information Guide to Depositary Receipts* (1995).

[6] See Cochrane et al. (1996) for a discussion of registration and trading of foreign securities in the United States including exemptions and key SEC accounting accommodations made. Biddle and Saudagaran (1992) and Frost and Kinney (1996) study disclosure choices among foreign registrants in the United States.

Table I
Depositary Receipt Programs by Type

Four different levels of American Depositary Receipt programs are available with various conditions on trading, registration requirements with the SEC (Securities Act of 1933), and reporting requirements (Securities and Exchange Act of 1934). More details are available from *An Information Guide to Depositary Receipts* by Citibank's Security Services Department (1995).

Item	No Capital Raising			Capital Raising with New Issue	
	Level-I	Level-II	Level-III	Rule 144A (RADR)	Global Offering
Description	Unlisted	Listed on major U.S. exchange	Offered and listed on major U.S. exchange	Private U.S. placement to qualified institutional buyers (QIBs)	Offer of in two or more markets; but not home market of issuer
Trading location	OTC Pink Sheet trading	NYSE, AMEX, or Nasdaq	NYSE, AMEX, or Nasdaq	U.S. private placement market using PORTAL	U.S. and non-U.S. exchanges
SEC registration	Registration Statement Form F-6	Registration Statement Form F-6	Form F-1 and F-6 for initial public offering	None	Private placement, as Rule144A or, new issue, as Level III
U.S. reporting required	Exemption under Rule 12g3-2(b)	Form 20-F filed annually	Form 20-F filed annually; short formsF-2 and F-3 used only for subsequent offerings	Exemption under Rule 12g3-2(b)	Private placement, as Rule144A or, new issue, as Level III
GAAP requirement	No GAAP reconciliation required	Only partial reconciliation for financials	Full GAAP reconciliation for financials	No GAAP reconciliation required	Private placement, as Rule144A or, new issue, as Level III

pensions, industry, and geographic segment information) and can be based on home country accounting practices. Since 1991, Canadian companies have been permitted to meet U.S. annual SEC reporting requirements with Canadian disclosure documents (under the auspices of the Ontario and Quebec Securities Commissions) by way of the Multi-Jurisdictional Disclosure System.[7]

II. Data

The initial sample of new listings in the United States includes all of the 317 exchange-listing Level II and III ADR applications that were successful for the period from 1976 to 1992. The sample and listing dates were obtained directly from the NYSE, AMEX, and Nasdaq Economic Research departments and were verified in publications such as the *NYSE Fact Book*, the *AMEX Fact Book*, *Moody's International Manuals*, and *Standard and Poor's Stock Reports*. To be included in the sample, the ADR program has to be the first U.S. listing for the firm (i.e., not a transition from RADR private placement to exchange-listed ADR) and has to have weekly (Friday closing) home-market stock price, exchange, and stock index data available.[8] Our primary data source for prices and exchange rates was Reuter's Exshare International Securities Database, accessed using Reuterlink™, its on-line data service. Returns are calculated as price changes without dividends. We cross-checked stock prices using various English-language sources, including *The Japan Times, Asian Wall Street Journal, Financial Times, Wall Street Journal*, and Datastream International. Canadian stock price information was obtained directly from the Toronto Stock Exchange/University of Western Ontario database. Listings before 1976 are excluded because of Reuter's Exshare database limitations.

The final sample consists of 153 listings from 11 countries in four regions of the world, including Europe, Canada, Asia, and Australia. Appendix A lists the firms by country with the associated listing date. The largest contingent is comprised of the 67 Canadian firms, all of which are ordinary listings, followed by the 36 U.K. issues, 26 from Europe (excluding the U.K.), 13 Australian issues, and 11 Asian listings (all but one from Japan). Table II provides summary statistics for the sample organized by home region, listing exchange, industry group, listing year, and type of ADR issue (i.e., Level III capital-raising or Level II non-capital-raising). Several facts are noteworthy. First, the accelerating trend for listings is visible with more than 54 new listings in the four-year period 1989 to 1992 in contrast to 11 new listings in 1976 to 1980 and 26 in 1981 to 1984. Most of the listings (82) occur on Nasdaq and this is dominated by many smaller, resource-based Canadian firms. Overall, all major sectors are represented. Cross-listed firms tend to be very large with an average capitalization of $2.5 billion, although the dis-

---

[7] See Multi-Jurisdictional Disclosure and Modifications to the Current Registration and Reporting System for Canadian Issues, Securities Act Release No. 6902 (July 1, 1991).

[8] Exchange rates are based on Friday, 10 a.m. midpoint quotes from Reuter's Exshare.

Effects of Market Segmentation and Investor Recognition   987

Table II

Descriptive Statistics for Global Firms Listing
on U.S. Exchanges, 1976–1992

Firms listing American Depositary Receipt programs as well as direct listings in the United
States with associated listing dates are obtained from the *New York Stock Exchange Fact Book*,
American Stock Exchange Fact Book, and American Stock Exchange and Nasdaq Economic
Research departments directly. New share issues are computed as a fraction of total shares
outstanding for 31 capital-raising Level-III ADR issues. Market capitalization values, information about type and sponsor institution of ADR program, and size of new issue for Level-III
ADRs are obtained from *Moody's International Manuals* (various issues). Data on shareholder
base are obtained from *Moody's Manuals* and supplemented with *Standard and Poor's Stock
Reports* (various issues). Sample of 153 firms screened for data on home-market weekly stock
price, local stock index values, and New York Friday, 10 a.m. midpoint quotes for home-market
exchange rate for 52 weeks before and after the listing date, all obtained from Reuter's Exshare
International Securities Database using Reuterlink on-line data service and supplemented with
various local periodicals. Data availability for certain variables is indicated in parentheses.

Home Region		Listing Exchange		Industry Group	
Canada	67	New York	60	Industrial	34
Australia	13	American	11	Resource	48
Europe ex U.K.	26	Nasdaq	82	Consumer	37
Asia	11			Financial	14
United Kingdom	36			Technology	12
				Utilities	8

Listing Years		Capital Raising		Capitalization	
1976–1980	11	Level-III ADR	31	Mean ($mills)	2,515.3
1981–1984	26	Non-capital raising	122	Maximum	53,221.0
1985–1988	62			Median	717.0
1989–1992	54			Minimum	3.5

New Share Issue (% of shares outstanding)		Shareholder Base (000s before listing)		Percent Change in Base (before/after listing)	
Mean	3.0%	Mean	52.9	Mean	28.8%
Maximum	12.6%	Maximum	740.3	Maximum	479.%
Median	2.1%	Median	10.0	Median	11.1%
Minimum	0.3%	Minimum	0.1	Minimum	−86.7%
Number	31	Number	145	Number	145

tribution is positively skewed with a median of only $717 million. By studying
the descriptions in *Moody's International Manuals* in the year immediately following listing, we also document that 31 of the issues were capital raising.

To proxy for changes in the shareholder base of each firm, data on the
number of registered shareholders for each security are collected prior to the
listing announcement and subsequent to listing. These data are obtained
directly from *Moody's International Manuals* for the year immediately preceding and the year following the recorded listing date, as available. Missing
observations are supplemented by *Standard and Poor's Stock Reports*.
Table II shows that for 145 of the firms for which data are available, the
mean number of registered shareholders is 52,900, although the sample is

strongly positively skewed with a median of only 10,000. The maximum of 740,000 shareholders belongs to Telefonica de Espana. On average, the change in shareholder base is positive at 28.8 percent with a median of 11.1 percent. The extreme outliers at 479 percent (Northern Telecom, Canada) and −86.7 percent (Petromet Resources, Canada) arise for firms with very low initial bases (fewer than 1,500 shareholders).

III. Market Segmentation Tests

A. *Global Market Segmentation, Cross-Listings, and Share Value*

Global cross-listings have interested the international finance literature because these securities overcome many of the regulatory restrictions, costs, and information problems that comprise barriers to investing in overseas securities. To the extent that these barriers influence how securities are priced in their respective markets, empirical researchers can evaluate the degree to which international capital markets are segmented or integrated. That is, in the context of an equilibrium model of expected returns, they ask whether market risk is "priced" differently in the two capital markets (see Black (1974), Stapleton and Subrahmanyam (1977), and Stulz (1981)). If markets are segmented, firms have an incentive to adopt policies to mitigate the negative effects of investment barriers and promote the positive effects of international diversification by direct foreign investment, mergers with non-U.S. firms, or dually listing their shares for trading on a non-U.S. capital market. Errunza and Losq (1985) and Alexander, Eun, and Janakiramanan (1987) refine the equilibrium models above for pricing shares of firms cross-listing abroad. These models predict that cross-listing shares between two segmented markets leads to a higher equilibrium market price for a given stock and a lower expected return. For example, consider the Errunza and Losq two-country model of "partial" segmentation in which investment barriers are asymmetric: country 1's investors can invest in country 2's securities, but country 2's investors are prohibited from investing in country 1's securities. They show that country 2's (eligible) securities are priced as if markets were completely integrated, but that country 1's (ineligible) securities command a "super" risk premium. If a company from country 1 cross-lists its shares in country 2, comparative statics show that the super risk premium disappears, the share price increases, and the expected return decreases.

Alexander et al. (1988) are the first to have studied price reactions for 34 firms from six different countries that were listed on either the NYSE, AMEX, or Nasdaq between 1962 and 1982. They demonstrate that the cumulative abnormal returns (CARs) for their non-Canadian benchmark sample of firms increase by an annualized 17 percent in the two years before listing and fall by an annualized 33 percent over the three years following listing. The CARs for the Canadian sample are considerably smaller in both periods, which they interpret as evidence consistent with the market integration between Canada and the United States. Foerster and Karolyi (1993) investigate a larger sample of 52 Canadian firms during the 1980s and find a much more dramatic reaction on the order of an annualized 21 percent run-up in the 100-day prelisting period and a 22 percent postlisting decline. They interpret this finding as evidence of segmentation between Canadian and U.S. markets, consistent with other findings by Booth and Johnston (1984), Jorion and Schwartz (1986), and Mittoo (1992).

In summary, previous research suggests that global cross-listing of shares can lead to a reduction in expected return on a security if the capital markets from which they originate are segmented completely or partially. If the segmentation hypothesis is correct, we should observe several patterns related to non-U.S. firms listing in the United States. First, we predict abnormal returns around interlisting should be positive. Second, abnormal returns around interlisting should vary across stocks by home market in ways related to differences in degrees of market segmentation. That is, firms from emerging markets are likely to experience larger abnormal returns than firms from developed markets.

B. Cumulative Abnormal Returns around Announcement versus Listing Dates

International asset pricing models suggest that when investors realize that barriers to investments are to be removed, expected returns should decrease as prices are bid up on the *expectation* of the removal of these barriers. Thus, in order to properly examine market segmentation hypotheses, we should examine price effects around interlisting *announcements*. A small number of studies have examined announcement effects in an international listing context. Lau at al. (1994) examine market reactions around the announcement of U.S. firms listing on overseas markets. Miller (1998) examines market reactions around announcements of international firms (primarily from Europe and emerging market countries) that interlisted on U.S. exchanges between 1985 and 1995, and Switzer (1997) examines announcements of Canadian firms that interlisted over the 1985 to 1996 period.

Although announcement dates are theoretically more appropriate than listing dates in order to test segmentation hypotheses, data collection presents some challenges, particularly for our sample of interlistings dating back to 1976. For example, one challenge relates to data sources. The most common data source for announcements is Lexis/Nexis, which includes hundreds of information sources. However, there are few relevant business data sources that precede 1980. For example, one of the main sources of information, Reuters Financial Service, is only available since January 1987. Another challenge relates to the determination of the announcement date, even if Lexis/Nexis accurately captures what is known in the market. For example, for some firms, markets have expected for years that a firm will eventually list in the United States; in some cases, a company spokesperson indicates that a firm is contemplating interlisting but the firm has not received board approval; and in other cases a firm has received board approval but has not

The Journal of Finance

received approval from the relevant exchange or securities commission. It is possible to have firms announce an intent to interlist without actually interlisting. For example, Grand Metropolitan announced, on November 1, 1989, that it was applying to list on the NYSE; on June 2, 1990, it announced a postponement in the listing; then on February 2, 1991, it announced again that it was seeking a NYSE listing—which finally occurred on March 13, 1991. All of these factors suggest that announcement dates may provide a noisy signal to the market.

Nonetheless, we gather as much data as possible related to announcement effects. We use Lexis/Nexis to obtain announcement dates for the 153 firms in our sample. Generally, the announcement date represents the earliest press release related to the eventual interlisting. We are able to identify 45 announcements,[9] the earliest of which is in 1982. Our sample of firms with announcements includes firms from Australia (6 firms), Canada (7), France (1), Italy (2), Japan (3), Netherlands (3), Norway (1), Spain (1), and the U.K. (21). Of the 45 firms, 32 listed on the NYSE, three on AMEX, and 10 on Nasdaq. For our sample, the mean (median) difference between the announcement date and the listing date is 70 (44) days.[10] The median across exchanges is 40 days for firms listing on the NYSE, 60 days for AMEX, and 65 for Nasdaq. Only nine announcement dates are more than 100 days prior to the listing date.

We compare results for both announcement and listing dates. In order to measure abnormal returns, we first estimate the (local) market model α and β for each firm (i.e., each firm's return relative to a local stock market index from Datastream International estimated during the 150-day prelisting period from day -250 to day -101). Abnormal returns are then calculated from days -100 to $+250$ as

$$\epsilon_{it} = R_{it} - [\alpha_i + \beta_{iL} R_{mt}^L], \tag{1}$$

where R_{it} is firm i's local currency return on day t.[11]

Cumulative abnormal returns from -100 days to $+250$ around both announcement and listing dates are presented in Figure 1, and statistical results are presented in Table III. Panel A of Table III examines announcement effects. There is strong evidence of a preannouncement run-up in prices. For example, in the preannouncement period between days -100 and -2, average daily abnormal returns are 0.11 percent and significant (t-statistic of 4.19). Around the announcement period (days -1 and 0), average daily ab-

---

[9] Details of dates along with the rationale cited for listing are available in an Appendix from the authors.

[10] Citibank (1995) estimates a 9-week horizon for a Level I ADR between establishing a program launch (U.S. counsel, depositary bank) and the start of Pink Sheet trading, a 14-week period for Level II or III ADRs. The RADR programs require only a 7-week period.

[11] We also examine tests using a two-factor IAPM and the Schipper and Thompson (1983) methodology, which we employ below. Results are quantitatively and qualitatively similar. We present the results above because they are most closely related to the methodology in other "announcement effect" studies.

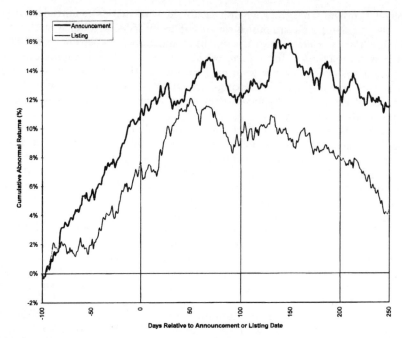

Figure 1. Cumulative abnormal returns around announcement/listing in the United States. Abnormal returns are computed for each firm based on market model risk adjustments using a local market index. Estimates are computed over days -250 to -101 relative to the identified announcement date for the U.S. listing. Daily abnormal returns are averaged across firms and cumulated. The sample includes 45 firms with identifiable announcement dates and stock and index prices are obtained from Datastream International.

normal returns jump to 0.21 percent. Although 53 percent of the firms experience positive abnormal returns around the announcement on day -1 (and 58 percent on day 0), there is a fairly large amount of variability. Consequently, the announcement effect results are not significant in our sample (t-statistic of 0.85). Subsequent to the announcement, average abnormal returns are not significantly different from zero.

It is possible that, because this analysis is based on event time, we may not capture time variation effects. For example, if markets have become more integrated over time, we might witness a decrease across time in abnormal returns around the announcement date. There is a need to develop new time-varying event methodology, but this is beyond the scope of the current paper.[12]

---

[12] There are other methodological issues as well. For example, event complexities including firms that signal intent to cross-list but do not actually cross-list could be incorporated in the event methodology (see Prabhala (1997)).

Table III
Abnormal Returns for 45 Firms around Announcement and Listing on U.S. Exchanges, 1981–1992

The market model is estimated for each firm relative to a local market index (Appendix B) during the prelisting period from day −250 to day −101. Abnormal returns are then computed for each firm based on market model risk adjustments. Daily abnormal returns are averaged across firms and cumulated. The sample includes 45 firms with identifiable announcement dates.

Event Period (days)	Average Daily Abnormal Return (%)	t-Statistic
	Panel A: Announcements	
(−100, −2)	0.1082	4.19**
(−100, −50)	0.1065	3.07**
(−49, −10)	0.1265	3.02**
(−9, −2)	0.0278	0.28
(−1, 0)	0.2057	0.85
(1, 10)	0.0388	0.55
(11, 50)	0.0291	0.63
(51, 100)	−0.0041	−0.11
(1, 100)	0.0135	0.49
(1, 250)	0.0010	0.06
	Panel B: Listings	
(−100, −2)	0.0711	2.74**
(−100, −50)	0.0388	1.09
(−49, −10)	0.0950	2.28**
(−9, −2)	0.1568	1.83*
(−1, 0)	0.3494	1.96*
(1, 10)	−0.0371	−0.41
(11, 50)	0.1169	2.44**
(51, 100)	−0.0546	−1.32
(1, 100)	0.0157	0.53
(1, 250)	−0.0157	−0.87

**,* indicate significance at the 5 and 10 percent levels, respectively.

Panel B of Table III examines listing effects. As in the preannouncement results, there is strong evidence of a prelisting run-up in prices. For example, in the prelisting period between days −100 and −2, average daily abnormal returns are 0.07 percent and significant (t-statistic of 2.74). However, around the listing period (days −1 and 0), average daily abnormal returns jump to 0.35 percent, almost twice as large as the announcement day effects. As well, 69 percent of the firms experience positive abnormal returns around the listing on day −1 (and 58 percent on day 0). Unlike the announcement effect results, these listing effect results are statistically significant (t-statistic of 1.96). Subsequent to the listing, average abnormal returns are −0.02 percent between days +1 and +250 but not significantly different from zero (t-statistic of −0.87).

Overall, results from Table III suggest there appears to be some information surrounding both the announcement of interlistings and actual listings. However, in addition to the recognition of the data collection challenges described above, these short-term results should be interpreted cautiously for other reasons. There may well be information dissemination (or leakage) prior to the announcement, between the announcement and the listing, at the listing date (with the removal of any remaining uncertainty about the listing), or even in the postlisting period when the information is actually disseminated to market participants. Thus, unlike the existing literature, which examines short-window results around announcement dates, we focus on the overall picture that emerges by examining longer periods around the listing. Consequently, the remainder of this paper focuses on results based on our larger sample of firms with listing dates using weekly returns for one year prior to listing and one year subsequent to listing.

C. Pre- and Postlisting Returns Performance

Summary statistics for weekly returns of the 153 firms around the listing dates are presented in Table IV. We report both mean excess returns—that is, in excess of risk-free rates and the associated Newey and West (1987) t-statistics in local currency and U.S. dollar-denominated terms for all firms and separately by region. The returns are computed in excess of weekly one-month Eurodollar quotes, which are obtained directly from Harris Bank's *Foreign Exchange Weekly*.[13] We compute average weekly returns before listing (weeks -52 to -1), around listing (week 0), and after listing (weeks $+1$ to $+52$).

The general pattern of excess returns is similar to that in other studies of interlistings, such as Alexander et al. (1988) and Foerster and Karolyi (1993). The returns increase by 0.38 percent per week in local currency (0.44 percent per week in dollars) during the period before listing, which is statistically significant. The cumulative return over the 12-month period corresponds to about 22 percent (26 percent). The excess returns are significantly positive during the listing week period, with an average return of 1.20 percent (1.24 percent) per week. After listing, the cumulative returns dissipate to a significant extent with an average weekly postlisting decline of -0.27 percent (-0.30 percent). This corresponds to an annualized cumulative return of -13 percent (-15 percent), which yields a net cumulative excess return of 7.5 percent (8.7 percent) over the entire two-year period. Given the similarity of our results using local currency and dollar returns, we only report local currency returns in subsequent analyses.[14]

To explain this returns pattern around the listing decision, Alexander et al. (1988), Foerster and Karolyi (1993), and many others propose the market segmentation hypothesis. These studies posit that the listing week

---

[13] We are grateful to Nelson Mark for providing us with these data.

[14] In an earlier version, we report all results using both local currency and U.S. dollar-denominated returns and find that the inferences from the two sets of results are qualitatively similar.

Table IV

Summary Statistics for Weekly Excess Returns of Global Listings around Listing Dates

Weekly (Friday close) returns for 153 listings are denominated in U.S. dollars and local currency terms using foreign exchange rates based on 10 a.m. (New York) midpoint quotes, all obtained from Reuter's Exshare International Securities Database using Reuterlink on-line data service and supplemented with various local periodicals. The returns are computed in excess of weekly one-month Treasury bill yields obtained from Harris Bank quotes. Means and standard deviations are computed separately across weeks $(-52, -1)$ before listing, (0) during listing, and $(+1, +52)$ after listing.

Stocks	No. of Observations	Local Currency		U.S. Dollar	
		Mean (%)	*t*-Statistic	Mean (%)	*t*-Statistic
Panel A: Before U.S. Listing (weeks -52 to -1)					
All	7062	0.3815	4.65**	0.4409	4.96**
Australia	659	0.8746	3.26**	0.8118	3.03**
Canada	3033	0.4152	2.60**	0.5359	3.00**
Europe ex. U.K.	1103	0.3966	3.04**	0.3649	2.82**
Asia	525	0.1524	0.81	0.0917	0.49
United Kingdom	1742	0.1956	1.75*	0.2883	2.58**
Panel B: During U.S. Listing Week (week 0)					
All	153	1.2026	1.65*	1.2404	1.71*
Australia	13	-0.1275	-0.08	-0.2071	-0.14
Canada	67	1.1463	0.75	1.2207	0.80
Europe ex. U.K.	26	2.5481	2.49**	2.4757	2.45**
Asia	11	0.7904	0.95	0.7325	0.89
United Kingdom	36	0.9419	1.18	1.0629	1.34
Panel C: After U.S. Listing (weeks $+1$ to $+52$)					
All	7681	-0.2651	-2.92**	-0.3035	-3.31**
Australia	674	-0.8594	-2.46**	-0.9500	-2.72**
Canada	3368	-0.4764	-2.76**	-0.5173	-2.99**
Europe ex. U.K.	1274	0.2051	1.63	0.1637	1.29
Asia	571	0.0026	0.01	-0.0649	-0.35
United Kingdom	1794	-0.0642	-0.48	-0.0670	-0.48

**, * indicate significance at the 5 and 10 percent levels, respectively.

returns should be positive overall and greater for firms for which the domicile market is more likely to be segmented from the U.S. market (e.g., emerging markets) and smaller for firms for which the domicile market is more integrated with that of the United States (e.g., Canada). Unlike the early Alexander et al. (1988) findings, we show in comparisons across different regions that the stock price reactions for the Canadian firms are at least as dramatic as most of the others. For example, the Canadian firms on average achieve an average prelisting stock price rise of 0.42 percent per week, equal to that of the entire sample. This contrasts with the largest average weekly rise for the Australian firms of 0.87 percent and with the insignificant run-ups for Asian firms. The large positive excess returns during the listing week for the Canadian firms is similar to that experienced by the U.K. firms but lower than that for the European (excluding U.K.) firms. Finally, the postlisting declines also exhibit considerable variation by region. The largest declines are for the Australian firms (−0.86 percent per week) and Canadian firms (−0.48 percent per week), yet for the Asian and European firms, the postlisting returns are positive.

D. Risk Adjusted Returns

In order to isolate patterns in expected returns around interlistings, existing studies, such as those by Alexander et al. (1988), Howe and Kelm (1987), Foerster and Karolyi (1993), and Lau et al. (1994), employ standard event study methodology in which expected returns are derived from the Sharpe–Lintner CAPM. This is a limiting approach for several reasons. First, the expected returns are proportional to a market covariance risk (beta) and the excess return on a benchmark portfolio, both defined relative to a domestic stock market index. In an international context, it seems appropriate for a firm listing in an overseas market to calibrate its exposure to overseas market risks in addition to domestic risks.[15] Second, these local and overseas market risks could be changing over time due to the interlisting itself or due to other firm-specific factors (e.g., changes in capitalization, new equity issues for Level III ADRs) that occur around interlistings. Third, using an International Asset Pricing Model (IAPM), such as that of Solnik (1974), where covariance risks are defined relative only to the world market portfolio, ignores local market risks that may impact prices of interlisting stocks from markets that are not integrated. Our objective is then to specify a returns generating model for these interlisting firms that captures both domestic and global risks and their changes over time.

To generate abnormal excess returns around the interlisting, we estimate a modified IAPM that captures both domestic and global market risk, where the former is computed relative to a local market index (Appendix B lists different indexes by local market) and the latter is computed relative to the weekly excess return on the Datastream International World Index.[16] We draw on the methodology of Schipper and Thompson (1983) in which we pool the cross-section and time series of returns to estimate our two-factor IAPM:

$$R_{it} = \alpha_i^{PRE} + \beta_{iL}^{PRE} R_{mt}^L + \beta_{iW}^{PRE} R_{mt}^W + \alpha_i^{LIST} D_t^{LIST}$$

$$+ \alpha_i^{POST} D_{it}^{POST} + \beta_{iL}^{POST} R_{mt}^L D_{it}^{POST} + \beta_{iW}^{POST} R_{mt}^W D_{it}^{POST} + \epsilon_{it}, \qquad (2)$$

---

[15] Empirical studies by Jorion and Schwartz (1986), Chan et al. (1992), and Dumas and Solnik (1995) focus on the pricing of domestic and foreign market risks as well as currency risks for stocks. See the survey by Stulz (1995).

[16] We chose the Datastream International World Index, denominated in U.S. dollars, because other well-known global indices, such as Morgan Stanley's Capital International and Financial Times Actuaries/Goldman Sachs indices do not extend back to 1976 when our sample begins.

where α_i's are constants (which we interpret as abnormal excess returns); β_{iL}'s are the coefficients on the local market excess return, R_{mt}^L; β_{iW}'s are the coefficients on the global market index excess return, R_{mt}^W; D_{it}^{LIST} is a dummy variable that equals one if observations are from the listing week (week 0) and zero otherwise; and D_{it}^{POST} is a dummy variable that equals one if observations are from the postlisting period (weeks +1 to +52) and zero otherwise. The returns are denominated in local currency and are defined in excess of the weekly yield of the one-month Eurodollar rate for U.S. dollar returns and in excess of weekly yields of one-month Euromarket rates for the Canadian dollar, U.K. sterling, German mark, Japanese yen, and French franc, where appropriate.[17] The advantage of this methodology is that we can measure the pre- and postlisting returns after adjusting for market covariance risks in addition to just the event-period abnormal returns using conventional event study methods. A distinct disadvantage is that by pooling cross-sectionally across the firms, we average the beta risk measures. Furthermore, the estimation and test periods are identical, which may not capture changing betas around the event period. However, in the next section, we compute these results separately by firm for the univariate and cross-sectional regressions and identify no major distortions or outliers that should generate concern about the pooled estimation.[18]

Table V presents results for the IAPM model regressions. We report the adjusted R^2 and robust t-statistics that are computed using Newey and West (1987) standard errors correcting for heteroskedasticity and serial correlation (up to six weekly lags). The final column reports a robust Wald test χ^2-statistic for the Chow test of structural break for the pre- and postlisting coefficients on the local and global returns.

Overall, we find in the prelisting period that the average beta on the local market excess return is close to one (1.03) and that of the global market beta is much smaller (0.22) but still significantly different from zero. By contrast, the postlisting local market beta drops considerably and significantly to 0.74 (a decrease of approximately 0.28) and the global market beta decreases from 0.22 to 0.12, but this change is not significant. The p-value for the Chow test for structural break indicates that the overall change is statistically significant. Our key finding here is that important changes in risk exposure result for firms interlisting their shares in the U.S. market: Exposure to the local market risk is diminished and exposure to global market risk has not significantly changed.

[17] Data were not available on Euromarket rates for each country from which sample firms originate. For local currency excess returns, we make arbitrary assignments, such as Euromark rates for Europe, except U.K. and French firms, Euroyen rates for all Asian and Australian firms, and Euro-Canadian dollar rates for Canadian firms.

[18] In an earlier version of the paper, we extend the model in two other ways: (a) to allow for currency risk with a separate factor related to foreign exchange returns and (b) to allow market risk factors (betas) to change with information variables related to macroeconomic conditions. See Shanken (1990) and Ferson and Schadt (1996). The results do not change qualitatively.

Table V
Market Model Regressions for Global Listings around Listing Date using Weekly Local Currency Excess Returns

We estimate IAPM market model regressions of firm excess returns on a constant, a local market index (Appendix B) excess return (in excess of a local/regional one-month Euromarket yield), R_{Mt}^L, and a global index (Datastream International World Index) excess return (in excess of the one-month U.S. Eurodollar yield), R_{Mt}^W:

$$R_{it} = \alpha_i^{PRE} + \beta_{iL}^{PRE} R_{mt}^L + \beta_{iW}^{PRE} R_{mt}^W + \alpha_i^{LIST} D_t^{LIST} + \alpha_i^{POST} D_t^{POST} + \beta_{iL}^{POST} R_{mt}^L D_t^{POST} + \beta_{iW}^{POST} R_{mt}^W D_t^{POST} + \epsilon_{i,t}.$$

The model is estimated with dummy variables to index the listing (D_i^{LIST} for week 0) and postlisting periods (D_i^{POST} for weeks +1 to +52) and associated coefficients are denoted with superscript *PRE* for prelisting, *LIST* for listing, and *POST* for postlisting periods. For excess returns, we employ Euroyen rates for Asian firms, Euromark rates for European (ex U.K.) firms, pound sterling rates for U.K. firms, Euro-Canadian dollar rates for Canadian firms, and Euromark rates for all others. Robust *t*-statistics are computed using heteroskedasticity-consistent and serially uncorrelated (lags = 6) standard errors using Newey and West (1987) procedures and reported below the coefficient estimates. A Chow test of the structural break in the coefficients before listing (weeks −52 to −1) and after (weeks 0 to +52), is reported as a χ^2 with associated *p*-value below the estimate.

| | Before U.S. Listing (weeks −52, −1) | | | Listing Week | After U.S. Listing (weeks +1, +52) | | | | |
	α_i^{PRE}	β_i^{PRE}	β_{iW}^{PRE}	α_i^{LIST}	α_i^{POST}	β_{iL}^{POST}	β_{iW}^{POST}	Adj. R^2	χ^2 (*p*-value)
All firms	0.0031	1.0259	0.2162	0.0029	−0.0053	−0.2835	−0.1023	11.24%	57.28
	4.14**	29.98**	5.03**	0.44	−4.64**	−5.53**	−1.44		0.00
Australia	0.0056	1.3602	0.0786	−0.0218	−0.0116	−0.5157	0.2211	18.88%	14.39
	2.59**	7.39**	0.60	−1.86*	−2.87**	−2.12**	0.85		0.01
Canada	0.0049	1.1664	0.2337	0.0023	−0.0092	−0.2019	−0.0317	6.36%	18.39
	3.17**	10.59**	2.57**	0.17	−4.06**	−1.31	−0.23		0.00
Europe (ex. U.K.)	0.0010	0.8719	0.0811	0.0064	−0.0001	−0.0848	0.0401	6.19%	7.315
	1.67*	41.99**	1.96*	1.21	−0.06	−2.28**	0.69		0.12
Asia	0.0003	1.2294	0.2153	0.0059	−0.0001	−0.8987	−0.2309	10.01%	35.53
	0.17	9.81**	1.77*	0.66	−0.02	−5.19**	−1.21		0.00
United Kingdom	0.0016	0.9998	0.1678	0.0081	−0.0017	−0.5245	−0.2496	14.04%	36.57
	1.64*	18.81**	2.93**	1.23	−1.06	−4.77**	−2.07**		0.00

**, * indicate significance at the 5 and 10 percent levels, respectively.

Even after we adjust for these changes in risk, however, interlisting firms still generate statistically significant abnormal returns, as measured by the α_i coefficients. In the prelisting period, firms earn 0.31 percent per week; in the postlisting period, firms lose 0.22 percent per week (calculated as the sum of α_i^{PRE}, 0.31 percent per week, and the α_i^{POST}, -0.53 percent per week). This suggests that the abnormal returns performance around interlistings is robust to changes in expected returns that are captured by shifts in risk exposure.

Table V also reports similar results by groups of firms according to home region. We find some important differences. First, the dramatic shift in local market betas is evident for the Australian stocks. β_L falls by 0.52 from 1.36 during the prelisting period to 0.84 during the post-listing period; β_W increases by 0.22 from 0.08 to 0.30, although the prelisting global beta is not significantly different from zero, nor is the change in the global beta. For the Canadian firms, the significant positive abnormal prelisting returns (0.49 percent per week) and negative abnormal postlisting returns (0.92 percent lower or -0.43 percent per week) obtain, as in Foerster and Karolyi (1993). Unlike other markets, however, neither the local market beta nor the global market beta change is significant during the postlisting period. Firms from the European and Asian subsample of ADRs retain the familiar increase in prelisting abnormal returns, but do not yield a significant decline in postlisting abnormal returns. The local market betas do drop significantly, by 0.08 from 0.87 to 0.79 for Europe and by 0.90 from 1.23 to 0.33 for Asia, and the global beta increases slightly for Europe but decreases for Asia, although neither change is significant. Finally, the U.K. ADRs generate negative postlisting abnormal returns, and significant declines in both local betas (by 0.52 from 1.00 to 0.48) and global betas (by 0.25 from 0.17 to -0.08). One possible implication of the significant decrease in local betas combined with the lack of significant increase in global betas suggests these firms appear to be successful in lowering their cost of equity, and hence cost of capital, by interlisting their stock on U.S. exchanges.

In order to observe the time series patterns in abnormal returns in event time, we compute estimates of the two-factor IAPM model using Ibbotson's (1975) Regression across Time and Securities (RATS) model. That is, we reestimate equation (2) pooled across all securities (and by regional groups), but in event-time on a week-by-week basis. We obtain estimates of the coefficients for each week τ, where τ runs from -52 to $+52$, and where the listing week corresponds to τ equal to zero. The cumulative values for the α_i's are computed. Figure 2 exhibits the results overall and by region. The cumulative abnormal returns pattern for the Australian and Canadian firms follow most clearly the prelisting run-up and postlisting decline. The drop for the Australian stocks occurs during week 5, whereas that for the Canadian stocks is more gradual. The cumulative abnormal returns for the European and U.K. firms follow a general increase for the entire pre- and postlisting period. The Asian ADRs demonstrate no discernible pattern at all.

Effects of Market Segmentation and Investor Recognition   999

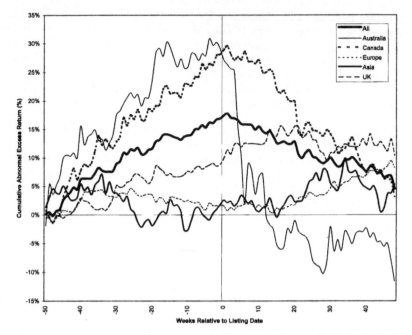

Figure 2. Cumulative abnormal excess returns for global listings in the United States by region. Cumulative abnormal excess returns are computed weekly using Ibbotson (1975) RATS (Regression Across Time and Securities) in event time using a two-index IAPM model for local currency excess returns with a local market index (Appendix B) and Datastream International's World Index. The intercept coefficients from each weekly regression are cumulated over the 52 weeks before and after listing. Data are obtained from Reuter's Exshare International Securities Database using Reuterlink on-line data service and supplemented with various local periodicals. The returns are computed in excess of weekly one-month Euromarket yields obtained from Harris bank quote sheets.

In summary, we compute measures of abnormal returns for a cross-section of global listings before, around, and following their U.S. listing. The pattern of a prelisting price run-up, listing week increase, and postlisting decline is robust even after accounting for statistically important risk changes around the listing. These abnormal return patterns also differ by region, though caution should be exercised as these regional subsamples are smaller. In the next section, we attempt to shed further light on these results by examining whether there are important differences in these abnormal returns that are related to firm-specific variables, such as the listing location, the industry group to which the firm belongs, or the type of listing.

E. Univariate Cross-Sectional Tests

In this section, we recompute weekly abnormal excess returns and betas for each firm based on 153 univariate time-series regressions as in equation (2). We cumulate across event time α's, as appropriate, to compute listing and postlisting abnormal returns and perform a series of cross-sectional tests based on the univariate abnormal returns and changing betas. Table VI reports dummy variable regression results of the abnormal returns and changing betas as the dependent variables with dummy variables as the independent variables based on different regions, exchanges, industries, and listing type. Average weekly abnormal excess returns are 0.15 percent in the prelisting period, 0.12 percent in the listing week, and −0.14 percent in the postlisting period. The fraction of firms with positive abnormal returns in the prelisting period is 61 percent versus 52 percent around listing and 50 percent in the postlisting period. The differences across regions indicate similar patterns to those uncovered above. When we test whether the regional differences are significant, we do not reject the null in the prelisting and postlisting period but reject the null in the listing period itself. When comparing the abnormal returns for global listings by exchange location, we find no significant differences on average. The NYSE listings seem to generate higher positive abnormal returns, not only in the prelisting period but also in the listing period as well as smaller declines than AMEX and Nasdaq firms following listing. However, the χ^2-statistics suggest the differences are not significant.

Industry differences are not an important factor in general. For the prelisting period, the abnormal returns increase consistently but differences range from as low as −0.27 percent per week for the technology stocks to 0.42 percent per week for industrial stocks. Similarly, the postlisting decline for the technology stocks is the highest, and contrasts with the postlisting increase observed for the utilities. The χ^2 test suggests the postlisting results are measurably different by industry at the 10 percent significance level. These postlisting returns results are consistent with earlier findings of differences across industry sectors in Foerster and Karolyi (1993) and complement those studies examining the important role of industrial structure in international diversification strategies.[19]

We also investigate whether there are possible confounding effects between industries and exchanges. For example, if technology stocks tend to list on Nasdaq, then any apparent differences across exchanges may actually be the result of differences across industries. To examine this, we rerun cross-sectional regressions including both industry and exchange dummies (to preserve space, results are not presented). We then test for differences across industries (after controlling for exchanges) and for differences across exchanges (after controlling for industries). In the prelisting period, abnor-

[19] Roll (1992), Heston and Rouwenhorst (1994), and Griffin and Karolyi (1998) debate the importance of industry and country factors in international stock returns. Recent evidence is also found in Karolyi and Stulz (1996).

Table VI

Mean Abnormal Returns and Changing Local and Global Beta by Variables Related to Home Region, Choice of U.S. Exchange, Industry Group, and Capital Raising

Abnormal returns are computed using regression model estimates of excess returns from before listing (weeks -52 to -1), listing week (week 0), and postlisting periods (weeks $+1$ to $+52$) for an IAPM model using excess returns of local market index and global index. Distributions of firms by region, U.S. exchange location industry group, and capital raising are provided in Table II. $\Delta\beta^{LO}$ and $\Delta\beta^{WO}$ are the differences between the prelisting and postlisting betas relative to the local market and global market, respectively. Abnormal returns are computed separately for each firm using local currency excess returns. χ^2 denotes a robust Wald test of the difference between the mean abnormal returns across different groupings. Tests for significance use Newey and West (1987) robust t-statistics. Wald tests and binomial Z-tests for percentage of positive/negative abnormal returns are indicated for significance at the 10 percent * and 5 percent ** levels, respectively.

Category	Abnormal Returns			Beta Changes	
	Prelisting α_i^{PRE} $(-52,-1)$	Listing α_i^{LIST} (week 0)	Postlisting α_i^{POST} $(+1,+52)$	Change in Local Beta $\Delta\beta_{iL}$	Change in Global Beta $\Delta\beta_{iW}$
Overall					
Mean	0.0015*	0.0012	-0.0014	-0.3209**	0.1349
Percentage Positive	60.78%**	51.63%	50.32%	39.86%**	53.59%
By region					
Australia	0.0052	-0.0276	-0.0016	-0.4904	0.1388
Canada	0.0034	0.0060	-0.0038	-0.1388	0.1910
Europe	-0.0055	-0.0179	0.0007	-0.3674	0.4536
Asia	0.0016	0.0099	0.0011	-1.0679	-0.0739
United Kingdom	0.0019	0.0135	0.0007	-0.3367	-0.1372
Adjusted R^2	3.25%	2.61%	2.98%	3.66%	2.21%
χ^2	5.52	12.29**	6.83	7.94*	5.886
By exchange					
NYSE	0.0027	0.0100	-0.0011	-0.4075	-0.0790
AMEX	0.0071	-0.0047	-0.0037	0.0268	0.0563
NASD	-0.0002	-0.0045	-0.0014	-0.3042	0.3021
Adjusted R^2	1.30%	0.71%	0.27%	0.75%	1.88%
χ^2	3.58	1.62	0.35	1.64	3.75
By industry					
Industrial	0.0042	-0.0029	-0.0001	-0.2508	-0.0990
Resource	0.0001	0.0026	-0.0034	-0.2974	0.2369
Consumer	0.0021	0.0079	-0.0007	-0.3407	-0.0037
Financial	0.0015	-0.0004	-0.0002	-0.4739	0.1097
Technology	-0.0027	-0.0145	-0.0042	-0.2866	0.8240
Utility	0.0011	0.0055	0.0031	-0.4510	0.1695
Adjusted R^2	1.08%	0.51%	2.22%	0.29%	3.23%
χ^2	5.85	1.21	10.47*	1.35	4.64
By level					
Capital Level (III)	0.0013	0.0025	0.0017	-0.3922	-0.0765
No capital Level (II)	0.0016	0.0009	-0.0023	-0.3028	0.1886
Adjusted R^2	0.04%	0.01%	1.62%	0.01%	0.63%
χ^2	0.02	0.02	7.22**	0.20	3.05*

**,* indicate significance at the 5 and 10 percent levels, respectively.

mal returns are not significant across industries, but are marginally significant across exchanges (with a χ^2 p-value of 0.103). During the listing week, abnormal return differences are not significant across either group. In the postlisting period, abnormal returns are significantly different across industries (with a χ^2 p-value of 0.004), but are not across exchanges.

Capital raising differences provide surprising results. One hypothesis suggested by Dharan and Ikenberry (1995) is that postlisting negative stock returns following Nasdaq and AMEX listings on the NYSE can be explained by managers of firms acting opportunistically in timing their listing. These managers, typically of smaller firms, strategically apply for listing just before a decline in performance. Dharan and Ikenberry refer to this as the opportunism hypothesis. They also offer this explanation for the equity issuance postlisting decline for U.S. initial public offerings (IPOs) and seasoned equity offerings (SEOs) uncovered by other studies, such as that by Loughran and Ritter (1995). One possible explanation for the postlisting negative abnormal returns for the ADRs around their listing in the United States is that the managers of these firms are timing their listing and equity issuance precisely when poor fundamental performance will follow. Our results in Table VI show that in the prelisting and listing periods both firms that raised capital through ADRs and those that did not experience positive abnormal excess returns and these returns are not significantly different across the two groups. However, in the postlisting period, capital-raising firms experience positive abnormal returns (weekly 0.17 percent, or annualized 8.84 percent) but non-capital-raising firms experience negative abnormal returns (weekly, −0.23 percent, or annualized −11.96 percent). The differences across the two groups are statistically significant. These results are contrary to findings in the IPO/SEO literature which show that firms that raise capital tend to experience subsequent negative abnormal returns. For example, Loughran and Ritter find a post-issue abnormal decline of 4.5 percent for IPOs in the first year and a decline of 6.3 percent for SEOs. Our results suggest global equity secondary offerings may differ from domestic equity offerings. A more extensive investigation of this issue is warranted, but is beyond the scope of this paper.

Table VI also presents results related to cross-sectional differences of changing local betas and global betas. Overall, firms experience a significant decline in local betas. On average, postlisting local betas are 0.32 below the level of prelisting betas. Furthermore, more than 60 percent of the firms experienced a decline. In contrast, world betas tend to increase by 0.13, on average, but only 54 percent of the firms experience an increase, and the postlisting beta is not significantly different from the prelisting beta. Changes in local betas are significantly different across regions. Canadian firms experience the smallest decrease in local betas, followed by U.K. firms; Asian firms experience the largest declines. Firms from Australia, Canada, and Europe experience increases in global betas; firms from Asia and the U.K. experience declines, although differences in global beta changes are not significant (χ^2 p-value of 0.210). There are no significant differences in either local or global beta changes across exchanges or industries. In fact, local beta changes are consistently negative across all industries and two of three exchanges. Both capital-raising firms and non-capital-raising firms experience local beta declines of similar magnitudes, but significant differences appear for the changing global betas. Capital-raising firms experience a decline in global betas, non-capital-raising firms experience an increase.

IV. Abnormal Returns, Betas, Liquidity, and Changes in the Shareholder Base

Although our findings on share price patterns around global cross-listings are generally consistent with the market segmentation hypothesis, we propose in this section two alternative hypotheses that associate the share price effects to changes in the underlying liquidity in the market for the shares and to changes in the shareholder base. Foreign firms seeking access to U.S. markets often cite these as two key factors in their decision to list abroad (see Karolyi (1998)) but they are just as likely to influence U.S. firms that may simply seek to change trading location (i.e., from Nasdaq to the NYSE). In fact, existing research on domestic listings, such as Christie and Huang (1993) and Kadlec and McConnell (1994), links the effects of listing choices on share prices, liquidity, and changes in the shareholder base to theoretical models developed by Amihud and Mendelson (1986) and Merton (1987). In this section, we follow these studies on domestic listings and describe the Amihud–Mendelson and Merton models, outline the new tests for global cross-listings, and present key findings.

A. Merton's (1987) Investor Recognition Hypothesis

Merton's (1987) capital market equilibrium is different from that of the Sharpe–Lintner CAPM in that investors consider only securities of which they are aware, an assumption about incomplete information. With this assumption, Merton shows that expected returns depend on factors other than just market risk. Specifically, the shadow cost of incomplete information for stock i is given as

$$\lambda_i = \delta \sigma_i^2 x_i (1 - q_i)/q_i, \tag{3}$$

where δ is the coefficient of aggregate risk aversion, σ_i^2 is the firm-specific component of the stock's return variance, x_i is the relative market value of the firm, and q_i is the size of the firm's investor base relative to the total number of investors. The relationship between the actual expected excess return of the stock, $E(R_i)$, and the expected excess return for the complete information case (where q_i equals 1), $E(R_i^*)$, is

$$E(R_i) - E(R_i^*) = \lambda_i E(R_i^*)/R_0, \tag{4}$$

where R_0 is the return on the zero-beta asset. The intuition behind the result is that since investors consider only a part of the opportunity set, full diversification is not possible and firm-specific risk is priced in equilibrium. Moreover, this firm-specific risk is weighted by the relative market value of the firm and its shareholder base. For firms with a relatively small shareholder base, these factors are likely to be very significant on average. Indeed, firms would have incentives to incorporate policies that actively expand the investor base of the firm's shares. For non-U.S. firms cross-listing their shares in the United States, we know that this is one of the primary motivations.[20]

We construct an empirical proxy for the shadow cost of incomplete information, λ_i, for each firm, following Kadlec and McConnell (1994). Specifically, we measure the change in λ around the interlisting by

$$\Delta\lambda_i = \sigma_{ei}^2 SIZE_i(1/SHR_{t+1} - 1/SHR_t), \tag{5}$$

where σ_{ei}^2 is the residual variance from our two-factor IAPM benchmark model regressions, as in equation (2); $SIZE_i$ is the U.S.-dollar market capitalization of the firm as measured by the price of the stock in week 0 and the number of shares outstanding, and is normalized by the level of the Datastream International World Stock index value in the listing week;[21] and SHR_t is the number of shareholders of record in the year before (t) and after $(t + 1)$ listing. The data on the number of shares outstanding and the shareholders of record are obtained from various publications of *Moody's International Manuals* in the year before and after listing. Due to data availability, our sample is pared down slightly to 145 firms.

In Section II and Table II, we demonstrate that firms experience an increase in their shareholder base by about 28.8 percent. The investor recognition hypothesis of Merton (1987) suggests that the abnormal returns experienced by firms during the pre- and postlisting period may be due to changes in the shareholder base, adjusted by the stock's residual variance and relative size. We follow Kadlec and McConnell (1994) and use cross-sectional regressions, such as

$$\alpha_i = \gamma_0 + \gamma_1 \Delta\lambda_i + e_{it}, \tag{6}$$

where α_i is the pre- or postlisting or listing week abnormal returns.[22] Given that $\Delta\lambda_i$ is negative for most firms with an increase in shareholder base, we expect that γ_1 will be significant and negative in the cross-sectional regressions.

[20] See Fanto and Karmal (1997) for a recent survey of corporate financial officers from overseas companies that listed their shares in the U.S. for the first time.

[21] We regress the capitalization value of each firm cross-sectionally on a constant and the value of the Datastream International World Index (where January 1, 1975, equals 100). The relative market value is computed as the residuals from this regression.

[22] Note that this estimation suffers from an error-in-variables problem. Due to the estimation error in $\Delta\lambda_i$, this would imply that the coefficient γ_1 is likely biased to zero.

Effects of Market Segmentation and Investor Recognition   1005

We also investigate a cross-sectional relationship between changing betas (both local and global) and changing shareholder base; that is, in separate regressions, we replace the dependent variable, α_i, of equation (6) with $\Delta\beta_L$ and $\Delta\beta_W$, respectively. Changing betas reflect changes in the assessments by the marginal investor of the domestic and global risk exposures of the firm and, as a result, changes in the market's expectation of its future returns. The Merton hypothesis would then predict a positive coefficient on $\Delta\lambda_i$ for these beta changes because an increase in $\Delta\lambda_i$ due to a larger investor base should be associated with a decrease in covariance risk and thus the cost of capital.

B. Amihud and Mendelson's (1986) Liquidity Hypothesis

Amihud and Mendelson (1986) develop an equilibrium asset pricing model in which gross returns are shown to be an increasing and concave function of liquidity. They proxy for liquidity using the bid-ask spread. In notational form, the gross return required by investor i on asset j is

$$E(R_j^i) = R_i^* + \mu_i S_j, \tag{7}$$

where R_i^* is the required spread-adjusted return and $\mu_i S_j$ is the expected liquidation cost (i.e., the investor's liquidation probability, μ_i, times the asset's relative spread, S_j). If spreads drop following listing, the lower expected returns required by investors should give rise to an increase in share value.

Unlike studies of the share price and liquidity impact of Nasdaq firms listing on the AMEX or the NYSE, no data on bid-ask spreads in home markets are systematically available for the cross-section of non-U.S. firms. In a domestic setting, Christie and Huang (1993) and Kadlec and McConnell (1994) show that Nasdaq listings on the NYSE enjoy uniformly lower spreads and that these changes are associated with abnormal returns for these firms around listing. We propose to test this liquidity hypothesis of Amihud and Mendelson (1986) indirectly by allowing the dependence of the abnormal returns in the prelisting, postlisting, or listing weeks themselves in the regression model of equation (6) to be differentially sensitive for NYSE, AMEX, and Nasdaq listings. We employ a series of controls associated with the size of the firm, whether it is a Level III capital-raising ADR or not, and, if so, the size of the new issue. We also investigate changing betas in a similar manner.

C. Multivariate Cross-Sectional Tests

Table VII presents the cross-sectional regressions of the abnormal returns. Four different models are examined using the abnormal returns as measured by the two-factor IAPM. We present regressions for the abnormal returns from the pre- and postlisting periods and for the listing weeks in

Table VII
Regressions of Abnormal Returns for Global Listings on Variables Related to Size, Shareholder Base, and Size of New Issue

Abnormal excess returns are computed for listing week (0) using an IAPM regression model and mean abnormal returns from the intercept of the same model for before listing period (weeks −52 to −1) and after listing period (weeks +1 to +52). Variables related to relative market capitalization (*SIZE*), change in shareholder base (*SHR*, for before and after listing), capital raising dummy (*ICAP*) and issue size (*ISSUE*) are as in Table II. Market incompleteness factor (Δλ) is from Merton (1987) based on Kadlec and McConnell (1994):

$$\Delta\lambda = (\sigma_\epsilon^2 SIZE)\cdot(1/SHR_{t+1} - 1/SHR_t),$$

where σ_ϵ^2 is the residual variance from IAPM model regression before listing period. Abnormal returns are computed separately using local currency and U.S. dollar denominated returns. R^2 is the adjusted coefficient of determination. *t*-statistics use Newey and West (1987) standard errors corrected for heteroskedasticity and serial correlation.

Variable	Prelisting Abnormal Returns				Listing Period Abnormal Returns				Postlisting Abnormal Returns			
	(1)	(2)	(3)	(4)	(1)	(2)	(3)	(4)	(1)	(2)	(3)	(4)
Constant	0.0015*	0.0020*	0.0021*	0.0014*	0.0013	−0.0022	−0.0019	0.0007	−0.0014	−0.0016	−0.0015	−0.0015
SIZE (10^{-9})	−0.0822		−0.0868		0.0538		0.0656		0.0315		−0.0423	
Δλ	−0.2401**		−0.2404**	2.2006	−1.2738		−1.2710	0.4640**	−0.4514**		−0.4450**	0.0283
ICAP		−0.0011	−0.0010*			0.0071	0.0069			0.0028*	0.0028*	
ISSUE (10^{-6})		0.0433	0.0516			−0.3023	−0.3088			0.0649**	0.0689**	
Δλ (AMEX)				−3.7026				−0.5525**				−0.0449
Δλ (NASD)				−2.3490				−0.4716**				−0.0319
R^2	0.24%	0.02%	0.27%	0.52%	0.24%	0.05%	0.29%	0.98%	1.36%	1.72%	3.03%	2.04%

**, * indicate significance at the 5 and 10 percent levels, respectively.

three panels. In each regression, we report the coefficient estimates, denoted as statistically significant based on robust t-statistics from Newey and West (1987) standard errors, and adjusted R^2.

The first regression shows that the abnormal returns around the listings are not significantly related to the market value of the firm, but are negatively related to Merton's market incompleteness factor. The coefficient on $\Delta\lambda$ is -0.24 for the prelisting period. During the listing weeks, we find that the relationship is still negative on $\Delta\lambda$ at -1.27, but the relationship is not significant. Finally, in the postlisting period, the coefficient on $\Delta\lambda$ is of the expected sign, -0.45, and statistically significant at the 5 percent level. These results are supportive of the Merton hypothesis and consistent with Kadlec and McConnell (1994).

When the size and Merton incompleteness factors are introduced into the regressions of abnormal returns, the intercept term is statistically indistinguishable from zero in the listing and postlisting periods. However, with R^2 measures at approximately one percent, it appears that these two variables cannot explain much of the cross-sectional variation in abnormal returns across the 145 firms. The explanatory power is likely low due to measurement errors in the incompleteness factor. Nevertheless, we interpret these multivariate cross-sectional regression results as consistent with the investor recognition hypothesis because $\Delta\lambda$ is generally significant and is consistently of the expected negative sign.

To gauge the robustness of these tests, we consider confounding influences of other firm-specific variables, such as the type of ADR issue. For example, we control for whether the ADR listing is Level III (capital-raising) and measure the size of the new issue. Regression (2) in Table VII demonstrates that the dummy variable for a capital-raising ADR (*ICAP*) is statistically significant and positive in the post-listing period. The positive *ICAP* coefficient in the postlisting period confirms our previous analysis presented in Table VI and suggests that the general postlisting negative abnormal return pattern is mitigated for firms that raise capital. Furthermore, the positive and significant *ISSUE* coefficient in the postlisting period suggests the postlisting decline is even more offset for larger issues. We combine the *SIZE*, $\Delta\lambda$, *ICAP*, and new issue variables in regression (3) and find that the statistical significance of the negative $\Delta\lambda$ and positive *ICAP* coefficient in the postlisting period is similar in the joint regression. As discussed earlier, this finding that capital-raising ADR issues yield positive abnormal postlisting returns is surprising given the U.S. IPO/SEO findings of Loughran and Ritter (1995).

To test the Amihud and Mendelson (1986) liquidity hypothesis, we allow the coefficient on the Merton incompleteness factor to interact with a dummy variable for the NYSE, AMEX, and Nasdaq. We know from Table VI that the average abnormal returns in any of the subperiods around interlisting are not different by exchange listing location. However, studies by Christie and Huang (1993) and Kadlec and McConnell (1994) show important liquidity effects for Nasdaq stocks listing on the NYSE. Regression model (4) indicates that the impact of changes in the shareholder base around listings for these firms does matter. In both the prelisting and postlisting periods, none of the coefficients are significant. However, in the listing period, the AMEX and Nasdaq $\Delta\lambda$ coefficients are significantly negative and the NYSE coefficient is significantly positive. If the NYSE is viewed as a more liquid market than the AMEX or Nasdaq, then these results are inconsistent with the liquidity hypothesis of Amihud and Mendelson (1986). More likely, these results represent only an indirect test of the liquidity hypothesis at best and should be interpreted with caution.

Finally, we examine the relationship between changing betas and shareholder base, as captured by $\Delta\lambda$. We repeat the four regressions described above using either the change in local betas or the change in global betas as the dependent variable. Results are presented in Table VIII. Coefficients are generally not significant, but the signs on $\Delta\lambda$ are positive, which implies that the decline in local and global betas is positively associated with an increase in shareholder base. To the extent that the decline in betas can be interpreted as a lowering of the firm's cost of equity, we find evidence once again consistent with Merton's investor recognition hypothesis. The only statistically significant results obtain for regression (4), which allows $\Delta\lambda$ to vary by exchange. In the case of both local betas and global betas, the NYSE coefficient is positive and the AMEX and Nasdaq coefficients are negative. This finding suggests that the overall statistical insignificance may stem from an averaging of the effect across exchanges: the lower betas, and potentially lower cost of equity, derive primarily from the NYSE cross-border listings. Again, the explanatory power of these cross-sectional tests is limited and results should be interpreted with caution.

V. Conclusions

We document the effect on share value and global risk exposures of a non-U.S. firm listing on U.S. exchanges. Our sample consists of 153 firms from 11 countries that listed their shares for the first time in the United States directly or as ADRs during the period from 1976 to 1992. We find that these stocks earned a significant average excess return of 19 percent during the year before listing, an additional 1.20 percent during the listing week, but incurred a significant average decline of 14 percent during the year following listing. We also find that a stock's market beta relative to its home market index declines dramatically from 1.03 to 0.74 on average, but its global beta relative to the world market index does not change significantly.

Existing studies have interpreted the dramatic patterns in share values around cross-border listings as evidence of market segmentation due to direct or indirect investment barriers. To the extent that a higher risk premium is built into the expected returns of such stocks as compensation for these investment restrictions, the cross-border listings in the United States overcome these barriers and their stock prices adjust accordingly. We find the evidence generally consistent with the market segmentation hypothesis. However, we uncover two other possible explanations for the abnormal return patterns for cross-border

Table VIII
Regressions of Changing Local and Global Betas for Global Listings on Variables Related to Size, Shareholder Base, and Size of New Issue

We estimate an IAPM market model regressions of firm excess returns on a constant, a local market index (Appendix B) excess return (in excess of a local/regional one-month Euromarket yield), and a global index (Datastream International World Index) excess return (in excess of the one-month U.S. yield). Changes in local and global betas are based on estimates from the prelisting period (weeks −52 to −1) and postlisting period (weeks +1 to +52). Variables related to relative market capitalization (*SIZE*), change in shareholder base (*SHR*$_t$ for before and after listing), capital raising dummy (*ICAP*), and issue size (*ISSUE*) are as in Table II. Market incompleteness factor (Δλ) is from Merton (1987) based on Kadlec and McConnell (1994):

$$\Delta\lambda = (\sigma_\epsilon^2\, SIZE)\cdot(1/SHR_{t+1} - 1/SHR_t),$$

where σ_ϵ^2 is the residual variance from IAPM model regression before listing period. Abnormal returns are computed separately using local currency and U.S. dollar denominated returns. R^2 is the adjusted coefficient of determination. *t*-statistics use Newey and West (1987) standard errors corrected for heteroskedasticity and serial correlation.

Variable	Changes in Local Betas				Changes in Global Betas			
	(1)	(2)	(3)	(4)	(1)	(2)	(3)	(4)
Constant	−0.3237**	−0.2963**	−0.2988**	−0.3401**	0.1330	0.1699	0.1695	0.1402
SIZE (10⁻⁸)	−0.4293		−0.3160		−1.0932*		−0.6912	
Δλ	0.2241		0.2229		0.1564		0.1525	
ICAP		−0.1014	−0.0930			−0.2307	−0.2170	
ISSUE (10⁻⁵)		0.6510	0.9599	14.236**		−1.8735	−1.2029	9.3731**
Δλ (AMEX)				−15.934**				−7.2099*
Δλ (NASD)				−13.879**				−9.3592**
R^2	0.38%	0.08%	0.44%	2.63%	0.39%	0.64%	0.87%	2.04%

**, * indicate significance at the 5 and 10 percent levels, respectively.

listings which stem from the larger shareholder base and the greater liquidity that these firms achieve upon listing in the United States. We show that a proxy for a market incompleteness factor, which captures the impact of a heightened level of investor recognition, is significantly related to the abnormal patterns in the pre- and postlisting periods. This market incompleteness factor derives from the incomplete information asset pricing model of Merton (1987). We also offer evidence that the statistical importance of this increased investor recognition is sensitive to the listing location of the non-U.S. firm. Finally, a surprising finding is that the postlisting decline of abnormal returns for these cross-border listings is mitigated for those firms that raise capital at the same time. This contrasts with the existing evidence on the long-run underperformance of equity issuances via IPOs and SEOs in the United States, and poses an interesting challenge for future research.

Appendix A. Sample Firms and Listing Dates

	Date (yr/mo/day)		Date (yr/mo/day)		Date (yr/mo/day)
Australia:		**Canada (continued):**		**Canada (continued):**	
Boral	920319	Giant Bay Res	870121	Scintilore Res	831007
Broken Hill Prop	870528	Gold Knight Res	841024	Sonora	860731
Central Pacific	810312	Goldex	890112	Sceptre Res	820402
Coles Myer	881031	Greenstone Res	890112	Softkey Softward	901001
FAI Insurance	880928	Granges	860618	Tudor	880304
Natl Australia Bank	880624	Healthcare	881110	Tee Comm	920828
News Corp	860520	Hemlo Gold	920115	Total Energold	880923
Orbital Engine	911204	Horsham	900115	Transcda Pipelines	850530
Pacific Dunlop	870702	Highwood Res	820226	Westburne Intl.	780510
Santos	810321	Corona	880729	Wharfe Res	830201
Southern Pacific	810312	Intl Platinum	890526		
Western Mining	900102	Intercity Products	780901	**France:**	
Western Pacific	890317	IPSCO	911217	Alcatel Alsthom	920520
		Intl Colin Energy	910515	LVMH Motet	871023
Canada:		Lac Minerals	850731	Societe Elf Aquitaine	910614
American Barrick	850125	Laidlaw	831021	Thomson	860723
Aber Res	890320	Loewen	900515	Total	911025
BCE Inc	760818	Magna Intl	840823		
BII Enterprises	920804	Mitel	810518	**Hong Kong:**	
Belmoral Res	880104	Mirtronics	861202	Hong Kong Teleph	881223
Bunker Hill	900530	MSR Explorations	830913	**Italy:**	
Central Fund Cda	860610	Minven Gold	891207	Benetton	890609
Centurian Gold	881003	Norcen Energy	890328	Fiat	890214
Consolidated Merc	860822	NHI Nelson	870626	Montedison	870716
Cornucopia Res	881003	Northern Telecom	751110		
Consolidated Prof	820127	Nova Corp	880613	**Japan:**	
Cineplex Odeon	870514	Newfield Mines	880314	CSK	830830
Cognos	870701	Nowsco Wells	770314	Hitachi	820414
Davidson Tisdale	850225	Petromet	880616	Honda	860523
Deprenyl	890808	Pegasus	820823	Kubota	761109
Dickenson Mines	810114	Pop Shoppes	770603	Makita	770125
Dreco Energy	900618	Quadra Logic	881025	Mitsubishi	890919
ECO Corp	900126	Quebec Sturgeon	830125	Pioneer	761213
Energex	870803	Rea Gold	850328	Sanyo	770401
Eastmaque Gold	870904	Repap Res	880202	TDK	820515
Fahnestock Vine	860828	SHL Systemhouse	850614	Wacoal	890428

(continued overleaf)

Effects of Market Segmentation and Investor Recognition   1011

Appendix A—*Continued*

	Date (yr/mo/day)		Date (yr/mo/day)		Date (yr/mo/day)
Netherlands		**Sweden:**		**United Kingdom (continued):**	
Aegon	911105	AB Electrolux	870701	Grand Metropolitan	910313
Ahold	910408	AB SKF	851025	Hanson	861103
Akzo	890508	ASEA AB	830815	Huntingdon Intl	890216
Oce Van Grinten	841101	AB Volvo	841203	Imperial Chemical	831101
Philips	870414			LEP Group	880930
		United Kingdom:		London Intl Group	901002
Norway:		Allied Irish Banks	890912	Medeva	910930
Hafslund Nycomed	920624	Attwoods	910412	Micro Focus Group	920526
Norsk Data	830210	Auto Security	920714	Natl Westminister	861022
Norsk Hydro	860625	Barclays	860909	Ratners Group	880713
		Bass	900216	Royal Bank of Scot	891016
		Beazer	870605	RTZ Corp	900628
Portugal:		BET	870806	Saatchi & Saatchi	871208
Banco Comercial	920612	Cable & Wireless	890927	Smithkline Beecham	890727
		Cadbury Schwepp	840911	Tiphook	911001
Spain:		Carlton Commun.	870130	Tomkins	881107
Banco Bilbao Vizca	881214	CRH	890710	United Newspapers	870828
Banco Central	830720	Danka Business	921217	Waterford Wedgwood	870128
Banco De Santader	870730	ECC Group	920430	Wellcome	920727
Empresa Electridad	880601	ELAN Corp	910103	Willis Corroon	901009
Telefonica Espana	870612	Glaxo Holdings	870610	WPP Group	871229

Appendix B. Local Market Indexes

Australia	All-Ordinaries (275)	Norway	FT-Actuaries-Norway
Canada	TSE-Western Index	Portugal	Lisbon BPA
France	CAC Broad Index	Spain	Madrid Gesant Index
Hong Kong	Hang Seng Index	Sweden	J-P Index (40)
Italy	BCI-Milan 260 Index	United Kingdom	FT-Actuaries UK
Japan	Topix Index	United States	Standard & Poor 500
Netherlands	Morgan Stanley Capital International		

REFERENCES

Adler, Michael, and Bernard Dumas, 1983, International portfolio choice and corporation finance: A synthesis, *Journal of Finance* 38, 925–984.

Alexander, Gordon, Cheol Eun, and S. Janakiramanan, 1987, Asset pricing and dual listing on foreign capital markets: A note, *Journal of Finance* 42, 151–158.

Alexander, Gordon, Cheol Eun, and S. Janakiramanan, 1988, International listings and stock returns: Some empirical evidence, *Journal of Financial and Quantitative Analysis* 23, 135–151.

Amihud, Yakov, and Haim Mendelson, 1986, Asset pricing and the bid-ask spread, *Journal of Financial Economics* 17, 223–249.

Bailey, Warren, and Peter Chung, 1995, Exchange rate fluctuations, political risk and stock returns: Some evidence from an emerging market, *Journal of Financial and Quantitative Analysis* 30, 541–562.

Baker, Kent, and Sue Meeks, 1991, Research on exchange listings and delistings: A review and synthesis, *Financial Practice and Education* 1, 57–71.

Bank of New York, 1996, *Global Offerings of Depositary Receipts: A Transaction Guide* (Bank of New York American Depositary Receipt Division, New York, N.Y.).

Barclay, Michael, Robert Litzenberger, and Jerold Warner, 1990, Private information, trading volume and stock-return variances, *Review of Financial Studies* 3, 233–253.

Bekaert, Geert, and Campbell Harvey, 1995, Time varying world market integration, *Journal of Finance* 50, 403–444.

Biddle, Gary, and Shahrokh Saudagaran, 1992, Financial disclosure levels and foreign stock exchange listing decisions, *Journal of International Financial Management and Accounting* 4, 106–148.

Black, Fischer, 1974, International capital market equilibrium with investment barriers. *Journal of Financial Economics* 1, 337–352.

Booth, Laurence, and David Johnston, 1984, The ex-dividend day behavior of Canadian stock prices: Tax changes and clientele effects, *Journal of Finance* 39, 457–476.

Campbell, John, and Yasushi Hamao, 1992, Predictable stock returns in the United States and Japan, *Journal of Finance* 47, 43–69.

Chan, K. C., G. Andrew Karolyi, and René Stulz, 1992, Global financial markets and the risk premium on U.S. equity, *Journal of Financial Economics* 32, 137–167.

Christie, William, and Roger Huang, 1993, Dissimilar market structures and market liquidity: A transaction data study of exchange listing, *Journal of Financial Intermediation* 3, 300–326.

Citibank Securities Services, 1995, *An Information Guide to Depositary Receipts* (Citibank NA, New York, N.Y.).

Cochrane, James, James Shapiro, and Jean Tobin, 1996, Foreign equities and U.S. investors: Breaking down barriers separating supply and demand, *Stanford Journal of Law, Business and Finance* 241, 19–32.

Dharan, Bala, and David Ikenberry, 1995, The long-run negative drift of post-listing stock returns, *Journal of Finance* 50, 1547–1574.

Dumas, Bernard, and Bruno Solnik, 1995, The world price of foreign exchange risk, *Journal of Finance* 50, 445–479.

Errunza, Vihang, and Etienne Losq, 1985, International asset pricing under mild segmentation: Theory and test, *Journal of Finance* 40, 105–124.

Fanto, James, and Roberta Karmel, 1997, Report on the attitudes of foreign companies regarding a U.S. listing, *Stanford Journal of Law, Business and Finance* 3, 37–58.

Ferson, Wayne, and Rudi Schadt, 1996, Measuring fund strategy and performance in changing economic conditions, *Journal of Finance* 51, 425–461.

Foerster, Stephen, and G. Andrew Karolyi, 1993, International listings of stocks: The case of Canada and the U.S., *Journal of International Business Studies* 24, 763–784.

Frost, Carol, and William Kinney, 1996, Disclosure choices of foreign registrants in the United States, *Journal of Accounting Research* 34, 34–58.

Griffin, John, and G. Andrew Karolyi, 1998, Another look at the role of the industrial structure of markets for global diversification strategies, *Journal of Financial Economics* 50, 351–373.

Gultekin, N. Bulent, Mustafa Gultekin, and Alessandro Penati, 1989, Capital controls and international capital market segmentation: Evidence from Japanese and American stock markets, *Journal of Finance* 44, 849–869.

Heston, Steven, and Geert Rouwenhorst, 1994, Does industrial structure explain the benefits of international diversification? *Journal of Financial Economics* 36, 3–27.

Howe, John, and Katherine Kelm, 1987, The stock price impact of overseas listings, *Financial Management* 16, 51–56.

Howe, John, and Jeff Madura, 1990, The impact of international listings on risk: Implications for capital market integration, *Journal of Banking and Finance* 14, 1133–1142.

Ibbotson, Roger, 1975, Price performance of common stock new issues, *Journal of Financial Economics* 2, 235–272.

Jayaraman, Narayanan, Kuldeep Shastri and Kishore Tandon, 1993, The impact of international cross listings on risk and return: Evidence from American Depositary Receipts, *Journal of Banking and Finance* 17, 91–103.

Effects of Market Segmentation and Investor Recognition 1013

Jorion, Phillippe and Eduardo Schwartz, 1986, Integration versus segmentation in the Canadian stock market, *Journal of Finance* 41, 603–616.

Kadlec, Gregory and John McConnell, 1994, The effect of market segmentation and illiquidity on asset prices: Evidence from exchange listings, *Journal of Finance* 49, 611–636.

Karolyi, G. Andrew, 1998, *Why Do Companies List Shares Abroad? A Survey of the Evidence and its Managerial Implications* (New York University Salomon Bros. Center Monograph, Vol. 7, no. 1, New York, N.Y.).

Karolyi, G. Andrew, and René Stulz, 1996, Why do markets move together? An examination of US–Japan stock return comovements, *Journal of Finance* 51, 951–986.

Lau, Sheila, David Diltz, and Vincent Apilado, 1994, Valuation effects of international stock exchange listings, *Journal of Banking and Finance* 18, 743–755.

Loughran, Timothy, and Jay Ritter, 1995, The new issues puzzle, *Journal of Finance* 50, 23–51.

McConnell, John, Hank Dybevik, David Haushalter, and Edward Lee, 1996, A survey of evidence on domestic and international stock exchange listings with implications for markets and managers, *Pacific Basin Finance Journal* 4, 147–176.

Merton, Robert, 1987, Presidential address: A simple model of capital market equilibrium with incomplete information, *Journal of Finance* 42, 483–510.

Miller, Darius P., 1999, The market reaction to international cross-listing: Evidence from depository receipts, *Journal of Financial Economics* 51, 103–123.

Mittoo, Usha, 1992, Additional evidence on integration in the Canadian stock market, *Journal of Finance* 47, 2035–2054.

Moody Investment Service, *International Manuals*, various issues, 1975–1993.

Newey, Whitney, and Kenneth West, 1987, A simple positive definite heteroscedasticity and autocorrelation consistent covariance matrix, *Econometrica* 55, 703–708.

Prabhala, N. R., 1997, Conditional methods in event studies and an equilibrium justification for standard event-study procedures, *Review of Financial Studies* 10, 1–38.

Roll, Richard, 1992, Industrial structure and the comparative behavior of international stock market indices, *Journal of Finance* 47, 3–42.

Sanger, Gary, and John McConnell, 1986, Stock exchange listing, firm value and security market efficiency: The impact of the Nasdaq, *Journal of Financial and Quantitative Analysis* 21, 1–25.

Schipper, Katherine, and Rex Thompson, 1983, The impact of merger-related regulations on shareholders of acquiring firms, *Journal of Accounting Research* 22, 184–221.

Shanken, Jay, 1990, Intertemporal asset pricing: An empirical investigation, *Journal of Econometrics* 45, 341–360.

Solnik, Bruno, 1974, Equilibrium in international asset markets under uncertainty, *Journal of Economic Theory* 8, 500–524.

Standard and Poor Corporation, *Stock Reports*, various issues, 1976–1993.

Stapleton, Richard, and Marti Subrahmanyam, 1977, Market imperfections, capital market equilibrium and corporate finance, *Journal of Finance* 32, 307–319.

Stulz, René, 1981, On the effects of barriers to international asset pricing, *Journal of Finance* 25, 783–794.

Stulz, René, 1995, International portfolio choice and asset pricing: An integrative survey; in Robert Jarrow, Vojislav Maksimovic, and William Ziemba, eds.: *Finance, Handbooks in Operations Research and Management Science, Vol. 9* (Elsevier-North Holland, Amsterdam).

Switzer, Lorne, 1997, Shareholder wealth effects of international listings: New evidence for Canadian stocks listed on the NYSE, Amex and Nasdaq 1985–96, Unpublished working paper, Concordia University.

Varela Oscar, and Sang Bin Lee, 1993, International listings, the security market line and capital market integration: The case of U.S. listings on the London Stock Exchange, *Journal of Business Finance and Accounting* 20, 843–863.

B
Liberalization and Political Risk

[11]

ELSEVIER

Journal of International Money and Finance
20 (2001) 43–69

Journal of
International
Money
and Finance

www.elsevier.nl/locate/econbase

Privatization, political risk and stock market development in emerging economies

Enrico C. Perotti [a,*], Pieter van Oijen [b]

[a] *Department of Finance, University of Amsterdam, Roetersstraat 11, 1018 WB Amsterdam, The Netherlands and CEPR*
[b] *Department of Finance, University of Amsterdam, Roetersstraat 11, 1018 WB Amsterdam, The Netherlands and Tinbergen Institute*

Abstract

This paper investigates whether privatization in emerging economies has a significant indirect effect on local stock market development through the resolution of political risk. We argue that a sustained privatization program represents a major political test that gradually resolves uncertainty over political commitment to a market-oriented policy as well as to regulatory and private property rights. We present evidence suggesting that progress in privatization is indeed correlated with improvements in perceived political risk. Our analysis further shows that changes in political risk in general tend to have a strong effect on local stock market development and excess returns in emerging economies. We conclude that the resolution of political risk resulting from successful privatization has been an important source for the rapid growth of stock markets in emerging economies. © 2001 Elsevier Science Ltd. All rights reserved.

JEL classification: G18; F30

Keywords: Emerging economies; Privatization; Political risk; Stock markets

1. Introduction

The rapid evolution of capital markets in developing countries has emerged as a major event in recent financial history. Portfolio flows to emerging countries rose tenfold from 1989 to 1995 (IFC, 1997) and kept rising until the recent crises. Local

---

* Corresponding author. Tel.: +31-20-525-4256; fax: +31-20-525-5285.
  E-mail address: enrico@fee.uva.nl (E.C. Perotti).

44   *E.C. Perotti, P. van Oijen / Journal of International Money and Finance 20 (2001) 43–69*

stock markets also grew considerably in size. The aggregate market capitalization of the countries classified by the IFC as emerging markets rose from US$488 billion in 1988 to US$2225 billion in 1996. Trading on these stock markets rose in similar magnitude, growing from US$411 billion to US$1586 billion in that period (IFC, 1997).

These remarkable developments followed a crisis period when foreign debt and large government deficits had undermined confidence in these economies. A critical policy change in many of these countries has been the establishment of large privatiz-ation programs. The known benefits of privatization are a reduction in public debt, improved incentives and efficiency,[1] and better access to capital. Sales to the private sector led to an inflow of foreign capital and technological transfers (Sader, 1995) and increased integration of local firms in international trade patterns.

The earliest extensive privatization plans were launched in the early 1980s in Chile and the UK. These programs were deemed successful and were mimicked by many developing and industrialized countries. From 1980 to 1987, a total of 696 privatiz-ation transactions were recorded by Candoy-Sekse (1988), of which 456 took place in developing countries. The importance of sales in developing countries thereafter increased significantly. Privatization revenues climbed from US$2.6 billion in 1988 to US$25.4 billion in 1996, amounting to US$154.5 billion over the whole period (World Bank, 1997, 1998). The privatization database of the World Bank reports more than 3000 transactions in developing countries.

While the privatization process in developing countries has been studied exten-sively, little attention has been given to its impact on the development of the local equity markets. The coincidence of the emergence of local stock markets and the progress of privatization begs the question to what extent these developments are related.

As many countries carried out privatization sales through offerings on the local stock exchange, sales certainly led to increases in market capitalization.[2] However, this direct effect of privatization does not account for much of the growth in local stock markets. Total sale revenue of US$154.5 billion in 1988–1996 represents only a small fraction of the increase in market capitalization over that period. In addition, many privatization transactions were not carried out through public issues and some took place in countries not classified by the IFC as an emerging market. Thus, although privatization appears to be associated with stock market development, the recent magnitude of market development by far exceeds their direct impact: thus there must have been both a reduction in discount rates and/or new private issues.

---

[1] For an assessment of welfare gains from privatization see Galal et al. (1994). For evidence on efficiency gains see Claessens and Djankov (1997) and Boubakri and Cossets (1998).

[2] In Chile, by 1993 the three largest companies listed on the exchange were all privatized firms. With a market value of over US$10 billion, they represented almost 25% of the market's capitalization. TelMex is easily Mexico's major listed firm, representing 18% of the market's capitalization in 1993. In Argentina the shares of YPF, Telecom and Telefonica added up to about 50% of total market capitalization in 1994. Around 30% of Malaysia's market capitalization in 1992 was contributed by privatized stocks. (Euromoney, 1993–4).

E.C. Perotti, P. van Oijen / Journal of International Money and Finance 20 (2001) 43–69   45

We study here how privatization sales may produce significant indirect benefits for local market development. Listings of large privatized companies provide substantial impact on trading liquidity while at the same time increasing investment opportunities for local investors to increase their portfolio diversification; these effects have a positive impact on the risk-sharing function of the market and lead to market deepening. This should hold particularly for developing countries, where local investors are not well diversified as a result of capital controls (Levine, 1991).[3]

Pagano (1993b) argues that firms seeking listings create an externality for other firms because their shares increase the potential for diversification for all investors. As the original owners incur some flotation costs but do not receive all the benefits of diversification, there will be an undersupply of new listings. Privatization may resolve this "low-listing trap" by adding diversification possibilities, encouraging both investment and listings by private firms.[4] In addition, an increase in overall liquidity due to new privatization-related listings can have a self-reinforcing effect on the willingness to hold shares, removing the local market from a "low-liquidity trap".[5]

These gains in market deepening and broadening could of course be the result of new private listings as well; there is no specific role here of privatization. In this paper we argue that the process of privatization itself, whenever implemented rigorously and consistently, leads to a progressive resolution of regulatory and legal uncertainty, and thus to a resolution of uncertainty over future policy. In particular, successful privatization results in a strengthening of property rights and institutional reliability which broadens the appeal and confidence in equity investment. As such, its impact is particularly relevant for emerging stock markets, whose legal systems are less developed.

Our argument is that prior to a sale, a government is uniquely motivated to establish a solid regulatory framework and to reduce ambiguity concerning private rights. Whenever the government uses the stock market to sell state-owned enterprises, the government also has incentives to facilitate stock market transactions. This may reverse a policy of discouraging private capital issues in order to fund the state's own funding needs. However, this process is neither instantaneous nor irreversible: after the sale there is some potential risk of a policy reversal (Perotti, 1995), particularly as many countries privatize at a time of difficult economic conditions and privatization hits entrenched political constituencies. Only as the commitment to the

---

[3] These local investors tend be less diversified because of capital controls. New listings due to privatization sales reduce the non-systematic risk of a local equity portfolio, and increase the willingness to invest in stocks, leading to higher valuation and trading.

[4] An objection to this view is that improving access by domestic investors to foreign financial markets would have an even stronger diversification effect and may thus lead to a similar acceleration in local listings.

[5] Pagano (1989) offers a theoretical interpretation of the externality effect of liquidity which is parallel in spirit to the diversification argument. In his model, participation by each trader reduces the volatility and increases the liquidity of the market for all other potential trades, and thereby induces more entry. This in turn reduces volatility and enhances liquidity, generating the potential for multiple, Pareto-ranked equilibria.

46   E.C. Perotti, P. van Oijen / Journal of International Money and Finance 20 (2001) 43–69

announced policy is sustained over time does a progressive resolution of legal and political uncertainty take place.[6] Equity investment, the residual bearer of such risks, thus becomes gradually more attractive as political risk is resolved over time. Unlike indirect benefits, the resolution of policy uncertainty is specific to privatization sales, and may occur even when privatization does not take place predominantly through public share offerings.

Our argument has two testable implications. First, the recent wave of privatization sales in developing countries should have altered the perceived political risks of these countries considerably, especially if governments have successfully implemented the announced privatization plans. Second, related shifts in political risk would have affected the attractiveness of equity investments and lead to stock market development.

In this paper we investigate these two implications in order to assess to what extent privatization contributes to the strengthening of local stock markets through the resolution of political risk. We first concentrate on how political risk has changed over the course of privatization in 22 emerging economies. We focus here on countries that have privatized extensively over a number of years after 1987, and use several quantitative indicators that proxy for our notion of political risk. We then assess the importance of political risk for stock market development in emerging economies by relating changes in stock market development proxies, such as market capitalization, traded value and excess returns, to changes in political risk.

We find that many emerging countries have gradually reduced their political risks during their period of sustained privatization. When privatization starts, credibility often is declining. Generally, it improves thereafter. This suggests that a sustained privatization policy represents a major political test which gradually resolves uncertainty over the political commitment to a market-oriented policy.

The second part of our analysis reveals that such changes in political risk are strongly associated 'with growth in stock market capitalization, traded value and excess returns. The economic impact of changes in political risk on stock market development appears large. These results suggest that the resolution of political risk through privatization has been an important factor in the recent emergence of the stock markets of developing countries.

The relevance of political risk for privatization that we document is consistent with results reported by Jones et al. (1998). They show that share allocation and pricing in initial public offerings (IPOs) from privatizations are sensitive to political considerations. Our result that political risk resolves gradually is also consistent with the puzzling findings that privatization IPOs appear to outperform matched control groups (Megginson et al., 1998). Perotti and Huibers (1998) attribute this result to the greater sensitivity of these stocks to political risk. They confirm that this effect vanishes after the IPO, as political risk gradually declines.

Our analysis on the influence of political risk on stock market development is also related to recent research on the link between the legal institutional framework and

---

[6] For a dynamic model of political risk resolution, see Cherian and Perotti (2000).

E.C. Perotti, P. van Oijen / Journal of International Money and Finance 20 (2001) 43–69   47

corporate finance. LaPorta et al. (1997, 1998) find that countries with a lower quality of legal rules and law enforcement have smaller and narrower capital markets and that the listed firms on their stock markets are characterized by more concentrated ownership. Demirgüç-Kunt and Maksimovic (1998) show that firms in countries with high ratings for the effectiveness of their legal systems are able to grow faster by relying more on external finance. Our analysis contributes to this literature by looking at the relation between stock market development and political risk, a measure of the quality of the institutional framework that supports the viability of external finance.

The results in this paper are also important from the perspective of economic growth. Levine and Zervos (1998) find that stock market variables such as market capitalization over GDP, traded value over GDP, and various measures of asset mis-pricing help to predict subsequent economic growth. There is a growing literature that further supports such linkages.[7] This suggests that countries have much to gain from privatization.

Our results also have implications for the analysis of market segmentation, of which political risk is viewed as one of the main causes. Emerging capital markets are believed to have grown largely as a result of decreasing segmentation. But this raises the question of why these markets have become progressively more integrated in the first place. Bekaert (1995) provides evidence that higher levels of political risk are related to higher degrees of market segmentation. Erb et al. (1996a) show that expected returns are related to the magnitude of political risk. They find that in both developing and developed countries, the lower the level of political risk, the lower are required stock returns.[8] Taken together with our results, it seems that political risk is a priced factor for which investors are rewarded and that it strongly affects the local cost of equity, which may have implications for growth.

The outline of the paper is as follows. In Section 2 we discuss the theoretical basis for the links between privatization, political risk and stock market development. In Section 3 we introduce our methodology and the political risk indicators that we use throughout the paper. Section 4 presents suggestive evidence that successful privatization gradually reduces political risk. Section 5 addresses the empirical relation between political risk and stock market development in emerging economies. We offer some concluding remarks at the end.

2. Privatization, political risk and stock market development

Is there something special about privatization sales? Do they provide some indirect benefits for stock market development, regardless of whether or not the privatized

---

[7] See Pagano (1993a,b) and Levine (1997) for an overview of the literature.

[8] In addition, Erb et al. (1996b) and Diamonte et al. (1996) find that changes in political risks are related contemporaneously to stock returns, using several quantitative indicators that proxy for the notion of political risk as outlined above. De Santis and Imrohoroglu (1997) report that emerging financial markets exhibit a higher conditional probability of large price changes than developed stock markets. There may be a role for political risk in explaining this difference in magnitude, as policy changes tend to have a large systemic effect.

48   *E.C. Perotti, P. van Oijen / Journal of International Money and Finance 20 (2001) 43–69*

shares are floated on the stock exchange? We will argue here that the *successful* transfer of important enterprises from state to private control has strong implications for the general perception of equity investment in emerging economies.

Privatization is an ideal test for political commitment to market-oriented reforms, as it severely tests the determination of policymakers to resist the political backlash after the sale is completed (Perotti, 1995). It involves a retreat of political forces from the governance of economic activity. As a consequence, politicians used to discretionary control over firms' activities see their capacity to reallocate resources sharply curtailed. In this shift of control rights to private owners lies an important cause of improved performance of firms under private ownership.[9] Although privatization in itself may help to strengthen the political forces in favor of market-oriented reforms (Bell, 1995; Biais and Perotti, 1999; Schmidt, 1997), after a sale no sovereign government can be fully restrained from altering policy. Therefore, only a sustained and consistent privatization policy establishes investors' confidence.[10]

In general, a successful privatization program requires institutional changes that contribute significantly to the strengthening of the legal framework underlying equity investment. However, private control and policy reforms must be maintained against any political backlash. As a consequence, market deepening will occur only as confidence builds up over time as a result of the actual progress of privatization and not upon its announcement. Thus our conjecture is that only the *actual implementation* of the privatization program contributes to the build up of confidence in a more reliable economic environment, leading to investment and trading. This may explain why privatization may be contemporaneous or even precede successful stock market development. Alternative benefits of privatization, such as improved risk sharing and increased liquidity of the market, would supply early anticipatory effects on market indicators.

There is a tradition of political risk even in developed economies. In the case of the Nippon Telegraph and Telephone sale, the firm was sold as a monopoly but was subsequently broken up, with a large fall in value (see Jones et al., 1998). Grandy (1989) offers some historical examples for the USA.

The political temptation to reverse policy after privatization is steep because areas traditionally under public ownership (utilities and infrastructure) were historical monopolies with major fixed sunk investments, which produce a long-term steady cash flow of revenues. Thus the profits represent considerable rents or quasi rents, which may arouse strong political opposition from, say, users.[11] Private investment in such

---

[9] The constitutional guarantee of property rights makes them residual with respect to contractual and legal obligations; thus, legislation may chip away at the owner's entitlement, but it can never fully expropriate them (Perotti, 1995).

[10] Demirgüç-Kunt and Levine (1994) maintain that whether public enterprise reform turns out to be a success or a failure depends more on the political commitment to change than on the initial state of the financial system.

[11] Such rents are also easily appropriable by other stakeholders, such as workers or domestic suppliers. In Brazil and Mexico salaries in the oil industry are several times as high as for the average manufacturing job.

E.C. Perotti, P. van Oijen / Journal of International Money and Finance 20 (2001) 43–69 49

industry has always been reluctant because of this heightened risk of de facto expropriation by ex post policy shifts.

Since investors understand the government's incentives to reallocate value or maintain entrenched rents, governments need to strengthen institutional rules protecting equity investment and prove over time that they intend to continue doing so. Thus the privatization process can only progressively establish credibility of announced reform policy, and thus leads only gradually to financial development.

The confidence-building hypothesis has been advanced by Perotti (1995), who shows that privatization sales need to be gradual (while securing immediate transfer of control) so that confidence on a stable policy towards privatized companies can be firmly established. Underpricing may also serve as a complementary signal of commitment. Perotti and Guney (1993) document that sale programs in twelve countries are initially gradual, even when retained stakes are explicitly targeted to be sold over a few years. Proceeds from privatization increase over time, suggesting gradual selling calibrated to build investors confidence. As policy credibility increases, larger initial sales become more common. They also document extensive underpricing, which on average is greater in privatization sales than in IPOs of private firms, and is especially larger for firms with substantial taxable rents, such as utilities, which are exposed to greater policy risk. Traditional asymmetric information explanations for underpricing such as those by Rock (1986) and Grinblatt and Hwang (1989) do not seem appropriate here, since these firms tend to be large and well known relative to private IPOs. Dewenter and Malatesta (1997) confirm that underpricing, while not always higher for privatization sales, is greater for firms subject to greater political risk.

Another source of evidence on the impact of privatization on the perception of political risk is provided by Sader (1993), who adds privatization sales to a specification proposed by Edwards (1990). His cross-section results over 21 countries indicate that privatization sales are a significant determinant of foreign direct investment. Moreover, the result is driven by the size of the program rather than the concentration of sales in specific industries, such as communications, which may be particularly attractive for foreigners.[12] Openness to foreign investment in privatization is also a good predictor of FDI.

A successful privatization program may also lead to a resolution of contractual and legal uncertainty relevant to capital markets, such as protection of minority shareholders.[13] While there may be resistance by established interests as well as listed firms to a significant improvement in such rules, the necessity for the government

---

[12] However, the size of privatization sales in utilities, other traditionally public infrastructures, financial institutions and mining interests turns out to be correlated with foreign interest. Sader's explanation, with which we concur, is that these are traditionally industries in which populist and nationalist politicians allowed limited possibilities for foreign and private investment. According to Sader (1993), the decision by the government to privatize in these areas is perceived by investors as a signal of a reduction in government intervention and restrictive regulations, which in turn improves the investment climate.

[13] Modigliani and Perotti (2000) show that a strong institutional framework of "rules of the game" is necessary to protect minority investors and thus to promote the development of security markets.

50   *E.C. Perotti, P. van Oijen / Journal of International Money and Finance 20 (2001) 43–69*

to attract foreign and domestic investors requires a reliable security commission, the promotion of greater accounting standards and more transparent disclosure rules, the availability of procedures to contest managerial decisions and appointment, and a reduction in the legal and fiscal rules which typically favor public sector borrowing. Additional steps often involve restrictions on dividend repatriation, foreign ownership and competitive entry.

Finally, it can be argued that privatization does create a firmer legal background for investors. Following a sale, policy reversals (re-regulation, taxation, entry deregulation, etc.) are based on arm's-length relations, thus subject to much greater public scrutiny. Consequently, privatization allows highlighted public debate and increased reliance on legal, as opposed to administrative, recourse. Heightened visibility of policy choices also contributes to reduced political risk.

In the next sections we explore empirically whether the progress of privatization is associated with a reduction in political risk and whether indeed political risk is important for stock market development. We expect political risk resolution to be particularly relevant for developing countries and we therefore focus on emerging markets. This also allows us to understand to what extend the resolution in political that resulted from sustained privatization contributed to the recent boom in emerging stock markets. Section 3 describes our methodology and introduces the political risk indicators that we use. We then analyze the impact of privatization of political risk (Section 4) and assess the importance of political risk for stock market development in emerging countries (Section 5).

3. Sample construction and methodology

We focus on developing countries with some privatization experience that are characterized by a minimally developed stock market. To be inclusive, we look at all the countries classified by the IFC as emerging markets. From this group of countries, we selected all markets for which there are data available in the *Emerging Stock Markets Factbook* from at least 1988 onwards. This leads to a sample of 31 countries.

In order to assess how sustained privatization influenced the development of these stock markets through a resolution of political risk, we chose to proceed in two steps. The first is to establish how political risk is related to privatization over the medium term. We require a sufficient history of privatization sales to ensure that our sample includes countries where privatization was maintained for at least some time. From the sample of 31 emerging economies, we select all those countries that have been engaged in substantial privatization sales for at least four years during 1988–1995. Using this criterion, there are 22 countries that can be classified as having a significant privatization policy.[14]

---

[14] There are only a few countries for which inclusion in either of the samples is ambiguous. We neglected Costa Rica and Uruguay for our initial sample of emerging stock markets because of incomplete data for the market capitalization or traded value on the stock market. For Israel, the World Bank reports 15 privatization transactions spread out over 1988 to 1995. We were unable to obtain information about

Our privatization data are obtained from the privatization database maintained by the World Bank, which records privatization transactions that took place since 1988. For all countries which privatized in 1988 or 1989 we rely on other sources to assign the beginning of the privatization program.[15] Most countries in our sample continue to privatize until 1995. The list of countries and years of start of the privatization program are in Appendix A.

Ideally we would test for a relation between privatization and political risk by classifying countries as a successful or an unsuccessful privatizer, but this would require a subjective judgement on the quality of each country's privatization policy. We instead use changes in perceived political risk as a summary statistics. While on average the programs in the sample were deemed successful, the sample does include countries for which the privatization process was stopped or slowed down due to political backlash.[16]

To assess how these privatization efforts have affected perceived political risk, we collect different quantitative measures of political risk. (See later for a discussion of these indicators.) For each country, we then determine how political risk has developed since the start of privatization, and contrast it with the development in the four years before privatization started. We also compare the political risk developments for our sample of privatizing countries with those in countries that did not privatize during 1988–1995.

Our second step is to test to what extent changes in political risk contribute to stock market development. For this part of the analysis we relate the stock market development in all of the 31 countries in our initial sample to changes in their perceived political risks. We use growth in market capitalization, traded value and number of listed firms as direct measures of stock market development as well as MSCI-world index adjusted returns.

We use five different quantitative indicators for political risk. All these ratings are indicators for country risk, of which political risk is only one of the sources. We wish to stress that our notion of political risk is much broader than the "political stability" concept that often underlies the use of the term "political risk" in standard textbooks. However, not all of the indicators we will use conform closely to our specific notion of political risk.

The first indicator is the so-called Country Credit Rating (CCR) constructed by the *Institutional Investor*. This indicator is based on information provided by leading

---

an explicit privatization policy in Israel or about privatization revenues for the years before 1988. Given the low number of transactions and the lack of data we excluded Israel as a privatizing country, but include it in our initial sample of emerging stock markets.

[15] The countries for which we relied on sources other than the World Bank privatization database are Chile, Jamaica, Malaysia and Mexico. The year of the start of privatization and the sales data for these countries are obtained from Hachette and Lüders (1993), Sader (1993), Galal et al. (1994) and Rodriguez (1992). For Brazil, we deviate from the procedure given in the text above to determine the start of privatization. In 1988, there was one large privatization transaction, followed by zero sales in 1989 and 1990. Sader (1993) reports that the sale in 1988 was incidental and that in 1990 a privatization plan was announced, with actual sales starting in 1991. We use this last year as the start of privatization sales.

[16] Turkey and Venezuela are prime examples during this period.

52   *E.C. Perotti, P. van Oijen / Journal of International Money and Finance 20 (2001) 43–69*

international banks and is constructed and published by the *Institutional Investor*. Bankers are surveyed to grade each country (developed as well as developing) on a scale of zero to 100, where the score of 100 represents the least chance of default. The survey is held every 6 months, includes 75–100 banks reporting their country ratings and was initiated in 1979. The survey results are published in March and September. The March survey is based on interviews gathered in November and December, and therefore reflects the opinion prevailing around the end of the year preceding the actual publication of the risk rating.[17]

To shed more light on the factors that bankers take into account in their rating, the *Institutional Investor* provides bankers with a list of nine factors. The bankers are asked to rank them in order of importance for their credit ratings. For the credit ratings of 1994, debt service, political outlook and economic outlook were considered as the three most important factors in rating emerging economies.[18] Bankers seem to care a lot about policy uncertainty in their ratings. Quotes in the *Institutional Investor* citing the motivations of the bankers for grading a country suggest that they are concerned about a government's attitude and ability to sustain a good economic policy.[19]

The forward-looking nature of the ratings, the large number of bankers interviewed and the explicit considerations for government policies make the CCR a very useful indicator.

The other three indicators were obtained from the commercial agency International Country Risk Guide (ICRG). This series was first constructed for 1984. ICRG classifies country risk into three different categories: political risk, financial risk and economic risk. Each indicator consists of different components of country risk, for which every country receives a score on a scale of 1 to 100. These different components are then weighted to construct the country's rating for each category. The components of each of these indicators and the weight of each component for the indicator are given in Table B1 of Appendix B.

The political risk indicator of ICRG, which is based on subjective analysis by its analysts, contains the components "Economic expectations vs. reality", "Economic planning failures", "Political leadership" and "Law and order tradition". These conform directly to our notion of political risk. However, most of the other components are more related to political turmoil, for which we expect no strong direct association with privatization.

The financial risk indicator is based on quantitative as well as qualitative information. It has three components that make this indicator worth considering. These

---

[17] An editor at the *Institutional Investor* confirmed that the March ratings are generally received during November and December.

[18] See Erb et al. (1996b) for the complete rankings.

[19] For example, "I think Jamaica's rise (in its rating) reflects not only good economic policies but also reduced scepticism about the Prime Ministers intentions, particularly in view of the populist policies during his previous stint as prime minister." (*Institutional Investor*, September 1990, p. 153) or "...I've got a low regard for their ability to follow any economic policy." (*Institutional Investor*, March 1989, p. 69).

E.C. Perotti, P. van Oijen / Journal of International Money and Finance 20 (2001) 43–69 53

are "Repudiation of contracts by the government", "Expropriation of private investments" and, somewhat less interesting for our purposes, "Losses from exchange controls". However, this indicator is partially based on historical information and may not be very forward looking. We consider this indicator a less attractive indicator for the type of political risk we wish to measure than the CCR and the ICRG political risk indicator.

The components of the economic risk indicator do not appear to be related to our notion of political risk as it seems to measure the financial capacity of the country. We include it in our analysis to compare its effect with the country credit rating.

4. Privatization and political risk in emerging economies

In this section we analyze whether political risk in emerging economies has improved as a direct consequence of the privatization programs. Within our sample of 22 emerging economies that we classified as having a privatization policy, we compare the development of our political risk indicators in the four years before privatization and during privatization. To further assess whether the development of political risk is indeed endogenous to the privatization process, we compare the changes in political risk indicators of the emerging countries we classified as privatizers with the simultaneous changes in developing countries that did not engage in privatization. As a final check, we analyze whether, within our sample of 31 emerging economies, privatization sales and political risk are directly related.

We first contrast the development in political risk before and during privatization. For each country that we classified as a privatizer we calculate the semi-annual (in case of the CCR) or monthly (in case of the ICRG) growth rates in the political risk. Note that a positive growth rate stands for a decrease in political risk. To fully exploit our data, we pool these percentage changes in one data set. Table 1 shows the average change in each of the indicators during the four years before privatization and for the period from the year in which privatization took off up to the end of the sample, which is 1995.

The CCR on average decreased in value in the four years before privatization, suggesting that deteriorating credibility may induce the establishment of a sale program. Political risk performance improves strongly during privatization: the implied yearly improvement is around 3.6%. We can reject that these two samples have a similar rate of improvement at the 1% confidence level. The ICRG political risk indicator exhibits a similar pattern; its average improvement during privatization, however, is at about equal to that of the CCR. We strongly reject the notion of equal rate of improvement in political risk as well. The ICRG financial and economic risk indicators behave differently. These ratings on average improved both before and during privatization, and their means are quite similar across periods. Taken together, these findings suggest that these two indicators are of a quite different nature than the CCR and the ICRG political risk indicator. The discrepancy in the behavior of

54   *E.C. Perotti, P. van Oijen / Journal of International Money and Finance 20 (2001) 43–69*

Table 1
Percentage improvement in political risk before and during privatization[a]

		Mean change (%)	Standard deviation	Minimum	Maximum	Number of observations
CCR (semi-annual)	Before privatization	***−1.21	5.85	−32.66	14.44	186
	During privatization	***1.80	5.45	−24.53	29.27	304
	t-value for equality of means:	***5.76				
ICRGPOL (monthly)	Before privatization	−0.04	1.90	−11.76	11.63	958
	During privatization	***0.31	2.55	−21.28	26.47	1824
	t-value for equality of means:	***3.74				
ICRGFIN (monthly)	Before privatization	***0.39	3.22	−18.75	20.00	958
	During privatization	***0.42	3.26	−13.79	80.95	1824
	t-value for equality of means:	0.24				
ICRGECO (monthly)	Before privatization	0.14	4.41	−29.17	37.21	958
	During privatization	***0.27	3.31	−23.53	27.66	1824
	t-value for equality of means:	0.90				

***Significant at the 1% level.

[a] CCR refers to the percentage improvements in the semi-annual *Institutional Investor* Country Credit Risk Rating. ICRGPOL, ICRGFIN and ICRGECO refer to percentage improvements in the monthly political, financial and economic risk indicators as constructed by the International Country Risk Guide agency. A description of these indicators is given in the text. The sample consists of 22 emerging economies that engaged in substantial privatization after 1987 (see Appendix A). The political risk improvements are pooled into one data set. "Before privatization" refers to the four years before the first privatization sales took place in a country. "During privatization" represents the years from the start of privatization up to 1995.

the CCR and the ICRG economic risk indicator supports our earlier contention that the CCR does not simply capture macro-economic developments.[20]

The development of the CCRs and the ICRG political risk indicator seem to confirm our hypothesis of a resolution of political risk through privatization. This raises the issue of the timing of the resolution of political risk. During what stage of privatization is the improvement in political risk realized? Note that if those providing the ratings believed that privatization will certainly be sustained, we would observe an

---

[20] We also performed non-parametric Wilcoxon rank tests and Mann–Whitney tests for these medians. These provided similar results.

E.C. Perotti, P. van Oijen / Journal of International Money and Finance 20 (2001) 43–69   55

immediate and stable gain in political credibility from the announcement of a privatization program.

We searched for such an announcement effect by looking at the political risk developments in the two years before actual sales started and compared it with their changes in the two years before. The development in political risk is almost identical in both periods; there seems to be no response in political risk trends at the announcement of privatization. This suggests that those providing the ratings have initially been very sceptical about government intentions and that they revised their beliefs as actual privatization progressed.

We then looked at the timing of the resolution during the period of actual privatization sales. If the uncertainty about a policy reversal would be fully resolved once the first sales went through, we expect to find that most of the improvement in political risk will be realized in the very early stages of privatization. The data show that this is not the case. The CCR and ICRG political risk indicators do improve significantly during the later stages of privatization, suggesting that political risk was only gradually resolved over the sale process.

Of course, the observed pattern in political risk may be due to factors other than privatization. For example, there may have been a change in perceived political risk over the last fifteen years shared by all non-OECD countries, independently of whether or not these countries engaged in substantial privatization.[21] To verify this, we constructed a benchmark for the development of political risk in countries that did not engage in privatization. We selected all countries that are classified as developing countries by the Global Development Finance CDROM of the World Bank, and removed all countries for which the privatization database reported some transactions. This resulted in a sample of 24 countries. Subsequently, we constructed a benchmark for each political risk indicator, equally weighting the countries. The semi-annual (in the case of CCR ratings) or monthly (in the case of ICRG ratings) growth rates of the ratings of each of the privatizing countries are then matched with those of the benchmark. This allows us to construct a series for the difference in political risk performance.

Table 2 reports the matched performance of the benchmark and the results of a *t*-test on the difference in the political risk development. Because the findings in Table 1 suggest no relation between privatization and the ICRG financial and economic risk indicators, we only report the results for the CCR and the ICRG political risk indicator.

Note first the results for the CCR indicator. The privatizing countries clearly outperform the benchmark during privatization, while their performance is quite similar before privatization. This strongly suggests that the CCR improvement that we

---

[21] This possibility is limited by the imperfect time overlap of the various privatization periods. For example, the year 1986 is classified as a year of privatization for Chile, Jamaica, Malaysia and Mexico while for the other countries, this year falls outside the sample or is classified as a year before privatization sales started. Nevertheless, 1992, 1993, 1994 and 1995 are all classified as years in which privatization was underway for all countries.

56   E.C. Perotti, P. van Oijen / Journal of International Money and Finance 20 (2001) 43–69

Table 2
Difference-tests between political risk developments of privatizing and non-privatizing countries before and during privatization[a]

		Mean change		t-value for the difference (1)−(2)	Number of observations
		Privatizers (%) (1)	Non-privatizers (%) (2)		
CCR (semi-annual)	Before privatization	−1.21	−1.65	1.08	186
	During privatization	1.80	0.69	***3.39	304
ICRGPOL (monthly)	Before privatization	−0.04	−0.01	−0.47	958
	During privatization	0.31	0.26	0.74	1824

***Significant at the 1% level.

[a] CCR refers to the percentage improvements in the semi-annual *Institutional Investor* Country Credit Risk Rating. ICRGPOL refers to percentage improvements in the monthly political risk indicator as constructed by the International Country Risk Guide agency. A description of these indicators is given in the text. The sample of privatizing countries consists of 22 emerging economies that engaged in substantial privatization after 1987 (see Appendix A). "Before privatization" refers to the four years before the first privatization sales took place in a country. "During privatization" represents the years from the start of privatization up to 1995. The benchmark "Non-privatizers" is determined by constructing an index for the average improvement in the ratings in all the developing countries that did not privatize during 1988–1995. Each semi-annual or monthly observation for the development of the rating of a privatizing country is paired with the improvement of the benchmark over that same period. A t-test is then performed to test the hypothesis that the series of the differences between the two are equal to zero.

reported in Table 1 is indeed endogenous to the privatization process. The ICRG political risk indicator outperforms the benchmark only slightly during privatization.

We also performed the non-parametric Wilcoxon signed rank test on the median of the difference series. This test may be especially useful for the ICRG political risk indicator because these ratings are updated quite infrequently while at the same time the magnitude of the revisions in the ratings can be quite dramatic.[22] Both of these characteristics undermine the validity of a t-test. The Wilcoxon test shows that the median difference in ICRG political risk performance during privatization is significant at the 5% level. These results offer some strong evidence that the evolution of the CCR risk indicator diverges between privatizing and non-privatizing countries during privatization. For the ICRG political risk indicator, the evidence is somewhat weaker.

---

[22] The ICRG political risk indicator responds dramatically to reductions in political instability. For example, Liberia's and Ethiopia's ICRG political risk rating rose by more than 200% between 1993 and 1995. In comparison, the improvement in the CCR ratings was below 50%.

It may be that political risk has recently improved in all emerging countries vis-à-vis other developing countries, irrespective of the privatization policies. The superior political risk performance of the privatizing emerging economies that we just documented would then fail to hold within our full sample of emerging countries.

To address this possibility, we decided to take a somewhat richer test. We first calculate the yearly percentage change in political risk in each emerging country. To capture the political risk resolution associated with privatization, we pool all yearly observations in one data set and regress the change in political risk on two different proxies for privatization. The first proxy we use is simply the revenue from privatization sales over GNP. The second one is a dummy that equals one if the country is classified as a privatizing country and the year of the observation is a year in which privatization sales took place. We also control for the main macro-economic developments by including the growth in GNP per capita, the growth in exports per capita and the real depreciation in the regressions. The data are obtained from the International Financial Statistics of the IMF and the World Bank Global Development Finance database.

We wish to stress that a contemporaneous linear relation between privatization sales (scaled by GNP) and changes in political risk is not entirely consistent with the hypothesis we have laid out in Section 2. Our argument is that privatization has a gradual and contingent impact, as investors watch actual deeds rather than policy statements. Privatization revenues are not an ideal proxy for the fulfilment of announced policy. Reform policies associated with privatization may be reversed over time and political risk should be more sensitive to the stock of privatized firms than to the current flow. Therefore, the resolution of risk may be fastest when privatization approaches its latest stage (even though sales may be slowing down) as investor confidence keeps climbing in view of the maintained policy vis-à-vis previously privatized firms. Because of these considerations, we also perform regressions with a dummy variable to proxy for privatization stages.

Table 3 shows the results of these regressions. The CCR rating is related positively to both measures of privatization and significant at the 1% level. The privatization dummy indicates that during privatization, the CCR rating improves by almost 3% every year, vis-à-vis the ratings of the other emerging economies. The ICRG political risk indicator has a weaker relation to privatization. The coefficient of the privatization dummy is close to significant at the 10% level and quite large in size. Note also that the ICRG political risk indicator is not very correlated with contemporaneous macro-economic developments, as opposed to the CCR ratings.

We conclude that there is apparently some evolution in the perception of political risk in countries engaging in sustained privatization programs relative to other developing countries. This is especially so when political risk is measured by the CCR. Our results support the view that privatization leads to a resolution of political uncertainty. At the same time, it seems that only actual implementation of privatization changes the perception of investors towards political risk.

In the next section we analyze how this reduction in political risk favors the development of equity investment in emerging countries.

Table 3
Privatization and political risk in emerging economies[a]

	Dependent variable: political risk			
	Country credit rating		ICRG political risk	
Constant	−0.00	−0.01	***0.02	**0.02
	(−0.44)	(−1.02)	(3.22)	(2.08)
Growth in GNP per capita	***0.18	***0.19	0.01	0.01
	(4.06)	(4.42)	(0.24)	(0.29)
Growth in exports per capita	0.05	0.04	0.05	0.04
	(1.35)	(1.14)	(1.30)	(1.14)
Real depreciation	0.02	0.02	0.02	0.02
	(0.65)	(0.81)	(1.02)	(1.08)
Privatization sales/GNP	***1.89		0.47	
	(3.45)		(1.24)	
Privatization dummy		***0.029		0.017
		(3.07)		(1.51)
Adjusted R-sq.	0.17	0.15	−0.00	0.00
N	306	306	298	298

***Significantly different from zero at the 1% level.
**Significantly different from zero at the 5% level.
[a] The sample consists of all countries classified as an emerging stock market by the IFC and for which the Emerging Stock Markets Factbook provides data on stock market capitalization and traded value on the stock market from 1988 on. This sample consists of 31 countries: the 22 countries we classified as privatizing (see Table A1 of Appendix A) and 9 additional countries. For the latter group of countries, we use data from 1988 to 1995. For the countries included in our sample of privatizing countries, we use data for the years as reported in Table A1 in Appendix A. The yearly data for the 31 countries are then pooled into one sample. The privatization sales dummy equals one if the country is classified as a privatizing country and the year of the observation is during the early or late stage of privatization (see Table A1 of Appendix A). t-values are calculated using White heteroskedasticity-consistent standard errors and are in parentheses.

5. Political risk and stock market development

This section addresses the empirical relation between stock market development and political risk in emerging economies. We use the IFC's emerging markets database to obtain these data for our initial sample of 31 countries. We study the following indicators of stock market development:

- yearly percentage growth in market capitalization over GNP
- yearly percentage growth in traded value over GNP
- yearly percentage growth in the turnover ratio which is defined as traded value over market capitalization
- yearly percentage growth in the number of listed firms

E.C. Perotti, P. van Oijen / Journal of International Money and Finance 20 (2001) 43–69   59

- the yearly average of monthly returns, where each monthly return is adjusted for the return of the Morgan Stanley Capital International-world index.[23]

Before we relate stock market development to changes in political risk, we first report how our measures of market development fare before and during privatization within our sample of 22 privatizing countries. Table 4 reports the summary statistics.[24]

The data indicate that the development of stock markets in the countries has been radical in all privatization periods. The average yearly growth in traded value over GNP exceeds 75% in both periods. The pattern confirms our earlier claim that the direct effect of privatization from public share issues can only account for a small fraction of the growth of these markets.

It is striking that our growth indicators for traded value, capitalization and the number of firms all peak before privatization. There may be several reasons for the incidence of the peak. The countries that are classified by the IFC as emerging markets are countries whose stock markets actually did emerge, so there may be a sample selection at the inclusion date. These markets often started growing from a very low initial level of market development; small absolute increases in capitalization or traded value then produce very high growth rates. Also, the announcement of privatization may induce higher market capitalization, traded value and new listings from the anticipation of risk sharing and liquidity benefits that are expected to result from

Table 4
Market development before and during privatization

		% Change	Standard deviation	Minimum	Maximum
Capitalization/GNP	Before privatization	47.11	116.87	−74.74	678.61
	During privatization	34.27	74.65	−66.01	402.83
Traded value/GNP	Before privatization	98.62	278.63	−72.28	1928.48
	During privatization	79.74	204.99	−76.89	2024.60
Traded value/capitalization	Before privatization	51.41	177.25	−78.64	1418.11
	During privatization	28.36	72.99	−77.62	322.53
Number of firms	Before privatization	9.71	31.32	−20.87	162.50
	During privatization	7.14	13.98	−18.82	120.00
MSCI-world index adjusted returns (monthly)	Before privatization	0.37	4.82	−12.43	10.02
	During privatization	0.72	4.19	−9.65	17.74

[23] We also used residuals from an estimated ICAPM model as a measure of stock market development. The results are similar to the results reported for the MSCI-world index adjusted returns reported here.
[24] For the traded value over GNP ratio, we removed the 1989 observations for Indonesia. In that year, the growth rate of the traded value over GNP equalled 11700%, which is more than five times as large as the second largest growth rate in the sample.

future sales. Perhaps importantly, some governments list the shares of state-owned enterprises on the stock exchange before actually selling them. This effect is not too pronounced, however, as it can at most explain the peak for the growth capitalization and the growth in the number of firms; early listings do not increase traded value and decrease the growth in traded value over capitalization.

We now turn to the final part of our analysis. Are changes in political risk important for stock market development in emerging economies? In order to assess this, we use our full sample of 31 emerging stock markets and link stock market development in these countries to changes in political risk. For our non-privatizing countries we use data for the years 1988–1995. For the countries that we classified earlier as privatizers, we use data for the years presented in Table A1 of Appendix A. We pool the yearly observations into one data set, which produces a sample of about 300 observations.[25] We then regress our different measures of stock market development in the improvements on political risk, using separate regression for each political risk indicator.

We use three control variables to capture general economic developments: real depreciation vis-à-vis the US dollar, growth of exports per capita and GNP growth per capita. We also include yearly privatization sales scaled by GNP; this term should capture any direct effect of privatization sales as well as contemporaneous risk sharing and liquidity benefits.

We perform regressions both with and without country dummies. Only in the regressions for the growth in the number of firms does the inclusion of country dummies seem useful. The adjusted R-squared increases by 10 percentage points, reflecting the erratic pattern of the number of listed firms across the different countries. Elsewhere the inclusion worsens the fit of the regression, measured by the adjusted R-squared. Table 5 reports the results of all the regressions, where we include country dummies only in the regression for the growth in number of firms.

Political risk proves to be an important factor for most measures of stock market development. The CCR is significant at the 1% level for the growth in capitalization over GNP and MSCI-world index adjusted returns. For the traded value over GNP regression, it is significant at the 5% level and it is borderline significant at the 5% level for the growth in number of firms regression. The ICRG political risk indicator is strongly related to growth in capitalization and traded value, as well as to returns. It is not significant, however, in the regression for the turnover ratio and the growth in the number of firms. The ICRG financial risk indicator is never significant at the 5% level but is always positively related with stock market development, with significance at the 10% level in the traded value and in the traded value over capitalization regression. In contrast, the ICRG economic risk indicator, which largely reflects macroeconomic variables, displays no consistency in the sign of its coefficient and is not significant in any of our regressions. Note that the coefficient for the privatization sales over GNP term is insignificant in all regressions, and generally

---

[25] In the regression on excess returns, the size of our sample is reduced to around 190 because the EMDB does not provide return data for all years and for all countries.

Table 5
Stock market development and political risk[a]

Panel A	Dependent variable: growth in market capitalization over GNP			
Constant	***0.25	***0.24	***0.23	***0.26
	(5.64)	(5.18)	(5.03)	(5.53)
Growth in GNP per capita	−0.54	−0.21	−0.27	−0.25
	(−1.23)	(−0.46)	(−0.58)	(−0.52)
Growth in exports per capita	*0.68	*0.66	0.58	*0.66
	(1.86)	(1.77)	(1.60)	(1.80)
Real depreciation	*−0.56	*−0.54	−0.45	−0.50
	(−1.72)	(−1.65)	(−1.30)	(−1.56)
Privatization sales/GNP	−2.78	0.05	0.78	−0.10
	(−0.82)	(0.02)	(0.27)	(−0.03)
Improvement in:				
Country credit rating	***1.89			
	(3.36)			
ICRG political risk		**1.04		
		(2.59)		
ICRG financial risk			1.02	
			(1.42)	
ICRG economic risk				0.45
				(0.81)
Adjusted R-sq.	0.05	0.02	0.04	0.01
Prob. F-value	0.00	0.04	0.01	0.14
N	301	292	292	292

Panel B	Dependent variable: growth in traded value over GNP			
Constant	***0.53	***0.49	***0.48	***0.54
	(5.25)	(4.50)	(4.20)	(4.95)
Growth in GNP per capita	−0.00	0.63	0.59	0.55
	(−0.00)	(0.53)	(0.49)	(0.43)
Growth in exports per capita	*2.91	*2.97	*2.84	**2.94
	(1.96)	(1.93)	(1.92)	(2.02)
Real depreciation	−0.65	−0.59	−0.40	−0.53
	(−1.21)	(−1.07)	(−.72)	(−0.98)
Privatization sales/GNP	−10.33	−4.18	−3.19	−4.63
	(−0.92)	(−0.42)	(−0.33)	(−0.44)
Improvement in:				
Country credit rating	**3.73			
	(2.42)			
ICRG political risk		**1.65		
		(2.03)		
ICRG financial risk			*1.79	
			(1.82)	
ICRG economic risk				0.89
				(0.38)
Adjusted R-sq.	0.04	0.02	0.03	0.02
Prob. F-value	0.01	0.04	0.02	0.06
N	301	292	292	292

(continued on next page)

Table 5 (*continued*)

Panel C	Dependent variable: growth in traded value over market capitalization			
Constant	***0.28	***0.28	***0.26	***0.28
	(4.43)	(4.17)	(4.00)	(4.31)
Growth in GNP per capita	0.18	0.29	0.25	0.30
	(0.38)	(0.60)	(0.52)	(0.60)
Growth in exports per capita	0.49	0.49	0.43	0.51
	(0.99)	(0.95)	(0.85)	(0.97)
Real depreciation	0.13	0.13	0.17	0.13
	(0.74)	(0.69)	(0.93)	(0.70)
Privatization sales/GNP	−0.68	1.01	1.24	1.28
	(−0.15)	(0.22)	(0.27)	(0.29)
Improvement in:				
Country credit rating	0.96			
	(1.55)			
ICRG political risk		0.28		
		(0.72)		
ICRG financial risk			*0.61	
			(1.95)	
ICRG economic risk				−0.10
				(−0.16)
Adjusted R-sq.	−0.00	−0.00	−0.00	−0.00
Prob. F-value	0.43	0.77	0.49	0.80
N	299	290	290	290

Panel D	Dependent variable: growth in number of firms			
Constant	***−0.10	***−0.10	***−0.12	***−0.10
	(−3.49)	(−3.29)	(−3.04)	(−3.10)
Growth in GNP per capita	0.14	*0.17	*0.16	*0.18
	(1.46)	(1.72)	(1.66)	(1.79)
Growth in exports per capita	0.08	0.08	0.06	0.10
	(1.13)	(1.09)	(0.84)	(1.21)
Real depreciation	−0.04	−0.04	−0.02	−0.04
	(−0.88)	(−0.74)	(−0.35)	(−0.78)
Privatization sales/GNP	−0.04	0.12	0.34	0.36
	(−0.05)	(0.14)	(0.42)	(0.46)
Improvement in:				
Country credit rating	*0.19			
	(1.94)			
ICRG political risk		0.15		
		(1.27)		
ICRG financial risk			0.20	
			(1.56)	
ICRG economic risk				−0.07
				(−0.99)
Adjusted R-sq.	0.15	0.14	0.15	0.13
Prob. F-value	0.00	0.00	0.00	0.00
N	294	285	285	285

(continued on next page)

E.C. Perotti, P. van Oijen / Journal of International Money and Finance 20 (2001) 43–69   63

Table 5 (*continued*)

Panel E	Dependent variable: MSCI-world index adjusted returns			
Constant	−0.002	−0.003	−0.003	−0.002
	(−0.60)	(−0.88)	(−0.69)	(−0.41)
Growth in GNP per capita	−0.009	0.021	0.020	0.016
	(−0.36)	(0.88)	(0.79)	(0.63)
Growth in exports per capita	0.004	0.007	0.007	0.003
	(0.20)	(0.31)	(0.30)	(0.15)
Real depreciation	***−0.073	***−0.064	***−0.061	***−0.061
	(−5.95)	(−4.81)	(−4.61)	(−4.46)
Privatization sales/GNP	−0.32	0.005	0.085	−0.030
	(−1.13)	(0.02)	(0.39)	(−0.12)
Improvement in:				
Country credit rating	***0.160			
	(3.83)			
ICRG political risk		**0.068		
		(2.26)		
ICRG financial risk			0.029	
			(1.12)	
ICRG economic risk				0.060
				(1.46)
Adjusted *R*-sq.	0.23	0.14	0.13	0.14
Prob. *F*-value	0.00	0.00	0.00	0.00
N	188	182	182	182

***Significantly different from zero at the 1% level.
**Significantly different from zero at the 5% level.
*Significantly different from zero at the 10% level.

ᵃ The sample consists of all countries classified as an emerging stock market by the IFC and for which the Emerging Stock Markets Factbook provides data on stock market capitalization and traded value on the stock market from 1988 on. This sample consists of 31 countries: the 22 countries we classified as privatizing (see Table A1 of Appendix A) and 9 additional countries. For the latter group of countries we use market development data from 1988 to 1995. For the countries included in our sample of privatizers we use market development data for the years as reported in Table A1 in Appendix A. The yearly data for the 31 countries are then pooled into one sample after which we regress our five different measures of stock market development on political risk improvement. The regressions for the growth in number of firms include country dummies. *t*-values are calculated using White heteroskedasticity-consistent standard errors and are in parentheses.

negative in CCR and ICRG political risk regressions. This is consistent with our earlier finding that stock market growth has been highest for our privatizing countries before the actual start of privatization sales.[26] Including country dummies in the regressions generally worsens the overall fit but increases the coefficient of the CCR and ICRG political risk indicators for the capitalization and traded value regressions, with little effect on the significance. The coefficient for the CCR equals 2.3 and 5.0

---

[26] Excluding privatization sales as a control variable provides similar results for the size and significance levels of the coefficients of the political risk indicators.

respectively after including country dummies, while the coefficient for the ICRG political risk indicator increases to 2.0 in the traded value regression.

The regressions also show that stock returns are strongly related to changes in the CCR and ICRG political risk indicator. This is remarkable, as it is quite difficult to find significant determinants of excess returns. Although the adjusted R-squares are especially high due to the inclusion of real depreciation, excluding this variable still produces an adjusted R-squared of 11% for the CCR regression. Our results for the relation between political risk and stock market returns are in line with those of Diamonte et al. (1996) and Erb et al. (1996b). Diamonte et al. find a strong contemporaneous relation between quarterly average returns and quarterly increases or decreases in the ICRG political risk indicator: emerging countries receiving upgrades are characterized by significantly higher average returns than those being downgraded. Erb et al., using the same measures of political risk as we do in our analysis, find that this relation between upgrades and downgrades holds as well for the CCR and the other ICRG ratings. In agreement with our results, these authors also find that among the four indicators, changes in the CCR and the ICRG political risk ratings display the most pronounced correlation with returns.

We checked for the presence of outlier effects by excluding countries with extreme market development patterns (Portugal and Indonesia) from our analysis; results are similar. In addition, we excluded all observations where the growth in stock market development was more than four standard deviations away from the mean. This reduces the size of the coefficients somewhat, but only affects the statistical significance for the ICRG political risk coefficient in the traded value regression, which becomes significant at the 10% level only. The pattern of significance remains the same for all other regressions. The coefficient for the privatization sales over GNP variable now has the expected positive sign, but it is still insignificant (even at the 10% level). We also included inflation in the analysis, but the results are almost identical.[27]

We find the differences in explanatory power among the different political risk indicators intriguing. The qualitative indicators that relate to the political process proved to be most valuable. The more quantitative indicators (ICRG financial and economic risk indicators) provided little evidence for an influence of these factors on market development.

It is possible that the more quantitative indices use conventional, backward-looking economic measures which are less informative on the underlying risk and opportunity factors than perceived risk and confidence. The differences between the significance of the CCR and the ICRG economic risk indicators confirms our earlier claim that the CCR is a valuable measure for the markets' perception of the credibility of government policy.

---

[27] The regressions in Table 3 show that growth in GNP per capita is positively related to the CCR rating. The results in Table 5 are not driven by the correlation between the CCR and growth in GNP per capita. Excluding this last variable does not affect the significance (or size) of the CCR coefficient in the regressions, other than that in the turnover ratio regression the CCR coefficient is now significant at the 10% level.

E.C. Perotti, P. van Oijen / Journal of International Money and Finance 20 (2001) 43–69   65

One may argue that it is possible that privatization only affects stock market development through direct listings and through the risk sharing and liquidity externalities of these listings, and that these benefits are picked up by our political risk indicators. We believe that our results indicate a direct causality running from political risk to stock market development. First of all, the importance of political risk for stock market development is established using a sample of privatizers and non-privatizers: around 40% of the observations are from countries that did not privatize or from periods more than two years before privatization started. We also find the gradual pattern in stock market development hard to explain only in terms of indirect risk-sharing benefits of new listings and increased trading and find that we attribute them to the gradual resolution of political risk. Since the stock market is a forward-looking indicator, if market conditions were expected to improve as a result of announced privatization sales, prices and trading volume should immediately anticipate these benefits.[28]

Finally, including privatization sales in our regressions captures any direct effect from share issues such as any anticipated risk sharing and liquidity benefits reflected in market development measures. Interestingly, the inclusion of privatization sales hardly affects the coefficients of political risk indicators or their significance. It is, therefore, unlikely that the political risk indicator simply picks up the effect of privatization sales on market development from channels other than political risk.

We conclude, therefore, that political risk improvements, correlated with the progress of a sustained privatization program, appear to be an important factor in the rapid development of emerging stock markets. Their economic significance is quite dramatic. The coefficient for the CCR in the traded value regression indicates that if political risk improved by 1% in a year, we expect that this led to an increase of nearly 4% for the traded value over GNP! From Table 3, we know that during years of privatization, the growth rate of the CCR was on average 0.029 higher in emerging countries that did privatize vis-à-vis those that did not. Combined with the regression results in Table 5, this implies that, on average, the yearly growth rate of traded value over GNP increased by 10.8 percentage points as a direct consequence of political risk reduction. Also, monthly stock returns were on average 0.46 percentage points higher during privatization because of the associated improvements in political risk, which indicates an extra return of almost 6% on an annual basis.

6. Concluding remarks

We have presented evidence that the resolution of political risk through sustained privatization has been an important source for the recent growth in emerging stock markets. It seems that sustained privatization has gradually strengthened the insti-

---

[28] Trading and diversification gains may also be incorporated gradually, of course, if there are fears that the privatization process may be halted or reversed; such concerns do belong to our definition of political and policy risk.

tutional framework by forcing a resolution of political and legal uncertainties which till then hinder equity market development. This ultimately leads to an increase in investor confidence. On average, this process seems to take place gradually as privatization proceeds.

An interesting empirical issue is the robustness of our results. Our sample may reflect a set of relatively successful privatizing countries, for which the early 1990s were a privatization stage, just when emerging stock markets generally performed quite well. However, our argument is that is no coincidence: emerging markets performed so well *because* they managed to convince many investors of their own reliability through radical economic reforms such as privatization. Ultimately, this is an empirical question which can be addressed at best when a longer historical experience becomes available.

It is possible that privatization, perhaps because it establishes more broad-based ownership, can by itself resolve political risk by helping to overcome political resistance to market reforms and their effect. Biais and Perotti (1999) develop a simple model of how a large privatization program may be designed so as to reduce political risk of future policy reversals. A market-oriented party may increase the probability of being re-elected by implementing a series of underpriced sales, where excess demand is rationed so as to ensure a broad diffusion of shareholding and to reward long-term holdings. A wide diffusion of shares may have the effect of shifting the preferences of the middle-class. This structural shift in the political equilibrium creates stable political support for market reforms and reduces political risk for equity investment, reducing the equity premium and increasing market capitalization. Jones et al. (1998) find significant empirical support for these conclusions by analyzing the pricing and share allocations affiliated with privatization sales.

In our view these observations and the results in our paper point to a strong potential for research developments in the area of political economy and corporate finance. Privatization, just like nationalization, has strong redistributive effects and tends to cause political conflict, the outcome of which is most informative for investors.

Acknowledgements

We thank Frank Sader, Sheridan Titman, and (especially) the referee for useful comments. The World Bank, Bert Scholtens, and the Master in International Finance Program at the University of Amsterdam supplied data, which we gratefully acknowledge.

Appendix A. Sample of privatizing countries

Table A1
Sample of countries that privatized and sample years

Country	Before privatization	Start privatization	End of sample
Argentina	86	90	95
Bangladesh	85	89	95
Brazil	87	91	95
Chile	81	85	95
Colombia	87	91	95
Greece	86	90	95
India	87	91	95
Indonesia	87	91	95
Ivory Coast	87	91	95
Jamaica	82	86	95
Malaysia	81	85	95
Mexico	81	85	95
Nigeria	85	89	95
Pakistan	86	90	95
Peru	87	91	95
Philippines	85	89	95
Portugal	85	89	95
Sri Lanka	85	89	95
Tunisia	84	88	95
Thailand	88	92	95
Turkey	84	88	95
Venezuela	86	90	95

Appendix B. Overview of the ICRG indicators

Table B1
Composition of the International Country Risk Guide indicators

	Weight
Political risk indicator	
Economic expectations vs. reality	0.12
Economic planning failures	0.12
Political leadership	0.12
External conflict	0.10
Corruption in government	0.06
Military in politics	0.06
Organized religion in politics	0.06
Law and order tradition	0.06
Racial and national tensions	0.06
Political terrorism	0.06
Civil war risks	0.06
Political party development	0.06
Quality of bureaucracy	0.06

(continued on next page)

Table B1 (*continued*)

	Weight
Financial risk indicator	
Loan default or unfavorable loan restructuring	0.20
Delayed payment of supplier's credits	0.20
Repudiation of contracts by government	0.20
Losses from exchange controls	0.20
Expropriation of private investments	0.20
Economic risk indicator	
Inflation	0.20
Debt service as a percentage of exports	0.20
International liquidity ratios	0.20
Foreign trade collection experience	0.20
Current account balance as percentage of goods and services	0.20
Parallel foreign exchange rate market indicators	0.20

References

Bell, S., 1995. Privatization through broad-base ownership strategies. World Bank Discussion Paper, Washington, DC.

Bekaert, G., 1995. Market integration and investment barriers in emerging equity markets. The World Bank Economic Review 9, 75–107.

Biais, B., Perotti, E.C., 1999. Machiavellian Privatization. CEPR Discussion Paper 2014, London.

Boubakri, N., Cossets, J.C., 1998. The financial and operating performance of newly privatized firms: Evidence from developing countries. Journal of Finance 53, 1081–1110.

Candoy-Sekse, R., 1988. Techniques of privatization of state-owned enterprises: vol. III. World Bank Technical Paper no 90, Washington, DC.

Cherian, J.A., Perotti, E.C., 2000. Option pricing and foreign investment under political risk. Journal of International Economics, forthcoming.

Claessens, S., Djankov, S., 1997. Politicians and firms: Evidence from seven central and eastern European countries. Mimeo, World Bank.

Demirgüç-Kunt, A., Levine, R., 1994. The financial system and enterprise reform. World Bank working paper, Washington, DC.

Demirgüç-Kunt, A., Maksimovic, V., 1998. Law, finance and firm growth. Journal of Finance 53, 2107–2137.

De Santis, G., Imrohoroglu, S., 1997. Stock returns and volatility in emerging financial markets. Journal of International Money and Finance 16, 561–579.

Dewenter, K.L., Malatesta, P.H., 1997. Public offerings of state-owned enterprises: An international comparison. Journal of Finance 52, 1659–1679.

Diamonte, R.L., Liew, J.M., Stevens, R.L., 1996. Political risk in emerging and developed markets. Financial Analysts Journal, 71–76.

Edwards, S., 1990. Capital flows, foreign direct investment, and debt-equity swaps in developing countries. NBER Working Paper No. 3497.

Erb, C.B., Harvey, C.R., Viskanta, T.E., 1996a. Expected returns and volatility in 135 countries. Journal of Portfolio Management 21, 32–48.

Erb, C.B., Harvey, C.R., Viskanta, T.E., 1996b. Political risk, economic risk and financial risk. Financial Analysts Journal, 29–46.

Euromoney (1993–4), Guide to World Equity Markets, and special supplements.

Galal, A., Jones, L., Tandon, P., Vogelsang, I., 1994. Welfare consequences of selling public enterprises: An empirical analysis. World Bank, Washington, DC.

Grandy, C., 1989. Can the government be trusted to keep its part of a social contract? New Jersey and the railways 1825–1888. Journal of Law, Economics and Organization 5, 249–269.

Grinblatt, M., Hwang, C.Y., 1989. Signalling and the pricing of new issues. Journal of Finance 44, 393–420.

Hachette, D., Lüders, R.J., 1993. Privatization in Chile: An Economic Appraisal. ICS Press, San Francisco, California.

IFC. Emerging Stock Markets Factbook. IFC, Washington DC, Various issues.

Institutional Investor. Various issues.

Jones, S.L., Megginson, W.L., Nash, R.C., Netter, J.M., 1998. Share issue privatizations as financial means to political ends. Journal of Financial Economics (in press).

LaPorta, R., Lopez-de-Silanes, F., Shleifer, A., Vishny, R.W., 1997. Legal determinants of external finance. Journal of Finance 52, 1131–1150.

LaPorta, R., Lopez-de-Silanes, F., Shleifer, A., Vishny, R.W., 1998. Law and finance. Journal of Political Economy 106, 1113–1155.

Levine, R., 1991. Stock markets, growth and tax policy. Journal of Finance 46, 1445–1465.

Levine, R., 1997. Financial development and economic growth. Journal of Economic Literature 35, 688–726.

Levine, R., Zervos, S., 1998. Stock markets, banks and economic growth. American Economic Review 88, 537–558.

Megginson, W.L., Nash, R.C., Netter, J.M., Schwartz, A.L., 1998., The long-run return to investors in share issue privatizations. Mimeo, University of Georgia.

Modigliani, F., Perotti, E.C., 2000. Security markets versus bank finance: legal enforcement and investors' protection. International Review of Finance, forthcoming.

Pagano, M., 1989. Endogenous market thinness and stock price volatility. Review of Economic Studies 56, 269–288.

Pagano, M., 1993a. Financial markets and growth: An overview. European Economic Review 37, 613–622.

Pagano, M., 1993b. The flotation of companies on the stock market: A co-ordination failure model. European Economic Review 37, 1101–1125.

Perotti, E.C., 1995. Credible privatization. American Economic Review 85, 847–859.

Perotti, E.C., Guney, S.E., 1993. The structure of privatization plans. Financial Management 22, 84–98.

Perotti, E.C., Huibers, F., 1998. The performance of privatization stocks in emerging markets: The role of political risk. Advances in Financial Economics (in press).

Rock, K., 1986. Why new issues are underpriced. Journal of Financial Economics 15, 187–212.

Rodriguez, F., 1992. The Mexican privatization programme: An economic analysis. Social and Economic Studies 41, 149–171.

Sader, F., 1993. Privatization and foreign investment in the developing world 1988–92. World Bank Policy Research Working Paper, Washington, DC.

Sader, F., 1995. Privatizing public enterprises and foreign investment in developing countries, 1988–93. Occasional Paper 5, IFC and World Bank, Washington, DC.

Schmidt, K., 1997. The political economy of mass privatization and the risk of expropriation. CEPR Discussion paper, CEPR, London.

World Bank, various years. World Debt Tables; External Finance for Developing Countries, World Bank, Washington DC.

C
Liberalization and Capital Flows

[12]

René M. Stulz

International Portfolio Flows and Security Markets

For most of the period following World War II, the economic significance of net capital flows was small and net portfolio flows were even less important (see Feldstein and Horioka 1980). Over recent years, net capital flows have become much larger, especially to developing economies. Net portfolio flows are now a major component of net capital flows. Table 5.12 gives various estimates of the main components of net capital flows for developing countries. From 1977 to 1982, average annual net cumulative portfolio flows to developing countries were negative (−$10.5 billion). In contrast, in the year before the Mexican crisis, net portfolio investment of $85.8 billion exceeded net foreign direct investment of $76.3 billion. After recovering from the Mexican crisis, net portfolio investment fell again with the Asian crisis. Net portfolio flows turned negative for Asian developing countries, but they were not as important in the 1990s for these countries as they were for Latin America. To find a period in history when net capital flows were possibly as important as in the 1990s, one has to go back to the beginning of this century. Strikingly, however, while net flows were comparable to the recent experience before World War I, there are two important differences. First, to use the expression coined by Eichengreen and Fishlow, the current era is the "era of equity finance," which started at the end of the 1980s when "an unprecented volume and share of capital flows to developing countries began to take the form of equity purchases by individual investors . . . through their institutional representatives" (1998, 24). Second, gross flows are dramatically larger today than ever before. A good example of this is the turnover in foreign exchange markets which exceeds one trillion dollars a day (Bordo, Eichengreen, and Kim 1998).

Part of this paper was written while the author was a Bower Fellow at the Harvard Business School. The author is grateful for comments from Warren Bailey, Geert Bekaert, Cam Harvey, Martin Feldstein, Anthony Richards, Linda Tesar, Ingrid Werner, an anonymous referee, and conference participants.

258   René M. Stulz

Table 5.12   Capital Flows to Developing Countries (billions of U.S. dollars)

A. Net Capital Flows to Developing Countries, 1977–94 (yearly average)

	1977–82	1983–89	1990–94
Total net capital flows	30.5	8.8	104.9
Net direct investment	11.2	13.3	39.1
Net portfolio investment	−10.5	6.5	43.6
Other	29.8	−11.0	22.2

B. Net Private Capital Flows to Emerging Markets

	1994	1995	1996	1997	1998[a]
Net private capital flows	133.6	147.3	190.9	131.8	87.6
Net direct investment	76.3	86.3	108.6	126.7	106.2
Net portfolio investment	85.8	22.2	52.5	51.8	38.0
Other net investment	−28.6	38.8	29.7	−46.6	−56.6

C. Net Private Capital Flows to Asia

	1994	1995	1996	1997	1998[a]
Net private capital flows	64.8	91.7	100.2	21.5	−18.3
Net direct investment	44.4	51.0	60.2	60.2	45.1
Net portfolio investment	11.5	10.0	10.1	7.5	−6.5
Other net investment	9.0	30.8	29.9	−46.3	−56.9

Sources: Panel A, Folkerts-Landau and Ito (1995); panels B and C, IMF, *World Economic Outlook and International Capital Markets* (Washington, D.C., 1998).
[a]Numbers are estimates.

   The increased relevance of net portfolio flows results first and foremost from the liberalization of financial markets in developing economies. This liberalization made it possible for investors from developed countries to invest in many emerging markets where previously they could not invest. As part of the liberalization, many countries engaged in large-scale privatization programs that increased the supply of equity from these countries. Even if investors from developed countries had kept their share of the capitalization of emerging equity markets constant, large capital flows would have taken place because of the increased capitalization of the emerging markets in which investors could buy securities as a result of the opening of markets and of privatization programs. However, investors also increased their share of the capitalization of emerging equity markets. The scope for further liberalization and privatization programs has narrowed, but large capital flows could result from increases in portfolio allocations to emerging markets. Currently, investors in major developed countries invest less than 1 percent of their assets in emerging markets. A 1 percent increase in this allocation corresponds to net capital flows of more than $120 billion.

Net portfolio flows should lower the cost of capital in many countries and facilitate the flow of capital to firms and countries that have the best investment opportunities irrespective of their locations. Overall, net portfolio flows should therefore be an engine of worldwide growth. This should be even more so because portfolio investments subject firms and countries to the discipline of capital markets. To attract and keep portfolio investments, firms and countries have to behave so as to maximize the value of these investments and are punished when they do not. As a result, firms and countries have greater incentives to invest efficiently. These arguments in favor of unrestrained portfolio flows are powerful, but many argue that they are flawed because investors are sometimes moved by "animal spirits" rather than rational thinking, so that portfolio flows have a dark side that can destabilize countries and reduce growth. The large net capital flows of the 1990s and the concomitant increase in the role of international investors in developing countries have led many to reconsider the benefits and costs of net portfolio inflows with some urgency.

The Mexican crisis has been an important cause of this reconsideration. It prompted many to worry about the stability of portfolio investments. Contrasting the Mexican crisis to the debt crisis of the early 1980s highlights why sudden changes in portfolio flows might be a source of concern. With the debt crisis, there were few key players in developed countries, their claims were illiquid, and they had strong incentives to work out solutions with the developing countries. With the Mexican crisis, coordination among portfolio investors was impossible. Even though collectively investors might have been better off committing funds to the Mexican government to resolve the crisis, individually each investor was better off selling out and could do so quickly because he was holding liquid securities. A number of economists have therefore argued that financing a country's growth through portfolio investment can expose it to sudden inflows and outflows that can destabilize an otherwise sound economy, force it into dramatic macroeconomic adjustments, and wreak havoc in its security markets. After worrying about the insufficient economic importance of net capital flows, some economists now worry that there might be too much portfolio investment. Sachs, Tornell, and Velasco aptly summarized this concern: "In today's world of fickle private capital movements, it is argued, large inflows leave a country exposed to the latest mood of Wall Street traders" (1996, 171). This leads economists such as Williamson to say that they "would not urge complete liberalization prior to (a) evidence that . . . controls have become completely ineffective (and hopelessly corrupting), or (b) the assurance that inflows will not be excessive" (1993, 14).

The Asian crisis has added fuel to this growing reconsideration of the benefits of capital flows. For instance, Stiglitz (1998) called for greater regulation of capital flows, arguing that "developing countries are more vulnerable to vacillations in international flows than ever before." Radelet and Sachs (1998) attributed the crisis to panic from foreign investors. Krugman (1998) summarized his view on the impact of capital flows in the East Asian crisis as follows:

"What turned a bad financial situation into a catastrophe was the way a loss of confidence turned into self-reinforcing panic. In 1996 capital was flowing into emerging Asia at the rate of about $100 billion a year; by the second half of 1997 it was flowing out at about the same rate. Inevitably, with that kind of reversal Asia's asset markets plunged, its economies went into recession, and it only got worse from there." He then went on to argue that the solution is to impose currency controls, finishing with an apocalyptic description of what would happen without them: "But if Asia does not act quickly, we could be looking at a true Depression scenario—the kind of slump that 60 years ago devastated societies, destabilized governments, and eventually led to war."

In this paper, we examine these concerns about the implications of net portfolio flows in light of the existing empirical evidence and theories of international portfolio investment. In section 5.2.1 we evaluate the impact of liberalization on equity valuations and on the cost of capital. In section 5.2.2 we address the issue of cross-country comovement in valuations and examine whether there is contagion in international financial markets. In section 5.2.3 we consider whether net portfolio flows can drive valuations away from fundamentals and make asset prices more volatile. Section 5.2.4 attempts to provide an assessment of the net benefits of openness to portfolio investment.

5.2.1   Capital Market Liberalization and Equity Valuations

The past twenty-five years in international capital markets have seen the dismantling of the restrictions on capital flows resulting from the two world wars. At the end of World War II, capital markets were essentially completely segmented. Because of restrictions on capital flows, investors mostly held assets from their home countries. International investment took the form of official capital flows. Some restrictions were soon lifted as currencies became convertible, but other restrictions were added periodically as governments in many countries tried to direct economic activity by reducing the role of markets. Since the 1970s, most of these restrictions have been removed. First, the markets of developed economies were deregulated. Countries removed obstacles to exchange rate transactions, agreed to tax agreements that reduced obstacles to international investment, and eliminated restrictions on foreign ownership that were often binding. Developing countries started to deregulate later than the developed countries, and many such countries have only taken timid steps in that direction. Nevertheless, many of these countries have eliminated obstacles to capital flows and promoted equity market deregulation actively.

Though economists in general are enthusiastic about the benefits of free trade in goods, they often seem surprisingly reluctant in their assessment of the gains from free trade in securities. For instance, Bhagwati (1998) stated: "This is a seductive idea: freeing up trade is good, why not also let capital move freely across borders? But the claims of enormous benefits from free capital mobility are not persuasive. . . . It is time to shift the burden of proof from those who oppose to those who favor liberated capital."[1] This is surprising because a country cannot take full advantage of the benefits of free trade in goods without full capital mobility. Capital mobility allows a country to produce more efficiently and enables the residents to bear fewer of the risks associated with domestic production. To understand these two effects of capital mobility, we consider a country with no capital flows that, for the sake of illustration, has a well-defined comparative advantage in producing coffee beans. We then consider the impact on that country of capital flow liberalization.

In the absence of capital flows, a country cannot have net trade flows. Consequently, residents have to bear all the country's risks. If they produce only coffee beans, any shock to the price at which they can sell coffee beans affects the country's income in direct proportion to the size of the crop. Any damage to the crop also affects the country's income directly. Since the price of coffee beans is quite volatile and crop yields can vary unexpectedly, the country's income would be quite volatile if it devoted all its resources to producing coffee beans. To avoid this volatility, the only solution in the absence of capital flows is to diversify production. This means that the country produces other goods even though it is less efficient at doing so. In the interest of smoothing its income, the country therefore limits the extent to which it takes advantage of the benefits of international trade.

In a country with a market economy, the channel through which production will be directed away from the coffee bean industry is the stock market. In the stock market, investors are rewarded for bearing risk with a risk premium. A stock's risk premium is the expected return of the stock in excess of the return of an investment that has no risk. For instance, the average annual risk premium on the U.S. stock market from 1926 to 1990 was 6.1 percent. Because coffee bean production leads to volatile returns, investors require a high risk premium to invest in that industry and a lower risk premium to invest in industries that provide diversification from the coffee bean industry. As a result, industries that provide diversification from the coffee bean industry are able to obtain capital at low cost. They can promise lower returns to investors because investing in them reduces portfolio volatility. The low cost of capital in industries that allow investors to diversify the return on their investments makes it possible for these industries to compete successfully against imports. As a result of this diversification effect, the country produces in industries for which it does not have a comparative advantage.

Consider now the impact on that country of allowing unrestricted capital flows and assume that there is no dark side to capital flows. Immediately, as investors learn that capital flows will be allowed, the risk premium in the coffee bean industry falls. As investors throughout the world invest in the country's coffee bean

---

1. Even before the recent crises, prominent economists advocated various kinds of taxes to limit international trade in securities in order to decrease speculative capital flows. See Summers and Summers (1989) and Tobin (1978).

production, they find that good events in that industry mostly offset bad events in their portfolios so that investing in coffee bean production actually reduces the risk of their portfolios. This means that the risks associated with coffee bean production are largely diversifiable internationally, so that the world capital markets require a much smaller risk premium to bear such risks and might require no risk premium at all. As the risk premium for the coffee bean industry falls, the country invests more in that industry. Simultaneously, the local industries that helped residents diversify their coffee bean production risks no longer offer that benefit to residents since residents can diversify internationally. Consequently, these industries may well contemplate an increase in their cost of capital and decreased investment. Once this process is completed, the country might specialize in the industry for which it has a comparative advantage.

We have shown that capital market liberalization leads to a reallocation of capital across industries. Obstfeld (1994) showed that this is not the whole story. Because the risks of a country's production can be diversified internationally after capital market liberalization, production technologies that were too risky before liberalization become advantageous because their risks can be diversified internationally. Hence, if riskier technologies are those with higher expected output, liberalization makes it possible for a country to shift to riskier production technologies and hence experience higher growth.

To have a better understanding of the transition from complete segmentation to a completely open capital market, it is helpful to use a numerical example. Suppose a country specializes in coffee bean production, the average annual value of the crop is $1 billion, and the annual volatility is $400 million. This means that each year there is a 5 percent probability that the country's income is below $340 million (assuming that the value of the crop is normally distributed). The country therefore experiences high income volatility. To simplify the discussion, let's assume that all the income accrues to capital. Because of the high volatility, suppose that investors require a risk premium of 10 percent for investments in the coffee bean industry and that the risk-free interest rate is 10 percent. This means that domestic residents are willing to invest in the coffee bean industry only if they expect to earn 20 percent annually, the sum of the rate that they receive on investments without risk plus the risk premium. The only way they can expect to earn 20 percent annually by investing in coffee bean production is if the value of the industry is the present value of a cash flow stream of $1 billion a year discounted at the rate of 20 percent. Consequently, the value of the coffee bean industry is $5 billion. An industry whose cash flows do not move with the cash flows of the coffee industry would have little risk for an investor heavily invested in the coffee bean industry and that investor would require a low risk premium to invest in that industry. Hence, that industry could raise funds promising an expected return to investors close to 10 percent. A dollar of annual average income from that industry is therefore worth $10.

Consider now the impact of an extremely successful liberalization, so that the risk of the production of coffee becomes a risk diversified in portfolios throughout the world. The risk premium on the coffee industry almost disappears, so that the present value of the perpetuity of $1 billion is now close to $10 billion. In other words, liberalization has a dramatic effect on the equity market capitalization. At the same time, however, the diversifying industry might now face a risk premium of 5 percent, so that its cost of capital increases from 10 percent to 15 percent. A dollar of average income in that industry falls from $10 to slightly more than $6. As with trade liberalization, not everybody benefits from capital market liberalization. However, as with trade liberalization, those who gain can compensate those who lose in such a way that everybody is made better off.

The decrease in the cost of capital has three effects on the coffee industry. First, it increases the value of the expected cash flows from existing investments since these expected cash flows are discounted at a lower rate. Second, it makes investments profitable that were not profitable at the higher cost of capital. Thus there will be an investment boom in the coffee industry. The third effect is that new investors will come to the industry and monitor firms in that industry.[2] These investors will have new ideas and will want to influence the actions of firms to make sure that their investments are profitable. Foreign investors will therefore improve corporate governance in the coffee industry, which will increase the value of the industry.

Our analysis of opening up security markets in a country has four empirical implications: (1) foreign investors acquire domestic securities; (2) domestic valuations increase; (3) the cost of capital falls; and (4) growth increases. We now consider the empirical evidence on these four implications. We focus on capital account liberalizations in developing economies both because of their intrinsic interest and because they constitute well-defined events.

Liberalization and Foreign Investment

Our analysis of liberalization assumes that foreign investors invest in the liberalized market rapidly. If this does not happen, no risk sharing takes place and asset prices do not increase. It is well known that holdings of foreign securities are small within portfolios of investors in developed countries.[3] Consequently, most of a developed country's equity is held by domestic residents. For instance, according to the NYSE 1996 fact book, foreigners held about 6 percent of U.S. equity at the end of the third quarter of 1996 (NYSE 1997, 59). This so-called home bias in portfolios implies that, even though portfolio flows have been large, domestic investors still have to bear a large fraction of the risks associated with domestic production. This limits the extent to which the cost of capital falls following liberalization.

Empirically, portfolio flows grow significantly as liberalization occurs. Kim

2. See Stulz (1999) for an analysis of the corporate governance benefits of globalization.
3. See Cooper and Kaplanis (1994), French and Poterba (1991), and Tesar and Werner (1994).

Table 5.13   Estimates of U.S. and Foreign Ownership for Selected
                    Emerging Markets

Country	U.S. Ownership (% of market capitalization)	Foreign Ownership (% of market capitalization)
Argentina	20	38
Brazil	6	–
Chile	4	17
Columbia	6	7
China	–	6
India	2	–
Indonesia	6	–
Malaysia	1	–
Mexico	21	25
Peru	–	38
Thailand	6	–
Venezuela	43	36

Source: Estimates of U.S. ownership are from Bekaert and Harvey (1999), who cumulate flow of funds data until the end of 1995. Estimates of foreign ownership are from Campollo-Palmer (1997).

and Singal (1993) documented that initially following liberalization there is a short period of net capital outflow, after which net capital flows turn positive and become large. This effect varies across countries. Liberalizations differ in degree across countries dramatically, so it is not surprising that foreign investors build larger stakes in some countries than in others. Table 5.13 provides estimates of U.S. equity investment and foreign equity investment in a number of emerging markets. For most countries, foreign ownership is difficult to estimate precisely. The table shows this vividly for Venezuela where the estimate of U.S. ownership exceeds the estimate of foreign ownership! Nevertheless, these numbers show that, on average, liberalization leads to substantial foreign equity holdings. These foreign equity holdings are generally large compared to foreign equity holdings in the United States. Consequently, the home bias has a somewhat different meaning for developing economies than for large developed economies. Because the capitalization of emerging markets is small, an investment corresponding to a small fraction of the capitalization of U.S. markets represents a large fraction of the capitalization of many emerging markets. One way to understand this is that in 1997 Bill Gates could have bought all the equity of Greece, Hungary, Jordan, Nigeria, Poland, Sri Lanka, Venezuela, and Zimbabwe—and would still have had $7 billion left to invest elsewhere.

Estimates of the Increase in Valuations Resulting from Liberalization

With our example, the capital market liberalization induces an increase in equity valuations and a decrease in the cost of capital, which leads to an in-

265   The Role of Equity Markets in International Capital Flows

crease in investment. Because of the home bias, the economic importance of these effects of liberalization is an empirical issue. It is relatively straightforward to look at stock market returns and evaluate whether they are unusually high at the time a country liberalizes. We will see that it is harder to figure out whether the cost of capital falls.

The large returns on emerging markets over the past fifteen years are well known. For instance, from December 1984 to December 1994 the real value of emerging market equity increased by 202 percent; in comparison, the S&P 500 increased by 93.5 percent. These large returns are in part responsible for the interest of portfolio managers in these markets. Since so many liberalizations took place during that period, the performance of emerging markets is consistent with the theoretical prediction of increases in equity valuations accompanying liberalization. However, stock market valuations are not affected by liberalization of capital flows only. Liberalization of capital flows is often accompanied by other events affecting the economy that liberalizes. For instance, the economy might have a new political regime that is market oriented and undertakes extensive domestic reforms that increase stock market valuations. Also, the performance of the stock market depends on how the economy is performing, so macroeconomic conditions have to be taken into account.

To assess the effect of liberalization on equity valuations, it is therefore important to pay close attention to other events that take place in the country that liberalizes its markets. This task is made more difficult by the fact that liberalization is rarely a one-shot event. Countries liberalize some aspects of their markets at one time and others at some other time. Henry (1999b) painstakingly identified individual economic reform and capital flow liberalization events that affected twelve emerging markets. Presumably, by the time the liberalization takes place, its effects are already incorporated in stock prices because investors have been aware of it for some time. It turns out that for the seven months preceding the first liberalization, equity returns are about 40 percent after adjusting for world market equity returns. However, once Henry (1999b) controlled for other events that affect these economies and for macroeconomic conditions, he concluded that the effect is on the order of 18 percent. He found an effect of 16 percent for subsequent liberalizations. This suggests a cumulative effect of about 37 percent.

The Impact of Liberalization on the Cost of Capital

The evidence of Henry (1999b) shows that capital flow liberalization has a large effect on equity valuations. In our earlier analysis, we argued that liberalization, by reducing the cost of capital, can have such an effect. The question that arises out of Henry's evidence is how large the impact of liberalization is on the cost of capital. Suppose that the reevaluation effect is 37 percent. In this case, the reevaluation takes $1 invested in a market and brings it to $1.37. This reevaluation captures all the effects of liberalization discussed earlier. Since the decrease in the cost of capital also makes new investments profitable, the

$.37 reevaluation is an upper bound on the impact of the decrease in the cost of capital. This upper bound implies that a country where the cost of capital for a project of typical risk was 20 percent now has a cost of capital of no less than 16.6 percent. In other words, the cost of capital of that country falls at most by 17 percent.

The sharp stock market increase associated with liberalization suggests that it might be straightforward to measure directly the impact of liberalization on the cost of capital. It turns out that this is not an easy task. The equity cost of capital is the expected return that investors anticipate from equity investments. As this cost falls, entrepreneurs can raise more funds for a project. Measuring the return that investors expect on equity is a difficult undertaking. One might be tempted to use past returns to forecast future returns. However, this strategy is not possible in the case of markets that undergo a liberalization. For such markets, the past returns are those appropriate for the segmented economy that no longer exists following liberalization. To complicate things further, past average returns for such markets are high for two reasons. First, segmented markets have higher risk premiums because domestic investors have to hold more domestic equity than they would in the absence of segmentation. Second, as discussed, liberalization boosts equity valuations as the cost of capital falls. Hence, the prospect of lower expected returns on equity has the paradoxical implication of increasing average returns on equity when measured over the liberalization period. This is because the expected cash flows on equity are discounted at a lower rate.

A second strategy to estimate the change in the cost of capital is to assume that following liberalization the expected return is determined by how the risk of equity is priced in global markets. To do this, one has to posit a model of how risk is priced in global markets and one has to assume that this model applies to equities of liberalized markets. For such an approach to make sense, one has to believe that it is reasonable to treat the world as if liberalized markets form one big market where capital flows freely across markets to equalize risk-adjusted returns. To proceed further, we therefore have to consider whether it is reasonable to think of the world of liberalized markets as one big market.

If investors can move capital freely across countries, they can diversify their portfolios internationally. This means that risks that are specific to small countries typically do not matter much in their portfolios. If their investments in one small country do poorly because of events specific to that country, their investments in another small country might be doing well. On balance, therefore, these risks offset each other. By diversifying internationally, investors can form a portfolio that has a lower volatility for a given expected return. Since investors would rather bear less risk than more, they should prefer this strategy. A reasonable measure of the gain that American investors can make by diversifying internationally was provided by DeSantis and Gerard (1997). They showed that as of 1994 a portfolio diversified internationally among ten major

267   The Role of Equity Markets in International Capital Flows

developed economies had the same volatility as a well-diversified portfolio of American equities but the annual expected return was higher by about 2.5 percent. Adding emerging markets to this portfolio would lead to further gains from diversification. For a portfolio to be well diversified internationally, however, its holdings have to be in the same proportions as the capitalization of securities from each country. A portfolio that holds the same proportion of the capitalization of each security in the world is called the world market portfolio. Hence, since emerging markets represent about 12 percent of world market capitalization, a well-diversified portfolio has an investment of about 12 percent in emerging markets.

An investor who holds a portfolio that is well diversified internationally measures the risk of a security by its contribution to the volatility of that portfolio. As the volatility of her portfolio increases, she bears more risk. Hence, she is only willing to hold a security that contributes significantly to the volatility of the portfolio if she receives enough of a reward in the form of a risk premium. A security contributes more to the volatility of her portfolio if that security moves more together with the other securities in the portfolio. Such a security has little diversification value since, if the portfolio performs poorly, that security is highly likely to perform poorly also. A security can have high volatility and yet have little co-movement with the portfolio. The investor will not be concerned about the volatility of such a security because most of the randomness of its return will be diversified away in the portfolio.

The part of the return of a security that cannot be diversified away is the part that moves with the return of the whole portfolio. Financial economists call this part of the return of a security its systematic risk. A simple model of the risk of securities in markets where capital flows freely is the international capital asset pricing model, which states that the return of a security in excess of the risk-free rate is equal to the systematic risk of that security times the risk premium on the world market portfolio.[4] The measure of the systematic risk of a security for a well-diversified investor is the degree to which it moves with the world market portfolio. For instance, if the world market portfolio has a 1 percent return, one can expect the U.S. market portfolio to have a 0.84 percent return while the Argentinian market portfolio is only expected to return 0.19 percent.[5] Consequently, the U.S. market portfolio has substantially more systematic risk than the market portfolio of Argentina and should earn a higher expected return. A security that covaries more with the world market portfolio must promise investors a higher expected return because it has more risk that investors cannot diversify away. With this model, the equity cost of capital is equal to the risk-free interest rate plus the systematic risk of the security times the risk premium of the world market portfolio. If we take the risk premium of the world market portfolio to be 6 percent, the Argentinian market portfolio

4. See Stulz (1995) for a detailed analysis of the theory and empirical tests of it.
5. These estimates are from Erb, Harvey, and Viskanta (1996).

would be expected to earn 1.14 percent in excess of the risk-free rate and the U.S. market portfolio 5.4 percent.

The international capital asset pricing model has been tested extensively with some degree of success, especially among developed countries. There is clear evidence that the returns of securities are related to their systematic risk. Countries whose markets covary more with the world market have higher equity returns on average, as predicted. At the same time, however, such a simple model has limitations. There are regularities that it cannot explain. For instance, it understates the required return from small firms and tends to overstate the required return from growth firms. Part of the difficulty for the model is that countries still have obstacles to capital flows. Nevertheless, the clear lesson from the empirical evidence is that, for countries whose capital markets are fairly open, the primary determinant of the valuation of securities is their risk as measured on international capital markets.

Like Argentina, most emerging markets have traditionally had little systematic risk. As these markets liberalize, the valuations of their securities are increasingly determined on international capital markets. As a result, valuations increase because the securities do not have much systematic risk. It is not the case, however, that these markets become completely integrated into world markets as soon as they liberalize. Liberalizations are generally partial, and there is always a risk that a country will adopt new restrictions on capital flows. Hence, the expected returns on emerging market common stocks are best described as a mix between expected returns determined on world markets and expected returns determined on local markets, with the mix changing over time.[6] If liberalizations were complete and credible and if there were no home bias, liberalizations would have a more dramatic effect on stock returns. Going back to our example where we argued that the empirical evidence suggests a fall in the cost of capital of 17 percent, one would expect the cost of capital to fall from 20 percent to about 10 percent rather than to 16.66 percent if the liberalized market became completely integrated into world capital markets. In this case, a liberalization would more than double equity valuations.

Bekaert and Harvey (1999) proposed a third approach to investigate the impact of liberalization on the cost of capital. They argued that the ratio of the dividend to the share price is a good proxy for the cost of capital. They then investigated how this proxy changes as a country liberalizes. Generally, they found that liberalization decreases the cost of capital by a relatively small amount (less than 100 basis points). Compared with the predictions one obtains from the applying the international capital asset pricing model, the estimates of Bekaert and Harvey (1999) are surprisingly small. Though the estimates implied by the work of Henry (1999b) are somewhat larger, they are also small compared to the predictions from the international capital asset pricing model. A plausible explanation is that the impact of liberalization on the

6. See Bekaert and Harvey (1995) for a model of how this mix changes over time.

cost of capital is limited because of the extent of home bias. If foreign investors do not buy the equity of liberalized countries, the cost of capital for that country does not decline.[7]

One last point should be made. As investors become better able to diversify their portfolios internationally, they bear less risk. If investors require more compensation to bear more risk, this means that the compensation for risk falls. Hence, greater globalization of capital markets implies a fall in the cost of capital everywhere because the risk premium on the world market portfolio falls.

The Impact on Growth

From our analysis, liberalization decreases the cost of capital. This should lead to an increase in growth because investment projects that were not advantageous before liberalization become advantageous afterward. Henry (1999a) provided direct evidence on this issue. He showed that liberalization induces an increase of 23 percent in private investment the year following liberalization and an increase of 24 percent the year after that. He also found that his estimate of the stock market effect of liberalization helps predict the increase in investment following liberalization.

We have seen that globalization increases stock market valuations, increases growth, and increases welfare. The question we have to address is whether there is a dark side of globalization that negates or even dwarfs these positive effects. We have proceeded as if capital markets work efficiently in allocating capital to its best uses. Instead, those concerned about capital flows are likely to believe Bhagwati's argument that "only an untutored economist will argue that, therefore, free trade in widgets and life insurance policies is the same as free capital mobility. Capital flows are characterized, as the economic historian Charles Kindleberger of the Massachusetts Institute of Technology has famously noted, by panics and manias" (1998, 8). The panics and manias are generally presumed to translate into contagion effects and volatility effects of capital flows. We therefore investigate the concerns about contagion in the next section and those about volatility in section 5.2.3.

5.2.2   How Do Changes in One Market Affect Other Markets?

With free capital flows, markets are connected. Investors who think that one market will have higher returns can move their investments to that market. Some have argued that this connection implies that markets move together more than they would if they were segmented. As investor sentiment changes in one large country, they argue, this change affects stock returns throughout the world irrespective of fundamentals. This view suggests that stock moves

---

7. See Stulz (1999) for a simple model showing the relation between the cost of capital impact of liberalization and the extent of home bias.

are contagious. To evaluate this claim, it is important to understand what moves stock prices. In section 5.2.1 we thought of stock prices as the present value of cash flows. Consequently, stock prices can change because expected cash flows change or because of changes in discount rates. The discount rate is the risk-free rate plus a risk premium. This means that the discount rate can change because of interest rates or risk premiums.

In global markets, the risk premium is determined globally. For instance, the risk premium on U.S. stocks is not determined in the United States alone. Chan, Karolyi, and Stulz (1992) documented that the risk premium on U.S. stocks and the risk premium on Japanese stocks are clearly connected, so that changes in the risk premium on Japanese stocks also affect the risk premium on U.S. stocks. This effect naturally induces co-movements in stock prices across the world, and it does not imply that investors are irrational or that stock prices disregard economic fundamentals. It does mean, however, that U.S. stock prices can change in circumstances where, if the United States were an isolated country, they would not change. We now examine stock price co-movements and whether they have changed as capital flows became less restricted.

Have Co-movements Increased over Time?

Much of the analysis of stock price co-movements has focused on one measure of co-movement, namely, the correlation of stock returns, which takes values between -1 and $+1$. Typically, well-diversified portfolios of U.S. stocks have a correlation close to one. Historically, however, correlations of foreign indexes with the U.S. market have been small, especially for emerging markets, where they often have been indistinguishable from zero. At the same time, though, these correlations change over time. This makes it difficult to figure out whether correlations are greater now than they used to be. This task is further complicated by the fact that these correlations are not well understood. Although many authors have tried to construct models that explain how they change over time and how they differ across countries, this literature has had little success. Table 5.14 provides a comparison of correlations of stock markets with the world market portfolio over two periods. One period is the sample period for which returns were available. The other period corresponds to the first five years of the 1990s (April 1990 to March 1995). Correlations have changed, but some increased and others decreased. The average correlation is .35 for the whole sample period and .41 for 1990–95. Hence, on average, correlations increased, but not by much. Many recent papers have looked at the issue of whether correlations have increased over time using sophisticated statistical techniques.[8] There is evidence of an increase in correlations, but the extent of this increase differs across studies and some studies do not report an increase. One important issue that affects the conclusions of the ex-

8. See Karolyi and Stulz (1996) for references.

Table 5.14   **Correlations between Countries and the World Market Portfolio (MSCI)**

Country	Source	Sample Start	Correlation	
			Full Sample	April 1990–March 1995
Argentina	IFC	October 1979	−0.01	0.12
Australia	MSCI	October 1979	0.52	0.49
Austria	MSCI	October 1979	0.30	0.54
Belgium	MSCI	October 1979	0.62	0.72
Brazil	IFC	October 1979	0.09	0.19
Canada	MSCI	October 1979	0.69	0.55
Chile	IFC	October 1979	0.07	0.12
China	IFC	April 1993	0.05	0.05
Colombia	IFC	October 1985	0.06	0.08
Denmark	MSCI	October 1979	0.51	0.63
Finland	MSCI	April 1988	0.47	0.51
France	MSCI	October 1979	0.65	0.73
Germany	MSCI	October 1979	0.56	0.66
Greece	IFC	October 1979	0.17	0.18
Hong Kong	MSCI	October 1979	0.43	0.47
Hungary	IFC	April 1993	0.45	0.45
India	IFC	October 1979	−0.05	−0.16
Indonesia	IFC	October 1990	0.12	0.25
Ireland	MSCI	April 1988	0.69	0.77
Italy	MSCI	October 1979	0.47	0.44
Japan	MSCI	October 1979	0.74	0.83
Jordan	IFC	October 1979	0.13	0.20
Malaysia	IFC	October 1985	0.41	0.47
Mexico	IFC	October 1979	0.24	0.29
Netherlands	MSCI	October 1979	0.75	0.77
New Zealand	MSCI	April 1988	0.39	0.56
Portugal	IFC	October 1986	0.41	0.62
Singapore	MSCI	October 1979	0.53	0.70
South Africa	IFC	April 1993	0.33	0.33
South Korea	IFC	October 1979	0.23	0.35
Spain	MSCI	October 1979	0.56	0.71
Sri Lanka	IFC	April 1993	0.01	0.01
Sweden	MSCI	October 1979	0.59	0.72
Switzerland	MSCI	October 1979	0.69	0.78
Taiwan	IFC	October 1985	0.22	0.33
Thailand	IFC	October 1979	0.27	0.34
Turkey	IFC	October 1987	0.06	0.05
United Kingdom	MSCI	October 1979	0.76	0.80
United States	MSCI	October 1979	0.77	0.70
Venezuela	IFC	October 1985	−0.08	−0.02
Zimbabwe	IFC	October 1979	0.08	0.11

Source: Erb, Harvey, and Viskanta (1996).

Note: IFC = International Finance Corporation. MSCI = Morgan Stanley Capital International.

isting studies is that some include the crash of 1987 and others do not. Over a short period of time in 1987, markets moved together by extremely large amounts. Including data from that period has the effect of increasing correlations. Hence one's conclusion about the evolution of correlations depends on whether or not one takes into account the crash. DeSantis and Gerard (1997) examined the correlation between the U.S. market and an equally weighted portfolio of nine other large developed markets. They used a statistical model to estimate monthly correlations. Their sample period was January 1970 through December 1994. The twenty lowest correlation estimates are all from before 1980. Sixteen of the twenty largest correlations are from after 1980. Their evidence shows that there is high correlation in periods of extremely low stock returns. Their average correlation is .56. However, the S&P 500 dropped by 29.42 percent from September to November 1987. They reported their highest correlation, .76, for that period. The second highest correlation they reported is during the period from January 1973 to September 1974, when the stock market dropped 45.06 percent. There is now considerable evidence that correlations are high in bear markets. It is difficult to attribute this to liberalization since correlations were high during the bear market of the 1970s also. This phenomenon creates concerns about the benefits of international diversification, however. Our analysis in section 5.2.1 argued that the benefit of international diversification is that some countries do well while others are doing poorly. If correlations are high during bear markets, this suggests that countries are more likely to do poorly at the same time, which reduces the benefits from international diversification.

What about correlations for emerging markets? In table 5.14 the average correlation for the emerging markets is .17 for the whole sample period, which is roughly half the average correlation for all countries and confirms that emerging markets have much lower correlations with the world market portfolio than developed economies. For 1990–95, the average correlation for the emerging markets is .22, which is still close to half the correlation for the whole sample. There is therefore an increase in correlations of emerging markets, but correlations among developed markets increased proportionally by roughly the same amount. In an interesting paper, DeSantis (1993) looked at the correlations of markets in the World Bank's emerging markets database over two periods. The first period was 1976–84 and the second 1984–92. He found that the average correlation is essentially the same for these two subperiods. Looking at the correlation of the United States with these markets, he found a slight increase. The average is a trivial .038 for the first subperiod and .132 for the second subperiod. The second subperiod contains the crash of 1987, however. Again, this evidence suggests a slight increase in correlations, but the increase seems slight enough that some might conclude there is no change. In a recent study, Bekaert and Harvey (1999) estimated a model that allows correlations between emerging markets and the world market to change over time. They then estimated correlations before and after liberalization. Out of seventeen emerging markets, they found the correlation with the world market to be higher for nine markets. This result seems to provide, at best, weak evidence that correlations increase after liberalization. We discuss below the increase in correlations during crisis periods. Adding the past two years, which correspond to a crisis period, to the samples of the studies discussed here would lead to higher correlation estimates.

Though there is little evidence of strong increases in equity return correlations before the Asian crisis, there is evidence of dramatic increases in correlations between bond yields. Goldstein and Folkerts-Landau (1994) provided correlations between ten-year yields in the seven largest developed economies and the U.S. ten-year bond yield. For the period 1970–79, the average monthly correlation excluding Canada is .41. This average correlation increases to .86 from 1980 to 1989 and to .88 from 1990 to 1994. Ilmanen (1995) showed evidence that there is a strong common factor in interest rate movements across developed countries. One view of this increase in correlations is that, as markets become more integrated, investors give little room to monetary authorities to pursue policies that lead to sharply divergent interest rate movements. It is unclear, however, why the growing integration of markets would affect nominal yields rather than expected real yields.

Is There Causation?

Many papers have been written trying to determine whether stock price changes in one market lead to stock price changes in another market. Initially, this research used monthly or weekly data. However, it quickly became apparent that such research is difficult to interpret. If prices adjust very quickly, there is little hope of finding relationships using infrequently measured data. If a shock to U.S. prices is transmitted to the rest of the world within twenty-four hours, this transmission is obscured by using monthly data. Weekly or monthly data might also yield spurious effects. Not all stocks trade frequently. Infrequent trading of some stocks can give the impression that one market leads another. To see this, suppose that the U.S. stock market drops by 20 percent during one month and one looks at whether this knowledge helps explain the return on foreign markets the following month. One would expect foreign stocks to fall contemporaneously to the extent that the U.S. stock market drop is brought about by some adverse event that affects the whole world. For instance, there could be bad news about the U.S. economy, which would reduce equity values throughout the world to some extent since firms would not be able to sell as much to the United States as expected. However, if some foreign stocks trade infrequently, the effect of bad news on their prices will be recorded only when they trade. Hence, if some foreign stocks do not trade when bad news occurs, they will record a drop subsequent to the drop in the United States, leading to the wrong impression that the U.S. drop caused the drop abroad, when in fact both drops were caused by the same bad news.

The difficulty of interpreting results using weekly and monthly returns has

8

led to the use of data of much higher frequency. Some of this research focuses on returns for periods when stock markets are open and periods when they are closed. Other research measures returns over even shorter periods of time. The opening hours for the U.S. and Japanese stock markets do not overlap. Over a twenty-four hour period, the Japanese market opens first and closes before the U.S. stock markets ever open. Japanese returns contain information about U.S. stock returns because the markets are correlated. A rough estimate is that a 10 percent increase in Japanese markets on average corresponds to a 3 percent increase in U.S. markets. However, all the information contained in the Japanese return during trading hours should be incorporated in U.S. stock prices at the time that the market opens in the United States. This means that the 10 percent Japanese market increase of our example should have no information about the U.S. market return during the U.S. trading day. The evidence is that most of the effect of the 10 percent Japanese market increase will be incorporated in U.S. stock prices by the time the market opens.

This research has also examined whether unexpected increases in volatility spill over across markets. The question asked is whether unexpectedly high volatility in the United States, when the U.S. market is open, leads to high volatility in Japan. This seems to be the case. It seems further that this effect is symmetric across the world: unexpected volatility in the United States leads to higher volatility in Japan, and unexpected volatility in Japan leads to higher volatility in the United States. One might be tempted to attribute this volatility spillover to the increased flow of capital and hence to the greater connections across markets. However, this literature finds greater evidence of spillovers in data before the crash of 1987 than after. One possible explanation is that many of the spillover effects documented in the literature were spurious, resulting from infrequent trading. There is substantial evidence that since the crash information has been incorporated in prices much faster, at least in the United States.

The problem with both the return and the volatility evidence is that it is consistent with two hypotheses that have dramatically different implications for the efficiency of financial markets. One hypothesis is that the Japanese and U.S. markets have common components, and spillovers reflect these common components. Under this hypothesis, spillovers show that markets incorporate information efficiently. The second hypothesis is that spillovers are the work of uninformed investors who overreact to news in one market, corresponding to a change in sentiment.[9] They become more risk averse following bad news and less risk averse following good news, regardless of the fundamentals of their own market. With this view, there is contagion. The lack of spillover reversals is evidence against the uninformed investor hypothesis. Lin and Ito (1994) devised an additional test that makes it possible to distinguish between the two hypotheses. They pointed out that uninformed traders who become

9. De Long et al. (1990) developed a theory of uninformed investors moved by sentiment and showed that such investors can affect asset prices in equilibrium.

275   The Role of Equity Markets in International Capital Flows

more or less risk averse trade to change their portfolios. Consequently, strong spillovers should be associated with high volume. They found no such evidence and argued that the evidence is more consistent with the view that markets impound information efficiently.

Contagion and Crises

We saw in the previous paragraph that there seems to be little evidence of contagion among developed markets under normal circumstances. However, we know that there are greater co-movements in bear markets. This could mean that there is contagion when it might be most damaging, namely, in periods of turmoil. There has been much discussion of contagion among emerging markets during the Mexican crisis and during the Asian crisis. Some have used this contagion to justify the help given to the Mexican government in 1994. For instance, Stanley Fischer states, "Of course, there was another justification: contagion effects. They were there and they were substantial" (quoted in Calvo, Goldstein, and Hochreiter 1997). Table 5.15 shows the performance of some emerging markets during January 1995. During that period, the markets performed poorly. Further, as documented in Calvo and Reinhart (1997), correlations among Latin American market equities and Brady bonds increased sharply around the crisis. Many have interpreted this as evidence of a contagion effect of the Mexican crisis. The view is that, as Mexico fell into its crisis, investors reassessed the prospects of emerging markets and grew pessimistic

Table 5.15   **Returns on Major Emerging Market Indexes during January 1995**

Country	Return (%)
Mexico	−22.2
Peru	−19.2
Brazil	−10.2
Chile	−6.9
Argentina	−5.8
Hungary	−21.1
Poland	−13
Turkey	−12.9
Pakistan	−13.4
Philippines	−13.2
China	−12.5
India	−12.2
Taiwan	−11.3
Hong Kong	−10.3
Thailand	−10.3
Malaysia	−9.2
Indonesia	−8.4
Singapore	−6.5
Sri Lanka	−2.3

Source: Khannah (1996).

even when there was no basis to do so. Flows to emerging markets slowed markedly immediately after the Mexican crisis, so that some have argued that this slowing was responsible for price drops. In the remainder of this section, we first discuss the economics of contagion and then examine some empirical evidence of the economic importance of contagion associated with the Mexican and Asian crises.

The traditional view of contagion has to do with banking panics. The idea is that a bank fails and depositors start withdrawing funds from other banks that are healthy, thereby weakening these banks. For emerging markets, the reasoning is similar, namely, that a shock in one market leads investors to withdraw funds from other markets because of irrational fears. It is certainly the case that some investors behaved that way. Stories of specific investors making obvious mistakes in their analysis of emerging markets have been repeated often.[10] Though such stories enliven conferences, they are irrelevant to an assessment of contagion. Market prices are the product of the actions of all investors, and the important question is whether aggregate outcomes are efficient. One would expect other investors to take advantage of the opportunities created by investors who panic. Hence, if there is plenty of arbitrage capital, contagion should not be a problem.

Unfortunately, the investment industry is organized in such a way that arbitrage capital to be used to take advantage of mispricings in emerging markets may be artificially scarce. Most investments in emerging markets are made by institutional investors. Typically, these investments are made because sponsors and clients designate emerging markets as an asset class in which they want to put funds. The investment industry responds to the demand for investment vehicles in an asset class by creating mutual funds and other investment vehicles. Consider now how institutional investors can react to lower stock prices brought about by panic selling from uninformed investors. Institutional investors who are not specialized in the emerging market asset class will find it difficult to suddenly start investing in emerging markets to take advantage of investment opportunities created by panicky investors. Institutional investors who are specialized in the asset class face a situation where their resources are weakened by the adverse shock that starts the contagion process and where they may find it difficult to liquidate assets to generate cash to exploit advantageous investment opportunities because of turmoil in the markets. Consequently, few institutional investors may be able to take advantage of the investment opportunities created by the actions of the uninformed investors. This lack of arbitrage capital creates a situation where valuations depend on the capital committed to an asset class and can create discrepancies between valuations across asset classes. For instance, Gompers and Lerner (1997) showed that valuations in the venture capital industry depend on the funds committed to the industry.

---

10. See, e.g., Wadhwani's comment in Calvo et al. (1997).

Institutional investors specialized in emerging markets face an additional problem that further limits their ability to take advantage of investment opportunities during periods of turmoil, namely, withdrawals of funds by clients. Shleifer and Vishny (1997) cogently argued that clients of institutional investors may not be able to easily assess whether an investment strategy is right and may therefore use short-term returns to guide their investment decisions. For instance, it may be quite difficult for the typical pension fund organization to assess the performance of an asset manager specialized in emerging markets. The manager may have a solid economic argument that explains why current valuations are too low and the best solution is to keep the portfolio unchanged. However, the client may find it difficult to assess whether this argument is correct and may simply change her allocation of funds to the manager based on his recent performance. Consequently, an institutional investor who thinks that stock prices are too low in a particular country may not be able to act on his judgment if his portfolio has done poorly because funds are being withdrawn. In fact, institutional investors may be forced by circumstances to aggravate the contagion rather than exploit it. Facing redemptions, they may have to liquidate assets in healthy countries because those markets are liquid and may therefore adversely affect capital flows in these countries. What creates the contagion in this case, however, is not an excess of speculative capital. Rather, it is that an insufficient amount of arbitrage capital is devoted to an asset class. The contagion arises because of a lack of investors who can provide liquidity to the institutional investors forced to withdraw from a country. Hence, leaders of emerging countries should not complain about the actions of hedge fund managers but rather should complain that there are too few hedge funds. As more institutional investors become authorized to shift funds between developed and emerging markets and across emerging markets, the possibility of contagion induced by forced liquidations of some institutional investors should disappear.

Contagion caused by panicky investors and forced liquidations is self-limiting in equity markets. As prices fall, it becomes more advantageous to hold on to an investment rather than liquidate it. However, in debt markets, the situation is more delicate for those who rely on short-term debt. If investors are reluctant to roll the debt over, promising higher yields may not solve the problem because these higher yields may imply too high a probability of default. As a result, a country or a firm might face a liquidity crisis and be forced to decrease investment because it was cut off from public markets. Obviously, firms and countries that find themselves in such situations chose an imprudent financing policy. Financing with short-term debt amounts to betting that one's credit will not deteriorate. Sometimes it does. When it does, those that finance with short-term debt face problems whether the change in the perception of credit quality is driven by contagion or not. If the change in credit quality is driven by poor economic prospects for a firm or a country, it should contract investment. However, if economic fundamentals are solid, contraction is not appropriate. Unfortunately, contagion can lead to costly liquidation of investments that represents a waste of resources.

When there are few creditors, they can get together and realize that the appropriate solution to a liquidity crisis is to restructure the debt. By doing this, the creditors make it more likely that they will be paid back. When the number of creditors is large, this coordination is no longer possible. A provider of liquidity of last resort can solve the problem by providing temporary loans. However, the existence of such a provider may lead to the problem in the first place. In the absence of such a provider, different funding strategies would be used to reduce the risk of a liquidity crisis. The existence of a provider of liquidity of last resort may also aggravate contagion. Presumably, the provider has limited resources; if these resources are deployed to help one country, they are not available to other countries. Consequently, a crisis in one country reduces the credit of other countries that might need the help of the provider of liquidity of last resort.

Empirical evidence derived by Calvo and Reinhart (1997) shows that the capital accounts of developing economies are negatively related to the U.S. ex post real rate of interest. This shows that there is a common factor in these capital accounts. The existence of common factors is not, however, evidence of irrational contagion. In the absence of a careful model that shows what the capital accounts of these economies would be in the absence of contagion, there is no way that correlations among capital accounts caused by the existence of common factors can be attributed to contagion. For instance, historically the U.S. stock market increases when interest rates fall. It could be perfectly rational for U.S. investors to invest more in developing economies when their wealth increases.

Contagion does not require changes in capital flows to sharply decrease the value of financial assets. This is because public information affects stock prices without trades in stocks. To see this, consider the Mexican crisis. All investors could observe the events taking place. When an adverse event has taken place, investors will not buy stocks at the prices prevailing before the event. On average, one would expect the price of the first trade taking place after the event to incorporate the information revealed by the event. At the very least, equity prices would reflect the event very quickly, and there is no reason for massive sales to take place for equity prices to reach their new value. If the stock price adjustment process is quick, it is very difficult to find evidence that information in one country caused markets in other countries to change value irrespective of fundamentals by trying to show that the change in one country preceded the other.

The literature often defines contagion to be an increase in correlations among country indexes in periods of crisis. The reasoning is that correlations among country indexes in noncrisis periods reflect fundamentals, so that if correlations during crisis periods are higher, this must reflect contagion. Rigobon (1998) showed why this reasoning is wrong. Correlations among security returns naturally increase when the volatility of a common factor that influences stock returns increases. For instance, if country indexes are related to the world market index, an increase in the volatility of the world market index implies that country indexes become more correlated with the world market index. Hence, comparing correlations among indexes for periods of different volatility would necessarily lead to the result that correlations are higher when volatility is higher. Consequently, higher correlations during crisis periods do not mean contagion. Forbes and Rigobon (1998) estimated correlation increases during the Mexican and Asian crises taking into account the natural increase in correlations during periods of high volatility. Using traditional estimates of correlations, they found that the correlation between Hong Kong and Australia was .356 during a period of stability and .865 during the Asian crisis period. The increase in correlation is statistically significant. Adjusting for the impact of the increase in volatility, they found the correlation during the crisis period between Hong Kong and Australia to be .561 rather than .865, and the correlation increase is not statistically significant. Looking at many countries, they found the same pattern, namely, statistically significant contagion when the estimate of the correlation increase ignores the impact of the volatility increase and statistically insignificant contagion otherwise. They found similar results looking at the Mexican crisis. For instance, the correlation between Mexico and Argentina was .382 during a period of stability and .859 during the crisis period when one ignores the impact of the increase in volatility. However, taking into account the impact of the increase in volatility, the correlation during the crisis period was .500 and is not significantly greater than the correlation during the period of stability. The analysis of Forbes and Rigobon showed that one cannot argue that the increases in correlations observed during crisis periods are evidence of contagion.

Using daily stock returns does not provide statistically significant evidence of contagion. Often, higher frequency data lead to more powerful tests. A recent study by Bailey, Chan, and Chung (1997) investigated the relation between changes in the peso-dollar exchange rate at half-hourly intervals from 21 December 1994 to 30 April 1995 and the returns of Asian and Latin American American Depository Receipts (ADRs) on the NYSE and country funds on the same exchange. They estimated the relation between the half-hour change in a stock and the contemporaneous change in the peso exchange rate as well as the change in the previous half-hour. Not surprisingly, they found a strong contemporaneous relation between the Mexican ADRs and the peso exchange rate, as well as a strong lagged relationship. However, they also found that a depreciation of the peso during a half-hour has a significant adverse effect on non-Mexican Latin American ADRs for the same period as well as for the next period. Essentially, a 1 percent depreciation of the peso is associated with a negative return on non-Mexican Latin American ADRs of -0.15 percent.

There is no effect on Asian ADRs. Looking at closed-end funds, they found a small but significant effect of peso depreciation on Asian country funds and a stronger effect on non-Mexican Latin-American country funds. A 1 percent depreciation of the peso is estimated to reduce the value of Asian country funds by 0.03 percent and the value of non-Mexican Latin American country funds by 0.18 percent. They also explored the impact of the intensity of news announcements on the volatility of ADRs and country funds. Again, they found that non-Mexican Latin American ADRs and country funds experience larger absolute returns when there is news about Mexico during a half-hour.

The findings of Bailey et al. (1997) provide evidence of a tequila effect on the NYSE. Unfortunately, the paper did not attempt to assess how much of the effect is due to information effects and how much is explained by the panic of uninformed investors. Lin and Ito (1994) argued that contagion associated with stock price decreases implies that high correlations are associated with high volume because uninformed investors liquidate their positions. Bailey et al. (1997) provided evidence that can be used to check whether contagion due to uninformed investors was important. They showed that news about the Mexican peso and other Mexican news had a strong effect on the volume of Mexican ADRs and closed-end funds. However, the same news had little effect on the volume of non-Mexican ADRs and closed-end funds, whether they were Latin American or Asian. From 21 December 1994 to 30 April 1995, Mexican news explained 5 percent of the variation in Mexican ADR volume and 9 percent in Mexican closed-end funds volume. In contrast, it explained nothing of the variation in Asian ADR or closed-end fund volume. For Latin American ADR and closed-end funds, Mexican news explained 1.1 percent of the variation in the volume of closed-end funds and 0.3 percent of the variation in volume of ADRs. Though it may be that using different measurement intervals would lead to different conclusions, this evidence is more supportive of the view that Mexican events provided useful information to markets rather than the view that a stampede of uninformed investors harmed valuations by sudden excessive cautiousness.

Another way to consider the economic importance of contagion was provided by Sachs et al. (1996). They examined the reaction of twenty emerging countries to the Mexican crisis. They argued that countries that suffered significantly from the tequila effect were weak to start with, in that they suffered simultaneously from a weak banking sector, an overvalued currency, and low reserves. In such countries, withdrawals of capital by foreign investors adversely affected the currency and endangered the banking sector as the value of foreign-currency-denominated liabilities increased in domestic currency. They argued that in the countries that did not suffer from these problems, the "Tequila effect left no hangover" (Sachs et al. 1996, 193). They found, however, no additional explanatory power in the magnitude and composition of capital flows before the crisis. In other words, large net portfolio flows did not make a crisis more likely.

281   The Role of Equity Markets in International Capital Flows

5.2.3   Flows and Asset Returns

In section 5.2.1 we saw that liberalization increases valuations and decreases the cost of capital. In section 5.2.2 we saw that there is little evidence of large increases in cross-country co-movements with liberalization and that, while co-movements are larger in bear markets, it is quite difficult to distinguish contagion effects from information effects based on evidence from stock returns. In this section, we address the issue of whether changes in valuations can be traced directly to flows. In other words, we try to understand how an additional dollar of flow affects valuations. This issue is at the heart of the concern of whether flows can push up equity prices irrationally only to bring them crashing when foreign capital withdraws unexpectedly. In this view, flows increase prices when they come in and decrease them when they leave. Further, they make prices more volatile because they come and go on a whim. From reading some commentators, it would seem that there is little debate about this issue. For instance, Dornbusch and Park argued that "there is ample evidence that financial market opening is likely to increase the volatility of asset prices" (1995, 39). The mechanism they had in mind is that foreign investors buy more as prices go up, engaging in what is called positive feedback trading. As they do this, prices keep increasing. Further, they also argued that the interest of foreign investors makes markets more liquid, thereby facilitating speculative trades.

A long tradition in financial economics argues that demand and supply shocks that do not convey information about fundamentals are unimportant. This tradition got its start with Scholes (1972). He showed very carefully that sales of large blocks of stocks have a negligible impact on the stock price when these trades are made purely for liquidity reasons. The reason is straightforward. If the equity of an individual firm becomes underpriced, investors can make money by buying it. Similarly, if equity is overpriced, those who own that equity can make money by selling it. Trades undertaken purely for liquidity reasons provide no information about the value of the equity for investors and hence do not change investors' assessment of the value of the equity. If investors suspect that a large trade is undertaken on the basis of information about the firm, then the large trade will naturally have an impact on the value of the equity as buyers will only buy at a price that protects them from the adverse information the seller has. In this view, the demand for securities is perfectly elastic at given prices as long as information about the securities does not change. This view implies that capital inflows or outflows have an impact on valuations only if they are undertaken because of information that foreign investors have that is not yet incorporated in prices.

Are there any reasons to suspect that foreign investors at times are better informed than domestic investors? This seems unlikely. As already mentioned, it is well known that investors do not take advantage of international diversification as much as simple models would suggest. There are many possible explanations for this phenomenon, but a leading one is that investors are less well informed about foreign securities than about securities of their own country. They are therefore concerned that when they buy equity from foreign investors, they buy the equity that foreign investors believe to be overvalued. A natural protection for investors who diversify internationally is therefore to invest in firms for which information is more easily available. Typically, large firms are the ones for which most information is available.

Unfortunately, data are lacking to test the hypothesis that foreign investors favor large firms. Japan seems to be the only country where data on holdings of equity by foreign investors are easily available at the firm level. Kang and Stulz (1997) demonstrated that foreign investors have a considerable bias toward large firm stocks in Japan. Dividing Japanese firms each year into five groups according to firm size, they found that foreign ownership in the smallest firms is 1.8 percent on average from 1975 to 1991; in contrast, ownership in the largest firms is 7.66 percent. This large difference in ownership between small and large firms is not completely attributable to the decrease in the information advantage of local investors as firm size increases. Most international investment is done by institutional investors. As reported by Falkenstein (1996), institutional investors prefer shares of large firms. These shares have lower transaction costs, are more liquid, and enable investors to make larger trades without affecting share prices. The overall preference of foreign investors for large firms suggests that large firms should have a lower cost of capital. For the case of Japan, Kang and Stulz (1997) found weak evidence that shares in which foreign investment is large have lower average returns.

The Mexican crisis offers another piece of evidence that foreign investors are at an information disadvantage. Whereas some have blamed foreign investors for Mexico's troubles, careful examination reveals quite a different story. Capital outflows from residents took place throughout 1994, following the assassination of the presidential candidate Colosio on 23 March 1994. In contrast, foreign investors were net buyers of Mexican equity even in December 1994.

Frankel and Schmukler (1996) found an interesting way to look at this issue. They investigated the returns of Mexican closed-end funds that trade in the United States. A closed-end fund typically trades at a price that differs from the value of the portfolio that it represents. The value of the underlying portfolio is called the net asset value (NAV) of the fund. Frankel and Schmukler (1996) reasoned that the price of a fund moves because of its U.S. investors whereas the NAV moves because of Mexican investors since the underlying portfolio is a portfolio of Mexican stocks that trade in Mexico City. They found that the NAV moves before the price of the fund and causes changes in the price of the fund. Their interpretation was that Mexico City moves Wall Street's assessment of Mexican stocks rather than the reverse.

If foreign investors are less well informed than domestic investors, they will be more sensitive than domestic investors to public announcements. First, public announcements are less likely to be news to domestic investors because they are insiders. Second, since foreign investors are less well informed, their assessment of a country is less precise and hence can be altered more by public information. This makes capital flows sensitive to news. Brennan and Cao (1997) modeled this phenomenon and provide supporting evidence. Note that this sensitivity to news implies behavior that is not too dissimilar to that discussed by Dornbusch and Park (1995). If investors react to news strongly, they buy when stock prices are increasing and sell when stock prices are falling. This makes capital flows correlated with contemporaneous returns. However, there seems to be no clear evidence in Brennan and Cao (1997) that investors practice a positive feedback trading strategy in that there is no evidence that high returns are followed by high flows rather than accompanied by high flows. Tesar and Werner (1993) also looked at the issue of the determinants of equity portfolio flows. Unfortunately, they only reported correlations. Nevertheless, their data set also provides evidence of a positive contemporaneous correlation between returns and flows for most Latin American countries and some Asian countries.

Several recent studies examined whether foreign investors are positive feedback traders, namely, whether they buy following positive returns and sell following negative returns. Bohn and Tesar (1996) found evidence of positive feedback trading using monthly data for a large number of countries. Using daily data of trades from the investors who use State Street Bank & Trust as their custodian, Froot, O'Connell, and Seasholes concluded that "there is very strong trend following in international inflows. The majority of the co-movement of flows and returns at quarterly intervals is actually due to returns predicting future flows" (1998, 18). Using data from Korea, Choe, Kho, and Stulz (1999) found strong evidence of positive feedback trading among foreign investors in that country in 1997. Surprisingly, however, the evidence of positive feedback trading is weak for the last three months of 1997 when the Asian crisis hit Korea. It seems implausible therefore that the trading practices of foreign investors had much impact on the crisis. Perhaps more important, positive feedback trading need not be destabilizing. For instance, if markets are slow to incorporate information into stock prices, positive returns can be expected to be followed by positive returns. Consequently, positive feedback trading is profitable, but investors who trade that way make markets more efficient rather than destabilizing them since they accelerate the incorporation of information into prices.

If domestic investors are better informed than foreign investors, they will hold more domestic shares on average. The reason is that foreign investors discount share prices relative to domestic investors since domestic investors tend to sell if they have adverse information that is not incorporated in asset prices. This means that foreign investors do not take as much advantage of international diversification as they would if all investors had the same information. This home bias resulting from information asymmetries implies that the cost of capital in the domestic country is higher than it would be in the absence of these asymmetries because domestic investors bear more risk. As flows leave the country because of bad news, equity prices fall because domestic investors have to hold more domestic shares. Inflows have the opposite effect. This means that in such a model flows have an impact on the cost of capital. It is also the case that information asymmetries between domestic and foreign investors increase equity return volatility. There is no reason for flows induced by new information to be destabilizing. As information is revealed, investors change their holdings, which has a permanent effect on prices.

When shares are sold by domestic investors to foreign investors, the shares become held by investors who are internationally diversified and who do not view domestic shares to be as risky as domestic investors do. Unexpected changes in investor composition affect equity prices for two reasons, one permanent and one transitory. The permanent reason is the one discussed in the previous paragraph, namely, that investors requiring a lower risk premium buy the shares. As foreign investors come to the domestic country, however, there might also be a transitory effect, which is that as they seek to buy the securities, they have to offer domestic investors an inducement so that they will sell. This compensation only affects prices in the short run, and its size depends on the liquidity of the markets. In very liquid markets, the compensation is trivial. As markets become less liquid, it might be substantial. This liquidity compensation has to be paid by investors who seek to buy, as well as by investors who seek to sell. If an investor wants to get out of a country quickly, she has to offer a discount on the shares she wishes to sell. As shown by Campbell, Grossman, and Wang (1993), this liquidity compensation creates reversals in stock prices. When a large group of investors wants to get out of stocks in a market, they have to provide compensation to buyers of their shares in the form of a larger short-term return. Buyers can only obtain this return by buying the shares at a temporarily low price. There is evidence for the United States that such an effect exists, but there is also evidence that it becomes much weaker over time as markets become more efficient.[11]

This liquidity compensation is a cost that investors pay to trade and it affects their trading strategies. In the extreme case, an illiquid market has a lock-in effect: the discount to be paid to get out is too high and therefore investors do not sell and ride out the bad times. Illiquidity can also keep investors out, however. Not surprisingly, international investors tend to hold securities for which this liquidity compensation is small, namely, securities of large firms. Though some have argued that liquid markets promote short-term horizons on the part of investors, which hurt economies, going even so far as to argue that the liquid markets of the United States were a source of competitive disadvantage for the

11. Froot and Perold (1995) documented that the short-term behavior of stock prices is different in recent years from what it has been historically. Yesterday's stock returns have much less information about tomorrow's stock returns than they used to. Gagnon and Karolyi (1997) showed that the volume-return relation is much weaker after the crash of 1987 than before.

285   The Role of Equity Markets in International Capital Flows

United States, it is important to remember that liquid markets facilitate purchases by investors. Investors who cannot sell in a country have no incentive to invest in that country.

We now look at the evidence of the impact of flows on returns. There is a paucity of empirical evidence at this point. Part of the reason for this is that good data on international flows are hard to find. Before turning to the international evidence, we first consider some evidence for the United States that uses high-quality data.

There is clear evidence from the United States that changes in the composition of investors can have a direct impact on the value of equity. Over the past twenty years, indexing has become tremendously important and the index chosen most often for index portfolios is the S&P 500. Consequently, when a stock joins the S&P 500, this immediately creates a demand for that stock from indexers. Standard and Poor's adds stocks to the S&P 500 based on public information, so that the fact that a stock is added to the S&P 500 does not reveal information about the true value of the stock. Further, indexers have to buy the stock irrespective of its price on the date that it joins the S&P 500. This means that no information is conveyed by the increased demand for the stock. According to the traditional finance model, there should be no price impact when a stock joins the S&P 500. Yet there is such a price impact. Shleifer (1986) and Harris and Gurel (1986) estimated this impact at 3 to 4 percent. Further, all the evidence suggests that this impact is permanent, corresponding to a decrease in the cost of capital for firms that join the S&P 500. The most sensible explanation for this effect is that the demand for the stock has increased. Existing investors in the stock do not have a perfect substitute for the stock that they are giving up if they sell, so that the total demand for the stock increases.

Adding a stock to the S&P 500 probably does not affect the overall demand for stocks. Rather, the existing demand gets redistributed across stocks and this redistribution has a price effect. One might argue that such an example understates the importance of changes in demand and that the situation of emerging markets facing an inflow of capital is more akin to what happens when new mutual fund money flows into the U.S. stock market. An inflow of mutual fund money is mostly money that was not invested in the stock market. In an interesting recent study, Warther (1995) argued that the impact of an unexpected flow of mutual fund money to the U.S. stock market is rather considerable. His estimates were that a 1 percent increase in mutual fund stock assets, which for his sample period corresponds to an inflow in the stock market of $4.57 billion, brings about an increase of 5.7 percent in stock prices. His concern was naturally whether this is a reversible price impact due to liquidity or a permanent price impact. Though he looked hard to find reversals, he was not successful. It appears that this effect is permanent. A plausible explanation is that a broadening of the shareholder base lowers the risk premium as risks are spread across more investors.

Flows move prices. One would expect this to be the case if the risk of stocks becomes spread across more investors. The alternative explanation is that flows move prices because they drive stock prices away from fundamentals. As investors flow into a market, they push prices up without regard for fundamentals, driven by some kind of feeding frenzy. Eventually, prices collapse. Clark and Berko (1996) attempted to distinguish between these two views in the case of Mexico. Mexico saw a dramatic increase in foreign ownership during their sample period. From 1989 to the end of 1993, foreign ownership of Mexican equities increased from a trivial amount to more than one-fourth of the Mexican market capitalization. Like Warther (1995), they found a strong effect of flows on returns. Their estimate was that an unexpected inflow equal to 1 percent of the capital of the market leads to a contemporaneous increase of 13 percent in prices. This estimate was actually smaller than Warther's (1995). They found no evidence of price reversals, suggesting that the impact of flows is permanent rather than transitory and cannot be explained by price pressure. They also found no support for the hypothesis of positive feedback trading. Therefore, their evidence is fully supportive of the investor base broadening hypothesis.

In an article discussing the difficulties of some Asian emerging markets, an economist at J. P. Morgan was quoted in the *New York Times* as saying: "One wishes the markets were less fickle." It could indeed be that flows have a permanent effect on prices but they are so volatile and fickle that, by coming and going, they keep inflicting shocks on prices. This is the concern often expressed about portfolio flows, that somehow equity investments are the wrong kind of investments for a country because they can leave a country rapidly. This view seems rather perverse in that, in the absence of contracting costs, there would be little reason to have direct foreign investment and all foreign investment would be portfolio investment. This suggests that portfolio investment is a more advanced and more efficient form of international investment. However, there are many ways to obtain financing through sales of securities. The risk of financing through short-term debt is that one might not like the conditions at which the debt can be refinanced. Portfolio flows should not be blamed when a country or a firm has chosen a financing strategy that leaves it exposed to refinancing risks.

Though well established, the view that portfolio investment is more fickle than other forms of investment seems to have little empirical basis. In a useful study, Claessens, Dooley, and Warner (1993) investigated the volatility of foreign direct investment, portfolio equity flows, long-term flows, and short-term flows for five developed economies and five developing countries. They also broke down flows by transactors, namely, foreign direct investors, banks, governments, and the private sector. The developing countries in their sample were Mexico, the Republic of Korea, Indonesia, Argentina, and Brazil. In all cases, they focused on net flows. Their results are surprising in light of the comments about fickle equity flows. They found no support for the notion that equity flows are somehow less stable than direct investment or official flows. They found that the label of flows provides no information about how they behave over time. Their conclusion was that "if presented with one time-series (statistics) only, one will likely be unable to tell the label of the flow" (Claessens et al. 1993, 26).

Liberalization opens the door to capital flows. These flows affect security prices. Another implication of the hypothesis that portfolio flows are excessively volatile is that portfolio flows increase the volatility of security returns. The risk-sharing hypothesis that predicts a decrease in the cost of capital suggests that opening up a country could well decrease the volatility of its security returns. Consider the example of our closed economy that has a comparative advantage in producing coffee beans. An adverse event that decreases the value of the coffee crop makes the country poorer. Suppose that poorer investors are more reluctant to bear risk. In this case, the adverse shock increases the risk premium and hence decreases stock prices even further. If this economy is an open economy, the adverse shock will be spread across investors throughout the world and hence will have only a trivial effect on the risk premium. With this analysis, opening up the economy decreases volatility. However, opening up the economy means that the risk premium on the coffee bean industry now depends on worldwide factors, so that shocks to the world risk premium affect the value of the coffee bean industry. If one thinks that risk premiums should be fairly stable on world markets, then opening up a country decreases volatility if investors who have become poorer are less willing to bear risk.

Let's consider the empirical evidence on volatility and liberalization. A number of different authors have examined this issue, using different approaches. Kim and Singal (1993) considered changes in volatility around liberalizations for a sample of sixteen emerging markets. In their study, they found that volatility in the first twelve months following a liberalization is not significantly different from volatility in the previous twelve months. However, they also found that after the first twelve months, volatility falls significantly on average. They provided other evidence that is consistent with an increase in volatility for some countries and no effect for most countries. Interestingly, the countries for which they found large significant increases were Argentina, Chile, and Mexico. Richards estimated volatility for emerging markets using weekly data and concluded that "the period 1992–1995, which saw foreign institutional investors playing a more significant role in emerging markets has been characterized by volatility that is marginally lower than the remainder of the sample period (1975 to 1992)" (1996, 473). His result is surprising in that it covers the period of the Mexican crisis. Bekaert and Harvey (1997) considered twenty emerging markets and examined stock return volatility before and after liberalization. Using a variety of approaches, they found in all cases that on average liberalization decreases volatility. The bottom line from these studies is that the claim that liberalization increases volatility is not supported by empirical evidence.

These volatility studies do not relate flows directly to volatility. Hamao and

Mei (1996) did this for the case of Japan using monthly data on equity purchases and sales by foreign investors. Foreign portfolio equity investment in Japan has been small over the past twenty years, peaking in 1984 at 10.31 percent but falling back to less than 5 percent in 1990. This means that evidence for Japan has to be viewed with caution on this issue. Nevertheless, they found that trades by foreign investors do not differ in impact on volatility from trades by other investors.

Folkerts-Landau and Ito (1995) computed volatility of emerging markets for periods that differ in the intensity of portfolio flows. Table 5.16 summarizes their evidence. They also showed evidence on the issue of whether a day of high volatility for the Dow Jones predicts high volatility the next day in an emerging market for periods where the nature of flows differ. Overall, their evidence is rather mixed. Mexican stock prices appear to be the least volatile when flows are most volatile. In contrast, however, the Hong Kong stock return volatility is higher when flows are most volatile. There seems to be evidence that local volatility is more strongly linked to the volatility of the Dow Jones in periods of more volatile flows. Models where foreign investors are less well informed than local investors and alter their holdings when they receive new information produce a positive relation between stock return volatility and flow volatility. However, in this case, this relation results mostly from flows and stock prices being driven by the same factors. The relation between flows and volatility would be a source of concern if it were due to temporary increases and decreases in stock prices. It is often argued that such temporary increases and decreases in stock prices can be the result of herding by institutional investors. The idea is that institutional investors behave alike, pouring in and out of stocks as a group. In the most detailed and careful study to date, Wermers (1998) investigated whether U.S. institutional investors herd and whether this behavior leads to temporary changes in stock prices. He found strong evidence of herding behavior, especially for smaller stocks. However, at the same time, he failed to find evidence that herding leads to temporary changes in stock prices. An increase in institutional ownership is associated with an increase in stock prices, but this increase appears to be permanent.

In a detailed investigation of the behavior of foreign investors in Korea in 1997, Choe et al. (1999) found that there is evidence of herding among foreign investors. Their data included all trades on the Korea Stock Exchange for 1997. For each trade, they had information on whether a party to the trade was a foreign investor and the country of origin of that investor. They showed that there is herding among investors from different countries. Further, herding measures for investors from the United States, though upward biased because of the nature of the data, seem extremely high. Surprisingly, however, they found that herding measures were smaller during the last three months of 1997, when the Asian crisis hit Korea, than before. To investigate whether foreign investors have a destabilizing effect on prices, they estimated the impact on prices of large purchases and large sales by foreign investors. They argued that

289 The Role of Equity Markets in International Capital Flows

Table 5.16   **Flows and Volatility of Stock Returns**

Country and Period	Volatility of Daily Returns	Local Volatility Divided by Volatility of Dow Jones	Correlation between Local Squared Return and Previous-Day Dow Jones Squared Return
Hong Kong			
Low inflow			
(Jan. 1988–Aug. 1991)	1.61	1.52	0.068
High inflow			
(Sept. 1991–Oct. 1993)	1.31	1.98	0.023
Volatile flow			
(Nov. 1993–July 1994)	2.33	3.68	0.150
Korea			
Low inflow			
(Jan. 1988–Dec. 1991)	1.51	1.42	0.055
High inflow			
(Jan. 1992–June 1993)	1.18	2.55	0.029
Volatile flow			
(July 1993–July 1994)	1.14	2.31	0.120
Thailand			
Volatile flow			
(Jan. 1988–Apr. 1991)	1.19	1.74	0.296
Moderate inflow			
(May 1991–Oct. 1992)	1.69	2.14	0.115
High flow			
(July 1993–July 1994)	1.17	2.66	0.103
Mexico			
Low inflow			
(Jan. 1988–Apr. 1990)	1.99	1.88	0.048
Volatile flow			
(May 1990–Jan. 1993)	1.57	1.76	0.324
More steady inflow			
(Feb. 1993–July 1994)	1.61	2.57	0.003

Source: Constructed from tables I.13 and I.14 of Folkerts-Landau and Ito (1995).

if foreign investors destabilize prices, they should start runs on prices. Instead, most of the price impact of trades by foreign investors is incorporated in prices within ten minutes and nothing else happens following trades by foreign investors. In other words, there is no evidence that foreign investors start runs on prices. Roughly, the impact of large trades by foreign investors in Korea is no different from the impact of large trades by institutional investors on the NYSE.

5.2.4 Conclusions

The empirical evidence shows that international portfolio flows have a beneficial effect on countries that liberalize, by decreasing the cost of capital in these countries and enabling residents to share risks with other investors. Portfolio inflows seem to have permanent positive effects on valuations. There is no strong empirical support for the view that portfolio flows increase the volatility of security returns or otherwise adversely affect the performance of equity markets. In particular, there is little evidence that the opening of countries has led to substantial increases in the co-movement of their stock markets with the world market. There is evidence that investors find information about one emerging market useful in their assessment of other emerging markets. However, proponents of the view that there is extensive irrational contagion across emerging markets have yet to prove their case.

Opening a country to portfolio flows makes the country better off by enabling it to share risks with foreigners and to lower costs of capital for its industries. It positions the country to receive more capital when the country's investment opportunities improve. The only way a country can take advantage of these benefits is by understanding fully that in a market economy foreign investors pursue the best investment opportunities available as they see them. They have strong incentives to identify all good investment opportunities carefully, because any opportunity they miss lowers the return on their portfolio. Their behavior makes investors as unlikely to be swept away by irrational contagion as to stay passive when governments try to maintain exchange rates and interest rates that are not sustainable.

References

Bailey, W., K. Chan, and Y. P. Chung. 1997. Depository receipts, country funds, and the peso crash: The intraday evidence. Ithaca, N.Y.: Cornell University. Unpublished paper.

Bekaert, G., and C. R. Harvey. 1995. Time-varying world market integration. *Journal of Finance* 50:403–44.

———. 1997. Emerging equity market volatility. *Journal of Financial Economics* 43:29–77.

———. 1999. Foreign speculators and emerging equity markets. Durham, N.C.: Duke University. Working paper.

Bhagwati, J. 1998. The capital myth. *Foreign Affairs* 77 (3): 7–12.

Bohn, Henning, and Linda Tesar. 1996. U.S. equity investment in foreign markets: Portfolio rebalancing or return chasing? *American Economic Review* 86:77–81.

Bordo, M. D., B. Eichengreen, and J. Kim. 1998. Was there really an earlier period of international financial integration comparable to today? NBER Working Paper no. 6738. Cambridge, Mass.: National Bureau of Economic Research.

Brennan, M. J., and H. H. Cao. 1997. International portfolio investment flows. *Journal of Finance* 52:1851–80.

Calvo, G. A., M. Goldstein, and E. Hochreiter. 1997. *Private capital flows to emerging markets after the Mexican crisis.* Washington, D.C.: Institute for International Economics.

Calvo, S., and C. M. Reinhart. 1997. Capital flows to Latin America: Is there evidence of contagion effects? In *Private capital flows to emerging markets after the Mexican crisis,* ed. S. Calvo, M. Goldstein, and E. Hochreiter, 151–71. Washington, D.C.: Institute for International Economics.

Campbell, J. Y., S. J. Grossman, and J. Wang. 1993. Trading volume and serial correlation in stock returns. *Quarterly Journal of Economics* 10:407–32.

Campollo-Palmer, C. 1997. Equity investment in emerging markets. Paper presented at the NYSE Conference on the Globalization of Financial Markets, Cancun, Mexico.

Chan, K. C., G. A. Karolyi, and R. M. Stulz. 1992. Global financial markets and the risk premium on U.S. equity. *Journal of Financial Economics* 32:137–68.

Choe, Y., B. C. Kho, and R. M. Stulz. 1999. Do foreign investors destabilize stock markets? The Korean experience in 1997. *Journal of Financial Economics,* forthcoming.

Claessens, S., M. Dooley, and A. Warner. 1993. Portfolio capital flows: Hot or cool? In *Portfolio investment in developing countries,* ed. S. Claessens and S. Gooptu, 18–44. Washington, D.C.: World Bank.

Claessens, S., and S. Gooptu, eds. 1993. *Portfolio investment in developing countries.* Discussion Paper no. 228. Washington, D.C.: World Bank.

Clark, J., and E. Berko. 1996. Foreign investment fluctuations and emerging market stock returns: The case of Mexico. New York: Federal Reserve Bank of New York. Working paper.

Cooper, I. A., and E. Kaplanis. 1994. Home bias in equity portfolios, inflation hedging and international capital market equilibrium. *Review of Financial Studies* 7:45–60.

De Long, J. B., A. Shleifer, L. Summers, and R. J. Waldman. 1990. Noise trader risk in financial markets. *Journal of Political Economy* 98:703–38.

DeSantis, G. 1993. Asset pricing and portfolio diversification: Evidence from emerging financial markets. In *Portfolio investment in developing countries,* ed. S. Claessens and S. Gooptu, 145–68. Washington, D.C.: World Bank.

DeSantis, G., and B. Gerard. 1997. International asset pricing and portfolio diversification with time-varying risk. *Journal of Finance* 52:1881–1913.

Dornbusch, R., and Y. C. Park. 1995. Financial integration in a second best world: Are we still sure about our classical prejudices? In *Financial opening: Policy lessons for Korea,* ed. R. Dornbusch and Y. C. Park. Seoul: Korea Institute of Finance.

Eichengreen, B., and A. Fishlow. 1998. Contending with capital flows: What is different about the 1990s? In *Capital flows and financial crises,* ed. M. Kahler. Ithaca, N.Y.: Cornell University Press.

Erb, C., C. Harvey, and T. Viskanta. 1996. Expected returns and volatility in 135 countries. *Journal of Portfolio Management* 22:46–58.

Falkenstein, E. G. 1996. Preferences for stock characteristics as revealed by mutual fund portfolio holdings. *Journal of Finance* 51:111–35.

Feldstein, M., and C. Horioka. 1980. Domestic saving and international capital flows. *Economic Journal* 90:314–29.

Folkerts-Landau, D., and T. Ito. 1995. *International capital markets: Developments, prospects, and policy issues.* Washington, D.C.: International Monetary Fund.

Forbes, K., and R. Rigobon. 1998. No contagion, only interdependence: Measuring stock market co-movements. Cambridge: Massachusetts Institute of Technology, Sloan School of Management. Working paper.

Frankel, J. A., and S. L. Schmukler. 1996. Country fund discounts, asymmetric information and the Mexican crisis of 1994: Did local residents turn pessimistic before international investors? NBER Working Paper no. 5714. Cambridge, Mass.: National Bureau of Economic Research.

French, K., and J. Poterba. 1991. International diversification and international equity markets. *American Economic Review* 81:222–26.

Froot, K. A., P. G. O'Connell, and M. S. Seasholes. 1998. The portfolio flows of international investors, I. Boston: Harvard Business School. Working paper.

Froot, K. A., and A. F. Perold. 1995. New trading practices and short-run market efficiency. *Journal of Futures Markets* 15:731–65.

Gagnon, L., and G. A. Karolyi. 1997. Information, trading volume and international stock market co-movements. London: University of Western Ontario. Working paper.

Goldstein, M., and D. Folkerts-Landau. 1994. *International capital markets: Developments, prospects, and policy issues.* Washington, D.C.: International Monetary Fund.

Gompers, P., and J. Lerner. 1997. Money chasing deals? The impact of fund flows on private equity valuation. Boston: Harvard Business School. Working paper.

Hamao, Y., and J. Mei. 1996. Living with the "enemy": An analysis of investment in the Japanese equity market. New York: Columbia University. Working paper.

Harris, L., and E. Gurel. 1986. Price and volume effects associated with changes in the S&P 500 list: New evidence for the existence of price pressures. *Journal of Finance* 41:815–29.

Henry, P. B. 1999a. Equity prices, stock market liberalization, and investment. Palo Alto, Calif.: Stanford University. Working paper.

———. 1999b. Stock market liberalization, economic reform, and emerging market equity prices. *Journal of Finance.* Forthcoming.

Ilmanen, A. 1995. Time-varying expected returns in international bond markets. *Journal of Finance* 50:481–506.

Kang, J.-K., and R. Stulz. 1997. Why is there a home bias? An analysis of foreign portfolio equity ownership in Japan. *Journal of Financial Economics* 46:3–28.

Karolyi, A., and R. Stulz. 1996. Why do markets move together? An examination of U.S.-Japan stock return co-movements. *Journal of Finance* 51:951–86.

Khannah, A. 1996. Equity investment prospects in emerging markets. *Columbia Journal of World Business* 31:32–39.

Kim, E. H., and V. Singal. 1993. Opening up of stock markets by emerging economies: Effects on portfolio flows and volatility of stock prices. In *Portfolio investment in developing countries,* ed. S. Claessens and S. Gooptu, 383–403. Washington, D.C.: World Bank.

Krugman, P. 1998. Saving Asia: It's time to get radical. *Fortune,* 7 September.

Lin, W.-L., and T. Ito. 1994. Price volatility and volume spillovers between the Tokyo and New York stock markets. In *The internationalization of equity markets,* ed. J. Frankel. Chicago: University of Chicago Press.

NYSE (New York Stock Exchange). 1997. *NYSE facts for the year of 1996.* New York: New York Stock Exchange, May.

Obstfeld, M. 1994. Risk-taking, global diversification, and growth. *American Economic Review* 84:1310–29.

Radelet, Steven, and Jeffrey Sachs. 1998. The onset of the East Asian financial crisis. Cambridge, Mass.: Harvard University. Working paper.

Richards, A. J. 1996. Volatility and predictability in national stock markets: How do emerging and mature markets differ? *IMF Staff Papers* 43:461–501.

Rigobon, Roberto. 1998. On the measurement of contagion. Cambridge: Massachusetts Institute of Technology, Sloan School of Management. Working paper.

Sachs, J. D., A. Tornell, and A. Velasco. 1996. Financial crises in emerging markets: The lessons from 1995. *Brookings Papers on Economic Activity,* no. 1:147–217.

Scholes, M. 1972. The market for securities: Substitution versus price pressure and the effects of information on share prices. *Journal of Business* 45:179–211.

Shleifer, A. 1986. Do demand curves for stocks slope down? *Journal of Finance* 41: 579–90.

293   The Role of Equity Markets in International Capital Flows

Shleifer, Andrei, and Robert W. Vishny. 1997. The limits of arbitrage. *Journal of Finance* 52:35–55.

Stiglitz, Joseph. 1998. Boats, planes and capital flows. *Financial Times,* 25 March.

Stulz, R. M. 1995. International portfolio choice and asset pricing: An integrative survey. In *The handbook of modern finance,* ed. V. Maksimovic and W. Ziemba. Amsterdam: North Holland.

———. 1999. Globalization and the cost of equity capital. New York: New York Stock Exchange. Working paper.

Summers, L. H., and V. P. Summers. 1989. When financial markets work too well: The cautious case for a securities transactions tax. *Journal of Financial Services Research* 3:261–86.

Tesar, L., and I. Werner. 1993. U.S. equity investment in emerging stock markets. In *Portfolio investment in developing countries,* ed. S. Claessens and S. Gooptu. Washington, D.C.: World Bank.

———. 1994. International equity transactions and U.S. portfolio choice. In *The internationalization of equity markets,* ed. J. Frankel. Chicago: University of Chicago Press.

Tobin, J. 1978. A proposal for international monetary reform. *Eastern Economic Journal* 4:153–59.

Warther, V. A. 1995. Aggregate mutual fund flows and security returns. *Journal of Financial Economics* 39:209–35.

Wermers, R. 1998. Mutual fund herding and the impact on stock prices. *Journal of Finance* 54:581–622.

Williamson, J. 1993. Issues posed by portfolio investment in developing countries. In *Portfolio investment in developing countries,* ed. S. Claessens and S. Gooptu. Washington, D.C.: World Bank.

World Bank. Various issues. *World debt tables.* Washington, D.C.: World Bank.

D
Liberalization and Diversification Benefits

THE JOURNAL OF FINANCE • VOL. LVI, NO. 2 • APRIL 2001

Testing for Mean-Variance Spanning with Short Sales Constraints and Transaction Costs: The Case of Emerging Markets

FRANS A. DE ROON, THEO E. NIJMAN, and BAS J. M. WERKER*

ABSTRACT

We propose regression-based tests for mean-variance spanning in the case where investors face market frictions such as short sales constraints and transaction costs. We test whether U.S. investors can extend their efficient set by investing in emerging markets when accounting for such frictions. For the period after the major liberalizations in the emerging markets, we find strong evidence for diversification benefits when market frictions are excluded, but this evidence disappears when investors face short sales constraints or small transaction costs. Although simulations suggest that there is a possible small-sample bias, this bias appears to be too small to affect our conclusions.

THE QUESTION OF WHETHER OR NOT an investor can extend his efficient set by including additional assets in his portfolio has recently received considerable attention in the literature. If extension of the efficient set is not possible for a specific mean-variance utility function, the mean-variance frontier of the benchmark assets and of the benchmark assets plus the additional assets intersect, that is, they have one point in common. If extension of the efficient set is not possible for any mean-variance utility function, the mean-variance frontier of the initial assets spans the frontier of the larger set of the initial assets plus the additional assets. These concepts are discussed by Huberman and Kandel (1987), who propose regression-based tests of the hypotheses of spanning and intersection for mean-variance investors. It is well known by now that a shift in the mean-variance frontier from adding assets to the investment opportunity set is tantamount to a shift in the volatility bounds of the kernels that price the assets under consideration (e.g., DeSantis (1994) and Bekaert and Urias (1996)) and that the issue is also very closely related to performance evaluation (see, e.g., Jobson and

* De Roon is from Erasmus University Rotterdam and CEPR, Nijman and Werker are from Tilburg University. Geert Bekaert, Feico Drost, Bruno Gerard, Pierre Hillion, Erzo Luttmer, Bertrand Melenberg, René Stulz (the editor), and an anonymous referee have provided many helpful comments and suggestions. We are also grateful to comments made by participants of the 1997 EFA meetings in Vienna and the 1998 AFA meetings in Chicago, and by seminar participants at INSEAD, the Norwegian School of Management, and the Stockholm School of Economics. The last author thanks the Humbold Universität zu Berlin for its hospitality during a time when part of this research was carried out.

Korkie (1988) and Chen and Knez (1996)). DeRoon, Nijman, and Werker (1997a) show how tests for spanning can be extended to allow for other utility functions, and to allow for the presence of nonmarketable risks.

Tests for intersection and spanning have been applied to numerous problems in the finance literature. A crucial assumption in almost all these applications is the absence of market frictions such as short sales restrictions and transaction costs. However, for many investors such frictions are important facts of life. The aim of this paper is to extend the tests for mean-variance spanning and intersection to take these market frictions into account.

The presence of transaction costs and short sales constraints is perhaps most predominant in the case of emerging markets. Using the Emerging Markets Data Base (EMDB) of the International Finance Corporation (IFC), both DeSantis (1994) and Harvey (1995) show that the mean-variance frontier that is based on well-developed Western markets only significantly shifts outward when the emerging markets are included. However, these results presuppose that there are no transaction costs or any other market frictions for both the developed and the emerging markets. Bekaert and Urias (1996) try to overcome this problem using returns on closed-end country funds, because the returns on these funds are attainable to investors. Based on emerging market country funds, Bekaert and Urias find only mixed evidence for the diversification benefits of emerging markets. Although the use of country funds adjusts for the effect of transaction costs and short sales constraints that investors face in emerging markets, it does not account for short sales constraints and transaction costs on the country funds themselves or on the benchmark assets.

Using industry portfolios, multinational corporation stocks, closed-end country funds, and American depository receipts, Errunza, Hogan, and Hung (1999) show that U.S. investors can create mimicking portfolios from U.S.-traded securities that are highly correlated with the IFC emerging markets indices. Their spanning tests show that for five out of the nine emerging markets that they study, direct investments in the emerging markets provide significant diversification benefits beyond diversified portfolios created from U.S.-traded securities. Errunza et al. (1999) do not consider short sales constraints or transaction costs on either the emerging markets or the U.S.-traded securities. Note that the effect of transaction costs will probably be smaller for the U.S.-traded securities than for the emerging markets, but that short sales constraints may cause the diversification benefits from direct investments in the emerging markets to be even stronger than suggested by the results of Errunza et al. (1999).

We provide direct evidence on the effect of transaction costs and short selling constraints on the diversification benefits of emerging markets by using the same IFC indices as in DeSantis (1994) and Harvey (1995), but incorporating these market frictions in our testing methodology. If frictions are ignored, we find that there are significant diversification benefits from adding emerging markets to an international stock portfolio that invests in the United States, Europe, and Japan. The evidence in favor of these diver-

sification benefits disappears when we take short sales constraints and investability restrictions into account, because in this case, for the three
geographical regions, the hypothesis of spanning cannot be rejected. This
effect is mainly due to the short sales constraints for the emerging markets
and not to the short sales constraints on the benchmark assets. Also, with
an investment horizon of six months and round trip costs of 0.5 percent on
the benchmark assets, we find that significant diversification benefits from
investing in the emerging markets are absent with only small transaction
costs on the emerging markets. Although our simulations suggest that there
is a possible small-sample bias in the asymptotic test, the magnitude of the
bias appears to be small.

The plan of this paper is as follows. In Section I we, first of all, formulate
the hypotheses of mean-variance spanning and intersection in the case of
short sales restrictions. Regression-based tests for these hypotheses are proposed in Section II. The empirical results on investing in emerging markets
are presented in Section III and in the final section we give some concluding
remarks.

I. Mean-variance Spanning With Short Sales Constraints

Consider a set of K assets, whose gross returns are given by the vector
$\mathbf{R}_{t+1}$. Investors can hold portfolios $\mathbf{w} \in C \subset I\!R^K$ such that $\mathbf{w}'\iota_K = 1$, where
ι_K is a K-vector containing only ones. The set of returns available to inves-
tors is therefore given by

$$X = \{R_{t+1}^P : R_{t+1}^P = \mathbf{w}'\mathbf{R}_{t+1}, \mathbf{w} \in C, \text{ and } \mathbf{w}'\iota_K = 1\}.$$

In case there are no market frictions, we have $C = I\!R^K$. If, in addition, the
Law of One Price holds, there exists a stochastic discount factor M_{t+1} such
that

$$E[M_{t+1}\mathbf{R}_{t+1}|I_t] = \iota_K, \tag{1}$$

where I_t denotes the information set that is available to investors at time t
(see, e.g., Duffie (1996)). In this paper, we will restrict ourselves to unconditional versions of equation (1) and to unconditional mean-variance spanning. Extensions of our results to the conditional case are straightforward
however (see, e.g., DeSantis (1994) and DeRoon et al. (1997a)). The stochastic discount factor $m(v)_{t+1}$ that has expectation v and that corresponds to a
mean-variance utility function, is a linear function of the asset returns:

$$m(v)_{t+1} = v + \boldsymbol{\alpha}'(\mathbf{R}_{t+1} - E[\mathbf{R}_{t+1}]), \tag{2a}$$

$$\boldsymbol{\alpha} = \text{Var}[\mathbf{R}_{t+1}]^{-1}(\iota_K - vE[\mathbf{R}_{t+1}]). \tag{2b}$$

From Hansen and Jagannathan (1991) we know that the discount factor given in equation (2) has the lowest variance of all stochastic discount factors with expectation v, that price $\mathbf{R}_{t+1}$ correctly. It is also well known that $\mathbf{w} = \boldsymbol{\alpha}/(\boldsymbol{\alpha}'\boldsymbol{\iota}_K)$ is a mean-variance efficient portfolio that has a zero-beta return equal to $1/v$.

Now consider the presence of market frictions such as short sales constraints and transaction costs. These can be dealt with by letting C be a particular subset of $I\!\!R^K$ and/or by adjusting the vector of returns $\mathbf{R}_{t+1}$ to reflect the frictions. In case of short sales constraints, $C = I\!\!R^K_+$, the nonnegative part of $I\!\!R^K$.[1] When there are short sales constraints on the portfolio holdings, the condition in equation (1) must be replaced by

$$E[m(v)_{t+1}\mathbf{R}_{t+1}] \leq \boldsymbol{\iota}_K, \tag{3}$$

where the inequality sign applies componentwise.

The mean-variance efficient frontier without short sales can be found by solving the problem

$$\max_{\{\mathbf{w}\}} \mathbf{w}'E[\mathbf{R}_{t+1}] - \tfrac{1}{2}\gamma\mathbf{w}'\,\mathrm{Var}[\mathbf{R}_{t+1}]\mathbf{w}, \tag{4}$$

$$\text{s.t. } \mathbf{w}'\boldsymbol{\iota}_K = 1 \quad \text{and} \quad w_i \geq 0, \quad \forall i,$$

where γ is the coefficient of risk aversion. From the Kuhn-Tucker conditions, mean-variance efficient portfolios $\mathbf{w}^*$ satisfy

$$E[\mathbf{R}_{t+1}] - \eta\boldsymbol{\iota}_K + \boldsymbol{\delta} = \gamma\,\mathrm{Var}[\mathbf{R}_{t+1}]\mathbf{w}^*,$$

$$w_i^*, \delta_i \geq 0, \quad \forall i, \tag{5}$$

$$\delta_i w_i^* = 0, \quad \forall i.$$

The vector $\boldsymbol{\delta}$ contains the Kuhn-Tucker multipliers for the restrictions that the portfolio weights are nonnegative. The Lagrange multiplier for the restriction that $\mathbf{w}'\boldsymbol{\iota}_K = 1$ is equal to η, the intercept of the line that is tangent to the mean-variance frontier in mean-standard deviation space.

Now take the mean-variance efficient portfolio for which $\eta = 1/v$, with v the expectation of a stochastic discount factor that prices $\mathbf{R}_{t+1}$ correctly subject to short sales constraints. Denote by $\mathbf{R}_{t+1}^{(v)}$ the L-dimensional subvector of $\mathbf{R}_{t+1}$ that only contains the returns of the assets for which the short sales constraints in equation (5) are not binding and let superscripts $^{(v)}$ refer to this subset. It is straightforward to show that the mean-variance efficient

---

[1] More generally, if we have a vector of lower bounds $\mathbf{w}_0$ on the portfolio weights, then we have that $\mathbf{w} \geq \mathbf{w}_0$ and $\mathbf{w} - \mathbf{w}_0 \in I\!\!R^K_+$.

portfolio in equation (5) is equal to the mean-variance efficient portfolio without short sales constraints of the assets in $\mathbf{R}_{t+1}^{(v)}$ only (see, e.g., Markowitz (1991)):

$$E[\mathbf{R}_{t+1}^{(v)}] - \frac{1}{v}\, \iota_L = \gamma^{(v)}\, \mathrm{Var}[\mathbf{R}_{t+1}^{(v)}]\mathbf{w}^{(v)} \quad \text{and}$$

$$(6)$$

$$E[\mathbf{R}_{t+1}] - \frac{1}{v}\, \iota_K + \boldsymbol{\delta} = \gamma^{(v)}\, \mathrm{Cov}[\mathbf{R}_{t+1}, \mathbf{R}_{t+1}^{(v)}]\mathbf{w}^{(v)},$$

where $\mathrm{Cov}[\mathbf{R}_{t+1}, \mathbf{R}_{t+1}^{(v)}]$ is the $K \times L$-dimensional covariance matrix of $\mathbf{R}_{t+1}$ and its subvector $\mathbf{R}_{t+1}^{(v)}$.

Because the mean-variance stochastic discount factor is a linear function of the mean-variance efficient portfolio, in case of short sales restrictions, the mean-variance stochastic discount factor that prices $\mathbf{R}_{t+1}$, $m_R(v)_{t+1}$, is equal to

$$m_R(v)_{t+1} = v + \boldsymbol{\alpha}^{(v)\prime}(\mathbf{R}_{t+1}^{(v)} - E[\mathbf{R}_{t+1}^{(v)}]),$$

$$(7)$$

$$\boldsymbol{\alpha}^{(v)} = \mathrm{Var}[\mathbf{R}_{t+1}^{(v)}]^{-1}(\iota_L - vE[\mathbf{R}_{t+1}^{(v)}]).$$

It is not hard to show that the stochastic discount factor as defined in equation (7) has the lowest variance of all pricing kernels that price $\mathbf{R}_{t+1}$ correctly, subject to short sales constraints. Therefore, in case of short sales constraints, the duality between mean-variance frontiers and volatility bounds still holds.

Next consider a set of N additional assets with return vector $\mathbf{r}_{t+1}$ besides the set of K benchmark assets with return vector $\mathbf{R}_{t+1}$. Mean-variance spanning of the assets $\mathbf{r}_{t+1}$ by the benchmark assets $\mathbf{R}_{t+1}$ occurs if the mean-variance stochastic discount factors that price $\mathbf{R}_{t+1}$ correctly also price $\mathbf{r}_{t+1}$, that is, if

$$E[m_R(v)_{t+1}\mathbf{r}_{t+1}] \leq \iota_N, \qquad (8)$$

holds for all values of v. Substituting equation (7) into equation (8), this is equivalent to

$$vE[\mathbf{r}_{t+1}] + \mathrm{Cov}[\mathbf{r}_{t+1}, \mathbf{R}_{t+1}^{(v)}]\mathrm{Var}[\mathbf{R}_{t+1}^{(v)}]^{-1}(\iota_L - vE[\mathbf{R}_{t+1}^{(v)}]) \leq \iota_N. \qquad (9)$$

The inequality sign in equation (8) reflects the fact that there are short sales constraints on $\mathbf{r}_{t+1}$. In the absence of short sales constraints on $\mathbf{r}_{t+1}$, the inequality becomes an equality. If there is only one value of v for which equation (8) holds, then there is intersection.

When taking transaction costs into account, it is useful to differentiate between the return on a long position in asset i, $\tau_i^\ell R_{i,t+1}$, and the return on a short position in asset i, $\tau_i^s R_{i,t+1}$ (see, e.g., Luttmer (1996)). Let $\tilde{\mathbf{R}}_{t+1}$ be a $2K$-dimensional vector, the first K elements of which are the returns on the long positions in the assets $i = 1,\ldots,K$, and the last K elements of which are the returns on the short positions in these same assets. Thus, $\tilde{R}_{i,t+1} = \tau_i^\ell R_{i,t+1}$ and $\tilde{R}_{i+K,t+1} = \tau_i^s R_{i,t+1}$. Considering $\tilde{\mathbf{R}}_{t+1}$ as the vector of returns on $2K$ different assets, transaction costs can now be handled by requiring that investors cannot go short in the first K assets ($C = \mathbb{R}_+^K$) and cannot go long in the last K assets ($C = \mathbb{R}_-^K$). Let $\tilde{m}_R(v)_{t+1}$ be the mean-variance stochastic discount factor that prices $\tilde{\mathbf{R}}_{t+1}$ correctly and let $\tilde{\mathbf{R}}_{t+1}^{(v)}$ be the L-dimensional subvector of $\tilde{\mathbf{R}}_{t+1}$ for which the constraints on the short and long positions are not binding. The notation is therefore analogous to the case of short sales constraints only. The mean-variance stochastic discount factor is now given by[2]

$$\tilde{m}_R(v)_{t+1} = v + \tilde{\boldsymbol{\alpha}}^{(v)\prime}(\tilde{\mathbf{R}}_{t+1}^{(v)} - E[\tilde{\mathbf{R}}_{t+1}^{(v)}]),$$

$$\tilde{\boldsymbol{\alpha}}^{(v)} = \text{Var}[\tilde{\mathbf{R}}_{t+1}^{(v)}]^{-1}(\boldsymbol{\iota}_L - vE[\tilde{\mathbf{R}}_{t+1}^{(v)}]). \tag{10}$$

In a similar way, we consider long and short positions in the N additional asset as $2N$ different assets. The returns on long positions in the additional assets are given by $(\tilde{\mathbf{r}}_{t+1}^\ell)_k = \tau_k^\ell r_{k,t+1}$, $k = 1,2,\ldots,N$, and the returns on short positions are given by $(\tilde{\mathbf{r}}_{t+1}^s)_k = \tau_k^s r_{k,t+1}$, $k = 1,2,\ldots,N$. The returns on the additional assets are then spanned by the benchmark assets if

$$E[\tilde{m}_R^{[j]}(v)_{t+1}\tilde{\mathbf{r}}_{t+1}^\ell] \le \boldsymbol{\iota}_N, \quad \forall j,$$

$$E[\tilde{m}_R^{[j]}(v)_{t+1}\tilde{\mathbf{r}}_{t+1}^s] \ge \boldsymbol{\iota}_N, \quad \forall j. \tag{11}$$

II. Testing for Intersection and Spanning

Absent short sales constraints and any other market frictions, the hypotheses of mean-variance intersection and spanning are equivalent to the condition that

$$E[m_R(v)_{t+1}\mathbf{r}_{t+1}] = \boldsymbol{\iota}_N, \tag{12}$$

for one value of v (intersection) or for all values of v (spanning). It is well known that in this case tests for intersection and spanning can be based on the regression

$$\mathbf{r}_{t+1} = \mathbf{a} + \mathbf{B}\mathbf{R}_{t+1} + \boldsymbol{\varepsilon}_{t+1}, \tag{13}$$

---

[2] In the portfolio problem with transaction costs, agents are prevented from taking simultaneous short and long positions in one asset, which would effectively create a long position in a risk-free asset with a negative return. Therefore, $\text{Var}[\tilde{\mathbf{R}}_{t+1}^{(v)}]$ is a nonsingular matrix.

with $E[\boldsymbol{\varepsilon}_{t+1}] = \mathbf{0}$ and $E[\boldsymbol{\varepsilon}_{t+1}\mathbf{R}'_{t+1}] = \mathbf{0}$. Intersection for a given value of v implies that $\mathbf{a}v + (\mathbf{B}\boldsymbol{\iota}_K - \boldsymbol{\iota}_N) = \mathbf{0}$, and spanning implies that $\mathbf{a} = \mathbf{0}$ and $\mathbf{B}\boldsymbol{\iota}_K - \boldsymbol{\iota}_N = \mathbf{0}$ (Huberman and Kandel (1987), Bekaert and Urias (1996)). Alternatively, GMM tests can be used to test for intersection and spanning (DeSantis (1994), Hansen, Heaton, and Luttmer (1995), Chen and Knez (1996)). As shown in the previous section, if there are short sales restrictions on the benchmark assets $\mathbf{R}_{t+1}$, the stochastic discount factor $m_R(v)_{t+1}$ is a linear function of $\mathbf{R}_{t+1}^{(v)}$ only, and if there are short sales restrictions on the additional assets $\mathbf{r}_{t+1}$, then the equality in equation (12) becomes an inequality. For a given value of v, the restrictions implied by intersection are given in equation (9). These restrictions are equivalent to the restrictions that in the regression

$$\mathbf{r}_{t+1} = \mathbf{a}^{(v)} + \mathbf{B}^{(v)}\mathbf{R}_{t+1}^{(v)} + \boldsymbol{\varepsilon}_{t+1}^{(v)},\tag{14}$$

it holds true that

$$v\mathbf{a}^{(v)} + (\mathbf{B}^{(v)}\boldsymbol{\iota}_L - \boldsymbol{\iota}_N) \leq \mathbf{0}.\tag{15}$$

Intuitively, since in case of short sales constraints, the mean-variance efficient portfolio of $\mathbf{R}_{t+1}$ for a given value of v consists of positions in only those assets for which the constraints are not binding, intersection requires that there is intersection at the unrestricted frontier of $\mathbf{R}_{t+1}^{(v)}$.

A Wald test can be used to test the inequality constraints in equation (15) (see, e.g., Kodde and Palm (1986)). Denote the left hand side of equation (15) as $v\boldsymbol{\alpha}_J(v)$, where $\boldsymbol{\alpha}_J(v)$ is the N-dimensional vector of Jensen's alphas of the assets $\mathbf{r}_{t+1}$ relative to the mean-variance efficient portfolio of $\mathbf{R}_{t+1}^{(v)}$ with zero-beta return $1/v$. The sample equivalent of $\boldsymbol{\alpha}_J(v)$ is $\hat{\boldsymbol{\alpha}}_J(v)$, and the estimated $N \times N$ covariance matrix of $\hat{\boldsymbol{\alpha}}_J(v)$, $\mathrm{Var}[\hat{\boldsymbol{\alpha}}_J(v)]$, can be obtained from the restricted covariance matrix of the OLS-estimates of equation (14), where the restrictions are given by $v\mathbf{a}^{(v)} + (\mathbf{B}^{(v)}\boldsymbol{\iota}_L - \boldsymbol{\iota}_N) = \mathbf{0}$. Following Kodde and Palm (1986), under the null hypothesis and standard regularity conditions, the test statistic

$$\xi(v) = \min_{\{\boldsymbol{\alpha}_J(v)\leq 0\}} (\hat{\boldsymbol{\alpha}}_J(v) - \boldsymbol{\alpha}_J(v))' \mathrm{Var}[\hat{\boldsymbol{\alpha}}_J(v)]^{-1}(\hat{\boldsymbol{\alpha}}_J(v) - \boldsymbol{\alpha}_J(v)),\tag{16}$$

is asymptotically distributed as a mixture of χ^2 distributions. For the case considered here, where we test whether there is intersection for the N assets $\mathbf{r}_{t+1}$, the probability of $\xi(v)$ exceeding a given value c is, under the null hypothesis, given by (see, e.g., Kodde and Palm (1986))

$$\Pr\{\xi(v) \geq c\} = \sum_{i=0}^{N} \Pr\{\chi_i^2 \geq c\}w(N,i,\mathrm{Var}[\hat{\boldsymbol{\alpha}}_J(v)]),\tag{17}$$

where $w(N, i, \text{Var}[\hat{\boldsymbol{\alpha}}_J])$ are probability weights.[3] Given the estimated covariance matrix $\text{Var}[\hat{\boldsymbol{\alpha}}_J(v)]$, the probabilities can be determined using numerical simulation, as proposed by Gouriéroux, Holly, and Montfort (1982). Alternatively, without calculating the weights, Kodde and Palm (1986) give expressions for an upper and a lower bound on the p values of $\xi(v)$.

Of course, when implementing the intersection test in empirical applications, it is usually the case that for a particular value of v, we do not observe which assets are in $\mathbf{R}_{t+1}^{(v)}$, but have to derive this information from the asset returns in our sample. It is shown in the Appendix that this does not affect the limit distribution of the Wald test statistic for the restrictions in equation (15) however, if v corresponds to an efficient portfolio where none of the weights in $\mathbf{w}^{(v)}$ is exactly zero (i.e., $w_i^* = 0$ and $\delta_i > 0$). If this latter situation occurs, then it is easily verified that the size of the test (conditional on $\mathbf{R}_{t+1}^{(v)}$) does not depend on $\mathbf{R}_{t+1}^{(v)}$, and hence the unconditional size equals the one chosen, which shows the validity of our test.

Glen and Jorion (1993) propose a test for intersection with short sales constraints based on the difference in Sharpe ratios[4] of the benchmark assets and the total set of assets. Unlike the test statistic in equation (16) however, their test does not yield a known distribution. Apart from this, our procedure has the advantage that we avoid the assumption that one of the assets is riskless and that the test can also be used to test for spanning.

Up to now, we considered tests for intersection. Spanning implies that the restrictions in equation (15) hold for all relevant values of v. Notice that for a given set of K asset returns $\mathbf{R}_{t+1}$, there is only a finite number of subsets with $L^{(v)}$ elements, $L^{(v)} \in \{1, 2, ..., K\}$, with $\mathbf{R}_{t+1}^{(v)}$ the $L^{(v)}$-dimensional vector containing the returns on the subset of the assets. Let $V^{[j]}$ be the set of those values of v for which the subset of assets for which the short sales constraints in the mean-variance efficient portfolios are not binding is the same, and denote the $L^{[j]}$-dimensional vector of returns for these assets as $\mathbf{R}_{t+1}^{[j]}$, that is, $\mathbf{R}_{t+1}^{[j]} = \mathbf{R}_{t+1}^{(v)}$ if and only if $v \in V^{[j]}$. Similarly, each variable or parameter that refers to the set $\mathbf{R}_{t+1}^{[j]}$ will be denoted with a superscript $[j]$. Because for $v \in V^{[j]}$ the mean-variance efficient frontier of $\mathbf{R}_{t+1}$ coincides with the mean-variance frontier of $\mathbf{R}_{t+1}^{[j]}$, the mean-variance frontier of $\mathbf{R}_{t+1}$ with short sales constraints consists of a finite number of parts of the unrestricted mean-variance frontiers of the subsets $\mathbf{R}_{t+1}^{[j]}$. It follows that the return on the additional assets $\mathbf{r}_{t+1}$ are spanned by the returns on the benchmark assets $\mathbf{R}_{t+1}$ if

$$E[m_R^{[j]}(v)_{t+1}\mathbf{r}_{t+1}] \leq \iota_N, \quad \forall j, \tag{18}$$

---

[3] The weights $w(N, i, \text{Var}[\hat{\boldsymbol{\alpha}}_J])$ are the probabilities that $(N - i)$ of the N elements of a vector with a $N(0, \text{Var}[\hat{\boldsymbol{\alpha}}_J])$ distribution are strictly negative.

[4] In fact, the test statistic in equation (16) can also be expressed in terms of Sharpe ratios. For details, see DeRoon, Nijman, and Werker (1997b).

where $m_R^{[j]}(v)_{t+1}$ is the mean-variance pricing kernel with expectation v that is linear in $\mathbf{R}_{t+1}^{[j]}$. If there are only short sales constraints on the benchmark assets $\mathbf{R}_{t+1}$ and not on the additional assets $\mathbf{r}_{t+1}$, the inequality in equation (18) becomes an equality. If there are only short sales constraints on $\mathbf{r}_{t+1}$ and not on $\mathbf{R}_{t+1}$, $\mathbf{R}_{t+1}^{[j]} = \mathbf{R}_{t+1}$.

If there are short sales constraints, then the mean-variance frontier of $\mathbf{R}_{t+1}$ consists of parts of the unrestricted mean-variance frontiers of the subsets of returns $\mathbf{R}_{t+1}^{[j]}$, $j = 1, 2, \ldots, M$, and $\mathbf{r}_{t+1}$ can only be spanned by the returns $\mathbf{R}_{t+1}$ if it is spanned by the M subsets of $\mathbf{R}_{t+1}$. If there are also short sales restrictions on $\mathbf{r}_{t+1}$, then the conditions in equation (18) imply that there is mean-variance spanning if and only if in the M regressions

$$\mathbf{r}_{t+1} = \mathbf{a}^{[j]} + \mathbf{B}^{[j]}\mathbf{R}_{t+1}^{[j]} + \boldsymbol{\varepsilon}_{t+1}^{[j]}, \tag{19a}$$

$$\mathbf{a}^{[j]}v + \mathbf{B}^{[j]}\boldsymbol{\iota}^{[j]} \leq \boldsymbol{\iota}_N, \quad \text{for all } v \in V^{[j]}. \tag{19b}$$

where $\boldsymbol{\iota}^{[j]}$ is an $L^{[j]}$-dimensional vector consisting of ones. The hypothesis that there is spanning can therefore easily be tested by using a multivariate regression of $\mathbf{r}_{t+1}$ on all $\mathbf{R}_{t+1}^{[j]}$ and using a Wald test for the restrictions in each of these regressions. Denoting $v_{\min}^{[j]} = \min_{v \in V^{[j]}} v$, and $v_{\max}^{[j]} = \max_{v \in V^{[j]}} v$, the restrictions in equation (19b) are satisfied if there is intersection for $v_{\min}^{[j]}$ and for $v_{\max}^{[j]}$, because in that case, there is also intersection for all the intermediate values of $v^{[j]}$. Therefore, testing for spanning comes down to jointly testing the restrictions:

$$\mathbf{a}^{[j]}v_{\min}^{[j]} + \mathbf{B}^{[j]}\boldsymbol{\iota}^{[j]} \leq \boldsymbol{\iota}_N,$$

$$\mathbf{a}^{[j]}v_{\max}^{[j]} + \mathbf{B}^{[j]}\boldsymbol{\iota}^{[j]} \leq \boldsymbol{\iota}_N, \tag{20}$$

for $j = 1, \ldots, M$. Again, a Wald test statistic for the inequality restrictions in equation (20) is asymptotically distributed as a mixture of χ^2 distributions. With transaction costs, testing for intersection or spanning is completely analogous to the case of short sales constraints, except that we have to take into account both negativity and positivity constraints.

The total range of v can be limited beforehand. An upper bound on v is obtained if we do not impose the requirement that investors should invest *all* their wealth in the available assets, but may choose to invest only part of their wealth, that is, $0 \leq \mathbf{w}'\boldsymbol{\iota} \leq 1$ (see also Luttmer (1996)). In effect, this allows for the possibility of taking long positions in a risk-free asset with zero net return. This implies that the upper bound for v is 1. If we move upward along the mean-variance frontier, v decreases until $1/v$ equals the intercept of the asymptote of the lines tangent to the mean-variance frontier. This intercept is equal to the expected return on the global minimum variance portfolio, $E[R_{t+1}^{GMV}]$, implying that the lower bound on v is given by $v = 1/E[R_{t+1}^{GMV}]$. Of course, these boundaries have to be adjusted in case there are short sales constraints and/or transaction costs on the benchmark assets $\mathbf{R}_{t+1}$.

The intersection and spanning tests presented here are closely related to the region subset test in Hansen et al. (1995), which is essentially a test for intersection. Hanson et al. (1995) estimate the minimum variance stochastic discount factor $m(v)_{t+1}$ under nonnegativity constraints (which induces a nonstandard limit distribution), in which case they end up with testing equality restrictions. On the other hand, our regression-based estimator is unrestricted with a standard asymptotic distribution, but we end up with more difficult inequality restrictions that have to be tested. This latter problem is well studied in the literature, however (see, e.g., Gouriéroux et al. (1982) and Kodde and Palm (1986)).[5]

To have an indication of the power of the spanning test with short sales constraints, Figure 1 presents the power as a function of the intercept $a^{[j]}$ in the spanning regression (19a). The figure contains the power function for the Wald spanning test statistics in the case where there are no frictions, in the case where there are short sales constraints for the new asset r_{t+1} only, and in the case where there are short sales constraints for both the new assets as well as for the benchmark assets. When there are short sales constraints on the benchmark assets, the test depends on the benchmark assets that are included in the segments, and hence the power function for the case of short sales constraints on all assets is shown when the elements in $\mathbf{R}^{[j]}$ are known as well as when they have to be estimated. The slope parameters are chosen such that in the case of short sales constraints, our test has maximum rejection probability in the null if the intercept $a^{[j]}$ is equal to zero.

For each value of $a^{[j]}$, the small-sample power is derived from a series of 1,000 simulations. In addition, for the case of no short sales, we also add the theoretical power of the spanning test, which may serve as a benchmark for the other tests.[6] For each simulation, 10 years of monthly data are generated and the empirical power for a size of 5 percent is determined. The benchmark indices are assumed to be the three stock indices used in the empirical application in Section III, where the data generating process for these indices is based on the summary statistics in Table II, assuming multivariate normality. For the new asset, the monthly standard deviation of the residual ε_{t+1} in equation (19a) is 10 percent, which is representative for the emerging markets that are analyzed in Section III. The figure plots the power for small values of $a^{[j]}$, because these appear to be the most relevant ones in the empirical application. Notice that $a^{[j]} < 0$, which is tantamount to a

---

[5] A detailed comparison between our test and the region subset test proposed by Hansen et al. (1995) is provided in DeRoon et al. (1997b). This comparison can be obtained from the authors upon request.

[6] We thank the referee for making this suggestion.

Short Sales Constraints and Transaction Costs 731

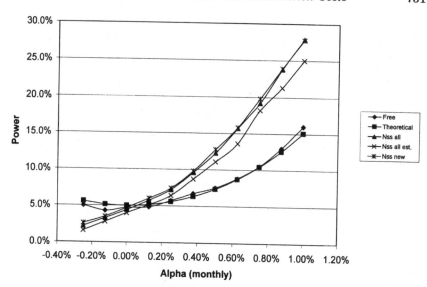

Figure 1. Power functions. The figure presents the power function as a function of the intercept in equation (19a). For each value of the intercept (Alpha), the power is derived from a series of 1,000 simulations with 120 monthly observations each, when the rejection rate is 5 percent. The theoretical power is presented (Theoretical) as well as the power for the test with no short sales constraints (Free), with short sales constraints on the new asset only (Nss new) and with short sales constraints on all assets (Nss all) in case the benchmark assets are known, and with short sales constraints on the new assets when the benchmark assets are estimated during the simulations (Nss all est.).

negative Jensen measure $\alpha_J(v)$ in our simulations, implies that there is spanning if there are short sales constraints. This explains the low rejection probabilities for negative values of $a^{[j]}$ in Figure 1.

As Figure 1 shows, the different tests are very similar with respect to power. Notice that, for the spanning test with short sales constraints on all assets, there is only a small difference between the power functions for the case where the elements in $\mathbf{R}^{[j]}$ have to be estimated and for the case where these elements are known. This confirms the result in the Appendix that shows that the limit distribution of the spanning test is not affected by the fact that the elements in $\mathbf{R}^{[j]}$ have to be estimated. For the case where the elements in $\mathbf{R}^{[j]}$ have to be estimated, the power is somewhat smaller than in the other cases though, suggesting that in this case, there may be a minor small-sample bias, which may lead to underrejection of the null hypothesis.

Table I gives rejection rates for the asymptotic critical values of the Wald test statistics with short sales constraints in several finite samples. In this table, we use the same data generating process that underlies Figure 1, in case $a^{[j]} = 0$, with 10,000 simulations. These rejection rates will also be used in the empirical analysis in Section III to incorporate the possible effects

732

Table I

Simulated Rejection Rates of the Wald Test Statistics

The table contains the rejection rates in finite samples of the Wald test statistics for spanning for several significance levels. p values are given for the spanning test when there are short sales constraints on the new assets only (nss new) and when there are short sales constraints on both the new assets and the benchmark assets (nss all). When there are short sales on all assets, the relevant subsets from the benchmark assets where the short sales constraints are not binding are estimated during the simulation. The p values are derived form a series of 10,000 simulations with 5, 10, 25, or 50 years of monthly data. The simulation assumes that the new asset is spanned by the three benchmark assets which are given in Table II.

	nss new			nss all		
Significance	0.100	0.050	0.010	0.100	0.050	0.010
5 years	0.099	0.050	0.011	0.083	0.042	0.008
10 years	0.096	0.050	0.009	0.089	0.044	0.008
25 years	0.100	0.051	0.010	0.092	0.046	0.010
50 years	0.097	0.049	0.010	0.097	0.049	0.009

of a small-sample bias. The first three columns of Table I show the rejection probabilities in finite samples using the asymptotic critical values, in the case where there are only short sales constraints on the new asset. From these numbers, it appears that the rejection rates in finite samples are almost indistinguishable from the asymptotic rejection rates. Therefore, in this case there does not seem to be a small-sample bias, and we can use the asymptotic test with confidence, even in samples as small as five years of monthly data. The last three columns show similar rejection rates in the case where there are short sales constraints on both the new asset and the benchmark assets. Here the elements $\mathbf{R}^{[j]}$ are not assumed to be known, but have to be estimated. For this case, there does seem to be a possible small-sample bias. The rejection rates are always smaller than the asymptotic ones and appear to be increasing monotonically with the sample size. The bias appears to be small, though, and for sample sizes of 10 years of monthly data, the rejection rates are close enough to the asymptotic ones for the test to be used with confidence. For the empirical analysis in Section III the large sample properties of the tests appear to be sufficiently informative, as the small-sample adjustment does not alter any of the conclusions.

III. Empirical Results for Emerging Markets

A. Data

We use 17 indices from the Emerging Markets Data Base of the International Finance Corporation. Monthly observations on the Global Indices are available over the period of January 1985 until June 1996, for six Latin

American countries, seven Asian countries, one European, one Middle Eastern, and two African countries. The Morgan Stanley Capital International (MSCI) Indices for the United States, Europe, and Japan serve as the benchmark assets. The dataset is therefore very similar to the ones used by DeSantis (1994) and Harvey (1995). For all these indices we use (unhedged) monthly holding returns in U.S. dollars. The indices for both the emerging markets and for the developed markets are calculated with dividends reinvested. All data are obtained from Datastream.

Bekaert et al. (1998) provide ample indications that the behavior of the emerging market returns might have been changing over time. One important reason for this is the many liberalizations that have taken place in the emerging markets (see, e.g., Bekaert (1995)), causing the emerging markets to become more integrated with the developed markets. Therefore, we focus on the diversification benefits that are offered by the emerging markets for the postliberalization periods only. Starting dates for the emerging markets data that we used (if different from January 1985) are given in Panel B of Table II. Results for the regions Latin America, Asia, and "Other" are based on data since the last liberalization in that region.

Some basic summary statistics for net monthly holding returns are given in Table II. Table II provides summary data on the three benchmark indices as well as for the emerging markets. In this table and the following, the emerging markets are organized according to their geographical region: Latin America, Asia, and Other. A quick look at the data reveals that the emerging markets indices are usually much more variable than the benchmark indices, but also have somewhat higher average returns. For the monthly holding returns we use, the average standard deviation of the emerging markets indices is 10.43 percent and the average expected return is 1.82 percent, compared with 5.54 percent and 1.46 percent for the benchmark indices. Also notice that there is substantial cross-sectional variation in the average returns of the emerging markets. The average correlation of the emerging markets with the developed markets (not reported in Table II) is only 0.09 whereas the correlation between the developed markets themselves is as high as 0.33.

B. Results for Spanning Tests With Short Sales Constraints

Based on the summary statistics, it may be conjectured that, in the absence of market frictions, many emerging markets yield diversification benefits relative to the benchmark indices for the United States, Europe, and Japan. Table III shows Wald test statistics for the hypothesis that the returns on these three indices span the returns for each emerging market. For each group, the first line shows the spanning test statistic and the associated p value in case there are no short sales restrictions on any asset. The joint tests for spanning for all the emerging markets within a geographical group show that spanning is always rejected at any confidence level. These results merely confirm the findings of, for instance, DeSantis (1994) and

Table II

Summary Statistics

Panel A provides summary statistics for monthly dollar returns on the MSCI Indices that serve as the benchmark assets. Panel B provides summary statistics for the IFC Emerging Markets Data Base. The overall sample period is January 1985 until June 1996, giving a total of 138 observations. For the emerging markets, if major liberalizations occurred in this period, only the postliberalization periods as indicated in the last column of Panel B are used.

Panel A: Benchmark Assets (January 1985–June 1996)		
	Avg. (%)	St. Dev. (%)
United States	1.38	4.16
Europe	1.58	4.91
Japan	1.43	7.55

Panel B: Emerging Markets (Postliberalization Periods)			
	Avg. (%)	St. dev. (%)	Liberalization
Latin America			
Argentina	Arg	3.16	17.42	Dec 1989
Brazil	Bra	2.91	14.12	Jul 1991
Chile	Chi	2.59	7.80	Apr 1990
Colombia	Col	3.18	11.33	Feb 1991
Mexico	Mex	1.96	9.92	May 1989
Venezuela	Ven	0.29	13.39	Dec 1990
Asia			
India	Ind	0.58	8.66	Nov 1992
Korea	Kor	0.49	7.68	Jan 1992
Malaysia	Mal	1.37	7.64	—
Pakistan	Pak	1.93	9.93	Feb 1991
Philippines	Phi	2.44	8.39	Nov 1991
Taiwan	Tai	1.47	11.22	Jan 1991
Thailand	Tha	2.39	8.69	—
Other			
Greece	Gre	2.11	11.81	—
Jordan	Jor	0.64	4.86	—
Nigeria	Nig	1.69	15.27	—
Zimbabwe	Zim	2.51	9.21	—

Harvey (1995), as well as those of Errunza et al. (1999). As noted before, however, the diversification benefits suggested by the first line in Table III may not be attainable to investors, because they may require short selling of the emerging markets indices, the benchmark indices, or both.

If we do not allow investors to go short in the emerging markets, while still retaining the possibility to sell the benchmark indices short, the conclusions are very different. The joint tests for spanning for Latin America and Asia no longer reject the null hypothesis in this case. It is only for the group Other that we still find significant diversification benefits from emerging markets. Notice that for the individual countries, the p values are often smaller than in the no-frictions case, because now a one-sided null distribution

Table III

Spanning Tests with Short Sales Constraints

The table presents test results for the hypothesis that there is mean-variance spanning of emerging markets by three benchmark assets, which are the MSCI indices for the United States, Europe, and Japan, after liberalizations in the emerging markets have taken place. For each emerging market, results are shown for the period after liberalization of the stock market has taken place, as reported in Table II. If there is no liberalization during the sample period, the entire sample from January 1985 until June 1996 is used. The numbers in the table are Wald test statistics. The numbers in parentheses are p values associated with the asymptotic distribution of the Wald test statistics.

Panel A: Latin America							
	Arg	Bra	Chi	Col	Mex	Ven	All
No restrictions							
Wald	2.12	2.28	4.38	5.14	1.02	1.85	18.12
(p)	(0.347)	(0.320)	(0.112)	(0.077)	(0.599)	(0.397)	(0.000)
No short sales of emerging markets							
Wald	0.76	0.85	3.52	4.01	0.93	0.01	5.60
(p)	(0.221)	(0.242)	(0.036)	(0.031)	(0.201)	(0.524)	(0.163)
			[**]	[**]			
No short sales							
Wald	0.27	0.40	3.51	4.01	0.85	0.01	5.03
(p)	(0.606)	(0.298)	(0.061)	(0.026)	(0.194)	(0.480)	(0.148)
			[**]	[**]			
Investable indices, no short sales							
Wald	0.27	0.38	3.94	4.43	0.95	3.78	5.57
(p)	(0.603)	(0.301)	(0.047)	(0.023)	(0.170)	(0.026)	(0.127)
			[**]	[**]			

Panel B: Asia								
	Ind	Kor	Mal	Pak	Phi	Tai	Tha	All
No restrictions								
Wald	3.16	3.33	0.74	4.42	3.19	1.31	4.60	16.50
(p)	(0.206)	(0.189)	(0.689)	(0.110)	(0.203)	(0.520)	(0.100)	(0.000)
No short sales of emerging markets								
Wald	0.12	0.12	0.05	1.95	2.72	0.70	3.28	1.33
(p)	(0.433)	(0.436)	(0.481)	(0.112)	(0.065)	(0.249)	(0.044)	(0.633)
					[*]		[**]	
No short sales								
Wald	0.12	0.13	0.05	1.67	2.67	0.55	3.25	1.30
(p)	(0.451)	(0.404)	(0.680)	(0.094)	(0.068)	(0.226)	(0.082)	(0.655)
					[**]		[**]	
Investable indices, no short sales								
Wald	0.21	0.18	0.97	2.03	1.63	0.53	0.61	3.11
(p)	(0.403)	(0.369)	(0.329)	(0.088)	(0.114)	(0.236)	(0.429)	(0.362)
				[*]				

Panel C: Other					
	Gre	Jor	Nig	Zim	All
No restrictions					
Wald	4.28	76.37	4.29	24.29	105.07
(p)	(0.118)	(0.000)	(0.117)	(0.000)	(0.000)
No short sales of emerging markets					
Wald	1.59	1.09	0.83	8.38	11.16
(p)	(0.125)	(0.186)	(0.227)	(0.001)	(0.013)
				[***]	[**]
No short sales					
Wald	1.58	1.08	0.83	8.31	11.08
(p)	(0.227)	(0.312)	(0.387)	(0.006)	(0.036)
				[***]	[**]
Investable indices, no short sales					
Wald	1.59	1.02	NA	3.21	3.25
(p)	(0.240)	(0.334)	NA	(0.105)	(0.391)
				[**]	

Significance levels based on simulated test statistics are given in square brackets: * = 10 percent, ** = 5 percent, *** = 1 percent. NA = Not available.

is the relevant one. For some individual countries, like Chile and Colombia, the outward shift of the estimated mean-variance frontier is big enough to reject the null hypothesis of spanning. For individual countries, the 5 percent critical value of the test statistic is determined by the χ_1^2 distribution. Even though the estimated outward shift that results from adding all six Latin American countries is even bigger, the joint test shows that this shift is not big enough for the resulting test statistic to exceed the 5 percent critical value, which is now determined by a mixture of χ_i^2 distributions, with $i = 1, 2, \ldots, 6$. A similar situation occurs for the Asian markets.[7] For both Latin America and Asia, the estimated diversification benefits mainly result from one or two countries only. There is too much sampling error in the data for the diversification benefits to show up in the joint tests. This also shows up in the estimated mean-variance efficient portfolio weights, which show that in case of short sales constraints, investors would mainly like to invest in Chile and Colombia (for Latin America) or in the Philippines (for Asia). These results can be obtained from the authors upon request. Finally, the use of the p values that are adjusted for small-sample bias as reported in Table I (and from similar simulation results for the joint tests) does not alter any of the conclusions.

It may be the case though, that the diversification benefits offered by the emerging markets depend on whether or not the portfolio of the benchmark assets contains short positions. To account for short sales restrictions on the benchmark assets as well, Table III also presents spanning tests in the case where there are short sales restrictions on both the emerging markets and the benchmark assets. These results are presented in the third line for each geographical group in Table III. Adding short sales constraints on the benchmark assets does not change the results. The Wald test statistics are similar to the case when there are short sales constraints on the emerging markets only, implying that there are no diversification benefits for the emerging markets of Latin America and Asia. For the group Other, the joint test still rejects the null hypothesis of spanning. Again, the conclusions do not change when we use the adjusted p values from Table I, even though in this case there may be a small-sample bias.

To shed some light on these results, Figure 2 shows the mean-variance frontiers for the benchmark assets and the Asian markets for the cases discussed above. From this figure, it is obvious that there is a big shift in the unrestricted frontier if the Asian markets are added to the three benchmark assets. Adding short sales constraints for the Asian markets causes the diversification benefits to be much less pronounced, as can be seen from the inward shift of the frontier, which is now segmented. According to the tests in Table III, this inward shift makes the difference with the frontier of the

---

[7] In addition to this, because the postliberalization periods are different for different countries, the joint test for the Asian markets is based on a smaller number of observations than the test for Thailand, for instance, which may result in a joint test statistic that is numerically smaller than the individual ones.

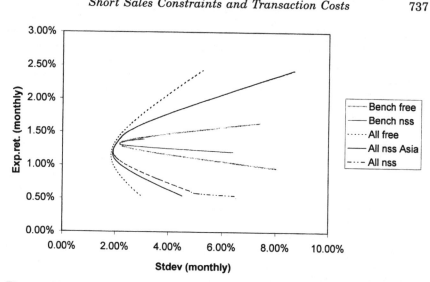

Figure 2. Mean-variance frontiers for the benchmark assets and Asia. The figure presents the unconstrained and segmented frontiers for the benchmark assets (Bench) and for the benchmarks plus the Asian markets (All) with (free) or with no (nss) short sales allowed.

benchmark assets insignificant. Finally, adding short sales constraints on the benchmark assets as well only makes a small difference in the frontiers. For the frontier of the benchmark assets, short sales constraints mainly make a difference for the inefficient part of the frontier and they put an upper limit on the efficient part. For the frontier of all markets together, adding short sales constraints on the benchmarks hardly makes a difference relative to the case where there are short sales constraints on the Asian markets only. Therefore, this figure illustrates that the main effect of short sales constraints operates through the emerging markets, as we also concluded from the results in Table III.

The results above show that adding short sales constraints considerably weakens the evidence in favor of emerging markets, except for the group Other. This latter result must be interpreted with some caution, because even for the emerging markets for which the null hypothesis is rejected, the diversification benefits may not be attainable, because of foreign ownership restrictions. Bekaert (1995) discusses several measures of the extent of foreign ownership restrictions in emerging markets. These measures suggest that these restrictions may be important for the countries for which the hypothesis of spanning is rejected (in particular for Zimbabwe). Thus, the diversification benefits suggested by Table III may be difficult or impossible to obtain.

To address this issue, the last line for each geographical group in Table III gives the results for the spanning tests in case the IFC Investable Indices are used instead of the Global Indices. The null hypothesis is again whether the emerging market indices are spanned by the benchmark assets in case there are short sales constraints on both the emerging markets and the benchmark assets. Joint tests for all emerging markets within a geographical group now never reject the hypothesis of spanning, including the group Other. This suggests that ownership restrictions for these countries are indeed binding.

C. Results for Spanning Tests With Transaction Costs

In this section, we consider the effects of transaction costs on the hypothesis that the mean-variance frontier of the benchmark indices spans the frontiers of the benchmark indices plus the individual emerging markets. We assume that investors face a round trip cost of 0.5 percent when trading the benchmark assets, and that they have a holding period of six months.[8] With a holding period of six months and a round trip cost of 0.5 percent on the benchmark assets, efficient portfolios consist of long positions in the MSCI Indices for the U.S., Europe, and Japan index or in the U.S. and Europe index only.

Our analysis focuses on the transaction costs that are needed to keep investors out of the emerging markets. In addition to paying transaction costs, investors are also not allowed to sell the emerging markets short and we use the IFC Investable Indices to incorporate possible ownership restrictions. Table IV presents levels of transaction costs in the emerging markets above which the hypothesis of spanning cannot be rejected at the 5 percent and 10 percent level, respectively. For instance, in the case of Argentina, a round-trip cost below 0.10 percent is needed to reject spanning by the benchmark assets at the 10 percent level. For Venezuela, for instance, spanning can never be rejected at the 10 percent level, no matter how low the transaction costs are, which is indicated as "NR." The estimates in Table IV suggest that with 0.5 percent round-trip costs on the benchmark assets and short selling restrictions on the emerging markets, transaction costs for the emerging markets need not be particularly high to keep investors out of these markets. Especially in the Asian markets, we often find that even in the absence of transaction costs on the emerging markets, spanning is not rejected. It is only in a few cases that a transaction cost of at least two times the level in the benchmark assets is needed to keep investors out of the market.

To get some further intuition about the importance of these transaction costs, the third line for each geographic group in Table IV gives an estimate of the actual round-trip costs in the emerging markets. These estimates are from Barings Securities and reported by Bekaert et al. (1998). The reported transaction costs are calculated from the percentage spread, which is the difference between the offer and bid price divided by the average of the offer and bid price for a security. For each country, the percentage spreads of

---

[8] Results for holding periods of 3 and 12 months are similar to those for 6 months and can be obtained from the authors upon request.

Table IV

Transaction Cost Bounds

The table presents estimated transaction cost bounds for the emerging markets in order to reject spanning of each emerging market by three benchmark assets at the 5 percent and 10 percent significance levels. The three benchmark assets are the MSCI indices for the United States, Europe, and Japan. The table assumes that there is a 0.5 percent round-trip cost on the benchmark assets and that there is a holding period of one month. The estimated transaction costs are in percentages. All results are based on the IFC Investable Indices for the postliberalization periods. The actual transaction costs are from Baring Securities as reported by Bekaert et al. (1996).

Panel A: Latin America						
	Arg	Bra	Chi	Col	Mex	Ven
10% bound	0.10	0.05	1.00	1.40	0.50	NR
5% bound	NR	NR	0.65	0.80	NR	NR
Actual tr. cost	1.55	0.85	3.93	1.00	0.93	NA

Panel B: Asia							
	Ind	Kor	Mal	Pak	Phi	Tai	Tha
10% bound	NR	NR	NR	NR	0.10	NR	NR
5% bound	NR	NR	NR	NR	NR	NR	NR
Actual tr. cost	1.50	NA	0.69	0.38	0.94	0.47	0.70

Panel C: Other			
	Gre	Jor	Nig	Zim
10% bound	NR	0.25	NA	1.20
5% bound	NR	0.10	NA	0.50
Actual tr. cost	0.48	0.58	NA	NA

NR = never rejected in the absence of transaction costs. NA = not available.

individual stocks are weighted by the capitalization of each stock within each country (see Bekaert et al. (1998)). Interestingly, except for Colombia, the actual transaction costs are always higher than the calculated 10 percent bounds in Table IV, and the actual transaction costs are in every case higher than the 5 percent bounds. This shows that, at least for a holding period of six months, the joint effects of transaction costs in the emerging markets, short sales constraints, a round-trip cost of 0.5 percent on the benchmark assets, and possible ownership restrictions make it hard to reject the hypothesis of mean-variance spanning.

IV. Concluding Remarks

In this paper, we show how regression techniques can be used to test for mean-variance spanning and intersection in the case where there are short sales constraints and/or transaction costs. When there are short sales constraints on the benchmark assets, the mean-variance frontier consists of parts of the mean-variance frontiers of subsets of the set of benchmark assets. If the benchmark assets are to span a new set of assets, there has to be spanning for each subset of the benchmark assets. This can be incorporated in regression-based tests for spanning, by using a multivariate regression in which the returns on the new assets are regressed on the returns of the relevant subsets of the benchmark assets. Short sales restrictions on the new assets require testing for inequality restrictions rather than equalities. Following the ideas presented in, for example, Luttmer (1996), transaction costs can be handled by looking at short and long positions in an asset as two different securities. Transaction costs can then be dealt with in the same way as short sales constraints.

There is substantial evidence available in the literature that suggests that, in the absence of market frictions, U.S. investors can benefit from including emerging markets assets in their well-diversified international portfolio of developed market assets. We try to shed some further light on this issue by testing whether emerging market indices are spanned by developed market indices when investors face short sales constraints and/or transaction costs. We find that, when accounting for short sales constraints and investability restrictions, the evidence in favor of diversification benefits of the emerging markets disappears, that is, for the three geographical regions, we can no longer reject the hypothesis of spanning. This is mainly due to the short sales constraints on the emerging markets. Although our simulations suggest that there is a possible small-sample bias in the asymptotic test, the size of this bias is small and does not affect our conclusions. Also, with a round-trip cost of 0.5 percent in the developed markets and a holding period of six months, only small transaction costs in the emerging markets are needed for possible diversification benefits to be insignificant.

Appendix: Proof of the Validity of the Test

In this appendix, we prove a simple but useful lemma. This lemma shows that the fact that we possibly use the incorrect regressions in our spanning and intersection tests (due to sample variation) is asymptotically negligible. Short sales restrictions on the benchmark assets are handled by testing for spanning and intersection on subsets of the available assets, where there is only a finite number of such subsets. The probability of choosing the right subsets tends to one and this turns out to be a sufficient condition for the validity of the tests. Suppose that we are given a finite number of Wald test statistics, $\xi(v^{[1]})_T, \ldots, \xi(v^{[M]})_T$, as defined in equation (16), where T is the sample size. Let the space of all possible values of v be partitioned in $V^{[1]}, \ldots, V^{[M]}$, with the interpretation that, depending on the value of the parameter v, one of the test statistics $\xi(v^{[1]})_T$ has desirable properties. Let j indicate the set $V^{[j]}$ to which $v^{[j]}$ belongs. If v_0 denotes the true value of v,

Short Sales Constraints and Transaction Costs   741

one would like to use the test $\xi(v_0)_T$, of course, but this is not possible, because v_0 is unknown. Assume, however, that we are given a parameter estimate $\hat{v}_T$, such that, under v_0

$$\Pr\{\hat{v}_T \in V^{[j]}\} \to 1, T \to \infty.$$

Now we have the following result.

LEMMA 1: *For each $c \in \mathbb{R}$, we have*

$$\lim_{T \to \infty} \Pr\{\xi(\hat{v}_T)_T \le c\} - \Pr\{\xi(v_0)_T \le c\} = 0.$$

Proof: The proof is very straightforward, using

$$\Pr\{\xi(\hat{v}_T)_T \le c\} = \sum_{j=1}^{M} \Pr\{\xi(v^{[j]})_T \le c \text{ and } v^{[j]} = \hat{v}_T\}$$

$$= \Pr\{\xi(v_0)_T \le c\} - \Pr\{\xi(v_0)_T \le c \text{ and } v_0 \ne \hat{v}_T\}$$

$$+ \sum_{v \ne v_0} \Pr\{\xi(v)_T \le c \text{ and } v = \hat{v}_T\},$$

and that the latter two terms converge to zero.   Q.E.D.

REFERENCES

Bekaert, Geert, 1995, Market integration and investment barriers in emerging equity markets, *World Bank Economic Review* 9, 75–107.

Bekaert, Geert, Claude B. Erb, Harvey, Campbell R., and Viskanta, Tadas E., 1998, Distributional characteristics of emerging market returns and asset allocation, *Journal of Portfolio Management*, Winter, 102–116.

Bekaert, Geert, and Michael S. Urias, 1996, Diversification, integration, and emerging market closed-end funds, *Journal of Finance* 51, 835–870.

Chen, Zhiwu, and Peter J. Knez, 1996, Portfolio performance measurement: Theory and applications, *Review of Financial Studies* 9, 511–556.

De Roon, Frans A., Theo E. Nijman, and Bas J. M. Werker, 1997a, Testing for spanning with futures contracts and nontraded assets: A general approach, CentER Discussion Paper 9683, Tilburg University.

De Roon, Frans A., Theo E. Nijman, and Bas J. M. Werker, 1997b, Testing for mean-variance spanning with short sales constraints and transaction costs: The case of emerging markets, CentER Discussion Paper 9807, Tilburg University.

De Santis, Giorgio, 1994, Asset pricing and portfolio diversification: Evidence from emerging financial markets, Working paper, University of Southern California.

Duffie, Darrel, 1996, *Dynamic Asset Pricing Theory* (Princeton University Press, Princeton, NJ).

Errunza, Vihang, Ked Hogan, and Mao-Wei Hung, 1999, Can the gains from international diversification be achieved without investing abroad? *Journal of Finance* 54, 2075–2107.

Glen, Jack, and Philippe Jorion, 1993, Currency hedging for international portfolios, *Journal of Finance* 48, 1865–1886.

Gouriéroux, Christian, Alberto Holly, and Alain Montfort, 1982, Likelihood ratio test, Wald test and Kuhn-Tucker test in linear models with inequality constraints on the regression parameters, *Econometrica* 50, 63–80.

Hansen, Lars Peter, John Heaton, and Erzo H. J. Luttmer, 1995, Econometric evaluation of asset pricing models, *Review of Financial Studies* 8, 237–274.

Hansen, Lars Peter, and Ravi Jagannathan, 1991, Implications of security market data for models of dynamic economies, *Journal of Political Economy* 99, 225–262.

Harvey, Campbell R., 1995, Predictable risk and returns in emerging markets, *Review of Financial Studies* 8, 773–816.

Huberman, Gur, and Shmuel Kandel, 1987, Mean-variance spanning, *Journal of Finance* 42, 873–888.

Jobson, J. D., and Bob M. Korkie, 1989, A performance interpretation of multivariate tests of intersection, spanning and asset pricing, *Journal of Financial and Quantitative Analysis* 24, 185-204.

Kodde, David A., and Franz C. Palm, 1986, Wald criteria for jointly testing equality and inequality restrictions, *Econometrica* 54, 1243–1248.

Luttmer, Erzo G. J., 1996, Asset pricing in economies with frictions, *Econometrica* 64, 1429–1467.

Markowitz, Harry M., 1991, *Portfolio Selection* (Blackwell Publishers, Cambridge, MA).

Part III
Real Effects of Financial Market Integration

A
Why Would Financial Liberalization Affect Economic Growth?

[14]

Risk-Taking, Global Diversification, and Growth

By Maurice Obstfeld[*]

This paper develops a continuous-time stochastic model in which international risk-sharing can yield substantial welfare gains through its effect on expected consumption growth. The mechanism linking global diversification to growth is an attendant world portfolio shift from safe low-yield capital to riskier high-yield capital. The presence of these two types of capital captures the idea that growth depends on the availability of an ever-increasing array of specialized, hence inherently risky, production inputs. Calibration exercises using consumption and stock-market data imply that most countries reap large steady-state welfare gains from global financial integration. (JEL F21, G15, O16, O41)

Standard models of international asset trade lack mechanisms linking an economy's long-run output growth rate to its financial openness.[1] Within such models, the gains from asset trade, at least between industrial economies, typically are estimated to be modest under common specifications of individuals' preferences. The contribution of this paper is a simple model of global portfolio diversification in which a link between growth and financial openness emerges very

[*]Department of Economics, University of California, Berkeley, CA 94720. I thank Matthew Jones for expert research assistance. In preparing this version of the paper I have had the benefit of detailed suggestions from three anonymous referees. Helpful comments were made by participants in research seminars at the Federal Reserve Bank of Minneapolis, the National Bureau of Economic Research Summer Institute, the Kiel Institute for World Economics, the University of British Columbia, UC-Berkeley, UC-Santa Cruz, the Wharton School, and the University of Michigan. All interpretations and any errors are, however, my own. The National Science Foundation and the Ford Foundation (the latter through a grant to CIDER at UC-Berkeley) provided generous financial support.

[1]Alternative theoretical models are proposed by Robert E. Lucas, Jr. (1982), René M. Stulz (1987), and Lars E. O. Svensson (1988). Recent attempts to quantify the welfare gains from international asset trade include Harold L. Cole and Obstfeld (1991), Enrique G. Mendoza (1991), Eric van Wincoop (1994), and David K. Backus et al. (1992).

naturally. Within that model, an economy that opens its asset markets to trade may experience an increase in expected consumption growth and a substantial rise in national welfare.

Recent analyses of economic growth due to Paul M. Romer (1986, 1990), Lucas (1988), and others explore mechanisms through which growth rates are endogenously determined by technological parameters, intertemporal preferences, market structures, and government policies. Extensions of these mechanisms to multieconomy frameworks, notably those contained in the treatise by Gene M. Grossman and Elhanan Helpman (1991), show that international trade in goods may accelerate or slow growth by shifting resources among alternative productive uses. The model set out below pursues this line of analysis, showing that a pure expansion of opportunities for trade across states of nature may itself promote resource reallocations favorable to long-term economic growth.

The paper's model supposes that each country can invest in two linear projects, one safe and one risky. This setup is a stylized rendition of the idea, developed by Romer (1990) and by Grossman and Helpman (1991), that ongoing growth depends on investments in supplying specialized, hence inherently risky, production inputs. Because risky technologies in my model have higher expected returns than safe ones, international asset trade, which allows each country to hold a globally diversified portfolio of risky investments, encourages all countries simultaneously to shift from low-return, safe investments toward high-return, risky investments. Provided risky returns are imperfectly correlated across countries, and provided some risk-free assets are initially held, a small rise in diversification opportunities always raises expected growth as well as national welfare.[2]

The basic theme of this paper recalls Arrow's (1971 p. 137) observation that "the mere trading of risks, taken as given, is only part of the story and in many respects the less interesting part. The possibility of shifting risks, of insurance in the broadest sense, permits individuals to engage in risky activities that they would not otherwise undertake."

Several recent papers have explored ideas related to those illustrated below. Jeremy Greenwood and Boyan Jovanovic (1990) develop a model in which financial intermediaries encourage high-yield investments and growth by performing dual roles, pooling idiosyncratic investment risks and eliminating *ex ante* downside uncertainty about rates of return. The analysis below shows, how-

ever, that even the former role of financial diversification can be an important spur to growth. The much simpler framework I choose allows closed-form solutions for an unrestrictive class of isoelastic preferences. As a result, quantitative welfare comparisons become simple, and links between preferences and growth are clarified.[3]

Valerie R. Bencivenga and Bruce D. Smith (1991) assume that financial intermediaries, by providing liquidity, encourage savings to flow into relatively productive uses. The random element in their model is not investment productivity, as below, but a preference shock that creates a demand for liquid assets. Because the payoffs on liquid assets, by definition, are relatively nonspecialized across dates and states of nature, the role of intermediaries in promoting more productive illiquid investments is another example of the mechanism emphasized in this paper.

Finally, Michael B. Devereux and Gregor W. Smith (1994) examine an explicitly multieconomy model of diversification and growth and illustrate how the risk reduction implied by diversification may promote or retard growth, with the outcome depending on assumptions about intertemporal consumption substitutability and the nature of uncertainty. Their analysis does not, however, allow for aggregate shifts in the global portfolio of risky assets. A special case of this paper's model, one in which countries initially hold no riskless assets and asset returns are symmetrically distributed, yields some of the main conclusions reached by Devereux and Smith.[4]

---

[2] With its linear technologies, this paper's model is a special case of the continuous-time stochastic model of John C. Cox et al. (1985). Their focus, however, is on asset pricing rather than on growth, and their assumptions on preferences are more restrictive than those entertained here. Similar stochastic models have been used to study effects, including growth effects, of fiscal or monetary policies (see Jonathan Eaton, 1981; Mark Gertler and Earl Grinols, 1982; Giancarlo Corsetti, 1991; Grinols and Stephen J. Turnovsky, 1992). Explicit production externalities of the type first posited by Kenneth J. Arrow (1962), and featured in much of the literature on endogenous growth, are not modeled here. Instead, endogenous growth springs from a constant private marginal product of investment, as in work of Hirofumi Uzawa (1965), Robert G. King et al. (1988), Robert J. Barro (1990), Larry E. Jones and Rodolfo Manuelli (1990), and Sergio T. Rebelo (1991). In endogenous-growth models based on Arrow-type externalities, the social marginal product of investment is effectively constant. Obviously, nothing in the present paper depends on the existence of literally risk-free assets; all that is needed is that relatively safe assets have relatively low expected returns.

[3] The Greenwood-Jovanovic assumption of a sunk cost of entering the financial intermediation network leads, however, to much richer dynamics than those that emerge from my model.

[4] The foregoing capsule review lists only a few papers that are especially relevant to the approach taken here to model the effects of uncertainty and financial markets on growth. A number of other related studies have appeared. See, for example, Giuseppe Bertola (1991), Thomas F. Cooley and Bruce D. Smith (1991), Harris Dellas (1991), Ross Levine (1991), and especially Gilles Saint-Paul (1992), who presents a formal

The paper is organized as follows. Section I describes a closed economy in which technological uncertainty follows a continuous-time diffusion process. Section II studies the closed economy's competitive equilibrium and shows how a reduction in uncertainty can spur economic growth. The section also explains the relationship among growth, consumers' risk aversion, and consumers' attitudes toward intertemporal substitution. The impact of global financial integration in a multieconomy world is studied in Section III. This section contains the paper's central results concerning international diversification, growth, and real interest rates. Section IV presents a pair of simple two-country examples to illustrate how some structural assumptions can lead to large welfare gains from financial integration, while others result in smaller gains of the type often found in contexts where long-run growth rates are exogenously determined.

Examples calibrated to international consumption and stock-market data are explored in Section V. Even when the reallocation of international capital stocks must occur gradually, the estimated gains from moving to a regime of perfect global financial markets can be large. Limitations of Section V's calibration exercise suggest, however, that the numerical welfare gains it implies should be viewed only as tentative indicators of the potential strength of endogenous growth effects. Section VI summarizes what has been learned.

I. Individual Choice in a Closed Economy with Uncertainty

The closed economy is populated by identical infinitely-lived individuals who face the choice between consuming or investing a single good. The economic decision interval has length h. At time t a representative

household maximizes the intertemporal objective $U(t)$ defined by the recursion

$$(1) \quad f([1-R]U(t))$$

$$= \left(\frac{1-R}{1-1/\varepsilon}\right) C(t)^{1-(1/\varepsilon)} h$$

$$+ e^{-\delta h} f([1-R]E_t U(t+h))$$

where the function $f(x)$ is given by

$$(2) \quad f(x) = \left(\frac{1-R}{1-1/\varepsilon}\right) x^{(1-1/\varepsilon)/(1-R)}.$$

In (1), E_t is a mathematical expectation conditional on time-t information, $C(t)$ is time-t consumption, and $\delta > 0$ is the subjective rate of time preference. The parameter $R > 0$ in (1) and (2) measures the household's relative risk aversion, and the parameter $\varepsilon > 0$ is its intertemporal substitution elasticity. When $R = 1/\varepsilon$, so that $f(x) = x$, this is the standard state- and time-separable expected-utility setup, which does not allow independent variation in risk aversion and consumption substitutability over time.

The more general preference setup assumed in (1) was proposed by Larry G. Epstein and Stanley E. Zin (1989) and by Philippe Weil (1989, 1990). There are two main reasons for considering such preferences. First, dynamic welfare comparisons that confound risk aversion and intertemporal substitutability can be misleading.[5] Second, one would like to answer the positive question of how preference parameters influence growth. The effects of intertemporal substitutability on growth have been analyzed extensively (e.g., Romer, 1990; Grossman and Helpman, 1991; Rebelo, 1991); the effects of attitudes toward risk have not.[6]

---

model of the link between technological specialization and markets for risk. Marco Pagano (1993) surveys this literature. Raymond Atje and Jovanovic (1993) present evidence of a positive cross-sectional association between national output growth rates and proxies that measure levels of domestic financial intermediation.

[5] For further discussion, see Obstfeld (1994).
[6] This paper will focus on the economy's behavior in the limit as h becomes infinitesimally small. When $R = 1/\varepsilon$, (1) implies that as $h \to 0$, $U(t)$ approaches the familiar expected-utility form,

$$U(t) = E_t \left\{ (1-R)^{-1} \int_t^\infty C(s)^{1-R} e^{-\delta(s-t)} ds \right\}.$$

Individuals save by accumulating capital and by making risk-free loans that pay real interest at the instantaneous rate $i(t)$. One unit of consumption can be transformed into one unit of capital, or vice versa, at zero cost. Capital comes in *two* varieties, however: riskless capital offering a sure instantaneous yield of r (a constant) and risky capital offering a random instantaneous yield with constant expected value $\alpha > r$. Therefore, individuals face a portfolio decision—how to allocate their wealth among the two types of capital and loans—as well as a saving decision. The fact that there is no nondiversifiable income (such as labor income) means that asset markets in this closed economy are complete.

The analysis is simplified by observing that, when $i(t) > r$, individuals wish to hold no safe capital and cannot go short in that asset. The opposite configuration $i(t) < r$ is inconsistent with equilibrium because it implies a sure arbitrage profit from borrowing for investment in safe capital. Finally, if $i(t) = r$, the division of an individual's safe assets between safe capital and loans is indeterminate.

Given this behavior of the interest rate, the individual's portfolio problem reduces to a choice over two assets only: risky capital and a composite safe asset offering the sure instantaneous real return $i(t)$. To simplify the derivations, I assume that the real interest rate is constant at level i. As the next section shows, the economy's equilibrium is indeed characterized by a constant real interest rate.

Let $V^B(t)$ denote the cumulative time-t value of a unit of output invested in safe assets at time 0 and $V^K(t)$ the cumulative time-t value of a unit of output invested in risky capital at time 0. Clearly $V^B(0) = V^K(0) = 1$. With payouts reinvested and continuously compounded, $V^B(t)$ obeys the ordinary differential equation

(3) $dV^B(t) = iV^B(t)\,dt.$

The stochastic law of motion for $V^K(t)$ is described by the geometric diffusion process

(4) $dV^K(t)/V^K(t) = \alpha\,dt + \sigma\,dz(t).$

In (4), $dz(t)$ is a standard Wiener process, such that $z(t) = z(0) + \int_0^t dz(s)$, and σ^2 is the instantaneous variance of returns.[7]

Per capita wealth $W(t)$ is the sum of per capita holdings of the composite safe asset, $B(t)$, and per capita holdings of risky capital, $K(t)$:

(5) $W(t) = B(t) + K(t).$

Equations (3), (4), and (5) imply that

(6) $dW(t) = iB(t)\,dt + \alpha K(t)\,dt$
$$+ \sigma K(t)\,dz(t) - C(t)\,dt.$$

Let $\omega(t)$ denote the fraction of wealth invested in risky capital. An alternative way to write (6) is as

(7) $dW(t) = \{\omega(t)\alpha + [1 - \omega(t)]i\}W(t)dt$
$$+ \omega(t)\sigma W(t)dz(t) - C(t)dt.$$

Epstein and Zin (1989) and Weil (1989, 1990) assume that time is discrete in their expositions of nonexpected-utility preferences. But continuous-time extensions by Svensson (1989) and Darrell Duffie and Epstein (1992) provide formulations that are readily applied to the problem of maximizing the continuous-time limit of $U(t)$ in (1) subject to (7) and an initial wealth endowment $W(t) = W_t$.

Let $J(W_t)$ denote the maximum feasible level of lifetime utility when wealth at time t equals W_t. Itô's lemma shows that in continuous time the stochastic Bellman equation resulting from maximizing $U(t)$ in (1) is

[7]Equation (4) implies that $V^K(t)$ is lognormally distributed: by Itô's lemma,

$$V^K(t) = V^K(0)\exp\{(\alpha - \tfrac{1}{2}\sigma^2)t + \sigma[z(t) - z(0)]\}.$$

Since $\mathrm{Var}[z(t) - z(0)] = t$, the expected growth rate of $V^K(t)$ is α, that is, $E_0 V^K(t)/V^K(0) = e^{\alpha t}$. The assumption of independently and identically distributed uncertainty is analytically convenient, but it compromises the model's empirical fit. For example, log U.S. consumption does not follow an exact random walk, as the model will imply. Independently and identically distributed uncertainty is in part responsible for the extreme equity-premium and risk-free-rate puzzles noted in Section V. Potentially, a linearized model such as the one proposed by John Y. Campbell (1993) could be used to approximate the effects of serially correlated shocks.

(8) $0 = \max_{\omega, C} \{[(1-R)/(1-1/\varepsilon)]C^{1-1/\varepsilon} - \delta f([1-R]J(W))$

$$+ (1-R)f'([1-R]J(W))[J'(W)(\omega\alpha W + [1-\omega]iW - C) + \tfrac{1}{2}J''(W)\omega^2\sigma^2 W^2]\}.$$

given by equation (8), above. [Recall the definition of $f(x)$ in equation (2). Time indexes henceforth are suppressed when they are unnecessary.] From (8), the first-order conditions with respect to ω and C follow:

(9) $J'(W)(\alpha - i) + J''(W)\omega\sigma^2 W = 0$

(10) $C^{-1/\varepsilon} - f'([1-R]J(W))J'(W) = 0.$

Equation (1)'s form suggests a guess that maximized lifetime utility U is given by $J(W) = (aW)^{1-R}/(1-R)$ for some constant $a > 0$. Given this functional form for $J(W)$, (9) and (10) simplify. Equation (9) now implies that demand for the risky asset is a constant fraction of wealth:

(11) $\omega = (\alpha - i)/R\sigma^2.$

Equation (10) becomes $C = a^{1-\varepsilon}W$, so that the consumption–wealth ratio also is a constant, denoted by μ. Substitution into (8) shows that

(12) $\mu = C/W$

$$= \varepsilon\{\delta - (1-1/\varepsilon)[i + (\alpha - i)^2/2R\sigma^2]\}$$

and confirms that the value function is

(13) $J(W) = [\mu^{1/(1-\varepsilon)}W]^{1-R}/(1-R).$

Consumption behavior depends on attitudes toward intertemporal substitution as well as toward risk, whereas portfolio choice, given the independently and identically distributed uncertainty assumed, depends only on risk aversion. When $R = 1/\varepsilon$, (11) therefore is unchanged, while (12) reduces to the formula derived by Robert C. Merton (1971) in the expected-utility case:

$\mu = (1/R)$

$$\times\{\delta - (1-R)[i + (\alpha - i)^2/2R\sigma^2]\}.$$

II. Closed-Economy Equilibrium

Equilibrium growth in this closed economy can now be described. Because the two capital goods can be interchanged in a one-to-one ratio, instantaneous asset-supply changes always accommodate the equilibrium asset demand given by (11). There are two types of equilibrium: one in which both types of capital are held and one in which only risky capital is.

The first type of equilibrium occurs when $(\alpha - r)/R\sigma^2 \leq 1$. In this case the interest rate i is equal to r, and the share of the economy's wealth held in the form of risky capital is, by (11), $\omega = (\alpha - i)/R\sigma^2 \leq 1$.

An alternative possibility, however, is that $(\alpha - r)/R\sigma^2 > 1$. Given this inequality, an interest rate of $i = r$ is impossible: it would imply that the closed economy, in the aggregate, wishes to go short in risk-free assets. The second type of equilibrium occurs in this case of an incipient excess supply of risk-free assets at an interest rate equal to r. In this equilibrium, the interest rate i rises above r until the excess supply of risk-free assets is eliminated, that is, until $\omega = (\alpha - i)/R\sigma^2 = 1$. The implied equilibrium interest rate is $i = \alpha - R\sigma^2 > r$. (This confirms the constancy of i that was assumed in the last section.)

The equilibrium interest rate helps to determine an equilibrium rate of economic growth. Equations (7) and (12) imply the wealth-accumulation equation

(14) $dW = [\omega\alpha + (1-\omega)i - \mu]Wdt$

$$+ \omega\sigma Wdz.$$

By (12) and (14), per capita consumption follows the stochastic process

(15) $dC = [\omega\alpha + (1-\omega)i - \mu]Cdt$

$$+ \omega\sigma Cdz.$$

Define g as the instantaneous expected growth rate of consumption:

$$g \equiv \frac{1}{C(t)}\left[\frac{E_t\,dC(t)}{dt}\right].$$

Equation (15) shows that g is endogenously determined as the average expected return on wealth, $\omega\alpha + (1-\omega)i$, less the ratio of consumption to wealth, μ.[8] Combination of this result with (11) and (12) leads to a closed-form expression for the expected consumption-growth rate,

$$(16)\quad g = \varepsilon(i - \delta)$$

$$+(1+\varepsilon)(\alpha - i)^2/2R\sigma^2.$$

In an equilibrium in which no riskless capital is held, the growth rate g can be expressed as

$$(17)\quad g = \varepsilon(\alpha - \delta) + (1-\varepsilon)R\sigma^2/2$$

which follows upon substitution of $\alpha - R\sigma^2$ for i in (16).

To gain some preliminary insight into the determinants of growth, consider the effects of a fall in σ. If the economy holds some risk-free capital, so that i may be held constant at r in (16) for small reductions in σ, the growth rate rises unambiguously. Equation (12) discloses that the effect of the fall in σ on the consumption–wealth ratio is ambiguous. The dominant effect on mean consumption growth, however, is that of the induced portfolio shift from risk-free to risky capital [equation (11)], which increases the average return to saving sufficiently to swamp any increase in the propensity to consume out of wealth. [The dominance of the portfolio-shift effect results from the specific isoelastic class of preferences assumed in (1).]

[8] Itô's Lemma, applied to equation (15), reveals the time-t consumption level to be

$$C(t) = C(0)\exp\left\{\left(g - \tfrac{1}{2}\omega^2\sigma^2\right)t + \omega\sigma[z(t) - z(0)]\right\}.$$

Note that for any $t > 0$, $E_0 C(t)/C(0) = e^{gt}$.

When all of the economy's capital is already in risky form, however, there can be no equilibrium portfolio shift for a closed economy. In this case equation (17) applies; it shows that a fall in σ raises growth when $\varepsilon > 1$ but lowers it when $\varepsilon < 1$. This is the result found by Devereux and Smith (1994). With the economy's production side held fixed, a fall in σ raises growth if and only if it lowers the consumption–wealth ratio. But a fall in σ now affects consumption by pushing up the real interest rate, $i = \alpha - R\sigma^2$. Since ε is the elasticity of intertemporal substitution, a rise in the real interest rate lowers C/W (and raises growth) when $\varepsilon > 1$, but raises C/W (lowering growth) when $\varepsilon < 1$.

The preference setup used in this paper allows an evaluation of the separate impacts of intertemporal substitution and risk aversion on growth. Consider intertemporal substitution first. In deterministic growth models, the rate of growth is determined by

$$g = \frac{1}{C(t)}\left[\frac{dC(t)}{dt}\right] = \varepsilon(i - \delta).$$

Thus, a rise in the intertemporal substitution elasticity ε raises growth provided i (the private rate of return to investment) exceeds δ (the rate of time preference).

In the present model with uncertainty, however, equation (16) can be written as

$$(18)\quad g - \tfrac{1}{2}R\omega^2\sigma^2$$

$$= \varepsilon\left[\omega\alpha + (1-\omega)i - \tfrac{1}{2}R\omega^2\sigma^2 - \delta\right].$$

The left-hand side of (18) is the *risk-adjusted* expected growth rate: the negative risk adjustment, $-\tfrac{1}{2}R\omega^2\sigma^2$, is proportional to the degree of risk aversion and to the instantaneous variance of growth. The right-hand side is the difference between the risk-adjusted expected rate of return to investment and the time-preference rate. We therefore have a result analogous to the certainty case. Since the portfolio weight ω is independent of intertemporal substitutability, a rise in the elasticity ε raises the expected growth rate whenever the risk-adjusted expected return on the optimal portfolio exceeds δ.

Equations (16) and (17) also reveal how the degree of risk aversion influences expected growth. The effect of lower R parallels that of lower σ. If some riskless capital is held, lower risk aversion is associated with higher expected growth; but if only risky capital is held, the effect of R on g is proportional to $1-\varepsilon$.

In either case expected economic growth is decreasing in the impatience parameter δ and increasing in α. The effect of a rise in the return on safe capital, r, is ambiguous when the economy is nonspecialized, because a rise in r diverts investment away from more productive risky capital.[9] Of course, a small rise in r has no effect when $i > r$.

When the economy holds both types of capital, the technological parameters α and σ influence the individual's lifetime utility only through their effect on the growth rate, g. This property of the model turns out to be useful in evaluating the growth effects of international asset-market integration. To prove it, I use (12) and (13) to calculate $J(W)$, the maximized value of the intertemporal objective U in (1):

(19) $J(W)$

$$= \left(\frac{W^{1-R}}{1-R}\right)\left(\frac{2\varepsilon\delta+(1-\varepsilon)(g+i)}{1+\varepsilon}\right)^{\frac{1-R}{1-\varepsilon}}.$$

Notice that because i is constant at r when some risk-free capital is held, the technology parameters α and σ influence lifetime utility only through their effects on g in that case.[10] Clearly an increase in g due to a rise in α or a fall in σ raises lifetime utility.

[9] For plausible parameter values, however, dg/dr is positive.
[10] Equation (19) follows from the observation that $\mu = [2\varepsilon\delta+(1-\varepsilon)(g+i)]/(1+\varepsilon)$. The condition $\mu > 0$ is required for the existence of an individual optimum.

For an economy specialized in risky capital,

$$J(W) = \left(\frac{W^{1-R}}{1-R}\right)(\alpha-g)^{(1-R)/(1-\varepsilon)}.$$

Given α and the preference parameters, changes in g can come about only through changes in σ when no riskless capital is held [see (17)]. As I have shown, a fall in σ may stimulate or depress growth in this case, despite its unambiguously positive welfare effect.

III. Growth Effects of International Economic Integration

All of the results above can be extended to a multicountry world economy. This extension yields predictions about the effect of economic openness on growth.

Let there be N countries, indexed by $j = 1,2,...,N$. Each country has a representative resident with preferences of the form specified in (1). However, preferences may be country-specific. Country j's representative individual has a relative risk aversion coefficient R_j, an intertemporal substitution elasticity ε_j, and a rate of time preference δ_j.

The rate of return on safe capital, r, is common to all countries (a condition relaxed in Section V). The cumulative value of a unit investment in country j's risky capital follows the geometric diffusion

$$(20) \quad dV_j^K(t)/V_j^K(t) = \alpha_j\,dt + \sigma_j\,dz_j(t)$$
$$j = 1,2,...,N.$$

Country-specific technology shocks in (20) display the instantaneous correlation structure

$$(21) \quad dz_j\,dz_k = \rho_{jk}\,dt.$$

The symmetric $N \times N$ covariance matrix $\Omega \equiv [\sigma_j\sigma_k\rho_{jk}]$ is assumed to be invertible.

My goal is to characterize a global equilibrium with free asset trade. The first step is to describe individuals' decision rules when they can invest in the N risky technologies described by (20) and (21) as well as in safe assets.

Let $\mathbf{1}$ denote the $N \times 1$ column vector with all entries equal to 1, let $\boldsymbol{\alpha}$ denote the

$N \times 1$ column vector whose kth entry is α_k, and let ω_j denote the $N \times 1$ column vector whose kth entry is the demand for country k's risky capital by a resident of country j. A generalization of the last section's argument (as in Svensson [1989]) shows that an individual from country j has the following vector of portfolio weights for the N risky assets

$$(22) \qquad \omega_j = \Omega^{-1}(\alpha - i^*1)/R_j$$

where i^* is the world real interest rate that all countries face.

The task of describing individual decision rules is simplified by the availability of a mutual-fund theorem identical to the one provided by Merton (1971) in a similar setting. Asset demands of the form in (22) imply that every individual will wish to hold the *same* mutual fund of risky assets. The ratio of risk-free wealth to wealth invested in the mutual fund is, however, an increasing function of investor risk aversion. What is convenient about the mutual-fund theorem is its implication that (11) and (12) remain valid, with α replaced by the weighted expected return on the risky mutual fund and σ^2 replaced by the variance of that weighted return.

Equation (22), as noted above, implies that the proportions in which individuals wish to hold the risky assets are independent of nationality. The $N \times 1$ vector of portfolio weights for the resulting mutual fund is

$$(23) \quad \theta \equiv \Omega^{-1}(\alpha - i^*1)/1'\Omega^{-1}(\alpha - i^*1)$$

where a "prime" (') denotes matrix transposition. Since the portfolio weights in (23) are constants, the analysis can proceed as if there is a single risky asset in the world with mean return $\alpha^* = \theta'\alpha$ and with return variance $\sigma^{*2} = \theta'\Omega\theta$.[11]

To envision equilibrium, imagine that N autarkic economies are opened up to free

multilateral trade. Since all types of capital may be freely transformed into each other, there can be no changes in the relative prices of assets, which are fixed at 1. Instead, available *quantities* adjust to balance demands, given the world real interest rate, i^*, and the technological parameters in α and Ω. For example, there may be an initial global excess demand for country 61's risky capital, in which case risky capital resident in country 61, K_{61}, expands under foreign ownership, while other countries' capital stocks shrink.

It will generally turn out that world investors desire to go short in some countries' risky capital stocks. Since this is not possible in the aggregate, these capitals will be swapped into other forms, and the associated activities will simply shut down. In equilibrium, the remaining $M \leq N$ risky capital stocks make up a market portfolio whose proportions are specified by the mutual-fund theorem.

Notice that individual countries can now go short in risk-free capital, that is, can invest a share of wealth greater than 1 in the global mutual fund of risky assets. They do this by net issues of risk-free bonds to foreigners. It may happen as in the closed-economy analysis above, however, that there is an *ex ante* global excess demand for the mutual fund. In this case, the world real interest rate, i^*, rises above r until the global excess demand for risky capital disappears.

More formally, assume that $M \leq N$ risky capital stocks remain in operation after

---

assets. Then by (22),

$$\omega_j^* = 1'\Omega^{-1}(\alpha - i^*1)/R_j$$

$$= \left[1'\Omega^{-1}(\alpha - i^*1)/R_j \right]$$

$$\times \left[\frac{(\alpha - i^*1)'\Omega^{-1}(\alpha - i^*1)}{(\alpha - i^*1)'\Omega^{-1}\Omega\Omega^{-1}(\alpha - i^*1)} \right]$$

$$= \frac{(\alpha - i^*1)'[\Omega^{-1}(\alpha - i^*1)/1'\Omega^{-1}(\alpha - i^*1)]}{R_j\theta'\Omega\theta}$$

$$= (\theta'\alpha - i^*)/R_j\theta'\Omega\theta$$

$$= (\alpha^* - i^*)/R_j\sigma^{*2}.$$

---

[11]For example, let the scalar quantity ω_j^* denote $1'\omega_j$, the share of country j's wealth invested in risky

trade is opened and that they are available in the positive quantities $K_1, K_2, \ldots, K_M$. To conserve on notation, let α now denote the $M \times 1$ subvector of mean returns and Ω the associated $M \times M$ covariance matrix of returns. Define the $M \times 1$ vector of mutual-fund weights θ by equation (23), $\theta \equiv \Omega^{-1}(\alpha - i^*\mathbf{1})/\mathbf{1}'\Omega^{-1}(\alpha - i^*\mathbf{1})$, and denote the fund return's mean and variance by α^* and σ^{*2}, respectively. Then an equilibrium must satisfy the conditions

$$K_j / \sum_{j=1}^{M} K_j = \theta_j > 0 \qquad \text{for all } j = 1,2,\ldots,m$$

$$\sum_{j=1}^{M} K_j = \sum_{j=1}^{N} (\alpha^* - i^*) W_j / R_j \sigma^{*2}$$

where θ_j is the jth component of θ and W_j is country j's wealth.

In an integrated world equilibrium, national consumption levels can grow at different rates on average despite the single risk-free interest rate i^* prevailing in all countries. Country j's mean growth rate is

$$(24) \quad g_j^* = \varepsilon_j(i^* - \delta_j)$$
$$+ (1 + \varepsilon_j)(\alpha^* - i^*)^2 / 2R_j\sigma^{*2}.$$

Given the world interest rate, country j grows more quickly the greater its tolerance for risk and the lower its degree of impatience. Subject to the condition discussed in the last section, an increase in willingness to substitute intertemporally also is associated with higher growth. Provided any risk-free capital is held in the world, $i^* = r$; but if not, a decrease in all countries' risk aversion implies a higher world interest rate and an ambiguous effect on growth.

Consider next the impact of economic integration on growth. The most straightforward case is that in which all countries hold riskless capital before integration and some continue to hold it afterward. In this case, countries share a common risk-free interest rate, r, both before and after integration. Equation (19), shows that the expected growth rate must rise in all countries. Why? Economic integration does not change any country's wealth because different types of

capital are costlessly interchangeable. In the present distortion-free setting, however, trade must raise welfare; and equation (19), shows that at an unchanged interest rate, welfare rises if and only if growth rises. The intuition behind this result follows from the discussion in Section II. International portfolio diversification encourages a global shift from (relatively) low-return, low-risk investments into high-return, riskier investments.

A similar argument, again based on equation (19), shows that any country whose risk-free interest rate falls upon integration with the rest of the world must experience increased expected growth. Growth can fall only in a country whose real interest rate rises. For such a country, however, the risk-reducing benefits of diversification necessarily outweigh the adverse welfare effect of lower expected growth. (Once again, the specific class of preferences assumed here is responsible for the strong predictions about growth described above.)

IV. Two Simple Examples

This section works out two numerical examples to show how the growth effects of international diversification can imply a large welfare payoff from financial integration. A number of applied studies (e.g., Lucas, 1987; Cole and Obstfeld, 1991; van Wincoop, 1994) take consumption growth to be exogenous in their evaluations of the costs of income variability. By comparing the welfare effects in the examples to the numbers a researcher would find if consumption growth were assumed to be exogenous, I can quantify the difference that endogenous consumption growth makes.

Example 1: Imagine a symmetric two-country world ($N = 2$) in which $r = 0.02$, $\alpha_1 = \alpha_2 = 0.05$, $\sigma_1 = \sigma_2 = 0.1$, and returns to capital are uncorrelated, $\rho_{12} = 0$. Preferences are the same in the countries, with $\varepsilon = 0.5$, $R = 4$, and $\delta = 0.02$. Under financial autarky, residents of each country hold a fraction of wealth $\omega = (\alpha - r)/R\sigma^2 = 0.75$ in the domestic risky asset. Equations (11) and (16) imply a mean consumption growth rate of $g = \frac{1}{2}(1 + \varepsilon)(\alpha - r)\omega - \varepsilon(\delta - r) = 1.6875$

percent. In both countries the risk-free real rate of interest, i, is equal to r (i.e., $i = 0.02$).

Now let the two countries trade. The optimal global mutual fund is divided equally between the two risky capitals. This portfolio's mean rate of return is $\alpha^* = 0.05$ with instantaneous return variance $\sigma^{*2} = (0.1)^2/2 = 0.005$. Each country's total demand for risky assets will now be $\omega^* = (\alpha^* - i^*)/R\sigma^{*2}$; it is simple to check that at a world real interest rate of $i^* = 0.03$, $\omega^* = 1$. Thus, financial integration leads to a rise in the real interest rate, from 0.02 to 0.03, and an equilibrium in which risk-free assets are no longer held. The increase in the world real interest rate reflects lower precautionary saving due to a reduction in the variability of wealth.[12]

From (24) one can calculate the expected consumption growth rate g^* in the integrated equilibrium. Equilibrium growth averages 2 percent per period, as compared with the rate of 1.6875 percent per period characterizing the situation prior to trade.

The present value of the welfare gain from economic integration can be calculated as an *equivalent variation*: by what percentage λ must wealth be increased under financial autarky so that people enjoy the same level of utility as under financial integration? Using (19) and (24), one finds that $\lambda = 0.371$, or 37.1 percent of initial wealth.[13] This is a very large welfare gain. It is derived from two sources: the opportunity to trade consumption risks *given* the stochastic process governing consumption growth, and the endogenous effect of this risk-sharing on the consumption-growth process itself.

Notice that this example assumes an instantaneous reallocation of capital from risk-free to risky uses. Such speedy adjustment would not be observed in practice. Instead, the shift in relative capital stocks would be spread out over time; the after-trade portfolio proportions just described would be reached eventually, but not in the short run. The welfare gain just calculated thus is more realistically viewed as the steady-state increase in wealth due to diversification; it provides no more than an upper bound on the short-run income effect.

Example 2: Consider an example in which (i) the induced growth effects of financial integration are essentially zero, and (ii) the variance of consumption is closer to the type of number characteristic of the richer industrialized economies. In this case, the welfare effects of financial integration will turn out to be much smaller than above. Let all parameters be as in the previous example, with the exception that now $\sigma_1 = \sigma_2 = 0.02$. Given this change, both countries hold only risky capital in the before-trade equilibrium, and their real interest rates will coincide at $i = 0.0484$. In each country, therefore, equation (16) or (17) gives $g = 0.0154$ as the expected growth rate of consumption.

Under financial integration, people hold a risky asset, the equal-shares mutual fund, with return variance half that of either country's capital and with a mean rate of return of 5 percent. In the pooled equilibrium the real interest rate is $i^* = 0.0492$, slightly above its level under autarky, and the growth rate of consumption declines very slightly, to $g^* = 0.0152$ percent. The equivalent-variation measure of the welfare gain from financial integration is now $\lambda = 0.0116$, or 1.16 percent of initial wealth.

The only difference between Examples 1 and 2 is that the variance of the risky-capital shock is 25 times larger in the first case than in the second. This leads to a welfare gain from financial integration that is about 32 times larger in the first case. Without knowing about endogenous growth, one might have guessed naively that the welfare gains

---

[12] The instantaneous variability of wealth falls from $(0.75)^2(0.1)^2 = 0.005625$ to $(0.1)^2/2 = 0.005$.

[13] For country j, the welfare gain λ_j is given by

$$\lambda_j = \left(\mu_j^*/\mu_j\right)^{1/(1-\varepsilon_j)} - 1$$

$$= \left\{ \frac{\left[2\varepsilon_j\delta_j + (1-\varepsilon_j)(g_j^* + i^*)\right]}{\left[2\varepsilon_j\delta_j + (1-\varepsilon_j)(g_j + i_j)\right]} \right\}^{1/(1-\varepsilon_j)} - 1.$$

TABLE 1—ENDOGENOUS GROWTH AND WELFARE COMPARISONS

Example	Welfare gain assuming exogenous growth (percentage of wealth)	Welfare gain assuming endogenous growth (percentage of wealth)
1	21.5	37.1
2	1.1	1.2

would be 25 times as great in the first example, not 32 times as great. The resulting underestimate of the gains from financial integration is economically substantial.

A more rigorous way to assess the contribution of endogenous growth is to ask what conclusion a researcher would reach in the examples above if he took the observed growth rate of consumption to be exogenous. The assumption that reducing economic variability does not greatly affect the growth rate of consumption has been typical in recent applied studies of the cost of consumption variability.

Equation (15) and Itô's lemma[14] imply that, under financial autarky, a researcher using annual data would observe the per capita consumption process

$$\log C(t) - \log C(t-1) = 0.0141 + v(t)$$

$$\sigma_v^2 = 0.00563$$

given the assumptions of Example 1, and the process

$$\log C(t) - \log C(t-1) = 0.0152 + v(t)$$

$$\sigma_v^2 = 0.00040$$

given those of Example 2. Taking the consumption growth rates as exogenous, the researcher might suppose that international diversification would halve each of the two variances above, leaving expected growth—which equals the regression constant plus $\frac{1}{2}\sigma_v^2$—unchanged. It is easy to compute the implied equivalent-variation measures of welfare gain, which are re-

ported in Table 1 (left-hand column) beside the true gains calculated earlier (right-hand column).[15]

In Example 2 the growth effects of international financial diversification are minimal. Thus, assuming exogenous consumption growth makes little difference to the answer. However, when larger growth effects are present, analyses that fail to account for them can be misleading. Under the parameters of Example 1, the true gain from financial integration is 73-percent higher than the number one finds ignoring the endogeneity of growth.

V. Examples Based on Global Consumption and Stock-Market Data

This section is devoted to two final examples of the gains from international financial integration. One example is based on actual consumption-growth data as reported by Robert Summers and Alan Heston (1991) in the Penn World Table (Mark 5), and the other is based on international data on stock-market returns. The welfare effects reported below should not be taken as a literal prediction about reality; they simply indicate that, when matched to some realistic parameters, the preceding model could imply very large gains from asset trade.

The first example considers an eight-region world consisting of North America, South America, Central America, East Asia, non-East Asia, Northern Europe, Southern Europe, and Africa. Within each region, real per capita consumption is a population-weighted average of national per

----

[14]See footnote 8. In what follows, $v(t)$ equals $\omega\sigma[z(t) - z(t-1)]$.

[15]The formulas for computing the welfare gains can be found in Obstfeld (1994) (see equation 11 in that paper).

TABLE 2—GLOBAL REGIONS AND THEIR CONSUMPTION PROCESSES, 1960–1987

A. *Mean and Standard Deviation of Annual Per Capita Consumption Growth Rate (Percentages):*

| | \multicolumn{8}{c}{Region} |
	NAm	SAm	CAm	EAsia	NAsia	NEur	SEur	Afr
g:	2.35	3.11	1.68	3.64	0.91	2.87	3.13	1.31
σ_v:	1.76	4.57	2.96	2.12	3.02	1.31	3.03	3.59

B. *Correlation Coefficients of Regional Per Capita Consumption Growth Rates:*

| | \multicolumn{7}{c}{Region} |
Region	SAm	CAm	EAsia	NAsia	NEur	SEur	Afr
NAm	−0.248	−0.113	0.393	0.117	0.366	0.118	−0.415
SAm		0.147	0.134	−0.467	0.440	0.391	0.139
CAm			0.365	−0.136	0.289	0.115	0.525
EAsia				−0.048	0.753	0.369	0.074
NAsia					−0.299	−0.166	−0.299
NEur						0.474	−0.035
SEur							0.321

Note: The regional groupings are as follows:
  North America (NAm): Canada, United States.
  South America (SAm): Argentina, Bolivia, Brazil, Chile, Colombia, Ecuador, Paraguay, Peru, Uruguay, Venezuela.
  Central America (CAm): Costa Rica, Dominican Republic, El Salvador, Guatemala, Honduras, Jamaica, Mexico, Trinidad.
  East Asia (EAsia): Hong Kong, Japan, South Korea, Malaysia, Philippines, Thailand, Australia, New Zealand.
  Non-East Asia (NAsia): India, Israel, Pakistan, Sri Lanka, Syria.
  Northern Europe (NEur): Austria, Belgium, Denmark, Finland, France, West Germany, Iceland, Ireland, Italy, Luxembourg, Netherlands, Norway, Sweden, Switzerland, United Kingdom.
  Southern Europe (SEur): Cyprus, Greece, Malta, Portugal, Spain, Turkey, Yugoslavia.
  Africa (Afr): Cameroon, Côte d'Ivoire, Kenya, Morocco, Senegal, South Africa, Tanzania, Tunisia, Zimbabwe.

capita consumptions. I use data spanning the period 1960–1987. Only countries with data available over this entire period, and with data quality of at least C− according to Summers and Heston (1991), are included.[16]

Equation (15) implies that the logarithm of per capita consumption follows a random walk with drift:

$$\log C(t) - \log C(t-1) = g - \tfrac{1}{2}\sigma_v^2 + v(t)$$

where $v(t) = \omega\sigma[z(t) - z(t-1)]$ and $\sigma_v = \omega\sigma$.[17] Table 2 reports the information one extracts by fitting this equation to the data: estimates of g and σ_v for the eight regions, as well as an estimate of the correlation matrix of regional consumption shocks. Be-

[16]National consumption per capita is measured at 1985 international prices as Penn World Table variable 3 times Penn World Table variable 6 (see Summers and Heston [1991 p. 362] for exact definitions). Consumption of nondurables and services would be a superior consumption measure for the purpose at hand, but data are unavailable for most countries.

[17]Recall that investments in a country's risky capital have cumulative payoffs that follow (4), and that ω denotes the share of risky capital in the optimal portfolio.

Table 3—Initial Portfolio Share of Risky Assets (ω), Expressed
as a Fraction, and Standard Deviation of the Annual Return
to Risky Investment (σ), as a Percentage

	Region							
	NAm	SAm	CAm	EAsia	NAsia	NEur	SEur	Afr
ω:	0.14	0.94	0.40	0.20	0.41	0.08	0.41	0.58
σ:	12.60	4.86	7.50	10.47	7.35	16.98	7.34	6.19

cause production shocks are the only source
of consumption uncertainty in the model,
the matrix in Table 2 is also the correlation
matrix of regional productivity shocks,
$z(t) - z(t-1)$. With perfect risk-pooling, all
entries in this correlation matrix would be 1.
The goal is to assess the welfare gains that a
shift to perfect pooling would yield.

The moments in Table 2 provide a basis
for calibrating the model empirically. However, any such attempt runs immediately
into two well-known problems: the equity-
premium puzzle of Rajnish Mehra and
Edward C. Prescott (1985) and the risk-
free-rate puzzle of Weil (1989).

To appreciate the equity-premium puzzle,
let i again be a country's risk-free rate. By
(11), the equity premium can be expressed
in terms of the consumption variance σ_v^2 as

$$(25) \qquad \alpha - i = R\sigma_v^2 / \omega.$$

Table 2 shows that, in most countries, the
variability of consumption growth is too
small to generate equity premia on the
plausible order of 5 percent per year without some combination of extremely high
risk aversion and a very low portfolio share
for risky assets. In an attempt to meet the
data halfway, I will assume that $R = 18$ and
that the equity premium is 4 percent per
year in all regions. Under these assumptions, (25) yields the estimates of ω reported in Table 3. (The ω values in Table 3
describe an initial allocation in which limited trade may occur, but in which economic
integration is incomplete.) With the exceptions of South America and Africa, where
the variability of annual consumption growth
is exceptionally high (standard deviations of
4.57 and 3.59 percent, respectively), these

portfolio shares for risky assets seem im-
plausibly low. I nonetheless use them to
infer estimates of $\sigma = \sigma_v / \omega$, the standard
deviation of the underlying annual produc-
tion shock. These, too, are reported in
Table 3.[18]

Table 3 highlights a counterintuitive empirical implication of the model. Equation
(11) implies that, for given values of the
equity premium and R, there is an *inverse*
relation between the observed variability of
consumption growth, $\sigma_v = \omega\sigma$, and the variability of the underlying technology shock,
σ: $\sigma = (\alpha - i)/R\sigma_v$. Thus, Table 3 suggests
that in those regions where the variability of
consumption growth is lowest, the variability of technology shocks is greatest. In
Northern Europe, for example, the standard deviation of the annual consumption
growth rate is only 1.3 percent (Table 2), yet
that of the return to risky capital is reck-
oned at 17 percent. Conversely, the corresponding standard deviation for risky capital held by South Americans is estimated to
be only 4.9 percent. The result could be
overturned if the equity premium had a
sufficiently strong positive cross-sectional
correlation with consumption variability; but
the empirical basis for such an assumption
has not been established. Risky nontradable
income, which is important in reality, would
also break the tight link between consumption variability and the riskiness of capital
investments.

Consider next the implications of the
risk-free-rate puzzle. Equation (16) can be

---

[18]Many would regard a value of $R = 18$ as being
unrealistically high. Shmuel Kandel and Robert F.
Stambaugh (1991) marshall arguments to the contrary.

TABLE 4—RISKLESS AND RISKY RATES OF RETURN, AS PERCENTAGES PER YEAR

	Region							
	NAm	SAm	CAm	EAsia	NAsia	NEur	SEur	Afr
i:	3.60	1.25	2.02	4.54	1.26	4.32	3.28	0.98
α:	7.60	5.25	6.02	8.54	5.26	8.32	7.28	4.98

TABLE 5—CHARACTERIZING EQUILIBRIUM UNDER GLOBAL FINANCIAL INTEGRATION:
FIRST EXAMPLE

A. *Equilibrium Shares in the Risky Mutual Fund:*[a]

	Region							
	NAm	SAm	CAm	EAsia	NAsia	NEur	SEur	Afr
Share:	0.105	0.225	0.098	0.101	0.205	0.000	0.207	0.058

B. *Other Characteristics of the Financially Integrated Equilibrium:*

Expected annual return on the risky mutual fund (α^*), percentage:	6.31
Standard deviation of mutual-fund annual return (σ^*), percentage:	3.41
Share of mutual fund in total wealth (ω^*), fraction:	0.85
World annual real rate of interest (i^*), percentage:	4.54
Expected annual growth rate of consumption (g^*), percentage:	4.37

[a]Shares sum to 0.999 because of rounding.

rewritten in the general form

(26) $g = \frac{1}{2}(1+\varepsilon) R\sigma_v^2 - \varepsilon(\delta - i).$

Given the low values for σ_v^2 suggested by Table 2, however, the mean growth rates g in the table cannot be matched unless some combination of the following is true: R is very large, ε is very large, δ is negative, or i is high. Maintaining the assumption that $R = 18$ and setting $\delta = 0.02$ and $\varepsilon = 1.1$, I compute region-specific risk-free interest rates that generate, through (26), the mean consumption growth rates reported in Table 2.

Table 4 reports these rates. Even though an unrealistically high intertemporal substitution elasticity ($\varepsilon = 1.1$) was assumed, the interest rates in the table are still on the high side for some of the regions, in line with the risk-free-rate puzzle. Notice that the risk-free rate is calculated to be relatively low in countries where consumption variability is relatively high. This pattern

results mainly from the low risk tolerance assumed earlier and reflects the precautionary motive for saving.[19] Mean national rates of return to risky capital are calculated as $\alpha = 0.04 + i$. For convenience, I report these rates in the second row of Table 4.

The numbers reported in Tables 2–4 allow computation of the covariance matrix of risky capital returns, and hence of the global equilibrium that would obtain after financial integration (recall Section III). Table 5 reports the equilibrium portfolio shares in the optimal global mutual fund of risky assets, along with the mean and standard deviation of the fund's annual return (α^* and σ^*), the share of the fund in global wealth (ω^*), the

---

[19]Consumption variability is highest in less-developed regions of the Western Hemisphere and in Africa. The low real interest-rate levels that these regions therefore display are consistent with the "financial repression" hypothesis of the economic development literature.

TABLE 6—GAINS FROM INTERNATIONAL FINANCIAL INTEGRATION,
AS A PERCENTAGE OF WEALTH

	Region							
	NAm	SAm	CAm	EAsia	NAsia	NEur	SEur	Afr
Gain:	124.5	237.6	299.1	22.6	478.4	61.1	98.8	463.4

prevailing world interest rate (i^*), and the common new world growth rate (g^*). Notice that Northern European capital disappears entirely from the world portfolio, essentially because it is highly correlated with East Asian capital (the correlation coefficient is 0.753 according to Table 2) but has a slightly lower expected return (Table 4). Equilibrium holdings of risk-free capital are located exclusively in East Asia.

A note of interpretation is in order at this point. The 1960–1987 data are already based on some international risk-sharing. For example, the high correlation between East Asian and Northern European log-consumption innovations probably reflects some cross-holding of capital. The nonappearance of Northern Europe in the optimal global portfolio therefore does not really mean that no Northern European capital is held in equilibrium. Prior to *full* market-pooling, East Asians already hold a portfolio that includes some Northern European capital; after pooling, it is this portfolio, rather than the one Northern Europeans hold, for which demand is positive. Nothing in the calculations requires literal autarky in the before-integration equilibrium.

Although the expected return on the global portfolio is significantly below that on East Asian capital, for example, global pooling does lead to a substantial reduction in risk (refer back to the second row of Table 3). In addition, the expected consumption growth rate rises everywhere. At 4.37 percent per year, equilibrium growth is substantially above even East Asia's initial high of 3.64 percent (Table 2). This sharp increase comes partly from a drop in the consumption-to-wealth ratio, but primarily from the shift of world wealth into riskier high-yield capital.

The gains from asset trade, reported in Table 6, are very large, ranging from 478.4 percent of wealth for non-East Asia to "only" 22.6 percent for East Asia. The uneven regional distribution of trade gains is easy to understand. Areas where returns initially are low gain disproportionately from access to more productive investment technologies. (These gains are especially large because of the assumed absence of diminishing returns to investment.) Naturally, the gains in Table 6 also reflect the advantages of worldwide risk-sharing.

For a given country, what share of the gain in Table 6 is due purely to the adoption of a new production technology, as opposed to the channels my theoretical model stresses? A simple measure of the gain from pure international technology transfer is the welfare effect, in a *deterministic* setting, of changing the average rate of return on domestic investment from $\omega\alpha + (1-\omega)i$ to $\omega\alpha^* + (1-\omega)i^*$. This experiment holds fixed the allocation of inputs to risky and riskless activities but moves the rates of return on those activities to expected world equilibrium levels.

Table 7 reports the resulting measures of welfare gain.[20] These gains are large in most

[20]Optimal consumption in a deterministic model with rate of return $\rho = \omega\alpha + (1-\omega)i$ is given by $C/W = \mu_d = [\varepsilon\delta - (\varepsilon-1)\rho]$. The coefficient μ_d^*, in which ρ is replaced by $\rho^* = \omega\alpha^* + (1-\omega)i^*$, governs optimal consumption after the technology transfer described in the text. The measure of welfare gain reported in Table 7 is $\lambda = (\mu_d^*/\mu_d)^{1/(1-\varepsilon)} - 1$. A more exact measure of the technology-transfer effect than the one used to construct Table 7 would be based on defining $\rho^* = \omega\alpha^* + (1-\omega)i^* + (\omega^* - \omega)[(\alpha^* - i^*) - (\alpha - i)]$. Making this change only reduces the numbers in Table 7, given the assumptions of the present example.

TABLE 7—GAINS FROM SWITCHING DETERMINISTIC TECHNOLOGIES,
AS A PERCENTAGE OF WEALTH

	Region							
	NAm	SAm	CAm	EAsia	NAsia	NEur	SEur	Afr
Gain:	43.3	106.7	154.4	−23.4	274.2	2.9	22.3	262.6

cases, but they are all far below the *total* gains shown in Table 6. The present example therefore implies large gains from diversification even after subtracting the gains from technology transfer.

The model unrealistically assumes that capital can relocate immediately; but allowing gradual adjustment could reduce the gains in Table 6 dramatically. A crude way to capture gradual adjustment is to suppose that after financial integration takes place, the current annual welfare gain converges toward the long-run annual gain implied by Table 6 at an instantaneous rate of γ percent. This convergence assumption means that the actual capitalized welfare gain, λ', is related to the measure λ in Table 6 by $\lambda' = \int_0^\infty i\lambda(1 - e^{-\gamma t})e^{-it} dt = \gamma\lambda /(i + \gamma)$. As a numerical example, suppose that the world real interest rate is 4.54 percent per year and that the annual rate of convergence, as suggested by the work of Barro et al. (1992), is 2.2 percent per year. Then the welfare gains from financial integration would be just under a third of those in Table 6 (and higher for lower interest rates). Such gains remain large.

A major shortcoming of this first example is that it must assume preference-parameter values that may seriously overstate both risk aversion and willingness to substitute consumption over time. Welfare gains even a twentieth as large as those in Table 6 would be significant, however, particularly for countries in the developing world.

A second numerical example of gains from financial integration is based on data on stock-market rates of return. As before, it is difficult to reconcile these data with aggregate consumption data within the class of models explored here. My procedure also assumes that stock-market returns are an

TABLE 8—STOCK-MARKET RETURNS AND IMPLIED
GROWTH RATES FOR GERMANY, JAPAN,
AND THE UNITED STATES, 1976–1992

A. *Mean (α) and Standard Deviation (σ) of Annual Risky Return and Implied Expected Annual Per Capita Consumption Growth Rate (g), as Percentages, and Implied Portfolio Share of Risky Assets (ω), Expressed as a Fraction:*

	Germany	Japan	United States
α:	9.10	12.79	6.72
σ:	28.35	28.07	12.41
g:	0.78	1.85	1.81
ω:	0.15	0.23	0.51
$\omega\sigma$:	4.25	6.46	6.33

B. *Correlation Coefficients of National Stock-Market Returns:*

	Country	
Country	Germany	Japan
United States	0.554	0.284
Germany		0.420

C. *Actual Annual Mean Growth Rate (g) and Standard Deviation (σ_v) of Consumption Growth Per Capita, 1976–1988:*

	Germany	Japan	United States
g:	2.09	3.06	2.49
σ_v:	1.80	1.40	1.82

accurate measure of the returns to risky investments.

In Table 8 I have used data on total annual stock-market returns, 1976–1992, to estimate α_j, σ_j, and Ω for a world of three countries: Germany, Japan, and the United States. The periodical *Morgan Stanley Capital International Perspective* publishes U.S. dollar indexes of stock-market value, including reinvested dividends. I deflated the dollar indexes for Germany, Japan, and the United States by the U.S. consumer price index (CPI) and used these data to estimate expected annual returns and return variances, along with the covariance matrix of annual returns.[21] Also shown in Table 8 are the before-integration mean consumption growth rates and portfolio proportions that (16) and (11) imply. The values shown for g and ω were derived on the assumptions that in all three countries, $R = 6$, $\varepsilon = 0.5$, and $\delta = r = i = 0.02$.

The implied average per capita growth rates in the table's upper panel are underestimates of the true growth rates, especially in the cases of Germany and Japan. The implied consumption-growth standard deviations ($\omega\sigma$) exceed the actual ones (σ_v) in the bottom panel by very wide margins in all three cases.[22] These results suggest that stock-market returns may be poor proxies for the aggregate returns to high-risk but productive investments.

In Table 9 I report the effects of full financial integration. If the data sample used here were typical, people would want to concentrate their stock portfolios (69 percent) in low-return but low-risk U.S. assets. The intermediate mean German risky return, coupled with the relatively high correlation of German with both U.S. and

TABLE 9—CHARACTERIZING EQUILIBRIUM UNDER GLOBAL FINANCIAL INTEGRATION: SECOND EXAMPLE

A. *Equilibrium Shares in the Risky Mutual Fund:*

	Germany	Japan	United States
Share:	0.00	0.31	0.69

B. *Other Characteristics of the Financially Integrated Equilibrium:*

Expected annual return on the risky mutual fund (α^*), percentage:	8.60
Standard deviation of mutual-fund annual return (σ^*), percentage:	13.84
Share of mutual fund in total wealth (ω^*), fraction:	0.57
World annual real rate of interest (i^*), percentage:	2.00
Expected annual growth rate of consumption (g^*), percentage:	2.84

C. *Gains from International Financial Integration (λ), as a Percentage of Wealth:*

	Germany	Japan	United States
Gain:	70.3	27.2	28.3

Note: The values reported above are based on the assumptions that $R = 6$, $\varepsilon = 0.5$, and $i = \delta = 0.02$.

Japanese returns (see Table 8), leads to an incipient negative demand for German assets. In equilibrium, therefore, no risky German assets are held. Average consumption growth rates increase in all regions.

The gains from trade remain substantial in this example; they are around 28 percent of wealth for Japan and the United States, and around 70 percent for Germany, which experiences the largest growth increase. Observe that the gains in Table 9 are expected to be smaller than those in Table 6 because I have now assumed smaller values of both R and ε. (Earlier I assumed $R = 18$ and $\varepsilon = 1.1$.) Realistic adjustment costs would suggest scaling down the gains in Table 9, as before.

VI. Conclusion

This paper has demonstrated that international risk-sharing can yield substantial

---

[21] By using the U.S. CPI to deflate dollar returns, I am implicitly assuming that German and Japanese investors evaluate the real returns on dollar assets as Americans do. The failure of the implicit assumption of relative purchasing-power parity (PPP) and the high correlation of nominal with real exchange-rate changes contribute to the spurious impression conveyed by Table 8 that all investors find German and Japanese real equity returns much more variable than American ones. A more detailed treatment would allow for deviations from relative PPP and thereby would recognize that investors in different countries may perceive different real returns on the same asset. In my 1989 paper I present evidence that international differences in consumption growth are systematically related to PPP deviations. The annual CPI data I use in Table 8 come from the first column of table B-56 in *Economic Report of the President* (Council of Economic Advisers, 1992).

[22] Empirical properties of per capita consumption growth rates were derived from the 1976–1988 data in Summers and Heston (1991). (See footnote 16 for details.)

welfare gains through its positive effect on expected consumption growth. The mechanism linking global diversification to growth is the attendant world portfolio shift from safe, but low-yield, capital into riskier, high-yield capital.

The model makes this theoretical point cleanly, but its empirical applicability is limited by several factors. One set of factors is related to the equity-premium and risk-free-rate puzzles familiar from U.S. data. Another, not entirely separate, issue is the probable importance of nontradable income risk. The model assumes a single consumption good and ignores the role of goods that do not enter international trade and the role of variation in real exchange rates. Finally, the absence of capital-adjustment costs and related capital-gains effects are drawbacks, except, perhaps, for analyzing comparative steady states. Further empirical and theoretical work is needed before accurate welfare evaluations can be made using models based on the one presented here. However, even welfare gains much smaller than those found in Section V above would be important.

REFERENCES

Arrow, Kenneth J. "The Economic Implications of Learning by Doing." *Review of Economic Studies*, June 1962, *29*(3), pp. 155–73.

_____. *Essays in the theory of risk-bearing*. Chicago: Markham, 1971.

Atje, Raymond and Jovanovic, Boyan. "Stock Markets and Development." *European Economic Review*, April 1993, *37*(3), pp. 632–40.

Backus, David K.; Kehoe, Patrick J. and Kydland, Finn E. "International Real Business Cycles." *Journal of Political Economy*, August 1992, *100*(4), pp. 745–75.

Barro, Robert J. "Government Spending in a Simple Model of Endogenous Growth." *Journal of Political Economy*, October 1990, *98*(5), Part 2, pp. S103–25.

Barro, Robert J.; Mankiw, N. Gregory and Sala-i-Martin, Xavier. "Capital Mobility in Neoclassical Models of Growth." National Bureau of Economic Research (Cambridge, MA) Working Paper No. 4206, November 1992.

Bencivenga, Valerie R. and Smith, Bruce D. "Financial Intermediation and Endogenous Growth." *Review of Economic Studies*, April 1991, *58*(2), pp. 195–209.

Bertola, Giuseppe. "Flexibility, Investment, and Growth." National Bureau of Economic Research (Cambridge, MA) Working Paper No. 3864, October 1991.

Campbell, John Y. "Intertemporal Asset Pricing without Consumption Data." *American Economic Review*, June 1993, *83*(3), pp. 487–512.

Cole, Harold L. and Obstfeld, Maurice. "Commodity Trade and International Risk Sharing: How Much Do Financial Markets Matter?" *Journal of Monetary Economics*, August 1991, *28*(1), pp. 3–24.

Cooley, Thomas F. and Smith, Bruce D. "Financial Markets, Specialization, and Learning by Doing." Rochester Center for Economic Research Working Paper No. 276, May 1991.

Corsetti, Giancarlo. "A Model of Taxation, Saving and Risk-Taking with and without Risk Disposal." Mimeo, Università di Roma, 1991.

Council of Economic Advisers. *Economic report of the President*. Washington, DC: U.S. Government Printing Office, 1992.

Cox, John C.; Ingersoll, Jonathan E., Jr. and Ross, Stephen A. "An Intertemporal General Equilibrium Model of Asset Prices." *Econometrica*, March 1985, *53*(2), pp. 363–84.

Dellas, Harris. "Stabilization Policy and Long Term Growth: Are They Related?" Mimeo, University of Maryland, February 1991.

Devereux, Michael B. and Smith, Gregor W. "International Risk Sharing and Economic Growth." *International Economic Review*, August 1994, *35*(4), pp. 535–50.

Duffie, Darrell and Epstein, Larry G. "Stochastic Differential Utility." *Econometrica*, March 1992, *60*(2), pp. 353–94.

Eaton, Jonathan. "Fiscal Policy, Inflation and the Accumulation of Risky Capital." *Review of Economic Studies*, July 1981,

48(3), pp. 435–45.

Epstein, Larry G. and Zin, Stanley E. "Substitution, Risk Aversion, and the Temporal Behavior of Consumption and Asset Returns: A Theoretical Framework." *Econometrica*, July 1989, *57*(4), pp. 937–69.

Gertler, Mark and Grinols, Earl. "Monetary Randomness and Investment." *Journal of Monetary Economics*, September 1982, *10*(2), pp. 239–58.

Greenwood, Jeremy and Jovanovic, Boyan. "Financial Development, Growth, and the Distribution of Income." *Journal of Political Economy*, October 1990, *98*(5), Part 1, pp. 1076–1107.

Grinols, Earl L. and Turnovsky, Stephen J. "Exchange Rate Determination and Asset Prices in a Stochastic Small Open Economy." Mimeo, University of Illinois, 1992.

Grossman, Gene M. and Helpman, Elhanan. *Innovation and growth in the global economy*. Cambridge, MA: MIT Press, 1991.

Jones, Larry E. and Manuelli, Rodolfo. "A Convex Model of Equilibrium Growth: Theory and Policy Implications." *Journal of Political Economy*, October 1990, *98*(5), Part 1, pp. 1008–38.

Kandel, Shmuel and Stambaugh, Robert F. "Asset Returns and Intertemporal Preferences." *Journal of Monetary Economics*, February 1991, *27*(1), pp. 39–71.

King, Robert G.; Plosser, Charles I. and Rebelo, Sergio T. "Production, Growth, and Business Cycles: II. New Directions." *Journal of Monetary Economics*, March/May 1988, *21*(2/3), pp. 309–41.

Levine, Ross. "Stock Markets, Growth, and Tax Policy." *Journal of Finance*, September 1991, *46*(4), pp. 1445–65.

Lucas, Robert E., Jr. "Interest Rates and Currency Prices in a Two-Country World." *Journal of Monetary Economics*, November 1982, *10*(3), pp. 335–59.

_____. *Models of business cycles*. Oxford: Blackwell, 1987.

_____. "On the Mechanics of Economic Development." *Journal of Monetary Economics*, July 1988, *22*(1), pp. 3–42.

Mehra, Rajnish and Prescott, Edward C. "The Equity Premium: A Puzzle." *Journal of Monetary Economics*, March 1985, *15*(2), pp. 145–61.

Mendoza, Enrique G. "Capital Controls and the Gains from Trade in a Business Cycle Model of a Small Open Economy." *International Monetary Fund Staff Papers*, September 1991, *38*(3), pp. 480–505.

Merton, Robert C. "Optimum Consumption and Portfolio Rules in a Continuous-Time Model." *Journal of Economic Theory*, December 1971, *3*(4), pp. 373–413.

Morgan Stanley Capital International Perspective. Geneva: Morgan Stanley, various issues.

Obstfeld, Maurice. "How Integrated Are World Capital Markets? Some New Tests," in Guillermo Calvo, Ronald Findlay, Pentti Kouri, and Jorge Braga de Macedo, eds., *Debt, stabilization and development: Essays in memory of Carlos Díaz-Alejandro*. Oxford: Blackwell, 1989, pp. 134–55.

_____. "Evaluating Risky Consumption Paths: The Role of Intertemporal Substitutability." *European Economic Review*, August 1994, *38*(7), pp. 1471–86.

Pagano, Marco. "Financial Markets and Growth: An Overview." *European Economic Review*, April 1993, *37*(3), pp. 613–22.

Rebelo, Sergio. "Long-Run Policy Analysis and Long-Run Growth." *Journal of Political Economy*, June 1991, *99*(3), pp. 500–21.

Romer, Paul M. "Increasing Returns and Long-Run Growth." *Journal of Political Economy*, October 1986, *94*(5), pp. 1002–37.

_____. "Endogenous Technological Change." *Journal of Political Economy*, October 1990, *98*(5), Part 2, pp. S71–102.

Saint-Paul, Gilles. "Technological Choice, Financial Markets and Economic Development." *European Economic Review*, May 1992, *36*(4), pp. 763–81.

Stulz, René M. "An Equilibrium Model of Exchange Rate Determination and Asset Pricing with Nontraded Goods and Imperfect Information." *Journal of Political Economy*, October 1987, *95*(5), pp. 1024–40.

Summers, Robert and Heston, Alan. "The Penn World Table (Mark 5): An Expanded Set of International Comparisons, 1950–1988." *Quarterly Journal of Economics*, May 1991, *106*(2), pp. 327–68.

Svensson, Lars E. O. "Trade in Risky Assets." *American Economic Review*, June 1988, *78*(3), pp. 375–94.

_____. "Portfolio Choice with Non-Expected Utility in Continuous Time." *Economics Letters*, October 1989, *30*(4), pp. 313–17.

Uzawa, Hirofumi. "Optimùm Technical Change in an Aggregative Model of Economic Growth." *International Economic Review*, January 1965, *6*(1), pp. 18–31.

van Wincoop, Eric. "Welfare Gains from International Risk Sharing." *Journal of Monetary Economics*, 1994 (forthcoming).

Weil, Philippe. "The Equity Premium Puzzle and the Risk-Free Rate Puzzle." *Journal of Monetary Economics*, November 1989, *24*(3), pp. 401–21.

_____. "Nonexpected Utility in Macroeconomics." *Quarterly Journal of Economics*, February 1990, *105*(1), pp. 29–42.

B
Measuring the Liberalization Effect on Economic Growth

[15]

ELSEVIER

Journal of Development Economics
Vol. 66 (2001) 465–504

JOURNAL OF
Development
ECONOMICS

www.elsevier.com/locate/econbase

Emerging equity markets and economic development [☆]

Geert Bekaert [a,b], Campbell R. Harvey [b,c,*],
Christian Lundblad [d]

[a] Columbia University, New York, NY 10027, USA
[b] National Bureau of Economic Research, Cambridge, MA 02138, USA
[c] Fuqua School of Business, Duke University, Durham, NC 27708, USA
[d] Kelley School of Business, Indiana University, Bloomington, IN 47405, USA

Abstract

We provide an analysis of real economic growth prospects in emerging markets after financial liberalizations. We identify the financial liberalization dates and examine the influence of liberalizations while controlling for a number of other macroeconomic and financial variables. Our work also introduces an econometric methodology that allows us to use extensive time-series as well as cross-sectional information for our tests. We find across a number of different specifications that financial liberalizations are associated with significant increases in real economic growth. The effect is larger for countries with high education levels. © 2001 Elsevier Science B.V. All rights reserved.

JEL classification: F3; G0; O1

1. Introduction

We present new evidence on the relation between financial equity market liberalizations and economic growth for a collection of emerging economies. We

[☆] This research was conducted while Lundblad was at the Board of Governors of the Federal Reserve System. The views expressed are those of the authors, and do not necessarily reflect the views of the Federal Reserve System.

[*] Corresponding author. Fuqua School of Business, Duke University, Durham, NC 27708, USA. Tel.: +1-919-660-7768; fax: +1-919-660-8030.

E-mail address: cam.harvey@duke.edu (C.R. Harvey).

466   *G. Bekaert et al. / Journal of Development Economics 66 (2001) 465–504*

find that average real economic growth increases between 1% and 2% per annum after a financial liberalization. Our results are robust across a number of different economic specifications. This analysis, of course, reveals no causality. However, even after we control for a comprehensive set of macroeconomic and financial variables, our financial liberalization indicator retains significance.

There is a substantial literature that tries to explain the cross-sectional determinants of economic growth. Barro (1991) and Barro and Sala-i-Martin (1995) explore the ability of a large number of macroeconomic and demographic variables to explain the cross-sectional characteristics of economic growth rates. More recent research in the growth literature has focused on the potential benefits of economic integration (the degree to which trade flows are free) and general financial development. For example, Rodrik (1999) examines the relation between openness to trade and economic growth with a standard cross-country regression methodology. With a proxy for the general openness to trade, the evidence suggests that the relation between economic growth and openness is statistically weak.

Following the development of endogenous growth models where financial intermediation plays an important role, there is also an interest in determining the influence of the financial sector on the cross-section of economic growth. King and Levine (1993) focus on several measures of banking development, and find that banking sector development is an important factor in explaining the cross-sectional characteristics of economic growth. Levine and Zervos (1998) explore the degree to which both stock market and banking sector development can explain the cross-section of economic growth rates. They find evidence in support of the claim that equity market liquidity is correlated with rates of economic growth. Additionally, they argue that banking and stock market development independently influence economic growth. They also find that there is little empirical evidence to support the claim that financial integration is positively correlated with economic growth.

Unlike previous work, we focus exclusively on the relation between real economic growth and financial liberalization. Our work is partially motivated by Bekaert and Harvey (2000) who examine the relation between financial liberalization and the dividend yield. While the dividend yield contains information about the cost of capital, it also houses information about growth prospects. A reduction in the cost of capital and/or an improvement in growth opportunities are the most obvious channels through which financial liberalization can increase economic growth. After finding reduced dividend yields for countries that undergo financial liberalization, Bekaert and Harvey also examine the relationship between economic growth and liberalization at very short horizons and find a positive association.

Our work is also distinguished by the extensive use of time-series as well as cross-sectional information. Indeed, the advent of financial liberalization suggests a temporal dimension to the growth debate that is not captured by the standard

G. Bekaert et al. / Journal of Development Economics 66 (2001) 465–504   467

cross-country estimation methodology. Typically, the growth literature focuses on either a purely cross-sectional analysis or a time-series dimension that is limited to at most three time-series observations per country.[1] We employ a time-series cross-sectional estimation methodology using Hansen's (1982) generalized method of moments (GMM). Our estimation strategy is considerably different from the existing literature in that we exploit the information in overlapping time-series data. Given the novelty of this approach, the econometric methodology is discussed extensively. Furthermore, we conduct several Monte Carlo experiments to assess the properties of our estimation strategy in this economic environment. Levine and Renelt (1992) discuss the caution one must exercise when interpreting cross-country regressions. They demonstrate that the estimated coefficients are extremely sensitive to the conditioning variables employed. For this reason, we also consider a variety of different specifications.

The paper is organized as follows. Section 2 introduces the variables we employ in our empirical work. Section 3 explains the econometric methodology, and discusses the results of a Monte Carlo analysis. Section 4 details the empirical results, and Section 5 concludes.

2. Financial liberalization and economic growth

Our empirical design is to explore the relation between real per capita GDP growth over various horizons and an indicator of official financial liberalization. The data are at the annual frequency from 1980 through 1997. We provide the official liberalization dates in the data appendix. These financial liberalization dates mainly represent the dates at which the local equity market was opened up to foreign investors. A detailed analysis of these dates and alternative sets of dates is provided in Bekaert and Harvey (2000).[2]

The set of variables that control for variation in economic growth rates across countries not accounted for by equity market liberalization fall into three categories: macroeconomic influences, banking development, and equity market development. More detailed information on the control variables, including data sources, are contained in the Data appendix.

The first set of variables is linked to the condition and stability of the macroeconomy: government consumption divided by GDP, the size of the trade sector divided by GDP, and the annual rate of inflation. We also include a human

---

[1] Some exceptions include Islam (1995) and Harrison (1996).
[2] A chronology of important events related to financial market integration is available on the Internet in the country risk analysis section of http://www.duke.edu/ ~ charvey.

468   *G. Bekaert et al. / Journal of Development Economics 66 (2001) 465–504*

capital variable, secondary school enrollment. Barro and Sala-i-Martin (1995) argue that government consumption divided by GDP proxies for political corruption, nonproductive public expenditures, or taxation. Bekaert and Harvey (1995, 1997, 2000) and Levine and Zervos (1998) employ the size of the trade sector as imports plus exports divided by GDP. This variable is employed as a measure of the openness of the particular economy to trade. Barro (1997) provides evidence suggesting a negative relationship between inflation and economic activity. Finally, Barro and Sala-i-Martin (1995) demonstrate the positive relationship between education and economic growth.

Following the evidence presented in King and Levine (1993), we include a control variable for the relationship between development in the banking sector and economic growth. In this capacity, we employ private credit divided by gross domestic product. King and Levine (1993) argue that this measure of banking development isolates the credit issued by private banks, in contrast to that issued by a central bank. Furthermore, Levine and Zervos (1998) provide evidence that the effects the banking sector and stock market development have upon economic growth are separate, and they use this variable to capture the former.

The focus of this paper is on the relation between economic growth and equity market liberalization. We examine three variables to proxy for the more general development of the equity market: a measure of equity market size, the log of the number of domestic companies, and equity market turnover as a measure of market liquidity. Both Bekaert and Harvey (1997) and Levine and Zervos (1998) use the ratio of the equity market capitalization to gross domestic product as a measure of the size of the local equity market. Large markets relative to the size of the economy in which they reside potentially indicate market development. Bekaert and Harvey (2000) employ the log of the number of companies as a measure of market development. Atje and Jovanovic (1993) and Levine and Zervos (1998) provide evidence for a strong relationship between economic growth and stock market liquidity, and, therefore, we employ value traded divided by market capitalization in this capacity.

2.1. Summary statistics

Table 1 describes the sample of 30 countries that we employ in estimation, classified as either emerging or frontier by the International Finance Corporation (IFC, 1997), for which there are annual data extending from 1980 to 1997. Table 2 presents the summary statistics for the macro economic variables. This includes average real per capita GDP growth rates across the 30 countries in our sample across two decades. For this variable, we provide means over the 1980s and 1990s, as well as for the full sample. The average growth rates differ substantially across time for many of the economies considered. Additionally, the rates of economic growth vary widely across the economies included. This paper focuses

G. Bekaert et al. / Journal of Development Economics 66 (2001) 465–504   469

Table 1
Sample specification
1980–1997 (30 countries).

Country	Liberalization	Country	Liberalization
Argentina	1989	Malaysia	1988
Bangladesh	NL	Mexico	1989
Brazil	1991	Morocco	1997
Chile	1992	Nigeria	1995
Colombia	1991	Pakistan	1991
Cote d'Ivoire	NL	Philippines	1991
Egypt, Arab Rep.	1997	Portugal	1986
Greece	1987	Sri Lanka	1992
India	1992	South Africa	1992
Indonesia	1989	Thailand	1987
Israel	1996	Trinidad and Tobago	NL
Jamaica	NL	Tunisia	NL
Jordan	1995	Turkey	1989
Kenya	NL	Venezuela	1990
Korea, Rep.	1992	Zimbabwe	1993

These countries are classified as emerging or frontier by the International Finance Corporation. Most of
the liberalization dates are from Bekaert and Harvey (2000). In addition, we designate a liberalization
when the IFC Frontier market is included into the IFC global index group. NL refers to not liberalized.

on the extent to which the time-series and cross-sectional differences can be
explained by differing states of financial liberalization of the equity market.

Fig. 1 presents evidence on the rates of economic growth both before and after
the official liberalization date. Of the 21 economies that undergo financial
liberalization in sample, 18 exhibit larger average GDP growth rates after the
official liberalization dates.[3] While this evidence implies no causality, it motivates
the exploration of the relationship between economic growth and equity market
liberalization. Tables 2 and 3 present average values for the various macroeconomic and financial, respectively, control variables across these economies. As the
average values of these control variables vary substantially in the cross-section, the
problem in examining the economic growth rates across these economies before
and after equity market liberalization is that the differences may be related to
phenomena not related to the liberalization itself, but captured by the control
variables. For example, in many countries macroeconomic reforms (including
trade liberalization) happened simultaneously or preceded financial liberalization
(see Henry, 2000a). Also, as Table 3 shows, the 1990s displayed a marked
increase in the size of stock markets of all countries. The number of domestic

---

[3] There are 24 countries that experience liberalizations in Table 1. However, for three of the
countries, Egypt, Israel and Morocco, the liberalization takes place in 1996 or 1997. Given our data
sample ends in 1997, these three countries are omitted from Fig. 1.

470   *G. Bekaert et al. / Journal of Development Economics 66 (2001) 465–504*

Table 2
Summary statistics for macroeconomic variables

	Argentina	Bangla-desh	Brazil	Chile	Colom-bia	Cote d'Ivoire	Egypt, Arab Rep.	Greece	India	Indone-sia	Israel	Jamaica	Jordan	Kenya	Korea, Rep.
Real per capita GDP growth (annual) US$															
1980–1989															
Mean	−0.021	0.017	0.008	0.025	0.012	−0.039	0.032	0.012	0.036	0.043	0.018	0.001	−0.001	0.005	0.063
Std. dev.	0.051	0.022	0.047	0.064	0.015	0.049	0.025	0.018	0.018	0.024	0.021	0.045	0.081	0.020	0.043
1990–1997															
Mean	0.036	0.032	0.006	0.058	0.020	−0.004	0.020	0.011	0.036	0.056	0.024	−0.001	0.003	−0.006	0.061
Std. dev.	0.052	0.010	0.034	0.025	0.014	0.036	0.016	0.013	0.024	0.012	0.015	0.022	0.056	0.020	0.016
1980–1997															
Mean	0.004	0.023	0.007	0.040	0.016	−0.024	0.027	0.012	0.036	0.049	0.021	0.000	0.000	0.000	0.062
Std. dev.	0.058	0.019	0.040	0.052	0.015	0.046	0.021	0.015	0.020	0.020	0.018	0.036	0.069	0.020	0.033
Inflation 1980–1997															
Mean	4.548	0.083	6.502	0.179	0.237	0.068	0.151	0.166	0.094	0.091	0.777	0.233	0.065	0.155	0.074
Std. dev.	8.506	0.041	8.696	0.082	0.040	0.064	0.052	0.057	0.024	0.030	1.071	0.176	0.062	0.105	0.068
Trade / GDP 1980–1997															
Mean	0.156	0.211	0.177	0.556	0.311	0.700	0.558	0.420	0.191	0.499	0.872	1.113	1.245	0.589	0.676
Std. dev.	0.022	0.043	0.022	0.074	0.040	0.095	0.115	0.025	0.046	0.040	0.100	0.160	0.171	0.089	0.064
Govt / GDP 1980–1997															
Mean	0.066	0.033	0.140	0.114	0.116	0.156	0.137	0.140	0.109	0.094	0.327	0.159	0.259	0.173	0.105
Std. dev.	0.037	0.011	0.042	0.019	0.022	0.021	0.033	0.009	0.008	0.015	0.044	0.031	0.021	0.015	0.006
Enrollment 1980–1997															
Mean	0.226	0.198	0.203	0.199	0.175	0.136	0.238	0.225	0.216	0.258	0.213	0.257	0.285	0.195	0.326
Std. dev.	0.023	0.016	0.022	0.043	0.016	0.052	0.057	0.029	0.016	0.022	0.022	0.067	0.066	0.018	0.038
PrivCredit / GDP 1980–1997															
Mean	0.212	0.118	0.493	0.488	0.292	0.340	0.293	0.395	0.254	0.296	0.615	0.307	0.602	0.295	0.572
Std. dev.	0.068	0.063	0.183	0.209	0.085	0.072	0.083	0.046	0.065	0.167	0.110	0.054	0.155	0.042	0.121

G. Bekaert et al. / Journal of Development Economics 66 (2001) 465–504   471

		Malaysia	Mexico	Morocco	Nigeria	Pakistan	Philippines	Portugal	South Africa	Sri Lanka	Thailand	Trinidad and Tobago	Tunisia	Turkey	Venezuela	Zimbabwe
Real per capita GDP growth (annual) US$																
1980–1989																
Mean		0.028	−0.002	0.021	−0.024	0.039	−0.007	0.029	−0.002	0.026	0.052	−0.010	0.010	0.018	−0.028	0.017
Std. dev.		*0.032*	*0.057*	*0.049*	*0.075*	*0.014*	*0.052*	*0.031*	*0.039*	*0.013*	*0.030*	*0.056*	*0.032*	*0.030*	*0.049*	*0.050*
1990–1997																
Mean		0.058	0.012	0.004	0.008	0.015	0.007	0.025	−0.010	0.040	0.058	0.011	0.030	0.030	0.011	0.001
Std. dev.		*0.006*	*0.040*	*0.067*	*0.026*	*0.023*	*0.023*	*0.017*	*0.021*	*0.010*	*0.032*	*0.072*	*0.022*	*0.050*	*0.038*	*0.056*
1980–1997																
Mean		0.041	0.005	0.013	−0.010	0.029	−0.001	0.027	0.032	−0.006	0.055	−0.001	0.019	0.023	−0.011	0.010
Std. dev.		*0.028*	*0.050*	*0.057*	*0.059*	*0.022*	*0.041*	*0.025*	*0.014*	*0.031*	*0.030*	*0.062*	*0.029*	*0.039*	*0.048*	*0.052*
Inflation 1980–1997																
Mean		0.037	0.479	0.065	0.289	0.089	0.128	0.128	0.126	0.129	0.055	0.095	0.069	0.631	0.358	0.180
Std. dev.		*0.023*	*0.378*	*0.034*	*0.222*	*0.029*	*0.108*	*0.079*	*0.057*	*0.032*	*0.043*	*0.041*	*0.019*	*0.247*	*0.265*	*0.087*
Trade / GDP 1980–1997																
Mean		1.400	0.366	0.550	0.588	0.350	0.622	0.685	0.714	0.508	0.671	0.787	0.842	0.341	0.491	0.534
Std. dev.		*0.329*	*0.122*	*0.041*	*0.219*	*0.020*	*0.169*	*0.043*	*0.083*	*0.058*	*0.161*	*0.112*	*0.083*	*0.091*	*0.074*	*0.141*
Govt / GDP 1980–1997																
Mean		0.145	0.095	0.167	0.136	0.127	0.095	0.156	0.095	0.182	0.111	0.161	0.164	0.102	0.096	0.191
Std. dev.		*0.021*	*0.010*	*0.012*	*0.031*	*0.018*	*0.015*	*0.018*	*0.011*	*0.025*	*0.016*	*0.050*	*0.008*	*0.019*	*0.022*	*0.032*
Enrollment 1980–1997																
Mean		0.341	0.195	0.225	0.178	0.152	0.227	0.270	0.251	0.207	0.336	0.196	0.265	0.210	0.192	0.184
Std. dev.		*0.061*	*0.026*	*0.020*	*0.044*	*0.016*	*0.040*	*0.036*	*0.029*	*0.043*	*0.062*	*0.050*	*0.039*	*0.048*	*0.033*	*0.034*
PrivCredit / GDP 1980–1997																
Mean		0.772	0.209	0.300	0.113	0.263	0.348	0.649	0.848	0.201	0.703	0.405	0.564	0.183	0.368	0.223
Std. dev.		*0.370*	*0.081*	*0.103*	*0.042*	*0.034*	*0.123*	*0.132*	*0.275*	*0.037*	*0.369*	*0.111*	*0.094*	*0.026*	*0.153*	*0.076*

Govt/GDP is the ratio of government consumption to GDP; Trade/GDP is the sum of exports and imports of goods and services measured as a share of GDP; Inflation as measured by the annual growth rate of the GDP implicit deflator or CPI if unavailable; Enrollment is the secondary school enrollment ratio; PrivCredit/GDP is private credit divided by GDP.

472   *G. Bekaert et al. / Journal of Development Economics 66 (2001) 465–504*

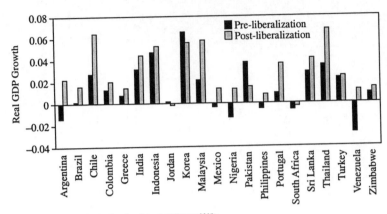

Liberalization dates from Bekaert and Harvey (2000).

Fig. 1. Real economic growth before and after financial liberalizations.

companies and turnover also increase for most countries. It is possible that these variables are correlated with our financial liberalization indicator. Consequently, we include in the regression specifications a set of variables, consistent with the existing growth literature, that control for variation in economic growth rates across economies and time potentially not accounted for by financial liberalizations.

3. Methodology

3.1. Econometrics framework

The primary quantity of interest is the growth rate in the real per capita gross domestic product (GDP):

$$Y_{i,t+k,k} = \frac{1}{k} \sum_{j=1}^{k} y_{i,t+j} \quad i = 1, \ldots, N, \tag{1}$$

where $y_{i,t} = \ln((\text{GDP}_{i,t}/\text{POP}_{i,t})/(\text{GDP}_{i,t-1}/\text{POP}_{i,t-1}))$, POP is the population, and N is the number of countries in our sample. Then, $y_{i,t+k,k}$ represents the annual, k-year compounded growth rate of real per capita GDP. In the growth literature, k is often chosen to be as large as possible. Our framework differs significantly in that we use overlapping data, facilitating the employment of the time-dimension in addition to the cross-sectional.

G. Bekaert et al. / Journal of Development Economics 66 (2001) 465–504   473

Our regression specification is as follows:

$$Y_{i,t+k,k} = \beta' \mathbf{x}_{i,t} + \epsilon_{i,t+k,k},$$ (2)

for $i = 1, \ldots, N$ and $t = 1, \ldots, T$. Denote the independent (right-hand side) variables employed, as discussed in Section 2, as $\mathbf{x}_{i,t}$. While the error terms are serially correlated for $k > 1$, $E[\epsilon_{i,t+k,k} \, \mathbf{x}_{i,t}] = 0$. The vector $\mathbf{x}_{i,t}$ includes the country-specific logged real per-capita GDP for 1980, which we call initial GDP hereafter. This variable is included to capture the "conditional convergence" discussed extensively in Barro (1997). To estimate the restricted system, consider the following stacked orthogonality conditions:

$$g_{t+k} = \begin{bmatrix} \epsilon_{1,t+k,k} & \mathbf{x}_{1,t} \\ \vdots \\ \epsilon_{N,t+k,k} & \mathbf{x}_{N,t} \end{bmatrix}.$$ (3)

With L the dimension of β, the system has $L \times N$ orthogonality conditions, but only L parameters to estimate. This procedure differs from ordinary least squares, as β is restricted to be identical across all countries, resulting in a system estimation that potentially corrects for heteroskedasticity across time, heteroskedasticity across countries, and correlation among country specific shocks (seemingly unrelated regression (SUR)). Define $\mathbf{Z}_t$, an $N \times (LN)$ matrix, as follows:

$$\mathbf{Z}_t = \begin{bmatrix} \mathbf{x}'_{1,t} & 0 & \cdots & 0 \\ 0 & \mathbf{x}'_{2,t} & \cdots & 0 \\ \vdots \\ 0 & 0 & \cdots & \mathbf{x}'_{N,t} \end{bmatrix}.$$ (4)

Then, one can rewrite the $(LN) \times 1$ vector of orthogonality conditions in the following manner:

$$g_{t+k} = \mathbf{Z}'_t \epsilon_{t+k},$$ (5)

where

$$\epsilon_{t+k} = \begin{bmatrix} \epsilon_{1,t+k,k} \\ \vdots \\ \epsilon_{N,t+k,k} \end{bmatrix}.$$ (6)

To derive the GMM estimator, it is useful to express these quantities in matrix notation.

Let

$$\mathbf{X}_i = [\mathbf{x}'_{i,t}], \quad \mathbf{Y}_i = [y_{i,t+k,k}], \text{ and } \epsilon_i = [\epsilon_{i,t+k,k}].$$ (7)

Table 3
Summary statistics for financial variables

	Argentina	Bangladesh	Brazil	Chile	Colombia	Cote d'Ivoire	Egypt, Arab Rep.	Greece	India	Indonesia	Israel	Jamaica	Jordan	Kenya	Korea, Rep.
MCAP / GDP															
1980–1989															
Mean	0.024	0.008	0.094	0.222	0.028	0.040	0.037	0.048	0.062	0.003	0.288	0.123	0.475	0.056	0.190
Std. dev.	0.016	0.007	0.054	0.087	0.009	0.007	0.016	0.027	0.019	0.007	0.145	0.088	0.074	0.001	0.213
1990–1997															
Mean	0.122	0.032	0.204	0.933	0.155	0.067	0.122	0.157	0.305	0.194	0.386	0.451	0.695	0.174	0.352
Std. dev.	0.052	0.035	0.110	0.291	0.066	0.028	0.081	0.034	0.101	0.129	0.222	0.250	0.120	0.123	0.124
1980–1997															
Mean	0.067	0.019	0.143	0.538	0.084	0.052	0.075	0.096	0.170	0.088	0.332	0.269	0.573	0.108	0.262
Std. dev.	0.061	0.026	0.098	0.413	0.078	0.023	0.069	0.063	0.141	0.128	0.184	0.241	0.147	0.099	0.193
Log(# of stocks)															
1980–1989															
Mean	5.417	3.983	6.272	5.403	4.890	3.185	5.379	4.744	8.264	2.939	5.410	3.662	4.540	3.994	5.945
Std. dev.	0.140	0.602	0.113	0.082	0.387	0.048	0.814	0.023	0.375	0.637	0.313	0.093	0.156	0.021	0.214
1990–1997															
Mean	5.083	5.089	6.319	5.557	4.766	3.318	6.488	5.152	8.370	5.250	6.119	3.864	4.646	4.021	6.566
Std. dev.	0.107	0.152	0.028	0.121	0.410	0.145	0.078	0.265	0.364	0.297	0.478	0.059	0.121	0.029	0.053
1980–1997															
Mean	5.268	4.475	6.293	5.471	4.835	3.244	5.872	4.925	8.311	3.966	5.725	3.752	4.587	4.006	6.221
Std. dev.	0.211	0.722	0.087	0.126	0.390	0.120	0.821	0.270	0.363	1.284	0.527	0.129	0.148	0.027	0.355
Turnover															
1980–1989															
Mean	0.267	0.008	0.502	0.057	0.100	0.028	0.064	0.041	0.495	0.091	0.524	0.065	0.122	0.022	0.692
Std. dev.	0.080	0.004	0.119	0.028	0.073	0.044	0.026	0.032	0.155	0.078	0.555	0.038	0.072	0.000	0.149
1990–1997															
Mean	0.320	0.091	0.514	0.089	0.085	0.019	0.118	0.283	0.322	0.480	0.700	0.109	0.182	0.028	1.503
Std. dev.	0.235	0.084	0.152	0.034	0.034	0.008	0.084	0.157	0.162	0.422	0.543	0.094	0.109	0.014	1.074
1980–1997															
Mean	0.291	0.045	0.507	0.072	0.093	0.024	0.088	0.149	0.418	0.264	0.602	0.084	0.148	0.025	1.053
Std. dev.	0.164	0.069	0.130	0.034	0.058	0.033	0.064	0.161	0.177	0.341	0.541	0.070	0.093	0.010	0.811

G. Bekaert et al. / Journal of Development Economics 66 (2001) 465–504   475

	Malaysia	Mexico	Morocco	Nigeria	Pakistan	Philippines	Portugal	South Africa	Sri Lanka	Thailand	Trinidad and Tobago	Tunisia	Turkey	Venezuela	Zimbabwe
MCAP/GDP															
1980–1989															
Mean	0.634	0.044	0.021	0.060	0.045	0.085	0.063	0.065	1.208	0.090	0.113	0.067	0.020	0.032	0.100
Std. dev.	0.166	0.030	0.003	0.028	0.014	0.076	0.087	0.009	0.301	0.100	0.044	0.003	0.017	0.008	0.070
1990–1997															
Mean	2.096	0.332	0.148	0.073	0.169	0.547	0.184	0.174	1.599	0.583	0.198	0.117	0.159	0.133	0.243
Std. dev.	0.971	0.105	0.110	0.028	0.050	0.331	0.089	0.052	0.400	0.319	0.144	0.074	0.079	0.053	0.098
1980–1997															
Mean	1.284	0.172	0.077	0.066	0.100	0.290	0.117	0.113	1.382	0.309	0.151	0.089	0.082	0.077	0.164
Std. dev.	0.981	0.164	0.096	0.028	0.072	0.322	0.105	0.065	0.392	0.333	0.107	0.054	0.088	0.062	0.109
Log(# of stocks)															
1980–1989															
Mean	5.366	5.246	4.322	4.573	5.872	5.080	3.860	5.146	6.318	4.629	3.491	2.565	4.821	4.548	4.041
Std. dev.	0.107	0.175	0.034	0.062	0.113	0.184	0.909	0.014	0.240	0.270	0.078	0.000	1.057	0.278	0.070
1990–1997															
Mean	6.097	5.282	4.037	5.101	6.494	5.222	5.164	5.327	6.494	5.842	3.283	3.017	5.134	4.477	4.128
Std. dev.	0.320	0.040	0.172	0.130	0.178	0.136	0.095	0.123	0.053	0.258	0.090	0.361	0.288	0.063	0.042
1980–1997															
Mean	5.691	5.262	4.195	4.808	6.149	5.143	4.440	5.226	6.396	5.168	3.398	2.766	4.960	4.517	4.080
Std. dev.	0.434	0.132	0.185	0.286	0.348	0.176	0.942	0.122	0.200	0.671	0.134	0.327	0.807	0.209	0.073
Turnover															
1980–1989															
Mean	0.151	0.629	0.044	0.006	0.123	0.221	0.066	0.012	0.048	0.384	0.095	0.050	0.031	0.043	0.077
Std. dev.	0.051	0.482	0.019	0.003	0.037	0.132	0.073	0.006	0.011	0.222	0.053	0.000	0.039	0.032	0.063
1990–1997															
Mean	0.556	0.386	0.131	0.013	0.334	0.274	0.328	0.113	0.087	0.768	0.085	0.080	0.996	0.237	0.082
Std. dev.	0.456	0.107	0.128	0.011	0.332	0.153	0.109	0.067	0.047	0.288	0.032	0.050	0.664	0.074	0.080
1980–1997															
Mean	0.331	0.521	0.083	0.009	0.217	0.245	0.183	0.057	0.065	0.554	0.090	0.063	0.460	0.129	0.079
Std. dev.	0.360	0.378	0.094	0.008	0.240	0.140	0.160	0.067	0.037	0.314	0.044	0.035	0.653	0.112	0.069

MCAP/GDP is equity market capitalization of the IFC index divided by GDP; log(# of stocks) is the log of the number of domestic companies in the IFC index; Turnover is the ratio of equity market value traded to the MCAP for the IFC index.

476   G. Bekaert et al. / Journal of Development Economics 66 (2001) 465–504

Also,

$$\mathbf{X} = \begin{bmatrix} \mathbf{X}_1 \\ \vdots \\ \mathbf{X}_N \end{bmatrix}, \quad \mathbf{Y} = \begin{bmatrix} Y_1 \\ \vdots \\ Y_N \end{bmatrix}, \text{ and } \boldsymbol{\epsilon} = \begin{bmatrix} \epsilon_1 \\ \vdots \\ \epsilon_N \end{bmatrix}, \tag{8}$$

where $\mathbf{X}$ is a $TN \times L$ matrix and $\mathbf{Y}$ and $\boldsymbol{\epsilon}$ are $TN \times 1$ matrices. Also, let

$$\mathbf{Z} = \begin{bmatrix} \mathbf{X}_1 & 0 & \cdots & 0 \\ 0 & \mathbf{X}_2 & \cdots & 0 \\ \vdots & & & \\ 0 & 0 & \cdots & \mathbf{X}_N \end{bmatrix}, \tag{9}$$

a $TN \times LN$ matrix. It follows,

$$\boldsymbol{\epsilon} = \mathbf{Y} - \mathbf{X}\beta. \tag{10}$$

Additionally,

$$\mathbf{g}_T = \frac{1}{T} \sum_{t=1}^{T} g_{t+k}$$

$$= \frac{1}{T} \{ \mathbf{Z}'(\mathbf{Y} - \mathbf{X}\beta) \}. \tag{11}$$

Employing this notation, the GMM estimator satisfies

$$\hat{\beta} = \arg\min_{\beta} \left[\mathbf{g}_T' \mathbf{S}_T^{-1} \mathbf{g}_T \right], \tag{12}$$

where $\mathbf{S}_T$ is the inverse of the GMM weighting matrix (see below). The First Order Condition associated with this optimum is as follows:

$$\frac{\partial \mathbf{g}_T'}{\partial \beta} \mathbf{S}_T^{-1} \mathbf{g}_T = 0. \tag{13}$$

Note that

$$\frac{\partial \mathbf{g}_T}{\partial \beta} = \frac{\mathbf{Z}'\mathbf{X}}{T}. \tag{14}$$

Hence, to set the first order condition to zero, we choose

$$\hat{\beta} = \left[(\mathbf{X}'\mathbf{Z})\mathbf{S}_T^{-1}(\mathbf{Z}'\mathbf{X}) \right]^{-1} \left[(\mathbf{X}'\mathbf{Z})\mathbf{S}_T^{-1}(\mathbf{Z}'\mathbf{Y}) \right]. \tag{15}$$

This is a well-known result from IV-estimators in a GMM framework. We optimally choose the GMM weighting matrix to minimize the variance–covariance

G. Bekaert et al. / Journal of Development Economics 66 (2001) 465–504

477

matrix of the estimated parameter vector; S_T is the estimated variance covariance matrix of $(\frac{1}{T}\Sigma_{t=1}^{T} g_t)$, taking all possible autocovariances into account:

$$S_T = \sum_{j=-\infty}^{\infty} E[g_{t+k} g'_{t+k-j}].$$ (16)

Using the identity matrix as the weighting matrix, first step parameter estimates are obtained as follows:

$$\hat{\beta}_1 = [(\mathbf{X'Z})(\mathbf{Z'X})]^{-1}[(\mathbf{X'Z})(\mathbf{Z'Y})].$$ (17)

Then, construct the first step residuals as follows:

$$\hat{\epsilon} = \mathbf{Y} - \mathbf{X}\hat{\beta}_1.$$ (18)

For the second step estimation, we use $\hat{\epsilon}$ to construct the optimal weighting matrix $\hat{S}_T^{-1}$. In the case of overlapping data $(k > 1)$, the residuals follow an $MA(k-1)$ process. This structure allows the consideration of four different specifications for the weighting matrix that facilitate increasingly restricted variance–covariance structures across the residuals in Eq. (2).

3.1.1. Weighting matrix I

The most general specification facilitates temporal heteroskedasticity, cross-sectional heteroskedasticity, and SUR effects.

$$\hat{S}_T = \frac{1}{T}\sum_t \mathbf{Z}'_t \epsilon_{t+k} \epsilon'_{t+k} \mathbf{Z}_t$$

$$+ \sum_{j=1}^{K}\left[1 - \frac{j}{K+1}\right]\left(\sum_{t=j+1}^{T} (\mathbf{Z}'_{t-j}\epsilon_{t+k-j}\epsilon'_{t+k}\mathbf{Z}_t + \mathbf{Z}'_t\epsilon_{t+k}\epsilon'_{t+k-j}\mathbf{Z}_{t-j})\right).$$ (19)

In order to ensure that the variance–covariance matrix is positive-definite, the Newey and West (1987) estimator is employed. $K(> k)$ is chosen to be 9, which is large enough to sufficiently capture the longer lagged effects and to ensure consistency. As the time dimension in our sample, T, is small, we do not consider this weighting matrix specification in practice. In the interest of parsimony, we consider three restricted variance–covariance structures.

3.1.2. Weighting matrix II

This specification facilitates cross-sectional heteroskedasticity and SUR effects, but not temporal heteroskedasticity. Define the $N \times N$ matrix $\hat{\Omega}_j$ as follows:

$$\hat{\Omega}_j = \frac{1}{T}\sum_{t=j+1}^{T} (\epsilon_{t+k}\epsilon'_{t+k-j}).$$ (20)

Then, the restricted variance–covariance matrix can be written as follows:

$$\hat{\mathbf{S}}_T = \frac{1}{T}\sum_t \mathbf{Z}_t' \hat{\mathbf{\Omega}}_0 \mathbf{Z}_t + \sum_{j=1}^{K}\left[1 - \frac{j}{K+1}\right]\left(\sum_{t=j+1}^{T}\left(\mathbf{Z}_{t-j}'\hat{\mathbf{\Omega}}_j\mathbf{Z}_t + \mathbf{Z}_t'\hat{\mathbf{\Omega}}_{-j}\mathbf{Z}_{t-j}\right)\right).$$

(21)

Given the small time dimension in our sample, the small sample properties of the estimator in this environment are questionable (see below). As a result, we restrict the non-diagonal terms of $\hat{\mathbf{\Omega}}_j$ to be identical:

$$\hat{\mathbf{\Omega}}_j = \begin{bmatrix} \hat{\sigma}_{11,j} & \hat{\sigma}_j & \cdots & \hat{\sigma}_j \\ \hat{\sigma}_j & \hat{\sigma}_{22,j} & \cdots & \hat{\sigma}_j \\ \vdots & & & \\ \hat{\sigma}_j & \hat{\sigma}_j & \cdots & \hat{\sigma}_{NN,j} \end{bmatrix}.$$

(22)

This structure greatly reduces the number of parameters in the weighting matrix structure, but retains some of the SUR flavor. When we refer to weighting matrix II in the estimation results section, this restricted form is employed.

3.1.3. Weighting matrix III

This specification facilitates cross-sectional (groupwise) heteroskedasticity, but neither temporal heteroskedasticity nor SUR effects. First, let the non-diagonal terms in $\hat{\mathbf{\Omega}}_j$ equal zero:

$$\hat{\mathbf{\Omega}}_j = \begin{bmatrix} \hat{\sigma}_{11,j} & 0 & \cdots & 0 \\ 0 & \hat{\sigma}_{22,j} & \cdots & 0 \\ \vdots & & & \\ 0 & 0 & \cdots & \hat{\sigma}_{NN,j} \end{bmatrix},$$

(23)

where $\sigma_{ii,j}$ is defined as follows:

$$\hat{\sigma}_{ii,j} = \frac{1}{T}\sum_{t=j+1}^{T}\left(\epsilon_{i,t+k,k}\,\epsilon_{i,t+k-j,k}'\right).$$

(24)

Given the restricted form for $\hat{\mathbf{\Omega}}_j$, let $\hat{\mathbf{S}}_T$ be determined as in Eq. (21). If GDP growth rates across the countries in our sample are idiosyncratic, then this assumption is plausible.

3.1.4. Weighting matrix IV

The final specification facilitates neither temporal heteroskedasticity, groupwise (country-specific) heteroskedasticity, nor SUR effects. In this case, the estimated parameters are equivalent to those obtained from a standard pooled OLS estima-

G. Bekaert et al. / Journal of Development Economics 66 (2001) 465–504   479

tion methodology, correcting for the MA residual structure. From $\hat{\Omega}_j$ defined in Eq. (23),

$$\hat{\sigma}_j^2 = \frac{1}{N}\text{trace}\left(\hat{\Omega}_j\right)\forall j. \qquad (25)$$

Then, define the restricted variance covariance matrix in the following manner:

$$\hat{\mathbf{S}}_T = \frac{1}{T}\sum_t \hat{\sigma}_0^2 \mathbf{Z}_t' \mathbf{Z}_t + \sum_{j=1}^{K}\left[1 - \frac{j}{K+1}\right]\left(\sum_{t=j+1}^{T}\left(\hat{\sigma}_j^2 \mathbf{Z}_{t-j}' \mathbf{Z}_t + \hat{\sigma}_{-j}^2 \mathbf{Z}_t' \mathbf{Z}_{t-j}\right)\right). \qquad (26)$$

Given the construction of the weighting matrix as in one of the preceding specifications, the GMM estimator is as follows:

$$\hat{\beta}_{\text{GMM}} = \left[(\mathbf{X}'\mathbf{Z})\hat{\mathbf{S}}_T^{-1}(\mathbf{Z}'\mathbf{X})\right]^{-1}\left[(\mathbf{X}'\mathbf{Z})\hat{\mathbf{S}}_T^{-1}(\mathbf{Z}'\mathbf{Y})\right]. \qquad (27)$$

The standard errors of $\hat{\beta}_{\text{GMM}}$ are determined from the variance–covariance matrix:

$$T\left[[\mathbf{X}'\mathbf{Z}]\hat{\mathbf{S}}_T^{-1}[\mathbf{Z}'\mathbf{X}]\right]^{-1} \qquad (28)$$

3.2. Monte Carlo experiment

We explore the finite-sample properties of the GMM estimator in this economic environment. We consider three separate Monte Carlo experiments, one for each of the latter three weighting matrix specifications, II, III and IV detailed above. We also started an experiment using the more general SUR specification of weighting matrix II in Eq. (20) but the finite sample properties of the estimator were quite poor.

3.2.1. Explanatory variables

The first step of the Monte Carlo exercise is to generate the right-hand side variables, $\mathbf{x}_{i,t}$. The first element of $\mathbf{x}_{i,t}$ is the logged initial real per capita GDP. We first identify the range for this variable in the observed data, and then draw a simulated initial GDP from a uniform distribution over this range for every country.

For the other right-hand side variables, we follow a very different strategy. The macro-economic and financial variables demonstrate significant serial and cross-correlation. We fit a restricted VAR to the following variables: government consumption to GDP ratio, trade to GDP ratio, inflation, secondary school enrollment, private credit to GDP ratio, market capitalization to GDP ratio, the logged number of domestic companies, and turnover. These are the control variables that we consider in our most general specification. As the time dimen-

480   *G. Bekaert et al. / Journal of Development Economics 66 (2001) 465–504*

sion, T, is small in our sample, we restrict the VAR coefficients to be identical across countries, but we allow for country specific intercepts. The restricted coefficient matrix, reported in the table in Appendix B, is estimated using pooled OLS (we also report the standard errors of the restricted VAR). Given the restricted VAR coefficients, for each country we begin the variables at their unconditional means from the observed data. We simulate $100 + T$ values from the VAR for each country, and discard the initial 100 simulated observations. Now, we have simulated observations for the right-hand side variables, $\mathbf{x}_{i,t}$, excluding the official liberalization indicator, to which we turn below.

3.2.2. The dependent variable

The real per capita GDP growth is determined according to the model as a function of the right-hand side variables, $\mathbf{x}$ and the residuals, ϵ. The null model is as follows:

$$\tilde{y}_{i,t+k,k} = \beta' \tilde{\mathbf{x}}_{i,t} + \tilde{\epsilon}_{i,t+k,k}, \tag{29}$$

with no official liberalization indicator included in the right-hand side variables. The β-vector comes from our growth model specification prior to introducing the indicator variables presented in Table 7. As there are three separate Monte Carlo designs, that is, one for each of the three weighting matrices under consideration, β is chosen from Table 7 for each of the three to reflect the particular weighting matrix under consideration. Given the use of overlapping data, the residuals follow an MA($k - 1$) process. To mimic this environment, we estimate a restricted MA($k - 1$) model for each of the residuals from the estimations performed in Table 7, depending upon the length k. The restriction lies in the fact that we jointly estimate the MA($k - 1$) process for each country, restricting the MA coefficients to be identical across countries. This restriction is motivated in precisely the same way the VAR's are restricted given the limited time series dimension. The restricted MA coefficients, reported in the table in Appendix B for $k = 2, \ldots, 5$, are estimated using quasi-maximum likelihood (QMLE) which assumes uncorrelated errors across countries and normal shocks in the likelihood function. Then, we construct the simulated residuals as follows:

$$\tilde{\epsilon}_{i,t+k,k} = \sigma_i \left(\sum_{j=0}^{k-1} \theta_j u_{t+k-j,i} \right), \tag{30}$$

where the $u_{t+k-j,\,i}$ are drawn from a standard normal distribution, σ_i is the estimated standard deviation for country i (given as the sample standard deviation of the residuals from the regressions reported in Table 7), and the θ_j are the cross-sectionally restricted MA coefficients, where $\theta_0 = 1$.[4] Notice that the error terms are independent of the right-hand side control variables.

---

[4] One extension is to allow the errors to be correlated. This would better reflect the SUR estimation structure, whereas the groupwise heteroskedasticity estimation structure is related to σ_i.

3.2.3. Official liberalization indicator

The construction of the liberalization indicator is very important to our Monte Carlo design. We generate series for each country that are zeros and ones, to mimic the properties of the observed liberalization indicator. First, we generate simulated liberalization dates drawn from a uniform distribution over the time series dimension, i.e. from 1 to T, for each country, so that each economy, as in our observed sample, liberalizes at some random time in our simulated sample. Then, the liberalization indicator values for that country are fixed at zeros prior to the simulated liberalization date and ones thereafter.

The next step is to estimate the model:

$$\tilde{y}_{i,t+k,k} = \beta' \tilde{\mathbf{x}}_{i,t}^{\star} + \tilde{\epsilon}_{i,t+k,k}, \tag{31}$$

where $\tilde{\mathbf{x}}_{i,t}^{\star}$ includes both the original control variables, $\tilde{\mathbf{x}}_{i,t}$, and the liberalization indicator. We retain the estimated coefficient on the liberalization indicator and the corresponding t-statistic. Under the null hypothesis of the constructed Monte Carlo model, this coefficient should not be significantly different from zero. We perform this procedure a total of 1000 times, for each of the three weighting matrix specifications. As can be seen in the table in Appendix C, we report the summary statistics for the estimated coefficient and the t-statistic. For weighting matrix IV, the asymptotic distribution appears to be a good approximation to the Monte Carlo distribution for the t-statistic. For weighting matrices III and IV, there appears to be some excess kurtosis in the t-statistic, indicating some differences from the asymptotic distribution. For all statistics, the small sample distribution is more dispersed than the normal distribution. We also report the 2.5% and 97.5% percentiles for comparison with the critical values we obtain in our regression specifications. For weighting matrices III and IV, these values are substantially larger than the ± 1.96 implied by the normal critical values. This indicates that 5% statistical significance is only reached for t-statistics larger than three (when k is larger than one). In all, the Monte Carlo analysis demonstrates that this econometric methodology is a reasonable strategy to evaluate the effect of liberalizations on GDP growth, provided we account for the finite-sample nature of the econometric environment.

4. Empirical results

4.1. The liberalization effect without control variables

Table 4 presents our estimates of the relation between real economic growth rates at various horizons and an official liberalization indicator and initial real per capita GDP without any additional control variables. Effectively, this is analogous

482   *G. Bekaert et al. / Journal of Development Economics 66 (2001) 465–504*

Table 4
Financial liberalization and economic growth—no control variables
30 Countries, 1981–1997.

	Horizon in years														
	Weighting matrix II					Weighting matrix III					Weighting matrix IV				
	$k=1$	2	3	4	5	$k=1$	2	3	4	5	$k=1$	2	3	4	5
Log(GDP)	0.0015	0.0014	0.0013	0.0013	0.0014	0.0016	0.0015	0.0014	0.0014	0.0013	0.0012	0.0014	0.0015	0.0017	0.0018
Std. error	(0.0003)	(0.0003)	(0.0004)	(0.0004)	(0.0004)	(0.0002)	(0.0003)	(0.0003)	(0.0003)	(0.0003)	(0.0003)	(0.0004)	(0.0004)	(0.0004)	(0.0005)
Official liberalization indicator	**0.0201**	**0.0189**	**0.0200**	**0.0194**	**0.0176**	**0.0193**	**0.0182**	**0.0191**	**0.0182**	**0.0163**	**0.0229**	**0.0220**	**0.0210**	**0.0183**	**0.0153**
Std. error	**(0.0035)**	**(0.0042)**	**(0.0051)**	**(0.0055)**	**(0.0058)**	**(0.0032)**	**(0.0044)**	**(0.0050)**	**(0.0051)**	**(0.0052)**	**(0.0042)**	**(0.0052)**	**(0.0060)**	**(0.0061)**	**(0.0062)**

The dependent variable is the growth rate of the real per capita gross domestic product. Log(GDP) is the log real per capita GDP level in 1980. The Official Liberalization variable takes a value of one when the equity market is liberalized, and zero otherwise. Weighting matrix II refers to a correction for cross-sectional heteroskedasticity and SUR effects; weighting matrix III refers to a correction for cross-sectional heteroskedasticity; and weighting matrix IV refers to a simple pooled OLS. All standard errors are robust, accounting for the overlapping nature of the data.

G. Bekaert et al. / Journal of Development Economics 66 (2001) 465–504 483

to exploring the mean growth rate before and after financial liberalization. Consistent with the evidence on the pre and post-liberalization average growth rates presented in Section 2, these estimates demonstrate a positive and statistically significant relation between financial liberalization and economic growth across a variety of specifications and horizons.

In each case, the estimated coefficient is presented when the GMM weighting matrix is constructed as in either specification II, III or IV in the previous section. Specification II is the most general that we consider in that it allows for cross-sectional heteroskedasticity and (restricted) SUR effects, whereas the latter two are more restricted versions. Regardless of weighting matrix specification, the estimated coefficient is positive and significant in all cases. The evidence implies that real GDP per capita growth rates increase following financial liberalization by anywhere from 1.5% to as large as 2.3% per annum, on average. For example, with a 3-year horizon using weighting matrix II, the impact on real economic growth rates is 2.0%. The evidence presented in Table 4 suggests that, on average, real economic growth rates increase roughly 1.9% per annum following financial liberalization.

Next, we present evidence on how this relation changes when additional variables are employed to control for various phenomena unrelated to the financial liberalization. Interestingly, the initial GDP appear to be positively related to the level of economic growth, in contrast to the convergence theory; however, much like the purely cross-sectional growth regressions, this relationship will change dramatically as additional control variables are added, lending credence to the concept of "conditional convergence" presented in Barro (1997).[5]

4.2. Allowing for control variables

The shortcoming of exploring the changes in real economic growth rates before and after financial liberalization is that the observed change may be related to various economic and political phenomena unrelated to the financial liberalization. For example, periods of financial liberalization may be contemporaneous with periods of political reform or economic restructuring. When estimating the relation between growth and financial liberalization, it is important to account for these potentially confounding effects. Consequently, we develop a hierarchical estimation strategy that evaluates the ability of incrementally increasing control groups to explain the cross-sectional and time-series characteristics of real economic growth.

First, we begin by estimating the relation between economic growth rates and several macroeconomic variables that are commonly employed in the literature to explain cross-sectional differences. Second, given the evidence presented in King

---

[5] The control variables potentially capture the differing steady state per capita GDPs across countries, and convergence is defined relative to these differing steady states. See Barro (1997).

and Levine (1993), we then add control variables which represent banking development. Third, we add equity market variables. These control variables encompass many of the variables deemed important in explaining the cross-section of economic growth rates in Atje and Jovanovic (1993) and Levine and Zervos (1998). Finally in Section 4.3, we add the official liberalization indicator, and reexamine the relation between financial liberalization and economic growth having controlled for unrelated effects using variables employed frequently in the literature.

In accordance with our tiered strategy, the first set of regressions we consider involve the use of three macroeconomic conditioning variables and a human capital variable: government consumption as a share of GDP, the size of the trade sector as a share of GDP, the annual inflation rate, and secondary school enrollment.

Table 5 presents evidence on the relation between these variables and economic growth. As before, we present the evidence obtained using the different GMM weighting matrix specifications. While the estimated relation between these variables and real economic growth is not entirely consistent across samples and estimation specifications, several patterns do emerge. First, as in Barro and Sala-i-Martin (1995), high levels of government consumption are negatively (significantly) related to economic growth rates, suggesting that the instabilities or taxation associated with government consumption are obstacles to economic development. However, this relationship is statistically insignificant for weighting matrix II. Second, the relation between the size of the trade sector and economic growth is statistically weak, and varies across the weighting matrix specifications which is consistent with the results in Edwards (1998) and Rodrik (1999). The relation between inflation and economic growth generally is mostly statistically insignificant and switches signs. Moreover, the measured effect is very small from an economic perspective. Additionally, secondary school enrollment is generally positively and significantly related to economic growth across all weighting matrix specifications. Finally, the relationship between initial GDP and economic growth is negative for weighting matrices II and III, indicating "conditional convergence" once these additional control variables are included.

Based upon the evidence presented in King and Levine (1993), we augment the previous set of conditioning variables by including a measure of banking sector development, the level of private credit as a share of gross domestic product. In Table 6, we present the regressions that include this measure. We find that the relation between the three macroeconomic variables, secondary school enrollment and initial GDP and economic growth is generally unaffected by the inclusion of private credit divided by GDP. Interestingly, the relation between banking sector development and real economic growth is fairly weak. Across the GMM weighting matrix specifications, the relationship is statistically insignificant, which is in sharp contrast to the evidence presented by King and Levine (1993) and Levine and Zervos (1998).

Table 5
Macroeconomic control variables and economic growth
30 Countries, 1981–1997.

	Horizon in years														
	Weighting matrix II					Weighting matrix III					Weighting matrix IV				
	$k=1$	2	3	4	5	$k=1$	2	3	4	5	$k=1$	2	3	4	5
Govt/GDP	-0.0593	-0.0277	-0.0204	-0.0030	-0.0014	-0.0760	-0.0711	-0.0543	-0.0304	-0.0232	-0.1469	-0.1457	-0.1396	-0.1308	-0.1201
Std. error	(0.0289)	(0.0274)	(0.0297)	(0.0302)	(0.0294)	(0.0312)	(0.0385)	(0.0352)	(0.0346)	(0.0327)	(0.0382)	(0.0465)	(0.0498)	(0.0494)	(0.0443)
Trade/GDP	-0.0035	-0.0063	-0.0117	-0.0206	-0.0208	0.0006	0.0023	-0.0021	-0.0091	-0.0118	0.0138	0.0211	0.0229	0.0213	0.0153
Std. error	(0.0061)	(0.0062)	(0.0065)	(0.0062)	(0.0062)	(0.0065)	(0.0083)	(0.0076)	(0.0074)	(0.0071)	(0.0083)	(0.0101)	(0.0109)	(0.0108)	(0.0099)
Inflation	-0.0006	-0.0001	0.0002	0.0004	0.0002	-0.0005	0.0001	0.0004	0.0004	0.0002	-0.0002	0.0006	0.0009	0.0010	0.0006
Std. error	(0.0008)	(0.0008)	(0.0007)	(0.0006)	(0.0005)	(0.0009)	(0.0008)	(0.0007)	(0.0006)	(0.0005)	(0.0007)	(0.0007)	(0.0006)	(0.0004)	(0.0006)
Enrollment	0.1907	0.2086	0.2131	0.2289	0.2194	0.1708	0.1658	0.1769	0.1885	0.1874	0.1077	0.0787	0.0598	0.0393	0.0712
Std. error	(0.0243)	(0.0248)	(0.0254)	(0.0234)	(0.0231)	(0.0255)	(0.0312)	(0.0283)	(0.0273)	(0.0265)	(0.0333)	(0.0402)	(0.0419)	(0.0404)	(0.0379)
Log(GDP)	-0.0018	-0.0031	-0.0033	-0.0037	-0.0034	-0.0010	-0.0012	-0.0017	-0.0021	-0.0022	0.0005	0.0008	0.0010	0.0016	0.0010
Std. error	(0.0009)	(0.0009)	(0.0009)	(0.0009)	(0.0008)	(0.0010)	(0.0012)	(0.0011)	(0.0010)	(0.0009)	(0.0011)	(0.0014)	(0.0014)	(0.0014)	(0.0013)

The dependent variable is the growth rate of the real per capita gross domestic product. Log(GDP) is the log real per capita GDP level in 1980. Govt/GDP is the ratio of government consumption to GDP; Trade/GDP is the sum of exports and imports of goods and services measured as a share of GDP; Inflation as measured by the annual growth rate of the GDP implicit deflator; Enrollment is the secondary school enrollment ratio. Weighting matrix II refers to a correction for cross-sectional heteroskedasticity and SUR effects; weighting matrix III refers to a correction for cross-sectional heteroskedasticity; and weighting matrix IV refers to a simple pooled OLS. All standard errors are robust, accounting for the overlapping nature of the data.

Emerging Markets

Table 6
Macroeconomic and banking control variables and economic growth
30 Countries, 1981–1997.

Horizon in years

	Weighting matrix II					Weighting matrix III					Weighting matrix IV				
	$k=1$	2	3	4	5	$k=1$	2	3	4	5	$k=1$	2	3	4	5
Govt/GDP	-0.0642	-0.0340	-0.0338	-0.0188	-0.0227	-0.0814	-0.0792	-0.0661	-0.0473	-0.0371	-0.1533	-0.1510	-0.1492	-0.1304	-0.1143
Std. error	(0.0301)	(0.0290)	(0.0307)	(0.0301)	(0.0277)	(0.0318)	(0.0388)	(0.0352)	(0.0339)	(0.0309)	(0.0385)	(0.0465)	(0.0486)	(0.0473)	(0.0455)
Trade/GDP	-0.0022	-0.0042	-0.0087	-0.0176	-0.0211	0.0003	0.0020	-0.0019	-0.0086	-0.0127	0.0119	0.0189	0.0229	0.0187	0.0143
Std. error	(0.0062)	(0.0064)	(0.0068)	(0.0064)	(0.0063)	(0.0066)	(0.0084)	(0.0077)	(0.0074)	(0.0071)	(0.0085)	(0.0102)	(0.0108)	(0.0105)	(0.0100)
Inflation	-0.0006	0.0000	0.0002	0.0004	0.0004	-0.0006	0.0000	0.0003	0.0003	0.0001	-0.0003	0.0004	0.0008	0.0009	0.0006
Std. error	(0.0009)	(0.0008)	(0.0007)	(0.0006)	(0.0005)	(0.0009)	(0.0008)	(0.0007)	(0.0006)	(0.0005)	(0.0007)	(0.0007)	(0.0006)	(0.0004)	(0.0004)
Enrollment	0.1855	0.1963	0.1960	0.2107	0.2175	0.1661	0.1562	0.1646	0.1746	0.1759	0.1000	0.0689	0.0313	0.0334	0.0231
Std. error	(0.0250)	(0.0255)	(0.0263)	(0.0245)	(0.0231)	(0.0259)	(0.0314)	(0.0285)	(0.0273)	(0.0262)	(0.0340)	(0.0404)	(0.0405)	(0.0389)	(0.0361)
Log(GDP)	-0.0015	-0.0028	-0.0029	-0.0033	-0.0033	-0.0008	-0.0010	-0.0015	-0.0021	-0.0023	0.0005	0.0007	0.0014	0.0012	0.0013
Std. error	(0.0009)	(0.0009)	(0.0010)	(0.0009)	(0.0009)	(0.0010)	(0.0012)	(0.0010)	(0.0010)	(0.0010)	(0.0011)	(0.0014)	(0.0014)	(0.0014)	(0.0013)
PrivCredit/GDP	-0.0022	0.0004	0.0038	0.0084	0.0073	0.0021	0.0055	0.0080	0.0130	0.0160	0.0098	0.0109	0.0118	0.0145	0.0208
Std. error	(0.0077)	(0.0085)	(0.0095)	(0.0097)	(0.0090)	(0.0079)	(0.0104)	(0.0101)	(0.0104)	(0.0100)	(0.0095)	(0.0116)	(0.0117)	(0.0111)	(0.0109)

The dependent variable is the growth rate of the real per capita gross domestic product. Log(GDP) is the log real per capita GDP level in 1980. Govt/GDP is the ratio of government consumption to GDP; Trade/GDP is the sum of exports and imports of goods and services measured as a share of GDP; Inflation as measured by the annual growth rate of the GDP implicit deflator; Enrollment is the secondary school enrollment ratio; PrivCredit/GDP is private credit divided by GDP. Weighting matrix II refers to a correction for cross-sectional heteroskedasticity and SUR effects; weighting matrix III refers to a correction for cross-sectional heteroskedasticity; and weighting matrix IV refers to a simple pooled OLS. All standard errors are robust, accounting for the overlapping nature of the data.

G. Bekaert et al. / Journal of Development Economics 66 (2001) 465–504   487

Levine and Zervos (1998) explore the degree to which banking and stock market development explain the cross-sectional characteristics of economic growth. They find that two measures of stock market liquidity are positively related to economic growth, and that stock market and banking development have separate effects upon growth. We employ equity market turnover as our development indicator. Additionally, they find a positive, but statistically weak, relationship between stock market size and GDP growth. We employ the number of domestic companies and the equity market capitalization divided by GDP as measures of stock market size. These variables can also proxy for market development.

In Table 7, we present the estimated regression coefficients when we add these three measures of equity market development to the control variables presented above, including the measure of banking development. The estimated relation between the macro economic variables and economic growth is qualitatively and quantitatively affected by the inclusion of the three equity market variables. The government/GDP and trade/GDP variables have now generally a larger sign, and are economically and statistically significant. The inflation effect has lost robustness across specifications. The enrollment variable is still important, but its effect is weaker both in an economic and statistical sense. The relation between initial GDP and economic growth is now negative and significant across almost all specifications. Additionally, the measure of banking development is now positively and significantly related to growth at longer horizons, which is consistent with the evidence presented in King and Levine (1993) and Levine and Zervos (1998). The coefficient on equity market size is generally negative and significant which is the opposite to what was expected. Additionally, the relation between the logged number of companies and the rate of economic growth is positive and significant. In accordance with the evidence presented in Levine and Zervos (1998), the relationship between turnover and economic growth is positive and significant in nearly all cases.

4.3. The liberalization effect with control variables

Having potentially controlled for unrelated phenomena by using the macroeconomic, banking sector, and equity market variables employed in the existing growth literature, we return to the relationship between economic growth and financial liberalization, where again the latter is measured using the official liberalization indicator. Table 8 presents the regressions with the financial liberalization indicator and all the control variables. The results in Table 8 show that the estimated relation between the control variables and economic growth are generally unaffected by the inclusion of the liberalization indicator. As before, the relation between economic growth and banking sector development is positive and significant only at longer horizons. The enrollment variable now proves fragile. However, it is striking that across all weighting matrix specifications, financial

488   G. Bekaert et al. / Journal of Development Economics 66 (2001) 465–504

Table 7
Macroeconomic, banking, and stock market control variables and economic growth
30 Countries, 1981–1997.

	Horizon in years														
	Weighting matrix II					Weighting matrix III					Weighting matrix IV				
	k=1	k=2	k=3	k=4	k=5	k=1	k=2	k=3	k=4	k=5	k=1	k=2	k=3	k=4	k=5
Govt/GDP	-0.1532	-0.1577	-0.1593	-0.1529	-0.1474	-0.1583	-0.1652	-0.1638	-0.1590	-0.1492	-0.1583	-0.1652	-0.1638	-0.1590	-0.1492
Std. error	(0.0329)	(0.0326)	(0.0324)	(0.0317)	(0.0303)	(0.0334)	(0.0335)	(0.0333)	(0.0324)	(0.0309)	(0.0334)	(0.0335)	(0.0333)	(0.0324)	(0.0309)
Trade/GDP	0.0241	0.0311	0.0334	0.0321	0.0306	0.0254	0.0337	0.0357	0.0342	0.0311	0.0254	0.0337	0.0357	0.0342	0.0311
Std. error	(0.0076)	(0.0078)	(0.0080)	(0.0079)	(0.0075)	(0.0077)	(0.0080)	(0.0081)	(0.0081)	(0.0076)	(0.0077)	(0.0080)	(0.0081)	(0.0081)	(0.0076)
Inflation	-0.0006	0.0001	0.0004	0.0005	0.0004	-0.0006	0.0001	0.0004	0.0005	0.0003	-0.0006	0.0001	0.0004	0.0005	0.0003
Std. error	(0.0009)	(0.0008)	(0.0007)	(0.0006)	(0.0006)	(0.0009)	(0.0008)	(0.0007)	(0.0006)	(0.0006)	(0.0009)	(0.0008)	(0.0007)	(0.0006)	(0.0006)
Enrollment	0.0638	0.0439	0.0292	0.0267	0.0196	0.0511	0.0250	0.0118	0.0126	0.0111	0.0511	0.0250	0.0118	0.0126	0.0111
Std. error	(0.0310)	(0.0309)	(0.0307)	(0.0298)	(0.0287)	(0.0307)	(0.0308)	(0.0308)	(0.0300)	(0.0288)	(0.0307)	(0.0308)	(0.0308)	(0.0300)	(0.0288)
Log(GDP)	-0.0016	-0.0020	-0.0022	-0.0023	-0.0023	-0.0015	-0.0019	-0.0022	-0.0023	-0.0023	-0.0015	-0.0019	-0.0022	-0.0023	-0.0023
Std. error	(0.0010)	(0.0010)	(0.0010)	(0.0010)	(0.0010)	(0.0010)	(0.0011)	(0.0011)	(0.0010)	(0.0010)	(0.0010)	(0.0011)	(0.0011)	(0.0010)	(0.0010)
PrivCredit/GDP	0.0029	0.0071	0.0117	0.0162	0.0220	0.0042	0.0098	0.0144	0.0186	0.0247	0.0042	0.0098	0.0144	0.0186	0.0247
Std. error	(0.0100)	(0.0100)	(0.0099)	(0.0098)	(0.0094)	(0.0101)	(0.0102)	(0.0102)	(0.0100)	(0.0096)	(0.0101)	(0.0102)	(0.0102)	(0.0100)	(0.0096)
MCAP/GDP	-0.0077	-0.0133	-0.0176	-0.0204	-0.0291	-0.0077	-0.0134	-0.0174	-0.0201	-0.0294	-0.0077	-0.0134	-0.0174	-0.0201	-0.0294
Std. error	(0.0056)	(0.0056)	(0.0053)	(0.0050)	(0.0051)	(0.0056)	(0.0058)	(0.0055)	(0.0051)	(0.0052)	(0.0056)	(0.0058)	(0.0055)	(0.0051)	(0.0052)
log(# of stocks)	0.0042	0.0049	0.0054	0.0054	0.0055	0.0045	0.0054	0.0058	0.0058	0.0058	0.0045	0.0054	0.0058	0.0058	0.0058
Std. error	(0.0010)	(0.0010)	(0.0011)	(0.0011)	(0.0010)	(0.0010)	(0.0010)	(0.0011)	(0.0011)	(0.0011)	(0.0010)	(0.0010)	(0.0011)	(0.0011)	(0.0011)
Turnover	0.0223	0.0184	0.0177	0.0143	0.0115	0.0221	0.0186	0.0180	0.0150	0.0119	0.0221	0.0186	0.0180	0.0150	0.0119
Std. error	(0.0055)	(0.0053)	(0.0055)	(0.0052)	(0.0053)	(0.0055)	(0.0054)	(0.0056)	(0.0054)	(0.0054)	(0.0055)	(0.0054)	(0.0056)	(0.0054)	(0.0054)

The dependent variable is the growth rate of the real per capita gross domestic product. Log(GDP) is the log real per capita GDP level in 1980. Govt/GDP is the ratio of government consumption to GDP; Trade/GDP is the sum of exports and imports of goods and services measured as a share of GDP; Inflation as measured by the annual growth rate of the GDP implicit deflator; Enrollment is the secondary school enrollment ratio; PrivCredit/GDP is private credit divided by GDP; log(# of stocks) is the log of the number of domestic companies; Turnover is the ratio of equity market value traded to the MCAP. Weighting matrix II refers to a correction for cross-sectional heteroskedasticity and SUR effects; weighting matrix III refers to a correction for cross-sectional heteroskedasticity; and weighting matrix IV refers to a simple pooled OLS. All standard errors are robust, accounting for the overlapping nature of the data.

liberalization is associated with a higher level of real economic growth. The evidence implies that real GDP per capita growth rates increase following financial liberalization by anywhere from 0.7% to as large as 1.4% per annum. Despite the large Monte Carlo critical values presented in the table in Appendix C, these estimates retain statistical significance at the 95% confidence level in many of the specifications considered.

Overall, the evidence presented in Table 8 suggests that on average real economic growth rates increase roughly 1.1% per annum following financial liberalization. This finding is consistent with that presented in Table 4, when no control variables are employed, suggesting the relation between financial liberalization and economic growth is robust across weighting matrix specifications and conditioning variables. Levine and Renelt (1992) demonstrate that the estimated coefficients in cross-country regressions require extreme caution in interpretation, as they are sensitive to the set of control variables employed. Consequently, the evidence presented in Table 8 strengthens the argument that financial liberalization explains an important part of the cross-sectional and time-series characteristics of real economic growth.

Surprisingly, the patterns in the coefficients across the different horizons suggest that the strongest growth impacts are experienced shortly after liberalization. For example, for weighting matrix III in Table 8, the coefficients for the 1- to 5-year horizons are: 0.0123, 0.0116, 0.0118, 0.0111, and 0.0081. This suggests that the total impact on economic growth over the 5-year period is 4.1%. Over half of the additional growth (2.3%) occurs in the first 2 years and 87% of the 5-year growth impact occurs in the first 3 years.

4.4. Robustness

We explore five experiments that are designed to test the robustness of the liberalization indicator effect on future economic growth.

First, we consider an alternative specification that allows for regional differences in the measured effect of financial liberalization on economic growth. In particular, the high level of economic growth observed in Latin American countries after the debt crisis may significantly affect the relationship between liberalization and growth discussed above. Although this higher growth after the "lost decade" may be due in part to financial liberalization, this is open to debate. Therefore, we explore whether Latin American countries drive our results by estimating the following regional regression equation:

$$Y_{i,t+k,k} = \beta' x_{i,t} + \delta_1(\text{lib indicator}_{i,t} \times \text{Latin}_i)$$
$$+ \delta_2(\text{lib indicator}_{i,t} \times (1 - \text{Latin}_i)) + \epsilon_{i,t+k,k}, \qquad (32)$$

where Latin_i takes the value of 1 if country i is a Latin American country, and 0 otherwise. This specification allow the relationship between financial liberalization

490　　　　G. Bekaert et al. / Journal of Development Economics 66 (2001) 465–504

Table 8
Liberalization and growth controlling for macroeconomic, banking and stock market development control variables
30 Countries, 1981–1997.

	Horizon in years														
	Weighting matrix II					Weighting matrix III					Weighting matrix IV				
	$k=1$	2	3	4	5	$k=1$	2	3	4	5	$k=1$	2	3	4	5
Govt/GDP	-0.1313	-0.1357	-0.1286	-0.1287	-0.1367	-0.1327	-0.1357	-0.1273	-0.1306	-0.1358	-0.1518	-0.1564	-0.1390	-0.1291	-0.1427
Std. error	(0.0332)	(0.0333)	(0.0327)	(0.0315)	(0.0300)	(0.0336)	(0.0339)	(0.0333)	(0.0321)	(0.0302)	(0.0396)	(0.0391)	(0.0421)	(0.0405)	(0.0384)
Trade/GDP	0.0259	0.0344	0.0399	0.0408	0.0395	0.0258	0.0345	0.0397	0.0411	0.0390	0.0297	0.0360	0.0361	0.0326	0.0283
Std. error	(0.0074)	(0.0075)	(0.0075)	(0.0072)	(0.0067)	(0.0074)	(0.0076)	(0.0075)	(0.0073)	(0.0068)	(0.0095)	(0.0093)	(0.0098)	(0.0097)	(0.0095)
Inflation	-0.0006	0.0002	0.0006	0.0007	0.0006	-0.0006	0.0001	0.0005	0.0006	0.0005	-0.0005	0.0003	0.0008	0.0007	0.0005
Std. error	(0.0008)	(0.0007)	(0.0006)	(0.0005)	(0.0005)	(0.0008)	(0.0007)	(0.0006)	(0.0005)	(0.0005)	(0.0007)	(0.0006)	(0.0004)	(0.0004)	(0.0005)
Enrollment	0.0613	0.0330	0.0108	0.0093	-0.0006	0.0562	0.0255	0.0040	0.0003	-0.0059	0.0194	0.0015	-0.0195	-0.0136	0.0147
Std. error	(0.0308)	(0.0313)	(0.0312)	(0.0303)	(0.0291)	(0.0306)	(0.0311)	(0.0311)	(0.0302)	(0.0289)	(0.0372)	(0.0361)	(0.0365)	(0.0351)	(0.0342)
Log(GDP)	-0.0026	-0.0028	-0.0034	-0.0036	-0.0034	-0.0024	-0.0027	-0.0033	-0.0035	-0.0034	-0.0025	-0.0029	-0.0026	-0.0025	-0.0030
Std. error	(0.0010)	(0.0010)	(0.0010)	(0.0010)	(0.0010)	(0.0010)	(0.0010)	(0.0010)	(0.0010)	(0.0010)	(0.0013)	(0.0013)	(0.0015)	(0.0015)	(0.0014)
PrivCredit/GDP	0.0025	0.0075	0.0112	0.0143	0.0252	0.0035	0.0086	0.0126	0.0157	0.0269	0.0068	0.0126	0.0093	0.0147	0.0265
Std. error	(0.0097)	(0.0097)	(0.0093)	(0.0092)	(0.0089)	(0.0098)	(0.0098)	(0.0095)	(0.0093)	(0.0090)	(0.0112)	(0.0110)	(0.0107)	(0.0103)	(0.0108)

MCAP/GDP	−0.0107	−0.0158	−0.0191	−0.0206	−0.0295	−0.0109	−0.0159	−0.0190	−0.0205	−0.0297	−0.0081	−0.0121	−0.0064	−0.0083	−0.0204
Std. error	(0.0054)	(0.0052)	(0.0047)	(0.0043)	(0.0046)	(0.0055)	(0.0053)	(0.0048)	(0.0044)	(0.0047)	(0.0068)	(0.0066)	(0.0058)	(0.0056)	(0.0077)
log(# of stocks)	0.0043	0.0051	0.0057	0.0058	0.0062	0.0044	0.0053	0.0059	0.0060	0.0063	0.0051	0.0059	0.0063	0.0060	0.0059
Std. error	(0.0010)	(0.0010)	(0.0010)	(0.0010)	(0.0011)	(0.0010)	(0.0010)	(0.0010)	(0.0010)	(0.0011)	(0.0015)	(0.0015)	(0.0017)	(0.0017)	(0.0016)
Turnover	0.0173	0.0133	0.0130	0.0125	0.0088	0.0168	0.0133	0.0125	0.0124	0.0090	0.0161	0.0128	0.0049	0.0041	0.0057
Std. error	(0.0057)	(0.0055)	(0.0056)	(0.0052)	(0.0054)	(0.0057)	(0.0056)	(0.0057)	(0.0053)	(0.0055)	(0.0068)	(0.0062)	(0.0050)	(0.0046)	(0.0052)
Official Liberalization Indicator	**0.0135**	**0.0119**	**0.0114**	**0.0107**	**0.0073**	**0.0123**	**0.0116**	**0.0118**	**0.0111**	**0.0081**	**0.0142**	**0.0138**	**0.0100**	**0.0072**	**0.0072**
Std. error	**(0.0034)**	**(0.0035)**	**(0.0036)**	**(0.0036)**	**(0.0034)**	**(0.0032)**	**(0.0033)**	**(0.0034)**	**(0.0034)**	**(0.0033)**	**(0.0046)**	**(0.0046)**	**(0.0044)**	**(0.0042)**	**(0.0044)**

The dependent variable is the growth rate of the real per capita gross domestic product. Log(GDP) is the log real per capita GDP level in 1980. Govt./GDP is the ratio of government consumption to GDP; Trade/GDP is the sum of exports and imports of goods and services measured as a share of GDP; Inflation as measured by the annual growth rate of the GDP implicit deflator; Enrollment is the secondary school enrollment ratio; PrivCredit/GDP is private credit divided by GDP; log(# of stocks) is the log of the number of domestic companies; Turnover is the ratio of equity market value traded to the MCAP and the Official Liberalization variable takes a value of one when the equity market is liberalized, and zero otherwise. Weighting matrix II refers to a correction for cross-sectional heteroskedasticity and SUR effects; weighting matrix III refers to a correction for cross-sectional heteroskedasticity; and weighting matrix IV refers to a simple pooled OLS. All standard errors are robust, accounting for the overlapping nature of the data.

492   *G. Bekaert et al. / Journal of Development Economics 66 (2001) 465–504*

and economic growth to differ across Latin American and non-Latin American countries.

Given the evidence presented in the first panel of Table 9 for these estimated regressions, the regional effect is negligible. If anything, the growth effect appears considerably weaker in Latin American countries relative to other countries. This suggests that the observed liberalization effect discussed above (and presented in Table 8) is not being driven by regional economic success in Latin America during our sample period.

Second, we examine the role of the government sector. Is it the case that the impact of liberalization on economic growth is determined by the size of the government sector? We create a variable, BigGov, that takes on the value of one if the country-specific median government spending to GDP ratio is greater than all countries' median government spending to GDP ratio. We run a regression similar to the regional regression above which splits the liberalization indicator into two pieces.

The results in the Panel B of Table 9 show that the financial liberalization variable retains it significance and magnitude for both sets of countries. The liberalization effect is 25 basis points larger for countries with smaller than median government sectors. However, the difference is not statistically significant. In unreported results, we also estimated a regression adding an interaction term (liberalization times the government sector to GDP ratio). The coefficient on the interaction term was insignificant, further strengthening the case that there is no relation between the size of the government sector and the impact of liberalization on real economic growth.

The third experiment examines the role of education. It is possible that countries with higher levels of education could stand to benefit more from financial market liberalizations than countries with low levels of education. Similar to the method for the size of the government sector, we created a variable, School, which takes on a value of unity if the country-specific median secondary school enrollment is greater than the whole sample median secondary school enrollment.

The results are presented in Panel C of Table 9. It is clear from these results that countries with high levels of education stand to benefit more from financial market liberalizations. For example, in the 3-year horizon for all three weighting matrices, the coefficient on the liberalization indicator is three times larger for countries with above median education levels. The results suggest that policy makers should not expect a large growth impact from liberalization if the country's education level is lower than the median in these 30 emerging markets. The Wald tests show that the difference between the two liberalization effects is statistically significant in the longer horizon regressions.

The fourth experiment focuses on early versus late liberalizers. Is it the case that most of the growth benefits occurred for the early liberalizers? This is possible if only limited capital from the developed world is available and that it

G. Bekaert et al. / Journal of Development Economics 66 (2001) 465–504 493

Table 9
The robustness of the growth–liberalization relation
30 Countries, 1981–1997.

	$k = 1$	2	3	4	5
	Weighting matrix III				
(A) Does one region drive the impact of liberalizations on economic growth?					
Govt/GDP	−0.1376	−0.1475	−0.1407	−0.1416	−0.1520
Std. error	(0.0336)	(0.0336)	(0.0329)	(0.0315)	(0.0294)
Trade/GDP	0.0261	0.0340	0.0384	0.0394	0.0386
Std. error	(0.0074)	(0.0075)	(0.0074)	(0.0071)	(0.0064)
Inflation	−0.0007	0.0002	0.0006	0.0007	0.0005
Std. error	(0.0009)	(0.0008)	(0.0007)	(0.0006)	(0.0006)
Enrollment	0.0549	0.0235	0.0042	0.0010	−0.0093
Std. error	(0.0306)	(0.0307)	(0.0305)	(0.0294)	(0.0279)
Log(GDP)	−0.0024	−0.0024	−0.0028	−0.0030	−0.0029
Std. error	(0.0010)	(0.0010)	(0.0011)	(0.0011)	(0.0011)
PrivCredit/GDP	0.0050	0.0095	0.0123	0.0145	0.0256
Std. error	(0.0098)	(0.0098)	(0.0094)	(0.0092)	(0.0088)
MCAP/GDP	−0.0114	−0.0159	−0.0186	−0.0197	−0.0290
Std. error	(0.0055)	(0.0053)	(0.0047)	(0.0043)	(0.0046)
log(# of stocks)	0.0045	0.0053	0.0058	0.0058	0.0063
Std. error	(0.0010)	(0.0010)	(0.0010)	(0.0010)	(0.0010)
Turnover	0.0175	0.0147	0.0145	0.0144	0.0120
Std. error	(0.0057)	(0.0055)	(0.0057)	(0.0054)	(0.0058)
Official Liberalization Indicator (Latin)	**0.0136**	**0.0081**	**0.0048**	**0.0014**	**−0.0004**
Std. error	**(0.0073)**	**(0.0084)**	**(0.0085)**	**(0.0082)**	**(0.0085)**
Official Liberalization Indicator (Non-Latin)	**0.0117**	**0.0107**	**0.0114**	**0.0116**	**0.0095**
Std. error	**(0.0033)**	**(0.0034)**	**(0.0037)**	**(0.0038)**	**(0.0038)**
P-value from Wald test, H0: Latin = Non-Latin	0.797	0.760	0.455	0.242	0.280
(B) Does the size of the government sector explain the impact of liberalizations on economic growth?					
Govt/GDP	−0.1309	−0.1276	−0.1169	−0.1230	−0.1304
Std. error	(0.0336)	(0.0341)	(0.0337)	(0.0326)	(0.0309)
Trade/GDP	0.0258	0.0346	0.0403	0.0419	0.0387
Std. error	(0.0075)	(0.0077)	(0.0078)	(0.0075)	(0.0071)

(continued on next page)

494   G. Bekaert et al. / Journal of Development Economics 66 (2001) 465–504

Table 9 (*continued*)

	k = 1	2	3	4	5
	Weighting matrix III				

(B) Does the size of the government sector explain the impact of liberalizations on economic growth?

	k = 1	2	3	4	5
Inflation	−0.0006	0.0002	0.0006	0.0006	0.0005
Std. error	(0.0008)	(0.0007)	(0.0006)	(0.0005)	(0.0004)
Enrollment	0.0566	0.0240	−0.0026	−0.0071	−0.0106
Std. error	(0.0309)	(0.0319)	(0.0322)	(0.0313)	(0.0300)
Log(GDP)	−0.0025	−0.0029	−0.0035	−0.0035	−0.0032
Std. error	(0.0010)	(0.0010)	(0.0010)	(0.0010)	(0.0010)
PrivCredit/GDP	0.0034	0.0083	0.0133	0.0169	0.0269
Std. error	(0.0098)	(0.0100)	(0.0098)	(0.0096)	(0.0092)
MCAP/GDP	−0.0109	−0.0158	−0.0194	−0.0215	−0.0303
Std. error	(0.0056)	(0.0054)	(0.0049)	(0.0045)	(0.0047)
log(# of stocks)	0.0044	0.0053	0.0060	0.0061	0.0061
Std. error	(0.0010)	(0.0010)	(0.0010)	(0.0010)	(0.0010)
Turnover	0.0166	0.0121	0.0108	0.0109	0.0080
Std. error	(0.0057)	(0.0056)	(0.0057)	(0.0053)	(0.0054)
Official Liberalization Indicator (Big Gov.)	**0.0128**	**0.0122**	**0.0119**	**0.0117**	**0.0080**
Std. error	**(0.0045)**	**(0.0047)**	**(0.0047)**	**(0.0046)**	**(0.0041)**
Official Liberalization Indicator (Small Gov.)	**0.0122**	**0.0127**	**0.0144**	**0.0134**	**0.0093**
Std. error	**(0.0039)**	**(0.0042)**	**(0.0045)**	**(0.0047)**	**(0.0049)**
P-value from Wald test, H0: Big Gov. = Small Gov.	0.920	0.926	0.681	0.792	0.829

(C) The influence of education on the relation between financial market liberalization and economic growth

	k = 1	2	3	4	5
Govt/GDP	−0.1283	−0.1322	−0.1218	−0.1256	−0.1338
Std. error	(0.0337)	(0.0336)	(0.0328)	(0.0313)	(0.0294)
Trade/GDP	0.0252	0.0341	0.0393	0.0406	0.0389
Std. error	(0.0075)	(0.0075)	(0.0075)	(0.0071)	(0.0065)
Inflation	−0.0005	0.0002	0.0005	0.0006	0.0004
Std. error	(0.0008)	(0.0007)	(0.0006)	(0.0005)	(0.0005)
Enrollment	0.0502	0.0138	−0.0051	−0.0093	−0.0166
Std. error	(0.0307)	(0.0309)	(0.0308)	(0.0296)	(0.0281)
Log(GDP)	−0.0023	−0.0026	−0.0033	−0.0034	−0.0033
Std. error	(0.0010)	(0.0010)	(0.0010)	(0.0010)	(0.0010)

G. Bekaert et al. / Journal of Development Economics 66 (2001) 465–504   495

Table 9 (*continued*)

	k = 1	2	3	4	5
	Weighting matrix III				

(C) The influence of education on the relation between financial market liberalization and economic growth

	k = 1	2	3	4	5
PrivCredit/GDP	0.0037	0.0097	0.0141	0.0174	0.0272
Std. error	(0.0098)	(0.0097)	(0.0094)	(0.0091)	(0.0086)
MCAP/GDP	−0.0105	−0.0154	−0.0190	−0.0209	−0.0298
Std. error	(0.0055)	(0.0053)	(0.0047)	(0.0043)	(0.0045)
log(# of stocks)	0.0045	0.0055	0.0060	0.0061	0.0065
Std. error	(0.0010)	(0.0010)	(0.0010)	(0.0010)	(0.0011)
Turnover	0.0165	0.0132	0.0122	0.0122	0.0095
Std. error	(0.0057)	(0.0055)	(0.0056)	(0.0053)	(0.0054)
Official Liberalization Indicator (+School)	**0.0140**	**0.0136**	**0.0144**	**0.0147**	**0.0118**
Std. error	**(0.0035)**	**(0.0037)**	**(0.0041)**	**(0.0042)**	**(0.0039)**
Official Liberalization Indicator (−School)	**0.0073**	**0.0033**	**0.0044**	**0.0032**	**−0.0015**
Std. error	**(0.0053)**	**(0.0054)**	**(0.0054)**	**(0.0053)**	**(0.0054)**
P-value from Wald test, H0: +School = −School	0.244	0.087	0.113	0.075	0.039

(D) Early versus late liberalization of financial markets and economic growth

	k = 1	2	3	4	5
Govt/GDP	−0.1242	−0.1175	−0.1056	−0.1030	−0.0752
Std. error	(0.0354)	(0.0370)	(0.0381)	(0.0370)	(0.0313)
Trade/GDP	0.0247	0.0340	0.0384	0.0388	0.0357
Std. error	(0.0079)	(0.0086)	(0.0092)	(0.0090)	(0.0088)
Inflation	−0.0006	0.0002	0.0007	0.0008	0.0007
Std. error	(0.0008)	(0.0007)	(0.0005)	(0.0004)	(0.0004)
Enrollment	0.0593	0.0276	0.0003	−0.0087	−0.0004
Std. error	(0.0316)	(0.0330)	(0.0343)	(0.0337)	(0.0318)
Log(GDP)	−0.0026	−0.0031	−0.0035	−0.0035	−0.0036
Std. error	(0.0011)	(0.0011)	(0.0013)	(0.0012)	(0.0012)
PrivCredit/GDP	0.0029	0.0085	0.0154	0.0200	0.0190
Std. error	(0.0100)	(0.0105)	(0.0111)	(0.0112)	(0.0103)
MCAP/GDP	−0.0102	−0.0148	−0.0155	−0.0152	−0.0222
Std. error	(0.0058)	(0.0060)	(0.0067)	(0.0069)	(0.0095)
log(# of stocks)	0.0044	0.0052	0.0054	0.0050	0.0046
Std. error	(0.0011)	(0.0011)	(0.0014)	(0.0015)	(0.0015)

(*continued on next page*)

Table 9 (*continued*)

	k = 1	2	3	4	5
	Weighting matrix III				
(D) Early versus late liberalization of financial markets and economic growth					
Turnover	0.0137	0.0094	0.0078	0.0072	0.0068
Std. error	(0.0064)	(0.0062)	(0.0066)	(0.0063)	(0.0060)
Official Liberalization					
Indicator (Early)	**0.0139**	**0.0136**	**0.0143**	**0.0161**	**0.0149**
Std. error	**(0.0037)**	**(0.0041)**	**(0.0047)**	**(0.0049)**	**(0.0050)**
Official Liberalization					
Indicator (Late)	**0.0139**	**0.0157**	**0.0181**	**0.0191**	**0.0265**
Std. error	**(0.0061)**	**(0.0078)**	**(0.0134)**	**(0.0205)**	**(0.0434)**
P-value from Wald test, H0: Early = Late	1.000	0.803	0.785	0.885	0.790
(E) Liberalization and growth excluding the financially oriented control variables					
Govt/GDP	−0.0507	−0.0397	−0.0280	−0.0272	−0.0403
Std. error	(0.0316)	(0.0324)	(0.0335)	(0.0327)	(0.0303)
Trade/GDP	0.0010	−0.0019	−0.0043	−0.0076	−0.0060
Std. error	(0.0063)	(0.0066)	(0.0068)	(0.0068)	(0.0070)
Enrollment	−0.0006	−0.0001	0.0002	0.0003	0.0002
Std. error	(0.0008)	(0.0007)	(0.0006)	(0.0005)	(0.0005)
Log(GDP)	0.1702	0.1821	0.1852	0.1834	0.1671
Std. error	(0.0250)	(0.0254)	(0.0265)	(0.0267)	(0.0272)
Inflation	−0.0018	−0.0024	−0.0028	−0.0029	−0.0025
Std. error	(0.0009)	(0.0010)	(0.0010)	(0.0010)	(0.0010)
PrivCredit/GDP	−0.0082	−0.0042	−0.0001	0.0069	0.0112
Std. error	(0.0077)	(0.0086)	(0.0094)	(0.0097)	(0.0093)
Official Liberalization					
Indicator	**0.0159**	**0.0157**	**0.0149**	**0.0127**	**0.0095**
Std. error	**(0.0030)**	**(0.0032)**	**(0.0034)**	**(0.0035)**	**(0.0036)**

The dependent variable is the growth rate of the real per capita gross domestic product. Log(GDP) is the log real per capital GDP level in 1980. Govt/GDP is the ratio of government consumption to GDP; Trade/GDP is the sum of exports and imports of goods and services measured as a share of GDP; Inflation as measured by the annual growth rate of the GDP implicit deflator; Enrollment is the secondary school enrollment ratio; PrivCredit/GDP is private credit divided by GDP; log(# of stocks) is the log of the number of domestic companies; Turnover is the ratio of equity market value traded to the MCAP and the official liberalization variable takes a value of one when the equity market is liberalized, and zero otherwise. Latin refers to an indicator that takes the value of one if the country is in Latin America. BigGov takes the value of one for the country has a larger than median gov/GDP ratio. +School takes the value of one for the country has a larger than median secondary school enrollment ratio. Early takes the value of one for countries that underwent a financial liberalization before 1991, the median liberalization date. Weighting matrix II refers to a correction for cross-sectional heteroskedasticity and SUR effects; weighting matrix III refers to a correction for cross-sectional heteroskedasticity; and weighting matrix IV refers to a simple pooled OLS. All standard errors are robust, accounting for the overlapping nature of the data.

G. Bekaert et al. / Journal of Development Economics 66 (2001) 465–504   497

has been exhausted by the early liberalizers. Given that the median liberalization date is 1991, we created an additional variable that identifies early versus late liberalizers. Regressions were run that split the liberalization variable into these two categories.

The results are presented in Panel D of Table 9. It is not the case that early liberalizations have more impact than late liberalizations. While the differences are small, the effect goes the other way. For most of the regressions, the late liberalization countries have a greater impact on economic growth. However, early liberalization still leads to a significant statistical and economic growth effect. The difference between the two effects is not statistically significant because the standard errors for the late liberalization countries are large due to the smaller number of observations available to estimate this coefficient.

The final experiment concerns the relation between the financial control variables and liberalizations. In particular, there are reasons to believe that market capitalization to GDP, the number of stocks in the index, and stock turnover, could be impacted by financial liberalization. Indeed, Bekaert and Harvey (2000), show that one of these variables, the number of stocks in the index, is significantly higher after liberalizations. The changes in the control variables could confound our analysis linking liberalization and real economic growth. Therefore, in the final panel in Table 9 we report estimates of the growth regression without any financial control variables. The significance for the coefficient on the liberalization indicator is not impacted when the financial variables are dropped from the regression and its magnitude drops by only 14 (31) basis points at the 5 (3)-year horizons. This suggests that only a small part of the financial liberalization can be accounted for by stock market development.

5. Conclusions

The goal of the paper is to explore the relation between financial liberalization and real economic growth. While considerable effort in the past has been expended on the economic and financial fundamentals that explain the cross-section of economic growth, we focus on financial liberalizations. We emphasize the time-series component of growth in addition to the cross-sectional relation. Our results suggest that financial market liberalizations are associated with higher real growth, in the range of 1% per annum. The impact of financial market liberalizations is robust to the inclusion of the usual set of control variables representing the macroeconomic environment, banking development and stock market development. In addition, the relationship between real economic growth and liberalization is not impacted if we control for the size of the government sector or examine early versus late liberalizers. We also find evidence that the impact of liberalization on growth is not a Latin American phenomena. We do find, however, that countries with a higher than average level of education, benefit much more from financial liberalization.

498   *G. Bekaert et al. / Journal of Development Economics 66 (2001) 465–504*

Although our empirical results are intriguing, they warrant further analysis. First, we have focused only on emerging financial markets. In the standard cross-sectional growth literature, larger cross-sections are used including developed countries. Second, dating financial liberalization is problematic (see Bekaert et al., 1999), and we should consider further robustness checks on the financial liberalization dates we consider.[6] Finally, the results remain inherently empirical. How do financial liberalizations result in higher economic growth? Bekaert and Harvey (2000) and Henry (2000a,b) provide evidence that the cost of capital may have decreased and investment increased after capital market liberalization. Comparing Tables 7 and 8 reveals that the turnover coefficient decreases when the liberalization indicator is introduced, suggesting perhaps a liquidity/efficiency mechanism for enhanced growth. Our new research, Bekaert et al. (2001), begins to carefully examine all of these important questions.

Acknowledgements

We have benefited from the comments of Rodolfo Apreda, Sebastian Edwards, Miguel Ferreira, Peter Henry, the participants at the NBER InterAmerican Seminar on Economics, December 2–4, 1999, in Buenos Aires, the 2000 European Finance Association Meetings in London, the 2001 American Finance Association Meetings in New Orleans and the suggestions of an anonymous referee.

Appendix A. Data appendix

In the system estimation described in the econometric methodology section, all data are employed at the annual frequency.

A.1. GDP growth

Growth of real per capita gross domestic product. Available for all countries from 1980 through 1997 from the World Bank Development Indicators CD-ROM.

A.2. Trade

Trade is the sum of exports and imports of goods and services measured as a share of gross domestic product. Available for all countries from 1980 through 1997 from the World Bank Development Indicators CD-ROM.

---

[6] We performed one robustness check reestimating the model without control variables using the 16 countries that Bekaert and Harvey (2000) show have breaks in their net capital flows. The results using this alternative indicator of liberalization are broadly consistent with what we have reported.

G. Bekaert et al. / Journal of Development Economics 66 (2001) 465–504   499

A.3. Government consumption

Government consumption divided by gross domestic product. General government consumption includes all current expenditures for purchases of goods and services by all levels of government, excluding most government enterprises. It also includes capital expenditure on national defense and security. Available for all countries from 1980 through 1997 from the World Bank Development Indicators CD-ROM.

A.4. Inflation

Inflation as measured by the annual growth rate of the gross domestic product implicit deflator. Available for all countries from 1980 through 1997 from the World Bank Development Indicators CD-ROM.

A.5. Secondary School Enrollment

Secondary school enrollment ratio is the ratio of total enrollment, regardless of age, to the population of the age group that officially corresponds to the level of education shown. Available for all countries from 1980 through 1997 from the World Bank Development Indicators CD-ROM.

A.6. Private credit

Private credit divided by gross domestic product. Credit to private sector refers to financial resources provided to the private sector, such as through loans, purchases of non-equity securities, and trade credits and other accounts receivable that establish a claim for repayment. Available for all countries from 1980 through 1997 from the World Bank Development Indicators CD-ROM.

A.7. Market capitalization

Equity market capitalization divided by gross domestic product. Equity market capitalization is from the *International Finance Corporation's* Emerging Stock Markets Factbook. The gross domestic product data are from the World Bank Development Indicators CD-ROM. Data are available from 1980 through 1997.

A.8. Number of companies

The log of the number of domestic companies covered taken from the *International Finance Corporation's* (IFC, 1997) Emerging Stock Markets Factbook. The data are available from 1980 through 1997.

500　　　G. Bekaert et al. / Journal of Development Economics 66 (2001) 465–504

Appendix B. Monte Carlo structure

Cross-sectionally restricted VAR used in Monte Carlo for constructing control variables

Dependent variable	Govt/GDP	Trade/GDP	Inflation	Enrollment	Priv Credit/GDP	MCAP/GDP	ln(# of stocks)	Turnover	Standard error of regressions
Govt/GDP	0.7988	−0.1783	−2.3019	−0.0852	0.1893	−0.1034	0.2191	0.3057	0.0140
Std. error	(0.0277)	(0.1190)	(4.0191)	(0.0423)	(0.1313)	(0.3332)	(0.4771)	(0.3251)	
Trade/GDP	−0.0167	0.8419	0.2663	0.0202	−0.0103	0.3277	0.0275	0.0625	0.0600
Std. error	(0.0072)	(0.0310)	(1.0478)	(0.0110)	(0.0342)	(0.0869)	(0.1244)	(0.0848)	
Inflation	0.0002	−0.0007	0.4115	0.0001	−0.0073	−0.0005	−0.0038	−0.0007	0.1727
Std. error	(0.0003)	(0.0012)	(0.0413)	(0.0004)	(0.0013)	(0.0034)	(0.0049)	(0.0033)	
Enrollment	0.0450	−0.1816	1.4580	0.7489	0.1481	−0.2998	0.2667	0.1919	0.0213
Std. error	(0.0176)	(0.0755)	(2.5479)	(0.0268)	(0.0832)	(0.2112)	(0.3024)	(0.2061)	
PrivCredit/GDP	0.0014	0.0711	3.7194	−0.0149	0.8204	0.0791	0.0378	−0.0271	0.0661
Std. error	(0.0058)	(0.0249)	(0.8395)	(0.0088)	(0.0274)	(0.0696)	(0.0997)	(0.0679)	
MCAP/GDP	0.0018	0.0358	−1.0816	0.0158	0.0640	0.6374	0.1365	0.0954	0.1679
Std. error	(0.0035)	(0.0148)	(0.5005)	(0.0053)	(0.0163)	(0.0415)	(0.0594)	(0.0405)	
log(# of stocks)	0.0043	0.0310	0.2683	0.0091	0.0158	0.0403	0.4857	0.0966	0.1638
Std. error	(0.0032)	(0.0136)	(0.4579)	(0.0048)	(0.0150)	(0.0380)	(0.0543)	(0.0370)	
Turnover	−0.0029	−0.0018	−0.1983	−0.0039	0.0124	0.0109	0.0633	0.8694	0.2404
Std. error	(0.0016)	(0.0067)	(0.2246)	(0.0024)	(0.0073)	(0.0186)	(0.0267)	(0.0182)	

To generate control (right-hand side) variables for our Monte Carlo, we estimate a VAR on Gov/GDP, Trade/GDP, Inflation, Enrollment, PrivCred/GDP, Log(# of stocks), and turnover, restricting the coefficients (reported) to be identical across countries but allowing for country specific intercepts (not reported).

Cross-sectionally restricted MA coefficient used in Monte Carlo for constructing residuals

	MA(1)	MA(2)	MA(3)	MA(4)
$k = 2$	0.778			
Std. error	(0.043)			
$k = 3$	0.786	0.494		
Std. error	(0.166)	(0.142)		
$k = 4$	0.695	0.498	0.337	
Std. error	(0.186)	(0.155)	(0.156)	
$k = 5$	0.900	0.685	0.317	0.008
Std. error	(0.289)	(0.301)	(0.339)	(0.294)

To generate the moving average structure of the dependent (left-hand side) variable in our Monte Carlo, we estimate an MA$(k-1)$ ($k = 2, \ldots, 5$) for the residuals from the estimations performed in Table 7, restricting the MA coefficients to be identical across countries. The estimation is performed using QMLE, assuming uncorrelated errors across countries and normal shocks in the likelihood.

Appendix C. Monte Carlo analysis

	Coefficient on Liberalization Indicator					T-statistic on Null Hypothesis					
	Horizon in years					Horizon in years					
Liberalization Indicator	k = 1	2	3	4	5	k = 1	2	3	4	5	N(0, 1)
Monte Carlo: 1000 replications (Weighting Matrix IV)											
Mean	0.0000	−0.0002	0.0000	0.0003	0.0002	−0.0050	−0.0426	−0.0018	0.0607	0.0362	0.000
Median	0.0001	−0.0002	0.0001	0.0002	0.0003	0.0373	−0.0486	0.0142	0.0355	0.0605	0.000
Std. dev.	0.0035	0.0047	0.0050	0.0053	0.0054	1.0169	1.1727	1.1301	1.1443	1.1404	1.000
Skewness	0.0312	0.0099	0.0539	0.0363	−0.1494	0.0355	−0.0248	0.0015	0.0768	−0.1244	0.000
Kurtosis	3.0587	3.0957	3.1887	2.8061	3.0049	3.0170	3.2067	3.1956	2.7769	3.0323	3.000
2.50%	−0.0069	−0.0092	−0.0099	−0.0101	−0.0112	−1.9710	−2.3223	−2.3009	−2.1631	−2.2771	−1.960
97.50%	0.0065	0.0092	0.0103	0.0105	0.0105	1.9040	2.2696	2.2023	2.2280	2.3086	1.960
Jarque–Bera	0.3056	0.3976	1.9689	1.7873	3.7216	0.2220	1.8831	1.5949	3.0569	2.6235	
Probability	0.8583	0.8197	0.3737	0.4092	0.1555	0.8950	0.3900	0.4505	0.2169	0.2694	
Monte Carlo: 1000 Replications (Weighting Matrix III)											
Mean	0.0001	−0.0001	−0.0001	0.0002	0.0001	0.0339	−0.0661	−0.0219	0.0953	0.0340	0.000
Median	0.0001	−0.0001	−0.0001	0.0001	0.0000	0.0660	−0.0470	−0.0372	0.0531	0.0151	0.000
Std. dev.	0.0025	0.0034	0.0035	0.0034	0.0036	1.0888	1.6476	1.6387	1.7479	1.7790	1.000
Skewness	−0.0055	−0.0992	−0.0667	0.0280	0.0206	−0.0294	−0.0790	−0.0266	−0.0166	0.0675	0.000
Kurtosis	3.0509	2.9859	3.0140	2.9323	3.0311	3.0403	2.9542	3.0376	3.0797	2.8988	3.000
2.50%	−0.0049	−0.0067	−0.0074	−0.0064	−0.0070	−2.0612	−3.2345	−3.2844	−3.2361	−3.2532	−1.960
97.50%	0.0049	0.0064	0.0070	0.0068	0.0069	2.1193	3.1524	3.2914	3.1836	3.2184	1.960
Jarque–Bera	0.1131	1.6469	0.7503	0.3216	0.1111	0.2122	1.1282	0.1771	0.3107	1.1869	
Probability	0.9450	0.4389	0.6872	0.8515	0.9460	0.8993	0.5689	0.9153	0.8561	0.5524	
Monte Carlo: 1000 replications (Weighting Matrix II)											
Mean	−0.0001	0.0001	0.0000	0.0003	0.0002	−0.0002	0.0250	−0.0168	0.0891	0.1017	0.0000
Median	0.0000	0.0000	0.0000	0.0000	0.0000	0.0000	0.0000	−0.0188	0.0817	0.0688	0.0000
Std. dev.	0.0027	0.0049	0.0065	0.0070	0.0077	1.2006	1.6480	1.6548	1.8059	1.8076	1.0000
Skewness	−0.0193	0.2424	0.1579	−0.0837	0.0925	−0.1564	−0.0301	0.0712	−0.0563	0.1424	0.0000
Kurtosis	3.5391	3.9869	3.2411	2.9376	2.8046	3.7899	3.5564	3.3945	3.1604	3.8650	3.0000
2.50%	−0.0040	−0.0099	−0.0126	−0.0138	−0.0152	−2.4329	−3.2895	−3.2882	−3.4898	−3.3569	−1.9600
97.50%	0.0039	0.0108	0.0132	0.0140	0.0162	2.3986	3.2754	3.2947	3.4111	3.5064	1.9600
Jarque–Bera	12.1708	50.3718	6.5785	1.3312	3.0155	30.0764	13.0491	7.3291	1.5998	34.5577	
Probability	0.0023	0.0000	0.0373	0.5140	0.2214	0.0000	0.0015	0.0256	0.4494	0.0000	

We report summary statistics for both the estimated coefficient on the Official Liberalization Indicator and the corresponding *t*-statistic from our Monte Carlo analysis for weighting matrices II, III, and IV. We also report 2.5% and 97.5% percentiles for comparison with the critical values we obtain in our regression specifications.

A.9. Turnover

The ratio of equity market value traded to the market capitalization. Both are available from the International Finance Corporation's Emerging Stock Markets Factbook. The data are available from 1980 through 1997.

A.10. Official Liberalization Indicator

The variable takes a value of one when the equity market is liberalized, and zero otherwise. Liberalization dates are based upon the chronology presented in Bekaert and Harvey (2000) for the markets covered by the International Finance Corporation's Global Indices. The dates are presented in Table 1.

References

Atje, R., Jovanovic, B., 1993. Stock markets and development. European Economic Review 37, 632–640.

Barro, R., 1991. Economic growth in a cross-section of countries. The Quarterly Journal of Economics 56, 407–443.

Barro, R., 1997. Determinants of Economic Growth. 1st edn. MIT Press, Cambridge, MA.

Barro, R., Sala-i-Martin, X., 1995. Economic Growth. 1st edn. McGraw-Hill, New York, NY.

Bekaert, G., Harvey, C.R., 1995. Time-varying world market integration. Journal of Finance 50, 403–444.

Bekaert, G., Harvey, C.R., 1997. Emerging equity market volatility. Journal of Financial Economics 43, 29–77.

Bekaert, G., Harvey, C.R., 2000. Foreign speculators and emerging equity markets. Journal of Finance 55, 565–614.

Bekaert, G., Harvey, C.R., Lumsdaine, R., 1999. Dating the Integration of World Capital Markets, Working Paper, Columbia University and Duke University.

Bekaert, G., Harvey, C.R., Lundblad, C., 2001. Does Financial Liberalization Spur Growth? Working Paper, Columbia University and Duke University.

Edwards, S., 1998. Openness, productivity, and growth: what do we really know? The Economic Journal 108, 383–398.

Hansen, L., 1982. Large sample properties of generalized method of moments estimators. Econometrica 50, 1029–1054.

Harrison, A., 1996. Openness and growth: a time-series, cross-country analysis for developing countries. Journal of Development Economics 48, 419–447.

Henry, P., 2000a. Do stock market liberalizations cause investment booms. Journal of Financial Economics 58, 301–334.

Henry, P., 2000b. Stock market liberalization, economic reform, and emerging market equity prices. Journal of Finance 55, 529–564.

IFC, 1997. Emerging Stock Markets Factbook 1997. International Finance Corporation, Washington, DC.

Islam, N., 1995. Growth empirics: a panel data approach. The Quarterly Journal of Economics 107, 1127–1170.

King, R., Levine, R., 1993. Finance and growth: Schumpeter might be right. The Quarterly Journal of Economics 108, 717–738.

Levine, R., Renelt, D., 1992. A sensitivity analysis of cross-country growth regressions. The American Economic Review 82, 942–963.

Levine, R., Zervos, S., 1998. Stock markets, banks, and economic growth. The American Economic Review 88, 537–558.

Newey, W., West, K., 1987. A simple, positive semi-definite, heteroskedasticity and autocorrelation consistent covariance matrix. Econometrica 55, 703–708.

Rodrik, D., 1999. Determinants of Economic Growth. Overseas Development Council, Washington, DC.

C
The Channels of Growth

[16]

ELSEVIER   Journal of Financial Economics 58 (2000) 261–300

JOURNAL OF
Financial
ECONOMICS
www.elsevier.com/locate/econbase

Finance and the sources of growth[☆]

Thorsten Beck[a,*], Ross Levine[b], Norman Loayza[c,a]

[a]The World Bank, Washington, DC 20433 USA
[b]Carlson School of Management, University of Minnesota, Minneapolis, MN, 55455 USA
[c]Central Bank of Chile, Santiago, Chile

Received 13 January 1999; received in revised form 27 July 1999

Abstract

This paper evaluates the empirical relation between the level of financial intermediary development and (i) economic growth, (ii) total factor productivity growth, (iii) physical capital accumulation, and (iv) private savings rates. We use (a) a pure cross-country instrumental variable estimator to extract the exogenous component of financial intermediary development, and (b) a new panel technique that controls for biases associated with simultaneity and unobserved country-specific effects. After controlling for these potential biases, we find that (1) financial intermediaries exert a large, positive impact on total factor productivity growth, which feeds through to overall GDP growth and (2) the long-run links between financial intermediary development and both physical capital growth and private savings rates are tenuous. © 2000 Elsevier Science S.A. All rights reserved.

JEL classification: G21; O16; O40

Keywords: Financial development; Economic growth; Capital accumulation; Productivity growth; Saving

[☆]We thank seminar participants at Ohio State University, the New York Federal Reserve Bank, Indiana University, Stanford University, and an anonymous referee for helpful suggestions. We thank Elena Mekhova for excellent support with the manuscript. This paper's findings, interpretations, and conclusions are entirely those of the authors and do not necessarily represent the views of the Central Bank of Chile, the World Bank, its Executive Directors, or the countries they represent.

* Corresponding author. Tel.: + 1-202-473-3215.

E-mail address: tbeck@worldbank.org (T. Beck).

262   *T. Beck et al. / Journal of Financial Economics 58 (2000) 261–300*

1. Introduction

Joseph Schumpeter argued in 1911 that financial intermediaries play a pivotal role in economic development because they choose which firms get to use society's savings (see Schumpeter, 1934). According to this view, the financial intermediary sector alters the path of economic progress by affecting the allocation of savings and not necessarily by altering the rate of savings. Thus, the Schumpeterian view of finance and development highlights the impact of financial intermediaries on productivity growth and technological change.[1] Alternatively, a vast development economics literature argues that capital accumulation is the key factor underlying economic growth.[2] According to this view, better financial intermediaries influence growth primarily by raising domestic savings rates and attracting foreign capital. Thus, while many theories note that financial intermediaries arise to ameliorate particular market frictions, the resulting models present competing views about the fundamental channels which connect financial intermediaries to growth. To clarify the relation between financial intermediation and economic performance, we empirically assess the impact of financial intermediaries on private savings rates, capital accumulation, productivity growth, and overall economic growth.

This paper is further motivated by a rejuvenated movement in macroeconomics to understand cross-country differences in both the level and growth rate of total factor productivity. A long empirical literature successfully shows that something else besides physical and human capital accounts for the bulk of cross-country differences in both the level and growth rate of real per capita Gross Domestic Product (GDP). Nevertheless, economists have been relatively unsuccessful at fully characterizing this residual, which is generally termed "total factor productivity." Recent papers by Hall and Jones (1999), Harberger (1998), Klenow (1998), and Prescott (1998) have again focused the profession's attention on the need for improved theories of total factor productivity growth. While we do not advance a new theory, this paper empirically explores one factor underlying cross-country differences in total factor productivity growth, namely differences in the level of financial intermediary development.

---

[1] Recent theoretical models have carefully documented the links between financial intermediaries and economic activity. By economizing on the costs of acquiring and processing information about firms and managers, financial intermediaries can influence resource allocation. Better financial intermediaries are lower cost producers of information with consequent ramifications for capital allocation and productivity growth (Diamond, 1984; Boyd and Prescott, 1986; Williamson, 1987; Greenwood and Jovanovic, 1990; King and Levine, 1993b). For a comprehensive exposition of the Schumpeterian view of growth, see Aghion and Howitt (1988).

[2] See discussion and citations in King and Levine (1994), Fry (1995), Bandiera et al. (2000), and Easterly and Levine (1999).

T. Beck et al. / Journal of Financial Economics 58 (2000) 261–300   263

While past research evaluates the impact of financial intermediary development on growth, we examine the relation between financial intermediary development and what we term the sources of growth. These sources include private savings rates, physical capital accumulation, and total factor productivity growth. King and Levine (1993a, b) show that the level of financial intermediary development is a good predictor of economic growth, even after controlling for many other country characteristics. Time-series studies confirm that finance predicts growth (Neusser and Kugler, 1998; Rousseau and Wachtel, 1998). One shortcoming of these papers is that financial intermediary development may be a leading indicator of economic growth, but not an underlying cause of economic growth. Recent industry-level, firm-level, and event-study investigations, however, suggest that the level of financial intermediary development has a large, causal impact on real per capita GDP growth (Rajan and Zingales, 1998; Demirgüç-Kunt and Maksimovic, 1998; Jayaratne and Strahan, 1996). Using both pure cross-country instrumental variables procedures and dynamic panel techniques, Levine et al. (2000) show that the strong, positive relation between the level of financial intermediary development and long-run economic growth is not due to simultaneity bias. This paper assesses the relation between financial intermediary development and (i) private savings rates, (ii) capital accumulation, and (iii) total factor productivity growth. While Levine et al. (2000) use a very similar data set and identical econometric procedures to study financial development and economic growth, this paper's major contribution is to examine the relation between financial intermediary development and the sources of growth.

Methodologically, this paper uses two econometric procedures to assess the relation between financial intermediary development and the sources of growth. While King and Levine (1993a) and Levine and Zervos (1998) examine this relation, their estimation procedures do not explicitly confront the potential biases induced by simultaneity or omitted variables, including country-specific effects. We use two econometric techniques to control for the simultaneity bias that may arise from the joint determination of financial intermediary development and (i) private savings rates, (ii) capital accumulation, (iii) total factor productivity growth, and (iv) overall real per capita GDP growth.

The first technique employs a pure cross-sectional instrumental variable estimator, where data for 63 countries are averaged over the period 1960–1995. The dependent variable is, in turn, real per capita GDP growth, real per capita capital stock growth, productivity growth, or private savings rates. Besides a measure of financial intermediary development, the regressors include a wide array of conditioning information to control for other factors associated with economic development. To control for simultaneity bias, we use the legal origin of each country as an instrumental variable to extract the exogenous component of financial intermediary development. Legal scholars note that many countries can be classified as having English, French, German, or Scandinavian legal origins. Countries typically obtained their legal systems through occupation or colonization. Thus, we take legal origin as exogenous. Moreover, La Porta et al., 1997, 1998; henceforth, LLSV) show that legal origin substantively accounts for cross-country differences in (a) creditor rights, (b) systems for enforcing debt contracts, and (c) standards for corporate information disclosure. Each of these features of the contracting environment helps explain cross-country differences in financial intermediary development (Levine, 1999). Thus, after extending the LLSV data on legal origin from 49 to 63 countries, we use the legal origin variables as instruments for financial intermediary development to assess the effect of financial intermediary development on economic growth, capital growth, productivity growth, and private savings rates.

These cross-country regression estimates have at least three drawbacks. First, they do not exploit the time-series dimension of the data. Second, these estimates may be biased by the omission of country-specific effects. Third, they do not control for the endogeneity of all the regressors. Therefore we also use a dynamic Generalized-Method-of-Moments (GMM) panel estimator.[3] We construct a panel dataset with data averaged over each of the seven 5-year periods between 1960 and 1995. We then use the GMM panel estimator proposed by Arellano and Bover (1995) and Blundell and Bond (1997) to extract consistent and efficient estimates of the impact of financial intermediary development on growth and the sources of growth. Relative to the cross-sectional estimator, this panel estimator has a number of advantages. Namely, the GMM panel estimator exploits the time-series variation in the data, accounts for unobserved country-specific effects, allows for the inclusion of lagged dependent variables as regressors, and controls for endogeneity of all the explanatory variables, including the financial development variables. To accomplish this task, the panel estimator uses instrumental variables based on previous realizations of the explanatory variables, referred to as internal instruments. Paradoxically, exploiting the time-series properties of the data also creates one disadvantage with respect to the cross-sectional estimator. By focusing on five-year periods, the panel estimator may not fully distinguish long-run growth relations from business-cycle ones. Thus, taking them as complementary, this paper uses two econometric procedures, a pure cross-sectional instrumental variable estimator and a GMM dynamic panel technique, to evaluate the impact of differences in financial intermediary development on economic growth, capital accumulation, productivity growth, and private saving.

This paper also improves upon existing work by using better measures of savings rates, physical capital, productivity, and financial intermediary development. Private savings rates are notoriously difficult to measure (Masson et al., 1995). As detailed below, however, we use the results of a recent World Bank

---

[3] By including initial income as an explanatory variable, growth regressions become dynamic in nature.

initiative that compiled high-quality statistics on gross private savings as a share of gross private disposable income over the period 1971–1995 (Loayza et al., 1998). We also use more accurate estimates of physical capital stocks. Researchers typically make an initial estimate of the capital stock in 1950, and then use aggregate investment data, coupled with a single depreciation rate to compute capital stocks in later years (King and Levine, 1994). The figures reported in this paper use capital stocks computed in this way because of data availability. Recently, however, the Penn-World Tables compiled disaggregated investment data into components such as machinery, transportation equipment, and business construction, and provided separate estimates of depreciation rates for each component. These data are available for only a subset of countries and years. Nonetheless, we confirm our results using capital stock estimates constructed using these disaggregated figures. Researchers typically define Total Factor Productivity (TFP) growth as a residual, or what remains when one calculates real per capita GDP growth minus real per capita capital growth times capital's share in the national income accounts, which is commonly taken to be between 0.3 and 0.4. Besides employing this traditional measure, we also control for human capital accumulation in computing TFP growth by using both the Mankiw (1995) and the Bils and Klenow (1998) specifications. Since these alternative productivity growth measures produce similar results, we report only the results with the simple, traditional TFP measure.[4] Finally, this paper also uses an improved measure of financial intermediary development. We measure financial intermediary credits to the private sector relative to GDP. This measure more carefully distinguishes who is conducting the intermediation, and to where the funds are flowing. Further, we more accurately deflate financial stocks than in past studies (e.g., King and Levine, 1993a, b). Finally, we check our results using the King and Levine (1993a, b) and Levine and Zervos (1998) measures of financial intermediation after extending their sample periods and deflating correctly.

We find that there is a robust, positive link between financial intermediary development and both real per capita GDP growth and total factor productivity growth. The results indicate that the strong connections between financial intermediary development and both real per capita GDP growth and total factor productivity growth are not due to biases created by endogeneity or unobserved country-specific effects. Using both the pure cross-sectional instrumental variable estimator and the system dynamic-panel estimator, we find that higher levels of financial intermediary development produce faster rates of economic growth and total factor productivity growth. These results are robust to alterations in the conditioning information set and to changes in the measure of financial intermediary development. Thus, the data are consistent with the

---

[4] Results with the other productivity measures are available on request.

Schumpeterian view that the level of financial intermediary development importantly determines the rate of economic growth by affecting the pace of productivity growth and technological change.

Turning to physical capital growth and savings, the results are ambiguous.
We frequently find a positive and significant relation between financial intermediary development and the growth rate of capital per capita. Nonetheless, the
results are inconsistent across alternative measures of financial development in
the pure cross-sectional regressions. The data do not confidently suggest that
higher levels of financial intermediary development promote economic growth
by boosting the long-run rate of physical capital accumulation. We find similarly conflicting results on savings. Different measures of financial intermediary
development yield different conclusions regarding the link between financial
intermediary development and private savings in both pure cross-section and
panel regressions. Thus, we do not find a robust relation between financial
intermediary development and either physical capital accumulation or private
savings rates. In sum, the results are consistent with the Schumpeterian view of
finance and development: financial intermediaries affect economic development
primarily by influencing total factor productivity growth.

The rest of the paper is organized as follows. Section 2 describes the data and
presents descriptive statistics. Section 3 discusses the two econometric methods.
Section 4 presents the results for economic growth, capital growth and productivity growth. Section 5 presents the results for private savings rates, and Section
6 concludes.

2. Measuring financial development, growth, and its sources

This section describes the measures of (1) financial intermediary development,
(2) real per capita GDP growth, (3) capital per capita growth, (4) productivity
per capita growth, and (5) private savings rates.

2.1. Indicators of financial development

A large theoretical literature shows that financial intermediaries can reduce
the costs of acquiring information about firms and managers, and lower the
costs of conducting transactions (see Gertler, 1988; Levine, 1997). By providing
more accurate information about production technologies and exerting corporate control, better financial intermediaries can enhance resource allocation and
accelerate growth (Boyd and Prescott, 1986; Greenwood and Jovanovic, 1990;
King and Levine, 1993b). Similarly, by facilitating risk management, improving
the liquidity of assets available to savers, and reducing trading costs, financial
intermediaries can encourage investment in higher-return activities (Obstfeld,
1994; Bencivenga and Smith, 1991; Greenwood and Smith, 1997). The effect of

better financial intermediaries on savings, however, is theoretically ambiguous. Higher returns ambiguously affect savings rates, due to well-known income and substitution effects. Also, greater risk diversification opportunities have an ambiguous impact on savings rates, as shown by Levhari and Srinivasan (1969). Moreover, in a closed economy, a drop in savings rates may have a negative impact on growth. Indeed, if these saving and externality effects are sufficiently large, an improvement in financial intermediary development could lower growth (Bencivenga and Smith, 1991). Thus, we attempt to shed some empirical light on these debates and ambiguities that emerge from the theoretical literature. Specifically, we examine whether economies with better-developed financial intermediaries (i) grow faster, (ii) enjoy faster rates of productivity growth, (iii) experience more rapid capital accumulation, and (iv) have higher savings rates.

To evaluate the impact of financial intermediaries on growth and the sources of growth, we seek an indicator of the ability of financial intermediaries to research and identify profitable ventures, monitor and control managers, ease risk management, and facilitate resource mobilization. We do not have a direct measure of these financial services. We do, however, construct a better measure of financial intermediary development than past studies and we check these results with existing measures of financial sector development.

The primary measure of financial intermediary development we employ is a variable called Private Credit, which equals the value of credits by financial intermediaries to the private sector divided by GDP. Unlike many past measures (King and Levine, 1993a, b), this measure excludes credits issued by the central bank and development banks. King and Levine (1993a, b) use a measure of gross claims on the private sector divided by GDP. But, this measure includes credits issued by the monetary authority and government agencies, whereas Private Credit includes only credits issued by deposit money banks and other financial intermediaries. Furthermore, it excludes credit to the public sector and cross claims of one group of intermediaries on another. Private Credit is also a broader measure of financial intermediary development than that used by Levine and Zervos (1998) and Levine (1998), since it includes all financial institutions, not only deposit money banks.[5]

---

[5] Credits by nonbank financial intermediaries to the private sector grow as proportion of total credits by the financial system to the private sector as countries develop. The level of development of these nonbanks is positively correlated with long-run economic growth. The correlation between private credit by nonbanks and real per capita GDP over the 1960–1995 period is 60%, and the correlation between nonbank credit to the private sector and growth is 30%. Both correlations are significant at the 1% level. Also, nonbank credits to the private sector are about equal to that of deposit money bank credits to the private sector in the United States, Sweden, Mexico, and Norway. Finally, across the entire sample, private credit by nonbanks accounts for about 25% of the Private Credit variable, but there is considerable cross-country variation.

Finally, unlike past studies, we carefully deflate the financial intermediary statistics. Specifically, financial stock items are measured at the end of the period, while GDP is measured over the period. Simply dividing financial stock items by GDP, therefore, can produce misleading measures of financial development, especially in highly inflationary environments. Some authors try to correct for this problem by using an average of financial intermediary balance sheet items in year t and $t - 1$, and then dividing that average by GDP measured in year t (King and Levine, 1993a). This however, does not fully resolve the distortion. This paper deflates end-of-year financial balance sheet items by end-of-year consumer price indices (CPI), and deflates the GDP series by the annual CPI. Then, we compute the average of the real financial balance sheet item in year t and $t - 1$, and divide this average by real GDP measured in year t.

While our measure Private Credit improves significantly on other measures of financial development, it would be valuable to construct a measure of financial intermediary development that identified credits issued by privately owned financial intermediaries. We could only obtain data, however, on 32 countries in scattered years over the 1980–1995 period, yielding a data set that is insufficient for the econometric procedures employed in this paper. Also, it would be valuable to incorporate measures of securities market development, as in Levine and Zervos (1998). Unfortunately, data on stock market activity are not available for a sufficient number of years or countries to perform this paper's econometric methods.

To assess the robustness of our results, we use two additional measures of financial development. One traditional measure of financial development used is Liquid Liabilities, equal to the liquid liabilities of the financial system, calculated as currency plus demand and interest-bearing liabilities of financial intermediaries and nonbank financial intermediaries, divided by GDP.[6] The correlation between Private Credit and Liquid Liabilities is 0.77, and is significant at the 1% level. Unlike Private Credit, Liquid Liabilities is an indicator of size. A second measure available is named Commercial-Central Bank, which equals the ratio of commercial bank domestic assets divided by commercial bank plus central bank domestic assets. Commercial-Central Bank measures the degree to which commercial banks or the central bank allocate society's savings. The correlation with Private Credit is 0.64, and is significant at the 1% level. The intuition underlying this measure is that commercial financial intermediaries are more likely to identify profitable investments, monitor managers, facilitate risk management, and mobilize savings than central banks.

We also used the variable Bank Credit, which equal credits by deposit money banks to the private sector as a share of GDP. This variable is a less

---

[6] Among others this measure has been used by King and Levine (1993a).

T. Beck et al. / Journal of Financial Economics 58 (2000) 261–300 269

comprehensive measure of financial intermediary development than Private Credit, because Bank Credit does not include nonbank credits to the private sector. Its correlation with Private Credit, however, is 0.92 and it produces very similar regression results, which are available on request.

2.2. Economic growth and its sources

To assess the impact of financial intermediary development on the sources of growth, this paper uses new and better data on capital accumulation, productivity growth, and private savings rates. This subsection describes our data on economic growth, capital per capita growth, and productivity growth. Appendix B presents a detailed list of the data sources used, and describes the construction of the data set employed in this study. The next subsection describes the saving data.

The variable Growth equals the rate of real per capita GDP growth, where the underlying data are from the national accounts. For the pure cross-sectional data, for which there is one observation per country for the period 1960–1995, we compute Growth for each country by running a least-squares regression of the logarithm of real per capita GDP on a constant and a time trend. We use the estimated coefficient on the time trend as the growth rate. This procedure is more robust to differences in the serial correlation properties of the data than simply using the geometric rate of growth (Watson, 1992). Using geometric growth rates, however, yields virtually identical results. We do not use least squares growth rates for the panel data because the data only represent five-year periods. Instead, we calculate real per capita GDP growth as the geometric rate of growth for each of the seven five-year periods in the panel data.

The variable Capgrowth equals the growth rate of the per capita physical capital stock. To compute physical capital growth figures for a broad cross-section of 63 countries over the 1960–1995 period, we follow King and Levine (1994). Specifically, we first use Harberger (1978) suggestion for deriving an initial estimate of the capital stock in 1950, which assumes that each country was at its steady-state capital–output ratio in 1950. While this assumption is surely wrong, it is better than assuming an initial capital stock of zero, which many researchers use.[7] Then, we use the aggregate real investment series from the Penn-World Tables (5.6, henceforth PWT) and the perpetual inventory method with a depreciation rate of seven percent to compute capital stocks in later years. To check our results, we also used disaggregated investment data from the PWT. Specifically, we consider four components of the investment series

---

[7] Alternative measures of capital growth based on assuming an initial capital stock of zero, tend to produce similar cross-country characterizations of capital growth, as discussed in King and Levine (1994).

independently, excluding the fifth component, residential construction: machinery, transportation equipment, business construction, and other non-residential construction. The capital stock number for each component, i, is then computed using the following formula:

$$K_{i,t+1} = K_{i,t} + I_{i,t} - \delta_i K_{i,t}, \tag{1}$$

where individual depreciation rates are used for the different categories. We again use Harberger's (1978) method for getting an initial capital stock estimate. We were only able to compute this alternative capital stock measure for 42 countries. Nonetheless, using this alternative measure does not alter any of the conclusions that follow.

By using alternative measures of capital growth in this study, a robustness check on our study emerges. The aggregate and disaggregated capital numbers have a correlation coefficient of 0.85. However, the disaggregated measure, which (i) focuses on nonresidential investment and (ii) uses more appropriate depreciation rates for each component of investment, produces quite different information on individual countries, which may influence the choice of capital stock measures in individual country-studies.

Our measure of productivity growth, Prod, builds on the neoclassical production function with physical capital K, labor L, the level of total factor productivity A, and the capital share α. We assume that this aggregate production function is common across countries and time, such that aggregate output in country i, Y_i, is given as follows:

$$Y_i = A_i K_i^{\alpha} L_i^{1-\alpha}. \tag{2}$$

To solve for the growth rate of productivity, we first divide by L to get per capita production. We then take log transformation and calculate the time derivative. Finally, assuming a capital share $\alpha = 0.3$ and solving for the growth rate of productivity per capita, we have

$$\text{Prod} = \text{Growth} - 0.3*\text{Capgrowth}. \tag{3}$$

2.3. Private savings rates

The data on private savings rates draw on a new saving database recently constructed at the World Bank, and described in detail in Loayza et al. (1998). This database improves significantly on previous data sets on saving in terms of country- and year-coverage and, particularly, accuracy and consistency. For example, Levine and Zervos (1998) have only 29 observations in their regressions analyzing the impact of financial development on saving. Here, we have 61 countries in the cross-section regressions. Furthermore, these new data on savings rates represent the largest and most systematic collection to date of annual time series on country saving and saving-related variables, spanning a maximum of 35 years, from 1960 to 1994, and 112 developing and 22 industrialized countries. These data draw on national-accounts information, and are checked for consistency using international and individual-country sources. Arguably, however, the main merits of the new World Saving Database are, first, the consistent definition of private and, thus, public sectors both across countries and over time and, second, the adjustment of private and public saving to account for the value erosion of private assets due to inflation. Therefore, the World Saving Database presents four measures of private saving, and their corresponding measures of public saving, according to whether the public sector is defined as either central government or consolidated state sector and whether saving figures are adjusted or not adjusted for inflation-related capital gains and losses. For the World Saving Database, the consolidated state sector includes, in addition to the central government, local governments and public enterprises.

The private savings rate is calculated as the ratio of gross private saving to gross private disposable income. Gross private saving is measured as the difference between gross national saving, calculated as gross national disposable income minus consumption expenditures, both measured at current prices, and gross public saving. In this paper, the public sector is defined as the consolidated central government. Using a broader measure of the public sector, instead of the consolidated central government, would be analytically preferable. This requirement, however, limits the sample size. Nonetheless, employing a broader definition of the public sector yields very similar results to those presented below. Gross private disposable income is measured as the difference between gross national disposable income and gross public disposable income, which is the sum of public saving and consumption.

Due to data availability, the sample for the private savings rate regression is slightly different from the sample used in the analysis of real per capita GDP growth, capital per capita growth, and productivity per capita growth. Specifically, we have data available from 1971–1995, so that we have five non-overlapping 5-year periods for the panel data set, and 25 years for the cross-country estimations.

2.4. Descriptive statistics and correlations

Table 1 presents descriptive statistics and correlations between financial development and the various dependent variables. There is a considerable variation in Private Credit across countries, ranging from a low of 4% in Zaire to a high of 141% in Switzerland. GDP per capita growth and capital per capita growth also show significant variation. Korea has the highest growth rates, both for real per capita GDP and for capital per capita, with 7% and 11%, respectively. Zaire has the lowest GDP per capita growth rate with − 3%, whereas Zimbabwe has the lowest capital per capita growth rate with − 2%. Private savings rates also show considerable cross-country variation. Sierra Leone has

Table 1
Summary statistics

Private Credit is credit by deposit money banks and other financial institutions to the private sector divided by GDP. Liquid Liabilities is liquid liabilities of the financial system, calculated as currency plus demand and interest-bearing liabilities of banks and nonbank financial intermediaries, divided by GDP. Commercial-Central Bank is assets of deposit money banks divided by deposit money bank plus central bank assets. These three variables are constructed using data from the International Financial Statistics. Economic Growth is the growth rate of real per capita GDP. GDP data are from Loayza et al. (1998). Capital Growth is the growth rate of physical capital per capita and is constructed using data from PWT 5.6. Productivity Growth is Economic Growth − 0.3* Capital Growth. Private Saving is the ratio of gross private saving and gross private disposable income. Data on Private Saving are from Loayza et al. (1998). The data are averaged over the period 1960–1995, with the exception of Private Saving, for which data are averaged over the period 1971–1995. The statistics for private saving and its correlation with the three measures of financial intermediary development are from a different sample. P-values are reported under the respective correlation coefficient.

Panel A: Descriptive Statistics

	Private Credit	Liquid Liabilities	Commercial-Central Bank	Economic Growth	Capital Growth	Productivity Growth	Private Saving
Mean	40.86	45.21	79.26	1.95	3.13	1.01	19.21
Median	27.81	41.02	83.89	1.98	3.11	1.15	19.98
Maximum	141.30	143.43	98.89	7.16	10.51	5.14	33.92
Minimum	4.08	14.43	23.72	−2.81	−1.84	−3.39	1.05
Std. Dev.	29.16	26.26	17.37	1.92	2.22	1.52	7.65
Observations	63	63	63	63	63	63	61

Panel B: Correlations

	Private Credit	Liquid Liabilities	Commercial-Central Bank	Economic Growth	Capital Growth	Productivity Growth	Private Saving
Private Credit	1.00						
Liquid Liabilities	0.77 0.01	1.00					
Commercial-Central Bank	0.64 0.01	0.59 0.01	1.00				
Economic Growth	0.43 0.01	0.56 0.01	0.46 0.01	1.00			
Capital Growth	0.34 0.01	0.36 0.01	0.25 0.05	0.71 0.01	1.00		
Productivity Growth	0.39 0.01	0.55 0.01	0.47 0.01	0.95 0.01	0.46 0.01	1.00	
Private Saving	0.75 0.01	0.65 0.01	0.73 0.01				1.00

a private savings rate of 1%, whereas Japan's rate is 34%. Notably, Private Credit is significantly correlated with all of our dependent variables.

3. Methodology

This section describes the two econometric methods that we use to control for the endogenous determination of financial intermediary development with growth and the sources of growth. We first use a traditional cross-sectional, instrumental variable estimator. As instruments, we use the legal origin of each country to extract the exogenous component of financial intermediary development in the pure cross-sectional regressions. We also use a cross-country, time-series panel of data and employ dynamic panel techniques to estimate the relation between financial development and growth, capital accumulation, productivity growth, and savings rates. We describe each procedure below.

3.1. Cross-country regressions with instrumental variables

To control for potential simultaneity bias, we first use instrumental variables developed by LLSV (1998). According to Reynolds and Flores (1996), legal systems with European origins can be classified into four major legal families: the English common law countries, and the French, German, and Scandinavian civil law countries. This classification scheme excludes countries with communist or Islamic legal systems. All four legal families descend from the Roman law as compiled by Byzantine Emperor Justinian in the sixth century, and from interpretations and applications of this law in subsequent centuries by Glossators, Commentators, and in Canon Law. The four legal families developed distinct characteristics during the last four centuries. In the 17th and 18th centuries, the Scandinavian countries formed their own legal codes. The Scandinavian legal systems have remained relatively unaffected from the far-reaching influences of the German, and especially, the French Civil Codes.

The French Civil Code was written in 1804, following the directions of Napoleon. Through occupation, it was adopted in other European countries, such as Italy and Poland. Through its influence on the Spanish and Portuguese legal systems, the legal French tradition spread to Latin America. Finally, through colonization, the Napoleonic code was adopted in many African countries, Indochina, French Guyana, and the Caribbean.

The German Civil Code (Bürgerliches Gesetzbuch) was completed almost a century later in 1896. The German Code exerted a great deal of influence on Austria and Switzerland, as well as on China and hence Taiwan, Czechoslovakia, Greece, Hungary, Italy, and Yugoslavia. Also, the German Civil Code heavily influenced the Japanese Civil Code, which helped spread the German legal tradition to Korea.

Unlike these civil law countries, the English legal system is based on common law, where the laws were primarily formed by judges trying to resolve particular cases. Through colonialism, it was spread to many African and Asian countries, Australia, New Zealand, and North America.

There are two conditions under which the legal origin variables serve as appropriate instruments for financial development. First, they have to be exogenous to economic growth during our sample period. Second, they have to be correlated with financial intermediary development. In terms of exogeneity, the English, French, and German legal systems were spread mainly through occupation and colonialism. Thus, we take the legal origin of a country as an exogenous endowment. Furthermore, we provide specification tests regarding the validity of the instruments. In terms of the links between legal origin and financial intermediary development, a growing body of evidence suggests that legal origin helps shape financial development. LLSV (1998) show that the legal origin of a country materially influences its legal treatment of shareholders, the laws governing creditor rights, the efficiency of contract enforcement, and accounting standards. Shareholders and creditors enjoy greater protection in common law countries than in civil law countries. French Civil Law countries are comparatively weak both in terms of shareholder and creditor rights. In terms of accounting standards, French legal origin countries tend to have company financial statements that are comparatively less comprehensive than the company financial statements in countries with other legal origins. Statistically, these legal, regulatory and informational characteristics affect the operation of financial intermediaries, as shown in LLSV (1997), Levine (1998, 1999), and Levine et al. (2000).

In the pure cross-sectional analysis we use data averaged for 63 countries over 1960–1995, such that there is one observation per country. The cross-country sample for private saving has 61 countries over the period 1971–1995. The basic regression takes the form

$$Y_i = \alpha + \beta \, \text{Finance}_i + \gamma' X_i + \varepsilon_i, \tag{4}$$

where Y is either Growth, Capgrowth, Prod, or Saving. Finance equals Private Credit, or in the robustness checks it equals either Liquid Liabilities or Commercial-Central Bank. In Eq. (4), X represents a vector of conditioning information that controls for other factors associated with economic growth, and ε is the error term. Due to the potential nonlinear relation between economic growth and the assortment of economic indicators, we use natural logarithms of the regressors in the regressions of Growth, Capgrowth, and Prod.

To examine whether cross-country variations in the exogenous component of financial intermediary development explain cross-country variations in the rate of economic growth, the legal origin indicators are used as instrumental variables for Finance. Specifically, assuming that the variables in vector Z are proper instruments in Eq. (4) amounts to the set of orthogonality conditions

276   *T. Beck et al. / Journal of Financial Economics 58 (2000) 261–300*

$E[Z'\varepsilon] = 0$. We can use standard GMM techniques to estimate our model, which produces instrumental variable estimators of the coefficients in Eq. (4). After computing these GMM estimates, the Hansen test of the overidentifying restrictions assesses whether the instrumental variables are associated with growth beyond their ability to explain cross-country variation in financial sector development. Under the null hypothesis that the instruments are not correlated with the error terms, the test has a χ^2 distribution with $(J\text{-}K)$ degrees of freedom, where J is the number of instruments and K the number of regressors. The estimates are robust to heteroskedasticity.

3.2. Dynamic panel techniques

The cross-country estimations help us determine whether the cross-country variance in economic growth and the sources of growth can be explained by variance in the exogenous component of financial intermediary development. There are, however, some shortcomings with the pure cross-sectional instrumental variable estimator. The use of appropriate panel techniques can alleviate many of these problems.

First, besides the cross-country variance, we also would like to know whether changes in financial development over time within a country have an effect on economic growth through its various channels. By using a panel data set, we gain degrees of freedom by adding the variability of the time-series dimension. Specifically, the within-country standard deviation of Private Credit in our panel data set is 15.1%, which in the panel estimation is added to the between-country standard deviation of 28.4%. Similarly, for real per capita GDP growth, the within-country standard deviation is 2.4%, and the between-country standard deviation is 1.7%.[8] Thus, we are able to exploit substantial additional variability by adding the time-series dimension of the data.

We construct a panel that consists of data for 77 countries over the period 1960–1995. We average the data over seven non-overlapping 5-year periods. The panel sample for private saving includes 72 countries and five 5-year periods between 1971 and 1995. The regression equation can be specified in the following form:

$$y_{i,t} = \alpha' X^1_{i,t-1} + \beta' X^2_{i,t} + \mu_i + \lambda_t + \varepsilon_{i,t}, \tag{5}$$

where y represents our dependent variable, X^1 represents a set of lagged explanatory variables, and X^2 a set of contemporaneous explanatory variables.

---

[8] The within-country standard deviation is calculated using the deviations from country averages, whereas the between-country standard deviation is calculated from the country averages. The fact that the between-country standard deviations in the panel are not the same as in the cross-section sample results from the different country coverage.

In Eq. (5), μ is an unobserved country-specific effect, λ is a time-specific effect, ε is the time-varying error term, and i and t represent country and 5-year time period, respectively.

We can now observe a second advantage of using particular panel techniques to estimate Eq. (5). In a pure cross-sectional regression, the unobserved country-specific effect is part of the error term. Therefore, a possible correlation between μ and the explanatory variables results in biased coefficient estimates. Furthermore, if the lagged dependent variable is included in X^1, then the country-specific effect is certainly correlated with X^1. Under assumptions explained below, we use a dynamic panel estimator that controls for the presence of unobserved country-specific effects. This approach produces consistent and efficient estimates even when the country-specific effect is correlated with X^1.

Third, the pure cross-sectional estimator that we use does not control for the endogeneity of all the explanatory variables. Instead, it only controls for the endogeneity of financial intermediary development. This approach can lead to inappropriate inferences. To draw more accurate conclusions, the dynamic panel estimator uses internal instruments, defined as instruments based on previous realizations of the explanatory variables, to consider the potential joint endogeneity of the other regressors as well. This method, however, does not control for full endogeneity but for a weak type of it. To be precise, we assume that the explanatory variables are only weakly exogenous, which means that they can be affected by current and past realizations of the growth rate but must be uncorrelated with future realizations of the error term. Thus, the weak exogeneity assumption implies that future innovations of the growth rate do not affect current financial development. This assumption is not particularly stringent conceptually, and we can examine its validity statistically. First, weak exogeneity does not mean that economic agents do not take into account expected future growth in their decision to develop the financial system. This assumption means that future, unanticipated shocks to growth do not influence current financial development. It is the innovation in growth that must not affect financial development. Second, given that we are using 5-year periods, the forecasting horizon for the growth innovation, that is, its unanticipated component, extends about five years into the future. Finally, we statistically assess the validity of the weak exogeneity assumption below.

Before describing the panel estimator more rigorously, note that the panel has a small number of time-series observations (seven), but the number of cross-sectional units is large (77 countries). Qualitatively, these are the characteristics of the data for which the specific panel estimator that we use were designed. Indeed, the panels used in microeconomic studies are usually much larger in the cross-sectional dimension, and a little shorter in the time-series one. The small number of time-series observations should be of no concern given that all the asymptotic properties of our GMM estimator rely on the size of the cross-sectional dimension of the panel.

Chamberlain (1984), Holtz-Eakin et al. (1990), Arellano and Bond (1991), and Arellano and Bover (1995) propose the General Method of Moments (GMM) estimator.[9] Arellano and Bond (1991) suggest to first-difference the regression equation to eliminate the country-specific effect, as follows:

$$y_{i,t} - y_{i,t-1} = \alpha'(X^1_{i,t-1} - X^1_{i,t-2}) + \beta'(X^2_{i,t} - X^2_{i,t-1}) + (\varepsilon_{i,t} - \varepsilon_{i,t-1}). \quad (6)$$

This procedure solves the first econometric problem, as described above, but introduces a correlation between the new error term, $\varepsilon_{i,t} - \varepsilon_{i,t-1}$, and the lagged dependent variable, $y_{i,t-1} - y_{i,t-2}$, when it is included in $X^1_{i,t-1} - X^1_{i,t-2}$. To address this correlation and the endogeneity problem, Arellano and Bond (1991) propose using the lagged values of the explanatory variables in levels as instruments. Under the assumptions that there is no serial correlation in the error term, ε, and that the explanatory variables X, where $X = [X^1 X^2]$, are weakly exogenous, we can use the following moment conditions:

$$E[X_{i,t-s} \cdot (\varepsilon_{i,t} - \varepsilon_{i,t-1})] = 0 \quad \text{for } s \geqslant 2; t = 3, \dots, T. \quad (7)$$

Using these moment conditions, Arellano and Bond (1991) propose a two-step GMM estimator. In the first step, the error terms are assumed to be both independent and homoskedastic, across countries and over time. In the second step, the residuals obtained in the first step are used to construct a consistent estimate of the variance-covariance matrix, thus relaxing the assumptions of independence and homoskedasticity. We will refer to this estimator as the difference estimator.

There are several conceptual and econometric shortcomings with the difference estimator. First, by first-differencing we lose the pure cross-country dimension of the data. Second, differencing may decrease the signal-to-noise ratio, thereby exacerbating measurement error biases (see Griliches and Hausman, 1986). Finally, Alonso-Borrego and Arellano (1999) and Blundell and Bond (1997) show that if the lagged dependent and the explanatory variables are persistent over time, lagged levels of these variables are weak instruments for the regressions in differences. Simulation studies show that the difference estimator has a large finite-sample bias and poor precision.

To address these conceptual and econometric problems, we use an alternative method that estimates the regression in differences jointly with the regression in levels, as proposed by Arellano and Bover (1995). Using Monte Carlo experiments, Blundell and Bond (1997) show that this system estimator reduces the potential biases in finite samples and asymptotic imprecision associated with the difference estimator. The key reason for this improvement is the inclusion of the regression in levels, which does not eliminate cross-country variation or

---

[9] The GMM estimator has been applied to cross-country studies, by, among others, Caselli et al. (1996), Easterly et al. (1997), and Fajnzylber et al. (1999).

intensify the strength of measurement error. Furthermore, the variables in levels maintain a stronger correlation with their instruments, as explained below, than the variables in differences, particularly as variables in levels are more serially correlated than in differences (see Blundell and Bond, 1997). However, being able to use the regression in levels comes at the cost of requiring an additional assumption. This requirement occurs because the regression in levels does not directly eliminate the country-specific effect. Instead, appropriate instruments must be used to control for country-specific effects. The estimator uses lagged differences of the explanatory variables as instruments. They are valid instruments under the assumption that the correlation between μ and the levels of the explanatory variables is constant over time, such that

$$E[X_{i,t+p} \cdot \mu_i] = E[X_{i,t+q} \cdot \mu_i] \quad \text{for all } p \text{ and } q. \tag{8}$$

Under this assumption, there is no correlation between the differences of the explanatory variables and the country-specific effect. For example, this assumption implies that financial intermediary development may be correlated with the country-specific effect, but this correlation does not change through time. Thus, under this assumption, lagged differences are valid instruments for the regression in levels, and the moment conditions for the regressions in levels are as follows:

$$E[(X_{i,t-s} - X_{i,t-s-1}) \cdot (\varepsilon_{i,t} + \mu_i)] = 0 \quad \text{for } s = 1; t = 3, \ldots, T. \tag{9}$$

The system thus consists of the stacked regressions in differences and levels, with the moment conditions in Eq. (7) applied to the first part of the system, the regressions in differences, and the moment conditions in Eq. (9) applied to the second part, the regressions in levels. Given that lagged levels are used as instruments in the difference regressions, only the most recent difference is used as instrument in the level regressions. Using additional differences would result in redundant moment conditions (see Arellano and Bover, 1995). As with the difference estimator, the model is estimated in a two-step GMM procedure generating consistent and efficient coefficient estimates.[10]

The consistency of the GMM estimator depends both on the validity of the assumption that the error term, ε, does not exhibit serial correlation and on the validity of the instruments. We use two tests proposed by Arellano and Bond (1991) to test these assumptions. The first is a Sargan test of over-identifying restrictions, which tests the overall validity of the instruments by analyzing the sample analog of the moment conditions used in the estimation procedure. Under the null hypothesis of the validity of the instruments, this test has a χ^2 distribution with $(J\text{-}K)$ degrees of freedom, where J is the number of

---

[10] We are grateful to Stephen Bond for providing us wih a program to apply his and Arellano's estimator to an unbalanced panel data set.

280 *T. Beck et al. / Journal of Financial Economics 58 (2000) 261–300*

instruments and K the number of regressors. The second test examines the assumption of no serial correlation in the error terms. We test whether the differenced error term is second-order serially correlated. By construction, the error term is probably first-order serially correlated. We cannot use the error terms from the regression in levels since they include the country-specific effect μ. Under the null hypothesis of no second-order serial correlation, this test has a standard-normal distribution. Failure to reject the null hypotheses of both tests lends support to our model.

4. Finance and the channels to economic growth

This section presents the results of the cross-country and panel regressions of real per capita GDP growth, productivity per capita growth, and capital per capita growth on financial development and a conditioning information set.

4.1. The conditioning information sets

To assess the strength of an independent link between financial development and the growth variables, we use various conditioning information sets. The simple conditioning information set includes the logarithm of initial real per capita GDP to control for convergence, and the average years of schooling as an indicator of the human capital stock in the economy. The policy conditioning information set includes the simple conditioning information set plus four additional policy variables that have been identified by the empirical growth literature as being correlated with growth performance across countries (Barro, 1991; Easterly et al., 1997). We use the inflation rate and the ratio of government expenditure to GDP as indicators of macroeconomic stability. We use the sum of exports and imports as a share of GDP and the black market premium to capture the degree of openness of an economy. In our sensitivity analysis for the cross-country regressions, we will also include the number of revolutions and coups, the number of assassinations per thousand inhabitants, and a measure of ethnic diversity. We cannot use the full conditioning information set in the panel estimations since there is not enough time series variation in the additional three variables.

4.2. Finance and economic growth

As noted in the Introduction, this paper's contribution is to investigate the relation between financial intermediary development and the sources of growth. We include this section on overall growth to motivate this inquiry. Levine et al. (2000) use identical econometric techniques to argue that financial intermediaries

T. Beck et al. / Journal of Financial Economics 58 (2000) 261–300   281

Table 2
Financial intermediation and economic growth

The regression equation estimated in columns 1 and 3 is Growth $= \beta_0 + \beta_1$ Initial income per capita $+ \beta_2$ Average years of schooling $+ \beta_3$ Private Credit. The dependent variable is the growth rate of real per capita GDP. Initial income per capita is the log of real per capita GDP in the first year of the respective time period. Average years of schooling is log of one plus the average years of schooling in the total population over 25. Private Credit is the log of credit by deposit money banks and other financial institutions to the private sector divided by GDP. The regression equation estimated in columns 2 and 4 is Growth $= \beta_0 + \beta_1$ Initial income per capita $+ \beta_2$ Average years of schooling $+ \beta_3$ Openness to trade $+ \beta_4$ Inflation $+ \beta_5$ Government size $+ \beta_6$ Black market premium $+ \beta_7$ Private Credit. Openness to trade is the log of the sum of real exports and imports of goods and nonfinancial services as share of real GDP. Inflation is the log of one plus the inflation rate, calculated using the average annual CPI data from the International Financial Statistics. Government size is the log of real general government consumption as share of real GDP. Black market premium is the log of one plus the black market premium. The regressions in columns 1 and 2 are cross-country regressions, with data averaged over 1960–1995, and using the legal origin of countries as instruments for Private Credit. The regressions in columns 3 and 4 are panel regressions, with data averaged over seven 5-year periods from 1960–1995, and using lagged values as instruments, as described in the text. The regressions in columns 3 and 4 also contain time dummies that are not reported. P-values calculated from White's heteroskedasticity-consistent standard errors are reported under the respective coefficient. The null hypothesis of the Hansen test is that the instruments used are not correlated with the residuals. The critical values of the Hansen test (2 d.f.) are: 10% = 4.61; 5% = 5.99. The null hypothesis of the Sargan test is that the instruments used are not correlated with the residuals. The null hypothesis of the serial correlation test is that the errors in the first-difference regression exhibit no second-order serial correlation.

	Cross-country data		Panel data	
	(1)	(2)	(3)	(4)
Constant	6.571	2.643	1.272	0.082
	0.006	0.527	0.250	0.875
Initial income per capita	− 1.971	− 1.967	− 1.299	− 0.496
	0.001	0.001	0.001	0.001
Average years of schooling	1.936	1.548	2.671	0.950
	0.008	0.078	0.001	0.001
Openness to trade		0.931		1.311
		0.042		0.001
Inflation		4.270		0.181
		0.096		0.475
Government size		− 1.207		− 1.445
		0.132		0.001
Black market premium		− 0.139		− 1.192
		0.914		0.001
Private Credit	2.215	3.215	2.397	1.443
	0.003	0.012	0.001	0.001
Hansen test	0.577	0.571		
Sargan test (p-value)			0.183	0.506
Serial correlation test (p-value)			0.516	0.803
Countries	63	63	77	77
Observations			365	365

exert a causal impact on long-run growth, but they do not investigate the links between financial development and productivity growth, capital accumulation, and private savings rates.

The results in Table 2 show a statistically and economically significant relation between the exogenous component of financial intermediary development and economic growth. The first two columns report the results of the pure cross-country regressions using the simple and the policy conditioning information set. Private Credit is significantly correlated with long-run growth at the 5% significance level in both regressions. The Hansen test of overidentifying restrictions indicates that the orthogonality conditions cannot be rejected at the 5% level. Thus, we do not reject the null hypothesis that the instruments are appropriate. The strong link between finance and growth does not appear to be driven by simultaneity bias. The variables in the conditioning information set also have the expected sign, except for inflation. Consistent with Boyd et al. (2000), we find that inflation affects growth by influencing financial sector performance. Specifically, when we omit Private Credit from the regressions in Table 2, inflation enters with a negative, statistically significant, and economically large coefficient. However, when we control for the level of financial intermediary development, inflation has an insignificant effect.

The results are economically significant. For example, Mexico's value for Private Credit over the period 1960–1995 was 22.9% of GDP. An exogenous increase in Private Credit that had brought it up to the sample median of 27.5% would have resulted in a 0.4 percentage point higher real per capita GDP growth per year. This result follows from $\ln(27.5) - \ln(22.9) = 0.18$ and $0.18*2.2 = 0.4$, where 2.2 is the smaller of the two parameter values on Private Credit in the cross-country regressions. This conceptual experiment, however, must be viewed cautiously, as it does not indicate how to increase financial intermediary development. Nonetheless, the example suggests that exogenous changes in financial intermediary development have economically meaningful repercussions.

The dynamic panel estimates also indicate that financial intermediary development has an economically large impact on economic growth. Further, the strong, positive link between financial development and growth is not due to simultaneity bias, omitted variables, or the use of lagged dependent variables as regressors. Columns 3 and 4 in Table 2 report the results of the panel regressions. Private Credit is significant at the 5% level with both conditioning information sets. The variables in the conditioning information set have significant coefficients, with the expected sign. Furthermore, our tests indicate that both our econometric specification and our assumption that the error terms display no serial correlation cannot be rejected. Thus, the pure cross-section, instrumental variable results and the dynamic panel procedure findings are both consistent with the view that financial intermediaries exert a large impact on economic growth.

4.3. Finance and productivity growth

The results in Table 3 show that financial intermediary development has a large, significant impact on productivity growth. The Hansen test for overidentifying restrictions shows that the data do not reject the orthogonality conditions at the 5% level. The variables in the conditioning information set have the expected sign, with the exception of the inflation rate, which reflects the close connection between inflation and financial intermediary development discussed above. To assess the economic magnitude of the coefficients, we continue to use Mexico as an example. Using the coefficient of 1.5 on Private Credit in Table 3, an exogenous increase in Mexico's Private Credit ratio over the 1960–1995 period, 22.9%, to the sample median, 27.5%, would have translated into almost 0.3 percentage points faster productivity growth per year over the 35 year period.

The results for the panel regressions confirm the pure cross-country estimates. The strong link between Private Credit and productivity growth is not due to simultaneity bias or omitted variable bias. The p-values for the Sargan test and the serial correlation test indicate the appropriateness of our instruments and the lack of serial correlation in the error term, ε.

4.4. Finance and capital growth

The empirical relation between financial intermediary development and physical capital accumulation is less robust than the link between financial intermediary development and productivity growth. The results shown in Table 4 indicate that Private Credit enters significantly at the 5% level in both the pure cross-country and the dynamic panel regressions. In the case of the cross-section estimator, we reject the Hansen test of overidentifying restrictions when using the simple conditioning information set. However, when we expand the conditioning information set, the cross-sectional estimator passes the specification test. Thus, Private Credit exhibits a strong, positive link with capital growth that does not appear to be driven by simultaneity bias. Nevertheless, other measures of financial intermediary development do not produce the same results. In the pure cross-section results, none of the other measures of financial sector development enjoys a significant link with capital growth as we discuss below in the subsection on sensitivity results. For completeness, we can get the other measures of financial sector development to enter with positive and significant coefficients in the capital growth equations by using alternative conditioning information sets. However, the other measures are not significant when using the simple or policy conditioning information sets.

The panel results are more robust. Financial intermediary development is positively and significantly correlated with capital accumulation when using alternative conditioning information sets and alternative measures of financial

284   T. Beck et al. / Journal of Financial Economics 58 (2000) 261–300

Table 3
Financial intermediation and productivity growth

The regression equation estimated in columns 1 and 3 is Productivity Growth $= \beta_0 + \beta_1$ Initial income per capita $+ \beta_2$ Average years of schooling $+ \beta_3$ Private Credit. The dependent variable is Productivity Growth, which is growth of real per capita GDP minus 0.3* growth of capital per capita. Initial income per capita is the log of real per capita GDP in the first year of the respective time period. Average years of schooling is log of one plus the average years of schooling in the total population over 25. Private Credit is the log of credit by deposit money banks and other financial institutions to the private sector divided by GDP. The regression equation estimated in columns 2 and 4 is Productivity Growth $= \beta_0 + \beta_1$ Initial income per capita $+ \beta_2$ Average years of schooling $+ \beta_3$ Openness to trade $+ \beta_4$ Inflation $+ \beta_5$ Government size $+ \beta_6$ Black market premium $+ \beta_7$ Private Credit. Openness to trade is the log of the sum of real exports and imports of goods and nonfinancial services as share of real GDP. Inflation is the log of one plus the inflation rate, calculated using the average annual CPI data from the International Financial Statistics. Government size is the log of real general government consumption as share of real GDP. Black market premium is the log of one plus the black market premium. The regressions in columns 1 and 2 are cross-country regressions, with data averaged over 1960–1995, and using the legal origin of countries as instruments for Private Credit. The regressions in columns 3 and 4 are panel regressions, with data averaged over seven 5-year periods from 1960–1995, and using lagged values as instruments, as described in the text. The regressions in columns 3 and 4 also contain time dummies that are not reported. P-values calculated from White's heteroskedasticity-consistent standard errors are reported under the respective coefficient. The null hypothesis of the Hansen test is that the instruments used are not correlated with the residuals. The critical values for the Hansen test (2 d.f.) are: 10% = 4.61; 5% = 5.99. The null hypothesis of the Sargan test is that the instruments used are not correlated with the residuals. The null hypothesis of the serial correlation test is that the errors in the first-difference regression exhibit no second-order serial correlation.

	Cross-country data		Panel data	
	(1)	(2)	(3)	(4)
Constant	3.527	− 1.189	2.473	− 1.611
	0.065	0.717	0.001	0.033
Initial income per capita	− 1.266	− 1.171	− 1.244	− 0.353
	0.001	0.001	0.001	0.001
Average years of schooling	1.375	1.241	3.043	1.174
	0.028	0.060	0.001	0.001
Openness to trade		0.956		1.337
		0.015		0.001
Inflation		3.223		− 0.415
		0.096		0.033
Government size		− 0.647		− 0.431
		0.286		0.088
Black market premium		− 0.191		− 1.003
		0.861		0.001
Private Credit	1.500	1.986	1.332	0.296
	0.004	0.021	0.001	0.001
Hansen test	2.036	3.472		
Sargan test (p-value)			0.205	0.401
Serial correlation test (p-value)			0.772	0.865
Countries	63	63	77	77
Observations			365	365

T. Beck et al. / Journal of Financial Economics 58 (2000) 261–300

285

Table 4
Financial intermediation and capital growth

The regression equation estimated in columns 1 and 3 is Capital Growth $= \beta_0 + \beta_1$ Initial income per capita $+ \beta_2$ Average years of schooling $+ \beta_3$ Private Credit. The dependent variable is the growth rate of physical per capita capital. Initial income per capita is the log of real per capita GDP in the first year of the respective time period. Average years of schooling is log of one plus the average years of schooling in the total population over 25. Private Credit is the log of credit by deposit money banks and other financial institutions to the private sector divided by GDP. The regression equation estimated in columns 2 and 4 is Capital Growth $= \beta_0 + \beta_1$ Initial income per capita $+ \beta_2$ Average years of schooling $+ \beta_3$ Openness to trade $+ \beta_4$ Inflation $+ \beta_5$ Government size $+ \beta_6$ Black market premium $+ \beta_7$ Private Credit. Openness to trade is the log of the sum of real exports and imports of goods and nonfinancial services as share of real GDP. Inflation is the log of one plus the inflation rate, calculated using the average annual CPI data from the International Financial Statistics. Government size is the log of real general government consumption as share of real GDP. Black market premium is the log of one plus the black market premium. The regressions in columns 1 and 2 are cross-country regressions, with data averaged over 1960–1995, and using the legal origin of countries as instruments for Private Credit. The regressions in columns 3 and 4 are panel regressions, with data averaged over seven 5-year periods from 1960–1995, and using lagged values as instruments, as described in the text. The regressions in columns 3 and 4 also contain time dummies that are not reported. P-values calculated from White's heteroskedasticity-consistent standard errors are reported under the respective coefficient. The null hypothesis of the Hansen test is that the instruments used are not correlated with the residuals. The critical values for the Hansen test (2 d.f.) are: $10\% = 4.61$; $5\% = 5.99$. The null hypothesis of the Sargan test is that the instruments used are not correlated with the residuals. The null hypothesis of the serial correlation test is that the errors in the first-difference regression exhibit no second-order serial correlation.

	Cross-country data		Panel data	
	(1)	(2)	(3)	(4)
Constant	8.448	8.349	− 1.273	5.694
	0.004	0.093	0.219	0.001
Initial income per capita	− 2.075	− 2.225	− 0.933	− 0.070
	0.001	0.001	0.001	0.701
Average years of schooling	0.663	0.628	0.985	− 0.340
	0.427	0.559	0.055	0.552
Openness to trade		0.245		− 0.448
		0.663		0.097
Inflation		4.196		0.445
		0.236		0.360
Government size		− 1.619		− 3.229
		0.082		0.001
Black market premium		0.304		− 0.748
		0.826		0.001
Private Credit	2.832	4.038	3.435	3.005
	0.006	0.012	0.001	0.001
Hansen test	6.747	3.039		
Sargan test (p-value)			0.166	0.316
Serial correlation test (p-value)			0.014	0.053
Countries	63	63	77	77
Observations			365	365

intermediary development. The test statistic for serial correlation, however, rejects the null hypothesis of no serial correlation at the 5% level when using the simple conditioning information set, and at the 10% level when using the policy information set. By including the private savings rate or lagged values of capital growth in the conditioning information set, however, we achieve three results. We eliminate the serial correlation, we find a positive impact of financial intermediary development on physical capital growth, and we obtain very similar coefficient estimates to those reported in Table 4. These results are available on request. We do not include the results here because we wanted to keep a uniform set of control variables across the growth and sources of growth equations. Since the resulting coefficient estimates are of similar magnitude and significance, we merely want to make the point that the serial correlation reflected in Table 4 is not biasing the results in a meaningful way.

The difference between the panel and cross-country results may reflect data frequency. While the long-run relation between capital accumulation and financial intermediary development is not robust to alternations in different measures of financial intermediary development, the short-term relation, which may reflect business cycle activity, is positive and robust.

4.5. Sensitivity analyses

Tables 5 and 6 present the coefficients on all three measures of financial development in the cross-country and panel regressions, respectively, using real per capita GDP growth as the dependent variable. The coefficient estimates for Liquid Liabilities and Commercial-Central Bank are significantly positive across both samples and both conditioning information sets. All regressions pass the different specification tests. We also run the regressions with the full conditioning information set in the cross-country sample and achieve similar results. These results strengthen the hypothesis of a statistically and economically significant causal impact of the exogenous component of financial development on economic growth.

The sensitivity results in Tables 7 and 8 further suggest that financial intermediary development exerts a positive influence on productivity growth. Tables 7 and 8 present sensitivity analyses of the productivity growth regressions with the three financial intermediary development indicators. In sum, the sensitivity results generally confirm our results with Private Credit. We find confirmatory evidence that greater financial intermediary development is associated with faster productivity growth, and that this positive link is not due to simultaneity, omitted variable, or lagged dependent variable biases.

Tables 9 and 10 present the corresponding results for capital per capita growth. Unlike Private Credit, Liquid Liabilities and Commercial-Central Bank

Table 5
Alternative measures of financial intermediary development and growth, using cross-country data

The regression equation estimated in Panel A is Growth $= \beta_0 + \beta_1$ Initial income per capita $+ \beta_2$ Average years of schooling $+ \beta_3$ Finance. The dependent variable is the growth rate of real per capita GDP. Initial income per capita is the log of real per capita GDP in the first year of the respective time period. Average years of schooling is log of one plus the average years of schooling in the total population over 25. Finance is either Liquid Liabilities, the log of liquid liabilities of the financial system divided by GDP, Commercial-Central Bank, the log of assets of deposit money banks divided by deposit money bank plus central bank assets, or Private Credit, the log of credit by deposit money banks and other financial institutions to the private sector divided by GDP. The regression equation estimated in Panel B is Growth $= \beta_0 + \beta_1$ Initial income per capita $+ \beta_2$ Average years of schooling $+ \beta_3$ Openness to trade $+ \beta_4$ Inflation $+ \beta_5$ Government size $+ \beta_6$ Black market premium $+ \beta_7$ Finance. Openness to trade is the log of the sum of real exports and imports of goods and nonfinancial services as share of real GDP. Inflation is the log of one plus the inflation rate, calculated using the average annual CPI data from the International Financial Statistics. Government size is the log of real general government consumption as share of real GDP. Black market premium is the log of one plus the black market premium. The regressions are cross-country regressions, with data averaged over 1960–1995, and using the legal origin of countries as instruments for Finance. *P*-values calculated from White's heteroskedasticity-consistent standard errors are reported. The null hypothesis of the Hansen test is that the instruments used are not correlated with the residuals. The critical values for the Hansen test (2 d.f.) are: $10\% = 4.61$; $5\% = 5.99$. There are 63 countries included in the sample.

Financial variable	Coefficient	*p*-value	Hansen test
Panel A: Regressions using the simple conditioning information set			
Liquid Liabilities	1.667	0.023	1.553
Commercial Central Bank	10.169	0.001	1.403
Private Credit	2.215	0.003	0.577
Panel B: Regressions using the policy conditioning information set			
Liquid Liabilities	2.173	0.020	2.393
Commercial Central Bank	9.641	0.021	2.350
Private Credit	3.215	0.012	0.571

do not have a significant impact on capital per capita growth in the cross-country sample. In the panel estimations, all three financial intermediary development indicators are associated with faster capital per capita growth. However, only in the regressions with Commercial-Central Bank is the null hypothesis of no serial correlation in the error term not rejected in all the specifications. Thus, while evidence suggests that financial intermediary development positively influences physical capital accumulation, the pure, cross-sectional relation between physical capital growth and financial intermediary development is highly dependent on the measure of financial intermediary development used.

Table 6
Alternative measures of financial intermediary development and growth, using panel data

The regression equation estimated in Panel A is Growth = β_0 + β_1 Initial income per capita + β_2 Average years of schooling + β_3 Finance. The dependent variable is the growth rate of real per capita GDP. Initial income per capita is the log of real per capita GDP in the first year of the respective time period. Average years of schooling is log of one plus the average years of schooling in the total population over 25. Finance is either Liquid Liabilities, the log of liquid liabilities of the financial system divided by GDP, Commercial-Central Bank, the log of assets of deposit money banks divided by deposit money bank plus central bank assets, or Private Credit, the log of credit by deposit money banks and other financial institutions to the private sector divided by GDP. The regression equation estimated Panel B is Growth = β_0 + β_1 Initial income per capita + β_2 Average years of schooling + β_3 Openness to trade + β_4 Inflation + β_5 Government size + β_6 Black market premium + β_7 Finance. Openness to trade is the log of the sum of real exports and imports of goods and nonfinancial services as share of real GDP. Inflation is the log of one plus the inflation rate, calculated using the average annual CPI data from the International Financial Statistics. Government size is the log of real general government consumption as share of real GDP. Black market premium is the log of one plus the black market premium. The regressions are panel regressions, with data averaged over seven 5-year periods from 1960–1995, and using lagged values as instruments, as described in the text. The regressions also contain time dummies. P-values calculated from White's heteroskedasticity-consistent standard errors are reported. The null hypothesis of the Sargan test is that the instruments used are not correlated with the residuals. The null hypothesis of the serial correlation test is that the errors in the first-difference regression exhibit no second-order serial correlation. There are 77 countries and 365 observations included in the sample.

Financial variable	Coefficient	p-value	Sargan set (p-value)	2nd order serial corr. test (p-value)
Panel A: Regressions using the simple conditioning information set				
Liquid Liabilities	2.093	0.001	0.227	0.522
Commercial Central Bank	4.763	0.001	0.246	0.712
Private Credit	2.397	0.001	0.183	0.516
Panel B: Regressions using the policy conditioning information set				
Liquid Liabilities	2.321	0.001	0.607	0.722
Commercial Central Bank	3.361	0.001	0.390	0.958
Private Credit	1.443	0.001	0.506	0.803

5. Finance and private saving

This section explores the impact of the exogenous component of financial development on private savings rates. As in the previous section, we will use both cross-country and panel samples, but a different set of conditioning information.

Table 7
Alternative measures of financial intermediary development and productivity growth, using cross-country data

The regression equation estimated in Panel A is Productivity Growth $= \beta_0 + \beta_1$ Initial income per capita $+ \beta_2$ Average years of schooling $+ \beta_3$ Finance. The dependent variable is Productivity Growth, which is growth of real per capita GDP minus 0.3* growth of capital per capita. Initial income per capita is the log of real per capita GDP in the first year of the respective time period. Average years of schooling is log of one plus the average years of schooling in the total population over 25. Finance is either Liquid Liabilities, the log of liquid liabilities of the financial system divided by GDP, Commercial-Central Bank, the log of assets of deposit money banks divided by deposit money bank plus central bank assets, or Private Credit, the log of credit by deposit money banks and other financial institutions to the private sector divided by GDP. The regression equation estimated in Panel B is Productivity Growth $= \beta_0 + \beta_1$ Initial income per capita $+ \beta_2$ Average years of schooling $+ \beta_3$ Openness to trade $+ \beta_4$ Inflation $+ \beta_5$ Government size $+ \beta_6$ Black market premium $+ \beta_7$ Finance. Openness to trade is the log of the sum of real exports and imports of goods and imports of goods and nonfinancial services as share of real GDP. Inflation is the log of one plus the inflation rate, calculated using the average annual CPI data from the International Financial Statistics. Government size is the log of real general government consumption as share of real GDP. Black market premium is the log of one plus the black market premium. The regressions are cross-country regressions, with data averaged over 1960–1995, and using the legal origin of countries as instruments for Finance. P-values calculated from White's heteroskedasticity-consistent standard errors are reported. The null hypothesis of the Hansen test is that the instruments used are not correlated with the residuals. The critical values for the Hansen test (2 d.f.) are: 10% = 4.61; 5% = 5.99. There are 63 countries included in the sample.

Financial variable	Coefficient	p-value	Hansen test
Panel A: Regressions using the simple conditioning information set			
Liquid Liabilities	1.787	0.002	0.253
Commercial Central Bank	5.853	0.001	0.092
Private Credit	1.500	0.004	2.036
Panel B: Regressions using the policy conditioning information set			
Liquid Liabilities	2.168	0.006	3.315
Commercial Central Bank	8.134	0.006	1.284
Private Credit	1.986	0.021	3.472

5.1. The conditioning information set

The set of conditioning information is selectively determined by various theories of consumption, including the classical permanent-income and life-cycle hypotheses and the more recent theories accounting for consumption habits, subsistence consumption, precautionary saving motives, and borrowing constraints (see Loayza et al., 2000). The variables included in the set of conditioning information for the saving regression are listed below.

Table 8
Alternative measures of financial intermediary development and productivity growth, using panel data

The regression equation estimated in Panel A is Productivity Growth = $\beta_0 + \beta_1$ Initial income per capita + β_2 Average years of schooling + β_3 Finance. The dependent variable is Productivity Growth, which is growth of real per capita GDP minus 0.3* growth of capital per capita. Initial income per capita is the log of real per capita GDP in the first year of the respective time period. Average years of schooling is log of one plus the average years of schooling in the total population over 25. Finance is either Liquid Liabilities, the log of liquid liabilities of the financial system divided by GDP, Commercial-Central Bank, the log of assets of deposit money banks divided by deposit money bank plus central bank assets, or Private Credit, the log of credit by deposit money banks and other financial institutions to the private sector divided by GDP. The regression equation estimated in Panel B is Productivity Growth = $\beta_0 + \beta_1$ Initial income per capita + β_2 Average years of schooling + β_3 Openness to trade + β_4 Inflation + β_5 Government size + β_6 Black market premium + β_7 Finance. Openness to trade is the log of the sum of real exports and imports of goods and imports of goods and nonfinancial services as share of real GDP. Inflation is the log of one plus the inflation rate, calculated using the average annual CPI data from the International Financial Statistics. Government size is the log of real general government consumption as share of real GDP. Black market premium is the log of one plus the black market premium. The regressions are panel regressions, with data averaged over seven 5-year periods from 1960–1995, and using lagged values as instruments, as described in the text. The regressions also contain time dummies. P-values calculated from White's heteroskedasticity-consistent standard errors are reported. The null hypothesis of the Sargan test is that the instruments used are not correlated with the residuals. The null hypothesis of the serial correlation test is that the errors in the first-difference regression exhibit no second-order serial correlation. There are 77 countries and 365 observations included in the sample.

Financial variable	Coefficient	p-value	Sargan set (p-value)	2nd order serial corr. test (p-value)
Panel A: Regressions using the simple conditioning information set				
Liquid Liabilities	0.663	0.001	0.124	0.841
Commercial Central Bank	2.388	0.001	0.242	0.965
Private Credit	1.332	0.001	0.205	0.772
Panel B: Regressions using the policy conditioning information set				
Liquid Liabilities	0.856	0.001	0.552	0.836
Commercial Central Bank	1.669	0.001	0.486	0.758
Private Credit	0.296	0.001	0.401	0.865

The level and the growth rate of private income have ambiguous effects on saving regressions, depending on whether the change in these variables is permanent or temporary. These ambiguous effects also occur depending on whether the change takes place within a generation or across generations. The same argument holds for the terms of trade, which can be considered an exogenous determinant of income. The level of income may have an additional,

Table 9
Alternative measures of financial intermediary development and capital growth, using cross-country data

The regression equation estimated in Panel A is Capital Growth $= \beta_0 + \beta_1$ Initial income per capita $+ \beta_2$ Average years of schooling $+ \beta_3$ Finance. The dependent variable is the growth rate of physical per capita capital. Initial income per capita is the log of real per capita GDP in the first year of the respective time period. Average years of schooling is log of one plus the average years of schooling in the total population over 25. Finance is either Liquid Liabilities, the log of liquid liabilities of the financial system divided by GDP, Commercial-Central Bank, the log of assets of deposit money banks divided by deposit money bank plus central bank assets, or Private Credit, the log of credit by deposit money banks and other financial institutions to the private sector divided by GDP. The regression equation estimated in Panel B is Capital Growth $= \beta_0 + \beta_1$ Initial income per capita $+ \beta_2$ Average years of schooling $+ \beta_3$ Openness to trade $+ \beta_4$ Inflation $+ \beta_5$ Government size $+ \beta_6$ Black market premium $+ \beta_7$ Finance. Openness to trade is the log of the sum of real exports and imports of goods and nonfinancial services as share of real GDP. Inflation is the log of one plus the inflation rate, calculated using the average annual CPI data from the International Financial Statistics. Inflation is the log of one plus the inflation rate, calculated using the average annual CPI data from the International Financial Statistics. Government size is the log of real general government consumption as share of real GDP. Black market premium is the log of one plus the black market premium. The regressions are cross-country regressions, with data averaged over 1960–1995, and using the legal origin of countries as instruments for Finance. P-values calculated from White's heteroskedasticity-consistent standard errors are reported. The null hypothesis of the Hansen test is that the instruments used are not correlated with the residuals. The critical values for the Hansen test (2 d.f.) are: $10\% = 4.61$; $5\% = 5.99$. There are 63 countries included in the sample.

Financial variable	Coefficient	p-value	Hansen test
Panel A: Regressions using the simple conditioning information set			
Liquid Liabilities	− 0.345	0.767	4.693
Commercial Central Bank	− 1.046	0.832	4.578
Private Credit	2.832	0.006	6.747
Panel B: Regressions using the policy conditioning information set			
Liquid Liabilities	0.511	0.562	4.605
Commercial Central Bank	1.018	0.755	4.722
Private Credit	4.038	0.012	3.039

positive impact on the private savings rate if a large share of the country's population is near subsistence consumption levels. Government saving, expressed relative to GPDI in our saving regressions, is another important variable, serving to account for Ricardian equivalence effects. The expected sign for government saving is negative, reflecting at least a partial private saving offset of changes in public saving. We include a measure of the real interest rate, which has well known negative substitution and positive income effects on consumption, resulting in an ambiguous sign in saving regressions. We include the inflation rate as a proxy for uncertainty, expecting a positive association

Table 10
Alternative measures of financial intermediary development and capital growth, using panel data

The regression equation estimated in Panel A is Capital Growth $= \beta_0 + \beta_1$ Initial income per capita $+ \beta_2$ Average years of schooling $+ \beta_3$ Finance. The dependent variable is the growth rate of physical per capita capital. Initial income per capita is the log of real per capita GDP in the first year of the respective time period. Average years of schooling is log of one plus the average years of schooling in the total population over 25. Finance is either Liquid Liabilities, the log of liquid liabilities of the financial system divided by GDP, Commercial-Central Bank, the log of assets of deposit money banks divided by deposit money bank plus central bank assets, or Private Credit, the log of credit by deposit money banks and other financial institutions to the private sector divided by GDP. The regression equation estimated in Panel B is Capital Growth $= \beta_0 + \beta_1$ Initial income per capita $+ \beta_2$ Average years of schooling $+ \beta_3$ Openness to trade $+ \beta_4$ Inflation $+ \beta_5$ Government size $+ \beta_6$ Black market premium $+ \beta_7$ Finance. Openness to trade is the log of the sum of real exports and imports of goods and nonfinancial services as share of real GDP. Inflation is the log of one plus the inflation rate, calculated using the average annual CPI data from the International Financial Statistics. Government size is the log of real general government consumption as share of real GDP. Black market premium is the log of one plus the black market premium. The regressions are panel regressions, with data averaged over seven 5-year periods from 1960–1995, and using lagged values as instruments, as described in the text. The regressions also contain time dummies. P-values calculated from White's heteroskedasticity-consistent standard errors are reported. The null hypothesis of the Sargan test is that the instruments used are not correlated with the residuals. The null hypothesis of the serial correlation test is that the errors in the first-difference regression exhibit no second-order serial correlation. There are 77 countries and 365 observations included in the sample.

Financial variable	Coefficient	p-value	Sargan set (p-value)	2nd order serial corr. test (p-value)
Panel A: Regressions using the simple conditioning information set				
Liquid Liabilities	3.667	0.001	0.192	0.013
Commercial Central Bank	8.848	0.001	0.258	0.172
Private Credit	3.435	0.001	0.166	0.014
Panel B: Regressions using the policy conditioning information set				
Liquid Liabilities	5.162	0.001	0.494	0.076
Commercial Central Bank	6.493	0.001	0.338	0.169
Private Credit	3.005	0.001	0.316	0.053

between saving and the inflation rate, consistent with a precautionary saving motive. This result would only be the partial effect of inflation on saving. The net effect of inflation on saving would also consider the negative effect of inflation on, among other variables, income growth.

We include several demographic variables. The first are the old-age and young-age population dependency ratios, defined, respectively, as the ratios of population under 15 years of age and over 65 year of age to total population. Including the dependency ratios helps account for life-cycle effects. The standard life-cycle hypothesis predicts a negative effect of dependency ratios on saving, whereas the permanent-income hypothesis predicts insignificance of either. The second demographic variable is the urbanization rate. Since agents engaged in agricultural activities face higher income uncertainty, economies more highly urbanized should have, other things held to be equal, lower private savings rates.

5.2. Regressions results

The results in Tables 11 and 12 do not suggest that financial intermediary development exerts a strong, positive effect on private savings rates. Whereas the coefficient on Private Credit is significantly positive in the cross-country regression, it is insignificant in the panel regression. The results for the cross-country regression indicate a small positive effect of financial development on private savings rates. To see this effect, note that Mexico's value for Private Credit over the period 1971–1995 was 21.7%. If this were exogenously raised to the sample median of 29.1%, the coefficient estimates in Table 11 indicate that Mexico's private saving would have increased only from 20% to 20.6%. The Hansen test of overidentifying restrictions indicates that the orthogonality conditions cannot be rejected at the 5% level, and that the instruments are therefore appropriate.

The panel estimations, however, indicate an insignificant impact of Private Credit on private savings rates. The econometric specification tests indicate that we cannot reject the null hypotheses of the appropriateness of the instruments and the assumption of no serial correlation of the differenced error terms. In sum, the results indicate that there is not a substantial economic impact of financial intermediary development on private savings rates. As shown in Table 12, alternative measures of financial intermediary development do not alter this conclusion.

6. Conclusions

This paper examined the impact of financial development on the sources of economic growth. We use two econometric methods. To assess the long-run impact of the exogenous component of financial intermediary development on the sources of economic growth, we use a cross-country sample with data averaged over the period 1960–1995, using the legal origin of countries as instruments. To exploit the time-series nature of the data, we create a panel data set and use recent dynamic panel techniques as proposed by Arellano and Bond (1991), Arellano and Bover (1995), and Blundell and Bond (1997). This procedure controls for the possible endogeneity of the regressors and for country-specific effects in dynamic, lagged-dependent variable models, such as growth regressions.

Table 11
Financial intermediation and private saving

The regression equation estimated is Private Saving $= \beta_0 + \beta_1$ Real per capita GPDI $+ \beta_2$ Growth rate of real per capita GPDI $+ \beta_3$ Real interest rate $+ \beta_4$ Terms of trade $+ \beta_5$ Old dependency ratio $+ \beta_6$ Young dependency ratio $+ \beta_7$ Urbanization ratio $+ \beta_8$ Government Saving $+ \beta_9$ Inflation $+ \beta_{10}$ Private Credit. The dependent variable is Private Saving which is the ratio of gross private saving and gross private disposable income. Real per capita GPDI is the log of real per capita gross private disposable income. Real interest rate is the log of one plus the real interest rate. Terms of trade is the log of the ratio of export and import prices. Old dependency ratio is the share of population over 65 in total population. Young dependency ratio is the share of population under 15 in total population. Urbanization ratio is the share of population that lives in urban areas. Government Saving is the ratio of gross public saving and gross private disposable income. Inflation is the log of one plus the inflation rate. Private Credit is credit by deposit money banks and other financial institutions to the private sector as share of GDP. The regression in column 1 is a cross-country regression, with data averaged over 1971–1995, and using the legal origin of countries as instruments for Private Credit. The regression in column 2 is a panel regression, with data averaged over five 5-year periods from 1971–1995, and using lagged values as instruments, as described in the text. The regression in column 2 also contains time dummies that are not reported. *P*-values calculated from White's heteroskedasticity-consistent standard errors are reported under the respective coefficient. The null hypothesis of the Hansen test is that the instruments used are not correlated with the residuals. The critical values for the Hansen test (2 d.f.) are: 10% = 4.61; 5% = 5.99. The null hypothesis of the Sargan test is that the instruments used are not correlated with the residuals. The null hypothesis of the serial correlation test is that the errors in the first-difference regression exhibit no second-order serial correlation.

	(1)	(2)
Constant	− 0.102	0.474
	0.387	0.001
Real per capita GPDI	0.041	0.000
	0.005	0.992
Growth rate of real per capita GPDI	1.378	0.531
	0.001	0.001
Real interest rate	0.172	− 0.101
	0.282	0.130
Terms of trade	− 0.024	− 0.029
	0.534	0.094
Old dependency ratio	− 0.313	− 0.940
	0.170	0.001
Young depencency ratio	0.012	− 0.300
	0.884	0.001
Urbanization ratio	− 0.073	0.107
	0.054	0.010
Government Saving	− 0.129	− 0.273
	0.527	0.001
Inflation	0.039	− 0.327
	0.733	0.001
Private Credit	0.085	0.021
	0.027	0.224
Hansen test	0.708	
Sargan test (*p*-value)		0.311
Serial correlation test (*p*-value)		0.335
Countries	61	72
Observations		247

T. Beck et al. / Journal of Financial Economics 58 (2000) 261–300   295

Table 12
Alternative measures of financial intermediary development and private saving

The regression equation estimated is Private Saving $= \beta_0 + \beta_1$ Real per capita GPDI $+ \beta_2$ Growth rate of real per capita GPDI $+ \beta_3$ Real interest rate $+ \beta_4$ Terms of trade $+ \beta_5$ Old dependency ratio $+ \beta_6$ Young dependency ratio $+ \beta_7$ Urbanization ratio $+ \beta_8$ Government Saving $+ \beta_9$ Inflation $+ \beta_{10}$ Finance. The dependent variable is Private Saving which is the ratio of gross private saving and gross private disposable income. Real per capita GPDI is the log of real per capita gross private disposable income. Real interest rate is the log of one plus the real interest rate. Terms of trade is the log of the ratio of export and import prices. Old dependency ratio is the share of population over 65 in total population. Young dependency ratio is the share of population under 15 in total population. Urbanization ratio is the share of urban population that lives in urban areas. Government Saving is the ratio of gross public saving and gross private disposable income. Inflation is the log of one plus the inflation rate. Finance is either Liquid Liabilities, liquid liabilities of the financial system divided by GDP, Commercial-Central Bank, assets of deposit money banks divided by deposit money bank plus central bank assets, or Private Credit, credit by deposit money banks and other financial institutions to the private sector divided by GDP. The regressions in Panel A are cross-country regressions, with data averaged over 1971–1995, and using the legal origin of countries as instruments for Finance. The regressions in Panel B are panel regressions, with data averaged over five 5-year periods from 1971–1995, and using lagged values as instruments, as described in the text. The regressions in panel B also contain time dummies. P-values calculated from White's heteroskedasticity-consistent standard errors are reported. The null hypothesis of the Hansen test is that the instruments used are not correlated with the residuals. The critical values for the Hansen test (2 d.f.) are: 10% = 4.61; 5% = 5.99. The null hypothesis of the Sargan test is that the instruments used are not correlated with the residuals. The null hypothesis of the serial correlation test is that the errors in the first-difference regression exhibit no second-order serial correlation.

Panel A: Cross-country data

Financial variable	Coefficient	p-value	Hansen test
Liquid Liabilities	0.075	0.102	3.106
Commercial Central Bank	0.896	0.338	1.370
Private Credit	0.085	0.027	0.708

Panel B: Panel data

Financial variable	Coefficient	p-value	Sargan test (p-value)	2nd order serial corr. test (p-value)
Liquid Liabilities	− 0.012	0.588	0.631	0.286
Commercial Central Bank	0.154	0.001	0.363	0.340
Private Credit	0.021	0.224	0.311	0.335

We find an economically large and statistically significant relation between financial intermediary development and both real per capita GDP growth and total factor productivity growth. Specification tests indicate that the robust, positive relation between financial development and both growth and productivity growth are not due to simultaneity bias or country-specific effects. This result is robust to the use of different estimation procedures, conditioning information sets, and indicators of financial development. The results, however, indicate an ambiguous relation between financial intermediary development and both physical capital growth and private savings rates. While there tends to be a positive link between financial intermediary development and both physical capital accumulation and private savings rates, these results are sensitive to alterations in estimation techniques and measures of financial intermediary development. This paper's results support the view that better functioning financial intermediaries improve resource allocation and accelerate total factor productivity growth with positive repercussions for long-run economic growth.

Appendix A. Data Appendix

A.1. Countries in the sample

1. Member of the cross-country sample for GDP, capital and productivity growth (63 countries)
2. Member of the panel sample for GDP, capital and productivity growth (77 countries)
3. Member of the cross-country sample for private saving (61 countries)
4. Member of the panel sample for private saving (72 countries)

Algeria (2)	El Salvador (1, 2, 4)	Kenya (1–4)
Argentina (1, 2)	Ethiopia (4)	Korea (1–4)
Australia (1–4)	Finland (1–4)	Lesotho (2, 4)
Austria (1–4)	France (1–4)	Luxembourg (4)
Bahamas (4)	Gambia (2–4)	Madagascar (3, 4)
Bangladesh (3, 4)	Germany (1, 2, 4)	Malawi (2–4)
Belgium (1–4)	Ghana (1–4)	Malaysia (1–4)
Belize (4)	Great Britain (1–4)	Malta (1–3)
Bolivia (1, 2)	Greece (1–4)	Mauritius (1–4)
Brazil (1, 2)	Guatemala (1–4)	Mexico (1–3)
Cameroon (2, 4)	Guyana (1, 2)	Morocco (4)
Canada (1–4)	Haiti (1, 2)	Myanmar (3, 4)
Central African Republic (2, 4)	Honduras (1–4)	Nepal (4)
Chile (1–4)	Iceland (3, 4)	Netherlands (1–4)
Colombia (1–4)	India (1–4)	New Zealand (1–4)
Congo (2)	Indonesia (2, 3, 4)	Nicaragua (2)
Costa Rica (1–4)	Iran (2)	Niger (1–4)
Cote d'Ivoire (4)	Ireland (1–4)	Nigeria (3, 4)
Cyprus (1–4)	Israel (1, 2)	Norway (1–4)
Denmark (1–4)	Italy (1–4)	Pakistan (1–4)
Dominican Republic (1, 2)	Jamaica (1–4)	Panama (1, 2)
Ecuador (1–4)	Japan (1–4)	Papua New Guinea (1–4)
Egypt (2–4)	Jordan (4)	Paraguay (1, 2)

Peru (1–3)	Sri Lanka (1–4)	Togo (1–4)
Philippines (1–4)	Sudan (2)	Trinidad and Tobago (1–4)
Portugal (1–4)	Swaziland (4)	United States of America (1–4)
Rwanda (2–4)	Sweden (1–4)	Uruguay (1–3)
Senegal (1–4)	Switzerland (1–4)	Venezuela (1–4)
Sierra Leone (2–4)	Syria (2–4)	Zaire (1, 2)
South Africa (1–4)	Taiwan (1)	Zimbabwe (1, 2, 4)
Spain (1–4)	Thailand (1–4)	

A.2. Data sources

The first eleven variables are from Loayza et al. (1998). These numbers represent National Account data that have been revised and cross-checked for consistency using international and individual-country sources.

1. Log level and growth rate of per capita GDP.

2. Log level and growth rate of per capita gross private disposable income (GPDI).

3. Private savings rates is the ratio of gross private savings and GPDI. Gross private saving is measured as the difference between gross national saving, calculated as gross national product minus consumption expenditure, both measured at current prices and gross public saving. GPDI is measured as the difference between gross national disposable income (GNDI), and gross public disposable income, which is the sum of public saving and consumption.

4. Capital stock numbers are constructed using data from Penn World Tables 5.6.

5. Government size is real general government consumption as share of real GDP.

6. Openness to trade is the sum of real exports and real imports of goods and nonfinancial services as share of real GDP.

7. Government saving is the ratio of gross public saving and gross private disposable income.

8. Real interest rate is defined as $\ln[(1 + i)/1 + \pi)]$, where i is the nominal interest rate and II the inflation rate. The inflation rate is the average of the current and year-ahead inflation.

9. Terms of Trade is the ratio of an export price index and an import price index.

10. Old and young dependency ratios are the shares of population under 15 and over 65, respectively, in total population.

11. Urbanization ratio is the share of urban population in total population.

12. Inflation rates are calculated using average annual CPI data from the International Financial Statistics (IFS), line 64.

13. The average years of schooling in the total population (25 years and over) come from Barro and Lee (1996). Data are taken for the initial year of the period.

14. Data on the black market premium are from World's Currency Yearbook; and Wood (1988).

15. Data on Private Credit are calculated using IFS numbers and the following method:

$$\{(0.5)*[F(t)/P\_e(t) + F(t-1)/P\_e(t-1)]\}/[GDP(t)/P\_a(t)], \tag{A.1}$$

where F is credit by deposit money financial intermediaries and other financial institutions to the private sector (lines 22d + 42d). If there are no data on 42d, we assume that the value is zero. GDP is line 99b, P_e is end-of period CPI (line 64) and P_a is the average annual CPI.

16. Data on Liquid Liabilities are calculated using IFS numbers and the following method:

$$\{(0.5)*[F(t)/P\_e(t) + F(t-1)/P\_e(t-1)]\}/[GDP(t)/P\_a(t)], \tag{A.2}$$

where F is liquid liabilities (line 55l) or money plus quasi money (line 35l), if liquid liabilities is not available. If neither liquid liabilities nor money plus quasi money are available, we use time and savings deposits (line 25). GDP is line 99b, P_e is end-of period CPI (line 64) and P_a is the average annual CPI.

17. Data on Commercial Central Bank are calculated using IFS numbers, using the following method:

$$DBA(t)/(DBA(t) + CBA(t)), \tag{A.3}$$

where DBA is assets of deposit money financial intermediaries (lines 22a–d) and CBA is central bank assets (lines 12a–d).

18. Data on legal origin are from La Porta et al. (1998) and from Reynolds and Flores (1996).

References

Alonso-Borrego, C., Arellano, M., 1999. Symmetrically normalized instrumental-variable estimation using panel data. Journal of Business and Economic Statistics 17, 36–49.

Aghion, P., Howitt, P., 1988. Endogenous Growth Theory. Massachusetts Institute of Technology Press, Cambridge, MA.

Arellano, M., Bond, S., 1991. Some tests of specification for panel data: Monte Carlo evidence and an application to employment equations. Review of Economic Studies 58, 277–297.

Arellano, M., Bover, O., 1995. Another look at the instrumental-variable estimation of error-components models. Journal of Econometrics 68, 29–52.

Bandiera, O., Caprio, G., Honohan, P., Schiantarelli, F., 2000. Does financial reform increase or reduce savings? Review of Economics and Statistics 82, 239–263.

Barro, R., 1991. Economic growth in a cross section of countries. Quarterly Journal of Economics 56, 407–443.

Barro, R., Lee, J., 1996. International measures of schooling years and schooling quality. AER Papers and Proceedings 86, 218–223.

Bencivenga, V., Smith, B., 1991. Financial intermediation and endogenous growth. Review of Economic Studies 58, 195–209.

Bils, M., Klenow, P., 1998. Does schooling cause growth or the other way around? Unpublished working paper, No 6393. National Bureau of Economic Research, Cambridge, MA.

Blundell, R., Bond, S., 1997. Initial conditions and moment restrictions in dynamic panel data models. Unpublished discussion paper, No 97-07. University College London.

Boyd, J., Levine, R., Smith, B., 2000. The impact of inflation on financial sector performance. Journal of Monetary Economics, forthcoming.

Boyd, J., Prescott, E., 1986. Financial intermediary-coalitions. Journal of Economic Theory 38, 211–232.

Caselli, F., Esquivel, G., LeFort, F., 1996. Reopening the convergence debate: a new look at cross-country growth empirics. Journal of Economic Growth 1, 363–389.

Chamberlain, G., 1984. Panel Data. In: Griliches, Z., Intriligator, M. (Eds.), Handbook of Econometrics. Elsevier, Amsterdam, pp. 1247–1313.

Demirgüç-Kunt, A., Maksimovic, V., 1998. Law, finance, and firm growth. Journal of Finance 53, 2107–2137.

Diamond, D., 1984. Financial intermediation and delegated monitoring. Review of Economic Studies 51, 393–414.

Easterly, W., Levine, R., 1999. It's not factor accumulation: stylized fact and growth models. Unpublished working paper. World Bank, Washington, DC.

Easterly, W., Loayza, N., Montiel, P., 1997. Has Latin America's post reform growth been disappointing? Journal of International Economics 43, 287–311.

Fajnzylber, P., Lederman, D., Loayza, N., 1999. What Causes Violent Crime? Unpublished working paper. World Bank, Washington, DC.

Fry, M., 1995. Money, Interest, and Banking in Economic Development. Johns Hopkins University Press, Baltimore, MD.

Gertler, M., 1988. Financial structure and aggregate economic activity: an overview. Journal of Money, Credit, and Banking 20, 559–588.

Greenwood, J., Jovanovic, B., 1990. Financial development, growth, and the distribution of income. Journal of Political Economy 98, 1076–1107.

Greenwood, J., Smith, B., 1997. Financial markets in development, and the development of financial markets. Journal of Economic Dynamics and Control 21, 145–186.

Griliches, Z., Hausman, J., 1986. Errors in variables in panel data. Journal of Econometrics 31, 93–118.

Hall, R., Jones, C., 1999. Why do some countries produce so much more output per worker than others? Quarterly Journal of Economics 114, 83–116.

Harberger, A., 1978. Perspectives on Capital and Technology in Less Developed Countries. In: Artis, M., Nobay, A. (Eds.), Contemporary Economic Analysis. Croom Helm, London.

Harberger, A., 1998. A vision of the growth process. American Economic Review 88, 1–32.

Holtz-Eakin, D., Newey, W., Rosen, H., 1990. Estimating vector autoregressions with panel data. Econometrica 56, 1371–1395.

Jayaratne, J., Strahan, P., 1996. The finance-growth nexus: evidence from bank branch deregulation. Quarterly Journal of Economics 111, 639–670.

King, R., Levine, R., 1993a. Finance and growth: Schumpeter might be right. Quarterly Journal of Economics 108, 717–738.

King, R., Levine, R., 1993b. Finance, entrepreneurship, and growth: theory and evidence. Journal of Monetary Economics 32, 513–542.

King, R., Levine, R., 1994. Capital fundamentalism, economic development, and economic growth. Carnegie-Rochester Conference Series on Public Policy 40, 259–292.

Klenow, P., 1998. Ideas versus rival human capital: industry evidence on growth models. Journal of Monetary Economics 42, 3–23.

La Porta, R., Lopez-de-Silanes, F., Shleifer, A., Vishny, R., 1997. Legal determinants of external finance. Journal of Finance 52, 1131–1150.

La Porta, R., Lopez-de-Silanes, F., Shleifer, A., Vishny, R., 1998. Law and finance. Journal of Political Economy 106, 1113–1155.

Levine, R., 1997. Financial development and economic growth: views and agenda. Journal of Economic Literature 35, 688–726.

Levine, R., 1998. The legal environment, banks, and long-run economic growth. Journal of Money. Credit, and Banking 30, 596–620.

Levine, R., 1999. Law, finance, and economic growth. Journal of Financial Intermediation 8, 36–67.

Levine, R., Loayza, N., Beck, T., 2000. Financial intermediation and growth: causality and causes. Journal of Monetary Economics, forthcoming.

Levine, R., Zervos, S., 1998. Stock markets, banks, and economic growth. American Economic Review 88, 537–558.

Levhari, D., Srinivasan, T., 1969. Optimal savings under uncertainty. Review of Economic Studies 36, 153–163.

Loayza, N., Lopez, H., Schmidt-Hebbel, K., Serven, L., 1998. World Saving Database. Unpublished working paper. World Bank, Washington, DC.

Loayza, N., Schmidt-Hebbel, K., Serven, L., 2000. What drives saving across the world? Review of Economics and Statistics 82, 165–181.

Mankiw, G., 1995. The growth of nations. Brookings Papers on Economic Activity, 275–326.

Masson, P., Bayoumi, T., Samiei, H., 1995. Saving behavior in industrial and developing countries. Unpublished working paper. International Monetary Fund, Washington, DC.

Neusser, K., Kugler, M., 1998. Manufacturing growth and financial development: evidence from OECD countries. Review of Economics and Statistics 80, 638–646.

Obstfeld, M., 1994. Risk-taking, global diversification, and growth. American Economic Review 84, 1310–1329.

Prescott, E., 1998. Needed: a theory of total factor productivity. International Economic Review 39, 525–551.

Rajan, R., Zingales, L., 1998. Financial dependence and growth. American Economic Review 88, 559–586.

Reynolds, T., Flores, A., 1996. Foreign Law Current Sources of Codes and Legislation in Jurisdictions of the World. Fred B. Rothman & Co., Littleton, CO.

Rousseau, P., Wachtel, P., 1998. Financial intermediation and economic performance: historical evidence from five industrial countries. Journal of Money, Credit, and Banking 30, 657–678.

Schumpeter, J., 1934. The Theory of Economic Development. Translated by Redvers Opie. Harvard University Press, Cambridge, MA.

Watson, M., 1992. A note on estimating deterministic trends in the presence of serially correlated errors. Unpublished working paper. Northwestern University, Evanston, IL.

Williamson, S., 1987. Financial intermediation, business failures, and real business cycles. Journal of Political Economy 95, 135–145.

Wood, A., 1988. Global trends in real exchange rates: 1960–84. Unpublished discussion paper, No. 35. World Bank, Washington, DC.

D
Income Distribution

[17]

ELSEVIER Journal of Empirical Finance 10 (2003) 217–248

Journal of EMPIRICAL FINANCE

www.elsevier.com/locate/econbase

Income inequality: the aftermath of stock market liberalization in emerging markets

Mitali Das[*], Sanket Mohapatra

Department of Economics, Columbia University, 420 West 118th Street, New York, NY 10027, USA

Abstract

Early research has documented that the large-scale equity market liberalizations of the last decade led the subsequent rise in aggregate equity indices, investment booms, capital flows and economic growth. An important and unaddressed issue is the normative question of whether and how these reforms shifted the distribution of incomes in the aftermath of equity market liberalization. In careful empirical analysis, we find a pattern indicating that income share growth accrued almost wholly to the top quintile of the income distribution at the expense of a "middle class" that we define as the three middle quintiles of the income distribution. A surprising finding is that the lowest income share remained effectively unchanged in the event of liberalization. These patterns are robust to the inclusion of a wide variety of controls for global shocks, country-specific factors, and contemporaneously implemented privatization and stabilization policies.
© 2002 Elsevier Science B.V. All rights reserved.

Keywords: Income inequality; Stock market; Liberalization

1. Introduction

In the latter half of the 1980s and the early years of the 1990s, the governments of over two dozen sovereign nations began to implement a wave of major economic reforms, which included capital account liberalization, privatization and/or a host of stabilization policies. This large-scale experiment has fuelled an active academic and popular debate on the causes and consequences of these reforms, in part because the aftermath of such reforms is important to nations which, to date, are considering liberalizing reforms. Empirical evidence on the consequences of these reforms will therefore be an important

* Corresponding author.
E-mail addresses: mitali.das@columbia.edu (M. Das), sm756@columbia.edu (S. Mohapatra).

0927-5398/02/$ - see front matter © 2002 Elsevier Science B.V. All rights reserved.
PII: S0927-5398(02)00025-7

218   *M. Das, S. Mohapatra / Journal of Empirical Finance 10 (2003) 217–248*

tool in assessing how best to implement similar liberalization policies in reform-minded countries.

In this context, a nascent but important body of empirical research has begun to emerge, analyzing important questions such as the relation of capital account liberalization to (i) emerging market equity prices (e.g., Bekaert and Harvey, 2000a,b; Kim and Singal, 2000; Henry, 2000a; Froot et al., 2001), (ii) liquidity (Levine and Zervos, 1998), (iii) private investment (Levine and Zervos, 1998; Henry, 2000b; Bekaert and Harvey, 2000a,b), (iv) equity flows (Bekaert et al., 2002) (v) and economic growth (Bekaert et al., 2001). This literature has found strong evidence that suggests capital account liberalization is associated with higher equity prices, lower cost of capital, investment booms, greater capital flows and higher growth.

To date, an important but unaddressed question in this literature is the issue of whether and how these reforms have shifted the *distribution* of incomes in the reforming countries. This is an important area of research for several reasons. For example, the finding in Bekaert et al. (2001) that average economic growth increased after liberalization raises normative issues about the allocation of the generated wealth. One would presumably evaluate the success of liberalizing reforms differently when average growth uniformly raised incomes for all quantiles of the distribution, from a finding that the average growth post-liberalization was only influenced by gains to the upper tails of the income distribution. For many countries that are still considering capital account liberalization, it is important to evaluate the benefits of market liberalization such as investment booms relative to the potential downsides of such policy reforms, so that future reforms may be tailored to alleviate any negative fallout from undertaking such economic reforms.

This paper takes a step in this direction by presenting the first set of results on the association of capital account liberalization with income inequality. In this paper, we heuristically and empirically describe the dynamics of the shifts in income distributions in a sample of 11 countries that undertook extensive economic reforms between 1986 and 1995[1]. Prior to our discussion of the empirical work, we consider various mechanisms that link capital account liberalization to income inequality. We do not intend these mechanisms to be causal in either direction, but to provide a framework in which the finding of an empirical link between the two variables should not necessarily be discarded as spurious.

We analyze income distribution changes by comparing the size of three income shares before and after liberalization, conditional on a set of country-specific factors, and contemporaneous global shocks. We study the share of GDP held by the top quintile, the lowest quintile, and a group we will henceforth refer to as the *middle class*, which represents the sun of the three middle quintiles. Because we track the changes in income shares which plausibly respond slowly to economic reforms (relative to equity prices or the dividend yield), we analyze movements in the distribution over the "short run" which we take as the first 2–4 years beyond the year of the first liberalizing reform. This aspect of the analysis is discussed in more detail when we present our methodological framework and the construction of event windows. We focus mainly on capital account liberalization, but also control for other reforms such as privatization and stabilization policies that were

---

[1] Data for the remaining countries are noisy and sparse. Details of the data are given in Section 2 of the paper.

M. Das, S. Mohapatra / Journal of Empirical Finance 10 (2003) 217–248   219

contemporaneously implemented. We will use the terms financial market liberalization, stock market liberalization and capital account liberalization synonymously for our purposes. Regression results in this study are given both for simple linear models as well as event-study models, which are somewhat incongruous in this context but useful nevertheless.

The principal findings of this research indicate systematic shifts in the income distribution in the first 4 years after a country's first liberalization reform. First, the raw data indicate that in the 11 emerging markets we consider, nine experienced a growth in the top quintile's share of income, and the mean share held by the top quintile rose by 1.3 percentage points. Second, one mildly surprising finding is that there is no discernible change in the mean income share of the lowest quintile. In the sample of 11 countries, four experience declines in the lowest quintile's income share, seven experience growth, and the mean share held by this group rises by 0.1%, which is statistically indiscernible from zero in regression analysis. This finding supports a recent finding in Dollar and Kraay (2001) that income growth of the poor is one-for-one with mean income growth of the population, which implies a constant income share for the poor. Based on these two strands of evidence and a basic adding-up theorem, there must be a reduction in the aggregate income share held by the middle class in the aftermath of capital account liberalization, and we find this to be the case. Specifically, in 9 of the 11 emerging markets in the sample, the aggregate income share of the middle class falls after liberalization. The raw data indicate a mean reduction of 1.45 percentage points in their share of income.

We test this pattern in careful regression analysis, to control for variations in domestic fundamentals, contemporaneous domestic and global business cycle effects, and country-specific effects. The regression results indicate that the income share of the middle class is strongly negatively associated with liberalization, and this relation persists in the presence of a wide variety of controls. In general, this finding is strongest for the 3rd quintile but holds statistically for the 2nd and 4th quintiles as well. In contrast, there is no statistically significant relation between liberalization and the income share of the lowest quintile in the presence of a rich set of controls. The empirical evidence for the upper quintile points to a positive and statistically significant relation between its income share and the event of liberalization, in accordance with the raw mean increases in their income shares. However, for certain regression specifications this relation attenuates. Because our regression estimates are sensitive to the choice of the regressor vector, we report a variety of results. We do not lend any causality interpretation to our results because of the well-known problems of identification. Instead, all of our results are presented as conditional correlations, and are open to varying interpretations, some of which we will discuss in the context of the regression results. It is important to stress that the described patterns hold for income shares. In the sample of emerging markets we consider, average income of the top quintile rose in all 11 nations, average income of the middle class as well as the lowest quintile rose in 10 of 11 nations.[2]

---

[2] The only exception is Nigeria, where the upper quintile's share of income after liberalization rose by 6.6 percentage points (a 13.6% increase), which is significantly higher than the mean increase of 1.3 percentage points in the upper quintile of all nations in the sample.

The key results obtained in this research complement, and should be viewed in the context of, some important research that precedes this, e.g., Levine and Zervos (1998), Henry (2000a,b), Bekaert and Harvey (2000a,b) and Bekaert et al. (2001). For instance, our finding that average middle class income share decreased while the average income share of the upper quintile simultaneously increased, coupled with the finding of Bekaert et al. (2000) that mean growth increased post-liberalization, indicates that the "pie grew" upon liberalization, but that the generated wealth was disproportionately allocated to the upper tail, suggesting a mean-increasing distributional shift. Without the result of Bekaert et. al., our finding could not reject the hypothesis that liberalization leads greater inequality with a mean-reducing distributional shift. The entire body of results jointly raises normative issues about capital account liberalization and the subsequent welfare of the population, and questions of the trade-off in mean income growth and the concomitant growth in inequality. Although the latter topics are of academic interest, they are not explicitly discussed here, but will be addressed in future research.

To better comprehend the dynamics of these shifts in the distribution post-liberalization, we complement the regression analysis with nonparametric tests of stochastic dominance of the pre-liberalization and post-liberalization income distributions. Logically, combining our results with that of Bekaert et al. (2001) yields a very precise set of null hypotheses. First, patterns of income levels described in the current research indicate that the average post-liberalization distribution of incomes should exhibit First Order stochastic dominance (FOSD) over the pre-liberalization distribution. Similarly, SOSD should be obtained. Second, the finding that liberalization on average raises mean income growth in Bekaert et al. (2000), coupled with our finding that this growth appears to be driven entirely by the upper quintile, indicates that we should not reject Lorenz dominance.[3] We provide formal tests of each of these hypotheses to provide a larger context for the results of our regression analysis.

An important issue that often arises in studying emerging markets phenomena is that of dating a country's first liberalizing reform. In this respect, our research was aided greatly by Bekaert and Harvey (2000a,b), and Henry (1999, 2000a), whose work has compiled official liberalization dates on overlapping sets of the sample of 11 liberalizing countries we consider.[4] Also useful to this paper is the work of Deninger and Squire (1996), which has assembled panel data on socioeconomic metrics for a large cross section of nations. Although the focus of this research is on the association of financial reforms with income

---

[3] Lorenz dominance, or mean-normalized second order stochastic dominance (SOSD) of income distribution y_1 over income distribution y_2 implies that any social welfare function that is increasing and concave in income will record higher levels of welfare in y_1 than in y_2; see Shorrocks (1983) or Litchfield (1999).

[4] As a referee has pointed out to us, the issue of dating liberalizing events is a somewhat unsettled matter in the literature. Bekaert and Harvey (2000a,b) and Henry (2000a) are some of the primary sources, and Kim and Singal (2000) is another. To limit the discrepancies that arise from using multiple sources, we have used data from Bekaert and Harvey (2000a,b) and supplemented these with data from Henry (2000a) for those nations not covered in the former. To verify the robustness of our results, we have re-estimated all models and reproduced the figures with data from Kim and Singal (2000). This analysis has revealed noticeable differences in only the individual country effects, and made the estimation less precise due to a much smaller set of nations in Kim/Singal (only 6 nations in their data set have corresponding income shares). The graphs, and alternative dates, are available upon request from us.

inequality, it is directly related to the vast literature in growth that has studied amongst other issues, growth and income inequality (some examples include Barro, 1990; Barro and Salai-Martin, 1995; Perotti, 1996; Banerjee and Duflo, 2000; Dollar and Kraay, 2001). This paper integrates some aspects of the growth research into studying emerging markets phenomena, by exploring income inequality in the aftermath of stock market liberalization.

We will focus on the share of income owned by the jth quintile as the dependent variable for the greater part of our empirical analysis (where $j=l$ represents the lowest, $j=h$ represents the highest quintile and, aggregating the three middle quintiles yields a "middle class" with $j=m$). One might consider studying the variation in the Gini coefficient of inequality to analyze income distributions pre- and post-liberalization; one drawback of this measure, however, is its inability to distinguish between distributions that are unequal in very different ways, e.g., thick-tailed at the upper end, versus thick-tailed at the lower. Furthermore, income shares are the relevant variable to analyze in studying relative gains, and in inferring the process of resource allocation in the liberalizing nation. Normative analyses about the welfare of the middle class whose income share falls in the event of capital account liberalization must therefore be tempered to allow for the possibility that the level of income in the middle class rises after liberalization. As indicated earlier, middle class income increased contemporaneously with the decrease in their share of national income in 10 of the 11 nations in our sample of liberalizing nations.

The remainder of the paper is organized as follows. In Section 2 we discuss the sample of emerging market nations in our study, provide some preliminary findings, and describe various mechanisms that link capital account liberalization with the observed changes in income shares. Section 3 describes our empirical methodology; results from both standard regression analysis and event study models are reported here. In Section 4, we discuss tests of stochastic dominance and Lorenz dominance, then describe the findings of our tests. Section 5 considers whether it is possible to give a causality interpretation to our findings. Conclusions follow. Appendix A details the data construction of this study, and the construction of some of our test statistics.

2. Capital account liberalization and income inequality

2.1. Sample of liberalizing and non-liberalizing nations

Listed in Table 1a, our panel data consist of 11 countries that underwent capital account liberalization between 1986 and 1995, and a sample of eight "control" countries that were subject to no major capital account reforms in this time period. The liberalizing countries are Brazil, India, Korea, Malaysia, Mexico, Nigeria, Pakistan, Philippines, Sri Lanka, Thailand and Turkey. Although over two-dozen sovereign nations implemented financial market liberalization in varying degrees in this time period, our sample is truncated for unavailability of income share data. For example, only pre-liberalization income share data are available for Chile and Morocco, while no income share data are available for other liberalizing countries such as Argentina, Taiwan and Venezuela. The control countries in our sample are Bangladesh, Cote d'Ivoire, Guatemala, Jamaica, Kenya, Niger, Sierra Leone and Trinidad and Tobago. The fact that these represent the same regions as the

222   *M. Das, S. Mohapatra / Journal of Empirical Finance 10 (2003) 217–248*

Table 1a
Sample of liberalized and non-liberalized countries

Liberalized countries	Liberalization date	T_i	Non-liberalized countries	T_i
Brazil	1988	13	Bangladesh	11
India	1986	13	Cote d'Ivoire	6
Korea, Rep.	1987	6	Guatemala	3
Malaysia	1987	4	Jamaica	9
Mexico	1989	5	Kenya	2
Nigeria	1995	5	Niger	3
Pakistan	1991	8	Sierra Leone	2
Philippines	1986	6	Trinidad and Tobago	5
Sri Lanka	1992	7		
Thailand	1988	7		
Turkey	1989	3		

The financial liberalization dates are based on Bekaert, Harvey and Lundblad (2001) and Henry (2000a). T_i indicates the number of years for which income shares are available for each country in the sample. National-level data on income shares of the various quintiles of the population were obtained from the High Quality Sample of Deininger and Squire (1996) and from the World Income Inequality Database (2000).
The minimal criterion for including a country in the sample was the availability of a minimum of one data point in each of the 5-year windows prior to and subsequent to liberalization.

liberalizing countries mitigates possible region-specific effects when comparing distributions between the liberalizing and control countries.

Annual income share data are compiled both from Deninger and Squire (1996) and the World Income Inequality Database (WIID). These data, which are available for T_i years for county i, yield an unbalanced panel for our data set. All stock market data, deflated by the price index, are taken from World Bank Database on Financial Structure and Economic Development (FSED). Country-specific data are obtained from the World Bank's Socio-economic Time Series Access and Retrieval (STARS) database, and rule of law data are from the IRIS data set. A description of the variables is provided in Appendix A. For dates of first capital account liberalization, we lean on the careful dating procedures developed by Bekaert and Harvey (2000a,b), and Henry (1999, 2000a). The liberalization dates are presented in Table 1a. Summary statistics of the key variables are in Table 1b. All data are measured at the annual frequency.

2.2. Mechanisms

There are a few important channels by which stock market liberalization could differentially affect different income groups in the population. Standard international asset pricing models (e.g., Stulz, 1995a,b) predict that global capital market integration may reduce the domestic cost of equity capital.[5] Although the domestic risk-free rate could rise above its autarky rate in the event of liberalization, research preceding ours indicates that the equity premium falls in the sample of 12 emerging markets we consider (see, for example, Tesar and Werner, 1998; Stulz, 1999; Bekaert and Harvey, 2000a,b; Henry,

---

[5] For instance, the presence of domestic investment opportunities could lead to net capital inflows that lower the riskless rate; and, greater risk sharing between domestic and foreign investors could result in reducing the risk premium (e.g., Errunza and Losq, 1985).

2000a). If equity market liberalization reduces the cost of equity capital, then holding future cash flows fixed, an immediate implication is an increase in the country's equity price index and, from a valuation perspective, capital gains in the liberalizing country at least over the short horizon. However, if participation in the stock market is segmented by income groups, then these gains will accrue only to those income groups that own equity, and ceteris paribus the measured response to liberalization will be higher for those groups whose income depends directly on the equity market. Although we have very sparse data on stock market participation in emerging markets, there is anecdotal evidence to strongly suggest that equity ownership is largely restricted to the upper income classes in the countries we sample (e.g., Beim and Calomiris, 2000).

Over the short horizon, stock market liberalization may also differentially impact the different income groups if access to credit markets is disparate within the population. By reducing the cost of capital, stock market liberalizations increase the net present valuation (NPV) of ongoing investments, while also rendering previous negative NPV projects feasible under a lowered cost of external finance.[6] Since there is evidence that growth is strongly positively associated with lowered cost of financing (see Rajan and Zingales, 1998), there will be a measured increase in income via entrepreneurial wealth and retained earnings following the event of stock market liberalization. However, if credit market imperfections limit lower income groups' access to credit, as in the models of Galor and Zeira (1993) and Ray (1998), such gains will be disproportionately allocated to the groups with better access to bank credit and external financing.

Capital account liberalization may also lead to distributional changes by affecting factors unobservable to the analyst. For example, the implementation of stock market liberalization might signal a change in domestic fundamentals that leads firms to expect a better environment for growth, as hypothesized in Bartolini and Drazen (1997). Improved expectations might be particularly strong for firms that are closely tied to the domestic government because they are in the best position to appropriate the gains from capital market integration, as implied by the rent-seeking models of Krueger (1974) and Bhagwati (1996). In particular, favored firms or investors may receive better information, or explicitly influence reforms that reap private benefits. To the extent that members of the upper income quintiles are tightly linked with the domestic governments, these factors should most strongly impact their income shares post-liberalization. Therefore, an a priori assumption is that the measured income of the upper quantiles will be inflated via this channel. If these groups undertake investments because they have private information of their prospects, then one would observe an increase in their mean income share even after controlling for contemporaneous increases in stock market valuation and investment. One might speculate, in the spirit of the Kuznets's (1955) inverted-U hypothesis,[7] that stock market liberalization leads to improvements in the upper tails of the distribution at the early stage of stock market development, while the lower quintiles gain over time.

The preceding discussion is intended to indicate possible links between liberalizing reforms and changes in income shares. We do not press on the issue of causality since

---

[6] Henry (2000b) finds evidence that stock market liberalization leads investment booms.

[7] Kuznet's hypothesis is an initial rise in inequality with economic progress and then a gradual fall as the benefits of growth permeate more widely.

Table 1b
Summary statistics for liberalizing countries

	Brazil	India	Korea	Malaysia	Mexico	Nigeria	Pakistan	Philippines	Sri Lanka	Thailand	Turkey
GDP per capita, PPP (current international $)											
Pre-liberalization											
Mean	4565.88	783.92	4110.91	3380.06	5230.02	769.90	1167.33	2374.05	1904.86	2096.13	3606.15
Std. Deviation	798.89	73.88	815.25	286.48	450.75	48.79	151.76	105.13	140.49	372.67	642.95
Post-liberalization											
Mean	5669.59	1292.65	8779.73	5419.37	6858.15	806.87	1662.13	2957.79	2700.13	4250.25	5118.65
Std. Deviation	267.48	119.03	1229.37	673.62	481.50	10.44	91.66	175.61	213.44	657.95	416.53
School enrollment, secondary (% gross)											
Pre-Liberalization											
Mean	35.80	34.96	88.50	52.22	55.90	28.82	19.36	65.58	72.34	29.96	42.86
Std. Deviation	1.33	2.68	4.95	2.68	0.42	3.49	2.02	1.82	1.46	1.09	2.20
Post-Liberalization											
Mean	40.17	41.27	90.95	57.52	54.78	N.A	25.60	71.15	74.73	33.25	50.58
Std. Deviation	2.22	3.27	1.47	0.73	1.96	N.A	0.00	3.16	0.59	5.71	3.94
General government consumption (% of GDP)											
Pre-Liberalization											
Mean	10.13	10.23	10.83	16.21	8.95	15.48	14.75	8.16	9.97	12.73	7.77
Std. Deviation	1.43	0.54	0.70	1.43	0.35	2.51	1.60	0.85	0.29	0.84	0.33
Post-liberalization											
Mean	16.46	11.66	10.35	14.18	9.70	9.59	12.72	9.16	10.14	9.68	11.70
Std. Deviation	2.52	0.34	0.37	0.76	1.37	1.55	0.91	0.86	0.83	0.34	1.39
Rule of law index											
Pre-liberalization											
Mean	3.82	2.70	2.76	4.54	3.22	2.38	1.82	1.00	0.36	3.00	3.00
Std. Deviation	0.25	0.48	0.43	0.51	0.44	0.91	0.40	0.00	0.50	0.00	0.00

Post-liberalization											
Mean	3.97	1.73	2.63	3.50	3.00	3.00	2.30	1.00	2.90	4.20	3.18
Std. Deviation	0.08	0.42	1.20	0.84	0.00	0.00	1.03	0.00	1.39	0.44	1.01
Private credit by deposit money banks and other financial institutions/GDP											
Pre-liberalization											
Mean	0.21	0.28	0.66	0.73	0.10	0.10	0.26	0.39	0.19	0.53	0.16
Std. Deviation	0.07	0.01	0.05	0.20	0.01	0.01	0.02	0.06	0.01	0.03	0.00
Post-liberalization											
Mean	0.25	0.28	0.86	0.81	0.23	0.08	0.23	0.19	0.22	0.77	0.13
Std. Deviation	0.06	0.03	0.11	0.11	0.09	0.00	0.01	0.02	0.02	0.16	0.00
Stock market capitalization/GDP											
Pre-liberalization											
Mean	0.12	0.04	0.07	0.58	0.04	0.05	0.06	0.05	0.09	0.05	0.02
Std. Deviation	0.04	0.01	0.02	0.04	0.02	0.01	0.01	0.02	0.04	0.02	0.00
Post-liberalization											
Mean	0.11	0.10	0.37	0.91	0.26	0.08	0.18	0.13	0.17	0.35	0.10
Std. Deviation	0.05	0.04	0.13	0.32	0.16	0.02	0.04	0.06	0.04	0.22	0.05
Stock market value traded/GDP											
Pre-liberalization											
Mean	0.06	0.02	0.05	0.07	0.04	0.00	0.01	0.01	0.00	0.03	0.00
Std. Deviation	0.04	0.01	0.03	0.03	0.04	0.00	0.00	0.00	0.00	0.03	0.00
Post-liberalization											
Mean	0.06	0.06	0.35	0.20	0.11	0.00	0.05	0.03	0.03	0.36	0.07
Std. Deviation	0.04	0.02	0.13	0.10	0.06	0.00	0.03	0.01	0.02	0.25	0.06

Summary statistics are for the 5 years prior to and the 5 years subsequent to liberalization.

226   *M. Das, S. Mohapatra / Journal of Empirical Finance 10 (2003) 217–248*

liberalizations are rarely implemented in a vacuum, as discussed in the next section. Rather, the above discussion intends to convey the notion that were liberalizations implemented exogenously, there are mechanisms by which they may directly or indirectly affect income shares. We will investigate the empirical links between income shares and liberalization in the next section. Prior to discussing the methodological framework employed in the regression analysis, we present some preliminary findings.

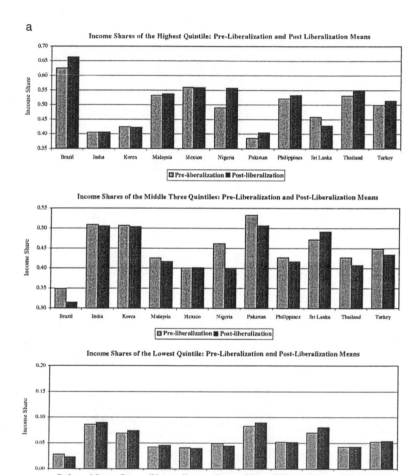

Fig. 1a. Income shares pre- and post-liberalization.

b

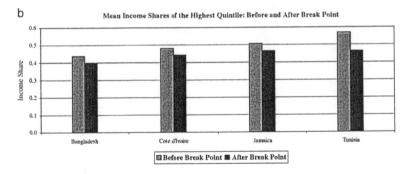

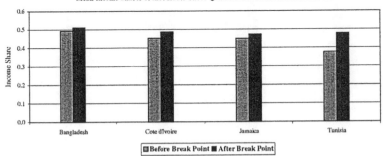

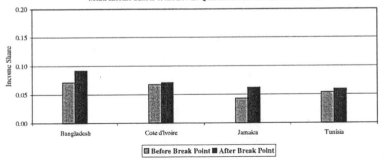

Fig. 1b. Income shares in non-liberalizing nations.

2.3. Preliminary findings

The central findings of this research are summarized in Fig. 1a. These graphs, which display mean income shares pre- and post-liberalization, reveal three main shifts in the

Table 2
Mean income shares and gini coefficents

Countries	Income share of top quintile		Income share of middle quintile		Income share of bottom quintile		Gini coefficient	
	Pre-liberalization	Post-liberalization	Pre-liberalization	Post-liberalization	Pre-liberalization	Post-liberalization	Pre-liberalization	Post-liberalization
Brazil	0.624	0.662	0.348	0.315	0.028	0.023	57.43	60.79
India	0.405	0.406	0.509	0.505	0.086	0.089	31.49	31.31
Korea	0.424	0.422	0.507	0.504	0.069	0.074	35.12	33.64
Malaysia	0.532	0.537	0.426	0.417	0.042	0.046	48.00	48.35
Mexico	0.559	0.559	0.400	0.401	0.041	0.040	50.58	51.34
Nigeria	0.490	0.557	0.462	0.400	0.049	0.044	42.46	50.60
Pakistan	0.385	0.405	0.532	0.506	0.082	0.089	32.17	31.19
Philippines	0.521	0.533	0.427	0.417	0.052	0.051	46.08	46.72
Sri Lanka	0.459	0.428	0.471	0.491	0.070	0.080	38.40	34.40
Thailand	0.531	0.550	0.427	0.407	0.042	0.043	47.40	47.22
Turkey	0.499	0.513	0.448	0.434	0.052	0.054	44.17	45.25

Four-year pre-liberalization and post-liberalization windows were used to calculate the income shares and gini coefficients.
For nations with fewer than 4 annual years of data, the maximum available years were used to construct the means.

M. Das, S. Mohapatra / Journal of Empirical Finance 10 (2003) 217–248   229

income distribution in the first 4 years after a country's first liberalization reform.[8] First, in almost all countries in the sample, income shares of the highest quintile increased in the 4 years post-liberalization. Second, there is a (weak) reduction in aggregate income shares of the three middle quintiles, in varying degrees, in the aftermath of stock market liberalization. Third, there is a mixed reaction for the lowest income group for our sample, as this share rose in some countries in the sample, and fell in other countries. In particular, the mean increase in the countries where the lowest income share rose is found to be statistically indistinguishable from the mean decrease in those countries where the lowest income share fell, making it difficult to detect any meaningful shift in their income share in the event of liberalization.

As a comparison, we also plot the income shares in non-liberalizing countries in Fig. 1b. Because there is no liberalization date, we pick the break point to be 1989 (which is the median liberalizing year in our sample) and compare income shares before and after 1989.[9] The idea of using a common break point has previously been studied by Levine and Zervos (1998). As Fig. 1b indicates, there is no striking pattern that emerges in income shares of non-liberalizing nations in this time period. Highest income quintiles both rise and fall after the breakpoint, and similarly for the middle income quintiles. The lowest quintile shares uniformly rise after the breakpoint.

The fact that income shares of the top quintiles grow, while those of the remaining quintiles shrink or remain stable, indicates a growth in inequality in the nations studied. Another way to examine whether inequality grew after liberalization is to examine the size of the well-known Gini coefficient of inequality before and after liberalization. This is done in Table 2 and the results corroborate our hypothesis.

The preliminary finding, based on Fig. 1a,b and Table 2, indicates that the income distribution is altered in the event of a liberalizing reform. We investigate this pattern more thoroughly in the context of regression analysis in the next section.

3. Empirical methodology

Two empirical strategies are used to study the empirical links between capital account liberalization and income inequality. In this section we attempt to uncover the relation between liberalization and income shares using regression analysis, and an event-study model that permits a diffused effect of liberalization on income shares. In the following section, we verify the changes in income distribution implied by the regression results, by tests of stochastic dominance and Lorenz dominance of the income distribution.

---

[8] Where possible the means are computed over the 4 years preceding and 4 years following the first year of liberalization. For those nations with fewer than 4 years of data before and after liberalization (see Table 1a), individual means are computed over as many observations available.

[9] We also tested this with alternate break points, with no substantive differences in the results to report.

3.1. Income shares and stock market liberalization

As indicated in the discussion of the mechanisms that link capital account liberalization to income inequality, valuation and capitalization changes in the local equity market after a liberalizing reform may be an immediate link between income shares and liberalization. Therefore, controlling for variations in equity markets across emerging markets, and over time within them, is expedient. We focus on two measures of equity market activity, which have been previously been considered (e.g., Atje and Jovanovic, 1993, Levine and Zervos, 1998; Bekaert et al., 2001). For an indicator of the activity in a local equity market, we use the actual dollar valuation of stock traded normalized by the local GDP. We also control for the size (or, financial sector development) of the local market using the equity market capitalization normalized by GDP.

The regression framework explicitly accommodates a delayed effect of stock market variables on income shares. As in Barro (1990) and Blanchard et al. (1993), both contemporaneous and lagged values of stock market and income variables will be utilized. Strictly speaking, the association of year t revaluations of the equity market with year t income shares is not "contemporaneous" in these data, because these data are annual averages.[10]

The first set of conditional correlations are obtained from estimating variants of the regression model:

$$Q_{jit} = \alpha_i + \tau_t + y \times \text{PostLiberalize}_{it} + X'_{it}\,\beta + \delta_1 \times \text{SMC}_{it} + \delta_2 \times \text{SMC}_{it-1} + \delta_3$$

$$\times \text{SMV}_{it} + \delta_4 \times \text{SMV}_{it-1} + \varepsilon_{it},$$

where

$$\text{PostLiberalize}_{it} = \begin{cases} 1 & \text{if year } t \text{ is year of or any year after } i\text{'s first capital account liberalization policy} \\ 0 & \text{otherwise} \end{cases}$$

i indexes the country, t indexes the year, SMC represents our measure of equity market size and SMV (an acronym for stock market valuation) will denote our measure of equity market activity described earlier. X is a vector of country-specific controls that include the contemporaneous and lagged values of the logarithm of per capita GDP, secondary school enrollment, government consumption, gross investment, and one measure of the "rule of law" as in Alesina and Rodrik (1995).[11] To partially capture differences in credit markets, a measure of banking sector development (measured by aggregate private credit normalized by GDP) is added as well. The liberalization indicator is included in addition to the year dummies to isolate the effects of liberalization from those of contemporaneous global or regional shocks.

---

[10] This accommodates the possibility that changes in the equity market earlier in the year are associated with income changes later in the year.

[11] The construction of this variable is detailed in Appendix A.

M. Das, S. Mohapatra / Journal of Empirical Finance 10 (2003) 217–248   231

Table 3a

Changes in income shares around financial market liberalization

	(A)			(B)		
	Q_h	Q_m	Q_l	Q_h	Q_m	Q_l
	(1)	(2)	(3)	(4)	(5)	(6)
PostLiberalize$_t$	0.036**	−0.031**	−0.0053*	0.057**	−0.048**	−0.009
	(0.013)	(0.011)	(0.003)	(0.0259)	(0.019)	(0.007)
LnGDP$_t$				0.206*	−0.210*	−0.006
				(0.177)	(0.117)	(0.084)
LnGDP$_{t-1}$				0.061	−0.082	0.020
				(0.236)	(0.371)	(0.072)
SMC$_t$				−0.293**	0.247**	0.045
				(0.146)	(0.109)	(0.044)
SMC$_{t-1}$				0.269	−0.184	−0.086
				(0.282)	(0.210)	(0.086)
SMV$_t$				0.243*	−0.216*	−0.023
				(0.141)	(0.148)	(0.061)
SMV$_{t-1}$				0.057	−0.081	0.025
				(0.498)	(0.176)	(0.151)
GovtConsumption				−0.001	0.001	0.001
				(0.005)	(0.004)	(0.001)
Secondary Enrollment				−0.002	0.001	0.001
				(0.002)	(0.001)	(0.002)
PrivateCredit				−0.077	0.060	0.015
				(0.182)	(0.136)	(0.055)
Rule of Law				0.082*	−0.070*	−0.011
				(0.051)	(0.038)	(0.015)
Terms of Trade				0.169	0.111	0.569
				(0.155)	(0.115)	(0.472)
Year Dummies	✓	✓	✓	✓	✓	✓
Country Fixed Effects	✓	✓	✓	✓	✓	✓
N	113	113	113	80	80	80

The dependent variable is the income share of the Q_j^{th} income group, where Q_h, Q_m and Q_l are defined in the text. The explanatory variables are: *PostLiberalize* for an indicator for liberalization, *LnGDP$_t$* and *LnGDP$_{t-1}$* for the current and lagged values of GDP respectively; *SMC$_t$* and *SMC$_{t-1}$* for the current and lagged values of normalized stock market capitalization respectively, and *SMV$_t$* and *SMV$_{t-1}$* for the current and lagged values of normalized stock market valuation respectively. The explanatory variables also include a measure of the banking sector development *Private Credit*, measures of secondary schooling, Rule of law, terms of trade, as well as country-specific dummies, and year dummies. The reported standard errors are heteroskedasticity-consistent (White) and reported in parentheses. * and ** respectively denote significance at the 10 and 5 percent error levels.

Panel (A) in Table 3a reports regressions of Q_j ($j=l$, m, h) on the liberalization indicator and a full set of year dummies and country-specific effects, yielding conditional mean differences in income shares pre- and post-liberalization. The results show a strong positive (respectively, negative) relationship between liberalization and Q_h (respectively, Q_m). In Column (1) the coefficient on PostLiberalize implies a mean increase of 3.6 percentage points in the income share of the highest quintile after liberalization. Column (2) indicates a mean decrease of 3.1 percentage points in the Q_m regression. In Column (3) the coefficient is significant, but at a much higher error level, pointing to a 0.5 percentage point increase in the income share of the lowest quintile. Together these results corroborate the pattern found in Fig. 1. However, these differences are larger in absolute value than the simple averages of income shares before and after liberalization, indicating that unobservable country-specific factors and contemporaneous global or regional shocks may be correlated with the decision to liberalize. This issue is further researched below where the regression model controls for coincidental implementation of major domestic reforms.

Panel (B) of Table 3a presents results when the above model is supplemented with a wide variety of controls for variations in equity market, banking sector and domestic fundamentals. These results show that while the basic pattern that emerged in Panel (A) persists in the presence of the additional covariates, the magnitude of that pattern is inflated with the additional controls, as evinced by the absolute value on PostLiberalize$_t$. Furthermore, the coefficient on PostLiberalize is no longer significant in Column (6). In Column (5), controlling for equity market size via SMC$_t$, the coefficient on SMV$_t$ is found to be negative and significant, suggesting that equity market activity is inversely associated with the middle class's share of income. Concurrently, the coefficient on SMV$_t$ is positive in Column (4), suggesting that the upper quintile's income share is affected by contemporaneous changes in equity revaluation. One possible mechanism for this finding is that greater equity market activity could plausibly reflect the greater willingness of participants to hold assets, and this leads to equity price appreciation, benefiting the upper quintile (who are the typical owners of equity in the sample we consider). The results reveal no statistical association between the lowest income quintile and equity market activity; correspondingly, the point-estimates on SMV$_t$ in the Q_h and Q_m regressions approximately sum to zero. Neither do the results reveal any statistical association between lagged values of equity market measures and income shares. Since liberalizations are associated with higher aggregate stock prices (Henry (2000a)), these results are consistent with a scenario in which the upper income quintile disproportionately participates in the equity market, accruing the capital gains from equity revaluation.

Some discussion of the additional regressors is warranted. We note that the measure of the banking sector development, PrivateCredit, is statistically insignificant in all specifications. Nevertheless, the central tendency of the estimator is positive for each of the Q_m and Q_l regressions indicating, perhaps, that banking sector development leads to better access for lower income groups, as discussed in Section 2.2. In a related vein, the coefficient on SMC$_t$ is worth further analysis. Suppose that growth in the financial sector is associated with greater stock market participation. Although we do not have data on participation, there is some casual evidence that participation is largely restricted to the upper quintiles in emerging markets (see Beim and Calomiris, 2000). Growth in the financial sector might therefore be associated with a greater share of the middle class' participation in the equity market, which would divert some fraction of the short-run capital gains from liberalization to the middle class. In this scenario, we would observe both, a positive coefficient on SMC$_t$ for the middle class, and a negative coefficient for the upper quintile. This is found to be the case in Columns (5) and (4), respectively.

In Table 3b we consider a small extension of the previous results by investigating how the income distribution is affected by differences in the strength of legal institutions/ government stability, by introducing the interaction Rule of Law×PostLiberalize. Essen-

Table 3b
Rule of law and liberation: different effects

	Q_h	Q_m	Q_l
	(1)	(2)	(3)
PostLiberalize	0.049** (0.0259)	− 0.038** (0.017)	− 0.007 (0.007)
Rule of Law	0.084* (0.051)	− 0.076* (0.038)	− 0.013 (0.015)
PostLiberalize × Rule of Law	0.009* (0.005)	0.013 (0.142)	0.010 (0.221)
Year Dummies	✔	✔	✔
Country Fixed Effects	✔	✔	✔

This table reports results for a regression that replicates the regression model in Table 3a, including all the regressors from Table 3a, plus an interaction between Rule of Law$_t$ and PostLiberalize$_t$. The reported standard errors are heteroskedasticity-consistent (White) and reported in parentheses. * and ** respectively denote significance at the 10% and 5% error levels.

tially, the hypothesis is that although stock market liberalization has been found to positively affect income shares, the efficacy of such liberalizing policies might depend on the perceived and actual stability of the government and other legal institutions. In Table 3b we find that this is indeed the case, although the hypothesis is statistically verified only for the top quintile. Specifically, we find that while a generic discrete jump in Rule of Law from 0 to 1 (i.e., anarchy to fully accountable) would result in a 8.2% appreciation in the top quintile's income share, a liberalized-induced jump in Rule Of Law would result in a larger 9.3% appreciation of the top quintile's income share. However, we are unable to statistically discern such a pattern for any of the other income shares.

3.2. Liberalization-induced changes in income shares

The results in Table 3a indicate that equity market revaluations affect income shares independently of liberalizing reforms, since the liberalizing indicator is a control variable in the estimated regression model. A legitimate question to consider is whether the association of income shares and equity market activity is systematically different prior and subsequent to liberalization. It is plausible that liberalization-induced revaluations in equity markets elicit different responses from investors than generic changes in equity market revaluations. This is plausible because the event of a liberalizing reform signals fundamental changes that lead firms to expect a better environment for growth, as discussed in Bartolini and Drazen (1997). For example, Henry (2000a) finds that private investment is differentially associated with liberalization-specific and generic changes in the rate of return.

To test this hypothesis, the above regression model was modified as follows:

$$Q_{jit} = \alpha_i + \tau_t + \gamma \text{PostLiberalize}_{it} + X_{it}' \beta + \delta_1 \text{SMC}_{it} + \delta_2 \times \text{SMC}_{it-1} + \delta_3 \times \text{SMV}_{it}$$

$$+ \delta_4 \times \text{SMV}_{it-1} + \delta_5 \times \text{SMV}_{it} \times \text{PostLiberalize}_{it} + \delta_6 \times \text{SMV}_{it-1}$$

$$\times \text{PostLiberalize}_{it} + \varepsilon_{it}.$$

The inclusion of the interactive variables permits a differential slope effect of equity market activity prior and subsequent to a nation's liberalizing reform. In particular, if

234 *M. Das, S. Mohapatra / Journal of Empirical Finance 10 (2003) 217–248*

liberalization-induced changes in stock market activity have fundamentally different implications for incomes from generic changes in stock market valuation, then we must find that $\delta_5 \neq 0$, and $\delta_6 \neq 0$. Estimated results are presented in Table 4.

The coefficients on both contemporaneous SMV_t, as well as its interaction with the liberalization indicator, are both statistically significant at the 10% error level, but of differing signs. In the Q_m regression, the coefficients δ_3 and δ_5 jointly indicate that while a generic 10% increase in equity market activity leads to a 2.8 percentage point decrease in Q_m, a liberalization-induced change of the same magnitude leads to a somewhat larger decrease of 3.5 percentage points. The results reject neither the hypothesis that $\delta_4 = 0$ nor $\delta_6 = 0$, indicating that changes in equity market revaluation in the preceding year have no statistically significant effect on Q_m. Similarly, the results indicate that a 10% increase in equity market activity tends to have a liberalization-induced increase in Q_h that is 2.6 percentage points higher than that for a generic 1% increase in trading activity. As with Q_m, there is no observed statistical association between the lagged measure of stock market activity and changes in the upper quintile's income share. The data also do not support any effects of changes in equity market activity before or after liberalization on the lowest income share.

A model of differential access to credit markets across income groups may reconcile the liberalization-induced slope effects found in Table 4. Since investment is (i) spurred after liberalization and (ii) more sensitive to liberalization-specific changes rather than generic changes in valuations (Henry (2000b)), liberalizing reforms are likely to lead to greater entrepreneurial wealth and retained earnings via the investment channel. However, as discussed earlier, segmented access to credit markets may result in these gains accumulating disproportionately to higher income groups. The differential slopes are also consistent with a story of the improved expectations after liberalizing reforms due, for example, to higher risk-sharing (see Bekaert and Harvey, 1995; Bartolini and Drazen, 1997). If liberalization does portend a differential association of changes in equity market valuations with income shares, then a differential association must also emerge between liberalizing nations and non-liberalizing nations. We test this hypothesis next.

Table 4
Liberalization-induced versus generic changes in stock market valuation

	Q_h	Q_m	Q_l
PostLiberalize	0.054* (0.028)	− 0.045** (0.020)	− 0.004 (0.006)
SMV_t	− 0.349** (0.165)	0.281** (0.122)	0.066 (0.052)
SMV_{t-1}	0.356 (0.318)	− 0.244 (0.233)	− 0.111 (0.100)
PostLiberalize × SMV_t	0.348* (0.213)	− 0.270* (0.163)	− 0.007 (0.046)
PostLiberalize × SMV_{t-1}	− 0.299 (0.332)	0.220 (0.245)	− 0.010 (0.069)
Year Effects	✓	✓	✓
Country Dummies	✓	✓	✓

The dependent variable is the income share of the Q_j^{th} income group (j=h,m,l). The explanatory variables include *PostLiberalize* SMV_t* which the interaction of *PostLiberalize* and *SMV_t* and *PostLiberalize* SMV_{t-1}* which is similarly defined as the interaction of its constituent variables. Country-specific dummies, year dummies, and all the control variables from Table 3a were estimated but are not reported for brevity. The reported standard errors are heteroskedasticity-consistent (White) and reported in parentheses. * and ** denote significance at the 10 and 5 percent error level, respectively.

3.3. Income shares in non-liberalization nations

A natural concern is that the results obtained in Tables 3a and 4 are driven, not by liberalizing reforms in the emerging markets, but rather by world or regional business cycle effects that are not adequately captured by year dummies.[12] If global economic changes are contemporaneously affecting all nations (or regional ones are affecting all nations in the particular region), including those that did not implement any reforms in this time-period, it may be difficult to conclude that liberalization has any statistical effect on income shares. Here we conduct a simple regression test to determine the validity of this alternative explanation.

$$Q_{jit} = \alpha_i + \tau_t + \gamma_1 \times \text{PostLiberalize}_{it} + \gamma_2 \times \text{NonLiberalize}_i + X'_{it}\,\beta + \delta_1 \times \text{SMC}_{it}$$

$$+ \delta_2 \times \text{SMC}_{it-1} + \delta_3 \times \text{SMV}_{it} + \delta_4 \times \text{SMV}_{it-1} + \delta_5 \times \text{SMV}_{it}$$

$$\times \text{NonLiberalize}_i + \delta_6 \times \text{SMV}_{it-1} \times \text{NonLiberalize}_i + \varepsilon_{it}.$$

where

$$\text{NonLiberalize}_i = \begin{cases} 1 & \text{if country } i \text{ has not undertaken any liberalization reform} \\ 0 & \text{otherwise.} \end{cases}$$

The indicator NonLiberalize, which does not vary over time in our sample, takes on the value 1 for the set of "control" nations listed in Table 1a. These controls should help mitigate the presence of unobservable regional differences between the controls and the liberalizing nations because both sets of countries represent the same world regions.

The results for variations of this model are given in Table 5. In Panel (A) we report results for a regression model with no interaction variables. In Column (1), the coefficient on NonLiberalize is positive but statistically insignificant, suggesting that the highest income quintile in control nations is approximately as well off as the same class in liberalizing nations. It is possible to reconcile this result with Fig. 1a and b. However, in Column (2) the coefficient on NonLiberalize is positive and statistically significant, indicating that the middle class in control nations actually fares better than its counterpart in liberalizing nations. A similar result is found for the lowest income quintile group in Column (3). In both Columns (1) and (2), PostLiberalize$_t$ is robust to the addition of the NonLiberalize indicator in both sign and magnitude.

In Panel (B) we extend the estimation idea of Section 3.2, by testing for differential slope effects in non-liberalizing versus liberalizing nations. Column (5) shows that the inclusion of the interactive variables reduces the magnitude as well as the statistical significance of NonLiberalize in the Q_m regression. Its statistical significance is retained in Column (6),

---

[12] Although Fig. 1b indicated no particular pattern in the change in income shares for non-liberalizing nations, that illustration was given for an arbitrary break point year (1989). Further, Fig. 1b is a useful summary of the data but does not control for country specific factors or year effects.

Table 5
Income shares in non-liberalizing nations

	(A)			(B)		
	Q_h	Q_m	Q_l	Q_h	Q_m	Q_l
	(1)	(2)	(3)	(4)	(5)	(6)
PostLiberalize	0.034*	−0.030*	−0.008	0.031*	−0.028*	−0.005
	(0.019)	(0.016)	(0.006)	(0.019)	(0.016)	(0.005)
NonLiberalize	0.301	0.247**	0.123*	0.260	0.223*	0.112**
	(0.193)	(0.125)	(0.069)	(0.201)	(0.131)	(0.044)
SMV_t	0.335**	−0.277**	0.066	0.206*	−0.199*	−0.007
	(0.111)	(0.085)	(0.052)	(0.121)	(0.126)	(0.036)
SMV_{t-1}	0.667**	−0.482**	−0.111	−0.056	−0.030*	0.033
	(0.243)	(0.186)	(0.100)	(0.404)	(0.235)	(0.055)
NonLiberalize × SMV_t				−0.284	0.203*	−0.019
				(0.188)	(0.089)	(0.054)
NonLiberalize × SMV_{t-1}				0.298	−0.129	0.386
				(0.732)	(0.123)	(0.216)
Year Effects	✔	✔	✔	✔	✔	✔
Country Dummies	✔	✔	✔	✔	✔	✔

The dependent variable is the income share of the Q_j^{th} income group (j=h,m,l). The explanatory variables include *NonLiberalize* which is an indicator of nations that experienced no liberalization policies, *NonLiberalize* SMV_t* which is the interaction of *NonLiberalize* and *SMV_t*, and *NonLiberalize* SMV_{t−1}* that is similarly defined as an interaction of its constituent variables. Country-specific dummies, year dummies, and all the control variables from Table 3a were estimated but are not reported for brevity. The reported standard errors are heteroskedasticity-consistent (White) and reported in parentheses. * and ** denote significance at the 10 and 5 percent error level, respectively.

where its magnitude is also slightly increased. Our primary interest is in the joint effect of the contemporaneous and lagged values of SMV and their interaction with NonLiberalize.

In Column (4), the results are somewhat robust to the inclusion of the interaction variable. The coefficient on SMV_t is significantly estimated at 0.206. While the coefficient on NonLiberalize×SMV_t is insignificant at conventional levels, something can still be said. The point-estimates indicate that a 10% increase in equity market activity (i) raises the upper quintile's income share in liberalizing nations[13] by 2.06 percentage points, but (ii) decreases Q_h by 0.78 percentage points in non-liberalizing countries; a result we qualify by stating that the obtained estimates are significant only at the 85th percentile.

In Column (5), NonLiberalize×SMV_t is estimated to be positive and statistically significant, while the coefficient on the contemporaneous variable SMV_t is estimated as negative and statistically significant. These results jointly indicate that (i) a 10% increase in equity market valuation results in lowering middle class income shares in liberalizing nations by 1.9 percentage points, but (ii) the same 10% increase in valuation is associated with an *increase* of 0.0045 (=0.2035−0.1991) percentage points in the middle class income share in non-liberalized nations. Although this is a statistically significant result, the implied numbers are economically less significant, i.e., they suggest that the change in middle class income shares is close to zero in non-liberalizing nations. The coefficients on

---

[13] The slope effect of a change in stock market valuation is given as $\delta_3+\delta_5 SMV$, or, a δ_3 change in liberalizing nations, and a $\delta_3+\delta_5$ effect in non-liberalizers.

M. Das, S. Mohapatra / Journal of Empirical Finance 10 (2003) 217–248   237

the lagged value of equity valuation, SMV_{t-1} as well as its interaction with the non-liberalizing indicator are estimated imprecisely, and cannot be distinguished from zero.

Overall, we find support for the hypothesis that increases in equity market activity are associated with income shares differentially in liberalizing versus non-liberalizing nations. However, this relationship is estimated less precisely and attenuates to zero for the highest income share Q_h.[14]

3.4. The staggered effect of liberalization

The next set of results is reported for models styled in the standard "event-study" specification pioneered by Eckbo (1983). Event study models are somewhat atypical for the current context because in contrast to changes in stock price valuations, we expect financial market liberalization to have continuous, diffused effects on income and income distributions, rather than discrete jump effects along the time line. Nevertheless, in keeping with some of the prominent themes in empirical finance, we begin with a simple specification, estimating variants of the model:

$$Q_{jit} = \alpha_i + \sum_{k=0}^{K} \text{PostLiberalize}_{it-k}\delta_k + X_{it}{'}\beta + \varepsilon_{it}$$

where the variable $\text{PostLiberalize}_{it+k}$ is now redefined as follows

$$\text{PostLiberalize}_{it+k} = \begin{cases} 1 & \text{if it is year } t+k \text{ after } i\text{'s first capital account liberalization policy} \\ 0 & \text{otherwise,} \end{cases}$$

and X constitutes a set of control variables used in Tables 3a–5 such as GovtConsumption, SecondaryEnrollment and Rule of Law. We replace the year dummies with a measure of regional GDP growth to account for some of the regional business cycle effects. The latter is a useful substitution, as the number of coefficients to estimate in this model increase linearly with the parameter K.[15]

The major statistical difference afforded by the event study analysis relative to the linear regression model is its accommodation of a staggered effect of liberalization on income shares for K periods beyond the first year of liberalization. Pooling all post-liberalization years together, as in Bekaert et al. (2000), is informative about mean differences before and after liberalization, but cannot separate the finer differences across these years. Although we experimented with a grid of values for $K=0, 1, 2,..., 6$, the reported results are for $K=4$ because the addition of every additional year beyond $K=4$ was found to have no power in explaining the variance in Q_j $(j=l, m, h)$.

[14] One might also directly test whether Fig. 1b is confirmed in the data by a simple regression of income shares on an indicator that takes on the value 1 for the breakpoint year or thereafter, and 0 otherwise. We find that such regressions are sensitive to the choice of the breakpoint year. Further, the breakpoint year is arbitrary and with no economic significance for these control nations so we do not report those results.

[15] One point of concern is that the number of regressors in this model will grow quite fast, limiting precision. To address this concern, we pared down the set of regressors in this model to those that we deem are the most important, from Table 3a. We find that making the relevant change makes our estimates more precise.

238 *M. Das, S. Mohapatra / Journal of Empirical Finance 10 (2003) 217–248*

Staggering the effects of liberalization could also be useful in speculating about the source of the changes in shares. For an extreme example, suppose the upper quintile's income were completely linked with the equity market. Then, based on the evidence in Henry (2000a) that liberalization leads a rise in emerging market equity prices, one would expect instantaneous changes in their income shares in the event of liberalization, and a coefficient on PostLiberalize$_t$ that is significantly different from zero. Alternatively, if the changes in income depend on realized profits from private investments, it is plausible that the measured response of liberalization is diffused over time, such that the coefficients on PostLiberalize$_{t+k}$ (k=1, 2,...) are different from zero, while the coefficient on PostLiberalize$_t$ is not.

Table 6 presents the results of estimating the model above. The first row, which presents robust regression estimates of the model above, indicates that in the year of liberalization the top quintile's share (Q_h) is positively affected, being 2.2% above its non-liberalization mean. This strand of evidence is consistent with the notion that gains to the upper quintile may be realized imminently after liberalization because of the instantaneous reaction of equity markets, whose valuation directly affects holders of equity. Because increases in one share must be offset by decreases in one or more of the other income shares, we expect coefficients on Q_m and/or Q_l to be negative, which is found to be the case in Columns (2) and (3). That these coefficients are statistically indistinguishable from zero could arise for two reasons. First, sharp declines within Q_m and Q_l in some countries may be offset by huge gains in Q_m and Q_l in others, leading to no observed change in an average (i.e., regression) sense in these income shares. This explanation would be consistent with the observed increase in Q_h and the absence of an estimated decline in Q_m and Q_l. An alternate explanation is that the offsetting declines are felt in narrower quantiles of the income distribution than we consider. To explore this possibility, the regressions are re-

Table 6
Staggered effects on income shares

	(A)			(B)		
	Q_h	Q_m	Q_l	Q_{m2}	Q_{m3}	Q_{m4}
PostLiberalize$_t$	0.022**	− 0.010	− 0.001	− 0.004	− 0.007**	− 0.002
	(0.006)	(0.012)	(0.002)	(0.005)	(0.003)	(0.004)
PostLiberalize$_{t+1}$	0.042*	− 0.029**	0.004*	− 0.008	− 0.014**	− 0.007
	(0.022)	(0.014)	(0.002)	(0.006)	(0.004)	(0.005)
PostLiberalize$_{t+2}$	0.024**	− 0.028**	0.002	− 0.006	− 0.011**	− .009**
	(0.008)	(0.012)	(0.002)	(0.005)	(0.003)	(0.004)
PostLiberalize$_{t+3}$	− 0.007	0.003	0.002	− 0.001	− 0.001	0.002
	(0.003)	(0.017)	(0.003)	(0.007)	(0.004)	(0.006)
PostLiberalize$_{t+4}$	0.004	− 0.011	0.005	− 0.005	− 0.003	− 0.007
	(0.003)	(0.017)	(0.003)	(0.007)	(0.004)	(0.006)

The dependent variable is the income share of the Q_j^{th} income group (j=h,m,l). Q_{m2}, Q_{m3} and Q_{m4} are the second, third, and fourth quintile, respectively, whose sum constitutes Q_m. The explanatory variables *PostLiberalize$_t$*, *PostLiberalize$_{t+1}$*, *PostLiberalize$_{t+2}$*, *PostLiberalize$_{t+3}$* and *PostLiberalize$_{t+4}$* are as defined in Section 3. Country-specific dummies were estimated but are not reported for brevity. Standard errors are heteroskedasticity-consistent (White), and are reported in parentheses. * and ** denote significance at the 10 and 5 percent error level, respectively.

M. Das, S. Mohapatra / Journal of Empirical Finance 10 (2003) 217–248   239

estimated on each of the three components that make up Q_m , i.e, the second, third, and fourth quintiles that we abbreviate as Q_{m2}, Q_{m3} and Q_{m4}. These results are reported in Panel (B) of Table 6.

We find that in the first year of liberalization, there is a statistically significant negative effect on the income share Q_{m3}, which is the center of the "middle class" income share, offsetting the rise in the income share of the top quintile. The point estimate suggests that the income share of this group fell 1.2 percentage points, while there was no significant effect on either Q_{m2}, or Q_{m4} . This finding reconciles the apparent lack of decline in the aggregate measure Q_m. It is also plausible that the observed gains to the upper quintile are driven by gains to a much narrower group than to the entire upper quintile; however, as there is no data on say, deciles, this hypothesis cannot be verified empirically.

The results of Table 6 indicate that while some movements in income shares are observed as early as the year of liberalization, much of the changes occur over the next 2 years and diminish thereafter. The results indicate that the upper quintile's income share is 4.2 and 2.4 percentage points larger than the sample mean in the first and second year after liberalization respectively, as seen by the coefficients on PostLiberalize$_{t+1}$ that and PostLiberalize$_{t+2}$. Contemporaneously offsetting these gains, the middle class income share falls 2.9 and 2.8 percentage points in the first and second years after liberalization respectively. In the first year after liberalization, the lowest income share, Q_l, also falls 0.4%. It is interesting to note that in the second year after liberalization where there is no discernible effect on Q_l, the gains to Q_h exactly offsets the reduction in Q_m. In each of the third and fourth years after liberalization there is no statistically discernible conditional mean difference in any of the income shares.

3.5. Contemporaneous reforms

One concern in empirically isolating the impact of capital account liberalization is that of controlling for the contemporaneous implementation of other economic or political reforms which might systematically influence the "climate" for growth. Henry (2000a) documents that, with very few exceptions, nations that undertook capital account liberalization coincidentally implemented stabilization and trade liberalization policies, accelerated privatization, and lifted restrictions on exchange rates. King and Levine (1993), Rajan and Zingales (1998), Levine and Zervos (1998) indicate that growth is strongly associated with development in the banking sector. Without controlling for coincidental domestic reforms or world business cycle effects that are themselves associated with changes in the income distribution, a regression framework would misrepresent the association of stock market liberalization with changes in income shares, if such co-movements are inadequately captured by year dummies.

To address this concern, the regression model in Section 3.1 is supplemented with additional controls for specific domestic reforms. Because we find in Table 6 that beyond the second year after liberalization the effects are insignificant both economically and statistically, we consider only the 2 years subsequent to the year of implementing capital account liberalization. Data on the other major domestic reforms in the emerging markets are from Henry (2000a). With these data, (for k=1, 2), we add indicator variables for stabilization policies (Stabilize$_{t+k}$), slackening of exchange rate restrictions (Exchange$_{t+k}$) and the implementation of privatization reforms (Privatize$_{t+k}$). These variables are defined analogously to PostLiberalize$_{t+k}$.[16], taking on the value of 1 if it is the $(t+k)$th year after the reform was implemented, and 0 everywhere else.

Results from estimating the modified regression model are given in Table 7. We find that relative to Table 6, the coefficient on the PostLiberalize$_{it}$ indicator becomes significant in the Q_m regression and its statistical significance is retained in the Q_h regression. Note that both these coefficients are more positive relative to their estimates in Table 6. This result is evidence that implementation of the other major domestic reforms is positively correlated to a liberalizing reform. We find that stabilization policies appear to have their strongest effect a year after they are implemented, as indicated by the significant coefficient on Stabilize$_t$. The results indicate that stabilization policies are in general beneficial to the lower income classes. Likewise, the effects of privatization reforms are felt with a year's lag as seen in the coefficients of Privatize$_{t+1}$ in both Columns (1) and (2). Privatization reforms, whose effects are an order of magnitude smaller than that of stabilization programs, are positively associated with the upper quintile, and negatively with the middle class. As with both the above policies, the easing of exchange restrictions also affects income shares with a lag; the results discern strong effects in both the first and second year after more lax exchange rate restrictions are implemented as seen in the coefficients of Exchange$_{t+1}$ and Exchange$_{t+2}$.

Table 7 indicates that it is important to control for contemporaneous domestic programs of stabilization, privatization policies and the easing of exchange rate restrictions. Importantly, the coefficients on the PostLiberalize indicators are statistically significant even after controlling for these other reforms, which themselves impact income shares. We infer that the implementation of the other major domestic reforms is positively correlated with capital account liberalization because of the direction in which the coefficients of the PostLiberalize indicators change relative to Table 6. In general, capital account liberalization appears to impact income shares contemporaneously and up to 2 years after liberalization, while other reforms have no contemporaneous effect.

4. Measures of stochastic and Lorenz dominance

The regression analysis presents evidence that higher income groups benefited unambiguously post-liberalization, with growths in their income share surpassing the

---

[16] These data are from Henry (2000a). "Stabilization programs" refers to programs enacted to require stricter and more transparent monetary policy, lifting of price and exchange rate controls, steps taken to prevent federal and state banks from money printing and "large" public debt rescheduling. Analogously, "privatization" is a term reserved explicitly for actual privatization of firms, and/or steps taken to accelerate privatization practices already in place including the enactment of official laws to permit private individuals into industries earlier reserved for the government, and the transfer of ownership to private individuals, including foreign ownership. "Exchange" refers to a significant easing of foreign exchange restrictions (e.g., easier profit remittance for foreign firms in Venezuela in 1989). Additional details are documented by Henry (2000a).

Table 7
Income shares, liberalization and concurrent reforms

	Q_h	Q_m	Q_l
PostLiberalize$_t$	0.016** (0.008)	− 0.017** (0.006)	− 0.001 (0.002)
PostLiberalize$_{t+1}$	0.022 (0.019)	− 0.031** (0.013)	0.009 (0.006)
PostLiberalize$_{t+2}$	0.051** (0.017)	− 0.05** (0.013)	0.003 (0.006)
Stabilize$_t$	0.022 (0.014)	− 0.026** (0.026)	0.002 (0.005)
Stabilize$_{t+1}$	− 0.084** (0.031)	0.056* (0.027)	0.024** (0.010)
Stabilize$_{t+2}$	0.002 (0.010)	0.001 (0.010)	− 0.0079 (0.003)
Privatize$_t$	− 0.037 (0.020)	0.040** (0.017)	− 0.0027 (0.007)
Privatize$_{t+1}$	0.041** (0.010)	− 0.033** (0.006)	− 0.008 (0.002)
Privatize$_{t+2}$	0.030* (0.018) *	− 0.011 (0.015)	− 0.017 (0.007)
Exchange$_t$	− 0.015 (0.016)	0.021 (0.011)	− 0.006 (0.004)
Exchange$_{t+1}$	0.046** (0.022)	− 0.036* (0.016)	− 0.011 (0.007)
Exchange$_{t+2}$	− 0.026** (0.011)	0.022* (0.010)	0.006 (0.004)
Country Dummies	✔	✔	✔

The dependent variable is the income share of the Q_j^{th} group (j=h,m,l). The explanatory variables *Stabilize*, *Privatize* and *Exchange* represent indicator variables for the implementation of stabilization programs, privatization policies and weakening of exchange rate restrictions, respectively. *Stabilize$_t$*, *Stabilize$_{t+1}$*, *Stabilize$_{t+2}$* are variables which take a value 1 during the year of liberalization, the year after liberalization, and 2 years after liberalization respectively and 0 everywhere else. The *Privatize* and *Exchange* variables are defined analogously. Country-specific dummies, and controls for *Regional GDP growth* (from year t to $t+1$), *Govt Consumption*, *Secondary Enrollment* and *Rule of Law* are also estimated but are not reported for brevity. ** and * denote significance at the 5 and 10 percent error level, respectively, and standard errors are White-consistent.

growth in mean income, while the middle class unambiguously suffered lowered income shares. However, as discussed earlier, this result must be qualified with the fact that with very few exceptions, income *levels* grew almost uniformly in all income classes in our sample. In this section, we revert to studying income levels using standard measures of stochastic and Lorenz dominance to empirically verify the shifts in income distributions from the pre-liberalization to post-liberalization era.

The three dominance measures discussed below are first order stochastic dominance (FOSD), second-order stochastic dominance (SOSD) and Lorenz dominance, also called mean-normalized second order stochastic dominance. Since the purpose is to compare inequality before and after financial liberalization, we are primarily interested in the concept of Lorenz dominance. However, comparisons using first- and second-order stochastic dominance are also presented since these give a broad picture of the mean changes in the income distribution during the process of financial liberalization. Based on the empirical finding from the regressions, we expect (i) the post-liberalization distribution to be characterized by FOSD and SOSD relative to the pre-liberalization distribution, while (ii) Lorenz dominance should not hold for the pooled sample of liberalizing countries. We use a method known as the "p-approach to dominance", where the measures of dominance can be expressed in terms of quantiles (Davidson and Duclos, 2000). Although income quintiles are a rough approximation to the actual income distribution, they are nevertheless useful in comparing the broad patterns of income distribution before and after liberalization.

Denote the cumulative distribution function of the inflation-adjusted incomes of the representative individuals prior to and subsequent to liberalization as F_A and F_B, respectively. F_B first order stochastically dominates (FOSD) distribution F_A if and only if $F_B(y) \leq F_A(y)$. Let I denote income. For the pth quintile, FOSD is equivalent to verifying whether $I_A(p) \leq I_B(p)$, i.e., whether the representative individual in each quintile is better off in the post-liberalization distribution than in the pre-liberalization distribution. SOSD is implied by FOSD. The test for SOSD entails verifying whether $CI_A(p) \leq CI_B(p)$, for each p, where $CI_A(p)$ and $CI_B(p)$ denote the mean cumulative income up to the pth quintile of distributions A and B, respectively. Fig. 2a and b illustrate the shifts in income distribution using these two measures of dominance for the combined sample of liberalizing countries before and after financial liberalization. The evidence seems to be overwhelmingly in favor of first-order (and hence second order) stochastic dominance. A similar exercise for individual countries yields similar results with FOSD holding for 10 out of the 11 countries, and mean inflation-adjusted incomes of each of the quintiles increasing by more than 5% in the 5-year window after liberalization.

A Lorenz curve plots the cumulative income share of the bottom p-quantiles of the population against p. Distribution B Lorenz-dominates distribution A if the Lorenz curve associated with distribution B lies nowhere below and at least somewhere above that of A. Equivalently, distribution B dominates distribution A if $CF_A(p) \leq CF_B(p)$, where $CF_A(p)$ and $CF_B(p)$ are the cumulative *income shares* up to the pth quintile of distributions A and B, respectively. Lorenz dominance can be interpreted as a shift in income distribution where the representative individual in the poorest p-quintiles receives a greater share of the income in the new state of nature after liberalization. We obtain Lorenz dominance for two and crossings for the rest nine liberalizing countries. Fig. 2c illustrates the absence of Lorenz dominance for the combined sample of liberalizing countries in the 5-year window after financial liberalization.

The simultaneous empirical observance of FOSD and the absence of Lorenz dominance reinforce our earlier conclusion that even though mean incomes increased for all the income groups post-liberalization, the gains from liberalization were not equitably distributed. The aggregate dominance results, combined with our regression analysis, make it highly likely that similar effects would be discernible at the micro-level as well for most of the liberalizing countries in our sample.

5. Can a case be made for causality?

Evidence from the regression analysis indicates that there are real statistical associations between the occurrence of liberalization and the income shares of the highest quintile and the "middle class". These relations persist statistically in the presence of controls for domestic fundamentals, world business cycle movements and country-specific factors. They are also robust upon controlling for contemporaneously implemented domestic stabilization and privatization reforms, and the easing up of exchange restrictions. The results indicate that the highest income quintile benefits at the expense of a large middle class. The lowest quintile's income share remains unaffected, mirroring a recent finding in Dollar and Kraay (2001).

M. Das, S. Mohapatra / Journal of Empirical Finance 10 (2003) 217–248   243

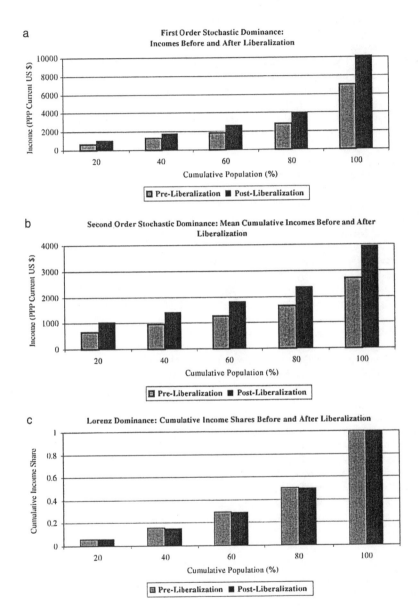

Fig. 2. (a) FOSD. (b) SOSD. (c)Lorenz Dominance.

244   *M. Das, S. Mohapatra / Journal of Empirical Finance 10 (2003) 217–248*

It is worth questioning whether the obtained results are simply a result of endogenous policy reforms that lead to the usual identification problem in cross-country regressions. Consider the following scenario. Suppose members of the upper quintile accurately predict a future positive shock to the marginal product of capital and, recognizing that foreign capital flows will have beneficial price effects on equity, influence policymakers to implement liberalizing reforms. Then, one would expect a rise in the upper quintile's income share due to the positive shock to the productivity of capital, and liberalization will have no causal role for their higher income share, although liberalization will be positively correlated with the upper quintile's income share. This scenario is consistent with our empirical findings. In this case, the liberalization indicator simply absorbs the effects of an unobserved variable representing expectations. In the absence of a convincing way to control for such a possibility, we do not press on a causal role for liberalization.

To this end, we temper our findings in the following ways. First, if the decision to implement liberalizing reforms was in correct anticipation of higher equity valuations in the future, then the obtained results must be different in magnitude than the true association between liberalization and the income shares. In particular, the documented statistical association between liberalization and the upper/middle income shares may be larger than the true association.

Second, even in the absence of endogeneity, all our estimates are obtained conditional on the world business cycle effects in place at the time of liberalization. As documented by Beim and Calomiris (2000) and Bekaert et al. (2002), the late 1980s and early 1990s saw an unprecedented rise in capital flows to emerging markets, at a time when global interest rates were fairly low. The rise in capital flows was linked to the expansion of international finance fuelled by deregulation in many parts of the world as well as technological advances in computing and risk analysis which supported the creation of global financial institutions. Therefore, out-of-sample predictions for future liberalizers based on our results, must be tempered to account for future global conditions, such as high world real interest rates, which may not facilitate large net flows to emerging markets.

On a related note, there may be an element of a "first-mover" advantage for the nations that liberalized first. It is plausible that for the first set of liberalizing nations, foreign investors discounted the importance of political uncertainties, judicial systems and the fragility of certain emerging market nations[17] when investing in these countries. Over time, there is likely to more learning for international investors about the nature of risk, as well as the political and legal institutions, in emerging markets. It is conceivable that such learning result in a more cautious approach to emerging market investments in the future. Under this scenario, one may observe a much less robust

---

[17] Chile, Brazil and Venezuela are examples of the liberalizing markets that are relatively fragile. These nations are heavily dependent on their undiversified export sectors, which makes their terms of trade highly sensitive to fluctuations in commodity prices which can lead to the deterioration of their debt or equity values (see Beim and Calomiris, 2000).

association of liberalization with incomes, or income shares than has been documented in this paper.

6. Conclusions

This paper presents evidence of a strong statistical association between the event of liberalization and income shares. The data strongly support a positive coefficient between liberalization and the highest income quintile's share of mean income, and a negative coefficient between liberalization and the middle class income share. For our study, the middle class represents the aggregate sum of the three middle quintiles. We find no evidence of any statistical association between liberalization and the lowest income quintile. Although the middle class "suffers" in the wake of a liberalizing reform while the upper quintile gains, this statement is true for income shares. We find that income levels in liberalizing nations almost universally rise after liberalization. We provide tests of stochastic dominance of the pre- and post-liberalization income distributions to complement our regression analysis.

The patterns we describe persist in the presence of a wide variety of controls for domestic fundamentals, world business cycle movements and country-specific factors. They are also robust to the addition of controls for contemporaneous domestic reforms. We find that equity revaluations affect income shares differentially before and after liberalizations. They also affect income shares differentially across liberalizing and non-liberalizing nations.

Because liberalizing and other major domestic reforms are rarely implemented in a vacuum, we do not press on causality. It is possible that endogenous policy decisions will attenuate some of the aforementioned correlations that we document. However, it is important to note that there are mechanisms which should relate capital market liberalizations to income shares under a wide variety of hypotheses that are true in emerging markets (e.g., differential access to credit markets, limited stock market participation, and the tight links between upper quintiles and policy makers). In any event, the patterns we describe should prove useful in the debate on emerging markets phenomena, and add to the research that analyzes the aftermath of capital account liberalization in emerging markets.

Acknowledgements

Geert Bekaert and an anonymous referee gave us very detailed, useful suggestions that have improved both the style and content of the paper. We also acknowledge useful conversations with Charles Calomiris, Peter Henry, Guido Kuersteiner, Atif Mian, Roberto Perotti and Edmund Phelps. Special thanks to Peter Henry, Geert Bekaert and Campbell Harvey for providing the liberalization dating procedure used in this paper. Part of this paper was written when the first author was visiting the Center for Basic Research in social sciences at Harvard whose hospitality is warmly acknowledged. Remaining errors are ours.

Appendix A. Data sources and variable glossary

Data source and variable name	Variable description	Detailed variable description
Deininger and Squire and WIID 2000		
Q_5	Income share of the highest quintile	Income share accruing to the highest quintile of the population. Income shares are constructed from reliable income or expenditure data referring to the (entire) national population.
Q_{234}	Income share of the middle three quintiles	Sum of income shares accruing to the middle three quintiles of the population.
Q_{m1}	Income share of the second quintile	Income share accruing to the second quintile of the population.
Q_{m2}	Income share of the third quintile	Income share accruing to the third quintile of the population.
Q_{m3}	Income share of the fourth quintile	Income share accruing to the fourth quintile of the population.
Q_1	Income share of the lowest quintile	Income share accruing to the lowest quintile of the population.
World bank database on financial structure and economic development		
SMC	Stock Market Capitalization/GDP	Stock market capitalization to GDP equals the value of listed shares divided by GDP. Both numerator and denominator are deflated appropriately, with the numerator equaling the average of the end-of-year value for year t and year $t-1$, both deflated by the respective end-of-year CPI, and the GDP deflated by the annual value of the CPI.
SMV	Stock Market Valuation/GDP	Stock market valuation equals the value of total shares traded on the stock exchange to GDP.
Private Credit	Private credit by deposit money banks and other financial institutions to GDP	Private credit by deposit money banks and other financial institutions to GDP equals claims on the private sector by both deposit money banks and other financial institutions divided by GDP.
WDI STARS 2000		
GDP	GDP per capita, PPP (current international $)	GDP per capita based on purchasing power parity (PPP). GDP PPP is gross domestic product converted to international dollars using purchasing power parity rates. An international dollar has the same purchasing power over GDP as the US dollar in the United States.
Govt. Consumption	General government consumption (% of GDP)	General government consumption includes all current government spending for purchases of goods and services (including wages and salaries).

M. Das, S. Mohapatra / Journal of Empirical Finance 10 (2003) 217–248 247

Appendix A (*continued*)

Data source and variable name	Variable description	Detailed variable description
Secondary Enrollment	School enrollment, secondary (% gross)	Gross enrollment ratio is the ratio of total enrollment, regardless of age, to the population of the age group that officially corresponds to the level of education shown.
Terms of trade	Terms of trade adjustment (constant LCU)	The terms of trade effect equals capacity to import less exports of goods and services in constant prices. Data are in constant local currency.
IRIS-3		
Rule of Law	Rule of law indicator	Rule of law contains annual values for the Rule of Law indicator (on a scale of 0–6) for the years 1982–1997, constructed by Stephen Knack and the IRIS Center, University of Maryland, from monthly data from the International Country Risk Guide (ICRG).

Notes: (1) WIID refers to the UNU/WIDER-UNDP World Income Inequality Database 2000. (2) WDI STARS refers to World Bank Socio-economic and Time Series Retrieval System CD-ROM 2000.

References

Alesina, A., Rodrik, D., 1995. Distributive politics and economic growth. Quarterly Journal of Economics 109, 465–490.

Atje, R., Jovanovic, B., 1993. Stock markets and development. European Economic Review 37, 632–640.

Banerjee, A.V., Duflo, E., 2000. Inequality and growth: what can the data say? NBER Working Paper, 7793.

Barro, R.J., 1990. Stock market and investment. Review of Financial Studies 3, 115–131.

Barro, R., Salai-Martin, X., 1995. Economic Growth, 1st ed. McGraw-Hill, New York, NY.

Bartolini, L., Drazen, A., 1997. Capital account liberalization as a signal. American Economic Review 87-1, 138–154.

Beim, D., Calomiris, C., 2000. Emerging Financial Markets, 1st ed. McGraw-Hill, New York, NY.

Bekaert, G., Harvey, C.R., 1995. Time-varying world market integration. Journal of Finance 50, 403–444.

Bekaert, G., Harvey, C.R., 2000a. Capital flows and the behavior of emerging market equity returns. In: Edwards, S. (Ed.), Capital Flows and the Emerging Economies: Theory, Evidence and Controversies. NBER, pp. 159–194.

Bekaert, G., Harvey, C.R., 2000b. Foreign speculators and emerging equity markets. Journal of Finance 55, 565–613.

Bekaert, G., Harvey, C.R., Lundblad, C., 2001. Emerging equity markets and economic development. Journal of Development Economics 66, 465–504.

Bekaert, G., Harvey, C.R., Lumsdaine, R., 2002. The dynamics of emerging market equity flows. Journal of International Money and Finance 21-3, 295–350.

Bhagwati, J., 1996. Political Economy and International Economics, 1st ed. MIT Press, Cambridge, MA.

Blanchard, O., Rhee, C., Summers, L., 1993. The stock market, profit, and investment. Quarterly Journal of Economics 108-1, 115–136.

Davidson, R., Duclos, J., 2000. Statistical inference for stochastic dominance and for the measurement of poverty and inequality. Econometrica 68-6, 1435–1464.

Deininger, K., Squire, L., 1996. A new dataset measuring income inequality. World Bank Economic Review 10, 565–591.

Dollar, D., Kraay, A., 2001. Growth is good for the poor. World Bank Policy Research Working Paper, 2587.

248   M. Das, S. Mohapatra / Journal of Empirical Finance 10 (2003) 217–248

Eckbo, B.E., 1983. Horizontal mergers, colllusion, and stockholder wealth. Journal of Financial Economics 11, 241–276.

Errunza, V., Losq, E., 1985. International asset pricing under mild segmentation: theory and test. Journal of Finance 40, 105–124.

Froot, K., O'Connell, P., Seasholes, M., 2001. The portfolio flows of international investors. Journal of Financial Economics 59, 151–193.

Galor, O., Zeira, J., 1993. Income distribution and macroeconomics. Review of Macroeconomic Studies 60, 35–52.

Henry, P.B., 2000a. Stock market liberalization, economic reform, and emerging market equity prices. Journal of Finance 55, 529–564.

Henry, P.B., 2000b. Do stock market liberalizations cause investment booms. Journal of Financial Economics 58, 301–334.

Kim, E., Singal, V., 2000. Stock market openings: experience of emerging economies. Journal of Business 73, 25–66.

King, R., Levine, R., 1993. Finance and growth: schumpeter might be right. The Quarterly Journal of Economics 108, 717–738.

Krueger, A.O., 1974. The political economy of the rent-seeking society. The American Economic Review 64, 291–303.

Kuznets, S., 1955. Economic growth and income inequality. The American Economic Review 45, 1–28.

Levine, R., Zervos, S., 1998. Stock markets, banks and economic growth. The American Economic Review 88, 537–558.

Litchfield, J., 1999. Inequality: Methods and Tools, Text for World Bank's Web Site on Inequality, Poverty and Socio-Economic Performance.

Perotti, R., 1996. Growth, income distribution and democracy: what the data say. Journal of Economic Growth 1, 149–187.

Rajan, R., Zingales, L., 1998. Financial dependence and growth. The American Economic Review 88, 559–586.

Ray, D., 1998. Development economics. Princeton University Press, Princeton, NJ.

Shorrocks, A.F., 1983. Ranking income distributions. Economica 50, 3–17.

Stultz, R.M., 1995a. The cost of capital in internationally integrated markets. European Financial Management, 11–22.

Stultz, R.M., 1995b. International portfolio choice and asset pricing: an integrative survey. In: Maximovic, V., Ziemba, W. (Eds.), The Handbook of Modern Finance. North Holland, Amsterdam, pp. 201–223.

Stultz, R.M., 1999. Globalization, corporate finance, and the cost of capital. Journal of Applied Corporate Finance 12, 8–25.

Tesar, L., Werner, I.M., 1998. The internationalization of securities markets since the 1987 crash. In: Litan, R.E., Santomero, A.M. (Eds.), Brookings-Wharton Papers on Financial Services. The Brookings Institution, Washington, DC, pp. 281–372.

World Income Inequality Database, 2000. User Guide and Data Sources. UNU-WIDER/UNDP.

Part IV
Contagion

[18]

ELSEVIER

Journal of International Economics 51 (2000) 145–168

Journal of
INTERNATIONAL
ECONOMICS

www.elsevier.nl/locate/econbase

On crises, contagion, and confusion

Graciela L. Kaminsky[a], Carmen M. Reinhart[b],*

[a]*George Washington University, Department of Economics, Washington, DC 20052, USA*
[b]*University of Maryland, School of Public Affairs, Department of Economics and NBER,
College Park, MD 20742, USA*

Received 8 December 1998; received in revised form 4 May 1999; accepted 26 May 1999

Abstract

Since the Tequila crisis of 1994–95, the Asian flu of 1997, and the Russian virus of 1998, economists have been busy producing research on the subject of contagion. Yet, few studies have examined empirically through which channels the disturbances are transmitted if there are, indeed, fundamental reasons for the spillovers we observe. We attempt to fill this gap by analyzing how both trade links and the largely ignored financial sector links influence the pattern of fundamentals-based contagion. We examine the role of international bank lending, the potential for cross-market hedging, and bilateral and third-party trade in the propagation of crises. © 2000 Elsevier Science B.V. All rights reserved.

Keywords: Contagion; Crises; Trade; Finance; Herding

JEL classification: F30; F32; F34

Earlier this year, so many families living in the fashionable suburb of San Pedro Garza Garcia invested in Russian bonds that it became known as San Pedrosburgo. Now this wealthy enclave feels more like Stalingrad...

The Wall Street Journal, November 18, 1998, on explaining why the Mexican stock market plummeted in August and September as leveraged investors faced margin calls.

*Corresponding author. Tel.: +1-301-405-7006; fax: +1-301-403-8107.
E-mail address: creinhar@wam.umd.edu (C.M. Reinhart)

0022-1996/00/$ – see front matter © 2000 Elsevier Science B.V. All rights reserved.
PII: S0022-1996(99)00040-9

146   *G.L. Kaminsky, C.M. Reinhart / Journal of International Economics 51 (2000) 145–168*

1. Introduction

No doubt, historians will remember the early 1980s as a period of systemic crisis in the emerging world. The Latin American countries, with their high debt burdens, fell like dominoes into an abyss of successive devaluations, banking crises, and deep and protracted recessions. Several countries in Asia were also deeply shaken. Yet, possibly, because much of the blame was placed on poor domestic policies and high real interest rates in the United States, little attention was given at the time to the possibility that financial crises could be contagious. After the Tequila crisis of 1994–95, the Asian flu of 1997, and the Russian virus of 1998, not to mention the Exchange Rate Mechanism Crisis of 1992 and 1993, economists are now producing a growing volume of research on the "new" subject of contagion.

Yet, contagion has been understood to be different things across different studies. Crises could be synchronous across countries because of a common adverse shock (i.e. a rise in world interest rates). But symmetric shocks are usually not included in most definitions of contagion. In an early study on the subject, Calvo and Reinhart (1996) distinguish between fundamentals-based contagion, which arises when the infected country is linked to others via trade or finance, and "true" contagion which is the kind that arises when common shocks and all channels of potential interconnection are either not present or have been controlled for. Most often, true contagion is associated with herding behavior on the part of investors – be it rational, as in Calvo and Mendoza (1998), or not.

Few studies have attempted to examine empirically the channels through which the disturbances are transmitted. In this paper, we attempt to fill this gap by analyzing how fundamentals-based contagion could arise due to both trade links and the largely ignored financial sector links. We examine the role of various creditors, including international banks and mutual funds, traders' potential cross-market hedging, and bilateral and third-party trade in the propagation of crises. Some of the conclusions that emerge from our analysis are:

- First, as other studies have suggested, we find evidence that contagion is more regional than global.[1] But evidence on the channels of transmission suggest there are dangers in extrapolating from history. While inter-regional trade in goods and services has not increased markedly in the past few years (a notable exception is Chile's rising trade with Asia), inter-regional trade in assets has skyrocketed. This makes it more likely that if Korean asset prices fall, so too will Brazilian asset prices.
- Second, susceptibility to contagion is highly nonlinear. A single country falling victim to a crisis is not a particularly good predictor of crisis elsewhere, be it in

---

[1]Eichengreen et al. (1996), Glick and Rose (1998), and Wolf (1997) all examined the scope for trade links.

G.L. Kaminsky, C.M. Reinhart / Journal of International Economics 51 (2000) 145–168 147

the same region or in another part of the globe. However, if several countries fall prey, then it is a different story. That is, the probability of a domestic crisis rises sharply if a core group of countries are already infected.

- Third, observational equivalence is a serious obstacle in understanding the channels of transmission. Is the regional complexion of contagion due to trade links, as some studies have suggested, or is it due to financial links – particularly through the role played by banks? Our results suggest that it is difficult to distinguish among the two, because most countries that are linked in trade are also linked in finance. In the Asian crises of 1997, Japanese banks played a similar role in propagating disturbances to that played by U.S. banks in the debt crisis of the early 1980s. Indeed, when we group countries in accordance with their exposure to a common creditor, knowing that there is a crisis in that core group has a higher predictive power than knowing that a country in the same bilateral or third-party trade clusters. The improvement obtained in forecasting performance of controlling for financial sector links in our sample is greater than the improvement gained by controlling for trade links.

- Fourth, an analysis of two potential victims of contagion, Argentina after Mexico and Indonesia after Thailand, indicates that financial linkages were the more likely culprits, given that both bilateral and third party trade links with the infected country were weak. In the case of Indonesia, it was also part of the same Japanese commercial bank borrowing cluster as Thailand.

The paper is organized as follows. Section 2 briefly reviews the theories of contagion and takes stock of the existing empirical evidence on these issues. Section 3 assesses the incidence of contagion across regions and time, while Section 4 attempts to discriminate across the various channels of transmission. Section 5 discusses some of the recent contagious episodes and concludes.

2. Theory and evidence: a review

Models of contagion have attempted to provide a framework that explains why a shock in one country may be transmitted elsewhere. Our review of this literature emphasizes the empirical implications of these models.

2.1. Defining contagion

As noted, the definition of contagion has varied considerably across papers. Eichengreen et al. (1996) focused on contagion as a case where knowing that there is a crisis elsewhere increases the probability of a crisis at home. This is the definition of contagion that we will explore in the remainder of this paper. Specifically, we control for a broad range of country-idiosyncratic fundamentals

148   *G.L. Kaminsky, C.M. Reinhart / Journal of International Economics 51 (2000) 145–168*

(i.e. real exchange rate, reserves, etc.) and for fundamentals which are common across countries (i.e., international interest rates). What we are really interested in are the possible links, be it through trade or finance, that give rise to "fundamentals-based" spillovers. Hence, our analysis does not directly speak to the issue of "animal spirits" or herding behavior.

2.2. Theories of contagion and their empirical implications

To explain why crises tend to be bunched, some recent models have revived Nurkse's story of competitive devaluations, which emphasized trade, be it bilateral or with a third party.[2] Once one country has devalued, it makes it costly (in terms of a loss of competitiveness and output) for other countries to maintain their parity. Hence, an empirical implication of this type of model is that we should observe a high volume of trade among the "synchronized" devaluers.[3]

Another family of models has stressed the role of trade in financial assets, particularly in the presence of information asymmetries. Calvo and Mendoza (1998) present a model where the fixed costs of gathering and processing country-specific information give rise to herding behavior, even when investors are rational. Kodres and Pritsker (1999) focus on the role played by investors who engage in cross-market hedging of macroeconomic risks. In either case, these models suggest that the channels of transmission come from the global diversification of financial portfolios. As such, they have the empirical implication that countries which have more internationally-traded financial assets and more liquid markets are likely to be more vulnerable to contagion. Cross-market hedging usually requires a moderately high correlation of asset returns. The implication is that countries whose asset returns exhibit a high degree of comovement with the infected country (such as Argentina with Mexico or Malaysia with Thailand) will be more vulnerable to contagion via cross-market hedges.

Calvo (1998) has emphasized the role of liquidity. A leveraged investor facing margin calls needs to sell (to an uninformed counterpart) his or her asset holdings. Because of the information asymmetries, a "lemons problem" arises and the asset can only be sold at a firesale price. A variant of this story can be told about an open-end fund portfolio manager who needs to raise liquidity in anticipation of future redemptions. In either case, the strategy will be not to sell the asset whose price has already collapsed but other assets in the portfolio. In doing so, however, other asset prices are depressed and the original disturbance spreads across markets.

One potential channel of transmission that has been largely ignored in the contagion literature but that is stressed in this paper is the role of common lenders,

---

[2]See Gerlach and Smets (1994) and Corsetti et al. (1998).

[3]As a story of fundamentals-based contagion, of course, this explanation does not speak to the fact that central banks often go to great lengths to avoid the devaluation in the first place.

G.L. Kaminsky, C.M. Reinhart / Journal of International Economics 51 (2000) 145–168 149

in particular commercial banks. U.S. banks had an extensive exposure to Latin America in the early 1980s, much in the way that Japanese banks did during the Asian crisis of 1997.[4] The behavior of foreign banks can both exacerbate the original crisis, by calling loans and drying up credit lines, but can also propagate crises by calling loans elsewhere. The need to re-balance the overall risk of the bank's asset portfolio and to recapitalize and provision following the initial losses can lead to a marked reversal in bank credit across markets where the bank has exposure.

The bulk of the empirical literature suggests that there is evidence of contagion, be it of the fundamentals-based spillovers or of the animal spirit, sunspot variety. Very few studies, however, have aimed at examining the possible underlying causes. Eichengreen et al. (1996) attempted to discriminate among a bilateral trade link channel and a "wake-up call hypothesis," where similarities to the crisis country in fundamentals lead investors to reassess the risk of the other countries. Glick and Rose (1998) studied these issues further in a broader country context, while Wolf (1997) sought to explain the pairwise correlations in stock returns by bilateral trade and other common macroeconomic fundamentals. All studies conclude that trade linkages play an important role in the propagation of shocks. Because trade tends to be more intra- than inter-regional in nature, some of these studies conclude that this helps explain why contagion tends to be regional rather than global. With a couple of exceptions, financial sector linkages have been largely ignored (see Baig and Goldfajn, 1998; Frankel and Schmukler, 1998; Kaminsky and Schmukler, 1999).

3. The incidence of contagion

In this section we examine the links among currency crises both globally and regionally. To proceed, we need to identify the dates of currency crises, gauge the odds of a crisis in a country when other countries are in turmoil, and control for the relevant economic fundamentals. Our sample is based on monthly data for 1970–1998 and it includes 80 currency crises episodes for a number of industrial and developing countries. The former include: Denmark, Finland, Norway, Spain, and Sweden. The latter focus on: Argentina, Bolivia, Brazil, Chile, Colombia, Indonesia, Israel, Malaysia, Mexico, Peru, the Philippines, Thailand, Turkey, Uruguay, and Venezuela. An analysis of transition economies in the aftermath of Russia would have provided useful insights on contagion channels, but our methodology requires sufficiently long time series so as to allow us to distinguish between what is the "normal" behavior of an indicator during "tranquil" periods

---

[4]European banks had also increased their exposure to Asia in recent years.

150   *G.L. Kaminsky, C.M. Reinhart / Journal of International Economics 51 (2000) 145–168*

and "anomalous" behavior during crises periods. The transition economies offer little capacity to assess what is normal.[5]

3.1. Definition of crisis

Most often, speculative attacks have been resolved through a devaluation of the currency or its flotation. But central banks can and do use contractionary monetary policies and sell their foreign exchange reserves to defend the currency. High interest rate defenses were not uncommon in the wake of the Asian and Russian crises, while Argentina lost 20 percent of its foreign exchange reserves in a few weeks following the Mexican peso crisis of 1994. Thus an index of currency crises should capture these different manifestations of speculative attacks, be they successful or otherwise. However, in the 1970s and early 1980s many of the countries in our sample had regulated financial markets with no market-determined interest rates. For this reason, our crisis index only incorporates reserve losses and depreciation. The index is a weighted average of these two indicators with weights such that the two components have equal sample volatility. This weighting scheme prevents the much greater volatility in the exchange rate (owing to several episodes of mega-devaluations) to dominate the crisis measure.[6] Because changes in the exchange rate enter with a positive weight and reserves enter with a negative weight, large positive readings of this index indicate speculative attacks. Readings that are three standard deviations above its mean are classified as crises. Less extreme readings (say two standard deviations from the mean), which we do not examine here, would identify periods of turbulence. The crises readings from this index do map well onto the chronology of events (i.e. devaluations, suspension of convertibility, etc.) for these countries.

3.2. Contagion: preliminary assessment

To examine whether the likelihood of crises is higher when there are crises in other countries, we begin by calculating the unconditional probability of a crisis. The unconditional probability that a crisis will occur in the next 24 months over the entire sample is simply the number of currency crises in the sample times 24 divided by the number of observations. As shown in Table 1, under the heading $P(C)$, these calculations yield an unconditional probability of 29 percent. We next calculate a family of conditional probabilities. If knowing that there is a currency crisis elsewhere helps predict a currency crisis at home, then, the probability of a

---

[5]Problems with limited data availability, particularly for financial indicators, precluded us from including countries in Sub-Saharan Africa. A full description of the data set is presented in Kaminsky and Reinhart (1999).

[6]See Kaminsky and Reinhart (1999) for details.

G.L. Kaminsky, C.M. Reinhart / Journal of International Economics 51 (2000) 145–168   151

Table 1
The incidence of global contagion: currency crises, 1970–1998

Proportion of other sample countries with crises (in percent)	Noise-to-signal ratio, N/S	Unconditional probability of a crisis	Probability of a crisis conditioned on crises elsewhere, $P(C\|CE)$	Difference between conditional and unconditional probability of a crisis, $P(C\|CE) - P(C)$
0–25	1.23	29.0	20.0	−9.0
25–50	0.64	29.0	33.0	4.0
50 and above	0.26	29.0	54.7	25.7
Memorandum items:				
Real exchange rate[a]	0.10	29.0	67.0	38.0
Imports	1.10	29.0	26.0	−3.0

[a] The real exchange rate is used as a comparison as it provides the best performance among the univariate indicators considered in Kaminsky and Reinhart (1999) and Kaminsky (1998). By contrast, imports were among the indicators which fared among the worst.

currency crisis, conditional on that information, denoted by $P(C|CE)$, should be higher than the unconditional one. The table also reports the noise-to-signal ratio for the various groupings.[7] The lower the noise-to-signal ratio, the more reliable is the indicator.

First, as regards the results presented in Table 1, at least at the global level, knowing that there is a single crisis elsewhere is not a particularly helpful piece of information for predicting a future crisis. This contrasts with the results presented in Eichengreen et al. (1996), who find stronger evidence of the predictive capacity of a crisis elsewhere variable. We suspect, however, that their results are influenced by the heavy representation of European countries in their sample. As we will discuss below, the pattern of contagion seems to be more regional than global in scope and the predictive ability of knowing that there is a crisis elsewhere depends importantly on where elsewhere happens to be. However, if one-half or more of the countries in the sample are having currency crises, this increases the likelihood of a crisis to 55 percent, or almost double the unconditional probability of crisis of 29 percent. Indeed, this result is similar to those found in some of the empirical papers on bank contagion. When the problem becomes that systemic, the chances of escaping unscathed are slim. Thus, it appears that the relationship between the probability of a crisis at home and the number of crises elsewhere is highly nonlinear.

We also examined these probabilities at the regional level (Table 2). There are three groups: Asia, which includes Indonesia, Malaysia, the Philippines, and Thailand; Europe, which encompasses the four Nordic countries in our sample

[7]For a detailed discussion of the construction of the adjusted noise-to-signal ratio see Kaminsky and Reinhart (1999).

152 *G.L. Kaminsky, C.M. Reinhart / Journal of International Economics 51 (2000) 145–168*

Table 2
The incidence and evolution of regional contagion: Asia, Europe and Latin America

Proportion of other sample countries in the region with crises (in percent)	Full sample: 1970 to 1998								
	Asia			Europe			Latin America		
	N/S	P(C)	P(C|CE)	N/S	P(C)	P(C|CE)	N/S	P(C)	P(C|CE)
0–25	1.37	26.8	19.8	1.37	28.6	14.7	1.29	29.4	18.3
25–50	1.30	26.8	15.3	0.58	28.6	32.3	0.77	29.4	30.8
50 and above	0.03	26.8	67.4	0.51	28.6	35.0	0.16	29.4	68.6

plus Israel, Turkey and Spain: and Latin America, which consists of Argentina, Bolivia, Brazil, Colombia, Chile, Mexico, Peru, Uruguay, and Venezuela. In all three regions the probability of crisis conditioned on crisis elsewhere increases sharply as the number of casualties rise. When the proportion of infected countries increases over the 50 percent hurdle, the conditional probability of crisis increases from about 27 percent to 67 percent in Asia; in Latin America it increases from 29 to 69 percent if half or more of the countries are in crisis.

3.3. Macroeconomic fundamentals

Naturally, an epidemic may arise when multiple individuals are exposed to a common virus. The global analogy to the common virus can be found in international interest rate fluctuations, which have had much to do in explaining the cycles in capital flows to emerging markets.[8] Since, in turn, abrupt swings in capital flows have done much to trigger currency crises we need to control for such common fundamentals as well as those that are country specific. The approach taken here follows the "signals" approach described in detail in Kaminsky and Reinhart (1999) and the construction of a composite leading indicator of currency crises outlined in Kaminsky (1998). A brief sketch of this methodology follows and the interested reader is referred to those papers for greater detail.

We begin by constructing a composite index that captures the fragility of the economy on the eve of crises. The index summarizes the behavior of 18 individual financial and macroeconomic time series. Each indicator may issue one or more

[8]See Calvo and Reinhart (1996).

G.L. Kaminsky, C.M. Reinhart / Journal of International Economics 51 (2000) 145–168   153

signals or warnings in the 24 months preceding the crisis.[9] For example, there may be an unusually sharp decline in foreign exchange reserves or in stock prices. If a signal is issued, it is assigned a value of one. Hence, if all 18 indicators issued a signal on a given month the value of the composite indicator would be 18 if all signals are weighted equally. However, as shown in earlier papers, the quality of the indicators is highly heterogenous.[10] For this reason, we weigh each signal by the inverse of the noise-to-signal ratio of the particular indicator that is issuing the signal. We can then construct a sample-based vector of conditional probabilities for currency crises. One set of probabilities will control for the macroeconomic fundamentals, denoted by $P(C|F)_t$, another set of probabilities will control for both the fundamentals and information about crises elsewhere, $P(C|F, CE)_t$, and a third, which we call the "naive" forecast controls for neither – hence, it is the simple unconditional probability of crisis. To assess the marginal contribution of knowing whether and how many crises are elsewhere we conduct a horserace between the naive forecasts, those that take into account the fundamentals, and those that also add information on crises elsewhere. To evaluate the average closeness of the predicted probabilities of crises and the actual realizations, as measured by a zero-one dummy variable, we calculate the quadratic probability score (QPS),

$$QPS^k = 1/T \sum_{t=1}^{T} 2(P_t^k - R_t)^2 \qquad (1)$$

where $k = 1, 2, 3$ refers to the indicator; P_t^k, refers to the probability associated with that indicator and R_t are the zero-one realizations. The QPS ranges from zero to two, with a score of zero corresponding to perfect accuracy. Table 3 reports the scores, for the naive forecasts, the forecasts on the basis of the macroeconomic fundamentals and the forecasts that also take into account information about crises elsewhere. The scores are given for the entire sample, as well as the regional

---

[9]Hence, we have the following two by two matrix,

	Crisis occurs in the following 24 months	No crisis occurs in the following 24 months
A signal is issued	A	B
No signal is issued	C	D

A "perfect" indicator would only have entries in cells A and D and a noise-to-signal ratio (calculated as [B/(B+D)/A(A+C)]) of zero.

[10]The noise-to-signals ratios for the indicators are given in Kaminsky and Reinhart (1999).

154   *G.L. Kaminsky, C.M. Reinhart / Journal of International Economics 51 (2000) 145–168*

Table 3
Contagion and the fundamentals: the quadratic probability scores 1970–1998

	Naive	Contagion	Fundamentals	Fundamentals and Contagion	Difference between columns (4) and (3) (in percent)
	(1)	(2)	(3)	(4)	
Full Sample	0.386	0.350	0.313	0.308	1.6
Asia	0.285	0.239	0.301	0.213	29.2
Europe	0.378	0.325	0.316	0.297	6.0
Latin America	0.380	0.334	0.304	0.289	4.9

groups. The main result that arises from this exercise is that adding information about crisis elsewhere reduces the prediction error, even after the fundamentals have been accounted for. The gains from incorporating information on crises elsewhere are highest for Asia (a 29 percent improvement in forecasting accuracy, shown in the last column). For Latin America and Europe, the gains are more modest and in the 5–6 percent range.

4. On the channels of transmission

We next turn our attention toward investigating what some of the international propagation mechanisms may be. Specifically, we consider four channels through which shocks can be transmitted across borders; two channels deal with the linkages among financial markets, be it through foreign bank lending or globally diversified portfolios, and two deal with trade in goods and services.

4.1. Common bank creditor

As discussed in Section 2, the studies that have attempted to analyze the channels through which contagion arises have found a prominent role for linkages on the basis of trade in goods and services. However, this line of enquiry does not speak to the fact that countries that engage in trade in goods and services typically also have strong connections through financial arrangements that facilitate trade – particularly through commercial banks. Just as there appears to be natural regional trade blocs, so there appear to be regional blocs that depend on a single common creditor country. This may help explain cross-border spillovers, since if a bank is confronted with a marked rise in nonperforming loans in one country, it is likely to be called upon to reduce the overall risk of its assets by pulling out of other high risk projects elsewhere – possibly in other emerging markets. Furthermore, it will lend less (if at all), as it is forced to recapitalize, provision, and adjust to its lower level of wealth.

Tables 4 and 5 present evidence on the incidence of regional borrowing arrangements from both the perspective of the borrower as well as the perspective

G.L. Kaminsky, C.M. Reinhart / Journal of International Economics 51 (2000) 145–168   155

Table 4
Banks: liabilities as a percent of borrower's total liabilities on the eve of the Mexican and Asian crises[a]

Borrower:	Liabilities to Japan		Liabilities to the United States	
	as of June 1994	as of December 1996	as of June 1994	as of December 1996
Asia average	37.2	30.1	12.8	12.2
China	39.5	32.3	1.9	4.9
Indonesia	54.0	39.7	7.7	9.5
Korea	29.4	24.3	10.0	9.4
Malaysia	40.2	36.9	11.3	10.5
Philippines	17.2	11.7	39.4	29.4
Thailand	56.8	53.5	7.1	7.2
Latin America average	7.1	5.2	28.8	26.3
Argentina	5.3	4.0	31.2	29.5
Brazil	10.6	7.6	22.7	27.1
Chile	8.8	5.2	31.2	27.9
Colombia	13.0	7.8	26.6	24.6
Mexico	7.3	8.7	34.2	28.4
Peru	7.5	2.9	15.9	17.4
Uruguay	0.7	0.8	35.2	30.2
Venezuela	3.7	4.2	33.3	25.6

[a] Sources: Bank of International Settlements, *The Maturity, Sectoral, and Nationality Distribution of International Bank Lending* and United States Treasury, *Treasury Bulletin*.

of the lender for Asia and Latin America. On the eve of the Thai crisis, 54 percent of Thai liabilities were to Japanese banks. Most of the other countries in the region, with the exception of the Philippines which has fared well by comparison, also depended heavily on Japanese commercial bank lending. From the perspective of the Japanese banks, Thai exposure was also not trivial. It accounted for the highest share of claims on emerging markets (22 percent) and more than twice that of China. As the Thai crisis unraveled, taking advantage of the short-term nature of their credits, Japanese banks began to call loans – not just in Thailand but all over the region. Commercial bank credit to the five affected countries (Indonesia, Korea, Malaysia, the Philippines, and Thailand) shifted from an inflow of over \$50 billion in 1996 to an outflow of \$21 billion in the following year. A regional liquidity crunch got under way.

While it is tempting to conclude that such transmission mechanisms are new to the global economy, they have been with us for some time. Mexico's share of U.S. claims on total claims on emerging markets was also the highest among emerging markets in 1982 and, like its Thai counterparts, it was also 22 percent (Table 5). Also like the Asian cluster, Latin American countries obtain their lion's share of their commercial bank credit from U.S. banks and like in the Asian crises, U.S. banks pulled out from Latin America at the time of the debt crisis.

156   *G.L. Kaminsky, C.M. Reinhart / Journal of International Economics 51 (2000) 145–168*

Table 5
Banks: liabilities as a percent of lender's total liabilities on the eve of the Debt, Tequila, and Asian Flu crises[a,b]

Borrower:	Liabilities to Japan		Liabilities to the United States		
	as of June 1994	as of December 1996	as of June 1982	as of June 1994	as of December 1996
Asia sub-total	53.6	67.3	10.1	18.1	24.4
China	9.7	10.3	0.1	0.7	2.1
Indonesia	11.7	13.0	0.2	2.6	4.1
Korea	9.9	14.3	5.4	5.2	7.2
Malaysia	3.9	4.8	0.2	1.7	1.8
Philippines	0.7	0.9	2.0	2.6	3.0
Thailand	14.6	22.1	0.4	2.8	3.9
Latin America sub-total	7.1	5.8	61.5	58.8	48.6
Argentina	1.2	1.1	8.4	10.6	10.2
Brazil	3.9	3.0	16.1	13.0	14.2
Chile	0.6	0.5	4.0	3.6	3.3
Colombia	0.8	0.8	1.9	2.5	3.2
Mexico	3.0	3.2	22.2	21.8	13.4
Peru	0.2	0.1	1.6	0.5	1.1
Uruguay	0.0	0.0	0.3	1.3	1.0
Venezuela	0.4	0.3	7.0	5.5	2.2

[a] Sources: Bank of International Settlements, *The Maturity, Sectoral, and Nationality Distribution of International Bank Lending* and United States Treasury, *Treasury Bulletin.*
[b] Notes: Lender's total claims represent the total claims on developing countries, excluding other BIS countries and offshore banking centers.

To step beyond the anecdotal evidence and systematically investigate whether common creditors (banks) are a possible channel of contagion, we clustered a subset of the countries in our sample into two groups – that group which borrows mostly from U.S. banks and that group which relies heavily on Japanese commercial bank lending. We could not identify a common European bank cluster in our sample. The first group encompasses most (but not all) of the Latin American countries in our sample and includes: Argentina, Brazil, Chile, Colombia, Mexico, Uruguay, and Venezuela. Bolivia and Peru were excluded as they have more heterogeneous sources of international bank credit. The Philippines, which has an exposure to U.S. banks that is about three times the average for Asia and comparable to many of the Latin American countries, is also included in this cluster. The Japanese bank cluster thus comprises of Indonesia, Malaysia, and Thailand. Had China and Korea been part of our sample, these would have been included in the Japanese bank cluster, as these countries relied on Japanese bank credit (Table 4).

Table 6 reports the results for the joint estimation of conditional and unconditional probabilities for the two banks clusters. We estimate these jointly as

G.L. Kaminsky, C.M. Reinhart / Journal of International Economics 51 (2000) 145–168   157

Table 6
Contagion and banking clusters[a]

Proportion of other sample countries in the region with crises (in percent)	Bank Clusters				
	N/S	P(C)	P(C|CE)	P(C|CE) − P(C)	[P(C|CE) − P(C)]/P(C)
0–25	1.507	31.5	19.2	−12.3	−39.0
25–50	0.903	31.5	28.4	−3.1	−0.9
50 and above	0.071	31.5	83.5	52.0	165.0

Quadratic Probability Scores					
	Naive	Contagion	Fundamentals	Fundamentals and Contagion	Difference between columns (4) and (3) and standard error[b]
	(1)	(2)	(3)	(4)	(5)
Score	0.394	0.291	0.304	0.245	−0.059* (0.017)

[a] Notes: An asterisk denotes significance at standard confidence levels. The Japanese bank cluster includes Indonesia, Malaysia, and Thailand. United States bank cluster includes Argentina, Brazil, Chile, Colombia, Mexico, the Philippines, Uruguay, and Venezuela.
[b] The standard error was estimated with robust methods.

disaggregation among the two clusters can be subject to small sample problems, in that the number of crises in the sub-sample is relatively small. The marginal contribution of knowing that a country in that cohort has a crisis does not add much information when there are few crises. However, once several countries in the cohort become infected, the conditional probability of a crisis jumps to 83.5 percent, well above the comparable conditional probability of 54.7 percent for a crisis elsewhere reported in Table 1 and the unconditional probability of 31.5 percent for the bank clusters.[11] These results suggest that perhaps much of what has been attributed to trade has to do with financial sector linkages. Furthermore, the QPS scores for forecasts that include information on both fundamentals and crises elsewhere in the bank cluster are significantly lower at all standard confidence levels than those that do not control for crises in the cluster (Table 6, column 5).

4.2. Liquidity channels, mutual funds, and cross-market hedging

While banks are important common lenders, they are not the only lenders to the emerging world. Portfolio flows to emerging markets surged in the early-to-mid-1990s. Hence, just as a commercial bank may call its loans to Malaysia after

---

[11] The crisis elsewhere criteria does not distinguish between being in a particular cohort or outside it.

158   *G.L. Kaminsky, C.M. Reinhart / Journal of International Economics 51 (2000) 145–168*

Thailand has a crisis, so can a diversified investor choose (or be forced by margin calls) to sell his or her Argentinean bond and equity holdings after Mexico devalues. Some of the models that stress this form of contagion were discussed in Section 2. In order to be of any consequence, however, this channel of transmission requires that there be sufficient asset market liquidity. If bond and equity markets are so underdeveloped that portfolio flows are trivial, then clearly this channel of transmission is not likely to be quantitatively important. In other words, if country's equity or bonds are not internationally traded to begin with, such liquidations are not a problem.

Table 7 provides a profile of emerging market mutual fund holdings on the eve of the Asian crisis. It is clear that there is a wide diversity of representation across markets, with Hong Kong, Brazil, and Mexico (in that order) being among the most highly represented (and also the most liquid) markets. It is noteworthy that two Latin American countries that did not even experience as much as a mild

Table 7
Emerging market mutual fund holdings[a]

Country	Major country holdings June 30, 1997	
	US$ billions	Percent
Total Asia	85.04	55.55
Bangladesh	0.03	0.02
China	3.74	2.44
Hong Kong	23.46	15.33
India	8.98	5.87
Indonesia	6.66	4.35
Korea	9.43	6.16
Malaysia	9.01	5.88
Pakistan	0.71	0.46
Philippines	3.68	2.40
Singapore	5.03	3.29
Sri Lanka	0.21	0.14
Taiwan	10.00	6.53
Thailand	4.11	2.68
Total Latin America	44.02	28.75
Argentina	4.56	2.98
Brazil	20.01	13.07
Chile	4.36	2.85
Colombia	0.81	0.53
Mexico	11.76	7.68
Peru	1.33	0.87
Venezuela	1.19	0.78

[a] Notes: The figures cover all dedicated emerging market funds – both regional and single country – that are registered or listed in a developed market (excluding the emerging market funds that are registered and traded in the emerging markets themselves).

G.L. Kaminsky, C.M. Reinhart / Journal of International Economics 51 (2000) 145–168   159

hiccup in their equity markets around the Mexican crisis are Colombia and
Venezuela (see Calvo and Reinhart, 1996), which are barely represented in the
mutual fund portfolios.

While there is broad variation across markets in the extent to which they are
represented in global investor's portfolios, there is also quite a degree of diversity
in the extent that asset price returns correlate across countries. Table 8, which
shows the pairwise correlations of stock returns (in US dollars) across selected
markets, provides evidence in this regard. For the sake of simplicity, we will
classify a pairwise correlation of 0–0.20 as low, 0.21–0.40 as moderate, and above
0.40 as high. Using these three grids it is easy to see that the highest correlations
among returns occur among the southeast Asian economies now mired in crises,
Indonesia, Malaysia. Philippines, and Thailand. It is also evident that high
intra-regional pairwise correlations are rare and that the highest correlation in
Latin America is between Argentine and Mexican stock returns.

Hence, on the basis of liquidity and correlation considerations, one would
expect a higher degree of cross-market hedging across the four southeast Asian
countries (although they are only moderately liquid) and among Argentina, Brazil,
Peru, and Mexico (two of which are comparatively liquid) and all four are
correlated. Yet, formally investigating this possible channel of interconnectedness
is fraught with difficulty. First, unlike the prevalence of bank lending, these
transmission channels are relatively recent, as emerging market funds and portfolio
flows to these countries were virtually nonexistent prior to the 1990s. Secondly,
there may be marked swings in the liquidity of these markets, as sovereign debt
can cease to be considered a liquid asset overnight.

With these shortcomings in mind, and taking the results as tentative, we formed
two clusters of countries that exhibited a high degree of comovement in their asset
returns. The first cluster includes the four southeast Asian economies in our
sample. South Korea, had it been part of our sample, would have excluded from
this cluster on the basis of its low historical correlations with the East Asia four.
For Latin America the high correlation cluster includes Argentina, Mexico, and
Peru. Needless to say, a shortcoming of these clusters is that they are based
entirely on recent correlations and give no weight to the role of market liquidity.
The joint conditional and unconditional probabilities for the high-correlation
groupings are reported in Table 9. In terms of the comparison between conditional
and unconditional probabilities, the conditional probability of this cluster at 80.4
percent (for the 50 percent and above category) is well above the unconditional
probability, although the improvement is not as substantial as that obtained from
the bank cluster. However, the QPS scores paint a very compelling picture – the
QPS scores that control for crises elsewhere in the cluster are significantly higher
than those that just control for fundamentals. Furthermore, the improvement in
forecasting accuracy is bigger than that obtained with the bank clusters. However,
it is important to be cautious about over-interpreting these results as the incidence
of portfolio flows and the widespread use of cross-market hedges has a much

160   G.L. Kaminsky, C.M. Reinhart / Journal of International Economics 51 (2000) 145–168

Table 8
Daily stock price index correlations: December 1991 to December 1996 (US dollars)[a]

Country	Arg.	Bra.	Chi.	Col.	Ind.	Kor.	Mal.	Mex.	Per.	Phi.	Rus.	Tha.	Tur.	Ven.
Argentina	1.00													
Brazil	0.37	1.00												
Chile	0.38	0.24	1.00											
Colombia	-0.01	0.15	0.02	1.00										
Indonesia	0.38	0.28	0.39	0.20	1.00									
Korea	0.09	0.00	0.20	0.13	0.10	1.00								
Malaysia	0.17	-0.09	0.12	0.02	0.50	0.20	1.00							
Mexico	0.56	0.36	0.34	-0.10	0.32	0.29	0.28	1.00						
Peru	0.44	0.40	0.45	0.21	0.22	0.32	0.14	0.53	1.00					
Philippines	0.35	0.05	0.25	0.24	0.63	0.09	0.61	0.30	0.29	1.00				
Russia	0.15	0.10	0.49	-0.14	-0.19	-0.19	-0.14	0.10	0.30	0.26	1.00			
Thailand	0.25	0.01	0.37	0.05	0.54	0.24	0.60	0.30	0.24	0.68	0.02	1.00		
Turkey	0.02	0.11	-0.07	-0.05	0.27	0.11	0.18	-0.04	-0.04	0.18	-0.39	0.14	1.00	
Venezuela	0.24	0.16	0.01	0.24	0.18	0.16	0.12	-0.06	0.012	0.32	0.22	0.09	-0.08	1.00

[a] Source: International Finance Corporation, *Emerging Stock Markets Factbook 1997.*

G.L. Kaminsky, C.M. Reinhart / Journal of International Economics 51 (2000) 145–168   161

Table 9
Contagion and high correlation clusters[a]

Proportion of other sample countries in the region with crises (in percent)	High correlation cluster				
	N/S	P(C)	P(C|CE)	P(C|CE) − P(C)	[P(C|CE) − P(C)]/P(C)
0–25	5.100	33.3	5.5	−27.8	−83.5
25–50	0.577	33.3	54.1	20.8	62.5
50 and above	0.389	33.3	80.4	47.1	141.4

Quadratic Probability Scores

	Naive	Contagion	Fundamentals	Fundamentals and Contagion	Difference between columns (4) and (3) and standard error[b]
	(1)	(2)	(3)	(4)	(5)
Score	0.381	0.186	0.343	0.158	−0.185* (0.014)

[a] Notes: An asterisk denotes significance at standard confidence levels. The Asian high correlation cluster includes Indonesia, Malaysia, the Philippines and Thailand. The Latin American cluster includes Argentina, Brazil, and Peru.
[b] The standard error was estimated with robust methods.

shorter history than bank lending in this sample and it is a phenomenon of the 1990s.

4.3. Trade links

Perhaps because trade in goods and services has a longer history in the post World War II period than trade in financial assets, or because of far better data availability, trade links have received the most attention in the literature on contagion. In this subsection we examine two types of trade links. The most obvious is bilateral trade among other countries and the infected country(ies). The second type of link is more difficult to quantify, which involves competition in a common third market. For the countries in Asia and Latin America in our sample, identifying a common third party is not a difficult task. The United States figures prominently in trade with Latin America (not unlike the bank credit clusters) and Japan figures prominently in Asian trade. However, all five crisis countries in Asia in 1997 also export extensively to Hong Kong and Singapore. While sharing a third party is a necessary condition for the competitive devaluation story it is clearly not a sufficient one. If a country that exports bananas to the United States devalues it is not obvious why this would have any detrimental effect on a country that exports semiconductors to the United States. Hence, clearly the composition of trade will play a key role in determining whether the third party trade links carry any weight. Previous studies that have examined the trade links have not addressed this issue altogether.

Tables 10 and 11 convey information about the extent of bilateral trade and third party trade on the eve of three crises episodes, the debt crisis, the Mexican peso crisis of 1994, and the Asian crisis of 1997. There are several features worth noting. As regards the most recent crises, it is hard to see bilateral trade as the force behind contagion. The share of exports that is destined to other Asian crises countries (including Korea) is not very large. For instance, Malaysia's exports to Indonesia, Korea, the Philippines, and Thailand combined only amount to 9 percent of its exports. For this reason we do not identify an Asian bilateral trade cluster. Understanding why Brazil and Mexico have been so adversely affected in the aftermath of the Asian flu is even harder as, on average only 2.3 percent of Latin American exports go to the Asian five. The most compelling case for bilateral trade links between the Asian crises countries and Latin America is

Table 10
Asia and Latin America inter- and intra-regional trade: exports to Asia[a]

Country	Exports to the rest of Emerging Asia[b]			Exports to the rest of Emerging Asia and China, Hong Kong, Japan, and Singapore		
	1982	1995	1997	1982	1995	1997
Asia Average	6.8	9.0	9.6	48.8	54.7	54.7
Indonesia	4.4	12.2	12.8	69.7	56.6	55.7
Korea	4.1	7.8	9.7	30.0	48.7	49.6
Malaysia	8.1	9.0	9.9	61.1	56.8	59.3
Philippines	8.0	9.8	7.7	40.2	41.7	40.9
Thailand	9.4	6.3	8.0	41.9	52.6	52.7

	Exports to Emerging Asia			Exports to Emerging Asia and China, Hong Kong, Japan, and Singapore		
	1982	1995	1997	1982	1995	1997
Latin America Average	1.2	2.3	2.0	9.0	10.5	8.7
Argentina	0.6	2.8	3.3	7.4	13.4	13.2
Brazil	1.8	4.6	3.8	10.7	17.5	14.4
Chile	1.4	8.3	9.9	16.1	33.7	37.5
Colombia	0.2	0.6	0.3	4.6	6.0	3.6
Mexico	1.4	0.2	0.1	8.8	2.4	2.0
Peru	3.2	5.8	4.1	21.1	26.0	23.6
Uruguay	0.2	1.4	1.4	3.4	11.7	10.1
Venezuela	0.3	0.1	0.1	5.1	2.7	1.9

[a] Source: International Monetary Fund, *Direction of Trade Statistics*.
[b] Other Emerging Asia includes those countries listed in the table.

G.L. Kaminsky, C.M. Reinhart / Journal of International Economics 51 (2000) 145–168   163

Table 11
Asia and Latin America inter- and intra-regional trade: exports to Latin America[a]

Country	Exports to Latin America			Exports to Latin America and the United States		
	1982	1995	1997	1982	1995	1997
Asia Average	2.4	2.4	2.5	20.7	21.8	21.7
Indonesia	4.2	1.4	1.1	20.0	18.1	17.5
Korea	3.1	4.7	4.7	31.9	24.0	21.0
Malaysia	0.3	1.6	1.5	12.0	22.3	19.8
Philippines	0.9	1.0	2.4	32.5	36.9	37.1
Thailand	0.2	1.0	0.9	12.9	18.7	20.6

	Exports to the rest of Latin America			Exports to the rest of Latin America and the United States		
	1982	1995	1997	1982	1995	1997
Latin America Average	19.8	18.9	20.4	50.2	66.1	71.3
Argentina	20.4	40.9	49.3	33.8	49.9	57.1
Brazil	15.6	23.0	27.7	36.1	41.9	45.4
Chile	19.4	19.2	16.8	41.0	33.1	32.5
Colombia	21.7	29.7	28.4	45.0	63.8	66.6
Mexico	8.8	5.6	6.0	61.2	89.9	91.6
Peru	11.0	17.1	18.2	42.0	34.4	44.4
Uruguay	30.5	53.3	56.0	38.3	59.3	62.0
Venezuela	39.5	33.6	33.8	66.3	82.8	85.4

[a] Source: International Monetary Fund, *Direction of Trade Statistics*.

clearly Chile, whose exports to Asia have been rising over time. Similarly, on the eve of the Tequila crisis only 1.7 percent of Argentine exports were destined for Mexico.[12] Yet clearly, important bilateral trade links are revealed in Tables 10 and 11. Most noticeable is the high level of bilateral trade among the Mercosur members (Argentina, Brazil, and Uruguay) and also Chile. Hence, a devaluation of the real would be expected to have important consequences for Argentina and Uruguay by way of trade – although it is important to remember that Argentina and Brazil are still relatively closed economies, with ratios of trade as a percent of GDP far below those recorded in the Asian and European countries in our sample.

The case for third-party trade links is much more compelling for some of the Asian countries. Table 12 shows that Malaysia and Korea, in particular, export many of the same goods to the same third parties. This leaves Indonesia largely unexplained. Third party trade also does not appear to account for the Tequila effects on Argentina and Brazil, whose exports have little in common with Mexican exports (see Table 13).

---

[12]These bilateral trade statistics are not reported in the tables but are available from the authors.

164   *G.L. Kaminsky, C.M. Reinhart / Journal of International Economics 51 (2000) 145–168*

Table 12
Composition of exports: Asian exports of top Thai exports (percent of exports, 1996)[a]

Description	Thailand	Korea	Indonesia	Malaysia	Philippines
Radio/amplifier parts	4.8	3.8	2.0	7.3	2.5
Semiconductors	5.3	15.4	0.3	18.0	9.1
Footwear	3.7	1.0	4.3	0.1	0.9
Calculation machines	4.6	0.7	0.5	6.6	1.0
Electric switches, relays, etc.	1.7	1.1	0.4	1.9	0.8
Computers and accessories	5.1	3.2	0.4	2.9	1.5
Jewelry	1.7	0.3	0.7	0.6	0.2
Televisions	1.7	1.5	0.1	3.0	0.4
Refrigerators	1.5	0.4	0.1	1.4	0.0
Shellfish	4.3	0.3	2.3	0.2	1.7
Rubber	4.4	0.0	4.2	2.2	0.2
Fish	1.4	0.2	0.2	0.1	0.7
Rice	3.4	0.0	0.0	0.0	0.0
Total	44.3	27.9	15.4	44.4	18.8

[a] Source: Statistics Canada, World Trade Database.

To examine these issues more formally, we constructed three trade clusters, a Latin American bilateral trade cluster which consists of the Mercosur members and Chile; a third-party Asian group, which does not include Indonesia as its structure of exports is very distinct from the others and; a third-party Latin group which includes Brazil, Colombia, Mexico, and Venezuela. These four countries

Table 13
The composition of exports: Argentinean and Brazilian exports of Mexico's top exports (percent of total exports, 1994)[a]

Description	Mexico	Argentina	Brazil
Oil	10.8	7.1	0.0
Automobiles	8.6	1.2	1.2
Insulated electric wire	4.8	0.1	0.1
Televisions	4.3	0.1	0.0
Engine parts	3.8	0.9	2.0
Automobile parts	3.4	2.6	2.9
Radio/amplifier parts	3.2	0.1	0.1
Electric switches, relays, etc.	3.2	1.3	0.3
Other electric machinery	2.7	0.0	0.1
Computers	2.0	0.3	0.2
Transportation vehicles	1.6	1.7	2.0
Semi conductors	1.5	0.0	0.2
Radios	1.5	0.1	0.7
Furniture	1.4	0.1	0.7
Electric power machinery	1.3	0.0	0.3
Total	54.1	15.6	10.9

[a] Source: Statistics Canada, World Trade Database.

G.L. Kaminsky, C.M. Reinhart / Journal of International Economics 51 (2000) 145–168   165

Table 14
Contagion and trade clusters[a]

Proportion of other sample countries in the region with crises (in percent)	Third party trade clusters					Latin American high bilateral trade cluster				
	N/S	P(C)	P(C|CE)	P(C|CE) − P(C)	[P(C|CE) − P(C)]/P(C)	N/S	P(C)	P(C|CE)	P(C|CE) − P(C)	[P(C|CE) − P(C)]/P(C)
0–25	1.51	27.6	21.8	−5.8	−21.0	0.53	37.4	29.3	−8.1	−21.4
25–50	1.54	27.6	21.3	−6.3	−22.8	2.34	37.4	15.6	−21.8	−58.3
50 and above	0.57	27.6	58.3	30.7	111.2	0.08	37.4	84.7	47.3	126.0

Quadratic Probability Scores	Naive	Contagion	Fundamentals	Fundamentals and Contagion	Difference between columns (4) and (3) and standard error[b]
	(1)	(2)	(3)	(4)	(5)
Score Third Party Trade	0.375	0.354	0.312	0.283	−0.029 (0.018)
Score Latin America bilateral trade	0.433	0.377	0.345	0.314	−0.031 (0.017)

[a] Notes: The Asian third party cluster includes Malaysia, the Philippines and Thailand. The Latin American third party cluster includes Brazil, Colombia, Mexico and Venezuela; the bilateral trade cluster includes the Mercosur countries plus Chile. Since there is little bilateral trade among the five affected countries no bilateral cluster is reported.
[b] The standard error was estimated with robust methods.

have the largest share of bilateral trade with the United States and some similarities in the structure of their exports. For instance coffee plays a prominent role in both Colombian and Brazilian exports while oil plays a similar role for Mexico and Venezuela and, to a lesser extent, Colombia. As with the bank and correlation clusters, we jointly estimate the conditional and unconditional probabilities for the third-party trade Asian and Latin American clusters. For bilateral trade, only the results for Latin America are reported, given that no Asian bilateral trade cluster was identified.

The results are reported in Table 14. The strongest results are those for the Latin American bilateral trade cluster, where the difference between the conditional and unconditional probability is 47.3 percent, which compares favorably with the results reported in Table 1, which are on the basis of crisis elsewhere and do not control for how elsewhere is defined. However, the third-party (and the bilateral) trade clusters do not compare favorably to the two financial linkages clusters results reported in Tables 6 and 9. Also, while the QPS scores decline when we control for crises elsewhere in the trade cluster, these improvements are not statistically significant when compared to the scores of the forecasts that control only for fundamentals. Hence, by these criteria, both types of trade clusters underperform the financial sector links previously discussed.

5. Recent episodes and conclusions

To sum up, our analysis suggests that susceptibility to contagion is highly nonlinear. Furthermore, when the number of crises in a given cluster is high, financial sector links via common bank lenders are a powerful channel of fundamentals-based contagion; the difference between the conditional and unconditional probability, $P(C|CE) - P(C)$, for the bank cluster is the highest at 52 percent (a 165 percent increase). This performance is followed by the high-correlation cluster $[P(C|CE) - P(C) = 47.1$, which represents a 141 percent increase], bilateral links $[P(C|CE) - P(C) = 47.3$, which is a 126 percent increase], and a less impressive performance by the third-part trade cluster $[P(C|CE) - P(C) = 30.7]$, which is only somewhat higher than the global crisis elsewhere results $[P(C|CE) - P(C) = 25.7]$. Besides these ordinal rankings, the QPS scores indicate an improvement in forecasting accuracy for all clusters; however, only in the case of the bank cluster and the high-correlation cluster are these improvements statistically significant at standard confidence levels. In the remainder of this final section we next turn our attention to two recent "contagious" episodes, the aftermath of the Mexican peso crisis and the floatation of the Thai baht. The aim is to assess through which channels these crises spread. We discuss both trade and financial links.

As regards the potential role of bilateral and third party trade linkages in these recent episodes, Malaysia would be the most closely linked with Thailand, with

G.L. Kaminsky, C.M. Reinhart / Journal of International Economics 51 (2000) 145–168   167

Korea and the Philippines having more moderate exposure. Trade can certainly not help explain Argentina and Brazil following the Mexican devaluation nor Indonesia following the Thai crisis. Exposure to Japanese banks, which pulled out rapidly across the region was common to all the affected countries except Hong Kong. While both Brazil and Argentina are in the same U.S. bank cluster as Mexico, banks were not at the heart of the problem in 1994 as they were in the early 1980s.

Most of the affected Asian countries, except Korea had high asset return correlations with Thailand, although none except Hong Kong had particularly liquid markets. The same is true of stock returns in Argentina, which have the highest correlation with Mexico of any country in the region. Here it is hard to separate cause and effect. A high correlation may reflect past contagion, but to the extent that current cross-hedging strategies use such historical correlations as a guide, it could be the vehicle for future contagion. In sum, it would appear that financial sector linkages, be it through banks of through international capital markets have much to say in how shocks are propagated in recent crises episodes, particularly for Argentina, Brazil, and Indonesia.

We have examined the incidence of contagion and some of the channels through which fundamentals-based contagion can arise. Some of the arrangements that have linked countries together are quite old – trade in goods and services and strong ties through a common bank lender – and can help shed light on earlier crises clusters, like the debt crisis of the early 1980s. Indeed, trade links and exposure to a common creditor appear to help explain the observed historical pattern of contagion. Yet, one should be cautious about extrapolation, as some of the channels through which shocks are transmitted are relatively new to emerging markets. After all, less than a decade ago there were only a handful of mutual funds that had any exposure to emerging markets to begin with. Cross-market hedges have become commonplace in emerging market trades. Clearly, these financial market channels need to be better understood and quantified if policymakers around the globe hope to develop a "financial architecture" that makes countries less crisis prone and susceptible to contagion.

Acknowledgements

This paper was prepared for the Duke University conference "Globalization, Capital Market Crises and Economic Reform." The authors wish to thank Patrick Conway, Alan Drazen, Aart Kray, Gian Maria Milesi-Ferretti, Vincent Reinhart, Roberto Rigobon, Jorge Roldos, Andres Velasco, two anonymous referees, and conference participants at *Globalization, Capital Markets Crises, and Economic Reform*, Arizona State University, the Bank of England, University of California, San Diego, and the World Bank for useful comments and discussion, Sergio

168   G.L. Kaminsky, C.M. Reinhart / Journal of International Economics 51 (2000) 145–168

Schmukler for kindly providing the data on mutual funds and Ian Anderson, Mark Giancola, and Ioannis Tokatlidis for superb research assistance.

References

Baig, T., Goldfajn, I., 1998. Financial Market Contagion in the Asian Crisis, International Monetary Fund, Washington, DC.

Calvo, G.A., 1998. Capital Market Contagion and Recession: an Explanation of the Russian Virus, University of Maryland, College Park, Maryland.

Calvo, G.A., Mendoza, E., 1998. Rational Herd Behavior and the Globalization of Securities Markets, University of Maryland, College Park, Maryland.

Calvo, S., Reinhart, C.M., 1996. Capital flows to Latin America: is there evidence of contagion effects. In: Calvo, G.A., Goldstein, M., Hochreitter, E. (Eds.), Private Capital Flows to Emerging Markets, Institute for International Economics, Washington DC.

Corsetti, G., Pesenti, P., Roubini, N., Tille, C., 1998. Structural Links and Contagion Effects in the Asian Crisis: A Welfare Based Approach, New York University, New York.

Eichengreen, B., Rose, A., Wyplosz, C., 1996. Contagious currency crises, National Bureau of Economic Research Working Paper, Vol. No. 5681.

Frankel, J.A., Schmukler, S., 1998. Crisis contagion, and country funds. In: Glick, R. (Ed.), Managing Capital Flows and Exchange Rates, Cambridge University Press.

Gerlach, S., Smets, F., 1994. Contagious Speculative Attacks, CEPR Discussion Paper No. 1055.

Glick, R., Rose, A., 1998. Contagion and Trade: Why are Currency Crises Regional?, University of California, Berkeley.

Kaminsky, G.L., 1998. Currency and banking crises: the early warnings of distress, International Finance Discussion Paper, Vol. No. 629, October, Board of Governors of the Federal Reserve System.

Kaminsky, G.L., Reinhart, C.M., 1999. The twin crises: the causes of banking and balance of payments problems, American Economic Review. Vol. 89, June.

Kaminsky, G.L., Schmukler, S., 1999. What triggers market jitters? A chronicle of the Asian crisis, International Finance Discussion Paper, Vol. No. 634, April, Board of Governors of the Federal Reserve System.

Kodres, L.E., Pritsker, M., 1999. A Rational Expectations Model of Financial Contagion, unpublished mimeograph, International Monetary Fund, Washington DC.

Wolf, H.C., 1997. Regional contagion effects in emerging markets, Working Papers in International Economics, Vol. G-97-03, Princeton University.

Part V
Other Issues

A
Corporate Finance

[19]

Financial Dependence and Growth

By Raghuram G. Rajan and Luigi Zingales *

This paper examines whether financial development facilitates economic growth by scrutinizing one rationale for such a relationship: that financial development reduces the costs of external finance to firms. Specifically, we ask whether industrial sectors that are relatively more in need of external finance develop disproportionately faster in countries with more-developed financial markets. We find this to be true in a large sample of countries over the 1980's. We show this result is unlikely to be driven by omitted variables, outliers, or reverse causality. (JEL O4, F3, G1)

A large literature, dating at least as far back as Joseph A. Schumpeter (1911), emphasizes the positive influence of the development of a country's financial sector on the level and the rate of growth of its per capita income. The argument essentially is that the services the financial sector provides—of reallocating capital to the highest value use without substantial risk of loss through moral hazard, adverse selection, or transactions costs—are an essential catalyst of economic growth. Empirical work seems consistent with this argument. For example, on the basis of data from 35 countries between 1860 and 1963, Raymond W. Goldsmith (1969 p. 48) concludes that "a rough parallelism can be observed between economic and financial development if periods of several decades are considered." Nevertheless, studies such as these simply suggest correlation. As Goldsmith puts it: "There is no possibility, however, of establishing with confidence the direction of the causal mechanism, i.e., of deciding whether financial factors were responsible for the acceleration of economic

development or whether financial development reflected economic growth whose mainsprings must be sought elsewhere." While Goldsmith is agnostic, other economists have expressed downright skepticism that financial development is anything but a sideshow to economic development. Joan Robinson (1952 p. 86) is representative of such a viewpoint when she claims "where enterprise leads, finance follows."

In an important recent paper, Robert G. King and Ross Levine (1993a) investigate the causality problem following a *post hoc, ergo propter hoc* approach. They show that the predetermined component of financial development is a good predictor of growth over the next 10 to 30 years. However, the skeptic could still offer a number of arguments against attributing causality.

First, both financial development and growth could be driven by a common omitted variable such as the propensity of households in the economy to save. Since endogenous savings (in certain models of growth) affects the long-run growth rate of the economy, it may not be surprising that growth and initial financial development are correlated. This argument is also hard to refute with simple cross-country regressions. In the absence of a well-accepted theory of growth, the list of potential omitted variables that financial-sector development might be a proxy for is large, and the explanatory variables to include a matter of conjecture.

Second, financial development—typically measured by the level of credit and the size of

* Graduate School of Business, University of Chicago, 1101 E. 58th St., Chicago, IL 60637. We thank George Benston, Marco Da Rin, Eugene Fama, Peter Klenow, Krishna Kumar, Ross Levine, Jonathan Macy, Colin Mayer, Canice Prendergast, Andres Rodriguez-Clare, David Scharfstein, Robert Vishny, and two anonymous referees for valuable comments. Jayanta Sen, Dmitrii Kachintsev, and Alfred Shang provided excellent research assistance. A preliminary study was supported by the World Bank. We gratefully acknowledge financial support from NSF Grant No. SBR-9423645.

the stock market—may predict economic growth simply because financial markets anticipate future growth; the stock market capitalizes the present value of growth opportunities, while financial institutions lend more if they think sectors will grow. Thus financial development may simply be a leading indicator rather than a causal factor.

One way to make progress on causality is to focus on the details of theoretical mechanisms through which financial development affects economic growth, and document their working. Our paper is an attempt to do this. Specifically, theorists argue that financial markets and institutions help a firm overcome problems of moral hazard and adverse selection, thus reducing the firm's cost of raising money from outsiders. So financial development should disproportionately help firms (or industries) typically dependent on external finance for their growth. Such a finding could be the "smoking gun" in the debate about causality. There are two virtues to this simple test. First, it looks for evidence of a specific mechanism by which finance affects growth, thus providing a stronger test of causality. Second, it can correct for fixed country (and industry) effects. Though its contribution depends on how reasonable our microeconomic assumptions are, it is less dependent on a specific macroeconomic model of growth.

We construct the test as follows. We identify an industry's need for external finance (the difference between investments and cash generated from operations) from data on U.S. firms. Under the assumption that capital markets in the United States, especially for the large listed firms we analyze, are relatively frictionless, this method allows us to identify an industry's technological demand for external financing. Under the further assumption that such a technological demand carries over to other countries, we examine whether industries that are more dependent on external financing grow relatively faster in countries that, a priori, are more financially developed.

This would imply that, ceteris paribus, an industry such as Drugs and Pharmaceuticals, which requires a lot of external funding, should develop relatively faster than Tobacco, which requires little external finance, in countries that are more financially developed. Consider, for instance, Malaysia, Korea, and Chile, which are moderate-income, fast-growing, countries that differ considerably in their financial development. Consistent with our hypothesis, in Malaysia, which was the most financially developed by our measures, Drugs and Pharmaceuticals grew at a 4-percent higher annual real rate over the 1980's than Tobacco (the growth rate for each industry is adjusted for the worldwide growth rate of that industry). In Korea, which was moderately financially developed, Drugs grew at a 3-percent higher rate than Tobacco. In Chile, which was in the lowest quartile of financial development, Drugs grew at a 2.5-percent *lower* rate than Tobacco. So financial development seems to affect relative growth rates of industries in the way predicted. We establish this result more systematically for a large cross section of industries and countries in the body of the paper.

Delving deeper into the components of growth, industry growth can be decomposed into the growth in the number of establishments and the growth in the average size of existing establishments. New establishments are more likely to be new firms, which depend more on external finance than established firms. So the growth of the number of establishments in industries dependent on external finance should be particularly sensitive to financial development. This is indeed the case. Our estimates suggest that financial development has almost twice the economic effect on the growth of the number of establishments as it has on the growth of the average size of establishments. This suggests that an additional indirect channel through which financial development could influence growth is by disproportionately improving the prospects of young firms. If these are typically innovators, they make possible Schumpeterian "waves of creative destruction" that would not even get initiated in countries with less-developed markets.

Let us be careful about what we find, and about what we have little to say. Our findings suggest that the *ex ante* development of financial markets facilitates the *ex post* growth of sectors dependent on external finance. This implies that the link between financial development and growth identified elsewhere may stem, at least in part, from a channel identified by the theory: financial markets and institutions reduce the cost of external finance for firms. Of course, our analysis suggests only that financial development liberates firms from the drudgery of generating funds internally. It is ultimately the availability of profitable investment opportunities that drives growth, and we have little to say about where these come from. In the imagery of Rondo Cameron (1967 p. 2), we find evidence consistent with finance as a lubricant, essential no doubt, but not a substitute for the machine.

Our paper relates closely to three recent papers that attempt to establish the direction of causation of the finance-growth correlation. Asli Demirgüç-Kunt and Vojislav Maksimovic (1996) also use micro-data to develop a test of the influence of financial development on growth. Using firm-level data, they estimate the proportion of firms whose rate of growth exceeds the growth that could have been supported only by internal resources. They then run a cross-country regression and find that this proportion is positively related to the stock market turnover and to a measure of law enforcement. There are two essential differences from our paper. First, their estimate of the internal growth rate of a firm is dependent on the firm's characteristics. While it is potentially more accurate than our measure of external dependence, it is also more endogenous. Second, they focus on between-country differences in the spirit of traditional cross-country regressions, while our focus is on within-country, between-industry differences. The latter is an important innovation in this paper.

Jith Jayaratne and Philip E. Strahan (1996) examine the liberalization of the banking sector in different states in the United States in recent years and show that this had a positive influence on a state's growth. Our attempt to correct for fixed effects is similar to theirs. They use differences in growth rates across the temporal shock of liberalization while we use differences between industries within a country to do so. Since they focus on a very nice natural experiment to provide identification, their methodology may be harder to apply to different countries or different questions. But the more important difference is that we focus

on providing evidence for a microeconomic channel through which finance is supposed to work rather than examining, as they do, the broader correlation between finance and growth.

Finally, Levine and Sarah Zervos (1998) study whether stock markets and banks promote economic growth. They find that measures of market liquidity are strongly related to growth, capital accumulation, and productivity, while surprisingly, more traditional measures of development such as stock market size are not as robustly correlated. They also find that bank lending to the private sector has a strong independent effect on growth. They focus on a richer set of measures of financial development and growth than we do, but their cross-country regression methodology is also more traditional. The two studies should be viewed as complementary—theirs providing information on a broader set of correlations, while ours details a mechanism.

In this paper, we start by describing the theoretical underpinnings of our work in Section I and then our measure of external dependence in Section II. In Section III, we present our data on financial development, country characteristics, and industry growth. In Section IV we set up our main test and discuss the results. We explore other tests and the robustness of our findings in Section V. Section VI concludes.

I. Theoretical Underpinnings and the Basic Test

A. *Theoretical Underpinnings*

There has been extensive theoretical work on the relationship between financial development and economic growth. Economists have emphasized the role of financial development in better identifying investment opportunities, reducing investment in liquid but unproductive assets, mobilizing savings, boosting technological innovation, and improving risk taking.[1] All these activities can

---

[1] Apart from the papers discussed below, see Valerie R. Bencivenga and Bruce D. Smith (1991), Gilles Saint-Paul (1992), King and Levine (1993b), Maurice Obstfeld (1994), and John H. Boyd and Smith (1996).

lead to greater economic growth. We do not have the space to go into all these theories [see Levine (1997) for a comprehensive recent survey] so we content ourselves with outlining the essential theoretical underpinnings for our test.

Jeremy Greenwood and Boyan Jovanovic (1990) develop a model where the extent of financial intermediation and economic growth are endogenously determined. In their model, financial intermediaries can invest more productively than individuals because of their better ability to identify investment opportunities. So financial intermediation promotes growth because it allows a higher rate of return to be earned on capital, and growth in turn provides the means to implement costly financial structures.

Equivalently, the model could be recast to show that financial development reduces the cost of raising funds from sources external to the firm relative to the cost of internally generated cash flows. External funds are generally thought to be costlier because outsiders have less control over the borrower's actions (see, for example, Michael C. Jensen and William R. Meckling, 1976) or because they know less about what the borrower will do with the funds (see Joseph E. Stiglitz and Andrew Weiss, 1981; Stewart C. Myers and Nicholas S. Majluf, 1984). Financial development, in the form of better accounting and disclosure rules, and better corporate governance through institutions, will reduce the wedge between the cost of internal and external funds and enhance growth, especially for firms that are most reliant on external financing.[2]

A second issue is how financial development takes place. Some economists take the

development of the financial market as exogenous to the model arguing that "differences in the extent of financial markets across countries seem to depend primarily on legislation and government regulation" (Bencivenga and Smith, 1991 p. 207). By contrast, Greenwood and Jovanovic (1990) have a "once-and-for-all" lump-sum cost of development and development is endogenous to their framework. From the perspective of our paper, it really does not matter whether legal and political or economic forces are responsible for financial development. Our focus is on whether the predetermined level of financial development affects growth. All we need for the stock of financial development to matter even when development is endogenous is that there be a cost to development (as in Greenwood and Jovanovic) or that financial development cannot happen instantaneously (as in reputational models of financial development such as Douglas W. Diamond, 1989). Either assumption seems plausible.

If financial development cannot take place at low cost and on the fly, the above theories would suggest that the a priori existence of a well-developed financial market should disproportionately improve the *ex post* growth rates of industries that are technologically more dependent on external funds.

B. *The Basic Test*

The most disaggregated comprehensive data on growth that we have for countries is at the industry level (data at the firm level, if available, is typically limited to large listed firms). Our hypothesis is that industries that are more dependent on external financing will have relatively higher growth rates in countries that have more developed financial markets.

Therefore, the dependent variable is the average annual real growth rate of value added in industry j in country k over the period 1980–1990. If we can measure industry j's dependence on external finance and country k's financial development, then after correcting for country and industry effects we must find that the coefficient estimate for the interaction between dependence and development is positive.

[2] In Greenwood and Jovanovic (1990), there are no moral hazard or asymmetric information problems at the level of the entrepreneur. The intermediary simply provides information about economywide trends that the entrepreneur cannot figure out for himself, enabling the entrepreneur to invest his own funds more productively. An equivalent formulation is to distinguish between savers and entrepreneurs. Absent financial development, savers can invest directly only in safe, low-return, government-sponsored projects, while financial development can reduce adverse selection, enabling savers to invest in risky (but often more productive) entrepreneurs.

The most effective way of correcting for country and industry characteristics is to use indicator variables, one for each country and industry. Only additional explanatory variables that vary both with industry and country need be included. These are industry j's share in country k of total value added in manufacturing in 1980 and the primary variable of interest, the interaction between industry j's dependence on external financing and financial market development in country k.

The model we want to estimate is then

$$(1) \quad \text{Growth}_{j,k}$$

$$= \text{Constant} + \beta_{1 \dots m} \cdot \text{Country Indicators}$$

$$+ \beta_{m+1 \dots n} \cdot \text{Industry Indicators}$$

$$+ \beta_{n+1} \cdot (\text{Industry } j\text{'s share of}$$

$$\text{manufacturing in country } k \text{ in } 1980)$$

$$+ \beta_{n+2} \cdot (\text{External Dependence of}$$

$$\text{industry } j \cdot \text{Financial Development}$$

$$\text{of country } k) + \varepsilon_{j,k}.$$

Of course, in order to estimate the model, we need appropriate measures of financial development and external dependence. This is what we will examine shortly.

Before proceeding, we point out that our study has one important advantage over recent cross-country empirical studies of growth.[3] That advantage is simply that we make predictions about within-country differences between industries based on an interaction between a country and industry characteristic. Therefore, we can correct for country and industry characteristics in ways that previous studies were unable to correct for, and will be less subject to criticism about an omitted variable bias or model specification.

---

[3] See, for example, Roger Kormendi and Philip Meguire (1985), Robert J. Barro (1991), Levine and David Renelt (1992), N. Gregory Mankiw et al. (1992), King and Levine (1993a), and Demirgüç-Kunt and Maksimovic (1996).

II. A Measure of Dependence on External Finance

A. *The Proxy for Dependence*

Data on the actual use of external financing is typically not available. But even if it were, it would not be useable because it would reflect the equilibrium between the demand for external funds and its supply. Since the latter is precisely what we are attempting to test for, this information is contaminated. Moreover, we are not aware of systematic studies of the external financing needs of different industries, either cross-sectionally or over time.[4]

We, therefore, have to find some other way of identifying an industry's dependence on external financing. We assume that there is a technological reason why some industries depend more on external finance than others. To the extent that the initial project scale, the gestation period, the cash harvest period, and the requirement for continuing investment differ substantially between industries, this is indeed plausible. Furthermore, we assume that these technological differences persist across countries, so that we can use an industry's dependence on external funds as identified in the United States as a measure of its dependence in other countries. While there are enormous differences in local conditions between countries, all we really need is that statements of the following sort hold: If Pharmaceuticals require a larger initial scale and have a higher gestation period before cash flows are harvested than the Textile industry in the United States, it also requires a larger initial scale and has a higher gestation period in Korea.

B. *How the Proxy Is Calculated*

We start by computing the external financing needs of U.S. companies over the 1980's. We use data from Standard and Poor's *Compustat* (1994) for this. *Compustat* does not contain a representative sample of U.S. firms, because it is limited to publicly traded firms, which are relatively large. Nevertheless, we

---

[4] Colin Mayer (1990) does look at external financing, but largely at the country level.

regard this as an advantage for two reasons. First, in a perfect capital market the supply of funds to firms is perfectly elastic at the proper risk-adjusted rate. In such a market the actual amount of external funds raised by a firm equals its desired amount. In other words, in such an idealized setting, the identification problem does not exist. But capital markets in the United States are among the most advanced in the world, and large publicly traded firms typically face the least frictions in accessing finance. Thus the amount of external finance used by large firms in the United States is likely to be a relatively pure measure of their demand for external finance.[5]

A second reason for using a database on listed firms is that disclosure requirements imply that the data on financing are comprehensive. For most of the paper, we will take the amount of external finance used by U.S. firms in an industry as a proxy for the desired amount foreign firms in the same industry would have liked to raise had their financial markets been more developed.

Next, we have to define precisely what we mean by external and internal finance. We are interested in the amount of desired investment that cannot be financed through internal cash flows generated by the same business. Therefore, a firm's dependence on external finance is defined as capital expenditures (*Compustat* # 128) minus cash flow from operations divided by capital expenditures. Cash flow from operations is broadly defined as the sum of cash flow from operations (*Compustat* # 110) plus decreases in inventories, decreases in receivables, and increases in payables.[6] Note that this definition includes changes in the nonfinancial components of net working cap-

ital as part of funds from operations. In fact, in certain businesses these represent major sources (or uses) of funds that help a firm avoid (or force it to tap) external sources of funds.[7]

Similarly, the dependence on external equity finance is defined as the ratio of the net amount of equity issues (*Compustat* # 108 minus *Compustat* # 115) to capital expenditures. Finally, the investment intensity is the ratio of capital expenditure to net property plant and equipment (*Compustat* # 8).

To make these measures comparable with the industry-level data we have for other countries, we have to choose how to aggregate these ratios over time and across companies. We sum the firm's use of external finance over the 1980's and then divide by the sum of capital expenditure over the 1980's to get the firm's dependence on external finance in the 1980's. This smooths temporal fluctuations and reduces the effects of outliers. To summarize ratios across firms, however, we use the industry median. We do this to prevent large firms from swamping the information from small firms; for instance, we know that IBM's free cash flow does not alleviate possible cash flow shortages of small computer firms.

C. *External Dependence for Different Industries*

In Table 1 we tabulate by International Standard Industrial Classification (ISIC) code the fraction of investments U.S. firms financed externally (first column) and the level of capital expenditures divided by net property plant and equipment (second column). We restrict our attention to those manufacturing industries for which we have value-added data from the

---

[5] Even if capital markets are imperfect so that the supply is not perfectly elastic, this methodology provides a reasonable measure of the relative demand for funds provided the elasticity of the supply curve does not change substantially in the cross section. By contrast, in a very imperfect capital market, the relative amount of funds raised may be a function not only of the demand for funds but also of factors that affect supply, such as the availability of collateral.

[6] This item is only defined for cash flow statements with format codes 1, 2, or 3. For format code 7 we construct it as the sum of items # 123, 125, 126, 106, 213, 217.

[7] It could be argued that interfirm trade credit should be viewed as a component of external financing. It is unclear how much of trade credit is used to reduce transactions costs and how much is used for financing. Much trade credit is granted routinely and repaid promptly and usually net trade credit for a firm (accounts receivable less payables) is small (see Mitchell A. Petersen and Rajan, 1997). This may be why trade credit is typically treated as part of operations in capital budgeting exercises. We adhere to this tradition.

United Nations Statistical Division (1993). Drugs and Pharmaceuticals emerge as the industry that uses the most external finance, with Plastics and Computing following close behind. Tobacco, on the other hand, generates the most excess cash flow and has negative external funding needs.

It is common wisdom in the corporate finance literature (though we were hard-pressed to find formal empirical studies of this phenomenon) that there is a life cycle in the pattern of financing for firms; firms are more dependent on external financing early in their life than later. Figure 1 supports the common wisdom. It plots the median financing and investment needs across U.S. firms as a function of the number of years since the initial public offering (IPO). Not surprisingly, in the year of the IPO, firms raise a substantial amount of external funds (especially equity). More interestingly, this continues — albeit on a smaller scale — up to approximately the tenth year. After that period, net equity issues go to zero and the usage of external finance fluctuates around zero. In the third and fourth columns of Table 1, we report the external dependence and capital expenditures for mature companies (firms that were listed for more than ten years), while the fifth and sixth columns are for young companies (firms that were listed for less than ten years).[8] This pattern appears to be fairly standard across different industries, though there are exceptions. All this suggests that very young firms are more dependent on external finance than older firms. This fact will provide an additional test of our hypothesis.

D. *Is the Dependence of U.S. Firms a Good Proxy?*

Much of our analysis rests on dependence of U.S. firms on external finance being a good proxy for the demand for external funds in other countries. We think this is reasonable for four reasons.

First, in a steady-state equilibrium there will not be much need for external funds, as Figure 1 shows. Therefore, much of the demand for external funds is likely to arise as a result of technological shocks that raise an industry's investment opportunities beyond what internal funds can support. To the extent these shocks are worldwide, the need for funds of U.S. firms represents a good proxy.[9]

Second, even if the new investment opportunities generated by these worldwide shocks differ across countries, the amount of cash flow produced by existing firms in a certain industry is likely to be similar across countries. In fact, most of the determinants of ratio of cash flow to capital are likely to be similar worldwide: the level of demand for a certain product, its stage in the life cycle, and its cash harvest period. For this reason, we make sure that our results hold even when we use the amount of internally generated cash, rather than the difference between investments and internally generated funds. We also check that the results hold when we use dependence as measured in Canada, a country which has well-developed capital markets but a very different banking system and industry concentration than the United States. Unfortunately, we do not have access to flow-of-funds data from any other countries, so we cannot venture further afield, but this methodology could, in principle, be used with dependence measured in any country with well-functioning capital markets.

Third, one might argue that the stage of the product life cycle that U.S. firms are in is likely to be different from that of foreign firms. Given that our sample is biased toward developing countries, one might think that the U.S. industry in the 1970's might be a better proxy for the position of developing countries in a product life cycle. For this reason, we also explore the robustness of our results to measuring

---

[8] We required that there be more than one observation in the industry for this variable to be computed. Even with this weak requirement we do not have data for some industries. Most notably there are insufficient young firms in the Tobacco industry.

[9] This amounts to saying that if the invention of personal computers increased the demand for external funds in the U.S. Computer industry, it is likely to increase the need for funds in the Computer industry in other countries as well.

TABLE 1—PATTERN OF EXTERNAL FINANCING AND INVESTMENT ACROSS INDUSTRIES
IN THE UNITED STATES DURING THE 1980'S

ISIC code	Industrial sectors	All companies		Mature companies		Young companies	
		External dependence	Capital expenditures	External dependence	Capital expenditures	External dependence	Capital expenditures
314	Tobacco	−0.45	0.23	−0.38	0.24	—	—
361	Pottery	−0.15	0.20	0.16	0.41	−0.41	0.13
323	Leather	−0.14	0.21	−1.33	0.27	−1.53	0.16
3211	Spinning	−0.09	0.16	−0.04	0.19	—	—
324	Footwear	−0.08	0.25	−0.57	0.23	0.65	0.26
372	Nonferrous metal	0.01	0.22	0.07	0.21	0.46	0.24
322	Apparel	0.03	0.31	−0.02	0.27	0.27	0.37
353	Petroleum refineries	0.04	0.22	−0.02	0.22	0.85	0.28
369	Nonmetal products	0.06	0.21	0.15	0.22	−0.03	0.26
313	Beverages	0.08	0.26	−0.15	0.28	0.63	0.26
371	Iron and steel	0.09	0.18	0.09	0.16	0.26	0.19
311	Food products	0.14	0.26	−0.05	0.25	0.66	0.33
3411	Pulp, paper	0.15	0.20	0.13	0.21	0.22	0.20
3513	Synthetic resins	0.16	0.30	−0.23	0.20	0.79	0.45
341	Paper and products	0.18	0.24	0.10	0.23	0.57	0.29
342	Printing and publishing	0.20	0.39	0.14	0.33	0.60	0.41
352	Other chemicals	0.22	0.31	−0.18	0.25	1.35	0.46
355	Rubber products	0.23	0.28	−0.12	0.21	0.50	0.32
332	Furniture	0.24	0.25	0.33	0.17	0.68	0.29
381	Metal products	0.24	0.29	0.04	0.25	0.87	0.34
3511	Basic excluding fertilizers	0.25	0.30	0.08	0.24	0.79	0.29
331	Wood products	0.28	0.26	0.25	0.23	0.34	0.40
384	Transportation equipment	0.31	0.31	0.16	0.28	0.58	0.31
354	Petroleum and coal products	0.33	0.23	0.16	0.26	−0.26	0.22
3843	Motor vehicle	0.39	0.32	0.11	0.33	0.76	0.32
321	Textile	0.40	0.25	0.14	0.24	0.66	0.26
382	Machinery	0.45	0.29	0.22	0.25	0.75	0.33
3841	Ship	0.46	0.43	0.04	0.34	1.05	0.56

TABLE 1—*Continued.*

ISIC code	Industrial sectors	All companies		Mature companies		Young companies	
		External dependence	Capital expenditures	External dependence	Capital expenditures	External dependence	Capital expenditures
390	Other industries	0.47	0.37	−0.05	0.28	0.80	0.49
362	Glass	0.53	0.28	0.03	0.28	1.52	0.33
383	Electric machinery	0.77	0.38	0.23	0.29	1.22	0.46
385	Professional goods	0.96	0.45	0.19	0.33	1.63	0.52
3832	Radio	1.04	0.42	0.39	0.30	1.35	0.48
3825	Office and computing	1.06	0.60	0.26	0.38	1.16	0.64
356	Plastic products	1.14	0.44	—	—	1.14	0.48
3522	Drugs	1.49	0.44	0.03	0.32	2.06	0.47

Notes: This table reports the median level of external financing and capital expenditure for ISIC industries during the 1980's. External dependence is the fraction of capital expenditures not financed with cash flow from operations. Cash flow from operations is broadly defined as the sum of *Compustat* funds from operations (item #110), decreases in inventories, decreases in receivables, and increases in payables. Capital expenditures are the ratio of capital expenditures to net property plan and equipment. Mature companies are firms that have been public for at least ten years; correspondingly, young companies are firms that went public less than ten years ago. The year of going public is the first year in which a company starts to be traded on the NYSE, AMEX, or NASDAQ. All companies is the union of mature and young firms plus firms for which the year of going public could not be determined (firms already traded on NASDAQ in 1972). All the information is obtained from the flow-of-funds data in *Compustat*, except for the SIC code which is obtained from the Center for Research on Securities Prices and then matched with the ISIC code.

the dependence of U.S. firms in the 1970's rather than in the 1980's. We also distinguish between dependence as measured for young firms in the United States (less than ten years from listing) and dependence for old firms (more than ten years from listing).

Last but not least, that we only have a noisy measure of the need for funds creates a bias against finding any interaction between dependence and financial development.

III. Data

A. *Data on Industries*

Data on value added and gross fixed capital formation for each industry in each country are obtained from the *Industrial Statistics Yearbook* database put together by the United Nations Statistical Division (1993). We checked the data for inconsistencies, changes in classification of sectors, and changes in units. The U.N. data is classified by Interna-

tional SIC code. In order to obtain the amount of external finance used by the industry in the United States, we matched ISIC codes with SIC codes.[10] Typically, the three-digit ISIC codes correspond to two-digit SIC codes, while the four-digit ISIC codes correspond to three-digit SIC codes. In order to reduce the dependence on country-specific factors like natural resources, we confine our analysis to manufacturing firms (U.S. SIC 2000–3999).

We would like data on as many countries as possible. The binding constraint is the availability of measures of financial development (specifically the availability of data on

---

[10] Not all the ISIC sectors for which the *Industrial Statistics Yearbook* reports data on value added are mutually exclusive. For example, Drugs (3522) is a subsector of other Chemicals (352). In these cases, the values of the broader sectors are net of the values of the subsectors that are separately reported. We follow this convention both for the data value added and for the financial data from *Compustat*.

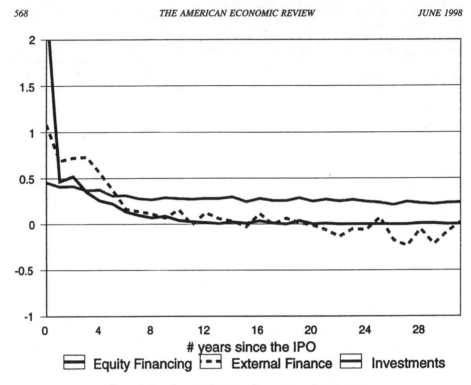

FIGURE 1. LIFE CYCLE OF EXTERNAL FINANCING AND INVESTMENTS

Notes: This graph plots the median level of external financing, equity financing, and investments in the United States across three-digit SIC industries as a function of the number of years since the IPO. External finance is the amount of capital expenditures not financed with cash flow from operations, reduction in inventories, or decreases in trade credit. Equity finance is the net amount of funds raised through equity issues divided by the amount of investments. Investment is the ratio of capital expenditures to net property, plant, and equipment. The IPO year is defined as the first year in which a company starts to be traded on the NYSE, AMEX, or NASDAQ. All the information is obtained from the flow-of-funds data in *Compustat*, except for the SIC code which is from the Center for Research on Securities Prices.

accounting standards). Since we also wanted data on equity market capitalization, we started with the 55 countries from the International Finance Corporation's (IFC's) *Emerging Stock Markets Factbook.* We dropped countries like Kuwait that did not report a stock market capitalization until the latter half of the 1980's. We could not use Hong Kong and Taiwan because data on these countries are not present in the International Money Fund's (IMF's) *International Financial Statistics* (IFS) volumes. We also dropped countries for which we did not have data from the *Industrial Statistics Yearbook* database that is separated by at least five years (notably, Swit-

zerland). Finally, Thailand is dropped because the U.N. notes that data from year to year are not comparable. The United States is excluded from the analysis because it is our benchmark. This leaves us with the 41 countries in Table 2.

We want to see if financially dependent industries are likely to be better off in countries with well-developed financial sectors. The availability of finance affects not just investment but also the ability to finance operations and sales through working capital. Therefore, the most appropriate measure of an industry being "better off" is the growth in value added for that industry, i.e., the change in the log of real value added in that industry between 1980 and 1990. Real value added in 1990 is obtained by deflating value added by the Producer Price Index (PPI). For high-inflation countries, spurious differences in value added may be obtained simply because the U.N. data are measured at a different point from the PPI. So, instead, we determine the effective deflator by dividing the growth in nominal value added for the entire manufacturing sector in the U.N. database by the index of industrial production (which measures the real growth rate in industrial production) obtained from the IFS statistics.

B. Data on Countries

The Gross Domestic Product, the Producer Price Index, the exchange rate, and the Index of Industrial Production are all obtained from *International Financial Statistics* published by the International Monetary Fund. Whenever a particular series is not available, we use close substitutes—for instance, the Wholesale Price Index if the Producer Price Index is not available. Data on a country's human capital (average years of schooling in population over 25) is obtained from the Barro-Lee files downloaded from the National Bureau of Economic Research web site (see Barro and Jong Wha Lee, 1993).

C. Measures of Financial Development

Ideally, financial development should measure the ease with which borrowers and savers can be brought together, and once together, the confidence they have in one another. Thus financial development should be related to the variety of intermediaries and markets available, the efficiency with which they perform the evaluation, monitoring, certification, communication and distribution functions, and the legal and regulatory framework assuring performance. Since there is little agreement on how these are appropriately measured, and even less data available, we will have to make do with crude proxies even though they may miss many of the aspects we think vital to a modern financial system.

The first measure of financial development we use is fairly traditional—the ratio of do-mestic credit plus stock market capitalization to GDP. We call this the *capitalization ratio*. We obtain stock market capitalization for all countries listed in the *Emerging Stock Markets Factbook* published by the International Finance Corporation, which contains data on developed countries also.[11] Domestic credit is obtained from the IMF's *International Financial Statistics*. Specifically, it is the sum of IFS lines 32a through 32f and excluding 32e. Finally, domestic credit allocated to the private sector is IFS line 32d.

Despite the virtue of tradition, there are concerns with this measure. Unlike domestic credit, stock market capitalization does not reflect the amount of funding actually obtained by issuers. Instead, it reflects a composite of retained earnings, the investing public's perception of the corporate sector's growth prospects, and actual equity issuances. One could argue that the amount of money raised through initial public offerings and secondary offerings is more suitable for our purpose. Unfortunately, these data are not widely available. At the same time, one cannot dismiss the capitalization measure in favor of actual financing too easily. The net amount raised from U.S. equity markets by large firms was negative in the 1980's (see, for example, Rajan and Zingales, 1995). So the actual amount raised may underestimate the importance of the stock market's role in providing price information and liquidity to investors. Market capitalization may be a better measure of the importance of the stock market in this respect. Since we are unsure about whether market capitalization is a reasonable proxy, we will check that the results are robust to redefining the capitalization ratio as the ratio of domestic credit to the private sector to GDP.

The second proxy for financial development we use is the accounting standards in a country. Unlike our first measure, accounting

---

[11] Stock market capitalization is measured at the end of the earliest year in the 1980's for which it is available, while Gross Domestic Product may value flows through the year. This may be a problem in high-inflation countries. We therefore measure GDP as the GDP in constant prices multiplied by the Producer Price Index where the base year for both series is five years before the year of interest.

TABLE 2—FINANCIAL DEVELOPMENT ACROSS COUNTRIES

Country	Accounting standards	Total capitalization over GDP	Domestic credit to private sector over GDP	Per capita income (dollars)
Bangladesh	—	0.20	0.07	121
Kenya	—	0.28	0.20	417
Morocco	—	0.41	0.16	807
Sri Lanka	—	0.44	0.21	252
Pakistan	—	0.53	0.25	290
Costa Rica	—	0.53	0.26	2,155
Zimbabwe	—	1.01	0.30	441
Jordan	—	1.16	0.54	1,109
Egypt	24	0.74	0.21	563
Portugal	36	0.82	0.52	2,301
Peru	38	0.28	0.11	842
Venezuela	40	0.34	0.30	3,975
Colombia	50	0.21	0.14	1,150
Turkey	51	0.35	0.14	1,081
Chile	52	0.74	0.36	2,531
Brazil	54	0.33	0.23	1,650
Austria	54	1.00	0.77	9,554
Greece	55	0.74	0.44	3,814
India	57	0.50	0.24	240
Mexico	60	0.39	0.16	2,651
Belgium	61	0.65	0.29	11,226
Denmark	62	0.56	0.42	12,188
Germany	62	1.08	0.78	12,345
Italy	62	0.98	0.42	6,460
Korea	62	0.63	0.50	1,407
Netherlands	64	0.91	0.60	11,155
Spain	64	1.02	0.76	5,087
Israel	64	1.18	0.67	3,573
Philippines	65	0.46	0.28	729
Japan	65	1.31	0.86	9,912

TABLE 2—*Continued.*

Country	Accounting standards	Total capitalization over GDP	Domestic credit to private sector over GDP	Per capita income (dollars)
France	69	0.70	0.54	11,337
New Zealand	70	0.59	0.19	7,490
South Africa	70	1.51	0.26	2,899
Norway	74	0.63	0.34	13,430
Canada	74	0.98	0.45	10,486
Australia	75	0.82	0.28	9,866
Malaysia	76	1.19	0.48	1,683
Finland	77	0.52	0.48	10,181
U.K.	78	0.78	0.25	9,600
Singapore	78	1.96	0.57	4,661
Sweden	83	0.79	0.42	14,368

Notes: Accounting standards is an index developed by the Center for International Financial Analysis and Research ranking the amount of disclosure in annual company reports in each country. Total capitalization to GDP is the ratio of the sum of equity market capitalization (as reported by the IFC) and domestic credit (IFS lines 32a–32f but not 32e) to GDP. Domestic credit to the private sector is IFS line 32d. Per capita income in 1980 is in dollars and is from the IFS.

standards reflect the potential for obtaining finance rather than the actual finance raised. Specifically, the higher the standards of financial disclosure in a country, the easier it will be for firms to raise funds from a wider circle of investors. The Center for International Financial Analysis and Research (CIFAR) creates an index for different countries by rating the annual reports of at least three firms in every country on the inclusion or omission of 90 items. Thus each country obtains a score out of 90 with a higher number indicating more disclosure. The Center for International Financial Analysis and Research, which produces this data, started analyzing balance sheets from 1983 onwards. However, its first comprehensive survey dates from 1990. We will use the accounting standards as measured in this study in much of the paper. The date of the survey raises concerns about endogeneity, but we believe such concerns are small to begin with, and can easily be addressed. First, accounting standards do not change much over

time. In 1995, the CIFAR published a study examining how accounting standards had changed since 1983. This study estimated the standards in 1983 and 1990 based on a subset of annual reports, and for a subset of countries that are in the comprehensive 1990 survey. The study finds the mean accounting standards for countries sampled both in 1983 and 1990 is the same at 65. The Wilcoxon signed rank test for equality of distributions fails to reject the equality of the distribution of accounting standards across countries in the two years. Finally, the correlation between the accounting standards in 1983 and 1990 is 0.75.[12] Nevertheless, we will instrument accounting standards with variables that predate the period of growth at which we are looking. Also, we will use the 1983 data to see that the results hold

---

[12] The regression estimates are not sensitive to dropping the few countries such as Denmark and Spain that changed accounting standards substantially.

TABLE 3—SUMMARY STATISTICS

A: Summary Statistics

Variable	Mean	Median	Standard deviation	Minimum	Maximum	Number of observations
Industry's real growth	0.034	0.029	0.099	−0.447	1.000	1242
Industry's growth in number of firms	0.012	0.007	0.071	−0.414	0.759	1073
Industry's growth in average firms' size	0.022	0.026	0.094	−0.536	0.410	1070
Industry's share of total value added	0.016	0.009	0.021	0.000	0.224	1217
Log per capita income in 1980 in dollars	7.870	7.971	1.344	4.793	9.573	41
Average years of schooling	5.900	5.442	2.829	1.681	12.141	41
External finance dependence (all firms)	0.319	0.231	0.319	−0.451	1.492	36
External finance dependence (old firms)	0.010	0.075	0.302	−1.330	0.394	35
External finance dependence (young firms)	0.675	0.673	0.643	−1.535	2.058	34
External finance dependence (1970's)	0.078	0.073	0.188	−0.450	0.542	35
External finance dependence (Canadian firms)	0.427	0.384	0.767	−0.802	3.512	27
Cash flow generated	0.173	0.198	0.112	−0.217	0.331	36
Investment intensity	0.298	0.278	0.095	0.161	0.600	36
Total capitalization over GDP	0.738	0.696	0.375	0.199	1.962	41
Domestic credit to private sector over GDP	0.377	0.302	0.201	0.069	0.856	41
Accounting standards	61.324	62.000	13.238	24.000	83.000	34
Accounting standards (1983)	65.393	68.500	11.426	39.000	81.000	28

B: Correlation Between Measures of External Dependence

	All	Old	Young	1970's	Cash flow	Investment
External finance dependence (all firms)	1.00	—	—	—	—	—
External finance dependence (old firms)	0.46 (0.01)	1.00 —	—	—	—	—
External finance dependence (young firms)	0.72 (0.00)	0.48 (0.00)	1.00 —	—	—	—
External finance dependence (1970's)	0.63 (0.00)	0.42 (0.01)	0.48 (0.00)	1.00 —	—	—
Cash flow generated	−0.91 (0.00)	−0.37 (0.03)	−0.55 (0.00)	−0.50 (0.00)	1.00 —	—
Investment intensity	0.81 (0.00)	0.28 (0.10)	0.64 (0.00)	0.63 (0.00)	−0.60 (0.00)	1.00 —
External finance dependence (Canadian firms)	0.77 (0.00)	0.36 (0.07)	0.58 (0.00)	0.37 (0.07)	−0.78 (0.00)	0.55 (0.00)

TABLE 3—*Continued.*

C: Correlation Between Measures of Financial Development

	Total capitalization	Market capitalization	Domestic credit to private sector	Accounting standards	Accounting standards 1983
Market capitalization over GDP	0.79 (0.00)	—	—	—	—
Domestic credit to private sector over GDP	0.67 (0.00)	0.21 (0.18)	1.00 —	—	—
Accounting standards	0.41 (0.02)	0.45 (0.01)	0.25 (0.17)	1.00 —	—
Accounting standards (1983)	0.27 (0.17)	0.39 (0.05)	−0.14 (0.50)	0.68 (0.00)	1.00 —
Per capita income	0.26 (0.09)	0.04 (0.80)	0.48 (0.00)	0.56 (0.00)	0.28 (0.16)

Notes: Industry real growth is the annual compounded growth rate in real value added for the period 1980–1990 for each ISIC industry in each country. The growth in the number of firms is the difference between the log of number of ending-period firms and the log of number of beginning-period firms. The average size of firms in the industry is obtained by dividing the value added in the industry by the number of firms, and the growth in average size is obtained again as a difference in logs. The industry's share of total value added is computed dividing the 1980 value added of the industry by the total value added in manufacturing that year. External dependence is the median fraction of capital expenditures not financed with cash flow from operations for each industry. Cash flow from operations is broadly defined as the sum of *Compustat* funds from operations (items #110), decreases in inventories, decreases in receivables, and increases in payables. External dependence has been constructed using *Compustat* firms between 1980 and 1990, except for Canada where we use *Global Vantage* (Standard & Poor's, 1993) data between 1982 and 1990. Accounting standards is an index developed by the Center for International Financial Analysis and Research ranking the amount of disclosure of companies' annual reports in each country. In Panels B and C the *p*-values are reported in parentheses.

in the subset of countries for which it is available.

Both our measures of financial development, accounting standards and the capitalization ratio, are tabulated for the different countries (see Table 2). While more-developed countries have better accounting standards, there are exceptions. For instance, Malaysia scores as high as Australia or Canada, while Belgium and Germany are in the same league as Korea, the Philippines, or Mexico. Portugal has among the worst accounting standards.

Before we go to the summary statistics, note that for a country's financial development to have any effect on industrial growth in that country we have to assume that firms finance themselves largely in their own country. In other words, only if world capital markets are not perfectly integrated can domestic financial development affect a country's growth. There

is a wealth of evidence documenting the existence of frictions in international capital markets: the extremely high correlation between a country's savings and its investments (Martin Feldstein and Charles Horioka, 1980), the strong home bias in portfolio investments (Kenneth R. French and James M. Poterba, 1991), and cross-country differences in expected returns (Geert Bekaert and Cambell R. Harvey, 1995). We have little else to say about this assumption other than noting that its failure would weaken the power of our test but not necessarily bias our findings.

Summary statistics and correlations are in Table 3. A number of correlations are noteworthy. First, the financial sector is more developed in richer countries. The correlation of per capita income in 1980 with accounting standards and total capitalization is 0.56 and 0.26 (significant at the 1-percent and 10-percent level, respectively).

Second, the correlation between our capitalization measure of financial development and accounting standards is 0.41 (significant at the 5-percent level for the 33 countries for which we have both data). However, the correlations between accounting standards and the components of capitalization differ. Accounting standards are strongly correlated with equity market capitalization (correlation = 0.45, significant at the 1-percent level) but not with domestic credit (correlation = 0.25, not significant). Domestic credit is credit offered by depository institutions and the central bank. One explanation of the low correlation is perhaps that institutions rely on their own private investigations, and credit from them is little affected by accounting standards. Another possible explanation is that when accounting standards are low, only institutions offer credit. But even though institutions benefit from improvements in accounting standards, other sources of finance become available, and firms substitute away from their traditional sources. We cannot distinguish between these explanations. It will suffice for our purpose that the overall availability of finance, whatever its source, increases with financial development.

IV. Financial Dependence and Growth

A. *Results From the Basic Regression*

1. *Varying Measures of Financial Development.*—Table 4 reports the estimates of our basic specification (1) obtained by using various measures of financial development. Since the specification controls for country-specific effects and industry-specific effects, the only effects that are identified are those relative to variables that vary both cross countries and cross industries. Thus, Table 4 reports only the coefficient of the industry's share of total value added at the beginning of the sample and the coefficient of the interaction between external dependence and different measures of financial development.[13] Since we use U.S.

---

[13] The dependent variable is the average real growth rate over the period 1980–1990. For some countries, how-

data to identify the external dependence, we drop the United States in all regressions.

We start with total capitalization as the proxy for development. As can be seen in the first column of Table 4, the coefficient estimate for the interaction term is positive and statistically significant at the 1-percent level (throughout the paper, the reported standard errors are robust to heteroskedasticity).[14]

The interaction term is akin to a second derivative. One way to get a sense of its magnitude is as follows. The industry at the 75th percentile of dependence (high dependence) is Machinery. The industry at the 25th percentile (low dependence) is Beverages. The country at the 75th percentile of development as measured by capitalization is Italy, while the country at the 25th percentile is the Philippines. We set the industry's initial share of manufacturing at its overall mean. The coefficient estimate then predicts that Machinery should grow 1.3 percent faster than Beverages annually, and in real terms, in Italy as compared to the Philippines. For comparison, the real annual growth rate is, on average, 3.4 percent per year. So a differential of 1.3 percent is a large number.

For each specification, we compute a similar number which is reported as the *differential in real growth rate* in the last row of each table. Of course, the countries at the 75th and 25th percentile vary with the measure of development, as do the industries at the 75th and 25th percentile with the measure of dependence.

The rest of the columns of the table include different measures of development. We in-

---

ever, data availability limits the period. For no country do we have data separated by less than five years. A potential concern is that we measure growth in value added rather than growth in output. Unfortunately, we do not have data for the latter. While we may not capture increases in productivity fully, we see no obvious way in which this should bias our results.

[14] We reduce the impact of outliers by constraining growth between −1 and +1. Three observations are affected. The coefficient estimates for the interaction coefficient are higher and still significant when we do not do this, though the explanatory power of the regression is lower. We also reestimate the same specification after winsorizing the 1-percent and 5-percent tails of the growth rate distribution obtaining virtually identical results (except that the explanatory power of the regression is still higher).

TABLE 4—INDUSTRY GROWTH AND VARIOUS MEASURES OF DEVELOPMENT

Variable	Financial development measured as					
	Total capitalization	Bank debt	Accounting standards	Accounting standards in 1983	Accounting standards and capitalization	Instrumental variables
Industry's share of total value added in manufacturing in 1980	−0.912 (0.246)	−0.899 (0.245)	−0.643 (0.204)	−0.587 (0.223)	−0.443 (0.135)	−0.648 (0.203)
Interaction (external dependence × total capitalization)	0.069 (0.023)	—	—	—	0.012 (0.014)	—
Interaction (external dependence × domestic credit to private sector)	—	0.118 (0.037)	—	—	—	—
Interaction (external dependence × accounting standards)	—	—	0.155 (0.034)	—	0.133 (0.034)	0.165 (0.044)
Interaction (external dependence × accounting standards 1983)	—	—	—	0.099 (0.036)	—	—
R^2	0.290	0.290	0.346	0.239	0.419	0.346
Number of observations	1217	1217	1067	855	1042	1067
Differential in real growth rate	1.3	1.1	0.9	0.4	1.3	1.0

Notes: The dependent variable is the annual compounded growth rate in real value added for the period 1980–1990 for each ISIC industry in each country. External dependence is the fraction of capital expenditures not financed with internal funds for U.S. firms in the same industry between 1980–1990. The interaction variable is the product of external dependence and financial development. Financial development is total capitalization in the first column, domestic credit to the private sector over GDP in the second column, accounting standards in 1990 in the third column, and accounting standards in 1983 in the fourth column. The sixth column is estimated with instrumental variables. Both the coefficient estimate for the interaction term and the standard error when accounting standards is the measure of development are multiplied by 100. The differential in real growth rate measures (in percentage terms) how much faster an industry at the 75th percentile level of external dependence grows with respect to an industry at the 25th percentile level when it is located in a country at the 75th percentile of financial development rather than in one at the 25th percentile. All regressions include both country and industry fixed effects (coefficient estimates not reported). Heteroskedasticity robust standard errors are reported in parentheses.

clude domestic credit to the private sector in the second column, accounting standards in the third column, and accounting standards from the 1983 subsample in the fourth column (for ease of presentation, accounting standards have been divided by 100 in the estimation). The coefficients are uniformly significant at the 1-percent level. The economic magnitudes—as measured by the differential in growth rates—are also similar except when development is measured by accounting stan-

dards in 1983. The magnitude in column four falls to approximately half of its level otherwise. The explanation for this fall is, perhaps, that the 1983 subsample, being based on just a few companies for each country, introduces significant measurement error.[15]

---

[15] When we instrument this measure (see next paragraph), the coefficient estimate goes up by 50 percent, suggesting the coefficient estimate is biased downwards by measurement error.

In the fifth column, we include both total capitalization and accounting standards. The coefficient for total capitalization is no longer different from zero and its magnitude falls to one-fifth of its level in the first column. Similar results are obtained when we replace total capitalization by domestic credit to the private sector (coefficients not reported). This suggests that accounting standards capture the information about development that is contained in the capitalization measures. For this reason, we will use accounting standards as our measure of development in the rest of the paper. The reader should be assured, however, that the results are qualitatively similar when capitalization measures of development are used.

Because of potential concerns about endogeneity, we will, however, instrument accounting standards with predetermined institutional variables. Rafael La Porta et al. (1996) suggest that the origin of a country's legal system has an effect on the development of a domestic capital market and on the nature of the accounting system. Countries colonized by the British, in particular, tend to have sophisticated accounting standards while countries influenced by the French tend to have poor standards. This suggests using the colonial origin of a country's legal system (indicators for whether it is British, French, German, or Scandinavian) as reported in La Porta et al. as one instrument. Also, countries differ in the extent to which laws are enforced. So we use an index for the efficiency and integrity of the legal system produced by Business International Corporation (a country-risk rating agency) as another instrument. As the sixth column of Table 4 shows, the fundamental interaction becomes even stronger in magnitude when we estimate it using instrumental variables.

Before going further, consider the actual (rather than estimated) effects of development on the growth of specific industries. In Table 5, we summarize for the three least-dependent and three most-dependent industries, the residual growth rate obtained after partialling out industry and country effects. The pattern is remarkable. For countries below the median in accounting standards, the residual growth rate of the three least-dependent industries is positive, while the residual growth rate of the

TABLE 5—EFFECT OF FINANCIAL DEVELOPMENT ON ACTUAL GROWTH RATES IN DIFFERENT INDUSTRIES

	Countries below the median in accounting standards	Countries above the median in accounting standards
Least financially dependent industries		
Tobacco	0.53	−0.60
Pottery	0.25	−0.30
Leather	0.77	−0.77
Most financially dependent industries		
Drug	−1.11	1.30
Plastics	−0.21	0.21
Computers	−2.00	1.80

Notes: This table reports the mean residual growth rate (in percentage terms) obtained after regressing the annual compounded growth rate in real value added for the period 1980–1990 on industry and country dummies.

three most-dependent industries is negative. The pattern reverses for countries above the median. Clearly, this suggests no single country or industry drives our results and the realized differential in growth rates is systematic and large.

2. *Varying Measures of Dependence.* —We now check that our measure of dependence is, indeed, reasonable. We do this in two ways. First, we check that past financing in a country is related to the external dependence of industries in the country. Second, we check that our result is robust to different measures of dependence.

Total capitalization is a (crude) measure of how much finance has been raised in the past in the country. If external dependence is a proxy for an industry's technological need for external finance outside the United States, then countries more specialized in externally dependent industries should have higher capitalization. We calculate the weighted average dependence for each country by multiplying an industry's dependence on external finance by the fraction that the industry contributes to value added in the manufacturing sector in 1980. We then regress total capitalization against weighted average dependence for the 41 countries in the sample. Weighted average dependence is strongly positively correlated with capitalization in 1980 ($\beta = 2.89$, $t = 3.06$). This suggests that our measure of dependence in the United States is related to the external financing used by industry in other countries.[16]

Next, in Table 6 we check that the results are robust to using the external dependence measured for the sample of young firms. Since Figure 1 suggests that most of the demand for external funds is expressed early on in the life of a company, it may be legitimate to expect this to be a better measure of an industry's financial needs. Regardless of how we measure financial development, the interaction effect is positive and statistically significant at the 10-percent level or better, and at the 5-percent level when we use instrumented accounting standards. The magnitude of the coefficient, however, is smaller (roughly a third of the one estimated in Table 4). In part, this reflects the higher level of the external finance raised by young companies. But even when we take this into account (see last row of the table), a difference, albeit smaller, persists. One possible explanation for this result is that young firms are not as important as mature firms in influencing the growth of the industry. We shall return to this issue in Section V, subsection A.

In Table 7, we undertake further robustness checks on our measure of external dependence. While we vary the measure of external dependence, we maintain as a measure of financial development a country's accounting standards, instrumented as above.

In the first column, external dependence is calculated restricting the sample only to mature firms (listed for more than ten years) in the United States. Our interaction variable is positive and statistically significant and the estimated differential growth rate (0.9 percent) is similar to that for the entire sample.

Next, we check whether there is persistence in dependence. If the pattern of financing in the United States in the 1980's is very different

from the pattern in the 1970's, it would be unreasonable to expect dependence to carry any information for other countries (especially developing countries that may use older technologies). The raw correlation between an industry's demand for external financing in the 1980's and its demand in the 1970's is 0.63. The coefficient estimate when dependence is measured by the demand for external financing in the 1970's is statistically significant, and the estimated differential growth rate is 0.9 percent.

Finally, it may be that our results derive from the peculiarities of the United States over the 1980's. Our method should work so long as we measure dependence in a country where financial constraints are thought to be small (so that we measure demand not supply). The only other country we have detailed data on flow of funds for is Canada. Canada is very different from the United States along important dimensions. Its banking system is more concentrated as is corporate ownership, and the composition of its industries is different. Nevertheless, the correlation between dependence measured in the United States and dependence measured in Canada is 0.77. As the third column of Table 7 shows, the coefficient estimate when dependence is measured using Canadian data is highly significant. What is especially interesting both in this table and Table 4 is that the economic magnitude of the interaction effect is generally similar despite variation in the measure of dependence and development used.

V. Other Tests

A. Decomposition of Sources of Growth

An industry can grow because new establishments are added to the industry or because existing establishments grow in size. The U.N. database also reports the number of establishments in an industry.[17] In our sample, it turns

---

[16] Of course, this raises the possibility of reverse causality which we will address later.

[17] An establishment is defined as a "unit which engages, under a single ownership or control, in one, or predominantly one, kind of activity at a single location." (*Industrial Statistics Yearbook* p. 4). This definition may not coincide with the legal boundaries of the firm, but is the only one available for such a large cross section of countries.

TABLE 6—INDUSTRY GROWTH AND VARIOUS MEASURES OF DEVELOPMENT
USING EXTERNAL DEPENDENCE MEASURED FOR YOUNG FIRMS

Variable	Financial development measured as					
	Total capitalization	Bank debt	Accounting standards	Accounting standards in 1983	Accounting standards and capitalization	Instrumental variables
Industry's share of total value added in manufacturing in 1980	−0.911 (0.287)	−0.904 (0.286)	−0.568 (0.234)	−0.616 (0.252)	−0.293 (0.149)	−0.571 (0.233)
Interaction (external dependence × total capitalization)	0.021 (0.012)	—	—	—	−0.004 (0.008)	—
Interaction (external dependence × domestic credit to private sector)	—	0.034 (0.019)	—	—	—	—
Interaction (external dependence × accounting standards)	—	—	0.046 (0.021)	—	0.045 (0.022)	0.058 (0.028)
Interaction (external dependence × accounting standards 1983)	—	—	—	0.038 (0.019)	—	—
R^2	0.283	0.283	0.341	0.236	0.415	0.340
Number of observations	1150	1150	1008	808	984	1008
Differential in real growth rate	0.6	0.5	0.4	0.2	0.1	0.5

Notes: The dependent variable is the annual compounded growth rate in real value added for the period 1980–1990 for each ISIC industry in each country. External dependence is the fraction of capital expenditures not financed with internal funds between 1980–1990 for U.S. firms which went public in the previous ten years belonging to the same industry. The interaction variable is the product of external dependence and financial development. Financial development is total capitalization in the first column, domestic credit to the private sector over GDP in the second column, accounting standards in 1990 in the third column, and accounting standards in 1983 in the fourth column. The sixth column is estimated with instrumental variables. Both the coefficient estimate for the interaction term and the standard error when accounting standards is the measure of development are multiplied by 100. The differential in real growth rate measures (in percentage terms) how much faster an industry at the 75th percentile level of external dependence grows with respect to an industry at the 25th percentile level when it is located in a country at the 75th percentile of financial development rather than in one at the 25th percentile. All regressions include both country and industry fixed effects (coefficient estimates not reported). Heteroskedasticity robust standard errors are reported in parentheses.

out that *two-thirds* of the growth is spurred by an increase in the average size of establishments, while the remaining third is accounted for by an increase in the number of establishments. The growth in the number of establishments is the log of the number of ending-period establishments less the log of the number of establishments in the beginning of period. The average size of establishments in the industry is obtained by dividing the value added in the industry by the number of

establishments, and the growth in average size is obtained again as a difference in logs.

Although the definition of establishments provided by the *Industrial Statistics Yearbook* does not coincide with the legal definition of a firm, there are three reasons why it is interesting to decompose the effect of financial development in its effect on the growth in the number of establishments and growth in the size of the existing establishments. First, since this statistic is often compiled by a different

TABLE 7—INDUSTRY GROWTH AND VARIOUS MEASURES OF EXTERNAL DEPENDENCE

	External dependence measured using		
Variable	Old firms	Firms in 1970's	Canadian firms
Industry's share of total value added in manufacturing in 1980	−0.625 (0.204)	−0.620 (0.205)	−0.610 (0.235)
Interaction (external dependence × accounting standards)	0.253 (0.063)	0.315 (0.127)	0.065 (0.023)
R^2	0.336	0.334	0.343
Number of observations	1035	1035	802
Differential in real growth rate	0.9	0.9	0.8

Notes: The dependent variable is the annual compounded growth rate in real value added for the period 1980–1990 for each ISIC industry in each country. External dependence is the fraction of capital expenditures not financed with internal funds by firms in the same industry during the 1980's. In the first column this ratio is computed only for companies that have been public for at least ten years. In the second column it is computed for U.S. firms during the 1970's. In the third column it is computed for Canadian firms during the 1980's. Also in the third column, data on U.S. industries are included while data on Canadian industries are dropped. The differential in real growth rate measures (in percentage terms) how much faster an industry at the 75th percentile level of external dependence grows with respect to an industry at the 25th percentile level when it is located in a country at the 75th percentile of financial development rather than in one at the 25th percentile. All regressions are estimated using instrumental variables and include both country and industry fixed effects (coefficient estimates not reported). Heteroskedasticity robust standard errors are reported in parenthesis.

body in a country from the one that produces the value-added data, this test provides an independent check on our results.[18] Second, the creation of new establishments is more likely to require external funds, while the expansion of existing establishments can also use internal funds. Thus, the effect of financial development should be more pronounced for the first than for the second. Finally, the growth in the number of establishments is more likely to be generated by new firms than the growth in the size of the existing establishments. Thus, the growth in the number of establishments should be more sensitive to the external dependence measured using young firms in the United States.

We then estimate the basic regression with growth in number of establishments and growth in average size as dependent variables. As Table 8 indicates, the interaction variable is statistically significant only when explaining

[18] The disadvantage is that the industry classification used by the body compiling the number of firms may differ from the industry classification used by the body compiling value-added data, resulting in an increase in noise.

the growth in the number of establishments. More important, the differential in growth rate suggested by the estimate is twice as large in the second column (the regression with growth in numbers as the dependent variable) as in the first column (the regression with growth in average size as the dependent variable).

This finding that the development of financial markets has a disproportional impact on the growth of new establishments is suggestive. Financial development could indirectly influence growth by allowing new ideas to develop and challenge existing ones, much as Schumpeter argued.

Recall that in the previous section, we found that the dependence of young firms was of lower importance (both statistical and economic) than the dependence of mature firms in explaining the relative growth of industries. One explanation is that the dependence of young firms in the United States is an accurate measure of the needs of new firms in that industry elsewhere, but only a noisy measure of the dependence of all firms. This seems to be the case. When dependence is measured for

TABLE 8—GROWTH IN AVERAGE SIZE AND NUMBER OF ESTABLISHMENTS

| | External dependence measured using | | | | | |
| | All firms | | Young firms | | Mature firms | |
Variable	Growth average size	Growth number	Growth average size	Growth number	Growth average size	Growth number
Industry's share of total value added in manufacturing in 1980	−0.620 (0.217)	−0.312 (0.154)	−0.635 (0.256)	−0.252 (0.179)	−0.624 (0.220)	−0.282 (0.152)
Interaction (external dependence × accounting standards)	0.051 (0.043)	0.115 (0.037)	−0.021 (0.029)	0.078 (0.024)	0.125 (0.055)	0.131 (0.041)
R^2	0.498	0.314	0.500	0.302	0.492	0.310
Number of observations	951	975	899	922	923	947
Differential in real growth rate	0.3	0.7	−0.2	0.6	0.4	0.4

Notes: The average size of establishments in the industry is obtained by dividing the value added in the industry by the number of establishments, and the growth in average size is obtained as a difference in logs between average size in 1990 and average size in 1980. The growth in the number of establishments is the log of the number of establishments in 1990 less the log of the number of establishments in 1980. The differential in real growth rate measures (in percentage terms) how much faster an industry at the 75th percentile level of external dependence grows with respect to an industry at the 25th percentile level when it is located in a country at the 75th percentile of financial development rather than in one at the 25th percentile. All regressions are estimated using instrumental variables and include both country and industry fixed effects (coefficient estimates not reported). Heteroskedasticity robust standard errors are reported in parentheses.

young firms, the interaction coefficient has a positive, statistically significant effect on the growth in the number of establishments, but a negative (and statistically insignificant) effect on the growth of the average size of existing establishments (third and fourth columns); when dependence is measured for mature firms, the interaction coefficient has a positive, statistically significant effect on both.

Since most of growth in value added is generated by an increase in the average size of existing establishments, the most appropriate measure of external dependence seems to be one that includes both the needs of new firms as well as the needs of existing firms. This is why in the rest of the paper we will use external dependence measured across all firms.

B. *Is the Interaction a Proxy for Other Variables?*

Do external dependence or financial development proxy for something else? In principle, there is a long list of sources of comparative advantage that may dictate the presence, ab-

sence, or growth of industries in a country. Our results, though, cannot be explained unless the dependence of industries on this source of comparative advantage is strongly correlated with their dependence on external funding *and* financial development is a good proxy for the source of comparative advantage. We rule out two such possibilities below.

Industries that are highly dependent on external finance—for example, Drugs and Pharmaceuticals—could also be dependent on human capital inputs. To the extent that financial market development and the availability of human capital are correlated, the observed interaction between external dependence and financial development may proxy for the interaction between human capital dependence and the availability of trained human capital. To check this, we include in the basic regression an interaction between the industry's dependence on external finance and a measure of the country's stock of human capital (average years of schooling in population over the age of 25). If the conjecture is true, the coefficient of the financial development interaction term

TABLE 9—ROBUSTNESS CHECKS

Variable	Human capital	Economic development	Above median	Below median
Industry's share of total value added in manufacturing in 1980	−0.386 (0.137)	−0.422 (0.134)	−0.437 (0.178)	−6.079 (1.932)
Interaction (external dependence × accounting standards)	0.191 (0.072)	0.149 (0.055)	0.161 (0.065)	0.161 (0.066)
Interaction 2 (external dependence × average years of schooling)	−0.002 (0.003)	—	—	—
Interaction 3 (external dependence × log of per capita income in 1980)	—	0.000 (0.005)	—	—
R^2	0.413	0.418	0.548	0.390
Number of observations	1006	1042	522	545
Differential in real growth rate	1.0	0.9	0.9	1.0

Notes: The dependent variable is the annual compounded growth rate in real value added for the period 1980–1990 for each ISIC industry in each country. The first column adds to the basic specification the interaction between external dependence and a country's human capital. The second column adds to the basic specification the interaction between external dependence and a country's level of economic development (log per capita income). The third column estimates the basic specification for industries that in 1980 were above the median industry in terms of the fraction they accounted for of value added in the manufacturing sector. The fourth column estimates the basic specification for industries that in 1980 were below the median industry in terms of the fraction they accounted for of value added in the manufacturing sector. The differential in real growth rate measures (in percentage terms) how much faster an industry at the 75th percentile level of external dependence grows with respect to an industry at the 25th percentile level when it is located in a country at the 75th percentile of financial development rather than in one at the 25th percentile. All regressions are estimated using instrumental variables and include both country and industry fixed effects (coefficient estimates not reported). Heteroskedasticity robust standard errors are reported in parentheses.

should fall substantially. As the coefficient estimates in the first column of Table 9 show, the coefficient on the human capital interaction term is small and not statistically significant, while the financial development interaction increases somewhat. This suggests that financial dependence is not a proxy for the industry's dependence on human capital.

Another possibility is that lower dependence on external financing in the United States simply reflects the greater maturity of the industry. An influential view of the development process is that as technologies mature, industries using those technologies migrate from developed economies to developing economies (see, for example, Rudiger Dornbusch et al., 1977). Since developing countries are more likely to have underdeveloped financial markets, the interaction effect we document may simply reflect the stronger growth of mature technologies in underdeveloped countries.

We already have results suggesting this cannot be the entire explanation. The interaction effect is present even when dependence is measured only for young firms in the United States. Furthermore, we can test if financial development is really a proxy for economic development in the regression. We include in the basic regression the interaction between the industry's dependence on external finance and the log per capita GDP for the country, in addition to our usual interaction term. As seen in the second column of Table 9, the coefficient of the interaction term falls from 0.165 (in the basic regression) to 0.149 but is still statistically and economically significant. The interaction between financial dependence and log per capita income is close to zero and not significant. The results do not suggest financial dependence is a proxy for technological maturity.

C. *Other Explanations: Reverse Causality*

Thus far, we have taken the state of financial markets as predetermined and exogenous. An alternative explanation of the development of financial markets is that they arise to accommodate the financing needs of finance-hungry industries.

The argument is as follows. Suppose there are some underlying country-specific factors or endowments (such as natural resources) that favor certain industries (such as Mining) that happen to be finance hungry. Then, countries abundant in these factors should experience higher growth rates in financially dependent industries and—as a result—should develop a strong financial market. If these factors persist, then growth rates in financially dependent sectors will persist and we will observe the significant interaction effect. But here it will result from omitted factors than any beneficial effect of finance.

On the one hand, the lack of persistence in country growth over periods of decades (see William Easterly et al., 1993) and the low correlation of sectoral growth across decades (see Peter Klenow, 1995) suggest that this should not be a major concern. On the other hand, our finding that capitalization is higher when the weighted average dependence of industries in the country is high indicates the argument is not implausible.

The results we already have should reduce concerns about reverse causality. By restricting the sample to manufacturing firms, we have reduced the influence of availability of natural resources. More important, the measure of financial development we use— accounting standards—is instrumented with predetermined variables that are unlikely to be correlated with omitted factors driving the growth of industries dependent on external finance. In fact, it should be less correlated with past financing than the capitalization measure, yet it explains future relative growth rates better.

However, we can also test the argument more directly. If an industry has a substantial presence in a particular country, it is logical

that the country has the necessary resources and talents for the industry. So by further restricting the sample to industries that are above the median size in the country in 1980, we reduce the problem of differences in growth stemming from differences in endowment. When we estimate the regression with this smaller sample (third column of Table 9), the interaction coefficient is virtually unchanged.

One way to make sense of all our findings without reverse causality driving the results is that financial markets and institutions may develop to meet the needs of one set of industries, but then facilitate the growth of another younger group of industries. Alfred D. Chandler, Jr. (1977) suggests this is, in fact, what happened in the United States. The financial sector, especially investment banks and the corporate bond market, developed to meet the financing needs of railroads in the mid-nineteenth century. The financial infrastructure was, therefore, ready to meet the financing needs of industrial firms as they started growing in the latter half of the nineteenth century. Similarly, Goldsmith (1985 p. 2) based on a study of the balance sheets of 20 countries writes: "The creation of a modern financial superstructure, not in its details but in its essentials, was generally accomplished at a fairly early stage of a country's economic development."

Again, we can test this possibility more directly. We estimate the effect of financial development only for industries that are small to start out with, and are unlikely to be responsible for the state of development of the financial markets. So we estimate the basic regression for industries that in 1980 were less than the median size in their respective countries. The coefficient of the interaction term is again unchanged (see column four of Table 9) even for these industries for which the economy's financial development is largely predetermined. We conclude that reverse causality is unlikely to explain our results.

D. *Other Explanations: Investment and Cost of Capital*

Investment opportunities in different industries may be very different. For instance, the

TABLE 10—CASH FLOW AND INVESTMENTS

Variable	Cash flow intensiveness	Investment intensiveness	Both	Both measured for 1980
Industry's share of total value added in manufacturing in 1980	−0.588 (0.201)	−0.653 (0.205)	−0.639 (0.205)	−0.639 (0.207)
Interaction (internal cash flow × financial development)	0.482 (0.153)	—	−0.261 (0.196)	−0.595 (0.295)
Interaction 2 (investment intensiveness × accounting standards)	—	0.623 (0.221)	0.443 (0.283)	0.800 (0.299)
R^2	0.343	0.345	0.345	0.344
Number of observations	1067	1067	1067	1035
Differential in real growth rate	−0.7	1.4	0.5	1.6

Notes: The dependent variable is the annual compounded growth rate in real value added for the period 1980–1990 for each ISIC industry in each country. Internal cash flow is the ratio of cash flow from operations broadly defined (see text) to net property plant and equipment for U.S. firms in the same industry. Investment intensity is the ratio of capital expenditures to property plant and equipment for U.S. firms in the same industry. The fourth column uses the cash flow intensity and the investment intensity measured for the year 1980. The differential in real growth rate measures (in percentage terms) how much faster an industry at the 75th percentile level of external dependence grows with respect to an industry at the 25th percentile level when it is located in a country at the 75th percentile of financial development rather than in one at the 25th percentile. All regressions are estimated using instrumental variables and include both country and industry fixed effects (coefficient estimates not reported). Heteroskedasticity robust standard errors are reported in parentheses.

Tobacco industry in the United States uses negative external finance (see Table 1) partly because investment opportunities in the Tobacco industry are small relative to the cash flows the industry generates. It may be that our measure of dependence on external finance proxies primarily for the investment intensity of a particular industry. Furthermore, the development of the financial sector may proxy for the overall cost of capital in that country (rather than the cost of external funds). The interaction effect then indicates that capital intensive firms grow faster in an environment with a lower cost of capital. Though this is a legitimate channel through which the financial sector influences growth, we are also interested in a different channel where the reduction in the incremental cost of external funds facilitates growth.

If investment intensity were all that mattered, and external finance and internal finance were equally costly, the cash internally generated by industries would be irrelevant in countries that are more financially developed. All that mattered would be the size of the required investment and

the cost of capital. By contrast, if there is a wedge between the cost of internal and external finance which narrows as the financial sector develops, industries generating lots of internal cash should grow relatively faster in countries with a poorly developed financial sector. As indicated in the first column of Table 10, they do. This is consistent with financial development reducing the cost of external finance. Of course, as is to be expected with both the "cost of capital" and "cost of external capital" hypotheses, industries that invest a lot also grow faster in countries with more-developed financial markets (second column). Unfortunately, when both interactions are introduced in the same regression, the coefficients are measured very imprecisely because of multicollinearity (cash flow intensity and investment intensity have a correlation of 0.73); so neither is statistically different from zero. However, the coefficient on cash flows is still negative and sizeable (accounting for a real growth rate differential of about 0.4 percent per year).

Multicollinearity results from our aggregating cash flows and investments over a decade.[19] Therefore, we estimate the same regression using a measure of cash flow intensity and investment intensity measured for just one year (rather than an entire decade). In the fourth column we report the estimates obtained by using the 1980 measures of cash flow and investment. Both the cash flow intensity and the investment intensity are statistically significant at the 5-percent level. We estimated (but do not report) the same regression using a 1985 measure and a 1990 measure. In both cases the results are similar and both coefficients are statistically significant at the 5-percent level.

VI. Conclusion

We develop a new methodology in this paper to investigate whether financial-sector development has an influence on industrial growth. In doing so, we partially circumvent some of the problems with the existing cross-country methodology highlighted by Mankiw (1995). First, it is difficult to interpret observed correlations in cross-country regressions in a causal sense. Here, we push the causality debate one step further by finding evidence for a channel through which finance theoretically influences growth. Also, since we have multiple observations per country, we can examine situations where the direction of causality is least likely to be reversed. A second problem with the traditional methodology is that explanatory variables are multicollinear and are measured with error. The combination of these two problems may cause a variable to appear significant when it is merely a proxy for some other variable measured with error. As a result, observed correlations can be misleading. By looking at interaction effects (with country and industry indicators) rather than direct effects, we reduce the number of variables that we rely on, as well as the range of possible alternative explanations. Third, there is the problem of limited degrees of freedom—there

are fewer than 200 countries on which the myriad theories have to be tested. Our approach partially alleviates this problem by exploiting within-country variation in the data. Our methodology, may have wider applications, such as testing the existence of channels through which human capital can affect growth.

Apart from its methodological contribution, this paper's findings may bear on three different areas of current research. First, they suggest that financial development has a substantial supportive influence on the rate of economic growth and this works, at least partly, by reducing the cost of external finance to financially dependent firms. We should add that there is no contradiction when the lack of persistence of economic growth (Easterly et al., 1993) is set against the persistence of financial development. Other factors may cause (potentially serially uncorrelated) changes in a country's investment opportunity set. Finance may simply enable the pursuit of these opportunities, and thereby enhance long-run growth. The paper does, however, suggest that financial development may play a particularly beneficial role in the rise of new firms. If these firms are disproportionately the source of ideas, financial development can enhance innovation, and thus enhance growth in indirect ways.

Second, in the context of the literature on financial constraints, this paper provides fresh evidence that financial market imperfections have an impact on investment and growth.

Finally, in the context of the trade literature, the findings suggest a potential explanation for the pattern of industry specialization across countries. To the extent that financial-market development (or the lack thereof) is determined by historical accident or government regulation, the existence of a well-developed market in a certain country represents a source of comparative advantage for that country in industries that are more dependent on external finance. Similarly, the costs imposed by a lack of financial development will favor incumbent firms over new entrants. Therefore, the level of financial development can also be a factor in determining the size composition of an industry as well as its concentration. These issues are important areas for future research.

---

[19] Early investments will generate later cash flows resulting in the correlation. Aggregating over a decade, however, will still give a reasonable estimate of the average demand for external funds even though it tells us less about the components.

REFERENCES

Barro, Robert J. "Economic Growth in a Cross Section of Countries." *Quarterly Journal of Economics*, May 1991, *106*(2), pp. 407–43.

Barro, Robert J. and Lee, Jong Wha. "International Comparisons of Educational Attainment." *Journal of Monetary Economics*, December 1993, *32*(3), pp. 363–94.

Bekaert, Geert and Harvey, Campbell R. "Time-Varying World Market Integration." *Journal of Finance*, June 1995, *50*(2), pp. 403–44.

Bencivenga, Valerie R. and Smith, Bruce D. "Financial Intermediation and Endogenous Growth." *Review of Economic Studies*, April 1991, *58*(2), pp. 195–209.

Boyd, John H. and Smith, Bruce D. "The Co-Evolution of the Real and Financial Sectors in the Growth Process." *World Bank Economic Review*, May 1996, *10*(2), pp. 371–96.

Cameron, Rondo. *Banking in the early stages of industrialization*. New York: Oxford University Press, 1967.

Chandler, Alfred D., Jr. *The visible hand: The managerial revolution in American business*. Cambridge, MA: Harvard University Press, 1977.

Demirgüç-Kunt, Asli and Maksimovic, Vojislav. "Financial Constraints, Uses of Funds and Firm Growth: An International Comparison." Working paper, World Bank, 1996.

Diamond, Douglas W. "Reputation Acquisition in Debt Markets." *Journal of Political Economy*, August 1989, *97*(4), pp. 828–62.

Dornbusch, Rudiger; Fischer, Stanley and Samuelson, Paul A. "Comparative Advantage, Trade and Payments in A Ricardian Model with a Continuum of Goods." *American Economic Review*, December 1977, *67*(5), pp. 823–39.

Easterly, William; Kremer, Michael; Pritchett, Lant and Summers, Lawrence H. "Good Policy or Good Luck? Country Growth Performance and Temporary Shocks." *Journal of Monetary Economics*, December 1993, *32*(3), pp. 459–83.

Feldstein, Martin and Horioka, Charles. "Domestic Saving and International Capital Flows." *Economic Journal*, June 1980, *90*(358), pp. 314–29.

French, Kenneth R. and Poterba, James M. "Investor Diversification and International Equity Markets." *American Economic Review*, May 1991 (*Papers and Proceedings*), *81*(2), pp. 222–26.

Goldsmith, Raymond, W. *Financial structure and development*, New Haven, CT: Yale University Press, 1969.

_____. *Comparative national balance sheets*. Chicago: University of Chicago Press, 1985.

Greenwood, Jeremy and Jovanovic, Boyan. "Financial Development, Growth, and the Distribution of Income." *Journal of Political Economy*, October 1990, *98*(5), pp. 1076–107.

International Finance Corporation. *Emerging stock markets factbook*. Washington, DC: International Finance Corporation, various years.

International Monetary Fund. *International financial statistics*. Washington, DC: International Monetary Fund, various years.

Jayaratne, Jith and Strahan, Philip E. "The Finance-Growth Nexus: Evidence from Bank Branch Deregulation." *Quarterly Journal of Economics*, August 1996, *111*(3), pp. 639–70.

Jensen, Michael C. and Meckling, William R. "Theory of the Firm: Managerial Behavior, Agency Costs and Capital Structure." *Journal of Financial Economics*, October 1976, *3*(4), pp. 305–60.

King, Robert G. and Levine, Ross. "Finance and Growth: Schumpeter Might Be Right." *Quarterly Journal of Economics*, August 1993a, *108*(3), pp. 713–37.

_____. "Finance, Entrepreneurship, and Growth." *Journal of Monetary Economics*, December 1993b, *32*(3), pp. 513–42.

Klenow, Peter. "Ideas vs. Rival Human Capital: Industry Evidence on Growth Models." Mimeo, University of Chicago, 1995.

Kormendi, Roger and Meguire, Philip. "Macroeconomic Determinants of Growth: Cross-Country Evidence." *Journal of Monetary Economics*, September 1985, *16*(2), pp. 141–63.

La Porta, Rafael; Lopez de Silanes, Florencio; Shleifer, Andrei and Vishny, Robert. "Law and Finance.'' National Bureau of Economic Research (Cambridge, MA) Working Paper No. 5661, 1996.

Levine, Ross. ''Financial Development and Economic Growth: Views and Agenda.'' *Journal of Economic Literature*, June 1997, *35*(2), pp. 688–726.

Levine, Ross and Renelt, David. ''A Sensitivity Analysis of Cross-Countries Growth Regressions.'' *American Economic Review*, September 1992, *82*(4), pp. 942–63.

Levine, Ross and Zervos, Sara. ''Stock Markets and Economic Growth.'' *American Economic Review*, June 1998, *88*(3), pp. 537–58.

Mankiw, N. Gregory. ''The Growth of Nations.'' *Brookings Papers on Economic Activity*, 1995, (1), pp. 275–310.

Mankiw, N. Gregory; Romer, David and Weil, David. ''A Contribution to the Empirics of Economic Growth,'' *Quarterly Journal of Economics*, May 1992, *152*(2), pp. 407–37.

Mayer, Colin. ''Financial Systems, Corporate Finance, and Economic Development,'' in R. Glenn Hubbard, ed., *Asymmetric information, corporate finance and investment*. Chicago: University of Chicago Press, 1990, pp. 307–32.

Myers, Stewart C. and Majluf, Nicholas S. ''Corporate Financing and Investment Decisions When Firms Have Information That Investors Do Not Have.'' *Journal of Financial Economics*, June 1984, *13*(2), pp. 187–221.

Obstfeld, Maurice. ''Risk Taking, Global Diversification, and Growth.'' *American Economic Review*, December 1994, *84*(5), pp. 1310–29.

Petersen, Mitchell A. and Rajan, Raghuram R. ''Trade Credit: Theories and Evidence.'' *Review of Financial Studies*, Fall 1997, *10*(3), pp. 661–91.

Rajan, Raghuram R. and Zingales, Luigi. ''What Do We Know About Capital Structure: Some Evidence From International Data.'' *Journal of Finance*, December 1995, *50*(5), pp. 1421–60.

Robinson, Joan. ''The Generalization of the Generat Theory.'' *The rate of interest and other essays*. London: Macmillan, 1952, pp. 67–142.

Saint-Paul, Gilles. ''Technological Choice, Financial Markets and Economic Development.'' *European Economic Review*, May 1992, *36*(4), pp. 763–81.

Schumpeter, Joseph A. *A theory of economic development*. Cambridge, MA: Harvard University Press, 1911.

Standard & Poor's. *Global vantage*. New York: McGraw-Hill, 1993.

———. *Compustat services*. New York: McGraw-Hill, 1994.

Stiglitz, Joseph E. and Weiss, Andrew. ''Credit Rationing in Markets with Imperfect Information.'' *American Economic Review*, June 1981, *71*(3), pp. 393–410.

United Nations, Statistical Division. *Industrial statistics yearbook*, Vol. 1. New York: United Nations, 1993.

B
Microstructure of Equity Markets

[20]

THE JOURNAL OF FINANCE • VOL. LIII, NO. 6 • DECEMBER 1998

International Cross-Listing and Order Flow Migration: Evidence from an Emerging Market

IAN DOMOWITZ, JACK GLEN, and ANANTH MADHAVAN*

ABSTRACT

Policymakers in emerging markets are increasingly concerned about the consequences for the domestic equity market when companies list stock abroad. We show that the effects of cross-listing depend on the quality of intermarket information linkages. We investigate these issues with unique data from the Mexican equity market. The impact of cross-listing is complex—balancing the costs of order flow migration against the benefits of increased intermarket competition. These effects are exacerbated by equity investment barriers that induce segmentation of the domestic equity market. Consequently, the benefits and costs of cross-listing are not evenly spread over all classes of shareholders.

THERE HAS BEEN A DRAMATIC INCREASE in the trading of foreign stocks as investors recognize the need for international diversification and as foreign companies seek to broaden their shareholder base and raise capital. As a result, the number of American Depository Receipt (ADR) listings on U.S. exchanges has also risen sharply. Though corporations view cross-listings as value enhancing, the changes in liquidity and volatility, and the cost of trading associated with order flow migration following cross-listing may adversely affect the quality of the domestic equity market. Such changes are especially important for emerging markets facing new competition from well-established, highly liquid markets abroad, and are the source of increasing concern among policymakers. There is also considerable academic interest in this topic, especially because the effects of cross-listing may be related to the

* Domowitz is from Northwestern University, Glen is with the International Finance Corporation, and Madhavan is at the University of Southern California. Financial support from the World Bank is gratefully acknowledged. Expert research assistance and several helpful suggestions were provided by Mark Coppejans. We thank Baizhu Chen, Harry DeAngelo, Vihang Errunza, Margaret Forster, René Garcia, Tom George, Andrei Kirilenko, Brian Pinto, René Stulz, and an anonymous referee for their helpful comments. We are also grateful to seminar participants at the University of Chicago, International Finance Corporation, London School of Economics, London Business School, University of Southern California, Vanderbilt University, Washington University, NYU Salomon Center Conference on Emerging Markets, and the SBF Paris Bourse Conference on Market Microstructure for their suggestions. Any errors are entirely our own. The comments and opinions contained in this paper are those of the authors and do not necessarily reflect those of the International Finance Corporation or the World Bank.

2001

degree of capital market segmentation.[1] We analyze these issues using new data on daily prices and volumes from 1989 to 1993 obtained from the Mexican Stock Exchange, the Bolsa Mexicana de Valores (BMV).

We develop a theoretical model to examine the impact of international cross-listing where investors acquire costly information. Our analysis highlights the importance of intermarket informational linkages or transparency. In particular, if intermarket price information is freely available, cross-listing results in an improvement in market quality. Intuitively, the provision of an alternative trading venue induces participation abroad by foreign investors who otherwise would not trade. With transparent markets, the increase in the total number of traders following cross-listing reduces spreads, increases the precision of public information, and increases liquidity in both markets.

In the opposite case, where intermarket information linkages are extremely poor, cross-listing reduces liquidity and increases volatility in the local market. Intuitively, cross-listing results in the diversion of informative order flow overseas, resulting in lower domestic market quality. The intermediate case, where information linkages are imperfect, is more complex. Heightened intermarket competition may narrow domestic market spreads, but order flow migration may result in lower domestic market liquidity and may increase price volatility. Our model provides a method to distinguish these outcomes from the data.

From an empirical perspective, the Mexican market is of particular interest. First, Mexico is an important emerging market, and previous studies of international listing have focused almost exclusively on large, liquid markets such as Britain, Canada, and Japan. Second, foreign listing is likely to have a significant impact on the domestic Mexican market because foreign investors (mostly U.S. nationals) account for more than 27 percent of holdings and up to 75 percent of trading in our sample period. Third, the BMV is open for trading during much of the time that United States equity markets are open. Consequently, an analysis of trading in Mexico provides a way to better understand the effects of international competition for order flow. Finally, as in many countries, Mexican companies issue multiple equity series that distinguish between foreign and domestic ownership. Because the diversion of order flow is likely to be manifested primarily in series open to foreign investors, this feature makes it easier to discern the effects of cross-listing.

Our empirical results demonstrate that the impacts of cross-listing are complex, reflecting the costs of order flow fragmentation as well as the benefits of increased intermarket competition. Specifically, we find that in those

---

[1] Karolyi (1996) provides an excellent survey of international cross-listing. See also Alexander, Eun, and Janakiramanan (1987, 1988), Chan, Fong, and Stulz (1995), Foerster and Karolyi (1993, 1994, 1996), Forster and George (1996), Howe, Madura, and Tucker (1993), Jayaraman, Shastri, and Tandon (1993), Jorion and Schwartz (1986), Kleidon and Werner (1996), and Urias (1994). Bekaert (1993), Eun and Janakiramanan (1986), and Stulz (1981), discuss equity investment barriers.

series open to foreign ownership, liquidity tends to decrease and price volatility increases, consistent with the migration of foreign investors. Interestingly, these effects appear to be mitigated by increased intermarket competition, which narrows spreads. Finally, although ADR listing is associated with positive excess returns, these benefits accrue largely to those series open to foreign investors prior to cross-listing. No such effects are present in a control group, indicating that our results are not driven by marketwide or macroeconomic factors. The fact that we find returns effects largely for shares already open to foreign investors might suggest that the cost of capital benefit of cross-listing is small. We do not want to push the interpretation of our findings too far, however. Consideration of the cost of capital also entails transactions costs and liquidity effects in both the domestic and foreign market, and the latter is not considered here, except for a very small subset of companies.

The paper proceeds as follows: The institutional features of the Mexican stock market and our data sources are described in Section I. A theoretical model to analyze the impact of cross-listing on the domestic market is developed in Section II. Section III contains our econometric methodology and results. Section IV concludes, and we offer some suggestions for future research.

I. Institutions and Data

A. The Bolsa Mexicana de Valores

The BMV, Mexico's only stock exchange, is a private institution owned by twenty-six Mexican-owned brokerage houses. The exchange operates from 8:30 a.m. to 4:00 p.m. local time (9:30 a.m. to 5:00 p.m. EST) from Monday to Friday, so that trading hours overlap to within an hour of U.S. markets. Orders are either sent to the BMV computer systems or worked by floor brokers through open outcry. Preopening orders can be entered by computer and are crossed automatically in a batch open, subject to certain price limits.

Our study focuses on twenty-five equity instruments issued by sixteen firms whose stock was traded as ADRs in the United States in 1993. Mexican equity instruments are of particular interest for our study in that each company may issue several different series of shares or tranches, each with different rights or shareholder bases. The major series are A, B, and C (or L and O) shares. For a nonfinancial company, series A shares may legally be held only by Mexican individuals or Mexican-controlled institutions. Shares have full voting rights and must collectively represent at least 51 percent of the voting shares.[2] Series B shares are open to all investors, regardless of

---

[2] Foreigners can participate through the Nacional Financiera trust where voting rights are stripped. In this case, the series designation changes to N or CPO.

nationality. Shares have full voting rights, but cannot collectively represent more than 49 percent of the voting shares.[3] Financial groups are not represented in the ADR sample.

Series C shares are open to all investors, but are limited to 30 percent of total capital. Companies also issue L and O series, which are available to all investors but carry limited or no voting rights. All series in our sample represent identical claims to the earnings of the firm.

Similar divisions are found in other countries (e.g., China and Thailand) where public policy seeks to restrict or control the foreign ownership of capital. They also may arise endogenously, as Stulz and Wasserfallen (1995) document for Switzerland. The divisions are important because they may induce internal equity market segmentation, as we describe below.

B. American Depository Receipts

Foreign companies wishing to trade equities (and debt) in the U.S. market often achieve this goal by issuing ADRs. The ADR represents shares held by a trustee in the Mexican market. The receipts, issued by a U.S. depository (Bank of New York, etc.), are then treated as U.S. securities for clearance, settlement, transfer, and ownership purposes. The depository is responsible for the payment of dividends (in dollars) to investors, for the distribution of information about the issuer, and for conversion between shares and ADRs.

The majority of ADRs, including those in our sample, are now sponsored by the issuer, which implies that the issuer has chosen a single depository to handle investor relations and that the costs associated with depository services are paid by the issuer. Alternatively, the issuer could leave the ADR unsponsored (although this is now rare), in which case investors are responsible for the costs of the depository's services.

There are four issue types. A Level I issue is the simplest and results in ADRs that are traded in the U.S. over-the-counter ("pink sheet") market. No new capital is raised and the issuer is not required to comply with U.S. Generally Accepted Accounting Principles (GAAP) or full SEC disclosure requirements. Twelve of the series in our Mexican sample are traded as Level I ADRs. Level II issues involve listing existing shares on a U.S. stock market, and although no new capital is raised, this involves compliance with U.S. disclosure and exchange requirements. None of our series are in this category. Level III issues involve a combination of exchange listing and raising new capital. In addition to the requirements of a Level II

---

[3] Both A and B shares can be further divided into fixed (1 or F) and variable (2 or V) shares, all of which carry equal rights. Under statute, a company must carry a minimum level of capital, the fixed part, which can only be changed by vote of shareholders at an extraordinary meeting. The variable part changes whenever rights are issued or the company decides to buy back shares.

issue, a prospectus must be prepared and additional SEC disclosure requirements must be met. Five of the series in our sample are Level III ADRs. Finally, ADRs can now be placed privately with qualified institutional investors (and new capital can be raised) with minimal disclosure requirements under the 144A rule. Trading in the 144A market takes place through a set of market specialists and the Portal quote system. Six of the series in our sample of Mexican shares are traded in the 144A market.

After issuance, the supply of ADRs varies over time with market conditions. When an existing ADR is sold by a U.S. investor, it can either be transferred to a U.S. buyer or can be canceled by the depository and converted back into the underlying share. Similarly, the demand for ADRs can induce the creation of new receipts from the underlying shares. The depository extracts a fee (generally $5 per 100 shares) for conversion. Given this connection between the ADR and the underlying share market, cross-border arbitrage should align the prices of the two securities (adjusted for the exchange rate) subject to transaction cost bounds imposed by the conversion fee and bid-ask spreads. Conversations with traders suggest that profitable arbitrage occurs when price differentials depart from theoretical bounds, possibly because of delays in observing prices and quotes in the other market, differences in the responsiveness of prices to news events, or price pressure caused by noise trading.

C. The Data

The data used in this study were obtained from the BMV, and until now have not been publicly available. The sample used here consists of daily observations on prices, returns, and share volumes of twenty-five equity series. These series represent sixteen firms over the period from September 1989 through July 1993, all of which experienced an ADR listing over the sample period. Additionally, we gathered data on nine non-ADR companies with similar trading frequencies and characteristics to form a control sample to check the validity of our results. On average, there were 828 trading days per series.

Company names, acronyms, series identifiers, and ADR series listing for the twenty-five stocks our sample are provided in Table I. Of the 25 series, eleven are A class (including fixed and variable) shares, nine are B class shares, and the remaining five are C, L, or O (nonvoting) shares. The majority of the ADRs in our sample are traded over-the-counter or in the 144A market. Of the stocks in our sample, only three are listed on an exchange and for these stocks we have data on trading in the U.S. market as well as in the domestic market.

Table II shows the date of ADR listing, the average daily trading volume (in shares), the standard deviation of daily price changes (a measure of volatility), and the number of trading days before and after ADR listing avail-

Table I

Sample Stocks and Series Type

The table contains the stock series key, names of companies, and series type (A, B, C, and O) by company in our sample for stocks traded on the Bolsa Mexicana de Valores. The ADR series listings are in brackets: OTC, over the counter; 144A, private issue under SEC rule 144A; NAS, Nasdaq; NYSE, New York Stock Exchange; GDR, global depository receipt. Series not in our sample are in parentheses. An asterisk indicates that the ADR raised new capital for the issuer.

Series Key	Company Name	Series
CEM	Cemex	A[144A]*, B[OTC]
CER	Internacional de Ceramica	B[OTC]
CIF	Cifra	A, B[OTC], C
COM	Controladora Comercial Mexicana	B[OTC]
EPN	EPN	A, (B[OTC])
FEM	Fomento Economico Mexicano	B[144A]
GCA	Grupo Carso	A[144A]
LIV	El Puerto de Liverpool	O, C[GDR]*
MAS	Grupo Industrial Maseca	A[OTC]*, B
PON	Ponderosa Industrial	A, B[OTC]*
SAN	Corporacion Industrial San Luis	A[OTC]
SYN	Grupo Synkro	A, B[OTC]
TEL	Telefonos de Mexico	A[NAS]
TMM	Transportacion Maritima Mexicana	A[NYSE]*, L[NYSE]*
TTO	Tolmex	B[OTC]
VIT	Vitro	O[NYSE]

able for analysis for each stock, grouped by series type.[4] The dates of ADR listing vary widely across the sample, with the earliest being EPN, listed in December 1989 and the most recent being TMM, listed in June 1992.

There is a wide range in trading activity and volatility across stocks. Overall, 62 percent of the series experienced some increase in volume, but this figure is not statistically significantly different from 50 percent. The figure is slightly higher for the A shares, at 67 percent. Higher volume is observed for 63 percent of the B shares, and for about 60 percent of all shares with foreign ownership rights prior to international listing. However, it is difficult to discern a pattern to the changes in volume and volatility following ADR listing. We turn now to a more formal analysis of this issue.

---

[4] We use the standard deviation of price changes as our volatility measure for consistency with the volatility measure used in model estimation, which, in turn, is based on the theoretical analysis to follow. Though this measure of volatility is highly correlated with the return variance, there are a few stocks where, because of differences in the way these measures weight outliers, the volatility patterns differ by whether we use the standard deviation of returns or price changes.

Table II

Volume and Price Volatility by Stock Series

This table contains the summary statistics for all stock series in our sample of stocks traded on the Bolsa Mexicana de Valores for which an ADR was introduced. The month and year of the ADR introduction is given under ADR Listing. Volume Prior and Volume After are average daily shares traded, in thousands, before and after the listing, respectively. Volatility Prior and Volatility After denote the average standard deviations of daily price changes before and after the listing. Days Prior and Days After are the number of trading days in the sample before and after the listing. Superscript a denotes scaling by 10^2. Panel A lists results for the series restricted to Mexican ownership domestically, Panel B for B shares, open to foreign ownership, and Panel C for other unrestricted series.

	ADR Listing	Volatility Prior	Volatility After	Volume Prior	Volume After	Days Prior	Days After
			Panel A: A Series				
CEM	5/91	0.204	0.697	444	343	409	551
CIF	1/91	0.073	0.197	893	847	336	624
EPN	12/89	0.005	0.005	349	955	70	760
GCA	10/91	0.405	0.731	16	720	312	444
MAS	4/92	0.228	0.229	291	513	431	311
PON	5/91	0.003	0.005	144^a	236^a	417	543
SAN	7/90	0.062	0.047	289	82	219	741
SANAV	7/90	0.054	0.045	462	269	219	741
SYN	6/90	0.035	0.098	137	54	192	768
TEL	5/91	0.090	0.213	6797	1539	415	545
TMM	6/92	0.480	0.492	46	88	73	270
			Panel B: B Series				
CEM	5/91	0.281	0.661	175	374	166	551
CER	4/91	0.048	0.137	8	36	387	573
CIF	1/91	0.073	0.218	699	2228	336	624
COM	2/92	0.044	0.059	1199	774	203	353
FEM	4/91	0.101	0.257	396	1186	387	573
MAS	4/92	0.217	0.235	301	664	431	311
PON	5/91	0.010	0.011	357	177	417	543
SYN	6/90	0.035	0.083	23	26	192	768
TTO	9/91	0.182	0.346	615	466	388	455
			Panel C: Other Series				
CIFC	1/91	0.026	0.063	2618	3979	61	624
LIVC	6/92	0.214	0.385	103	480	685	275
LIVO	6/92	0.211	0.327	47	220	685	275
TMML	6/92	0.472	0.499	91	60	73	270
VITO	11/91	1.100	1.811	150	457	547	413

II. The Analytical Framework

A. The Model

Consider a domestically traded stock for which trading takes place sequentially at prices posted by floor traders or marketmakers. Both foreign and domestic investors can trade the stock; we extend the model below to discuss the impact of equity investment barriers in the form of ownership restrictions. Let n_d represent the number of domestic traders in a given day, n_f denote the number of investors who are foreign nationals seeking to trade in the domestic market, and let $N = n_d + n_f$ denote the total number of (actual, as opposed to potential) traders, where we suppress the time subscript for notational convenience.

We assume that arrivals of both domestic and foreign investors are governed by independent Poisson distributions with (possibly time-varying) parameters θ_d and θ_f, respectively. The choice of a Poisson distribution to model trader arrivals is a natural one since it arises in the limit from a more primitive model of the behavior of individual traders, as shown below. Using the properties of the Poisson process, the total number of traders arriving in a day of unit length follows a Poisson process with parameter $\theta = \theta_d + \theta_f$.

A.1. Security Prices and Trades

Following Glosten and Milgrom (1985), we assume trade size is one unit. Let x_k denote the desired order of trader k (who arrives at calendar time t_k), where we adopt the convention that $x_k = +1$ for a buy, -1 for a sell, and 0 if the trader chooses not to trade. Let $p_k(x_k)$ denote the stock's price as a function of the order and let μ_k denote the expected value of the asset at the time of the kth trade of the day from dealers' viewpoint based on the past history of trading. We assume that the quotation function is public information, and that the marketmakers' conditional expectation of the asset's value can be inferred from their quotes. This will indeed turn out to be the case.

To model the behavior of traders, we assume that trader k receives idiosyncratic human capital income, denoted h_k. At time t_k, trader k obtains a private information signal regarding the current value of the asset. Denote by y_k the *deviation* of the asset's fundamental value and the conditional mean based on public information. Thus, the expected value of the asset, given public information and the private signal y_k, is $y_k + \mu_k$. Let ρ^2 denote the variance of this estimate. We assume that investors maximize mean-variance expected utility functions, where a denotes the risk-aversion parameter. The investor's expected utility, u_k, conditional on entering the market is

$$u_k = (\mu_k + y_k + w_k - p_k(x_k))x_k + \mathrm{E}[h_k] - a\rho^2 x_k^2 - a\sigma_h^2, \qquad (1)$$

where $w_k = -2a\mathrm{cov}(h_k, v_k)$ is the covariance between the asset's fundamental value (denoted by v_k) and the trader's idiosyncratic income. The term w_k reflects the additional value trader k places on the asset as a hedge against fluctuations in other income. The potential diversification benefits accruing from holding the risky asset create both information and liquidity motives for trade. The trader's optimization problem, given the prevailing quotes in the market, is to choose the optimal order $x_k \in \{-1, 0, 1\}$ to maximize expected utility, u_k.

As in Glosten and Milgrom (1985), the price facing trader k is $p_k(x_k) = \mu_k + sx_k$, where s represents both the order processing cost element of the bid-ask spread as well as any rents accruing to dealer market power. Note that dealers' conditional mean valuations can be inferred from the quotation function, as previously conjectured. Previous research suggests that this spread element is inversely related to the expected trading frequency, and we write $s = s(\theta)$, where $s'(\theta) < 0$. Dealers are ex post rational, that is, they set quotes that recognize the information conveyed by trade. We write the conditional valuation of the stock μ_k as $\mu_k = \mu_{k-1} + \lambda x_k$, where λ captures the information content of the trade. Formally, $\mathrm{E}[y_k|x_k = 1] = \lambda$ and $\mathrm{E}[y_k|x_k = -1] = -\lambda$. Higher perceptions of information asymmetry (in the form of more accurate private information signals y_k or less dispersion in liquidity motivations w_k) are manifested in higher values of λ.

An investor who, having gathered information, "arrives" planning to trade (as described below) may elect not to do so if the costs of trading exceed the possible expected profits and diversification gains. Using equation (1), the trader will place a buy order if $y_k + w_k > s + a\rho^2$, a sell order if $y_k + w_k < -s - a\rho^2$, but will not trade otherwise. Let ζ denote the probability that a trader, upon arrival, chooses not to trade where $\zeta = \mathrm{Prob}[x_k = 0] = \mathrm{Prob}[s + a\rho^2 > |y_k + w_k|]$. Observe that nontrading is an increasing function of s, the spread, and $a\rho^2$, the term capturing risk aversion.

A.2. The Entry Decision

Prior to making a decision about whether or not to trade, a potential trader must decide whether it is worth gathering information about fundamentals. Let c_k denote the idiosyncratic cost for agent k to obtain information in the domestic market; we assume that information is observed only after c_k is incurred. Thus, a potential trader will gather information only if the ex ante gain in terms of possible realized expected utility exceeds his or her costs of acquiring information. Let q denote the unconditional probability that a randomly selected potential trader's expected utility exceeds his or her costs of gathering information. The probability that a randomly selected potential trader will trade is given by a Bernoulli distribution with parameter q. The Poisson distribution for investor arrivals thus follows as the limiting case (with large numbers of potential investors) of independent Bernoulli trials. The parameters of the Poisson distribution for each investor group, θ_d and θ_f, are inversely related to the average costs of information acquisition for domestic and foreign investors. Formally, we can write $\theta_d = \theta_d(c_d)$, where c_d is the average cost of information acquisition for domestic investors, and $\theta_d(c_d)$ is a decreasing function of c_d. A similar expression holds for θ_f.

2010   *The Journal of Finance*

A.3. Price Dynamics and Volume

Using the fact that the expected number of arrivals in a given "day" is θ, the expected daily volume can be written as

$$E\left[\sum_{k=1}^{N} |x_k|\right] = (1 - \zeta)(\theta_d + \theta_f), \tag{2}$$

which is an increasing function of the arrival probabilities and a decreasing function of the spread element s, the degree of risk aversion a, and the variance of investor's priors regarding fundamental value, ρ^2. The price change from the opening price to the close of the day is given by

$$p_N - p_0 = \lambda\left(\sum_{k=1}^{N} x_k\right) + sx_N, \tag{3}$$

where p_0 denotes the opening price, which is determined in a batch market. In equation (3), the enclosed term represents the cumulative order imbalance, and the last term represents the effect of bid-ask bounce. Observe that the larger the parameter λ, the greater the impact on prices of a given order imbalance. Thus λ can be interpreted as an inverse measure of market liquidity.

We assume that the opening price is the sum of the previous day's closing price plus an innovation, ϵ. The innovation ϵ captures the effects of overnight information flows regarding changes in fundamental value, and is distributed with mean 0 and variance σ_ϵ^2, where the variance term is inversely related to θ. This assumption follows naturally from a more primitive model of the evolution of beliefs. For example, suppose the number of analysts following the stock, m, is roughly proportional to the mean number of investors likely to trade the stock (i.e., $m = \kappa\theta$, where $\kappa > 0$ is a constant), and each analyst independently obtains a noisy signal about the deviation of the value of the underlying asset from the previous close. Let τ^2 denote the variance of each analyst's signal, so that $\sigma_\epsilon^2 = \tau^2/\kappa\theta$; that is, the variance of public information is inversely related to the number of market participants. It is clear that the desired result would hold even if analyst forecasts were correlated, as long as the correlation were not perfect. Alternatively, recall that the market opens with a single-price batch auction, so that ϵ can be thought of as the difference between the previous day's close and the opening auction price. Given the presence of liquidity motivated traders, the opening price is a noisy but unbiased signal regarding fundamental value. If liquidity shocks are less than perfectly correlated, the variance of ϵ will decline with the number of traders.

The close-to-close price movement from day $t - 1$ to day t is given by $p_N - p_0 + \epsilon$. Using equation (3) and the properties of the Poisson distribution, the variance of *intraday* price changes is $\sigma^2(p_N - p_0) = \omega + \lambda^2(1 - \zeta)(\theta_d + \theta_f)$, where $\omega = (s^2 + 2\lambda s)\sigma^2(x_N)$. Observe that ω is an increasing function of the spread s and a decreasing function of market liquidity, measured by λ^{-1}. The variance of successive changes in closing prices is then

$$\sigma^2(\Delta p) = \gamma + \lambda^2(1 - \zeta)(\theta_d + \theta_f), \tag{4}$$

where $\gamma = \omega + \sigma_\epsilon^2$.

Equation (4) has a natural economic interpretation. Specifically, price volatility has two components: The first component, γ, represents the volatility arising from the bid-ask bounce plus the variance of overnight public information. The second component, $\lambda^2(1 - \zeta)(\theta_d + \theta_f)$, represents the volatility induced by microstructure frictions including information asymmetry. Using equation (2), we see that this term is proportional to expected daily volume, where the proportionality coefficient is inversely related to market liquidity. Information asymmetry is not essential for this result; we would obtain an identical representation if marketmakers faced inventory carrying costs.

B. The Impact of International Cross-Listing

Suppose now that the risky asset is cross-listed on a foreign market. Let $P_k(X_k)$ denote the price quotation function in the foreign market at time t_k as a function of the trade, X_k, with the same signing convention as above. The impact of cross-listing will depend on the extent to which price information in the two markets is observable—that is, the quotation transparency. Formally, suppose that at the time of trade k, domestic marketmakers observe a signal about the prevailing price *quotation* function in the other market of the form $P_k(X_k) + Q_k$, where Q_k is a random variable with precision (the inverse of the variance) χ. The parameter χ is a summary measure of transparency that captures the quality of intermarket information linkages regarding quotes and prices. Note that the quotation function is, by assumption, a sufficient statistic for the underlying conditional mean beliefs in the other market so that transparency in this context is distinct from trade reporting. We discuss below three cases corresponding to different levels of transparency.

B.1. Market Integration ($\chi = \infty$)

With perfect quotation transparency, the precision of the signal regarding the foreign market, χ, is infinite and information on prices and quotes in both markets is freely available at all times. Denote by C_k the ex ante cost of entering the ADR market for investor k, and let c_k denote the cost of entering the domestic market. We assume that $C_k < c_k$ for some investor k, since otherwise there will be no gain to opening the foreign market. In this case, cross-listing will induce investors with high entry costs who would not otherwise enter the domestic market to gather information and enter the foreign market. Let Θ denote the trading intensity in the foreign market, and let θ^* denote the post-cross-listing intensity in the domestic market. The entry of new traders implies that the combined trading intensity in both markets increases following cross-listing, that is, $\Theta + \theta^* > \theta_d + \theta_f$.

Since there is a one-to-one mapping between dealer quotations and beliefs, dealers share common beliefs irrespective of their geographic location and trading histories. Costless arbitrage ensures that the price facing trader k is equalized across markets, so that $p_k = P_k = \mu_k + s^* x_k$, where s^* denotes the post-ADR order processing element of the spread. Our model suggests that $s^* < s$—in other words, that ADR listing decreases the spread. Intuitively, the spread element s is negatively related to the frequency of trading, which increases with the entry of new traders. This also occurs if integration lowers the costs of marketmaking services or if intermarket price competition reduces or eliminates any rent elements contained in s.

Since $\lambda = E[y_k | x_k = 1] = E[y_k | y_k + w_k > s + a\rho^2]$ is an increasing function of s, it follows that λ decreases following cross-listing, implying more liquidity and greater depth. We would obtain similar results if λ were interpreted as arising from inventory control costs instead of asymmetric information, because such costs are positively related to the expected time between trades and hence inversely related to the arrival rate. As the probability of trading is decreasing in s, and trading intensity increases, equation (2) shows that expected total volume will increase. However, the distribution of volume between the two market centers is a function of trading costs in the foreign market. It is possible, for example, that some traders who would otherwise trade domestically find it cheaper to trade abroad, so that volume in the domestic market falls. Such volume movements have no economic impact on security prices in an integrated market where the geographic distribution of trading volume is irrelevant.

Finally, it is likely that participation by new investors will reduce both elements of base-level volatility. Specifically, both γ (because s and λ fall) and the variance term σ_ϵ^2 may decrease. The latter occurs either because opening prices are more informative (represent more efficient aggregation of investor beliefs) or because the increase in trading activity induces entry by analysts who gather additional information. For example, the total number of analysts now following the stock is given by $\kappa(\Theta + \theta^*)$, which is greater than before cross-listing, and the variance of public information is now given by $\tau^2/\kappa(\Theta + \theta^*)$, which is less than that before cross-listing. In summary, when markets are informationally linked, entry by new investors following cross-listing improves standard measures of market quality in both domestic and foreign markets.

B.2. Fragmentation ($\chi = 0$)

The polar opposite case occurs when the precision of intermarket price information signals is zero ($\chi = 0$), that is, markets are not informationally linked. International cross-listing results in a migration of investors away from the domestic market for those investors for whom $C_k < c_k$, causing the trading intensity (and hence expected volume) in the local market θ to decline. The decrease in the expected number of market participants need not be confined to foreign traders, for some domestic investors may also find it cheaper to trade in the United States. The combined volume in both markets may increase with the entry of new investors into the ADR market. Even so, without quotation transparency the diversion of order flow abroad results in less efficient prices and lower market quality in the domestic market.

The decrease in expected trading activity should increase spreads in the domestic market because trading intensity decreases. Further, because λ is an increasing function of s, it follows that λ increases following cross-listing, reducing liquidity. Similar results would obtain if λ also captured inventory control costs inversely related to the arrival rate, θ, of traders.

Finally, trader migration increases both the base-level volatility term ω (because s and λ rise) and the variance of overnight public information flows σ_ϵ^2 in the domestic market. The latter occurs either because opening prices are less informative or because less information is gathered by domestic analysts. In summary, in the absence of quotation transparency, order flow migration following cross-listing lowers the standard measures of market quality in the domestic market.

B.3. Partial Fragmentation ($0 < \chi < \infty$)

When domestic marketmakers observe foreign prices with noise ($0 < \chi < \infty$), imperfect information linkages may result in *partial fragmentation*, where the effects of cross-listing are concentrated in some segments of the equity market. Such effects are likely to be exacerbated by internal market segmentation induced by barriers such as foreign ownership restrictions. In particular, Stulz and Wasserfallen (1995) show that ownership restrictions can induce segmentation between the assets held by foreign and domestic investors. If foreign investors currently trading in the domestic market obtain the greatest reduction in trading costs by moving abroad (as seems likely), the loss of order flow primarily occurs in the B series shares where foreign ownership is especially significant. In turn, the diversion of order flow in the B shares is likely to decrease market liquidity as marketmakers face higher inventory carrying costs.

The presence of arbitrageurs who observe intermarket prices and trade simultaneously exacerbates this problem. Let b denote the magnitude of transactions costs associated with arbitrage. An arbitrageur who has access to intermarket quotes will buy the domestic stock if $P_k(X_k = -1) - p_k(x_k = 1) - b > 0$ and sell if $p_k(x_k = -1) - P_k(X_k = 1) - b > 0$. From the viewpoint of a domestic marketmaker, there is a positive probability that the price in the foreign market reflects more recent information. This is especially so when trading activity in the ADR market greatly exceeds that of the domestic market (e.g., Telefonos de Mexico) so that price discovery essentially takes place abroad. Thus, with arbitrage present, the adverse selection costs of domestic dealers increase, so that λ rises and liquidity falls.

Conversely, transactions costs may fall in those segments of the equity market facing foreign competition (i.e., B series) as domestic marketmakers cut spreads in an attempt to retain order flow. To see this, recall that the probability a trader will buy or sell is given by $1 - \zeta$, which is inversely related to the spread element s. If the costs of information acquisition are identical in the two markets, a trader will direct the order to the market with the lowest spread. The threat of potential competition from foreign markets may induce domestic dealers to reduce s to remain competitive even as their adverse selection costs increase because, other things equal, an investor will trade in the market where $\lambda + s$ is the lowest. Such competition will be observed in the B series shares (assuming that s contains rent elements) which are open to foreign investors, but not necessarily in A shares where the migration of foreign investors is not a factor. No such effects are observed in the pure fragmentation case considered above because quotations in the other market are not observed by a trader at the time of order placement, eliminating dealers' incentives to compete on the basis of price.

The impact of cross-listing on fundamental or base-case volatility in the partial fragmentation case is more complex. If intermarket information links are poor or if new investors in the foreign market have low quality information signals, base-level volatility will tend to increase. This occurs because the variance of the public information signal σ_ϵ^2 regarding overnight information flows increases as domestic trading intensity falls. In the case of Mexico, the small lack of complete overlap of trading hours with U.S. markets may contribute to this effect. It is also possible that exposure to a new, foreign factor may cause an increase in base-level volatility. For example, the covariance term w_k can lead to differences in valuations between foreign and domestic investors. Time variation in this factor may result in additional price volatility after cross-listing, because the market price represents an average of foreign and domestic valuations.

Alternatively, if intermarket information links are relatively good and the new investors participating in trading in the foreign market contribute significantly to price discovery, base-level volatility will fall as information aggregation improves. The net impact of cross-listing on the volatility of information flows is thus an empirical issue.

III. Empirical Results

A. Estimating the Changes in Liquidity and Volatility

Recall from equation (3) that price movements reflect two components: (i) base-level volatility arising from imperfect public information, and (ii) transitory volatility arising from trading frictions and information asymmetry. The latter term is the product of volume and a parameter that is inversely related to market liquidity. Given data on prices and volumes, we estimate jointly the changes in volatility and liquidity around ADR introduction. We proxy for the unobservable price variance term on day t with the squared price change on that day. When the number of traders is large, the cumulative price movements are approximately normal, and the expected absolute daily price change is proportional to the standard deviation of daily price changes. It also seems economically plausible that fundamental (or base-level) volatility may be related to price movements on the previous day. Accordingly, we estimate:

$$(\Delta P_t)^2 = \gamma_t + \delta_t(\Delta P_{t-1})^2 + \lambda_t V_t + \eta_t, \tag{5}$$

with time-varying parameters given by

$$\gamma_t = \gamma_0 + \gamma_1 ADR_t$$

$$\delta_t = \delta_0 + \delta_1 ADR_t$$

$$\lambda_t = \lambda_0 + \lambda_1 ADR_t, \tag{6}$$

where V_t is the volume on day t, ADR_t is a dummy variable taking the value 0 if date t is before the ADR listing and 1 otherwise, and η_t is the error term. Here, γ_t represents the base-level volatility, δ_t captures any dependency between current and past volatility, and λ_t reflects the responsiveness of price to volume. We expect that current volatility is likely to depend on past volatility, so that $\delta_0 > 0$.

Under integration, the ADR listing increases the flow of public information, reducing price volatility and increasing market liquidity, so that λ_1 and γ_1 are negative. Under fragmentation, the ADR listing decreases liquidity and increases price volatility so that λ_1 and γ_1 are positive. The partial fragmentation case implies a reduction in liquidity for those segments of the equity market where migration is most likely to occur.

We estimate the time-varying parameter model in equations (5) and (6) using generalized method of moments (GMM) estimators. Table III contains the coefficient estimates, with corresponding autocorrelation-heteroskedasticity consistent standard errors in parentheses, for all twenty-five series in the sample grouped by series type. There are several results of interest. First, the estimates provide support for the decomposition of price volatility provided by the theoretical model. In particular, the base-level volatility coefficient γ_0 is positive in all but one case (the exception is virtually zero), and the coefficient on volume λ_0 is positive in twenty-three of twenty-five cases as predicted.

Second, the median coefficient estimate of the base-level volatility coefficient γ_0 is 0.007 (the mean is 0.057) and the median coefficient γ_1 is 0.024 (the mean is 0.286), implying a dramatic increase in base-level volatility following the ADR listing. This increase is observed in twenty-one of the twenty-five series. In particular, fundamental volatility increases in thirteen of the fourteen series open to foreign ownership (i.e., the B, C, L, and O series) and in all nine of the B series shares, at generally high levels of

The Journal of Finance

Table III

Generalized Method of Moment Estimates

This table contains coefficient estimates and heteroskedasticity-consistent standard errors (in parentheses) for the model

$$(\Delta P_t)^2 = \gamma_t + \delta_t(\Delta P_{t-1})^2 + \lambda_t V_t + \eta_t$$

$$\gamma_t = \gamma_0 + \gamma_1 ADR_t$$

$$\delta_t = \delta_0 + \delta_1 ADR_t$$

$$\lambda_t = \lambda_0 + \lambda_1 ADR_t.$$

The model is estimated by generalized method of moments, with equations for multiple stock series within a single company estimated jointly. The series represent all stocks traded on the Bolsa Mexicana de Valores for which an ADR was introduced. The variables ΔP_t and V_t are price change and volume (tens of millions of shares), respectively. The variable ADR_t is equal to zero prior to the date of the ADR listing and is one thereafter. Superscript a denotes scaling by 10^3. Panel A lists results for the series restricted to Mexican ownership domestically, Panel B for B shares, open to foreign ownership, and Panel C for other share series open to foreigners.

Series	γ_0	γ_1	δ_0	δ_1	λ_0	λ_1
			Panel A: A Series			
CEM	0.031	0.516	0.149	0.009	0.745	7.956
	(0.009)	(0.104)	(0.084)	(0.100)	(0.215)	(2.789)
CIF	0.007	0.048	0.054	0.005	−0.004	0.013
	(0.002)	(0.007)	(0.048)	(0.061)	(0.003)	(0.015)
EPN	0.015^a	−0.003	−0.012	0.010	0.001	0.016
	(0.008)^a	(0.014)	(0.021)	(0.021)	(0.000)	(0.009)
GCA	0.159	0.280	0.015	0.321	9.697	−6.488
	(0.067)	(0.187)	(0.031)	(0.091)	(6.957)	(7.456)
MAS	0.050	0.024	0.100	−0.018	0.982	0.281
	(0.011)	(0.019)	(0.076)	(0.111)	(0.442)	(0.572)
PON	−0.001^a	0.021^a	0.012	−0.119	0.063	−0.280
	(0.002)^a	(0.005)^a	(0.018)	(0.073)	(0.036)	(0.571)
SAN	0.006	−0.003	−0.011	0.060	0.001	0.033
	(0.001)	(0.001)	(0.032)	(0.047)	(0.001)	(0.010)
SANAV	0.005	−0.002	0.141	−0.078	0.000	0.009
	(0.001)	(0.001)	(0.064)	(0.075)	(0.001)	(0.004)
SYN	0.001	0.008	0.102	0.026	−0.002	0.066
	(0.000)	(0.002)	(0.095)	(0.167)	(0.001)	(0.049)
TEL	0.007	0.092	0.333	−0.320	0.003	−0.014
	(0.002)	(0.011)	(0.125)	(0.123)	(0.002)	(0.025)
TMM	0.280	0.005	−0.003	0.111	18.21	−8.422
	(0.090)	(0.107)	(0.073)	(0.080)	(3.925)	(7.585)

International Cross-Listing   2017

Table III—*Continued*

Series	γ_0	γ_1	δ_0	δ_1	λ_0	λ_1
			Panel B: B Series			
CEM	0.114	0.475	−0.066	0.205	0.098	4.457
	(0.025)	(0.089)	(0.032)	(0.061)	(0.063)	(1.741)
CER	0.002	0.015	0.048	0.045	0.714	0.173
	(0.001)	(0.003)	(0.049)	(0.079)	(0.264)	(0.445)
CIF	0.005	0.070	0.110	0.024	0.025	−0.012
	(0.001)	(0.012)	(0.093)	(0.120)	(0.019)	(0.034)
COM	0.001	0.004	0.130	−0.048	0.019	0.005
	(0.000)	(0.000)	(0.085)	(0.095)	(0.006)	(0.016)
FEM	0.018	0.093	0.075	0.126	0.007	−0.023
	(0.002)	(0.012)	(0.055)	(0.100)	(0.018)	(0.028)
MAS	0.038	0.030	0.182	−0.072	0.808	−0.214
	(0.009)	(0.017)	(0.088)	(0.108)	(0.281)	(0.373)
PON	0.010[a]	0.013[a]	0.194	−0.101	0.001	0.001
	(0.002)	(0.003)	(0.058)	(0.092)	(0.004)	(0.000)
SYN	0.001	0.003	0.027	0.051	−0.004	0.853
	(0.000)	(0.001)	(0.043)	(0.072)	(0.008)	(0.424)
TTO	0.045	0.074	0.209	−0.113	0.053	2.656
	(0.006)	(0.037)	(0.114)	(0.134)	(0.055)	(0.809)
			Panel C: Other Series			
CIFC	0.001	0.006	0.119	−0.022	0.001	−0.001
	(0.000)	(0.001)	(0.171)	(0.175)	(0.000)	(0.001)
LIVC	0.027	0.159	0.149	−0.141	2.020	−0.653
	(0.006)	(0.033)	(0.073)	(0.087)	(0.142)	(0.334)
LIVO	0.045	0.050	0.095	0.075	0.792	1.031
	(0.007)	(0.023)	(0.050)	(0.114)	(0.212)	(1.034)
TMML	0.026	−0.052	−0.058	0.133	21.50	15.63
	(0.143)	(0.158)	(0.043)	(0.055)	(16.46)	(27.40)
VITO	0.555	5.267	0.109	−0.101	82.49	−84.48
	(0.302)	(1.164)	(0.060)	(0.063)	(27.28)	(27.40)

statistical significance. Though previous studies (see, e.g., Jayaraman, Shastri, and Tandon (1993), and Karolyi (1996)) document an increase in the return variance following international listing, our analysis shows that the change in volatility is due to factors unrelated to volume, that, in fact, the change is the result of changes in the information structure. The coefficient δ_0, which captures the sensitivity of current volatility to past volatility shocks, is positive in twenty-one of the twenty-five cases, as expected, and does not change in any systematic way after cross-listing.

Third, the shifts in the liquidity coefficients following ADR listing are differentiated by series type. In six of the eleven A series shares (which are restricted to Mexican nationals), cross-listing is associated with a decrease in liquidity (i.e., λ_1 is positive), and in three of those six the decrease is statistically significant at the 1 percent level. By contrast, of the five cases where liquidity increased in A series shares, none is statistically significant. In the B shares, which are open to both foreign and domestic investors, the evidence for a reduction in liquidity upon cross-listing is far more compelling. Indeed, in the B series shares, liquidity falls in six of the nine cases, four of which are statistically significant at the 1 percent level, and of the three cases where liquidity increases, none is statistically significant. The changes in liquidity in the remaining five series (C, L, and O) do not exhibit a systematic pattern.

We also perform some tests to ensure that our results are not driven by potential nonlinearities in the volatility-volume relation. A common diagnostic method to detect nonlinearities is to examine the pattern of residuals. Misspecification would be manifested in the form of serial correlation in the residuals. For example, if the true relation were concave, the predicted volatility on a high-volume day is too high, generating a negative residual. Because high-volume days are likely to be clustered in time, this form of misspecification will result in serial correlation in the residuals. However, Lagrange multiplier tests for serial correlation in the residuals of the model fail to reject the null of no serial correlation in all but two cases in the sample. On this basis, if there is some nonlinearity, it must be minor, relative to the linear relationship predicted by theory. Estimates of various semiparametric nonlinear models also support our use of a linear specification.[5]

In summary, our results thus far suggest that ADR listing is associated with a general increase in base-level volatility unrelated to volume. There is evidence of reduced liquidity in the form of an increased sensitivity of price variability to volume, especially in the B series shares, which were open to foreign ownership prior to the international cross-listing. For the case of shares for which ownership was restricted to residents of the home country prior to ADR listing, as with shares with limited voting rights, the results are inconclusive.[6] These findings reject the integration hypothesis, but are consistent with both fragmentation hypotheses discussed above.

B. Computation and Testing of Implicit Spreads

Our model suggests that cross-listing may induce changes in the bid-ask spread. Unfortunately, without quotation data we cannot directly make inferences about the bid-ask spread. Roll (1984) uses the covariance in suc-

---

[5] Models estimated using squared volume, for example, produce the same qualitative results as reported here. Other nonlinear alternatives are tried, with the same result. We also conduct direct tests for nonlinearity, as exposited in Granger (1995), and cannot reject the null of a linear model in all but two cases.

[6] The precise series (A, B, etc.) for which the ADR is listed appears not to matter in the analysis. We match the precise series for eleven companies: CEM (B), CIF (B), SAN (A), PON (B), GCA (A), MAS (A, B), SYN (B), TEL (A, L), LIV (C), VIT (O), leaving us with five companies for which we can differentiate between ADR and non-ADR series, the results for which contribute no additional information to the analysis.

cessive price changes to make inferences about the size of the bid-ask spread when bid-ask quotations are unavailable. We use a related approach by George, Kaul, and Nimalendran (1991) (GKN) which offers several extensions to Roll's model, including adjustments for potential serial correlation in returns. Our approach to estimation differs slightly from GKN in the way we adjust for autocorrelation and by our use of GMM to jointly estimate the underlying parameters of the implicit spread. The GMM technique is attractive for several reasons, but most importantly because we can construct a new statistic to test the change in implicit spreads following the ADR listing. Since the GKN procedure is well known, we will concentrate in this section on the development of this test statistic.[7]

The modified GKN estimate of the spread can be written as $S = 2\sqrt{-\psi(\Gamma)}$ where ψ is the covariance between returns at times t and $t + 1$. The vector Γ contains parameters relating to the GKN prefiltering process, as well as the mean and variance of the adjusted returns. Let the subscripts 0 and 1 denote before and after ADR introduction, respectively. The change in the implicit bid-ask spread following the ADR listing is $h(\psi_1, \psi_0) \equiv S_1 - S_0$, where $s_1 = 2\sqrt{-\psi_1(\Gamma)}$ and $S_0 = 2\sqrt{-\psi_0(\Gamma)}$. The hypothesis of interest is whether the change in spreads is equal to zero:

$$H_0: h(\psi_1, \psi_0) = 0. \tag{7}$$

We estimate the vector Γ using GMM; Hansen (1982) proves that the GMM estimate, ψ_Γ^G is consistent and asymptotically normally distributed under very weak conditions. Standard arguments imply that the statistic

$$h(\psi_1^G, \psi_0^G)^2 \Sigma^{-1} \tag{8}$$

is distributed as χ^2 (1) under the null hypothesis of equation (7), where Σ is the (scalar) variance of $h(\psi_1^G, \psi_0^G)$. A series of mean-value expansions yields

$$\Sigma = \nabla_\psi h(\psi_1, \psi_0)' \nabla_\Gamma \psi(\Gamma)' \Omega_\Gamma \nabla_\Gamma \psi(\Gamma) \nabla_\psi h(\psi_1, \psi_0),$$

where $\nabla_\psi h$ and $\nabla_\Gamma \psi$ are the gradient vectors of $h(\psi_1, \psi_0)$ and $\psi(\Gamma)$, respectively, and Ω_Γ is the variance-covariance matrix of the estimated vector Γ. This expression can be used to compute the test statistic in expression (8) given GMM estimates of the spread before and after ADR introduction, computed in the standard way.

Information with respect to the tests of changes in implicit spreads after ADR listing is provided in Table IV. The difference in spreads across the two periods is reported with the computed significance level of the test against the null hypothesis of a zero difference in the spread. The estimated spread

---

[7] Estimates of bid-ask spreads based on indirect methods such as the GKN model may be subject to misspecification biases as shown by Jones and Lipson (1995).

2020 *The Journal of Finance*

Table IV

Tests of Spread Equality across ADR Listing

This table contains the differences in the implicit bid-ask spread after the ADR listing less the implicit spread before the ADR listing, denoted as ΔS, using the method of George, Kaul, and Nimalendran (1991). Prob(ΔS) is the significance level for a test against the null hypothesis of zero difference in the spread following the ADR listing.

Series	A		B		Other	
	ΔS	Prob(ΔS)	ΔS	Prob(ΔS)	ΔS	Prob(ΔS)
CEM	−0.004	0.083	−0.095	0.003	—	—
CER	—	—	0.034	0.001	—	—
CIF	0.016	0.042	−0.003	0.076	−0.001	0.521
COM	—	—	0.000	0.822	—	—
EPN	0.000	0.837	—	—	—	—
FEM	—	—	−0.001	0.177	—	—
GCA	−0.135	0.001	—	—	—	—
LIVO	—	—	—	—	−0.032	0.015
LIVC	—	—	—	—	−0.036	0.007
MAS	−0.018	0.123	−0.021	0.050	—	—
PON	0.001	0.180	0.001	0.410	—	—
SAN	−0.007	0.175	—	—	—	—
SANAV	−0.004	0.215	—	—	—	—
SYN	−0.002	0.696	−0.013	0.067	—	—
TMM	−0.018	0.774	—	—	−0.003	0.899
TTO	—	—	−0.005	0.055	—	—
VIT	—	—	—	—	0.000	—

decreases in seventeen of twenty-two series that experienced changes sufficient to allow computation of the significance level. These decreases tend to be concentrated in series that allowed foreign ownership prior to the ADR introduction. Specifically, of the thirteen series open to foreign ownership where spreads did change, there was a decrease in ten series, seven of which were statistically significant at the 10 percent level. This is especially surprising because one component of the spread, captured by the adverse selection parameter λ, tended to also increase. This suggests that the decrease in spreads reflects a general decline in the order-processing element of the spread (s in our model), perhaps reflecting increased intermarket competition.

The decline in spreads for share issues open to foreign ownership, associated with a decrease in liquidity and an increase in return volatility unrelated to volume, is not consistent with the fragmentation hypothesis, but fits the partial fragmentation hypothesis. Indeed, Foerster and Karolyi (1994), in their study of cross-listed Canadian stocks, find that changes in trading costs are related to both domestic and foreign volume. Such effects are most likely to be observed in issues open to foreign investors, because these investors are probably the most likely to obtain lower transaction costs in U.S. ADR markets.

There is additional support for the partial fragmentation hypothesis. Domowitz, Glen, and Madhavan (1997) examine the prices of a different sample consisting of *purely domestically* traded Mexican stocks subject to ownership restrictions that distinguish between individual and institutional investors and between foreign and domestic investors. They find price differentials between restricted and unrestricted stock (in a manner predicted by Stulz and Wasserfallen (1995)), which suggests that these investment restrictions can cause segmentation. If this were not the case, the partial fragmentation hypothesis clearly could not explain our findings.

C. Stock Price Effects

To investigate the effects of ADR listing on domestic stock prices, we form equally weighted portfolios of the underlying Mexican shares for 101 trading days around the listing day of ADRs listed from December 1989 through June 1992. The portfolios considered are: (i) All shares, (ii) A Series Shares, (iii) B Series Shares, and (iv) Level III ADRs (shares for which additional equity capital was issued upon listing.) We estimate the daily excess return, computed as the residuals from the standard market model estimated from the earliest day for which observations are available by stock up to 51 days *prior* to the listing date (day 0). Shares with fewer than 75 days of data prior to day −51 are excluded from the portfolios.

Table V contains the average daily cumulative excess returns, in percent, for the five portfolios considered. The figures in parentheses represent the significance levels for a statistical test that cumulative returns are zero. Although the cumulative excess returns for all shares are positive from day −40 onward and total 6.77 percent by the date of listing, these returns are not statistically significantly different from zero. The breakdown by series type shows that the excess returns for all shares derive largely from the B shares. Indeed, by day 0, the cumulative excess return is 14.4 percent and this is statistically significant at the 10 percent level. By contrast, the A shares show smaller positive excess returns and the cumulative returns are not statistically significant. There is little evidence of any systematic price effects associated with Level III ADRs, possibly because any benefits from cross-listing are spread over longer periods or are anticipated further in advance. Indeed, Foerster and Karolyi (1996) find significant abnormal returns for a portfolio of 160 foreign firms in the year prior to cross-listing.

D. Economy-Wide Effects

The effects we attribute to international cross-listing may reflect economy-wide economic or political effects (see, e.g., Bailey and Chung (1995)) over the sample period. To investigate this issue, we gather data on nine companies traded on the BMV for which there are no associated ADRs listed over the sample period with comparable trading volume and market capitaliza-

Table V

Cumulative Excess Returns around ADR Listing

This table contains average daily cumulative excess returns, in percent, for equally weighted portfolios of the underlying Mexican shares for 101 trading days around the listing day of ADRs listed from December 1989 through June 1992. Significance levels for a test that cumulative returns are zero are given in parentheses. Daily excess returns are computed as the residuals from the standard market model, estimated from the earliest day for which observations are available by stock up to 51 days prior to the listing date. Mexican shares with fewer than 75 days of data prior to day 51 before listing are excluded from the portfolios. Each column head signifies the portfolio considered: All shares, A shares, B shares, and Level III (shares for which additional equity capital was issued as part of the ADR listing).

Day	All Shares	A Shares	B Shares	Level III
−50	−0.10	−0.09	−0.16	0.08
	(0.93)	(0.96)	(0.88)	(0.90)
−40	1.49	2.46	2.96	0.54
	(0.71)	(0.57)	(0.48)	(0.92)
−30	3.56	2.89	7.22	4.05
	(0.53)	(0.62)	(0.21)	(0.48)
−20	5.35	5.19	9.82	3.91
	(0.44)	(0.45)	(0.17)	(0.62)
−10	6.69	4.61	13.3	4.65
	(0.37)	(0.54)	(0.09)	(0.53)
0	6.77	4.86	14.4	4.75
	(0.41)	(0.56)	(0.09)	(0.60)
+10	6.35	4.71	17.2	1.41
	(0.48)	(0.61)	(0.07)	(0.89)
+20	5.50	2.97	16.9	2.34
	(0.55)	(0.72)	(0.10)	(0.78)
+30	6.80	3.15	19.6	1.79
	(0.50)	(0.73)	(0.07)	(0.86)
+40	5.12	1.46	18.8	−2.01
	(0.63)	(0.88)	(0.11)	(0.83)
+50	2.62	−1.93	17.9	−3.26
	(0.79)	(0.92)	(0.15)	(0.75)

tion to our ADR sample.[8] Series A, B, C, and O shares are represented in the control group, as well as disparate industries including brokerage, chemicals, banking, paper, and steel.

We analyze these series with respect to base-volatility changes, liquidity shifts, price effects, and potential impacts on returns. Equations (5) and (6) are first estimated for all nine series, but with the dummy variable for ADR introduction set in the middle of the period over which ADRs were introduced. We also estimate the same equations using intervention analysis, a

---

[8] The control companies are Grupo Industrial Alfa (Series A, holding company); Quimica Borden (Series B, chemicals); Grupo Bursatil Mexicano (Series C, brokerage); Corporacion Mexicana de Aviacion (Series C, holding company); Banco Internationale (Series B, banking); Kimberly Clark de Mexico (Series A, cellulose and paper); Multibanco Comermex (Series B, banking); Banca Serfin (Series B, banking); and Tubos de Acero de Mexico (Series O, steel).

procedure that uses a likelihood ratio test to detect statistically significant periodic shifts in volatility and liquidity. Under both approaches, we cannot reject the hypothesis that there are no changes in base-level volatility and liquidity for all series at reasonable levels of significance. Indeed, significance levels ranged from a low of about 0.80 to 0.99. Price changes are more pronounced in the ADR sample, with a positive price change that is 56 percent greater than for the change for control group (computed using a midpoint date), but these differences are economically small. We find no differences in the level of returns between the ADR sample and the control group. These results indicate that our results are unlikely to be the result of economy-wide effects. These results also suggest that the negative effects on liquidity documented for some ADR stocks had no significant spillover effects to non-ADR stocks.

E. The U.S. ADR Market

The U.S. ADR market provides an additional perspective on our results. As shown in Table I, most of the ADRs in our sample are traded in the 144A market (where qualified institutional buyers can trade securities that do not meet strict disclosure requirements) or in the over-the-counter market. Because transactions in informal upstairs markets need not be disclosed, they do not appear on the ticker tape, and hence data are unavailable for these securities in public databases. We obtain information on trading volumes for three of the ADRs traded in the United States for which such data are available. These stocks are actively traded and account for the majority of market value of the sample. We use the U.S. ADR data to directly measure the extent to which cross-listing results in a broadening of participation abroad.

Table VI contains summary statistics on BMV-listed share returns and their corresponding U.S.-listed ADR returns in issues for which trading information in both markets is available. The table also contains the details of statistical tests of equality of average daily returns. The average returns in the two markets are very similar but are generally not *identical*, suggesting that there are opportunities for profitable cross-country trading. Our conversations with traders in Mexico and the United States suggest that this is the case, which is consistent with our presumption that the two markets are not perfectly transparent. It is also possible that the differences in average daily returns between the two markets reflect nonsynchronous trading (since the opening and closing times in Mexico and the United States do not perfectly overlap), the effect of currency movements that affect dollar-denominated returns, or bid-ask bounce.

We are also interested in the extent to which the U.S. markets divert order flow away from the domestic markets. Following Foerster and Karolyi (1994), we compute three summary statistics about the gains in order flow and total volume in shares for which information is available for trading in

Table VI

Summary Statistics on Returns

This table contains summary statistics on Bolsa Mexicana de Valores (BMV)-listed share returns and their corresponding U.S.-listed ADR returns in issues for which trading information in both venues was available. The first three rows contain average daily percentage returns on the BMV, prior- and post-ADR introduction, and percentage returns for the U.S. ADR, respectively. The remaining rows contain statistical significance levels for tests of equality of average daily returns. "6 mos" denotes a test based on daily returns measured over the six months before and/or after the month of ADR introduction. For example, BMV = BMV denotes a test of equality for shares traded on the BMV before and after ADR introduction; BMV = BMV (6 mos) tests returns for equality over the six-month period before and after the ADR month.

	VIT O	TMM A	TMM L
BMV prior	0.22	0.16	0.21
BMV post	0.04	0.28	0.26
U.S. ADR	−0.06	0.34	0.32
BMV = U.S.	0.94	0.85	0.83
BMV = U.S. (6 mos)	0.98	0.85	0.83
BMV = BMV	0.11	0.48	0.78
BMV = BMV (6 mos)	0.33	0.68	0.87
BMV prior = U.S.	0.08	0.34	0.56
BMV prior = U.S. (6 mos)	0.32	0.60	0.73

both the U.S.-listed ADR and the underlying Mexican share on the BMV. Specifically, Table VII shows the percentage gain in daily order flow in Mexico after ADR introduction in the United States (termed "Order Flow"), computed as the ratio of average daily dollar volume post-ADR listing to average daily volume prior to listing, less one. We also compute U.S. Flow, the ratio of the average daily dollar volume in the U.S. ADR market to the average daily volume traded on the BMV, less one. This statistic captures the size of the U.S. market relative to the prelisting domestic market. The percentage gain in total volume postlisting is the sum of U.S. Flow and Order Flow.

Order flow is negative for TMM L shares, suggesting order flow migration. For VIT O shares and TMM A shares, however, order flow is positive, indicating a net increase in volume. Interestingly, the U.S. market appears large relative to the pre-listing domestic market. This is consistent with our hypothesis that the increase in fundamental volatility is due to the shift to price discovery abroad. Overall, volume rose in three stocks, the exception being TMML which experienced a modest decline in total volume. In summary, the results from the ADR market provide some evidence consistent with order flow migration, but it is difficult to discern a general pattern given the limited sample available to us. The most comparable study, by Foerster and Karolyi (1994) for Canadian stocks, also finds considerable variation in the extent of order flow migration across companies.

International Cross-Listing 2025

Table VII

Gains in Order Flow across Markets after ADR Listing

This table contains three summary statistics relating to gains in order flow and total volume in shares for which information was available for trading in both the U.S.-listed ADR and the underlying Mexican share on the Bolsa Mexican de Valores (BMV). The column marked Order Flow contains the percentage gain in daily order flow in the Mexican market after ADR introduction in the United States, computed as the ratio of average daily dollar volume prior to ADR introduction to average daily dollar volume post introduction, less one. The column marked U.S. Flow contains the ratio of the average daily dollar volume in the U.S. ADR market to the average daily dollar volume traded on the BMV prior to ADR introduction, less one. The column marked Total Flow is the percentage gain in total volume after ADR introduction, computed by summing the first two columns, plus one.

Stock	Order Flow	U.S. Flow	Total Flow
VIT O	67%	−86%	81%
TMM A	177%	−76%	201%
TMM L	−24%	−90%	−14%

IV. Conclusion

Despite the rapid increase in the number of internationally cross-listed securities, relatively little is known about the impact of such actions on the domestic market. This topic is especially important for emerging markets that are smaller and less liquid than the foreign market where cross-listing occurs. Our theoretical analysis highlights the importance of intermarket information linkages in determining the impact of international cross-listing on measures of domestic market quality including the precision of public information, market depth, and bid-ask spreads.

We use data from the Mexican equity market to distinguish empirically between the possible effects of cross-listing on domestic market quality predicted by our theoretical analysis. The Mexican market offers a unique opportunity to analyze questions relating to intermarket competition. The domestic market faces direct competition from U.S. ADR markets during exchange hours, and foreign ownership restrictions allow us to better understand the potential effects of order flow migration by foreign investors following cross-listing.

We demonstrate that the traditional dichotomy between market integration and fragmentation is inappropriate in considering the effects of foreign listing. Rather, international listing embodies aspects of both the benefits from increased intermarket competition and the costs of order flow diversion. In general, ADR introduction is associated with an increase in the variance of public information flows unrelated to the volatility induced by changes in liquidity and trading activity. This is not consistent with market integration. These effects are especially concentrated in those equity series open to foreign participation prior to cross-listing. Such series also show a reduction in liquidity manifested by a heightened sensitivity of price variability to volume, possibly the result of the migration of foreign investors. However, such shares also experience a decline in the implicit bid-ask spread following ADR introduction, which is consistent with increased competition among domestic liquidity providers to retain order flow following cross-listing.

Our analysis suggests several new directions for further analysis. First, our findings suggest that corporate governance issues may play an important role in a firm's decision to cross-list its stock because the costs and benefits of cross-listing are not uniformly distributed across all share series. For example, consider a closely held company where controlling ownership is concentrated in the A series shares. Following cross-listing, the costs associated with order-flow migration (in terms of liquidity and price volatility) will largely accrue to other series where trading occurs, whereas the benefits (in terms of increased ability to access international capital markets) accrue to the firm as a whole.

Second, the effects of cross-listing are likely to vary systematically across securities and across nations. For example, the extent to which intermarket competition can reduce spreads depends on intramarket competition among domestic dealers, which in turn may differ with market capitalization. Similar remarks apply to companies in nations where, by virtue of geography or technology, intermarket information linkages are of high quality.

Finally, the impact of foreign equity ownership restrictions is an important public policy issue; our results suggest that such restrictions are sources of intramarket segmentation, but do not explain why such restrictions may be binding. These are topics for future research.

REFERENCES

Alexander, Gordon, Cheol S. Eun, and S. Janakiramanan, 1987, Asset pricing and dual listing on foreign capital markets: A note, *Journal of Finance* 42, 151–158.

Alexander, Gordon, Cheol S. Eun, and S. Janakiramanan, 1988, International listings and stock returns: Some empirical evidence, *Journal of Financial and Quantitative Analysis* 23, 135–151.

Bailey, Warren, and Y. Peter Chung, 1995, Exchange rate fluctuations, political risk, and stock returns: Some evidence from an emerging market, *Journal of Financial and Quantitative Analysis* 30, 541–561.

Bekaert, Geert, 1993, Market segmentation and investment barriers in emerging equity markets, Working paper, Stanford University.

Chan, Kalok C., Wai-Ming Fong, and René M. Stulz, 1995, Information, trading, and stock returns: Lessons from dually-listed securities, *Journal of Banking and Finance* 20, 1161–1187.

Domowitz, Ian, Jack Glen, and Ananth Madhavan, 1997, Market segmentation and stock prices: Evidence from an emerging market, *Journal of Finance* 52, 1059–1085.

Eun, Cheol S., and S. Janakiramanan, 1986, A model of international asset pricing with a constraint on the foreign equity ownership, *Journal of Finance* 41, 897–914.

Foerster, Stephen R., and G. Andrew Karolyi, 1993, International listings of stocks: The case of Canada and the U.S., *Journal of International Business Studies* 24, 763–784.

Foerster, Stephen R., and G. Andrew Karolyi, 1994, Multimarket trading and liquidity: A transaction data analysis of Canada-U.S. interlistings, Working paper, Ohio State University.

Foerster, Stephen R., and G. Andrew Karolyi, 1996, The effects of market segmentation and illiquidity on asset prices: Evidence from foreign stocks listing in the U.S., Working paper, Ohio State University.

Forster, Margaret M., and Thomas George, 1996, Pricing errors at the NYSE open and close: Evidence from internationally cross-listed stocks, *Journal of Financial Intermediation* 5, 95–126.

George, Thomas, Gautam Kaul, and M. Nimalendran, 1991, Estimation of the bid-ask spread and its components: A new approach, *Review of Financial Studies* 4, 623–656.

Glosten, Lawrence R., and Paul Milgrom , 1985, Bid, ask, and transaction prices in a specialist market with heterogeneously informed agents, *Journal of Financial Economics* 14, 71–100.

Granger, Clive W. J., 1995, Modelling nonlinear relationships between extended memory variables, *Econometrica* 63, 265–279.

Hansen, Lars P, 1982, Large sample properties of generalized method of moment estimators, *Econometrica* 50, 1029–1084.

Howe, John, Jeffrey Madura, and Alan Tucker, 1993, International listing and risk, *Journal of International Money and Finance* 12, 99–110.

Jayaraman, Narayanan , Kuldeep Shastri, and Kishore Tandon, 1993, The impact of international cross listings on risk and return: The evidence from American Depository Receipts, *Journal of Banking and Finance* 17, 91–103.

Jones, Charles M., and Marc L. Lipson, 1995, Continuations, reversals, and adverse selection on the Nasdaq and NYSE/AMEX, Working paper, Princeton University.

Jorion, Philippe, and Eduardo Schwartz, 1986, Integration versus segmentation in the Canadian stock market, *Journal of Finance* 41, 603–616.

Karolyi, G. Andrew, 1996, What happens to stocks that list shares abroad? A survey of the evidence and its managerial implications, Working paper, University of Western Ontario.

Kleidon, Allen, and Ingrid Werner, 1996, U.K. and U.S. trading of British cross-listed stocks: An intraday analysis of market integration, *Review of Financial Studies* 9, 619–664.

Madhavan, Ananth, 1995, Consolidation, fragmentation, and the disclosure of trading information, *Review of Financial Studies* 8, 579–603.

Roll, Richard, 1984, A simple implicit measure of the effective bid-ask spread, *Journal of Finance* 39, 1127–1139.

Stulz, René M., 1981, On the effects of barriers to international asset pricing, *Journal of Finance* 25, 307–319.

Stulz, René M., and Walter Wasserfallen, 1995, Foreign equity investment restrictions, capital flight, and shareholder wealth maximization: Theory and evidence, *Review of Financial Studies* 8, 1019–1057.

Urias, Michael, 1994, The impact of security cross-listing on the cost of capital in emerging markets, Working paper, Stanford University.

C
Stock Selection of Equity Markets

[21]

THE JOURNAL OF FINANCE • VOL. LIV, NO. 4 • AUGUST 1999

Local Return Factors and Turnover in Emerging Stock Markets

K. GEERT ROUWENHORST*

ABSTRACT

The factors that drive cross-sectional differences in expected stock returns in emerging equity markets are qualitatively similar to those that have been documented for developed markets. Emerging market stocks exhibit momentum, small stocks outperform large stocks, and value stocks outperform growth stocks. There is no evidence that high beta stocks outperform low beta stocks. A Bayesian analysis of the return premiums shows that the combined evidence of developed and emerging markets strongly favors the hypothesis that similar return factors are present in markets around the world. Finally, there exists a strong cross-sectional correlation between the return factors and share turnover.

THERE IS GROWING EMPIRICAL EVIDENCE that multiple factors are cross-sectionally correlated with average returns in the United States. Measured over long time periods, small stocks earn higher average returns than large stocks (Banz (1981)). Fama and French (1992, 1996) and Lakonishok, Shleifer, and Vishny (1994) show that value stocks with high book-to-market (B/M), earnings-to-price (E/P), or cash flow to price (C/P) outperform growth stocks with low B/M, E/P, or C/P. Moreover, stocks with high return over the past three months to one year continue to outperform stocks with poor prior performance (Jegadeesh and Titman (1993)). The evidence that beta is also compensated for in average returns is weaker (Fama and French (1992), Kothari, Shanken, and Sloan (1995))

The interpretation of the evidence is strongly debated.[1] Some believe that the premiums are a compensation for pervasive risk factors, others attribute them to firm characteristics or an inefficiency in the way markets incorporate information into prices. Yet others argue that the premiums may be biased by survivorship or data snooping. A motivation for examining inter-

---

* Yale School of Management, Yale University. I thank Geert Bekaert, Steve Buser, John Chalmers, Ken French, Campbell Harvey, Theo Nijman, N. Prabhala, Jeremy Stein, Raman Uppal, and seminar participants at 1999 ASSA Meetings, the Berkeley Program in Finance, Dartmouth, the 1998 European Finance Meetings, the Harvard Business School, H.E.C., Ohio State University, M.I.T., the 1998 NBER Summer Institute, Indiana University, Tilburg University, the University of Illinois at Urbana-Campaign, the University of Southern California, the University of Virginia, and Yale University for helpful discussions and comments. Part of this research was conducted while I was visiting M.I.T.

[1] Participants in this debate include Berk (1995), Daniel and Titman (1997), Fama and French (1996), Haugen and Baker (1996), Kothari et al. (1995), Lakonishok et al. (1994), Lo and MacKinlay (1990), Loughran (1997), and MacKinlay (1995).

national markets is that, to the extent that these markets move independently from the United States, they provide independent samples to study return premiums. In this spirit, a number of researchers have recently shown that size, value, and momentum also help to explain the cross section of average returns in developed equity markets outside of the United States.[2]

This paper examines the sources of return variation in emerging stock markets. From the perspective of collecting independent samples, emerging market countries are particularly interesting because of their relative isolation from the capital markets of other countries. Compared to developed markets, the correlation between most emerging markets and other stock markets has historically been low (Harvey (1995)), and until recently many emerging countries restricted investment by foreign investors. Interestingly, Bekaert and Harvey (1995) find that despite the recent trend toward abolition of these restrictions and the substantial inflows of foreign capital, some emerging equity markets have actually become more segmented from world capital markets. A large portion of the equity capital of emerging economies is held by local investors who are likely to evaluate their portfolios in light of local economic and market conditions (Bekaert and Harvey (1997b)). Therefore, the relative segmentation of emerging markets provides a unique opportunity to examine cross-sectional variation of stock returns: If the return factors in a group of relatively isolated markets are the same as those found in developed markets, it becomes more likely that the factors are fundamentally related to the way in which investors set prices in financial markets around the world.

Market segmentation and low correlations *across* emerging market countries do not preclude structure to the individual stock returns *within* these markets. For example, suppose that emerging markets are effectively segmented from world markets, and that a domestic version of the Capital Asset Pricing Model (CAPM) holds in each country. Under these conditions high beta stocks are expected to outperform low beta stocks in each country, as long as betas are measured relative to the appropriate local market portfolios. Therefore, one expects to find similar risk exposures driving expected stock returns in segmented and integrated markets, with the qualification that if markets are segmented the risk exposures are measured relative to local benchmarks, and the prices of risk are determined locally rather than in global markets.

The paper attempts to answer two sets of questions. The first set of three questions concerns the existence of return premiums: (i) Do the factors that explain expected return differences in developed equity markets also describe the cross section of expected returns of emerging market firms?

---

[2] For example, Fama and French (1998) report a value premium in a sample of 13 developed markets, and Heston, Rouwenhorst and Wessels (1999) and Rouwenhorst (1998) document a return premium for beta, size, and momentum in European countries. Haugen and Baker (1996) examine 12 return factors in five developed countries. Chan, Karceski, and Lakonishok (1997) compare return factors in three developed countries.

Local Return Factors and Turnover in Emerging Markets 1441

(ii) Are the return factors in emerging markets primarily local or do they have global components as well? (iii) How does the emerging market evidence contribute to the international evidence from developed markets that similar return factors are present in markets around the world?

The second set of questions relates to the interpretation of the return factors. Daniel and Titman (1997) argue that the return premiums in the United States are related to firm characteristics, rejecting the linear multifactor interpretation of Fama and French (1996). One firm characteristic that is of particular concern to investors in emerging markets is liquidity. For example, if growth stocks are on average more liquid that value stocks, the value premium may in part reflect a compensation for the lower liquidity of value firms. This motivates the final two questions of the paper: (iv) Is there a cross-sectional relationship between liquidity and average returns in emerging markets? (v) Are the return factors in emerging markets cross-sectionally correlated with liquidity?

Little is known about the answers to these questions, as few papers have studied individual stock returns in a broad sample of emerging markets. There is some conflicting evidence on the first question: Fama and French (1998) and Patel (1998) document a premium for small firms and value stocks in 17 emerging market countries; Claessens, Dasgupta, and Glen (1998) report a premium for large firms and growth stocks in an earlier sample of 19 emerging markets, in addition to a premium for beta and share turnover.[3] Harvey (1995), Bekaert et al. (1997), and Bekaert and Harvey (1995, 1997a) have studied the influence of local and global factors on expected returns and volatility in emerging markets (question (ii)), but these studies have been conducted at the aggregate country level, whereas this paper is concerned with the cross section of individual stock returns in countries.

The findings can be summarized as follows. In a sample of 1705 firms from 20 emerging markets, taken from the Emerging Markets Database (EMDB) of the International Finance Corporation (IFC), I find that the return factors in emerging markets are qualitatively similar to those documented for many developed markets. The combination of a small number of stocks in some countries and the high volatility of returns often precludes precise measurement of return premiums in individual countries, but averaged across all emerging markets, stocks exhibit momentum, small stocks outperform large stocks, and value stocks outperform growth stocks. There is no evidence that high beta stocks also outperform low beta stocks, nor do I find that average returns are related to liquidity, as measured by share turnover. The results for value and size confirm findings by Fama and French (1998) and Patel (1998), but differ from Claessens, Dasgupta, and Glen (1998). A Bayesian analysis of the return premiums shows that, unless one has strong prior beliefs to the contrary, the combined evidence from developed

---

[3] Anchour et al. (1998) look at the performance of individual stocks in emerging markets using portfolios sorted on a large number of firm characteristics, but the sample includes only three markets.

and emerging markets strongly favors the hypothesis that value, momentum, and to a lesser extent size are compensated for in average stock returns around the world.

Two empirical observations suggest that the return factors of emerging markets have a strong local character: their correlation across emerging markets is on average low, and the exposure to global risk factors cannot explain their average returns. There is no evidence that the factor correlations are higher among countries within particular geographical regions such as Latin America, Asia, or Europe/Africa/Middle-East. And although the co-movement between emerging market country returns may have increased over time (Bekaert and Harvey (1997b)), I find little evidence that this is also true for the factors that drive individual stock returns within these markets.

Although share turnover cannot explain differences in average returns in emerging markets, there are strong cross-sectional share turnover patterns in the local return factor portfolios. Stocks with high beta, small market cap, high past medium-term return, or high book-to-market have higher average turnover than stocks with low beta, large market cap, poor past performance, or low book-to-market. This seems at odds with a simple liquidity explanation for the return premiums.

The remainder of the paper is organized as follows. Section I gives a description of the data. The next section presents the average returns of the local return factor portfolios and their correlations. The third section evaluates the international evidence that similar factors are compensated in markets around the world. The evidence of the relationship between average returns and turnover is presented in Section IV. The final section gives a summary of the conclusions and provides directions for future research.

I. Data Description

As of April 1997 the Emerging Markets Database of the IFC contains data on more than 2200 firms from 31 emerging markets, but not all are included in the sample. Eleven countries are excluded because of insufficient return histories, which leaves 1705 firms in the 20 countries that the IFC tracks for at least seven years. For some firms monthly closing prices and dividends are available dating back to 1975. Starting at various points during the 1980s the IFC expanded its reporting to include monthly time series for price-to-book ratios, price-earnings ratios, market capitalization, trading volume, and the number of days per month that a stock is traded. It is important to note that the EMDB does not represent a random sample of emerging markets firms. There are two main sources of bias. First, the IFC uses several criteria to select stocks for its global indices. In order of importance these are: trading activity in terms of value of shares traded during a review period, total market capitalization coverage, and industry diversification. The EMDB is therefore biased toward larger and more frequently traded issues. Second, in mid-1981 when the IFC started constructing indices for 10 emerging markets, it collected available return information back to 1975, which introduces a survivorship bias into the pre-1982 returns (see Harvey

(1995) for a detailed discussion). For this reason firms are included in this study only after their respective countries enter the IFC database, which has the effect of excluding the backfilled returns.[4]

In addition to survivorship and stock selection bias there are several other data issues to confront. First, there are missing values in the time series of firm characteristics used to form portfolios such as size or book-to-market. A firm is excluded from a characteristic portfolio if the relevant ranking information is missing in a particular month, but remains in the sample otherwise. Second, there appear to be data errors. These vary from zero entries in cases where the database carries insufficient significant digits, to a computed total firm return that exceeds 100,000 percent per month. In light of the high volatility of emerging markets and lacking an independent data source, it is difficult to reliably identify data errors but for a few isolated cases of miscalculated stock splits ratios. Except for these few corrections, the reported results are based on all observations as reported in the database.

Total returns are calculated as the sum of the dividend return and price appreciation, using prices scaled by a "capital adjustment factor," which the IFC computes to correct for price effects associated with stock splits, stock dividends, and rights issues. Many emerging markets have firms with multiple classes of shares carrying different ownership restrictions. Firms with multiple share classes are treated as a single value-weighted portfolio of the outstanding equity securities.

Table I presents some summary statistics for the resulting sample. The first columns confirm one of the well-known facts about emerging markets: Between 1982 and 1997 average returns in emerging markets were high relative to most developed markets, both in local currency and in U.S. dollars (Harvey (1995)). Measured in U.S. dollars, average returns range from 0.17 percent in Jordan to 5.30 percent per month in Argentina, and average returns exceed 2 percent per month in 11 of the 20 sample countries. Emerging markets have also been more volatile than developed markets. Argentina has a standard deviation of almost 30 percent and is one of eight countries for which the historical standard deviation exceeds 10 percent per month. Goetzmann and Jorion (1999) argue that the survival of emerging markets can induce a positive correlation between ex post average returns and volatility. This survivorship bias may in part explain the high ex post correlation of 0.90 between the mean and standard deviation of the country returns measured in U.S. dollars.

The next columns show that there is considerable cross-sectional variation in median firm size, book-to-market, and trading intensity across markets.[5] Median firm size measured as the natural logarithm of the market value of equity in U.S. dollars varies from 2.81 in Zimbabwe to 6.14 in Taiwan, which

[4] Backfilled returns are used to get preliminary estimates of momentum and beta that are used to rank stocks in the first month that a country enters the sample.
[5] The distribution of these firm characteristics is skewed, and the ratios are especially sensitive to outliers. For these reasons, I compute monthly medians across firms in a country and report the time series average of these monthly medians.

Table I

Summary Statistics of Emerging Markets Firms, 1982:1–1997:4

The table gives for each country the number of firms in the sample, the starting date for the return data, the average return, and the standard deviation of the return of the equally weighted index of the sample firms, both in local currency (LC) and U.S. dollars (USD). Returns are expressed as percentage per month between the starting date and April 1997. The last four columns give summary statistics for median firm size, median book-to-market value (B/M), median monthly turnover, and median trading activity of the sample stocks in each country. The medians are computed by month across firms, and the table reports the time series average of these monthly medians. Size is measured as the log of the market value of equity in U.S. dollars. Turnover is computed as the number of shares traded in a month as a percentage of the number of outstanding shares at the beginning of the month. Days traded is expressed as the number of days that a stock trades in a month. Information on B/M, turnover, and days traded is not available before 1987.

Country	Number of Firms	Starting Date	LC Return		USD Return		Median Size	Median B/M	Median Turnover	Median Days Traded
			Mean	Std. Dev.	Mean	Std. Dev.				
Argentina	49	8201	16.50	42.92	5.30	29.82	4.08	1.58	3.00	20.58
Brazil	87	8201	19.35	26.67	4.27	20.17	4.97	1.62	1.82	20.28
Chile	59	8201	3.41	8.30	2.12	8.63	4.84	0.71	0.49	19.70
Colombia	34	8601	4.41	9.60	3.01	9.33	4.44	0.94	0.43	15.02
Greece	69	8201	2.24	9.71	1.40	9.91	4.02	0.51	1.51	20.25
Indonesia	114	9001	0.96	7.13	0.62	7.18	4.82	0.51	2.42	16.55
India	15	8201	1.92	9.50	1.14	9.04	4.76	0.40	1.88	18.09
Jordan	66	8201	0.56	4.57	0.17	4.78	3.30	0.67	1.79	18.29
Korea	179	8201	1.34	7.55	1.22	7.78	5.19	0.75	8.13	24.36
Malaysia	184	8601	1.63	9.15	1.60	9.06	5.64	0.43	1.89	20.59
Mexico	98	8201	6.00	12.93	3.05	13.86	5.17	0.90	2.74	18.75
Nigeria	38	8601	4.15	5.09	2.05	15.84	3.59	0.53	0.04	16.13
Pakistan	118	8601	1.74	7.00	1.05	7.05	2.97	0.51	0.44	15.22
Philippines	58	8601	3.17	10.83	2.92	10.69	4.51	0.45	1.78	20.50
Portugal	45	8901	0.77	6.14	0.63	6.74	4.93	0.72	1.34	18.89
Taiwan	119	8601	2.80	13.95	3.11	14.27	6.14	0.35	30.22	23.77
Thailand	120	8201	1.27	8.60	1.21	8.65	5.04	0.46	3.48	20.47
Turkey	64	8901	8.73	18.97	4.36	19.48	4.94	0.35	4.29	20.80
Venezuela	20	8601	5.43	12.35	2.98	13.62	4.76	0.61	0.84	17.06
Zimbabwe	28	8201	3.75	9.64	2.24	9.78	2.81	1.15	0.29	9.85

means that the median firm in Taiwan is almost 30 times larger than the median firm in Zimbabwe. Median B/M ratios range from 0.35 in Turkey and Taiwan to 1.62 in Brazil. The final two columns report liquidity measures for the sample stocks. Liquidity, as measured by the median number of days per month that a stock trades, is fairly uniform across countries and exceeds 15 in all countries except one. The monthly share turnover ratios show considerably more dispersion across markets. With a median monthly turnover ratio of 0.04 percent, Nigeria is one of six countries with turnover ratios below 1 percent. By contrast, Korea and Taiwan have monthly share turnover ratios of 8.13 and 30.22 percent respectively, and the median ratio has regularly exceeded 100 percent per month in Taiwan. These observations suggest that the median stock in most countries trades frequently, but the volume can be relatively small. The next section describes the cross-sectional relation between these characteristics and average returns by emerging market.

II. Local Return Factor Portfolios

It is standard practice in empirical finance to study return premiums by comparing the returns of portfolios that are formed by sorting stocks on observable firm characteristics or estimated risk exposures.[6] We rank stocks by country on local beta, size, prior six-month return, book-to-market, and turnover. At the beginning of each month, stocks for which the relevant ranking information is available are grouped by country into three portfolios (top 30, middle 40, and bottom 30 percent). The portfolios are equally weighted and are rebalanced every month. Unless stated otherwise, the conclusions are unaffected by the equal weighting of the factor portfolios. Throughout the paper I report the full sample postranking returns of the top and bottom portfolios, expressed in U.S. dollars. Choosing the U.S. dollar as a numéraire serves to make the average portfolio returns comparable across countries, but does not affect the excess returns of top minus bottom portfolios within countries because these excess returns correspond to investment strategies that take simultaneous unit dollar long and short positions, and therefore to a first approximation take no net position in any country or currency.[7]

---

[6] An alternative methodology is to run Fama–MacBeth (1973) monthly cross-sectional regressions to examine return premiums. Although these regression slope coefficients sometimes have the interpretation of portfolio excess returns, they do not constrain the portfolio weights to be positive. Because short selling is a serious problem in emerging markets, I choose to compare the return of equally weighted portfolios.

[7] The equivalence between average dollar and local currency excess returns is exact for log returns and only approximate for the reported simple returns. Also, country neutrality does not mean that the spread portfolios have no exposure to the local market. For example, the excess returns on portfolios sorted on local beta are expected to be positively correlated with the local market.

A. *Local Beta and Size*

For each stock a monthly preranking local beta is estimated by regressing its local currency return on the local currency IFC Global (IFCG) index return of the country to which the firm belongs. One lag of the index return is included to allow for a delayed response due to nonsynchronous trading. A minimum of two years and up to five years of historical returns prior to the time of ranking are used to obtain preranking betas. The choice of benchmark merits some discussion. Because the primary focus of the paper is on local factors and not market integration, the IFCG country indices are used instead of the narrower IFC investable country indices, or a "world" market index that includes developed markets. Harvey (1995) has shown that the correlations between emerging country returns and the world market are close to zero, and it seems unlikely that a global beta is informative about the cross section of expected returns. In Section II.C, I examine the extent to which these local beta portfolios share a common component with global factors.

The left half of Table II summarizes the average postranking returns of the beta-sorted portfolios by country. There is no clear relation between average returns and preranking local betas in emerging markets. In approximately half of the countries the high beta portfolio outperforms the portfolio of low beta stocks, but the excess return is never significantly different from zero. The last two rows of Table II show that the difference between the returns of beta-sorted portfolios that are diversified across all 20 emerging markets is not significantly different from zero, both in the case where stocks are equally weighted and where countries are equally weighted.

The high volatility of emerging market returns raises two concerns about the power to detect differences in average returns. First, the preranking betas may be poorly estimated, and what is designed as a sort on beta is effectively a sort on estimation error that is uncorrelated with the postranking average returns. The next two columns of Table II show that this is not the case. The full sample postranking beta of the high-beta portfolios exceeds the beta of the low-beta portfolios in 18 countries, and in 13 countries by more than two standard errors. The second concern is that it may be difficult to accurately estimate average returns over relatively short time intervals. However, the *t*-test applies to the return *difference* between two portfolios that are strongly positively correlated. The sample correlations between the two beta-sorted portfolios range from 0.44 to 0.94 across countries. As a consequence of diversification, the sample correlation between the two internationally diversified beta portfolios reported in the next to last row exceeds 0.90, and the standard error of the average excess return of −3 basis points (bp) is only 18 bp per month. This is small in absolute terms, but needs to be put in perspective against the difference between the postranking betas, which averages 0.22 across countries. Suppose that a local version of the CAPM holds in each country and that the true risk premium for beta averages 12 percent per annum across markets, or 100 bp per month. The expected excess return of two portfolios that differ in beta by 0.22 is

Table II
Average Returns of Beta- and Size-Sorted Portfolios

At the beginning of each month all stocks with at least two years of return history are ranked by country based on historical beta into three groups: High (top 30 percent), Medium (middle 40 percent), and Low (bottom 30 percent). Preranking betas are computed in local currency relative to the IFC Global index of that country, using two to five years of monthly historical returns, depending on data availability. Columns 3–5 give the average return on equally weighted portfolios of low (L) and high (H) beta stocks and the HML-β excess return, measured in U.S. dollars and expressed in percentage per month. $t(\ )$ is the mean excess return divided by its standard error. The next two columns give the postranking betas of the HML-β excess return, and the betas divided by their standard errors. The final four columns summarize the returns of size-sorted portfolios. At the beginning of each month all stocks with available ranking information are sorted by country into three groups based on market value of equity measured in U.S. dollars: Big (top 30 percent), Medium (middle 40 percent), and Small (bottom 30 percent). Columns 10–12 report the average return on equally weighted portfolios of small (S) and big (B) stocks, and the average SMB excess return. The last two rows report data for an equally weighted portfolio of stocks of all 20 markets and for the cross-country average, an equally weighted average of the 20 country excess returns. The standard errors are computed using the Newey–West correction for heteroskedasticity and autocorrelation.

Country	Start	Average Returns of Beta Portfolios				Postranking Betas		Start	Average Returns of Size-Sorted Portfolios			
		Low-β	High-β	HML-β	t(HML-β)	HML-β	t(HML-β)		Small	Big	SMB	t(SMB)
Argentina	8201	5.40	4.82	-0.58	-0.63	-0.10	-2.98	8201	7.30	3.47	3.84	2.54
Brazil	8201	3.44	3.56	0.12	0.13	0.08	1.89	8201	5.00	3.25	1.76	1.33
Chile	8201	2.65	2.41	-0.24	-0.43	0.06	0.71	8201	2.22	1.91	0.31	0.61
Colombia	8701	2.83	1.97	-0.86	-1.30	-0.11	-1.56	8601	2.60	3.29	-0.68	-0.79
Greece	8201	1.96	1.30	-0.66	-1.05	0.14	2.36	8201	1.42	1.38	0.04	0.07
Indonesia	9201	1.46	2.33	0.87	1.77	0.47	5.94	9001	0.22	0.69	-0.46	-0.80
India	8201	1.38	0.83	-0.56	-1.60	0.30	6.71	8201	0.89	1.24	-0.35	-0.89
Jordan	8201	-0.13	0.68	0.80	1.96	0.34	3.47	8201	0.02	0.35	-0.34	-0.79
Korea	8201	1.13	1.16	0.03	0.07	0.09	1.61	8201	1.39	1.07	0.32	0.51
Malaysia	8701	2.23	2.19	-0.04	-0.08	0.34	5.34	8601	1.84	1.42	0.43	0.60
Mexico	8201	2.81	3.29	0.47	0.54	0.39	5.58	8201	4.63	2.24	2.39	2.17
Nigeria	8701	4.34	1.87	-2.47	-1.57	0.23	0.67	8601	1.62	2.22	-0.59	-0.62
Pakistan	8701	1.32	0.96	-0.36	-0.80	0.28	4.99	8601	0.70	1.11	-0.42	-0.75
Philippines	8701	1.15	2.46	1.32	1.36	0.27	2.83	8601	3.56	3.33	0.23	0.29
Portugal	8901	-0.06	0.82	0.88	1.54	0.32	3.32	8901	0.34	1.08	-0.74	-1.61
Taiwan	8701	2.81	3.03	0.22	0.42	0.09	2.65	8601	3.57	2.90	0.68	0.81
Thailand	8201	1.05	1.30	0.26	0.31	0.55	6.66	8201	0.52	1.90	-1.39	-2.39
Turkey	8901	4.85	4.97	0.12	0.12	0.26	4.39	8901	4.84	4.12	0.72	0.59
Venezuela	8701	1.77	2.63	0.85	0.83	0.40	4.47	8601	3.85	2.48	1.37	1.41
Zimbabwe	8201	2.39	1.58	-0.81	-1.06	0.09	0.92	8201	3.28	1.42	1.85	1.95
All 20 markets		2.14	2.11	-0.03	-0.17				2.42	1.73	0.69	2.88
Cross-country average		2.22	2.15	-0.08	-0.43				2.60	1.90	0.70	2.96

$100 \times 0.22 = 22$ bp per month, which is only about one standard error from the sample average premium. The conclusion is therefore that although there is no evidence that local beta risk is compensated in average returns, the power of the test is probably low due to difficulties in achieving sufficient spread in the postranking betas.[8]

The last columns of Table II give the returns on size-sorted portfolios. Although the size premium is only significant in a few individual countries, an internationally diversified portfolio of small stocks has significantly out-performed a portfolio of large stocks by approximately 69 basis points per month ($t = 2.88$) when securities are equally weighted or by 70 basis points ($t = 2.96$) when countries are equally weighted. The strong performance of small stocks has not been uniform: Of the five countries with the largest size returns, four are from Latin America, and only in 12 of the 20 countries have size returns been positive. A nonparametric Wilcoxon Signed Rank Test (SRT) on the 20 small (S) and big (B) average returns does not reject equal performance of small and big firms at the 10 percent level. Unreported results show that the performance of small stocks cannot be attributed to a negative correlation between beta and size. Of the 20 country-specific small minus big (SMB) excess return portfolios, 14 have a negative beta with respect to their respective IFCG indices. The average correlation between the SMB portfolios across countries is only 0.01, which suggests that most of the country-specific excess return variance can be diversified internationally. The low correlation of size-sorted portfolios across emerging markets is similar to the international evidence for developed markets reported by Heston et al. (1995), who conjecture that if most of the variance in size returns can be diversified internationally, the size premium is perhaps a reward for the lower liquidity of small stocks. Although a direct measure of liquidity, such as the bid-ask spread, is not available in the EMDB, the database provides information on share turnover. As will be shown in Section IV, the median turnover of the stocks in portfolio S is higher than in portfolio B. This does not reflect a positive association between turnover and average returns in emerging markets, but is a consequence of the sample selection criteria used by the IFC. Instead, the interesting finding is that even among stocks that are screened based on the total value of trading volume, small stocks earn a return premium over large stocks in emerging markets. This seems to be at odds with a simple liquidity explanation of the size premium.

B. Momentum and Value

Momentum or relative strength portfolios are formed by ranking stocks in each country on prior six-month return. As shown in Jegadeesh and Titman (1993) and Rouwenhorst (1998) for developed markets, momentum returns

[8] It is conceivable that a larger spread on beta can be obtained by constructing the beta-sorted portfolios from only the extreme preranking beta deciles. Because these portfolios have fewer securities, they are not as well diversified and the power of the means test is attenuated by a larger standard error of the average excess return.

Local Return Factors and Turnover in Emerging Markets   1449

accrue gradually over a period of up to one year after ranking. Contrary to the beta- and size-sorted portfolios, it is important to select a holding period that is longer than one month. For ease of comparison with earlier papers a holding period of six months is chosen. And similar to Jegadeesh and Titman, I report the monthly average return across six strategies, each starting one month apart to handle the issue of overlapping observations. To attenuate the effect of bid-ask bounce the portfolios are formed one month after the end of the ranking period. The positions initially weight stocks equally and are not rebalanced during the holding period. Return outliers are potentially a problem in the formation of momentum portfolios because momentum strategies select stocks based on extreme prior performance. For this reason I exclude at each ranking date the extreme five percent of the prior six- month return distribution in the portfolio formation.[9]

The first columns of Table III show that on average past Winners (W) outperform Losers (L) in 17 of the 20 countries (Wilcoxon SRT p-value < 1 percent), and the average WML (Winners minus Losers) excess return is more than two standard errors away from zero in six countries. Implemented simultaneously across all 20 emerging markets, the WML excess return averages 0.39 percent per month ($t = 2.68$) if stocks are equally weighted, and 0.58 percent per month ($t = 3.96$) when countries are equally weighted. The statistical significance of the returns to these internationally diversified momentum portfolios is again a result of the low pairwise correlation between the momentum returns of individual countries, which averages -0.007 across all 20 emerging markets and never exceeds 0.25 for individual country pairs.

At first glance, the average momentum returns in emerging markets seem lower than those reported for developed markets by Jegadeesh and Titman (1993) and Rouwenhorst (1998).[10] However, the W and L portfolios in these studies contain only stocks from the top and bottom 10 percent of the prior return distribution, but the emerging markets momentum portfolios include stocks from the top and bottom 30 percent. Since the evidence for developed markets indicates that the strength of return continuation increases with past return, the coarser sort attenuates the documented momentum effect for emerging markets.

The remaining columns of Table III report the average returns for portfolios ranked on book-to-market. The stocks of firms with low B/M are commonly referred to as growth stocks, as opposed to value stocks which sell at high B/M multiples. The table shows that high B/M stocks have outperformed low B/M stocks in 16 of 20 countries (Wilcoxon SRT p-value < 1 percent). Although the return differences are not always significant for individual countries, the average excess return of an internationally diversified high

[9] The results are qualitatively similar, although slightly weaker, if these extreme observations are included.

[10] Jegadeesh and Titman (1990) report an average excess return of about one percent per month in the United States, and Rouwenhorst (1998) documents a similar return for a diversified European portfolio.

Table III

Average Returns of Momentum and Book-to-Market Portfolios

Momentum portfolios are formed by sorting all stocks with available ranking information at the beginning of each month t on prior six-month return between month $t - 7$ and month $t - 1$. After excluding the top and bottom five percent, stocks are assigned to three equally weighted portfolios: Winners (top 30 percent), Average (middle 30 percent) and Losers (bottom 30 percent). Positions are held for six months and are not rebalanced during this interval. Columns 3–6 report the average return of the Loser (L) and Winner (W) portfolios, the average Winners minus Losers (WML) excess return, and the t-statistic of the mean WML excess return. Book-to-market (B/M) portfolios are constructed as follows: At the beginning of each month all stocks with available ranking information are sorted by country based on B/M into three groups: High (top 30 percent), Medium (middle 40 percent) and Low (bottom 30 percent). Columns 8–11 report the average return on equally weighted portfolios of low (L) and high (H) B/M stocks, the average High minus Low (HML-BM) excess return, and the t-statistic of the mean excess return. The reported returns are expressed in U.S. dollars as percentage per month. All is the equally weighted portfolio of stocks from all 20 countries. The cross-country average portfolio weights all countries equally. The standard errors are computed using the Newey–West correction for heteroskedasticity and autocorrelation.

Country	Average Returns of Momentum Portfolios					Average Returns of Book-to-Market Portfolios				
	Start	Losers	Winners	WML	t(WML)	Start	Low-BM	High-BM	HML-BM	t(HML-BM)
Argentina	8201	5.51	4.72	-0.79	-0.95	8701	4.73	6.41	1.68	1.08
Brazil	8201	4.21	4.22	0.01	0.01	8701	2.46	6.40	3.94	2.34
Chile	8201	1.23	2.60	1.37	3.18	8801	2.10	3.17	1.07	1.74
Colombia	8601	1.90	3.99	2.09	3.27	8701	1.96	1.60	-0.36	-0.40
Greece	8201	0.59	2.35	1.76	4.95	8701	1.61	2.92	1.31	1.68
Indonesia	9101	0.65	0.41	-0.24	-0.61	9001	0.24	1.34	1.11	1.57
India	8201	0.84	1.35	0.51	2.02	8701	1.13	1.18	0.05	0.08
Jordan	8201	-0.35	0.90	1.25	3.63	8701	0.02	0.09	0.06	0.15
Korea	8201	1.32	1.34	0.03	0.08	8701	0.17	1.75	1.58	3.99
Malaysia	8601	1.52	1.66	0.14	0.39	8701	1.49	2.52	1.02	2.37
Mexico	8201	2.48	3.01	0.52	0.89	8701	2.47	3.86	1.39	1.17
Nigeria	8601	1.76	3.18	1.43	1.79	8701	2.71	2.96	0.25	0.19
Pakistan	8601	0.82	1.10	0.28	0.84	8701	1.12	1.07	-0.05	-0.08
Philippines	8601	2.69	2.85	0.16	0.33	8801	1.11	1.62	0.51	0.77
Portugal	8901	0.02	1.19	1.16	2.11	8901	0.97	0.37	-0.60	-0.93
Taiwan	8601	3.05	2.58	-0.47	-1.39	8701	2.72	3.73	1.01	1.42
Thailand	8201	0.93	1.63	0.70	1.58	8701	2.00	0.44	-1.56	-1.80
Turkey	8901	4.04	4.51	0.48	0.73	8901	3.41	6.27	2.86	1.60
Venezuela	8601	2.68	2.71	0.03	0.05	8701	2.27	3.54	1.27	0.93
Zimbabwe	8201	1.94	2.69	0.75	1.23	8701	1.48	3.80	2.31	1.86
All 20 markets		1.74	2.13	0.39	2.68		1.70	2.42	0.72	3.35
Cross-country average		1.86	2.44	0.58	3.96		1.90	2.83	0.93	3.68

Local Return Factors and Turnover in Emerging Markets   1451

minus low B/M excess return (HML) is 0.72 percent per month ($t = 3.35$) if stocks are weighted equally, or 0.93 percent per month ($t = 3.68$) if countries are weighted equally. Unreported results show similar excess returns for portfolios sorted on earnings-to-price. The excess return of equally weighted B/M portfolios translates to an estimated value premium of 9.00 percent per annum, which is close to the historical averages of 7.60 percent reported by Fama and French (1998) for developed markets between 1974 and 1995. They report a value premium of 16.91 ($t = 3.06$) for B/M-sorted portfolios that are value-weighted and diversified across 17 emerging markets between 1987 and 1995.

C. *Emerging Market Return Factors: Local or Global Risks?*

The previous sections show that on average across emerging markets small stocks outperform large stocks, past medium-term winners outperform medium-term losers, and value stocks outperform growth stocks. Are these return factors predominantly local, or do they have common regional or global components as well? Panel A of Table IV examines the return factor correlations among emerging markets and within geographical regions, and Panel B presents the sensitivity of the internationally diversified emerging markets return factors to a set of global risk factors. The first entry in Panel A shows that the pairwise correlation between the excess returns of the 20 beta-sorted portfolios averages 0.02 across all markets. The remainder of the first column shows a similarly low average correlation for the other return factors. The next columns show that the correlations are not appreciably higher among members of the same regional IFC indices. Even between the geographically concentrated emerging markets of Latin America, the average sample correlation between the return factors never exceeds 0.03. The right-hand side of Panel A gives average sample correlations for the last five years of the sample. During this period most emerging markets had relaxed barriers to cross-border investment, which can lead to an increase in the correlations between country market returns (Bekaert and Harvey (1997a, 1997b)). This is illustrated by inspecting the last line of Panel A, which give the average correlations between the IFCG country index returns. The average estimated pairwise correlation between the IFCG country returns is 0.18 over the last five years, compared to the full sample correlation of 0.10. However, there is no clear increase in the correlation between the local return factors. This suggests that the factors that influence country performance are distinct from those that drive expected return differences within markets. In conclusion, the correlation evidence suggests that the cross-sectional differences between expected returns are primarily driven by local factors.

The easiest way to assess the influence of global components would be to run a multiple regression of the local return factors on their global counterparts. However, global momentum, and size returns are not readily available. Panel B gives the coefficients of a simpler regression that includes the

Table IV
Correlation between Emerging Markets Factor Portfolios and Global Factor Exposures

Panel A gives the average pairwise correlation between the local excess return factor portfolios of emerging markets. The second column gives the average cross-correlation for all 20 markets. The next three columns give the average correlation by region: Latin America (Argentina, Brazil, Chile, Columbia, Mexico, and Venezuela), Asia (India, Indonesia, Korea, Malaysia, Pakistan, Philippines, Taiwan, and Thailand), and EMEA (Europe/Middle East/Africa: Greece, Jordan, Nigeria, Portugal, Turkey, and Zimbabwe). The last row of Panel A gives the correlations between the IFC Global country index returns of the sample countries. Panel B reports the results of regressing the factor portfolios that are diversified across 20 emerging markets on the Morgan Stanley Capital International world excess market return, $R_M - r_f$, and the global Fama–French (1998) High minus Low Book-to-Market Portfolio (HML-BM). Due to data availability, the full sample results in Panel B end in 1995. All returns are measured in U.S. dollars.

Panel A: Correlation between Emerging Markets Factor Portfolios

Portfolio	Full sample: 1982–1997:4				1992:4–1997:4			
	All Markets	Latin America	Asia	EMEA	All Markets	Latin America	Asia	EMEA
HML-β	0.02	0.01	0.05	0.06	0.03	0.03	0.10	0.06
SMB	0.01	0.03	0.02	0.02	0.01	0.06	0.06	0.03
WML	−0.01	−0.02	0.01	−0.05	0.01	0.05	0.01	−0.09
HML-BM	0.01	0.00	−0.01	0.06	0.04	0.07	−0.01	0.13
Global IFC index returns	0.10	0.04	0.20	0.08	0.18	0.19	0.32	0.12

Panel B: Factor Exposures to Global Risk Factors

$$R_{i,t} - r_{f,t} = a + b \left[R_{M,t} - r_{f,t} \right] + c \text{ HML-BM}_t + e_{i,t}$$

	Full sample: 1982–1995							1991–1995						
	a	$t(a)$	b	$t(b)$	c	$t(c)$	R^2	a	$t(a)$	b	$t(b)$	c	$t(c)$	R^2
HML-β	−0.15	−0.73	0.08	1.57	0.16	1.61	0.02	−0.31	−1.17	0.08	0.94	0.45	3.37	0.18
SMB	0.86	3.41	−0.06	−0.98	0.08	0.66	0.08	0.26	0.83	−0.33	−3.41	0.12	0.77	0.19
WML	0.36	1.92	0.05	1.05	−0.10	−1.13	0.04	0.24	1.52	0.08	1.59	−0.21	−2.61	0.17
HML-BM	0.91	4.37	−0.06	−1.28	0.11	1.11	0.19	0.98	3.45	−0.07	−0.84	0.02	0.16	0.19

Local Return Factors and Turnover in Emerging Markets 1453

excess returns of the Morgan Stanley Capital International (MSCI) world market portfolio and the book-to-market portfolio of Fama and French (1998) as independent variables.[11] Over the full sample, approximately half of the estimated global exposures are negative, and none of the factor portfolios have significantly positive loadings on the global risk factors. As a consequence, it is not surprising that the global risk factors are unable to explain the mean returns of the emerging markets return factors. With the exception of the momentum factor, the intercepts of the regressions are close to the raw excess return reported in Tables II and III.[12] Over the last five years of the sample, the intercepts are insignificant for momentum and size, not because of increased explanatory power of the global risk factors, but because the raw momentum and size premiums are lower during this period. The combined evidence from the correlations and the exposure regressions provides further evidence that during much of the sample period emerging markets have been isolated from world markets.

III. A Bayesian Interpretation of Return Premiums around the World

Table V summarizes the average emerging markets factor premiums, as well as their counterparts from the United States and other international developed markets reported elsewhere in the literature.[13] The fact that qualitatively similar factors play a role in both financially integrated markets and in countries with segmented capital markets makes it more likely that the premiums are fundamentally related to the way in which financial markets set prices. However, despite the large *t*-statistics in Table V, some individuals may still be skeptical about the presence of these risk premiums because of their prior beliefs about the distribution of the returns before examining the data. For example, based on reading the extensive literature on (weak form) market efficiency, someone may have strong prior beliefs that momentum strategies, which trade stocks based on their most recent six-month price history, are equally likely to return positive or negative profits. How would this "skeptic" update his prior beliefs after consecutively examining the momentum premiums for the U.S., international, and emerging markets reported in Table V?

[11] I thank Ken French for making these data available, in addition to the time series for SMB and HML-BM portfolios for the United States and for international markets outside of the United States, which will be used in Section III. A detailed description of the methodology used to construct these series can be found in Fama and French (1996, 1998).

[12] Adding the SMB and WML excess returns from the United States as regressors does not affect the results.

[13] The HML-BM returns for the United States and international markets are from Fama and French (1998), as well as the time series for SMB. The SMB for Europe and WML returns for the United States and Europe are from Heston, Rouwenhorst, and Wessels (1999) and Rouwenhorst (1998). They are constructed in the same way as the size and momentum returns in emerging markets.

Table V

Return Premiums around the World

The table summarizes a sample of international evidence on return premiums around the world. The U.S. return premiums for size and book-to-market (B/M) represent the excess return of small over large stocks (SMB) and the excess return of high over low B/M stocks (HML-BM) from Fama and French (1996, 1998) updated through 1997. U.S. and European WML momentum returns are from Rouwenhorst (1998). They are calculated as the excess return of a portfolio of stocks with highest prior six-month return (Winners) and a portfolio containing the stocks with lowest prior six-month performance (Losers). Winners and Loser portfolios contain the top and bottom three deciles of the prior six-month return distribution. The International B/M return premium is the excess return of an international portfolio of high B/M stocks from 12 developed markets outside the United States and a portfolio of low B/M stocks from those same countries, as reported in Fama and French (1998). The size premium for Europe is the excess return of small and large stocks, averaged across 12 countries in Europe, reported in Heston, Rouwenhorst, and Wessels (1999). The emerging markets premiums represent the average across 20 emerging markets. The table gives for each sample the average return and the t-statistic of the sample mean. The bracketed t-statistics are computed as the average difference between the return premium in the United States or International/Europe and the premium in emerging markets (during the period that the samples overlap), divided by the standard error of the difference. The standard errors are computed using the Newey–West correction for heteroskedasticity and autocorrelation.

	United States			International[a]/Europe[b,c]			Emerging Markets		
Premium	Period	Mean	t-statistic	Period	Mean	t-statistic	Period	Mean	t-statistic
Size (SMB)	6307–9712	0.23	1.62 [2.96]	7901–9512	0.29[c]	3.67 [2.36]	8201–9704	0.70	2.96
Momentum (WML)	8001–9512	0.64	3.02 [−0.31]	8001–9512	0.67[b]	6.33 [−0.65]	8201–9704	0.58	3.96
Value (HML-BM)	6307–9712	0.41	3.28 [2.70]	7501–9512	0.50[a]	3.13 [1.47]	8701–9704	0.93	3.68

[a] Source: Fama and French (1998).
[b] Source: Rouwenhorst (1998).
[c] Source: Heston et al. (1999).

Local Return Factors and Turnover in Emerging Markets   1455

Bayes' Rule provides a natural framework to analyze how the combination of prior beliefs and information obtained by sampling the data influences individual beliefs. If an individual's prior belief about the mean return premium, μ, is given by the probability density function $P_0(\mu)$ and the likelihood of observing a sample premium $\bar{x}$ is $P_x(\bar{x}|\mu)$, Bayes' Rule states that the probability density function that describes the posterior beliefs about the mean return premium after observing the data, $P_1(\mu|\bar{x})$, is proportional to $P_x(\bar{x}|\mu)P_0(\mu)$. Assuming normal distributions for prior beliefs and the sample means, the distribution for the posterior mean will also be normal.[14] In this case the mean of the posterior distribution μ_1 is simply a weighted average of the prior mean μ_0 and the sample mean $\bar{x}$:

$$\mu_1 = \frac{w_0 \mu_0 + w_x \bar{x}}{w_0 + w_x}, \tag{1}$$

where the weights w_0 and w_x are the precisions (inverse of the variances) of the prior and sample means. The precision of the posterior distribution is $w_1 = w_0 + w_x$.

Suppose there is an investor who is skeptical about the ability of past returns to predict future returns and, before examining the data, believes that the average excess return of momentum investing is not different from the excess return of two random portfolios with the same number of securities. To characterize the distribution of these prior beliefs he takes the same 18 years of monthly data from the United States that were used to compute the momentum returns in Table V and he constructs two random "momentum" portfolios. The difference between the average returns of these portfolios is close to zero with a standard error of 0.06 percent per month. The actual sample average excess return of momentum strategies in the United States is 0.64 percent per month with a standard error of 0.217 percent. Using equation (1), the skeptic's posterior beliefs after observing the U.S. evidence would be given by a normal distribution with a mean of 0.046 and a standard deviation of 0.058. Defining the odds ratio as the probability that the average return premium is positive divided by the probability that the average return premium is negative, the skeptic would update his prior odds ratio of 1 (even odds) to about 7:2 in favor of a positive momentum premium. How would the European and emerging markets evidence further alter these beliefs? If the U.S. and European samples were independent, it would be possible to simply use the posterior distribution obtained from the U.S. data as the prior distribution before observing the European sample mean, and find a new posterior distribution by substituting the European sample moments into equation (1). However, momentum strategies are correlated across countries (Rouwenhorst (1998)). To account for the covariance

---

[14] With 15 to 30 years of monthly data available, the distributions of the sample means are likely to be close to normal.

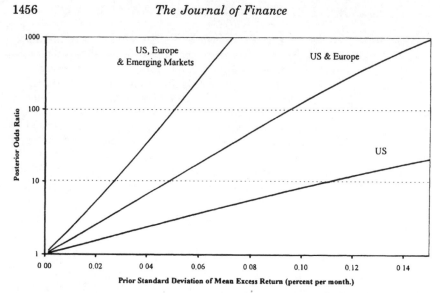

Figure 1. Posterior odds ratio of a positive momentum premium. The posterior odds ratio is defined as the posterior probability that the mean excess return of momentum investing (WML) is positive divided by the posterior probability that the mean return premium is negative. The figure plots the posterior odds ratio for an individual with prior beliefs that the mean return is zero, as a function of the standard deviation of these prior beliefs. The three lines show how this individual updates his prior beliefs using Bayes' Rule, after consecutively observing the sample average excess returns to momentum investing in the United States, Europe, and Emerging Markets.

between the regional sample means, I update the skeptic's initial prior beliefs using the sample means and standard deviations of two momentum portfolios that combine the information from the United States and the international data: The first portfolio combines stocks from both the United States and Europe, the second portfolio is diversified across all three regions. Regions are weighted equally. By forming portfolios across regions, the dependence between the regional returns will be reflected in the sample variances of the combined portfolios.[15] Updating the initial prior beliefs using the sample means of these internationally diversified momentum portfolios increases the posterior odds of a positive momentum premium to about 18:1 and 265:1 respectively. Figure 1 illustrates how the posterior odds are affected by changes in the precision of the prior beliefs. The posterior odds ratios are increasing in the standard deviation of the mean of the prior distribution: As an individual's prior beliefs become more diffuse, more weight will be placed on the information provided by the sample. Therefore, Fig-

---

[15] To the extent that the portfolios combine time series of different lengths, the variance of the internationally diversified portfolios will be heteroskedastic, even if the regional returns are not. For this reason, a correction for heteroskedasticity is used to compute the standard errors of the average returns that are diversified across regions.

Local Return Factors and Turnover in Emerging Markets   1457

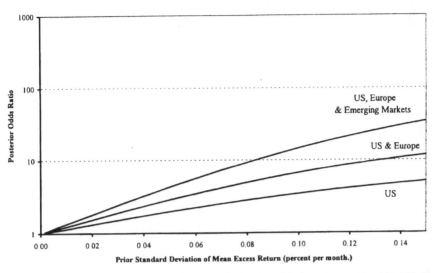

Figure 2. Posterior odds ratio of a positive size premium. The posterior odds ratio is defined as the posterior probability that the mean excess return of size portfolios (SMB) is positive divided by the posterior probability that the mean return premium is negative. The figure plots the posterior odds ratio for an individual with prior beliefs that the mean return is zero, as a function of the standard deviation of these prior beliefs. The three lines show how this individual updates his prior beliefs using Bayes' Rule, after consecutively observing the sample average excess returns of size portfolios in the United States, Europe, and Emerging Markets.

ure 1 shows how confident an individual has to be about his prior beliefs that the mean return of momentum investing is zero, in order for the posterior odds not to exceed a certain ratio.

Figures 2 and 3 show the posterior odds ratios for the size and value premiums. If the same distribution is used to characterize the prior beliefs about size and value premiums, the empirical evidence gives posterior odds ratios of 2.3, 3.4, and 5.6 (size) and 6.5, 14.1, and 34.3 (value). In the case of value investing, the emerging markets evidence influences the beliefs of the skeptic by more than doubling the posterior odds that the return premium for value and momentum is positive, and the posterior probability of a positive value premium exceeding 95 percent. The posterior probability of a positive size premium exceeds 95 percent for investors whose prior standard deviation of the mean premium exceeds 0.12 percent per month.

One of the motivations for examining international samples is to address the potential data-snooping bias in U.S. data. An investor who has prior beliefs that the true return premiums are zero, and that the reported premiums for the United States are the outcome of repeated data snooping, may choose to discard the U.S. evidence entirely and only examine evidence from international developed and emerging markets to update his priors. Unreported results show that if the standard deviation of his prior beliefs about

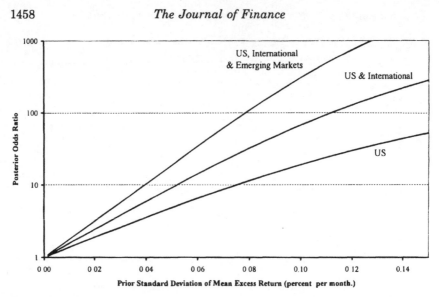

Figure 3. Posterior odds ratio of a positive value premium. The posterior odds ratio is defined as the posterior probability that the mean excess return of High minus Low Book-to-Market portfolios (HML-BM) is positive divided by the posterior probability that the mean return premium is negative. The figure plots the posterior odds ratio for an individual with prior beliefs that the mean return is zero, as a function of the standard deviation of these prior beliefs. The three lines show how this individual updates his prior beliefs using Bayes' Rule, after consecutively observing the sample average excess returns of Book-to-Market portfolios in the United States, Europe, and Emerging Markets.

the mean exceeds 0.08 percent per month, the posterior odds ratio after observing only the international and emerging markets evidence will exceed 20 for each of the return premiums (size, momentum, and value). The conclusion is that unless investors have strong prior beliefs to the contrary, the combined evidence from developed and emerging markets favors the hypothesis that size, momentum, and value are compensated for in average returns around the world.

IV. Share Turnover and Emerging Market Stock Returns

Despite the evidence that similar return factors are compensated for in average returns around the world, an important question remains unanswered: What is the (economic) interpretation of these premiums? Fama and French (1996) interpret the premiums as a rejection of the CAPM in favor of a linear multifactor model of returns. By contrast, Daniel and Titman (1997) show that the premiums in the United States are not related to factors exposure, but instead to firm characteristics. One firm characteristic that is of particular interest to investors in emerging markets is liquidity, and work by Amihud and Mendelson (1986), Hu (1997), Chalmers and Kadlec

Local Return Factors and Turnover in Emerging Markets 1459

Table VI
Average Returns of Turnover Portfolios

At the beginning of each month all stocks with available ranking information are ranked by country into three groups based on share turnover: High (top 30 percent), Medium (middle 40 percent) and Low (bottom 30 percent). Turnover is measured as the number of shares traded in a month as a fraction of the total number of shares outstanding at the beginning of the month. Columns 3–6 report the average return on equally weighted portfolios of High (H) and Low (L) turnover stocks, the average HML-T excess return. $t(\ )$ is the mean excess return divided by its standard error corrected for heteroskedasticity and autocorrelation.

Country	Start Date	Average Returns Turnover Portfolios			
		Low-T	High-T	HML-T	t(HML-T)
Argentina	8701	7.21	5.20	−2.01	−0.90
Brazil	8701	3.91	2.85	−1.07	−0.97
Chile	8701	2.86	2.84	−0.02	−0.04
Colombia	8701	2.00	2.71	0.71	0.90
Greece	8701	1.65	2.80	1.14	1.45
Indonesia	9001	−0.38	1.46	1.84	3.88
India	8701	0.75	1.45	0.70	1.15
Jordan	8701	0.27	0.47	0.20	0.34
Korea	8701	0.97	1.08	0.11	0.19
Malaysia	8701	1.54	1.86	0.32	0.50
Mexico	8701	3.17	2.83	−0.35	−0.48
Nigeria	8701	3.16	1.74	−1.43	−2.08
Pakistan	8701	1.51	1.00	−0.50	−1.12
Philippines	8801	1.36	1.35	−0.01	−0.01
Portugal	8901	0.14	0.91	0.76	1.52
Taiwan	8701	2.90	2.87	−0.03	−0.04
Thailand	8701	0.63	1.26	0.62	0.91
Turkey	8901	3.62	4.77	1.15	0.92
Venezuela	8701	3.01	3.77	0.75	0.64
Zimbabwe	8701	1.97	3.02	1.06	1.12
All 20 markets	8701	1.97	2.11	0.14	0.72

(1998), and Datar, Naik, and Radcliffe (1998) suggests that liquidity is compensated for in expected returns. If small stocks, past medium-term winners, and value stocks are on average less liquid than big stocks, past medium-term losers, and growth stocks, the reported premiums in emerging markets may simply be a compensation for their relative illiquidity.

To examine the potential confounding influence of liquidity, I study the cross section of returns and share turnover. Two questions are of interest: Is there a difference in the average returns of turnover-sorted portfolios? If so, is it possible that a "turnover premium" indirectly drives the returns of the factor portfolios? The returns of turnover-sorted portfolios are summarized in Table VI. There is little evidence of a difference between the average returns of portfolios formed by ranking stocks based on prior turnover. The return on high turnover portfolios exceeds the return on a portfolio of low turnover stocks in 12 of the 20 countries studied, and the absolute value of the *t*-statistics for the equality of means exceeds 2 in only two countries, which is only slightly higher than can be expected purely by chance. Averaged across all 20 markets, the excess return of high turnover stocks is insignificantly different from the return on low turnover stocks ($t = 0.72$). These results are much weaker than the findings of Claessens et al. (1998) who report a positive association between average returns and turnover in 17 of 19 markets in an earlier and shorter sample.

By contrast, Table VII shows that there are strong turnover patterns associated with the local factor portfolios of emerging markets. For example, the average median turnover of small stocks is higher than the turnover of the large stocks in 15 of the 20 countries. As pointed out previously in Section I, this is in part a consequence of the sample selection criteria used by the IFC: For a small stock to clear the sample selection hurdle in terms of total value of shares traded, it has to have higher turnover than a large stock. However, size is not the only factor that is associated with turnover. Average turnover is positively associated with beta in 19 of 20 countries, with value in 14 of 20 countries, and momentum in 16 of 20 countries. The results for beta- and size-sorted portfolios are consistent with the findings reported by Lo and Wang (1997), who find in a cross section of U.S. firms that individual stock turnover is positively related to beta and residual standard deviation, and negatively related to firm size. The sample selection bias that leads to the negative cross-sectional correlation between size and turnover may indirectly be responsible for the turnover patterns in the other factor portfolios. For example, high B/M firms are on average smaller than low B/M firms in all 20 markets, and this size-bias likely contributes to the turnover differences between value and growth portfolios. However, size cannot explain the turnover of beta-sorted and momentum portfolios. The relationship between beta and turnover is particularly strong. This is despite the fact that high beta stocks are larger than low beta stocks in 14 of 20 markets, which would attenuate the positive turnover difference between beta-sorted portfolios. A possible explanation is that high beta stocks are on average more volatile, and more sensitive to portfolio rebalancing by investors. At first glance, the turnover difference between momentum portfolios is the weakest among the four factors. However, unreported results show that past Losers are on average smaller than past Winners in all markets, and this size bias is likely to attenuate differences in turnover. Interestingly, the median turnover of the Losers is lower than the turnover of the median stock in 18 of the 20 countries. This somewhat surprising considering the fact that Losers are on average small, and that Losers (as well as Winners) tend to be more volatile than the average stock in a country, because ranking on past return is correlated with volatility. Odean (1998) attributes the low turnover of Losers in the United States to a disposition effect whereby investors are more reluctant to realize losses than take gains. Whether similar turnover patterns are associated with momentum strategies in other developed markets is not known. If so, these data can potentially suggest an

Local Return Factors and Turnover in Emerging Markets 1461

Table VII
Turnover Characteristics of Local Factor Portfolios

The table summarizes the median turnover of individual stocks, of country-factor portfolios that are formed by sorting stocks on local beta, size (market value of equity), momentum (past 6-month return), and book-to-market. For each portfolio the median turnover is computed by month, and the table reports the time-series average of these monthly medians, and the average difference between medians by country. The third column (Full) gives the average median turnover of all stocks in a country. The following columns give the average turnover of the stocks in the country-factor portfolios. The last row is the equally weighted portfolio of stocks from all 20 countries. t( ) is the average divided by its standard error, corrected for heteroskedasticity and autocorrelation. Turnover is measured as the number of shares traded during a month expressed as a percentage of the total number of shares outstanding at the beginning of that month.

Country	Start	Full	Beta			Size			Momentum			Book-to-Market		
			Low-β	High-β	t(HML-β)	Small	Big	t(SMB)	Losers	Winners	t(WML)	Low-BM	High-BM	t(HML-BM)
Argentina	8701	3.00	2.64	3.01	1.42	2.40	2.81	-1.52	3.61	2.85	-2.29	2.91	4.29	4.19
Brazil	8701	1.82	1.16	2.38	9.20	2.73	1.17	5.67	2.25	1.69	-1.87	1.26	2.52	6.80
Chile	8701	0.49	0.41	0.71	3.96	0.51	0.63	-2.34	0.45	0.56	2.01	0.59	0.60	0.12
Colombia	8701	0.43	0.53	0.45	-2.31	0.53	0.48	0.77	0.42	0.49	1.96	0.38	0.48	2.49
Greece	8701	1.51	1.40	1.56	0.70	2.28	1.44	3.45	1.40	1.61	1.76	1.90	1.49	-3.15
Indonesia	9001	2.42	2.07	3.05	4.97	2.77	2.16	2.15	2.51	2.11	-3.17	2.13	3.18	4.54
India	8701	1.88	2.27	2.94	1.96	2.48	2.12	1.25	2.00	2.34	1.68	1.59	2.45	3.21
Jordan	8701	1.79	1.18	1.91	2.30	4.82	0.86	4.20	1.26	2.50	2.69	4.16	1.07	-4.08
Korea	8701	8.13	6.99	8.67	2.82	13.09	6.39	5.40	7.70	8.77	1.46	8.54	8.06	-1.28
Malaysia	8701	1.89	0.87	3.28	6.80	4.79	0.92	5.93	2.06	1.83	-0.64	1.76	2.45	1.69
Mexico	8701	2.74	1.77	4.05	6.35	2.01	3.42	-6.12	2.53	3.29	3.28	3.24	2.38	-2.74
Nigeria	8701	0.04	0.05	0.05	-0.60	0.04	0.05	-1.69	0.04	0.04	0.78	0.04	0.04	-1.62
Pakistan	8701	0.44	0.25	0.62	7.71	0.53	0.47	0.65	0.45	0.47	0.43	0.04	0.52	2.59
Philippines	8801	1.78	1.35	3.64	4.14	3.30	1.44	4.04	1.76	1.92	0.53	0.37	1.45	-0.94
Portugal	8901	1.34	1.37	1.69	3.02	1.38	1.46	-0.75	1.21	1.60	2.84	1.55	1.45	4.39
Taiwan	8701	30.22	22.20	38.18	4.29	53.39	12.16	7.41	28.94	32.47	0.78	23.86	37.16	1.49
Thailand	8701	3.48	2.66	4.76	3.47	5.20	2.81	2.23	3.19	3.77	1.58	3.09	3.94	2.51
Turkey	8901	4.29	4.42	4.57	0.24	11.58	2.69	6.53	3.86	5.04	1.69	4.18	8.16	1.48
Venezuela	8701	0.84	0.67	1.83	2.84	1.57	1.42	0.28	0.89	1.21	0.98	0.95	1.37	3.30
Zimbabwe	8701	0.29	0.26	0.34	2.27	0.54	0.22	3.92	0.31	0.35	0.86	0.25	0.57	3.30
All 20 markets		1.74	1.10	2.14	12.46	2.30	1.40	9.41	1.62	1.78	2.38	1.62	1.89	5.89

interesting dimension for distinguishing between various models that attempt to explain return continuation (Hong and Stein (1997), Daniel et al. (1998) and Berk, Green, and Naik (1998)).

The conclusion is that turnover is positively associated with the same attributes that explain cross-sectional differences in average returns. Absent a dynamic theory that links returns to trading activity, these patterns are difficult to explain. However, the empirical evidence suggests that common factors may drive the cross section of returns and turnover, which provides an interesting challenge for theoretical models to explain. And a practical implication of these findings is that portfolio managers who seek to increase their exposure to the return factors in emerging markets can do so without simultaneously increasing their positions in relatively illiquid (low turnover) securities.

V. Conclusion

This paper examines the cross section of returns in 20 emerging markets using return data of 1750 individual stocks. The first conclusion is that the return factors in emerging markets are qualitatively similar to those in developed markets: Small stocks outperform large stocks, value stocks outperform growth stocks and emerging markets stocks exhibit momentum. There is no evidence that local market betas are associated with average returns. The low correlation between the country return factors suggests that the premiums have a strong local character. Furthermore, global exposures cannot explain the average factor returns of emerging markets. There is little evidence that the correlations between the local factor portfolios have increased, which suggests that the factors responsible for the increase of emerging market country correlations are separate from those that drive the differences between expected return within these markets. A Bayesian analysis of the return premiums in developed and emerging markets shows that, unless one has strong prior beliefs to the contrary, the empirical evidence favors the hypothesis that size, momentum, and value strategies are compensated for in expected returns around the world. Finally, the paper documents the relationship between expected returns and share turnover, and examines the turnover characteristics of the local return factor portfolios. There is no evidence of a relation between expected returns and turnover in emerging markets. However, beta, size, momentum, and value are positively cross-sectionally correlated with turnover in emerging markets. This suggests that the return premiums do not simply reflect a compensation for illiquidity.

REFERENCES

Amihud, Yakov, and Haim Mendelson, 1986, Asset pricing and the bid-ask spread, *Journal of Financial Economics* 17, 223–249.
Anchour, Dana, Campbell R. Harvey, Greg Hopkins, and Clive Lang, 1998, Stock selection in emerging markets: Portfolio strategies for Malaysia, Mexico, and South Africa, *Emerging Markets Quarterly* 2, 38–91.

Local Return Factors and Turnover in Emerging Markets   1463

Banz, Rolf W., 1981, The relationship between return and market value of common stocks, *Journal of Financial Economics* 9, 3–18.

Bekaert, Geert, Claude Erb, Campbell R. Harvey, and Tadas Viskanta, 1997, What matters in emerging markets investments?, *Emerging Markets Quarterly* 1, 1–30.

Bekaert, Geert, and Campbell R. Harvey, 1995, Time-varying world market integration, *Journal of Finance* 50, 403–444.

Bekaert, Geert, and Campbell R. Harvey, 1997a, Emerging equity market volatility, *Journal of Financial Economics* 43, 29–77.

Bekaert, Geert, and Campbell R. Harvey, 1997b, Foreign speculators and emerging equity markets, Working paper 1441, Graduate School of Business, Stanford University.

Berk, Jonathan, 1995, A critique of size related anomalies, *Review of Financial Studies* 8, 275–286.

Berk, Jonathan B, Richard C. Green, and Vasant Naik, 1998, Optimal investment, growth options, and security returns, *Journal of Finance*, forthcoming.

Chalmers, John M. R., and Gregory B. Kadlec, 1998, An empirical examination of the amortized spread, *Journal of Financial Economics* 48, 159–188.

Chan, Louis K. C., Jason Karceski, and Josef Lakonishok, 1997, The risk and return from factors, mimeo, University of Illinois.

Claessens, Stijn, Susmita Dasgupta, and Jack Glen, 1998, The cross section of stock returns: Evidence from emerging markets, *Emerging Markets Quarterly* 2, 4–13.

Daniel, Kent, David Hirshleifer, and Avanidhar Subrahmanyam, 1998, Investor psychology and security market under- and overreactions, *Journal of Finance* 53, 1839–1885.

Daniel, Kent, and Sheridan Titman, 1997, Evidence on the characteristics of cross-sectional variation in stock returns, *Journal of Finance* 52, 1–34.

Datar, Vinay T., Narayan Y. Naik, and Robert Radcliffe, 1998, Liquidity and stock returns: An alternative test, Working paper, London Business School.

Fama, Eugene F., and Kenneth R. French, 1992, The cross-section of expected stock returns, *Journal of Finance* 67, 427–465.

Fama, Eugene F., and Kenneth R. French, 1996, Multifactor explanations of asset pricing anomalies, *Journal of Finance* 51, 55–84.

Fama, Eugene F., and Kenneth R. French, 1998, Value versus growth: The international evidence, *Journal of Finance* 53, 1975–2000.

Fama, Eugene F, and James MacBeth, 1973, Risk, return and equilibrium: Empirical tests, *Journal of Political Economy* 81, 607–636.

Goetzmann, William N., and Philippe Jorion, 1999, Re-emerging markets, *Journal of Financial and Quantitative Analysis*, forthcoming.

Harvey, Campbell R., 1995, Predictable risk and return in emerging markets, *Review of Financial Studies* 8, 773–816.

Haugen, Robert A, and Nardin L. Baker, 1996, Commonality in the determinants of expected stock returns, *Journal of Financial Economics* 41, 401–439.

Heston, Steven L., K. Geert Rouwenhorst, and Roberto E. Wessels, 1995, The structure of international stock returns and the integration of capital markets, *Journal of Empirical Finance* 2, 173–197.

Heston, Steven L., K. Geert Rouwenhorst, and Roberto E. Wessels, 1999, The role of beta and size in the cross-section of European stock returns, *European Financial Management* 5, 9–27.

Hong, Harrison, and Jeremy C. Stein, 1997, A unified theory of underreaction, momentum trading, and overreaction in asset markets, Working paper, Sloan School of Management, MIT.

Hu, Shing-yang, 1997, Trading turnover and expected stock returns: The trading frequency hypothesis and evidence from the Tokyo stock exchange, Working paper, National Taiwan University and University of Chicago.

Jegadeesh, Narasimhan, and Sheridan Titman, 1993, Returns to buying winners and selling losers: Implications for stock market efficiency, *Journal of Finance* 48, 65–91.

Kothari, S. P., Jay Shanken, and Richard G. Sloan, 1995, Another look at the cross-section of expected returns, *Journal of Finance* 50, 185–224.

Lakonishok, Josef, Andrei Shleifer, and Robert W. Vishny, 1994, Contrarian investment, extrapolation and risk, *Journal of Finance* 49, 1541–1578.

Lo, Andrew W., and A. Craig MacKinlay, 1990, Data-snooping biases in tests of asset pricing models, *Review of Financial Studies* 3, 431–467.

Lo, Andrew W., and Jiang Wang, 1997, Trading volume: definitions, data analysis and implications of portfolio theory, Working paper, Sloan School of Management, Massachusetts Institute of Technology.

Loughran, Tim, 1997, Book-to-market across firm size, exchange, and seasonality: Is there an effect?, *Journal of Financial and Quantitative Analysis* 32, 249–268.

MacKinlay, A. Craig, 1995, Multifactor models do not explain deviations from the Capital Asset Pricing Models, *Journal of Financial Economics* 38, 3–28.

Odean, Terrance, 1998, Are investors reluctant to realize their losses?, *Journal of Finance* 53, 1775–1798.

Patel, Sandeep A., 1998, Cross-sectional variation in emerging markets equity returns January 1988–March 1997, *Emerging Markets Quarterly* 2, 57–70.

Rouwenhorst, K. Geert, 1998, International momentum strategies, *Journal of Finance* 53, 267–284.

Name Index

The International Library of Critical Writings in Financial Economics

DATE DUE